JUDGEMENT IMPAIRED

BY MICHAEL HUGHES

FIRST EDITION

PUBLICATION DATE: 10TH OCTOBER 2005

Mike Mre GORING, OXON 29⁴/08

GW00724505

JUDGEMENT IMPAIRED

JUDGEMENT IMPAIRED
*Law, Disorder and Injustice to Victims
in 21st century Britain*

Michael Hughes

Hande-Cuffe Publications Limited

Published by Hande-Cuffe Publications Limited
Copyright © 2005 by Michael Hughes

No reproduction without permission
All rights reserved

The right of Michael Hughes to be identified as author of this work
has been asserted by him in accordance with the
Copyright, Designs and Patents Act, 1988

Design and Artwork by Stephen Green Print & Design

Printed in Great Britain by Antony Rowe Limited
Chippenham, Wilts SN14 6LH

ISBN 0-9550397-0-3

DEDICATIONS

To my much-missed Mum and Dad – Alf Hughes and Marjorie Hughes nee Hancock – for giving to me that greatest of all gifts – the gift of life itself. A mother who sacrificed hours and hours of her own leisure and relaxation time to read to myself and my siblings for extended periods of time.

To my maternal Grandparents, Charles and Fanny Hancock nee Rumbold – who cherished me, loved me and spoilt me whenever possible and annually laid on the most sumptuous feasts for the entire extended family on Boxing Days, at their Haverstock Hill home, Hampstead, London, NW3. Charles spent a full term as a Police Constable in the Metropolitan Police, and walked everywhere thereafter.

To one of their sons, my Uncle John, who hardly went anywhere without me, and who managed Oakeshotts Provisions Store in Englands Lane, London, NW3 – until forced into early ill-health retirement. Also to his wonderful wife Barbara who, with John, always made me, her nephew, feel really special.

To another one of my maternal Uncles, my Mum's brother Stanley Hancock, in whose footsteps I followed after leaving school – firstly the Royal Marines and later the Police. He had served in the Palestine Police until the Force was disbanded in 1948, and had the honour of taking part in the final Royal Inspection Parade by King George the V1th at Buckingham Palace. He later emigrated to Canada with his brother Arthur, and both were much missed in their absences as they found new territory to explore in the vast wilds of Canada.

To Stan Hancock's wife Lillian, whom he met whilst she nursed him in hospital out there. Through meeting Lillian, they created my wonderful 'Canadian Cousins' – Julie, Nancy and Wayne – and never to forget Julie's twin sister Deborah, who was unlucky enough to not survive an operation in a Canadian Hospital – and who is missed so much.

To my first-born child Jacqueline ('JAX') – for whom I curtailed my promising Royal Marines career - as I was serving on LST 3516 HMS Striker in the Persian Gulf and was refused compassionate leave to fly home and be present at her birth in Brentwood, Essex. Therefore I prematurely left the

Corps and just about made it home via Bahrain in time for her birth. This wonderful girl – of whom I am so proud – had to endure the grief and trauma of losing her first child, Eleanor, at the age of just 2 weeks – Baby Eleanor's loss was the first infant death in living memory throughout our extended families. However Jax bravely survived this tragic ordeal and later brought Pelham into the world – who fully understands that Eleanor would have been his loving older sister, had she survived.

To my son David, of whom I am also so proud of his achievements in life – and, as the author of several books of his own, gave me every encouragement and assisted with the laborious editing of this book. With his wife Zahida (Ida) – a lovely girl from Croatia – they were later to present us with grandchildren Harrison (Harry) and Genevieve (Jenna) – cousins to Pelham – all three of whom became the lights of my life.

This cool dude of a son has carved an amazing niche for himself in his creative working life – very busy male lead singer in a Tribute Band – interviewer of international movie stars - author of several books – creative movie writer – there could never be enough hours in a day for this young man!

To Liz, who helped make it all possible - by bringing Jackie and David into the world - and with whom I once shared some wonderful experiences.

To Jane, who shared with me around 20 years of her young life – being 20 years younger – who could never ever, to her great credit, see anything bad about anyone – and taught me not to be judgemental.

All of these fine people, in their own separate ways, left their individual marks on me – contributing in no small measure to my most interesting and exciting journey through life.

Having experienced in my own lifetime, the pain, suffering and anguish caused when my first-born grand child, Eleanor, was tragically taken from us at the tender age of just 2 weeks – for medical reasons not fully understood even to this day – I dedicate this book to Eleanor's memory.

In a book of this nature, no Dedications section would be complete without mention of four others of God's so-innocent, beautiful children – who were tragically taken from their loving parents, without warning – because of man's inhumanity to man. None of us – so remote from the scenes – can ever possibly imagine the shock, horror and awful realisation of the unbelievable truth – that their much-loved and cherished child had been taken away from them – not accidentally – but through deliberate acts at the hands of 'human beings' whom right-thinking people see as perverse monsters. Therefore, this book which highlights the current existence of such dreadful people – many of whom are still at large on our streets – is specially dedicated to the memories of Holly Wells, Jessica Chapman, Sarah Payne and James Bulger. May God support their brave parents as they awake to face each new day with such emptiness in their hearts.

ACKNOWLEDGEMENTS

Teachers at the Royal Liberty School, Hare Hall, Gidea Park, Romford, Essex, Mr 'Nick' Nicholson, Mr Harry Askew and Mr Guy, all of whom helped to run the Army Section of the school's CCF – Combined Cadet Force – who by their inspiration, dedication and guidance, were instrumental in setting me on the initial path that would lead me into an enjoyable military career.

Bandmasters Peter Richardson and Dick Bouchard - both of whom came from military backgrounds – who recruited me as a founder member of what was then known as the Romford British Legion Boys Band, meeting at Pettits Lane School, Romford, and were inspirational role models in keeping young boys off the streets, and bringing welcome and much-needed discipline into their young lives. These two respected and revered Bandmasters went on to become great achievers in the youth military-style Band world, each as Directors of Champion, World Class, Youth Marching Bands. They were both later rewarded with individual insignia in the British Empire division.

To then-Corporal, Royal Marines, Maurice Ford and his instructor-partner Corporal 'Willy' Carr, RM, Drill Leaders at the Depot, RM, Deal, Kent. Maurice went on to be a Senior 'First Drill' Warrant Officer at Eastney Barracks, Portsmouth, whilst 'Willy' Carr was later Commissioned as a Royal Marines Officer. These 2 highly-trained, dedicated and inspirational individuals took myself – and the rest of no. 673 Squad Royal Marines, by the scruff of the neck in 1957, and by their inspirational leadership, military professionalism and by personal example – took responsibility for a crowd of young tearaway ragamuffins and 'Teddy Boys' etc., aged 17+ years – shouted at us, 'bullied' us, shaped and moulded us, working absolute miracles in turning us all into proud young Royal Marines, experts in precision drill etc. – all in the short space of just three months – being phase one of our nine months total recruitment training. Both of these Drill Leaders went on to be very high achievers in their chosen careers in that elite body known worldwide as HM Royal Marines.

Later in my life, along came Police Sergeant Ken Watkins, of Oxford City Police, and Mike Humberston, then a Police Sergeant in Essex Constabulary, both of whom were Instructors at No. 5 District Police Training Centre at Eynsham Hall, near Witney, Oxfordshire. These two wonderful men took us all through initial Police training for approx 13 weeks and were an inspiration to us all, bringing great interest and realism into the often-boring different aspects of our Law training.

In addition, former Guardsman, Police Sergeant Harry Fuller of Essex Police, our Drill instructor, motivated us to greater things on the Eynsham Hall parade ground. However he was never able to properly cope with the fact that former Royal Marines and Sailors, carried out their foot-drill the *correct* way – *without* stamping their booted feet so hard that their knees almost reached their chins – whilst coming to attention, standing at ease, or marking time etc. In spite of this minor 'inadequacy', Harry Fuller, at our eventual Police Recruit Squad Passing-Out Parade, in which we marched up and down the Drive and the Parade Ground, normally to the sound of his very loud and scratchy 'British Grenadiers' or 'Colonel Bogey' record, respected me enough and was kind enough to play instead – 'A Life On The Ocean Wave' – the Regimental Quick March of HM Royal Marines – for our Pass-Out. That was a high honour for me and I have never forgotten it – thank you so much Harry for that kind gesture.

To Christine from Sheffield Drive, Harold Hill who was my 'first love'. We saw each other from time-to-time whilst I was home on leave from the Royal Marines, as well as corresponding by post. However one day whilst I was cold, wet and miserable, guarding my slit trench on Dartmoor in driving rain, whilst on my Junior NCO's promotion course – my morale almost at rock bottom as our Royal Marines instructors sought to undermine our confidence – and break our spirits by forever attacking our defensive positions – both by night, and day – I opened a soggy letter from Christine and found, to my horror that she had sent me a much-dreaded 'Dear John' letter! However the ultimate 'insult' was yet to come – Christine had ditched me for a Royal Navy Sailor, from the Senior Service! Tragically, as she was such a sweet girl, I don't think I ever saw her again, so 'Jolly Jack' must have carried her off into the sunset.

Then there was Maggie, whom I met at my first job in London on leaving school. In our amazing sophistication, belying our young ages of 16 years plus, together we took in just about every Theatrical Musical in London's West End. However our short-term, very enjoyable boy-girl relationship was doomed to failure, as Maggie found a job overseas, whilst I was posted to 40, Commando RM, in Malta for 18 months. Therefore all of those miles got in the way and, unfortunately at the time – that was the end of that.

No 'Acknowledgements' section would be complete without a mention for my long-term buddy, Bill Blackmore, and his wife Sylvia. Bill hailed from Norbiton, near Kingston On Thames, Surrey. We met when we both joined the Royal Marines at Deal on the same day in 1957. So I have known him now for 48 years. Like me, Bill had an Uncle who was a *serving* Royal Marine, also stationed at Deal, a Colour Sergeant. Later, Bill was to achieve the exact same rank as a PTI – Physical Training Instructor – known colloquially as a 'club-swinger'. We appeared in the 1958 Royal Tournament together in a Cliff Assault demonstration, and were then both posted to Malta – he to 45, Commando RM, at one end of the Island, and myself to 40, Commando RM at the other end. We used to meet up for 'big eats' in Valetta together. We are still in touch to this day and amazingly, live within 20 minutes drive of each other. We take turns to host meals and cards and cryptic crossword schools at each others homes. Over the last 12 months or so, being computer illiterate when I made a start on researching etc for this book, Sylvia has become my 'Computer Mentor' and takes pride in being able to speak words of wisdom down the telephone line, so as to help get my PC up and running again. Furthermore, she's not a bad cook, too!

My final personal acknowledgement is for David Petley from Brentwood, Essex – Dave and I were at school together, and both enjoyed our membership of the school Cadet Force, Army Section and had some amazing times together at Cadet Camps during school holidays etc. I have now known this guy for an unbelievable 54 years – We B & B at each other's homes as often as possible and I also get on well with his very pleasant wife Sonia. We have all holidayed together in Cyprus several times.

I have one last general tribute to pay to a particular branch of Society – these men and women, who totally unselfishly, dedicate their own personal lives – and put themselves in personal danger almost daily – to allow us all to sleep peacefully and undisturbed in our beds at night. They self-sacrifice, carry on regardless of largely undue criticism from armchair experts – somehow manage to keep up their determination to succeed, and their morale – in the face of continual, daily lack of support from by far the majority of the present Judiciary in the United Kingdom – due to lenient, inappropriate and ill-conceived sentencing – and placing the 'rights' of *criminal offenders*, over and above those of the actual *victims* of the crimes. What a crazy world we are all living in these days – the world is 'on its head', many right-thinking people claim!

These brave heroes, produce brilliant responses in the face of modern budgetary constraints – keep a stiff upper lip in spite of the constant challenges to their personal integrity, in the witness box – from money-grabbing 'fat-cat' defence lawyers, whose clients are almost always funded through Legal Aid. To all of the currently serving and former colleagues of mine, who are, or were *'IN THE JOB'* – <u>keep up the good work.</u> Thousands of law-abiding citizens and victims of crime right across the United Kingdom, appreciate your daily efforts and know that life would be intolerable without all of *YOU* special people on their side! I say this from a position of great strength - as I've *'been there and done that'*.

One person who is in 'The Job' stands head and shoulders perhaps – above the rest of his thousands of male and female colleagues up and down the country. This guy's leadership is totally inspirational and motivational – not just to his own colleagues – but to the entire population of the UK who know full well how to conduct themselves properly, and are right-thinking and law-abiding. This man's name must be on everyone's lips, as he crusades and issues his daily proclamations from his Middlesex offices, as he comments and leads the all-out war against criminals and crime, and stands up for the 'underdogs' within the Criminal 'Justice' System viz: the victims. This guy is so huge in personality, drive and sheer enthusiasm, that I personally compare him to Sir Winston Churchill – without whom, it is claimed, we would have succumbed to the Nazis in WW2. The person I'm thinking of, must be loathed by all liberal judges and magistrates in the land – as well as Mr Blair and former Home Secretary Mr David Blunkett, whom he must regularly embarrass. He fights his own personal war against crime every single day of his life. Serving British Transport Police Constable, and Director, The Victims of Crime Trust, MR NORMAN BRENNAN. To his great credit, he even took the most desperate step of once writing a personal letter to HM The Queen - a copy of which appears in Judgement Impaired.

PC Norman Brennan
British Transport Police
Director, The Victims of Crime Trust

FOREWORD

"*Judgement impaired* illustrates in detail the many injustices imposed on victims and society as a whole, not just by the criminal element, but also by members of the judiciary, whose general attitude is to give repeat offenders a licence to re-offend time and time again; until their criminal behaviour becomes so ingrained that they are destined for a career in crime with little chance of turning back.

This book is written by someone who has hands-on experience in front-line policing and the devastation that is caused by those who break society's laws.

Reading this book will allow you to see through the eyes of a police officer the uphill fight for justice. It details why it is the very criminal justice system itself, to which we all look for protection, that fails us all so badly."

Norman Brennan,
Director, The Victims of Crime Trust,
British Transport Police Constable
of 26 years service

August 2005

INTRODUCTION

In recent years, FEAR has been the emotion most felt by many people in this country, almost on a daily basis. This is particularly so in the case of the elderly and infirm, disabled and other vulnerable people. If we look at a period of, say, the last 5 years, the fear level has increased even more. Many people would consider that it is at an all-time-high. This has caused many people who can afford it, to fit extra locks, bars, grilles, closed circuit television (CCTV) cameras, panic alarms, security gates, door chains etc in the hope of increasing their peace of mind. In other words, insofar as personal and household budgets will allow, turning the homes into a 'Fort Knox'. However taking some or all of these precautions can only go towards increasing one's peace of mind whilst inside the home.

For most of the general public, the place where fear can be experienced mostly, as they go about their normal business, is on the streets. Lives can be changed forever by becoming unwillingly involved in all kinds of street crime. Robbery, which includes personal violence to steal handbags, mobile telephones, wallets (so-called 'muggings') and now even private motor cars, known as 'car-jackings'. As regards the latter, in very recent times there have been fatalities and therefore what started out as attempts to deprive somebody of their cars by force, have turned into murders. Roaming the streets, particularly in Inner City Areas - there are very many persons who are 'high' on drugs of many kinds, or through glue sniffing, or in drink. These people can be absolutely desperate as to where their next 'FIX' is coming from, and when the mood takes them, or they are experiencing 'cold turkey', nothing but nothing will stand in their way to raise the funds required to finance their habit. This street violence has been extended in recent times to include very serious motoring offences such as causing death by dangerous driving, driving whilst disqualified, without insurance or without a driving licence and failing to stop after an accident. There is a quite high chance that offenders responsible for some of these crimes, are drug users, racing to meet their supplier or dealer, as they are desperate for their next 'fix'. Furthermore, there have been reported many offences of this nature committed by illegal immigrants, some of whom have swiftly returned to their own countries immediately afterwards, to evade detection and capture. Some of these real-life case studies will be reported later in this book. Several years ago, when the current Government came to power, it had been a much-publicised special feature of 'New Labour's' election manifesto that the breakdown of law and order would be dealt with quite adequately. In fact the expression used was: 'We will remove the fear from victims and transfer that fear onto the perpetrators of the crimes', or words to that effect. There must be thousands of people around the country who are still worrying and wondering, probably on a daily basis in some cases, when this is actually going to happen.

The Government is currently attempting to change the constitution of the country, which includes getting rid of the last unelected members of The House of Lords. There is also a serious attempt to introduce a new 'Supreme Court' situation, whereby Crown Court and High Court Judges would be appointed by a special panel of lawyers etc - but to include lay persons too.

This latter proposal is being strongly resisted by the Lord Chief Justice of England and Wales, Lord Woolf. He has declared that such a serious and dramatic change to the present Criminal Justice System would necessitate the finding by the Government of multi-millions of pounds. The author's private assertion is that there is no need to change the present system at all, as sufficient powers and penalties are already in position, and have been for years. The problem appears to be one of Judges and Magistrates being perceived to only take into consideration the rights of the offender, with scant or no apparent regard at all for the victims' rights. My purpose is to demonstrate throughout this book that it is within the power of the Judiciary to change things for the better, virtually overnight. Judges and Magistrates appear to be 'getting it wrong' far too often in the way they dispose of cases, and it is my intention to include and highlight many examples of this in some detail. This will all be presented in a totally balanced way, leaving the reader to form his or her own opinions - and to come to a personal decision as to what is the best way forward .

I shall attempt to illustrate matters through the carefully researched and documented real-life cases, supplemented with my own every-day experiences from my 20 years plus spent working within the Criminal Justice System, which I know will add interest as well as supplying you with some 'insider information'. For ease of reference, the book is divided into the format of creating separate chapters, (but listed as 'Counts of an Indictment') to deal with the various types of crimes which are continuing to cause grave concerns. However it is inevitable that some types of crime will overlap with others, because of course, some criminals do not stick to a single method of operating. (known as 'modus operandi' or 'MO'.) Whilst researching for this book, I had occasion to read a book recently published, by a top lawyer, Baroness Helena Kennedy, QC. Over the years I have enjoyed her appearances on Television Chat Shows and as a panellist during many live debates, and respected her views. I am also aware that she Chairs very many Public Committees, and I respect her too for all of that. Her book is entitled, *JUST LAW - 'The Changing Face Of Justice - And Why It Matters To Us All'*. The front cover indicates that the following subjects are dealt with inside:

EQUALITY

FAIRNESS

RESPECT

DIGNITY

CIVIL LIBERTIES

On completion of reading my own copy of *Just Law*, I made the judgement that Baroness Kennedy, QC, its author, who of course, as a Baroness, now sits in the House of Lords, had written it very much in a spirit of liberalism, and from the point of view of an eminent, top-class, high-earning lawyer – which of course she is. Her experiences obviously included acting as defence counsel on many occasions throughout her long and full career. I felt it was overall biased in favour of the 'much-aligned, offender' - and how he or she suffers within the criminal justice system, by being deprived of liberty etc. I felt there was scant regard for the actual victims of crime. I also found that *Just Law* took longer to read than I would have liked. This was because Baroness Kennedy, QC had utilised the following obscure words and phrases within her text:

EVANESCENT	*CONTEXTUALISE*
SYNCHRONICITY	*TABULA RASA*
COMMUNITARIANISM	*RESILED*
MANICHAEN DIVIDE	*CODA*
INCULPATORY	*EXORIATION*
FECUND	*HEGEMONY*
POSITING	*EXECRABLE*
ELISION	*AMELIORATIVE*

On reflection - I suppose it's just me! I'll bet you have nearly all of the above words within your personal vocabulary. Although I am an avid cryptic crosswords fan, I found that almost none of the above words or phrases could be easily deciphered or interpreted. Therefore my enjoyment of the book was interrupted and delayed by having to frequently put it down and visit my bookcase, to look up their meanings in the various dictionaries and a thesaurus. However, through persisting with her book to the end, I learnt a useful lesson in *how to communicate easier with your target readership*. I now hope that all the thousands of eventual readers of *Judgement Impaired* will be able to enjoy a totally uninterrupted read, as I have tried very hard to avoid *gobbledegook*, *double Dutch* and *legal-speak* and to deal only in plain speaking throughout. If I'm totally wrong altogether about that, I guess it will be due to the fact that my own judgement was - and still is perhaps - impaired.

In conclusion, I have enough researched Law and Order media etc material left over to make an almost immediate start on *Judgement Impaired - Volume 2* - It's only fair to warn my readers too, at this early stage, that a secret admirer is already considering making me a quite substantial offer for *Judgement Impaired - The Movie* - but right now I'm keeping all my options open - and my size eleven-and-a-half flat feet firmly on the ground.

Throughout the book you will come across press cuttings of court reports concerning some of the cases I was involved in during my service as a Police Officer in the 60s and 70s which I hope will add to your enjoyment.

Do have a good read - and tell all of your friends that there is now real HOPE on the horizon, for a safer and, who knows? - a possible better world, with more opportunities for our safety - and plenty of 'BANGING-UP' time for our mutual enemies. Most right-thinking people in this country know that Michael Howard is right - PRISON WORKS! - The criminal can only harm himself inside jail - not US!

Mike Hughes March 2005

IN THE JURISDICTION OF THE VICTIMS OF CRIME AND LAW-ABIDING CITIZENS' CENTRAL COURT OF CRIMINAL INJUSTICE CONCERN IN THE UNITED KINGDOM

CASE NO :   THURS - 05 – 05 – 2005

IN THE MATTER OF THE PROLONGED FAILURE OF THE BRITISH LABOUR GOVERNMENT - UNDER THE RIGHT HON. MR TONY BLAIR, PRIME MINISTER - HIS HOME SECRETARY - HIS CABINET AND PARTY MEMBERS - TOGETHER WITH MOST MEMBERS OF THE SO-CALLED 'JUDICIAL POLITICALLY-ELITE' - ON DIVERS DATES BETWEEN 1997 AND 2005 - TO JOINTLY AND SEVERALLY DELIVER ITS GENERAL ELECTION PARTY MANIFESTOS OF 1997 AND 2001 - IN SO FAR AS CHIEFLY - THE MATTER OF LAW AND ORDER IS CONCERNED - AND SECONDLY - IN SOME OTHER AREAS ALSO CAUSING CONCERN.

PLAINTIFFS: ALL OF THOSE RIGHT-THINKING AND LAW-ABIDING MEMBERS OF THE BRITISH PUBLIC, AND THE COUNTLESS VICTIMS OF CRIME SINCE 1997.

FIRST DEFENDANTS: MR TONY BLAIR - PRIME MINISTER – HIS CABINET AND THOSE MEMBERS OF THE LIBERAL 'POLITICALLY-ELITE' JUDICIARY

SECOND DEFENDANT: MR DAVID BLUNKETT, MP - FORMER HOME SECRETARY

THIRD DEFENDANTS: ALL OF THOSE MEMBERS OF THE CRIMINAL FRATERNITY CURRENTLY CONSPIRING TO STEAL, COMMIT BURGLARY, DEAL IN DRUGS, OR OTHERWISE INTERFERE WITH THE RIGHT OF LAW-ABIDING, RIGHT-THINKING PEOPLE TO GO ABOUT THEIR DAILY BUSINESS WITHOUT FEAR OF HARASSMENT, MOLESTATION OR INJURY.

INDICTMENT

*THIS INDICTMENT AGAINST EACH
AND ALL OF YOU DEFENDANTS,
CONSISTS OF 24 COUNTS,
AS FOLLOWS:*

LEARNED CLERK'S TRIAL RECORD DOCUMENT

CASE NO: 5953/ 05

LEARNED COURT CLERK:

TRIAL JUDGE:

COUNSEL FOR PROSECUTION:

JUNIOR:

COUNSEL FOR DEFENCE:

JUNIOR:

STENOGRAPHER FIRM:

STENOGRAPHER NAME:

JURY BAILIFFS:

DOCK OFFICERS:

LIST DOCK OFFICERS VARIATIONS & DATES:

PLEAS ENTERED ON:

JURY SWORN ON:

JURY MEMBERS EXCLUDED ON OBJECTION:

JURY MEMBER(S) DISCHARGED ON:

1997 LABOUR PARTY GENERAL ELECTION MANIFESTO

We will be tough on crime and tough on the causes of crime

- **Fast-track punishment for persistent young offenders**
- **Reform Crown Prosecution Service to convict more criminals**
- **Police on the beat not pushing paper**
- **Crackdown on petty crimes and neighbourhood disorder**
- **Fresh parliamentary vote to ban all handguns**

Under the Conservatives, crime has doubled and many more criminals get away with their crimes: the number of people convicted has fallen by a third, with only one crime in 50 leading to a conviction. This is the worst record of any government since the Second World War - and for England and Wales the worst record of any major industrialised country. Last year alone violent crime rose 11 per cent.

We propose a new approach to law and order: *tough on crime and tough on the causes of crime*. We insist on individual responsibility for crime, and will attack the causes of crime by our measures to relieve social deprivation.

The police have our strong support. They are in the front line of the fight against crime and disorder. The Conservatives have broken their 1992 general election pledge to provide an extra 1,000 police officers. We will relieve the police of unnecessary bureaucratic burdens to get more officers back on the beat.

Youth crime

Youth crime and disorder have risen sharply, but very few young offenders end up in court, and when they do half are let off with another warning. Young offenders account for seven million crimes a year.

Far too often young criminals offend again and again while waiting months for a court hearing. We will halve the time it takes to get persistent young offenders from arrest to sentencing; replace widespread repeat cautions with a single final warning; bring together Youth Offender Teams in every area; and streamline the system of youth courts to make it far more effective.

New parental responsibility orders will make parents face up to their responsibility for their children's misbehaviour.

Conviction and sentencing

The job of the Crown Prosecution Service is to prosecute criminals effectively. There is strong evidence that the CPS is over-centralised, bureaucratic and inefficient, with cases too often dropped, delayed, or downgraded to lesser offences.

Labour will decentralise the CPS, with local crown prosecutors co-operating more effectively with local police forces.

We will implement an effective sentencing system for all the main offences to ensure greater consistency and stricter punishment for serious repeat offenders. The courts will have to spell out what each sentence really means in practice. The Court of Appeal will have a duty to lay down sentencing guidelines for all the main offences. The attorney general's power to appeal unduly lenient sentences will be extended.

We will pilot the use of compulsory drug testing and treatment orders for offenders to ensure that the link between drug addiction and crime is broken. This will be paid for by bringing remand delays down to the national targets.

We will attack the drug problem in prisons. In addition to random drug testing of all prisoners we will aim for a voluntary testing unit in every prison for prisoners ready to prove they are drug-free.

Victims

Victims of crime are too often neglected by the criminal justice system. We will ensure that victims are kept fully informed of the progress of their case, and why charges may have been downgraded or dropped.

Greater protection will be provided for victims in rape and serious sexual offence trials and for those subject to intimidation, including witnesses.

Prevention

We will place a new responsibility on local authorities to develop statutory partnerships to help prevent crime. Local councils will then be required to set targets for the reduction of crime and disorder in their area.

Gun control

In the wake of Dunblane and Hungerford, it is clear that only the strictest firearms laws can provide maximum safety. The Conservatives failed to offer the protection required. Labour led the call for an outright ban on all handguns in general civilian use.

There will be legislation to allow individual MP's a free vote for a complete ban on handguns.

Labour is the party of law and order
in Britain today

2001 LABOUR PARTY GENERAL ELECTION MANIFESTO

Ambitions for Britain

Fulfilling Britain's great potential
The Prime Minister sets out his vision
for Britain's future

Investment and reform
Key measures for public service reform

1 Prosperity for all
How we expand our economy and raise our living standards

2 World-class public services
How investment and reform will improve public services

3 A modern welfare state
How we help people into work and provide security for those who can't work

4 Strong and safe communities
How we tackle crime and renew our society

5 Britain strong in the world
How we make foreign policy work for Britain and the wider world

The choices for Britain
A lot done, a lot to do, and a lot to lose
25 steps to a better Britain

Our key steps for a second term

The contract delivered

How Labour has fulfilled its first-term promises
Five pledges for the next five years

Economic pledge
1 Mortgages as low as possible, low inflation and sound public finances. As we deliver economic stability not return the economy to Tory boom and bust

Schools pledge
2 10,000 extra teachers and higher standards in secondary schools As we invest in our schools not make reckless tax cuts

Health pledge
3 20,000 extra nurses and 10,000 extra doctors in a reformed NHS As we improve NHS care for all not push patients into paying for operations

Crime pledge
4 6,000 extra recruits to raise police numbers to their highest ever level as we tackle drugs and crime not cut police funding

Families pledge
5 Pensioners' winter fuel payment retained, minimum wage rising to £4.20 As we help hard-working families not the privileged few

Built on five achievements since 1997

- Typical mortgage £1,200 less than under the Tories, inflation lowest for '30 years'
- The best ever results in primary schools
- 17,000 extra nurses now in the NHS
- Crime down ten per cent
- One million more people in work and a new Children's Tax Credit

This manifesto contains the details of our plans for the future of Britain. If you would like to find out more about our policies, join the Labour Party or make a donation to Labour's election fund, please call 08705 900 200 or visit our website at www.labour.org.uk

Renewing public services: criminal justice reform

New Labour believes that crime can only be cut by dealing with the causes of crime as well as being tough on criminals.

We plan the most comprehensive reform of the criminal justice system since the war, to catch, convict, punish and rehabilitate more of the 100,000 persistent offenders. Our ten-year goal is a modernised criminal justice system with the burglary rate halved.

We will now:

- overhaul sentencing so that persistent offending results in more severe punishment.

- reform custodial sentences so that every offender gets punishment and rehabilitation designed to minimise reoffending.

- reform rules of evidence to simplify trials and bring the guilty to justice.

- introduce specialist, late-sitting and review courts to reflect crime patterns and properly monitor offenders.

- establish a new Criminal Assets Recovery Agency to seize assets of crime barons and a register of dealers to tackle drugs.

- introduce a victims' bill of rights providing legal rights to compensation, support and information.

Prime Minister Tony Blair

David Blunkett

"Bad men need nothing more to compass their ends
than that good men should look on and do nothing"

*(Attributed to John Stuart Mill on 1st February 1867,
during his inaugural address on being installed
as rector of St Andrews University, Scotland)*

COUNT 1

BURGLARY

Section 9, Theft Act 1968

*(1) A person is guilty of burglary if-
he enters any building or part of a building as a trespasser and with intent
to commit any such offence as is mentioned in subsection (2) below: or
having entered any building or part of a building as a trespasser he steals
or attempts to steal anything in the building or that part of it or inflicts or
attempts to inflict on any person therein any grievous bodily harm*

*(2) The offences referred to in subsection (1) (a) above are offences of
stealing anything in the building or part of a building in question, of
inflicting on any person therein any grievous bodily harm or raping any
woman therein, and of doing unlawful damage to the building or anything
therein.*

*A person guilty of burglary shall on conviction on indictment be liable to
imprisonment for a term not exceeding fourteen years.*

I consider that Burglary is the crime which affects most law-abiding citizens across the country on a daily basis. This is possibly because most burglars are *opportunists*, often driven by the urgent requirement for funding their drugs habit, by illegally taking possession of everyday valuable items such as personal computers, plasma screens, television sets, video recorders, cash & jewellery etc. Most of these items are easily converted into hard cash by their sale for a fraction of their true value, to dishonest shopkeepers, jewellers, second hand shop owners etc or by disposal, usually after dark, to friends, associates or even strangers in a public house. In fact anyone who has ever had the time to sit in the public gallery of courts across the land, will know that when a burglar elects for trial by jury at a Crown Court, or is committed to one for trial - by a Magistrates Court, the most frequently offered defence 'story' is that the item(s) were bought from an *unknown man in a pub*. In fact this 'defence tale' has become predictable but laughable. If you watch the faces of individuals seated in the jury box, they will smile when the defence counsel makes reference to this unidentified, unknown man from the pub – this tells me straight away that this is not the first time the person who smiled, has sat on a jury. It is only funny in the telling however – it is no joke in the serious business of criminal trials for the same old 'stranger in the pub' tale to be tossed into the pot of defence 'evidence' – That old chestnut tale has worn very thin and magistrates and judges show their displeasure when it comes up yet again. Tragically for many victims of burglaries, there is no such thing as a 'professional jury' and some ordinary members of the public who are called for Jury Service are very naïve.

They may lead very simple and ordinary lives in which their view of what happens in the world outside their home environment, is largely influenced by the goings-on in their favourite soap operas, such as 'East Enders', 'The Bill', 'Coronation Street' or 'Neighbours'. Therefore the situation regularly is encountered whereby jurors are by no means 'streetwise' and give *the benefit of the doubt* leading to acquittal for an offence of say, burglary, to a person who, unbeknown to them, has a list of criminal convictions for burglary and probably other offences too, 'as long as your arm'. On occasions, Crown Court Jurors show visible surprise, shock or horror when, after they have acquitted a person, they remain in Court whilst the Judge sentences the defendant for an offence to which he pleaded guilty prior to the Jury being sworn-in, and for which they were not required to try him, and then hear about possibly his many previous convictions for the same type of offence for which they have just acquitted him. There was a time when Jury men and women were required to be persons of substance, or at least own their own home, and often complaints are made about the youth, demeanour or conduct in court of a particular juror, who these days need only be aged a minimum of 18 years. It used to be claimed that Snaresbrook Crown Court in East London/Redbridge area, had the highest acquittal rate in the country. At the time, it was said that the reason for this was because Snaresbrook Crown Court's jury catchment area included a large area of docklands, in its original state prior to redevelopment, and being Inner City dwellers, a high proportion of selected Jurors would never find anyone guilty of any crime whatsoever. Indeed, before Jury Selection Rules were tightened up, some Jurors were *themselves* convicted criminals. No doubt the reader will have his or her own ideas about the truth of this. There was a time in the late 1970's, when I was a CID officer stationed at Ilford, Essex, where Crown Court cases could be dealt with at many venues. These included the Central Criminal Court (Old Bailey), many Crown Courts within the Greater London area and on occasions, even as far away as Chelmsford or Basildon in Essex.

I was once co-opted onto a Metropolitan Police crime squad based at Woodford Police Station. A uniform police inspector was in overall charge of the squad, which was made up entirely of uniform officers working in plain clothes, with CID assistance from myself. One of the officers had been employed for quite some time as what was then known as a 'home beat officer'. This normally meant that he lived on his 'patch' and spent most of his working days on it. This meant that he was a very visible presence in his police uniform and people who worked or lived on his 'ground' would pass the time of day with him, and even, if his luck was in on a good day, 'tell him stuff', in confidence of course! When he was seconded on to the Woodford Crime Squad, as it was then known, this gave him 'the edge', as he had been monitoring and passing on to the local police (intelligence) 'Collator', details of the movements of a small team of men who in his words, 'Had never done a day's work in their lives'. I'll just refer to this team as Brian, Harry and George, who lived on, or frequented Bob's 'patch'. Over the years, colleague Bob had accumulated a whole heap of intelligence about these men. It was therefore decided that the 'team' would be targeted by our Crime Squad. Brian and George were very, very professional burglars and to their great 'credit', so far as I can recall, violence towards any of their victims had never been reported. For this reason, once we started to uncover more and more facts about them, we actually developed a kind of healthy respect for them and their ice-cool nerve which had allowed them to 'live off the fat of the land' for far too long. Brian appreciated and enjoyed the finer things in life and actually drove around in either a Jensen Interceptor or Aston Martin DB5 sports car, my money is on the Jensen, which had a huge wrap-around rear window. We discovered that Brian appeared to have small fortunes secreted away in various Banks, under false names, of course. He had indulged his passion for flying and underwent the requisite number of lessons and tests to proudly earn his Private Pilot Licence (PPL).

Brian had an older brother called Harry, who ran a local business with a van, carrying out painting & decorating jobs, small building works and suchlike. Harry's line of business proved to be a considerable asset to Brian. We suspected that, being in the business of working in peoples' homes, Harry was well-placed for passing onto Brian details of any homes which Brian might wish to 'visit' when a suitable chance presented itself. The third member of the 'gang' was George, who seemed to have just been a long-term friend of Brian, or possibly an old school mate. Prior to our being given the task of targeting the team, we had long known that Brian and George very much enjoyed travelling around, visiting & enjoying the more rural parts of the country. They had been found together at all hours of the day or night, mainly the night, or in the early hours, dressed in trainers and track suits, jogging along keeping fit and breathing the fresh country air. It quickly came to the attention of various police forces in the Home Counties and even Regional Crime Squads, that Brian and George travelled great distances from their home areas, to indulge their need for the healthy activity of jogging. (Most people do this in their own home areas). Sometimes they were taken in for questioning but invariably released without charge quite quickly, as nothing could then be proved against them. However they often received special mention in police intelligence bulletins which were normally circulated inter-Force. Intelligence had been extracted from these bulletins and elsewhere and quite a bank of knowledge was either being carried around in my colleague Bob's head, within his notebook or at the Collator's office for the Police Division or Sub-Division in which he worked. Brian, almost all through his own efforts, had become one of life's winners, quite self-sufficient. However there was a void in his life as he had no steady female companion with whom to share the fruits of his labour. Until he found Rosemary.

We never found out how he found her, but she proved to be an absolute godsend to him, in fact, later on, he could hardly live without her. She was to prove very beneficial to Brian, as she was employed by one of the largest firms of insurance brokers in the country, possibly now defunct, which had its local, if not Head Office in the Gants Hill, Ilford area. Although she was employed as a policy renewal typist, her life too, was soon to change for the better, at least in the short term. We never did find out whose idea it was, but Rosemary decided that whilst typing out the insurance policy renewal notices, it would be of assistance to Brian if somehow she could acquaint him with her work. This could only be for the better and would lead to a better understanding of the daily stresses and strains of her being office-bound, and therefore a fuller and more meaningful relationship could develop. She obtained an extra sheet of carbon paper and before long, she was to find herself typing up an *extra* flimsy copy of each insurance policy renewal notice. Brian was interested to see the flimsy copies and marvelled at how items for contents insurance of high or special value and/or valuable possessions attracting higher annual premium surcharges, were neatly entered up on the documentation by Rosemary – with scarcely a single character of mis-typing. Sometimes, Brian was shrewd enough to observe that additional references were made on the renewal notices as to whether floor or wall safes were installed at the home, and the location of these, plus, what type of burglar alarm, if any, were installed! It must have been at this stage that Brian became aware of Rosemary's potential for remaining not just his girl friend, but a new and full member of his team as well!

As we now know, Brian put his Private Pilot's Licence to good use as often as possible. Naturally he was obliged to carry air navigational charts as part of his essential flying kit, under the terms of his PPL, The Civil Aviation Act, 1949 and The Civil Aviation (Licensing) Act 1960. Being ultra-cautious by nature, Brian got into the habit of also carrying in his flight bag, ordnance survey maps of whichever area of the country he decided to over-fly on a particular day, together with every pilot's aid to flight, his binoculars. He may have even carried a camera of some sort, so as to take shots of places of interest he flew over en route, but I cannot be sure of the latter after the passage of time. Places of interest, so far as Brian was concerned, would include Country Mansions, very old, isolated and sometimes listed buildings, Museums, that kind of property.

Naturally all of this took place in the Pre-Computer Age so Bob and I and the rest of the team members had to resort to creating our own Card Index System, kept in long boxes, of postcard-width dimensions, to create a log of Brian's teams' movements and sightings. These days, such a boring, monotonous job as writing out in long-hand a dated postcard containing positive and/or suspected sightings, country wide, of Brian, Harry, George and Rosemary, would be programmed into a computer database by a super-fast typist in next to no time, but we had no other choice. However the monotony of writing out details of the sightings of the team members under the headings of where, when, what time, place, which car, clothing worn, top-value premises burgled recently nearby, YES/NO, etc. soon paid off and made the task that much more exciting and fulfilling. And so the card index grew rapidly. Within a year or two we had Burglar Brian, George, brother Harry and girlfriend Rosemary , 'done up' like the proverbial 'kippers'.

The way they worked was like this. Hiding their means of transport at a respectable distance from the intended target property, probably inside a wood or copse, they would rummage around inside the grounds until a ladder was found. George and Brian would then brazenly reach up with the ladder and coolly smash the burglar alarm bell-box from its wall-mounting. Another way of preventing the bell from ringing was to squirt polystyrene-type foam, thick oil or even treacle or sawdust into the bell-box. All of these methods, of course, contained and trapped the internal bell-hammer so it could not strike the outer casing or vibrate against the internal bell-dome, thus arousing the occupants from their deep slumber. Brian and George would at first lie low to watch for lights coming on inside the property, and listen for the barking of dogs etc, until they were sure the coast was clear. They would then enter the dwelling by whichever means was found to be most appropriate or relevant at the time. You can rest assured that Brian ensured that he and George never forgot to wear gloves. This wasn't so much to protect them from the chilly night air but more because Brian had once read a book about a careful professional burglar forgetting to put on his gloves - and being tragically arrested after leaving one of his fingerprints behind. One thing which really excited the team was if they found items of *solid silver* which had been in the owners' family for centuries, handed down from generation to generation. They were not too fussed or particular as to what form or shape the solid silver heirlooms took. It mattered not to Brian and George, as they were in touch with a jeweller/market trader who was an expert at melting down the silver into unidentifiable form, so the items from the Family Heritage were gone for ever – totally unidentifiable in their reduced-to-scrap metal format. They were long-in-the-tooth enough not to hang onto their ill-gotten gains for long, nor to attempt to transport it too far or too soon. In fact it was their usual habit to bury the stolen goods in a hole in the grounds of the house, or in a nearby field. They were far-sighted enough to keep a metal-detector at Brian's home, or one of his homes. This was so that, after a respectable period of time had passed since the burglary, they could return to the scene and quickly identify the burial place and, usually under cover of darkness, retrieve the goods for onward transmission to the dishonest-handling jeweller. As stated earlier, Brian, and George would always wear their jogging kit for these outings, in an attempt to hoodwink the Police. However, unfortunately for the pair, some Police Officers take a whole lot of hoodwinking, or may just give the impression that they have been hoodwinked! Phone calls and telex messages would soon be generated, together with official pocket book entries duly dated, timed and signed. Believe it or not, Brian and George would on occasions have the audacity to supply false names and addresses to the Police!

One day, Brian and his brother Harry bought a Jaguar motor car from a man who lived not too close to them, in the Ilford area. They paid for the purchase of the car in cash, to the tune of £8,000 as I recall. It did not escape the attention of Brian and Harry, shrewd business men, that the vendor of the Jaguar car placed the £8,000 in cash in his briefcase before thanking them and seeing them safely off the premises, ensuring that he had handed over the vehicle logbook. Believe it or believe it not, that very same night Brian 'crept' into the vendor's home overnight and took back that huge amount of money, which was a small fortune at the time. By now you will appreciate that the two criminals were shrewd enough not to have arranged the appointment time to view the Jaguar car, until the Banks were well and truly closed, leaving the vendor 'high and dry,' with nowhere to securely lodge that huge amount of cash overnight. On another occasion, we believe that Brian alone, 'crept' into the home of the manager of a petrol filling station in the Ilford area, who lived some distance away from his workplace. Whilst the manager was deep in sleep with his wife in the bedroom, Brian boldly tiptoed in and 'borrowed' the keys to the filling station, from either the bedside table or the manager's trouser pockets. Brian was a 'creep' in more than one sense of the word! He returned to the garage, entered using the keys from the manager's bunch and opened up the floor safe behind the counter. The safes were provided so that as soon as the till content reached a pre-determined level, the assistant would place a roll of paper money and associated documentation into a cylindrical tube with a cap. (Similar tubes to those used in the old department stores, which linked the points of sale to the cashier's office via overhead tubular trunking, possibly vacuum-operated or by compressed air.) Even in those days, the plastic tubes containing the money were actually pre-drilled. Apparently this was to prevent a burglar achieving partial safe lid removal in the floor, from pouring water into the cavity to float the money containers to the floor level and beat a hasty retreat.

Having had a successful nights work thus far, Brian placed an electric drill beside the floor safe, having drilled through the safe 'door' and lock mechanism, to make it look as if a different 'MO' had been utilised to 'crack' the safe, thus hoping to fool both the proprietor and staff, as well as the Police. 'Bold-as Brass' Brian then returned swiftly to the manager's home and crept back into his bedroom, replacing the garage keys in the trousers pocket, or on the bedside table. Nerves of steel, had our Brian. On another occasion, Brian and Rosemary gave false identity particulars to the manager of the local (Ilford) branch of The Property Owner's Building Society. Through this criminal deception offence, they succeeded in purchasing a second property in the area, mortgaged to the Building Society. Rosemary was installed in this house. It became a place which provided some useful additional storage space for current and future ill-gotten gains, and the team's extensive burglary toolkit etc. What today we might refer to as a 'safe house'. Later, quite separately to all of the burglary charges which would soon be preferred, once our extensive mortgage fraud enquiries had been completed, Brian and Rosemary were jointly charged with the fraud offences. When questioned, I'm fairly sure that they both made full admissions of guilt to the mortgage fraud and this was most useful as it gave us a 'holding charge' with which to have at least Brian remanded in custody and taken off the streets in the interim, for the benefit of all home owners in the Home Counties! Brian also made a full admission about the mortgage deception to his solicitor and subsequently to his barrister ,who would represent him at the Crown Court trial or appearance, at which he had indicated that he would plead 'Guilty' all along. I recall that when the case was first called, we all had to travel all the way to Chelmsford Crown Court, Essex for the disposal of the case. Looking around the Court List beforehand we noticed that a certain Judge had been allocated to deal with Brian and Rosemary's case. I can even recall the name of the Judge, but suffice to say that as far as I am aware, he was the only Peer of the Realm who then sat as a Judge at Chelmsford Crown Court, formerly known as Essex Assizes, which was high enough to warrant a 'red' Judge (wears red robes, not purple) and was also used as an Essex Court of Quarter Sessions. When the case was called Brian entered the Court from the lower level custody area. Before the Court Clerk could put the counts of the indictment to Brian to note his pleas, Brian called over his barrister for a short huddle out of earshot to the rest of us. To our absolute amazement, Brian's barrister stood up and addressed the Judge. He explained in open Court, with apparent difficulty in getting his words out clearly, that he had become professionally embarrassed and sought His Lordship's permission to withdraw from the case, which was granted.

Afterwards we were disgruntled and very angry to learn what had actually transpired, so as to cause the defence barrister to require *release* from the case. Apparently, Brian had taken one look at the Judge, recognised him and *was personally 'embarrassed'* himself, as he feared the Judge had a reputation for *harsh* or *severe* sentencing. Therefore Brian, in a sudden fear of *extended* liberty deprivation, made a snap decision to 'play the system', changing his plea from 'GUILTY' to 'NOT GUILTY'. (Naturally his defence barrister had prepared his case and his speech for His Lordship, on the basis of a 'GUILTY' plea, leaving him with no other choice than to withdraw from the case!) In due course, the entire Woodford Crime Squad, plus lots of uniformed backup, borrowed from other police stations in the area, dog handlers etc, met up for the long-awaited Pre-Dawn Raid briefing. This included who would be going to which of the several addresses for which search warrants had been obtained and which radio call signs had been allocated to which of the search teams. Additionally, maps of the expected scenarios, indicating front and rear access points, barking dogs likely to give advance warning of our approach, together with photographs of each of the Main Players in the criminal gang, were issued. This happy day for us was to become the culmination of approx 2 years of really hard, mostly boring work, undertaken mainly indoors away from fresh air, as we patiently collated all of the intelligence, of which there was reams – therefore adrenalin levels were unusually high. Thanks to all of the material contained within our precious card index system, each card having been meticulously filed in precise date order, bearing its precious bits of vital information as to the movements or location or sightings of each of the gang members, the actual post-arrest interrogations would be an absolute 'doddle'. This was because we were in the very strong position of having exact details of their movements over a long period of time, at, or close to the scenes of most of their burglary offences, virtually Home Counties-wide. The whole Police case presented an unassailable, comprehensive record of their recent criminal activities, on a large scale over time. We had so much evidence against them that it mattered not whether they remained silent or answered 'no comment' to every one of our questions. It turned out to be an exciting and wonderful day for all concerned, but a dreadful day for Brian and Co.! Police vans scuttled backwards and forwards carrying huge loads of stolen property, including oddments of top quality furniture, family heirlooms etc. Overall we recovered from the several addresses used by the burglars, mainly frequented by Brian, George, Rosemary and his brother, the following amazing collection of housebreaking implements and associated accessories:

US style doctor's hands-free headband battery light.

Several flattish tobacco-type tins containing soap and/or wax with integral key impressions.

A real sniper's telescopic sight with laser 'red spot' facility ensuring positive 'hits' every shot.

A crossbow and several crossbow bolts (A very lethal weapon indeed!)

All shapes and sizes of torches.

Various masks, balaclavas, woolly hats, dark glasses, gloves of all kinds & sizes etc.

Large cash sums.

Multi-Bank statements of accounts opened in false identities, for concealing proceeds of crimes from Police.

False documents for various motor vehicles.

Brian's Private Pilot's Licence, flight case, binoculars etc.

Several picklocks and skeleton key sets or bunches.

Huge assortment of large and small house breaking tools, such as jemmies and case openers.

Brace and bits and tins of multi-size drill bits.

Cameras.

In fact the largest collection of burglary tools that most of us had ever seen. Additionally we recovered so many items of property stolen during the team's many burglaries that we were obliged to hold a Crimewatch-style 'Aladdin's Cave' display over a whole weekend, for burglary victims to attend and identify all kinds of property stolen from their homes. This exercise generated a whole host of previously unknown burglary victims, opening up a whole new world of additional charges for the burglary team to account for, or to have them 'TIC' (Taken into consideration) at later Court appearances. You will recall that whilst describing to you the kind of burglaries which Brian and Co. specialised in, I was careful to mention that as far as I can recall, violence was never shown to, or used against any person. In fact they were careful enough to take all precautions possible to avoid coming in contact with people at all. The only exception to this 'avoid contact' rule of Brian's was when he stole the petrol station keys from the manager's bedroom, used them for his unlawful purposes and then had the gall and sheer presence of mind to replace them in the sleeping manager's bedroom! You will appreciate that Brian committed separate offences of burglary that night, at both the petrol station and at the manager's house. The end result, justifying all of our boring, laborious efforts, was that the whole team went to jail. Brian personally received 12 years imprisonment. This included the jeweller/market trader who had received, or as it is now known, dishonestly handled all of the stolen jewellery and solid silver items etc.

Let's just consider some of the possible traumas experienced and involved in a typical house burglary, for a minute or two:

You arrive home and your heart stops. You can't get your key to turn the front door lock because burglars have put the catch of the lock down, to stop you taking them by surprise before they are ready to leave with as many of your valuables as possible. You go round the back and find broken glass everywhere, inside and out, they've smashed their way in (Sometimes they'll scrape the putty out and remove the glass intact to avoid noise). You don't know whether they're still inside your home or have already fled with your property. Your heart is beating '19 to the dozen'. Plucking up the courage to go inside, perhaps, you try to call the Police but they've cut the telephone wires, or just ripped them out of the walls. There's a dreadful smell in the house that you left immaculate and fresh when you went out. You track down the smell and to your horror, you find someone has defecated on your carpet (some burglars do this for spite, others because they have been under such stress from being where they shouldn't – and the fear of sudden discovery – that they lose control of bodily functions). You find your settee seat and back cushions all slashed and in tatters as they frantically searched for cash and valuables etc. There is broken glass all over the floor and possibly blood from where they cut themselves on entry (possibility of identifying them here, as blood will lead to a DNA identification in most cases, these days). Not finding as much property as they had hoped, they have smashed all your family photographs and frames from the sideboard; in sheer spite. In the kitchen, they've gone into the larder, pantry or cupboards and thrown everything around, looking for cash hidden in empty jars, biscuit tins etc. Every kitchen drawer is upended onto the floor, ketchup, mayonnaise, eggs etc may have been squirted or thrown around. You may even slip over and hurt yourself unless you're very careful. All up the stairs and on the landing etc are mucky footprints where they've tramped the muck from the kitchen floor around. If they didn't find as much 'loot' as they had hoped, they may have put the plugs in and left your sink and/or bath taps running to overflow situation. You can bet your life they've had every carpet up and moved every picture or wall mirror, looking for floor and wall safes.

You're desperate to call Police or your loved ones for help on your mobile telephone, but by now you are shaking so much from shock, fear and apprehension, you can't manage to press the right keys. Your heart sinks. You wonder if you'll ever feel safe enough to close your eyes to sleep again at night. How on earth can you ever get your beautiful home back to how it was before this outrageous invasion of your privacy, which has already destroyed your peace of mind forever? If you are a woman, you head for your bedroom and find all of your not-so-expensive jewellery thrown around. Your underwear drawers are emptied out on the bed, some of your finer pieces may have been taken as trophies to 'show the lads'. All your best jewellery, it's safe to say, you will never see again, some of this will have been in your family for 'donkeys years' and of such sentimental value and irreplaceable. You won't even miss some items for days or even weeks or months. Your fragrances, hand and moisturising creams are squirted everywhere, beds totally in tatters where they've slashed your pillows and bedding and mattress, looking for your life savings in cash, they had hoped. Some pillow cases will be missing – used as a quick-use tote bag to cart your possessions away. In the old days, the Police would have been able to have sent someone round to make sure the burglars aren't hiding in the loft and to prepare a list of all the damage, value of stolen property, descriptions of it etc.,and questioned you as to whether it could have been someone you know or once knew. However that's all gone forever, apparently. If you call in the Police Station tomorrow though, you can have a *Police reference number* to enter up on your burglary insurance claim form! You go to the garage to fetch the vacuum cleaner. The garage is empty, the car has gone, you left the car keys on the hook in the hall. Your husband catches the train or bus to work. When you try to phone him at work, you're put on the Call Centre carousel menu and lose precious time trying to press the right option number to speak to a human being. (You would give anything at this stage to have Lords Woolf, Irvine and Faulkener, Tony Blair or David Blunkett walk in and see the state of the place!) Absolute nightmares – all too frequent occurrences these days. If you're cynical, you'll be wondering what sort of security situations Lord Chancellors and Lord Chief Justices have at home - Razor wire, 10feet high walls, electronic gates, movement detectors, armed Police, Panic Buttons, guard dogs, direct-to-nearest-Police Station alarms, PIR searchlights etc.

Two Appeal Court judges have been accused of "delivering a slap in the face to victims of crime" after letting a disgraced antiques dealer escape from justice without paying a penny of his fine for handling stolen goods. Lawrence Perovetz had tried to make thousands of pounds selling heirlooms worth a total of £130,000 after they were stolen from the Earl of Chichester and another family, by a gang of professional burglars. Perovetz's original trial judge decided to be lenient, after hearing that his wife was suffering

from cancer and that he may have committed the offences to help pay for her treatment in America! He walked free from Salisbury Crown Court in March 2003 with an 18-month *suspended* jail sentence, a £4,000 costs order against him and a £25,000 fine. Mr Justice Fulford and Mr Justice Aikens, however, have decided that this was not lenient enough. After hearing in

Mr Justice Fulford   Mr Justice Aikens

May 2004 that Perovetz had no money, and that his previous good reputation had been *ruined*, they quashed his fine completely. The verdict has stunned the Earl of Chichester. He said, "He's better off than you or I if we overstayed on a parking meter or drove at 35mph in a 30mph zone. They could have reduced the fine to, say, the £40 we pay for overstaying on a parking meter. Instead, they quashed it completely, and the man walks away totally free with no punishment. What a grievous insult to the thousands of cancer victims and their families who struggle and suffer to stay honest. What a slap in the face to the victims of crime and the police. The police see days and weeks of effort in the fight against crime go for nothing. How deeply depressing for the victims of burglaries. They often don't report break-ins because they think nobody will be caught. Then they see that when the police do manage to catch someone for a related crime, some half-witted judges decide to let them off. I sincerely hope that they retire."

Lord Chichester lost antiques worth about £1million, most of them collected by his grandfather in the 1900's, when the thieves broke into his home at Little Durnford Manor on Salisbury Plain, Wiltshire, in June 2002. The raiders tore down a curtain and used it to carry away heirlooms including rare Meissen porcelain figurines, vases and bowls, two clocks and 27 18th century gold snuffboxes. Perovetz, a 53-year-old Briton who had been living in Florida, was arrested on a business trip to England in July 2002, after selling four of the snuffboxes, worth a total of £80,000, and a silver peacock and silver ladle stolen during another burglary in Witney, Oxfordshire. The antiques trade had been warned to look out for the missing items, and a dealer who bought from Perovetz in good faith, contacted the police when he realised that they had been stolen. Perovetz denied the offences but was convicted of two counts of handling stolen goods by a jury at Salisbury Crown Court. He received Legal Aid throughout the five-day trial and his subsequent appeal. The antiques, later valued at £130,000, were the only items recovered from the burglaries, leaving stolen property worth £1.87million still missing. Wiltshire police had to spend nearly a year disproving Perovetz's lies about acquiring the antiques from an American vendor. They used telephone and computer analysis and liaised with the Special Branch to prove that his story was a fabrication. One Wiltshire officer said that he could not be openly critical of judges. "A lot of hard work went into that man. We have the greatest sympathy for his wife and accept that he no longer has a good reputation. It's just disappointing that he does appear to have had the biggest part of his punishment removed."

Perovetz worked in the family firm H. Perovetz, a central London silver dealership until the company was dissolved in 1995. Shortly after he moved with his family from north London to Florida, to secure the best treatment for his wife, who had breast cancer and had been told that she had 18 months to live. He was unavailable for comment but his solicitor said: "I appreciate that people lost property but he spent nine months awaiting trial on stringent bail, unable to leave the country, unable to see his wife who was undergoing gruelling chemotherapy and radiation treatment. He has been subjected to a suspended term of imprisonment, which is a punishment. He has not escaped justice; he has not got away scot-free." Asked whether he felt remorse for his crimes, she said: "I don't think I can answer that question. He still maintains that he is innocent. He is currently in the US caring for his wife, who sadly has a very short time to live." Norman Brennan, the director of the Victims of Crime Trust, said: "I despair of Appeal Court judges. They should get their acts together and ensure that those who cause devastation to the law-abiding public by their criminal behaviour, are told in no uncertain terms that they will not be tolerated." When contacted by the *Sunday Telegraph*, Mr Justice Aikens, 55, said: "I cannot possibly make any comment on particular cases." Mr Justice Fulford, 51, was unavailable for comment.

In sharp contrast to the way Brian, George and team conducted themselves, I should inform you about the criminal conduct of a man named Mark Patterson aged 42 years, a drug addict. Apparently, presumably some time in 2003, Patterson is reported in the national press as having armed himself with a meat cleaver in order to burgle the house of a neighbour. By virtue of his possession of the meat cleaver, Patterson had upgraded the seriousness of his actions from 'bog standard' burglary, serious enough in itself – to AGGRAVATED BURGLARY, which carries more severe penalties, viz: life imprisonment. This case was only finalised at Court this year, 2004 and was very widely publicised at the time. The Judge could have sentenced him to Life Imprisonment for this, particularly as Patterson had 58 previous convictions! However his barrister must have made out a really good case to the Judge, for imposing a non-custodial sentence on this occasion. You can just imagine the public outcry and utter despair experienced by the victim of the meat cleaver burglary, when Judge Israel Goldstein merely ordered Patterson to seek drugs rehabilitation treatment. Reportedly His Honour had been swayed by hearing that the defendant had 'FOUND SALVATION IN POETRY!

Needless to say, Patterson was back at the Crown Court 4 months later. He had been recalled after failing to take what was described in Court as his 'golden opportunity.' He had failed to turn up for a drugs treatment course. It was also revealed in Court that the day before this latest Court appearance, he had been arrested on suspicion of robbery – a charge later dropped after a witness withdrew. This time, a different Judge jailed Patterson for three and a half years. At this stage, perhaps we should not be too hard in condemnation of the original Judge Israel Goldstein, as the sentence he imposed on Patterson followed new **guidelines** issued by the Lord Chief Justice of England and Wales, Lord Woolf. He had advised Judges to make greater use of community sentences, viz: non-custodial sentences. Later on I will advise you in some detail of LCJ Woolf's guidance, in which he was fully supported by the former Lord Chancellor, Lord Irvine, in creating what was to become known as "THE BURGLARS' CHARTER." This was destined to become controversial nationwide and was to spell the end of peace of mind for thousands of home dwellers.

The next burglary case review had an absolutely appalling headline on an **inside** page of the *Daily Express* newspaper dated 4th February 2004. Readers might well wonder why it was not banner-headlined on the **front page**.

Dad's throat slashed by intruder in his garage
Horror as family sleep upstairs

The tragic victim of this horrendous burglary, which soon ended in murder, was a wealthy property developer aged 57 years, whose detached family home was in Ormskirk, Lancashire. (Coincidentally, about 8 years ago my Ford Granada motor car, fitted with an alarm, which I had owned for hardly 1 month, was stolen from a hotel car park near Preston in broad daylight. It had only been parked there for 1 hour approx. It was quickly found by Police, dumped at Ormskirk, minus all 4 doors, stereo, the entire boot contents and was written off at once by the insurance company. At the time it was the best car I had ever had. When my wife saw its condition after recovery, she was soon in tears.) Apparently the victim returned home from a night out at his golf club and disturbed the intruder. He was found lying in a pool of blood in his garage, having been bludgeoned with a blunt instrument and had his neck repeatedly slashed. The assailant escaped from the scene in the deceased's BMW motor car. At the time, the victim's wife and daughter were upstairs asleep in bed. His wife slept on until 5.30am and then dialled 999 to report her husband missing. However at 10am that morning, her sister decided to check the garage and it was then she was confronted by the dreadful scene. The actual murderous attack is thought to have occurred around midnight. This vicious attack took place just weeks after a report revealed that the number of house burglaries committed by ARMED AND VIOLENT criminals, **had soared by 75% over the last decade.**

To give you an idea of the true picture, reportedly in the year of 1991 almost 1,980 such violent burglaries were recorded across England and Wales. By 2002 this figure had increased to 3,475. (These figures are extracted from Home Office official statistics) Many readers will no doubt be thinking, "Where's it going to end?"

Take a look at this table, representing the criminal actions of just one man:

Avon and Somerset	274 burglaries
Devon and Cornwall	80 burglaries
Dorset	80 burglaries
Wiltshire	7 burglaries
Grand total since 1999	**441 burglaries**

(This means there were at least 441 victims)

The above grid shows the appalling record of house burglaries by a serial burglar who carried out all of the above offences, he claims, to finance his lavish lifestyle, and what is described as his 'gigantic' cocaine and brandy habit. He lives in Bridgewater, Somerset and I hope that's nowhere near you. His name is John Bale, aged 40 years and he claims to have 13 children! He had been on the run for some time but was eventually recognised whilst he was at a *Holiday Inn Express* at Taunton, Somerset. When a CID officer tried to arrest him for the burglaries, he threw a decanter at him! However there was no mention of a further charge of assault with intent to resist arrest, or even one of assault on police. (The missile doesn't actually have to come in contact with the intended victim for it to be an assault) You may think this man is a particular form of 'low life', as he preys on the homes of elderly people while they are out. His shocking record goes right back to 1978, so you can imagine how skilled he has become at his chosen 'craft'. When first arrested for this awful catalogue of house burglaries, after being recognised by Detective Constable Darren Lipscomb, Bale initially denied all charges. However he was then presented with DNA evidence (of which more later) and decided to lead Police Officers around his former 'hunting grounds', recalling what he stole and where, as far as possible. One old lady lost a diamond ring left to her by her mother. Since he has been in custody, burglary figures have dropped significantly in the areas in which he used to operate. Naturally he caused great distress to his victims over this long period, especially so, given their ages, frailty and vulnerability. This case clearly illustrates, you might think, how 'hit and miss' some parts of the Criminal Justice System are, and on the whole unfair to victims. Just taking the case of John Bale alone, can you imagine a scenario where all or most of the 400 odd elderly victims are packed tightly as sardines into the Courtroom at Taunton Crown Court, hoping perhaps for some compensation or restitution to be awarded to them? Also wondering, perhaps, if they would be allowed to address the Judge for a minute or two, to explain the awful effects this man's dreadful behaviour had upon them personally? You can see that this would be totally impossible to administer and the Courtroom is probably far too small to contain them all anyway. Can there be any fairness or actual justice within the Legal System for people like these innocent Senior Citizens, most of whom would have been too weak and frail to resist if they had caught Bale red handed? You might wish to reflect on that important point. When he was brought up before the Judge, Bale admitted just one count of dishonest handling of stolen goods, (The old offence of 'receiving' under The Larceny Act 1916), and 4 counts of burglary, that's all. (They are normally referred to as 'specimen charges', you may well consider that Police charge sheets in the Taunton area should be considerably increased in size, to allow for more than just 5 charges to be written down or typed up)

However Bale asked for a further 325 house burglaries to be TIC, which I've already explained. In Court, Prosecuting Counsel Sean Braunton is reported as informing the Judge that, "These offences caused great distress to the victims." Defence Counsel Patrick Mason said, "This is a man who has only spent 6 Christmases in the outside world. (Pass the tissue box please!) but underneath all of that is an intelligent and caring individual. He could have made a great deal of his life." Members of the 'Jury', you might well put a different interpretation of the words 'intelligent' and 'caring', if one of your loved ones had been one of this man's victims, wouldn't you? As time goes by in life, if you are aware of what's happening around you, or you sit in on Crown Court cases in the public gallery, there is a chance that you may not believe what you are hearing from Defence Counsels' and Solicitors' mouths. Why don't you try it some time? You may well be fooled into thinking you are at the theatre watching a **farce**. In the event, Bale was jailed for 5 years, so that's him off the streets for two and a half years, or less, unless he decides to appeal against the severity of the sentence, which he is fully entitled to do, of course – Almost certainly whilst Legally Aided!

In July 2002, the home at Virginia Water, Surrey of veteran celebrity entertainer Bruce Forsyth was burgled. A team of 3 men used violence on Mr Forsyth's live-in housekeeper, Cora Gumarang, aged 48 years. Although she is so short that she hardly comes up to Bruce's shoulder, she was repeatedly, viciously and brutally punched around the face by one of the attackers to facilitate the speed of the burglary, and to make her keep quiet. She has had to undergo, probably painful - reconstructive facial surgery. Bruce himself was away on holiday at the time but his wife and son were all asleep upstairs when the unlawful entry was made. However they apparently woke up after hearing all of the commotion. The gang fled with thousands of pounds worth of jewellery, including Mr Forsyth's wife's wedding ring and diamond engagement ring. By using the awful violence on his housekeeper, the team of burglars aggravated their frightening crime and upgraded it to the offence of robbery, which is far more serious.

By far the most high-profile case of burglary in recent years was that on the secluded and partially derelict farmhouse owned by farmer Mr Tony Martin, in East Anglia. The case has been so well documented, almost world-wide it seems. An apparently terrified Mr Martin, unlawfully in possession of a shotgun, fired at or near 3 burglars inside his house and possibly heading towards him. One of them, a 16 year old boy called Fred Barras was killed. Another burglar named Fearon, with a criminal record 'as long as your arm' was wounded in a leg. Presumably the 3rd team member decided to make himself scarce. There was an immediate public outcry when Mr Martin was arrested and indicted for the murder of the youngest burglar. Apparently to the utmost amazement of most people, Mr Martin was **convicted** of the murder and there being no other penalty available under the law, he was sentenced to Life Imprisonment. When many people heard about the verdict and sentence on the news or in the papers they could hardly believe their eyes and ears. It was claimed that relatives of the dead boy, members of the travelling fraternity, had sat in the public gallery of the court, staring intimidatingly at the members of the jury during the trial. A very longstanding principle had been overturned at a stroke by the jury's decision to convict for murder, as it had been open to them to convict Mr Martin of the lesser crime of manslaughter. This principle, which had been held up as strong and appropriate and undeniable, was 'an Englishman's home is his castle.' I recall a fairly similar case which happened literally years ago. A retired Royal Naval officer kept his old naval sword in the room not too far from his front door. One day, some sort of intruder entered and refused to give way or back off, whereupon the occupier 'ran him through' with the sword, killing him outright if my memory serves me well.

As far as I recall, the swordsman was either tried for murder and acquitted, or never tried at all, probably because it was considered he was acting in self defence. There have also been similar cases where no action was taken or a verdict of 'not guilty' delivered. Sitting in his cell at Bullingdon Prison, near Bicester, Oxon, Mr Martin was swamped with letters of support and the public outcry lingered on for a long time. Eventually, possibly bowing to public pressure, I recall the Lord Chief Justice headed up an appeal at the Court of Criminal Appeal in London and Mr Martin's murder conviction was set aside and one for manslaughter was substituted. Instead of the Life Imprisonment sentence, he received a sentence of 5 years imprisonment and after approx 3 years, was recently released. (Early in 2004) Further public outcry was initiated when he was at first refused release on parole, as his probation officer or a parole panel, decreed that he was 'not remorseful enough'. He may also have indicated that he would take the same course of action again, if necessary. Who could blame him for having that kind of mind-set? Had his firearm been properly licensed, the outcome might have been totally different. Due to the fact that most people around the country have followed the case with such interest, as well as it having been so well documented, I will make no more mention of it at this stage.

In a *Times* article, there was a report of a very fast-acting householder who disturbed a burglar, photographing him with a digital camera as he broke in through a glass door. As the burglar ran away from the burglary, at Topsham near Exeter, the home owner quickly e-mailed the 2 shots of him he had taken, to Police, who identified and arrested him within minutes of the break-in! The burglar, David Leaman, aged 43 years, then had 43 previous convictions and had been jailed 12 times before. Fortunately for the victims, you may be pleased to hear, this happened in April 2001, so Leaman was jailed for 3 years. You may not have overlooked the fact that Leaman's record of convictions matches the number of years in his life! However cynical readers will no doubt be thinking, "Oh yes, but what about all of the other burglaries etc. for which he was never caught, or never owned up to at each arrest?"

In March 2004 at a house in Hythe, Hampshire, the home of regular foster parents was ransacked by a youth of 17 years named Andrew Williams. The owners had given Williams the run of their home whilst he stayed with them temporarily, as they had done to approximately 100 other young people over the years, as temporary foster parents. They had even given him spending money and allowed his girlfriend to stay in their home. Apparently whilst armed with an air gun, he led a hooded gang in a raid on their home, after deactivating the burglar alarm, a skill he had acquired on a Duke of Edinburgh Award Scheme weekend! The gang of 4 were all locked up by Southampton Magistrates, Williams being sent down for 18 months. What a way to repay such a caring couple who had treated him as if he were one of their family!

At Prestbury, Glos, in early May 2004, former builder Ray Safe, 84, collapsed with a suspected heart attack after thugs slit the throats of nine of his beloved racing pigeons. Mr Safe, who keeps a total of 200 pigeons in his garage, also had his car stolen during the burglary. A friend who asked not to be named said, "I went round to his house to make sure he was OK. He's a bit deaf and only found out what had happened when his dog started barking. We went into his garage and there was blood all over the place.

It was just so cruel." Mr Safe's stolen car was later recovered after a police chase and two youths aged 17 and 20 have been charged with burglary offences, as Mr Safe recovered at home.

A brave 75-year-old pensioner, Joan Rice, from Poole, Dorset was disturbed by a burglar in her flat during the early hours one morning. She bravely got up to find out what was going on, arming herself with a metal tea tray before entering her spare room. There she encountered the burglar wearing gloves and a balaclava helmet. Mrs Rice crept up behind him and hit him over the head with her tea tray. While he staggered around in a daze, she then battered him 5 more times about the head and body. Caught off-guard by the unexpected onslaught, the burglar then pushed her to one side to flee the flat. He had earlier stolen a ladder from a building site to climb up into her flat through an open window. Prosecuting counsel at Bournemouth Crown Court read to the judge a Crime Impact Statement from the plucky OAP. In it she said, "I can still feel his gloves on my face when he pushed me back. I feel I was victimised because of my age." A statement from Mrs Rice's GP was also read to the court. He said, "She was shocked, agitated and angry. She suffered bruising to both arms and her right shoulder." Mrs Rice had caught serial burglar Cavin Engel, 58, rifling through her possessions. He had at least eight previous convictions for similar offences. Although Engel must have thanked his lucky stars at the time, after escaping from the flat, police had great pleasure in feeling his collar at a later date, after DNA from his blood on the metal tray due to the cut head, was traced back to him. Paul Hester, defending Engel, who pleaded guilty, told the judge that, despite his previous convictions, Engel was a "vulnerable" man and was facing having his home repossessed. Judge John Harrow told Engel, " This must have been a terrifying experience and she is still affected by what happened." Engel was sentenced to 4-years imprisonment.

Teenaged lottery-winner Callie Rogers, 17, was distraught to learn that her mother had been attacked by a knife man in her home at Workington, Cumbria, which Callie had bought her from her lottery winnings. Her mother had been knifed on the hands – defensive wounds – during a fight with a burglar and was rushed to hospital. Armed police and paramedics had been called to the scene and police later raided a house nearby and arrested Paul Dryden, 35, in connection with the stabbing. He was due to appear at West Allerdale Magistrates Court on a holding charge of grievous bodily harm.

Police were quickly on the trail of burglar Kevin Skelly, 27, of Manchester. They simply followed a trail of footprints he left in the frost after leaving his victim's flat and returning to his nearby home. Officers discovered a haul of valuables, including watches and jewellery in his bedroom and loft. He admitted three burglaries and dishonestly handling stolen goods. It was the third time that Skelly had been convicted of burglary. At Manchester's Minshull Street Crown Court he was jailed for five and a half years.

In May 2004, soccer legend Jack Charlton fell victim to a couple who stole a key to sneak into his hotel room during the night whilst he was asleep. He awoke to find £150 in cash was missing but his credit cards were still in his wallet. Jack, also a former Ireland football team manager said, "It is a very uncomfortable feeling to know that someone has been creeping around your bed in the middle of the night. I'm only glad I was on my own." He was staying at the Village Hotel in Hearsall, Coventry, after speaking at the Unipart Football Club annual dinner in nearby Tile Hill.

Jack said that staff played back for him a hotel security video showing a man taking his key from reception, then another showing the couple entering his room. Police have arrested a man and a woman and were questioning them. The hotel said they were not its employees.

Fed-up Steven Lowe, 33, a chef and his wife Zhoe, of Halton Moor, Leeds, have installed 41 locks at their home after a spate of break-ins. They have 5 locks on some windows – as well as metal grilles on the front and back doors and some other windows, and 80 feet of barbed wire around their garden. It takes him 20 minutes to lock up at night. Stephen said, "It feels like a jail. When we watch *Bad Girls* or *Prisoner Cell block H*, we know how it feels. But at least we feel a bit more safe. We shouldn't have to keep doing this, to look after our home, but it's the only way." They spent around £1,000 turning their council semi into a mini-Fort Knox after four daylight breakings in 3 months. Even an exterior security light and sensor have been stolen. Son Zach, 8, had his bedroom trashed and his PlayStation and VCR stolen. Stephen said, "It's really upset me, but more so Zhoe and Zach, who now hides his toys for fear he'll have them stolen again. My son has told me he hates me for bringing him here. We're living in a fortress and don't know how much more we can take. It's no way to live and we want out."

Whilst I was working on CID at Ilford Police Station, there came a time when a uniformed police officer approached us in the CID office, in confidence and 'marked our card' as to the suspicious behaviour, every tour of night shifts, of one of his colleagues. This particular officer drew attention to himself by always wearing his black leather police issue gloves, on night duty, regardless of the weather. Furthermore, where possible, he seemed to favour being out on the streets, in a police car, patrolling **on his own**, rather than being doubled-up with a uniformed colleague. Another strange habit he had developed was not to return to the police station to take his refreshments break, halfway through the shift, as did his colleagues, on a staggered rota. Our informant, the uniformed colleague, together with most if not all of the rest of their 'relief', (team of officers who nearly always worked together, following the earlies, lates and night duty shift patterns), had spent quite some time recently, attending burglaries at local petrol stations, other than all-night opening ones. Normally just cash or some chocolate bars etc had been stolen. In the CID office we had of course noticed this recent trend of overnight petrol station burglaries, as of course we were detailed to investigate some of them, and had been plotting them on a map, as well as the house burglaries. Well to cut a long story short, as a result of the valuable piece of intelligence supplied to us by our trusted uniformed colleague, whenever the suspect's 'relief' was on night duty, we started 'staking-out' petrol stations, by two officers hiding-up inside the darkened premises. Every officer 'in the know' was aware that it was just a matter of time before 'the trap was sprung'. Sure enough, within a week or less of the surveillance operation being set up, the 'bent' PC was caught red-handed, having broken into one of the petrol stations on our 'manor.' As he shone his torch around to get his bearings, he must have had, deservedly, a terrible shock when the torch beam fell on the two waiting officers. Although I was not personally present on the night he was captured, I will remember his opening sentence when he must have realised the game was up. He was reported to have said, "Well you know who I am, but who the devil are you?" One of the CID officers replied, "I'm Detective Sergeant so-and-so and you're now being arrested for burglary." He later pleaded guilty to this burglary and I think several others, claiming he had committed the crimes because he and his wife were in trouble with their financial affairs. As you can imagine, the Crown Court Judge made an example of him, because of his trusted position as a police officer. I recall he received approximately 18 months imprisonment (immediate as opposed to having part of the term suspended) You can just imagine the contempt which he must have been shown, both by Prison Officers and by other inmates of the jail! Everybody working at the Police Station, both uniformed and CID staff, were extremely pleased to be able to put that nasty series of incidents behind them. Naturally, from the date of his arrest, the crime clear- up figures improved.

Retired Army Major Timothy Clarke was so tormented by the fear of being burgled that he committed suicide, an inquest heard. The former soldier, hailed as a loyal husband and devoted father, grabbed a double-barrelled shotgun, strode into a nearby field and shot himself. Major Clarke, 46, was plagued by thoughts of intruders after thieves raided his country home. In the end, his paranoia spiralled so far out of control that he could bear it no longer. Major Clarke, a caring father of two, had left a note for his wife Jean at their home in Chedworth, Gloucesershire. The tragedy was described at the Cirencester hearing where Mrs Clarke, 42, paid tribute to her husband and father of their sons Sebastian, 10 and Freddie, 8. She said, "I believe that his illness was sudden – something snapped inside him. He was tormented by concerns that the premises would be burgled. He was a special person who was very loyal, had great vision and a wicked sense of humour and who was meticulous in the way he organised his life and his work. We had lots of fun and laughter." James Clarke, the Major's uncle, said: "Tim avoided parties and became increasingly paranoid about security. He had recently been on holiday and had talked of suicide. His wife became concerned. He was a true gentleman with strong principles and enormous physical courage. If he hadn't gone into the Army he could have been an actor as he had a fantastic memory and could mime people wonderfully." A report by a pathologist into Major Clarke's death revealed there were no traces of either drugs or alcohol in his body. Cotswold Assistant Coroner Sally Scanlon told the grieving family: "I conclude that Mr Clarke took his own life. This was a great personal tragedy for all of you." A verdict of suicide was recorded. Major Clarke was born into a military family. He went to the Royal Military Academy, Sandhurst and joined the Gloucestershire Regiment, serving in Germany, Cyprus and Northern Ireland and Kenya, before marrying in 1986. His final posting was at Catterick, N.Yorkshire, after which he retired to take over the family home at Chedworth. He maintained his military links by joining the Territorial Army and commanding the Cirencester Squadron of the Royal Gloucester-shire Hussars. But his rural idyll was shattered after their Cotswold home was burgled.

Britain's most prolific burglar was behind bars after looting hundreds of homes and stealing property worth an astonishing £1.25 million. Dean Ward, 27, left a trail of destruction during a two-and-a-half year crime spree to fund his heroin addiction. After pleading guilty to one charge of burglary and one of aggravated burglary, he asked a judge to take a staggering 225 other offences into consideration. The court was told that after breaking into people's houses, Ward hunted for the keys to high-performance cars such as Audis and BMWs parked in the driveways. Along with homes, he also targeted shops, stealing thousands of packets of cigarettes. Such was his desperation for a daily fix, he also broke into fashion stores to steal designer clothes, which he sold in pubs around his home town of Bradford, West Yorkshire. His one-man spree was only brought to an end when he made a mistake during a break-in at a vicarage in Bradford. Ward smashed a window and stole the TV set, video and some food from the kitchen, but left behind a finger-print, through which police eventually tracked him down.

Forensic evidence also linked him to another burglary after he broke into a home and took a knife from a butcher's block, before going upstairs and using it to threaten the terrified owner. Ward was jailed for eight years at Bradford Crown Court. The court heard that while stealing items valued in total at £1.25 million, he also caused £116,000 worth of damage to the properties he ransacked. Sentencing him, Judge Linda Sutcliffe, said: "I can honestly say, quite frankly, that I have never before in my experience, both on the Bar and on the Bench, seen a schedule like it." During one incident, unemployed Ward confronted an off-duty woman police sergeant with a knife after she tried to stop him from stealing a neighbour's car. Ward, who has previous convictions for burglary and robbery, confessed to all the offences after leaving fingerprints at the vicarage at St Stephen's Church, in West Bowling, Bradford. The former vicar of St Stephen's, the Rev Charles Barber, said: "This sort of petty crime is a menace to the community and I am very pleased that Dean Ward has been caught and punished by the courts." Mr Barber, who previously served as a prison chaplain, added: "I hope and pray that his time in prison will help him build a profitable life." Ward's barrister, Mark Fletton, told the court the serial burglar committed the crimes to pay for his long-term heroin addiction but added that he now wanted to get off the drug. He said: "This young man is now showing a considerable turn-around in the way he intends to live. All his intentions are focused on trying to get himself right and sort it out. It is perhaps rare for matters to be admitted quite on the scale this man has done." After the case, Detective Inspector John Armitage said: "Dean Ward was a prolific burglar who today received his just desserts for this crime spree. When your home is broken into it is extremely distressing, and I hope his victims can take some comfort in the sentence that has been given. Painstaking detective work has gone into this investigation. It is fair to say that this man was a one-man crime wave across West Yorkshire. It shows that West Yorkshire Police and our partners in the criminal justice system will do everything in our power to bring people who cause such misery to justice." Police estimate that £250,000 worth of items stolen by Ward have still not been recovered.

Nine men were charged by police following raids on suspected "Hanoi" burglars. This is when a house is broken into specifically for the keys to steal a car parked outside. Six men from Bradford, two from Dewsbury and one from Leeds appeared before Leeds Magistrates Court. The operation by West Yorkshire Police was launched after a four-month investigation into 60 burglaries across the country, which led to the theft of high performance vehicles worth more than £1.2 million.

Marathon runner Danny Scott leapt into action when a sneak thief targeted his home. Superfit Danny, aged 47, a long-distance runner for 30 years, heard a burglar and sprang into action as the thief fled through the back door. He slipped on running shoes and set off in hot pursuit along the street outside his home in Worksop, Notts. He said: "I didn't think twice about chasing after him, it was just an instinct to protect my home and family and to get back whatever he had taken." He ran for almost a mile before catching the teenager, who was later arrested. Danny, a meter reader, has been a member of Worksop Harriers for more than 30 years and has competed in seven London Marathons. "My wife had just nipped out and I was in the living room when I heard a noise. I slipped on my running shoes and set off after him. I knew there would not be a problem in catching him although he had a head start and was around 400 yards in front. "I ran through an alleyway and over a bridge and I soon chased him down - I've run in seven London marathons, all in under three hours. "He might have been much younger and he could have run for miles and I would still have caught him. I managed to catch up with him at his own house and so I was able to give his home address to the police who arrested him." Danny's mobile phone, car keys and house keys as well as cash were taken in the theft. Police confirmed that a man had been arrested in connection with the burglary and had been released on police bail

I must draw from my bank of memories to tell you about a small team of shop burglars in the Grays, Essex division of Essex Constabulary, which was the first Police Force I joined on completing my military service. This particular team of 2, sometimes 3 shop burglars had been tearing our ground apart for quite some time. We actually knew who they were but in those days we lacked the resources to mount an ongoing surveillance operation. Full details of their identities, descriptions, known motor vehicles etc had been circulated around our own Force and to those Forces which abutted onto our boundaries. Their MO was to attack off licences and shops, (mainly newsagents) from the rear. They invariably used an old fashioned carpenter's hand brace and bit, which made much less noise than an electric drill of course. They would drill a series of about 1 inch holes, in a square pattern, until they could push through the resulting loose wooden panel and squeeze through into the premises. They always had with them large hessian sacks to carry away the large cartons each containing 200 cigarettes. We knew about the sacks because on the odd occasion they had been disturbed by the waking occupier and had just raced for their van to make good their escape, leaving behind partly-filled sacks. On this particular occasion I was driving one of the local police area cars with my buddy Pc Roger Brotherton as my observer/ radio operator. We were driving along the main A13 London to Southend road, not too far from the Dartford Tunnel, on night duty. Under these circumstances, police car crews are vigilant for lots of reasons, seeking persons who are disqualified drivers, drunken drivers, stolen cars, missing persons, especially children etc. Traffic was very heavy in both directions at Grays as this is a particularly busy stretch of road, all day and half the night too. All of a sudden we spotted two of the burglary team driving in their van, in the opposite direction to us. We could tell from the way they were dressed in dark clothing, woolly hats etc that they were probably 'tooled up' and on a mission. We did not switch on the blue flashing light so as not to alert them. Because of this, it seemed an eternity before there was a break in the oncoming traffic large enough to allow us carry out a 'U' turn across the dual carriageway and get after them. As it turned out, we suspect that they had spotted our police car before we saw them, so they quickly took the first left turning they came to and entered quite a long straight road which ran right along into the Grays town centre. We gave chase and Roger, craning his neck in his seat, had seen which way they had driven. Having a faster vehicle than their old van, we soon caught them up and pulled them over, Roger calling for backup over the only radio we had in those days, connected to Chelmsford Police HQ information room. Other units arrived on scene and we quickly moved the two men away from each other, out of earshot, whilst we questioned them individually. Surprise, surprise, they both projected a picture of innocence - but having been caught in an unprepared state, they could not give a good account of themselves and their respective stories did not tally. Neither could they account for why they were travelling **away** from the direction of their homes. On searching their messy old rusty van, we found one or two items which could be construed as 'house breaking implements' by police officers with nasty suspicious minds! As we privately chatted, Roger told me that at one stage, just as we had drawn level with them during the rapid overtake, he felt he had seen an arm go out of the window on the passenger side of the van.

We therefore arranged for our colleagues to separately take them to the nearby police station for further questioning. Roger and I then had some inspiration and carried out a basic police manoeuvre which meant turning our car round and returning to the junction with the A13 road, at which they had been out of our sight for a very short time. We then slowly drove along the road, checking the grass verges, gutters and house gateways, for any incriminating items which the villains might have quickly discarded whilst out of our sight. Boy, did we get lucky!

We found a brace and bit stuck almost upright into a section of grass verge by its drill bit, almost still vibrating from the force of its rapid deployment by the burglars! A bit further along, we found 2-3 very large Hessian sacks folded together, intended for rapid carriage away of the cigarette cartons. As real luck would have it, it had been raining ever since we had first taken the police car out around 2200 hours. The sacks, apart from a few spots of rain, which had landed on them in the short time it took us to pull over the criminals with help from colleagues, were virtually bone dry! They were kept in custody overnight at Grays Police Station, in separate cells, out of shouting distance to each other. The next morning, the scenes of crime officer (SOCO) ran a microscopic search over the van, tools and their clothing. As a result he discovered that in the rear of their van was a very thin dusting of fine flour, from the (flour) sacks, which meant he had physically *put* the sacks *back* into the van rear, supported later by a detailed report from a forensic scientist at the Metropolitan Police Forensic Science Laboratory in London. In due course, once all the evidence had been gathered together, we were able to charge the 2 shop breakers with the offence of 'going equipped for burglary.' This is the updated offence by virtue of The Theft Act 1968. Under the old Larceny Act 1916, we would have charged them with 'possessing housebreaking implements by night.' Subsequently they appeared before a Judge at Essex Quarter Sessions, or its modern title of Chelmsford Crown Court, Essex and if my memory serves me well, they each received a 3-year term of imprisonment. The Chief Constable of Essex decided that Roger and I had done a good job that night and all the 'brace and bit' shop breakings had ceased, therefore he awarded us one of his commendations, which went down rather well on our personal file. However what mattered most, far more than our personal kudos, was that 2 really annoying, persistent criminal, 2-bit shop breakers had been taken out of circulation for a while, and at last were out of our hair! Shopkeepers in the area could get a good night sleep again too. The guys in the CID office thought we were the 'cats whiskers' for ages afterwards.

High up on the roof of the Central Criminal Court (Old Bailey), in London, is a well-photographed statue of a lady carrying a pair of scales, the so-called 'scales of justice'. By the time you have finished reading this book, you may well feel that it's high time the scales were taken down and remade and replaced. My contention is that those scales which served the public for so many years in the old days, are now tipped so far in favour of defendants as to make a mockery of them, hence my front cover illustration.

Turning now to the 'guidance' instructions to Judges and Magistrates, set out by Lord Woolf, the most Senior Judge in the land. You will observe that there are very serious implications for all of us, particularly the old and frail and people living on their own, as the LCJ launched his 'words of wisdom', described by cynics as a 'softening-up process.' Lord Woolf issued his new 'guidelines' for sentencers, which include both Judges and Magistrates, whilst delivering the Rose Lecture in Manchester in October 2002. He stated that the "punitive approach" to fighting crime by imposing ever-tougher jail sentences had failed. He went on to say, "Over-reliance on jail sentences has led to an overcrowding problem in prisons, which is a 'cancer' at the heart of the Prison Service," he warned: "that undermines its efforts to **reform and rehabilitate offenders**, and contributed to disturbances such as the then recent riots at HMP Lincoln," he said. He called for a more "holistic" approach to criminal justice, with more use of community-based penalties, restorative justice and drug treatment for minor offenders. Jail should be reserved for serious and violent criminals, he said – which would free the Prison Service to concentrate on rehabilitation work

The Lord Chief Justice's comments were **welcomed** by the Home Office, which was expected to extend the use of community penalties in the Criminal Justice Bill, in the then forthcoming Queen's Speech. But Lord Woolf warned that the changes must be backed by more money for the Probation Service, which has the job of supervising the offenders in the community. He accepted that Judges must bear some blame for the increasing prison population. However, he said they were reacting to pressure from politicians. "There is a continuous upward pressure, and very rarely any downward pressure, on the level of sentences," he said. "The upward pressure comes from public opinion and the media, the government of the day and Parliament. The prison estate has a finite capacity," he said.

"If you insist on trying to take in through the front door more prisoners than a prison can hold, without letting the necessary number out of the back door, a prison will simply explode. This is what happened during the (HMP) Strangeways series of riots. It is also possibly what happened at (HMP) Lincoln last week." He said that Martin Nearey, the Director-General of the Prison Service, (Now known as The Commissioner Of National Offender Management Services)

LCJ Lord Woolf

attributed the problem to 'mischief makers.' "However, I am sceptical as to whether mischief-makers can result in the loss of a prison, if they are not able to make mischief in fertile ground." He also said the various agencies within the criminal justice system needed to "pull together" more. Lord Woolf said the sentencing 'starting point' of up to 18 months in prison no longer applied and Courts should impose a community sentence in the first instance. But that must be an effective punishment which would tackle the offender's underlying problems, such as drug addiction. Opposition parties (Conservatives, Liberals etc) were said to have *welcomed* the LCJ's ruling. The Police Federation's spokesman, Mr

Rod Dalley, said, "This is another example where the **offender** and not the **victim** is being put at the **centre** of the criminal justice system's concerns. We are concerned at both the timing and message it sends to burglars who may not yet have done their 'Christmas shopping". The Association of Chief Police Officers (ACPO) said the news would come as a shock to some victims of burglary, and would 'strike fear' into others. The MP for Nottingham North said the LCJ's decision bore no reality to the lives of victims of burglary. "I am very much in support of community sentences where appropriate, but this sends a very bad signal to constituencies like mine, that **the ultimate sanction** for first-time burglars is being removed. There has to remain the threat that **any burglary can result in a prison sentence**. Within about a month, in January 2003, the then Lord Chancellor, Lord Irvine, gave his backing to the LCJ's recent rulings. He said: **"The public sees nothing wrong in**

Lord Derry Irvine

burglars escaping jail, even for their second offences." Supporting the **lenient** approach prescribed the previous month by Lord Woolf, he said: **"I don't accept that people are disturbed at first-time burglars or even second-time burglars – where there are no aggravated elements in the burglary – not going to prison."** Asked about Lord Woolf's ruling in the guideline judgement, he said that he had **no difficulty** in agreeing with the LCJ on that. He insisted in a BBC interview that people had less faith in imprisonment than tabloid newspapers suggested. **"In other words, I think that people are more worldly-wise, better informed, than some of the critics of the Lord Chief Justice credit."**

In an attempt to put the Court of Appeal's recent burglary guide lines in context, the then Lord Chancellor claimed that Lord Woolf and the other Judges sitting with him had "sanctioned very substantial sentences of imprisonment for the three burglars whose appeals were in front of them", and that this had been "largely ignored." (However, like his £300 plus per roll wallpaper to refurbish his private quarters supplied by the state, to go with his Lord Chancellor's antiquated appointment, he 'got it wrong.' In fact there were **two** burglars before the Court of Appeal just before that Christmas [2002] and both had their sentences **cut**. William McInerney, aged 22 years, who had 19 previous convictions for a total of 39 offences and who had at one stage asked for 49 other burglaries to be TIC, had his five-year sentence **reduced** to 3.5 years).

Stephen Keating, aged 33 years, with 12 previous convictions, for which he had served two terms of imprisonment, had a four-year sentence **reduced** to three years. His Probation Officer was quoted as saying: "He had clearly poor coping-mechanisms for his offending," but did not assess him as presenting a serious risk of harm to the public. You might take the view that, had they been asked, the Police may well have taken the opposite view, since they are at the front line of having to catch these people who just cannot stay out of other people's houses! Bill Cash, the Tory MP who shadowed Lord Irvine's department in the Commons, called on the Home Affairs committee to examine how the new burglary guidelines would operate in practice. "These guidelines have not been debated in Parliament. They concern the safety of the public and their confidence in the judicial system," he said. Mr Cash pointed out that someone breaking into a house could not be sure there was nobody at home. "These guidelines do not provide a sufficient deterrent in such cases", he said. Sir David Calvert-Smith, QC, the Director of Public Prosecutions, said the new guidelines would not discourage the Crown Prosecution Service from bringing cases to court. "Burglary is still sufficiently serious to prosecute, even if it leads to a community punishment." The only difference he saw was that more burglars would be tried by magistrates, so fewer cases would be dealt with in the Crown Courts, which have heavier sentencing powers." The Isle of Wight MP, Mr Andrew Turner took rather a different stance in the ongoing controversy over the matter, which many sceptics are convinced was designed *to reduce the prison population*, as jails are *bursting at the seams*, rather than encouraging repeat offenders to respond to community sentences. Mr Turner said that *Parliament*, not Judges, should retain the last word on sentencing guidelines for criminals. He accused Ministers, high-placed lawyers and the Judiciary, of being out of touch with people's wishes in their treatment of burglars and running away from their responsibility to explain their policies to the electorate. Even a first or second time burglar who steals electrical goods or personal items, causing damage and mess to the house, and trauma to the victim, would get a community penalty rather than 9 to 18 months in jail. He went on to say: "This announcement shows how out of touch the Senior Judiciary can be with public opinion. The Lord Chief Justice talks about the theft of high-value goods – but for people I know who have been burgled, it is the loss of possessions of great sentimental value, and the fact that ones home has been violated, that matters. This announcement was sneaked out the day Parliament rose for the Christmas recess and Ministers ran away from giving interviews on the subject. That smacks of cowardice by Judges and Ministers alike – they knew what they were planning was unpopular and wrong, and, like guilty children they hid from the consequences. This is not the first time this has happened – Judges are allowing their office to be abused, Ministers to downgrade the penalties Parliament allows for crimes. There (was) a Criminal Justice Bill before Parliament at the moment, **and I**

shall examine carefully whether measures can be included to prevent Judges defeating the will of Parliament."

In the first paragraph of Mr Andrew Turner MP's article above, he was largely echoing what the then Chief Constable of Thames Valley Police, Sir Charles Pollard, once had to say. He was a guest speaker on BBC's *Question Time* programme on BBC TV on Thursday evenings, hosted by David Dimbleby, which is my favourite TV programme of the week as it is so topical. There are 4-5 panellists and they have no idea at all as to what questions will be asked by the audience. The questioner had asked about the severe breakdown in law and order under the Tory Government which was then in power. Sir Charles Pollard held up above his head a huge glass ashtray to make his point. He said: "The trouble is this – up here in this 'hot air balloon' are Senior Judges, Ministers, 'Do-gooders', Human Rights activists etc., floating around in the atmosphere way above our heads. They are totally out of touch with reality and what's going on in the REAL WORLD. Nobody ever breaks into their homes or steals from them etc." (Or words to that effect).

This vivid demonstration and Sir Charles' simple explanation as to the root of the law and order breakdown problem, went down so well with the audience, that he all but received a standing ovation! He obviously had so much insight that he was able to put his finger straight on the cause of the problem, much to the audience's delight, as well as mine. After all the years since he made his point on *Question Time*, I have never seen such a responsive audience, which showed its acceptance with great gusto.

On a lighter note, after this pretty *heavy* chapter on burglary and its implications for the victims of the present and future burglaries, I must draw your attention to this article taken from *Police Magazine* March 2003. It was headed up by a photograph of the Lord Chief Justice in his long wig and all of the colourful paraphernalia of his High Office. The banner headline, of course in bold, heavy type, reads:

WHO'S AFRAID OF THE WIG CLAD WOOLF?
Not the burglars, that's for sure

A few weeks ago, LCJ Woolf delivered an angry rebuke to the media for, in his opinion, giving the public a totally wrong impression of his latest guidelines on sentences for burglars. These 'inaccuracies', he says, could seriously harm the public by reducing, without justification, their confidence in the criminal justice system. Let's read that again, "their confidence in the criminal justice system." What confidence? In which world do the noble Lords Woolf and Irvine, and their colleagues on the bench, reside? Irvine, who sprang to the defence of the Lord Chief Justice when the storm broke, insists that the public is quite happy with the way the courts are doling out their idea of justice. The (former) Lord Chancellor claims that his research shows that, when carefully questioned, the views of ordinary citizens are in line with the decisions of judges. If the people who are most responsible for dispensing criminal justice really believe that, the rest of the nation can only despair.

REMISSION

Is Lord Woolf seeking to put the minds of citizens at rest when he points out how prison sentences no longer mean what they say? He explains that 'a prisoner sentenced to 18 months in gaol is likely to serve a quarter of that time in gaol.' A prisoner serving 12 months starts off with six months automatic remission, then gets a further 90 days, off during which he is on "home (detention) curfew." (HDC – a "tag") If that prisoner spent any time in custody before being convicted, he is likely to be out of gaol before he had had time to settle in! It reminds us of 'Del Boy Trotter', " Ere, never mind 12 months, never mind six, call it three, alright?" Lord Woolf's "explanation" of his policies reiterated his view that a burglar not violent, or a persistent offender should get a community punishment. But he also gave the game away. "Such a policy," he said, "has the added bonus of relieving the overcrowding in prisons." This is what the government and the judiciary are really about.

CRISIS

It is quite conceivable that the present crisis in the prisons will lead to yet another round of prisoners in police cells, and if the worst scenario occurs, riots. This is why judges and magistrates are under pressure from the top, urging them to use prison as a last resort. The public know it, and certainly the criminals know it. What was that about the fear of detection being the greatest deterrent to crime?

But what faith can be put in the current alternatives to prison? Selective statistics suggest that re-offending rates are lower among offenders who do not receive custodial sentences. Such comparisons are meaningless unless enough is known about the activities of offenders when at liberty. The burglar who is caught every time he breaks into a home is either incompetent or desperately unlucky. The only time we can be *sure* that a burglar isn't burgling, is when he is in custody (unless he's on home leave). Does the Lord Chief Justice have the faintest idea of the reality on the ground? Has he noticed that the National Association of Probation Officers is planning industrial action, because its members have reached the end of their tether?

In the last 5 years the caseloads of probation officers have doubled –

while their numbers have gone up by less than 10 per cent. The service cannot attract recruits in Britain, so it is advertising vacancies in South Africa, Australia, and throughout Europe. Meanwhile the Probation Service in the most pressured areas is near to total collapse. Cases are delayed because there is no one to complete court reports, a vast number of community orders are ineffective because there is no one to supervise the offenders. Some inner-city probation offices have a 30 per cent vacancy rate While Government Ministers might dismiss mere anecdotal evidence, one reliable story sums up the true situation. A consultant employed by the government to examine the state of the criminal justice system confided recently to a senior probation officer that in his professional opinion, the criminal justice system was on the verge of collapse, and he could not understand why it had not already done so.

STRUGGLE

The answer may lie in the efforts of committed people in all the relevant agencies, who wage a constant struggle to keep the system going as long as they can. Lord Woolf's indignation with the media was over the top. His lengthy explanation of what he said, and what he meant to say, did little to reassure those who live in fear of crime, and especially burglary. It is true that he recognised the trauma that victims go through, but as he acknowledges, he has sought to change the emphasis in sentencing. He wants to provide better protection for the public and at the same time reduce the use of custody. Most people would say that the two things are, in practice, incompatible with each other. Lord Woolf insists burglars should only be sent to prison when it is necessary, and then for no longer than necessary. This is not a message that lessens the apprehension of the citizen who knows that his home is no longer his castle."

Cambridgeshire Police have advised motorists to take their car key bunches to bed with them at night! Apparently burglars have difficulty in starting up modern cars as they are fitted with immobilisers. It seems too many home owners are leaving their keys on the hall table, on hooks visible through the letter box or nearby windows etc. Burglars then break in to grab the keys and swiftly abscond in high-value cars parked outside on the drive or in the street. I remember reading about a wave of burglary and car crimes near to my own home area, where criminals used innocent-looking canes or poles with hooks on the end, to lift keys off wall hooks and out of wall-mounted key safes, via the letter box or ground floor left-open windows. However it seems that even with your car keys bunch in the bedroom with you overnight, you would not be safe from ice cool 'creeper' burglars like *Brian* whom I previously described.

Some years ago when I was stationed at Ilford in Essex, which was on J division Metropolitan Police, I was a CID officer. Ilford was an area of high-density population, bed-sits everywhere and many rather large houses. Most of our working day in CID was spent in attending house burglaries, after initial visits by our uniformed colleagues had taken place.

Our job included interviewing the occupier, any possible witnesses, knocking on doors either side or over the back, seeking information about sightings of strangers in the vicinity, unusual noises or strange vehicles seen in the area etc. We were also responsible for obtaining from the burglary victim, as soon as possible, a comprehensive list of the stolen items with values, identifying marks etc. We would then advise a special department at the Yard of the full details, in case a burglar was found in possession of the stolen goods. That way the goods could be traced back to their burglary of origin, the arresting officer could have a happy day, but the burglar would not be going straight home on that occasion! Also, on return to the police station, we would raise a teleprinter message for circulation to all police stations in the area, with details of the stolen property.

Essex Police had a an excellent system in place to increase our chances of catching burglars. Each area patrol car, dog van, CID car etc kept in the glove compartment a small loose leaf book which could easily and quickly be amended where necessary. I don't know whose brainchild this was but because of it, our arrest rate for burglars caught at or very close to the scene, was improved considerably right across the county. It had long been known that criminals of most types listened-in to police messages radioed to cars. (I had in part been brought up on them, as my grandfather who served in the Metropolitan Police for approx 30 years, in the Hampstead, Kentish Town and Stoke Newington areas of London, was still addicted to listening to the calls going out from Scotland Yard information room, at home years later, and explained to me what was going on during my frequent visits, as I lived nearby. The Police Service gets that kind of grip on you, almost as if you're frightened of missing something that's going on near where you live, even if you can no longer do anything about it.) Our burglar alarm 'code books' as they were known, were very important to us and you were in big trouble if you couldn't account for one that had been in your possession on the car. The normal old-fashioned type home and shop burglar alarms just used to ring the moment they were activated by an intruder or some external innocent source, birds, rodents, strong winds etc. thus scaring burglars away before we could get there, in most cases. Insurance companies were slowly allowing to be introduced a type of alarm which did not immediately kick off and warn the intruder that he had been tumbled, but instead kept silent for just a few minutes whilst alerting a police station or a security firm known as a Central Station Alarm monitoring facility. Obviously this gave the nearest police units just a very few minutes advantage to race to the scene and hopefully catch the burglars red handed on site, before the external audible alarm was triggered and began ringing on the actual premises. Different-length silent delays were in place according to the size of the perceived threat at a particular premises and the value of the goods etc. the alarm was protecting. Sometimes insurance companies would agree to a slightly longer delay than normal, as persuaded by the Crime Prevention Officer, particularly if it was in a remote rural location or the approach roads were rugged or very winding so as to slow down approaching police cars. Under the old system, the burglars would keep one ear to their portable transistor radio or crystal set, whilst they attacked the premises. Obviously they would normally know the address of where they were and could recognise the fact that particular police vehicles had been deployed in their direction, and therefore it was time to make tracks! More often than not, they had a keen advantage and could either lie low in the area or make a run for home. When an operator at the Information Room at Police HQ at Chelmsford wanted to direct a police unit to a premises listed in the 'code book', he would simply call the local or nearest unit by its call sign and transmit the message, for instance, "Hello Golf Alpha Two from 'VG', CODE G-Golf 39, did you receive?"

Usually the driver would acknowledge receipt of the message because the observer/operator beside him would be frantically in a panic under the following stressful circumstances:

1) Scrabbling about in the foot well searching for the all-important 'code book'.
2) Rummaging through the patrol car's leather brief case for the said book.

3) Trapping his fingers in the glove compartment lid as the frustrated driver tried to help.

4) Searching for his dropped torch so he could look up page 39 in the book, with some haste to prevent the driver's oncoming apoplectic fit.

The relevant page in the book was full of very useful information as follows:

Address of premises and possibly name of occupier.

Best approach for first police unit on scene.

Known hazards on site, such as ponds, ditches, walls with broken glass tops etc.

Likely escape route(s) by fleeing bandits.

Possible venues where criminals' vehicles parked.

How long silent alarms ran before giving audible warning of police approach.

Useful approaches by supplementary police units arriving.

Nearest Police Station to the venue willing and ready to receive prisoners.

Presence and possibly the breed(s) of any guard dogs kept by the owners.

The Sunday Telegraph Nov. 7 2004

Naturally to a burglar listening-in to the Police Radio Frequency, at the 'code G-GOLF 39' alarmed premises, the Information Room operator's words meant nothing at all, so he and his team could carry on with their criminal activities for a short time until the bell clapper or klaxon was tripped at the end of the allowed silent delay. This type of encrypted message proved to be a wonderful source of prisoners and brought many a proud smile to the faces of Essex Police Officers for quite some time. In the fullness of time, as the insurance companies came to appreciate that the system actually worked and bore 'fruit' in the shape of higher arrest levels and more valuables recovered etc., they very slightly extended the delay periods, to give us a better chance and to help with crime clear-up rates.

Personally, as a Police Probationer in Grays Division of Essex, when I was first detailed as a trainee area car observer/operator, I couldn't have had a better tutor than PC "Wacker" Hughes (no relation) from Liverpool, who ran his area car like a finely tuned military unit. He used to pass on wonderful tips such as *make sure you can find that 'code book' within 5 seconds of the call coming out* etc. He was so professional and good at his job that he would go to great lengths to disguise the fact that we were in a police car, at night creeping around the backs of factories, office blocks, banks etc. The actual

The Sunday Telegraph Oct. 24 2004

police radio mounted in the central console had very small red and green pilot lights which advised you that it was switched on and in which mode it was operating etc. " Wacker" trained me, as we crept around as I've just described, to make sure our faces couldn't be seen in the glow from the radio pilot lights on the dashboard, by holding one of my police gloves against the radio fascia. How's that for professionalism? What an amazing coach and trainer and what an impressive number of arrests he must have

had throughout his full police career!

Before we leave this pretty hefty chapter on **BURGLARY**, as I'm pretty sure that in this country at any one time, there are more **victims of burglaries** than any other crime I can think of, affected by **FEAR**, I would like to share with you some views of others, who have

The Sunday Telegraph

commentated publicly. The first is a featured article by Mr John O'Connor who is a former Commander in the Metropolitan Police and was Head of The Flying Squad. His article appeared in *The Daily Express* on 9th February 2004 and was headed-up:

As US research reveals the worst detection rates in the West
THE LAW MUST TAKE ACTION ON OUR DISMAL CRIME FIGURES

The Sunday Telegraph Oct. 31 2004

"It will come as no surprise to the thousands of crime victims and police officers in the United Kingdom that American research has shown we have the worst crime detection in the western world. From 889,000 burglaries last year (2003) only 26,300 offenders were convicted – a lamentable detection rate of less than 3 per cent. There are 3 areas of blame for this state of affairs : the police, the judiciary and the Home Office. Ask any solicitor or agency that has day-to-day dealings with the police and they will tell you the same depressing story – *morale is shot to pieces and the average copper does no more than he has to*. There is a prevailing culture that the less you do, the less likely you are to get into trouble.

Going the extra mile without overtime is considered by many officers to be the height of stupidity. Conversely, the quality and education of our police force is higher than at any time in its history. The problem is poor leadership. A former Metropolitan Police Commissioner, asked by

The Sunday Telegraph Nov. 28 2004

the Commons Home Affairs select committee: "What percentage of your force is corrupt?" answered: "Up to two per cent". In real terms that is around 500 men and they are not going to be in charge of horse brasses or community affairs – they are going to be front-line detectives. Then there are allegations of institutional racism. Morale is not the only problem. The true plight of the public's suffering under burgeoning crime rates has been camouflaged by the police and Home Office. A US Justice Department-backed report has looked at our conviction rates and exposed the deception that has been practised on the public for years. It is not just creative accounting - blue-sky thinkers in the police service have come up with ingenious methods to improve the figures without actually arresting anyone. How about 10 burglaries in a block of flats being recorded as one burglary with 10 losers? Only in the unlikely event of somebody being arrested is it 10 separate burglaries. One crackpot scheme was sending a police officer to interview a convicted burglar in prison and persuading him to admit offences he may or may not have committed. The crimes were treated as solved and written off. It is surprising that judges and magistrates have not picked up on "consideration offences" (TICs) : Before sentencing, a burglar could admit to all the crimes he said he had committed and they would be taken into account. In the Metropolitan Police, most active detectives had a good working relationship with the Solicitors'Department and, in the more serious cases, with the Director of Public Prosecutions.

The fictional American TV series *Law and Order*, where police officers are regularly seen in conference with the district attorney, is not unlike the way things used to be here. The advent of the Crown Prosecution Service changed all that. Cases were routinely thrown out without discussion and a chasm developed between the two agencies. The CPS tended to see itself as independent and did not attract the highest quality of prosecutors. The standard of police evidence dropped dramatically, while up went the number of cases thrown out through administrative incompetence.

Things are starting to improve but there were 10 wasted years. Home Office interference with sentencing can also have a detrimental effect on the crime figures. Locking up burglars and thieves is not just about

The Sunday Telegraph

The people have spoken

Our campaign to grant home owners an unqualified legal right to fight back against burglars who invade their property has struck a chord with politicians, The Home Secretary has accepted the need for a "rebalancing of the law" in favour of home owners, as has the leader of the Opposition.

Both, however, have equivocated on whether a wholly fresh law is needed. Yet the response of the public has been markedly less ambivalent than that of the politicians. When tackling an intruder under the existing law, an individual, if he wants to escape prosecution or a civil suit from the burglar, can only use what the police and the Crown Prosecution Service deem to be "reasonable force". The people of Britain do not want a "rebalancing" of that law. As our poll today shows, an overwhelming majority of people believe that the current law is completely inadequate. They believe that householders should have the unqualified right to use force against an intruder in their homes.

This is not a party political issue, or one that appeals only to so-called "Right-wingers". Support for a change in favour of home owners cuts across the political spectrum. People between 18 and 24 years old are as enthusiastic about restoring rights to home owners as are people aged over 65. Poorer citizens show as much, if not more, commitment to the right to fight back than their richer neighbours. Yet the politicians, normally so sensitive to issues with great popular support, seem ... to do anything about ...

citizens sufficiently to prevent the commission of all violent crimes.

As long as individuals are left with any degree of freedom at all, some will choose to commit burglary and other violent crimes. It is the politics of fantasy to suppose that it is possible for the police to prevent that from happening – but it is the politics of folly to base the criminal law on that fantastic supposition.

The police jealously guard what they conceive to be their monopoly of the legitimate use of force. It produces the absurd situation we saw last week, when officers entitled to carry guns in London handed in their weapons because two of their number were suspended for shooting dead an unarmed man going about his lawful business. If an ordinary citizen did such a thing, the police would be the first to insist that he should be tried for murder. We do not suggest the two police officers should be prosecuted: we only call for parity between the police and the people. If the police are entitled, when they believe their lives are threatened, to take lethally offensive action, then so should home owners.

Politicians and lawyers also say that any change to the law that explicitly entitles home owners to tackle intruders will lead to more innocent people being accidentally killed or hurt. That is a genuine risk. But that risk has to be weighed against the certainty that there will be fewer burglaries if burglars know that home owners are free to take action against them.

As we reported last week, when the American state of Oklahoma introduced a law permitting home-owners to take whatever ... they believed to be necessar ... ... just in ...

It is the politics of fantasy to suppose that the police can prevent burglary and violent crime

The Sunday Telegraph

punishment. It provides welcome relief for the public when these people are not out on the streets committing further offences. It is quite common practice for the Home Office to advise judges and magistrates that the prisons are full, and please will they find alternative punishments. Burglars are let off from custodial sentences and the whole process of crime and detection recommences. Perhaps the establishing of a multi-agency task force to deal with serious and organised crime can go some way to re-establishing credibility in British justice. This is probably the best idea yet to come from this Government. It should go further. When Chief Officers fail to perform, they should be sacked. The cornerstone of improvement has to be the police, and Chief Officers must be made accountable for results. Most are hidebound by fear of corruption, but should realise they are in the risk management business. The police must go on the offensive, with the full backing of senior officers. Most officers are too busy keeping their heads down to avoid the whistle blowers waiting to report a politically incorrect comment in the canteen. They also have to live with the crackpot out-pourings of some Chief Constables with mad ideas on drugs and motorists. Support your local copper, he needs it."

This next comment was in the form of a letter published in *The Mail on Sunday* in March 2004, under the bold headline,

The law must protect us, not the criminal

"In the past few years I have seen the rise of a disturbing attitude to victims of crime – that they should just shut up and take it. But why should law-abiding members of the community be victimised twice – once by the criminal and again by our legal system, just for trying to uphold the very laws that are supposed to protect us? I foresee the day when a woman who has been raped will be arrested for injuring her attacker while trying in vain to defend herself. If individuals choose to step outside the law to commit crime, they do not deserve protection from within the law. And if they sustain injuries while committing crime – whether from those defending themselves and their property, or just from a rusty nail in a fence – on their own heads be it. I am neither condoning nor promoting vigilantism, but the letter of the law is now being used by those breaking the law to kill the spirit of the law, and this, as well as the criminal, must be stopped."
Name and address supplied

(How on earth did that anonymous person manage to reflect so clearly, the contents of our minds?)

Here is a comment by Rachel Baird, Home Affairs Correspondent of *The Daily Express*, published on 7th January 2004:

13,000 WILL BE SPARED PRISON

Fury over full-up jails

"Thousands of criminals must be kept out of jail to stop the prison population soaring," Ministers announced. They hope to divert 13,000 burglars, car thieves, drug users and minor offenders from custody over the next six years and fine them or impose community punishments instead. The Home Office insisted it was not 'going soft on crime,' and said the move would help reduce re-offending. But Shadow Home Secretary David Davis warned MPs, "The House will need to be reassured that fines and community penalties will not be used to replace custodial sentences merely because the Home Secretary has already filled our jails. Does he still believe that punishment should fit the crime, or does he believe it should fit the number of empty cells?" The proposals were announced as a report, ordered by Tony Blair, warned that the justice system is failing "to bear down sufficiently on serious, dangerous and highly persistent offenders." The report, by businessman Patrick Carter, said only the most dangerous and persistent criminals should be jailed. Others should get toughened-up community punishments. Prisons minister Paul Coggins said the number behind bars could not be allowed to continue rising – from 72,300 now to an estimated 93,000 in 2009. But Norman Brennan, director of the Victims of Crime Trust, said this was "contemptible to victims of crime and law-abiding members of the public." Tory MP Ann Widdecombe, a former Shadow Home Secretary, insisted: "The answer to over-crowding in our jails is to build fresh jails."

(I would love to know which way the consensus of opinion amongst my readers is going!) Barely 2 weeks later, the same *Daily Express* Home Affairs Correspondent published this article under the frightening-to-some bold headline,

EXPLOSION OF VIOLENT INTRUDERS

"Burglaries by armed and violent intruders have rocketed 75 per cent in just over a decade leaving householders asking: 'Is anyone safe in their homes?' One in 200 burgled families now suffers the ordeal of confronting an intruder wielding a gun, knife or some other weapon in their home. The devastating figures emerge from one of the most comprehensive studies of burglary ever carried out in Britain.

The report has renewed demands for a "Tony Martin Law" allowing home owners to defend their property from criminals, using whatever means necessary. Supporters of the Norfolk farmer jailed for shooting dead a teenage burglar, said the sharp rise in violent break-ins strengthened the case for a new law spelling out the right to defend your home. And they demanded longer prison sentences for those convicted of these crimes. Malcolm Starr, Tony Martin's spokesman said, "If they were behind bars for longer, I believe it would serve as a deterrent and make them think again about doing this for a living. But none of the main political parties appear to be worried about the electorate – the people that put them into power." He added, "I think the party that jumps on the bandwagon and takes tougher action against burglars will be the one that wins the next election." Amid warnings that criminals are resorting to greater violence during break-ins because of better home security, the Home Office released a raft of figures cataloguing the worrying rise of violent Britain. The number of violent offences leapt by 17 per cent last summer, with almost 250,000 woundings, assaults and other violent offences between July and September 2003. Rapes, paedophile crimes and other sex attacks also rose eight per cent

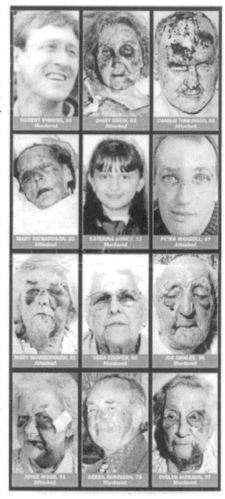

Helpless victims who have been assaulted in their own homes
The Sunday Telegraph Oct. 24 2004

compared with the previous year, to reach 14,000.

And the number of gun crimes recorded by police across England and Wales hit 24,070 in 2002-3, a worrying seven per cent increase over 2001-2.

Armed thugs committed almost 3,500 house burglaries in 2002-3, up 75 per cent since 1991, the Government figures show.

Victims of violent break-ins included TV star Cilla Black, whose 22 year old son Jack had a knife held to his throat during a burglary last August. (2003). Ministers played down the latest statistics, saying that some of it was due to new police counting methods – and more victims coming forward to report crimes against them. They also emphasised that the total number of crimes of all kinds is static, at around 1.5 million offences between July and September last year. But Shadow Home Secretary David Davis retorted, "No amount of Home Office spin can hide the fact that violent crime is soaring." Mark Oaten, Liberal Democrat home affairs spokesman said, "The rise in violent crime is surely a sign that the binge drinking culture is getting out of hand." But the Home Office stressed that the risk of being burgled was at its lowest for 20 years and that in 2002-3 there were just over 4,000 aggravated burglaries (including non-domestic burglaries) out of a total of 889,000 break-ins. The figures show the number of non-violent burglaries falling 3 per cent to 104,000 across England and Wales. Car crimes were down eight per cent to 222,000. But vandalism was up seven per cent and drug offences up two per cent.

The following table may give see-at-a-glance clarification to the above-mentioned latest figures:

Violent burglary in the home over last decade	**+ 75%**
Violence against the person	**+ 17%**
Sexual offences	**+ 8%**
Robbery	**- 2%**
Domestic burglary	**- 3%**
Thefts of and from vehicles	**- 8%**
Vandalism	**+7%**
Drug offences	**+2%**

A new Act of Parliament known as the Powers of Criminal Courts (Sentencing) Act 2000 came into being. The most important part of it to BURGLARY VICTIMS appears to have been Section 111.

This required the (Crown) Court to impose a sentence **of at least 3 years** for a third or subsequent burglary conviction, unless (regrettably there is always an unless, working in the **offender's** favour, you might be thinking!) there were specific circumstances that made the sentence unjust.

Would you believe that my research indicates that hardly any judges ever implemented this important string to the bow of police officers and victims of multi-burglaries etc? At the time it created very wide publicity indeed and many people saw this as at least a step in the right direction, to attempt to drastically reduce the dreadful burglary figures. This subsequently found to be hardly-ever used concept, quickly became known as

THREE STRIKES AND YOU'RE OUT

This might well prompt you to ask "Who is actually running this country's Criminal Justice System?" Throughout the whole, protracted period of my researching for *Judgement Impaired*, I had not come across a single reference **anywhere**, to **any** Crown Court Judges who had imposed the minimum sentence of **three years** to a burglar who qualified under the THREE STRIKES AND YOU'RE OUT doctrine. I therefore wrote to my Member of Parliament, Boris Johnson MP, asking him to look into it for me. He then raised the matter by writing directly to then-Home Secretary David Blunkett, who delegated it to the appropriate Home Office Minister, Baroness Scotland QC

She raised her own enquiries and the results are recorded verbatim as follows:

Home Office
The Right Hon Baroness Scotland of Asthal QC
MINISTER OF STATE
5O Queen Anne's Gate, London SW1H 9AT
0870 000 1585

Boris Johnson Esq. MP
House of Commons
London
SW1A 0AA

27 OCTOBER 2004

Reference: M1391174

Thank you for your letter to David Blunkett of 17 September 2004 on behalf of Mr M Hughes about law and order issues. I am replying as the Minister responsible for this area of the law.

It is certainly the Government's responsibility to ensure that the courts have the powers they need to deal with the offenders who appear before them, and this is a responsibility that we take very seriously.

Within the broad statutory limits set by Parliament, sentences in individual cases are a matter for the courts alone, taking into account all the circumstances of the offence and the offender, including all mitigating and aggravating factors. The independence of the courts is an important principle and the Government is not able to interfere in

– or comment on – the sentences passed in individual cases. It is ultimately the judge's decision what sentence to pass within the legal boundaries. However, I can inform you that the maximum penalty available to the court in the case of Lee Hughes (International footballer – convicted fatal hit-and-run drink-driver) was 10 years as this incident happened in November 2003. The new maximum penalty of 14 years applies to all offences committed on or after the 27 February 2004.

The Government recognises that there needs to be a consistent set of guidelines that cover all offences that should be applied whenever a sentence is passed.

This excludes murder, which reflects the special place that it occupies in the criminal justice system, and also the special requirements a framework for sentencing for murder must fulfil. We need to work to eradicate the wide disparity in sentencing for the same types of offences and the public's mistrust of the system that comes partly from inconsistent sentencing.

The Criminal Justice Act 2003 sets out proposals, which with the help of the judiciary, has established the Sentencing Guidelines Council (SGC). The Lord Chief Justice chairs the SGC, and it is responsible for setting guidelines for the full range of cnminal offences.

The Home Office is committed to improving the criminal justice system, so that it becomes one that is respected and in which all members of the public have full confidence.

You also asked about the 'three strikes and you are out' procedure. As part of the Government's crime reduction strategy to tackle domestic burglary, section 111 of the Powers of Criminal Courts (Sentencing) Act 2000 – which is still in force – provided for the imposition of a mandatory minimum three year prison sentence for adult domestic burglars convicted for a third time. The court has discretion not to impose the minimum custodial sentence of three years if it is of the opinion that there are particular circumstances, which relate to any of the offences or to the offender, which would make it unjust to do so in all the circumstances.

The Home Office holds the details shown on the attached Annex A. The identity of the trial judges is not included in the statistics available to the Home Office.

Best wishes

Patricia

BARONESS SCOTLAND QC"

04 17:34 FAX +44 20 7273 3094   HOME OFFICE

Annex A

Sentencing under Powers of Criminal Courts (Sentencing) Act 2000

4.55 Sections 109 and 110 of the Powers of Criminal (Sentencing) Act 2000 came into force on 1 October 1997. They were originally enacted as sections 2 and 3 of the Crime (Sentences) Act 1997 although the 1997 Act has now been consolidated into the Powers of Criminal Courts (Sentencing) Act 2000. The section provides that the court shall impose a mandatory life sentence on an offender convicted of a second serious offence and a sentence of at least 7 years for a third class A drug trafficking offence if the offender:
was 18 or over when he committed the offence;
committed the offence on or after 1 October 1997;
in the case of the drug offence had previously been convicted of two other class A drug trafficking offences in England and Wales; and had been convicted of the first serious offence or one of the drug offences, in the United Kingdom before he committed the second.

4.56 Section 111 came into force on 1 December 1999. Again it was originally enacted as section 4 Crime (Sentences) Act 1997. This section provides that the Crown Court shall impose a sentence of at least three years for a third domestic burglary if the offender:
was 18 or over when he committed the offence;
committed the offence on or after 1 December 1999;
had previously been convicted of two other domestic burglary offences in England and Wales; one of those offences has been committed after conviction for the other; and both of the previous domestic burglaries had been committed on or after 1 December 1999.
The court has a discretion not to impose these sentences if it is of the opinion that there are exceptional circumstances relating to either of the offences or to the offender which justify its not doing so.

4.57 Table 4G shows persons sentenced under these provisions, as notified to the Home Office since 2000 (when the Crown Court computer system was updated to recognise these offences).

Table 4G Persons sentenced under the Powers of Criminal Courts (Sentencing) Act 2000, 2000-2002

England and Wales   Number of persons

Year	Section 109 Life for second serious offence	Section 110 Minimum 7 years for third class A drug trafficking	Section 111 Minimum 3 years for third domestic burglary
2000	57	2	-
2001	51	1	6
2002	44	-	2

Those are the results supplied by the Home Office Minister. You will appreciate that within this **Burglary** chapter, we are only interested in those quoted figures in the right-hand column above. Therefore columns 2 and 3 should be disregarded completely. The first thing that caught my attention was that **not a single Crown Court Judge implemented the minimum 3 years sentence** throughout the whole of the year 2000.

Baroness Scotland QC, Home Office Minister, advises us the new 'three strikes and you're out' legislation was actually brought into effect – or 'implemented' – on 1st December 1999. In layman's terms, the law actually came into force on that date. This tells us that, in spite of all the long, drawn-out hard work that had gone into its drafting etc. – and having passed safely through the House of Commons, then the House of Lords, then back to the Commons, **at least once**, then finally given the Royal Assent when Her Majesty signs the Bill, converting it into an Act of Parliament – not a single Crown Court Judge in 2000 (New Millenium Year) – it's first full year in existence – could be bothered, or chose **not** to sentence a serial domestic burglar to the minimum sentence of 3 years. The mind boggles as to how many serial burglars would have **qualified** for that important minimum sentence, under the conditions set out by Baroness Scotland QC above. What a complete and utter waste of time and money, for so-called *Learned Judges* to ignore it or totally disregard it! We should also bear in mind that, as the Act was so newly-introduced, just 1 month before the year 2000, the Police and/or the Crown Prosecution Service might have been at fault in failing to draw it to the Judge's attention, if 'their' burglar currently on trial at a Crown Court, 'fitted the bill'. Naturally Magistrates Courts are excluded from being able to impose a sentence of 3 years, as they are limited to just a period of six months maximum imprisonment. Referring back to the table again, we see that only **six** Crown Court Judges saw their way clear to handing down the 3 years minimum to serious burglars throughout the whole of the year 2001.

So much for the *Will of the People*, expressed in our *democratic* society through the ballot box, via freely-elected House of Commons MPs, being totally ignored – possibly through contempt by Judges taking a stand to show everyone who really runs the country? As regards the stated six Judges who did take the trouble to exercise their increased sentencing powers in 2001, it's a pity Baroness Scotland QC was unable to name them in the above table. Had she done so, I would certainly have given each of them a special mention in the *In Praise of the Judiciary* chapter. When we look at the fact that only **two** Judges utilised their new, increased sentencing powers in burglary cases, in the whole of 2002 – which happened to be a good year for burglars, but a bad year for householders and victims – the reader surely must agree it helps me in my quest to lay the responsibility for the greatest failure in the criminal justice system, firmly at the door of the Judiciary. I rest my case! To swiftly illustrate the point, just return to the above table 4g for one last time. What do you notice about it? Amazingly, as we have passed ever deeper into succeeding years of the Labour Government under Prime Minister Tony Blair, ALL of the figures, in all three columns, have reduced – year-on-year! Whatever happened to his much-publicised pre-General Election promises, *Tough on crime – tough on the causes of crime*, and *We will transfer the FEAR from the crime victims, back onto the perpetrators of the crimes*. Oh really? Whilst steaming into possibly his third consecutive 4-years term in Government, the Prime Minister is certainly leaving it a bit late. Even this close to the next election, purported to be in May 2005, as I draft this chapter in November 2004, I'm sure he's left it far too late. He just seems to be fixated with the War in Iraq, 'poodling' along behind President George Bush, and extending public house and clubs licensing hours and arranging for Las Vegas-style gambling casino complexes to be constructed. Not a word about getting Prince Charles to lay the first bricks in the one dozen or so new prisons we so desperately need. By the time you have finished being updated on what is going on behind the scenes, you might well be asking about what you personally could do to change things, and overturn all of the injustices happening in the Courts every day. Injustices to victims of course, is what I am referring to. My suggestions would be to tell everyone you know to purchase and read this book – then, armed with the arsenal of information it contains, as to what's wrong, you can lobby your MP to find out whereabouts in the Priority Order of his Party's Manifesto, does the breakdown in Law and Order come? – and cast your next vote accordingly.

Just in case you have any doubt left in your mind, as to how to recognise the Learned Establishment Figures who are behind it – if you pass them in the street – and by their ineffective, lenient and inappropriate sentencing policies, allow the criminals of this country of ours to literally create thousands of new victims of crime, each day that passes, here are a few positive identification tips:

Some of us will have seen them making their long, primary-school-like crocodile processions into the Royal Courts of Justice in London on special or ceremonial occasions. Just to remind you, in case you are unfamiliar with their dress codes, these are basic minimum dress-standards for our High Court Judges:

>*Shoulder-length wig.*
>
>*Ceremonial regalia, including cape.*
>
>*White or black panti-hose.*
>
>*Knee breeches. (Pronounced 'BRITCHIES')*
>
>*Patent leather buckled shoes.*
>
>*Carrying white gloves.*
>
>*Posy of flowers known as a 'nosegay.'*
>*(In case of horrible smells during great plagues)*

If you saw one on foot, on his way to the Law Courts, passing through the old Covent Garden Market area, now a street live entertainment centre, on his way back from *MacDonalds*, you might be forgiven for confusing the colourful traditional, intimidating garb of a High Court Judge with that of a street clown.

Remember too, that if one happens to challenge you – for sniggering, they must be politely and respectfully addressed as either *My Lord*, or *Your Honour*.

Burglars have "no rights" to protection, declared a minister who broke ranks. Home Office Minister Paul Goggins spoke out as the row continued to rage over Tony Blair's refusal to strengthen the law in favour of householders. He said: "The burglar has no rights. The burglar is in the wrong." Previously, the Government's top lawyer has insisted burglars deserve protection from their victims and "don't lose all rights" when they break into homes. Attorney-General Lord Goldsmith said: "We must protect victims and law-abiding citizens. But we have to recognise that others have some rights as well. They don't lose all rights because they're engaged in criminal conduct." Mr Goggins' comments came as he sat face-to-face with a householder who had to wait nine months to discover if he would be prosecuted for fighting back against an intruder with an Indian club. Derek Godfrey-Brown, a pensioner, struck the intruder on the leg, breaking his tibia, as the man lunged towards him. Mr Godfrey-Brown, of Okehampton, Devon, was immediately arrested and charges of grievous bodily harm were only dropped weeks before he was due to stand trial. Sitting opposite Mr Goggins in the studio of ITV's *This Morning* he said: "As far as I know, the burglar got away Scot-free. That was the sickening thing." The Minister admitted that Mr Godfrey-Brown had suffered an ordeal and, under guidelines issued earlier this week in a pamphlet, he should not have been prosecuted. He added: "The person wrong in Derek's story is the burglar. He should not have been there." Mr Goggins' frank admission that burglars should have "no rights" was last night welcomed by victims' groups. But Norman Brennan, director of the Victims of Crime Trust, said, "It is all very well for the minister to say burglars have no rights but the public will want to see it in black and white. "It should be enshrined in law and then the public will be reassured."

Mr Blair's refusal to alter the law to offer protection to home owners who use all bar "grossly disproportionate force", again dominated Prime Minister's Questions in the Commons. Conservative leader Michael Howard said the leaflet drawn up by police and lawyers "only adds to the confusion" about what levels of violence were allowed.

A Police Chief dramatically stepped into the row over the right to fight back against burglars by explaining exactly what he would do if confronted by an intruder. Bob Quick, newly appointed Chief Constable of Surrey, admitted he would act first and think about the consequences later. Mr Quick was spelling out his plans for policing in the county when he was asked about his attitude to the current debate on tackling burglars. He said: "I have a family to protect and if I found an intruder in my home I would incapacitate him first and ask questions later." Mr Quick spoke as Labour MPs were accused of running scared of a public backlash against their refusal to tighten the law. In a cynical pre-election ploy, the Party's high command allowed a Conservative Bill giving homeowners the right to use all but "grossly disproportionate force" to pass its first Parliamentary hurdle. But Ministers admit they do not want the Householder Protection Bill to become law and will attempt to quietly kill the legislation in a Westminster committee room. The tactic was deployed to save Labour's rattled MPs from having to publicly oppose a measure which has massive backing among voters. The MPs faced being confronted on the election trail by opponents pointing out that they had let down homeowners desperately worried they could face charges, just for defending their home and property. The Tories, who saw the Bill passed by 130 votes to four yesterday, last night accused the Labour MPs of being "soft". Shadow Home Secretary David Davis said: "The vote reflects the overwhelming support for changing the law to make it favour the householder, not the criminal. "We think the law needs to be changed so that burglars will be deterred from burgling and people will feel safe defending their property. The fact that Labour MPs didn't even turn up to vote on this important Bill demonstrates their whole approach to protecting people from crime - talking tough but acting soft."

The Tories are now seeking to capitalise on the chaos in the Government's ranks with a new nationwide poster campaign. The posters, written in a childish hand, say: "The law should protect me, not burglars!" Labour MPs had lined up to dismiss Patrick Mercer's Bill during its second reading in the Commons yesterday. Home Office Minister Paul Goggins said a change in the law - which allows the use of only "reasonable force" - was unnecessary as current regulations already struck a fair balance. He admitted: "Being burgled is a very frightening experience and householders who react instinctively and attack intruders will only be prosecuted if they use very excessive force. "What the law does not permit is an act of retaliation. Punishment of criminals is a matter for the courts." Tony Blair originally indicated he would back a change in the law. But, after talks with lawyers, he made a dramatic U-turn to insist the current legislation is "sound". In a statement last night, Mr Goggins made it clear the Tory Bill would be killed off eventually. He said: "The failings of this Bill will become apparent in committee."

On 12th January 2005, Tony Blair turned his back on millions of home owners by refusing to give them greater rights to fight back against burglars. In a staggering U-turn, which defies overwhelming public opinion, the Prime Minister refused to back Tory proposals to give people stronger powers to use physical force to protect their homes and families. Instead of better protection from prosecution for home owners who defend themselves, they will be given pamphlets on how far they are allowed to go under the law as it stands. Mr Blair's about-turn, confirmed by his Home Secretary Charles Clarke, comes just weeks after he promised that householders would be allowed to use maximum force against violent intruders. In a devastating blow to anxious householders, Mr Blair now believes the existing law is *sound*. Last night opposition MPs and anti-crime campaigners accused ministers of flying in the face of public opinion. The extraordinary reversal was slipped out just hours before Tory MP Patrick Mercer introduced his private Bill to toughen the law in Parliament.

The Daily Express has led the way in crusading for the law to be beefed up in favour of victims of crime. At present the law says "reasonable force" can be used by householders, but campaigners complain that too many are subject to police investigation of their actions. But Mr Clarke said: "I have concluded that the current law is sound. I have come to the conclusion that this guidance and clarification will ensure that the current law is properly understood and implemented, and that therefore no change in the law is required." Norman Brennan, Director of the Victims of Crime Trust, said public faith in Mr Blair was now shot to pieces. He said: "Tony Blair has promised time and time again to make the public safer and to crack down on those who blight people's lives. But the sad fact is that every promise he makes is broken." Mr Blair's official spokesman last night insisted: "This is not something the Government has decided willy-nilly. "What is important is that we have taken advice from those at the sharp end of enforcing the law. We do not legislate simply for the sake of satisfying an opinion poll." But Shadow Home Secretary David Davis said the Government had flown in the face of compelling evidence for change. He added: "Police officers, the public and even professional burglars have said they think a change in the law would shift the balance towards the victims and away from the criminal. "Just this morning, 99 per cent of people said they should have the right to defend their homes, and only a few weeks ago Tony Blair acknowledged that a change is necessary. "Labour have shown yet again that their promises to be tough on crime are all talk." Calls for action have gathered pace after a series of high-profile burglaries, including the murder of financier John Monckton who was stabbed to death by intruders at his London home in November.

The issue has been a hot topic since farmer Tony Martin shot dead a teenage burglar at his remote farm in 1999. Rocker Ozzy Osbourne, 55, last year also grappled with a burglar during a raid at his country mansion near London. The TV star said he feared suffering the same fate as the late Beatle George Harrison, who was stabbed by an intruder at his mansion in rural England in 1999. The outgoing London police chief Sir John Stevens, the most senior officer, is among those backing a change in the law. He said last year: "My own view is that people should be allowed to use what force is necessary to defend themselves and that they should be allowed to do so without any prosecution." Mr Blair appeared to back a change in the law during Prime Minister's questions last month. He told MPs: "I think in the light of recent concern, it is worth looking at whether we don't have to clarify the law so that we send a very, very clear signal to people that we are on the side of the victim, not the offender." Mr Mercer wants the law changed to protect householders unless they have used "grossly dispro-portionate" force when tackling intruders. But his Bill now stands little chance of becoming law without Government backing. He yesterday accused Ministers of playing "political football" with an important issue. Mr Mercer said: "I am extremely disappointed. It seems that the Home

Secretary is flying in the face of public opinion." The Tory MP added that he had been inundated with letters from the public, police – and even criminals - supporting his campaign. He said: "I can only assume that this incredibly important subject which ought to stand above party politics, has been reduced to a political football. "If this was a Labour private members Bill, I am sure it would go through without hindrance. I hoped that the Government would stand above this sort of thing." But Mr Mercer refused to back down and a full debate on his Bill is now scheduled for the beginning of February. He said: "I am going to continue to make the point. This is public opinion speaking. I am amazed the Home Secretary is choosing to ignore this." Malcolm Starr, a spokesman for Norfolk farmer Tony Martin, added: "The Government should wage war on the criminals and parasites of society. "It should ensure the criminals are afraid not of being injured by a householder but fearful of the police, courts and prisons." Mr Blair abandoned his pledge to the public, after the intervention of his most senior lawyer, the Attorney-General Lord Goldsmith, QC. Last night Lord Goldsmith said: "I welcome the decision to provide householders with clearer information and reassurance of the protection given by the current law." The Association of Chief Police Officers also said it supported the status quo. Last year, 2004, 402,000 households suffered the agony of a burglary – which means one in every 50 homes is broken into every year. Research shows that, once the burglar escapes, there is little chance they will be brought to justice.

Under Labour, the detection rate for the crime has halved. Last year, it stood at only 13 per cent.

Labour was braced for a public backlash on 24th January 2005 after suffering a double blow on crime. Ministers face allegations they have gone "soft" by allowing up to 33,000 criminals who would have been jailed to remain at large. And, in a separate blow to the Government, new figures out today are expected to show a surge in alcohol-fuelled violence, with more than a quarter of a million attacks logged in only three months – 2,800 every day. Three years ago the Home Office estimated the prison population – currently 73,700 - could reach almost 110,000.

But yesterday the number of people expected to be locked up in 2011 was dramatically revised downwards to between 76,000 and 87,500. The Conservatives claimed the Government had told judges to hand out softer penalties because they did not have enough prison places to be tough on law-breakers. Crooks will also be released early – with all bar the most dangerous offenders automatically freed half way through their sentence. The Treasury has refused to hand over the cash to fund any more than 80,000 prison places and, for the first time, judges have been told they must keep this in mind when deciding if a criminal should go to jail – or be given a community punishment. Shadow Home Secretary David Davis said: "Our prisons have experienced massive problems with overcrowding under Labour."

Home owners frightened of crime, plan to spend as much as £13billion this year, £823 for every home, improving the security of their properties. A report by *Sainsbury's Bank* claims two-thirds of householders intend to fork out up to thousands of pounds on alarms, locks, outside lighting and even guard dogs. The survey confirms that safety in the home has become a major problem. The Government is trying to reduce this problem by instructing judges to take the limited prison capacity into account when they hand down sentences. "At the same time as the deterrent of prison is reduced by these shorter sentences, the number of crimes recorded by police continues to rise. "So far, 3,600 crimes have been committed by criminals let out early on Labour's early release scheme. "That's 3,600 extra victims as a direct result of Labour's attempts to reduce prison over-population." The Government insisted that, under new "public protection sentences", sexual and violent offenders whom the Parole Board considers a significant threat, will never be released. It also said 1,500 persistent burglars were expected to be jailed for a minimum of three years each under a "three strikes and you're out" sentencing policy.

Tony Blair recently admitted there was "real public concern". Robert O'May, from the bank, said: "This is good news in terms of reducing burglaries and increased security *can* also mean lower home insurance premiums." More than half of prospective homebuyers said the decor was irrelevant compared to security. But Prisons and Probation Minister Paul Goggins admitted there would be "increased use" of community penalties. Mr Goggins insisted he was confident the public would accept the new sentencing regime, even though it will see some prisoners released earlier than at present. Mr Goggins said they would be more closely supervised.

"If there's any reason that they are not complying with the license conditions, they can be recalled to prison right up until the end of their sentence, which is an enhancement on the current position. "The most dangerous and most serious can be subjected to indeterminate sentences and not allowed back into the community until the Parole Board say so. "We think the balance between greater penalties for the more serious offenders, lesser penalties for the less serious combined with greater supervision and stronger powers to recall when taken together, are a very credible package."

Today's quarterly crime figures cover July, August and September last year, when police attempting to crack down on drunken yobs fighting in town centres made more than 4,000 arrests.

In a survey carried out for the BBC's *Breakfast* programme, the public delivered a damning verdict on extended drinking hours licences, due to be phased in from next month. Some 67 per cent of those questioned thought the new legislation would lead to an increase in anti-social behaviour. Three-quarters of home buyers rated good security an essential factor in their decision to buy a house. It even ranked above the quality of the neighbourhood and the area's local facilities. Nick Clark, of the show, said: "Security has moved up the agenda. If you want to sell your home, quickly upgrading your security systems will be a major help."

The BBC was under fire on 3rd March 2005 after secretly giving £4,500 of licence payers' cash to the burglar who raided farmer Tony Martin's home. The decision to pay Brendan Fearon, a career criminal with 36 convictions, for an interview was branded "disgusting and despicable" by friends of Mr Martin, victims' groups and MPs. Mr Martin,who was also interviewed for a documentary about the night he shot and killed Fearon's accomplice Fred Barras, did not receive a penny. As politicians reacted with horror to the revelations, BBC bosses last night desperately sought to justify their actions. One insider said: "We did pay Mr Fearon, yes. He received £4,500 but that reflects the time we spent filming with him and background research. "What our guidelines say is that ordinarily we do not pay convicted criminals but in some extraordinary cases where there is huge public interest, as there clearly is here, this can be waived. Tony Martin didn't receive any payment because he didn't ask for one. Mr Fearon did." But the BBC's protestations were greeted with astonishment by victims of crime organisations and politicians. Mr Martin's MP described the decision to pay Fearon as a flagrant abuse of licence payers' money. Tory Henry Bellingham, who represents North West Norfolk, said he would be protesting to Culture Secretary Tessa Jowell and BBC chairman Michael Grade. "It is mind-blowing that this is happening at a time when the BBC's future is being debated," he said. "It is a quite extraordinary decision. The corporation should be conducting itself with probity and balance when its charter is on the line." Norman Brennan, director of the Victims Of Crime Trust, said: "What does it say about the BBC when it is happy to fritter away £4,500 of honest taxpayers' money paying a convicted criminal? "It is because of decisions like this that the BBC may find itself being challenged over the licence fee. It should stick to what it does best, making hard-hitting programmes such as *Panorama*, but should not be helping convicted criminals make money from their crimes." Mr Martin was jailed for murder in April 2000, sparking a public outcry and resulting in a change in the law governing how much force householders can use to protect their homes from intruders. He was sentenced to life imprisonment but that was reduced to five years for manslaughter and he was released after three years. The reclusive farmer's close friend Malcolm Starr said the BBC's decision to pay Fearon was despicable. "It absolutely stinks doesn't it? Tony will be gobsmacked and very angry. I took him to be interviewed and he sat with these people for three hours and didn't receive a penny.

"He is not money-motivated but I'm pretty sure they said they could not pay him anyway because he was a convicted criminal. "And yet they have paid Fearon £4,500, disgusting, completely despicable. They have taken advantage of Tony's good nature and to pay this man is outrageous." Political parties also reacted with astonishment to the BBC's decision. Shadow Culture Secretary John Whittingdale said: "We are strongly oppposed to criminals profiting from their crimes. People should be punished for their crimes, they shouldn't benefit from them. "If the BBC has allowed a criminal to profit from committing a crime it is even more serious, the BBC is financed by the public, and people will be very concerned about their licence fee being used for this purpose." At the time of the burglary at Mr Martin's Norfolk farm, Fearon, who was born in Newark, Notts, already had 33 convictions for assault, burglary and theft. His first court appearance came at the age of 14. By the age of 22 he had been given a three-month prison sentence after a string of dishonesty offences. He was sent to prison again at the age of 24 and again at 27 after being convicted of wounding. Now 34, he was recently released after being jailed for heroin dealing. His criminal career spans three decades. After he was jailed for three years for conspiring to burgle Mr Martin, Fearon threatened to sue the farmer for the injuries he received during the bungled raid on his isolated farmhouse. Fearon was vilified for using legal aid to attempt to sue his victim. But after a further public outcry he later dropped the controversial £15,000 damages case. It was just as Mr Martin was released from custody after serving two thirds of his five-year term for manslaughter that Fearon finally dropped the civil action. While an official BBC spokesman last night refused to comment on the amount of the payment involved, the corporation stood by its decision. The spokesman said: "The BBC's guidelines are very clear that payments to convicted criminals are only justifiable when there is exceptional public interest in what a contributor has to say and where there is no other way of obtaining such a contribution.

"Given that Mr Fearon is the only person apart from Tony Martin who is alive and a witness to what happened, and because there is currently public controversy about householders' rights to protect their homes from intruders, it is extremely important that the public hear the fullest possible account of the events that led to the death of 16-year-old Fred Barras and the imprisonment of Tony Martin. "We believe that what Mr Fearon has to say is a contribution which will ensure that the programme is properly balanced and as full a picture as is possible. "The fact that Mr Fearon was paid will be made clear to viewers in the programme. In the end it is for viewers to weigh up the credibility of what he has to say.

COUNT 2

PAEDOPHILIA

The words paedophile and paedophilia would seem to be words which have only recently entered common usage. *The Collins Paperback English Dictionary* first published in 1986, offers this definition :

> **Paedophilia** *n. the condition of being sexually attracted to children – paedophile or paedophiliac n., adjective.*

Anyone who has ever studied in depth what is known as *case law*, will be aware of various tricks, deceptions etc. which some defendants, including sexual predators, have used to justify their claim that consent was lawfully, or in good faith, obtained. One such well-documented case was that of a choirmaster who had sexual intercourse with a young girl whose parents had entrusted her to his care. He convinced the girl that by having intercourse with her, it would enhance her singing voice. Fortunately, he did not get away with that one, and was convicted of rape.

As a child, I was personally sexually abused. I was under the age of 11 when, with my family, I moved away from North London and took up residence in Romford, Essex. We had been living in Rhyl Street, Kentish Town, London, NW5, within easy walking distance of London Zoo, and the currently extremely popular modern market at Camden Lock. My younger sister and I, through our parents' encouragement, became regular attendees at St Silas' Church, NW5. We became very keen and could hardly bear to miss a church service or Sunday school. Additionally, I became an altar *server*, assisting the Priest and of course, wearing a cut-down surplice and cassock. Over time, my sister joined the church-based brownie pack, whilst I became a member of their cubs-pack and later, the scouts group. The sexual abuse took place whilst I was either a wolf cub or a very young boy scout. There was an adult, single, male member of the church congregation, apparently well-thought of, who lived very nearby and used to assist with the cubs and scouts. His full-time occupation was with *W.H.Smith*, the chain of newsagents, running one of the old, brown-painted kiosks with a metal roller shutter, found on practically every station in those days, where travellers bought their newspapers, magazines, cigarettes, etc. Through church and youth activities, at my young age, he befriended me and used to get me to *help* him at his place of work, at Chalk Farm underground station, on the Northern Line.

He was a very cunning and careful paedophile, as many of them are. When it was time to close the newsagent kiosk, which he ran single-handedly, he would pull down the roller shutter and then lock it from the inside using the attached bolts. He would then take an old penny coin from his pocket or the till drawer, and wedge it into the inside of the letter box mechanism, so that nobody, such as underground railway staff, could take him by surprise by peeping through and discover what he was up to.

He would then undo his trousers, as well as my short ones, and expose his penis. He would have his handkerchief standing by whilst he encouraged me to rub his penis. Then he would increase his own sexual desires by fondling me down below and at the same time, showing me black and white photographs of naked men and women, pictured in a magazine called *Health and Efficiency*. Obviously I trusted him and cannot recall being scared at all, but was too young to grasp the reality of what he was up to. These indecent assaults took place on a regular basis, I think on Saturdays, when there was no school. I recall his name to this day, but all I am prepared to say as regards identification, is that at the time, he lived just a few minutes walk from our church, in Prince of Wales Road, near the local landmark, *The Mother Shipton* public house. He swore me to secrecy, somehow, in such a way that I never told a soul about his dirty tricks until much later when I disclosed the information to my wife.

Committing this series of sexual assaults to paper for the first time, in 2004, I was given to wonder if this individual had any other young victims within the church/Sunday school/youth activities framework, bearing in mind boy scouts and cubs used to leave home to attend youth camps, with Mum and Dad's blessings, and trust that their offspring would be soundly looked after in both body and mind, by the adult staff. In more recent years, the fact that I too, had once been a victim of sexual abuse has helped me to empathise and bond with persons I have encountered, at the various workplaces within the criminal justice system. These include so-called *self-harmers*, some of whom have stated that they self-harm because they have been victims of sexual abuse. I have been able to try to motivate them to try to *rise above* their self-pitying and negative line of thought, which can virtually consume them at times, by suggesting that those *bad* memories can be put behind them, and that if I could do it, so can they.

This seems an appropriate time to raise the subject of regular or serial sexual predators and how they find their young, innocent victims. The following list includes some occupations or persuasions which are very relevant:

1) Members of the clergy, particularly Roman Catholic priests and even Nuns;
2) Scout Leaders & other male leaders of youth groups;
3) School teachers;
4) Male nurses in hospital and engaged on community visits;
5) Employers of young people, such as milkmen, mobile ice cream salesmen etc.;
6) Child-minders, baby-sitters and au pairs, which can often be of the male gender;
7) Doctors;
8) Military instructors;
9) Driving instructors;
10) Care home staff, particularly where vulnerable & those with learning difficulties reside.

Years ago, whilst working on CID at Ilford, Essex within the MPD (Metropolitan Police District), I had great personal pleasure and satisfaction in assisting to put a serial paedophile out of action, behind bars for quite a long time.

This notorious individual was a habitual paedophile, although that term was not in common use in those days, as evidenced by his long list of previous convictions. On his last conviction, prior to his arrest for what I am about to reveal, he had been released prematurely from a previous prison sentence, deciding to settle in the Ilford area. Somehow, through repeated advertising in appropriate areas and media, he formed a juvenile train spotting club. (In those days, like stamp collecting, it was a major hobby for school children, we certainly had one at my old school and I was an enthusiastic member. We carried special pocket-sized books to tick off every locomotive spotted, by its registration number, and compared our engine sightings to date.) Over time, as the club membership grew, he would arrange weekends away and overnight stays at major train-spotting venues around the country, such as Crewe, York, Reading etc. Regrettably, gullible parents were drawn into allowing their young lads to go with this evil man, which gave him a quite large *pool* of potential victims, from whom he would select, in turn, those to share his personal bed or tent. Over time, he built up a boxed card index system of club members. Each boy had his own index card, (or even 2 cards in some cases), containing all normal member details, name, address, age, birth date, physical description etc. It would also contain details of the perpetrator's own sexual preferences in relation to that particular child, as well as the innocent child's own preferences, if applicable. Times and dates of specific events and types of sexual activity were carefully recorded, together with, where possible, victim photographs in various poses and states of undress, sometimes two or more *train spotters* depicted together in the same photograph. (These were mostly taken by using a Polaroid camera, to avoid detection at a photo lab.)

As the investigation progressed and the stockpile continued to mount, an increasing number of boys were interviewed at the police station with their parents. The sheer scale of this man's sexual predation became quite horrifying. One day, working the late shift, I was posted to the first floor of Ilford police station, where the divisional surgeon (police doctor) had his own mini-surgery including examination couch, rubber gloves, specimen receptacles, cotton buds, blood-testing hypodermic syringes etc. My job was to empathise with and attempt to reassure the parents waiting in line with their son(s) outside the police doctor's room, and to comfort them. As each young lad left the room after his rectum had been forensically examined in front of one or both of his parents, it was immediately evident, by the expression on the parents' faces, whether they had received good news or bad whilst inside the room. This miscreant was subsequently convicted of multi-cases of buggery and indecent assault and sentenced to seven years imprisonment. As you can imagine, the sexual predator's meticulous record-keeping in his card index system, played a major part in his eventual downfall. A classic case of *documentary evidence* being used in an investigation and trial, to good effect.

Many police officers and prison officers consider that, no sooner has a jailed serial paedophile settled into his new prison cell, than he is formulating his plan for his intended actions with his next victims, upon his release from custody. Some believe that the police should use satellite surveillance devices or the services of GCHQ listening and monitoring department of the Home Office, at Cheltenham, to watch and log the movements of, and communications between, convicted paedophiles. Others are of the opinion that, after conviction for serious offences such as these, and corruption of innocent lives, they should be chemically *castrated* so as to prevent, hopefully, the chance of their ever re-offending again. Still others feel that life imprisonment is the only way to protect citizens from their actions.

It is likely that you will have come across examples of *soft sentencing* from within your own experience, from what you have seen and read in the media, and from what others have told you. The International Police's recent *Operation Ore* has been a robust, ruthless and expertly-co-ordinated attack on organised paedophiles, with vigorous, well-planned, dawn raids on suspected paedophiles. In mid-April 2004, some results of *Operation Ore* successes were released. The detectives nationally employed were then in possession of a new list of 1,000 names of suspected internet paedophiles. Names, e-mail addresses and credit card details were handed over to British police officers, after the American authorities smashed a mammoth pay-per-view pornographic website. As I mentioned earlier, some of the men have already been prosecuted , but are now known to have **re-accessed** the depraved images on the website, which netted its originators literally millions of dollars worth of subscriptions. One senior police officer was reported as saying: "This new list proves that, for some people, rehabilitation is simply not an option. They need to be stopped and the only way to do that is to use tougher sentences both as a punishment and a deterrent. A small minority of the names we came across during *Operation Ore* are returning to haunt us."

The maximum sentence for possessing an indecent image of a child is five years in jail, but many paedophiles get off much more lightly. Ironically, this is often because investigations are so thorough that the accused plead guilty straight away, and receive reduced sentences for their co-operation. For example, in September 2003, Neil Bower, a 32-year old health and safety consultant, admitted possession of nearly 3,000 images on his home computers, but walked free from a court in Manchester so he could undergo therapy. In October 2003, a former police officer, Alexander McArthur, 30, from Argyll, Scotland, escaped jail despite having 5,613 images in his possession. He was sentenced to 300 hours of community service and ordered to attend a sex offenders treatment course. The National Crime Squad says 102 children have been identified and saved from sexual abuse, or further abuse, as a result of *Operation Ore*. The youngsters, aged between two and thirteen, made complaints about adults after they were arrested. Some children have been taken into care after making allegations against their own parents. Others reported on people in positions of responsibility, such as teachers. *Operation Ore* was launched in 2002, when 7,250 British subscribers were identified. Of those, 4,100 addresses were searched, 3,500 people were arrested, 1,670 have been charged and 1,230 convicted, 27 of whom were serving police officers.

Among those identified as having accessed child porn on the internet was *The Who* guitarist, Pete Townsend. He was put on the Sex Offenders' Register but not charged, as he had not **downloaded** illegal images. He told police he had looked at the images for research purposes. In fact this celebrity was shown in great detail in the TV series I mentioned earlier. His London home had been staked out for some hours, not just by police officers but also by international journalists, anxious for a good story and accompanying photographs. He fully co-operated with police throughout and was not spared the slightest modicum of embarrassment because of his celebrity status. He was pictured in a police video turning out his pockets on the chargeroom counter, the same as everyone else. The scale of the internet website for paedophiles proved to be enormous. Police in Fort Lauderdale, Florida and the former Soviet state of Belarus, came into possession of the names of 27,000 people worldwide who had paid to download sick images of children, via two firms who had set up the websites. It is currently feared that police will struggle to cope with the huge list of new names of British offenders. The backlog for examining computer hard drives is growing. Some hard drives take literally months to properly investigate, as paedophiles grow ever more adept at covering their tracks. Mr Jim Gamble, Assistant Chief Constable of the National Crime Squad, refused to comment on the new list or the repeat-offenders claims.

He said: "The fact that more than a hundred children in the UK alone have been identified and removed from areas of abuse is good news, but it is a statistic we cannot celebrate. Many offenders had thousands of images on their systems." Another senior source said: "We have uncovered every kind of child abuse against girls and boys, some babies of 18 months. Many had been raped or subjected to other gross sex acts by members of their own families. It is heartbreaking." In mid-April 2004 a 37-year old man from Dorking, Surrey was arrested under suspicion of sexually abusing three children in America. At the same time in Dallas, Texas, the FBI arrested the 25-year old mother of three children, aged nine, seven and four. The couple allegedly met over the internet in 2003 and the man, who has not been named, flew to America several times to stay with the family.

On 24th July 2004 a former civil servant, Alan Green 51, from Ryde, Isle of Wight, appeared at Portsmouth Crown Court. (Coincidentally, this is the crown court at which disgraced Judge David Selwood, with his child pornography hobby, presided, until he was forced to resign on 'ill health' grounds.) This defendant claimed he had downloaded pornographic pictures of children from the internet as research for a novel. He was arrested after a neighbour tipped-off police that he had pictures of naked teenage girls hanging on his walls. When detectives seized his computer, they discovered 170 indecent images of young children, as well as pornographic stories. Judge Price branded Green 'a danger to children' and sentenced Green to nine months imprisonment. Perhaps you are wondering what manner of sentence Judge David Selwood would have passed in that very same crown court barely two months previously.

In 2002, a serving prison officer at HMYOI Huntercombe, Oxfordshire, Steve Holt, from the Bicester area of Oxon, was sentenced to 12 years imprisonment after being convicted of having sexual relations with his own children. It is thought that his wife reported the allegations to police after the children, or one of them, informed their mother of what had taken place. Holt is thought to have been an ex-regular soldier.

Thomas Titley, a 46-year-old paedophile from Walsall, West Midlands, was jailed for pervertedly abusing two young boys in a sex dungeon at his flat. He lured a 7-year old child to his flat after meeting him with his mother, encouraged the boy to strip naked and help him to dig in his basement to make a dungeon, like the one used by *Buffalo Bill* in the movie *Silence of the Lambs.* He then enticed the poor child into the pit, put a carpet over their heads and abused him. He trapped the boy in the hole despite knowing that he was terrified of the dark. When police raided the flat following a tip-off, they found the child cowering in a garden dog kennel, where he had been told to hide. Titley also lured the youngster's eight-year old friend into his makeshift dungeon with promises of cigarettes and alcohol. The secret of the pit's existence emerged only two years later when the seven-year old 'freaked out' and began sobbing uncontrollably after his mother lifted a carpet while decorating his bedroom. Memories of the abuse came flooding back and the boy poured out the details of his ordeal.

Titley, driven by urges he knew he could not control, had returned to preying on children after he was freed from a four-and-a-half year jail term imposed for paedophile offences in 1996. The prosecution said at the more recent trial at Wolverhampton Crown Court in March 2004: "Titley said he knew one of the boys was frightened of the dark, because the child began screaming when he couldn't get out of the hole. The boy also remembered being in the hole on his own after the defendant covered the top." Titley admitted three charges of indecent assault and six of gross indecency at a hearing in November 2003. He also admitted four charges of child abduction, one of false imprisonment and one of breaching a sex offender's order. After the case, Chief Inspector Glover said: "The fact that this man could treat a seven-year old boy in this way is beyond belief. These sorts of things will stay with the lad for ever." Titley admitted to Judge Robert Orme that he was a menace to children, asking to be locked up for a very long time. Judge Orme, jailing Titley for life, said: "You will not be freed until those responsible are satisfied you are no longer a risk. Nobody knows what the long-term effects on these boys will be. We can only pray that they recover from the damage."

In April 2004, John Kinsey, 46 years, a former novice monk denied indecently assaulting three lads aged 14 to 16 years, in the 1980's at Belmont Abbey, Hereford. He groped them as they learnt bell-ringing and altar duties. Kinsey, from Cardiff, later became a Roman Catholic priest. Judge Andrew Geddes said to Kinsey: "You abused their trust. The damage you have done is incalculable". He sentenced him to five years imprisonment.

In early March 2004, Ian Taylor, 38, formerly of Walgrave, Northants, was jailed for abusing five teenaged girls in his care at a care home. He was found guilty of rape and indecency of two girls aged 10 and 11. He had admitted indecently assaulting two girls between 1985 and 1990 at the council care home at Tiffield, Northants. Judge Patrick Eccles, QC told Taylor: "Each girl went there emotionally vulnerable and each of them was preyed upon by you." He was jailed for 15 years.

In the same month of 2004, school governor and father-of-two Christopher McCoy, 45, was jailed for storing 21,000 photographs of children being sexually abused on his computer. He was snared by a Canadian detective posing as a 13-year-old girl during an internet chat room exchange. She contacted local police who arrested McCoy after finding the photos, which he swapped with other paedophiles. His computer, which also held 200 short, depraved films, was kept in his house he shared with his wife and children aged 10 and 13. He admitted 20 charges of possessing, storing and distributing indecent photographs. At Minshull Street Crown Court, Manchester, McCoy, of Partington, was jailed for three and a half years.

In February 2004, the Crime team of *The Sun* daily newspaper published the results of a survey they had carried out on dangerous or high risk sex offenders. They have headed up the list of published offenders 'BEASTS ON THE LOOSE' and refer to them as 'THE DIRTY DOZEN', which you may think is quite appropriate. Unfortunately, for legal reasons, it is not possible to actually *name and shame* them at the moment, in case one or more has already re-offended and awaiting trial, which might be prejudiced. They can go wherever they like, free to prowl around seeking new victims. Police are routinely alerted to the men and told to monitor their movements as best they can. However with all of their custodial sentences complete, officers are powerless to act until another offence has been committed. Michael Hames, ex-head of New Scotland Yard's Paedophile Unit warned, Police and other agencies try to monitor these people, but surveillance is phenomenally expensive and cannot be maintained indefinitely. When police are withdrawn, there is a serious risk that they will re-offend. They have been released after convictions for assaults on boys, girls and women. They are among scores across Britain who are set free routinely, as their sentences end. But their risks of re-offending have been placed at 'serious', 'high' and 'very high.' Many of them are being supervised by the Probation Service and living at hostels. They are subject to night curfews, but roam free by day.

The 12 include one fiend caged for eight years for a catalogue of sex abuse against a girl of 14 years. He was also convicted of the manslaughter of another teenager and was seen dancing on her grave. Another of the freed beasts has been diagnosed with a severe personality disorder and has vowed to rape a woman. Yet another is a serial paedophile whose convictions include 15 indecent assaults on a young lad and seven indecency counts. While inside, paedophiles go on sex offenders' programmes, intended to address their offending behaviour. But there is evidence that they swap fantasies with other offenders, about what they'd like to do when they are free.

Following the abduction and murder of eight year-old Sarah Payne in 2002 the Government vowed to tighten legislation, but parents are still not allowed to know any details of perverts lurking in their area. Schools are seldom alerted unless a suspected paedophile is posing a threat.

The following table gives details of the 'Public Enemies Nos. 1-12:

BEAST 1 Sex attacker aged 28 Risk Factor: VERY HIGH

Freed from jail in December 2003 and vowed to rape a woman. A South London man with convictions for indecent assault, stalking and robbing women. Drink and drugs problems & severe personality disorder.

BEAST 2 Paedophile aged 45 Risk Factor:VERY HIGH

Wanted for recall to prison after going missing from a Hampshire probation hostel. Assessed as being a 'very high' risk of re-offending against children. History of 'grooming' children with learning difficulties.

BEAST 3 Paedophile aged 48 Risk Factor: HIGH

A menace who cannot stop re-offending. Convictions include 15 offences of indecent assault on a boy and seven of indecency. Travels into London by bus and trains but barred from going near schools or playgrounds.

BEAST 4 Child killer aged 48 Risk Factor HIGH

Twisted fiend, got eight years for a catalogue of sex abuse against a girl of 14. Served only five and is free despite fears he could kill. Was convicted of the manslaughter of another 14-year-old girl as part of a suicide pact. Formerly housed in a hostel with other paedophiles in Stratford, East London, he once played out a mock execution on a boy, by forcing him to kneel with his head over a bucket while he wielded an axe.

BEASTS 5 and 6 Paedophiles aged 22 and 18 Risk Factors SERIOUS

This sick pair are COUSINS who invited two 13-year old boys to an address in South West London and put them through a hideous and humiliating ordeal. The boys were first of all forced to undress at knifepoint. They were then ordered to perform degrading sex acts on each other while being beaten at the same time with a belt. The cousins were convicted of incitement to rape, indecent assault and false imprisonment. They were each sentenced to four-and-a-half years but were released after serving just 30 months behind bars. Both were put on the sex offenders register for life, and ordered to stay away from the Westminster area where the offences were committed, but the evil pair have since threatened to go back.

BEAST 7 Child rapist aged 36 Risk Factor SERIOUS

Released from HMP Wormwood Scrubs after serving 18 months for raping his seven-year-old nephew. Has been released on three previous occasions but failed to sign the sex offenders register. Several experts said he poses a serious risk of harm to young boys. Police warned: "It is vital we don't lose contact with him until he's housed."

BEAST 8 Serial paedophile aged 47 Risk Factor HIGH

This fiend was branded a 'prolific' paedophile who was convicted of more than 30 offences on boys in Northern Ireland. He was also charged with a similar offence on a youngster in Bayswater, West London. He is currently on the loose with his whereabouts last listed as being at an address in Greenford, Middlesex.

BEAST 9 Child rape and kidnap aged 64 Risk Factor SERIOUS

This pervert has previous convictions for rape, abduction and indecent assaults on children under 14. He has also committed robbery and a string of assaults and sexual offences. He was living

in temporary accommodation in Paddington, West London and is listed as 'a very dangerous man.' Worried experts described him as 'violent and mental'.

BEAST 10 Child sex attacker aged 51 Risk factor HIGH

This despicable pervert indecently assaulted his nine-year-old niece and forced her to drink his urine. He has been rated 'highly likely' to re-offend. This man is now believed to be living rough in central London, but he has visited the Haringey and Stoke Newington areas and has found work as a decorator.

BEAST 11 Rapist aged 35 Risk Factor VERY HIGH

This sex offender was released from high-security Whitemoor jail in Cambridgeshire after serving 15 years for two counts of rape and one of possession of an imitation firearm. He was living in a hostel in Kilburn, North London. A report on him stated and warned, "He is at very high risk of repeat offending."

BEAST 12 Rapist aged 50 Risk Factor HIGH

Branded a 'predatory and violent' offender who attacks lone women at night, this man was jailed for 'life' in 1984 for six rapes, indecent assault, grievous bodily harm and robbery. Now he is given 'rehabilitation leave' every 2 months and can roam about unescorted for a week at a time. He was due to stay in a hostel in Beckenham, Kent.

You may recall the much-publicised case of the 33-year-old ex-US marine who *groomed* a British girl aged 12 years via an internet chat room. Toby Studabaker sparked an international manhunt after abducting the girl and fleeing with her to Paris. He was finally captured in Germany in July 2003 and extradited back here to Britain. The couple were depicted on CCTV screens in airport departure lounges etc. The Afghan war veteran from Michigan, USA, pleaded guilty to child abduction and to inciting a child to commit gross indecency, at Manchester Crown Court on 2nd April 2004. Sentencing him to four-and-a-half years, Mr Justice Leveson told Studabaker: "What you did from your home in the United States was to groom an impressionable child into a relationship, with the result that she practised a deception on her family, left her home and travelled with you to France and then on to Germany." The nature and tone of some of your communications, including so-called cyber sex, demonstrates that you, then 32 years old, were intent on sexual intimacy with a girl you knew to be 12. Although the internet can be a force for very great good, it is not always so, and its abuse can slip under the guard of parents who are not aware what their children can get involved in while on the web. Where use of the internet has been involved, harsh sentences will be passed, particularly in relation to the grooming of children." Studabaker has also been indicted in Michigan,USA by a grand jury, on charges that include transporting a child across international borders for sexual exploitation. Any jail term imposed by a US court could be added to his current British jail sentence.

During mid-April 2004, at his home in the Winchester area of Hampshire, a top Crown Court Judge, David Selwood, the Resident Judge at Portsmouth Crown Court, was arrested over the nationwide/international *Operation Ore* child pornography allegations. The married father of four, who boasts an illustrious military record and a lengthy entry in *Who's Who?* was interviewed at Eastleigh police station, near Southampton. He was quizzed by detectives over allegations of possessing indecent images of children and released on police bail pending further inquiries. At his £500,000 home in leafy Magdalen Hill, Winchester, the curtains remained drawn, and the senior judge refused to talk to reporters about the allegation, when he answered his intercom.

Judge Selwood, 69, would only say: "Thank you for your enquiry, but I am afraid that I am not in a position to say anything at the moment." The former Army Major General had been listed to sit in Court 1 at Portsmouth Crown Court on Thursday 22nd April 2004 but did not attend. He was due to preside over the trial of Francis Snook, 70, of Portsmouth, accused of indecent assault. Legal argument was instead heard by Judge Roger Hetherington.

A Portsmouth Crown Court spokesman confirmed: "Judge Selwood has not been at work due to illness. We are not expecting him in next week either." A Hampshire police spokeswoman said: "The police can confirm that a man was arrested at an address in Winchester on Wednesday in connection with a countrywide paedophile operation. The man was interviewed at a police station in Hampshire and has been subsequently released on bail pending further enquiries." Judge Sellwood has been married for more than 30 years to his wife Barbara, with whom he has three sons and a daughter. In *Who's Who?* the judge lists a distinguished military career dating back to 1957, when he was a 2nd Lieutenant on National Service. He held military posts in the legal services in Germany and Cyprus before being appointed Director of Army Legal Services in the Ministry of Defence in London from 1990 to 1992. The son of a naval commander, he had been a circuit judge in Hampshire since 1992 and resident judge at Portsmouth Crown Court since 1996. He is also an author of the *Crown Court Index*, a respected legal publication which gives advice on crown court issues.

Judge Selwood has presided over a number of high profile cases at Portsmouth Crown Court. In 2001 he called a teacher who ran off with a 15-year-old schoolgirl, 'Every parent's nightmare.' He jailed Paul Tramontine, then 33, for 18 months, after hearing that the girl's mother could never forgive him. He also made headlines the same year after a legal loophole meant he had to free a man from jail who was branded 'Britain's most dangerous paedophile.' A spokesman for the Department for Constitutional Affairs said: "We can confirm that he is not currently sitting. We cannot comment on anything which may or may not be pending with this individual."

On 1st June 2004 it was announced publicly on BBC South TV news that Judge Sellwood was being retired prematurely on health grounds! (What?, No court case? Why on earth not?) I wouldn't mind betting that, like me, certain questions sprang to your mind as you read this report:

1) Did Judge Selwood receive the early morning sledge hammer knocking on his door?

2) Were police covering the rear as well as the front of his house in case he ran off?

3) Was his computer seized by police? How many vile images were downloaded or inspected by him?

4) Was he handcuffed behind his back?

5) Was he videoed for the continuance of the national *pay-as-you-view* child porn TV documentary?

6) At the police station, was he allowed his single phone call and did he turn his pockets out?

7) In 1992, did he walk straight into his Army-to-Judiciary career change under *The Old Pals Act?*

8) In the last few years, has he sentenced any other *pay-as-you-view* child porn offenders?

9) If so, could they have been members of a paedophile ring to which he might have belonged?

10) If the answers to questions 1-6 above are 'No', we have a *one law for rich, another for poor* scenario.

On the front page of the *Daily Express* newspaper dated 14th July 2004, beside a picture of him in his wig and robes, appears the following banner headline:

**Was this paedophile let off with a soft sentence
because he is a Crown Court judge?**

The main full-page article on page 11, carries two eye-catching, bold banner headlines:

(1) OUTRAGE AS HE WALKS AWAY WITH COMMUNITY ORDER

(2) Paedophile judge is let off with just a slap on the wrist

As this serious case of a senior judge, who was still sitting as 'judge-in-charge' at Portsmouth Crown Court, when he was arrested for downloading indecent images of young boys on his computer, is of such national importance and with far-reaching implications as to what goes on in the dark, murky world of paedophilia, I will now supply you with a verbatim report of the case, straight from the *Daily Express*.

> Children's charities hit out at *soft justice* yesterday after a former judge was given a 12-month community order for downloading indecent images of young boys. Experts condemned the sentence as 'little more than a slap on the wrist' and demanded a major overhaul of punishments for internet paedophiles. The NSPCC said: "Behind these indecent images are real children who will have suffered immense trauma. Receiving or downloading abusive images of children perpetuates its production and reinforces the cycle of exploitation. It is important to send out a strong warning to everyone, including those in all walks of life and professions that they cannot remain anonymous and escape the law, by using the internet to access abusive images of children." David Selwood, 70, looked relieved as he emerged from Bow Street magistrates court in central London, holding hands with his wife Barbara.
>
> He resigned recently as a £110,000 a year judge at Portsmouth Crown Court. He was once head of the Army's legal service, holding the rank of major general (This is just two ranks below the very top rank – Field Marshal), and gave advice to the SAS. While sitting as a judge in 2002, Selwood jailed an internet paedophile for seven years for having hundreds of indecent images of girls on his computer. He told Paul Hobbs, of Fareham: "Those who search for and download images of this kind create a market which encourages the abuse of young girls." Selwood admitted 12 counts of making indecent images of boys, aged from eight to fourteen, and one count of possessing 75 indecent pictures in his computer. The father of four was arrested at his £500,000 home in Winchester, Hants, after detectives were tipped off by US investigators that he was using his credit card to download pay-per-view paedophile websites. The court heard yesterday that the images were considered to be 'level one' – the least serious of the 5 categories of child pornography.

District Judge Timothy Workman was restricted by court sentencing guide-lines in punishing Selwood. He dismissed an application by Richard Hallam, defending, to give a conditional discharge. But legal experts said a 12-month community rehabilitation order was hardly a more severe penalty. Selwood was excused working in the community as part of the Order because of his age and health. He will also not have to attend a programme for sex offenders.

Mr Workman told the court: "The defendant is a man who until now has had an exemplary record, and who has throughout his career in both the Army and in the law, provided long and distinguished public service. He is entitled to credit for pleading guilty at the earliest opportunity and for his co-operation throughout with the police investigation. The commission of these offences and the convictions now recorded are undoubtedly a personal tragedy to him and his family." Selwood was put on the sex offenders' register for five years at a hearing last month. A senior lawyer involved in child porn prosecutions said: "This is little more than a slap on the wrist. The sentencing guidelines urgently need to be looked at again.

"A year's community rehabilitation order in cases like these simply does not represent an effective deterrent." Children's charity *Childline* welcomed the prosecution. Detective Chief Superintendent Jon Hesketh, who led the investigation said: "Mr Selwood disgraced the position of authority he held as a crown court judge." Despite calls that he should face severe financial penalties, Selwood will receive a £35,000-a-year pension plus a lump sum, thought to be around £75,000. He also has a substantial Army pension. Meanwhile, nine people were arrested by detectives and questioned at a London police station yesterday as part of the *Operation Ore* inquiry into child pornography on the internet.

On 1st July 2000, 8-year-old Sarah Payne from Hersham, Surrey, went missing while visiting her grandparents in Kingston Gorse, in Sussex. She had been playing in a field with her older brother. A massive search began and we saw thousands of images of her distraught parents, Sara and Michael Payne. There was very close media scrutiny in the area and the Forensic Science Service (FSS) was invited to help by Sussex police. It wasn't long before a local man on the sex offender's register became a police suspect but, at that early stage, there was no evidence. The suspect, Roy Whiting, was brought in for questioning, his van he used for work was seized and forensically examined, as of course was his clothing etc. Sarah's decomposing body was found on 17th July 2000.

Following a targeted approach, the FSS made their first breakthrough in December 2000, when a link was made between fibres found on Sarah's shoe and Whiting's red sweatshirt. Further forensic examination, patiently undertaken, produced more damning evidence than the original fibres on her shoe. This included fibres from Whiting's van, fibres in Sarah's hair from her grave site, and DNA tests proving that a hair found on the red sweatshirt had been one of Sarah's. A total of more than 500 individual items were submitted to the FSS laboratories. Over 20 forensic experts were employed. These were qualified and skilled in the fields of pathology, archaeology, entomology, geology, environmental profiling and oil/lubricant analysis. In all, a thousand personnel were involved in the major crime investigation, costing in excess of £2million.

The forensic evidence examined in *Operation Maple*, as it became known, rested on a combination of work on DNA and the fibres. When Sarah's body had been found on 17th July, she had no wounds from assault and in addition, her poor body was badly decomposed making identification difficult. Her DNA profile was obtained via one of her muscles and, fortunately, her mother Sara had saved one of Sarah's milk teeth, which proved to be an exact match to the muscle DNA. Shortly after Sarah had disappeared whilst at play, her brother Lee had noticed a white Ford Transit type van being driven along the lane. It transpired that Roy Whiting had purchased a white Fiat Ducato van a week before Sarah disappeared.

When police seized it, they took possession of all of its contents, which included a red sweatshirt, a pair of socks, a check-pattern shirt, a clown-patterned curtain and a petrol receipt, which proved that Whiting had been only a few miles away from where Sarah's body was discovered, on a certain day. Police also found that internal protective plywood panelling, installed by the van's previous owner, in the back of the van, had been removed. Furthermore, the rear doors had been removed. The fact that the fabrics of the seats on the driver's and passenger's sides of the cab differed also proved to be significant. The only piece of Sarah's clothing to be found was a black shoe with a Velcro fastening, which had trapped a total of 350 separate fibres. Some of these fibres of blue polyester and cotton, proved to match those on her school sweatshirt. All of the fibres were carefully gathered one-by-one under a microscope with a fine pair of tweezers and retained under sellotape for security against future loss. At a later stage, when a forensic scientist was examining the sellotaped 'tapings' from the red sweatshirt and the clown curtain, she became aware that the sweatshirt fibres were unusually dark red and that they easily became separated from the garment. When she next examined the fibres which had been carefully retrieved from the velcro shoe fastening, she saw that four of these were the same shade of dark red as those of which the red sweatshirt was constituted. She then inspected and compared, under a powerful microscope, a fibre from the Velcro and one from the sweatshirt, they proved to be a perfect match, thus scientifically and forensically linking Sarah to the van. After discovering this match, all of the fair hairs from the clown-curtain were sent for DNA comparison with the sweatshirt. A total of 40 hairs had been found and gathered, but only one from the 40 gave a positive result, a full DNA matching profile.

The red sweatshirt had been recovered from the front seat of the suspect's van. From this, tapings were made of fibres and hair, and screened for bodily fluids, such as saliva, semen and hair. Sweatshirt tapings were also examined for blue fibres of the type from which it was thought Sarah's dress had been made. All of the taped fair hairs were prepared for DNA and the collar and cuffs were also tested and found to give a full and perfect full profile to match Whiting's. From the site at which Sarah's body had been abandoned, two balls of her hair were retrieved. A number of fibres were retrieved from the hair balls and from the body bag. From one of them, fibres were found that matched the red sweatshirt and Whiting's socks. In the second clump of hair from the grave, fibres matched the sweatshirt, socks, and a single fibre from the passenger seat in the front cab of the van. One sock fibre and one from the driver's seat were also found in the body bag.

During all of the careful and thorough inspections of all of the fibres, a number of different blue polyester cotton fibres were found on several items. These were thought to have originated from Sarah's dress, although it had been impossible to obtain what is known as a 'control' sample fibre, for comparison. Sarah's friend with whom she had been playing on the day of her disappearance, had worn the same type of dress as Sarah, but it was green in colour. Forensic examination of fibres taken from the green dress showed similarities to the blue polyester cotton fibres. In all, 25 'patchy' blue polyester fibres were found on Sarah's silver-coloured jacket, which was known to have been worn over the missing dress. These were found to match nine fibres which had been found on the red sweatshirt. The same type of fibres were found in one of the hair masses retrieved from the body bag, and in the pocket of Whiting's jeans. Additionally, three blue polyester, textured fibres were found on Whiting's red sweatshirt, matching the same number in Sarah's hair. The enormity of the huge sequence of forensic tests carried out in the investigation by the FSS team between December 2000 and November 2001, can be judged by the fact that the team carried out 128 separate thin-layer chromatographic tests, 461 individual microspectrophotometry tests and 23 infrared spectroscopy tests.

During Whiting's subsequent trial, his female defence barrister had attempted to discredit the FSS team in a number of ways, making the following claims:

1) The red sweatshirt had been contaminated during its first-ever examination.

2) 2 hairbrushes had been taken from the Payne family home and sent to the Forensic Laboratory.

3) A Sussex Police SOCO had put them in a tube and then in a bag on the floor.

4) The seal was intact but some adhesive was exposed & human & animal hairs adhered from the carpet

During cross-examination, the defence team argued that as a result of the above factors, a 23cm long hair belonging to Sarah, had at first transferred onto the bag containing the red sweatshirt, and then onto the sweatshirt itself, when it was removed from the transport bag for its first examination in the lab. However it was shown that this examination had been completed before the hairbrushes were removed from the police exhibits store and no leaked orange adhesive from the bag seal had been found in Sarah's hair when it was tested. Whilst giving evidence in court, one of the FSS team witnesses had told the jury that it was unlikely that contamination had occurred in the manner suggested by the defence. Undertaking work on forensic exhibits from both the victim and the suspect did in fact provide opportunities for cross-contamination, even though normal rigorous and precise anti-contamination procedures had been followed. Even so, forensic examinations relating to items from the suspect, and from the victim, took place on totally different floors at the laboratory.

The evidence in respect of the fibres was less important. The defence argued that there were few fibres and that, in any case, the fibre tests are not as discriminating as DNA tests. However, the FSS team member was able to point out that although each type of fibre on its own, may not be rare, when taken together, the combination of the collection of fibres could provide very strong evidence indeed, in much the same way as 20 common *segments* of the *barcode* of the DNA, combined to give a very rare profile. Sarah Payne's mother, Mrs Sara Payne, over the years since her daughter's life was lost to Roy Whiting, has proved to be an inspiration to most people right across this country. She has bravely campaigned tirelessly to attempt to have legislation introduced, part of which to be known as *Sarah's Law*, but so far without success. In December 2001, Roy Whiting's jury found him guilty of the murder etc. of Sarah Payne. Mr Justice Richard Curtis sentenced him to life imprisonment and told Whiting that it was one of those exceptionally rare cases when he could recommend that his life sentence should mean life. This is known as a *whole-life tariff*.

Since Whiting's conviction for his horrific murder of Sarah Payne, and his subsequent disposition of her body, he has been attacked in jail by another inmate. His face was slashed in more than one place, probably using a razor blade embedded into a toothbrush handle, after warming it to soften the plastic. The convict who slashed Whiting was later placed on trial for the attack, during the summer of 2004. At the time of researching this feature in April 2004, Whiting is confined in HMP Wakefield in Yorkshire. The BOV (Board of Visitors), now known as the IMB (Independent Management Board) at HMP Wakefield, very recently made a very important, serious, and as they saw it, helpful recommendation to the Governor of that prison, which hosts Whiting and many others of a similar nature. They recommended that from then on, Whiting and other major and serial predating criminals currently incarcerated in Wakefield jail, should be addressed by Prison Staff as 'Mr Whiting' etc. This may well be adopted across the entire HMP establishment, although actual enforcement on a day-to-day basis may prove to be most difficult.

In fact the Prison Service liberal Directing Staff at HM Prison Service HQ, in London, have been trying to implement this *common courtesy* innovation for many years, commencing when Mr Martin Narey was its Director General. He has now moved on to be elevated to a most senior position where he commands not just the Prison Service but the Probation Service too, as Commissioner for National Offender Management Services. Although the title sounds American, it is unlikely that certain prison procedures from that continent will be adopted here in the UK, namely:

1) Convicts being moved around and delivered into USA courthouses wearing body belts of strong leather with attached handcuffs and ankle chains, to prevent attempted escape and injury to judges etc.
2) Court security staff wearing handguns at their belts.
3) Rear-of-courthouse visits areas behind glass or strong Perspex to prevent drugs ingress etc.
4) Dressed in bright orange jumpsuits for ease of identification.
5) Being forced to work on hard labour-type *chain gangs*, repairing roads etc.

One paedophile recently became the first person in Britain to be banned from all contact with children under the new child sex laws. Wheelchair-bound Kevin Fisher, 44, of Bristol, faces jail if he approaches a child or goes within 100 metres of a school or playground. He is also prevented from entering a house when a child is present, working with children, or photographing them. Fisher is the subject of a Sexual Offences Prevention Order. Bristol Crown Court in May 2004 was told that Fisher was exposed as a pervert while working as a technician at an internet café. Staff became concerned because they had seen him looking at images of undressed and swim-wear-dressed children. Judge Simon Darwall-Smith sentenced Fisher to nine months imprisonment.

On 11th June 2004, Mthokozisi Zondo, 28, an asylum seeker, was jailed at Cardiff Crown Court for trying to snatch a two-year-old girl away from her mother in *Argos Superstore*. The little girl was just two feet away from her mother when this man tried to lure her away. He was spotted by the shocked mum who reached for the toddler's hand, only for the paedophile to seize the screaming girl's wrist. An aunt, who was also on the trip to buy jewellery in Cardiff, said a *tug-of-war* ensued before the man, from Zimbabwe, walked off. The girl's mum told Cardiff Crown Court: " I heard someone saying 'Come on, come on.' A man was whispering and walking towards her, making beckoning signals. He grabbed her wrist and tugged. I took her other arm and pulled her towards me." Prosecutor Sue Ferrier said: "This is not a kind man with a healthy interest in children. It takes just seconds to take a child that age away from her parents. What happened is every parent's nightmare." Father of 4 Zondo claimed he was being friendly.

He denied attempted child abduction but was found guilty and the judge jailed him for 3 years. After serving his sentence he will be deported.

At Winchester Crown Court in June 2004 a perverted police surgeon was found guilty of drugging, sexually abusing and filming two 11-year-old girls at his home. Experts are trying to crack the master codes on his computers amid fears he has videoed other children as he assaulted them. But police say it could take 20 years to unlock the dark secrets hidden in the disgraced doctor's computer files. He was condemned for committing the 'grossest breach of trust a doctor could ever commit,' after he was convicted of raping one 11-year-old girl and molesting another. It then emerged that this wicked man found a job as a police doctor in Hampshire, despite standing trial in Sussex in 1995 for sexually assaulting girls aged 15 and 8. He was cleared by a jury and loose vetting procedures allowed him to secure the post of a forensic medical examiner, which brought him into contact with crime victims, many of them vulnerable children or single mothers. The lapse has parallels with the case of Soham double child killer Ian Huntley, who got a job as a school caretaker despite a history of sex allegations involving young girls. Dr. Robert Wells, 52, was told by Judge Keith Cutler: "The evidence has revealed the sinister and secret traits of your character and the jury has found you to be a dangerous sex offender. These convictions will send a shiver down the spines of many now fearful that your examination of them, some of them probably vulnerable or abused, gave you some perverted pleasure that no doctor should enjoy. The criminal behaviour reflected in this trial is deeply disturbing and will no doubt have an impact on society's regard and trust of the medical profession. It is difficult to think of a more deliberate and gross breach of trust." Wells, a father of four, was found guilty of two charges of rape and three of indecent assault on one of the 11-year-olds, and of taking an indecent photograph of her. He was also convicted of indecently assaulting and drugging the other 11-year-old girl and illegally administering drugs to her sister, aged five.

He was cleared of indecently assaulting the five-year-old. During the trial, Stephen Parish, prosecuting, described Wells as a 'Dr. Jekyll and Mr. Hyde' character and a 'serial paedophile.' He lured one of the 11-year-olds, known as Girl B, and her five-year-old sister, to his home in Southampton and gave them *Angel Delight* and milkshakes laced with date rape drugs. He is believed to have taken *Viagra* before attacking his victims. When Girl B fell unconscious, he filmed her as he indecently assaulted her. Their mother alerted police when the girl appeared 'spaced out' after Wells dropped the sisters back home. Officers seized his computers and discovered film of him abusing another 11-year-old, Girl A,in a camper van. Police also found evidence that he had accessed paedophile websites. Girl A told the court that Wells had rubbed baby oil over her and raped her 'five or six times.'

The attacks, in the autumn of 2002 and winter of 2003 took place in his flat or his camper van. Wells took off her Harry Potter pyjamas and swapped them for a maid's outfit or basque before abusing her. Medical examinations proved the girl had been raped. Traces of the sleeping drug temazapan, also used as a date-rape drug, were found in her hair. The court heard that Wells assaulted Girl B and her sister after persuading their mother to leave them in his care on 25th February 2003. After a trip to Marwell Zoo, he took them to his flat where he fed them both drugged *Angel Delight* desserts. He assaulted Girl B as she slept, filming the attack. Hospital tests revealed that Girl B had significant amounts of benzo diazepine, a powerful sedative, in her blood. Wells had administered a potentially lethal dose. Her little sister had been given temazapan.

The girls would have been knocked out by the drugs which would also have caused them to suffer amnesia. Police seized drugs and a biscuit barrel in which Wells stored them. They also found a timetable for picking the sisters up from the railway station, going to the zoo, drugging them and the abuse of the older girl. Other notes gave times and the words *Angel Delight* and *Viagra*, plus indications that what had happened had been filmed. The pervert's calculating approach to the sexual abuses appalled the judge. He told Wells: " You wrote a chilling programme of the days activities. It clearly refers to you feeding the girls temazapan and set your plan to film the older girl naked and indecently assault her."

Twice divorced Wells, who also had a private practice in Brighton, denied the charges. In a bizarre defence, he claimed he had framed himself for fake sex attacks. Wells claimed he wanted to kill himself with a lethal injection because he was depressed and in financial difficulties. He wanted to make sure no one would miss him by faking the sex crimes. But he did not go through with the suicide after receiving letters of support. Detective Inspector Sara Glen, who led the investigation, said: "It has been a very harrowing case. The components are awful and sufficient to leave these girls as very damaged people. Wells used his expert knowledge of drugs and forensics to cover his tracks. He also used expert computer knowledge to encrypt files on his computer. Wells did not co-operate at all during the investigation and would not reveal the code, which we suspect may hide more movie files. We appeal for anyone else who believes they have been abused by Wells to come forward."

Wells, a doctor for 27 years, was subsequently suspended by the General Medical Council, banned indefinitely from working with children and placed on the sex offenders' register for life. Wells obtained work with Hampshire Police in October 2001 via an agency, *Primecare*. He was made forensic medical examiner even though his past was known to the neighbouring Sussex force. A spokeswoman for *Primecare* said that Wells had worked for them since 1979 and it had completed all the checks required. At the time, guidelines required police only to check locally, and not other areas a person had lived in. Vetting procedures have since been improved. Judge Keith Cutler jailed Wells for 15 years.

A perverted Scout leader lured a nine-year-old boy into his bedroom and made him watch sickening child porn. Steven Castle, 41, who was trusted implicitly by parents, gloated while the stunned and bewildered lad was confronted with horrific images of young children being forced to have sex. Castle, who had conned the boy into thinking he would be getting computer lessons, then allowed a network of paedophiles to chat with the boy on the internet. He also bombarded the boy by e-mail with more disgusting pictures from his vast collection of child porn. He also sent innocent pictures of unsuspecting uniformed cubs in his care to a worldwide network of lusting perverts. One scout group member who cannot be named for legal reasons said: "Everyone was totally shocked. Steven was always so good with children. No one had any idea he was involved in this type of thing. A lot of the children have since left the cubs because the parents are worried. It's totally sick to expose a young child to such horrific photographs. He has corrupted this child's mind." Parents also fear that pictures of their children will be circulating round the secretive internet world of paedophiles for ever. The cubs, photographed on camping trips and during games organized by Castle, were clothed in their uniform shorts, shirts and woggles.

One appalled ex-friend said, "His life revolved around children and everyone thought he loved them. Every Sunday he would spend hours on his computer planning the games the Scouts would play next week. He also organized many camping trips with the children. He was very protective of them and got on very well with all the parents and no one can believe what he did." Castle, who was involved with the scouts for seven years and was also a bus driver for disabled children, traded photos of uniformed cubs with other sex fiends across the world in return for their porn pictures. When police raided his home at 8am he was chatting on-line to four other perverts. Police discovered he had a huge collection of images of teenage boys having sex with younger girls. There were pictures of children aged between two and sixteen years engaged in indecent acts with other children and adults. Other depraved pictures showed girls being dragged around by a leash and then forced to have sex with men. At Southwark Crown Court he was jailed for (just) four years. He has also been banned from ever working with children again, must never enter an internet chat room, never talk to a child on-line and never download internet files with any child content. However enforcement of these orders in future may be most difficult, if not impossible, due to already-overstretched police resources.

Two of Castle's mates who swapped pictures with him are also behind bars. Robert Wood, 24, of Dewsbury, West Yorks, is serving 42 years in Thailand for taking pictures of himself having sex with boys under 15 and then distributing them on the internet. Raymond McDonagh, 42, of Holloway, North London, is serving 10 years for having 12,000 images on his computer. Detective Sergeant Steve Quick, who helped to nail Castle, said: "Paedophiles feel secure behind certain types of computer software. But this is not foolproof and we have ways of tracking them down." The Scout Association said: "We now carry out stringent vetting of all adults who work with young people."

A married religious education teacher was jailed for 16 months at Doncaster for having an affair with a 14-year-old girl who developed a crush on him. Mike Hardy, 47, of Scarborough, slept with the girl after she sent him a valentines card and held his hand during a school trip. The couple had sex twice a week for six months before the girl's parents alerted police. He was Head of Year at a school in Hull and admitted five specimen charges of unlawful sex. The girl was in court and wept when he was jailed. His defence counsel told the court: "It's his foolish mistake, he accepted a girl's crush on him."

Head PE teacher Irvin Gale, 52, sent a series of explicit text messages to a 14-year-old female pupil. One message read: "I'm just getting into a hot bath with a glass of red wine. Wish you were here, kiss, kiss, kiss." He sent the seedy messages to the girl, who cannot be named, between April and June 2003. Bristol Crown court heard that when confronted with them he resigned. Gale pleaded guilty to a charge of abusing a position of trust. He was given a three year conditional discharge and ordered to sign on the sex offenders' register.

A paedophile who posed as a former police officer to abuse and rape boys, was convicted of 21 charges at Exeter Crown Court in May 2004. Robin Woods, 59, preyed on young lads aged seven to fifteen for 25 years, after luring them with sweets, beer, videos and shooting trips. He turned his Exmouth home into a playground. One 13-year-old victim suffered learning difficulties. Woods was jailed for life.

Mechanic Brian Darwent, 42, of Rotherham, faked suicide in a bid to escape justice for molesting children. He went missing on the day he should have been sentenced in 2003. He had dumped his car at the Humber Bridge and left two suicide notes saying he was going to jump off. He evaded police for 5 months before he was caught, when police found a van he was driving was insured in his real name, yet registered in the false name of Brian Green. At Sheffield Crown Court on 13th May 2004 he was jailed for four and a half years. He had admitted indecently assaulting a boy of eight and a girl of ten dating back to 1989. He also admitted perverting the course of justice by faking suicide.

An infant school teacher caught with 95,000 child porn images pleaded guilty to 42 charges and was jailed for seven years. Bachelor Martin Taylor, 39, of Hucknall, Notts, was described by Judge Dudley Bennett at Nottingham Crown Court as a 'genuinely evil paedophile.'

His collection of child porn images was discovered by police probing a fire at his home. Neighbours had smelt smoke and called the fire brigade. PC Phil Musson said: "His computer exploded." He had been a teacher at Butlers Hill infant school in Hucknall.

Ex-school director John Keeler, 59, from Somerset, was jailed for a string of sex assaults after being deported from Cambodia for similar offences. He was branded a 'manipulative predator,' who groomed his victims as objects of love. Police said later: "Young people worldwide will be safer as a result of this." In 2000 he had been jailed in Cambodia for 3 years for making indecent videos of girls as young as eight. Later he was deported and arrested on return to UK. His trial in Cambodia was seen as a test of the country's bid to stop a flood of foreign paedophiles. Earlier in 2003, Cambodia had banned Gary Glitter, who was jailed for four months in 1999 for possessing child porn. At Taunton Crown Court he was convicted of 21 counts of indecency involving three girls under 16 and was jailed for 15 years.

Stephen Mertens, 53, an ex-Tory Party official, went on the run after repeatedly raping a six-year-old girl. He was arrested for the attacks in May 1990 while he was secretary of Hackney and South Shoreditch Conservative Association in East London. Anthony Orchard, prosecuting at the Old Bailey, said the arrest came after the little girl victim revealed her ordeal to a friend. But Mertens jumped bail and set up home in Bristol with his wife, using a false name. He was arrested for another matter in July 2003 and police matched him to DNA evidence. Mr Orchard said police had also discovered e-mails in which he boasted of having sex with young girls. Mertens admitted two counts of rape. Two further charges of indecent assault and a further two of indecent assault on another girl, were ordered to lie on the file. On 20th July 2004 he was sentenced to ten years imprisonment. His victim, now aged 24 years, was present in court at the Old Bailey to see him sentenced.

It was revealed in July 2004 that British computer users try to access child porn sites on the internet up to 400,000 times a day. New internet *blocking* technology has exposed the true extent of the lust for sickening images. *British Telecom* has run secret trials of its *Cleen Feed* software on its own web service for three weeks. Over that time it stopped more than 230,000 attempted hits on the illegal sites, averaging about 10,000 requests a day. But *BT*'s 2.8million internet customers account for just a tenth of the 27.5million who use the web in the UK and it is believed that the real figure is astronomical. Shy Keenan, who runs the internet child victims' organization *Phoenix Survivors Group*, said: "This is a major step forward by *BT* in the battle to stop paedophiles, but it is only the tip of the iceberg. We estimate there are as many as 400,000 hits a day in Britain, of people trying to access these sites."

BT's figures have provided the first concrete evidence of the massive extent of web paedophilia. The *Internet Watch foundation* called them 'staggering.' It supplied a list of 15,000 sites with child porn to *BT* and adds about 80 sites a week to the list. *BT* has now offered to help other internet service providers block access to the sites by their own customers. Home Office Minister Paul Goggins said he was "deeply shocked" by BT's findings and urged other companies to take up *BT*'s offer of help. A police spokesman called *BT*'s figures "extremely disturbing" and called for efforts by other ISP's.

The Sun newspaper's Online correspondent, Jonathan Weinberg, said:

"About 99 per cent of illegal web material is hosted outside the UK. *BT* has done well, but until bodies like the EU get together to act, this tide of filth will continue."

Serving Police Constable Lee Doggett, 24, of Northumbria Police, was caught red-handed by police colleagues as he indecently exposed himself to girls as young as ten, as he performed a sex act whilst holding a pornographic magazine in a play area. Doggett exposed himself to girls as they walked to school in Cramlington, Northumberland, and was immediately arrested by police who had been keeping watch on him.

At Newcastle Crown Court, Doggett was convicted of outraging public decency and indecency with a child. Although Doggett's lawyer Paul Greaney, defending, argued that no attempt was made to touch any of the girls, Judge Tim Hewitt told Doggett, his behaviour was "obscene" and jailed him for six months.

The Queen's former choir-master was branded a predatory paedophile at Reading Crown Court on 25th August 2004, for attacking children in his care. Jonathan Rees-Williams, 55, who served the Royal Family at Windsor, abused victims as young as nine years of age, over a period of 14 years. He attacked them in churches, at his home and on coaches and trains. Rees-Williams, of Bristol, was convicted of 18 charges of indecent assault and jailed for five years. He was given a further three months imprisonment for possessing 127 obscene images of children on computers. None of the assaults related to his time as organist and choirmaster at St George'Chapel, Windsor. He resigned in 2002. The children concerned were his music students. A legal expert said the *predatory paedophile* could have been given ten years.

In September 2004 a pensioner was jailed for three-and-a-half years after admitting a series of sex attacks on a teenager more than thirty years ago. Retired electrician Frank Newberry, 66, preyed on a 13-year-old girl between 1972 and 1973 while he was teaching her horse riding at a stables. Newberry, a married father of two, forced the girl to have sex with him and sexually assaulted her on a regular basis over a year, after befriending her family so that he could give her lifts to and from the stables. Police traced him to Bedfordshire after a two-year probe which began when Newberry's victim, now a 45 year old mother of two, contacted Scotland Yard in 2002.

Newberry, from Royston in Herts, admitted four counts of indecent assault at Wood Green Crown Court in North London. The judge ordered a further four counts of rape to remain on the file, but sentenced him on the basis he repeatedly forced the girl to have sex with him.

A top tennis coach has been arrested after a former child prodigy claimed she was raped by him. Christopher Dunkley, 57, currently separated from his wife, has been accused of sexually assaulting the girl when she was 16. He was held by police after his alleged victim, now in her 20's, made written statements claiming he raped her when he was her tennis coach. She claims one assault occurred in the grounds of a school after a coaching session. Dunkley, a performance development officer for Hertfordshire Lawn Tennis Association was arrested after going voluntarily to a police station. He was bailed to a later date pending furthr police enquiries. The alleged victim still works in the game and has been seen with some of the world's top players. Dunkley has denied the allegations. A spokeswoman for the LTA said: "We have taken immediate action to suspend Mr Dunkley's coaching licence until this case is resolved."

Quite a few years ago a disgusting, serial-paedophile named Sidney Cook, went to a fair or circus at Wokingham, Berkshire, and kidnapped an innocent young lad called Mark Tildesley, who had gone there on his own on his bike, from his home only about one mile away. His parents were frantic with worry and their distress continued for very many years. Nationwide publicity was generated. Eventually it all came out. It turned out that Cook and possibly other members of his paedophile ring, had taken poor Mark to a caravan parked in a field not too far from where the circus or fair was parked. There, it is thought that Mark was drugged and then passed around the assembled sexual predators, who gang-raped him in turn. It is difficult to comprehend the poor lad's fear, apprehension and ongoing suffering until they finally murdered him. His battered body was never found and therefore his parents were denied closure, as they were unable to give him a proper Christian burial. As far as I know, the only visible reminders to passers-by in Mark's old home market town of Wokingham, of his former existence, are that the field from where he was abducted has been renamed *The Circus Field*. A very well-equipped swimming pool and leisure complex has been erected on the site. Using specially imported huge timbers from Scandinavia, the building complex has actually been designed and constructed to look exactly like a circus 'big top' tent. Additionally a wooden bench has been installed there, at the field corner. The bench bears an inscribed plaque to Mark Tildesley's memory. Another member of the ring of Paedophiles came clean years later and supplied useful information, as a result of which the Metropolitan Police, with the assistance of other police forces, made a huge sweep and arrested many of the paedophiles and murderers. One of them, whose name escapes me, was himself murdered in jail by another prisoner, therefore you might think that justice was done and seen to be done in his case.

Several other young boys had been abducted over the years by this unwholesome mob. One boy, again on his bike, was thrown into the back of a motor car, bicycle too, and, it is believed, taken to a paedophile ring gathering in a block of council flats in the Hackney area of East London. This boy too, was passed around the pitiless group and later taken to the Bristol or Gloucester area of the West Country, his wretched body being dumped on a golf course.

A millionaire dubbed Britain's worst paedophile was jailed for life on 4th October 2004, after sexually assaulting thousands of young boys over 40 years. Victims clapped and cheered as pervert William Goad, 60, was warned he may never be freed because he poses such an extreme danger to children. Businessman Goad once boasted of abusing 142 boys in a single year and even urged one youngster to snatch a five-year-old boy off the street for him. One of his victims was only eight when he raped him in front of another man during a camping trip. Others were assaulted up to three times a week for three years. Two of the pervert's victims have killed themselves and several others have attempted suicide. One young man summed up the devastating impact of being one of Goad's long-term victims. He told police: "Sometimes I wished he'd killed me rather than leave me with the torture, memories and nightmares." Goad, who ran shops and market stalls, lured vulnerable youngsters into his clutches by offering them money, toys, sweets and drink. His home, equipped with pool table and computer games, would attract at least ten boys aged between 13 and 16 almost every day. He even paid a £50 'finder's fee' to victims to introduce him to their young friends, Plymouth Crown Court was told.

Wealthy Goad guaranteed the boys' silence by threatening to harm their mothers, or giving them cash, up to £150 each. He admitted 14 specimen charges of buggery and two of indecent assault. Judge William Taylor told the monster: "The boys were attracted to you by your wealth, your apparent kindness and the facilities to be found at your home, which was a magnet for youngsters who went there seeking excitement, money or drugs. You used money, drugs and the offer of jobs to purchase sexual favours. Some boys were groomed while others were effectively raped soon after they met you. I am in no doubt you pose an ongoing and serious danger to young men and will do so for an indeterminate time." Goad will have to serve at least six years and six months before he can apply for parole. But Judge Taylor told him: "You will not be released until authorities are satisfied you no longer pose any threat to children. In your case life may well mean just that."

Some of Goad's victims spoke of their delight at seeing their tormentor jailed for life. As he was led to the cells one shouted 'Beast' the name they called him after his sex attacks. David Batcup, defending, had told the court that Goad was a sick man who needed a heart by-pass operation while awaiting trial. When the barrister said Goad might die in prison, a victim shouted: "Good, the sooner the better!" Later another victim said: "I hope he rots in hell, he ruined so many lives." A man who was a child when Goad abused him, said: "My life is worthless because of that bastard. A lot of us have turned to drink and drugs and crime to shut out what the beast did to us. He should never be let out of jail. I hope he has it rough in prison. Some of his victims might be in there and could get to him and get revenge for us. That would be the sort of justice he should understand, picking on a weak vulnerable victim." Goad's first known attacks date back to 1965, which means it is likely he has abused thousands of children. When police started closing in on him he fled to Thailand where they fear he carried on abusing children.

Finally arrested after returning to Britain on a false passport in 2003, Goad falsely accused victims of attempting to obtain compensation from him. He had been in court three times for indecent assault in the past but each time was let off with a light sentence. In 1972, he was put on probation and put on a sex offenders rehabilitation course. He was given suspended sentences in 1980 and 1987. He was said to have preferred boys with blonde hair and blue eyes aged between 13 and 16, but at least one of his victims was as young as eight. Martin Meeke, QC, prosecuting said Goad groomed victims by offering them well-paid jobs in his shop and inviting them back to his home. "Goad has been a voracious, calculating, predatory and violent homosexual paedophile for 40 years," added Mr Meeke.

Boys who went to his comfortable home in Plymouth were treated to sweets, cash, pool and games. Mr Meeke said: " It was a lure or a magnet for these young boys, who seem always to be on hand." The earliest charge against Goad involved a boy of ten who was attacked between 1965 and 1967. He met the youngster through a camping club. The boy's character completely changed after he was raped by Goad. His school work suffered and he later turned to drink and drugs. He was plagued by nightmares and contemplated suicide. As Goad was taken to a high security, segregated cell, it emerged how he destroyed the lives of victims with relentless sexual abuse and threats of violence to keep them silent. Everything he did was directed at meeting boys. He employed them at his shops and market stalls, owned two houses overlooking school playgrounds and ran a camping club. Mr Meeke added: "Police conducted a huge enquiry and they understand that there has not been a single defendant with more victims than this man."

The son and heir to the Earl of Caithness, a family friend of Prince Charles, was put on the sex offenders' register after being convicted of having under-age sex. Alexander James Berriedale, 23, who holds the title of Lord

Berriedale, was spotted having sex with his 15-year-old girlfriend at a beauty spot near Wick, Highlands. The town's Sherriff Court heard he still has a relationship with the girl, who has turned 16. She attended court in support of Berriedale, who was also put on probation for a year. His father is a former Paymaster General and Privy Counsellor to the Queen.

A man who rescued a three-year-old girl from a stranger trying to abduct her, was hailed as 'an absolute hero' by her father. Rescuer Stuart Wilson acted as Martine Emerson, three, was being led away in broad daylight yards from her home. She had been playing with her brothers and sisters in a quiet, suburban street when a man approached and took her hand. As trusting little Martine walked off by his side, Mr Wilson gave chase. He earned the tearful gratitude of Martine's shaken parents after grabbing the girl back and returning her home unharmed. Mr Wilson, a 20-year-old electrician, lives a few streets away from Martine's home but was working on a house four doors from theirs in the Vange district of Basildon, Essex, when the drama unfolded. Mr Wilson said: "I heard a couple of children shouting and screaming. One of them told me a little girl had been taken away by a strange man. I jumped into my car and drove up the road where I saw the man leading her along by her hand. As I pulled up beside him, we caught each other's glance and then he tried to run with her. He then picked her up under one arm and started to run towards woodland. I chased after him and shouted to him to leave her alone. He realized I was close to him and dropped her. Mr Wilson said the man ran off towards Basildon golf club. "I thought about chasing after him but I decided it would be better to get her back to her parents as soon as possible. You can imagine their relief. The little girl was very confused. She didn't seem confused but I think she was too young to understand what had happened." Martine's father Darren Emerson, a 35-year-old construction worker said: "I owe everything to Stuart. Martine is a trusting and friendly girl. I was sat in my front garden and didn't even realize what was going on until I heard the screech of Stuart's car driving off. He is an absolute hero who probably saved my daughter's life." Police are hunting the attacker, described as white, in his 20's, around 5ft 10 ins tall, of stocky build with short brown hair.

A leading criminal lawyer faced a long jail sentence after being caught downloading hardcore child pornography. Former policeman John Temple's life was in ruins after he admitted 34 offences involving sexual images which he then distributed to other internet perverts.

Detectives who raided his home and legal chambers said some of the 3,700 images were among the most serious they had encountered. One depicted abuse on a baby thought to be just 10 months old, a month older than Temple's own baby at the time. Other pictures showed youngsters having sex with adults and yet more fell into the most serious category of obscenity, touching on sado-masochism and bestiality.

Police said that Temple, a former Royal Navy recruit and North Yorkshire police officer, played a 'commanding role' in the distribution of the pictures. Temple, 46, is living apart from his wife Deborah, 39, a former police officer, and their children, aged four and 16 months. Their £315,000 five-bedroomed detached house in a village near Durham is up for sale. Temple was granted bail on condition he lives in Scarborough with his father James, a retired fireman, pending sentence. When he appeared at Liverpool Crown Court on Wednesday 5th January 2005, he admitted 16 offences of making indecent images, 17 of distributing them and one of possessing more than 3,700 images on his computer, between January 2000 and May 27 last year. The maximum sentence he faces is 10 years. His arrest came after detectives were tipped off by the National Crime Squad as part of the long-running *Operation Ore* inquiry. In 2003, at the Appeal Court in London, Temple successfully got a convicted paedophile's sentence for possessing and taking indecent photographs of children, reduced from eight years to just three.

The apparent suicide of a naval commodore under investigation on child pornography allegations has focused attention on a huge British police investigation into internet paedophiles, in which 32 other suspects are believed to have taken their lives. *Operation Ore* was launched when American investigators supplied credit card details of 6,500 Britons who entered a US pay-per-view web *portal*, called *Landslide*, to gain access to around 300 websites carrying child abuse images.

The commander of British forces on Gibraltar, Commodore David White, who was found dead in his swimming pool at the weekend, was an *Ore* suspect. The former submariner was 51 and single. Brought up in Kent, he was educated at Eton. Since 2002, more than 3,700 people identified from the US list have been arrested in Britain. Some 4,300 premises have been raided in the hunt for computers. More than 1,800 people have been brought before the courts, with some jailed and many getting non custodial sentences. More than 500 others have been cautioned by police, after admitting offences. Their numbers have swollen the Sex Offenders' Register. The remainder of those arrested, around 1,400, are on police bail while computers are 'interrogated'. Around 900 further cases are at the pre-arrest stage. Hundreds more on the US list, distributed to British forces after work by the National Crime Squad (NCS), have yet to be examined. The inquiries have cost the British police millions of pounds. Though US authorities shut down the *Landslide* operation to which British 'customers' paid up to £21 a month for *platinum* membership, giving access to sexual images of children, only hundreds of subscribers have been investigated in America. However, Germany, Switzerland, Italy, Belgium and Australia are working through their full lists, like Britain. British suspects include lawyers, doctors, teachers and police officers. Pete Townsend, the guitarist with The Who, was cautioned. Many, even though they may not go to prison, have faced shame and professional disgrace.

Some question whether *Operation Ore* has been justified.
Key questions are:

- Were the Landslide images real? Police say they were real children, some very young. There is a high suicide rate among victims of abuse.
- Who decided they were indecent and illegal? In Ore cases, a child was classed as someone under 16, though the law has since changed.
- Has the operation prevented abuse? The 3,700 arrests have so far generated 109 British cases where children considered at risk were removed to safety.
- Could suspects have come across the sites accidentally? Police say that to access the Landslide child images, you had to give e-mail and credit card details.
- Could investigations have been conducted in secret, without arrests? Anecdotally, at least one police force has contacted those on its Ore list to warn "we know who you are, stop it". However, most believe it is impossible to gauge the risk that individuals might pose to children without arresting and investigating.
- Could police have been quicker, and more sensitive? The length of time taken by some forces to work through the Ore lists is seen as unacceptable. Police say they are aware of the trauma for suspects and tread warily.

A top Royal Navy officer quit as the Queen's Harbour Master, as he appeared in court charged with a string of child porn offences. Commander Tom Herman, 48, is accused of possessing 173 pornographic photographs of children under the age of 16 between December 2003 and November last year. He also faces 20 charges of making indecent images of children. Herman was arrested two months ago after Ministry of Defence police raided his cottage in Titchfield near Fareham, Hants, and seized computer equipment. He was formally charged when he answered bail last week. Herman spoke only to confirm his name, age and address during the five minute hearing at Fareham Magistrates' Court. But Caroline Busst, representing Herman, indicated that he would plead not guilty to all the charges. Herman was granted unconditional bail and the case was adjourned.

Making indecent images of children carries a maximum Ten year sentence. Possessing indecent images could lead to five years in prison. After the hearing it emerged that Herman had decided to step down from his role as Queen's Harbour Master. A Royal Navy spokesman said: "Commander Herman is no longer Queen's Harbour Master and has been granted a reappointment at his request. He will be given another appointment in the Royal Navy in the area, which will be less onerous. This will allow him to face these charges." Herman had headed a 28-strong team based in Portsmouth, and his duties are now being undertaken by his deputy, Lieutenant Commander Tim Gibson. Herman, a father of three, met his wife Amanda in 1981 when she was a Naval Nursing Sister in the Royal Naval Hospital at Haslar, Hants. He became Queen's Harbour Master in 2002. The historic title, personally approved by the Queen, meant he was responsible for guarding the British fleet at its Portsmouth home. He was awarded the OBE in 1999 for his part in planning and executing the submarine element of the Kosovo campaign. He is a submariner and specialist navigator with nearly 30 years' service, having commanded two subs - HMS Opossum and the ballistic missile sub HMS Renown. Herman accompanied Prince Andrew on a tour of Naval headquarters when the Royal travelled to Portsmouth to take a look at new equipment in May 2003. As the Harbour Authority for Portsmouth Harbour and the Eastern Solent, the Queen's Harbour Master and his staff of 28 carry out a significant number of duties each year. They ensure that the 156,000 yearly shipping movements under their control each year are safely carried out, and with minimum impact to the surrounding area. The QHM has responsibility for all shipping, military and commercial, that is in Portsmouth Dockyard.

A paedophile who built up Britain's biggest collection of child pornography walked free from court because of a legal loophole. Married father-of-five John Harrison, 55, amassed a library of more than a million sickening images, including photographs of babies. But the computer expert, caught after a worldwide police operation, escaped a maximum ten-year sentence. New laws which came into force in January 2001, raised the maximum term for Harrison's crimes from three to ten years. But Judge John Burke QC, at Minshull Street Crown Court in Manchester, was powerless to use the tougher legislation because the charges date back to 1997. Harrison was jailed for two-and-a-half years after he admitted conspiracy to distribute indecent images and making and possessing pictures. But because he had already served 16 months on remand, more than half his sentence, he was allowed to walk free. Norman Brennan, from the *Victims of Crime Trust*, said: "Every parent in Britain will be in total shock and disbelief over this. How many depraved images did he need to go to prison, two million or three? When will the punishment ever fit the crime in this country?" Michelle Elliot, from children's charity *Kidscape*, said: "I am hugely concerned by this. There are a million images of children yet this man has walked free."

Harrison, who was also a foster carer, built the collection while working for a US paedophile web-site known as *The Brotherhood of Sharing*, the court heard. As well as storing the images, he helped to run internet bulletin boards for paedophiles. Police who raided his home in Denton, near Manchester, found images on his computer of adults having sex with children, sadism and bestiality. James Rae, prosecuting, said: "It is physically impossible to put before the court an accurate figure for the amount of images involved. "But Harrison has accumulated the largest private library of obscene images of children that has yet to be recovered in the United Kingdom. He had well over a million images." Harrison was seized with 65 others worldwide in 2003 after the arrest of notorious US paedophile Earl Webster Cox, known as 'The Master' of the website ring. He was given 30 years in the US. Harrison worked as an administrator, assessing new images. Paedophiles accessed the restricted site to swap images, which were described as 'absolutely horrific' by detectives. Judge Burke told him: "It is because people like you derive twisted gratification from these disgusting images that these children, some babes in arms, are treated as slaves and routinely defiled by their depraved keepers." Harrison, who has to sign the Sex Offenders' Register for life, refused to comment as he fled into a taxi, attempting to cover his face with a coat.

Paedophiles and sex offenders will sit lie detector tests to ensure they have lost their sick urges, David Blunket has stated. Those who lie about their habit will automatically be sent back to jail or refused parole. Satellites will also keep tabs on offenders 24 hours a day. The Home Secretary's crackdown will delight millions of parents. Tony Blair has told police officers: "Where there are prolific offenders, even when they come out of prison again, it's important they are tracked and monitored. We can make sure these people realize they've got a choice every single day. They can either go straight or go back inside again." Mr Blunkett said: "We are talking about really modern technology and we are testing it. It won't just pick up whether a person is lying. It will be a major deterrent. People can rest more securely in their beds."

Lie detectors, known as polygraphs, proved successful in tests and new versions are less susceptible to rogue results, they work by reading changes in body temperature, blood pressure and breathing. Sex offenders will be asked if they have kept away from kids, and if they still have sick urges. Experts say they are 90 per cent accurate, but results are not admissible in

UK courts. The Home Office's pilot is running in 14 counties. Mr Blunkett wants the proposed law to be put before judges. Convicted perverts will have to carry a mobile phone linked to a satellite tag on their ankle. The satellite is connected to a call centre and if the link breaks an alarm will go off. It will ensure paedophiles don't go anywhere near schools or parks or other exclusion zones. The technology was developed for charging vehicles on toll roads. Mr Blunkett's announcement, two weeks before the European parliament and town hall elections, sparked a political row. Ministers are barred from unveiling new policies during an election campaign. A spokesman for the *Association of Chief Police Officers* said he was 'optimistic' about the plan. Sex crime expert Ray Wyre, a leader in the field for 27 years, said: "Sex offenders can't now just disappear when they have been released."

Convicted paedophile Matthew Brereton, 34, from Dunstable, Beds, has been using a chat room provided by internet service provider AOL, to air his views. A spokesman for AOL said that if a user broke their code they could be banned.

Richard Brunstrom, Chief Constable of North Wales, has blasted a 'ludicrous' gap in the law which lets out perverts likely to reoffend after they have served their sentences. A particular sex offender, who cannot be named, is so dangerous that experts forecast that he will kill someone, is set to be freed from jail by a legal loophole. The prisoner is one of several thought to be a risk to the public but who can't be kept locked up because they are not mentally ill. Mr Brunstrom said, "We are waiting for him to kill somebody so that we can arrest him. But he is received (back) into society, which does not make sense to me. We are failing to protect citizens. We should rethink whether these people are allowed out in society." But the Home Office said that new provisions under the Criminal Justice Act would block their release.

A spokeswoman said: "New sentences for dangerous offenders will be geared towards public protection, and will ensure they are assessed by the parole board and in serious cases are not released until their level of risk is assessed as manageable in the community."

(**Author's note:** *My own conclusions are that there is great diversity and inconsistency of sentencing from Court to Court for similar degrees of offending by paedophiles. I am absolutely amazed that former Resident Judge at Portsmouth Crown Court, Mr David Selwood, who engaged in downloading of child pornography on his personal computer, whilst still in Judicial Office, and was eventually arrested by police working on international Operation Ore, was not committed to a Crown Court for trial* *or sentence, by the District Judge at Bow Street Magistrates Court. This meant he was singled out for a minor community rehabilitation order punishment, giving rise to apparent confirmation of the old adage 'One law for the rich – another for the poor." The man was an absolute hypocrite and had previously jailed at least one sexual offender for engaging in the self-same disgraceful hobby in which he himself indulged. I am further amazed that the Crown Prosecution Service did not submit an immediate appeal to the effect that former Judge Selwood's sentence was far too lenient.)*

Readers may be astonished that, in the enlightened world in which we live these days, people in high places, colloquially referred to as 'The Politically Elite', in this case the lay members of the Independent Management Board (Formerly 'Board of Visitors') at HMP Wakefield, took it upon themselves to dictate that serious, murdering paedophiles like Roy Whiting and Ian Huntley, should be addressed by HM Prison staff as 'MR WHITING' and 'MR HUNTLEY', or by their first names or nicknames. This should be viewed in contrast with the recent case of a prison officer with very many years of loyal service, who was dismissed for 'gross misconduct,' having been overheard and reported for referring to adult male prisoners as 'convicts' and a meal time as 'feeding time.' He later took HM Prison Service to an Employment Tribunal. During the course of the Hearing, he referred to a dictionary definition of the word 'convict', as 'a person serving a prison sentence.' From my personal experience working on the landings in a juvenile prison for six years (ages 15-18yrs), viz: 'at the sharp end,' I have experienced many displays of modern liberalism and can reiterate the popular expression, 'This is political correctness taken far too far.' Some examples of this liberalism in HM Prison Service establishments will be reported elsewhere in this book.

A paedophile has been given £5,500 compensation by European judges because of the length of time his case took to come to court. Barrister Rupert Massey, 59, who was jailed for sexually abusing three young boys, complained legal delays had caused him stress. Even though Massey himself stretched out proceedings by electing for a lengthy committal process, then pleading not guilty, judges at the European Court of Human Rights in Strasbourg sided with him. They awarded the paedophile £2,748 in damages and £2,748 costs.

One of Massey's victims who was awarded only £6,000 compensation for all the suffering he experienced because of the pervert, spoke of his disgust at the ruling. Dave Meek, now 41, waived his right to anonymity to demand: "I want to know how the European Court of Human Rights can justify insulting me in this way." Meek, who was eight when he was abused by Massey, said no one considered the stress he had endured as the case dragged on for five years. Where was the European Court when I was sat at home tearing my hair out because of yet another adjournment in the case? Three of us had to go through the stress of the court case and I had to talk about the most intimate details what happened to me. Most people would not be able to imagine what it is like to be abused in the first place, let alone give evidence in court." Mr Meek, who received £6,000 from the Criminal Injuries Compensation Board, added: "This judgment defies logic and all justice. "The people that matter, the victims, the police and the prosecutors were never consulted over his claim for money and that can't be right."

Peter Saunders, of the *National Association for People Abused in Childhood*, said: "A convicted child abuser receiving compensation seems perverse. By pleading 'not guilty' he made it a lot worse for his victims." Oxford-educated Massey, who was also an actor and appeared in the John Cleese film Clockwise, befriended his victims on a beach in Poole, Dorset. After gaining their trust, he took them to his home where he abused them. The offences took place between 1971 and 1985 but Massey was not arrested until one of the boys made a complaint to Dorset police in 1995. Massey was eventually charged in December 1997 with 16 counts of indecent assault.

Massey chose a time-consuming old-style committal hearing, to see if he had a case to answer and pleaded not guilty at his trial, which had to be moved to Wolverhampton because he was too well-known in Dorset. The trial started in November 1999 and he was found guilty the following month. Mr Justice Poole jailed him for six years, saying his victims had suffered "moral corruption and emotional damage."

After Massey lost an appeal against his convictions, he applied to the European Court of Human Rights. In its judgment, the court said: "Criminal proceedings lasting nearly five years exceeded the reasonable time requirement of guaranteeing a fair trial in Article 6.1 of the European Convention on Human Rights. It is reasonable to assume that the applicant suffered some distress and frustration."

A magician spanked a schoolgirl with his magic wand before having sex with her, a court heard. Children's entertainer Eric Blackledge, 62, showed her where he made his wands then allegedly hit her on the bottom with a cane. The girl, who is now 25, told a jury that Blackledge, who used the stage name Eric Black, 'spanked' her in the shed he used as his magic workshop. Cardiff Crown Court heard she developed a 'crush' on Blackledge and had sex with him when she was 14.

Prosecutor Richard Twomlow said: "He told the girl he had fallen in love with her. But there was a great gap between their ages. "He said he would wait until she was 14 then he would have sex with her." After having initial doubts, the girl went to his house and they had full sexual intercourse on his bed." Mr Twomlow said Blackledge performed at schools and functions and went to people's homes for parties. Blackledge, of Porthcawl, South Wales, admits having sex with the girl when she was over 16 but denies indecent assault. The trial continues.

COUNT 3

VIOLENCE
IN THE STREET, CLUBS AND PUBS

A furious chef went on a Basil Fawlty-style rampage, smashing up a restaurant and threatening staff with a knife, after he was asked to cook more food. Hotel workers and customers were terrified when overworked Peter Grice went berserk with waiters who refused to stop taking orders. The 23-year-old caused £20,000 worth of damage after he threw a fire extinguisher through a glass door, wrecked the kitchen, threatened staff with a knife, smashed chairs and pictures and chucked a printer out of an office window. His manager was so scared he barricaded himself in the hotel's bar. After his rampage, he calmly rode off on his bicycle. Grice, of Wellington Street, Gloucester, was jailed for six months on 1st March 2005 after pleading guilty to affray and criminal damage at the city's Crown Court. Judge Jamie Tabor said: "I am picturing myself enjoying a meal at the pub and then out comes a kitchen manager going berserk, and it must have been terrifying."

Grice went on his rampage at Twigworth Lodge Hotel, Twigworth, on January 14th in scenes reminiscent of John Cleese's madcap hotel manager in sitcom *Fawlty Towers*. He had asked waiters to stop taking orders because the kitchen, which he had managed for five months, was overworked. The manager refused to let them, saying many of the 200 customers were still waiting for food. He then tried to suspend Grice, setting off the tirade. The manager fled when Grice threw a chair. The chef then returned to the kitchen and hurled a fire extinguisher through a glass door. The manager barricaded himself in the bar while Grice continued smashing things in the kitchen as staff tried to hold him. Mary Harley, prosecuting, said they let him go when Grice picked up a knife and threatened them and the manager with it. "Staff and customers were petrified," she said. "He then rode off on his bike." Giles Nelson, defending, said Grice only became violent in the high-pressure environment of the service industry, adding: "He realises his behaviour was disgraceful." He added that Grice, who is now working night shifts at *Tesco*, would miss the birth of his child in May if he went to jail. But Judge Tabor told Grice the public would expect nothing other than jail. He added: "I think your sentence should be short so you have the opportunity to see a doctor about the extraordinary loss of temper you suffer from."

On 1st May 2004 in the early hours of the morning at Hove, East Sussex, there took place an apparent 'Kenneth Noye'-style road rage killing. A 25-year-old man was repeatedly stabbed in the street after a three car pile-up. The victim was pronounced dead at the scene, after paramedics had fought to keep him alive as he lay on the grass of the central reservation of a dual carriageway. As the suspected killer tried to escape, an on-looker dialled 999, police sealed-off the area and a man was taken into custody for questioning, believed to be one of the drivers. Police said that the victim will not be identified until after a post mortem has been carried out, and that the attack was 'appalling'. One elderly resident in the area, who did not want to be named, said: "I heard cars colliding and then saw young men gesticulating aggressively in the street. I went back to bed but it was awful to hear later that a young man had died in such dreadful circumstances.

In the last few years this sort of disturbance in the street has become almost commonplace on Friday and Saturday nights." Another local resident spoke of being woken up by a group of girls in the street frantically shouting: "Call the police, call the police!" Several days later, two Albanian

---

ANGELO'S ARGUMENT OVER HIS BUS FARE ENDED UNHAPPILY —IN THE DOCK

EVERY TIME Angelo Laudat took a 69 bus from Woolwich Ferry to his home in Canning Town he paid 7½p fare.

But on Saturday night the conductor charged him 10p. An argument between Laudat and the conductor Emil Baruxakis followed, magistrates at East Ham court were told on Tuesday.

The situation became violent and Mr. Baruxakis received a split lip and his glasses were broken in the fracas that followed.

Laudat, of Florence street Canning Town, was charged with assault causing bodily harm, disorderly behaviour and unlawful damage.

DIFFICULT

A 29-year-old labourer, he told the court his domestic situation was difficult and he had had a few drinks before he got on the bus.

"I fell asleep and the conductor woke me. He told me the fare from Woolwich Ferry to Canning Town supermarket was 10p

"I said I had paid 7½p the other times I had made the same trip. He disagreed and would not give me 2½p change from the 10p I gave him.

"I stood up and we argued then he punched me before I punched him. I feel ashamed of what I did because he is a much older man than me and I apologise to him and the court for what I did."

Magistrate Mr. Alan Davis told Laudat: "You have got to be made to realise that attacking what is virtually a public servant will not be tolerated by this court.

"There are too many attacks on public servants and I am going to deal with you with a prison sentence."

Laudat was sentenced to three months' imprisonment on the first charge of assault and the charge of unlawful damage run concurrently.

The sentences were suspended for a year. He was also fined a total of £40 on both charges.

The charge of disorderly behaviour was dismissed.

nationals were arrested and remanded in custody to appear at Lewes Crown Court later in the year.

UPDATE: In June 2004 I was fortunate enough to be able to attend the D-DAY + 60 memorial events in Normandy, France. Whilst I was watching a Royal Marines Band march off after a war memorial parade and service at Ouistreham, I was approached by 4-5 former fellow Royal Marines, who are now in a Sussex Police Force, stationed at Gatwick Airport, employed as armed 'machine gunners' in an anti-terrorist and airport security role. They had recognised my Corps tie and my green beret. These serving police officers advised me that the above incident, after close investigation, was found not to have been caused due to Road Rage at all. In fact, all parties involved were from Eastern Europe and the attack was thought to be over a drugs deal. No doubt we will hear the full facts of the case in due course, as it will be widely publicised as it comes to trial.

A woman watched in horror as a man killed her fiancé with a bayonet during a row over noise. A Crown Court trial result from Norwich has not yet been released. Amy Cottrill, 21, tried to staunch the flow of blood from her fiance's wounds, where the 2-foot long bayonet with a sword handle had punctured his lungs during the assault. Neighbour Melvin Sullivan, 45, had used the fearsome weapon on Michael Bailey, 28, after allegedly complaining that the couple had returned home noisily at two am one day in June 2003. Apparently victim Mr Bailey went out into the street bare-chested and told Sullivan to come out, shouting: "You may bully everyone else in the street but you're not going to bully us." Amy was led from the courtroom in tears after being asked to say how Michael was stabbed. Sullivan, of Wisbech, Cambs. is claiming self-defence.

An elderly man walking his dog in the Mayhill area of Swansea was attacked and tormented by a gang of stone-throwing yobs and collapsed and died. Retired lorry driver Trevor Griffiths, 63, had been the target of youths near his home after he stood up to them. As he took his Great Dane dog for an evening walk, the six-strong gang pounced on him again. He is thought to have died from a heart attack. Friends and neighbours said that Mr Griffiths had been terrorised by the gang for months, because he refused to be intimidated by them. A neighbour said: "Kids were throwing stones at him and taunting him just before he collapsed. It was a regular occurrence. These little yobs made his life very unpleasant, I suppose because he was the only one to stand up to them. Everyone knows who these people are, but we're afraid of them. Trevor was a gentleman, a pillar of the community. We will get the dog re-homed." The latest information is that two youths have been questioned by police but released without charge.

Four doormen aka 'Meeters and Greeters' (previously known as 'bouncers'), have denied strangling a man to death in a popular nightspot at Slough, Berks. Stevie McClean, 45, Robin Breakspear, 44, Oliver Atkinson, 22, and Rizwan Choudry, 36, are all accused of the manslaughter of Spencer Munyengeterwa, who died following an alleged incident at the *Assembly* pub on High Street, Slough, in the early hours of August 10th 2003. In court the four men spoke only to confirm their names and plead not guilty, and Judge Stanley Spence, of whom more later, released them on conditional bail and their trial date was set for 5th July 2004.

SOLDIER ON CHARGE OF MALICIOUS WOUNDING, FINED

A 29-year-old Birmingham man has appeared in court, charged with the attempted murder of a three-year-old boy who was stabbed in the chest. James Pinsent was remanded in custody. Police had been called to Brindley Drive, Birmingham where they found the injured child. The boy was treated at Diana Princess of Wales Birmingham Children's Hospital but fortunately his injuries are not thought to be life-threatening.

A drunken landscape gardener waved a chainsaw at 30 terrified strangers outside a nightclub, after being refused admission as the club was closed. Lee Sharkey, 23, of Oxford, then fetched the chainsaw from his vehicle and returned to the nightclub with it. He started it up, revved it and then brandished it over his head. He finally put down the chainsaw when a police officer threatened to use a CS gas spray on him. At Swindon Crown Court in May 2004 Sharkey admitted Affray and was jailed for 12 months.

A man was shot dead in the street after a row between two cyclists in the Handsworth area of Birmingham in early May 2004. Elija Fagan, 24, was riding along on his bike when he got into an argument with another man, described as black, wearing a black T-shirt and black jeans and riding a mountain bike. Police said he was shot by the other cyclist, who then pedalled away. Mr Fagan managed to struggle along for a few yards before slumping to the ground. He was taken to hospital but died from his injuries. A post mortem examination revealed that he had been shot in the stomach. Let's hope that his violent assailant is behind bars soon, for the protection of all peaceful and right-thinking and law-abiding residents of Birmingham.

The father of a two-year-old girl was bitten, punched and knifed on his own doorstep, when neighbours discovered he was noting details about their noisy parties and yobbish behaviour in a diary, Minshull Street Crown Court, Manchester was told. Victim Martin Brierley, in his 20's, from Oldham, Lancs, was stabbed in the back and upper chest, after being accused of being a 'grass'. He had been logging details of their anti-social, rowdy 3am parties on the advice of his local council, after being left 'at the end of his tether'. But his neighbours flew into a rage when he threatened to report them. They found out about his 'diary of despair' and attacked him twice within 24 hours. The jury was played a recording of a 999 call to police made by Mr Brierley during the second incident, as his brother Peter tried to keep the four men out of the two-bedroom flat. Peter Brierley was heard to take the telephone and tell the operator: "There's four of them, they've stormed in my brother's. It looks like they've bit some of his fingers, bit his fingers off. They think he's a grass because he's been writing anti-social behaviour down. Hang on, hang on, I think he might have been stabbed in the chest, just above his arm."

Susan Klonin, prosecuting, said the attacks took place in September 2003, nine months after the victim moved into his home in Oldham. "On one side was a young woman called Rachel who appeared to have frequent noisy visitors. They were drinking and caused disturbances. Martin was at the end of his tether. He frequently had his two-year-old daughter go to stay with him. He decided to complain to Oldham Council who told him to keep a diary of anti-social behaviour." Victim Mr Brierley told the court: "There were people going to see Rachel next door until 3am and taking drugs and listening to music. We have to work all week and did not need that. I complained to the council and they gave me a booklet to fill in." Michael Stein, 34, who lived next door but one, and Michael Marler, 44, who lived upstairs, became concerned that they were being reported to police, Miss Klonin said.

MAN, 26, ADMITS ASSAULTING PC's

A MAN who has twice been convicted of assaulting policemen pleaded guilty to a similar charge at East Ham Court.

Labourer James Donovan, of Jersey-road, Canning Town, also pleaded guilty to a charge of being drunk and disorderly and to a third charge of causing wilful damage.

Donovan, 26, was fined a total of £80, ordered to pay £7.88 costs and given a six-month prison sentence, suspended for a year.

The court heard that on October 2 Donovan was seen to leave a pub in Albert-road, Canning Town. When questioned by Pc Michael Hughes the defendant became violent. During the ensuing struggle Pc Hughes shirt was torn.

Donovan told the court that Pc Hughes had grabbed his arm. "He tried to screw it off and I resisted," he added.

The first attack occurred when Mr Brierley caught Marler's son scratching his father's name on the front door. Marler then emerged, calling Mr Brierley a 'grass'. His 21-year-old nephew, Wayne Marler, punched Mr Brierley in the head. The following day, Mr Marler asked his brother to come over as he was afraid to be alone. Michael Marler again confronted him, threatening to kill him. He summoned Wayne Marler and his friend, Paul Clegg, 17. Stein went along and offered to help them. The gang forced their way into Mr Brierley's flat and trapped him in the kitchen. "Wayne gets stuck under Martin in the fight and then starts biting his fingers. Martin manages to get his finger in Wayne's eye to make him stop and Wayne runs off. Martin Brierley then realises that he has been stabbed." said Miss Klonin. All of the gang, from Oldham, denied violent disorder and assault, Wayne Marler alone also denies unlawful wounding, so we can have a pretty accurate guess that he was the man who did the stabbing.

Under the influence, man went berserk

UNDER THE influence of a mixture of drugs and drinks, labourer Brian Coleman went berserk during an argument with his father on returning home.

Because of his behaviour, his sister called for Police assistance. But Coleman assaulted the two officers who arrived and kicked and dented their patrol car, Grays Justices were told on Friday.

Prosecutor Mr. Anthony Cranfield said one of the officers, P.c. Michael Hughes, was off duty for 10 days as a result of the incident.

Coleman (22), of Hamble Lane, South Ockendon, admitted assaulting P.c. Hughes causing him bodily harm, assaulting P.c. Brian Freeman and causing £5 worth of wilful damage to the Police car. He was fined a total of £35 and ordered to pay £5 for the cost of the damage.

Mr. Cranfield said Coleman arrived home the worse for drink. He had also been taking drugs prescribed by a doctor. His father spoke to him, an argument developed and defendant went berserk.

When Police arrived, Coleman threw a suitcase at P.c. Hughes and then lunged at the officer. He swung several punches, two of which landed on the upper part of the constable's body. Coleman was also kicking out violently.

The officers managed to get him out of the house but accused kicked P.c. Hughes and also assaulted P.c. Freeman. He then kicked the driver's door of the Police car, causing a dent and also dented the bodywork with another kick.

P.c. Hughes received cuts and bruises to the left shin, multiple bruises and a swelling to his calf and bruises to the chest. He was off duty for 10 days, said Mr. Cranfield.

P.c. Freeman had bruises to his arm and back.

Coleman told Juices: "I cannot remember a lot of what happened through taking drink at the same time as the pills he doctor prescribed."

Vipaul Prasannae, 41, a father of three, was walking through the foyer of Wembley Park tube station, N. London at 11am one Sunday morning in April 2004, when he accidentally bumped into a young boy aged about 10 years. The boy yelped in pain, whereupon a man in his 20's accompanying the child, possibly his father, savagely hit Mr Prasannae in the face. The force of the blow knocked him to the ground and his head hit the pavement. He was rushed to hospital fighting for his life and placed on a life support machine, meanwhile British Transport Police scanned CCTV camera footage in the hope of identifying the attacker (In fact the very sad news is that Mr Prasannae did not make it, but his assailant has been identified and subsequently charged with his murder in May 2004).

A bride's big day was wrecked when she was forced to walk down the aisle with two black eyes and a broken nose. The honeymoon was cancelled because both she and the groom were on police bail. Amy Exley's problems started a week before the wedding in July 2003, when her husband-to-be, Chris, returned from Iraq where he was serving as a lance corporal in the Royal Logistics Corps. A fracas started on the steps of an Indian Restaurant and Amy, 24 was punched in the face. Chris, 22, became involved in a fight with an off-duty-police officer. In the scuffle Chris bit off the end of the PC's nose and was charged with causing grievous bodily harm. Despite her injuries, Amy was determined that the wedding would go ahead. "I was punched so hard I blacked out and came round in the ambulance on the way to hospital. My nose was shattered and badly swollen and both of my eyes were black. But I didn't contemplate cancelling the wedding, as I was so in love with Chris and wanted to be his wife."

Charges against the police officer were later dropped but at Leeds Crown Court, Chris was jailed for 15 months. Tearful Amy, who has since had plastic surgery on her nose, added: "My husband is now in prison and the policeman is back on duty, I think it is disgraceful." Chris has been discharged from the Army and Amy, who was arrested but never charged, has moved back in with her parents, in Wakefield, Yorks. Her mother Angela said: "They are not going to be together for their first wedding anniversary. It has all been horrendous. It should have been the happiest occasion, but it broke my heart." Although reference was made in the court report to the plastic surgery on Amy, there was no mention of any plastic surgery involved in replacing the end of the police officer's nose bitten off by ex-Lance Corporal Chris.

Passenger struck Policeman

WHEN P.c. Michael Hughes stopped a car in Calcutta Road, Tilbury, a passenger got out and started arguing. When as'ed to get back in the ca: he struck the Policeman's arm, then continued to struggle and punched th officer several times and threw him to the ground

These facts were told to Justices at Grays on Wednesday when Joseph James Conroy (37), of Hillcrest Avenue, West Thurrock, pleaded guilty to assaulting a Policeman.

Conroy, who told the Court he had been out to a Christmas dance with his wife and "must have had a drink too much," was fined £5 with three guineas costs.

After being charged, Conroy apologised to P.c. Hughes and shook hands with him.

A drunken man who accidentally shot himself in the testicles with a sawn-off shotgun was jailed for five years. David Walker, 28, went home to get the gun, after arguing with a friend over whose round it was, during an all-day drinking session. He stuffed the sawn-off shotgun down his trousers, but inadvertently pulled the trigger. Sheffield Crown Court heard that Walker crawled 200 yards home after the accident in Dinnington, South Yorks. He admitted possession of an illegal firearm, an offence that now carries a minimum five-year jail term. Police have refused to confirm whether or not his drinking partner, when told by Walker that he was going home to fetch his gun, to settle the argument, replied: "You wouldn't have the balls to pull the trigger."

On 15th February 2005, the son of a Tory MP was given a four-year jail sentence for smashing a night-clubber over the head with a champagne bottle. David Amess, 20, had been found guilty of wounding with intent to cause grievous bodily harm (which carries a maximum penalty of life imprisonment). He used the bottle as a 'club' when plumber Paul Trussler accidentally trod on his foot at a nightclub in Southend-on-Sea, Essex. His 54-year-old father, also called David Amess, is MP for Southend West. The MP, once private secretary to Edwina Currie and Michael Portillo, comforted sobbing relatives in the public gallery as his son was led to the cells. Later a family friend said: "The family is absolutely heartbroken by what has happened to their son." During his trial in December 2004 a jury heard how Amess Jnr, a father, lashed out at Mr Trussler while drinking with friends. At Chelmsford Crown Court Judge Charles Gratwicke told him: "Your behaviour that night was disgraceful. This was a deliberate act done by you with the intention of causing Mr Trussler serious bodily harm. You swung that champagne bottle like a club, bringing it down onto his head. It was fortunate that it did not break and he was fortunate not to have more serious injuries. These courts have consistently said that those who behave in the manner you did on that night, can expect to receive an immediate and substantial prison sentence to mark the social abhorrence of those who behave in this manner, and also to deter others from behaving this way."

The young father of one was trying to impress a woman when he struck his victim at *Talk* nightclub in Southend in May 2004. Earlier defence lawyer Sarah Foreshaw pointed out that Amess Jnr had already served nine weeks in custody on remand. She appealed for his release, saying the victim, who received a four-inch gash to the head, had not suffered 'major injuries'. Of his time on remand, she said: "Mr Amess is a troubled man. He was self-harming, sometimes literally punching himself on to the floor and sometimes cutting and burning himself. On one occasion he even drank disinfectant. This is a man who has real problems. He's frightened of inmates and keeps himself to himself and there are concerns about his psychiatric state." She added: "My client has been living with his uncle but his father is here today and would welcome his son back. He intends to assist him while he undergoes intensive psychotherapy. He has had a troubled life and suffered many pressures as a result of the media attention his father's profession has brought on the family. During his trial Amess Jnr claimed Mr Trussler had punched him and he acted in self-defence. The family were said to be considering an appeal. Mr Amess Senior is MP for Southend West.

COUNT 4

HOMICIDE

The killing of a human being by a human being. It may be:

1) *Criminal – murder, manslaughter.*
2) *Justifiable.*
3) *Excusable.*

Murder is when a person of sound memory and of the age of discretion unlawfully kills any reasonable creature in being under the Queen's Peace, with malice aforethought, either express or implied, so as the person dies of the injury inflicted within a year and a day after the same. Mandatory sentence – Life Imprisonment.

For many people, the taking of another's life, deliberately and premeditatedly, is the ultimate crime. Nowadays, the terrible crimes of murder in this country have become so frequent and common-place that they rarely make front-page news any more. This is a terrible indictment on our society. It seems that many people who over-indulge in drugs and alcohol, lose all reason, and reach a certain stage where they cease to act rationally, or indeed, like human beings at all. To this day, there are many groups of people and individuals who constantly campaign for the restoration of the death penalty, which was abolished in 1965, but it does seem that there is no likelihood of its ever being restored. People are even being murdered these days in the course of comparatively lesser crimes, such as to steal a car by force, now known by the 'soft' term of 'CAR-JACKING'.

Whilst I was serving in Essex Police, I recall that an elderly lady named Tilly, who lived in an alms house in the village of South Weald, near Brentwood, Essex, was murdered by a young man whom she had befriended, although I cannot recall how they came to meet. It was Tilly's habit, week in and week out to walk to the local sub-post office in the village and purchase a 'block' of savings stamps, which presumably, she took home and, after licking the backs, stuck them into a book supplied for that purpose. One unfortunate day, poor Tilly was found dead and it was obvious she had been murdered. I don't think the motive for the murder was necessarily clear in the first few days or weeks after her death. However, eventually, the youth whom she had befriended was arrested, charged and later convicted of her murder.

The prime exhibit, found in his possession, was a 'block' of savings stamps, of some financial worth. The important thing was that when the block of stamps from the murderer's possession was forensically examined, it was found that the block of stamps was an exact 'mechanical fit' with the original whole sheet of stamps sold to 'Tilly' previously by the sub-postmaster.

A 'mechanical fit' in this particular case means that the perforations on the remainder of the sheet of stamps still in the sub-postmaster's possession, lined up absolutely perfectly with those of the block of stamps found in the possession of the wicked murderer, and therefore must have been stolen from Tilly by the murderer. This awful murder was a local scandal with huge publicity generated at the time, as Tilly had lived in the village of South Weald for most or all of her life, and was well-loved as a local character. Everyone in the small village and its small surrounding hamlets breathed again, once that dreadful youth was taken into custody and sentenced to Life Imprisonment.

At the time of the 'Tilly' murder, I was working in another police division of Essex and so I had no actual personal dealings with the case. However years later, by which time I had transferred to the Metropolitan Police, coincidentally I worked on another murder squad involving stamps, this time actual postage stamps.

An elderly man ran a small stamp shop on the Ilford High Road, which had remained much as it had been when it first opened, as though time had stood still within its four walls. The owner provided a really good service, as philately,or stamp collection as a hobby had a far greater following in those days than it does today. One day, the poor man was found dead in the shop and the murder was quickly solved and the perpetrator brought to justice. Unfortunately that was the end of the stamp shop and many enthusiasts had to travel further afield to pursue their exciting hobby.

In the Metropolitan Police in those days, of course there was no information technology or computers. The Met had a very good procedure for investigation of murders, which had been honed to perfection over very many years. It was a well-known fact that if a murder had not been 'cleared-up', viz: solved, within 3 days, as a general rule you were in big trouble. This was because most murders then, and it's probably still the same today, were committed by somebody who knew the deceased in some way. Perhaps as a relative, work mate, friend or associate, neighbour, business partner and suchlike.

When a 'suspicious death' was reported, quite often by ambulance staff or uniformed police who had been called to the scene, a 'squad' of CID officers from the local area, and sometimes from surrounding areas, would be drafted-in, or to use the modern equivalent, deployed on to the squad. A senior police officer, usually of the rank of detective chief inspector or higher, would be assigned to the case. An 'incident room' would be set up at once in the most convenient police station and armies of Post Office Engineers, as they were then called, would move in with miles of telephone cable and set up at least several additional lines, for the sole use of the murder squad. These would soon be up and running, which was imperative, as there would be much telephoning in and out to be done. One or more walls of the 'murder incident room' would carry large scale maps of the area, photos of the victim, suspects and 'dodgy' witnesses etc., photos of footprints, clothing or items still un-recovered, pictures of motor vehicles and interesting venues where known events had occurred prior to, or since the murder.

An 'office manager', which was his title, would be appointed, he was usually a First or Second Class detective sergeant who had probably undertaken the task several times before. His job could be quite boring as he would rarely see the light of day. It was his job to 'hold the fort' and make sure the rest of the staff were kept on their toes. Probably the task he spent more time on than anything else, was reading as quickly as possible all the hand-written, lengthy statements which 'the troops' were spending most of their time out of the office, in creating. The important thing was to find out as much as possible about the deceased as quickly as possible and commit it all to paper in the form of written statements.

The office manager would then have each statement typed up by one or more typists and would then make quite a few copies of each one, filing them in separate folders for allocation as follows:

1) Officer in charge of investigation.
2) His deputy, usually a detective inspector or first class sergeant CID.
3) Office copy.
4) Copy in chronological order.
5) Copy with witnesses in alphabetical order.
6) A few spare copies, which officers popping in and out could swiftly read and acquaint themselves with the latest developments.

An essential item at the hub of the murder squad room would be a huge, old-fashioned blackboard and easel, like most of us remember from school, complete with coloured chalks and eraser pad. This board was headed-up in huge lettering, 'A C T I O N S'. Below this heading, every CID officer, and sometimes co-opted uniform officers, would have their name listed at the left of the blackboard. Against your name would be a series of numbers which got longer and longer as the enquiry developed. The 'actions' listed against your name were cross-referenced to the all-important 'ACTION BOOK', which was raised, updated and maintained by the office manager. Normally only the senior investigating officer or the office manager would create and enter up 'actions' in this book. 'Actions' varied from quite simple routine, but important tasks , such as 'ascertain the registered owner of green Rover motor car, index no. GVK 142'. More importantly, another 'action' would state, 'trace and interview as a matter of utmost urgency, Basil Thompson, believed to be the last person to have seen the victim alive'. Every time you arrived back and checked in at the murder room with your completed or uncompleted 'actions' you would endorse the appropriate space in the 'action book', update the office manager personally and hand him your written statement or documentation to prove the 'action' was completed, or still pending, and the likely period of time before finalisation. Whilst there, you would put a chalk line through your completed actions and in your official pocket book, record the full details of the latest 'actions' allocated to you.

Hopefully too, you would make time to grab a ring binder containing a spare copy of all of the written statements taken to date, and quickly read the fresh ones which had appeared since you last looked. This was in case another witness revealed details or made mention of some part of one of your personal 'actions', which might mean you had to tackle the job in a different way. Furthermore, each officer on the murder squad needed to know exactly how far the investigation was progressing on a day-to-day basis. Off you would fly again, sometimes alone, other times with another officer or two, to sort out the next 'action(s)' in priority order. If you were very lucky, you made the time to go to the toilet whilst you could.

If you were using your private car on official police business, it was important to re-zero your odometer so that you did not sell yourself short when you submitted your next private car mileage expense claim! Unfortunately there were never enough police vehicles to go round, so sometimes you used theirs, sometimes your own.

One 'major' murder enquiry I once worked on was the gangland murder of William ('Billy') Moseley, who hailed from, or had frequented the Islington and Camden areas of London, as well as most of Her Majesty's Prisons, at one time or other in his life. This swiftly became known as 'The Torso In The Thames' murder. At the time I was still a very junior CID officer, an 'aide to CID' or 'TDC' (Temporary Detective Constable) and I felt highly honoured to have been 'hand-picked' by the 'Governor' (Senior Investigation Officer) or one of his assistants. In this case the 'Guv' was a Detective Chief Superintendent, who was the senior detective on 'Outer K Division'. ('K' Division was so large and spread out geographically that it had been divided into two halves, known as ' inner' and 'outer' 'K'.)

A male 'bird watcher' had been up and about early, pursuing his hobby on the foreshore at Rainham, Essex when he spotted what he at first thought to be the carcass of a dead sheep, washed up by the tide of the River Thames. However he was suspicious so fortunately he reported it without delay. It was quickly retrieved and found to be human remains, a large part of the torso of the late Billy Moseley.

From that moment on, 'Thames Division' of the Metropolitan Police, together with Kent Constabulary, who policed the opposite side of the river, were alerted and within the space of a few days, several other body parts were found, either floating in the river, or washed up on its banks. In our official pocket books, murder squad detectives, kept a diagram of the human body and every time a fresh, or different body part was discovered, we shaded in the appropriate section. This way, from day to day, we always had a good idea of which parts of the deceased were still outstanding. This murder squad operated from a major incident suite at Romford Police Station, which was purpose-built. However there came a time when we had to close off at the halfway point of the huge room, the folding doors which allowed two major incidents to be run concurrently. (This was because another criminal, George Brett, and his young son, had suddenly vanished off the face of the earth, on Romford's police ground, never to be seen again.)

A post mortem was held by a Home Office pathologist, at a local hospital. This was to be the first of many post mortem examinations. This was because every time a fresh body part was found, it was preserved forensically and then deposited in the same deep freeze section of the hospital mortuary as the torso itself. Therefore a 'jigsaw' was slowly being assembled, body part by body part, on the mortuary body tray. You can imagine the condition and stench of the torso after it had been frozen, defrosted and thawed out and re-frozen several times! There were several suspects in the case, one of whom turned out to be the victim's half brother, who it was claimed, was the 'friendly face' present at the (criminals') MEET, to which Billy Moseley was lured. I am not sure, after all of these years, whether it was at this 'meet' that the death sentence was just decided upon, or whether he was in fact executed there and then.

He was a very large man and we were told that he always kept a large offensive weapon, such as a baseball bat, close at hand in his car, which I think was a 3.5 litre Rover. He had always held down a reputation for being able to look after himself. More and more body parts were being retrieved. I don't think the hands were ever found, due to making identification by finger prints almost a certainty. Bizarrely, the head did not turn up until after a long Old Bailey trial, at which at least two persons were convicted, including Billy's half brother or step brother, Bobby Maynard. When the head was found, inside a bag dumped in a gents lavatory, it scotched an earlier rumour that it had once been brought to the sea surface caught in a large fishing net, and was apparently thrown back, probably in sheer shock by the fishermen. I believe that during the trial, this theory was put to the test and I understand that scientific experts in the movement of tides actually appeared as expert witnesses at The Old Bailey.

A man who knew the victim very well became a very useful assistant to our murder squad and gave very long witness statements. Naturally, what he had to say generated masses of 'actions'. As time went by, most of the police officers working on the squad, became increasingly frustrated with the way it was being progressed by the Detective Chief Superintendent in charge. This was quite unusual, as massive enthusiasm is normally present and a determination by most squad members to get the case 'solved' and the perpetrators brought to justice as soon as humanly possible, was normally paramount. Top suspects, as identified to us by our star witness, arrived at the police station and were apparently interviewed alone in his office by the top investigator. He was seen in a passageway upstairs one day, shaking hands with the main suspect and actually thanking him for coming in. One of our colleagues who entered the Detective Chief Superintendent's office before this interview was completed, took in some refreshments on a tray. He reported back to us afterwards that the scene inside the office was 'more like tea at the vicarage' than a murder enquiry.

Difficulty was being experienced in making a positive identification of the torso and subsequently-found other body parts, as being those of Billy

Moseley. However thanks to the ongoing help from the witness I referred to earlier, we discovered that Moseley had, at one time, suffered with the skin disease dermatitis. An urgent 'action' had been created in the 'action book' to try to track down a dermatologist who had once treated Moseley.

He had then operated from a consulting room in Holloway Road, North London, in what had been the Royal Northern Hospital years before. Subsequently this medical man was tracked down and he attended at the hospital where the body remains were still being preserved, in a mortuary drawer. Once again the torso had to be, at least partially thawed so that the dermatologist could make his examination, accompanied by the Pathologist and at the very least, the Detective Chief Superintendent in charge of the case. Plus an official police photographer. The Dermatologist had previously indicated that if he were allowed to view the torso with the help of an ultra-violet lamp, he would recognise his own handiwork, from when he had treated Moseley, by somehow removing surface layers of skin, as if treating serious facial acne. Sure enough, he recognised his own work pattern in the correct place on the body and this was then taken as firm and positive, strong evidence that the body parts were those of Billy Moseley, which of course we had long suspected, virtually from day one.

The suspected motive for his murder was that he was thought to have broken a golden rule amongst villains. This being that if a criminal within your close circle of friends and associates is imprisoned, although you are expected to look after the welfare of his wife or partner and children whilst he is in jail, at all costs you must not have relations with his wife or partner. Moseley was suspected of having done this forbidden act and once sufficient evidence came to the hands of the cuckolded male, the death sentence was passed and carried out.

Moseley had been a 'career criminal', as we call them in the criminal justice system. He had started off, like most school children, with very small scale shoplifting. When he realised that he had become very skilled at it, he became a professional shop lifter and mainly acted as fast getaway car driver, using the motorways to swiftly disappear with firstly, arms full and then latterly, car boots full, of high value merchandise, such as leather jackets and suits. Later he graduated to more lucrative methods of raising maximum cash advances for swift, over-in-a-few-minutes raids on banks. He was said to have specialised in reversing a flat-backed lorry or large van up to the outside windows of bank managers' offices. Fully armed, with huge sledge hammers and probably bolt croppers for the protective window bars, he and his accomplices would crash through an office window in this way, terrorising the bank manager with sawn-off shotguns etc., forcing him to have large cash amounts etc. brought in from other parts of the bank, to his office, netting Moseley and associates fast, rich profits. However, he and his team were well aware of the huge jail sentences which were passed (in those days), but viewed the prospect of liberty-deprivation as a calculated risk worth taking. There came a time when I was allocated an 'action' to attempt to trace and interview a criminal named 'Mickey Cornwall.' In the Islington and Camden areas of North London, Cornwall had grown up with Billy Moseley and they had become lifelong friends, as well as ultra-skilled professional criminals. I made my initial enquiries and discovered that within the last few weeks, I had just missed Cornwall. He had been released from a prison in either Norfolk or Suffolk and his forwarding address had not been accurately supplied to the prison authorities on discharge, or a false, misleading address had been tendered. I was forced to make the rounds of all last-known addresses and virtually every public house in the Islington area, leaving word that, should Cornwall surface, I had to see him, or at least speak to him, on a very important matter. So I left my telephone number and extension for Romford police station at each address I visited.

Eventually, Mickey Cornwall did contact me by telephone there. His opening words were: "Will I need a 'mouthpiece?'" (solicitor) I advised him that would not be necessary and soon I interviewed him by appointment at Romford police station. I swiftly updated him as to why we sought his help. In a long witness statement of 12 pages or more, he summarised how he had grown up since childhood with Moseley, in fact they had 'done everything together', as he put it. As he knew only too well how capable 'Billy' was of taking care of himself, he really could not believe that some kind of serious harm had befallen him. I assured him that at this time, we were virtually certain that 'Billy's' remains found to date, were currently resting in our deep freezer. Mickey Cornwall's parting words to me as we shook hands at departure were: "I still can't believe that you've got Billy there, but I owe him so much, if it turns out to be him for sure, I won't rest until I find out who did this to him."

Tragically, Mickey Cornwall went away and attempted to do just that. He deliberately entered some sort of a relationship with the daughter of a major 'player', poking his nose in where it wasn't wanted. He must have known the risks he ran, attempting to 'infiltrate' the gang when they well knew that he was more or less Billy Moseley's 'soulmate'. Within the space of about 2-3 weeks since his visit to Romford police station to supply his witness statement to me, to assist the investigation, there was very bad news. Cornwall had been found dead in a shallow grave, somewhere in the county of Hertfordshire, which was outside our police area, with bullets between the eyes. The local Regional Crime Squad had become involved. However, in our district of the Metropolitan Police was a very senior officer, known as

'The Grey Fox'. His full title was Commander Albert Wickstead, known as 'Bert' Wickstead, and he was very well respected, as a 'gangbuster', having been responsible for breaking up several London area gangs, involved in kidnapping, torture, extortion etc.

Bert Wickstead's reputation went before him and no doubt many officers clamoured to be seconded onto one of his squads, which invariably operated from (close to his home) Loughton police station in Essex, which was almost at the end of the Central Line and close to Epping Forest. To cut a long story short, Bert managed somehow to take over the investigation of what had now become a double murder, obviously with the full cooperation of the Hertfordshire Constabulary. One of Mr Wickstead's first tasks, I understand, was to take over the murder squad and 'sideline' the DCS who had been running the case up until then. I say 'I understand' because just after Cornwall's visit to see me at Romford, I had finally passed a police promotion board. I was then 'promoted' to be a fully-fledged detective constable instead of a *temporary* one. At the Old Bailey murder trial, I recall that at least two men, including Moseley's half brother or step brother, Bobby Maynard, were convicted and sentenced to life imprisonment. They have both featured in several TV documentaries over the years, and have lost several criminal appeals. As far as I know, they are still imprisoned to this day, as no doubt the trial judge set a high tariff for their minimum sentences.

Some time after this, in the Goodmayes area, on J Division, a very attractive and well-liked married woman was killed and found on the stairs of her home. From the start, we suspected that a young window cleaner, whom she and her husband had previously trusted, had murdered her after she arrived home and caught him in her purse.He was interrogated for hours and we carried out the full range of set-piece enquiries and involved forensic scientists etc. We really thought we had got him at one stage. However an identification parade was held and unfortunately, an important witness failed to pick him out. As you can imagine, this gave the only suspect in the case, the young window cleaner, the increased confidence to carry on *denying* that he had killed the lady. There was no other option other than to let him go at that time, whilst we continued our enquiries while he was back home on police bail.

At the time, we suspected that he may have raped her, or had sexual relations with her, probably after death. However, unlike these modern times, DNA linking had not then been discovered, so were forced to manage without it. We were later able to prove that this most unsavoury character had actually *stabbed* the poor woman to death. He then cleaned the knife and had the coolness or presence of mind to return the weapon to the kitchen drawer. (Over the years, I have noticed that returning knives used in murders to kitchen drawers is quite a common practice.) He was later found guilty of her murder and received the mandatory life sentence.

In the vast area of London covered by the Metropolitan Police with its then complement of approx 20,000 officers, you were in big trouble if a murder was not 'wrapped-up' within about 3 days, which normally meant the victim had been killed by a complete stranger or a travelling criminal from miles away, during a chance encounter, or deliberately targeted by a hired outsider.

I worked for a short time only, as it was more or less solved with an arrest on the day of discovery, on a *double* murder in the Ilford area. A married woman who ran a local business in connection with the building trade, was found by her husband to be involved in a lesbian relationship with her aunt, whose home was on our 'manor'. Apparently he had intercepted or come across some very explicit 'love letters' between them, which was all the evidence he needed. He had tried quite hard by reasoning with his wife, and possibly her Aunt, to terminate the relationship, but to no avail. One day, the Aunt was found dead in her kitchen, with the dinner actually cooking on the hob. She had been battered to death with a 'blunt instrument.' Tragically for him, the Aunt's teenaged nephew, younger brother to the Aunt's female lover, was off from school, having broken his leg in a skiing accident. He was in another ground floor room at his Aunt's house that day, working on his school home work. As, if he had lived, the poor young lad could have testified that his brother-in-law had been present in the house that day, he too was bludgeoned to death. Once we learnt of the background and the possible motive, the hunt was on for the husband of the Aunt's lover. We 'got lucky' straight away when we discovered that, unusually, he had not turned in for work that day. He was arrested the same day and took the arresting officers to some kind of rubbish dump in the Southend area of Essex, where the murder weapon was recovered. This proved to be such an 'open and shut' case that the murder squad personnel could be swiftly reduced, leaving just the DI, the office manager and one or two other officers, to 'tie up the loose ends.'

On another occasion, with a detective sergeant, we were on night duty CID patrol in an unmarked police car. We were given a radio message to urgently attend a house at an address in Dagenham, Essex, which comes under the umbrella of Greater London, covered by the Metropolitan Police. On arrival at the house, an ambulance was just racing away. We instructed a uniformed PC to preserve the scene of crime and to literally allow NO ONE into the house until he heard from us. We followed the ambulance to the hospital where a 'crash' trauma team was standing by in readiness. It transpired that a man had walked into the front office at Dagenham police station and placed a gun on the station officer's desk, claiming to have shot his wife. He was obviously taken into custody immediately, searched and processed until the full facts of the case became known.

Back at the hospital, my colleague and I were allowed to be present in the trauma area of the A & E Department, whilst the very experienced nursing team did their jobs. Most readers have probably seen what goes on in real-life situations in such TV series as *Trauma*, which was on BBC 1. The medical 'crash' team fought like crazy to keep this poor woman, who was in her late 30's, alive. This included use of the high-voltage electric paddles to shock the heart into resuming its normal beating-pattern. These attempted life-saving procedures lasted about an hour and a half. Whilst it was going on, one of the nursing sisters said quietly to me: "I bet this lady comes from a beautifully-kept home." I said: "How could you know that?" She said: "Look at her beautifully-kept toe nails, they tell me everything about her."

Unfortunately, she did not make it. Not many people survive one or more bullets in the head. So we had a murder on our hands. Once somebody dies under suspicious circumstances, each police officer who comes in contact with that person in life, or after death, for the sake of continuity of evidence, takes on the temporary role of 'coroner's officer'. He or she must stay with that body until there is a chance to hand over the responsibility of proving the identity of that person, along the chain of persons who will be involved with it, right through to the inquest and even beyond. This is to ensure that there can be no mistake or accidental or careless 'body-switching' or incorrect identification. In the case of this poor woman from Dagenham whose husband had just murdered her, we summoned a trusted firm of undertakers from the local police 'approved' list, who arrived at the hospital and took away the body in a light-weight, easily-manageable coffin called a 'shell'. This was in the days before purpose made body bags were available.

We followed them to the public mortuary, took possession of what few valuables she had with her, marked the body at a toe with a tie-on label containing her full name, date of birth, date of death etc.

We then wheeled her over to one of the deep freeze compartments and using the inbuilt trolley raise/lower mechanism, lined up the stainless steel tray on which she lay, with an available empty shelf, and eased the tray in. We then filled out an identifying ticket with her personal details as before, and placed the ticket in the deep freeze door at the appropriate level, as part of the continuation of evidence routine. Finally we entered up her details yet again on the large 'Body Identification Board' fixed to the mortuary wall and released the undertakers. On a later date, having made a statement of what actions we had taken to date, we returned to the mortuary and identified the body to the pathologist at the post mortem, often remaining to witness the unpleasant laborious but essential task.

There is only one sentence for murder prescribed by law and that is the mandatory LIFE IMPRISONMENT. Therefore, in theory, it should be impossible for a High Court Judge to be criticised for imposing a weak sentence.

As regards the crime of *manslaughter*, the maximum sentence for this is also LIFE IMPRISONMENT, although it is very rarely awarded. In fact many High Court Judges are criticised for awarding what many relations of dead victims, and others, regard as totally inadequate sentences, in that, as they see it, the sentence by no means fits the crime. Usually, only 'red Judges', viz: those who are senior enough to wear red robes, rather than purple, are authorised to deal with murder cases. These Judges are normally known by their titles of 'Mr Justice Soames' or 'Mrs Justice Reynolds' etc.

In early 2004, Exeter Crown Court heard a case against an elderly former RAF pilot, Alan Wickenden, 67 yrs, who had allegedly beaten his wife to death with an iron bar, when she refused to go along with his wishes to sell the marital home so as to relieve the serious debts situation they were in. Amazingly, passers-by witnessed the killing, which took place in a layby. The defendant, aged 67 years, tried to flee on a bicycle but was taken into custody by the passers-by. When police searched his home at Down St Mary, Devon, they found his pre-prepared 'blueprint' for the crime, which was set out on 2 sides of A4 paper, like a shopping list, as follows:

1) Secretly buy second car.
2) Hire bicycle.
3) Train times.
4) Where to hide the push bike ready for the getaway.
5) Which car to take to the layby.
6) Cut grass in churchyard just before taking wife to her death.
7) Fake breakdown in mower to give alibi for sudden disappearance and return to churchyard.
8) Feign puncture in car tyre at layby.
9) Cycle back to station and catch train home.
10) Return to churchyard.

Three months before the unlawful killing, Mr Wickenden took out a £250,000 life insurance policy on his wife. The Judge, Mrs Justice Hallett told the defendant: "It was not a spur of the moment reaction to a nagging spouse. Your plan to kill your wife was the way you saw of getting out of financial difficulties."

His barrister told the court: "The defendant felt they needed to move to a more modest property to release capital to support them in their declining years. Mrs Wickenden could not face it. Whenever the issue was raised, she would blame him for the financial disaster in Majorca. (Loss of £450,000 15 years previously when a boatyard he bought in Majorca went bust.) It was a constant bone of contention."

The Judge sentenced him to four years imprisonment after the defendant had admitted manslaughter by reason of diminished responsibility, after psychiatrists said he had become depressed by money pressures.

No doubt you have all seen the way that banks and finance houses bombard us all with huge advertisements of 'unlock the equity in your home and release capital you can utilise today', which are most often aimed at elderly people, whom you might think are most vulnerable to this kind of approach. There can be no doubt that Mr Wickenden was sorely tempted to respond to an advertisement like this, and when his wife refused to go along with his plan, she paid the ultimate penalty.

Two months after Ian Madden, aged 54 years, and his wife Lynn, aged 38 years were divorced, he discovered she was seeing a new man, after hacking into her emails. He threw a rope around her neck and throttled her. Then he left the body in the house, hanging from the rafters, to look as if she had committed suicide, with the two children of the marriage still in the house. He returned to the house next morning, as if nothing had happened, to collect his children, pretending that he had just found the body. In the meantime, his five-year old son stumbled across the 'awful spectacle' of his mother hanging there. As he thought she was asleep, he found a knife and placed it near her side so that she could cut herself free when she 'woke up'.

Judge Geoffrey Rivlin said to Madden: "One dreads to think of the life-long torment you have inflicted upon the children and upon Lynn's family and friends." Madden had been found guilty of murder by a jury at Southwark Crown Court, in London, in March 2004. Sentence had been postponed for psychiatric reports. He had denied murder but police found defensive scratch mark wounds on the defendant's neck, where his poor wife had fought for her life. Madden, of Greenford, West London, was sentenced to life imprisonment and it is reported that Madden gasped in the dock, as the Judge said he should serve a minimum of 18 years.

A man who was driven to distraction by his neighbour's prolonged DIY drilling sessions, finally snapped and stabbed him to death. Christopher Hoyland, 42, called at George Evans's house on the day he was drilling holes in a party wall, plunging a knife into his neck. Hoyland had been keeping a log of all the dates and times of the annoying drilling noises etc., in a diary and on 'post-it' notes. The prosecution told Teesside Crown Court that the knife blow was 'a purposeful and aimed thrust' into the victim's neck. Afterwards, Hoyland tried to create an alibi, by visiting his sister's house to walk the dog. His wife and two children later left him. He was sentenced to life imprisonment for the savage murder.

In June 2003, Aaron Spencer, 21, from Islington, and his friend O'Fill Allen, 20, from Finsbury Park, beat to death business man Orlando Thompson, 31, with two baseball bats. At the Old Bailey in March 2004 they were both convicted of murder and sentenced to life imprisonment. The victim had been lured to his death at a 'honey trap' meeting by their accomplice, Tara Icar, 18, from Islington, the stepdaughter of a gynaecologist. She had pleaded guilty to conspiring to cause bodily harm to victim Mr Thompson, whom she claimed had raped her. As she was jailed by Judge Paul Focke, bizarrely, she giggled. The Judge snapped: "Please don't laugh." Icar then burst into tears and wept through the rest of the Judge's remarks. He then said to her: "You have shown little remorse for what happened. Your only concern was what happened to your boyfriend."

She was jailed for 30 months. A question springs to mind. As this was a joint enterprise in which Tara Icar played an essential part in luring the victim to his eventual death, why was she not convicted of murder too? Was this a decision by the jury, or did the Crown Prosecution Service, in formulating the counts on the indictment, consider they had 'less than a 50 per cent chance of conviction' in Icar's case? (This 'yardstick' utilised by the CPS is a serious bone of contention between themselves and the Police, as too many serious cases are either downgraded to lesser offences, or worse still, *not proceeded with at all.*)

At Newcastle Crown court in April 2004, a 15-year old boy was convicted of manslaughter after a prank went wrong. Michael Timperley, 15 yrs, the victim, was locked inside a rubbish skip after burning paper had been thrown inside. The victim's mother wrote to the court to ask for mercy. The Judge, Mr Justice Henriques, said he had to give a 'commensurate sentence' for such a serious offence. He sentenced the boy to four years detention, which will be served in a Young Offenders Institution.

An environmental campaigner stabbed his friend to death and left his body to be eaten by maggots. Police only discovered the victim, James MacFarlane's corpse after 19 days, when the bugs started falling from a light below the flat he shared with his killer. Keith Newnham, 41, later admitted murder, saying his friend, aged 32, had threatened him with a knife in a drunken row. Anti-roads protestor Newnham 'just snapped', snatched the weapon and stabbed the victim five times, in Glastonbury, Somerset.

Amazingly he had informed police: "I was not worried about him stabbing me." The Judge told him: "You lost your temper with a drunken man and took up a weapon and stabbed him." At Bristol Crown Court, Judge Neil Butterfield sentenced Newnham to life imprisonment with a minimum tariff of 12 years.

Two father and son 'career criminals' shot dead a have-a-go-hero as he tried to stop them fleeing an armed robbery. Derek Elener, 65, and son Barry Elener, 42, gunned down Tasawar Hussain, 36, after he bravely pursued their getaway car after a £40,000 raid on a travel agent's in Bradford, West Yorks. On 12th March 2004 at Leeds Crown Court, after a four-week trial, Mr Justice Wakerley told them: "You have indicated not a jot of remorse for what you did." He sentenced them both to life imprisonment for murder.

At Bury St Edmunds Crown Court on 6th April 2004, a landlord and his odd-job man admitted the manslaughters of Michael Frosdick, 19, and Keith Reynolds, 17. They both died when they were overcome by fumes from a faulty second-hand gas fire in their rented flat. Wealthy Stanley Rogers, 62, and Barry Stone, 39, both of Great Yarmouth, were involved in the offences. Rogers financed the deal and hired Stone to install the fire, to save money. Landlord Rogers was jailed for five years and told to pay £5,000 costs. Stone, the handyman, was jailed for three years.

Curtis Rowe, 33, of Enfield, was jailed for seven years in April 2004 after admitting he had killed a neighbour, Peter King, 51, who 'made his life hell'. The Old Bailey heard he had hit Mr King with an iron bar, stabbed him and then set him alight.

Rapist Jason Dockrill, 34, of Stratford, East London was jailed for life for murdering Suvi Aronen, 23, a university student from Finland. Her death cries were heard by her parents in a phone call. The judge called him a 'sadistic predator' who would remain a danger to women all his life. Cries of 'Yes' came from the public gallery as the Old Bailey jury found him guilty. He bludgeoned her to death near Wanstead Common, East London. The attack came as her parents rang her mobile from their home in Finland. The Recorder of London told Dockrill: "You are a predator whose motivation was sexual and sadistic." Suvi's parents said in a statement: "A major part of our ability to live a happy life died with Suvi." Dockrill had denied murder but admitted manslaughter through diminished responsibility. He had assaulted three other women before killing Suvi.

A Sikh elder who strangled a pregnant mother in front of her 19-month-old son, after she spurned an arranged marriage, was jailed for life. Anita Gindha, 22, who eloped with another man and was happily married, was just two weeks from the birth of her second child when she was murdered by Palwinder Dhillon, 65, at her home in East London in February 2003. Dhillon, from Walsall, West Midlands, had denied murder.

Jason Ward, 22, of Mansfield, robbed 87-year-old Gladys Godfrey at her bungalow in Mansfield in April 2001. Eighteen months later he returned to rape her and broke her neck through strangulation, and left 23 other injuries on the frail old lady. She had fractures to her neck, jaw and six ribs, her face was so bruised it was almost black, and her scalp had been pulled back. The prosecutor told Nottingham Crown Court: "Clumps of her hair were on the floor and there were spatters of blood around the front room. Mrs Godfrey was found in her bedroom, naked from the waist down."

Factory machinist Ward was jailed for life and will serve at least 22 years. The judge said he was 'a very dangerous young man' who had never explained his actions. Cheery Mrs Godfrey had a walking frame to move around her bungalow in Mansfield, after hip and knee replacements. In April 2001, a man slipped into her home in the early hours and indecently assaulted her. She beat him off with a lemonade bottle and scratched his face.

After her death in September 2002, police re-examined the first attack. Fingernail scrapings from the assault made a DNA match with a sample from the murder. Ward volunteered to take a DNA test 15 months after the killing, and it matched. His defence lawyer said: "He wanted to be caught." He had a history of mental problems, including anxiety and hallucinations. He admitted indecent assault, burglary, rape and murder.

A girl of 15 and two 17-year-old boys were remanded in custody by Sheffield magistrates, charged with murdering 17-year-old Terry Lee Hurst, whom police believe was attacked with farm scythes. His body was found with stab and slash wounds near Bolsterstone reservoir, Stocksbridge, South Yorks. He was last seen alive the previous day carrying camping equipment, with a small group nearby.

You may well consider that this is one of the most horrendous double murders you have ever heard of, due to the fact that a police 999 operator was able to record in the greatest detail, the frantic cries for help from a terrified woman, whose husband was about to murder her. On 18th November 2003, Alan Pemberton, 48, a millionaire accountant, from Hermitage, near Newbury, Berkshire played a game of golf on a golf course near to his home. He had been made the subject of a court injunction to prevent him going to the former matrimonial home, where he had a history of domestic violence against his estranged wife, Julie Pemberton. He arrived at the £975,000 house armed with a shotgun and a large bag of cartridges.

His 17-years-old student son William was on the drive and appears to have made an attempt to keep his crazed father from hurting his mother, who was inside the house. The 16-minute transcript of the 999 call for help from Julie Pemberton, was played at the inquest into her death and that of her son William. She is telling the operator that her husband has a gun and her son William is outside.

The coroner was told that, in the months before her tragic death, she was so terrified that her husband would kill her that she and her brother gave police all of her kitchen knives and Mr Pemberton's air rifles. Death threats had been received via text messages, phone calls and via the children, for up to a year before her death. Mrs Pemberton's brother, Frank Mullance told the inquest that he had a record of a specific threat to Mrs Pemberton from her husband. In it he said: " Laura and Will are going to be orphans and it is your fault." Another threat said: "You have ruined my life. You will have to face the consequences."

This is an extract from Mrs Pemberton's last few words with the 999 operator before she was murdered:

Julie Pemberton: "I am in Slanting Hill, Hermitage, I got an injunction. My husband is out there with a gun and my son is there. He has a gun and he's let off some shots. My son is out there with him, I have an injunction, he is not supposed to come within 50 metres of the house. (shots are heard)   Oh my God."

Operator: "What is your address?" (Mrs Pemberton gives the address, there is a bang then a cry)

Julie Pemberton: "Oh God, has he hurt my son? He's come through the window. Please come quickly." (Large bang and Mrs Pemberton is heard screaming)

Operator: "Officers are on the way."

Mrs Pemberton: "He's breaking down the door. He is letting off shots. He is coming in. Oh my God, please help me. I am going to die. He has fired through both windows. I can hear him shouting and screaming. My son is with him. He is going to get me. I think he is in the house. I can hear him. Please help me."

(The operator asks her to describe the house, which apparently was quite new and possibly not yet marked on maps of Hermitage)

Mrs Pemberton: "Oh my God, please help me!"

Operator: "Where is he now?"

Mrs Pemberton: "I do not know. I am hiding in a cupboard. Oh God, he is here. Please help me!"

Operator: "Can you hear your son at all?"

Mrs Pemberton: "No. It is all quiet. He's killed my son. Oh my God!"

Operator: "How many shots has he fired?"

Mrs Pemberton: "About a dozen. I can hear him coming. It has gone quiet. I heard another bang. He is letting off guns. He is banging down the door. Please help, my son could be dead. Oh God, I have about one minute before I die. Oh my God, help me. (Two large bangs are heard) I can hear him bashing the glass. He is coming in now, he is coming. Oh my God! I can hear him! He is coming through! Oh my God help me! I am hiding in the store room. He will catch me! He is coming! Here he comes! Here he comes! Oh my God he's come!"(Mrs Pemberton says she cannot lock the store room door) He is coming now!"(The door is heard opening and a male voice says, 'You whore!' Mrs Pemberton cries out. Then the line goes dead.)

Mr Pemberton then apparently turned the shotgun on himself and died at the scene. Penny Cook, Mr Pemberton's lover at the time of the shootings, told the inquest that he may have been influenced by a similar tragedy in the same village just a year earlier, after she found a newspaper cutting in his possessions. She was left more than £300,000 in life insurance policies signed over by Mr Pemberton in the month before the shootings. She said that he was fully aware he was going to carry out the killings. He had written a note saying: "By the time you read this I will have undertaken a pretty callous act for which I know I will be severely berated. No one quite knows the grief and shock I have suffered as a result of the action of my darling wife, my need for revenge is overpowering, as I discussed, I have become obsessed." The Pemberton's daughter Laura, was spared, as she was away at university at the time of her father's murderous spree.

On Good Friday in April 2000, the naked body of sports student Sara Cameron, 23, from Earsdon, N. Tyneside, was discovered, the day before she was about to travel to Australia, where she had secured a dream job at the Sydney Olympics. It transpired that she had been murdered during a sexual attack. Her killer remained at large, undetected, for several years.

During the early part of 2003, a man was arrested after a domestic dispute culminating in his damaging a neighbour's door. Police routinely took a DNA swab of mouth cells whilst he was in custody, and scientists later matched his DNA with that found on semen on Sara's naked body. Michael Robinson, 30, a bus driver, was re-arrested and charged with her murder. In October 2004, Robinson was jailed for life at Newcastle Crown Court by Mr Justice Henriques, who stated that he was 'exceptionally dangerous'. He ordered that Robinson should serve a minimum of 17 years.

It transpired that even Robinson's own family knew about his violent tendencies, describing him as a moody loner, heavy drinker and cannabis addict. They also reported that in the past, he had been known to kill family pets. The court was told that on the night she died, Sara had been out with friends for a farewell drink before flying off to Australia for the Olympics and to commence her new job. Robinson had selected her as a target, following her late-night from a railway station. Sara was subjected to a horrific sexual attack in a field, just 100 metres from her home. Paul Worsley QC, prosecuting, said: "For four years the defendant lived with a guilty secret. His secret was that on April 21st 2000, he had strangled a young female student and at some point he had stripped her naked and tried to rape her. Having removed all of her clothing, he sought to destroy it, then took elaborate steps to conceal his involvement in the killing. For four years he showed no remorse and breathed not a word of what he had done and moved from the area." The judge told Robinson, that the last minutes of his victim's life 'must have been terrifying, painful and humiliating'.

A teenager obsessed with satanism was facing life in jail after being convicted of the 'truly evil' ritual murder of his girlfriend. Luke Mitchell, 16, who was a fan of goth rock star Marilyn Manson, was found guilty on a jury's majority verdict of killing 14-year-old Jodi Jones. Jodi was stripped, tied up and stabbed to death with all the hallmarks of a ritual killing. She went missing after going to meet her boyfriend in June 2003. Hours later, her naked and mutilated body was found close to her home. Her death bore similarities to the Black Dahlia murder of 1940s Hollywood actress Elizabeth Short. Manson has painted graphic images depicting the US killing.

During the trial, the prosecution attempted to prove that Manson's work was connected to Jodi's murder. The High Court in Edinburgh was shown a Manson DVD bought by Mitchell. It featured two girls tied together and struggling as hoods were placed over their heads. Mitchell, who was 14 when he killed Jodi, denied murdering her in woods near their homes in Dalkeith, Midlothian. But the judge, Lord Nimmo Smith, told him yesterday: "It lies beyond any skill of mine to look into the black depths of your mind. "You have been convicted of a truly evil murder – one of the most appalling crimes that any of us can remember – and you will rightly be regarded as wicked."

The murder verdict was met in court with cries of 'Yes' and applause from the public gallery. Jodi's mother, Judith wept when the verdict was announced. Mitchell's mother Corinne hung her head. The judge told Mitchell, who will be sentenced in three weeks' time, that he would face 'detention without limit of time'. He added: "What you did was to subject Jodi to a horrible death and one can only hope it was mercifully quick. There must, however, have been a time before she became unconscious when she knew that you, her boyfriend, whom she held in affection and trust, and whom she left joyfully to meet, had turned into a fiend. She was loved by her family and you have left them bereft." Sentence was deferred for background reports to help determine the minimum period Mitchell will have to serve before being considered for release. The trial began on November 18 2004, making it the longest single accused murder trial in Scottish legal history. The jury of women and seven men took five hours to reach their decision.

'Lady in the Lake' killer Gordon Park was locked up for life after evading justice for almost 30 years. The cold-hearted 61-year-old schoolmaster slumped forward in the dock as he was found guilty of murdering his wife Carol and dumping her mutilated corpse into one of England's deepest lakes. Park could well die in prison as he will serve at least 15 years behind bars for what has become one of the most infamous cases in British criminal history. As the bespectacled grandfather sat in shock with his head in his hands, members of his family, including his third wife Jenny, 60, burst into tears at the verdict. The jury had taken only seven-and-a-half hours to reach its verdict, after a trial which started more than two months previously.

Sobbing too, but for different reasons, was Carol's brother Ivor Price, 66, who has waited 29 years to see justice done for his sister. He wept and then collapsed. Later, the deeply religious former shipyard clerk said: "I knew that he would get his just deserts, either in this world or the next. I thank God I have lived to see the day when justice has been done." Park, a keen amateur sailor, thought he had got away with the perfect crime by dumping his wife's body from his yacht into Coniston Water, in the Lake District. But when her remains were found 25 metres below the surface by pleasure divers, 21 years later, it triggered an incredible police investigation, which took another seven years to assemble enough pieces of the jigsaw. It ended on 28th January 2005 at Manchester Crown Court. Only Park, a father of three from Barrow-in-Furness, Cumbria, knows what really happened the night in July 1976 when he murdered his wife. But the trial heard an overwhelming mass of forensic and circumstantial evidence that Park was the killer. Shortly after the body was first discovered in August 1997, Park was charged with murder. Proceedings were dropped because the Crown Prosecution Service said there was not enough evidence to convict.

Undaunted, police continued investigating until the authorities had the confidence finally to put Park in the dock. Some of the evidence came from two prison inmates who claimed that the teacher confessed to his crimes when he was under huge emotional pressure on remand, after his first arrest in 1997. One of them, fellow prisoner Michael Wainwright, said Park told him, 'She deserved it' and added that he caught her with another man in the marital bed at the family home. Another witness came forward to reveal that she recognised Park's face from an incident in 1976, when she and her husband clearly remembered an almost identical figure sailing a boat on Coniston, and watching from their car as he tipped a large, heavy object over the side. The husband had joked: "I hope that's not his wife."

Gordon Park appeared a most unlikely killer, a softly-spoken pillar of the community, portrayed by his defence team as a quiet, calm man, 'a big softie' according to his son Jeremy. But while the mild-mannered father won the respect and sympathy of friends, family and neighbours, struggling to raise his children and to hold down a responsible job on his own, he hid a dark, terrible secret. Beneath the calm exterior was a ruthless control freak with the potential to erupt, and that is what led to Carol's death.

They think the couple, who had an unhappy marriage and had both had several affairs, even indulging in wife-swapping, argued on the night Carol died. Park was almost certainly driven into a jealous rage by his wife's infidelity when he killed her at *Bluestones*, the little cottage he built himself in Leece, a village about 20 miles from Coniston.

In an attack of extraordinary ferocity, Park smashed his wife's face to pieces with an ice axe to hide her identity. He then trussed and wrapped her body before dumping it in the water. He waited six weeks before reporting her missing, and said he thought she had left him for another man as she had done on previous occasions. But this time, Carol made no attempt to get in touch or ask about the children she adored. Some of the evidence against Park included the complex system of yachting knots used to tie her up. The body was also weighed down with rocks, whose unusual geology was completely different from the stones around the lake, but which matched perfectly those used to build his cottage.

After the first murder charge was dropped, Park accepted £50,000 to tell a Sunday newspaper his story, which was full of self-pity and denial. He insisted: "I am not a violent person. I don't believe in violence. I would never dream of hitting anyone, especially a woman, no matter what provocation." He added: "I must have sailed over her body dozens of times." Park showed almost no emotion during the trial even as the most gruesome details of his wife's murder and mutilation were revealed. Each lunchtime, after hearing the day's evidence of how he bludgeoned his wife to death, he would leave the court, open his sealed plastic lunch box, carefully unwrap the foil around his home-made sandwiches and calmly sip tea from his silver vacuum flask.

Park was supported by his third wife Jenny, 60, his son Jeremy, 34, younger daughter Rachel, 33, and family friends. After the verdict Detective Superintendent Keith Churchman, the man who ended the murder hunt, said: "Most people who kill their partner tend to be immediately remorseful. But Park was very different. He has gone beyond the act of killing his wife. He has done something to dispose of the body, probably more than most people would do in the circumstances."

Passing sentence, Mr Justice Combes, said: "I have to take into account the terrible concealment of the body that has inflicted so much suffering on so many people. The court's sympathies go out to all those who held Carol Park dear." She was an intelligent, vivacious and attractive young teacher with a zest for life and a mother's indulgent devotion to her children. He was a strait-laced, domineering schoolmaster regarded as a fastidious 'control freak'. They could not have been more different. So when Gordon Park could no longer take his wife Carol's flighty ways, or the affairs she had, to escape the tedium of a loveless marriage, his iron will snapped in an eruption of appalling violence.

Others had witnessed intense arguments between the couple, with Gordon pinning Carol's arms down or sitting astride her on the floor. But nothing matched the unparalleled butchery that occurred on a sweltering July night in 1976, as their three children slept nearby in the Lakeland cottage, that Park had built with his own hands. He attacked their mother so savagely with an ice axe from his climbing kit that he obliterated her face. She put up such a spirited defence that the bones in her hands were smashed into tiny pieces. She ultimately drowned in her own blood.

Park dragged his wife's body, still in its blue baby doll nightdress, to the garage, where he trussed her up in a foetal position, with a complex system of knots he had learned as a skilled sailor. A keen outdoorsman, he stuffed her in one of his old rucksacks and two bin bags. He then created a makeshift body-bag from 30-year-old Carol's pinafore dress, tying the shoulder straps together at one end, and, with meticulous preparation, punching 14 holes through the hemline at the other end, to thread through a drawstring. Police believe he may then have waited a week, keeping the body in a freezer, before the opportunity came to dump it. They also believe Park used two sticking plasters to keep Carol's eyes closed. One officer said: "With the remains, we recovered two sticking plasters, each of which contained traces of Carol's eyelashes. "What we think must have happened was that he used them to close her eyes. Without them, she must have been staring up at him every time he opened the freezer." When the time was right, he left the kids at home in Leece, a village near Barrow-in-Furness, while he stealthily made the half hour, 20-mile trip to Coniston Water. He sailed on to the lake where he often took her in his own *Sailfish 505*, and tipped Carol's body into the dark, icy water. The next day he callously took the children on a trip to Blackpool. And he waited six weeks before reporting his wife missing, later admitting to police: "It sounds a bit calculating, doesn't it?"

Detective Sergeant Geoff Huddlestone, who grilled Park after his arrest in 2004, told how he coolly tried to unsettle officers. He said: "When we went to arrest him at home we had to wait until he came out of the shower, and then he came out and stood in front of us, stark naked. It was bizarre, as if he was sending out the message, 'You don't bother me'." He never showed a flicker of emotion, nor the slightest hint of remorse."

Detective Chief Inspector Keith Churchman, who finally cornered the killer, said Park's arrogance 'shone through' during the interviews. But the people he really feels for are the Park children. He said: "Park lied to his children that their own mother had abandoned them. I have the greatest sympathy for them, because their life was also based on a lie. Then they discover their father is a murderer. They probably learned more about their mother during the course of the trial than they knew from the last 30 years."

Carol had at least two lovers, but tragically, during one separation from Park, he was awarded custody of the children. One of her lovers, Teesside teacher David Brierley, now 60, lived with her in 1974 until the prospect of losing the children for good forced her to go back, to her death. Mr Brierley said: "Carol was shattered. It broke her heart and she cried for days. She was being torn apart. She simply could not live without her children."

Carol Park's oldest daughter opened her heart to tell how having two mothers murdered had blighted her life. In 1969 Carol's sister Christine Price, 17, was tied up and strangled by a boyfriend who was later given life jail for the killing. Christine's 18-month-old baby, Vanessa, was adopted by the Parks and raised as their own. But Vanessa was less than nine years old when her adoptive mother vanished, and it would be decades before Carol's body was found in Coniston Water.

The discovery was doubly devastating for someone who had already lost a mother in violent circumstances. "You can't imagine the sense of shock," said Vanessa, 36, a former cleaner, now a divorced mother-of-two, at her home in Barrow. "It was only then that I knew for sure that she was never coming back. I don't think I will ever get over having two mums murdered. I think about it all the time. My proper mum was taken from me but I was lucky in that I found another one. She loved me and raised me as her own, and I loved her. Then she was taken from me too. It's just too cruel for words."

On 17th February 2005, murdered Charlotte Pinkney's parents appealed for her killer to be kept behind bars until he tells police where he left the teenager's body. Robert Pinkney and Sara McKee hit out as scaffolder Nicholas Rose was convicted of murdering the pretty 16-year-old during a sex attack. Rose, 23, denied murdering Charlotte, and her remains have never been found, despite a year-long search of countryside near her home in Devon. As Judge Graham Cottle jailed him for life with a minimum sentence of 20 years, her parents demanded Rose stays locked up unless he speaks. In a joint statement, the divorced couple said: "No punishment will ever fit this terrible crime. We hope no release from prison will ever be considered, at least until our precious girl's remains have been returned to us and we can finally find some peace." They added: "We have waited 11 torturous months since our daughter's murder to gain some public acknowledgement of her death. The perpetrator has been finally exposed for what he is, and shows neither remorse or sense of responsibility."

After the verdict, the judge told Rose, of Ilfracombe, Devon: "You concealed her body and disposed of it well outside the area which was searched, and as a consequence to date it has not been found. "You continue to harbour that dreadful secret as to where you took her and in so doing you deprive her parents of the opportunity of a proper burial for their child. This is the most serious aggravating feature in this case because her parents can never rest until they know what happened to their child."

Exeter Crown Court heard that Charlotte met Rose at a party in February 2004 and left with him in a car with a friend, Dean Copp. He said when they dropped him off the pair were kissing. It is thought Rose killed her after she refused sex. Paul Dunkels QC, prosecuting, said her blood was found in the car and in one of Rose's trainers. He was also seen with the car near where Charlotte's bag was found and was also spotted cleaning the vehicle. The court also heard the youngster lived a double life between her family and boyfriend Gus O'Brien, 42. Friends described her as a 'social' drug user who enjoyed wild nights out. Detective Chief Inspector Tony Carney, who led the inquiry, called on Rose to give Charlotte's parents 'closure'.

The terrifying threat posed by knife-wielding thugs was exposed on 30th January 2005 as figures revealed Britain's mounting death toll from the menace. Nearly a third of the 858 violent deaths reported in 2004 involved a sharp instrument, as the knife became the criminals' murder weapon of choice. Such killings have risen by 18 per cent since Labour came to power, and by 30 per cent in the past decade. And according to victim groups, a child is stabbed to death every two weeks. In all last year there were 240 murders where a sharp instrument was the weapon. Guns claimed 77 lives. The Government was facing renewed demands to tighten laws and punish those caught carrying blades with the same severity as those found holding guns.

The families of victims, politicians and pressure groups all called for a radical overhaul after the findings were revealed in a Home Office report.

Pupil Luke Walmsley was stabbed to death by 16-year-old bully Alan Pennell at Birkbeck Secondary School in North Somercotes, Lincolnshire, in November 2003. His mother Jayne said yesterday: "To stab somebody is a very personal crime. Unless something is done they seem to have no deterrent." Turning her fire on the Government, she added: "Measures have to be introduced. I think if it was one of their children or a member of their family and one of their children had been murdered, measures would have been brought in within a year, but of course we are Joe Public." The rising trend in knife crime over the past decade comes as the total number of murders in Britain, involving all types of killing, fell for the first time since 1996. The Youth Justice Board has said that up to 300,000 of Britain's 10 million pupils take knives into class, even though it is now a specific criminal offence. Most claim they are for 'self-defence'. Figures for London show that one in six muggings involves someone carrying a knife.

The Conservatives called for the maximum penalties for carrying knives in public to be increased. Shadow Home Secretary David Davis said yesterday: "Knife crime, like gun crime, has risen steeply under Labour and this trend looks set to continue." Norman Brennan, director of the *Victims of Crime Trust*, said he would raise the 'biggest petition Britain has ever seen' if the demands were ignored. He said: "These appalling figures confirm that knife crime has spiralled out of control, but the Government is not listening. I, along with the relatives of many tragic victims of knife culture, gave them warning in December we would no longer stand for it."

Former Home Secretary David Blunkett forced through a crackdown on gun crime, raising the *minimum* penalty for carrying a gun to five years' imprisonment. But he resisted pressure for a similar five-year penalty for carrying a blade over three inches, which the Trust insists would reduce knife crime by 75 per cent. It also wants to see a six-month minimum jail term for carrying shorter blades, or three months for juveniles. The Home Office's latest Homicide and Gun Crime report revealed that the number of deaths caused by firearms is three times lower than with blades. Guns were responsible for nine per cent of the 858 murders, compared with 28 per cent with knives. Mr Brennan is backed by the families of other knife victims, including 15-year-old Kieran Rodney-Davis, who was stabbed to death for his mobile phone on a housing estate in Fulham, west London, and Bernard Heggarty who was stabbed in east London last August while on a lunch break. Also in London, Colin Igwe was knifed in the chest in September 2003, after three youths jumped out of a car, and attacked him and Richard Taylor, father of murdered schoolboy Damilola, has labelled current knife laws as having 'no effect at all'. Britain's most senior police officer made his own call for action against the 'extremely worrying' fashion for carrying knives.

Sir John Stevens, the now retired commissioner of the Metropolitan Police, said he supported officers carrying hand-held scanners for use in schools, outside pubs and clubs and other trouble hotspots. In London alone, figures revealed an 18 per cent rise in knife-related crime last year (2004). Knives were used in 6,600 crimes in London in the 12 months to May 2004, of which 80 per cent were carried out by teenagers.

The Home Office has raised the minimum age for carrying a knife from 16 to 18. Officials have said widespread consultation will be needed before any decision can be taken on toughening the penalty for carrying a knife. A spokeswoman said there were no plans to make carrying a knife as serious an offence as carrying a gun. "We are looking at adding certain types of knives to the list of banned offensive weapons and giving head teachers the power to search pupils."

The grandmother of a toddler left alone at home in a flat with his dead father for three days, branded his killers 'inhuman' on 4th March 2005. Betty Marshall spoke after a man appeared in court charged with the murder of her son Scott, 45, who was battered to death while his three-year-old son Abraham was in the flat. She said: "My tears for Scott are gone. Whoever did this, I want them put away for a long time. Nobody who was human would leave a child alone for two days."

Mrs Marshall is now taking care of Abraham, who was sobbing and in a distressed state when relatives called at Mr Marshall's flat in Kingsdown, Bristol. His sister, Tania Lovewell, said the family would struggle to come to terms with his loss. Breaking down in tears, she said: "Scott was a much loved father, brother and uncle and will be missed by each and every one of us. Not a day will pass without one or all of us thinking of him. He was unique and gave to each of us a different aspect of his personality. Abraham will now be cared for by his close and loving family." Mrs Lovewell said that Mr Marshall had been struggling to get over the death of his partner Lisa, who died two years ago from cancer. He was due to be the best man at the wedding of his friend Marc Davit later this year.

A tearful Mr Davies said: "He was the most wonderful person I've met in my life. He was a loving father and a wonderful friend. "He was a big fan of loud music and loved the band *Radiohead*."

At a police press conference, Mr Marshall's daughter Jennifer Hobbs appealed for witnesses to come forward. Detective Superintendent Nigel Woods, who is leading the investigation, said the case was now focused on recovering a camcorder and silver metallic box. "Fortunately this is an isolated but tragic incident," he said. "It has left the family devastated and the young son Abraham orphaned. We are appealing for local people who have seen either the camcorder or the silver case since Tuesday. "These are vital to the investigation and we need to recover them. We would ask people who may have seen them to get in contact." Mr Woods said Abraham had recovered well after his ordeal in the flat with his father's body. "We understand that the child was there for some time. It was distressing but he is now with his family, he's fit, well and healthy. The child has had a torrid time but fortunately he has survived, and survived well, and his life is a normal as it can be in the circumstances."

James Long, 27, from the Clifton area of Bristol, has been charged with the murder of Mr Marshall and was remanded in custody by magistrates in the city. He is due to appear at Bristol Crown Court on March 11.

A young gunman who celebrated his execution-style shooting of a dad of three by writing a rap lyric on it, was jailed for 25 years on 25th February 2005. David Gaynor, 19, wrote: "I will kill you in front of your family." Police believe Gaynor took the line from ex drug dealer and rap superstar 50 Cent, the Old Bailey heard. Gaynor was convicted of attempting to murder carpenter Douglas Mullings, 32, in May 2004. Mr Mullings who had confronted a gang of youths outside his home in Tottenham, North London, was left paralysed.

Chilling new TV footage will reveal the utter contempt that Britain's most notorious serial killer Harold Shipman showed towards the police. The pictures, seen exclusively by the *Sunday Express*, show the GP responsible for the deaths of more than 250 patients, with his back to the investigating officers in the interview room while being interrogated. In the film, *To Kill And Kill Again*, to be shown on ITV. Shipman refuses to answer questions and remains silent with his arms folded.

West Yorkshire detectives were questioning him about the deaths, which took place on one day in 1975, of three of his terminally ill patients in Todmorden, where Shipman had worked after qualifying as a doctor. He would later move to a surgery in Hyde, Greater Manchester. The GP is shown a photograph of each victim, but fails to respond. One of the detectives says: "For the benefit of the tape, Harold Shipman's eyes are closed and he won't look at the photographs at all." Consultant psychologist Paul Brittan tells the programme: "Shipman is showing his contempt for the police and contempt for their lack of medical knowledge. He is trying to manipulate the process. He has also lost count of how many people he has killed. He has no idea that he has killed these people."

To Kill And Kill Again features another interrogation in which Shipman is interviewed about the death in Hyde of former mayoress Kathleen Grundy, 81. Asked whether he injected her with a lethal dose of diamorphine, Shipman says: "No. And you tell me that people in Hyde don't have access to drugs. I think you should talk to your drug squad." He claims Mrs Grundy, whom he was treating for irritable bowel syndrome, was a drug addict. The detective says: "Do you really expect me to believe that a well-respected, elderly lady like Mrs Grundy gave herself a fatal overdose of drugs?" Shipman: "Yes. I'm sure you're aware that drugs like morphine, heroin and pethidine all cause constipation."

But as the film points out, it was Shipman who had an addiction to pethidine since medical school. Later in the interview, the police say that after poisoning Mrs Grundy in her home with diamorphine, he changed her medical records on the computer. Shipman breaks down and crawls about the floor of the interview room. Shipman's killing spree went undetected but local people had their suspicions. Funeral director Alan Massey said: "We used to say, 'It's another one of Shipman's'."

Shipman subsequently hanged himself in prison, thus defeating the ends of justice. In August 2005 the Prisons and Probation Ombudsman, Mr Stephen Shaw, published his long-awaited report into the circumstances of Shipman's death by suicide. He concluded that no HMP staff were to blame and that Shipman's suicide could not have been prevented.

The widow of killer GP Harold Shipman has been awarded £35,000 of taxpayers' money. Primrose Shipman, totted up the sum in legal bills for the inquiry into her husband's 284 murders. He last practised in Hyde, Greater Manchester. Mrs Shipman, 55, gave three hours of evidence at the inquiry, but couldn't remember details about the deaths of two patients. The money dwarfs that paid to the families of the victims, who got an average of £11,460 each. The inquiry has cost nearly £21million. Norman Brennan, of the *Victims of Crime Trust*, said the payment to her "will leave a very bad taste in the mouths of the families of Shipman's victims."

What is wrong with our judiciary? How could Judge Thomas Crowther justify handing out a paltry sentence of two-and-a-half years to Craig Swann, a 21-year-old kick boxer, who killed William Bird with a single, brutal punch? Mr Bird was out walking with two friends and asked Swann to dismount from his bicycle while on a footbridge. Swann rode off laughing after the attack and was later heard bragging in a local pub. Mr Bird leaves a wife, children and grandchildren. Their lives will never be the same again. He, at 67, was enjoying his retirement.

On the day of the attack he had been to a rugby match and no doubt looked forward to many more pleasant outings. A vicious, mindless thug has robbed him of all that. Surely, natural justice calls out for tough punishment, yet time and again judges hand out wilfully perverse and liberal sentences which enrage public opinion. Drink-drivers who kill, paedophiles, career burglars who shatter their victims' confidence, many face nothing more than a few months inside before they are free to hurt again. What are these highly paid, jumped-up lawyers playing at? Do they feel some peevish need to assert independence from the public they serve, and the Government which they suspect of impinging on their authority? Or maybe it's that *proximity* to the dregs of society has warped their sense of what is right and proper.

Daily Express, 5th March 2005, Editorial

COUNT 5

ROBBERY AND THEFT

Section 8 Theft Act 1968

A person is guilty of robbery if he steals, and immediately before or at the time of doing so, and in order to do so, he uses force on any person or puts or seeks to put any person in fear of being then and there subjected to force. A person guilty of robbery, or of an assault with intent to rob, shall on conviction on indictment be liable to imprisonment for life.

Section 1 Theft Act 1968

A person is guilty of theft if he dishonestly appropriates property belonging to another with the intention of permanently depriving the other of it; and "thief" and "steal" shall be construed accordingly.

A person guilty of theft shall on conviction on indictment be liable to imprisonment for a term not exceeding ten years.

When I was working on CID at Romford I became quite envious of a more senior colleague who had recently been transferred in from the Stoke Newington area of London, on another Metropolitan Police Division. This is a very popular residential area with members of the Jewish faith, particularly Orthodox. In those days, the males signified their reverence and precise religion by wearing dark or black homburg or trilby hats over their skull caps, grey, very dark or black overcoats or raincoats, white, tie-less shirts done up at the collar, and sometimes highly decorated waistcoats, black trousers and shoes, wore very full-beards and very prominent 'ringlets' at the sideboards level. The men often had pocket watches and chains with fobs attached to their clothing. Even young males wore the skull caps and 'ringlets.' They were obviously very devout people, whose weekends, I believe, began on Friday nights and from then on, right through their Saturday 'Sabbaths', they must not carry out any work, not even the effort of switching-on a light, I believe. At that time, they almost all drove around in massive Volvo estate cars, and Volvo motor dealers must have 'cleaned-up' in that area for many years. I mention this because for the local criminal 'hoods,' it became very fashionable to rob these people in the street. The word 'mugging' was not then in use. They were seen as an 'easy-touch' as they were a very peace-loving, law-abiding race, minded their own business and very much kept themselves to themselves in close-family units, with close-community ties. It was plain and simple robbery or assault with intent to rob, maximum penalty, as I mentioned earlier, Life Imprisonment.

In the Stoke Newington area, I recall the pavements were very wide and therefore the 'robbing-ground' was very spacious, with loads of room for all. There came a time when crime figures analysis revealed that it was time for specific, direct action to be taken against the low-life criminals who crawled out from under their damp stones, normally when the daylight began to fade, as dusk and darkness creates artificial courage for cowards. In those days their brains were not addled by cannabis, heroin and crack cocaine, and frontal lobotomy NHS operations, had even longer waiting lists than in today's climate. My Romford colleague 'Mick', pre-transfer to outer K division, and his police buddies, approached the Orthodox Jewish community and succeeded in obtaining some relevant garments etc and presented themselves, in pairs of course, as 'easy, soft targets' on those wide Stoke Newington pavements. Can you imagine the sheer shock, surprise, horror and possible immediate-change-of-pants required when our intrepid, innocent-looking 'Orthodox Jew' colleagues swiftly turned the tables on the low life and felt their collars, for a very rapid frog-march or 'Hurry-Up' wagon trip to Stoke Newington police station? Wouldn't you have just loved to have been standing in a shop doorway or at a bus stop nearby, to witness such a happy event? Some of the first offenders arrested during this quite short police operation 'put their hands up' to some of the earlier crimes of that nature, improving the all-important robberies 'clear-up' rate. However the main benefit to local police AND the Orthodox Jewish community, was that the word soon got round that serious liberty-loss was looming on the Stoke Newington horizon, and the attacks swiftly petered-out. Personally, at the time I would have just loved to have been part of that exciting police operation. To 'take out' the 'no-hopers', put them where they deserved to be, thus making the streets much safer for all, and adding to the adrenalin-run 'buzz', that made up for the losses when you were too unfit through smoking to be able to run fast enough to catch the little darlings, on which your intended rapid rise to Commissioner of the Metropolis so much depended.

Frail, partially-sighted, 94-year-old, war hero Eddie Poole from Wincobank, Sheffield, who served on the front line with Montgomery in N. Africa during WW2, was badly beaten up in his bungalow as he attempted to fight off a thug, who fled with £135. The trauma forced widower Eddie to move from his beloved home into sheltered accommodation. He is still suffering nightmares about his ordeal. In December 2003 he answered a knock at his front door and a mindless thug knocked him to the floor and dragged him by his legs into the kitchen. When Eddie, who has difficulty walking unaided, tried to defend himself by grabbing the leg of his attacker, he was kicked in the chest. As the robber fled with his money, Eddie managed to shuffle into the kitchen and set off an attack alarm to seek help.   On Christmas Eve, detectives were able to arrest a 34 year-old man, who strongly protested his innocence and denied robbery, but was kept in custody for four months. But he walked free when the charges were dramatically dropped by the Crown Prosecution Service, on the day his trial was due to start at Sheffield Crown Court. Richard Sheldon, prosecuting, told the court there was 'insufficient evidence' to take the case forward.

The victim's son, Brian Poole, 70, said he was disgusted that the case had been allowed to drag on. "It is hard to put into words how I feel. I don't blame the police, but somewhere along the line someone has got it wrong. The two detectives on this case worked their socks off and there was a great response from the public. For the case to fall down at this stage is very distressing. We have never been consulted or asked about the decision. My father is still not well following the attack. He has nightmares and is jittery. I shudder to think what he will say when I tell him his suspected attacker has walked free.

"He keeps saying, if his attacker is not sent to jail, he thinks he will be terrorised by him. I am very, very bitter about this, and all the family is as well. Everyone has been so concerned. Even his old regiment, based in Germany, sent him a donation and asked to be kept informed. He stated too, that he is 'in the dark' about why charges had been dropped and was seeking an explanation." South Yorkshire police stated that they are not looking for anyone else in connection with the attack. Detective Inspector Steve Williams said: "This was a horrendous attack on an elderly man in his home. Police carried out a thorough and vigorous investigation. Unfortunately the Crown Prosecution Service decided not to offer any evidence. They will provide an official explanation to the victim and his family. Police officers have been in touch with the family. The investigation into the incident is now at an end unless any new evidence comes to light." A CPS spokeswoman said: "This is a case which always presented a number of evidential difficulties. It became apparent at court, following discussions which involved the prosecution and defence counsel, the reviewing lawyer and the police, that there was insufficient evidence to provide a realistic prospect of conviction."

To me, this sounds as if it would have been a case of just the victim's word against that of the cowardly perpetrator, with little or no supporting independent evidence. On the other hand, a Bench of magistrates and later, probably a Crown Court Judge after his committal for trial, found that there was sufficient available evidence to keep the suspect 'banged-up' in custody for 4 months awaiting trial. One consolation to Eddie and his family and to the public at large in the Sheffield area, was that if the suspect was guilty, whilst in custody he could not commit further vicious attacks during that 4 months. We will never know for sure the answer as to the suspect's guilt or otherwise, if he was guilty, then a serious miscarriage of justice has been done, but of course, there is no right of appeal by the prosecution, police or victim under these circumstances.

One really frustrating feature of the case for me personally, is that I am well aware, as a former serving police officer, that in the 'old days', the case would have been allowed to run its proper course at the crown court, and the final question of guilt or innocence would have been established in a jury room, not in an air-conditioned CPS office! Instead, bureaucrats who have never been victims of crime themselves, apparently toss a coin in the air or play a game of coinage 'spoof' as to the chances of a conviction being secured. After reading this book, you may find it as bizarre, amazing and almost incredible, that in our so-called 'best-in-the-world', much admired British Criminal Justice System 'lottery', that the 'chips' are so often stacked against the innocent victim. Now you will appreciate why I felt compelled to try to redress the balance by researching and writing this book!

In early May 2004 a murder investigation was launched after an 82-year-old woman was knocked to the ground near her home in Wanstead, East London. The mugger ran off with her handbag. The victim was taken to hospital with a fractured leg and shoulder but died later. Her son David, in his 50's, said: "I am completely cut to pieces, he mugged her for the bag and then came back for a bus pass."

Police in the Stoke-on-Trent area are hunting for a callous group of youths who robbed a 31-year-old blind woman of her white stick. The woman, although badly shaken, was not seriously hurt in the broad daylight attack at Longton. The victim told police that one of the group of up to five youths was wearing Lynx Phoenix scent deodorant, which she recognised. Police said: "The youths asked her the time and she let them hear her talking watch. They stole her white cane and the watch and made taunting remarks as they pushed her into the road." A female bus driver drove her to a police station.

Richard Benamara, 17, of Langton Green, Kent, disguised in a balaclava and brandishing a knife, went to the Texaco service station in his village in October 2003 and threatened a male member of staff. He pointed the knife at a Mr Kumar shouting: "Give me the money." Mr Kumar fled to a secure office and from there watched on CCTV as Benamara climbed over the counter, picked up a bin liner and put cigarettes in it. He also stole cash from the till, as well as Mr Kumar's mobile phone. When questioned by police, Benamara replied: "You're joking, I wouldn't have gone back to the same place." The court was told that was a reference to an earlier, similar robbery at the garage when £415 in cash and £300 worth of property was stolen. Prosecuting counsel said Benemara first started committing offences when he was just 12 years old. The youth stood handcuffed in the dock as the judge told him that his recent crimes were "in a different league."

Judge McKinnon told the court that it was in both Benemara's interest and the public interest that he used his time in custody to straighten himself out. He said: "You need sorting out inside, with intensity." Benemara had pleaded guilty to the second robbery and asked for the second one to be TIC (A bizarre way of dealing with it, I would have charged him with both robberies!). His barrister told the court that Benemara now had an 'insight' into what he had done (Whatever that might mean!). "He knows the tariff for knifepoint robberies of small shops" (All robberies and assaults with intent to rob carry life imprisonment as a maximum, as do causing GBH with intent and attempted murder, which are relevant to this chapter). He was sentenced to three years in a Young Offenders Institution.

Readers may be interested to learn that prisoners in the court dock are not routinely handcuffed. A special application form has to be completed and handed to the judge or magistrates before the prisoner is 'put up' or brought up into the dock, requesting permission and setting out the grounds for the request. The grounds could be one or more from the following list:

1) *Is a known escaper from custody; from jail, court rooms or custodial areas, prison vans etc.*

2) *Known to be very violent or made threats to harm a judge or magistrates bench, or Police.*

3) *His associates, family, friends in court may attempt to assist his escape.*

4) *The seriousness of the offences with which charged.*

5) *The length of prison sentence which he is likely to receive for his present criminal offences.*

Home DIY TV addicts will be interested to learn that TV presenter Lowri Turner, (apparently named by her parents after 2 famous artists) has been robbed in the street for the second time in 12 months. On this occasion it took place at 9.15pm as she was walking home, when her attacker struck. A youth appeared at her side and grabbed and yanked her handbag away from her. The strap broke and he almost broke her fingers too, as they were locked around it. Terrified Lowri, 39, ran to her sister's house nearby and called the police. She said: "When they arrived I was barely making sense due to the shock. My confidence is shaken. I'd just managed to build it up after the first mugging. For months I froze if I heard the sound of feet behind me. I asked people to walk me home after dark and always wore flat shoes. I even stopped wearing make-up, as if by making myself unattractive I might repel muggers." She is now planning to quit her home in NW London for somewhere safer to bring up her sons aged three and one.

TV news reader Jan Leeming was attacked in the BBC Television Centre newsroom at Wood Lane, Shepherds Bush in 1987, whilst she was actually on her way to read the news, by 4 youths who had stormed in. The evening news had to be re-scheduled due to the interruption. Readers may recall witnessing the 'live' attack as the news went out. One of the attackers was Richard Green, now aged 34, from London. He had sprayed ammonia into her eyes and mouth before grabbing her handbag containing £23 and leaving her screaming for help. She was rushed to hospital with injuries to her mouth, nose, lips, and her right eye.

The attack attracted national attention, as Jan Leeming was one of the first women to read the national TV news. Green was sentenced to five years imprisonment for the attack at the time. With others, Green has now been arrested for an even more horrendous and callous attack on a 52-year-old man in his own home, in the Glasgow area of Scotland, which of course has its own Criminal Justice System, quite separate and different to ours. On this occasion Green was accompanied by Edward Guiller, 38, from Greenock and Thomas Edgar, 20, from Preston. A jury at the High Court in Glasgow heard that their victim, Robert Devine, had been tortured for hours before he died from 70 injuries. He had been stabbed, kicked and stamped on by the 3 vicious criminals. All three were convicted of his savage murder. They were all jailed for life. The judge, Lady Paton, ordered that Guiller and Edgar should serve 12 years before being able to approach the parole board. However in Green's case, because of his 'atrocious' criminal record, he must serve a minimum of 15 years.

In April 2004 on the 10.17pm train from Victoria to Bognor Regis, West Sussex, four mindless cretins battered into unconsciousness a lone businessman, father of three, aged in his 30's, who was travelling in a first-class compartment. They showered him with foam from a fire extinguisher, wrenched from its fixture. As he tried to defend himself by wrestling the fire extinguisher away from them, they beat him over the head with it. He was later found unconscious by rail staff and rushed to hospital in a waiting ambulance, when the train stopped. The images of all four thugs were recorded on CCTV cameras, with quite remarkable clarity, so it may just be a matter of time before British Transport Police track them down and bring them to 'justice.' The victim had gashes in his head stitched,and spent the night in hospital. A BTP spokesman said: "The poor guy was travelling back from a hard day's work, reading his book when he was set upon. He was hit very hard. These lads were on the train spraying everyone, and we understand they assaulted another male, although he has not come forward. The victim is anxious to bring his attackers to justice. He was pretty shocked afterwards. I think his reaction was one of compete disbelief that it could have happened." Hopefully they will be recognised, identified and arrested for this unprovoked series of vicious assaults, which could easily have ended in murder, particularly if the victim had a thin skull.

An 87-year-old woman was robbed in a packed *Marks & Spencer* store in Broad Street, Reading, by two teenage girls, who punched another woman as she tried to help her. Police are shocked by the audacity of the robbers who struck whilst the store was full of customers and staff. The pensioner had just put her handbag in a trolley when the thugs pounced. In the struggle she was knocked to the ground and could not hold onto her bag, which contained credit cards and £120 cash. The other woman bravely stepped-in to assist and stop them, but one of the girls lunged forward and punched her in the chest. The girls then ran through the store with the bag and made their escape. Staff immediately came to the assistance of the two pensioners, and though they were not badly hurt, they were deeply distressed and badly shaken. CCTV footage was being examined. The attackers were described as European or Indian, wearing headscarves and aged between 16 and 18 years.

Another blind person was beaten up by a mugger who stole his white stick. The victim, 21, was in a bus station phone box when he was hit twice in the face and knocked to the ground. His suitcase was also stolen. One police officer said: "How callous can you get? To take advantage of a blind person in this way is beyond belief." Police think the robber, in Gloucester in April 2004, may have been a junkie who chose his victim so he could not be identified.

(I'm finding it hard work to keep up my reportage of all this dreadful violence, as fast as I draft it up for the book and think the end of that chapter is in sight, another host of violent material comes to hand from various sources. It just goes to show what a violent country and violent world we live in.)

A frail pensioner aged 84, a former Red Cross nurse who then spent 20 years of her life counselling violent offenders, suffered a vicious attack by a thug in broad daylight in Penzance, Cornwall. She was rushed to hospital with six broken ribs and a cut head in what police have described as 'an extremely nasty attack.' The grandmother of four, who lost £20 in the attack, said: "He probably thought that he had killed me." To me, it sounds like a miracle that she was not killed, it only needed one or more of her six broken ribs to puncture her lungs or other vital organs, for that to have been the case. From a personal viewpoint, I'd say from experience, that kind of over-the-top violence had all the hallmarks of a frenzied attack by some dreadful out-of-control crack cocaine or heroin addict, desperate to raise immediate funds and race to his drugs dealer to secure his next fix.

Jamie McLaughlin, 30, held up his local *Blockbusters* video store at Weybridge, Surrey at knifepoint and took £80 worth of goods. However he was captured after a sharp-eyed *Blockbusters* assistant noticed that McLaughlin had left his *Blockbusters* membership card on the counter when fleeing. He pleaded guilty and was sentenced to 45 months imprisonment.

On 21st July 2004, a thief who took part in Britain's biggest diamond robbery was convicted at the Old Bailey. Nebojsa Denic, drew and discharged a Magnum handgun during his attempt to escape. Clint Eastwood fans will recall that a bullet fired from a Magnum hand gun can purportedly pass right through the engine block etc. of a car. He was held by some very brave security guards and a woman was hit by the powerful bullet, but lived to tell the tale. A second man, Milan Jovetic, assisted in the robbery, during the £23million raid on *Graff's* jewellers in Central London in June 2003. Both were members of the Pink Panther Gang, so-called because some stolen gems were hidden in a tub of face cream, as in the movie *The Return Of The Pink Panther*. Denic was jailed for 15 years and Jovetic received a sentence of five-and-a-half years. I wonder if you can imagine the feelings of absolute rapture and bliss, and the excitedly-beating heart and broadest of smiles on the face of the police officer who looked thoroughly inside that innocent-looking tub of face cream? I certainly can! One of the magic moments in your police career, when the sudden rush of adrenaline makes up for all the horrible recent experiences in the down-side of 'THE JOB'!

OPERATION BOSTON: Joint Flying Squad and Security Express anti-cash-in-transit and bullion van robbery surveillance operation. Each of these suspects appeared to be taking a keen interest in the movements of the Security Express van and crew members at various locations in the London area

I was once engaged on *Operation Boston*, a joint *Security Express* bullion/cash-in-transit/Flying Squad surveillance operation. Security Express had been plagued by what its Insurers appeared to feel was too high volume in robberies from both bullion and cash-in-transit vans,

Whilst about to make a delivery in Westow Hill, Crystal Palace, S. London, the driver was approached by the suspect shown, who had been standing on the opposite side of the road, but suspiciously came over on the apparent pretext of asking for directions

as well as attacks on crew members whilst pedestrianised for 'across the pavement' deliveries & collections.

For several months, Security Express vehicles based at a certain depot, were the subject of the surveillance operation described above. Each individual delivery vehicle, whether carrying bullion or cash-in-transit, was shadowed from its depot by a motor car and motorcycle team.

At each stop for deliveries or collections, the surveillance team would keep close watch from a discreet distance, following crews on foot if necessary, ready to call for urgent Police assistance and, using telephoto lensed cameras, record the ongoing action in the event of an attempted raid on the vans or walking crew members.

Whilst in 'convoy' following these vehicles at a discreet tactical distance around London and the Home Counties, as they delivered and collected their cash consignments, we were in radio contact with the van crew and with base. We also kept the crews on foot under close surveillance, as they

OPERATION BOSTON:
Puffer jacket man

made the pedestrian journeys during which they were at their most vulnerable to attack.

One day, this man in the 'puffer' jacket at London Bridge station, apparently closely watched the *Security Express* crew arrive and park at the bus stand,whilst they serviced automatic teller machines, deep inside the station. He then followed them along a deserted platform until they entered a 'staff-only' area, where he dare not follow them. On their return, he followed them again, laden with their large (now empty) cash boxes, back to their van.

We then moved as a convoy to the next pickup/dropping-off point approximately one mile away near Elephant and Castle. As I parked our car in a side street ready to observe the crew's actions at a nearby bank on the main road, amazingly the *puffer jacket man* reappeared in the same street, and approached our car, walking along the pavement from behind us.

As I had been unable to obtain a clear, full-frontal photo of this man in good daylight, at London Bridge station, it was essential that I took this opportunity to do so. Whilst still facing my front,so as not to attract this 'suspect's' attention, I took the shot by aiming my telephoto lens at the driver's offside door mirror of my parked car as I still sat in the driving seat. He was oblivious to my actions.

Whilst acting suspiciously at London Bridge station, as he followed the *Security Express* crew on foot with their laden money boxes, he had been totally unaware that my colleagues and I had been keeping **him** under surveillance, as he apparently watched, and certainly followed the crew.

This type of camera 'mirror' shot, can also be taken by aiming the camera at the car *interior* mirror to capture on film a suspect approaching from behind. However it is essential to have a pristine clean and condensation-free rear window for this to be successful.

Security Express was subsequently taken over by *Securitas*, a

Scandinavian company.

To my knowledge, neither the puffer-jacketed robbery 'suspect', nor any of the other photographed suspects pictured here, were ever caught in a robbery - However it was very necessary to photograph them at the time, in case they were engaged in reconnaissance and/or planning for future attacks at or near the venues shown.

A multi-million-pound Heathrow Airport crime syndicate suspected of robbery, money-laundering and cocaine smuggling has been smashed by Police and Customs. A 200-strong task force arrested 12 men and 2 women in raids across the Home Counties. The suspects include airport workers on average wages, who allegedly enjoy 'inexplicable wealth' living in expensive houses and driving luxury cars.

Investigators seized several vehicles, including a Ferrari and a Porsche. Alleged criminal assets including luxury homes in Cyprus and Spain are likely to be frozen. Police said that the arrests included "foot soldiers as well as significant players." Four of the men arrested are suspects over a £4.7 million cash robbery at Heathrow in February 2002. In that lightning raid, two men posed as British Airways staff and ambushed a security guard as he loaded a van with boxes of foreign currencies from a BA flight from Bahrain. The terrified guard was handcuffed and the fortune in cash, packed into eight large plastic crates, was switched to a stolen BA Renault Mastervan. The robbers drove out of the airport then transferred the cash to another vehicle and set fire to the Mastervan.

The latest raids also netted three people alleged to have been involved in a £100million bullion robbery at the airport in May 2004. Seven men have already been charged over that robbery. Three suspects now held are linked to huge imports of cocaine passing through the airport. They will also be questioned about the alleged laundering of profits from drug trafficking. The arrests were hailed as a triumph for *Operation Grafton* (do you get it, graft-on?) a joint initiative by the Metropolitan, Surrey and Thames Valley police forces and Customs and Excise. Since it was launched in March 2003, *Operation Grafton* teams have arrested more than 100 people and seized stolen property, including bullion, cash and computer chips, worth £150million. The operation has already cut high-value thefts at the airport by 73 per cent. Each year, tens of millions of pounds of goods, including bullion, currency and electrical items are stolen after arriving at Heathrow, which handles 200 high-value shipments every day. Customs Director of Investigations Paul Evans said that the arrests sent a powerful message to gangs based in and around the airport. He warned: "If you are engaged in crime, you are going to be caught." Metropolitan Police Assistant Commissioner Tarique Ghaffur said: "There have been some serious career criminals operating in and around the airport making a good living."

Five members of a gang who savagely attacked scores of commuters "for kicks," robbing them of their phones and small change, were jailed for a total of 25 years at Middlesex Guildhall Crown Court on 1st September 2004. The 'steamers' operated as a pack of animals, swarming through trains, Tubes and buses in London, terrifying and robbing their victims. Some used street tags such as Killer, Bastard, Packman and Driller. Operating in groups up to 50 strong, in two weeks in September 2003, the gang, known as Lords of Stratford crew, committed at least 12 robberies. "We believe there are many more victims we don't know about," said one police officer in the case. The five, including four juveniles, were sentenced to five years each for three separate counts of conspiracy to rob. Jerry McPherson, 17, from Wood Green, Dennis Barrette, 16, of Ilford, Michael Silcott, 17, of Stoke Newington, (Brother or son of Winston Silcott?) and Francis Oshane, 16, of Hackney Wick, were all given five years detention. Michael Onward, 21, of Ilford, was jailed for five years. Silcott had nine previous convictions and Oshane eight. Silcott, whose convictions include threats to kill and burglary, had only just been released from detention when he was arrested. Oshane had served four months for attempted robbery.

Sentencing them at Middlesex Guildhall Crown Court, Judge Henry Blacksell QC heard the thugs were "in it for the kicks and thrills". "It is part of the distressing aspect of this case that the attacks were so casually carried out," he told them. "Anyone who had the misfortune to be out and about was at risk. You all understood the dreadful fear and injuries. You enjoyed the humiliation. You picked on people who were weak and vulnerable. Not content with taking their property, you beat them up." The gang were described by one victim as "a pack of wild animals." Specialist welder John Tovey thought he would die, as he was repeatedly kicked in the head when 20 of the thugs attacked him on the train from Camden to Stratford. He was robbed of his mobile, but then three of the gang savagely beat him up. His eyesight was permanently damaged and he was forced to give up his £70,000-a-year job. Another victim, student Katie Tyler, 19, was going to visit her boyfriend when she was attacked by ten 'Lords' who stole her phone. She was held in a headlock, repeatedly punched and left covered in blood. "I felt like it was going on for ever," she said. "They were animals, there was nothing human about them at all." One woman victim was repeatedly punched and suffered a serious sex assault during an attack.

At the end of April 2004, the Government published the latest crime figures which do not make good reading at all. They reveal that violent offences such as hooliganism and assault rose 11 per cent in the final three months of the year 2003. At the same time, violence against the person, which we are dealing with in this chapter, increased 13 per cent, while 'minor' assaults rose by 20 per cent. Ministers tried to play down the rise in violent crime by dismissing much of the increase as 'low-level thuggery'. But they did announce a summer crack-down on under-age binge drinkers in a bid to put an end to 'no-go city centres' and 'reclaim the streets' for law-abiding people.

Sex offences increased by six per cent, while criminal damage and vandalism rose ten per cent in 2003, compared with the same period in 2002, the British Crime Survey revealed. But there was an 11 per cent fall in burglaries, a seven per cent decline in robbery and a ten per cent drop in car crime. Overall figures remain the same. The results follow news that the Metropolitan Police has had spectacular success in reducing crime in London. There, burglary has fallen to 1975 levels and street crime is down four per cent. The Met. Deputy Commissioner, Sir Ian Blair, said the results showed the positive effect of having more officers on the beat. The figures were also hailed as 'encouraging' by Home Office Minister Hazel Blears, despite the rise in violent crime. The Government and police have announced plans to name-and-shame pubs, clubs, off-licences and shops, as part of a campaign to beat under-age drinking, which will include 'stings' using children to buy alcohol from suspected outlets. Irresponsible traders could also lose their licences. Ms Blears said: " Out-of-control drinking can turn a night out into a nightmare. 70 per cent of weekend night admissions to hospital casualty departments are due to alcohol and in 50 per cent of violent crimes the attacker is intoxicated."

The Government is cracking down on irresponsible landlords who encourage binge-drinking, we are going to put an end to no-go city centres."

(**Author's note:** *You may think there is hypocrisy involved here, given that the Government, in October 2004, in the face of very serious binge-drinking problems already leading to street violence, is intent on extending Licensing Hours!*)

Rick Naylor, president of the Police Superintendents' Association of England and Wales said: "Alcohol-fuelled violence in town and city centres on Friday and Saturday nights has become the norm. The police and other emergency services are fed up with clearing up the broken bodies, broken glass, discarded kebabs and vomit which seems to follow every Friday and Saturday. Paul Cavadino, chief executive of crime reduction charity *Nacro* (National Association For The Care and Resettlement Of Offenders) welcomed the new strategy, but said ministers should look more at prevention, education and treatment of offenders. But Dr Ruth Henig of the

Association of Police Authorities, warned that Chancellor Gordon Brown needed to meet a £250 million shortfall in funding or there could be fewer police officers in future. Jan Berry, chairman of the Police Federation of England and Wales, said the Government was right to ease closing-time restrictions to stop last orders binge-drinkers, but called for a ban on happy-hour promotions.

The hard-line Police Chief in a gun-ridden heartland of crime has ordered a controversial zero-tolerance policy. With the support and help of the local community, Commander Richard Quinn, Metropolitan Police, in charge of Lambeth, South London, has identified crime 'hot-spots', shutting down three pubs, including bulldozing one of them, which had become magnets for criminals. Now other Police Chiefs around the country are set to follow his bold, tough approach to stop crime and murders before they happen. With 149 murders in the last ten years, Commander Quinn will have his work cut out, but he is determined to reverse the tide of killings in his south London borough. When interviewed about his plans he said: "This sends a very clear message that we will not tolerate this kind of behaviour in our community and if you do, we will close you down. If I know a pub landlord is allowing criminal activity they won't get a second chance and the public are behind us all the way on this."

He described how, when he first arrived in the borough, intelligence revealed that drinkers in *The Green Man* and *The Duke of Wellington* were 'armed and dangerous' and involved in tit-for-tat rivalry. The gangs had turned the areas surrounding the pubs into the 'Wild West' and the losers were locals whose lives were made miserable. Mr Quinn's biggest fear was that innocent victims would be caught in the cross-fire, and it was only a matter of time before a hapless passer-by would be killed. One couple escaped a near-miss while sitting in their car outside *The Duke Of Wellington* in Brixton. Their windscreen was shattered in a drive-by shooting and it was only by good luck that they escaped unhurt.

Since then, the *Duke Of Wellington* has been closed down and its rival, *The Harrier* in nearby Herne Hill, has been reduced to rubble. *The Green Man* in Brixton has also been closed down. Many were injured and Richard White died when he was shot twice in the neck outside *The Duke of Wellington*. Two gunmen were jailed for 24 years for their part in the turf war. Commander Quinn explained how he ordered the managing agents of all three pubs to Lambeth Police Headquarters in Brixton and told them they had to call time. They all agreed to shut for eight weeks but only *The Duke of Wellington* looks set to re-open, as a smart organic pub.

If the pubs had not closed, Commander Quinn would have gone to court in an attempt to force them to shut, but he discovered that the licensees were also being ruthlessly intimidated by the gangsters. He said: "One licensee, a woman, was clearly trying her best but she was being intimidated. We went down to the pub with her that day and boarded up the premises, and we did the same to the other two pubs. Now local people can venture past without fear for their lives. Most of these shootings were linked to lifestyles of the people involved and were connected to drugs, organised crime, or disrespect and stupidity. The steps we have taken have allowed us to dismantle that activity. Pubs are very often the very heartbeat of a community, where people relax and play dominoes but the less strong licensees can become targets for ruthless individuals. There are also many very good landlords whom we support." With their favourite meeting places closing, many of the gangsters attempted to take over neighbouring pubs, but Commander Quinn and his officers were there first to ensure that they couldn't get a foothold, and they were shown the door instead. He is determined that this is a long-term, rather than a short-term solution and in recent weeks he has posted armed checkpoints around his borough, with automated licence number recognition systems to dissuade gun criminals from entering. Now he is threatening to use new licensing laws to shut down any landlord who does not crack-down on the anti-social behaviour. Scotland Yard recorded 211 murders between 1st April 2003 and 31st March 2004, compared with 195 in the previous 12 months, a rise of 7.5 per cent. But in Lambeth, Commander Quinn is expecting to announce soon a ten per cent drop in shootings.

I expect everyone at some time or other has seen those huge, long-wheel-based white box vans with the brand name 'SNAP-ON TOOLS' printed everywhere, together with the name of the actual franchisee or salesman. Most often you see them parked in the street near large car main agents or car repair workshops. I believe *Snap-On* is a Canadian firm and they appear to be very strong over here. The spanners etc. are claimed to be totally unbreakable and a suitable money back or instant replacement guarantee used to be in force. Motor mechanics buy these very expensive tools by paying weekly, and that's why you see the white vans parked up near motor premises, the drivers are collecting the weekly payments. Mechanics can buy anything from a single small spanner to huge tool display cabinets on wheels, nearly as big as a Ford Transit van. One day when I was stationed at Ilford on CID, I was allocated a crime for investigation, which our uniformed colleagues, who had received details of the theft, at the station office counter, thought was a bit fishy. The driver of one of these *Snap-on Tools* white vans, Harry, reported that he had parked his van in a car park in Ilford and when he returned several hours later, the vehicle had totally disappeared. The value of the contents of the box van, in spanners etc. of all shapes and sizes plus the huge mobile tool chests, ran into thousands of pounds. Routinely, I contacted the *Snap-On Tools* area manager, who came over to see me quite swiftly when he heard the news. Surprise, surprise, the vehicle and its very high value load of tools etc., had been stolen just one day before the quarterly stock take. However, I was well aware that life is full of such coincidences!

After hearing from the area manager, what a van driver's typical day would consist of, and being given details of all of Harry's customers' names and addresses etc., my colleague Bernie and I, after a brief conference, decided it was time to meet Harry. He turned out to be a very pleasant little chap in his late 20's or early 30's and he lived in the Southend-on-Sea area, Essex. We had no recording equipment for interviewing suspects in those days, so everything had to be written down in long hand.

It turned out that Harry had been on his rounds of the garages, making fresh sales and collecting monies from previous ones, which had taken up most of the morning. He had then parked up in a local car park, had some lunch and then gone to watch a matinee screening of one of the *Godfather* film epics in the afternoon. Afterwards, he had gone for a relaxing 'massage' at one of the 'massage parlours' on the Ilford High Road. As the interview progressed, we tied Harry down as closely as possible to all of his timings and made notes of the full details of his movements around Ilford, right up until the dreadful moment his heart sunk, after finding his van had been stolen. We obtained a full list of the van's contents from Harry, as far as he could remember them. He was unable to refer to his stock list as this had been left in the vehicle, on his clip board I think. There was nothing else we could do for the time being, so we thanked Harry for being so helpful and allowed him to go. Later the same day, the van was found by police parked at the side of a house in Leyton, East London, only about half an hours drive away from Ilford, where Harry had left it parked. We were quite dismayed to hear that its entire contents of top quality, unbreakable, market-leading brand of tools was missing. We raced over there to have a look at the vehicle in situ and to await the arrival of the scenes of crime officer (SOCO). Whilst looking around the outside of the vehicle, Bernie and I kept our hands in our pockets (All the best sleuths do this so as to remember not to touch anything, thus possibly spoiling a finger print or other mark.).

At this point, a wonderful elderly gentleman approached us and identified himself as the person who had reported to police that, unusually, the van was parked at the side of his house. He was also able to supply us with an approximate time the vehicle must have been abandoned there, as he was very ill and rarely went out, except to the hospital. In fact although he could walk very slowly with difficulty, an oxygen cylinder was kept beside his easy chair and in his bed room, for when he found he could no longer breathe unaided. He took us to the rear of the van, in which the rear access door into the back was fitted. It turned out that this fantastic witness had been some sort of mechanical engineer all of his life until his health had gone. Indicating the scuff marks and crumpled metal sections on the back door and its frame, he gave us a crash course in physics, with particular emphasis on the laws of leverage. He showed us how, if you wanted to force open a rear door on a van like Harry's and you applied leverage say, with a large screwdriver, jemmy or case opener, at point A, certain consequential resulting damage would occur at point B on the doors surround or frame. To prove his point he used his own lever near the marks and went through the motions of lever pressure being applied, but without actually touching the vehicle at all. Therefore, he was convinced that the damage to the back door and surround was 'rigged'. That was good enough for Bernie and me. We immediately arranged for the box van to be hoisted onto a low loader and transported to the Metropolitan Police Forensic Science Laboratory in Lambeth, London.

In the meantime, we made ourselves known to the manager of the Ilford cinema where '*The Godfather*' film was showing. He took us up into the projection room and for the first time ever, I saw that the entire contents of a cinema's programme, including adverts, news items, forthcoming attractions etc. were all edited and spliced together and laid flat, horizontally on a huge turntable called, for obvious reasons, a 'cake stand.' The projectionist, was able to give us, from his records and programme details, fairly accurate times of what was happening on the screen and when. We needed this important information, as Harry said he had wandered into the main feature, '*The Godfather,*' whilst it was part way through, and had given us the approximate time, together with what was happening on-screen. When the film finished, as was par for the course in those days, he stayed in his seat until the film was run through again, to the part where he had come in, and gave us the approximate time for this, which more or less checked out. Somewhat sceptically, Bernie and I, without warning, adjourned to Harry's massage parlour and interviewed the receptionist and Harry's actual 'masseuse'.

They both showed us around the premises and showed us the (assisted) showers, steam room, 'blue' film video player areas and the lists of available 'facilities' and 'extras', which Bernie and I, in our utter innocence, found to be quite bizarre! To complete the tour, we were shown the main salon set aside for individual 'massages'. This was divided up into separate cubicled areas by stud partition walls and pull curtains. With practised eyes we noted the contents of 'massage' tables and side furniture and waste bin locations, in case we were later required to prepare a 'plan drawing' for court. Harry's 'masseuse' remembered him quite well and was able to 'alibi' him for the approximate period he had told us he'd spent there. In the meantime, we had arranged for a police traffic motor cyclist to run through on the ground, via various routes, approximate distances and times to drive between Ilford and Leyton, where the van had been found 'abandoned', logging his findings in case it was later required in evidence. When the *Snap-On Tools* area manager heard that all of the tools had been stolen from the van, he went ballistic! In due course, after re-interviewing Harry, armed with a precision report from a physicist at the Forensic Laboratory confirming the staged 'damage' to the vans back door, as witnessed by the observant elderly gentleman at Leyton, we charged Harry with the theft of his load of tools, which did not go down at all well with Harry. Whilst we had the advantage of still having Harry in custody at Ilford, pending our enquiries, we had taken the precaution of arranging for Essex Police to visit Harry's home at Southend and give it 'the once over,' but regretfully, nothing was found.

My next task was a very unusual one, an absolute 'one-off', as I was required to carry out a procedure which most police officers, even in a full 25 or 30 years career, would not have the opportunity to take part in. When it became time for Harry to be committed for trial at a Crown Court by local magistrates, prosecution witness statements had to be served on Harry and his lawyer and the court etc. However, before we reached this stage, it had been necessary, with the elderly gentleman's permission, for us to contact his local medical practitioner to enquire as to his patient's prognosis. As it turned out, we discovered that the poor man was very ill indeed and the outlook was not good, but the doctor felt that he was up to being interviewed at home. In case the poor man did not survive long enough to be able to personally give evidence at Harry's Crown Court trial, we all attended at the elderly witness's house in Leyton. The following persons were present whilst we took from him, what is known as 'a statement from a person dangerously ill':

A court clerk.

Prosecuting Counsel.

Defence counsel.

Defendant Harry.

The court clerk's assistant, to write everything down in statement form.

The elderly witness and his wife, oxygen bottle at the ready.

Myself and Bernie.

On completion of the witness statement, Harry and his barrister were given the opportunity to cross examine the witness, and the questions and answers were incorporated into the written statement, from here on in to be referred to by its correct legal term, deposition. Our wonderful, hawkeyed old gentleman then had the deposition read over to him by the court clerk. The gentleman then swore on oath and signed to the effect that its contents were entirely true to the best of his knowledge and belief. On completion, we relaxed for a few minutes as the old gentleman's wife played an active part by producing tea and biscuits. Had the old gentleman died before the trial, his deposition could have been read out to the jury, carrying as much weight as if he had personally given the evidence before them, although there was no need as it turned out, as Harry never disputed even one grain of his evidence.

In due course Harry stood his trial in an old prefabricated court room building at 'Snaresbrook Crown Court sitting at Woodford' as 'satellite' courts became known. Much earlier on I referred your attention to the then supposed highest acquittal rate in the country of Snaresbrook Crown Court. You've already guessed the disappointing ending! After all of our hard work, Harry's jury gave him the benefit of the doubt and he was acquitted. Whether or not that jury was 'so satisfied as to be sure', in accordance with Judge Barrington Black's lecture point, as to Harry's innocence, we will never know, and only Harry knew the whole truth of the matter anyway. Bernie and I, though thoroughly disappointed (again!) consoled ourselves with the thought that we knew something the jury hadn't been entitled to know, the fact that Harry had previous convictions for theft!

Here's another unfortunate sign of the times for you, regarding theft, under the banner headline in the *Daily Express* (Page 26) of 25th February 2004:

FRAIL PENSIONER, 83, CLUNG TO HIS CAR AS THUG SPED OFF

"Detectives appealed for help in catching a carjacker (Car thief to you and me!) who dragged a frail pensioner 100 yards down a road. Sid Gratwicke, 83, had part of his scalp ripped off and a collar bone smashed, after trying to stop the thug stealing his D-reg Ford Escort from a petrol station. The pensioner's arm became trapped as the thief sped off, causing his head to scrape along the concrete. The accident happened within sight of Holbeck police station in Leeds. Speaking from his hospital bed, the retired lorry driver said: "The pain was hellish. I lost a hell of a lot of blood. All that for an old banger." Det. Inspector Mick McDermott said: "It is fortunate the injuries were not more serious."

One night at Ilford police station, I was working quite late with a colleague on the late shift, 0900-2200 hrs, which we were obliged to work on alternate days. Across the road from the police station was a large multi-storey building and behind it was an old cinder car park where police parked their cars when there were spare spaces for this. It was quite dark, after 10pm, as I left the police station and crossed the road to collect my car to drive home. A youth stood in the street at the corner of the dark alleyway beside the building, that led to the car park. For some reason, I noticed that the further I walked into the alleyway, the louder this youth was whistling. When I turned the corner at the end of the alleyway and headed towards where I had parked my car, I found out why the lad was whistling. He was the look-out. My then car was a Ford Corsair 2000E saloon with an automatic gearbox. Unusually, the automatic gearbox shift indicator quadrant was mounted over the steering wheel, giving the impression the car had a 'column change' manual gearbox. I immediately saw, in the half-darkness, that the car interior light was switched on, because the front passenger door was wide open. Standing near my car, quick-thinking and pretending to be urinating, were youths nos. two and three. Fortunately for me, given the darkness of the scenario, my police colleague entered the car park soon after me to get his car to drive home too.

Instead, I handed him one of the two car thieves and we marched them to the police station after locking up my car. Both youths, predictably, protested their innocence. My colleague lead the way into the police station and as he did so, I heard but did not see a metallic 'clink.' My buddie then paused for a second to bend down and pick up the bunch of car door and ignition keys which, in the darkness, his prisoner had tried to discard un-noticed. His prisoner was seen first by the Sergeant in charge (Station Officer) so I waited in a charge room ante- room with my prisoner, who kept on asking me what this was all about. I tried to keep the conversation to a minimum until later, when everything could be written down word-for-word for the court, if required.

When the time came I entered the charge room with my prisoner and explained the brief circumstances of what had transpired in the car park to the Station Officer. He then said to my prisoner: "Is that right, what the officer has just told me?" The young lad said: "No." The Station Officer said to him: " OK, turn your pockets out on the desktop please." At this stage, the Sergeant and I almost fell about laughing! The second object that the prisoner pulled from his pocket and placed on the table was my black plastic, Metropolitan Police issue torch, about 10 inches long. I examined it closely and could hardly contain myself as I handed it to the Station Officer. Burnt into the plastic casing of the torch near the on/off button was my Metropolitan Police 'warrant number,' '161223'. (My grandfather's warrant no. was '104159' which means that 57,064 people joined the Metropolitan Police between he and me!) This is like a regimental number issued to you when you first join the 'Met', and it identifies you for ever and you never forget it, I always kept the torch in the central console/arm rest lift-up storage box for cassettes, in my car. Needless to say, the lads, confronted with the evidence, appeared at court next day and pleaded guilty to attempted theft of (my) a motor vehicle. There were three of them in the dock together, as we had also managed to track down *Whistler*, the look-out at the corner of the alley way. We found out that the only reason that my car had not yet been driven away by them ,was the fact that it looked like a column-change gear change lever for a manual gearbox, so they had been unable to figure it out before my timely arrival! As I had a personal interest in the case, being the near-victim, I was not allowed to present the case to the magistrates myself. I think they were each sentenced to a two years Probation Order for first offences, and all went home after court with their irate parents.

At the other end of the scale of theft is the case of Colin Sadd, 41, a contract cleaner from Southey Green, Sheffield. Sadd has behind him a 30-year career as probably Britain's most obsessive, but thoughtful car thief.   He appeared to worship motor cars (other peoples' of course) and instead of vandalising one he had taken without permission, by crashing it or setting fire to it, he would just go for a run in it and then wash and polish it before leaving it for the owner to find once he'd finished with it. At Sheffield Crown Court in April 2004, Sadd admitted 5 charges of stealing two Vauxhall Astras, a Rover MGZR, a Ford Mondeo and a Renault Laguna. He asked for 31 similar offences to be TIC. Defence barrister Guy Watt told the court that psychiatrists thought it could take years to cure his compulsive disorder, but he was not mentally ill. Judge Alan Goldsack told Sadd: "You do not gain financial benefit, but having driven cars around you dump them with the keys still in. It makes you feel worthwhile and you like to give the impression you are a business man, with an expensive car." The Judge also said that in view of medical opinion, no short-term treatment would work, and Sadd's 155 previous convictions, mostly for car theft which had begun at age 11 years, meant he had no choice but to impose a long sentence. Judge Goldsack then sentenced Sadd to 6-years imprisonment.

Many people, including Sadd's latest victims, would probably agree that was a good result. However, one shouldn't 'count one's chickens' as the defendant's solicitor would not yet have had the time to utilise the Court of Criminal Appeal procedure, funded by Legal Aid from the Public Purse, of course.

Here is a tragic real-life case, which I am transcribing directly from two separate newspaper articles. Both are from the *Daily Express*, the first dated 14th February 2004, reported deep inside on page 30, the second dated 17th February 2004, from page 19. (Sadly, in spite of the sheer tragedy of the circumstances, which you will hear, the newspaper Editor and publishers decided not to give the two stories as much prominence as you might think the stories warranted)

ASYLUM SEEKER FLEES AFTER CRASH KILLING OF MUM-TO-BE

A refugee accused of killing a pregnant teacher and her unborn baby in a car crash has fled to Germany after being released on bail. Police revealed that Sri Lankan fugitive Ratnam Yogan flew to Berlin from Stansted airport a week ago, three days before he was due to appear in court. A manhunt led by Interpol was launched when it emerged that the 29-year old landed in the German capital at 10pm local time and promptly disappeared. Yogan, of East London, denied causing the deaths by dangerous driving of Deborah Peaty, 26, and her baby, at a recent hearing. He was remanded on bail to Northampton Crown Court for a pre-trial hearing last week but failed to appear and a warrant for his arrest was issued.

Inspector Geoff Gascoigne of Northamptonshire Police said, "We opposed the bail conditions but unfortunately the judiciary decided otherwise. Yogan's failure to turn up is costing us a lot of time and money, trying to bring him back to justice." Yogan came to Britain as an asylum seeker and was granted indefinite leave to remain in August (2003), two months before the fatal crash.

Three days later, as I stated, the Daily Express ran a follow-up article on the same fatal accident case, as follows:-

WHY DID HE GET BAIL? WHY DID HE STILL HAVE HIS VISA? MUM'S FURY AT RUNAWAY ASYLUM SEEKER

The family of a pregnant teacher killed in a car accident were furious after it emerged a second refugee involved in the case has fled after a court granted him bail. Deborah Peaty and her unborn child died on her way home from school when her car was involved in a collision with a BMW, allegedly driven by Sri Lankan Ratnam Yogan. Yogan, 29, of East London, vanished after boarding a flight to Berlin, when he should have been in court entering a plea to two charges of causing death by dangerous driving and one of conspiring to pervert the course of justice. Deborah's family were angry after learning that Yogan's co-accused, failed asylum seeker Pushparajah Sinnappayal, has also vanished.

He appeared at Northampton Crown Court but *was granted bail despite losing a second asylum appeal in December (2003) and being due for deportation*. Detectives revealed that he had gone missing when he failed to report to police daily as part of his bail conditions. Police are now watching ports and airports across the country in a bid to prevent 25-year old Sinnappayal following Yogan abroad. In a statement, Deborah's parents Bill and Marge Peaty, and boyfriend Jason Leach, spoke of how both they and the police had objected against bail. It read: "From the beginning, we and the police opposed bail. Our worst fears have now been realised as, to be honest, we always suspected they would be. We are angry and frustrated that the authorities did not take their travel visas from them, as we understand they were supposed to. If it were not for this, they would probably still be in the country." Detectives believe that Sinnappayal, who was charged with conspiring to pervert the course of justice, may be hiding among London's Tamil community or in Leicester. Deborah, 26, from Daventry, died before she reached hospital after the collision last October, near Pottersbury, Northants."

The two *Daily Express* articles were accompanied by tragic photographs of Deborah at graduation, wearing her mortar board, and of Deborah's red car after the death crash.

You may feel that important questions should be asked here.

1) *How could anyone in authority grant bail knowing the full circumstances?*

2) *Why was the visa not taken from the subject, to prevent the chance of absconding?*

3) *When will the Judiciary consider victims first and offenders second?*

4) *One offender was due for deportation, how can he be given bail?*

5) *Should the Judiciary foot the bill for tracing and returning the offender to custody?*

The next theft report, which I was personally involved in, began with some parents from the Rainham area of Essex, policed by the Metropolitan Police, on Outer K division. One of them reported that their baby in its carry cot had been abducted, but from the outset we didn't believe them. In fact quite early on in the investigation they were separately interviewed and we seized their clothing, which was placed into brown paper bags and sent to the MP Forensic Science Laboratory in London. Meanwhile we dressed the parents in the white suits. Within a few hours, after a massive police hunt, the baby was found safe and well, still in its carry cot, in some bushes at Harrow Lodge Park, Hornchurch. Had it not been found before nightfall, there was a high probability of the child being attacked by foxes, that were known to frequent this quite large parkland. Samples of soil, leaves, plants including weeds and pollen were forensically gathered by the SOCO from the bushes where the child had been found. No admissions were ever made about this by the parents but we strongly suspected that one or both of them had personally 'dumped' the poor child there, possibly as a 'cry for help' (the old catch-all cliché)

Sure enough, in due course, a forensic scientist from the ever-busy forensic lab, sent through her written report. She referred to the fact that pollen etc had been found on the clothing of one of the parents. This pollen etc. was exceedingly rare and could only be found in that part of Hornchurch and a very few other places dotted around the country. However this exciting development in forensic evidence was, in itself insufficient to warrant charging the parents with abandoning the child in the park, in the absence of an admission or confession.

That decision was taken by MP Solicitors Department. In the meantime the parents had been released without charge, pending further enquiries, forensic tests etc. Many people may not be aware of the vast store of what are known as 'control samples,' which are kept in the various Home Office forensic laboratories, for future comparisons. These 'control samples' would include specimens of automobile manufacturers paint coating layers, showing rust proofing, various under coatings, primers, top coats etc for just about every car still in use, from which actual makes and models etc. can be identified from just a paint chip left at the scene of a hit and run accident, for instance. The same applies to headlight, fog and tail light glasses as well as car fixed and opening windows and windscreens etc. Electronic microscopes and spectrograms can show the actual thickness of the individual coats of paint in a small fragment. Such technology can even disclose at what angle a glass from a vehicle headlamp was actually struck, as 'striation' marks reveal clues at to how the glass actually shattered (A bit like the 'tell-tale' ripples in the sea or a pond when you throw in a pebble and the series of concentric circles is created).

Similar 'control samples' for other materials, will be available for reference purposes in the Labs, including textiles, footwear etc. and hundreds of everyday objects too numerous to mention here. Anyway, the poor abandoned child was safely recovered and as far as I know, lived happily ever after and everything went quiet again.

There came a time when a postman whose postal delivery round included several blocks of the old eyesore multi storey, flat-topped, concrete flats allocated to council tenants, attended the local police station at Rainham. He reported that whilst he left bundles of undelivered mail and small packages in his mail bag on the bike's carrier, every Tuesday, whilst he went upstairs, calling at umpteen floors, he was finding missing items on his return. The flats had far too many floors for him to be able to carry the whole heavy bag around with him, upstairs and down, as invariably the lifts were not working. I was stationed at nearby Hornchurch police station at the time and a small team, about six of us, all would-be detectives known as 'Aides to CID' or just plain 'aides', was assigned to check out the mystery of the missing mail.

The following Tuesday turned out to be the worst weather Rainham had experienced for many a day. It was 'blowing a gale' with very heavy downpours of rain and all drivers know what happens to visibility through the windscreen and side windows due to condensation etc., under such conditions. We climbed into our non-descript-van, known to us as the 'nondo' or 'nondy'. The Met. Police had a whole fleet of these vans, of all makes, shapes and sizes and they were frequently moved around within the Force, division to division, so that individual vans did not become well-known in particular areas, and could therefore be recognised by local criminals. These vans were well-equipped. Inside was a desktop of sorts for resting your logbook etc. on. There was a Met. Police radio system, complete with headphones, for keeping the noise down and the inside wall and door panels were lined with dark-painted wood or fibreboard for warmth and sound insulation. There was a facility for improving the quality of two-way radio traffic between the van's occupants and the local police stations and other mobile colleagues, by plugging into a special dedicated aerial connection. The windscreen wipers and washers could be controlled from inside the back of the van, which was obviously screened-off from the driving compartment, like most vans - but also fitted with a door to the back - itself fitted with more drop-down or sliding observation ports. Extra ventilation slits had been installed for all-round visibility as far as possible and these were covered on the inside by drop-down flaps of wood or strong waxed textile and press studs etc. Narrow gauge metal mesh matting was installed inside the observation slits so that your eyes could not be seen by passing pedestrians.

Cut into the rear floor area was the all-important access to the road surface for when nature called! In fact just a hole cut in the floor, like the lavatories in Oriental airports (It was never a good idea to set out on a possibly long period of surveillance in these vans if you had been to the pub recently, for obvious reasons!). Several of us were in the back of this 'nondo' and one of our colleagues drove us to the location near the tower blocks, as arranged, got out, locked the cab and walked away, giving the appearance of his just parking up an empty van, to interested onlookers. Unfortunately, our colleague, the van driver, had parked the van where we could not even see the relevant tower block, never mind the postman's bike! There was nothing we could do, except pray, as we did not have a spare set of keys to the van. As our colleague was locking up the van from the outside at the driver's door, we had banged on the side to attract his attention, but unfortunately the sounds of the wind howling and the battering rain had muffled our efforts.

Weeping wife tells of 'forged' confession

A YOUNG wife claimed last week that she was forced to confess to a crime she did not commit under threats from police.

Jean Hanmore alleged she signed a statement admitting dishonestly handling four dresses because police said they would bring her husband and children to the station where she was being questioned.

Hanmore, 28, of East-close Rainham, wept as she told her story to Hornchurch Court. She pleaded not guilty to handling he dresses.

Police told th court that a search was made of Hanmore's bedroom and four dresses believed to be part of a batch stolen in March, were found.

'UNDER THREATS'

Said Det. con. Michael Hughes: 'When the dresses were found we asked Hanmore to go to Rainham police station, but her husband demanded that he called his solicitor and left his Alsatian dog in front of the door to prevent us leaving.'

He added that after questioning at the station Hanmore signed a statement saying she knew the dresses were stolen when she bought them.

But Hanmore claimed the statement was made under threats. 'It was getting late and I was worried about my children.

'I was told that unless I signed the statement they would fetch my husband and children to the station.'

She was found guilty and fined £50 with £19.50 costs.

It proved to be a terrible day for staring through the observation slits, as the wind and driving rain kept on making our eyes water! At one time, we had a brief sighting of the postman arriving in the area with his bike, but as it turned out, it was all we saw or heard of him, until a few minutes later when he banged on the side of our van. This made us all 'jump,' as you do when something unexpectedly happens and you can't see it coming. 'Postman Pat' followed up his banging on the side with the immortal, anguished cry, "THE * * * * * * * * BAG'S GONE!

At this juncture, six hearts sunk in unison and there were several sharp intakes of breath and pulse-rates quickened in horror, as the adrenalin kicked-in. Teeth, already 'chattering' from the cold inside the van, as the gale blew through the observation slits, almost flopped to the floor in some cases! Oh boy, every 'aides' nightmare had befallen us, the precious Royal Mail, in transit in HM The Queen's name, had disappeared, and no prisoner forthcoming to account for it! However 'help' was at hand and this was the first time in my entire life and police career that I had utilised what is now known as 'logical thinking' in my then finest hour to date.

I advised my assembled colleagues that within the last 15-20 minutes, a woman whom I recognised, had walked past my observation slit wearing a fur coat. Shortly afterwards, she had walked back past my observation post *carrying* the fur coat, in spite of the fact that it was 'tipping it down' with rain. However, due to the excitement and stress of anticipating all of us being returned to uniform duties by tomorrow morning, for professional incompetence, I had been unable to link in my mind the two sightings of the woman at the time. To cut a long story short, we used our radios to recall our mate Jim, the 'nondo' driver from the police station to collect the van and take it to one of the tower blocks and meet us there, after we had got an officer at base to make a quick inspection of the local electoral roll and advise us of the result of that. We then went to a certain address on a certain floor of one of the tower blocks and, without a search warrant, entered the flat almost literally on 'a wing and a prayer' and little else, except intuition.

Fortunately, the door was opened to us by, you've guessed it, Mrs 'Child-Dumper.' On entering the main bedroom, there, sitting up in bed in his winceyette pyjamas was Mr 'Child-Dumper.' He had a mug of tea in one hand and a paper knife in the other, as he slit open the next envelope from a pile on the bedcover near his plate of toast. Beside the bed, on the floor was a small pile of opened envelopes, some of which had once contained post office giro cheques which were not made out as payees to Mr and Mrs 'Child-Dumper.' As it transpired, the couple were later found to have been carrying out their criminal conduct for a couple of weeks beforehand, stealing other residents' benefit giro cheques and cashing them in later by deception. Tuesday was the all-important day of arrival of the cheques, as you will know from the post office queues you have patiently stood in on many occasions.

Meanwhile back at the tower block, some of us had to sink just about as low as you can get, to finish the job, seeking to recover additional opened brown envelopes from the huge joint-use 'wheely-bins' at ground level, accessed at each storey via a 'chute flap.' Although we had special protective gloves for this disgusting task, it was absolutely obnoxious. As you can imagine, the vast container was full of fish heads, old cans, used sanitary towels, condoms etc., as well as last night's vin de loo and chicken chow mien debris and containers, used nappies, apple cores, broken glass and the horrible rest of it. Whilst we were doing this, the others were guarding the two prisoners in their flat and our intrepid van driver, who was not having a good day at all, managed to get the 'nondo' van stuck part way up the spiral vehicular access to various floors of the multi-storey flats building - due to the poor turning circle of the van's steering mechanism. All did not end well there either, because of various political decisions made, which displeased us intently, higher up the chain of command. Our team of 'aides' had hoped that Mr and Mrs 'Child-Dumper' would be committed to the Crown Court for the serious offence(s) of interfering with HM The Queen's Mail, but in the event, they pleaded guilty at the local magistrates court and therefore were only lightly sentenced.

The whole days work, had produced a successful conclusion, although not quite on the scale of the Great Train Robbery, and the whole team lived on to fight another day in our precious plain clothes, instead of being returned to uniformed duties!

This next one, from the Daily Express on 25th March 2004 takes some believing too.

EVIL SONS STEAL CREDIT CARD OFF THEIR DEAD DAD
Laughing brothers on 4-day bender after his funeral

Two twisted brothers who used their dead father's credit card for a four-day drinking session, started just hours after his funeral, left court laughing. Magistrates were told the pair were full of shame and remorse for the cynical crime, which broke their mother's heart. But by the time the 'despicable' pair walked free into the street, Craig and Carl Nicholson seemed to think their crime was just a joke. They roared with laughter shortly after a court was told how 25-year old Craig stole the plastic card and its PIN number from his mother Sue's kitchen table, soon after laying his father Frank to rest. He withdrew £100 cash from an automatic dispenser and used it to buy booze from an off-licence. Then he told his brother, 24, what he'd done and they gleefully used the card to fund a booze tour of pubs and clubs. They spent £180 over counters and took a further £400 from ATMs in the street. When they appeared before magistrates in South Shields, they claimed they took the cash only because they were grief-stricken and wanted to drown their sorrows. But their angry mother has disowned her boys and said their father would be turning in his grave.

Mrs Nicholson, 51, had taken on her 65-year old husband's Barclaycard after he died in June last year (2003) following a long illness. But while she was grieving she was saddled with the debt because of her selfish sons, and was horrified when she learned what had happened. "I have washed my hands of them, to me they no longer exist," she said at her home at Hebburn, Tyne and Wear. "I really don't care what happens to them now. They have left me hurt and upset. They have made my life a misery and they made my husband's life a misery."

She spoke after watching from the public gallery as Craig, from Newcastle, and Carl, from Wallsend, appeared in the dock. Craig admitted theft from a dwelling, theft from cash machines and obtaining property by deception. Carl pleaded guilty to obtaining by deception and theft from ATMs. When the brothers first appeared in court, the bench chairman Anne-Marie Darke, warned them they could go to jail. She said: "This matter is one of the most despicable to come before this bench. You were stealing your mother's credit card on a day she was trying to cope with the trauma of your father's death." The brothers, who are serving community punishment orders for unrelated matters, had their sentences adjourned until September (Six months away – swift justice?).

Their solicitor Kyle Patterson said: "Both of these boys have expressed significant degrees of remorse and today ask me to issue a public, unequivocal apology to their mother." He said that at the time the pair had been trying to "drink themselves into oblivion."

Questions arising:

1) *What is the point of delaying sentencing for six months after their guilty pleas have been entered, to these awful crimes?*

2) *From their obvious level of intelligence, would they really know the meaning of unequivocal?*

3) *What are the risks of criminals like these re-offending within the next 6 months?*

4) *How much suffering and anxiety will their mother endure in the meantime, whilst the sons still have their liberty in the community?*

5) *If commission of these wicked thefts & deceptions by the brothers put them in breach of their community service orders, what action do you suppose the bench will take against them in respect of the breach?*

A callous thief stole a pensioner's wallet as he lay trapped in his upturned car after an accident. The low-life criminal climbed into the upturned vehicle posing as a paramedic, before calmly taking the pensioner's wallet from his pocket and walking off. The 74-year-old victim's car had rolled over after a collision with another vehicle on Broad Green, in Wellingborough, Northants. The thief, who was white and in his late 20's, walked off quickly towards the town centre before the emergency services arrived. The victim, from Essex, was not badly injured, police said.

Thieves in London have come up with a different way to pocket-pick or steal purses, what is known in the Police as distraction-theft. In a small team they target a person walking away from a cash point machine having just withdrawn cash. They then 'accidentally' squirt mustard or tomato ketchup onto the victim's clothing from a squeezy bottle.

They then draw the victim's attention to the offending stain and start helping to clean it off, meanwhile another team member picks your pocket or rifles your handbag while you are distracted. I don't suppose you would relish this happening to you, so be on your guard before, during and after your cash point transactions. Particularly beware of someone being 'in-your-space' behind you, standing too close so as to be able to memorise your pin number. Also, never, but NEVER respond to a notice at the cash

point stating it is 'closed for maintenance' and 'please use the temporary facility over there' – type of notice.

If you are intending to withdraw cash in the very early hours of the morning, beware of the

Theft of ATM from HSBC branch at High St, Goring-on-Thames, Mothers Day, 6th March 2005 (Florist damaged next door)

tractor-crew or JCB-crew waiting nearby with a strong chain and hook as if about to rescue a broken-down car and tow it away. In fact as soon as you turn your back, they will hitch-up to the cash point machine and drag it out of the wall and cart it off to a quiet location, before cutting it open etc. Therefore I suggest you stand clear, concealed in the shadows and at least write down or try to remember the vehicle number. If you don't have a pen, use your lipstick or mascara brush, useful ready-use emergency kit these days, you too Gents, if you use the stuff! You never know, the bank may reward you for your trouble if you were instrumental in bringing the offenders to justice.

Speaking of cash point machines, hundreds of shoppers recently 'cashed-in', or 'cashed-out' as the case may be, at a *Tesco* store in North Cheam, Surrey. A huge queue built up outside the store as the out-of-control cash point machine of the *Royal Bank of Scotland* issued £20 notes instead of tenners, for a total of 5 hours. One *Tesco* shopper said: "It was like the gold rush, the word spread like wildfire, the machine was chucking out free money. They must have loaded the £10 section with £20 notes by mistake. Everyone agreed each individual should only make three transactions and then move to the back of the queue." (Sounds more like a parlour game, but wearing my old police hat I'd call it, 'Conspiracy to Defraud The Bank', serious enough to only be tried at a crown court, so don't be tempted!)

Apparently the machine only stopped when all the money had gone.

Police are now examining from Tesco's records and CCTV cameras, normal shopping and spending habits of customers at that store on that day, to see who used a huge, deep trolley instead of their shallow one! (Only joking, but did you know they can monitor absolutely everything about your likes and dislikes around the store, from their copy of your till receipts? Their excuse is that it tells them current trends and indicates best-selling items and what to re-order in huge quantities and what to discontinue etc. Some people would say that 'Big Brother' has struck again.)

Turning now to the bank that gives you 'XTRA', meaning the *Halifax*. Customers queued all night at a *Halifax* machine at Urmston, Manchester, after discovering that a £20 'bonus' was being delivered with each withdrawal transaction. It was the third time in a week that bank cash machines had been plundered.

Alert *Halifax* staff arriving for work next morning, saw the unusually-long early morning queue at the machine, plus the porta-potties, blankets, thermos flasks, camping stoves and 400 transaction slips blowing about on the pavement, and quickly realised something was wrong, especially as the massive queue was there one minute and gone the next! Apparently the best racket, if you had a £250 per day limit, was to make ten withdrawals of £10 and you could make £500 profit on the spot. However *Halifax* staff, after tea and bacon butties, knuckled down and swiftly calculated that only £65,000 had been taken overnight. *Halifax* refused to say whether or not it would try to reclaim the cash. I'd love to watch the re-run of the inbuilt security camera film showing all of the greedy and guilty customers licking their lips with delight at their new-found change of fortune, it would do well on a *candid camera* TV prog.

Cunning choc-a-holic criminals have used a new type of deception to part long-distance lorry drivers from their high-value loads. Whilst the driver is enjoying his *Sun* newspaper and his 'second-mug-of-tea-free' in 'The Greasy Spoon' transport café or motorway service area, they unscrew and remove his lorry rear number plate. They then tail him off until a quiet stretch of road is reached, whereupon they drive beside him holding up his 'lost' number plate. Naturally he is very grateful at its recovery by Good Samaritans and pulls over to reattach it to the vehicle. Whilst he is doing so, a 'samaritan' jumps into the cab and drives off with 25 pallet-loads of Cadbury chocolates, value £55,000 destined to be sold by the bar miles away later that day, at half-retail-price, to grateful but unsuspecting, panting and sweating starving 'weight-watcher' clients, leaving the Hackney Town Hall after a 'marathon' punishment session, with the risk of the extra hazard of being mugged on the way home.

In May 2004 at the world-famous John Radcliffe Hospital in Oxford, raiders stole surgical equipment valued at £160,000, this being the latest theft in a series of hospital raids, others targeted were in Hampshire and Sussex. A police theory is that this equipment is being 'stolen-to-order' then sold on to Third World countries. Police stated the obvious, by being quoted as saying: "They would not have any use except in the medical world."

Mr Tony Hill, 40, from Bournemouth, in April 2004 offered a £1,000 reward after super-cool thieves, using a large crane, lifted his two-ton, £10,000 Sundance hot tub from his garden into the street, wrecking the garden in the process. Neighbours actually saw the criminals in the act of the theft, but assumed they were delivery men. Mr Hill said: "I'm furious, it's the sheer audacity, to steal my tub in daylight". Apparently a large hole was left in the garden. Police are looking into it.

A callous window cleaner was caught red-handed stealing cash from an elderly customer as she made him a cup of tea. Nicholas Sims repeatedly dipped into the purse of the vulnerable 86-year-old woman. But the family of the frail pensioner, who lives alone, installed a CCTV camera after becoming suspicious when money began to go missing. They knew their mother could not be spending it because the old lady suffers from dementia and rarely leaves the house. But the mystery was solved when Sims, 61, was caught stealing from the woman after calling for her window-cleaning money. He was seen to remove her purse three times and hide it under his coat. He would go out the front door so that she wouldn't see him stealing the money, before returning her purse. After the third incident, the victim's family took the film footage to the police and Sims was identified and arrested.

Sims, of Clevedon, Somerset, was charged with three offences of taking a total of £30 and denied them all, despite being caught on camera. But magistrates in Weston-Super-Mare found him guilty and he was jailed for nine months, with an order that he must serve no less than half the sentence. After the hearing, daughter Susan Hopegood, 56, of Bristol, said:"I pay for her bills, so she does not need to spend any money. I would leave her £15 in her purse so she could have some change, but on several occasions I went round to see her, it was all gone." Mrs Hopegood said the family then decided to install the CCTV. She added: "Sims would have a cup of tea and ask for £4.20 for cleaning the windows. When she discovered that she didn't have any money because he had just taken it, he would arrange another time to come back and take even more money from her."

A Magistrate who found a Rolex watch and then invented an elaborate cover story to pretend it was his, has been convicted of theft. Geoffrey Rowlett, a magistrate for more than 30 years, picked up the £3,200 lady's watch in a *Tesco* supermarket and gave it to his wife Margaret as a present for her 60th birthday. But when he took the *Rolex Oyster* for repair, a jeweller found it had been reported lost or stolen in January 2002. Mr Rowlett claimed he had bought it in a Portsmouth bric-a-brac shop. Southampton Magistrates Court fined him £600 with £400 costs. Rowlett, 67, of Poole, has now been suspended by Dorset Magistrates Courts. When last heard of, he was still doing his time, a sentence of lifetime embarrassment.

A temporary postman went on a £29,000 spending spree, after stealing more than 100 credit cards and cheque books from envelopes, a court heard. Yasir Darr, 24, stole the mail sent from banks and building societies, to buy designer clothes, motorbikes, a BMW car and a lap-top computer. He also bought gifts for his five-year-old son. Darr, who worked for the Royal Mail for just 12 weeks, withdrew up to £3,500 in cash on one card. More than 60 credit and debit cards and 50 cheque books, with PIN numbers and passports, were found stashed in a suitcase at his home in Southsea, Hampshire. Darr was taken on as a postman at the Royal Mail offices in Portsmouth in June 2004 while on a summer break from his studies at the city's university. The scam only came to light when a man who was expecting a bank card, contacted the Post Office when it failed to turn up.

Portsmouth Crown Court heard that Darr, who is in his final year of a Latin and American studies degree, had student debts of £10,800. He could not resist the temptation to start stealing, but had not paid back any of his student loan with the stolen cards. Recorder Peter Barrie said: "These offences look like greed." Barrister David Jenkins told the court: "You could say that, but he was depressed and they were a way of alleviating his depression." Darr pleaded guilty to two thefts, three counts of obtaining property by deception, two charges of attempting to obtain property by deception and one of receiving stolen goods. He also asked for 41 other matters to be taken into consideration. Recorder Barrie adjourned sentencing for a psychiatric report on Darr but warned him this did not mean he would avoid going to jail. He said: "I want you to know that for my part, I think you should be in custody, but I want to make sure the court knows as much about you as possible." Case officer Detective Constable Andy Wilson said of Darr's thefts: "This is a man in a position of trust who abused the system."

A mother and daughter were jailed after wrecking the hunt for toddler Ben Needham, by stealing from his heartbroken grandparents. Alison Jarvis, 23, and her mother Joan, 49, took £23,000 that the youngster's family had raised to fund their desperate search for him. Eddie and Christine Needham had hidden the cash under their bed at their home near Market Rasen,

Lincs, ready for use at a moment's note if there were any sightings of their grandson. But the Jarvises, of Wrexham, North Wales, sneaked into their home and made off with the fund after Alison had endured a bitter break-up with one of Ben's uncles, Lincoln Crown Court heard. Ben's family said the hunt for the toddler, who vanished on the Greek holiday island of Kos 13 years ago, had been set back 10 years. Speaking after the Jarvises were each jailed for three years and nine months, Ben's mother Kerry, 32, said: "This has had a devastating effect. We know Ben is still out there but what has happened has made us lose track of him." Police in the UK recently made a fresh bid to trace Ben, from Sheffield, who would now be 14, by issuing an image of how he might look now, but authorities in Greece have scaled down searches for the youngster.

A gang of thieves who stole millions of pounds worth of luxury cars in six months has been smashed by police. The raiders targeted Mercedes Benz E class models, brazenly taking them from outside their owners' homes using low-loader trucks. Police believe that more than 1,000 cars valued at £3.5million were stolen. Scotland Yard confirmed that 17 people, all of them Nigerian, have been arrested on suspicion of conspiracy to handle stolen cars and money-laundering, following raids across Essex. The gang stole the cars in north London, taking them to unregistered salvage yards in Essex where they were stripped and the parts shipped off to west Africa. It is believed the cars were being sold off as spare parts or, in some cases, being rebuilt as taxis. *Operation Resolution* followed a lengthy investigation by the Yard's stolen vehicle unit after the interception of two ships at Tilbury docks, which contained stolen parts from 38 Mercedes. Det Insp Charlie McMurdie yesterday said police were alerted to the gang's operations when they found the stolen vehicle recovery rate was only five per cent in north London, compared with the normal 45 per cent.

"We were finding six,seven, eight vehicles being stolen in one area in one night," she said. In November last year officers recovered the parts belonging to approximately 18 Mercedes, and last month parts from a further 20 Mercedes in containers at an Essex dockyard. "This was brazen vehicle theft on a large scale, primarily in the north London area and primarily Mercedes Benz E class, because they are not fitted with an immobiliser. The thieves were completely blatant. They used specialist tools and perhaps tow trucks to remove them, because there was never any sign of smashed glass found around the missing car." She added: "Unlicensed and unregistered salvage yards are allowing this crime to happen. This raid is part of a clampdown on those operations. We found numerous VAT and Inland Revenue breaches. All of those arrested were Nigerian. Only two of them had a National Insurance number. The raids will have a significant impact on vehicle crime in London."

Assistant Commissioner Tarique Ghaffur, head of the Met's Specialist Crime Directorate, said: "This operation demonstrates our ongoing commitment to tackling serious and organised crime which impacts upon London. We are committed to removing unlicensed motor salvage operators which will reduce the opportunity for the disposal of stolen vehicles." *Operation Resolution* was supported by officers from Essex Police and various agencies, including Customs. The arrested men were taken to various police stations in Essex and later bailed.

Some hotel guests take shampoo and soap, some may even sneak away with a towel, but one couple stole the entire shower unit, it emerged. The pair, a man in his 50s and a woman in her 20s, had spent the night in a four-poster bed at the 17th century *Globe Hotel*. After they checked out of the £70-a-night en suite room, staff found that the shower had gone from the wall. The couple had even turned off the water before disconnecting it. Liz Hodges, owner of the *Globe Hotel* in Topsham, near Exeter, Devon, said the pair, who paid cash, had left her with a £300 bill for the shower and damage. She added: "I have never experienced anything on this scale before. I just cannot believe someone would do this." Devon and Cornwall Police said the theft was 'particularly unusual'.

A senior policeman who was convicted of selling stolen bicycles on the internet escaped jail on 25th February 2005. Inspector David Humphrey, dubbed 'Gorgeous George' because of his flashy dress sense, used the auction site *eBay* to sell bikes worth hundreds of pounds. He was found guilty of nine counts of handling stolen goods and two of false accounting, after the owner of one of the stolen items recognised his £700 custom-built machine being advertised. Inside Humphrey's home in Wimbledon, south London, police found 10 bicycles worth up to £1,500 apiece. Humphrey, who was with the Royal Parks Constabulary for 20 years before his arrest, claimed he bought the bikes for cash and in good faith from Brick Lane market, London, a notorious hot spot in the stolen bicycle trade. But he was sentenced to a 220-hour community punishment order at Kingston Crown Court. Burly Humphrey, who is 6ft 2in tall, was married to a model and is said to have led a charmed life in the police.

In 1999 he was stabbed by a suspected thief in Regent's Park after spotting the man apparently trying to break into a parked car. Humphrey gave chase and caught the robber and in the ensuing struggle fell to the ground with stab wounds to his abdomen. He was found after radioing for help, and the stabbing led Humphrey to retire. The officer had earlier asked for body armour but not been given any. As a result he won a six-figure compensation settlement. Despite this he returned to the force shortly afterwards, paying back most of the money, but he quit the force before being convicted. But the officer drew criticism from colleagues thanks to his so-called flashy lifestyle and ability to emerge unscathed from career-threatening scrapes. One officer said: "He got promoted, not sacked, after being caught drink driving, and stayed in the job even after he had to report losing his police radio in *Wimbledon* while he was supposed to be on duty in *St James's Park*. He always landed on his feet. We used to call him 'Gorgeous George' because he wore such flash clothes and thought he looked like George Michael." Humphrey recently split from his Texan-born wife, Holly Scott, a former model who appeared in Guinness advertisements in the Nineties. They have a seven-year-old son. (Wouldn't you just have given anything to be a fly on the wall at his Police Discipline Board when they told the *ex* Inspector 'On your bike!')

SWIFT JUSTICE

In those days there were no ridiculously long delays between first appearance at court and eventual final disposal. Swift justice was the order of the day. About 75-80% of cases were disposed of on day one at court. When we charged somebody with an offence, if they were suitable for bail to be granted, i.e. were not of 'no fixed abode' (NFA) and their proper address had been established by a police visit or electoral roll check, the Station Officer would release them on 'Police Bail'. This meant the prisoner would sign an official form to say that if he failed to appear at court next morning at 10am, he would pay The Queen whatever sum of money had been set for his bail, according to the severity of the offence charged. If he did fail to appear, the Justices would issue a warrant for his arrest and Scotland Yard would place his details on a special register, in case he was stopped in the street by police for any reason, after coming to notice.

If the defendant had not indicated to you in advance whether his intention was to plead guilty or not guilty, the arresting Officer, or the Officer in charge of the case, would ask for the charge(s) to be put to the defendant. This was the cue for the court clerk to read to the prisoner in the dock, from the court's copy of the charge sheet, details of what the police had charged him with. If he pleaded guilty, as most people on first appearances seemed to do in those days, the court clerk would say to the officer: "Brief facts please, Officer." The officer would then read from a 'brief' he had prepared himself, to acquaint the bench of magistrates with what criminal behaviour had led to his arrest, and the circumstances of it. On completion, the court clerk would ask: "Anything known?" At this stage the officer would hand up to the court clerk and magistrates, individual copies of his list of criminal convictions, if any. When the bench had had time to scan the list of convictions, the officer would be invited to read them aloud, taking the magistrates through the brief 'MO' of each conviction, with values etc. and the court sentences awarded for each conviction. Following-on from the convictions lists would be 'antecedents'. These would have been prepared by the officer in the case at the police station after the prisoner had been charged.

We had pre-printed antecedent forms and basically filled in the gaps on each page as to his declared educational background and work record etc., details of which could only be confirmed in very serious cases, as you would then have more time. The magistrates would have copies of these which you would have handed up with the criminal conviction sheets. The magistrates would thank the officer and then retire to their special room, for tea, biscuits and cake and also to decide what to do with the prisoner. Occasionally they would summon the clerk from the court and he would then carry his huge legal reference books, such as *Stone's Justices Manual* and *Archbold's Criminal Pleadings* out of court to the bench retiring room, as the intricacies of the law are far too complex to be carried round in a simple court clerk's head.

At this juncture, the prisoner would be chewing his nails, mopping his brow or asking passing court officials: "What do you reckon?", or "Will I go down?" or otherwise apprehensively contemplating his immediate future. Prior to retirement, the clerk would have asked him if he had anything to say to the Bench. This was normally his only chance to 'grovel' to them, unless he intended to elect trial by jury, of which more later. When the bench returned with their thirst quenched, they would get him to stand up in the dock and then 'weigh him off', as it was colloquially known, meaning sentence him. At this moment there would usually be Police 'Courts Officers' aka 'Jailers,' standing by the dock enclosure, in case the defendant wanted to fight, lambaste the Justices or try to escape. If the bench felt they needed to know a bit more about the prisoner than they already did, they would adjourn the case for a short time until they could track down the duty Probation Officer, to have a few words with him, perhaps as to his suitability for Probation supervision, or his ability to pay a fine, if the latter had not been covered during 'Brief Facts' by the officer in the case.

It was most rare in those days for a case to be adjourned to another date, unless the prisoner had pleaded 'not guilty' or the magistrates decided to commit him to quarter sessions (now crown court) for sentence, or for trial. Therefore, swift justice was delivered and the prisoner could get on with his life, without being hassled by a solicitor to change his plea to 'not guilty', as happens all too often these days, as everybody knows. There would be a different procedure of course, if when asked, the prisoner had replied, 'Not guilty.' Sometimes, this would be the first occasion when the officer in the case knew of this. In my experience, most people, on arrest, once they realise that 'the game is up' when their collar 'is felt' (arrested), are inclined to want to confess and confide in the nice police officer as to the (almost) full extent of their offending behaviour.

They seem to feel a bit better to have 'got it off their chest'. However, once they have had the benefit of time before that vital first court appearance, all sorts of gremlins seem to attack them.

These include:

1) *Next door neighbours with cauliflower ears and GBH convictions.*
2) *'Lower deck lawyer' Uncle George from no. 22, who once sat as a jury foreman.*
3) *Ex-docker, ex-merchant seaman Wally Thomas, well used to sailing close to winds.*
4) *Widow Beaney from the 'Queens Head' snug, who had been a 'bookies runner.'*

Almost certainly, one or more of the above will have got wind of the prisoner's intention to plead 'guilty' to his crimes, and pull out all of the stops to make him change his mind.

Amazingly, this prisoner who, full of guilt and remorse, feeling morally duty-bound to face up to his crimes by pleading 'guilty' to each of them, has been approached and 'got at' and influenced by one or more of the persons on the above list, and/or that days Duty Lawyer, scampering from Court to Court, puffing and blowing as he dealt out his official business cards, trying to shepherd each and every prospective client towards his lucrative *Legal Aid*-only practice, all within the short space of time overnight, since the defendant's release on bail by the police! Therefore we must return to court now, as he enters the dock, having been brow-beaten to 'welsh' on his long voluntarily-given statement under caution, which amounted to a very full confession, by his friendly, well-meaning lay advisors, or Mr Rich from Messrs Grabbitt, Gotit and Keepit. This prisoner answers in a now-confident firm and meaningful 'not guilty' when asked to plead by the court clerk. The officer in the case hides his embarrassment behind a short fit of coughing and then asks the court to remand the case for legal representation. This is the cue for the court clerk and bench to scramble through their diaries there and then, or to retire to their room with diaries for more tea and cake, this time sharing it with the court clerk.

On return, the adjournment or remand date is mutually agreed. The plea-changing prisoner has fulfilled his obligation to HM The Queen, without owing her a penny, by surrendering to the court at the appointed date and time, as stipulated in his police bail notice, effectively terminating it. What's required now is for the magistrates to decide whether this prisoner can be trusted to comply with the terms of fresh bail, which they may set for him, if they decide not to remand him in custody. They will ask the officer in the case whether there are any objections to the granting of bail and if so, what are they and why? The officer will then take the witness stand and the oath and state his reason(s) for opposing bail, or otherwise. It will depend on how long this particular stage of the proceedings takes, as to whether the bail decision should be debated over yet more morning coffee or not.

I am of course, describing how things used to be run under the old unwritten maxim of 'swift justice.' In those days, police supplied their reasons for opposing bail which may have included one or more of the following:

1) Seriousness of the offence(s).
2) Likely to abscond.
3) Seriousness of the punishment the prisoner could reasonably expect to receive.
4) May attempt to contact and interfere with witnesses.
6) Reason to believe he may harm himself, therefore for his own protection.
7) Has previously failed to appear or comply with the terms of bail.
8) Likely to commit further offences whilst on bail.
9) Likely to approach and/or intimidate prosecution witnesses.

Nowadays, liberalism appears to have taken over, in favour of the offender, rather than the victim(s) or their representatives, viz: the police in most cases. This seems to have caused the entire bail process and procedure to have been 'turned on its head.'

Under the terms of The Bail Act 1976, it appears to me that it specifies that ALL PERSONS should be granted bail *unless* certain conditions or factors apply, which appears to be the reverse of how things were in my day. To be honest, you would find all the minute details of the whys and wherefores as to whether bail should be granted or not, to be thoroughly ponderous and boring, so I will spare you all of that.

However it would be remiss of me if I had failed to bring to your attention the kind of terrible implications for the victim(s) or their (surviving) relatives which are manifest in the all-too-frequent situations where the Judiciary, in their supposed wisdom, get it very badly wrong, with catastrophic effect.

Just to finalise the procedure that Metropolitan Police officers used, to deal with their own cases in court, usually next morning following the arrest, in the days before the oft-criticised *Crown Prosecution Service* was introduced. As I stated earlier, if the prisoner could NOT be granted bail for one or more of the reasons we have already discussed, he would be kept overnight in the cells of the police station in whose area he had been arrested, or the next nearest police station, if, for instance, the cells were already full, as we routinely never doubled-up prisoners. You may well have asked yourself already, how on earth could we have discovered a prisoner's list of previous convictions so rapidly, as to be in possession of them by the time the court opened next morning, usually around 10 am? Well in those days the Metropolitan Police seemed to have a virtually foolproof fast track system and this is how it worked.

Once the prisoner had been charged, the very next task was for us to take his fingerprints, thumbprints and palm prints on special forms. These would be attached to special Metropolitan Police criminal record office descriptive forms. Full particulars of his name, address, date of birth, date and time of arrest, the offence(s), his modus operandi(s), value of property involved etc. were completed. (On any subsequent convictions in the fullness of time, these descriptive forms, or an extract from them, would be utilised to inform magistrates and judges of details of the 'old' previous convictions, from possibly years ago.) Many prisoners, particularly habitual criminals, try to prevent courts hearing about the true and full extent of their past history, for obvious reasons. Therefore, they may supply a false name each time they are arrested, particularly if they are travelling criminals, moving from one police area to other police areas, where they are not known to police, and therefore may not be recognised and identified under their real name.

The way the system works is as follows:

After his very first conviction, a Criminal Record Office (CRO) file was raised in the (full) name the criminal supplied to police on arrest. The same name would have been entered up on his fingers, thumbs and palm prints forms, for continuity. (Later the officer in the case would have notified the criminal record office of the sentence he received at court, in the greatest of detail, with the date and court specified.) Now the criminal record office descriptive form and finger etc. prints forms were collected overnight by 'despatch vans' and swiftly delivered at New Scotland Yard.

Throughout the night, police finger print officers (FPO's) and civilians trained in the same post, would classify the prisoners' prints into loops, whirls and ridge patterns etc and then check them against outstanding finger prints found at scenes of unsolved crimes. It may well be the case, that when this routine finger print search is carried out in future, the finger print experts at the Yard would advise you that all is not as it appears. The criminal may have given his name as 'Frederick Jones' the first time ever he was arrested. He would therefore be convicted in that name (unless acquitted) and police would notify the Yard of the full details and open his criminal record in that name.

Now it could well be that 'Frederick Jones' was given a Probation Order, Conditional Discharge or a suspended prison sentence at last conviction, and one or more of these could still be effective and 'hanging over his head.' Therefore, as our 'Fred' doesn't want the police or the court to know about that, which will nearly always result in a harsher treatment this time, he tells the police he is 'Wilfred Thomas' instead. However 'Frederick Jones', alias 'Wilfred Thomas,' unfortunately lacks 'insider knowledge' of the CRO system.

Overnight, finger print experts wearing their thick-lensed glasses from years of squinting at finger print loops and whirls etc., will classify the NEW finger prints and discover that 'Wilfred Thomas' is in fact 'Frederick Jones', CRO number ???????/ 82. These details, plus his previous convictions in the first ever name he gave on first arrest, will be telephoned through to the officer in the case at his police station or the appropriate court, in time for the offender's appearance and poor old 'Fred' will have failed to beat the system on this occasion, and all because of his finger prints! Furthermore, his full frontal and side view photographs would have been taken at the time of arrest and forwarded to Scotland Yard with the fingerprints and descriptive form.

Research indicates that nearly one million people will become victims of green-fingered thieves in the year 2004 as the cost of garden thefts hits a record £400million. It is estimated that 800,000 homes will be targeted by criminals who will get away with everything from power tools to garden furniture. As spending on gardens rockets to £5 billion, research shows that the value of the average theft from a garden has reached £500. It also shows that people are spending more on their gardens because they are seen as extra 'rooms' which can dramatically increase a property's value. However this makes them more attractive to thieves. Examples of surging crime include an entire lawn being stolen and then turning up at a car boot sale as turf, and a 6ft X 4ft pond complete with 17 fish, all gone missing. The main items targeted by thieves include bicycles, pots and containers, power tools, lawn mowers, clothes and washing, garden furniture, tools and plants. Robert O'May, of *Sainsbury's Insurance*, which commissioned the survey of 500 home owners said: "The popularity of gardens has been increased by television programmes such as *Ground Force*. It is important that people protect the valuables in their garden." Tips to foil thieves include marking items with a postcode, joining a neighbourhood watch scheme, putting (noisy) gravel on paths, fitting security lighting and planting prickly shrubs.

Securicor Security ran a survey, the results of which indicated that we are rapidly becoming a 'nation of shoplifters'. Nearly a quarter of all adults questioned during the survey, think that stealing from shops is 'no big deal.' 17 per cent admitted shoplifting, 40 per cent knew someone who had and 24 per cent believe stealing from large retailers was less damaging than from small shops. A *Securicor* spokesman said: "These figures are a major concern for UK retailers, who already face an average loss of almost £3,000 per year per outlet from shoplifting. It is most prevalent in the South-East and East Anglia, with the lowest rates in Yorkshire and Humberside.

I recall that when I was a TDC based at Romford, we noted that most major stores like *Marks & Spencer* had far too many double-door entrance/exits, without having sufficient staff to monitor movements in and out at each door. They also regularly displayed one of their most expensive items of merchandise, leather jackets, far too close to the doors.

Individual items were not tagged then, neither were doors fitted with alarm signal receivers and it was not unknown for career criminal shoplifters to rush through the double doors with huge double-arms full of leather jackets etc, and be lost in the market crowds very quickly. There at Romford we had a full-time police shoplifting squad who were on the go virtually all day long, on market days and weekends, specially at 'Sale' times and Christmas. Patient police and store detectives, acting in pairs would not 'pounce' on shoplifters at the first observed instance of theft, or attempted theft. It was much more rewarding to follow them from store-to-store and after a while, when you finally decided to 'strike', you would find they were carrying whole huge bags full of stolen items, from *Debenhams*, *M & S*, *Woolworths*, *BHS*, *Littlewoods* etc.

Once at the police station we would endeavour to track down their parked cars and, if successful, we would be rewarded with the discovery of hundreds of pounds worth of stolen merchandise that they had already accumulated, and stored in the car boot, before catching our eyes. This way, they could not claim, in court, that it was a 'one-off' venture. Particularly as they were unable to produce proofs of purchase, viz : receipts. Between us we also developed a very basic 'early-warning' system, whereby descriptions of suspects were circulated from store-to-store, the more watchful eyes on the case the better. Some ultra-greedy shoplifters used to return to *M & S* the following week, when the heat had died down, and queue at the customer service or refund counter, asking for a refund on previously-stolen items as they had 'changed their minds,' or 'it didn't fit', or 'the colour looked different when viewed in proper daylight'. When caught, these persons were charged with the original thefts and additionally offences of attempted or criminal deceptions, as the gear wasn't legally theirs in the first place.

Eventually *Marks & Spencer* and other stores got wise to this and developed elaborate receipts and 'kimbell' tags. What made our job easy of course, when confronting shoplifters with their exposed shopping bag contents on the charge room desk, was that, although they would protest their innocence until they were 'blue-in-the-face', they were unable to produce a single receipt for payment, therefore the trap was fully sprung in our favour. It was at this stage that the colour of their faces changed from pink to red, as they realised the game was up. This triggered very dry mouths, rivers of sweat between shoulder blades and sad eyes spasmed into auto-irrigation mode!

Often women would have their children with them as 'cover', whilst others made it look as if they were pregnant, to hide property in their false 'bump'. In those days we routinely searched the house and/or business premises of every single shoplifter, very often finding 'Aladdin's Caves' with mobile dress and gown rails of displayed goods in dress-size order, which had literally been 'stolen-to-order'. Very big business indeed and a specialist skill of many gangs of travelling criminals. Store detectives and security staff need eyes everywhere these days. Many criminals are guilty of the offence of 'going equipped for theft,' by wearing devices such as limply-hanging false arms, trousers with pockets one metre deep, and long-skirted women wearing elasticated-waist multi-skirts containing endless, deep pockets, where selected items of plunder are swiftly secreted from view. However these days there are good, sophisticated, concealed CCTV cameras with zoom lenses and ceiling glass domes, which conceal rotating cameras but give the appearance of emergency lighting fixtures. One time, whilst routinely searching a female shoplifter's home at Rainham, Essex, we found that the bath was almost full to the brim with rum of almost 100% proof, which would have been lethal if not drastically diluted-down before drinking. We called in HM Customs to take over that part of the enquiry, and it was that Agency which tested the bath rum as to its proof, so as to calculate the customs duty payable. Meanwhile I got covered in dust, dirt, fluff, fibreglass loft insulation and spiders' webs, whilst searching the prisoner's loft, hoping to discover the usual aladdin's cave of previously stolen merchandise.

COUNT 6

DRUGS
THE SCOURGE OF OUR MODERN SOCIETY

Fairly early on in my police career in the Essex Constabulary, in the late 60's, we had quite serious drugs problems within Grays Division in the South Ockendon and Aveley council estate areas of Essex, not very far from the Dartford Tunnel. These estates were built as London overspill areas. Unfortunately for the ordinary law-abiding residents of those areas, two different kinds of drugs-using communities quickly sprang up. Firstly, there were the *hippy* types in their flowing floral, loose-fitting clothing and driving around in psychadaelic-painted cars, who held cannabis-smoking parties, funded by the benefits system of the day. They tended to sit around on the upstairs floors, leaning on large cushions or bean bags, passing around cannabis joints or *spliffs*, drinking cider and rapidly addling their brains. Due to being practically *out of their heads* most of the time, their reactions were very slow, and when we arrived with a small posse on the doorstep, someone would stagger down the stairs, assuming we were further arriving party-goers, and let us in. It was just as well that they did, as sledge hammers, hydraulic door-frame-splitters and tubular metal ram-rods had not yet been adopted as essential a part of a constable's *appointments*, as his handcuffs, truncheon and official pocket book and whistle were then known. It was a cinch and we swiftly seized ashtray contents, mini-weighing scales, king size Rizlas and lumps of dark brown cannabis resin looking exactly like pieces broken off a *kit-kat* chocolate bar. Naturally there was plenty of *grass*, herbal cannabis, lying around as well. If you were extra lucky, you might even find some rapidly-growing, lovingly-tended cannabis plants in the greenhouse or on the bedroom window sill. Full-time drugs squads were formed on divisions, with a central control at Police HQ at Chelmsford. Quite a few officers cut their teeth on this new drugs menace and quickly enhanced their police careers and obtained rapid promotion.

The second type of drugs menace, then in its infancy, were amphetamines etc known as *speed* and *party-poppers*. These peoples' eyes almost popped out of their sockets and the eyeballs were almost all pupil. The drug-users *buzzed* their lives away, but, unlike the *hippies*, they had fast reactions and all of the evidence in the form of pills, capsules or tablets, were swiftly flushed down the toilet or sinks at the first inkling of *The Bill* wishing to join the party. Amazingly, homes of drugs dealers and major drugs users these days, are converted into Fort Knox-type buildings, by the addition of secondary, inner-door prison-type metal-barred grilles, sophisticated alarms and PIR sensors and Rottweiler and/or Pit-Bull Terrier, police-flesh-ripping guard dogs. You will no doubt have seen real-life police documentaries where a multi-storey block of flats with a major drugs dealer living on the 7th floor, had reinforced his front entrance door so well, that specialist police teams had to risk their lives by *abseiling* down the outside from the 13th floor, like the Iranian Embassy assault by the SAS, crash through the not-so-well-guarded windows and let in the rest of the drugs search teams from the inside.

Bizarrely, but essentially, so as not to lose pills etc. being flushed down toilets and sinks, like we used to, police now unhitch sections of the drain pipes and foul water pipes so everything cascades onto the pavement and not much is lost or wasted. Quite a lot of developments have taken place in police forces over the years, and as we know, modern drugs dealers even target young kids in the school playgrounds.

My most recent involvement with drugs was when, with a colleague, I was acting as dock officer at Andover Magistrates Court. The custody area there is very antiquated, and so insecure that until just after the event I am about to describe, any members of the public could just wander unchallenged, round to the rear of the court buildings, look through the windows and wave or signal to defendants locked in the all-bars custody areas. No individual cells were provided. Locked in the barred area, with floor to ceiling bars, were two career-criminal prisoners, serving time at HMP Winchester for burglary and drugs offences. On this particular day we had brought them to the court at Andover on fresh charges in relation to the possession and suspected dealings in drugs, which they had not admitted prior to their last conviction for the current sentence. I was entering up some records of the days events in an official book when I happened to look up and glance in the direction of the two prisoners. They were standing on the wooden bed/bench, facing the back windows and holding up a piece of A4 - size lined paper. This made me look towards the rear windows and I saw that members of the public were looking in. I shooed them away from the windows and approached the barred area and asked one of the prisoners to pass the note through the bars to me. He shook his head in refusal and tore the note into many pieces, some of which he scattered on the floor. After they had been further remanded by the court we loaded them into the prison van for return to HMP Winchester. But before we set off, I swept out the part of the custody area they had occupied and preserved the floor litter and debris. This included a paper coffee cup which contained soggy paper pulp in the bottom, together with stubbed dog ends. On arrival at HMP Winchester we filled out the necessary disciplinary forms to place the two prisoners on Governor's Report for failing to carry out a lawful order, viz: 'Hand over the note you were holding up towards the windows.' I was too busy to look at the cell debris that day so I took it home with me that night.

Everything had to be dried out to preserve it, as it was too fragile in its wet condition. Believe it or not it took my wife and I almost a week of our spare time to carefully piece together the micro-fragments of the cell note. It was such a fiddly, painstaking operation that I sympathised greatly with our predecessors, the Egyptologists trying to unravel the hieroglyphics found inside the pyramids many years before us! Eventually through still more extreme patience we were able to paste those fragments which had the slightest trace of biro ink on them. The completed work read 'PASS HASH WHEN WE COME OUT!' We were bright enough to appreciate the significance of this message meant for their nosy-parker accommodating relatives at the windows of the custody area. When this development was communicated to The Governor, HMP Winchester, he held an Adjudication and they both pleaded guilty to the charge. He awarded them some extra days to be added on to the end of their current sentences, so all's well that ends well. Unfortunately, the Human Rights do-gooders somewhere on the Continent, who meddle with everything British today, have since decreed, in their great wisdom, that UK Prison Governors are breaching the prisoners' Human Rights, by topping up or extending the sentences being currently served by the offenders. This is a great backward step, discipline-wise in UK prisons now, as only panels of visiting magistrates or judges can award EXTRA DAYS for breaches of Prison Discipline. Previously, I believe that a Governing Governor in a jail could award a maximum of an additional

28 extra days, but even then, there was provision for Mr Jailbird to keep his head down for a while, and then apply to have the extra days order rescinded, for 'good' behaviour.

As a result of the sharp-eyed devotion to duty I had displayed in the Andover Magistrates Court custody area on that day, I received a special award. This consisted of three rolls of one-way transparency security film to be affixed to the rear windows of the custody office. However I was not given long to bask in the reflected glory of my award, as it was seized by my Line Manager, who felt that he would make a neater job of it than me! However, I am pleased to report that as a result of my personal vigilance on the day in question, potential drugs couriers are no longer able to peer into the custody area at that particular magistrates court.

The falling cost of cocaine, and an increased use by young professionals, has doubled the number of deaths caused by the drug, says new research. There were 87 cocaine-related deaths in the UK in the first half of 2003 compared to half that in the first half of 2002. A gram of cocaine now costs £40 in May 2004, compared to £70 in the year 2000. Many young professionals take the drug believing it to be safe. But doctors warn it can trigger heart attacks, strokes and depression. Experts fear a fashion for mixing cocaine with other drugs is also causing more deaths. Dr Fabrizio Schifano, of St Georges Medical School, in Tooting, South London, last year warned of more deaths among young ecstasy users.

The world's first portable drugs testing kit could be in use soon in the UK, by the end of the year 2004, if current police trials cause it to be recommended. German makers, *Draeger Safety*, said the £4,300 device called, aptly enough *DrugTest*, will enable traffic officers to carry out on-the-spot drug tests among motorists. It is claimed that the shoebox-sized kit can detect even the smallest traces of drugs including heroin, ecstasy, cocaine or cannabis, within only 15 minutes. It works in a similar way to breathalysers with motorists suspected of drugs abuse being asked to blow into a small pipe. Accident estimators say around 10,000 people a year are killed and 25,000 seriously injured within the Europeant Union because of motorists on drugs.

Home-testing kits that will allow parents to check if their children are taking drugs are to go on sale in chemists at the end of May 2004. However, a parents' group warned that they could destroy trust within the families, and the Home Office advised parents to think twice before using them. The kits, which will sell for £12 each over the counter, can give a positive or negative result from a urine sample within seconds. They test for cannabis, cocaine, amphetamines, ecstasy, heroin and Diazepam. The makers claim that they are 99.98 accurate. John Mullee of Hunter Diagnostics said,

"Every responsible parent has a niggle about drugs. Nobody knows for sure what their kids are doing." Margaret Morrissey of the National Confederation of Parent Teacher Associations said, "Youngsters will see it as a big threat." The Home Office said that parents needed to "consider very carefully" the effect that a test would have on their relationship with a child.

Drug tests for teens cannot be the answer

"Communication between generations has always been a problem. Now it seems to have broken down irrevocably. Hot on the heels of the distressing story of the 14-year-old-girl whose abortion was organised by her school without her parents' knowledge, comes a brand new product. It costs £12. It's available from your chemist, 11,000 have already been sold in Ireland. What is it? To our shame, the home drug-testing kit is designed for parents to use on their children. You merely demand a urine sample from your child, immerse the dipstick provided and, Hey Presto, you'll find out if he or she has been abusing cocaine, ecstasy or amphetamines. I use the word 'merely' with heavy irony. Asking for a urine sample from my children has never featured highly on my list of preferred parental activities. Demanding to see their finished homework? Absolutely. Asking them to tidy up the filthy mess in their bedrooms? Definitely. Beseeching them to wear cycling helmets, write thank-you letters and be polite to crotchety relatives? All the time. But make a trip to the chemist because the trust between myself and my own flesh and blood, has evaporated so completely that I need to test their urine to find out if they are on drugs? What a woefully tragic scenario. The very existence of this kit raises all manner of agonisingly uncomfortable questions.

Do we really keep so little track of our children, are we really so unaware of their normal speech and behavioural patterns, that we need to resort to scientific testing to find out what they're up to? Are we so chronically incapable of inspiring confidence and communication in our teenagers that they embark on drug use without reference or deference to us? What of the morality of taking urine samples from our children? They are sure to be unwilling and uncooperative. Practically speaking, the issue's cloaked in embarrassment. Do we barge into the bathroom and insist? When does this amount to bullying and invasive treatment by parents? Why stop there? By logical progression we are veering towards relationships ultimately permitting us to extract blood or DNA samples and stools for home culture. Where will such unethical procedure end? Random drugs tests may be standard for competing athletes but for parents who suspect drugs may be a problem, I can't think of a more alienating less conciliatory process. When the Education Secretary said British children were starting school aged five, unable to hold or listen to a conversation, he highlighted a devastating trend. Fractured families, grazing at different times, plugged in isolation to computers and surfing the net in silence, have lost the art of conversation. Parents must revive the skill of sharing, shaping, informing and appraising their children's lives simply by taking the time to talk to them. Otherwise, a ghastly spectre looms of families rotating around in utter ignorance of each other's thoughts, feelings and fears and desperate parents swooping on their children clutching £12 drug-testing kits."

Vanessa Feltz, TV presenter, Daily Express columnist, 18th May 2005

(**Author's note:** *How would Vanessa reconcile her views above, with seeing across the national media, tragic photos of the body of a young drugs-addicted girl crouched on the floor of a drugs den, which her devastated parents declared should be widely publicised as a stark warning to others?*)

Drug users committing crimes to feed their habits are being targeted as soon as they are arrested, to get them into treatment and away from a cycle of crime and drug addiction, through an innovative Government scheme. A £46.2 million intensive package of measures to combat drug-related crime is being phased-in to 30 of the worst affected areas. The package is an end-to-end, joined-up process that is providing support and treatment to rehabilitate offenders, from the moment they are identified as drug users, through to the end of their sentences and beyond it. It is an ambitious, innovative programme aiming to get offenders off drugs and out of trouble. A key element of the scheme is compulsory drug testing to identify heroin, crack and cocaine addicts who steal to fund their habits. The tests, for offenders charged with offences such as burglary, shoplifting and vehicle crime, ensure that problematic drug users are identified early and offered appropriate treatment. A Home Office Minister explained that the Government's package to combat drug-related crime includes community sentences, rehabilitation and aftercare, all of which have been proven to deliver results. For every £1 spent on treatment, £3 is saved in the criminal justice system, that is why we are spending record amounts on the fight against drugs – £1.2 billion in 2004, including £503million on treatment alone. Property crime like robbery and car crime is going down, but still remains a problem, fuelled by class A drugs. Drugs can tear communities apart and make thieves and villains out of those who would, under normal circumstances, be law-abiding citizens.

A red-card zone is being set up in the London Borough of Lambeth to eradicate drug dealing and anti-social behaviour. Police can now exercise new powers to clean up public spaces in Brixton blighted by drunkenness, cannabis use and abusive behaviour. The crackdown, prompted by public concern, will see police move people on under the Anti-Social behaviour Act, if their actions are deemed likely to deter other people from enjoying the area. Det. Superintendent David Zinzan said: "We want to make Brixton a safer and more pleasant place for people to live and work." Rachel Heywood, chairman of the Brixton Area Forum said: "Local people have a right to live, work and play without feeling intimidated by loutish behaviour." Three pubs linked to gun crime in the area have already been closed down under local police chief Dick Quinn's controversial zero tolerance policy.

Young professionals who use cocaine as a recreational drug are developing holes in their brains, a leading expert has found. Three-dimensional scans by neurosurgeon Dr Peter Harvey have revealed the appalling damage done by the drug to blood vessels. Tests have shown that the users' ability to think clearly has been impaired by cocaine and the worst cases could result in a fatal brain seizure caused by restricted blood flow. The findings are alarming because cocaine is the weekend drug of choice for high-flyers in their 20's and 30's. They do not consider themselves addicts, and see it as a relatively *safe* recreational drug. Studies have already revealed that cocaine causes damage to the heart, increasing the risk of heart attacks. The latest evidence is the first to show definitively that cocaine also harms blood vessels in the brain.

Dr Harvey, previously Consultant Neurologist at the Royal Free Hospital in NW London, and now in private practice in Harley Street, recently treated three cocaine users with affected brains. Two of the patients were City businessmen in their 40's, who had used the drug weekly or fortnightly for about ten years. The third was a professional woman in her thirties who used it occasionally at weekends. Dr Harvey said: "The brain scans I have carried out show holes in the brain which have been caused by cocaine use. In an acute case this could cause a possible brain seizure which could result in death. In the first case he dealt with, an MRI scan showed the patient's brain to be normal, but a Spec scan, which uses radiography to monitor blood flow around the brain, revealed an abnormality. The scan is three-dimensional and you could clearly see holes in the brain from the arterial damage caused by the cocaine use. These holes are not present in a brain with no history of substance abuse." Dr Harvey sent the patient to see a neurological psychologist, who found his thinking capacity was considerably impaired. The doctor added, "This came as a shock to the patient, as he did not feel as though the drugs had affected his work or memory." He believes many more people may be suffering from the condition and have not sought medical help. Further recent research shows one in ten people being treated for chest pains at a leading heart hospital, have used cocaine. Doctors are seeing many 30-year-olds whose hearts resemble those of someone twice their age. Hospital staff are being forced to delay looking after other sick patients in order to deal with suspected heart attacks caused by drug abuse. According to the independent Drug Monitoring Unit, cocaine use has more than doubled in Britain over the past seven years – 1997-2004, as its price dropped to about £40 a gram from £100 in the early 1990s.

A company behind a revolutionary instant drugs test is to float on the stock market. A device made by Cozart can detect heroin and cocaine use in just three minutes by testing saliva. Cannabis takes a little longer with the machine, shaped like a mobile phone, and ecstasy needs up to 12 minutes. Five different drugs can be identified at a time from one saliva sample. The *RapiScan* is being tested by the Home Office at 130 police stations in England and Wales. It would save police time and money in two ways, said Dr Chris Hand, managing director of Cozart, which has 58 staff at Abingdon, Oxon. He told the City pages of *The Sun* newspaper: "With the current tests, a police officer has to *watch* a suspect provide a urine sample, as drug users tend to adulterate their sample or switch it. With our equipment there is no need to observe the suspect in this way, which saves time. Secondly, the test is done on the spot and the results are there very quickly." Cozart will be valued at around £27million in the shares flotation, in which it is raising £6.75million from outside investors. This would help finance international expansion. The drug buster is already being used by police in Italy, Australia and Germany. Dr Hand, who founded Cozart with his accountant brother Philip, 11 years ago, said: "Our product will hopefully break the cycle, as the Government puts it, between drug use and crime." The brothers will get £1.5million cash after the share issue and their joint holding will be valued at £8.18million. The way the hand-held *RapiScan* works is that a sample is collected from an absorbent pad in the suspect's mouth. This pad is put into a disposable cartridge, where chemical tests detect precisely which drugs have been taken. The cartridge is placed into the *RapiScan*, which translates the test results and prints them out on paper.

New research has confirmed that smoking cannabis can trigger mental illness. Six months after the Government downgraded it to a Class C drug, researchers at one of America's most respected institutions, the Yale University School of Medicine, have established a link between its use and schizophrenia. In a series of tests, 22 people who were not cannabis users, and who were in good physical and mental health, received intravenous injections of Delta-9-THC, the main active chemical ingredient in cannabis, and were tested for any ill-effects over a three-day period. They reported schizophrenia-like symptoms, including altered perception, anxiety, euphoria, impaired verbal fluency, lack of concentration and memory loss. Some participants had difficulty in carrying out simple intelligence tests, such as finding words with the same letter in under 60 seconds. They also complained of hallucinations and obsessive suspicion of people around them. The findings, reported in the American Journal of Neuropsychopharmacology, come only six months after Britain liberalised the law on cannabis. There are fears the change has led more young people to try the drug, because they believe it is harmless and that they are unlikely to be prosecuted.

Official figures claim more than three million people in the UK use cannabis regularly and a third of 15-year-olds have tried it. Consultant Psychiatrist Professor Robin Murray said earlier this year that up to 80 per cent of new psychiatric patients had a history of smoking the drug. The latest US research was welcomed by British scientists. Dr Alan Young of Newcastle University, said: "It is not only bad for your physical health, like smoking an unfiltered cigarette, but also for your mental well-being. It is not true, as some claim, that it is a benign substance." The number of young people and adults injecting illegal drugs in major cities is as high as 1-in-50, experts have learned. A study focusing on London, Liverpool and Brighton, estimated that between 1-in-50 and 1-in-80 people aged between 15 and 44 injected drugs regularly. The researchers said this made the problem as common as diabetes and more common than chronic diseases such as epilepsy.

According to the study in the Journal of Epidemiology and Community Health, injecting drug-users were more likely to die from their habit in Brighton. Overall, around one per cent of injecting drug users die from an overdose each year. But in Brighton, not only were there higher rates of drug users, but two per cent died from an overdose. The researchers, from Imperial College and Liverpool John Moores University, gathered their information from drug treatment centres, referrals after police arrest, and syringe exchange schemes. In London, the team concentrated on 12 boroughs. They estimated that rates of injecting drug use among 15 to 44-year olds were two per cent in Brighton, 1.5 per cent in Liverpool and 1.2 per cent in London. Routine statistics on problem drug use did not accurately reflect the actual prevalence in the population, they warned.

The drug epidemic in Britain's jails has forced prisoners to put signs on cell doors saying 'No Salesmen' in a desperate bid to deter dealers, it has been revealed. A report by the Prison Reform Trust said smuggling drugs inside prison had become an organised racket. Dealers were using cleaners and auxiliary staff to sneak hard drugs inside to tap into the captive market of inmates. Other tricks include throwing tennis balls stuffed full of heroin or crack cocaine over prison walls.

The report's author, Enver Solomon said that at Wealstun Prison in Yorkshire, some dormitory doors had notices saying *'No Salesmen'*. The Trust reveals that, at the worst prisons, one in every three inmates is now testing positive for drugs. The jail with the highest recorded drug use was Kirkham in Lancashire, which had a rate of 34 per cent. This was followed by Armley, Leeds, (30.5), Winchester (28.5), Liverpool (28.3) and Risley, Cheshire (26). Nationwide, the percentage of positive tests was 12.3 per cent, missing the Government's target of ten per cent. In a speech to the Prison Service annual conference, Director-General Phil Wheatley admitted facing 'significant operational challenges'. He added: "These centre particularly around drug dealing in prisons, which appears to be coming much more organised and we will have to find ways of responding to this increased determination and sophistication on the part of drug dealers." The Reform Trust blamed prison overcrowding for many of these problems.

On 1st August 2004 the prison population in England and Wales stood at 75,146, an increase of 1,235 in the past year. At the end of July 2004, 83 of the 138 prisons in England and Wales were overcrowded. The number of serious assaults was higher than targeted and there were 92 suicides, including five at Nottingham and four each at Preston, Durham and Blakenhurst in Worcestershire. Shadow Home Secretary David Davis said: "Not only is crime increasing on our streets under Labour, it is also rising in our prisons. The Home Secretary has failed to ensure the capacity of the Prison Service properly reflects the level of prison population. It's simple maths, and his do not add up." A Prison Service spokesman said: "I don't think the Prison Reform Trust has recognised the improvements we have made in the past year. In the light of the fact that the prison population has been quite high, we believe progress has been good."

Arrests for cannabis possession have dropped by a third, after the drug was reclassified from Class B to the less serious Class C in January 2004, new figures have revealed. Home Office insiders said police can now spend 200,000 extra hours every year fighting hard drugs. A Whitehall source added: "Their time is much better spent tackling those peddling Class A drugs like heroin." The charity Drugscope welcomed the figures but a spokesman said: "People should not be misled into thinking that cannabis use has dropped by 33 per cent." A quarter of 16 to 24-year-olds use the drug, more than twice the world average.

Reclassification means they are unlikely to be arrested if caught.
(**Author's note:** *I was greatly heartened to hear that police officers have*

an extra 200,000 hours per year to continue the uphill struggle against hard-drugs dealers.

However, I am worldy-wise enough to realise that, even as I type, some obscure civil servant in the Importance Of Filling In Forms Department of the Home Office, is gleefully working on the design and creation of some additional, fresh statistical police forms, so that the spare 200,000 hours per year of police time, can be put to, as he sees it, better use.)

Sniffer dogs are being used to search tens of thousands of school pupils for drugs. The dogs are regularly used in more than 100 secondary schools in England and Wales. Police in 12 regions have taken up the scheme launched by Kent officers. Fifteen other forces are considering similar drives. At the Heart of England School in Solihull, West Midlands, Head Teacher Annette Croft said: "Sniffer dogs are a very mellow, humane response to the threat of drugs." Parents are asked to sign a letter of consent for the searches. Pupils whose parents refuse are searched by hand. But Drugscope charity magazine editor Harry Shapiro said: " It seems unhelpful. It causes distress and distrust."

A Drugs Counsellor was arrested at a top-security jail for allegedly trying to smuggle cocaine to an inmate in her bra. The 41-year-old civilian worker was stopped after going through checkpoints with two bags of drugs strapped to her breasts. The woman had been giving advice at Full Sutton jail, near York, which has serial killer Dennis Nilsen, 58, among its inmates. (Also, serial-family-killer Jeremy Bamber is housed there and is currently suing HM Prison Service for failing to look after him properly, after his throat was slit by another prisoner, requiring 28 stitches in hospital.) The drugs are thought to be cocaine with a street value of several thousand pounds. Prison officers were tipped off in advance, but allowed the woman to pass through the security checks before searching and arresting her. She was held in custody at the prison until police arrived. She was strip-searched and taken to a local police station to be interviewed. Tests are being carried out and the suspect was released on bail pending scientific analysis. Full Sutton prison was opened in 1987 and holds 608 inmates. It is described by officials as housing some of Britain's *most difficult and dangerous criminals.*

A teenager threatened to slash his own mother's throat after becoming violently addicted to *harmless* cannabis, a court was told. Adam Gregory, 19, flew into a rage when he woke up one day and could not find his *weed,* which the Government recently down-graded to a Class C drug. He chased his mother Judith, whom he thought had hidden his daily *fix,* around the family home and threatened her with a kitchen knife. He later fled the house in his boxer shorts, and was found by police curled up in a ball in the street sobbing. He was ordered to a rehab clinic after the judge at Minshull Street Crown Court, Manchester said he should take a six-months course to conquer his cannabis addiction. His mother, in her 40's, was too upset to comment. The Government downgraded cannabis from Class B to C even though some doctors believe it is linked to mental health problems and is more likely to cause anxiety, depression and schizophrenia. The court heard that the drug was at the *root* of Gregory's problems. Of the confrontation with his mother at the home in Timperley, near Altrincham, prosecutor Justin Hayhoe said: "He said 'where have you put it, my weed?' He grabbed his mother by the dressing gown and pulled it tight around her throat and shook her. He was screaming and shouting, gritting his teeth. He was described as manic and wild. He went back upstairs where there was more banging before he declared *someone else* must have moved the drugs. He then smashed a family photo frame before holding a chair above his head as if to throw it at his mother. He was heard rummaging in a kitchen drawer before returning with a knife and telling his mother: "Tell me where it is. I'm going to cut your throat." She tried to get away but Gregory pressed the weapon against her throat. She described her son as being *totally out of control.* When police found him after fleeing the house, he said: "I'm sorry, my head's in bits." He had pleaded guilty to affray and criminal damage.

(**Author's note:** *He had appeared at the crown court wearing a hooded jacket, as worn by many criminal youths these days, the hood being worn in the up position, even on the hottest days. Surely they aren't trying to hide their faces? This style of jacket with hood is banned in prisons.*)

Julian Halloran, 39, of Port Talbot, South Wales, was so proud of his personal cannabis crop that he photographed it and took the film to be developed at *Tescos*. On 24th March 2004 he appeared at Swansea Crown Court, which was told that Halloran had invested in a hydroponic system to grow cannabis with a street value of £27,500. The judge jailed Halloran for 15 months, after he admitted producing and possessing the drug.

(**Author's note:** *Hydroponic – a method of cultivating plants by growing them in gravel etc. through which water containing dissolved inorganic nutrient salts is pumped.*)

British teenager Michael Connell, 19,of Bury, Greater Manchester, who smuggled 3,400 ecstasy tablets into Thailand, avoided the death penalty by pleading guilty to the charges. He was jailed for 99 years instead. He was arrested at Bangkok International Airport in November 2003 with the drugs concealed in jars of face cream in his luggage. His father Derek Connell, a 48-year-old taxi driver said: "I'm devastated. He's naïve and has learning difficulties, so he was the perfect target for drug dealers who need someone to do their dirty work. I believe he did this to pay off a small debt."

A boy of nine was forced to listen as gangland assassins shot dead his mother's boyfriend at his home. Andrew "Bo" Boland, 35, was shot in the chest as he pleaded for his life in what police believe was a drugs-related murder. The distraught boy and his 12-year-old brother, who had hidden in the kitchen, were questioned by police. Boland died after the nine-year-old opened the door to two masked men. One pointed a pistol at his head and said: "Go upstairs or I'll shoot you." As the boy fled, the killers demanded money before shooting Boland in front of his lover, Angela, aged 33. Two men aged 23 and 26, were arrested after the killing in Stretford, Manchester, and then bailed. Two other men aged 28 and 26 were being questioned by police, who said: " Andrew was involved in the supply of cannabis."

A woman held a blood-filled syringe to an 11-month-old boy's throat to force his mother to hand over cash and jewellery. The unnamed victim of the street-junkie, aged 20, in Pontefract, west Yorks, said: "I was terrified for my baby. This thief must be caught quickly."

A soccer star has been arrested by police probing a £250,000 drugs find. Coventry City striker Onandi Lowe, 30, and a woman believed to be his girlfriend, were interviewed by police who stopped his car. Undercover detectives found a package containing cocaine worth £250,000. The Jamaican international and the woman aged 24, were arrested as they drove near Lowe's home in Rushden, Northants. They were taken to Wellingborough police station and later released without charge. Later, Coventry City football club said: "Onandi Lowe has informed the club that he has been arrested in connection with the possession of the package containing an illegal substance."

A crack cocaine baron who ran a £170 million drugs empire was jailed for 25 years at Kingston Crown Court. Lincoln White, 39, lived quietly in the UK, driving a battered Peugeot 206. But he bought property in Jamaica and banked his cash in the Cayman Islands. Police seized 10.9 kilos of crack cocaine from him in 2003, their biggest ever haul. Judge Edward Southwell told White, of Dulwich, South London: "You played for the highest stakes with arrogance and those stakes must now be met." White was convicted of conspiracy to import and supply drugs.

Grandma Pat Brailsford, 59, of Stapenhill, Staffs, used some judo tips her son had taught her to trap a crook. She got him in a headlock, wrapped her legs around his, and refused to let go. "He kept shouting 'Get off!' but I wouldn't", she said. She had found the drugs suspect hiding from police in her garden. A PC said: " Pat fought like a tiger."

Customs officers seized cannabis with a street value of £3.5million from a lorry that arrived from France by ferry. The 1.3ton stash was found at Poole, Dorset, concealed in commercial air conditioning units. The British driver was interviewed but later released. Customs said: "It was excellent work by one of our teams."

A pigeon breeder caught trying to smuggle cocaine worth £80,000 across the Channel in a cage of racing birds was jailed for 18 months. French Customs Officers who stopped John Gerard, 45, on a motorway near Calais, found a bag containing 3 lbs of the drug in a crate of flapping pigeons. Gerard, of South London, who had pleaded not guilty, told a court in Dunkirk: "The man who sold me the pigeons in Belgium said it was a bag of bird seed."

A gifted young athlete died after taking a cocktail of prescription drugs at a pal's party. Michael Edwards, 16, and three teenaged girls were rushed to hospital after bingeing on the medicines which they found in a bathroom cabinet. The girls, all aged 16, survived but doctors were unable to save Michael, who excelled as a sprinter. Police have launched a probe into the party in Aberaeron, West Wales, which took place while the owners of the house were away. Five youngsters, including the son of the house owners, have been arrested and released on police bail. The local detective inspector said: "The drugs belonged to the parents of one of the children. This is a warning not to meddle with prescribed drugs."

An uninsured driver who killed a mother-of-four while high on crack cocaine has appeared at Northampton Crown Court. Lee Robins, 22, slammed his car into the wall of a pub after a 3-day cocaine and cannabis binge, killing his friend and passenger Joanne Woods. Robins, who had never taken his driving test, fled after the crash in 2003, leaving critically injured Miss Woods behind. She later died in the ambulance en route to the hospital. Robins turned himself in to police after the smash, vowing he would never drive again. But within weeks of killing Miss Woods, who had 4 daughters aged 9 to 16, he was back behind the wheel and was arrested for dangerous driving. Judge Charles Wide told Robins: "You got into a car and drove it with a passenger when you were completely incapable of driving. You had been on a drug-fuelled binge and taken crack cocaine and cannabis." His erratic driving had been caught on CCTV cameras, which showed him smashing into a bicycle rack outside the pub when he failed to slow for a bend, sending him careering into the wall of the *Crown and Cushion* pub, Wellingborough, at high speed. Robins admitted causing his friend's death by dangerous driving and was sentenced to three years consecutively (following-on) with three years he was given in December 2003 for dangerous driving, burglary and other offences committed just weeks after the fatal smash. He was also banned from driving for 15 years.

Pupils at Eton College, Windsor accused teachers of sneaky tactics, after four boys found with traces of drugs in their hair were expelled. The sixth-formers claim hair samples were taken for tests after they admitted under an *amnesty* that they had taken drugs. On the stroke of midnight on 23rd May 2004, 800 boys at the top college took part in a *midnight howl*, a traditional demonstration of disapproval. For 10 minutes they screeched and hooted from the windows of the £20,000-a-year school in sympathy with their expelled pals. The four boys had locks of hair snipped off by Deputy Head Master Dr Robert Stephenson. A source at Prince William and Prince Harry's old school said: "All 4 had voluntarily gone to their Housemasters to say they had taken drugs in the past and had voluntarily signed a contract with the school to stay off them. As part of that contract they get counselling and also agree to random drugs tests. They had all stopped smoking dope because they knew they might have to give a urine sample at any time, and failing the test would mean they were out on their ear. But instead the school pulled a flanker and insisted on them having a hair test. The boys quite rightly pointed out that they had admitted taking drugs in the past and that traces of cannabis would remain in the hair until it grows out entirely. Not surprisingly they all tested positive. They feel they have been victimised for admitting a problem and seeking help, and that others in the same position in the future will not come forward to seek help. Everyone is very angry that Eton has dealt with them in this way." Pupils have threatened more protests unless Head Tony Little takes notice. Two of the boys were in Godolphin House, one was in Durnford House and one in Walpole House. They were expelled last week and packed their bags on Saturday morning. Three of the boys were in the Upper Sixth and will be allowed to return to take their A-levels. The fourth boy was in the Lower Sixth and must find another school. During his time at Eton, Prince Harry was put on notice of random drug testing after admitting to his father Prince Charles that he had smoked cannabis when he was 16. Harry admitted puffing on joints at Highgrove and a local pub, when he went off the rails in booze and drug binges, but was spared expulsion as it wasn't done at Eton. Insiders at the school estimate at least a third of the Sixth Form smoke cannabis. Eton heads were unavailable for comment. (NB: *Nine boys have*

*been suspended until the end of term at £19,000-a-year Bryanston School,
Dorset, after being caught sharing a joint.)*

A distraught mother hit out after a drug-fuelled learner driver was leniently
punished, after killing her 14-year-old daughter in a horror smash. Gareth
Frost, then aged 17, had taken two ecstasy tablets and smoked cannabis
before climbing behind the wheel of a car he had bought minutes earlier for
just £50. A court heard that Frost crashed the Metro into a lamp post at
70mph. It skidded for 50 yards and flipped onto its roof, killing Jade Foster,
who was a passenger,instantly. Frost and three other teenagers escaped with
minor injuries. After he was sentenced for causing death by dangerous
driving, an angry Mrs Lisa Forster said: "He should have got ten years." Mrs
Forster, 35, from Maltby, Rotherham, who has three other children said:
"He'll be walking the streets again in 15 months but I've got a life sentence.
I will never see my pretty daughter again. She was only 14, with her whole
life ahead of her, and it's been snatched away. She was killed by somebody
who had taken drugs and was driving a car that wasn't fit to be on the road.
He hasn't even passed his test. Even the police have said they are amazed
how light the sentence was. It was said in court that he showed remorse and
regretted Jade's death, but I haven't had a word from him, not even a simple
sorry. I made myself go to court every time he appeared. It was agony, but
I wanted to see the boy who took my daughter's life. I have never seen an
ounce of remorse from him in court."

Mrs Forster told how on the night her daughter was killed, she thought
Jade was sleeping over at her best friend's house. But she went out with her
friends and one of them knew the driver, so they thought it would be fun
having a ride in his car." Sheffield Crown Court was told that Frost, 18, from
Wickersley, Rotherham, had bought the car on 21st June 2003. He had
taken two ecstasy tablets, cannabis and a small amount of alcohol before
meeting the group of teenagers. Witnesses said the car was swaying from
side to side before it skidded off the road and hit a lamp post outside the
Lumley Arms pub in Maltby. Jade suffered serious head injuries and died at
the scene. Frost, who admitted causing death by dangerous driving, was
banned for three years and given just two and a half years youth custody.
The learned Judge Robert Moore in his wisdom told Frost: "You have taken
away one life and ruined the lives of two families." Acting police inspector
Graham Sayner said later: "The maximum sentence in a case like this is ten
years and he was given a quarter of that. I'm sure Jade's family will not be
happy with that."

Student Jack Elliott, 17, died at a party after taking the biggest overdose of
ecstasy ever recorded, an inquest was told. Friends said they thought he had

taken at least 11 tablets of the drug. But a post-mortem examination revealed he had a level of ecstasy of 10,420 milligrammes per litre of blood. The pathologist said: " There is a case of 7,720mg per litre of blood and this was found in a patient who had allegedly taken 42 tablets. It is impossible to say how many tablets he had actually taken, but at the very least he had taken 11." The inquest heard that the A-level student, who died of multiple-organ failure, had been *desperate* to get hold of the drug. He met up with friends at a pub in his home village of Curdridge, near Southampton. Later there was an all-night party at the £500,000 family home of one of his friends. Detective Constable Martyn Allen told the Winchester inquest that Jack had bought a bag of 20 tablets with a friend, before going out for the night. "Jack had already had four whiskies and a pint of lager and smoked cannabis at the party. The friends were dancing to music and taking ecstasy. By the time of Jack's death it would appear he had taken 11 tablets. At 6am the following day, two of Jack's friends found him on the floor and noticed the blotchy colour of his skin. They had put him on a sofa earlier after finding him shaking and shivering. An ambulance was called and Jack was pronounced dead at the scene." The inquest was told that all of Jack's friends were arrested and one was charged with drug offences. Elspeth Cook who had been at the party said: "I am aware that Jack had taken nine tablets on one occasion. It was at New Years Eve and he had been on his own and had taken them throughout the day. We were shocked." The student, at Peter Symonds College, Winchester, had been due to go to Oxford Brookes University. Coroner Grahame Short said: "It was a tragic waste of a young life." and recorded a verdict of accidental death.

Police in Liverpool have celebrated the seizure of a huge shipment of cannabis worth £35 million. Seven suspects were questioned after 7.2 tonnes of the drug were found hidden inside marble fireplaces on two freight containers. The massive shipment, packed in brick-size slabs, was seized in raids at Seaford Docks in Liverpool. A Customs & Excise spokesman said the haul, believed to come from Morocco, was the biggest ever in Merseyside. He added: "We're very pleased. This is going to hit a lot of people in the criminal world hard and is the result of good intelligence." Customs carried out the raid with Merseyside Police's Middle Market Drugs Unit, after a long-running operation. Detective Chief Inspector Mark Matthews, head of the MMDU said: "This is another successful operation against organised drug-traffickers operating within Merseyside. We're working hard to reduce drug availability on our streets and to arrest the dealers."

A criminal who tried to go straight by having his face covered with tattoos, including the words *'Shame on me'* is back in jail. Nigel Clack, 43, a career criminal, of Witnesham, Suffolk, who has 56 convictions for robbery, assault and theft, said tattoos would make him go straight because he would be so easily recognised. But Clack, a drug addict, punched a deaf man and broke his jaw. And sure enough, police instantly recognised him from the description. Clack was jailed for 12 months at Ipswich.

The father of a former public school boy who masterminded a £50 million cocaine empire, blamed his son's teenage cannabis smoking for his descent to international criminal. After Julian Whiteway-Wilkinson, 32, from the fashionable part of London's East End, was jailed for 12 years, his father Juan, 53, an antique dealer and property developer, condemned the pot-taking craze among the young. But as his son was taken to prison, his once-estranged father vowed to stick by him. He said: "I think anybody would be shocked by what has happened. It goes totally against all my own values. I'm very disappointed he has taken this route in life. Julian is a very strong character. I'm sure he will be okay and he will have full family support behind him." His son's two public school-educated accomplices were also sent to prison with him. James Long, 31, a former merchant banker, was jailed for nine years and jazz pianist Tom Connell, 30, was sentenced to eight years. The three men had admitted conspiracy to supply cocaine. A fourth member of the gang, state-educated cable engineer Milroy Nadarajah, 32, admitted the same charge and was sentenced to seven years. The court heard that champagne-swigging 'Jules' Whiteway-Wilkinson ran the drugs racket like a *white-collar business*. Customers for their top-quality cocaine, ecstasy and cannabis were said to include London City high-fliers and leading figures in the showbusiness and music industries. The gang had luxury homes in the East End of London, drove top-of-the range cars and spent fortunes on their girlfriends, foreign holidays and their passion for antiques. Mr Whiteway-Wilkinson said his son's cannabis habit took hold when he was a sixth-former at the £18,000-a-year Blundell's School in Devon. The millionaire businessman, who is separated from his wife, said: "It's most unfortunate, it's not a nice thing to happen. I did have my suspicions that all was not well before, but I have not spoken to my son for a long time. I didn't know anything about it. Julian is a well-loved boy who has gone off the rails. I think what started Julian off of was taking cannabis in his late teens and paying for the habit by selling to his friends. It has got out of control. He has not been helped by having a non-united family. Things haven't worked out in that direction." His son's drugs racket lasted for at least a decade but was finally smashed in September 2003 in a joint operation by the Metropolitan Police and Customs Officers. Detectives hope to confiscate £4.5million from the gang. But it is believed that the racketeers may have salted away fortunes in overseas bank accounts ready for when they are released. In one year alone, Whiteway-Wilkinson and his accomplices grossed £6.9million.

Norwich Crown Court was told that a gang trying to smuggle cocaine into Britain from Columbia, stitched £126,000 worth of the drug into the stomachs of two dogs. But the plot was uncovered when the Labradors were seen to be acting strangely and were checked by a vet at Amsterdam's Schipol airport,while waiting for a flight to Stansted. X-rays showed 21 packets of cocaine weighing 2.5lbs had been implanted into their stomach cavities. One of the dogs had to be put down because the packets had fused to its abdominal wall. Sophia McPherson, 24, a student, Gregory Graham, 27, of Harrow, Middx, Kaye Chapman, 20, also of Harrow and Glenroy Kentish, 28, of Hitchin, deny conspiracy to import the drug between September and October 2003. The court heard how Dutch customs officials contacted the Metropolitan Police, who set up a *sting* to find those collecting the dogs once they reached Stansted. A woman calling herself Kerry Williams, who the prosecution claims was Chapman, contacted an undercover police officer about picking up the animals. The jury was told McPherson was taken to the airport by Graham, with whom she had been having a relationship, and was arrested. Graham and Kentish were picked up in a nearby lay-by and Chapman was arrested later. McPherson told the court she was collecting the dogs as a favour to her boyfriend.

The finalisation of the above case actually took place at Kings Lynn Crown Court on 1st September 2004. Gregory Graham was sentenced to ten years imprisonment and Kaye Chapman was sentenced to seven years imprisonment.

It has emerged that Harold Shipman charmed a female pharmacist into unwittingly helping him stockpile enough heroin to kill 800 patients. From the day he set up his GP surgery in Hyde, Greater Manchester, Shipman set out to *chat up* and befriend Ghislaine Brant who worked at the chemist's next door. His ploy worked, and between 1992 and 1998, he got his hands on more than 24,000 milligrams of diamorphine, the pharmacological equivalent of heroin, without suspicion. A 30mg dose is fatal to someone not used to the effects of the powerful painkiller. Mrs Brant, 47, was criticised for failing to question Shipman's demands for large quantities of the drug, and for not reporting him to the Authorities. In the fourth report from the Shipman Inquiry, chairman Dame Janet Smith said Mrs Brant had 'lost her professional objectivity' when dealing with the family doctor who, during that time, used the drug to murder at least 143 of his patients. She recommended an overhaul of the laws relating to controlled drugs and called on the Government to establish a Drugs Inspectorate to prevent a case like Shipman recurring. Dame Janet said Shipman, who killed at least 215 people over 23 years, stole the diamorphine by prescribing it for patients who did not need it, or by over-prescribing it. Because there was little regulation surrounding such dangerous drugs, his activities were allowed to go unnoticed. However, she said, Mrs Brant should have picked up on an *unusual* pattern when Shipman prescribed 14 single 30mg ampoules in the names of 13 different patients over a seven-month period in 1993. Mrs Brant told the enquiry: "I would check up sometimes but out of interest rather than mistrust. There was always a plausible explanation." Dame Janet said Mrs Brant trusted Shipman implicitly: "He almost certainly groomed her", she added. "He chatted her up, he flattered her, he asked her advice. I've no doubt that Shipman deliberately set out to win her confidence and deceive her." Mrs Brant's husband Ian said: "My wife has been totally devastated by this." Dame Janet also criticised Detective Constable Patrick Kelly, whose job it was to inspect chemists in Hyde during the 1990's, for not noticing the unusual prescriptions. She concluded that if either he, or Mrs Brant had reported Shipman, it is likely lives could have been saved. Shipman, 57 was jailed for life in 2000 for 15 murders. He committed suicide in his jail cell in January 2000.

Jailed boxing champ Nicky Booth, 24, opened his heart from prison to reveal how drug addiction led him into a squalid life of crime. Booth invited the *News of the World* to visit him at Ashwell Prison in Rutland to reveal why he plunged in to the sordid world of crack cocaine and ended up jailed for burglary. But the former British and Commonwealth bantamweight champion vowed: "I'm clean now and I want my titles back. I'll never, ever take drugs again. If anybody comes near me offering stuff when I'm free, I'll knock them out." Booth wants his dramatic fall from grace to serve as a grim warning to fellow fighters. He confessed how he squandered £30,000 on crack. He was sucked into an underworld of drugs dealers and hardened criminals, and turned to burglary to feed his addiction.

Booth sat in the visitors' area at Ashwell, where he is serving a two-year sentence for theft, and admitted: "Prison was the best thing that could have happened. Coming here has saved my career and made me realise I have to start a new life from scratch. I never want to come back inside. When I come out the only thing I will have is the bag that I'll be carrying my clothes in. All my savings and ring earnings have gone. But now all I think about is boxing again. Getting back in the ring is what drives me on." Booth's world fell apart when he was sentenced to two years imprisonment in May 2004 for theft and burglary. And he admitted: " I can't even remember anything about the crime which led to my conviction. I just pleaded guilty. Under the drugs' influence, I didn't have any fear about what I did. Sometimes I was like a zombie. I got in with some bad company and I am certain it would have become even worse. I learned there were guns to be had and I could easily have got into that, but that would have led to a five or ten-year stretch. There were crack houses and dealers everywhere. I just had to walk a couple of minutes from my house to find drugs. But I hate myself for all the trouble and stress I have caused my parents. I'm ashamed of what I did to my mum and dad, yet they have stuck by me. I don't want to do anything else to let them down, especially mum as she has a heart problem. But I haven't got any friends anymore, I'm on my own now. I have decided I'm going to look after number one and aim to secure a future for my four-year-old daughter Paris. I split from her mother last year after six years together. That made me really low. I suppose she could see what was coming. I'd become fed up with boxing and wasn't training with enthusiasm. A fight I desperately wanted with Johny Armour kept falling through and that got me annoyed. I'm normally extrovert but instead I was feeling depressed and started going out. The first puff of the crack pipe that was handed to me was to cheer me up. It didn't do anything but I still tried another one, and that's how it started. It can take a week, a month or a year but once crack gets to you, you're hooked. There's no escape and you don't care about anything else. It was £5 or £10 for a hit and it soon adds up when you go from one buzz to wanting another, I got through thousands. I knew some working girls who were making £300-£400 a day. They would spend it on drugs and then give me some. Luckily, my trainer kept my Lonsdale Belt I won outright when I was British champion, and wouldn't let me accept the £8,000 I was offered for it. I went from having massive highs to having my chin on the floor. I had spells of anxiety and used to take sleeping tablets to calm me down. Now I can tell a crackhead from 100 yards." Booth also revealed that he only stopped taking crack a week before his last fight. That was back in September 2003, a WBU bantamweight title clash against Nathan Sting in Booth's home town of Nottingham. Booth, who followed in his brother Jason's footsteps in 2000 by winning a British title, admitted: "I didn't want to go through with it. I felt like it wasn't me in there. I had come off the crack a week before I fought. I had been told it clears from your system in two days but my heart wasn't in the fight." Booth lost in 12 rounds and only eight months later he lost his freedom as well. But now he is determined to get back in the ring, even if it means fighting with an electronic tag on his ankle. He said: "I am training 24/7 inside and the support I've had here has been tremendous. I've even dreamed of being allowed to box while tagged. If I could fight at 8.30pm, I'd be finished by 9.30pm, enough time to beat my curfew."

Many people right across this country, if not throughout the world, will perhaps be delighted to hear that *Royal Love Rat*, aka *The Cad*, disgraced former Household Cavalry Officer James Hewitt, has apparently received his comeuppance at last. During the evening of 22nd July 2004, he was seen in the company of a TV presenter in Central London restaurants and bars, by a press photographer. The pair appeared to be on a fashionable 'binge-drinking' session. The photographer could hardly believe his luck because he was able to record for posterity a whole montage sequence of photographs. Included were images of Hewitt, former lover of Princess Diana for several years, engaging in ordering by mobile telephone, a supply of packeted white powder, thought to be cocaine. The photographer, or one of his colleagues, made several calls to the police, one of which was eventually answered by a small squad of CID officers with uniformed back-up. Hewitt was publicly searched in the street and the suspected drugs were found in his pocket. He and his girlfriend were handcuffed and led away to a local police station where they spent the night, in separate cells of course. Next day when they were sober, they were interviewed and later released on bail whilst the white powder is scientifically analysed. He, for being found in possession of Class A drugs, and his TV presenter girlfriend, on suspicion of supplying him with the suspected cocaine. Hewitt's awful facial expressions in his embarrassment at being caught apparently red-handed, will bring a smile to many people around the world who were disgusted with the way he dealt with the aftermath of Lady Diana's death, viz: earning fortunes from spilling the beans and giving away all the special between-lovers secrets, to say nothing of internationally attempting to auction their love letters to the highest bidder! No doubt the member of the paparazzi who secured these priceless, real-live action images, will earn a small fortune from them once they are syndicated around the world.

The girlfriend concerned was Alison Bell, a former girlfriend of Prince Edward. On the day following his arrest for possession of suspected cocaine, he was again pictured in the national press, this time with a different blonde on his arm. They first visited the bars where he had been arrested the night before. (well, police had seized his white powder stocks, maybe he needed more!) They then attended a huge Game Fair at Blenheim Palace, Oxon, where the national press and 109,000 *Hooray-Henries* found him again. This time he was wearing his Calvin Klein *shades*, a huge Stetson-type 10-gallon straw hat and an eye catching suede or chamois waistcoat, perfect for leathering-off a stretch limousine on a Sunday morning! You and I would have been too ashamed to be seen in public so soon, would have kept a low profile and de-greased the oven or mended the dripping tap in the utility room, too embarrassed even to pick up the ringing telephone without first monitoring the voices on the ansafone. On the other hand, Hewitt might have just been following the advice of world famous Publicist Mr Max Clifford, to brazen it out as a picture of innocence, until he had been proven guilty in a court of law. The Household Cavalry, his old Regiment, must be cringing and hanging their heads in shame. No wonder one of their troopers was injured in falling off his horse and probably denting his shiny breastplate as well as his pride, at the 2004 Trooping The Colour ceremony. He must have spotted Forced-To-Resign-Ex-Major James Hewitt in the crowd, forcing involuntary arm movements on the reins, and his black charger horse to shy. Speaking personally, as a former Royal Marine, Hewitt's parents must have disowned/disinherited him after all of his antics in recent years, his father is a former Royal Marines Officer, so I can just imagine what they must be going through.

UPDATE: Subsequently Hewitt escaped jail, as the police and CPS appeared to have decided that the quantities of cocaine found in his possession, were insufficient to warrant possession with intent to supply, but deemed as *for own, personal use,* or words to that effect.

A brilliant young scientist who turned to drug dealing because he was bored with research work, has appeared at Newcastle Crown Court. Millionaire's son Frazer Goodwillie, 24, of Heaton, Newcastle, was found in possession of cocaine, cannabis, ecstasy and £20,000 in cash, when police raided the £200,000 town house bought for him by his parents. His lawyer said that Goodwillie had been a model son and student, but after completing his master's degree in natural science, he found research work at Newcastle University 'dispiriting and empty' and he turned to drugs. The court heard that he would use his expensive Toyota 4 x 4 to deliver drugs to various customers at their homes over a period of several months. He admitted nine drugs charges, including possessing cocaine with intent to supply. Further court action could see him stripped of every penny and possession which his illegal drug trafficking brought him. A confiscation hearing will be held in September 2004, and Goodwillie has been ordered to hand over all details of his assets, including bank accounts which remain frozen. I will try to report the result of what happens there to Goodwillie, God willing. Judge Guy Whitburn jailed him for just three and a half years and said: "It's very unusual for the courts to deal with somebody like you. You are highly educated and come from a devoted and affluent family. It has to be shown that those who, like you come from a background where you have had every advantage, will be dealt with severely."

(**Author's note:** *That might be Judge Whitburn's idea of 'being punished* *severely', and made an example of, but it's not mine, is it yours? If you are cynical, like me, I'll bet you are chuckling to yourself, wondering just what sort of pre-sentence lecture Judge Guy Whitburn would have delivered to disgraced Judge David Selwood, We can of course, predict, with some certainty, that the sentence would have been a low-key, non-custodial, community penalty one, delivered under the Old Pals Act.)*

Lord Freddie Windsor, 24, wayward son of the Duke and Princess Michael of Kent, once confessed to snorting cocaine. His mother stated publicly that she was 'blown away' and their lives were thrown into disarray, when son Freddie, 28th in line to the throne, admitted taking the cocaine at university. He was found slumped on the steps of a club in the year 2000. He admitted snorting cocaine and apologised to his Royal parents, vowing never to touch it again. Princess Michael said that she had always been a strict parent to Freddie and his sister, Lady Gabriella. "My children have always been very anti-drugs so when my son was accused of taking cocaine in his first year at Oxford I was blown away." She said that Royal Rebel Freddie was talking against drugs when challenged by a group of people who would not listen to him because he had not tried the drug. He took the cocaine to silence them, his mother claimed. She said she believed him because: "he has never lied to us". Freddie is now studying to be a solicitor, after abandoning plans to become a barrister. He also writes a rock column for the Tatler.

On the 22nd July 2004 a woman was accused of drugging four City businessmen and stealing tens of thousands of pounds of property from them. Selina Hakki, 37, of Bow, East London, appeared at London's Middlesex Guildhall Crown Court. She stands charged with four counts of administering a stupefying or overpowering drug, Rohypnol, with intent to enable herself to commit theft. She also faces four further counts of theft. She allegedly 'stupefied' the 4 men with the so-called date-rape drug. Once they had been 'overpowered', she pocketed high-value watches, clocks, clothes and a video camera. She also took cigars, aftershave, a backpack, cash held in money clips, and bottles of wine and champagne from them, it is claimed. Hakki is accused of slipping the drugs into her alleged victims' drinks after meeting them at bars and hotels in London's wealthy Mayfair. Her alleged victims, named as John Estill, Volker Vogler, Henry Okereke and Alexander Jovy, are all expected to testify against her at the crown court in December 2004. The smartly dressed defendant spoke only to confirm her name and address, at the short remand hearing. She denied all of the charges against her. Judge Simon Smith released her on conditional bail until 13th December 2004. Until then she must remain on bail on condition that she resides at her home address. She must also observe a nightly curfew between the hours of 9pm and 7am. As she appears to have played for high stakes in deliberately selecting MAYFAIR as the venue, if convicted, she is going to need more than a 'Get Out Of Jail Free' card and will almost certainly 'Go to jail – Move directly to jail – without passing 'GO' or collecting £200!

On the very next day after Selena Hakki's remanded court appearance for those very serious charges reported above, a STUDY was launched to try to determine the true extent of drug rape. Apparently nine police rape centres will use analysis of suspicious drinks and victim questionnaires to compile statistics on the crime. The Roofie organisation, which was set up to help victims of drug rape, says it has received around 6,000 calls from both women and men since 1997. But Detective Chief Superintendent Dave Gee, from Derbyshire, who is spearheading the initiative, said: "At present there is a lack of valid data showing the prevalence of this kind of offence. There is no definitive test to identify specific drugs in drinks or bodily fluids." I wish them every success in their STUDY . I would have found it particularly interesting, even at this early stage, to have seen a breakdown of Roofie's 6,000 telephone calls to date, broken-down into year-by-year figures from 1997 to date, and as to the numbers of male and female callers. However, it's almost certain that major drugs manufacturing companies and their equipment suppliers are already going all-out to be the first providers of Mr Gee's 'definitive test' device.

UPDATE: In the Crown Court on 17th January 2005, Hakki sobbed in the dock after the jury found her guilty of doping businessmen with the sedative date rape drug Rohypnol. The evidence included the fact that her DNA was found on cigarette butts from cigarettes she had smoked in the flats, together with her fingerprints having been found on a glass. She became the first woman to have been convicted in the UK of administering the drug to men, with the intention of robbing them, in her case.

It was reported in the national press on 28th August 2004 that ten members of the Queen's Troop of ceremonial bodyguards are to be sacked for failing random drugs tests. The soldiers, all from the Household Cavalry Mounted Regiment, were caught in a dawn raid on their Knightsbridge Barracks in Hyde Park. Testers carried out urine tests on the 146-strong unit and found ten members were positive. The ten, among them at least one woman, have been confined to barracks. Two are said to be contesting the results. The 870-strong regiment is responsible for ceremonial duties at state and royal occasions, effectively working as bodyguards for the Queen. A Ministry of Defence spokeswoman confirmed: "The 10 soldiers have been confined to their barracks and are facing discharge."

On Tuesday 12th May 2004, Home Secretary David Blunkett provoked an angry backlash after telling the public not to 'grumble' about drug dealers and anti-social behaviour. He was accused of 'living in cloud cuckoo land' after telling long-suffering communities that they could not blame the police for the scourge. He said the public should take responsibility for the problems in their areas, rather than 'grumbling' at the authorities. He told the Association of Chief Police Officers' conference: "The days have gone when we could blame someone else." He said the police now have the powers to close down drug dens, impose curfews and temporarily shut rowdy pubs. But he added that police action should be "matched by a response from the community who, instead of grumbling, will see themselves as in partnership with the police, overcoming what is happening in every community in this country, a breakdown of respect, a breakdown in the culture of belonging." But Liberal Democrat Home Affairs spokesman Mark Oaten said: "The Home Secretary is living in Cloud-Cuckoo Land if he thinks that law-abiding citizens are going to take on violent drug dealers. It is the police's job, not the public's job, to rid communities of this scourge." Mr Blunkett went on to recall his childhood in Sheffield. He said: " We didn't have the scourge of drugs, the needles on the street." But Shadow Home Secretary David Davis said the Government had failed to resolve the problems surrounding alcohol and crime. He claimed that the charge of drunk and disorderly was rarely used, that under-age drinking was ignored and that only a few pubs had been closed for repeated offences. "The Government has made no effort to encourage the police to use the powers they already have to deal with drink-fuelled crime and has no answer as to how policing will change with the relaxation of opening hours. A wait-and-see attitude will not do."

The full cost of organised drug crime was revealed for the first time – a £20,000 kilogram of heroin would lead to a staggering 220 burglaries, as addicts stole to pay for their fix. The cost to the community caused by the single kilogram was estimated at £250,000, as the British 'FBI' announced a team of top lawyers to target gangster bosses. Details of the specialist team of prosecutors were outlined by the Attorney General, Lord Goldsmith. They will work with the new Serious Organised Crime Agency staff, right from the start of an investigation all the way through to presenting the case in court. They will also be responsible for implementing new powers to bring previously untouchable gangland bosses to justice. Under the Serious Organised Crime and Police Bill, the new prosecutors will be able to issue disclosure notices, which compel people to answer questions if they have information of 'substantial value' to an investigation. They will also be able to offer suspects immunity from prosecution or a reduced sentence if they become a supergrass or turn so-called 'Queen's evidence' by testifying against their partners in crime. Lord Goldsmith said the prosecutors were a vital part of the Government's new strategy to combat organised crime, which costs Britain £20billion a year. "The decisions by those involved in prosecuting organised crime have a real effect on the lives of the British people," he said. He added: "We want to make the UK one of the least attractive locations in the world for organised crime to operate. Prosecution is a vital part of our strategy. It is the way to put criminals out of circulation for a long time and confiscate their assets. Above all, prosecution is the way to increase the personal risk for criminals, especially the criminal kingpins."

The new specialist cadre will be drawn from the existing ranks of prosecutors and from trial lawyers in private practice. They will be based within the Crown Prosecution Service and the Revenue and Customs Prosecution Office when it is established later this year. The Director of Public Prosecutions, Ken Macdonald, said prosecutors had to abandon 'timidity' and 'wield every new weapon' available to tackle the growing menace of organised crime. He said: "Organised criminals, alongside terrorists, pose the greatest challenge to law enforcement agencies, prosecutors and the wider criminal justice system. Organised criminals are resourceful, well-financed and innovative in their exploitation of new opportunities, new criminal markets and new technologies. "We must be creative in developing robust prosecution structures to respond powerfully to the new challenges." The 5,000-strong crime agency will attempt to crack down on drug gangs, people-traffickers, major fraudsters and internet paedophiles.

She is known as much for her violent outbursts as for her catwalk skills, and supermodel Naomi Campbell has finally given a reason for her famous short fuse – cocaine abuse. "You become short tempered, you know," says statuesque Campbell, who has been known to use her staff as target practice. "What is very scary about cocaine is that you start to feel too confident and you start to feel indispensable." Now 34 and resolutely clean, the Streatham-born mannequin says she feared her drug use would kill her. "Something would have happened, some self-destructive thing," she says in a candid US television interview "I mean, there are kids now having heart attacks at 21." *Narcotics Anonymous* regular, Campbell first took cocaine around 10 years ago. "No one forced me. I did it because I wanted to," she says. 'It wasn't fun for long. I was very, very low, to the bottom of the barrel because of that drug. Your little charm goes. The little glow in your face goes. It's a very nasty drug." Her employees would no doubt agree. Three years ago police were called after her maid Millicent Burton claimed she slapped her. About the same time, her personal assistant Simone Craig accused Campbell of holding her hostage in a hotel, hitting her and hurling a phone at her. She was also accused of using her mobile as a missile in 1998 by assistant Georgina Galanis, who said she'd hit her with it and threatened to throw her from a moving car. Campbell was charged, pleaded guilty and ordered to attend anger management classes. In 1993 her US agent Elite wrote in an open letter: "We do not wish to represent Naomi Campbell any longer. No amount of money or prestige could justify the abuse imposed on our staff and clients." Campbell says she now has a constant battle to stay off cocaine. "I don't want to be in that pain again," she says. "But there's always a moment when you want to self-destruct and I don't know what it is."

COUNT 7

SCHOOLS
CRIMES INVOLVING PUPILS, STAFF AND PARENTS

I can't recall a single case of violence occurring in my infants, juniors, or primary schools, all of which were in north London. The closest I came to it was on a cold winter's day in Fleet Road, Hampstead when we made a playground 'slide' on the ice. When it was time for me to have my second go, I was racing halfway along it when another boy decided to kneel down across the slide, right in my path. The result was predictable, I was catapulted into the air, carried out an involuntary double somersault and landed on my head on the hard playground tarmac. I was rushed to the Royal Free Hospital, Hampstead and kept in bed in the Childrens' Ward for several days, suffering from concussion, and subsequently discharged with little or no after effects. The boy responsible received a ticking-off from the duty playground-minding teacher and that was the end of that. No threats to sue the Education Authority, no racing round to the boy's house by my parents threatening to burn their house down, no police involvement, no ruler taps on the open hand or thigh slap for the boy, no erection of razor wire fences and electronic gates, pupil swipe cards, CCTV cameras – none of that was required because common sense and respect for others prevailed, and had been drilled into teachers and pupils alike, in those days.

What a happy world it was then, but successive governments over the years have allowed liberalism and indiscipline to prevail in schools and everywhere else.

Later on, between the ages of 11 and 16 years, I was lucky enough to have passed my 'Scholarship' and attended a grammar school for boys in the Romford area of Essex. The school had very strict discipline regimes in place, involving the ultimate sanctions of receiving the cane from the Head or Deputy Head. Other staff members punished unruliness by issuing orders to *write out lines*, such as *I must behave in class at all times* etc., 50 or 100 times or more. One maths teacher dictated a *line*, or rather a *paragraph* which ran into four-five lines of an exercise book, to be written out the designated number of times. The only way to cope with this imposition was to secure three or more pens together with string or elastic bands! Some other male teachers imposed corporal punishment, by literally *boxing your ears*. One absolute sadist, a french master, if you offended, even by just not listening, would stride purposefully over to your desk. Whilst you were seated, he would take hold of the hair of your sideboards, shake your whole head and neck and slowly drag you to your feet, and then all of the way down again to the seated position. I was a recipient of this *barbarism* at least once, so I can still recall the extreme pain level. This really was what is now described as *cruel and inhumane treatment*, as your head hurt and your eyes literally watered, for just about the rest of the lesson. When you saw this cruelty being applied to another boy, there was a hushed silence in the classroom. I have to admit it was an effective deterrent to us all, to behave ourselves in his lessons.

This school had the advantage of running its own CCF (Combined Cadet Force) with Army, Naval and RAF sections. With friends I joined the Army section and received my uniform and was disciplined by some school masters who were officers and wore the appropriate uniforms with pips or stars on the epaulettes.

We paraded often and went away on Army courses in the school holidays, attended Army camps under canvas and received all the appropriate badges and promotional stripes etc. All of this gave us a great sense of purpose in life, and a spirit of discipline and comradeship and kept us off the streets. Concurrently to this, I joined a local boys marching band at Romford, and received yet another uniform for my mother to press. Sometimes, on occasions such as Remembrance Day parades, I was undecided as to which unit's uniform to put on, so as not to let the other side down. Membership of these military-style organisations, as a child and youth, later steered me into joining the Royal Marines on a regular engagement. Here I received the best discipline training of my life – and never looked back.

Whilst I was stationed at Hornchurch police station, attached to CID, we had been plagued with many cases of serious burglaries, thefts and vandalism at local schools, all of which had to be thoroughly investigated. We plotted the attacks on the schools on a chart, which revealed the approximate days, dates and times of day when the schools were being raided. Eventually, one of our uniformed colleagues, who was a Home Beat officer, picked up a strong lead. This developed into a major clear-up of almost every single offence which had taken place. A huge round-up of schoolboys took place, and we all shared in the glory and the hard work in having them all processed and eventually brought to court. The clear-ups had snowballed because each child arrested, became anxious to mitigate their criminal liability by naming other boys who had not yet been interviewed or arrested, and so it went on. The amazing thing was that all of the boys were quite gentle-natured, and with very supportive parents in all cases, in stark contrast to some parents of today, who race up to the school and confront, or even assault the teaching staff! Two of the boys were the children of two now-famous male stand-up comedians. Unfortunately, one of those latter boys later committed suicide using a shotgun.

Please read on to compare what used to happen in schools, to what happens now, in the years 2004 and 2005.

Furious teachers are threatening to strike because their school has been told it must take back a teenager who was kicked out after attacking a member of staff. This is the latest in a long line of school decisions being overturned by appeal panels, despite pledges by the Government to back the teachers. Ta'Lisha Edwards, 14, was permanently excluded from Becket comprehensive, a Roman Catholic school in Wilford, Nottingham, for slapping a teacher on the arm and being abusive. An independent appeal panel's decision to overturn the head teacher's ruling has now led to staff refusing to teach her, and may end in an official industrial dispute. More than 1,000 pupils will be affected if the 63 teachers go ahead with the move. The teachers say that their authority is being undermined and safety jeopardised. At least 10 teachers are refusing to teach the girl and are looking for support from the rest of the staff. All will be balloted about the next move and unions are not ruling out the possibility of strikes. The local education authority says Ta'Lisha could be moved to a different school if the dispute grows. It added, "We are liaising with the school and the family to agree a way forward." But their actions might prove to be too little too late after all three of the main teaching unions slated the appeal panel decision for undermining teachers. The NUT's Brian Helliwell said, "Ta'Lisha's expulsion was a *last resort* following a series of unacceptable incidents. The exclusion had not *come out of the blue*. He added, "These appeal panels don't know anything about schools or education. Teachers and pupils have a right to be free of violence." Ta'Lisha's mother Cecilia, 42, claimed her daughter was the victim, not the troublemaker and was only guilty of "cheek." Mrs Edwards added: "My daughter loved going to school, now I have to force her to go. She is due to start GCSEs in September and there's no compromise yet about her proper education." Ta'Lisha allegedly slapped a male teacher on the arm and shouted a torrent of abuse during a lunch break disturbance. Her family appealed against the punishment, arguing it was too harsh. The panel agreed.

Since the end of the half-term holiday, Ta'Lisha has been banned from classes, after teachers refused to have her in their lessons. Instead they have prepared study material for her and marked her work, leaving her supervised by an assistant. Ta'Lisha said: "It's not fair, I want to stay at the school. If I'm not taught by the teacher concerned then fair enough, but I don't see why all the teachers should get involved." Unions have long been critical of the appeals system, arguing it undermines Heads' powers. National Association of Head Teachers general secretary David Hart said: " The appeal panels are increasingly acting irresponsibly and this is yet another example. They are making outrageous decisions and I can understand why teachers are up in arms. They show pupils they can assault teachers with impunity. These panels don't live in the real world."

A man was fighting for his life after he was attacked while attending a school reunion in the car park at Belmont School in Chiswick, W.London. Richard Walters, 20, was hit over the head with an 8-foot wooden stake, after he and some friends had been in an argument with a group of teenagers.

A school bus carrying children as young as 11 was raided for drugs by police with sniffer dogs, at the Oldbury Wells School, Bridgnorth, Shropshire, just before 9am on 11th June 2004. More than 20 officers were waiting for the bus to arrive at the school. The 40 pupils on board were offered an amnesty from arrest, if they handed over any drugs before being escorted off the bus and filmed by police CCTV. Officers, acting on information that some children were selling-on drugs to other pupils, carried out searches in the grounds of the 1,000-pupil, mixed school. No drugs were found but police later claimed the operation had been a success.

A Head Teacher called in police when 100 pupils rioted after they were told they could not wear shorts. The 14 and 15-year-olds staged a demo after their request to ditch long trousers during hot weather was refused. When the protest spilled out of Rhyl High School, North Wales, onto the street, Head Mike Williams called in the police. Mr Williams said, "It wasn't a protest, it was a riot." Eight pupils were suspended. Joanne Dalziel, whose 13-year-old daughter Paige took part in the demo said, "The head over-reacted."

A gang of 50 screaming schoolgirls clashed with police at a train station as an operation to check tickets spiralled into chaos. Passengers watched in disbelief as the girls, aged between 12 and 17, turned on eight British Transport police officers *like a pack of screaming banshees*. In what was described as *a scene out of St Trinian's gone wrong*, one girl attacked an officer with an ironing board, as the police found themselves pressed as they tried to stop the group boarding a train. The battle broke out when pupils arrived at the station to find the hapless officers waiting to check tickets. Around 50 girls, who police say had no tickets, tried to rush the platform to board a waiting train at New Beckenham station in South London, while friends held the doors open. Officers tried to stop the crowd and violence erupted when two of the girls were grabbed. While one attacked with the ironing board, others leapt on the back of officers as they tried to arrest others. Girls already on the train pulled communication handles to stop it leaving. They were all pupils from Cator Park School for Girls, and were wearing a uniform of grey skirts, white blouses and blazers. Detective inspector Karl Skrzypiec said: "It was a very volatile situation, like something out of St Trinian's gone wrong. These girls were like screaming banshees. There was a huge amount of swearing, scratching, kicking and pushing. They were screaming so much abuse the officers couldn't use their radios to call for back-up. We managed to get the two arrested girls to a police van. They were screaming that they were going to be raped." Met police reinforcements arrived on the scene during the incident, as did Merrill Davies, Head of the 1,300 pupil school, and they managed to calm the furore. Ms Davies said: "The school is investigating what happened. If the behaviour of any girls fell below the high standard we expect of them, we will be taking firm action involving their parents." Mr Skrzypiec denied the officers had been racist or heavy-handed. He said: "The girls perceived it to be a racist attack. I can only surmise it was because most of them were black. But anyone without a ticket wasn't allowed on the platform. I think the officers showed remarkable restraint when confronted by the situation." But former teacher John Fowler said: "If the police hadn't been there, there wouldn't have been a riot. You don't treat teenage girls like that, certainly not in south London. Officers are examining CCTV footage to try to identify the ringleaders. The two arrested girls have been bailed.

A teenager who lost her voice after being bullied at school has spoken for the first time in 19 months. Sarah Fisher, 17, was reduced to whispering after being tormented by a group of 12 bullies at her old school. But her voice suddenly came back as she sat at home with boyfriend Liam Gooderham, 18. She says she can now finally put the past behind her and get on with her life. "It's really strange to have my voice back again. When I answered the phone again for the first time yesterday it was a very weird but very good feeling. I don't think about the bullies any more as so much has changed in the last year. Getting my voice back is the last step. I have finally beaten them. I didn't need any medication to cure the problem, I just needed to calm down and relax," she said. Sarah's mother Maria, a 37-year-old trainee teacher said, "Sarah came running up the stairs and said, 'I can talk' in a normal voice. It was an incredible feeling. The only trouble is that ever since that moment she hasn't shut up." Sarah says she was the target of endless name-calling and shoving at Horndean Technology College in Hampshire. Verbal attacks culminated in an e-mail from a bully who wanted to repeatedly run her down and watch her *head explode*. Sarah, of Clanfield, Hants, went to see a counsellor and attended speech therapy sessions in an attempt to get her voice back. But the torment continued when she returned to school. Despite police warning one of the bullies, the abuse went on and Sarah's mother removed her from the college. The teenager is now studying at Chichester College of Arts and Technology. She is doing AS-level exams in chemistry, human biology and music. Experts said her vocal chords were not damaged but she was psychologically stopped from speaking for fear of being bullied. At the time of the bullying, the Head Teacher of Horndean Technology College, Glen Strong, said, " We have a very strict bullying policy at the school and take it very seriously."

A teacher endured two years of hell at the hands of violent pupils as young as seven, who left her permanently disabled. Jo Redmond, 51, was punched in the stomach, hit with a fire extinguisher, urinated on and regularly thumped, kicked and spat on by groups of youngsters. She lost several teeth after being tripped by a pupil, one of her wrists was left *virtually useless* after being slammed in a door and she was cut taking a weapon, made from pencils and a piece of glass, from a pupil. Her injuries forced her to take early retirement and she was awarded £92,500 compensation in an out-of-court settlement with her employers – one of the biggest awards of its kind. They cannot be named for legal reasons and have not accepted liability. Mrs Redmond spoke out for the first time about her experiences, as fellow teachers warned that there is now *a culture of accepted violence* in many schools. The Association of Teachers and Lecturers' annual conference in Bournemouth heard that Head Teachers are failing to report incidents for fear of bad publicity. A survey of union members found that fewer than one in three violent incidents in schools is reported to police. Conference delegates called for all assaults to be reported. Mrs Redmond, who has more than 20 years experience working with special needs children, was employed for the last two years of her career at a Greater London school for children aged seven to fourteen with emotional and behavioural problems.

She said: "I was kicked, I was spat at, I had things thrown at me. I was assaulted when I tried to prevent children's work being destroyed. I was punched and urinated on. I suffered a severe wrist injury and now my left wrist is virtually useless. Some of these children were physically bigger than me. Sometimes it was individual children, sometimes it was groups of two or three at a time. There were things occurring on a daily basis. I got the impression that we were expected to accept it." Elizabeth Greed, a teacher at Lavington school in Devizes, Wiltshire, told the conference, "There is a culture of accepted violence in schools. We should be able to do a job without the risk and fear of abuse." And one teacher said he was asked by the chairman of his school governors to drop a criminal claim against a parent who broke down a door during an attempted assault. Phil Baker, 55, suffered post-traumatic stress as a result of the incident and left the school he had worked in for 27 years. He was given an undisclosed package. He told the conference he had refused to drop the action, but when the case came to court, the parent was given a conditional discharge and fined £100 for damaging the door.

Armed with CS gas, a truncheon and wearing a stab and bullet-proof vest, Police Constable Peter Jones is ready to patrol his beat – in a school. His role is to round up truants and arrest pupils who commit crimes during school hours. He patrols not only the school corridors but also the £40,000, 6ft-high, prison-style steel fence being built around Hengrove School in Bristol to keep pupils *in*. He is assisted by a bank of 24-hour CCTV cameras. PC Jones has already arrested nine pupils at the school, which has the sixth-worse attendance in the country, according to latest Government figures. At least 150 schools in England and Wales regularly employ police officers in direct response to the increasing number of attacks on teachers. According to unions, more than 5,000 staff are punched, kicked or verbally abused by pupils and parents every year. And staff at almost one in ten secondary schools fear pupils may be taking guns into class-rooms, according to *SecEd*, a newspaper for teachers. Dr Rona Tutt, president of the National Association of Head Teachers, said: "Heads feel forced to go down this route. We would never have dared dream that something like this could happen a few years ago. The idea of having police patrolling in schools has become acceptable and that is very sad. It is a terrible indictment of society." Explaining his role, PC Jones said: "When the kids arrive I'm on the school gate greeting them and making sure there is no trouble outside.

I've also made myself known to the local shopkeepers so they can call me if they see pupils truanting. I have had to arrest pupils for minor theft offences. I do carry the full police uniform, which includes CS spray and a truncheon, but fortunately I have never had to use them." The Home Office has given £30,000 funding as part of the Safer Schools Initiative to pay for PC Jones. Headteacher Stephen Murtagh said: "Having a uniformed officer had a positive effect on pupils. We still have high levels of absence but PC Jones has helped raise the awareness of pupils who might be either victims of crime or be on the border of criminal behaviour."

Mike Wilson, 53, of Balderton, Nottinghamshire, teaches religious education at the nearby Grove School. He lives with his wife Alison, also 53, a part-time music teacher. Three years ago, in 2001, he was the victim of an unprovoked attack by a pupil at his school, which left him with three broken ribs. He said: "It had been a long day and I was late for a meeting. I was on my way out and as I passed one of the boys, he lashed out at my chest. I was carrying a hard ring binder and the boy hit me so hard that the ring binder jammed into my ribs. Then he just ran off down the corridor. I was in pain and shock and all I could do was shout out after the boy, who was about 15, and tell him that I'd be reporting the incident the next day. I had no idea why he had attacked me so viciously. Later, I discovered that he had just come from the Head Teacher's office where he had been told off about a previous incident. Clearly upset about being disciplined, he'd lashed out at the first figure of authority he could find. Unfortunately that was me. I didn't realise until later how badly injured I was. When I got up the next morning, I couldn't move my left arm and there was a searing pain across my chest. I thought I was having a heart attack. I went to the doctor and he could tell from the pain I was in that the blow had broken three of my ribs. It took me weeks to fully recover, and as a member of the NASUWT teaching union, which runs an *Enough is Enough* campaign against violence towards teachers, I was determined to make sure the boy didn't get away with it. I reported the incident and the next day he was asked to leave school. The irony is that the school has a good reputation for discipline and, as someone who's taught there for 33 years, I'm known for maintaining firm discipline. This incident showed me that this sort of incident can happen to anyone, not just new or vulnerable teachers, and can still occur in some of the best schools. The local branch of our union recently carried out an anonymous survey of schools in the Nottinghamshire area, and discovered 63 recent examples of physical violence towards teachers. We lost count of the number who had suffered from extreme verbal abuse. Sometimes the attackers can be as young as 6 or 7. As many incidents go unreported because teachers are too upset to come forward, many victims have to face the horrible reality of teaching a class that contains a child who has assaulted them. The main problem is that, increasingly, children seem to regard this sort of violence as acceptable or normal. Partly, I blame television, which appears to be getting more violent all the time, while offering no real positive role models for kids."

Melanie Symonds, 46, has been teaching French and German for 12 years, for the past five at a church secondary school in West Sussex which she prefers not to name. She says: "I was walking down a corridor with children queuing on one side when I felt a terrible thump in my lower back. I knew who it was, a boy I had excluded from my class because he had disrupted lessons so badly. He was nearly 16 and 6ft tall, almost a foot taller than me. He had hit me with his heavy schoolbag and, when I turned around, he was lounging against a door grinning insolently. I was shaken and told him to go to the Deputy Head's office. My back hurt and I wanted to sit down and cry but I had to carry on teaching. The next day I saw an osteopath who told me the injury would heal but that it could have been much worse. I was sure that the boy would be appropriately disciplined, but the Deputy Head told me that he had denied everything, so it was my word against his – a boy who has been excluded three times, once for assaulting another pupil in a lesson in a fight over a girl. I was told that it was my responsibility to find witnesses because according to government guidelines, you have to have them to prove an assault. That's why teachers are so vulnerable. If you are accused of even touching a child you are guilty until proven innocent, but it seems that pupils are innocent until they admit to doing something wrong. The more often these attacks happen the more courage it takes to do the job. I came into teaching with a sense of vocation but my experience has really disillusioned me. At my last school we would regularly be told to f*** off. In the end you pretended not to hear it because you knew nothing would be done to punish them. I'm just grateful that I wasn't assaulted there, it was like a zoo. There were drug-addicted ex-pupils coming back to settle old scores. One child tried to throw himself off some railings on to a concrete floor 10 feet below and his friends had to talk him down."

Andy Mather, 28, is a science teacher at a school in Bolton in Greater Manchester, where he lives with his fiancée Estelle, 31, an electronics assembler, and her children aged 15 and 6. In 1997 he was the victim of violence at a school in Oldham. He says: "At the time of the attack, I was only 21 and had two days left of my teacher-training placement. I'd just got into a car with a female colleague, who'd offered me a lift home, when we saw a nasty fight at the school gates. One 15-year-old boy was beating and kicking another boy who was trapped by a railing. I went over and shouted at the boys to stop. I knew that I wasn't allowed to touch either of the boys or I would be accused of assault, but it would have been negligent to ignore the fight. All I could do was ask them to stop but as soon as I did, the attacking boy swore at me and started hitting me repeatedly in the face. A sports teacher came out and tried to help. He had a cricket bat in his hand. But instead of stopping, the aggressive child just turned on the sports teacher, punching him in the head and stealing his bat. He then ran after the other boy with the bat in his hand. The boy who was being attacked ran inside, but the other boy ran after him still brandishing the bat. The police were called. Thankfully, the boy who was being chased hid somewhere in the school and the aggressive boy was calmed down and the bat taken off him. Because the boy who had assaulted me was on study leave, the school could do little but ban him from doing his GCSEs at the school. He was also given a police caution for assault. It was a stark introduction to teaching. One of the main problems is that children have so many rights. They know how to threaten you with them and they know how difficult it is for us to do anything."

Killer Winston Silcott has sparked outrage by giving a talk to pupils as young as 12 about crime. Silcott, 44, who was convicted then cleared on appeal of the murder of PC Keith Blakelock, was part of a group who spent an afternoon working with children at Aylward School in Edmonton, North London. But Aylward's Head Teacher, John Keller, said he had no warning that Silcott, who served 18 years in jail for an unrelated killing, would be involved and insisted he would not have given permission for the visit had he known. Career criminal Silcott was invited into the school as part of the Haringey Peace Alliance's *Inside out* scheme. The school is only a mile from the Broadwater Farm estate in Tottenham, North London, where PC Blakelock was hacked to death during riots in 1985. Accompanied by HPA members including former policeman Bill Burns and convicted armed robber Steve Akorsa-Acquah, Silcott spoke to youngsters aged 12 to 14 who, it is feared, might join street gangs. Mr Keller said: "These were the sort of kids who could join a gang out there on the streets. Because of their discussions, it happened to be with Winston this time, they will now not join a gang. He was talking about the circumstances of being in prison and what can happen to get you there, not necessarily his guilt or otherwise, more to do with his life and choices he'd made." But Mr Keller had no idea that Silcott would be among the the HPA group. "In hindsight, had I known the sensitivity of the person coming we might have had to react differently. I talked to the chairman of governors and we agreed that we were disappointed that we didn't know that Winston was coming." Enfield Council leader Michael Rye, who is also a full-time teacher, said: "I was shocked to find out about this. I think it shows very poor judgement in allowing this man into the school. Winston Silcott is a convicted murderer but he has never admitted any responsibility for his crimes. He's certainly not a suitable role model for children." An NUT spokesman said: "There are surely more suitable people to bring into schools to work with kids." Silcott refused to comment on the row, but HPA chairman Pastor Nims Obunge said: " The project aims to highlight the negative implications of prison life to deter people at risk of offending. It does not make ex-offenders into role models. They are there as a warning." Silcott was convicted in 1987 of PC Blakelock's murder but cleared on appeal in 1991. In the meantime he had been jailed for the unrelated murder of amateur boxer Anthony Smith in 1984. He was released in October 2003 and plans to appeal against that conviction.

(**Author's note:** *You may remember seeing pictures of Silcott on pre-jail release short leave, wandering unaccompanied in shopping crowds. Whilst in jail he grew his beard almost unbelievably long, swearing that he would cut it off when his innocence had been proved. It was so long that he had to carry the beard around in a bag on his chest. In the photograph of Silcott accompanying the above press article, he is shown wearing an ordinary short bushy beard, although his innocence of the murder of the boxer has never been established. Silcott is about 6ft 4ins tall, so he stands out in a crowd. Whoever involved him in lecturing to young children in schools must be nuts. A serving or retired prison officer or probation officer could have made an excellent role model for these lectures, rather than a convicted murderer!*)

A school with one of the worst reputations in Britain has been forced to scour the world to find teachers brave enough to work there. A Deputy Head from Moorside High School in Swinton, Greater Manchester, had to fly to Canada to sign up new recruits. Paul Simpson had planned to find teachers in Australia, but a recruitment trip to Brisbane had to be scrapped because so few Australians applied for the jobs. So now Mr Simpson has found the 11 volunteers he needs in Toronto and they will be flown to Swinton for a week's training before the start of term in September 2004. It's easy to see why teachers are reluctant to work at Moorside. Around one in six of the 70 staff quit every year. Two years ago, 22 pupils and a teacher needed hospital treatment after an arson attack in which someone set fire to a stairwell. There is always a risk of violence, but not just among the pupils. Because of the danger of parents attacking teachers, mothers and fathers are not allowed into the school without an appointment. On any day, around 70 pupils don't turn up for lessons. Its truancy rate is five times the average.

Inspectors from the schools' watchdog Ofsted gave it a damning report. They told how the classrooms used by the 1,250 pupils were cramped and covered in graffiti, with plaster flaking off the walls and ceilings. But the report's greatest criticism was of the staff. It said: "Teaching was often dull, it did not inspire the pupils or expect enough of them." The leadership and management of the school by senior staff was described as *unsatisfactory*, though the inspectors did praise the efforts of the Headmaster Graham Rollinson. But in March 2004, Mr Rollinson, 51, who is married, resigned amid allegations he had been caught using a school computer to send indecent images of naked men, including himself, to staff at another school he used to work at. Despite everything, Mr Simpson is confident he has now found 11 good teachers from Canada capable of coping with life at Moorside. "We were extremely impressed by the quality of the candidates, they are all eagerly awaiting the challenge of teaching in another country," he said. He recruited four English teachers, half the department, three science teachers, plus staff for drama, technology, maths and PE. The Canadians have accepted 12-month contracts that could become permanent posts after that. A new Head has been appointed. Jill Baker, director of education and leisure at Salford City Council, said: "The advantage of looking further afield for a supply of good quality teachers, means we can counter the shortage facing many schools across the UK." But a spokeswoman for the National Union of Teachers said it was a short-term measure that would not solve Moorside's problems. "We believe that dropping teachers from abroad into a challenging school is not a great idea. If the management at this school is poor, as the Ofsted report suggests, the Canadians won't stay to work there long, just like the British teachers they are replacing."

Jennifer Abbot, 58, a teacher at a special school, lived *the life of a celebrity* by stealing more than £150,000 from the school funds of the Lancasterian School for Disabled Children, at Didsbury, Manchester. She indulged herself on holidays to Mauritius and the Caribbean and on designer goods. Meanwhile 90 children at the school had to endure leaky roofs and old books because of an apparent lack of school funds. Whilst acting as manager for the school's £1.5million budget, Abbot forged signatures on 157 cheques. The money she stole found its way into 26 separate bank accounts. At Manchester Crown Court she pleaded guilty to 20 counts of theft amounting to £150,000. Judge Martin Rudland told Abbot, "You acted in a scheming, dishonest, manipulative, calculated and cynical way. You went to Mauritius and took a friend with you. You spent it on Caribbean cruises and on trips in limousines, on highly expensive goods, with everything associated with the celebrity lifestyle. You took from the funds for a life you were using, as some sort of anaesthetic or comforter for other problems." Gordon Cole, prosecuting, said, "This defendant systematically stole money from the school. She manipulated the school computer system, placing false orders and forging signatures. She had total responsibility and was given special training on how to use the computer systems. The ramifications for the school were that the school roof needed repairing but could not be, because of lack of funds. Some rooms required ramps and there were difficulties purchasing books and other equipment." The court heard that Abbot, who has no previous convictions, suffers from severe depression and had attempted suicide a number of times. Her solicitor, Dennis Talbot, told the court that in her defence, £100,000 of her and her husband's money had gone as well. "This isn't just treating stolen money as though it meant nothing. It was her own money that was going as well. This is a woman who is behaving peculiarly. It is not just theft to live the high life. There is something wrong here. Her remorse could not be more deep." Judge Martin Rudland wasn't having any of that, apparently, no doubt he had heard it all many times before, out of the mouths of barristers and solicitors. On 23rd July 2004, he sentenced Abbot to a period of two years imprisonment. Not too high a price to pay by Abbot, after an investment of £150,000 of taxpayers' money!

Sinister Alan Pennell, 16, a moody teenager who rarely smiled, has been unmasked as a binge-drinking bully obsessed with knives and violent films. He had a long history of vicious attacks on his schoolmates. He was often in trouble with the law. Pennel, who boasted about his collection of knives, had been warned for assaulting a police officer. The spotty youth with a vicious temper was a timebomb waiting to explode, say experts. He had five incidents of violent behaviour logged on his record at Birkbeck School in North Somercotes, Lincs. The violence became more severe with each attack until he finally plunged his favourite flick-knife into the heart of 14-year-old Luke Walmsley, who instantly bled to death on the floor outside a school classroom, in November 2003. At Nottingham Crown Court on 27th July 2004, Mr Justice Goldring ruled that Pennell should be detained for life after he was convicted of Luke's murder, during a long, hotly-contested trial. He said the murder had been so savage that he could order the ban on naming Pennell to be lifted, because of *very legitimate public interest*. After the case, Luke's tearful mother Jayne, 41, said: "He was just an evil boy who was a bully. He bullied children. It was always younger children. He rode in a pack. He is a true bully. The older boys often picked on Luke because he was big for his age, and very sporty and clever. It was the same group all the time and Pennell was always among them. Some children take their own lives because they are being bullied. But Luke was killed because he dared to stand up to the bullies in his school." Pennell was raised by his father after his mother was killed in a car crash when he was six. She and her new partner had been 3 times over the drink-drive limit. As time passed, the boy would spend his time swigging lager or vodka and skulking around a local recreation ground. He would often have knives hidden in his belt. They came from a collection he kept in his bedroom. They included a machete with a foot-long blade, a flick-knife with a seven-inch blade, and a Swiss Army knife. He kept even more knives in a Portakabin in the garden where he hung around with his mates. When he was not in his den, Pennell loved to watch X-rated films, glorying in the scenes of violence. In real life, his love of violence was increasing.

The incidents on his school record included grabbing one pupil around the neck, being unruly on the school bus and grabbing another student around the throat. In the months before Luke's tragic death, Pennell was twice warned by police. He was reprimanded for jumping on the back of a constable who had gone to his house to arrest his sister's boyfriend. He was also given a final warning for punching another pupil from his school three times in the face, leaving him with a loose tooth and a swollen lip. Fellow pupils remember him as a monster. They could never recall him smiling, except once. When teacher Mrs Carol Mortimer confronted him after the stabbing of Luke, he held the blood-covered knife behind his back. She said later: " I took it off him. He was very calm, with what I would call a slight smile on his face, a smile without emotion." During his trial, the court heard from various pupil witnesses that he made various threats that he was going to 'get' Luke, or words to that effect. Whilst in the witness box giving evidence on his own behalf, under quite brisk cross-examination, he insisted that he simply "held" the knife towards Luke and that Luke had "walked on to it". He demonstrated his version of the knife action to judge and jury. The pathologist found that the thrust of the knife into Luke's chest had been so forceful that marks were made on his skin in the shape of some screws let into the flick-knive's hilt. Anyway the jury weren't having any of that and probably weren't too impressed with his 'not guilty' plea, given the huge strength of the prosecution's case. Furthermore, Luke's parents had to suffer the daily stress of the trial, so Pennell could have spared them all of that additional suffering. We will probably never know whose idea it was for the not guilty plea to be entered. Was it at his own insistence? Did his solicitor frame the defence case around a not guilty plea? Or was the plea made on his counsel's advice? After the jury found him guilty of the savage murder, his barrister, Sasha Wass,QC, told them how her client had been *gutted* by Luke's death but she said: "In our submission, there is much more to it. He is someone who has difficulty expressing his feelings. He has very, very deep feelings about the incident on November 4th 2003." Detective

Sergeant Sean Baxter said the stabbing was "a cowardly act." He added: "I am satisfied with the sentence because for a lad of his age (16) to get a minimum term of 12 years is quite high. He doesn't actually get out after 12 years, he has to show some remorse. It was an unprovoked, callous and cowardly attack, while Luke Walmsley stood no chance whatsoever."

Later, after conviction, his defence lady barrister had the absolute nerve and cheek, in front of the dead boy's parents, to ask the judge not to NAME the killer, as that would *add* to his already severe sentence. She said that *naming* Pennell would involve unnecessary vilification and punishment in addition to his 12 year custodial sentence. Can you really believe she said that? These lawyers are literally a law unto themselves. Pennell's QC should feel ashamed of herself after opposing the judge's intention to be about to name and shame Pennell.

A violent gypsy threatened to mow down his childrens' Head Teacher in his car after driving up to the school and challenging her to "RUN". Bare-knuckle boxing champion Eli Frankham, who is 6ft 5ins and weighs 21 stone, faces jail after admitting harassing Head Teacher Rachel Voss and dinner lady Jane Plumb, who needed police protection afterwards. Terrified Mrs Voss, of 176-pupil Anthony Curton School in Norfolk, told magistrates of one occasion when Frankham arrived at her office unannounced. She said he told her, " I have told my missus to do you, and if she does not do you, I will." Frankham, heir to the title King of the Gypsies, made headlines when he was accused of intimidating jurors by glaring at them during the trial of farmer Tony Martin, who shot dead a 16-year-old burglar from a travelling family. The court at Kings Lynn heard how Frankham and his wife Vanessa threatened and intimidated Mrs Voss over a month. It began after Mrs Frankham complained about their children being bullied. Gwen Wallace, prosecuting, said: "Mrs Frankham spoke with Mrs Voss and she twice physically pushed her out of the way. She was shouting and abusive to Mrs Voss and the police were called. The situation worsened when Mrs Voss excluded three of the Frankham's children from a football tournament for bad behaviour. At one stage, she and dinner lady Jane Plumb were so concerned about threats from the Frankhams that they had to be escorted home by police. But events took *a far more sinister tone* after Mrs Voss suspended the Frankham children on 23rd March 2004 over an alleged incident at the school. Mrs Voss wrote to Mr & Mrs Frankham informing them of the suspension. But at the end of the day, when she was shutting the school gates she saw Eli Frankham outside in a silver car. "He revved the car and shouted, 'Go on, run'." said Miss Wallace. "She ran back and called the police." Mrs Voss said she received at least eight calls from Mrs Frankham on 27th March. Miss Wallace said another teacher, Gail Coates was also sworn at. She said the behaviour of the Frankhams was "thoroughly unpleasant." Frankham, of Walpole St Andrew, admitted harassing Mrs Voss and abusive behaviour to another staff member. He was made the subject of an ASBO banning him from intimidating staff. Full sentencing was adjourned for a month, but he was warned that he could be jailed.

UPDATE: His wife was given a 180 hour community punishment order after she admitted harassing Mrs Voss, and abusive behaviour towards two other staff. She was also given a three year ASBO. On 27th September 2004, Frankham was sentenced to a total of 18 weeks imprisonment and also made the subject of a 5-years ASBO.

The parents of two children who were repeatedly allowed to miss school were jailed on 28th September 2004. Georgina Corby, 32, and her estranged husband John, 37, were each sentenced to three months because their son and daughter missed school on 104 days out of a possible 118 between January and April 2004. It is the first time that both parents of a truant child have been jailed. The couple, who separated in March 2004, were called in by the Headmaster of West Leeds High School, in Armley, Leeds, at the beginning of 2004 and promised the situation would improve. But within two weeks, son John, 14, and daughter Samantha, 16, were absent again. Despite further meetings between the parents and education officials, the children attended barely half their classes that term. At a previous hearing at Leeds Magistrates Court, the couple were found guilty of knowingly failing to ensure that their children attended school. However on 28th September 2004, presiding magistrate Eric Drake told them he had no option but to send them to prison. He said, "Children have a right to have an education, and parents have a responsibility to ensure that a child attends school to receive that education." Both parents were ordered to serve two months on the latest charge and another month for similar offences which had been suspended for similar offences in December 2003. Mrs Corby, a mother of four, sobbed as she was sentenced. Steve Culleton, defending, had told the court that Samantha was taken into her father's care after the couple's separation, and she now boasted a near-100 per cent attendance record. But brother John, living with his mother, continued to skip school. Mr Culleton attacked the Government for sending truants' parents to prison at all. He said: "This is political legislation. It's not about improving the lot of a child or to improve the lot of society, it's here to give some impression that the Government is actually doing something. From where I'm standing, I can't see that they are actually doing anything." After the court hearing, a spokesman for Education Leeds said the authority was liaising with Social Services over the welfare of the two teenagers. No decision had been made about who would look after them. In recent months, Yorkshire Education Authority has cracked down on parents of truant children, threatening more than 300 with court action.

On 8th November 2004, Deputy Headmaster David Morgan, 42, a father-of-two, from Spotborough, near Doncaster, appeared at Leeds Crown Court. He was convicted of stroking the bottoms of five girl pupils aged around eight, in 19 indecent assaults over a period of time. The offences took place at a junior school in the Wakefield area, West Yorkshire. One frightened girl reported the matter to her parents, stating that Morgan did 'naughty things' to her, in front of her friends in class. He had started abusing the young girls in his care around December 2003, but it was stated that most offences took place in 2004, between February and April. The prosecution counsel, Patricia Doherty, told the court about one of Morgan's victims, whom he had assaulted on eight occasions. "She described Morgan tapping her bum, and said he was putting his hands down pants and getting confident." When interviewed by police, the girl told them: "I feel scared when he does these naughty things." Another girl told officers: "He goes up my skirt and touches my bum on my cheek." Judge Alistair McCallum told Morgan: "You abused children in your trust. It was a huge breach of trust and I wish I wasn't sitting here today having to address someone like you in this way. There is no way that I can avoid sentencing you to prison. I shall give you the maximum credit for your plea of guilty, but the least possible sentence that I can impose on you is one of five years." Morgan, a teacher for 10 years, had been given credit for pleading guilty at an earlier hearing in September 2004, which meant that none of his very young victims had to suffer the ordeal of testifying against him. He was told by the judge that he would be eligible for release after two-and-a-half years and would then be placed under close supervision. He was placed on the Sex Offenders' Register for life and disqualified from working with children ever again. Defence Counsel Bryan Fox had said his client was deeply sorry for his actions, and was anxious that he should make a public apology to all of those affected by his conduct. Morgan had been dedicated to his job and a future Headmastership had been well on the cards, until the current unlawful matters came to light. On 26th April 2004, Morgan had been suspended from his post and had since resigned.

It was revealed on 10th September 2004 that a fifth of all state schools have been attacked by arsonists and other vandals over the summer holidays. Thousands of children arrived for the first day of term to find burned-out classrooms, flooded science labs and broken windows. A survey by arson experts ADT found that middle schools were the worst hit, with 24 per cent reporting incidents. At secondary schools it was 21 per cent and primary and infant schools 15 per cent. ADT's Peter Lackey said: "The increasing number of arson attacks is a very serious situation. There is the need for real action to combat this problem." Each year, more than 2,000 schools are damaged by fire, with 70 per cent started deliberately during the long summer holidays or dark winter evenings when school grounds are deserted. Another 2,700 are hit by vandals. Security experts put the cost at around £100million, equivalent to employing an extra 3,750 teachers.

A teacher with 25 years experience went *totally loopy* and shot at youths she believed had been subjecting her to a campaign of abuse, a court was told. Linda Walker, 47, was *bright red in the face* when she confronted the teenagers before returning to her home nearby to fetch a gas-powered pellet pistol and air rifle. Then she fired the Walther CP88 pistol up to six times into the pavement at the feet of one of the gang who was *tipsy* and had convictions for burglary, theft and criminal damage, a jury heard. Police were called and after she was arrested she told them she had gone "totally loopy" after being called "every name under the sun" by the boys including "loser" and "fat ugly c**t". Before the incident in Urmston, Greater Manchester, last August, Walker, a teacher at a school for children with behavioural difficulties, had encountered a catalogue of problems with yobs and complained to police. She claimed she had also received an abusive phone call alleging her son was homosexual, and had been targeted by vandals who damaged her garden shed. Matters came to a head when she and her partner, fellow teacher John Cavanagh, 56, noticed a washing up bottle on the roof of their car parked on their drive at 12.30am. "Linda Walker decided whoever had done it lived nearby and so she rushed outside," prosecutor Mike Leeming told Minshull Street Crown Court, Manchester. She saw a group of youths about 250 yards away, and claimed to have seen one of them placing a traffic sign in the road, causing an obstruction. "She jumped to the conclusion that they were in some way responsible for the plague of problems she had had at her house, though there was not a shred of evidence to support this conclusion," added Mr Leeming. Before opening fire she told the group: "Look, I've got some guns here and that's what you will get if you come to my house again." He said one of the youths was Robert McKiernan, then 18, who was convicted in November 2003 of burglary, theft and criminal damage after breaking into his former school to steal chocolate. He was returning home from a night out when Walker came up to the group. She was red in the face screaming "psychos" and "tossers" and accused them " without a shred of evidence".

Before leaving the house she phoned police and said: "I'm going over to that field over the road. I've got an air rifle and a pistol and I'm going to shoot them." Cavanagh then arrived, stood very close to the boy and claimed he had seen him placing the sign in the road. "Robert was very frightened at this point because two adults had confronted him with two firearms," said Mr Leeming. "Walker then discharged the pistol five or six times into the pavement close to Robert's foot. "He wasn't struck by any of the pellets but you can imagine the potential injuries if an accident had occurred." Mr Leeming told the jury. "Linda Walker told police how she had 25 years experience working as a teacher dealing with children with special needs, so you might think she could deal with confrontational situations better than this. But she said she was fuming mad when she saw the bottle on the car and was called all the names under the sun. She told them she was acting in self defence. "She said she went totally off her head, totally loopy and went out to intimidate the boys. She said it was a highly-charged situation and she just lost it."

Giving evidence McKiernan, now 19, said he had earlier had four cans of lager and while tipsy was not drunk. He bumped into a friend, Nicolas Violett, now 16, as Walker approached shouting. "I was scared at first but then I thought she isn't going to shoot me, she wants to threaten me," he said. "My friends ran off again but I stayed. I hadn't done anything wrong. I was scared by the looks on their faces and by the two guns. She fired the pistol at the pavement near my foot about six times and I was scared because even if she hadn't meant to hit me, she might have by accident. "When the police arrived and told her to put the guns down, she didn't straight away but then did when they asked again. She seemed shocked that she was the one in trouble." Walker, who claims she acted in self defence, denies possessing a firearm with intent and affray. Cavanagh, who is also accused of confronting the youths, denies affray.

UPDATE: The conclusion to the case was that Mrs Walker was sentenced to 6 months imprisonment by the Crown Court judge. Just to apparently rub salt in the wounds, Mrs Walker appealed and a single Judge allowed her appeal to proceed with an early appeal date. However, amazingly, he refused bail in the interim, so that Mrs Walker had to remain in jail!

Tearaway pupils got more than they bargained for after terrorising an elderly couple, they were caught red-handed by the principal and his deputy lying in wait behind a garden shed. College principal Keith Ballance and vice-principal David Cheshire planned their stakeout after receiving a plea from two pensioners. A couple aged 68 and 72 had faced a daily ordeal of stone-throwing by vandals from Tamarside Community College in

Plymouth. But the pupils behind the attacks, aged 13 to 14, walked straight into the ambush. "We decided on direct action and left school early so we could hide behind this couple's garden shed," said Mr Ballance, 50, who joined the college as principal three years ago. "When we heard the sound of stones on glass, I dashed out from our hiding place to confront three lads, one of whom still had stones in his hand." Mr Cheshire, 56, who has taught at the school for 27 years, followed fast on the heels of his athletic, footballing boss. "Mr Ballance hurtled down the path like a blur and nabbed the three boys," he said. "To say they were stunned to see us would be an understatement. "Mr Ballance gave them a serious talking to and marched them inside the house to face their victims." It is not the first time the pair, dubbed Batman and Robin by pupils, have used their hands-on approach to improve community relations. Father-of-two Mr Cheshire added: "Often it's the only way to catch pupils who are misbehaving. I've hidden in houses and burst through front doors." The pupils behind the stone-throwing are going to help their victims by doing gardening and maintenance jobs as punishment. Beat bobby PC Kevin Morely said: "This demonstrates the school's willingness to improve the quality of life for local residents."

Two hundred pupils abandoned their lessons after a headmaster banned kissing, cuddling and holding hands. They staged a mass sit-in in a field, claiming the ban was ridiculous because it prohibited friends from holding hands or hugging. Eight pupils were suspended for being defiant and rude to staff, the school said. The crackdown was set out in a memo to teachers which was read to 900 secondary pupils at Warneford School, in Highworth, Wiltshire. The Headmaster of the mixed comprehensive, John Saunders, insisted the ban was designed to cover inappropriate behaviour and to maintain discipline. "We are reminding pupils of a rule that already exists. It is clearly not appropriate for pupils to be blatantly kissing or cuddling about the school, the same rules apply in any workplace." Students plan to petition school governors to get the ban lifted, said 15-year-old Kim Cullinane. "I admit kissing in school is not appropriate but saying we can't touch each other is too much" she added. "At 16, you can get married, so to say you're not allowed to touch one another is ridiculous. There's a lot of anger." Her mother, Sandra, said, "It's archaic. I don't see how they can enforce it."

A Headmaster was threatened with a Dunblane-style massacre in a series of terrifying e-mails which forced the school to be closed. One message warned: "This is a jihad now, we have enough AK-47s and Uzi 9mms to do the job. Call the cops and you forfeit 10 more lives." Another threatened: "You will cause the deaths of staff and kids at your school and the whole world will know that you could have stopped it." The campaign of terror started after Anthony Gatenby, 38, accepted an innocent *peck* on the cheek from a four-year-old girl when he went to pick up his son at the end of lessons. Headmaster Jim Green heard about the incident and warned it was inappropriate. Unemployed decorator Gatenby promptly threatened to return to Haydn Road Primary in Sherwood, Nottingham, with guns and shoot Mr Green. Nottingham magistrates were told that the school had to be shut four times and security guards brought in as a result of the threats. As *hysteria* gripped the school, the shrubbery in the grounds was even trimmed back so there would be no cover for a would-be gunman. Gatenby, who moved to Sherwood from Taunton a year ago with his wife, Jane, and son Brendan, four, denied harassing Mr Green.

The magistrates, who found him guilty of the charge at an earlier hearing, spared him from jail but banned him from the school for two years. He was also banned from contacting Mr Green or his staff for the same period, sentenced to two years' community rehabilitation and ordered to attend an anger-management course. The chairman of the bench, Keith Stanyard. told Gatenby: "This is a very serious matter, whatever was thought to be the provocation, you cannot take a situation like this into your own hands, particularly in a school environment." The earlier hearing was told that the threats began after a member of the nursery staff at the school saw a girl peck Gatenby on the cheek. But the e-mails, which claimed to come from a friend of Gatenby, were not used as evidence, as it could not be proved who had sent them. Mr Green told magistrates that on the day he confronted Gatenby he had to call police to eject the furious father on two occasions. The school then broke up for Easter, but on its first day back Gatenby, who by then had already been banned from the premises, rang up. Mr Green said: "He said he was going to come to my office because he wanted a meeting with the person he described as his accuser. He said 'I'm going to report you for child abuse, and I'm going to take more extreme measures. I've got a handgun. I'm going to shoot you'. He delivered it in a calm, calculated voice. It made me fearful. I put the phone down and dialled 999, put the staff on alert and locked the gates." Gatenby was arrested when he arrived at the school minutes later, but the threatening e-mails began arriving after he was released on bail. Mr Green said: "When the contents became known hysteria spread through the school. At times some of my staff have broken down in tears. "The pressure had been very difficult to take. Parents were demanding to know what was going on and if we could guarantee their children's safety." Speaking after the case, Gatenby insisted: "I never threatened anyone and I still don't believe Jim Green lived in fear. Is it a crime to get a peck on the cheek from a child?" Martin Smalley, defending, told the court: "Something that started with a kiss has turned into a nightmare as far as Mr Gatenby is concerned., it was an entirely innocent act on the part of a four-year-old girl and matters just snowballed."

Parents have been warned to monitor their childrens' use of the internet after two girls, aged 13 and 14, put explicit photographs of themselves on the web. Both girls are pupils at Cefh Hengoed Community School in Swansea. Deputy head teacher Geoff Brookes said: "The children understand the technology but do not understand the consequences."

On 9th February 2005 a music teacher was jailed for having sex with pupils after he sent them naked pictures of himself. Two girls had shown their breasts to him at the end of the school prom to celebrate finishing their GCSE courses. The teacher, David James, 32, sent three girls, aged 16 and 17, naked pictures of himself from his webcam. And at his home he received topless pictures of the girls. Prosecutor Tom Crowther said: "Each of the girls was musical and were involved in extra-curricular musical productions with James. "But his interest went further than that and became sexual. He split up with a girlfriend and described himself as lonely. "But rather than face the indignities and uncertainties of meeting new people, he turned to a group of girls who regarded him with respect and affection. In the girls' GCSE class, his conduct began to be inappropriate. "Two of the girls were regular visitors to his home, which many would regard as odd. "He said they exposed their breasts to him at the school prom. But instead of discouraging it, he pursued it. "One of the girls was an assistant to him, turning his pages as he played the piano at a school production. He asked her to show him her breasts and she did. This was in school and a request by a respected teacher and confidant. "On another occasion the two girls washed his car and he invited them into his home where he photographed them topless."

Cardiff Crown Court heard that computer enthusiast James gave the girls his e-mail address. Mr Crowther said: "He received topless photos and used his own webcam to send naked pictures of himself to the girls." The court heard James had sex with two of the girls after they finished their exams. "He took both to bed and had sex with each one," said Mr Crowther. "He would have been twice their age and was still their music teacher. "As far as one of the girls was concerned, it was a single incident. "But he commenced a relationship with the other girl. She would visit his home two or three times a week and stay over on Saturday nights. "He followed her on a family holiday in Spain and had sex with her there. "He didn't think of her as his girlfriend but she bought him presents, sent him cards and allowed him to make films of her sexual activity. James stored these films in a hoard of home-made pornography." Police seized James's computer and discovered more than 80 pictures and films featuring the three girls. Mr Crowther said: "Perhaps, inevitably, rumours went around the school and James was formally warned. But there was nothing more than rumour upon which the school could have acted. "But a police investigation was launched and James was arrested and charged." Bachelor James, of Pentwyn, Cardiff, admitted six counts of abusing a position of trust and one of sexual activity with a child by a person in a position of trust. Michael Mather-Lees, defending, said: "He has been frank in accepting that there was no excuse for getting into the situation. It has destroyed his life and his career. "All three girls stated this was consensual and willing and they participated in this without force." Judge Christopher Llewellyn-Jones told him: "As a teacher, you owed them and their parents duties and responsibilities. "It's difficult to imagine a graver breach of trust than for a teacher to engage in sexual activity with those who are in their charge." James was jailed for 20 months and ordered to register as a sex offender for 10 years. He was also banned from working with children for life.

A headmaster at a school for the disabled stole £178,000 from the kids' charity and then hoped to pay it back by winning the Lottery. Stanley Johnson, 66, ripped off the Devon and Exeter Spastics Society for 20 years. He spent the cash on home improvements and holidays. As his scam continued he started putting £50 bets on the Lottery hoping for a win. The fiddle was exposed when a new headmaster took over. Johnson, of Pinhoe, Devon, admitted theft at court in Exeter. He was jailed for 30 months.

On 12th February 2005 it was announced by Senior Staff at St Martins School in Essex, that they have launched a ground-breaking internet scheme known as 'Gateway'. During the school working day, each pupil is monitored by Staff and details input into the School computer up to 5 times per day. Staff input details as to whether each pupil is present at school all day, at each scheduled lesson, their progress in various subjects, their attitude and behaviour etc. Parents at home can then log in to the school's 'Gateway' website and monitor their child's details on screen. This should lead to reassurance for parents as to the child's safety, early warnings of truancy, poor performances etc. Many other schools are expected to follow the scheme.

A sixth-form schoolboy hanged himself after suffering months of bullying by younger pupils. Tormented Oliver Sabine, 17, had his nose broken, five bicycles stolen and was frequently intimidated in dark alleyways surrounding his school. His body was found hanging from a tree in the back garden of his family's large 1930s semi-detached home. His distraught mother, Shirley Owen, 43, told an inquest that Oliver's school failed her son. Ms Owen said she warned of his mental frailty, adding: "I don't think they believed that Oliver was suicidal." She said she confronted Oliver's head of year to press home how vulnerable he was. "He didn't seem to be taking it too seriously, so I said I'm really worried Oliver is going to kill himself." But the vital information never reached Richard Green, the headmaster of 1,500-pupil Waingel's Copse Secondary School in Woodley, Berkshire. He was never made aware that Oliver had been diagnosed as suffering from *modest to severe* depression. Even though Oliver was bullied, depressed and in therapy, Mr Green told the inquest the pupil never came to his attention. Ms Owen told the hearing in Windsor, Berks, that her son's plight was obvious. She said: "He was pushed off his bike, he was assaulted, his nose was broken." Constant threats and taunts meant he was reluctant to go to school, or even socialise with friends. Ms Owen told the inquest: "Friends would come and call for him and he would not go out." None of the bullies was named during the inquest, but most were said to be younger than Oliver. They picked on him because he stood out from the crowd and had a low sense of self-esteem. The coroner heard that reporting the assaults to police resulted in arrests and cautions, but no expulsions. Ms Owen, who has two other sons, Henry, 17, and Charlie, 14, told the inquest she felt let down by the way the school handled the bullying, in particular by one boy. Headmaster Mr Green accepted he was a remote figure for many in the huge school. But he denied that teachers had been told Oliver was suicidal. He told the coroner that, if they had known, appropriate action would have been taken. Recording a verdict of suicide, Berkshire Coroner Peter Bedford criticised the way Ms Owen's concerns apparently failed to reach the headmaster.

Britain's top Catholic boarding school was at the centre of a drugs scandal on 11th February 2005 after 21 boys were suspended for cannabis use. The pupils from Ampleforth College have been questioned by police and will be cautioned as the result of an investigation into drug use at the school. The boys were sent home from the £20,000-a-year independent school for three days at the beginning of the week. The suspension will be followed by counselling and random drug testing. The headmaster, Father Gabriel Everitt, said: "Some may regard cannabis as a soft drug, widely tolerated for recreational use by much of society. That is not the view here. "It can be vastly more powerful than what was available a generation ago. Our attitude is uncompromising. "We regard any form of drug-taking as a very serious breach of discipline and we are conducting a rigorous investigation into all the circumstances of this discovery." Ampleforth College is set in an idyllic location on the edge of the North Yorkshire Moors near Helmsley. It takes boys from age 13 to 18 and girls in the sixth form. Its ethos is to educate the intellectually gifted. The college's teachings are based on the Benedictine tradition that the sons of the rich and influential should receive an education to ensure an elite place in society. Former pupils include actors Rupert Everett and Colin Firth, Tory deputy leader Michael Ancram, Radio 4 Today presenter Edward Stourton and former England rugby international Lawrence Dallaglio. Two years ago, a monk quit the school after he had a sexual relationship with a pupil. Father Christian Shore, 53, admitted *improper physical conduct* with a sixth former. The school hit the headlines again after another monk was charged with 16 counts of indecent assault which allegedly took place at a feeder school more than 30 years ago. Father Piers Grant-Ferris, 71, was charged following a police investigation into alleged abuse at Gilling Castle Preparatory School, Ampleforth, where he worked as a teacher. The alleged assaults date back to a period between the late 1960s and the mid 1970s. His connection with Gilling Castle School, which has now closed, ended in 1975.

A Deputy Head's future was in doubt last night after he was convicted of kerb-crawling. John Hurst, 53, picked up a prostitute in a red light district after an evening's birdwatching. The churchgoer claimed he naively allowed her into his car believing she needed a lift. But magistrates convicted him of soliciting for sex after hearing she was a known vice girl in Doncaster, south Yorkshire. Primary school boss Hurst told police who stopped him: "I've never done it before. I promise you it will be the last." Hurst, from Epworth, told Doncaster JPs he offered the girl a lift after getting lost. He said: "When I realised she might be a prostitute I was torn between fear, panic and embarrassment." His solicitor admitted the verdict was "likely to end his career". He was given a 12-month conditional discharge and ordered to pay £300 costs.

Teacher Gavin Lister wrecked his marriage and career because of his love for a teenage schoolgirl. A court heard shaven-headed Lister, 32, became so obsessed with the girl that he sent her 302 text messages in a month. She sent him 850. Cheryl Williams, prosecuting, said: "In late December 2004, the relationship between them became close, initially by e-mail and chatroom, and by text messaging and conversation between the two of them, and also furtive kissing." Ms Williams added: "He knew it was wrong but could not stop." Lister was charged on January 17th 2005 but continued to send e-mail messages, including one that said: "It doesn't matter that you're a teenager. "I might as well be in prison. I might as well be dead. At least then I'd be out of the way, unable to hurt you. "I can't be cut out of your life, I won't let myself. What I've done is wrong and I will be punished for it." Lister pleaded guilty to engaging in sexual activity with a girl between the ages of 13 and 15 and abusing a position of trust, at Peterborough magistrates' court. He met the girl at the prestigious King's School in Peterborough when he started teaching PE in September 2004. Lister, of Parnwell, Peterborough, also admitted breaching his bail conditions. Tim Devas, defending, said: "This young man is not a paedophile. It's quite clear that this defendant fell in love with this girl. It's illegal, it's unlawful and he was in a position of trust. "The opportunity to take this much further and make this into a much more serious offence, was there on offer. Mr Lister did not take it any further." Magistrate Wendy Sayers told Lister: "The offences are so serious that you should receive a greater punishment than we can impose." He will now be sentenced at Peterborough Crown Court. Speaking after the case, his wife Clare, 35, said she had only become suspicious when she found hundreds of text messages to one number on his mobile phone bill, and e-mails on his laptop. She then went on the internet and discovered he had left messages on the Friends Reunited website and football forum 24/7. On 24/7 he wrote: "New Year's resolutions: break up with wife, find someone new." After he had been arrested, Lister left this message on Friends Reunited: "Fell out of love 18 months ago. Met someone else, but unlikely to go anywhere. May go missing for a year or more." The couple and her three children had moved to Peterborough from Sydney, Australia, last summer to start a new life.

New Education Secretary Ruth Kelly will unveil a zero tolerance approach to children who disrupt lessons. Schools will be told they can throw pupils out of class who talk back to teachers. Heads will also be told they should ban mobile phones from classrooms. Ms Kelly will use a major speech on school discipline to say the bar needs to be lowered on the level of bad behaviour acceptable in class. She wants to follow up a 25 per cent cut in pupils expelled or suspended for the worst violent and abusive conduct, with an end to minor disruptions that stop other children learning. Heads will be told to get tough and follow the example of schools where rigid discipline has already seen exam results rise. Ms Kelly will also fire a warning shot at parents of disruptive pupils, saying they must take responsibility for combating unruly behaviour. Schools will be given more choice about what they can do with teenage troublemakers but they will also be given more advice on what has worked in other schools. Ministers want clear policies throughout Britain enforced rigorously and consistently so that pupils and teachers know where they stand. A source in the Department for Education and Skills told the *Sunday Express*: "We want to redraw the line on bad behaviour. There needs to be zero tolerance." Ms Kelly will stress the need for central and local government to work together to provide teachers with the support they need, against pupils who sometimes make false claims of assault against staff who tackle the troublemakers. The source added: "Parents have a right for their children to receive an undisrupted education but they also have a responsibility to help tackle bad behaviour. "Exclusions are down by 25 per cent since 1997 but that is no comfort to the parents of pupils whose lessons are disrupted by others. We have to deal with other behaviour and disruptions that wear teachers down. That means tackling pupils who have no respect for others and won't buckle down and follow rules. "The Secretary of State wants to support schools in redrawing the line. Some children need help. Others need to be told where the line is and what punishment will follow if they break the rules." The zero tolerance approach will be welcomed by the teaching unions, which have threatened to strike over plans by Charles Clarke, Ms Kelly's predecessor, to make every school accept tearaways.

Foul-mouthed football and television celebrities have been condemned for inspiring a generation of out-of-control playground yobs. As discipline in the classroom hit an all-time low, teachers blamed some stars for the appalling behaviour of the country's youth. It was also revealed that the number of failing schools has soared by 18 per cent, while a tenth of all schools are not improving fast enough. At the same time, the shameful behaviour of millionaire footballers, whose vile televised obscenities are watched by millions of impressionable children, came under attack. Fans who tuned in to Manchester United's clash with rivals Arsenal, were treated to a record number of swear words by players idolised by young fans. The disgraceful antics of some of Britain's most prominent role models came as teachers voiced concern that such outbursts had contributed to collapsing standards of classroom behaviour. Education watchdog Ofsted revealed that pupil behaviour in secondary schools is now at its worst ever, with one in ten suffering *unsatisfactory* conduct. Headteacher Gareth Davies, 47, is particularly concerned about the influence of stars and television. He said: "Young children model their behaviour on their role models and if they are spitting and swearing on TV it sets a terrible example. "The playground language of many children is quite appalling and is upsetting to those who are routinely subjected to it. "Today's culture means that bad language is heard everywhere from the football field to street conversation." Mr Davies has now written to parents at his school, Ysgol Frongoch primary in Denbigh, north Wales, urging them, to curb their offsprings' tongues in what he labelled a *nationwide problem*. He warned parents that their children watch television unsupervised in their bedrooms long after the 9pm watershed. He said in his letter: "It is a problem and will not go away unless we work together to tackle this issue and let children know that we all find bad language unacceptable." Education psychologist Kairen Cullen, who works in north London schools, said pupils' actions reflected their wider experiences. The deteriorating state of children's behaviour was echoed by Ofsted, which revealed standards at their lowest ever. Of all secondary schools inspected last year, nine per cent had pupils with *unsatisfactory or worse* behaviour, the highest figure since the watchdog began in 1992. Just 68 per cent showed *good or better* behaviour, the worst since 1992 and a drop from 76 per cent when Labour came to power in 1997. In another stinging verdict on the education system, the annual report of Chief Inspector David Bell also revealed that 332 schools were on *special measures* by last summer, 50 more than the previous year. Over the last three years, 1,000 schools have failed to make sufficient improvement following inspections. MPs and teaching groups last night demanded tougher punishment for classroom yobs and more power to teachers.

Nick Seaton, chairman of the Campaign for Real Education, said: "Most parents will think it is a very damning report on the trend in state education. "There is a general lack of punishment in schools. Teachers can not cope in lots of instances and they are leaving the profession. We need more powers of punishment and stricter discipline all round." Mr Bell said the trend was "worrying" and stressed: "It is right that we continue to keep a focus on this matter because young people are unlikely to learn as much as they should if their time at school is being disrupted by the behaviour of others." Shadow Education Secretary Tim Collins said the report showed "a vital pillar in our schools system is crumbling badly." He said, "Conservatives are convinced schools that perform poorly in their teaching assessment are those with the worst discipline." He also accused the Government of ignoring the issue for nearly eight years and only picking it up because of the likely election.

Teachers themselves have painted a grim picture of life in the class room in an online chat room for the *Times Education Supplement*. One, who was threatened with having their car brakes cut, wrote: "There's mob rule in the corridors and gangs running riot." Another said: "I rang a mother to tell her that her son had told me to '**** off' and she seemed flabbergasted that I was informing her of something so trivial." Mr Bell pledged to revisit schools with poor behaviour within a year of inspection, and warned those with *satisfactory* ratings not to rest on their laurels. He also urged politicians not to indulge in short-term policies on schools ahead of the expected general election. In Mr Blair's first speech as Labour leader in opposition, he said: "To parents wanting their children to be taught in classrooms that are not crumbling, to students with qualifications but no university place, let us say 'The Tories have failed you. We are on your side. Your ambitions are our ambitions'." In a Fabian Society pamphlet in 1995 a year later, he wrote: "On education, we seek excellence for all and not just a few. We must tackle the third of schools that are poor or failing." A year later Mr Blair wrote: "We need the commitment to excellence at the top to permeate all the way down." In his last conference speech before becoming Premier, he said: "Ask me my three main-priorities for government, and I tell you - education, education, education." But he admitted only last July it was a "scandal" that a quarter of 11 year olds left primary school without a sound grasp of the three Rs.

Soccer ace Wayne Rooney is inspiring foul-mouthed copycat yobs with his four-letter word tirades, a leading headteacher claimed on 23rd February 2005. Pupils follow the star's bad behaviour, believing they can get away with angry outbursts, as referees are *too soft* on the £20million striker, said Dr Chris Howard, a member of the National Association of Head Teachers. Children see Rooney getting away with yobbish behaviour and believe they can. Teachers are facing it in the classroom and police face it on the street. It's just gnawing away at us." The criticism was sparked by a Premiership football match earlier this month in which Rooney, 19, launched into an astonishing verbal attack on referee Graham Poll. But the official merely gave Rooney a yellow card and told the fiery player to calm down. The foul behaviour was highlighted by the *Daily Express* in a report revealing how Britain's schools are now overrun with foul-mouthed pupils. Earlier in February 2005, education watchdog Ofsted revealed that behaviour in secondary schools is at its worst ever, with one in ten suffering problems caused by *unsatisfactory* conduct. Dr Howard, head at Lewis Boys School in Pengam, Gwent, where former Labour leader Lord Neil Kinnock was a pupil, added: "Young people behaving like Wayne Rooney are increasingly finding themselves in front of an exclusions panel." Teachers now regularly face physical and verbal abuse, including the widespread use of the F-word and other sexually explicit language, he said.

More than 100 obscenities in a single football match left tens of thousands of family viewers shocked during the evening of 2nd February 2005. Fans who tuned in to Manchester United's clash with Arsenal on Tuesday saw players, idolised by millions of children, mouthing a record number of swear words. Even before the 90 minute game, captains Roy Keane and Patrick Vieira had to be pulled apart in the tunnel when the United star warned: "I'll get your f******g legs". Worst offender was Wayne Rooney. He was seen mouthing abuse with 10 swear words coming in less than a minute when he was booked. Fans who focused on the 19-year-old using *Sky's PlayerCam* feature were shocked by a series of close-ups. By the 48th minute, referee Graham Poll had enough and he gave Rooney a yellow card. But even that failed to stop him. *Sky Sports* said it made strenuous efforts to ensure audible swearing was not transmitted: "There was one word that may have been audible, in the tunnel, for which we apologised on air." Dr Adrian Rogers, of Family Focus, said: "They could make it a red card for an expletive. Perhaps there is a case for a tape to be played back to the Director of Public Prosecutions."

On Wednesday 2nd February 2005, the handful of outstanding schools dubbed the "magnificent seven" by the head of Ofsted, put their success down to strict discipline and respect. One primary and six secondary schools were praised by Chief Inspector of Schools David Bell as the only ones to get top marks in inspections three times in a row. Mr Bell said: "These magnificent seven epitomise the characteristics of effective schools, strong leadership, and very good achievement brought about by the best of teaching." One of them, The Downs School in Compton, Berks, is a mixed comprehensive of 1,000 pupils. But headmaster Graham Taylor said: "We have very traditional discipline. The pupils know from the outset what the rules are. We have a strict uniform policy, it's part of the culture. The pupils know it when they step out of line." Richard Bilous, acting head of Woodlands Junior in Tonbridge, Kent, the only primary school on the list, said: "It's not always easy. We've got 380 children. Adults, when they come here, are respected. It's an expectation here that the children behave with respect. It's automatic now." Many of the 1,250 pupils who join Gable Hall comprehensive in Corringham, Essex at the age of 11, have poor literacy and numeracy skills. But headmaster John King said they are given challenges to help realise their potential. He added: "We addressed the discipline problem long ago. Once you have a structure in place you have to give the kids what they need and give them more responsibility." The other schools are Henrietta Barnett in Hampstead, north London, Colyton Grammar in Devon, Oxted School in Surrey and Heckmondwike Grammar in West Yorkshire.

Teachers are reluctant to discipline unruly pupils because they are frightened of breaking the law, it was claimed in July 2004. Union boss Barry Mathews attacked the declining standards of behaviour in children and hit out at the obsession with exam results and the power of television. Mr Matthews, chairman of the Professional Association of Teachers, said that while *it does no one any good to look back*, youngsters had too much freedom, which made it hard to control them. He told the union's annual conference in Bournemouth: " I have had many discussions with teachers and parents who find it difficult to impose discipline. They are concerned with breaking the law and finding themselves in trouble for applying what they consider to be appropriate disciplinary action to a child that steps out of line." As a boy, it was made clear to him where the boundaries of acceptable behaviour lay. But new laws and the ban on corporal punishment made the task of imposing discipline more difficult for teachers and parents. He said: "As a child I knew there were certain actions that could reap unfavourable rewards. I did not enjoy having the cane (having the cane in those days was normal) or having to stay in after school, any more than the next person, but I knew that if I stepped out of line I could be subjected to some kind of punishment." He was not calling for the return of the cane, but called on teachers to find new methods of *control* in an era when too many children were not given boundaries. Teachers now faced having their authority questioned by both pupils *and* their parents." Mr Matthews also demanded that governors and authorities stop reversing schools' attempts to discipline children by expelling or suspending them. He said: " How can we impose discipline if, when we do take a particular course of action, the authorities are lenient and do not support teachers' professional judgements. I do not think it is helpful when a teacher or school applies a form of discipline only to have it overruled by a board of governors or a local authority." He added that Labour's focus on exam results meant that *little or no attention* was given to children's well-being. When he was young, children were *required to lie on a mat and rest, even sleep for half-an-hour every day after lunch* in the school hall. " I am concerned we are in an age when it would appear that getting a certificate or diploma is the most important requirement", he said. "But," he asked: "Do we need bricklayers with degrees or practical ability? What value is there to have a shop assistant with a degree who does not have customer skills?" Mr Matthews warned of the power of TV on children. "For some, television provides the sense of community through soaps and such programmes, and has taken over their personal relationships."

The number of schoolchildren taking drugs, including heroin, crack and cocaine, has almost doubled since Labour came to power. An alarming new study highlighting the figures will embarrass the Government, which recently placed its *new war on drugs* at the heart of the election campaign. It will also concern Tony Blair, who has been keen to demonstrate his personal commitment to tackling the youth drug problem. In a controversial move, the Prime Minister recently gave his support to random drug testing in schools, introduced in the first state school last week. Mr Blair also announced harsher penalties for dealers operating at school gates. The figures, compiled by top drugs expert Dr Russell Newcombe, of Liverpool John Moores University, show that last year more than 25 per cent of all children aged between 11 and 15 had taken illegal drugs. In 1998, the year after Labour came to power, the figure was 14 per cent. Figures suggesting regular use also showed a huge rise from seven per cent in 1998 to 12 per cent of children last year. Dr Newcombe said the Government's drug education strategy did not prevent children using drugs, "it just tells them about the risks." His conclusions have been seized on by the Tories, who say Labour's drug education policy is failing because it gives youngsters a mixed message. Dr Newcombe said the street price of illegal drugs has fallen so low that hard drugs are more affordable than ever. He added: "The market is saturated and drugs are cheap and easy to get hold of. Young kids get them from older kids and then graduate to using dealers." The increase in use among the young is reflected in the adult population, according to Dr Newcombe's findings, due to be published later this year in a book, *Drug Misuse In Britain.* They show that since 1998 every form of drug abuse has risen, except for LSD and speed, which have been replaced by Ecstasy and cocaine.

There are now about five million illegal users in the UK and half a million dealers.

In some parts of the country the cost of a line of cocaine is less than a glass of wine. A tablet of Ecstasy can cost as little as £1. There are even areas where dealers operate dial-a-drug services, delivering to customers' homes in just half an hour. Dr Newcombe said: "The supply has become much more organised as dealers compete for trade. We need an urgent review of drugs policy. Why is the Government carrying on with something which simply hasn't worked? "Things are just going to get worse." He said: "The Government had put too much emphasis on heroin addicts and their crimes which does not help people with other drug problems." Shadow Home Secretary David Davis said: "Labour has acknowledged the damage that drugs do. However, typically, its approach has been characterised by broken promises and failed initiatives." A spokeswoman for the Government's National Committee for Prevention of Addiction said tackling drugs had been a "massive priority" for Labour, which had succeeded in getting more people into drug rehabilitation. She said money had been poured into such schemes and further funds had been pledged. But Peter Stoker, of the National Drug Prevention Alliance, said: "It's not enough for a treatment agency to say we're processing more people. It's the quality of the outcomes which is important and the number of people with drug problems is still sky-high." Meanwhile, the *Sunday Express* can reveal that the comprehensive school which last week introduced Britain's first state school random drug testing policy, has at least three pupils who are heroin addicts. Insiders at Abbey School in Faversham, Kent, said that one of the three 15-year-olds has been using heroin since he was 12 years old. Head teacher Peter Walker insisted: "This school doesn't have a worse drugs problem than anywhere else. The Government's drug education strategy is not as we would want. We want to see if drug testing helps."

About half of schoolchildren aged between 11 years and 16 years have been victims of violence or aggression, a recent study has revealed. One in five know someone who carries a knife. About 33% have been victims of bullies, whilst the figures for children who have been abused by a stranger in the street is about one in four, the same as for those children whose mobile phones have been stolen from them. These figures were calculated after a joint survey by the charity *Crime Concern* and *Norwich Union* insurance company. A total of 550 children were canvassed for their responses during the survey. Around 50 per cent sought tougher sentences of imprisonment for perpetrators.

Violent gangs are running amok at one in five secondary schools, a shock report, revealed on 1st March 2005. An alarming number of schools reported gang culture was widespread among their pupils. And 40 per cent of them disclosed that pupils were bringing weapons into the playground or classroom at least once a term, said the Office for Standards in Education. Inspectors found about half of schools thought *gang behaviour* among feuding groups of pupils was an issue, with 20 per cent describing the problem as widespread. The report will further increase public concern about discipline in state secondary schools, with growing complaints from teaching unions about assaults on staff. Ofsted said drug abuse was *a daily challenge* for some older teenagers. It said: "In most secondary schools there are drug-related incidents at least once a term." The report warned: "In one in five of the secondary schools visited, gang culture is perceived to be widespread, although few schools had firm evidence of it. "There were instances of the carrying of knives and other potential weapons reported in less than half of the secondary schools and pupil referral units (where expelled pupils are taught) and in about half of the colleges visited." Chief Inspector of schools David Bell said: "Although the large majority of schools are orderly places where children behave well, it is worrying that unsatisfactory behaviour has not reduced over time. "Unsatisfactory behaviour by a minority of pupils causes nuisance and distress and disrupts the learning of others."

The main problems with badly behaved pupils is with low-level disruption rather than serious violence, Ofsted said. Drug abuse is worse in colleges and pupil referral units than secondary schools. About 30 per cent of schools reported pupils carrying weapons once a term and about 10 per cent said weapon-carrying incidents happened twice a term. Pupils in about 50 per cent of secondary schools *self-harm*. Schools Minister Stephen Twigg said: "We are supporting schools in showing zero tolerance to any bad behaviour. Permanent exclusions are 25 per cent lower than 1997 and, as Ofsted acknowledges, pupil behaviour is good in most schools most of the time." A spokesman for the Department for Education and Skills said it was important to tackle perceptions "even where there is little evidence". He went on: "We fully back heads in taking robust action against any violent behaviour, including permanent exclusion. Most pupils don't carry knives in or out of the classroom. There are 6.7 million pupils in England's 24,000 schools. There were 57 convictions last year for possession of a knife on school premises." He added that ministers had implemented "a zero tolerance policy" on drugs in schools. "We have equipped heads with a wide range of tools to tackle drugs through education, detection and deterrence, up to and including drugs testing for pupils and one-strike permanent exclusion for dealing in drugs."

England's top education official blamed parents and heads for the Government's failure to stop children, 500,000 a day, missing school. Sir David Normington, permanent secretary at the Department for Education and Skills, said it was *very disappointing* truancy rates had not reduced, but some head teachers were failing to apply strict rules while many parents condoned truancy. Three weeks ago the National Audit Office savaged Sir David's department for failing to reduce truancy despite spending £885million on improving behaviour and cutting absence. Sir David made his comments to the Commons Public Accounts Committee as police and education welfare officers launched a countrywide crackdown on truancy. Thousands of hardcore truants and their parents will be tracked down and punished. The pupils will be dragged back to the classroom and their parents will get penalty notices if they are found with them.

A boy of six was so terrorised by a school bully he threatened to kill himself with a kitchen knife. Over two years Ross Tonks broke two pairs of glasses, cut his eye, split his lip and was bruised all over by his tormentor. His nightmares got so bad he could not sleep, yet when his mother, Rosemary, complained to the school she was told nothing could be done as there were no witnesses. "I felt I was making him go to school to be hit," she said, "but they were telling me if I didn't take him to school I would get into trouble. "We kept promising Ross it would stop but we were telling him lies because it went on for two years." One day after Mrs Tonks insisted he went to school, Ross grabbed the knife in the kitchen of their home in Bedworth, Warwickshire. "He was screaming and crying," said Mrs Tonks, 41. "He came into the kitchen and I said I would let him calm down. When I went in he had got this knife out of the kitchen drawer and he said 'I don't want to be here any more'. I froze on the spot and said 'Put the knife down and please come to mum'. I held my arms out and he came running to me." His family claims St Michael's Church of England Primary School in Bedworth, and Warwickshire County Council, failed to take adequate steps to address the problem. Mrs Tonks said: "I pleaded for help but I wasn't getting any. The school said they didn't class it as bullying. "I got in contact with the governors and had some meetings with the LEA but I felt I hit a brick wall with them." No-one at Warwickshire County Council was available for comment. Ross, now aged eight and who featured in a BBC documentary on 28th February 2005, has since moved to St Giles Primary School in Bedworth, where he is thriving. The Government now wants all schools to sign an anti-bullying charter. Earlier this month a pioneering scheme in which pupils getting bullied can directly text police was launched in Warwickshire. Called *text2talk*, the drive will be monitored by the Home Office for a possible national roll-out.

On 2nd March 2005 a muslim schoolgirl claimed a human rights victory which signals the end of traditional school uniform. The Court of Appeal ruled that a headmaster had been wrong to exclude Shabina Begum from school for wearing a *head-to-toe* jilbab dress. Muslim leaders and MPs expressed dismay at the decision, which has huge implications for schools. They will now be expected to respect a pupil's right to wear traditional religious dress rather than punish them if they refuse to wear a blazer, shirt and tie. Ghayasuddin Siddiqui, leader of the Muslim Parliament of Great Britain, said: "This may be a human rights issue but we need to understand the fundamentalist agenda, which is ultimately that women should stay at home. "If this means that this girl and others will be able to go to school in the jilbab I will be saddened. The fundamentalist agenda is that we should have nothing to do with the non-Islamic world, and this will have gained currency and momentum today." The Tories said head teachers must not lose the right to decide their own school uniform policy. Parents should have sufficient choice to find a school where the jilbab is allowed rather than challenge in court those which do not, they argued.

Shadow Education Secretary Tim Collins said: "This case yet again reflects the way in which the Human Rights Act is unduly restricting the freedom of head teachers to run their schools in their own way. "The Conservative Party is already reviewing the Human Rights Act and its negative effects in many fields and this latest ruling further strengthens the case for fundamental change or repeal." Shabina, whose case was originally presented by human rights lawyer Cherie Blair, accused the head teacher and governors of Denbigh High School in Luton, Bedfordshire, of denying her the "right to education and to manifest her religious beliefs." The teenager had worn the shalwar kameez - trousers and a tunic - from when she entered the school at the age of 12 until September, 2002. But she was sent home after telling the school she was going to start wearing the full-length jilbab, which leaves only the face and hands exposed, launching a series of court cases. Lord Justice Brooke, Vice-President of the civil division of the Court of Appeal, ruled yesterday that the school had unlawfully excluded her, unlawfully denied her the right to manifest her religion and unlawfully denied her access to suitable and appropriate education. He called on the Department of Education to give schools more guidance on complying with their obligations under the Human Rights Act. The judge quoted one of the sayings of prophet Mohammed which states: "Whenever a woman begins to menstruate, it is not right that anything should be seen except her face and hands."

Shabina, now 16 and attending a school where the jilbab is allowed, declared the victory was "for all Muslims who wish to preserve their identity and values despite prejudice and bigotry." She added: "The decision of Denbigh High School to prevent my adherence to my religion cannot unfortunately be viewed as merely a local decision taken in isolation. "Rather it was a consequence of an atmosphere that has been created in western societies post 9/11, an atmosphere in which Islam has been made a target for vilification in the name of the war on terror." A spokesman for the Children's Legal Centre, which also represented Shabina, warned: "This will have wide-ranging consequences for freedom to manifest religious beliefs and will have a significant impact on school dress codes." Shabina's local education authority, Luton Borough Council, said that all schools would now be advised to take pupils' religion into account when imposing uniform rules. Denbigh High School said the case had been lost on a technicality and the school was proud of its multi-racial policy. It was ordered to pay costs to the legal aid authorities which funded Shabina's appeal. The school's barrister, Simon Birks, said this would be the equivalent of paying for a teacher for a year. A Department of Education spokesman said: "We will study the ruling carefully."

Many young Muslims wear a shalwar kameez, a traditional trousers and tunic outfit, to school. This was worn by Shabina until September, 2002, and her headmaster raised no objection. A jilbab is an ankle-length gown worn by some Muslim women who seek to cover their arms and legs, but not faces or hands. This was refused by the school. Shabina said wearing the jilbab is a religious act in itself. The shalwar kameez may meet the need for modest dress but it is also worn by people from other faiths. The school's management at no stage objected to Shabina wearing an Islamic headscarf known as a hejab and many of its pupils do so. The Jilbab is banned in French schools along with all other *ostensible religious symbols*. Arguing Shabina's case, Cherie Booth QC said effectively banning some outfits while allowing others was to say some beliefs are more valid than others. She said countries were entitled to impose a set dress code for everyone, as France has, or respect diversity and allow pupils to express their religious beliefs, but not both. Other forms of religious dress are allowed in British schools, including the shalwar kameez previously worn by Shabina.

"I am deeply saddened at yesterday's ruling in the Court of Appeal that upheld Muslim schoolgirl Shabina Begum's right to wear the jilbab to school as a matter of her *human rights*. As a Muslim who has been subjected to the horrors of having my and my family's human rights abused by Arab governments, I find today's court ruling disturbing and a gross misuse of the European Convention on Human Rights. What Shabina wants to wear outside her school is a matter for her and I respect her right to do so. However, what she wears for school should be subject to the school regulations and I fear that yesterday's ruling will open the floodgates to spurious demands. If I wanted to walk around naked in central London, this ruling in effect would permit it. Luton's Denbigh High School, where Shabina was a student until she was suspended for not respecting the school's dress code, had devised a code with local Muslim clerics that was acceptable to the majority of students, 79 per cent of whom are Muslims. Her demand to wear the jilbab, a head-to-toe gown, was rejected not on religious or cultural grounds but primarily for safety reasons. The school did not single her out for her Muslim beliefs, it merely wanted her to comply, as all the other students do, with its uniform regulations. Also, it did not want the wearing of the jilbab to be seen as a way of being a *better Muslim*, creating a competition in piousness in which one can imagine many young girls would wish to take part. Shabina's recourse to the courts was wholly inappropriate and undermines the fundamental principles of human rights legislation. She must have missed some schooling in pursuit of the claim, which is a tragedy in itself. Let us not forget that human rights legislation was created to protect all of us from religious or cultural discrimination, arbitrary detention, torture and government tyranny. Its purpose was to protect and enable minorities and individuals to seek Justice when their fundamental rights were denied or withheld. It is absurd to use the Act in the way that Shabina has, for it undermines genuine cases of human rights violations. It trivialises what human rights are about and in this particular instance undermines one of the principal tenets of Islam, tolerance towards the society of which you are part.

Orphaned two years ago, Shabina's life has been tinged with tragedy and it might well be that she needs to reaffirm her cultural and religious identity by adhering to a very strict interpretation of Islam. Nevertheless, she is a British subject who enjoys all the benefits of a British national; health, education, freedom of speech, the right to practice whatever faith she wants and the right to wear what she wants. These are liberties that are denied in Bangladesh, from where her family came, and in most Islamic countries, where the consequences of practising them would result in imprisonment and torture. As a Muslim and a Palestinian who lives in this country, I feel passionately that Islam has been hijacked by Islamic fundamentalists for political purposes. Islam is an important religion that advocates understanding and acceptance. To a large degree, it gives women many rights, although it falls short of giving them equality, with traditionalists demanding their subjugation. My daughter Soraya wears clothes typical of most British teenagers, which might horrify the more traditional members of the Islamic community. But, more importantly, I teach her that what is important in life is respect and understanding. When she was eight, I arranged special lessons with one of London's leading Muslim clerics. After three lessons she came home in tears because he was insisting she cover herself from head to toe – at eight! I had a huge row with this man and said: "I want you to teach my daughter the principles of love and compassion, the basic tenets of Islam, not about clothes." Not long afterwards, this revered cleric left his wife and ran off with a Moroccan dancer. While I don't deny that there is prejudice towards Muslims, I do feel that there is a small Muslim minority that wants to take us back to the Middle Ages. Because they do so under the banner of religion, the Government has been reluctant to address the underlying causes that create such extreme views, for fear of being labelled anti-Islam. Britain is not a perfect society, but it is a multi-racial society that embraces and celebrates the diversity of all of us. Shabina should reflect on the fact that this country allows all of us to retain our culture, our religion and our tradition. In repressive regimes those rights are denied and I fear that the political correctness of this present government will erode many of the freedoms we take for granted in Britain. We need to talk about religion and the havoc that it can cause and we need to have more inter-faith dialogues. We need our religious leaders to speak to their communities to reconfirm the need for acceptance and respect towards others who follow different faiths. To deny religion as a salient factor in many of today's conflicts the world over is akin to leaving a bomb ticking away, a bomb that will surely explode and take away the language of human rights. Shabina might have won her right to wear the jilbab to school, but it's a hollow victory for human rights, for Islam and for all of us, as it has undermined the purpose of the Act and made it a tool for frivolous claims."

Mona Bauwens, Palestinian Writer   Daily Express Feature

COUNT 8

RAPE AND SEXUAL OFFENCES

Commander Brian Moore, Metropolitan Police in mid-April 2004 advised that police are launching the largest 'cold case' review of gang rapes, after it was revealed there is an average of one attack every day in London. Scotland Yard detectives will re-examine 2,000 unsolved cases and victims who have stayed silent will be urged to come forward and report attacks. The review decision comes in the wake of an interim study conducted by the Metropolitan Police, which revealed that a hard core of muggers carry out an alarming number of gang rapes in London, although there have been similar crimes in Birmingham and Manchester. Many of these teenage rapists take part in the sickening assaults as part of initiation ceremonies, to be accepted by gang members. A total of 2,607 rapes were reported in the Met area last year, up 4% on 2002. Only 25% of perpetrators were identified and only a fraction of the number successfully prosecuted. The figures showed that 49% of the alleged attacks were committed by black males and 13% by Asians. Half the victims were under 21, more than 50% of the assaults involved 3 or more attackers and a high proportion of the victims were white females.

The Met has a dedicated rape investigation and victim care team called Operation Sapphire. Its Head, Commander Moore said: "We will examine every case reported to us in the last five years to find out every trend, pattern and common thread between each assault. We are determined to discover what changes need to be made to the way we analyse cases, prosecute them and support the victims, as well as how we can best prevent such rapes." He added: "The most important thing is to get the message across to women out there who have not come forward to report serious sexual assaults of the past. If victims wish to tell us about their experience, we are prepared to just listen. If they want us to start investigating and try to catch the perpetrators , we will do that too.

One of the most brutal gang attacks of recent years took place in the summer of 2000, when 37-year old Delphi Newman, a visitor to this country, was raped on the towpath of the Grand Union Canal in West London, by a gang of five boys and one girl. After the Old Bailey trial, the victim waived her legal right to anonymity, to reveal the full brutality of the attack. Mr Moore is determined that after *Operation Sapphire's* review, police will be able to lessen the chance of such cases taking place. He said: "We have six dedicated officers who will compare all the new information to that received over the past decade." His predecessor, John Yates, who was recently promoted to Deputy Assistant Commissioner, sparked a debate in January 2004 about political correctness, when he explained in a Radio Four broadcast, why the Met no longer used the term "gang rape" and instead labelled these attacks as "group rapes". He said: "It is not the ethnicity that counts here, it's the way we treat the victim. Gang rape suggests groups of feral youths roaming London. That is not the case. Group rape, by our definition, is when two or more people are present or aware of the conspiratorial element of the attacks. It's not less nasty, it's less emotive."

Senior Scotland Yard officers are well aware that black youths are disproportionately involved in rape cases and are treading carefully, because the issue is fraught with political dangers. Dr. Tony Sewell, a lecturer at Kingston University in London and a columnist for the black newspaper *The Voice* said: "Because of the guilt they had in the past, the police have become too politically correct. What's the difference between a gang rape and a group rape? For young men, the gang takes over. In school, teachers don't discipline these boys. They're frightened of being accused of being racist."

During my 14-years police career, I was never required to become involved in the investigation of a rape case. The nearest I came to it was once when I was stationed at Upminster. A woman with two sons of school age, who was married to a quite violent criminal, made an allegation that he had forced her into allowing him to have anal intercourse with her. The case papers were submitted to Solicitors Department for advice and were returned marked NFA (No further action), as there was no other evidence in support and corroboration of her story. In other words, it was a case of one person's word against the other. At court, the case would never have even got off the ground, therefore her cruel and brutal husband could not be charged with the offence, which is looked upon as being very akin to rape. In some peoples' eyes, the act is viewed as despicable, unnatural – and disgusting.

Here are some recently dealt with cases of rape, the first was heard at Norwich Crown Court in February 2004.

Anthony Millgate, 45, over a 3-hour period, raped his female victim nine times. She later discovered that she was in fact his third victim, making Millgate a serial rapist. When she heard the full story of his criminal past, she expressed horror that he may be released to rape yet again. It emerged in court that in 1983, Millgate was sentenced to 8 years imprisonment for rape. He was released, but in 1989 struck again and this time was sentenced to 12 years imprisonment for rape. He attacked his latest victim in October 2003. When arrested, he told police he should never have been released to commit his latest horrific attack. Judge Philip Curl sentenced Millgate to two life sentences and told him that he must serve at least nine years.

You will no doubt be horrified to hear about the awful offences committed by the following sex-crimes beast, who had also been released from jail too early, thus giving him the opportunities to strike again.

Matthew Thomas, 43, snatched a mother of two off the street and raped her in a flat, where he had already murdered another woman. After kidnapping her as she left work, he repeatedly raped her during a two hour ordeal. As her nightmare unfolded in the lounge of the flat, this latest victim had no idea that the body of murdered Collette Magee, 44, was lying just feet away from her in the kitchen. Thomas had stabbed her to death just a few hours beforehand, at her flat in Luton, just 6 days after she had married her second husband. The court heard that the amazing courage displayed by the rape victim, aged 45, saved her life. When her husband called her on her mobile phone, she was able to give him a cryptic clue that she was in trouble. Eventually she gained her captor's confidence to such an extent that he allowed her to leave with him when he left the flat. At Luton Crown Court, Thomas pleaded guilty to the murder of Collette Magee, kidnapping the second woman and twice raping her. He also pleaded guilty to a further offence of indecently assaulting her. The offences happened just two months after Thomas had been released from a 16-year jail term for a string of sex offences. He had then gone to live in a hostel in Luton.

The Judge, Mr Justice Beatson, sentenced Thomas as follows:

The murder of Collette Magee – Life imprisonment.

Kidnapping the second victim – 8-years imprisonment.

Each of two rapes on the second victim – two sentences of life imprisonment.

Indecent assault on the second victim – five years imprisonment.

The Judge ordered that Thomas must serve a minimum of 16 years, as he is 'a high risk to the public'. We will probably never know what other serious offences Thomas committed, prior to murdering Collette Magee, nor how she must have suffered.

As you progress through this book, reading about these awful people who are all-too-often set free too early, you may like to keep in mind that, in reality, most criminals are really unlucky if they are arrested and convicted 'first time out'. Many would have you believe that they have only committed the actual offences for which they have just been convicted. However you have also heard of the reality of the matter, through the high number of TIC offences, which some criminals admit to. It would certainly be a more perfect world as far as the police are concerned, if they could make an arrest every single time a criminal committed yet another offence!

At Oxford Crown Court in March 2004, Clare Newson, 19, from Banbury, pleaded guilty to attempting to pervert the course of justice. She had pretended that she had been raped. She wept as she was sentenced to six months in a young offenders institution.

An Old Bailey judge has praised an 11-year-old girl who fought off a man who tried to rape her at knife point. He also backed her campaign to be rehoused because of the terrible memories. Scott Lockett, 32, of Peckham, crept in when her parents were out but the screaming girl battled back, the court heard. Judge Jeremy Roberts said: "It was only due to her courage that you fled." Lockett was found guilty of aggravated burglary with intent to rape and was jailed for 11 years. The girl wrote describing her ordeal and her fight for Peckham council to find a new home. The judge said: " It is most unfair if the council are unable to rehouse the family." He said her letter should be sent to the council with his comments.

Teenager Lance Smit, 18 went on a week-long terror rampage in Tooting, South London, attacking six women in total. He climbed a drainpipe and sneaked into a bedroom where a 29-year old teacher was sleeping. When she told him to take her handbag, he said: "I don't want that, I want sex." He threatened to kill her before raping her. He then snatched £10 and fled. In the space of eight days, Smit attacked and robbed five women, threatening them all with a knife. One victim was attacked in a park in front of her two-year old child, a second was pregnant and a third was a teenage student. He was arrested after police mounted a large-scale surveillance operation. He admitted rape, false imprisonment, assault, kidnap and robbery. Judge Jeremy Roberts, at the Old Bailey, told Smit: "It is hard to think of a worse experience than for a young woman to be woken in the night to find a strange man with a knife in her bedroom and who then proceeds to rape her." Smit was sentenced to life imprisonment.

This next report you may consider is just about as bad as it gets, almost beyond the imagination. It is essential to report it in detail so that you will know the whole story of what this dreadful person has been capable of.

His name is Andrezej Kunowski, 48 years, whose dreadful criminal career commenced in Poland, when he was 17 years of age.

June 1973 – Grabbed a neighbour's daughter aged 17, bundled her in some bushes and raped her. He was jailed for 3 years.

July 1977– Attempted murder and attempted rape of a 24-year old woman whom he strangled into unconsciousness, passers-by stepped in to save her.

April 1978 – Attempted rape after grabbing a 22-year old woman by the throat and throttling her. Raped a 27-year old woman, grabbing her by the throat.

June 1978 – Raped and robbed a 22-year old woman by grabbing her throat and bundling her into bushes.

1st July 1978 – Raped a 16-year old girl.

21st July 1978 – Raped a 12-year old girl.

4th August 1978 – Raped and robbed a 19-year old girl and grabbed her by the throat.

August 1978 – Raped a 22-year old woman as he tried to strangle her.

6th September 1978 – Rape and robbery of a 20-year old woman involving strangulation.

8th September 1978 – Attempted rape of a 17-year old girl, again by grabbing her neck.

20th September 1978 - Rape of a 17-year old girl by grabbing her neck.

October 1978 – Raped and robbed 17-year old and 20-year old girls.

20th October 1978 – Rape and attempted robbery of a 28-year old woman involving strangulation.

21st October 1978 – Attempted rape and strangling of a 30-year old woman.

7th November 1978 – Attempted rape of a 19-year old girl.

9th November 1978 – Raped a 21-year old woman by grabbing her by the throat.

14th November 1978 – Raped a 15-year old girl by grabbing her from behind by the throat.

29th November 1978 – Raped an 11-year old girl.

14th December 1978 – Attempted rape of a 16-year old girl involving strangulation.

22nd December 1978 – Raped and abused an 11-year old girl.

25th January 1979 – Theft of a car.

26th January 1979 – Robbed a 41-year old woman and tried to strangle her with his bare hands. Attempted robbery of a 36-year old woman. Raped and robbed a 20-year old woman by trying to throttle her with his hands.

24th February 1979 – After being sentenced, forced a male cell-mate into oral sex.

1st March 1979 – Still in prison serving 15 years for previous offences, male-raped, another cell-mate.

25th April 1979 – Escaped from prison.

May 1979 – Forgery of a Polish identity card.

7th May 1979 – Raped a 13-year old girl in her flat and tried to throttle her. Demanded, money and jewellery.

8th May 1979 – Threatened to kill a child with an axe as he tried to escape arrest.

18th August 1979 – Second escape from prison.

19th August 1979 – Stole a Fiat 126 motor car.

22nd August 1979 – Stole another Fiat 126.

24th August 1979 – Various road traffic offences.

21st March 1980 – Theft of clothing.

1985 – Given 15 years for those crimes and another 15 years for attacks he carried out in Warsaw, but only served 6 years.

1991 – Released from prison for good behaviour.

15th October 1991 – Tried to defraud unemployment benefit.

12th August 1992 – Raped an 11-year old girl.

1993 – Arrested for the rape of two girls in Warsaw before escaping whilst awaiting trial.

1995 – Arrested again but jumped bail when he was freed to visit hospital for a hip operation.

1996 – Arrived in the UK.

9th May 2003 – Jailed for 9 years at the Central Criminal Court for raping a 23-year old Korean student in London in September 2002. Offences included three rape charges and false imprisonment.

31st March 2004 – Sentenced to 'whole life' imprisonment for the murder by strangulation of 12-year old Katerina Koneva in May 1997.

As you can see from the above catalogue of heinous crimes, Kunowski is a dreadful man who will stop at nothing to get his wicked way. He was described by the officer in the most recent case, Detective Chief Inspector David Little as 'Probably the most dangerous, and certainly the most prolific, sex offender I have ever come across'.

Extreme liberalism within the Polish criminal justice system over the years, played its part in allowing this man to run wild. (You may take the view that our own criminal justice system is fast catching up with how Poland was, after all the awful things you have been reading about in this book and from your own knowledge of life.) Just to summarise Kunowski's awful history of sex crimes and near-murders by strangulation, in almost every case.

He was first imprisoned for rape in Mlawa, Poland in 1973. He twice fled prison before being jailed for 15 years for the string of rapes in nearby Ciechanow. He was sentenced to another 15 years for the attacks in Warsaw. In just nine months in 1978, he carried out 15 rapes. Victims were frequently sexually abused after arriving home alone and being choked senseless. But the Polish courts in their liberalism, allowed the jail terms to be served concurrently instead of consecutively and he only served six years, being freed in 1991. Two years later he was held for the rape of two girls in Warsaw, but fled while awaiting trial. In 1995 he was arrested again for the rape of a girl of 10 in Warsaw. This time he jumped bail after a judge allowed him to be freed unsupervised to have a hip operation.

A year later, he entered Britain as a tourist using forged Portuguese documents, free to continue his reign of terror in a new country. In May 1997, he killed Macedonian-born Katerina Koneva, aged 12, when she returned to her empty home at Iffley Road, Hammersmith, West London. You probably remember reading or hearing about the horrific case. Pushing his way into the property, Kunowski throttled the beautiful child with a cord, in a sexually-motivated attack. As the girl slipped into unconsciousness, her father arrived home and found the front door open and the living room door barricaded with a chair. Unaware that his daughter was breathing her last, he rushed to the front door as Kunowski jumped out of a window. He escaped in a hijacked car after pulling a knife. Her father raced back to the house and made frantic efforts to cut the ligature around Katerina's neck, but the cord was too tight and, presumably, he was in fear of cutting her throat with the knife he was using. Three other girls aged about 12 years were stalked in the Hammersmith area around the time of Katerina's murder.

A month later, Kunowski was held for theft in Hereford and handed over to Immigration Officials. They discovered he was an illegal 'over-stayer'. But even though his fingerprints had been sent to 125 countries, he was not linked to his past record or Katerina's murder. He then spent two months in an immigration detention camp in Oxford and was released after applying for residence. When his application was refused, he again vanished. Astonishingly, even though he was a hunted killer and illegal immigrant, he was given a life-saving NHS heart bypass operation in the year 2000. In 2001 he stopped a woman in the street in West London and told her: " I know where you live, I murdered a young girl in Iffley Road, four years ago." The following year he was again tracked down and ordered to be deported, but (not surprisingly, given his record!) he failed to turn up for the deportation order to be carried out. A few days later, he was arrested for raping a 21-year old Korean girl he lured to his bedsit, in Acton, West London. The student had arrived in Britain only a few weeks earlier. In a three-hour ordeal, she was bound, throttled and raped. After Kunowski was jailed for nine years, it was discovered that his DNA matched the DNA of a single hair found in packaging containing Katerina's cardigan at the time of her death.

During his three-week trial at the Old Bailey, he denied murder. However he was convicted by a jury after two-and-half hours deliberation. Judge Peter Beaumont said to Kurnowski: "I would be failing in my duty if I did not ensure you spend the rest of your life in prison." (Many judges do 'fail in their duty' as you will know through reading this book – However Judge Peter Beaumont is obviously not one of them.) Although Judge Beaumont has, quite rightly, in most sensible peoples' minds, set a 'whole life' tariff of imprisonment for Kurnowski, it is far too soon for us to sympathetically draw comfort. There has been insufficient time for the Appeals Court process to be explored by those defending him. Furthermore, you can guarantee that before long, some of 'the usual suspects', such as the Human Rights officianados will be 'snapping at the heels' of whoever is the Home Secretary of the day, so as to give Kurnowski some 'light at the end of the tunnel' by a definite release date being set.

You will appreciate that some of Kurnowski's victims can never have 'light at the end of the tunnel', Commenting on this case after Kurnowski's latest conviction, a Home Office spokesman said: "It's a matter of great concern that a criminal with such a serious history managed to get into this country and that his background was not uncovered when he came to our attention. All suspected asylum seekers are now electronically fingerprinted on entry. These details are then fed into a European index which would alert us to criminal activity."

As a footnote to the above case, a 19-year old Polish girl, identified only as 'Ania', flew to London from her Warsaw home to give evidence in this trial, but was prevented by a legal ruling. (No doubt through a defence move that the trial must be scrupulously fair to the defendant, but the victim's rights and those of her family must count for nothing!) She would, had she been allowed to testify,have told the court and jury that at the age of 10 years, in 1995, in Warsaw, Poland, she had been targeted by Kurnowski after she came home from school. He claimed to know her father and forced his way into the flat. She said: "I was very afraid of him and did what he told me to do, but I started to scream. He covered my mouth with his hand so I could barely breathe. When the man entered my room and I followed him in, he asked me if I could keep a secret. He told me to kiss him but I didn't want to, and then he started to choke me." 'Ania' said she was raped on her sofa bed. "Then he tied up my hands and my feet with telephone wire." He left after stealing some money. A DNA profile from the bed matched Kurnowski's by a factor of one in a billion.

Coincidentally, this next sexual pervert is also an immigrant to this country, this time born of a Polish father and a German mother. His name is Antoni Imiela, 50 years, who worked in maintenance on this country's railways. This gave him the independence and freedom to move around the country. We are told, presumably by the police officer in the case or his defence counsel at the trial, that he spent his first six years in a refugee camp in Lubeck, West Germany. In 1960 the family moved to Newton Aycliffe, County Durham, where the defendant was bullied at school and dubbed a Nazi. His welder father, Anton, apparently thrashed and humiliated his son, punishments included shaving his head. He also informed another family member that his father had also sexually abused him. When his mother, Elfriede, a cleaner, fled to Germany after a nervous breakdown, it is claimed that this event triggered his future life of crime.

At school in nearby Bishop Auckland, he was a troubled teenager. He fought and stole, raided the school tuck shop and later confessed to burgling every single house in a street. He was sent to Borstal at age 17 years. In February 1987 he held up a post office in Darlington with a sawn-off shotgun and escaped with £10,000. He fled abroad and blew the cash from the robbery, before walking away empty-handed from a fresh post office raid in October 1987. In the next 2 months he carried out six robberies, once leaving a man with serious head injuries before fleeing with £8,000. On 5th January 1988 he slipped through an armed police cordon before giving himself up at his partner's home the following day. In May 1988 at Teesside Crown Court he was jailed for 14 years. After serving just nine of the 14 years, he was released and settled down into an apparently normal life after getting married, moving into his wife's former council house in Appledore, Kent and working full-time earning good money. But at the relatively late stage in life, aged 47 years, he was to start the continuance of his earlier criminal career. He was on course to become eventually known as the 'Trophy Rapist'.

These are the very serious criminal offences he committed against members of the female gender, in chronological order:

15th November 2001 – Rape of a 10-year old girl in Ashford, Kent.

11th July 2002 – Rape of a woman aged 30 years, in Redhill, Surrey. (On the same day) – Rape of a woman aged 26 years, in Putney, SW London.

16th July 2002 – Rape of a woman aged 18 years, in Woking, Surrey. (2 counts)

6th August 2002 – Rape of a woman aged 52 years, in Wimbledon.

7th August 2002 – Rape of a woman aged 26 years in Epsom, Surrey.

6th September 2002 – Rape of a girl aged 13 years, near Woking, Surrey.

25th October 2002 – Rape of a girl aged 14 years, in Stevenage, Herts.

21st November 2002 – Kidnap, indecent assault and attempted rape of a 10 year old girl.

Imiela became known as the 'Trophy Rapist' because he stole clothing from his victims. His attacks struck fear into women and young girls in Southern England. His first and youngest victim, now aged 12 years, has said she would like to kill him for what he put her through during his attack. She finds that she is still unable to sleep at her home, after Imiela threatened to go there and kill her if she reported him. She has blocked the memory of her ordeal but suffers flashbacks and nightmares that leave her terrified of the dark, more than two years later.

She said: "Jail is not good enough for him, I want to kill him for hurting me." Her father said: "I think even death is not punishment enough for what he's done. But I would still kill him if I got my hands on him. He threatened that he knew where she lived and would come back for her if she told anyone about the attack. The only time she has had a good night sleep is when she has stayed at someone else's house, because he wouldn't know where she is, even though he's in jail." He added: "Jail is a soft option for a beast like him. He wouldn't even look me in the eye in court, because he knows he hasn't even got the decency to spare the victims the ordeal of a harrowing court case, by just admitting what he's done."

The victim, from Ashford, Kent, was outside a youth club she helped to run, when he struck. He had been out drinking with workmates in Swanley, Kent but stated he had only drunk two pints. The girl had noticed Imiela talking to her from across the street. At this time, he was just a couple of miles from his home address at Appledore, Kent. The girl said: "I watched him trying to talk to me and talking to himself, pretending he was beckoning a dog by saying, 'Come on then.' The next thing, he was running across the road towards me. I just froze and couldn't move. When he reached me, he grabbed me, put a hand over my mouth, picked me up and ran off." Imiela lay her down in some bushes, stripped her down to her T-shirt and one sock, and when a couple passed nearby, he said, 'Pretend I'm your Dad.' The girl said: "But I didn't want to because I know who my Dad is." Her father added, "It shows just how sick and depraved he is. She thought he was going to kill her. How can he pretend to be her father behaving like that?" The victim's mother said: "She told him he was drunk. She said she was only 10 and was too young and innocent for him, but his only response was to torment her, saying, 'Shut up' or 'Be quiet' and 'Don't tell me you haven't done this before'." The girl added: "I thought he was going to kill me. I remember thinking 'I want to hurt you like you're hurting me'." Imelia then told her he would take her home so that he knew where she lived and could come back for her if she told police. The girl said: "He grabbed my orange T-shirt and asked if he could take it. Then suddenly he just ran off, telling me to count to 500. I did it, I was so scared, but I missed a few numbers on the way so I could get away as quickly as possible." She went to a nearby house and said: "Can you help me, I've just been raped?"

In early March 2004 at Maidstone Crown Court, Mr Justice Owen told Imiela: "You have been convicted on overwhelming evidence of an horrific series of rapes. You attacked unsuspecting victims, overwhelming them with brute force and in most cases, with threats to kill, dragging them into the undergrowth. Most thought they would die at your hands. You subjected them to humiliating and degrading sexual acts culminating in rape. In many cases you asked your victim to respond to you, saying such things as, 'tell me how much you like it, tell me how big and strong I am'. In a grotesque parody of a formal relationship, you displayed a chilling contempt to your victims, exemplified in the case where you took the mobile telephone from

your victim and phoned her mother. You are a ruthless, sexual predator."
Mr Justice Owen sentenced Imiela to seven life imprisonment sentences for
the rapes of four women and three girls aged from 10 to 52. He was also
given concurrent sentences of 10 years, seven years and 12 years for the
kidnap, indecent assault and attempted rape of the 10-year old brave little
girl we just heard about. The jury were discharged after failing to reach
verdicts over the double rape attack against the 18-year old victim from
Woking, Surrey, in July 2002. Those charges were ordered to remain on file.

You may well be thinking, if you are above a certain age, that at this stage
of Imiela's trial, Mr Justice Owen should have been reaching for the black
cap. Amazingly, Imiela's wife, Christine intends to stand by him. She is
quoted as saying: "I don't know how I'll feel once this has all blown over, but
at the moment I think I would have him back, yes. I don't believe my
husband is guilty, I just think he's sick and needs help. He must have
committed the crimes, because he can't have just innocently been in all
those places at the time all the offences were carried out."

Not surprisingly, you might think, after the trial, Imiela's stepdaughter,
now aged 22 years, came forward for interview and stated that when she
was 16-years old, he pursued her for sex too. She said: "Within the first year
of him moving into our house, I noticed his dangerously short temper. I
started feeling like he was watching me. He made me feel uncomfortable if
I wore a short skirt or a little top. But despite his violent mood swings I
never believed for a second that he was the evil monster the police were
searching for. Now I realise how close I had been to becoming one of his
victims. Since then I've had nightmares about him attacking me. I imagine
him holding my arms and trying to kiss me. He disgusts me and after what
he's done he deserves everything he gets."

The case of rapist and murderer Graham Coutts, 35 years, from Brighton,
was widely publicised in February 2004. Coutts was the man who
downloaded from the internet awful images of women with rope nooses or
other various ligatures around their throats. He claimed that in order for
him to 'get off' during sexual intercourse, it was essential that his female
partners were partially asphyxiated by ligatures. At least one of his previous
partners was able to confirm this, claiming that she had to eventually stop
seeing him as he put her in so much fear, by insisting on the partial
asphyxiation during sexual intercourse. On the fateful day, a well-loved and
respected lady who taught people with learning difficulties, Jane Longhurst,
31 years, somehow finished up in his company at his flat. She had a regular
boyfriend of her own, Coutts was the partner of her best friend. As poor
Jane never lived to tell the tale, we only have, from the trial and a TV
documentary, the version of events supplied by Coutts.

Somehow, after she had phoned his flat, presumably to speak to her best friend, who was not at home, Coutts lured her to the flat. It seems that nobody will ever know whether consexual sex took place, or whether Coutts raped Jane. What is known is that he used a ligature around her neck and her death was caused by strangulation. Whether it was deliberate because he intended to murder her, or if he just went too far by over-tightening the ligature during his bizarre sexual performance, will always remain a mystery. Suffice to say that, once he found that he had killed his victim, he placed her body in a huge rented storage box, together with some of her clothing and, bizarrely, a used contraceptive. He was then pictured on CCTV transporting the box, which became Jane's temporary coffin, out of the storage warehouse. He had been obliged to do this as the body was deteriorating into putrefaction, with the resultant tell-tale smells and fluids leakage. At one point, he was clearly pictured on CCTV wiping up spilled bodily fluids from the floor near a lift. He then transported the body to some remote wasteland, where he set it on fire, obviously hoping that it would never be found, or at least be unrecognisable.

The storage warehouse records and the in-place CCTV cameras recorded that he visited the storage compartment on several occasions. Due to the presence of the used condom, the police seemed convinced, apparently, that he may well have had sexual intercourse with his unfortunate victim, on at least one occasion after her death, viz: whilst her body was still in storage. Jane's poor mother, sister and the rest of the family and friends, will never know the whole truth and can only guess at the degree of suffering she must have experienced at the hands of sexual pervert Coutts. In an effort to come to terms with the horror of it all, and to assist with the grieving process, her mother is now strongly campaigning to have internet websites depicting strangulation-type sexual behaviour, including murder, rape and even necrophilia scenarios, shut down.

After the trial, Coutts was observed in police interrogation video clips as being absolutely perverse and pathetic, being unable to give an account of himself and his behaviour and worst of all, being unable or unwilling to provide crucial answers. Coutts was sentenced to life imprisonment at Lewes Crown Court, having caused victim Jane's family additional and unnecessary suffering, by pleading 'not guilty' to the counts on the indictment. There is no doubt whatsoever that whilst serving his sentence of imprisonment, he is going to have to 'watch his back' against summary justice being carried out by other inmates, for a long, long time.

Another furious person came forward to illustrate how murderer Coutts had previously defeated justice, by convincing a Bench of three elderly women magistrates that his alleged 'creepy' behaviour was quite innocent.

Georgina Langridge, now aged 51, told how in 1997, she had a disturbing brush with the future killer at a swimming pool in East Grinstead, Sussex. Mrs Langridge reported that she was in a changing cubicle at the pool, wrapped in only a towel, when she spotted a video camera lens pointing at her. She said: "After a swim, I took my costume off and walked through the changing rooms with just a towel around me. I spotted something in the corner of my eye. I thought it was a snorkel at first. I yelled 'creep, pervert!' I chased him and caught up with Coutts (Whom she recognised in reports of the current trial) as he tried to stash his video camera in a hold-all." Coutts was arrested and at the local magistrates court hearing, Coutts was allowed to cross-examine her, during her evidence. The magistrates cleared him, giving him the benefit of the doubt, after he told them he entered the pool area to check on the swimming times and took his video camera in with him so it would not be stolen from his car.

Sussex police explained that as Coutts was acquitted, the police record would have been 'weeded' from their system and destroyed, six months after the court case.

It was reported in March 2004 that a convicted rapist, civil rights activist Delroy Lindo, 44 years, is to receive £85,000 compensation from police, after claiming his family were victims of an 'orchestrated campaign of intimidation' by officers. Lindo, the best friend of murderer Winston Silcott, had hoped to receive £1million after suing Scotland Yard for racial harassment. The former housing official complained that, over an eight year period he was arrested 37 times and charged with 18 offences – none of which resulted in convictions. Officers insisted they were provoked into arresting Lindo. His case was highlighted by Left-wing newspapers, who ignored his extensive criminal record and portrayed him as a 'model' citizen. They also failed to mention that he is wanted in the US over allegations of domestic violence. It has emerged that after a four-year legal battle, Lindo and his wife Sonia had reached an out-of-court settlement in which they will receive £85,000 from the Met. The pay-out has enraged senior officers who regard father-of-three Lindo as a 'professional police baiter and hater'. Critics believe Met Chiefs have again buckled under the pressure of political correctness. The black activist has an appalling criminal record and does not hide his hatred of the police. Three years ago a Scotland Yard report listed his 17 criminal convictions, including rape, grievous bodily harm, actual bodily harm, theft, handling stolen property and criminal damage. It also revealed how he held his wife at knifepoint at their North London home, in March 1996. Lindo was arrested and bound over and fined £100 for breach of the peace.

The report controversially accepted this led to 'negative stereotyping', and, as a result, 'a disproportionate number of reactions' from local police. It said Lindo was 'partly instrumental' in the worsening relations with officers and at times his behaviour was 'arguably provocative.' The report concluded that there was no evidence of an 'organised conspiracy' against the Lindos. However it did find the Met guilty of harassment – which left many officers furious with their senior colleagues for condemning them without hearing their side of the story. They claim their rights to a fair hearing were sacrificed in the interests of appeasing a vocal black minority, intent on taking advantage of the Met's sensitivity on race issues. But the report rejected the assertion that Lindo was targeted because of his links to the defence campaign for Silcott, who was convicted and then cleared of the murder of PC Keith Blakelock during the Broadwater Farm riots in 1985.

Silcott was released from prison last year (2004) after serving a life sentence for murdering a boxer, and remains a close friend of Lindo. Scotland Yard said in a statement on 22nd March 2004 that: "The Met can confirm that after a period of consultation with Mr and Mrs Lindo, we have reached a settlement regarding their civil action against the MPS. It has been reached without any admission of legal liability, and the Met denies any organised conspiracy of harassment against the Lindo family. However the Met accepts it has not always got everything right in its interactions with the family between 1992 and 2000, and regrets any distress this may have caused." The enquiry report was written by Assistant Commissioner Tarique Ghaffur, the most senior ethnic officer. Glen Smyth, chairman of the Metropolitan Police Federation said: "I hope relationships between Mr Lindo and local police improve and he does not engage in the sort of behaviour he was criticised for in Mr Ghaffur's report." In 1984 Lindo was jailed for raping a typist on the day he returned from his honeymoon. Silcott had been best man at his wedding.

World-renowned concert pianist Brian Parnell, 66, of Hornsey, appeared at Wood Green Crown Court on 2nd June 2004. He had been convicted of child sex offences involving 'sex tourism', in an elaborate 'sting' set up by Scotland Yard's paedophile squad. The pianist had tried to lure a boy for sex in Sri Lanka while he was on tour with an opera company, but was confronted by investigators as he was about to play in a concert. Police later arrested him at his London home. Seven witnesses travelled to London from Sri Lanka to give evidence at his trial. He was jailed for just two years.

Turning now to matters of a sexual nature in which I personally took part in the investigations, during my 14-year police career. I have already told you about the murder squad I worked on in the Ilford area where the female victim was probably raped, but certainly murdered by her window cleaner.

My first-ever case was whilst I was a uniformed police officer stationed at Tilbury, Essex, a well-known busy dockland area. I was fresh out of Police College, Eynsham Hall, near Witney, Oxon., which was then known as 'No. 5 District Police Training Centre'. My head was still full of important legal definitions and powers of arrest, which had to be learnt word-perfect by walking around the Police College grounds in your lunch hour, repeating them out loud, over and over again, ad nauseum. I was on night duty at Tilbury and had probably only just finished 'learning beats' under the supervision of an experienced constable. I saw a man about 50 yards ahead of me, in the semi-darkness, standing on the opposite pavement of busy Dock Road, Tilbury, looking up at a house opposite. His body language made him suspicious. As I crept closer and closer to him, hugging the shop doorways, I saw that I had spotted my first ever 'flasher.' He was intently gazing up at a lighted window in which a fully-clothed woman was doing her ironing, apparently oblivious to his presence in the street below. At this important stage of my new career, I was mentally trying to call to mind under what circumstances I could arrest a man who, 'with intent to insult a female, was wilfully, openly, lewdly and obscenely exposing his person,' which was a summary offence, as against the more serious felonies and misdemeanours.

As luck would have it, I was carrying my Police Diary which was more or less a compulsory purchase at Police Training College! The diary contained lists of definitions and tables of Police Powers of Arrest, set out in columns with an alphabetical block capital against each one. The columns of the table included such scenarios as:

1) Found committing, name and address refused, or suspected false.
2) Only if in possession of a warrant.
3) Accompanied by a Breach Of The Peace. Etc, etc.

Quickly flicking through the diary to the *Powers of Arrest* table, by shaded torchlight in a shop doorway, to my supreme delight I was reassured by the diary page that although this man was only committing a 'summary offence,' Her Majesty The Queen had vested in me the power to arrest this awful man and deliver him up, for justice to take its course. Amazingly, I was able to get right up close to him, approaching from directly up front, without him being aware of my presence, as he was so engrossed in what he was doing!

I promptly took him into custody, by gripping his arm, after a brief bodily search to ensure that he was not carrying anything with which he could harm myself, himself or anyone else. Immediately prior to the moment of arrest, I had, of course, observed his exposed and erect penis and his hand movements, vital evidential factors for the court case. I think he was probably unable to understand my formal arrest and caution conversation, as he turned out to be a Swedish seaman from a merchant navy ship berthed at Tilbury Docks. He pleaded guilty at Grays Magistrates Court next morning and received a monetary penalty. I had needed to contact the woman who was ironing at her window to ascertain if she had, firstly, seen him, secondly, been aware of what he was up to and thirdly, been insulted by his actions. Once again my luck was in as I received a very welcome 'triple-Yes.'

As Temporary Detective Constables (TDC's) whilst based at Romford on 'Outer K' division, Metropolitan Police, we mainly 'cut our teeth' on shoplifters in the large department stores, shops and market stalls (on Wednesday and Saturday market days). Patrolling the stalls in the market meant we were also vigilant to detect what had been known since time immemorial as 'bustle-punchers'. These were horrible men who were attracted like magnets to market stalls run by persons like noisy Fred, who was born with a loud microphone grafted to his throat. He offered, (every single market day), 'totally unrepeatable' special offers. In the crowd around his stall, and other stall-holders like him, would be his 'plants.' These are supposed, but never innocent-looking, male and female staff, who are always the very first to raise their £5 note (supplied by Fred) at arms length, to 'assure' genuine would-be 'punters' that these are truly the best bargains of all time. Whichever stall-holder had the loudest sound speakers, or could shout the loudest without becoming hoarse, it is written, would secure the largest audience of mugs, sorry, customers around the stall. In the old days of my youth, Romford was a very well-known cattle market, holding stocks of pigs, sheep, cattle, chickens etc, but I stop short of drawing an analogy between these and the potential customers gathered around Fred's stall!

The dreaded 'bustle-punchers' knew just which days to report for duty at Romford Market, as I said, Wednesdays and Saturdays. Because of them, needing as many prisoners' names logged in the rear of our official, A5 sizes, hard backed, blue covered CID diaries, as it was possible to cram in each week, we TDC's too, were attracted to the market place, like moths around a flame or light at night. It became our sworn and bounden duty to 'nail' as many 'bustle-punchers' as humanly possible and competition between us, and patrolling uniformed colleagues, was very fierce.

Definition: *BUSTLE-PUNCHER. A person of the male gender who, attracted by a large, distracted crowd around a market stall, pushes or thrusts the front of his body against the rear of female customers (and even children of course) in the crowd, so as to receive sexual stimulation and gratification.*

Anyway, no names-no pack drill, suffice to say that, on both market days at Romford, there was rarely a shortage of 'bustle-punchers' and absolutely never a shortage of shoplifters. Really, with 'bustle-punching', it was a bit of a grey area, simply because most ladies or girls, perhaps not convinced that the offender's behaviour was anything other than 'accidental', would rarely want to assist us. Although the police station was literally just up the road, a few minutes walk away, it meant, for the witnesses, losing at least a couple of hours of their precious shopping time, whilst making a written statement to Police about the incident. Later on, too, they may have been required to attend court at Havering Magistrates Court, which abuts Romford police station. This all meant, in practice, that invariably two would-be fully fledged CID officers would arrest Mr 'B-P' and charge him with 'conduct likely to cause a breach of the peace', for which he might be lightly fined and then Bound Over to be of good behaviour in future and to Keep The Peace, in the sum of money of whatever the court set, for a period of (usually) 12 months. Obviously, if he were in breach of the Binding Over Order within the next year, he would be hauled up back before the court in respect of the breach. In those days, the usual definition of 'The Peace' was 'The Queen's Peace,' or shortly, 'The Peace' is the normal state of society, and any interruption of that peace and good order is a 'Breach Of The Peace.'

The same procedure in the store, police station and at court was once used by myself in the case of a man my colleague and I watched from a vantage point inside the department store. He got his kicks by hanging around at the bottom of a rising escalator, looking up the women's skirts. I must admit, it's a terrible shock to the system, the prisoner's that is, when the dreaded hand falls on your shoulder and

another on your forearm, as you start to enter 'feigned innocence' mode. In this particular case he was convinced of his innocence enough as to wrestle himself to the ground, cracking his head, but admitted the offence by the time he appeared at court. He too, was Bound Over to Keep The Peace.

We also were always on the look out for male 'flashers', who of course frequent all parks, open spaces and proximities of schools. We really felt we had made good arrests when we were able to detect these people and bring them to justice, who were and always will be, absolutely disgusting pests. These days, most of them seem to frequent pedestrian walkways and underpass tunnels, as well as parklands and open spaces, swing parks etc. In the Hornchurch area, at a place near a school called Roneo Corner, we made a good arrest one morning. Schoolgirls who had been exposed to, made a complaint about a man sitting at the kerbside in a particular make of car, on certain weekdays. The very first time we went after him, there he was at his usual parking spot, covering his exposed penis with a newspaper or magazine, which he would lift so that passing young girls could see his person. His feet didn't touch the ground and he was in the charge room at the police station with hardly a chance to 'please adjust your dress before leaving'. (As was always displayed on a sign in gents' lavatories.) This particular man was just so ashamed of his conduct and was absolutely terrified about confronting his wife when he got home. He really could not explain what came over him, he told us and the magistrates. I wonder what he told his wife?

There came a time when I was finally selected to be upgraded to Detective Constable and transferred onto 'J' division at Ilford. I was working the night shift with two colleagues in a plain Hillman Minx, posted as what was known as 'Night Duty CID'. We covered most of the Division all night, dealing with serious matters, which quite often meant making arrests at *The Ilford Palais* on Ilford High Road, for GBH, Affray, Indecent Assaults etc., the usual products of late-night drunkenness by thugs and yobs (Nothing's changed over the years!). We would carry out as many enquiries as were possible within the club or dance hall venue, which normally resulted in our finding that approx 150 club-goers and dancers were all in the lavatories at the time of the disturbance and had therefore seen nothing. Where possible, we would seize and preserve evidence and the crime scene, and arrange for the forensics to be done, finally leaving everything for the day staff to sort out next morning. Obviously, this kept CID staff overnight 'call-outs' to a minimum, so it was a good scheme.

One night, I was in the night duty CID car with two male police colleagues. We had been asked to keep an eye on a male public lavatory on Wanstead Flats, East London, a large open space with grassland, ponds etc, frequented by family groups during daylight hours. At night, reports indicated that the public toilet was being used for 'cottaging', viz: homosexuals loitering and frequenting the premises for unlawful sexual acts, or picking up to engage in the unlawful acts elsewhere. These people were real pests, as for heterosexual law-abiding males, they found it most embarrassing and even threatening, on entering to use the urinal or wc, only to find persons present who appeared to be intending to 'stay the night'. On this particular night, in virtually total darkness, from a 'safe' surveillance position, we parked our police car on the flat, open ground, not too far from the nearest cars, which either contained genuine heterosexual courting couples, or homosexuals enjoying a liaison with a male partner, possibly recently just been introduced at the gents lavatories, which were now within our sights. We shared a pair of official police binoculars and, for a while, watched the comings and goings by the toilets, in the darkness, in the distance as best we could.

There came a time when two people left the toilets together and walked to a nearby parked car. We saw the interior light go on and then off, confirming that the couple had indeed entered the car. We gave them two-three minutes, before driving the police car a bit nearer to the scene, so as to be able to facilitate the impending planned arrests. The colleague who was driving that night, remained in our car. The other two of us, carrying our police torches, approached the 'suspect' car and, at a signal, I wrenched open the front drivers' door as my colleague swiftly pulled open the rear nearside door. Naturally, the interior light came on to illuminate the scene, so our torch beams were not required. Our pulses raced with the adrenalin generated by the occasion, as we saw that one person was lying right on top of the other. However, to our utter surprise and abject horror, our hearts sunk, as it dawned on us both that the person in the uppermost position, was a WOMAN! You can just imagine how fast we slammed their car doors and beat a hasty retreat to our official car, which fortunately for us, already had the engine running. Naturally, in the darkness, our red faces could not be seen.

We couldn't imagine who was the most disappointed, us for having been deprived of our intended arrests for 'cottaging', or the apparently innocent heterosexual couple whom we had disturbed in the most shocking, unannounced manner of our arrival.

The woman had been wearing jeans and a white shirt, which is why she had appeared to us, at our distant vantage point, as a man. Several hours later, we plucked up the courage to return to the scene and swept the front of the lavatory building with our main beam headlights. It was then, and only then, that we dutifully observed that there were quite separate entrances for both women and men. This brought home to us the importance of the old military doctrine: "Time spent in reconnaissance is time well-spent."

Nicola Lowrie, her fiancé Richard Dyke, Laura Waghorn and her fiancé Nick Barnes had celebrated Richard's 20th birthday at his bedsit. Then a knock at the door turned a fun-filled evening into a night of terror as the four were subjected to horrific sex attacks by a knife maniac. The brave couples reveal for the first time how their friendship has helped them to survive the nightmare. Richard lowers his eyes as he recalls the run-up to the nightmare: "We didn't have much money so we planned a cheap night in. We just chilled out, drank wine, ate nibbles and watched telly. Some time after midnight we all hit the sack."Then at 4am, someone banged violently on the front door of Richard's bedsit and was shouting. Still half asleep and wearing only a pair of boxer shorts, Richard opened the door to find his neighbour, Daniel Owen. Richard, a care worker, says: "His face was twisted and he was screaming something about us keeping him awake. Suddenly, he lunged towards me and tried to stab me with a knife he was holding. The blade was five inches long with a razor-sharp edge.

I shouted for help but Owen pushed me back into the bedsit and slammed me against a wall. He was a bouncer in a local pub and twice my size. But it was like he was possessed. He seemed to have the strength of ten men." Laura and Nick were lying on the sofa and 35-year-old Owen looked lustfully at Laura, who was wearing only bra and knickers. Laura says: "There was an expression on his face which I can only describe as pure evil. He was in a rage and a terrifying sight. He used his aggression and size to dominate everyone in the room. We felt helpless."

Owen ordered the men to lie face down on the floor. Then, in a cold voice, he said, to Laura: "Take off your clothes." The barmaid, 19, recalls: "I was shaking with fear, but said 'No'. He said, "Do it or I'll kill the other two" I knew he meant it. He raped me while my fiancé and my friend lay just four feet away. I was numb with fear and shock". Nick, 25, a factory worker, says: " Owen was terrifying. He seemed high on drugs and had a maniacal look on his face. It was obvious he was looking for a reason to kill somebody. So when he started touching Laura, although it sickened me and every part of me wanted to scream 'No', I called to her gently and said, 'Do what he wants'. Laura was raped with a knife to her throat. He then turned to Richard and forced him at knifepoint to commit a sex act on him. Richard says: "He told me, 'Do it now or you're dead.' His sinister black eyes told me I had no choice."

Owen then raped Laura once more, performed an unnatural sex act on her and assaulted her with a bottle. She says: "It just went on and on. I remember trying not to think about what he was doing to my body. I looked towards Nick and mouthed, 'I love you'. He mouthed, 'I love you too.' It gave me a lot of strength. No matter how much pain Owen caused my body he would never be able to touch my thoughts." Then Owen brutalised Nicola, 20, an office administrator. She says: "I knew what was going to happen. He raped me, went back to rape Laura, then raped me again. As he forced himself on me he whispered, 'I've fancied you a long time'." Richard says: "I could barely watch as that monster violated the woman I love. I wanted to go for him, to make him stop. But the knife was still pressed against Nicola's throat. The moment I made a move towards him he'd have killed her."

The beast was still not finished. He forced the men to watch the women they love suffer again. He made the girls touch each other and Richard perform a sex act on Laura, his friend's partner, warning, "Do as I say. One of you, all of you, I don't care how many I kill."

By 6am the four friends were at breaking point. Laura was injured, both girls were in terrible pain and sobbing uncontrollably. Richard was traumatised and Nick, who'd been ordered to have sex with Richard, was in a near catatonic state of shock. The two friends were so traumatised they could not do what Owen wanted. But knowing they would die if they didn't give into his perverted demands, they simulated having sex together. Then, suddenly, Owen ordered them all to sit down. He paced around, telling them his troubles almost as if they were friends. Nicola recalls: "He said his marriage had broken up and he didn't see enough of his kids. It felt like, despite everything he'd just put us through, he wanted US to feel sorry for HIM." Then the aggression flooded back. He threw Richard on the floor and pressed the knife between his shoulder blades. Nicola screamed: "Don't kill him! Leave him alone, I beg you. I love him and want his children!" Unbelievably, her plea seemed to work. Owen stormed onto the landing and yanked at the loft hatch to reveal a rope noose. Laura says: "We stumbled to the doorway and saw Owen put the noose around his neck. Then he climbed onto the banister." Richard adds: "He couldn't jump so I asked if he wanted help to get down. I didn't want to save his life. I wanted him to pay for what he'd put us through. I kept thinking, 'if he kills himself, he will have got away with it'." Owen had demanded the four take the batteries from their mobile phones. Now he took Nicola's car keys and fled. The friends looked at each other in disbelief. Nicola says: "We were thinking 'is it finally over? Have we really got through all this alive?'."

Richard looked at his watch. It was 8.30am. Their ordeal had lasted more than four hours. Then they spotted a mobile phone battery Owen had dropped. Richard dialled 999. Their horror was finally over. Nick says: "As a man, I felt I should have been able to protect the woman I love. But Owen was a maniac. If I had tried, we would probably all be dead."

Owen was arrested the same day. On 17th May 2004 he was convicted of four charges of rape, four of false imprisonment and one of indecent assault. He was jailed for life and his name added to the sex offenders' register. The court heard he had previous convictions for attempted rape, indecent assault and robbery following attacks on two prostitutes. But because he wasn't on the register before, he was allowed to get his job as a bouncer. The judge told Owen he was "The manifestation of pure evil."

Today, in July 2004, Laura still gets terrible nightmares and Richard and Nicola are on anti-depressants. Richard says: "It's been difficult to resume a normal sex life. One of us would get a flashback of some horrible moment. But we just took things very slowly. Our love has healed so much. At Nick and Laura's wedding Richard will be best man and Nicola a bridesmaid. Richard and Nicola set a date for July 2005. Nicola says: "We went to hell and back but we refuse to let that monster turn us into victims for the rest of our lives." Nick adds: "Owen did some terrible things that night that have left us all damaged and traumatised, but not defeated."

A stalker who preyed on 60 women threatening rape and murder, has been jailed for eight years at Winchester Crown Court. Mark Brown, 30, spent thousands of pounds bombarding his victims with text messages and mobile phone calls. He travelled 200 miles to call a terrified woman outside her home, saying he could see what she was wearing and would break in to slit her throat. Police caught the farm worker at home in Rodmersham, Kent, after a victim came forward, prompting them to scour records of his four mobiles. While in jail before being found guilty, he continued calling victims using a jail phone card.

A rape victim survived three terrifying months as a sex slave and endured five days reliving every agonising moment in the witness box. Susan McDonald was interrogated in court by the monster, crack cocaine addict Milton Brown, who had subjected her to appalling abuse. He was jailed for 21 years, but the horrors never left her. Susan was found dead in her flat in West Norwood, South London, surrounded by empty bottles of pills. But her family hit out at the open verdict recorded at the inquest into her death. Speaking outside Southwark Coroner's Court in London, Susan's mother, Sandra Harris said: " We are not satisfied with the verdict. Susan never recovered from what happened to her, she was never the same. I am very angry about that." Susan had bravely described how she was repeatedly raped and savagely beaten with a pool cue and a wooden plank covered with nails. But she triumphed in the end and one of Britain's most notorious rapists was jailed.

A law change, partly prompted by her harrowing courtroom experience, later banned rapists from cross-examining their victims. Brown, 50, was jailed at Knightsbridge Crown Court in 1997 for attacking former girlfriend Susan, raping a widow and sexually assaulting a graduate. The jury heard how he beat his ex-lover so badly, she was in excruciating pain every time she breathed. He even attacked her with a rusty horse pick, and swept aside her anguished cries for a doctor. Mrs Harris has accused the justice system of abandoning her daughter as soon as Brown, a convicted child molester, was found guilty. She said: "Susan would be alive now if she had help. She just couldn't block out the terrible things that happened to her. I tried to get her as much help as I could but she found it difficult to open up. Her mental scars never healed. My daughter never got over the barbaric abuses she suffered. She reached rock bottom. It struck us how ill she was when she came round for dinner last Christmas. She was so feeble and weak. It was as if she was about to fall over. She just sat in the corner talking gibberish to herself. It was desperately sad for a mother to look at that. That was the last time I saw her."

The inquest heard that Susan was taking Diazepam and was prescribed Methadone in a bid to get her off her heroin addiction. Her stepfather, Stephen Harris, said of Brown: "It is outrageous. When he comes out he won't even be on the sex offenders' register. Susan suffered so much, now she is dead." Susan was prescribed 55 milligrammes a day of Methadone and 60 milligrammes a day of Diazepam. Bus driver Mr Harris added: "It troubles us that her prescription was for very high doses of anti-depressants. We can't understand why." Coroner Selena Lynch said: " She may have died from an accidental overdose, there is nothing to suggest suicide. But she may have died from natural causes. With her lifestyle and the drugs she was taking, that could have happened."

A serial sex attacker known as the *Night Stalker* could finally be caught after 16 years, thanks to a DNA breakthrough. He has carried out 94 burglaries, four rapes and 28 indecent assaults in London and the home counties since 1988, targeting elderly women. Three attacks in the past four months are feared to have been carried out by him. But detectives hope DNA evidence from these assaults, applied to a breakthrough detection technique, could lead to his arrest.

An 84-year-old woman in Bromley, south-east London, had her home broken into and £1000 stolen in September. On October 8, an 81-year-old lady was attacked in a sexually motivated assault at her home in Welling, Kent. On November 20 an 80-year old man in Croydon, south London had his home broken into, although detectives believe this may have been a mistake. The attacks match the technique used by the *Night Stalker*, who would strike dressed in a black balaclava and catsuit. DNA was recovered at the scene of the Bromley attack, and police hope they can use a new forensic technique, *ancestral DNA*, to catch him. Scientists have broken down the DNA and established that the man is from the Caribbean. Now police have flown there to carry out voluntary DNA testing, hoping to work out where he comes from and whittle down a list of suspects to 200. Detective Superintendent Simon Morgan said of the investigation: "There may be links down the generations between our suspect and the countries of the Caribbean."

He said of the latest attacks: "The first two incidents are in new areas for him. The man has a conscience and I would appeal to that. I have been to the funeral of seven of his victims and all their health deteriorated since the attacks. This illness that gives him an unhealthy interest in elderly women is treatable and I would ask him to come forward so we can help him."

The *Night Stalker* is believed to be a light-skinned black man with a south London accent. He enters the homes of elderly women in the early hours, cutting the electricity and removing light bulbs before striking. There is a £40,000 reward for information leading to his arrest.

2005 UPDATE: *Night Stalker* case: Detectives hunting Britain's worst serial sex attacker have revealed he is harbouring a longstanding grudge over the death of his mother. The cold-blooded rapist dubbed the *Night Stalker* strikes at the homes of elderly women and has left pensioners terrified they could be his next target. He told one of his victims of his distress at his mother's death four-and-a half years ago and said he blamed the Government for letting her down. The well-spoken offender, who has hinted on three occasions he has links with the Brighton area, may have a mother fixation like Norman Bates in the Hitchcock film *Psycho*. Now police, who have been hunting him for 12 years, are expecting groundbreaking DNA techniques could reveal his ancestry within the next fortnight, eventually leading them to him through his grandparents and parents. They hope an unusually long 15-minute slot on BBCs *Crimewatch* will give them the breakthrough they need to uncover the identity of the maniac, who has struck five times in the past five months. They think he may have tried to sell gold coins stolen during one attack and are also hoping for new leads from a glove containing the DNA of an unknown woman that he left behind at another crime scene.

Three of his victims have gone to their graves haunted by the trauma of his crimes, and detectives fear that if they do not catch him a victim will die during an attack. He carefully cuts the electricity and phone lines to stop victims from raising the alarm. At one home he spent an hour carefully chipping out a lock and has also removed entire window frames to get at his victims. During a recent attack in Sanderstead, Surrey, he even created a camouflage screen to prevent passers-by from seeing him as he struggled to get into the home of an 82-year-old woman. One theory is that he is such a proficient burglar that he may have had training from an experienced crook. All the *Night Stalker's* attacks have been in the south-east. His reign of terror began in October 1992 with the rape of an 84-year-old woman in Croydon, Surrey. Most assaults have been in Croydon and Orpington, but a number have also taken place in Coulsdon, Warlingham, Forest Hill, Catford, Dulwich and Sidcup.

Detective Chief Inspector Will O'Reilly, who is heading the hunt, said: "This is a man who is meticulous in his planning. He has no fear, and will often spend hours trying to get into the homes of his elderly victims. He only targets elderly people on their own and is careful about the homes he chooses. He always burgles private owner-occupied properties never nursing homes. We are determined to catch this man but we really need public help, so I hope people will watch the *Crimewatch* appeal. I am sure there is someone out there who could have a vital piece of information which will lead us to him." In October 2004 a former teacher spent four-and-a-half hours persuading him not to rape her at her home in Shooters Hill, south London. On Wednesday's *Crimewatch* the brave pensioner explains how she used mental control to talk him out of the attack, questioning what his mother would think of his behaviour. A month earlier police found a gortex-type glove at the home of an 84-year-old victim in Bromley, south London. Two burglaries in Lea a week before and a burglary in West Wickham have also been linked to him.

The rapist is known to be a light-skinned black man aged between 25 and 45, and about 5ft 10ins tall. He disguises his face with a Balaclava and often wears a large heavy coat, even in summer. Police believe he may be a motorbiker or a minicab driver as he always makes a quick getaway. He wakes victims by shining a torch directly in their eyes. Though he can appear compassionate, at other times he shows little regard for his victim or their age. Last year, 2004, an 88-year-old retired bookkeeper who was attacked in her bungalow in Orpington, Kent, found the strength to relive her harrowing ordeal. She described how she was watching late-night television in bed when a hooded man appeared. He told her that if she kept quiet and handed over her money, she wouldn't get hurt. But after taking £60 from her purse, he assaulted her so violently that she passed out. When she came to, he raped her a second time, ignoring her anguished pleas. Describing the attack, the victim revealed: "I said, 'No, please, can't you go and get a prostitute? Why pick on old ladies?'." She said that afterwards she lay there for hours not knowing if he was still in the bungalow. Had she not managed to activate her personal alarm, she would almost certainly have bled to death.

The *Night Stalker* has been profiled as a gerantophile, a man who loves older women and may have formed a loving relationship with an elderly relative, not necessarily through choice. Although he has left his DNA after several assaults, no match has yet been found on Britain's national DNA database, which contains samples taken from everyone arrested since 1995. Described as 'forensically aware', though he does not use condoms, he has never left fingerprints and tries to prevent victims from getting a good look at his face. Police originally compiled an initial list of about 21,000 'persons of interest', using information about previous offenders, the location of assaults and names received after appeals to the public. In a bid to learn more about his behaviour they have consulted a range of 'Cracker-style' forensic profilers. And they have even turned to the only other known similar offender, who used to prey on elderly people in the Eastbourne area, as they try to understand the man they are hunting. But senior detectives now believe a new 'ancestral profiling technique' may very soon lead them to the rapist, after they turned for help to a high-tech research company in Florida.

Scientists there can test for 177 DNA 'markers', essentially, genetic fingerprints, compared to the 10 normally used in the UK's national database. They discovered the rapist's genetic make-up is 82 per cent Sub-Saharan African, 12 per cent Native American and six per cent European. And now they have tracked down his ancestry to a handful of Caribbean islands, Trinidad, Tobago, St Lucia and St Vincent. Thirty DNA samples taken from these islands are currently being analysed and should lead police closer to the brute's family. Rewards totalling £40,000 have been offered for evidence leading to his arrest. Anyone with any information should ring *Crimestoppers* on Freephone 0800 555 111 or call the actual police incident room on 020 8649 1556.

Two illegal immigrants who smuggled women into the country and forced them into prostitution have been jailed. Taulant Merdanaj, 28, and Elidon Bregu, 19, are the first people in Britain to be convicted of people trafficking. The men, both Albanians, lured two Lithuanian women to the UK promising them legal work as nightclub waitresses. But on arrival the women, aged 21 and 24, were bundled into a car and driven to Sheffield's red light district, Attercliffe.

Merdanaj and Bregu confiscated their passports and mobile phones and imprisoned them in a flat for two months. The women were told they must work as prostitutes to repay the cost of the flights and were put to work every night for two months in a massage parlour called the 160 Club. They were subjected to sex attacks, escorted to work and never left alone.

Police raided the flat in September after a tip-off and arrested the men, who have been in Britain for an unknown period. At Sheffield Crown Court Merdanaj, of no fixed address, was found guilty of 13 offences including trafficking people into and within the UK for sexual exploitation, three counts of rape, two charges of causing or inciting prostitution and two counts of false imprisonment. He was jailed for 18 years. Bregu, who was cleared of two counts of rape, was found guilty of trafficking people within the UK for sexual exploitation and two offences of false imprisonment. He was jailed for nine years.

Mr Justice Bullimore said: "There is ruthlessness in both of you, so the sentences must be long to warn others this conduct will not be tolerated." The new Sexual Offences Act 2003 came into force in May 2004 and includes for the first time, offences relating to human trafficking. Judith Walker, Chief Crown Prosecutor for South Yorkshire, said after the hearing: "We view this new legislation as an important step forward in protecting vulnerable women who are deprived of their freedom and are trafficked. Detective Superintendent John Parr, who headed the police investigation, said: "We suspect the Albanians were part of a gang but we are pretty satisfied we have got the two main players. "These women came to the UK thinking the streets were paved with gold and would have proper jobs. Instead they were forced to work as prostitutes. The new law has made it easier for us to prosecute such criminals."

A convicted rapist is facing life in prison for raping a frail elderly woman. Wayne Gaskin, 38, pleaded guilty to attacking the 85-year-old victim in his van after offering her a lift home. Gaskin, of Bradford, West Yorks, who had previously been convicted and jailed for rape and indecent assault on girls under 16, in Sheffield seven years ago, was told he now faces an automatic life sentence. He was remanded in custody to await a psychiatric report. Detective Inspector Gerry O'Shea, who led the investigation, described the latest attack as: "thoroughly sickening".

A village doctor who threw a two-day champagne party after he was cleared of groping a patient, was unmasked as a serial sex pest. Vakil Singh, 59, was found guilty of indecency by the General Medical Council after he fondled three women in his surgery. The hearing came nine years after he was acquitted of indecently assaulting another woman, following a trial at Enniskillen Crown Court in North Ireland.

The not guilty verdict sparked a major celebration by Singh's patients in the village of Gortin in County Tyrone. They gave him a reception and a victory parade to his local pub. At the time of his acquittal Singh, a father of three, sobbed with his wife Agia as he told his supporters: "I had feared my life and career were in ruins." But on 21st January 2005 the GMC hearing in Manchester was told that the GP had been groping women over a 12-year period dating back to 1990. One woman had her breasts fondled during a home visit after she complained of vomiting and diarrhoea. On another occasion, Singh unbuttoned a patient's dress and touched her breast when she complained of an inflamed nose. Another woman who complained of tiredness following an ectopic pregnancy, had her buttocks felt before Singh exposed her breasts and touched her nipples. The GP exposed a third woman's breasts and touched them when she complained of suffering breathing difficulties.

The GMC found Singh guilty of conduct which was 'inappropriate, indecent and an abuse of his professional position'. It is considering whether the charges amount to serious professional misconduct. If it does, Singh could be struck off. The hearing was told that the doctor was advised by medical colleagues in 1999, to offer female patients a chaperone if proposing to carry out intimate examinations. None of the three women was offered one, or given any adequate explanation of why he touched their private parts. During the 1996 court case, a 22-year-old woman claimed Singh touched her breasts after she consulted him about a sore leg during a home visit. She alleged Singh told her: "You are a pretty girl, will you give me kisses?" But the jury took an hour to find him not guilty after a busload of patients travelled 40 miles every day to support their GP. The young woman left the village after making her claims.

A college student was gang-raped in a car by three men after being abducted off the street while using a cash point machine. The 16-year-old girl was about to return home when a man grabbed her from behind and bundled her into a car with darkened windows. Three other men were in the vehicle which was driven to a car park at the National Sports Centre in Crystal Palace, South-East London where three of the four men raped her. After her ordeal, the victim escaped by jumping out as she was being driven elsewhere. A Scotland Yard spokesman said the girl was abducted at 5.30pm near her home in Crystal Palace and was forced into a dark green car, possibly a VW Golf. It was not until 6.45pm that she managed to run to safety. Her attackers are all described as black men aged around 20. The victim is white and was wearing a white coat. Police described her as: "your average 16 year old" and said she had been left deeply traumatized. Investigating officer Detective Inspector Nick Downing said the teenager had been snatched off the street in an 'apparently opportunist and brazen attack'. Footage from CCTV cameras covering the car park and the route taken by the rapists is being studied. DI Downing said: "The victim is your average 16-year-old. I would not call her street-wise at all, and all her attackers are believed to be older than her. She is a vulnerable teenager who found herself in one of the most horrific situations anyone could be in. She was snatched off the street on her way home from a cash point and she certainly did not know any of her attackers.

"She was in a car, which was possibly stolen, with darkened windows so no one could see in and they have taken her to the darkest, most remote point of the overflow car park. It is not clear which of the three occupants partook, whether it included the man who originally snatched her. She was not seriously physically injured but she is very traumatised. We are working with her and her family in terms of counselling to avoid prolonging an ordeal she should never have had."

DI Downing said the original motive for abducting the girl may have been robbery. He said: "This was early evening and it was quite brazen. "There is no suggestion they had been stalking her. There is no suggestion of drink, drugs or weapons being involved. They said nothing of significance to her. "Robbery is the more common motive for attacks among youths of their age. But nothing was stolen. The location where she was taken was a quiet road, so that was not going to create too much risk for them. But they took her to a car park and there is always going to be the possibility of people there. The traffic at that time of day was busy and slow-moving. She was in a busy street when she took the opportunity to escape. They certainly did not let her out and she has done well to escape. Someone must have seen her getting out of the car, wearing what was quite a striking white coat, and running away."

He said it was possible the men had struck before. He said: "It may mean they have been there before. But we don't want to alarm women in the local community and we hope this was an isolated incident." Officers are appealing for any witnesses to contact South Norwood Sapphire Unit.

A ruthless madam convicted of forcing hundreds of eastern European girls to work as sex slaves in the UK has been ordered by a judge to pay back almost £1 million. Asylum seeker Guinara Gadzijeva ran a £1.2 million racket by luring young girls to Britain with promises of domestic work before forcing them to have sex with up to 40 clients in 24-hour shifts. She banned the girls, who had already paid human traffickers £20,000 to get to the UK, from having mobile phones and forced them to pay the bills for the brothels, including council tax.

Gadzijeva, a Lithuanian national, who was herself once a prostitute, operated brothels in London's Mayfair and Soho, keeping girls prisoner by charging up to £450 a day rent with £75 'maid charges'. The girls were forced to have sex with clients for as little as £10 a time. But after being convicted of a string of offences, Gadzijeva and her husband Venthasalam Muruganathan have now been ordered by Judge Dawn Freedman to pay back £932,448.10, after a confiscation hearing at Harrow Crown Court.

It is the second biggest vice confiscation issued by a British court since wheelchair-bound madam Josephine Daly was ordered to pay back £2million in 2000. Gadzijeva thought nothing of spending £2,000 on a night out at the Park Lane Hilton and lavishing £17,000 on furniture, while the girls she exploited suffered in the brothels, one of which contained a torture chamber. Despite making a fortune, the husband and wife team led outwardly humble lives in suburban Acton, west London, and drove economy Japanese cars. Police said the main aim of the prostitution racket was to stash money away in safety deposit boxes and send it back to Lithuania, probably as part of a larger criminal enterprise. Gadzijeva first came to Britain in 1997 and applied for asylum but was deported the following year when she was found working as a prostitute. Within weeks she re-entered the country and set up her lucrative vice racket. In February 2000 she married Muruganathan, who has indefinite leave to remain and the couple have a young daughter living with relatives in Lithuania. After their arrest police discovered £650,000 cash left in safety deposit boxes in Knightsbridge and St John's Wood. In February 2004, Gadzijeva was jailed for six years and Muruganathan for three years. He has since been released from prison.

Detective Constable Martin Griffiths, of Scotland Yard, said: "It is amazing that in the 21st century we still have forms of slavery and the sentences these people get do not reflect the gravity of their crime." Gadzijeva was ordered to pay back £520,788.50 from a total benefit from prostitution of £537,155.37. Muruganathan, jailed for living off prostitution, was ordered to pay back £411,659.60 from a total benefit of £666,115.01. The couple, both 37, have nine months to pay the money or face a further two years in jail.

Ministers have dropped plans for a drug-test kit to tackle the problem of people being raped or robbed after their drinks are spiked. The move has angered campaigners who are battling the spiralling problem of drug rape in pubs and clubs. Former Home Secretary David Blunkett and Trade Secretary Patricia Hewitt ordered research into ways of protecting people from sex attackers using the date-rape drugs Rohypnol, GHB or Ketamine, but Home Office Minister Caroline Flint has revealed that plans for a special swizzle stick to test for spiked drinks have now been axed. The decision comes after a woman was jailed for doping and robbing wealthy businessmen by spiking their drinks with Rohypnol. Mother-of-two Selina Hakki, 37, of Bow, East London, was sentenced to five years. Mrs Flint said the Government had commissioned research two years ago into a device which could be used to detect drugs in drinks. Under the plan, bar staff would have been required to put the swizzle stick in all drinks which would change colour if drugs were present. But she said: "Due to the difficulty of producing a satisfactory device, the project is not being continued."

The revelation is a bitter blow to charities who estimate that more than 2,000 people a year are attacked. Graham Rhodes, founder of the Roofie Foundation, which helps the victims of drug rape, said: "Ministers have got their heads stuck in the sand. We get about 1,000 calls a year from people who believe they have been raped after their drinks were spiked and that is just the tip of the iceberg. Many other people's drinks are spiked before they are robbed or simply because they are the victims of a cruel prank." In the worst cases, drinks are drugged to allow criminals to film their unsuspecting victims for porn movies. Liberal Democrat home affairs spokesman Mark Oaten said: "The Government should start analysing how big a problem this is before they rule out further research into ways of detecting if drinks have been spiked by these drugs. This is a growing problem and must be taken seriously." But a Government spokesman said it had proved impossible to find one 'catch-all' test for all potential drugs.

Police are collecting data for the first time on rapes involving drugs under a pilot scheme which is expected to be extended nationwide. And the Home Office is to issue new guidelines to pubs and clubs on how to combat illegal drugs. Mrs Flint said the guidelines would include 'a section on drug-assisted assault' but warned that devices to test for spiked drinks could 'provide a potentially dangerous false reassurance'. Anyone caught spiking a drink could face up to five years in jail. Police have advised drinkers to follow a number of simple rules to avoid being caught out. They include not leaving drinks unattended and not accepting drinks from strangers.

In conclusion, we have the disgraceful, totally unacceptable situation in the United Kingdom, that the actual CONVICTION RATE of male rapists, is expressed as a percentage, almost in single figures. This is a shocking indictment on the UK Criminal Justice System. We obviously have very serious flaws in the way our evidence in such cases is tested in Courts during Rape trials. From my own career in the Police Service, I can recall so many occasions when Judges, at the request of Defence Counsels, granted the temporary exclusion of the entire Jury from the court room. This is normally when Defence Counsels wish to pursue a particular point of law, or test a piece of 'contentious' evidence which is about to be given. In the latter case, a 'trial-within-a-trial' is held, whilst the Jury are in their room, temporarily relaxing or watching TV. The witness(es) may be asked to give their evidence, or certain aspects of it, and the Judge is required to rule on whether or not it is admissible in law. If the Judge decides in favour of the point or points, the Jury is then called back in, and the trial resumes.

Experience as a former (cynical) Police Officer soon opened my eyes to the facts that some Judges seemed to be 'frightened of their own shadow'. They would almost always, and still do to this day, bend over backwards to be seen to be totally fair to the accused, thereby disallowing large chunks of the Prosecution's case. Therefore the Jury often have to make their deliberations on fragmented, and therefore confusing tracts of evidence. Defence Counsels and all Judges really go to town on emphasing the offender's Human Rights, as well as other rights. However, the poor victim's rights are hardly ever mentioned or considered at all.

Therefore, the evidence is stacked against the *victim* being able to enjoy proper, fair, so-called 'justice' in this country. Many law-abiding citizens consider that important cases, if not all criminal ones, should be decided on 'the balance of probabilities', rather than 'to be so convinced that you are SURE'. Readers unfamiliar with our British criminal 'justice' system, which has not been at all clarified, strengthened or enhanced during the tenancy of Mr Tony Blair's Government, in spite of their 1997 and 2001 General Election Manifestos, (which the reader is reminded are set out, so far as they relate to Law and Order at the very start of this book) may wonder how, in this troubled modern world, one can ever be 'SURE' about ANYTHING. You only have to consider the total uncertainty which abounds in modern times, right across the whole world, when maniacal, fanatical, brain-washed suicide bombers abound, striking indiscriminately and totally without warning, seeking maximum casualties from every single detonation of their lethal body belts. Readers have probably seen images in the media whereby young toddlers, even of pre-playschool age, are pictured posing for family snaps, in their 'suicide bomber' belt-packs and brandishing either real or mock-up rifles and hand guns etc.

By the time you have finished reading this book, I am sure that it will have been well and truly spelt out to you that Mr Tony Blair's Government has totally failed to deliver on law and order. As I finalise my draft manuscript, in April 2005, he is currently being described as follows:

'A liar'

'A Prime Minister who makes his own agenda, without Cabinet consultation'

'A Top politician who misleads the Electorate at every opportunity'

'An opportunist'

'Exaggerating, enhancing and/or twisting the facts, to serve his own ends'

'Being desirous of surrounding himself with 'cronies' from his past life'

'Allowing the Judiciary, to over-rule the wishes of Parliament, especially LCJ'

'A waster of funds from the Public Purse, by employing Armies of advisers'

'A Master spin-doctor'

'Uncaring attitude to military & civilian victims of recent and modern warfare'

Furthermore, readers may well have wondered over the last eight years of his Government's tenancy, how he could have allowed, or put up with the continual public embarrassment, caused by the fact that his own wife of many years, in her capacity as our equivalent of the American 'First Lady', constantly challenges the current law, particularly in relation to HUMAN RIGHTS matters. In fact I'm sure that the average 'man on the Clapham omnibus', must be totally convinced that her own Barristers' Chambers - known as 'Matrix', actually specialises in human rights.

Most people are by now well aware that, apart from being Mrs Cherie Blair, wife and mother, she is a qualified Queen's Counsel, and often sits as Mrs Cherie Booth, QC, a Recorder (part-time or junior Judge) in important cases in High Courts. (Readers who have followed the modern TV series on BBC television, in which actor Martin Shaw plays an excellent part as High Court Judge Sir John Deed, will by now be quite familiar with the ups and downs of Court Room life. Speaking as a person who has worked within the Criminal 'Justice' System for in excess of 20 years, I find it to be an excellent, so true-to-life series, so believable. Also, Martin Shaw carries off the red-robed and bewigged male lead to absolute perfection, I would say, as 'one who knows').

On 14th March 2005 I heard about a really sad and sobering statistic. Apparently the current conviction rate for male rapists is a staggering five per cent, that's all. I suspect a working party should be set up at once to investigate that serious, countrywide problem.

COUNT 9

VIOLENCE & OTHER CRIMINAL OFFENCES BY SELF-STYLED 'CELEBRITIES', PROFESSIONAL FOOTBALLERS AND SUPPORTERS

There was a time during my police career with the Metropolitan Police when I lived and worked quite near to West Ham Football Club. This was at the time when Bobby Moore, Geoff Hurst, Frank Lampard and Trevor Brooking were in the team. On-pitch violence was almost unheard of in those days and most people remember these four West Ham players with great pride, as well as the way they conducted themselves on the pitch, as real gentlemen I would say. Regrettably, however, those peaceful days of soccer enjoyment are long gone. But even then, there was plenty of violence *on the terraces* of West Ham, particularly in the area known as 'The North Bank.'

I used to attend nearly all home games at Upton Park football ground, always in police uniform, sometimes detailed to attend there as part of my usual police duties and also on my rest days. This was known as 'voluntary duty' or overtime. Unfortunately, we didn't get to see much of the football matches because we stood with our backs to the pitch, facing the terraces, to watch out for trouble amongst the crowds and keep order. Right at the front of the terraces was a low, solid concrete wall and young children were encouraged to stand near and against this wall, both for safety and to have an uninterrupted view of the game. Disabled persons in wheelchairs were also permitted to watch the match from the vicinity of the wall.

As now, all the hooligans, thugs and yobs, whose entrance fees were as important to the Club as anyone else's, congregated together, mainly on the North Bank. Supporters of 'away' teams were encouraged to view the game from the South Bank or other areas. The favourite provocative 'war cry' of the day, to incite violence, from the North Bank 'supporters' to the visiting supporters, was 'You'll Never Take The North Bank!'

A favourite trick of the mindless thugs at the uppermost terraces of the North Bank, was for a whole group of them to suddenly, without warning, push hard against some spectators in front of them. They had no chance to stand their ground, over-balanced and were forced to lean forward quite violently, trying to support themselves against the innocent supporters in front of them. The end result was what we would now describe as 'the domino effect', and the main force of the violent momentum was thrust against the young lads right at the front, who were jammed up against the concrete wall, which had only ever been built as a token sign to discourage pitch-invasions.

Sometimes these poor kids were hurt, sometimes not, but they were certainly shaken-up, frightened and often at least winded. We did not have enough CCTV cameras in those days, otherwise 'action replays' of the camera tapes would have soon helped us to identify the ringleaders, cowardly cringing at the back, smugly feigning innocence. Women too, even in those days, took part in singing all the vile songs, adapted with swear words from popular songs such as 'You'll never walk alone' from the musical *Carousel*. These girls could swear with the best of the men and youths. I can still see the face of one woman in her late 20's who always arrived early enough to occupy a spot immediately above the players' tunnel. If she had not liked what she saw, at half time or end of the match, she would lean down and rain blows on unsuspecting departing players, or the referee, and verbally abuse them with her foul mouth. It was obvious to regular staff such as stewards, West Ham players and police officers, that this horrible woman's mother had never 'made her wash out her filthy mouth with carbolic soap'.

Over time, I almost came to hate the regular offenders, our police powers were quite restricted in those days, but naturally we would arrest serious troublemakers if we could spot them. These would not just have been persons engaged in what is now referred to as 'violent disorder', but the usual sex offenders too, drawn to dense crowds like a magnet, with their apparently almost uncontrollable urges to touch people with anonymous hands, when they thought they might get away with it. Later on, when my own son grew up and wanted to watch a professional game of football, I took him to Fulham to watch a match in which Chelsea were playing. As we approached the stadium from the street, we had to scatter as mounted police were engaged in a Crimean War Battle of Balaclava-type charge against seriously violent thugs engaged in a huge affray with opposing side supporters. As it turned out, this proved to be the one and only time my son and I ever attended a professional football match together. He had seen enough and must have feared for his personal safety, as much as I had. In sharp contrast, as a child, an uncle of mine who lived in Highbury had taken me onto the terraces at Arsenal Football Club. As I leaned on the steel terrace bar I felt totally at peace and thoroughly enjoyed the game, being able to watch the players on the pitch for the entire 90 minutes, undistracted by hooligan elements, as there were none, in those calm and peaceful days, when so-called 'professional' footballers did not spit on the pitch all of the time, or earn more than Prime Ministers.

To this day, I despair of learning of what takes place both on and off the pitch, although nothing surprises me any more. It comes to something when H.M. The Queen presents a once-respected Order of the British Empire award to the likes of David Beckham, whose knighthood is only in the concept stage at the moment. What a hero! What a role model for young lads of impressionable ages! Tattooes being added to his body at a fast rate, dressing scruffily like 'Kevin' on the Harry Enfield comedy shows, torn jeans, different 'girlie' hairstyles almost every week, weighed down with so much gold jewellery that he is terrified to wander near a scrap-metal yard with an electro-magnetic probe and doesn't even known his four times table! Should England tremble, or what?

Even if you choose to watch the sport at home on TV there's no way you can avoid all the spitting on the grass, swearing and rude gesticulating, kissing and hugging, and that's just the players on the pitch! From the stands you will swiftly learn all of the words of the foulest songs you can imagine, punctuated by the mindless spectator who has smuggled in an instrument which blasts off 'dot-dot-dot-dash-dot, dash-dash' like a passenger liner's foghorn every few minutes! Yes, there is one of these irritating and noisy persons in attendance at every single football match. How do they manage to get past security checks and searches, given the size of these plunger-operated fog horns? The answer is, the device is hidden under the clothing, concealed under the over-hang of the beer belly. On being cursorily searched by Security Staff or Police Officers at the entry turnstiles, the owner squeezes hard for those few moments of searching, thus trapping the instrument in the crevice formed by skin and flesh folds.

Using this well-practiced method, the fog hornist's hands are temporarily free, permitting him to assume the 'spread-em, hands up' position. After all, no Police Officer or Security Guard worth his salt, would wish to rummage from beer belly skinfold to skinfold, in the face of haletosis of the mouth, and under-arm detritus, birds nests and blackheads etc. unless wearing a Nuclear, Biological and Chemical total-seal suit, and sucking a Fisherman's Friend!

(**Author's note:** *As you have guessed correctly, I have 'been there – done that'!*)

Disgraced former England International soccer star Gary Charles yelled at photographers after a judge spared him a return to prison. As he left Derby Crown Court he shouted: "At the end of the day I go back to my big mansion and your lives don't mean s***." Charles, 33, had been warned he faced jail after he grabbed a woman's breast and threatened to beat her up. He was sent to the cells for a day after interrupting Judge Andrew Hamilton at that court. But the judge spared him custody. Charles, of Stretton, Derbys, promised to beat his alcoholism. He admitted common assault but was cleared of indecent assault. He was ordered to pay £500 compensation and £2,600 costs and a 9pm to 5am curfew was imposed. Last year Charles was found sitting in his own filth as his car blocked a road.

The Ipswich Town and England Under 21 footballer, Darren Bent, was arrested after allegedly shooting at a boy with a BB gun. He is said to have produced the gun after being bothered by a group of children near his home. A boy aged 12 was allegedly hit in the back by a ball bearing fired from the gun, near a play area in Kesgrave, near Ipswich. Bent, 20, was arrested on suspicion of possessing an imitation handgun with intent to cause violence. He was quizzed by officers before being released without charge on police bail pending enquiries.

England football star Steven Gerrard, 23, of Blundell Sands, has been fined £1,000 for driving his sports car carelessly on a suburban road. Police stopped the Liverpool captain as he drove through Bootle, Merseyside, in his £25,000 Audi Cabriolet. He admitted driving without due care and attention. He had to pay £55 costs and received five penalty points.

His Liverpool team mate Milan Baros plans to appeal against a £500 fine and three penalty points for failing to provide information after a speeding incident.

Footballer Terrell Forbes, 22, a defender with Second Division team QPR, accused of the gang-rape of a 15-year old, is out on bail to help his team's promotion chase, a court has heard. Forbes was freed from custody by the High Court, the Old Bailey was told. He can play in away games but must be taken home by QPR staff after all matches. Other High Court bail conditions are that he must report to police daily, stay at home in New Cross, south London under a curfew when not playing, and lastly he is not allowed to contact any of his co-accused.

The son of a policeman responsible for monitoring football hooligans was filmed hurling at least 6 rocks at officers. Portsmouth fan Ben Upton, 17, was part of a mob which turned on police after they were kept away from rival Southampton supporters. The prosecution counsel told the court: "Experienced officers described it as the worst violent disorder they had dealt with." Upton, of Portsmouth, was flanked in court by his parents. Judge John Woollard, sitting at Portsmouth Youth Court told Upton: "When you were throwing missiles, you saw it as sport." Upton was sent to a Young Offenders Institution for eight months. He was also banned from English and Welsh football grounds for six years.

Pop star Lee Ryan left court a sadder but wiser man after being convicted of smashing photographers' cameras outside a London night club, but he was cleared of assault. The 'Blue' singer was found guilty of two counts of criminal damage after he lashed out at a pack of photographers as he left the 10 rooms nightspot in London's West End, damaging the cameras of freelancers David Abiaw and Conor Nolan. Ryan claimed that he had been trying to protect himself and 23-year-old brunette Tanya Mills, whom he had met inside the club, from the media scrum. He was ordered to pay a total of £500 compensation for the damage he caused to the cameras. But District Judge Caroline Tubbs imposed no separate penalty and made no order for costs.

Ryan, 20, made no comment as he left the court, smiling. But he was said by his mother Sheila, who had sat in court throughout the trial, to be 'extremely relieved'. During the two-day trial at Horseferry Road magistrates court, Ryan admitted hitting the cameras. But he denied assaulting the photographers. Clearing him of assault, District Judge Tubbs told the court: "Mr Ryan is entitled to the benefit of the doubt in relation to this matter." She said that Ryan admitted kicking Mr Nolan's camera and the photographer became 'understandably irate'. She added: "I do find he came close to Mr Ryan and Mr Ryan pushed him in the chest. He was demonstrating by his actions that he did not wish to fight. In the circumstances Mr Ryan believed Mr Nolan was going to take physical action against him. That contact, that force, was reasonable. I do find that he was acting in self-defence and I am dismissing the charge of assault on Mr Nolan." But MS Tubbs found him guilty of the two counts of criminal damage, saying: "I accept that Mr Ryan was concerned not only for his own situation on that occasion, but also that of Miss Mills. I do not find that his actions in breaking the camera or pushing and kicking was reasonable in the circumstances of that night." Outside the court his lawyer Nick Freeman said: "He is extremely relieved today. He had behaved reasonably that night. He wants to get on with his career and move forward." Ryan's mother added: "Lee has held himself with dignity throughout the whole process."

Although I wasn't present at the nightspot venue, or in court, it sounds to me as if minor celeb Mr Ryan is in the wrong line of business, having acted more like a 'professional' footballer than a singer in a group.

David Beckham shocked his legions of young fans with a foul-mouthed rant at a linesman during Real Madrid's soccer match on Sunday 16th May 2004. He yelled, 'Hijo de puta' Spanish for 'son of a whore'. It is considered the ultimate insult in Spain. Legendary *SunSport* columnist John Sadler reflects on the outburst: "The shaved haircut, the snarling anger, the raging expression and the irresponsible, deeply offensive language. The image was all-too depressingly familiar. It could have been just another example of an England football hooligan spewing his defiance of authority, his ignorant disregard for right and wrong, in the direction of a police officer or overwhelmed bar-tender. But this time we were looking at pictures of David Beckham, the England captain, on television and in newspapers, on the very day manager Sven Goran Eriksson was to name his squad for the European championships. He was aiming his abuse at a linesman who flagged for hand-ball and a penalty from which already relegated Murcia took a two-goal lead against Real Madrid. Despite time to control himself after defender Ivan Helguera had been penalised and the spot-kick converted, Beckham made it his business to pursue the linesman, say his nasty little piece and receive the appropriate red card.

We can only wonder what Bobby Moore would have made of it had he still been with us. The England Captain who led our World Cup winners in 1966, and had the presence of mind to wipe his hands before accepting the trophy from the Queen. On second thoughts, we have no need to wonder. The timing of Beckham's outburst could not have been worse. For his club, who had to play for 55 minutes without him and, not so surprisingly, failed to avoid humiliating defeat. Or for England, who run the risk of rejection from Euro 2004 if their notorious fans resort to the hooligan behaviour for which they have become infamous and detested abroad. Some will be quick to sympathise with Beckham, insisting that his loss of temper and dignity was a symptom of the stress and anguish of his recent, turbulent private life. Sorry but that won't wash. David Beckham is 29 years old, one of the world's richest sportsmen, paid in the region of £100,000 a week.

I'm afraid there are certain forfeits involved with such wealth and celebrity status and sympathy is not one of them. Especially for the Captain of England on the eve of a major tournament that is likely to attract to Portugal anything between 40,000 and 80,000 supporters from these shores. Beckham, quite rightly, has been portrayed as the ideal role model for youngsters and older football fans alike. He has at times gone public with his condemnation of the hooligans and bravely sided with some of the punitive measures to eliminate the problem. He has worked on his own self-discipline. Against considerable provocation he has emerged intact from the trauma of his sending-off in the World Cup finals of France 1998.

Had his dismissal on Sunday been suffered for a mis-timed tackle or two innocuous yellow cards, it could have been regarded as nothing more serious or damaging than a hazard of the job, something that can happen to anyone. But the nature of his offence left no room for excuse and every reason for concern. Because it sent out exactly the wrong message to those who have no hesitation in shaming the image and reputation of their own country. It symbolised utter disrespect and contempt and could have awful implications among the yob elements who survive attempts to prevent troublemakers travelling. Plenty will escape the net. The good people of Portugal should brace themselves for such visitors. They are the ones who will have looked at those pictures of a raging Beckham and seen some kind of perverted justification for their own intentions.

They are the ones who will have seen nothing but cause for doubling their admiration of the Captain. More's the pity because Beckham's breakdown in control came on a weekend of unprecedented celebration in England. Of Arsenal's dazzling Premiership triumph that swept them through an entire season without defeat. An Arsenal team who have cleaned up their image during the course of an historic season. A group of outstandingly talented players who have learned to cut out the kind of ill-mannered intimidation of officials, that brought such disgrace to Beckham. Everyone has admired Arsene Wenger's remarkable team since that black day of mass misconduct at Old Trafford early in the season. Everyone has been in awe of their class and impregnable composure. Even those who support their arch-rivals Tottenham. Why, even the fans of relegated Leicester stayed behind at Highbury to applaud them at the weekend and, heaven knows, they have suffered for months. In appreciating Arsenal's extraordinary championship, football fans throughout the land have come to recognise success can taste sweeter still if it is achieved with style and a refusal to be lured into distracting, distasteful side-issues. It is to be hoped England's players and more particularly, England's followers, adopt Arsenal's amended code of conduct in Portugal. And not the latest example offered by England's Captain.

A 14-year-old schoolgirl has become the first female ever to be locked up for football hooliganism. Felicity Thorpe, of Southsea, Hants, admitted violent disorder and a court heard she had thrown up to 20 missiles at police, which was more than any of the men in the wild mob had hurled. But hardened officers in the case stated that what shocked them just as much was the fact that Thorpe was accompanied by a 10-year-old boy accomplice. She was filmed inciting violence after a clash between fans of Premiership football rivals Portsmouth and Southampton. The boy, who cannot be named for legal reasons, has been handed a referral order for his part in the riot, becoming Britain's youngest ever football hooligan. Portsmouth magistrates saw CCTV images of Thorpe, who nibbled nervously on her fingernails throughout the hearing, throwing stones during running battles lasting three hours between police and gangs. She admitted violent disorder after being detained in *Operation Market*, which has so far resulted in 47 yobs convicted for the violence outside Portsmouth's Fratton Park stadium in March 2004. Police, their dogs and horses were injured, cars were trashed and shops looted, when a 300-strong mob turned their anger on police riot officers, after they foiled a bid to attack Southampton fans. They had aimed to ambush the away supporters following Portsmouth's victory, but officers were prepared for them and prevented the two groups clashing.

Incensed, the two groups turned their anger on the police and sparked the violence which shamed the football club and the city. They ripped up metal fencing and blockaded Fratton Road, marching on police lines while hurling missiles at the officers. Other yobs tied a rope across Fratton Road so mounted police could not charge the crowd and began pelting riot squads. Thorpe, dressed in a Portsmouth shirt, was seen with the boy, captured on police video cameras, ducking under the rope and hurling missiles at police and regularly disappearing to re-arm herself. She later went quietly when arrested at her care home, wearing the latest England football shirt.

In court, she bowed her head and whispered: "I'm sorry for what I've done." Also banning her from football grounds for six years, magistrate Paul Thompson said: "This offence is so serious that only a custodial sentence is appropriate. You need to get this into your head, the community of which you are a part will not put up with that sort of behaviour." Detective sergeant Gary Cable, who interviewed the girl after her arrest, said outside the court: "It was surprising to see her in the trouble because all the other offenders have been men. She didn't throw just one missile. She was recorded throwing between 15 and 20 missiles at officers. That was a lot more than were thrown by men who have been jailed over the incident. She obviously had a clear disregard for the safety of police and the members of the public that were in the area." The girl's mother Annie, who is divorced from her father, said her daughter was 'not a monster or a thug'. She admitted that her behaviour 'had spiralled out of control' but said, she was 'not brought up to be like this. Deep down my daughter is a real softie'. Home Office figures reveal that only five of the more than 2,300 Football banning orders involve females. Before Thorpe, the youngest was 16.

Former Leeds and Wales footballer Mark Aizlewood, 44, has been fined £1,500 at a Cardiff magistrates court for attacking an attractive BBC reporter. He grabbed presenter Jane Harvey, 32, round the neck and pushed her down a flight of stairs. She was interviewing him for BBC Wales consumer affairs programme *X-Ray* when he 'went berserk' and tried to grab the camera tape. Ms Harvey said: "It was terrifying. He said, 'Get out of my office girl, you're not stitching me up'." Aizlewood, who also played for Charlton and Cardiff, was being quizzed over complaints about a foreign soccer trip for youngsters.

England soccer star Trevor Sinclair, 31, the Manchester City winger, of Lower Witherington, Cheshire, has been arrested on suspicion of assaulting his wife Natalie. He is believed to have rowed with her after a party at 2am one morning. He has been released on police bail pending further enquiries. The couple, who have two children, were not available for comment, but friends called it 'a storm in a teacup'. Sinclair had joined his club in a £2.5million deal.

West Ham football star Tomas Repka has been arrested over an alleged feud. The Czech International defender was quizzed by detectives over claims that he was harassing a 46-year-old man. Repka, who has cultivated a hard-man image on the pitch, was detained after walking into a police station in East London with his solicitor. It follows an accusation made to police by the alleged victim on 19th July 2004. Repka was released on bail and must report back to police later in the year. He lives with his wife and two children in Woodford Green, East London. The £20,000-a-week central defender, who has won 42 caps for the Czech Republic, was signed by West Ham for a record £5.5million from Fiorentina in 2001. He has been at the centre of flare-ups with opponents, spectators and even his team mates.

Celebrities and Premiership football players rubbed shoulders with football hooligans at the premiere of a film that glories in soccer violence. *East Enders'* Barbara Windsor, actress Daniella Westbrook, 'Bond' girl Rachel Grant and presenter Kirsty Gallagher, with rugby-playing boyfriend Paul Samson, were among those present at the London screening of *The Football Factory*. It proved a shock for some of them. The film, which employed known hooligans as advisers, charts the activities of a group of Chelsea FC thugs. Barbara, 66, said: "I did not realise how controversial it would be. The film tells the story about what is actually happening. Unfortunately this is what happens, young men want to feel alive. Perhaps we should bring back National Service."

Fears have been expressed that the film, which has opened across the UK, will incite copy-cat violence at this summer's European Football championships in Portugal. Despite the controversy, a host of household names turned up to support the premiere alongside convicted football hooligans. Chelsea stars including John Terry and Wayne Bridge partied at the after-show bash alongside hooligans, some of whom have been banned from Euro 2004. Of the 16 thugs who 'worked' on the film, few would reveal their identities. But one former Millwall hooligan, who gave his name as Wheeler, dismissed the controversy. He said: "I can't believe it has caused all this fuss, it's reality, a few people punching each other. It isn't a big deal." But the film's star confessed he was expecting violence to mar the European Championships. Danny Dyer, 26, attending with his girlfriend Joanna said: "It's going to go off, no two ways about it. This is the big stage for hooligans." Julie Kirkbride, Shadow Culture Secretary said: " It's grossly irresponsible for film-makers to glorify mindless violence."

(**Cynical author's note:** *no mention of celebrity arch-thug Vinnie Jones being present – perhaps he was elsewhere 'air-raging' in mid-Atlantic!*)

Critic Martin Evans' note to the above report, headed-up 'Hooligans will just revel in it', reads as follows:

> *If ever the violent, mindless, anti-social, yobs who have done so much to ruin English soccer needed a clarion call, 'The Football Factory' is it. Hooligans the length and breadth of the country will view it and pour out of cinemas with renewed vigour. The film, based on John King's much deeper and more complex novel, does not just glorify football hooliganism, it attempts to justify it as a harmless pastime for those who enjoy living life to the full. Centred on a small 'firm' of Chelsea thugs who get their kicks brawling with like-minded gangs, the film follows Tommy Johnson, played by Danny Dyer, who is haunted by premonitions of his own downfall. While scenes of violence make up only a relatively small part of the film, when they do appear they are graphic and disturbing. Far more worrying is the portrayal of hooliganism as a force for camaraderie and true friendship. While few sane people will be able to understand the attraction of wanton violence, the appeal of feeling part of a loyal and tight group will not be lost on many young impressionable football fans. And the timing of the film's release will do nothing to help keep the coming European championships free of*

violence. There is an argument to suggest that films like this merely reflect reality. But 'The Football Factory' goes beyond that, joyously revelling in its subject. Few could argue that the film is not powerful, but sadly its message is that football violence is alive and thriving.

England football star Wayne Rooney will not be charged with assault after a 23-year-old woman claimed he spat in her face. She said the Everton player spat at her at Manchester club *Ampersand* in February 2004. Rooney, 18, was interviewed by police. But a Crown Prosecution Service spokeswoman said there was not enough evidence for a 'realistic prospect of conviction'. Rooney's agent Paul Stretford, said the woman's complaint was 'fatuous and entirely false'. The player was having a night out with friends following a match against Manchester United when the woman complained.

An England fan has become the FIRST soccer yob to be prosecuted in this country using foreign film footage. Neil Coyle, 39, of Chatham, was banned for four years from following England or his Premiership team Chelsea abroad. It came after Swiss police handed over a video of him running riot in Zurich just 24 hours before England played Liechtenstein in March 2003. At the time, Coyle escaped arrest. But 5 months later the boozy yob was held while trying to get into England's game with Croatia at Ipswich. Coyle denied being drunk but was fined £200 by Ipswich magistrates. They also issued the banning order after watching the amazing 24-minute tape of the Zurich aggro involving 100 fans. Police commented: "This case sends a clear message to hooligans that no matter where they travel, they will be tracked down." Two thousand thugs have been banned from Euro 2004 in Portugal.

A boy of 10 has become Britain's youngest suspected football hooligan after being arrested following a Premiership riot. He was held by police investigating violence which marred Portsmouth's derby match victory over Southampton at Fratton Park in March 2004. The boy, from neighbouring Gosport, was picked up by the police *Operation Market* team which was set up to investigate the riot. He was allegedly caught on camera throwing stones at police after the game. Acting detective Sergeant Cable said: " We were pretty amazed at the age of this young man. We have never come across someone this young involved in this sort of violence. As part of our investigations we have had two officers looking through video evidence and one tape identified a small lad who was throwing missiles towards officers. He was named and identified by a police officer as he has received previous warnings and reprimands, although not for anything that is football related. He lives with his foster parents and was arrested by appointment with them and with a solicitor present.

When he was interviewed by us he fully admitted that he had been there on the day in question. This boy was seen coming to the front of the crowd after the game on a number of occasions and throwing missiles. He was with known football hooligans but no one was forcing him to be there. He could have left at any time and walked away from it all. He was part of that group and he is being treated in the same way as everyone else." On 28th May 2004, Nicholas Hawkins, prosecuting at Portsmouth Youth Court said: "He said he was not sorry for his actions because the police deserved it." The youngster had admitted violent disorder.

The boy wiped away tears as Judge John Woollard imposed an order banning the boy from every football ground in England and Wales for the next three years. He was also ordered to report to a Youth Offending Team (YOT) for nine months. A 14-year-old girl, the first female to be arrested in the operation, is also accused of throwing stones at officers. In the same operation, officers arrested seven men from in and around Portsmouth. They were all questioned by the police's dedicated football intelligence unit at Southsea police station. All were released on bail without charge to report back to the station on June 21st. Police have viewed more than 100 hours of surveillance footage recorded by Portsmouth city council's CCTV cameras and by officers with hand-held cameras. They have vowed to identify and prosecute as many offenders as possible.

Southampton football midfielder star Fabrice Fernandes, 24, appeared at Bow Street Magistrates Court, London on 18th May 2004 accused of jumping nine red traffic lights in his Porsche car, during a high-speed police chase through London. He denied dangerous driving, drink-driving and failing to stop for police. Magistrates bailed him to reappear at the same court on 29th June 2004.

In May 2004 at Lincoln Crown Court, the mother of TV's *Holby City* star Kelly Adams, admitted attempting to kill her own mother, aged 80 years. Sheila Brimblecombe, whose daughter plays maternity nurse Mickie Hendrie, tried to suffocate frail Joan Baker. She admitted having crept into her home, pinched her nose, put a hand over her mouth and urged her mother 'Die, damn you, die'. She then thrust a pillow over her face. The court heard that Brimblecombe 'lost her mind' after becoming depressed over the break-up of her second marriage. She told police she had been 'greatly hurt' by her marriage breakdown. Her mother told police that she had noticed that her daughter had been behaving strangely.

On the night of 6th December 2003 she awoke to find herself on the floor being punched by her own daughter. She of course recognised her own daughter's voice and said to her 'Stop it, you'll be done for murder'. A neighbour then rushed to help but Brimblecombe, obviously 'thinking on her feet', claimed that her mother had 'had a turn'. She then told her mother: "You had a nightmare." At the time, both women were living in the same village of Waddington, near Lincoln, but Brimblecombe has moved to Bedford (Where there happens to be a prison, but for male adult offenders only). Judge Michael Heath was told by the victim that she and her daughter were now reunited, and that she did not want her daughter to be jailed, although the offence of attempted murder carries life imprisonment. In adjourning the case, presumably so that modern-day judges can see extensive, costly reports, Judge Heath assured Brimblecombe: "You are not going to prison."

This next, long-running domestic violence case has almost become its own 'soap' series. During research, I have accumulated more than enough reports about it, to include it with almost its own full chapter. You've probably guessed already that I'm referring to the relationship between TV actress Leslie Ash and her ex-professional footballer husband, Lee Chapman. At this time the matter is still unresolved but you'll recall that one Sunday morning Leslie Ash was rushed to hospital with quite serious injuries. She remained in hospital for a few days and then went home. Within a very short time she became partially paralysed, particularly in her legs, so she returned to hospital. There it was thought she may have contracted the MRSA disease, which is said to be hospital-specific in that it is caused through nurses and doctors allegedly not washing their hands properly, often enough or, most importantly, between patients. If true, it takes some believing, doesn't it?

Tragically, quite a few people have entered hospitals for quite simple operations, have contracted MRSA, and many have died. The current Leader of the Opposition, Michael Howard, MP, QC states that he actually lost his own mother-in-law in this way. Returning to the Leslie Ash v Lee Chapman saga. Naturally perhaps, practically the whole country is in fullest sympathy with Leslie Ash, who is very popular, but quite recently lost a few brownie points when she had her lips injected with botox or collagen, in vanity, finishing up with bloated lips which distressed her immensely, as the way she then looked became known as the 'trout pout'. There is still much speculation as to whether her husband inflicted her most recent injuries on her deliberately in a domestic violence scenario. However poor Leslie is still sticking to her original story that she fell out of bed during 'rough sex.' Her own sister strongly claims that Leslie is in denial, and claims to have seen Lee Chapman assaulting her sister quite badly in the past. Current and former employees of the couple have also come forward willing to testify that Lee Chapman is virtually a 'serial wife beater', but this he seriously denies. Allegedly the couple are even prepared to sue all the 'witnesses', including Leslie's own sister, over this. Whilst we are totally in sympathy with what has happened to Leslie and wish her a very speedy recovery and return to work, many people are quoting the old adage, 'There's no smoke without fire'. Although the police originally held-off from interviewing Lee Chapman, it appears that they have changed their minds over that. In the meantime, the whole boring saga is being placed on the back burner by myself and I will update as and when the final episode has been played out.

UPDATE Police have advised Lee Chapman that there is no longer any requirement for him to comply with the conditions of his police bail. They have decided that he cannot be prosecuted, in the absence of sufficient evidence. From the sheer repetition of stories about them constantly reported in the media, if you're a cynical person, as I'm sure I am, you may well be of the opinion that some so-called 'professional' footballers appear to be addicted to violence, both on and off the football pitch.

I recall that many years ago football pundit and supremo, Jimmy Greaves actually married a girl who lived next-door to my parents house, in the Romford, Essex area. Whilst he was courting his future wife, Irene from next-door, he actually used to go outside onto the green and play football with my brothers and the other kids 'on the block'. Irene was the daughter of an apparently successful haulage contractor, next door to the house my siblings and I had been brought up in. As time progressed and Jimmy became ever-more successful, as a professional footballer, he appeared to suffer from what cynics now refer to as 'George Best disease', viz: alcoholism.

During my police service with the Metropolitan Police, I was once temporarily stationed at the small Upminster police station and at other times had to cover the Upminster police area from other stations. By then I also lived in the area myself. Upminster is at the far eastern end of the underground District Line. I was a CID officer by then, but uniformed colleagues quite regularly it seemed, attended at Jimmy and Irene's marital home in the Upminster area. I believe this was through being called there by Irene as she had suffered domestic violence from Jimmy. I can't say how long this went on for, some years it seemed at the time. I often saw him driving around the 'manor' as BMW cars were quite rare in the UK in those days. Naturally Jimmy displayed his hard-earned wealth by purchasing the registration plate 'JPG 1' for the BMW. Irene often took county court injunctions out against Jimmy, which then had to be personally served on him. In those days there were very few court bailiffs or process servers around, so it was left to the police to serve Jimmy with the necessary legal documentation, to stay his hands from violence etc., until the next impending court date. As I am no football fan I don't happen to know whether Jimmy is over his alcoholism problem or not.

Football 'legend' Stan Bowles, 55, from Brentford, was arrested in mid-May 2004 accused of assaulting an ex-wife. He was interrogated after police had called at his home. Three-times-divorced Bowles admitted he 'scuffled' with third wife Diane Bushell when she confronted him outside a betting shop. The 1970's Queens Park Rangers soccer ace was held for eight hours at Hounslow police station, then released with a caution, after admitting common assault, which usually means the skin and flesh was unbroken, blood probably didn't flow, just shock, hurt feelings and minor bruising, I would imagine. Police described the injuries as superficial and having been caused in the street. (Bowles is allegedly as much a 'legend' as a heavy drinker, gambler and womaniser, as David Beckham is, for spitting on the football pitch whilst I'm watching football highlights with my meal. The latter is also 'legendary' for his bizarre bodily tattoos, full-bodily-hair waxings, and for his uncertainty as to whether he is a boy or a girl, as manifested in his bizarre hairstyles and female vanity-adornments.) As for Bowles, he later said that he could not remember what the row was about. He states that in his estimation he has 'blown' more than £500K in betting shops. He said: "We were always arguing. It could have been about anything. My hand 'accidentally' went out and I must have struck her." ('Must have' struck her? What does this mean? Was someone else manoeuvring his fist for him?) In 1992 Bowles was Bound Over in a magistrates court, to Keep the Peace, after his then ex-girlfriend accused him of assaulting her. I shall await the result of this latest assault case with bated breath.

The next angry 'celebrity' professional footballer in the news for alleged violence is ex-England striker Stan Collymore. In mid-May 2004 he was 'lying-low' after being released on police bail, having admitted to having had a 'bust-up' with his estranged wife, Estelle, 26. Collymore's agent, Simon Kennedy said: "Stan and his wife were involved in a domestic argument which took place over the weekend. There was an argument that became heated. The result of this was police involvement, but at no time did the argument resort into a level of physical intimidation, or any form of threat.

"Stan is adamant that he is completely innocent and he's quite happy to go in front of a court of his peers and prove that, at any time." Collymore was arrested after allegedly threatening to kill his wife Estelle at her parents' home in Heath Hayes, Staffs. He is also accused of attacking her £15,000 mini and threatening to burn down the house. He has been charged with causing criminal damage, behaving abusively, threatening to kill and threatening to cause damage. The ex-Liverpool player was remanded on police bail to Mid-Staffordshire magistrates court, where it now seems that the charges were 'dropped' or 'not proceeded with' after Collymore's solicitor had addressed the court. He agreed to be Bound Over in the sum of £500. Estelle moved from their £1million home to live with her parents, taking their daughter Mia, three years, with her, after Collymore was caught watching and joining couples having sex in a car park. The 'dogging' scandal also cost him his job as a pundit on BBC Radio Five Live. If I remember, isn't this the Stan Collymore who publicly beat up TV presenter/weather girl Ulrika Johnson a few years ago?

Blackburn Rovers football manager Graham Souness has been arrested over a fight with his ex-wife's husband, over the alleged failure of the latter to properly discharge his parental responsibilities. Apparently Souness came away from the row at Wilmslow, Cheshire, with his wrist in a plaster cast. The ex-husband, fashion tycoon Jonathan Levy was also injured during the row. He has facial and head injuries.

Former *Sky* TV presenter Frank Partridge, 50, appeared before High Wycombe magistrates court and was convicted of common assault after a two-day trial. He had punched in the face and thrown a glass of water over his former girlfriend of 17 months, Pamela Downs, 49, a TV continuity worker, when she told him she wanted to break-off the relationship. Miss Downs had told the court that she had ripped-up a photo of Partridge. He then burst into her office, hurled the glass of water at her, then chased her, 'terrified' into the garden. He hit her above her left eye and she then fell onto the patio injuring her back. Partridge, who was working for London's LBC Radio at the time, had denied the charge. Under cross-examination, Miss Downs told the magistrates she was very afraid of him. "He blacked my eyes, cut my face and suffocated me with a pillow. He had abused me for the previous 17 months, verbally, psychologically and emotionally. This was a fist too far."

Partridge was sentenced to 180 hours of community service and ordered to pay £175 compensation and £500 costs. He stated that he would be appealing against the conviction, which he thought was a civil matter rather than a criminal one. In 2001 Partridge had been sacked by *Sky* TV for slapping across the face his co-presenter Kay Burley. You may well consider that here is a man in the public eye who cannot keep his hands to himself, where members of the opposite sex are concerned.

A professional cricket player appeared at Preston Crown Court on 12th July 2004 charged with knifing his lover to death. Bevan Willians, 27, a talented club cricketer, stabbed his lover Melanie Horridge, 25, twenty-four times, as she pushed her four-month-old son in his buggy, because she had threatened to expose their secret affair. As the brute murdered the mother-of-three, his own 10-month-old daughter also sat in another pram nearby.

Three teenagers discovered Miss Horridge's body on the floor in a pool of blood, after hearing the screams of her baby, the court was told. Williams flew into a rage after Melanie Horridge threatened to tell his other girlfriend about their relationship. As she made the short walk to a phone box from her mother's house in Chorley, Lancs, she suffered horrific knife wounds to her face, head, neck, mouth and hands. She was also left with a fractured spine and bruising to her head and legs. The teenagers who found Miss Horridge at 7.30pm, alerted neighbour Arif Khansaheb, who tried in vain to resuscitate her and she was pronounced dead an hour later in hospital.

Preston Crown Court had heard how West Indian Williams, from Tobago, arrived in Britain six years ago, in 1998, to play for a team in Cambridgeshire, before moving to Euxton Cricket Club in Lancashire as their professional. At the time of the murder he was preparing to sign for nearby West Leigh Cricket Club. Williams and Miss Horridge had a child in 2001 but the relationship fizzled out. Problems flared when they met again and twice had casual sex in February 2004. Miss Horridge gave Williams an ultimatum to ditch his girlfriend Kirsty Charnock, or she said she would call at her place of work to tell her about the affair, the court was told. Keith Thomas, defending Williams, said he was 'desperate' when he saw Miss Horridge in the alleyway on 27th February 2004. "A scuffle ensued, his recollection thereafter is not the best. He is unable to explain his loss of control and what happened next. He had significant feelings of anxiety and anger with regard to what might happen." David Pickup, prosecuting, said the teenagers originally thought they had found a coat in the snow-covered alley. "The baby was in the pram and there was a figure laying face down on the ground."

Williams was sentenced to life imprisonment after pleading guilty to murder. He handed himself in to police the morning after the killing and officers discovered his daughter's pram covered in blood at his home. The judge, Mr Justice Brian Leveson, recommending he serve a minimum of 11 and a half years before being considered for parole, rejected Willams' claim that he used a knife which had been discarded, near the murder scene. He said: "I'm sure you had a knife on you and had previously carried a knife, and in the heat of the moment you decided to use it with terrible consequences. You snuffed out the life of another human being, depriving her children of their mother." At the time of the murder, Miss Horridge's sister Michelle, 33, said her younger sister would do anything to help anyone. "My mum has lost her daughter, we have lost a sister and our best friend. Our children have lost a loving auntie and, most important, three children are left without a mother. My sister suffered at the hands of a sick and evil person who had no consideration for her or her children."

Miss Herridge's two remaining children aged three and two, including Williams's child, are now being cared for by her relatives, who were too upset to comment after the trial. Tragedy has struck the family before, Miss Herridge lost a baby son Joshua in a cot death six years ago.

The father of England football star Jamie Carragher was banned from all football grounds in the UK on 16th February 2005. Gary Carragher spent the night in cells after being arrested for being drunk while watching his son play in England's game with Holland. He was allegedly thrown out of his VIP seat by stewards at Villa Park, Birmingham and later held by police after trying to get back into the stadium. Carragher, 50, from Crosby, Liverpool, appeared before magistrates in Birmingham to plead not guilty to a charge of trying to enter a sports arena while drunk. Ian Till, defending, urged magistrates not to ban Carragher from football grounds while he waited for his trial. "He follows his son across the country and it would be unfortunate to deny him this opportunity." he said. But senior magistrate Rama Joshi told Carragher that as a condition of bail he would not be able to enter any football ground in the UK.

A former football chairman has branded today's soccer stars as liars and 'total scum', it was reported on 12th February 2005. Entrepreneur Sir Alan Sugar said most of Britain's professionals 'would be in prison' if they had not become full-time players. In an extraordinary outburst the former chairman of Tottenham Hotspur said: "They don't know what honesty or loyalty is." He went on: "They're the biggest scum that walk on the planet and if they weren't football players most of them would be in prison, it's as simple as that." The boss of electronics firm *Amstrad*, who still owns a 13 per cent share in Spurs after his resignation as chairman in 2001, said people should not believe a word that comes out of footballers' mouths and that players were only interested in themselves. He added: "If something doesn't go right, they'll go behind you and stab you in the back. If you ever had to go into the trenches and had to rely on people,don't ever rely on footballers." Sir Alan stars in *The Apprentice*, a reality TV show on BBC2, which gives high-flyers the chance to work for him for a year. A Tottenham Hotspur spokesman replied: "These comments reflect Alan Sugar's personal views and not those of the club. "But it is puzzling that he said those things, as he still regularly comes to home matches." And Gary Mabbutt, who was captain at Spurs during much of Sir Alan's time as chairman, said: "It's unnecessary and derogatory and an astonishing statement. Perhaps, when he took over, he didn't realise what he was letting himself in for. People are entitled to their opinions but the bottom line is it's hard to take these comments seriously." And he added that if Sir Alan's outburst had come on April 1st it would have been accepted as a joke.

Early evening football matches at weekends could be banned after drunken violence on and off the pitch marred Saturday's tense FA clash between Everton and Manchester United. The match, marking the first return of striker Wayne Rooney to his former boyhood club since his controversial £27million transfer, was shamed when United keeper Roy Carroll was hit by a coin thrown by a yob. And trouble flared after the match when Everton fans tried to break through a police cordon escorting some of the 6,000 United fans back to Liverpool's city centre. The violence led to 33 arrests, mostly for public order offences. Five police officers were injured as youths attempted to stone the away supporters with masonry and rubble. Merseyside Assistant Chief Constable Mick Gianassi, said that the late kick-off was a factor in the violence because it allowed people to drink more. "It just provides the opportunity to drink before and after the game and quite clearly drink is a factor in violence." But he added that trouble would have 'broken out regardless' with more than 300 fans 'intent on causing trouble'. Before the game, both clubs and the police were concerned when the kick-off was switched to 5.30pm so the BBC could show the match live.

Sports Minister Richard Caborn warned: "We may well have to rethink the 5.30pm kick-off. We know it is done predominately for television, but we might have to reflect on that. There are now a lot more people returning to football and it is a minority of fans who are bringing the game into disrepute and we have to deal with that." He added that it was up to police and the clubs to consider whether games of high tension should be played earlier. One Manchester United fan described how the violence erupted after the game, which United comfortably won 2-0. He said: "One thing led to another. We were being escorted back to our trains and they came out of the darkness throwing things. Unfortunately some of our supporters responded and things went to pot from there."

But the Football Association insisted proper consultations had been followed. FA media head Adrian Bevington said: "We work with all the relevant parties, including the police, when arranging kick-off times and we have never arranged a time without full agreement. We have of course seen many FA Cup ties played at 5:30 successfully without any problems in recent years."

Merseyside Police have launched an inquiry and are examining TV footage to try and identify the coin-throwing culprit. They are also examining other missiles, thought to be a golf ball and mobile phone, which are believed to have been thrown at United players. Chief Constable Bernard Hogan-Howe said: "I will be asking for a report to review the full facts of the violence on Saturday. I will also be urging a review of the behaviour of both sets of supporters and talking to the BBC about the kick-off time for future games here." Everton spokesman Ian Ross said if the fans who threw the missiles are identified they would be banned from Goodison Park for life. He added: "The police did a magnificent job. The trouble occurred away from the ground and apart from the one missile incident, the game passed off very peacefully. The trouble appears to have been pre-meditated and who knows whether the kick-off time had any bearing. These people are not football supporters, they are men of violence. But they are still there and everybody must continue to be vigilant." And ACC Gianassi added: "We police society and one of the issues we have to deal with is the commercial interests of football clubs and the desire of people to watch football late in the afternoon.

Everton are bracing themselves for a £50,000 fine from the Football Association as Manchester United goalkeeper Roy Carroll claimed he feared for his safety after being struck by a coin during the FA Cup fifth round tie at Goodison Park. Sports Minister Richard Caborn has suggested Saturday evening kick-offs may have to be re-examined after 33 Everton and United fans were arrested and five police injured following clashes in the streets of Liverpool after the game.

Sunday 20th February's much-anticipated FA Cup derby between Burnley and Blackburn was marred by three pitch invasions and further missile throwing. One Burnley fan ran on towards the end of the 0-0 draw at Turf Moor and raised his fists towards Blackburn midfielder Robbie Savage. He knocked the helmet off a policeman then lashed out at a policewoman before being finally restrained and arrested. Blackburn manager Mark Hughes fears such incidents could have more serious consequences. He said: "Given the amount of stewarding and policing, for three fans to encroach on to the field was appalling. It should be looked at." But Everton have most to lose. An urgent probe into the flashpoint will be stepped up today as the club feared a heavy punishment for the latest example of crowd violence.

Carroll fell clutching his head after being hit during the second half of United's 2-0 victory and is believed to have told officials, including police and referee Rob Styles, he was worried for his well-being. The Northern Ireland goalkeeper has also alleged Everton stewards laughed in his face when he outlined his concerns. Hampshire official Styles has included the incident, along with reference to two other episodes in which objects, thought to include a golf ball and a mobile phone, were thrown onto the pitch, in his match report. The FA is likely to hit Everton hard, having warned them as to the future conduct of their supporters after pitch invasions against Portsmouth and Liverpool. Everton have been swift to condemn the latest incident and spokesman Ian Ross said: "At least 99.9 per cent of our fans behaved, but we have been let down by one complete moron who has disgraced the name of this football club. We have apologised to both Mr Carroll and to Manchester United. We are hopeful of identifying the culprit and if that person is charged by the police and convicted, we will look to implement a life ban." Sports Minister Caborn, meanwhile, told BBC Radio 5 Live's Sportsweek: "We know the Saturday 5.30pm kick-off is predominately television, but we might have to rethink."

COUNT 10

HIT-AND-RUN & OTHER DRIVING OFFENCES

As a uniformed Police Constable based at North Woolwich, by the Woolwich Ferry, in the MPD, I was required to deal with whatever type of incident presented itself. One day I was patrolling on foot towards the end of the 'early' shift (6AM – 2PM) when I was advised that there was a serious road accident in North Woolwich Road, London, E16. On arrival I found a scene of mayhem and horror, which had been brought on by a blatant piece of very dangerous driving by a most impatient driver, who had 'carved-up' the driver of an articulated lorry, which was driving towards Canning Town. The lorry was freshly fully-laden from the nearby Royal Docks. The impatient, unknown driver of the car, who was never identified as he or she sped away afterwards, failing to stop - had pulled out to overtake the lorry with scant regard as to whether it was safe to do so and whether there was *room* to do so. Whilst actually alongside the quite long towing unit and trailer bearing a container, this speeding driver, who could not possibly have put enough thought into his intended actions, must suddenly have realised that he had made a grave error.

Ahead of him, outside a public house which lay back from the road, was a large concrete central refuge or 'island' with 'keep left' signs to warn drivers. The road at this point, being at a main docks approach area, was wider-than-normal and therefore the 'island' had been installed to assist pedestrians to cross the road. Instead of backing off, i.e. slowing down or stopping and giving way, the dangerous driver, determined to complete his overtaking manoeuvre no matter what, increased his speed, approaching an ever-diminishing gap between the front of the lorry and the central refuge. The lorry driver, assessing the situation realised that he was confronted with no choice but to brake hard, to prevent his lorry slamming the overtaking car into the central refuge, with serious consequences. As he did so, the inevitable happened and the lorry jack-knifed. The loaded trailer and container, through centrifugal force, wanted to carry on in the previous straight ahead direction of travel, but instead, was pushed around to the right with deadly speed and lethal force.

At that moment, travelling in the opposite direction, was a car being driven at normal, safe speed by a male driver who had been to work that morning but, it was later found, had without permission left work before the end of his shift and was on his way home. The massive force generated by the combined weight of the lorry's containerised trailer, as it slewed across the opposite carriageway, must have been about the equivalent of the innocent driver's car having slammed into a concrete motorway bridge at motorway speeds. He was killed instantly, as the human frame is incapable of sustaining such tremendous forces as that. The fire brigade and an ambulance were very soon on scene but it was far too late for medical help.

As you can imagine, it was a bloody and horrific scene, so much so that fire fighters had to hold up huge tarpaulins to shield the carnage from public view, whilst their colleagues cut away the remains of the car so that the deceased's body could be extricated. In the meantime, with police colleagues, I searched for potential witnesses, starting at the public house opposite, outside which the tragedy had occurred. It was a bright, sunny day and many local employees were taking their lunch hours at the pub, eating and drinking at the outside chairs, tables and benches supplied by the brewery. At least some of these people were facing the main road and from these, you would expect that one or more of them would have seen just what happened. Attention must have been drawn to the scene opposite, at least by the great shrieking noise as the brakes of the articulated lorry were rapidly employed. In fact most readers are probably aware that the ultra-efficient air-braking systems of lorries and large vans, mean that they can almost stop on a sixpence. The outcome was, that the relations of the driver killed instantly right outside that pub on a bright sunny day, were never to find out who had caused the tragic loss of their loved one, as not a single witness from the public house clientele would admit to having seen anything at all. Neither was anyone else who had stopped to offer assistance on realising the enormity of the impact, been able to advise us of the make, model or registration number of the car, the driver of which had caused that poor man's death by extremely dangerous driving. To this day, there is no doubt in my mind that the offending, impatient driver must have had his eyes drawn like a magnet to his interior mirror and could not have resisted at least a glance to see what had taken place behind him, as he sped away. Therefore, he was also guilty of failing to stop after an accident and probably could have been construed as having 'hit and run', like some of the other examples of abysmal driving that I shall tell you about next, even though his vehicle did not actually make contact with either the central refuge, the lorry or the innocent deceased's motor car.

Prior to the introduction of the breath test/blood sample procedures, it was the devil's own job to convict a driver of 'driving under the influence of drink or drug', under section 6 of the old Road Traffic Act 1960. If a police officer suspected that a motorist was guilty of that offence, somehow he had to arrest the driver, take care of his car and get him to the police station. This was extremely difficult then, as there were no personal radios carried by patrolling beat officers and hardly any (unvandalised) public telephone boxes, with which to call for help. In the meantime, the prisoner's adrenalin was coursing through his veins due to the shock of being arrested. Also, as the time was elapsing whilst the officer attempted to get him to the police station, the prisoner could be rapidly sobering-up, unless he was paralytic, as in some cases.

On arrival at the police station, the sergeant, most of whom were 'little tin gods' in those days, if he was not already present, had to be contacted somehow and asked to return at once. You then had to convince the sergeant, not that he was *now* unfit to drive his car through drink or drugs, but that *he was in that condition at the time you stopped him*, possibly ages beforehand. But the ordeal for the by now sweating arresting officer was by no means over yet. If the sergeant agreed with you as to his condition, it was then necessary to summon the Police Surgeon. Sometimes these were just ordinary GP's who supplemented their NHS salaries by being contracted to assist the Police Forces with their professional opinions as to sobriety matters. If the Police Surgeon was still out on his GP rounds and uncontactable, you were in really big trouble and had to try other Police Surgeons. Once you finally were honoured by his presence at the station, he commenced a question and answer examination as to how much food had been eaten and how long ago, how much to drink and when the session finished etc., what a palaver!

The doctor then carried out his own 'fitness' tests on the prisoner and made his immediate verbal report to the sergeant. If he certified that chummy was indeed unfit to drive etc., you thanked your lucky stars and could then get on with the all-important paper work and reception into the station, searching, advise relatives, bring in his vehicle, obtain urine samples by trans-pouring gallons of water from one container to another, endlessly flushing the toilet chain and running water down the sink, attempting to make an unwilling prisoner fill the blessed officially-labelled urine container, for onward transmission to the Lab for scientific analysis.

On one difficult occasion at Tilbury I had a Scottish prisoner who was a full-time merchant seaman. For some minutes as he was attempting to pee, I thought he was swearing at us, in fact he was using the nautical term for urinating (Often over the ship's side!) 'PUMP SHIP, PUMP SHIP!' Before you settled him down to sleep it off in the cell, you had to remove his shoe laces, belt and tie so that he could not harm himself, before placing him in the 'recovery' position to avoid him choking on his own vomit.

Prior to leaving the station, the Police Surgeon would certify the prisoner's condition, so far as being fit to drive was concerned, and complete his all-important expenses claim form, not necessarily in that order! All of the above events had to take place in the correct order at the Police station and were based on the assumption that one or more of the following series of events did not take place, delaying your progress, immediately after you effected your arrest on the street:

1) Prisoner struggling or fighting like mad to escape. Your struggle to handcuff him/her.

2) Calling upon innocent passers-by to assist his escape from lawful custody by assaulting you.

3) Full-bladdered prisoner, after a 'skinful', demanding to pee in the street there and then.

4) Producing from his pocket a further beer or spirits bottle and attempting to drink from same.

5) Attempting to cram into his mouth old pork pie or sandwich fragments, so as to attempt to alter body metabolism.

6) Screaming for his mother, wife or help from the Almighty.

7) Difficulty in securing his car and contents against theft/being hit by other traffic in the dark etc.

In one quite extraordinary case, whilst on early shift, pre-breathalyser era, I arrested a man driving his car home on a Sunday morning, who was still ultra-drunk from the night before and not willing to come quietly. In fact he tried to drive away with me stretched across his lap as I struggled to reach across him and remove the ignition keys, the ignition lock being in the centre-dashboard position as was fashionable in that era. As luck would have it, he was so drunk that I was able to settle him down in the back seat of his car whilst I drove his car to the police station.

Readers, take great care when drinking too much whilst out socialising. When you set out to drive to work next morning a random breath test procedure on your way to work could have you convicted for driving with excess alcohol in your body, as your metabolism had not had a sufficient number of hours to break down the alcohol, particularly so in the absence of little or no food consumed with, or after all the drink!

Once the breathalyser was perfected abroad and approved and introduced in the UK, it made our lives much easier. In my own case, once I became an area car driver at Grays Division, in Essex, it was easy to spot drivers potentially over the limit by simply following them along the ever-busy A13 London to Southend road. 'Suspects' would tend to 'lane-wander', cross double-white lines, drive too slow or too fast, nearly hit the kerb, over or under-steer, commit 'moving traffic offences' or cause accidents en route. Naturally the presence of 'cats-eyes' lane markers on multi-laned busy roads, made it a piece of

CAR MOVED OFF WITH POLICEMAN LEANING THROUGH THE DOOR!

WHILE a Policeman was talking to a car driver and leaning through the car door, the car moved off carrying the officer with it. He was practically sitting in the driver's lap.

The driver appeared in Court last week pleading guilty to driving under the influence of drink. He was Ralph Walton (51), barman, of Lampits Hill, Corringham, who was fined £30, disqualified from driving for 12 months and was ordered to pay costs of over £9

The Court heard that the incident occurred at about midnight and the Police officer's attention was drawn to the car because it had driven up on to a traffic island at the junction of Feenan Highway and St. Chad's Road, Tilbury.

The officer went over to the car and opened the driver's door; there was a strong smell of drink and it was obvious to him that Walton, the driver, had been drinking.

As he spoke to Walton the car began to move forward across the road taking the officer with it. The officer had to wrench the steering wheel to the right to prevent the vehicle running off the road into a ditch.

Unfit

Walton was arrested and taken to Tilbury Police Station, where he was examined by a doctor and found to be unfit to drive through drink. A test showed that there was the equivalent of eight pints of beer in his bloodstream.

Walton told the Court that he was not usually a heavy drinker, but he had had some bad news that evening.

cake for suspect-identification. When we had our black Austin Cambridges with a two-candle-power revolving blue light on the roof, we struggled to even catch up with most traffic, as it took forever to progress through the manual gearbox, even up to say, 50mph. On occasions we had to almost 'will' a driver to slow down to allow us to overtake him, even when we had made the decision to 'pull him', as we needed to get in front of him so the observer/operator could pull down the 'POLICE STOP' roller blind!

However, eventually that was all to change for the better when Traffic Patrol Officers were issued with Lotus Cortina super-fast cars and less-fortunate colleagues like me had to make do with Ford Mark 2 Cortinas with 1600cc engines instead. These white-painted patrol cars really turned our lives around. They were fitted with short, stubby gear levers for rapid gear-changes, 4-candle-power blue lights and best-of-all, amazing Pirelli Cinturato tyres, which stuck to the road like the proverbial 'toffee-to-a-blanket', particularly at high speed around bends! (These are the tyres on the car in the TV commercial ad which screeches to a halt on the very edge of a US skyscraper roof). We could almost 'fly' along the A13 road and their introduction in the late-60's must have almost halved the time it took us to arrive at an accident or incident.

Whilst on night duty at Grays in the EPD (Essex Police District), during the early hours of the morning, as was often necessary on a busy weekend night, I had dropped-off my co-driver, as we often shared the driving, at the police station for his refreshment break of 45 minutes. The plan was that he would then have relieved me for my meal-break. This was a cold and frosty night with white frost clearly visible on some road surfaces, in other words, be aware of tendencies to skid if you weren't careful and beware of hard-braking around bends or coarse or violent steering, which are skid-inducible. Alone in the area car, I parked up on a closed petrol station at Daneholes roundabout, a local landmark. Before long, a car came flying along the road from Southend direction, heading for London, the next town after Grays being Rainham, Essex, almost on the EPD/MPD border.

This car successfully negotiated the roundabout and then accelerated to a fast speed along the dual carriageway. Naturally I gave chase to see what the male driver was up to. My job was doubly difficult through being alone, as I wanted to keep both hands on the steering wheel at all costs under those slippery road conditions, particularly around bends, as Pirelli Cinturato tyres can't work miracles on snow, ice, oil, grease or frost. However to call for assistance or 'back-up', as you know if you're a fan of '*The Bill*', you need to grab and hold onto the fitted police radio mike and/or your personal radio handset to alert the station and your mobile colleagues to give you a hand. You also need to have the bandit car's index number checked against the active stolen car register.

Eventually, getting towards Rainham, which had a fairly major traffic-lights junction, I succeeded in drawing alongside the car. He had known I had wanted him to pull over for some miles, as the blue light had been visible in his interior mirror, had he been one of those drivers who ever looked in it, to see who or what was behind! Along this final stretch of the A13 road, lit by high sodium lamp posts, the white frost was more visible than ever. To my horror, as I drove beside him, I glanced at the speedometer only to find that we were travelling at just over 90mph! He pulled over before the traffic lights, where my buddies were waiting for a chance to get to him. He got out onto the grass verge without speaking, just shrugging his shoulders. Naturally he qualified for a free breath test after that display of abysmally dangerous driving. As I walked past his car to get the kit for this, I glanced through the rear window of his car. You will understand that I could hardly believe my eyes when I saw that his son, aged about 8-10 years, was curled up asleep on the back seat!

The breath test proved positive and he was later charged with excess alcohol, dangerous driving, failure to stop for police and a whole range of other offences. These later caused him a second-mortgage-worth of court-imposed fines, endorsements and disqualification. I hope he learned his lesson. Cost to me, increased stress-level and mega-hunger pangs through a maniac-induced, much-delayed meal-break!

In this other case, which I did not personally deal with, but in which I got to see the official police photographs afterwards, a teenaged car thief caused his own death in Grays, Essex, by driving the stolen car too fast around a serious bend. Due to his driving inexperience and previous absence of driving lessons and driving test, and having failed to ask the car owner if he could use it, he 'ran out of road'. He crashed into a small wooded area and rammed a fence. This was a fence made of chestnut stakes as used by countless local councils to separate the gardens of individual council houses. One of these sharpened chestnut stakes impaled him, killing him instantly. I can assure you the accident scene was not a pretty sight and his loved ones were unable to identify and bid him farewell at the council mortuary chapel until the 3-4ft stake had been removed. Unusually, only the perpetrator came to physical grief in this particular case. More often than not, the statistics seem to indicate that others are hurt or killed but the person carrying out the dangerous driving survives.

A man aged 31 was killed crossing a road in Dalston, Cumbria as two motorists raced through a village. Claire Brumwell and Frankie Hodgson, both aged 19-years were driving side-by-side at speeds of up to 80mph, presumably in what is commonly known as 'a burn up'. The deceased was killed as Hodgson swerved to the right of a 'keep left' bollard. Brumwell pleaded not guilty to causing death by dangerous driving at Carlisle Crown Court, whilst Hodgson pleaded guilty. The prosecution claimed that they were equally to blame for causing the tragic, needless death of Mr Little.

At Teesside Crown Court on 5th March 2004, Paul Lee, 25, of Gateshead, admitted causing death by dangerous driving over the Christmas Holiday Break on 27th December 2003 at West Cornforth, County Durham. Tests proved that Lee had been taking drugs the night before at a club. Traces of amphetamines, cocaine, ecstasy and cannabis were found in his blood. As he drove along, he bragged to a friend that his car could 'fly'. He then drove down a hill at 60mph in a 30mph speed zone. So fast was he travelling that the car became *airborne* for 45 feet before ploughing into a young family out for a walk. The car slammed into a buggy killing eight-month-old Callum Taylor. Little sister Lottie, 21 months, was also in the tandem buggy, but survived. At the time of the tragedy, Lee was disqualified from driving, the driving ban having been imposed for his third conviction for dangerous driving. In addition to his plea of guilty to the offence of causing the baby's death by dangerous driving, he admitted driving whilst disqualified and without insurance. He was banned from driving for just 6 years but the judge sentenced him to eight years imprisonment on the major count of the indictment.

These road races seem to take place more often than we normally hear about. In April 2003 Steven Hoggett, 19, from Murton, County Durham and Csaba Nemeth, 22, from Sunderland, were taking part in a race with each other, in their cars near Sunderland. They drove at speeds of up to 100mph as Hoggett tried to keep up with his workmate Nemeth. In doing so, Hoggett hit the moped of father-of-four Mr Derek Miller, 59. Mr Miller died instantly. On 23rd February 2004 at Newcastle Crown Court, both men were convicted of causing death by dangerous driving by racing and each sentenced to three years and 9 months. After the case, Mr Miller's widow stated that in her opinion the sentences should have been doubled. What is your opinion? Did the judge carry out his job properly on this occasion? Do you agree that their sentences should be doubled? Have you noticed all of the inconsistencies in sentencing, up and down the country?

The newspaper headline in this next case reads, **ANOTHER HIT-RUN MADMAN IS FREED**. Daniel Wilkinson, 23, had taken a car without consent (known as 'TWOC', previously known as 'JOYRIDING') and drove into a 12-year-old boy, Jack Willis, who was walking home from a football match, then fled the scene, at Illingworth, West Yorks. The car belonged to Wilkinson's girlfriend.

This was obviously one of those common cases where you lend your car to a friend who has no business using it for various reasons, on the understanding that, if he is caught, you will say *that he did not have your permission to take it*. The alternative for you is that you are summoned for aiding and abetting the offence of 'no driving licence and no insurance', which could seriously affect your relationship with your own car insurance company if they found out (Such as by reading the court report in the local newspaper). At Calderdale Magistrates Court, Wilkinson admitted taking the car without consent (to spare his girlfriend's blushes etc?) driving without a driving licence and insurance and failing to stop after an accident. To his credit, Wilkinson had turned himself into the police after seeing a picture in the local paper of little victim Jack, 12, in hospital with his broken arm and leg. Like me, you are probably wondering whether it was at Wilkinson's girlfriend's suggestion that he was good enough to give himself up into custody, as no doubt she was feeling some guilt for having 'lent' him the car in the first place.

Victim Jack is expected to be off school for at least five months in recovery, after enduring a 4-hour operation to pin his shattered thigh bone. His mother said after the case: "Anyone who runs down a child and leaves them lying unconscious in the road should go to prison. It should be as simple as that. He has just walked free. Our family has been through hell." Magistrates Chairman Mr Robin Kempster told Wilkinson he had escaped prison by a 'knife edge'. "We are dealing with a matter here which could easily have turned into tragedy." He sentenced him to 240 hours community service and banned him from driving for 2 years. Tory David Davis, a Hull MP, called for 'longer sentences' for car maniacs.

A road menace who refused to fix his dangerous brakes was jailed for eight years on 23rd August 2004 for killing two school friends in a horrific crash. Lee Elton, 28, was 'showing off' by speeding at 70mph when he ploughed into a car taking Christian Leyden and Anthony Hughes, both 16, home from football practice. Elton, a salesman, got behind the wheel knowing his brakes were faulty and lost control, despite desperate pleas from his young passengers to slow down, a court heard. Christian and Anthony were being driven home by Anthony's mother when Elton mowed into her Ford Focus, sending it flying through the air and into a lamp post. It came to rest upside down. The boys, born just two days apart, had known each other since nursery and had been 'inseparable' at school. They died at the scene as firemen fought to free them from the wreckage in Oldham, Greater Manchester.

Elton began his sentence after pleading guilty to two charges of causing death by dangerous driving. He had told car enthusiasts in an e-mail that the brake system in his 12-year-old Rover 827 was 'absolutely knackered'. Judge John Burke QC, sentencing Elton at Minshull Street Crown Court, Manchester said: "You snuffed out the lives of two much-loved and very promising young boys and dealt their families a devastating blow. You were showing off by all the signs, the car was of some age, the MOT had run out and the ABS (anti-lock brakes) were out of action and you had known that for some time. Your passengers were begging you to slow down to no avail."

Nick Clarke, prosecuting, said that had Elton been travelling at 30mph with working brakes he would have stopped short of the Focus. Such was his grossly excessive speed that his own passengers were screaming at him to slow down and he continued to go faster and faster. Because the ABS brake system was not working, the car ploughed into the Focus which was lifted into the air. Elton and his passengers escaped from the crash without serious injury. So did Anthony's mother, Kathleen Hughes, 57, who had been waiting to turn right at a junction when the Rover smashed into her.

Seven ambulance crews went to the scene which onlookers described as 'complete carnage'. Mark Fireman, defending Elton said: 'He understands he cannot go back in time and undo what he has done, but his feelings of remorse are true and genuine. He has not only taken two lives but ruined his own. Whatever happens to him and his family it pales into insignificance compared to the family of the two boys". Elton, of Oldham, was also banned from driving for ten years.

A car thief has been given free membership to a £50-a-month health club at taxpayers' expense. He committed up to 50 offences a week and has served time for breaking into cars and garages. His free gym pass was issued under a probation service scheme to 'reintegrate' criminals into society. It offers luxury facilities including a 20ft pool, steam room and state-of-the-art gym. The idea is being tried in Bristol and Taunton, Somerset before going nationwide later in 2004. Throughout Avon and Somerset 220 criminals will benefit by Autumn but not all will be given free gym passes. Tory MP Adrian Flook said: "It's an insult to victims of crime." Local sceptic Mike Hughes said: "Who is picking up the tab for provision of a new security guard or cutting-edge CCTV system, to keep watch on the locker-rooms where innocent, law-abiding health club members stow their clothes and valuables whilst enjoying the facilities?"

Lee Jones, 24, of Bournemouth, had hung up his mobile telephone shortly before he swerved into the wrong lane and hit an oncoming car, Bournemouth magistrates were told. As a result, James Phillip, 28, and his passengers Mark Pitman, 18 and Suzanne Manning, 23 were all killed instantly. Two other passengers survived but are still recovering from their injuries. The five had been taking part in a national volleyball championship in Bournemouth and were on their way to get something to eat. Jones admitted driving without care and attention. The Crown Prosecution Service said it did not have enough evidence to bring the more serious charge of causing three deaths by dangerous driving, which carries a maximum penalty of 10 years imprisonment.

The presiding magistrate, Margaret Field, said the court's powers of sentencing were restricted by the law. She told the defendant Jones: "You have accepted responsibility and no doubt your conscience will bear the burden of this for the rest of your life. This offence is very serious but we are bound to apply the law, which does not allow us to impose a custodial sentence for what you have done. Furthermore, the law is such that we are generally asked to consider how badly you were driving rather than the consequences of your driving, but the fatalities are too important to ignore in this case."

After the case, Mr Pitman's sister said: "We have got to live without our loved ones while Jones has to live without his licence. The law has to be changed so that people who kill on the roads can be given custodial sentences. There really can't be justice until this happens." Magistrates had been told that Jones had been driving to a wine bar. He made a telephone call 20-25 seconds before a member of public dialled 999, but police could not prove that he had been on his mobile at the time of impact. The court heard that his Rover 620 was travelling at about 60mph, 20mph over the 40mph speed limit and that his car was 1.1 metres (about 4ft 3 ins) over the opposite carriageway. Jones was given a breath test which proved to be negative. The volleyball players' Renault 19 was split in two by the impact. Mr John Revell, the Chief Crown Prosecutor for Dorset said: "There were exhaustive enquiries made by Dorset Police, but when all of the evidence was looked at there was nothing to suggest any dangerous driving." (I would have thought that having your car 1.1 metres over the centre white line while speeding at 60mph in a 40mph limit area went some small way towards dangerous driving. What is your view?). The magistrates had fined Jones the sum of £1,500 (maximum fine £2,500) and banned him from driving for 5 years. Jones has lodged notice of appeal against sentence.

In January 2004 at Reading Crown Court, Simon Teesdale, 33, from Slough, Berks., (It used to be in Bucks, but the powers-that-be moved it, together with Sandhurst, once Surrey, now also in Berks!) admitted causing death by dangerous driving and having no driving licence (as he was a diabetic it had probably been suspended). Whilst driving in a diabetic trance, meaning he was driving on 'auto-pilot', he mounted the pavement and mowed down a 16-year old victim, killing him. Teesdale's 10-week-old daughter was in the car when the accident occurred. His Honour the crown court judge, in his wisdom, sentenced Teesdale to just 18 months imprisonment (Maximum penalty as we've just read, 10 years). The family of the young victim, Usman Akhtar, described the 'lenient' sentence as 'a slap in the face,' claiming that

Teesdale could be out of jail after just 9 months.

A father killed his own 14-year-old son Lee, in a high-speed crash on a trip to the seaside, Lincoln Crown Court was told. Stephen Johnson, 41, was overtaking a line of traffic at up to 94mph in his Toyota MR2 sports car when he lost control on a bend. He hit an oncoming car and his son died of his injuries. A mother and her five-year-old daughter in the other car were also injured. The court heard that the boy, who lives with his mother, was on an access visit with his father in May 2003, heading for a day out at Skegness when the tragedy occurred. Johnson's speed was estimated at between 79 and 94mph.

Witnesses said the sports car was going so fast that the engine appeared to be screaming as it overtook a row of cars before trying to cut in at a right-hand bend. Johnson braked sharply but the wheels locked and he lost control, skidding sideways and into the oncoming traffic. Johnson's barrister told the court that his client could remember nothing of the crash. "Putting aside the tragic loss, the most difficult thing that he has had to do is accept that he was the sole cause of the accident. He accepts that he has condemned all of those involved, to a life living with that loss. He does not know how to live with himself. Whatever happens to him today cannot be as bad as what he has to bear, not only for the last 10 months but for the rest of his life." Judge John Milmo told Johnson: "Your son died of head injuries because of the way in which you drove dangerously. One of the drivers could not believe your stupidity in trying to overtake when you did. I share her obvious amazement at the way in which you were driving." The judge said he was satisfied that Johnson was 'riddled with remorse'. He then sentenced Johnson to four years imprisonment. Outside court, Johnson's ex-wife, the boy's mother said: "The sentence has not been important to me. The law decides what happens to Stephen, but it was not easy for me seeing Lee's dad being sent to prison today for what he has done. However, he drove dangerously and anyone who drives dangerously in that manner can destroy lives. Let it be a lesson to other people."

A Red Cross volunteer driver forced to break the speed limit when a passenger had a fit in his vehicle, has appeared before magistrates at South Somerset. Good Samaritan Ivon Flagg, 70, a retired medic, was driving two cancer patients to hospital when one woman began to suffocate after swallowing her tongue. Mr Flagg broke the 30mph speed limit by driving at 42mph on the A37 in Lydford, Devon in September 2003, as he tried to find somewhere to pull over so that he could treat the woman. However the magistrates fined him £70. It does not say in the article if he was caught by a speed camera or in some other way.

Although we are quick enough to criticise magistrates and judges in their normal under-sentencing mode, you might think that a conditional discharge for 12 months would have been more appropriate in this particular case, wouldn't you? After all, he was on a life-saving mission at the time. I do hope he will appeal against the sentence and win the appeal.

A teenager's reunion with his long-lost father ended in tragedy when they were both killed in the same motorcycle crash. Samuel Turvey died on his 17th birthday riding pillion on a superbike being driven by his father Peter Cassidy. Plymouth Coroner Nigel Meadows warned about the dangers of driving under the influence of drink and drugs, after hearing from the pathologist that Mr Cassidy had alcohol, cannabis, cocaine and amphetamines in his system. A police expert said the bike's speedometer was 'frozen' at 83mph after the crash, but marks on the road suggested it had been travelling at about 50mph. Samuel had decided to track down his real father in 2001 and the pair had become very close over the following couple of years. Peter Cassidy, 40, had taken Samuel for a birthday ride on the back of his 1300cc Kawasaki motorbike, around the country lanes near his home in Kingsbridge, Devon when they crashed into a hedge.

Samuel's mother Joanne, who is remarried said: "It was destiny that they met up again after 15 years and it is destiny that they will be together forever. It was the first birthday I have ever spent without seeing Sam. I spoke to him in the morning and I knew he was so happy and was having a wonderful time with his dad. It gives me comfort to know that he was so happy on his last day." Samuel, who lived in West Mersea, Essex had told his mum that he wanted to meet his real father, who was vice-president of a Plymouth motor cycle club. By coincidence, half an hour later, Mr Cassidy had called Sam's mother saying that he wanted to make contact with his son he had not seen since he was a newborn baby. The coroner said: "The drink and drugs must have impaired his ability to ride the motorcycle, but I cannot resolve to what extent." Verdict: Accidental death.

A Catholic priest who was **FOUR TIMES OVER THE DRINK-DRIVING LIMIT** on Christmas Day 2003, had been celebrating at a friend's house. He had drunk an Irish coffee which was much stronger than he thought. He was Father Colin Murphy, 56, of St Patricks RC Church in Chislehurst, Kent. In spite of being four times over the limit, which made him a fatal-accident-waiting-to-happen, he 'escaped' a custodial sentence by the learned Bench at Bromley Magistrates Court, in their wisdom. Instead, they banned him from driving for 18months. Obviously his prayers had been answered.

A bridegroom spent his wedding night behind bars after being arrested for drink-driving as he travelled home from the evening wedding reception.

Stephen Wallace, 41, from Hull, East Yorks, was **TWICE OVER THE LEGAL LIMIT**. He and his bride Julie, had returned home from their afternoon reception for a nap before the evening festivities. But the couple overslept and were late for the party at their local pub, so Wallace decided to drive. He admitted drink-driving and driving without a driving licence or insurance. Hull magistrates banned him from driving for 16 months.

In Camberley, Surrey, Sean Huntroyd, 30, callously ran down PC Roy Teague, then drove off at 60mph with the officer clinging to his car roof by his fingertips. For this horrific dangerous driving, he was jailed for nine years at a crown court. However during a brief spell at top-security Belmarsh prison, South London, he was disciplined for fighting. Within a month of receiving his nine year jail sentence, he was moved to a jail near his home, Coldingley Prison, which is rated as low security and has a 'soft' regime. Furious police and prison officers now fear that Huntroyd will be freed after only serving half of his sentence. Low security jails like Coldingley are normally used to train convicts for jobs before release. At his trial, the trial judge said that he should have been tried for attempted murder rather than attempted GBH (This is a major criticism of the Crown Prosecution Service, which is responsible for assessing the evidence and accurately formulating and preparing the most appropriate counts to appear on the indictment.). A source at HMP Coldingley said: "It was a shocking crime. People are angry that he's on such a cushy number." (There was a time when I frequently visited this jail, which used to have a whole series of 'air-lock' open air security areas with separate gates, so that authorised vehicles can only progress through the establishment one short step at a time and only one inner set of gates can open at a time. It has a huge laundry operated by inmates under HMP staff supervision, which is professionally run and supplies an excellent laundry service to other HM Prisons as well as to local hospitals and other commercial concerns. Whilst progressing through the various entry stages of this prison, I once saw an inmate walking through the grounds with a huge creature sitting on his outstretched arm. On enquiring of a local prison officer, I was told it was an eagle owl, which is a very large bird indeed. Apparently within the jail is a separate inner section which is converted into a wildlife conservation area or sanctuary for birds etc. However I was unable to ascertain who was responsible for carrying out 'slopping-out' procedures within that serene environment and no chain-gangs breaking stones here then!)

Pop star Dane Bowers, 23, former singer with *Another Level* group, (No, neither have I!) has been banned from driving for 16 months for **BEING TWICE OVER THE DRINK-DRIVING LIMIT**. He was spotted by police, driving erratically and veering across the road in Romford, Essex as he returned to his home in Purley, near Croydon after a disco. He pleaded guilty to driving with excess alcohol and told the Bench at Havering Magistrates Court: "There's no real excuse. It's a pretty stupid thing to do. I'd had a bad day and thought I would be OK to drive home. I am ashamed. In a way I'm glad they pulled me over so I did not have to drive home drunk." Bowers, whom we are amazingly delighted to hear, once had an affair with mega-boobs model Jordan, was also fined £400.

Jobless Christopher Till, 24, a father of two from Messingham, North Lincs, an uninsured driver, left a cyclist to die after crashing into him whilst high on drink and drugs. He slammed into the rear of 64-year-old experienced cyclist Alan Taylor at almost 60mph, as he was crossing a line of traffic which had stopped to allow him to pass. Impatient Till, who had drunk two pints of strong lager and smoked two cannabis joints at a birthday party, and who has never had a driving lesson or taken a test, got tired of waiting for the cars to clear, so he overtook them on the inside and ploughed straight into Mr Taylor. Victim Mr Taylor was thrown into the air, crashing into the Ford Escort's windscreen before landing in the gutter. With Till's wife screaming hysterically and their young child in the vehicle, he did not even brake. Instead, he tore away from the scene, dumping the car and throwing away the keys. All he would admit later was that his road skills may have been 'a bit rusty' and that he had been driving with just one hand on the wheel. Mr Taylor's wife Gill, 62, said: "I will never forgive him. I cry every night, I have lost a soulmate." Till admitted driving whilst disqualified, driving without insurance and failing to stop after an accident. He was also convicted of causing death by dangerous driving. Passing sentence at Hull Crown Court, Recorder Stuart Brown, QC said Till had been 'grossly irresponsible.' He jailed him for six years. At the time of causing this dreadful tragedy in September 2003, Till was already serving a two-year driving ban over a high-speed pursuit by police.

Another drink-driver's plan to avoid a court appearance backfired when he sent a phoney sick-note to his solicitor. Retired businessman Norman Preston, 59, of Bispham, Lancs, claimed he was too ill to appear in court. In fact he was heading off on holiday to Mexico, but he faxed the note as he checked-in for the holiday trip and the note carried the airport address. The learned magistrates at Llandudno, North Wales, in their wisdom, heard that he already had two drink-driving convictions. They sentenced him to a community rehabilitation order, ordered him to pay £75 costs, disqualified him from driving for five years and fined him a further £175 for failing to surrender to his bail.

The families of two young nannies killed by an uninsured drink-driver have condemned the British Justice System after he received a pathetically-short sentence at Lewes Crown Court in February 2004. Relatives of Vicki Browne, 19, who looked after TV star Zoe Ball's son, said they were disgusted that killer Graham Travers is likely to be freed from jail in three years time, despite killing two women and maiming a third. Vicki's mother Tarnyar Browne sobbed: "The sentence was an act of sheer stupidity and an insult to us all. We accept that none of this was intentional but five-and-a-half years is not acceptable. The family feels cheated. We expected justice for the death but what we have got is an insult. Is this all Vicki's life was worth?" Mrs Browne said the family would urge the Crown Prosecution Service to take the case to the Court of Appeal in a bid to get the sentence increased. Vicki and Natalie McCabe, 20 accepted a lift home from the 21-year-old barman in a borrowed Ford Mondeo after a night out. The killer was **ONE-AND-A-HALF-TIMES OVER THE DRINK-DRIVING LIMIT**, had no driving licence and no insurance. As he drove at speed along the seafront in Hove, East Sussex, he hit a barrier. The third passenger, Becky Fish, 20, survived the crash but had to have a leg amputated. Coward Travers crawled from the wreckage and ran off after the horrific crash in October 2003. Passing sentence, Mrs Justice Rafferty told him: "Your driving was an exercise in arrogance. Like a petulant child you indulged your temper, but you did so using that most dangerous of weapons, a motor car. It is not accurate to say you have ruined three lives, since you have blighted many more. They include those who loved, and still love them and those who loved you. Nothing this court can do can right your wrongs." Outside court, Natalie's grieving parents called for a change in the law to punish killer drivers more severely. Flanked by supporters wearing T-shirts with the words, 'You don't need a licence to kill,' Jane McCabe said: "He had no right to be behind a wheel in the first place.

The whole law needs to be changed. Driving licences and insurance documents should be displayed in car windscreens at all times." Her husband Ray said Travers should have been jailed for at least eight years, the maximum is 10 years. Travers, of Portslade, East Sussex, admitted causing two deaths by dangerous driving and having no insurance or driving licence. In jailing him, Mrs Justice Rafferty was 'guided' by current sentencing policy and had to give the driver 'credit' for his guilty plea and the 'one-off' nature of the offence. A leading barrister said: "The judge has to work within sentencing guidelines and give the defendant credit for pleading guilty. If he had fought it and he was convicted, she would have jailed him for seven or eight years. Bad as this case is, there are even worse cases, particularly by repeat offenders. Five-and-a-half years is a stiff sentence when the maximum is 10."

(*Who is he trying to kid? The entire Legal Profession seem to have been brainwashed into totally ignoring what the public want to see and hear! Presumably this brainwashing at first takes place in Law Schools up and down the country and is then perpetuated in post-graduate courses, continuation training and through employment in Solicitors firms and Barristers' Chambers. This apparent brainwashing seems similar to that apparently undergone by trainee Probation Officers, who give the impression of wording their pre-sentence reports on offenders to magistrates and judges as if they should be kept out of jail at all costs regardless of their long previous convictions history.*)

Round-the-world heroine, yachtswoman Tracey Edwards MBE , has been convicted of drink-driving after being found that she was **TWICE ABOVE THE LIMIT**. An off-duty police officer saw her meandering from lane-to-lane before mounting a verge along the A419 road near Swindon in her Cherokee Jeep, in August 2003. He alerted colleagues who tracked down her vehicle and stopped her. She tried to explain away the erratic driving by saying she had been trying to answer her mobile phone. She had been driving home from a charity lunch at the time, having drunk just two small glasses of white wine and one glass of champagne during the four-hour lunch. Swindon magistrates heard that she was careful about what she had to drink as she was aware that she had to collect her four-year old daughter after the lunch. She was fined a total of £240 including costs and banned from driving for 16 months. She was also offered an option of reducing her driving ban by four months by completing a drink-driving rehabilitation course. It was stated in court that she was found to have 78mg of alcohol in 100ml of breath, but no mention was made during the evidence of how many sheets she had been to the wind.

This case too, has a nautical flavour to it. Andrew Bartlett, 37, the Master of a 680-ton dredger craft, *The Donald Redford*, apparently failed to spot a 124-years-old pier at Hythe in Hampshire, whilst on his way out to sea. He navigated straight through it, leaving a 50 foot hole and causing £308,000 worth of damage, resulting in it being out of use for several months. Shortly before the accident, coastguards became alarmed as they watched the vessel veer erratically on their harbour radar computerised monitor screen, which I happened to see with interest when it was shown on BBC South TV news. When they radioed his ship, they noted that his voice was slurred. Additionally one of his crew had pointed out that the dredger was veering to one side, but the captain replied: " F*** off, it's none of your business."

Bartlett tried to correct the ship's course, but continued to steer towards the pier. Moments later it smashed into the wooden structure. Hythe Pier was built in 1880 at a cost of £7,000. In 1922 its electric train service was opened and is now Britain's oldest pier railway. Four hours after the collision, Bartlett was breathalysed and found to be **ALMOST THREE TIMES OVER THE DRINK-DRIVE LIMIT**. Bartlett, of Portsmouth, admitted endangering lives by being drunk in charge of the vessel and causing damage to the pier, after downing six pints of lager. At Southampton Crown Court on 19th March 2004, Captain Bartlett was jailed for eight months.

At Peterborough Crown Court in May 2004, a devastated family wept as a drink-driver admitted killing their teenage daughter in a Christmas Day crash in 2003. Student Amy Gonzales, 18, died four weeks after the crash, just hours after opening her eyes for the first time since the tragedy. Craig Smith, 22, from Eaton Socon, Cambridgeshire, admitted killing Amy by dangerous driving and driving with excess alcohol. More than 20 of Amy's friends and family, wearing sunflower buttonholes, packed the public gallery shouting 'killer' as Smith stood in the dock. Amy's mother Melanie, 43, began sobbing after her daughter was mentioned during the emotionally-charged hearing. Her boyfriend Paul Ray attended, still on crutches after the accident. The court heard that Amy had bought a kebab with Paul, 21, when she was hit by Smith's BMW in the town's High Street at around 1am on Christmas Day, after attending a church midnight mass with her family. A subsequent breath test revealed that Smith was **ONE-AND-A-HALF-TIMES THE LEGAL LIMIT**.

A have-a-go mother is in intensive care after a driver who had just knocked down a moped rider ran her down as he fled. Tracie Ward, 30, from Borehamwood, had been about to set off on a family fishing trip with her boyfriend and two daughters when she saw a car smash into the 16-year-old boy on the moped. The driver tried to make off, leaving the boy injured in the road. Tracie's boyfriend, Steve Beevor, 46, rushed over and grabbed the steering wheel as she ran round the front of the car, screaming: "Stop! Please stop!" But the driver revved up and mowed her down. She careered off the bonnet and was left lying in a pool of blood in the road, at Borehamwood, Herts. As detectives appealed for information about the driver of a green 'Fiat Punto style' car, Tracie had emergency surgery for a fractured leg, collar bone, ribs, pelvis and vertebrae, and a punctured lung. Her condition at Hospital was described as 'serious but stable'. The moped rider was understood to have a dislocated jaw and bruised legs. Mr Beevor said: "We saw the driver hit the motorcyclist, then,cool as you like, try to drive around him. The security guard at the *Co-op* shop next door ran over and punched the glass out of the driver's window. I dived in to try to get the guy's keys and he was dragging me along. I realised Tracie had run around the front of the car when I heard her repeatedly banging on the bonnet, begging him to stop. I shall never forget how calm he was as he suddenly accelerated. There is no doubt in my mind that he knew what he was doing. Her little girl watched as this animal just drove over their mother. I could hear her go under the front wheels, then roll into the middle as he drove the back ones over her as well. I saw a lad on a motorcycle and we chased after him but he got away. To tell the truth, if I had caught up with him I would probably be up for murder. Tracie has had a very hard life but it looked like she was turning a corner before this happened. She had found a new place to live and we were very, very happy." One of Tracie's daughters has a tumour on her neck. But the family had recently heard from Great Ormond Street Children's Hospital that it was now treatable at home.

An RAF pilot died while high on drink and drugs after driving his crashed sports car two miles with a useless front wheel. The behaviour of Flight Lieutenant Simon Trimble, 32, was completely out of character, his estranged wife told the inquest. The pilot, who had just returned from special forces helicopter duties in Iraq, was **FOUR TIMES OVER THE DRINK-DRIVE LIMIT** and had traces of cocaine and amphetamines in his body. He had been at a party at RAF Odiham, Hants, and was 'more than merry' when he left to drive 12 miles home to Lower Farringdon. The Basingstoke inquest heard he crashed twice, the first time a front wheel was torn from its mountings, but he then drove another two miles before hitting a tree. Just five days before his death on 9th May 2004, the special forces pilot was handed his squadron's new standard by Prince Charles at a 90th anniversary celebration. North Hampshire coroner Andrew Bradley recorded a verdict of accidental death.

Les McKeown, 48, the lead singer of Seventies pop heart-throbs the *Bay City Rollers*, has appeared in court and denied crashing his car and fleeing the scene while **MORE THAN TWICE THE DRINK-DRIVE LIMIT**. It is the latest blow to hit him and he now faces a trial after pleading not guilty to three counts of driving with excess alcohol, failing to stop at the scene of an accident and driving without insurance. He is accused of having 75 mgs of alcohol per 100ml of blood when his silver Volvo collided with a Honda Civic in Dalston, North London at 5pm on 8th July 2004. The legal limit is 35mg. He will stand trial at the same court, Thames Magistrates Court, on 8th December 2004.

Daniel Beldom, 18, from Wraysbury, Berks, has been charged with killing his two pals after a stolen Porsche ran out of control on a motorway. He appeared before a special court charged with two counts of causing death by dangerous driving and other offences to be considered later. He was arrested in his hospital bed after the high-speed crash which happened on a slip road joining the M25 and the M4 near Slough. His two friends, Ricky Loveridge, 25, and Ali Malik, 26, died at the scene. The Porsche had allegedly been stolen from Hampton Court.

A car passenger's frantic final words before he was killed in a high-speed crash were recorded on a friend's mobile phone. Tony Withington was heard screaming to uninsured driver Dave Gough, 31, of Darrington, West Yorks, 'Dave you're gonna lose it here!' A few seconds later their car skidded and hit a wall. Father-of-two Mr Withington, 43, suffered serious head injuries and died in hospital. Leeds Crown Court was told that he had phoned an unnamed friend to complain about Gough's driving but was diverted to voice mail. The sound of the car's engine racing could be heard in the recording. The two men had been out drinking together in June 2003 and later Gough had given Mr Withington a lift to get some cigarettes from a garage. Gough, who broke an arm and a leg in the crash, told police he had three pints of lager, two bottles of beer, four glasses of wine and two Jack Daniels. Gough admitted causing his friend's death by dangerous driving, driving with excess alcohol, driving whilst disqualified and without insurance. Judge Kerry MacGill told Gough that he accepted that he was full of remorse and jailed him for six years. Mr Withington, of Carleton, West Yorks, was a former branch secretary of the National Union of Mineworkers.

The uncle of a three-year-old girl who was not wearing a seat-belt when she was killed by his car airbag, will not be prosecuted. Little Zoe Moran died after a Vauxhall Corsa driven by her uncle, David Moran, 27, was in collision with a Ford Focus at Litherland, Merseyside in November 2003. A spare tyre which had been lying loose on the back seat, smashed into the front passenger seat causing the airbag on Zoe's side of the car to inflate. Tragically it caught her under the chin and broke her neck. She also suffered a fractured skull in the accident. In early 2004 an inquest recorded a verdict of unlawful killing. Mr Moran, who had claimed that both he and Zoe were wearing seatbelts, was prosecuted for driving without a driving licence as well as driving without insurance. At the time he was condemned by Merseyside police for 'gross negligence' and told that they were considering whether or not to bring a charge of manslaughter. The case would have been the first of its kind in this country, because, as most people are aware, airbags are a relatively new feature of modern cars. However, the CPS has made the decision not to pursue it. Their spokesman said: "We have looked at the circumstances surrounding the case and decided not to take any action." What tragic loss of such a young girl and how on earth will her parents deal with her uncle's irresponsibility in setting out with Zoe in the car without lawful documentation, together with possibly failing to safely install her in the car for the journey?

A mother was killed when her car was hit by a driver who was allegedly speeding away from the scene of an attempted murder. Caroline Murphy, 39, from Stotfold, near Hitchin, Herts., died in hospital hours after the collision with the man, who was believed to have been driving away from the incident at his home. The man, who was seriously injured in the accident, was in custody after being charged with causing death by dangerous driving and the attempted murder of his partner. The unnamed woman was in a stable condition at Lister hospital in Stevenage. Mrs Murphy's husband and her four children were devastated. Mr Murphy said: "Caroline's death has left a huge gap in all our lives and words cannot express our feelings of loss."

She was driving towards a railway bridge near her home when her silver Vauxhall Tigra was hit by an estate car driven by the man. His car collided with a support for the bridge, veered across the road and hit her car. Emergency services received several 999 calls and two ambulances and two fire engines rushed to the scene. The accident occurred in broad daylight at 1pm. Fire fighters used special equipment to cut free the two drivers. Caroline, an office administrator, was removed from her car on a spinal board after suffering multiple injuries, but died at nearby Lister hospital as surgeons battled desperately to save her. The man was trapped in his overturned car for 30 minutes and suffered serious chest injuries. Caroline's husband added: "Caroline loved everyone, most of all her family, and all she ever wanted was to be loved back. She meant the world to everyone, family, friends and colleagues alike, and was always at the centre of laughter and fun. We'll particularly miss her infectious laughter. She was very precise in everything she did and was always immaculately turned out." The driver responsible was remanded in custody to appear at Luton Crown Court.

A young mother with drink-driving convictions, who killed her three-year-old son in a car crash appeared before Reading Crown Court on 9th July 2004. Tara King, 26, of Reading, had drunk two glasses of wine and taken anti-depressants after smoking cannabis the night before. Then she strapped her son, Lee Caterall, into a front car seat and set off to a friend's house for lunch. Lee, who had survived a previous car crash with his mother at the wheel, begged to sit in the front, the court was told. Prosecutor Nicholas Syfret told the court that another driver reported seeing King's car over the white line between Bracknell and Crowthorne in Berkshire.

Moments later King failed to negotiate a tight bend and hit a tree, causing 'massive damage' to Lee's side of the car.

The little boy was thrown out onto the road. Passers-by found King sitting at the wheel asking: " Where am I?" In court she admitted causing death by careless driving. Martin Jackson, defending, said King's mental health was now 'fragile'. He added: "Miss King is in the invidious position of being both the defendant and the principal mourner." The judge sentenced her to two-and-a-half years imprisonment.

(**Author's note:** *I lived very close to this road for 16 years. The road is called Nine Mile Ride and is literally nine miles long, through a forest, with all kinds of traffic hazards such as sudden, very narrow, hump back bridges, deer and serious, blind bends, fallen trees or branches. It was not at all unusual to pass abandoned cars just inside the forest edge, where drivers travelling too fast had 'lost it' on sudden bends.*

Several years ago a man in his late 20's or early 30's was driving along this same road when he was distracted by his mobile phone conversation. He caused a fatal car crash and became the very first driver to be convicted of causing death by dangerous driving through mobile phone distraction, after police examined his mobile phone printouts, proving that he was actually in mid-conversation at the exact moment of impact. As I recall it, he had denied being on his mobile phone at the time, realising the awful implications of what he had done, together with the likely penalty.).

An estate agent is facing up to 14 years in jail for killing a teenager while drink-driving for the third time. Shamsi Ahmed, 43, of Newcastle had been arrested for his second case of drink-driving just nine weeks before he killed moped rider David Ross, aged 16 years. Ahmed was **MORE-THAN-ONE-AND-A-HALF-TIMES-OVER-THE-LIMIT** when his Rover 216 car smashed into the back of the moped, sending the youngster sprawling across a dual carriageway near his home in Cramlington, Northumberland. David had been on his way home on Christmas Eve 2003 after delivering presents to neighbours and friends. His mother Christine sobbed as she watched Ahmed admit causing her son's death by dangerous driving and drink-driving. Judge John Milford adjourned sentence for reports, warning Ahmed: "The sentence I am going to pass upon you inevitably is a substantial prison sentence." Outside Newcastle Crown Court, Mrs Ross, who lived alone except for her only son David, said: "I am so angry. He has taken him away, he will never know how that feels." John Sparrow, of the Campaign against Drink Driving, said: "If ever there was a case for that maximum sentence to be used it is this one." Ahmed had been banned for three years just one month earlier in respect of his second drink-drive conviction. Road safety campaigners say that Ahmed deserves the maximum penalty, increased in April 2004 from 10 to 14 years.

UPDATE: On 17th January 2005 Judge John Milford sentenced Ahmed to just five-and-a-half years, eight-and-a-half years short of the recently increased 14 years imprisonment. This was in spite of the fact that it was Ahmed's *third* conviction for drink-driving in a short time.

A failed asylum seeker jailed for the hit-and-run killing of nine-year-old Callum Oakford is to have his punishment reduced. The two year sentence for Kamel Kadri, 38, after he knocked over the boy while speeding and left him to die, has already prompted fury. However The Crown Prosecution Service noticed that the judge had exceeded his powers with the punishment for motoring offences and using a false passport. As a result, the Algerian will be out of prison in less than a year, taking into account time on remand and good behaviour. Callum's mother, Lynn, from Worthing, West Sussex was said to be 'deeply upset' by the news. "This just adds insult to injury" said a close family friend. "He got a light sentence in the first place, let alone having it reduced. She has been let down by everybody." Kadri had been jailed for a total of eight months for failing to stop and failing to report an accident, and 16 months for the passport offence, by Judge Anthony Thorpe. But a legal technicality means Kadri can only be jailed for a maximum of six months for the motoring offences. The CPS said that was the maximum possible sentence regardless of how many he committed. This ruled out the judge's action in imposing consecutive four-month terms for each crime, making eight months. As a result the Algerian will serve less than three months for the motoring offences. Callum died after being hurled into the air by Kadri's vehicle as he crossed the A259 in Ferring, West Sussex, with his brother Sam, 12, and a friend on New Years Day 2004. Kadri, who had no licence, insurance or MOT, fled the scene and abandoned the car. He was initially arrested for causing death by dangerous driving, which carries a maximum jail sentence of 14 years, but was charged with lesser offences, thus considerably reducing the judge's sentencing powers. His plea for asylum failed in September 2002 and he was living illegally in the UK at the time of the crash.

Judge Anthony Thorpe was so annoyed about it that he wrote a letter to *The Times*, as follows:

> *Sir, my recent encounter with a failed asylum seeker driving an unlicensed, untaxed car with no MOT which killed a young boy, has made me realise what a serious problem we have with these cars on our streets. I suggest a two-stage way of addressing the problem.*

Abolish the annual car tax, which would save a fortune when the Driver and Vehicle Licensing Agency is slimmed down, and recoup the lost tax by adding 1p or 2p to a litre of fuel. Make insurance companies issue a swipe card each year. A motorist would have to display the card on his windscreen, and more importantly, he could not fill his fuel tank until he had swiped the card at the pump. I appreciate this would not deal with any lack of MOT but it would be a start to identify these rogue cars.

Many people, apart from Judge Thorpe, have been campaigning for many years to abolish the car tax and pay revenue via a few pence extra per litre, over and above the greedy Chancellor of the Exchequer Gordon Brown's existing massive fuel tax on each litre. Recently, at the Kent County Show, I discussed this with some staff manning a DVLA tent. Although they appreciated that many DVLA jobs would be at stake if the system was changed, a major advantage of the current scheme is that, at least once or twice every single year, before you can tax your car, you have to produce for inspection a valid insurance certificate and MOT. I thought they had made a valid point and had probably been asked the same question thousands of times before.

Amongst all the gloom and doom that inevitably surrounds reports of horrendous bad driving, here is a case of hit-and-run that, for a change, had a happy ending for the victim and her family and friends. On 19th June 2004, near her home in Morden, South London, a very pretty twelve-year-old girl, Jodie Duffin, was mown down by a people carrier, which stopped only briefly before driving off from the scene, as passers-by watched in horror. Jodie was rushed to hospital and was immediately hooked-up to a ventilator, barely clinging to life. Immediately after the collision, hospital staff had warned Jodie's parents, Robert and Amanda, to prepare for the worst. She had received massive head injuries in the crash and her parents were told that, even if she survived, she might be permanently brain-damaged and unable to speak. In an effort to track down the man who had left their daughter for dead, they allowed a harrowing photograph showing Jodie in intensive care at St George's Hospital, Tooting, SW London, to be published. She had 18 lines linking her to a ventilator and was heavily sedated.

A fortnight later there was a break-through. Jodie's mother, Amanda Duffin, 40, a bank cashier, said: "The first time we knew she was coming round was after two weeks, when the nurses said if she could hear them to squeeze my hand. I felt this slight squeeze. My dad was on his knees crying. Jodie's first words were 'sorry' to her dad. We hadn't been sure if she would talk again." Her husband Robert, 41, a self-employed builder, added: "The consultant in intensive care said she wouldn't bother looking at scans again because according to the scan, Jodie shouldn't be here." She moved out of intensive care and into a room in a children's ward. Mr Duffin then said: "A couple of days ago she walked back down to intensive care and the nurses were near enough crying, they were so happy. They can't believe the progress she's made. To get this far should have taken months."

He said the last month had been a nightmare for the couple and their other children Kim, 15, Harry, 10 and Bobby, 7. Jodie meanwhile, remembers nothing of her ordeal but is sure of one thing: "I'm going home" she declared. She is a keen gymnast and dancer. While she has a slight weakness of movement on the left-hand side of her body, it is hoped this can be rectified with physiotherapy. A hospital spokesman said: "Her condition is stable and she is recovering well." Jodie's father added: "They didn't think she would make it through the night. Now they are saying she might be home at the weekend. They are calling her 'the little miracle'." What a happy ending to a terrible near-tragedy and a tribute both to the love of Jodie's parents and family, and the skill and dedication of the NHS doctors and nurses who helped to save Jodie. A 31-year-old man has been arrested in connection with the hit-and-run incident.

Car thieves wanted by the police were invited to appear on a fun TV show, then arrested in front of the TV cameras. The wanted men turned up by invitation, to take part in a Go-Kart race as part of the sting operation. They thought they were being given the chance to show off their driving skills in front of viewers. As part of the trick they were also offered the chance of winning a top-of-the-range car and meeting former Formula One world champion Nigel Mansell, in the fake game show. But instead, having passed through several stages of the game, and stood close to some life-sized figures of Nigel Mansell, they were introduced to police armed with warrants for their arrest, at Middlesbrough Football Club's Riverside Stadium. DI Colin Tansley said: "It was a surprise to them and the reactions were quite funny. One offender was so stunned when told he was being arrested that he asked the officer: "Is this a joke?" The officer replied: " If it was, I would have started with 'I say, I say, I say'!" He added: "I am happy to do this to bring people to justice." Police said offenders who ignored community penalties imposed by courts were targeted and that the men were trapped by the lure of easy money."

The operation was caught on camera for *McIntyre's Big Sting* on Channel Five on 6th April 2004. I was warned about this and managed to video the programme as I was out. Next morning I had the time of my life seeing the facial expressions of the goons as they passed into the final chamber. Some of them were wanted by the courts for **jumping bail**. Guess what happened to some of them, on appearing before the magistrates, you've guessed it, they got **fresh bail** from the learned magistrates, in their great wisdom! I give up!

A man who was jailed for causing death by dangerous driving in 2003 has escaped going back to prison for driving while disqualified in Romford. Elo Quincy Okpokpor, 22, of Arnold Road, Dagenham, pleaded guilty to driving while disqualified, driving without due care and attention and without insurance after being caught by police in Victoria Road, Romford. Okpokpor was found guilty at Snaresbrook Crown Court in September 2003 of causing death by dangerous driving and having no driving licence or insurance, and was sentenced to two years in prison, although he served less than a year and was disqualified from driving until September 2007. But facing another stint in jail, an emotional Okpokpor told Havering Magistrates Court: "I know I have made a mistake and I'm sorry about it. A custodial sentence would ruin my life and what I have done to try and get past what happened. I beg the court please don't do it to me."

Earlier, Prosecutor, Miss Hough, had told the court how two police officers had spotted Okpokpor driving the wrong way around a mini-roundabout from South Street into Victoria Road. Mr Okpokpor was taken to Romford Police Station where it was discovered he was disqualified from driving. Miss Hough added: "He stated to the police the reasons why he was disqualified from driving. He also stated that he would not drive again and that he thinks about the person he killed everyday."

Miss Thompson, defending, said her client had enrolled in a multi-media course at London's Metropolitan University and was doing everything he could to get on with his life following his previous sentence. She said: "Mr Okpokpor should be spared custody. He should be given full credit for his early guilty plea and from his demeanour the court can see how remorseful he is." Okpokpor was given a community punishment and rehabilitation order for two years and was also ordered to do 80 hours unpaid community work during the next 12 months. He was also ordered to attend the *Think First* programme, pay £70 costs by February 15th 2005 and given nine penalty points.

A jealous woman driver who mowed down a beauty queen was jailed for 15 months on 4th February 2005. Sonja Oliver, 33, ploughed her BMW into brunette Brooke Cameron, 20, after spotting her outside a nightclub. Miss Cameron survived the accident but her arm was left hanging on by a few tendons. The *Miss Wales* finalist told yesterday how two years of 'bitchiness and back-biting' led to veterinary nurse Oliver accelerating towards her in a fury. She said: "I have seen Sonja around for a few years, she's made it clear she doesn't like me even though I've never even spoken to her. She made snide remarks in a restaurant just because I have nice fingernails. She said, 'Look at her, who does she think she is with her acrylic nails?" I have avoided her ever since. She is trouble and has made it quite clear she doesn't like me. There has been a lot of bitchiness and back-biting. But never in my worst nightmares did I think she despised me enough to drive a powerful car at me." The student was leaving a nightclub with friends when she saw blonde Oliver behind the wheel of a friend's silver BMW. She said: "She was honking the horn and revving up, I just thought it was typical of her so I turned my back. The next thing I knew the car was on top of me." Miss Cameron was dragged under the car before it smashed into the back of a van outside the *Bane* nightclub in Pentre, South Wales. It was only the towbar on the van that stopped her head from being crushed between the two vehicles. Oliver fled the scene, leaving shocked revellers to gently lift the car off Miss Cameron. "They pulled me out by my arm but it was so smashed up it was just hanging on," she said. "I was screaming in pain, I had a head injury and I knew my arm was in a state. It was so bad they wouldn't let me see it." She was told she was just millimetres away from having her arm amputated and underwent two operations at Royal Glamorgan Hospital in Llantrisant, then needed plastic surgery on her damaged elbow. It was five weeks before she dared to look at her shattered elbow and then she cried for four hours. Doctors have told her she will always have limited use of her arm and the scars will never go. Her confidence was shattered and her dreams of becoming a model were over. But her family and friends encouraged her not to give up and just six months later she qualified for the *Miss Wales* finals. "I didn't tell the competition organisers about my injury and my scars," she said. "I wore a long sleeve dress and put my left hand over my elbow." She was a runner-up in the contest and has been encouraged to enter again next year.

Ms Cameron came face-to-face with her attacker in a courtroom when Oliver was found guilty of unlawful wounding and dangerous driving. Oliver, of Penrhiwfer, near Tonyrefail, South Wales, had downed a pint of lager in one go just before climbing into the BMW. As well as being jailed, the single mother was disqualified from driving for three years by Judge Gerald Price QC at Cardiff Crown Court. He told her: "I have no doubt that you were in a party mood that night and that was the cause of your offending. You had too much to drink and when you saw that BMW, you fancied yourself to get in, put on loud music and sound the horn. I have no doubt that you fancied driving it. You ploughed into a crowd of people. Your victim Brooke Cameron suffered an ugly and unpleasant injury which has left her scarred and with some disability. It is frankly a miracle that a more serious injury wasn't caused. Someone could have been killed."

Miss Cameron is now trying to put the horrific night behind her and is continuing her studies in criminology at the University of Glamorgan. She had planned to join the police but could be rejected on medical grounds because of her injury. She said: "What happened that night will stay with me for the rest of my life. I only have to look at the horrific scars to remember how close I was to losing my arm altogether." She added: "I don't care what happens to Sonja, I just hope I never see her again."

Three teenage girls died while taking part in a high-speed race through a city centre on 18th February 2005. Police believe the girls, two aged 16 and one 17, were duelling with another vehicle carrying three men, when they lost control of their Citroen Xsara and smashed into a tree in the centre of Hull early in the morning. The men were in a Citroen Saxo which also hit a tree. Two of them, both 17, were arrested at the scene on suspicion of causing death by dangerous driving. The third man, aged 23, fled the scene of the crash but was arrested later on the same charge. A man aged 21 and a woman of 18, who were in the Xsara with the three girls, were fighting for their lives in hospital after being cut from the wreckage. The man lost a leg in the smash.

On 18th February 2005, a drunk driver who almost killed a teenage girl avoided jail because magistrates were left with no other choice. Mark Stockdale, 30, was **THREE TIMES OVER THE LIMIT** when he ploughed into Roxanne Kehoe, 17, pinning her against a shop window in Darwen, Lancs. She is still in hospital. Stockdale was banned for just two years, fined £200 and ordered to pay £300 compensation after admitting drink-driving, the usual sentence for such a charge. Blackburn magistrates asked why he had not faced a more serious charge and were told by the prosecution it was because Lancashire Police had not advised the CPS on the case. Roxanne's stepfather John Kehoe, 27, fumed: "Our legal system is one big joke."

All the victims are believed to be from the Hull area. Police are still investigating who was behind the wheel of both cars at the time of the crash. A Humberside Police spokesman said: "Both vehicles were believed to be travelling north when the collision occurred. "The Citroen Xsara hit a tree, collided with a fence and then hit another tree. The Citroen Saxo also hit a tree." The road, a busy commuter route, was closed in both directions while the accident was investigated. The spokesman said: "The area is being treated as we would a crime scene." Family liaison officers spent the day looking through the debris for personal items which could help to confirm the victims' identities.

A rookie bus driver was jailed for 12 months on 11th February 2005 for killing a woman cyclist on a notorious death trap cycle lane, as a judge criticised transport chiefs. As Michael Duncan started his sentence, Judge Simon Davies urged transport officials to cut out 'superfluous bureaucracy' to prevent future tragedies. Vikki McCreery, 37, was crushed under the wheels of Duncan's five-ton single-decker bus as he was looking the other way crossing London's Blackfriars Bridge. He had only received his bus driver's licence 52 days earlier. Australian-born Mrs McCreery, married for just a year, died almost instantly when she was hit by the bus in May last year, Inner London Crown Court was told.

After the tragedy the *Daily Express* mounted a crusade to highlight the scandal of how cyclists were forced to use thin strips of road between major traffic lanes near the newspaper's offices. Judge Simon Davis, who has cycled the route, said: "I have no doubt that the layout on that bridge that day was a contributory factor. It is not appropriate for me to make comments about what I hope for the future of the lay-out of that bridge, save to say this, if there is anything positive that I can hope for that might emerge from this case, it is that those advisers get on with the job and continue through what may otherwise be superfluous bureaucracy, to ensure that at least on that part of the road in London this never happens again." He told the court: "You may take it that I'm well acquainted with this route. I've cycled this route and taken the number 100 bus."

Duncan, 22, of Edmonton, north London, had admitted causing death by dangerous driving. Andrew Espley, prosecuting, said that had the defendant been looking where he was going, the accident would never have happened. "She was in front of him for a total of 23 seconds before the collision and it occurred because he was not looking where he was going," he said. Michelle Rawcett, defending, said it was only the third time he had driven that route. Mr Duncan was not confident with the number 100 route. He had expressed his concern to his line manager. Instead of receiving sympathy or being assigned to a different route he was more confident with, he was simply informed to take a map with him and do his best. He was told that if he did not comply then his employment would be terminated." Miss Fawcett said Duncan was driving a full bus and looking to the right to try to change lanes when he collided with the cyclist at between 26 and 29mph. It was then that he hit Mrs McCreery in the bus operated by *Stagecoach*.

Jailing Duncan for 12 months, Judge Davis called it 'a lapse, a momentary dangerous error of judgement'. Duncan was also banned from driving for two years after which time he must take an extended test. Mrs McCreery's husband, Sandy, a lecturer at Middlesex University, sat at the back of the court. The couple had been planning a family together. The judge read part of a letter from Mr McCreery which read: "I know what I had with her was unique and irrevocable." Mr McCreery, who scattered his wife's ashes over a favourite spot in her native Australia, refused to comment after sentence.

After Mrs McCreery's death, Ralph Smyth, of the London Cycling Campaign, said of the Blackfriars Bridge layout: "It is designed like an urban motorway for speeds of 50 mph. Until the design is changed radically it will remain a blackspot."

On 11th February 2005, angry relatives condemned traffic laws after a killer driver escaped with a fine after claiming his second victim in six years. Neil Honnor, 30, walked free after admitting driving carelessly when he knocked down and killed 23-year-old barman Andrew Moorcroft. The court heard that he was travelling at more than 50 mph in a 40 mph zone. Honnor had previously been sentenced to three years for causing death by dangerous driving while over the drink limit and uninsured. He was released after 16 months but was soon spotted behind the wheel again, even though still banned, and was jailed for four months. But the law prevented Liverpool magistrates from jailing him for his latest offence. Careless driving carries a maximum punishment of a £2,000 fine and lifetime disqualification. They fined Honnor £400 and banned him for three years.

A new offence of causing death while a disqualified driver is being considered and could lead to stiffer sentences. Six years before the accident in which Mr Moorcroft died, taxi driver Honnor, of Huyton, Liverpool, killed 49-year-old Geoffrey Bahner in a hit-and-run incident while over the drink-drive limit and uninsured. Families of the two dead men spoke of their anger at Honnor's lenient treatment. Mr Moorcroft's mother Lynn, from Broadgreen, Liverpool, said: "How is it possible to go to prison for killing one person but then kill another and practically get away with it?" Mr Banner's sister-in-law, Linda Lea, said: "He only got 16 months for killing our Geoff but it looks like he has got away with it this time."

An evil drink-driving yob was caged after leaving a pal to burn to death in a crashed car. Nathan Rowe, 19, ignored the pleas of three terrified passengers as he sped down a country lane at 70mph. He was high on drugs and swigging from a can of strong lager. When he smashed head-on into a tree, the coward fled the burning wreck by clambering over a paralysed girl passenger. And instead of helping his friends from the mangled car, he fled, leaving his unconscious mate Robert Morris, 17, to be burned alive. Sick Rowe then tried to blame the accident on his dead pal. But on 13th January 2005 he was jailed for eight-and-a-half years. Judge Adrian Lyon told him: "It is difficult to imagine a more serious case. One of the other passengers was lucky to get out of the car, it was absolutely no thanks to you. You climbed over her."

Manchester Crown Court heard that Rowe, who bought the old K-reg Citroen ZX car for just £80, had no driving licence, tax or insurance. The tragedy happened in Dunham Massey, near Altrincham, Cheshire, on 2nd September 2004. Rowe, of Partington, Greater Manchester, took Robert for a late-night spin after smoking cannabis and drinking lager in a pub. They picked up three 19-year-old girls to 'accompany them', Sian Dempsey, Tanya Higson and Stacey Povey. Sian and Stacey squashed on to the front passenger seat.

Prosecutor Adrian Farrow told the court: "The manner of his driving caused the girls to be frightened and unnerved as his speeds reached 70 miles an hour." At one point the car mounted the pavement and he narrowly missed hitting two girls walking. Robert screamed at Rowe to slow, but he ignored him, saying: "I have been driving for years, I am not going to kill you." An eye-witness described the car going 'stupidly fast' round a bend. Rowe lost control of the car and it ploughed in to a tree, knocking Robert unconscious. Sian was left trapped after breaking her spine in the impact. The car burst into flames but as the passengers shouted at Rowe for help, he clambered over Sian and fled. Luckily, Sian was dragged from the car by the other two girls. But they were unable to save Robert.

Cowardly Rowe got a lift home after running to a nearby house and claiming he had been beaten up. When police later arrested him, angry Rowe said: "I am the one that got beaten up and I get arrested?" The sick liar later suggested Robert had been driving. Robert's family burst into tears as Rowe finally pleaded guilty to causing death by dangerous driving, driving without a licence, driving without insurance, failing to stop after an accident and failing to report an accident.

Rowe was jailed and also banned from driving for 15 years. He had been in court five times for taking cars without consent. He was first cautioned by police in 1998 when he was just 12. Outside court Robert's father Mike, 37, said: "Justice has been done." PC Dave Holmes, of Greater Manchester Police, praised the bravery of Tanya and Stacey. He said: "Despite their own injuries they climbed back into a burning vehicle." Sian spent four weeks in hospital and is permanently affected by the injury.

On 6th January 2005 a 13-year-old boy was named and shamed as Britain's youngest drink-driver after being caged for four months. Baby-faced Jon Smee, who is 4ft 10ins, was drunk and barely able to see over the wheel of a stolen Ford Mondeo when it crashed into a kerb after a high-speed police chase. Before officers arrested him, he had raced down the wrong side of a 30mph road at 70mph without lights on, narrowly missing a pedestrian. The chase came to an end when he crashed and burst a front tyre of the car, but even then officers had to run after him to make the arrest. It was only when they caught the schoolboy that they realised he was a child.

A breath test later revealed that Smee, of Salford, Greater Manchester, had 50 microgrammes of alcohol in 100 millilitres of breath. The legal limit is 35mg. Despite his age, the tearaway has a history of offending and had already been banned from driving twice at the time of his latest offence on November 1st 2004. Although he cannot legally drive until 17, he was still banned as a juvenile. He had also received an anti-social behaviour order after a terror campaign against staff at his local *McDonald's*.

Five weeks before the drink-driving offence, Smee had walked free with a supervision order for car theft and vehicle interference. At Salford youth court, district judge John Finestein took the unusual step of allowing Smee to be named. He said: "It is difficult to underestimate the risks you have posed not just to your life but also to other people's lives. You had no ability to control a car. It is a miracle that you did not seriously injure, or even kill, yourself or other people. I hope this will send out a message to others that drinking and driving at any age is a very serious offence and that a prison sentence will follow."

Smee had admitted drink-driving, driving while banned, aggravated vehicle taking, breaching an ASBO and supervision order and driving without insurance. The teenager, who arrived at court smoking, will serve his sentence in a detention centre. He also received a four-year driving ban. In mitigation, defence solicitor Mike Gee said Smee realised he has let his family down and is now back at school. Greater Manchester Police Chief Inspector David Bleackley said: "This is the first time I have heard of anyone so young being prosecuted for drink-driving and it is appalling to think that this youngster was driving around the streets whilst under the influence of alcohol."

Former athlete Steve Cram begged a court to let him keep his driving licence so his lover wouldn't have to chauffeur him to visit his children. He claimed his estranged wife Karen would hit the roof if he turned up with his new love Alison Curbishley, also a star runner, at the wheel. But JPs ignored his plea and handed 43-year-old Cram a six-month road ban and a £60 fine. He already had nine penalty points for speeding.

Police stopped Cram's silver Mercedes because it was crammed with too many passengers, the court was told. He had four people in the back seat, one lying across the laps of the others, and a front seat passenger. The maximum number in the car, including the driver, should have been five.

Cram, a BBC sports commentator, who admitted carrying excess passengers, told magistrates at Newcastle upon Tyne that a ban would make it very difficult for him to see his children Josie, 15, and Marcus, 12, who live with their mother. He said he now lives in the Northumberland village of Ryal, three miles from the nearest town and he would have to rely on taxis and trains. His solicitor Zoe Passfield said Cram was staying at a Newcastle hotel last July when he and friends decided to go for a meal. He volunteered to drive because he was not drinking.

She said: "There were a large number of them so he asked some of them to make alternative arrangements. The remaining passengers wanted a lift and he felt it impolite to ask just one person to get out. "Mr Cram was legally advised that he had a defence to this charge but he is not a man who wants to get away with things."

An international athlete who smashed a driver's jaw in a violent road rage attack has escaped a jail sentence. Hefty Daniel Baptiste, 19, who has represented the UK in shot-put and discus, broke his victim's jaw in two places with one punch. Jatinder Virdee was unable to talk or eat properly for weeks afterwards and needed two metal plates to pin his shattered face together. Baptiste and two pals attacked city worker Virdee and his passenger after a minor bump between their cars in the early hours. Virdee was trying to protect his passenger who had been kicked unconscious when Baptiste lashed out. He was ordered to do 240 hours community service and pay £2,500 to his victim. His friends were jailed for up to 15 months at Snaresbrook Crown Court, London.

A drunk-driver who was **FOUR TIMES OVER THE LIMIT** and swigging vodka when he was stopped by police, escaped jail on 17th May 2004, sparking fury among campaigners. Richard Dark, 55, forced pedestrians to run for safety when he mounted a pavement. But he told Exeter JPs he was 'afraid' of going to jail and could not do community work because of a broken hip. Jobless Dark, of Exeter, who admitted dangerous driving and driving with excess alcohol, got a three-year ban. Campaigner Mike Jobbins said: "It doesn't deter others."

A drink-driver who killed his wife and unborn son in a car crash said he deserves to be executed, after pleading guilty on 7th June 2004 to causing their deaths. Paul McDonald, 32, and wife Sharon, who was seven months pregnant with their sixth child, had been on a pub crawl before the fatal accident. Despite being **TWICE THE DRINK-DRIVE LIMIT**, the chef still got behind the wheel of his Fiesta and tried to drive them and a 17-year-old friend home. But on the way he ploughed into the back of a lorry parked by the side of the road near Barnsley in South Yorkshire. He and his friend escaped with minor injuries but Sharon, also 32, was much more seriously injured and had to be cut from the wreckage. Surgeons at Barnsley District General Hospital carried out an emergency caesarean to try to save the unborn child. But Sharon and the child died.

Petty criminal McDonald, who had been married to Sharon for 10 years, was later shown pictures of the 3lb 15oz baby, who they had intended calling Keian. He pleaded guilty to causing death by careless driving at Sheffield Crown Court. Sentencing was postponed until the end of the month while medical reports are prepared, after the judge heard he had attempted suicide three times since the accident on December 12 last year. Speaking after an earlier hearing, McDonald, of Barnsley, said: "I pray every night that I will die, and I wake up every morning and curse. It never gets easier. There's no judge in the country that can make me feel worse. I have lost everything. I wish there was capital punishment for what I did. I wish it was me that had died and not them." Inspector Trevor Tindle, of Yorkshire Police, said: "This was a quite tragic case. He is full of remorse and of course he blames himself. It has been a difficult case to investigate but I hope people take notice of the consequences of drinking and driving."

On 1st March 2005 the grieving parents of a 12-year-old boy mown down by an illegal immigrant were outraged after the drink-drive killer was jailed for just two months. Zambian Aaron Chisango was **ONE AND A HALF TIMES OVER THE LEGAL DRINK-DRIVE LIMIT** after consuming a litre of whisky, had no licence or insurance and may have been speeding when he hit Jamie Mason. Jamie's mother Hayley, 41, and stepfather Steve Leighton, 44, spoke of their disgust after learning that Chisango had repeatedly been refused permission by the Home Office to stay in Britain. Their anger deepened when Chisango appeared before Wolverhampton magistrates and an original charge of causing death by dangerous driving was reduced through lack of evidence of driving with excess alcohol. The couple are now campaigning to tighten driving laws. They have the support of local MP Ken Purchase and plan to take the case directly to Home Secretary Charles Clarke. Chisango, 27, arrived in Britain in 1998 and applied to stay when his visa expired. He was turned down but appealed to an adjudicator who backed the Home Office's refusal. A new appeal to a tribunal is pending. Post Office worker Mrs Leighton, from Wednesfield, near Wolverhampton, said: "I blame the Government. The asylum system is shambolic because they seem determined to protect the rights of immigrants over us who live here." Mrs Leighton said she was 'disgusted and outraged' at Chisango's sentence. She added: "I cannot believe he has walked away scot-free. When I heard the decision I was sick to the bottom of my stomach. I don't think I will ever get over this. Even if they deport him he will have a new life, but ours is in ruins."

Service engineer Mr Leighton said: "The punishment that this man received was a pathetic and lenient slap on the wrist. "Chisango should never have been in the country, never mind in that car. The legal system has let us down. He never faced a charge which in any way reflects the gravity of what he did." Both parents paid tribute to Jamie, who was a pupil at Wednesfield High School. He loved ice hockey and soccer. He supported Wolverhampton and Newcastle and played for a local youth team. His mother said: "Jamie was a big-hearted boy who would go to the ends of the earth to help you out. He was a perfect gentleman." Labour MP Mr Purchase said: "Chisango has used the asylum system, put in place to protect people, to stay in this country for as long as he could. Sadly, he seems to have outmanoeuvred the authorities. The outcome is a massive injustice. He should not have been driving any car."

Jamie had been crossing the road just behind his half-sister Tracy, 31, on January 8 as they walked towards their car for a trip out. His uncle Scott Mason, 43, said: "Tracy got across the road. Jamie hesitated. Tracy said that by the time she got to the other side, he was up in the air. The car had hit him. Jamie died of a broken neck. They said in court no competent driver could have stopped in the time he had. But when you see a child beside the road, you automatically slow down." Magistrates heard that Chisango, a qualified mental health nurse, had studied at the University of Central England in Birmingham. He lived with his sister in Telford, Shropshire, but before the accident had stayed with friends in Wolverhampton. That evening he had drunk almost a litre of whisky. Chisango was also banned from driving for 12 months. Having already served time on remand, he is due to be released in days.

A Home Office spokesman said that they could not comment on individual cases but added: "The Government will seek to remove all those who have no legal business to remain in the UK as soon as possible. We can't remove individuals from the UK while they are exercising their rights against a refusal decision".

Police have launched a fresh crack-down on drink-driving that could treble the number of convictions. Police officers using sophisticated new equipment will be able to tell with one roadside test whether a driver is over the limit. Until now, some motorists who were on the borderline have escaped conviction because by the time they took two more tests at a police station, as required under rules dating back to 1977, their alcohol reading had fallen below the legal limit, due to the passage of time and the body's metabolism breaking-down the alcohol. The new roadside test will ensure they do not escape justice. Officers will be allowed to breathalyse, charge and bail motorists at the roadside, using machines that have the same accuracy as a blood test.

The Home Office also plans to provide police with roadside equipment capable of testing drivers for drugs such as cannabis, heroin and crack cocaine. The moves, part of David Blunkett's war on anti-social behaviour, were welcomed by Police chiefs and Motoring Organisations. Experts predicted that the new campaign could treble the 100,000 drivers a year who end up in court for driving over the limit. The current system uses the hand-held breathalyser as the first check in the street. Home Office officials hope to have the new equipment in use within twelve months from April 2004, provided Ministers can push it through the crowded Parliamentary programme.

The drugs test equipment could take up to two years or more to introduce, because of the technological advance required. An observer reported that the police should be able to 'hit' three times as many people, or more, as they will not have to keep going back to the police station. A spokesman for the Association of Chief Police Officers said: "As long as the new breathalyser equipment is totally accurate, the majority of motorists will support a building-up of procedures on the roadside against drunk drivers. If it means the Police can target more drunk drivers, and get them off the road, that's got to be good for road safety, it's a positive step. But if there are borderline cases, we advocate that those drivers are taken to the police station for second checks to verify the readings. We're fully behind this initiative, the benefits are enormous in being able to deal with offenders at the scene without the need to arrest." Anyone caught over the limit will be obliged to leave their car at the roadside, as they currently are. Now you know why all of those cars you pass in ditches and on the grass verge have 'POLICE AWARE' stickers on them.

Uninsured drivers are being stopped in their tracks by a senior police officer who has pioneered a zero-tolerance policy in which illegal cars are seized and crushed. The crusade has led to 350 cars, or 70 per month, being destroyed in the first five months of its operation. Now the scheme, which is being piloted in Leeds, is set to be adopted nationally after impressing the Home Office. The man behind it is Inspector Justin Pedley, of West Yorkshire Police, who says it has already led to a drastic reduction in the number of cars being stopped without insurance. There has also been a dramatic fall in other crimes such as burglaries, which have gone down by 40 per cent in the areas where the scheme is being operated. Inspector Pedley agreed that the measure was draconian but asked that it be judged on results. "It's a constant battle we're fighting against this underclass of drivers. We think this is the most effective way of stopping them." He said that there had been a massive reduction in the number of crimes on his Leeds City and Holbeck beat, some slashed by more than half. Besides the drop in burglaries there has been:

1) a 68 per cent fall in the number of motorists making off without paying for petrol.

2) a 16 per cent drop in the theft of motor vehicles.

3) a 40 per cent drop in thefts from motor vehicles.

The initiative comes as the Association of British Insurers told ministers to 'get tough' by confiscating cars of illegal motorists, whose accidents cost £500 million a year. There are more than two million uninsured drivers on Britain's roads. Even if caught they often escape prosecution or are fined between £150 and £200, much less than it costs to insure a car.

Since September 2003, officers in Leeds have stopped and questioned motorists they believe may be dodging car insurance. If a driver is caught without cover, officers immediately remove the offender's vehicle from the road. The vehicle is towed to a massive car pound in the city where the driver can pay £105 plus VAT, along with a £12-a-day charge, to release the car once they have produced valid insurance cover. Or the drivers can disclaim the car completely, condemning the vehicle to be crushed. Inspector Pedley said success of the project was due to a wider clampdown in Leeds. "We are targeting criminal use of vehicles, without a car, they cannot move around and commit these crimes."

A Home Office spokeswoman said: "West Yorkshire police are to be congratulated on an excellent operation with impressive results." More power to Inspector Pedley's pulling the car-crusher mechanism's lever elbow, and let us hope the exciting project swiftly extends across the country. However we should not hold our breath, Lord Chief Justice Woolf and his thousands of 'Human Rights' lawyer cronies have apparently not got wind of this scheme yet!

In January 2004, the Government's alleged 'war on the motorist' took a dramatic turn as Home Office statistics showed that 5,000 more motorists than burglars were sent to prison in just one year. An astonishing 15,059 drivers were given custodial sentences in 2002, while just 10,184 burglars were jailed. Martin Narey, the then Prisons and Probation Chief had warned that jails are 'overrun' with drivers clogging up cells. Brian Gregory, chairman of the Association of British Drivers, slammed the figures and blamed the huge rise on the government's 'pathological hatred' of drivers. He said: " It seems that terror groups which place bombs in bins and blow people to pieces get an amnesty but drivers face jail." He warned that motorists would take their revenge at the next general election. Of the 15,059 jailed, 2,200 were for the most serious offences such as causing death by dangerous driving, dangerous driving and drink-driving resulting in injury. This means that almost 3,000 more drivers convicted of minor motoring offences were jailed, than burglars. AA statistics also showed that the number of drivers sent to prison to await trial has shot up by more than 400 per cent since 1992.

Ernie Harbon, 62, a painter and decorator from South Normanton, Derbyshire, refused to pay a fine and accept three penalty points after he was caught driving at 38mph in a 30mph zone by a speed camera. He claimed there were no speed-limit signs on the quiet A6007 road in Derbyshire. Magistrates upped his fine to £400 and issued a warrant for his arrest. Ernie declared: " I have nothing to lose but my freedom and I'm prepared to make a stand on this."

Yet the courts have repeatedly failed to get tough on serious crime. In 2003, child molester Christopher Harris walked free from Norwich Crown Court after assaults on girls aged nine and ten. Pervert doctor Charles Bartlett escaped with a rehabilitation order at Cardiff Crown Court after amassing a huge child porn collection. These January 2004 prison statistics for England and Wales came as the number of burglars convicted fell from 58,660 in 1992 to 32,462 in 2002. A Home Office spokesman said: "The Home Secretary has stated many times in the past that prison should be used for serious criminals." Magistrates have three options when sentencing drivers. They can either impose a fine, a driving ban or a custodial sentence, even though studies show that courses to address driver behaviour are more effective.

Here is a 'Letter-Of-The-Day' published in the *Daily Express* on 4th May 2004, written by Lyndon Herring of Ashbourne, Derbyshire, which I hope you will find topical and interesting.

> *Your story ('Fury at 40% leap in speed camera fines', May 1st) surely points to the need for a change in policy. Despite this increase in offences, and the prospect of three million convictions this year, the annual fatality rate remains stubbornly constant at around 3,500. Despite the proliferation of cameras, the policy has not been effective. The real risks of death and mayhem on our roads are caused by young, inexperienced drivers, elderly motorists who ought to have been 'medically retired' and a hardcore criminal element who drive unroadworthy vehicles, untaxed, uninsured and often under the influence of alcohol or drugs.*
>
> *Surely the money raised by speed cameras would be better spent on real traffic police officers patrolling our roads and feeling the collars of the real culprits?*

Well I have to say I very much agree with the correspondent except as regards reference to those who should be 'medically retired', of whom I have found very little, or no offending behaviour at all during my research for this chapter, perhaps surprisingly.

The following is a letter I received from bereaved parents Eileen and George whose son was killed by a 'hit and run' driver.

Brentwood, Essex.
30th January 2004

Dear Mike,

Apologies for the delay in answering but we have been away for eight days, a very good reunion.

Regarding your request, there is so much we could say as you know but perhaps the following might help.

In 1977 we lost our son, aged twenty two in a hit and run accident. I think the word accident is too sweeping. The driver had no tax, no insurance and received legal aid to help him. We had nothing. Our son was completely innocent, killed whilst out working, going about his normal duties.

The driver received a fine, which was an insult to the memory of our son, and banned from driving for a few years. We presume he is driving around now, continuing with his life, perhaps with a family, grandchildren etc.

We have been sentenced to a lifetime of sadness and loss. Who knows what grandchildren we might have had, what joys we have missed? Christmas, Mother's and Father's days, birthdays, all these have come and gone with sadness.

The loss has affected our health and also our daughter's outlook on life. We must remember the loss affects the whole of the family.

When someone is killed suddenly like that there is no time to say goodbye, to tell them you love them. It is made so much worse and makes one bitter and resentful even after all this time, that such a low value was put on our son's life.

Hope that helps.

Best wishes,

Eileen and George.

COUNT 11

CRIMINAL DAMAGE

Under the Criminal Damage Act 1971, sec 1(1) 'a person who, without lawful excuse, destroys or damages any property belonging to another, intending to destroy or damage any such property, or being reckless as to whether any such property would be destroyed or damaged, shall be guilty of an offence.'

Where the damage is caused other than by fire, the offence is punishable by imprisonment for 10 years. The Act does not specifically define 'destroy' or 'damage.'

Where fire is used, viz: arson, the maximum penalty becomes life imprisonment.

For approximately 15 years I lived in an almost idyllic, rural scenario in Wokingham, Berkshire, in a very old farm cottage, surrounded by at least 40 acres of fields, bushes and trees which all belonged to the proprietors of an adjacent equestrian centre. Some of the views were stunning and marred only by a few huge electricity pylons in the distance. The area teemed with wildlife, mostly rabbits, which commit serious damage to crops, young saplings, garden flowers and shrubs, most of which they bite off at just above ground level and then abandon, for the plants to die. Huge damage was caused right across the fields, which formed part of the equestrian centre, much of which had been given over to a professionally constructed cross-country course. With the large amount of high-speed horses and riders competing in the 3-day events, there was a huge risk of horses putting their feet down the vast number of rabbit holes, breaking limbs and inevitably having to be destroyed on site by a vet. For this reason, the land owners employed amateur, frustrated, would-be SAS soldiers to patrol the area from time-to-time. They would appear just before dusk dressed in their army surplus store DPM's. (Disrupted Pattern Material), or camouflage clothing. The 'uniform' for rabbit-stalking covered them from head-to-toe, from the DPM baseball cap right down to their elasticated-at-the-ankle gannex trousers. The boots of course, must comply too, so they were purchased from the huge olive green marquees with the union flag flying, seen at every medium to large outdoor market or car boot sale, second-hand ex-paratroopers boots for £40.00. Watching these guys prepare for 'battle' with the rabbits used to make us chuckle at times, as they took it so seriously. We would joke amongst ourselves that even their underpants or boxers were of DPM, for when they needed to take a leak, as rabbits are known for being very sharp-eyed, even in the dark.

They were armed with either very high powered air rifles and/or shotguns, as the 'SAS' often hunted in small groups. Basically they did a good job for all local residents as well as the land owners, as rabbits really are very destructive. Naturally we all kept indoors once we heard their guns going off, as we never knew if they had spent hours in the pub beforehand, gaining the courage through drink to overcome their natural fear of the dark.

The only bad news about living there, in the heart of the country, was that access was quite difficult at times. This was due to there being only a very narrow, much-potholed farm track as the only vehicular access route to our cottages. The track had high hedges on both sides and had never been effectively maintained or managed by the land owners. It was just about wide enough for a single horsebox to pass, but even then it would scrape its sides on the vegetation on either side. Certainly it was impossible for even two cars going in opposite directions to pass each other, due to the narrow width of clear track space. Those few residents who lived at the rural end of the track, had complete, unrestricted vehicular and pedestrian access rights along the track, filed with the deeds of our homes, in the *Woolwich Building Society* vaults.

Naturally there were loads of horses liverying, showjumping, dressaging, cross-countrying and hacking, in addition to generating massive quantities of horse manure. In later years, the quite inconsiderate land-owners dug a huge pit at the inner end of the track and hedgerow, bang opposite one of our neighbour's front door. This became the main horse manure dump and you can imagine the smell on a hot summers day with your windows open and trying to enjoy BBQ's with friends and neighbours, to say nothing of buzzing flies and even rats and mice, which enjoy the heat generated by fermenting hot manure, and ammonia-soaked stable floor debris of straw,

Chapel Green, Wokingham, Berks

hay and shredded paper. A man who lived miles away on a farm at Hook, Hampshire, just off the M3 motorway, travelled all that way with a huge modern tractor and trailer, to empty the manure heap and cart it away, presumably for fertilising the farm land at Hook. This part of the chapter on criminal damage is being illustrated by photographs so you will 'get-the-picture' quite literally in due course. The photo above proves that there was ample space near the inner end of the track, by a farm gate, where a piece of land was used as a car park by equestrian customers and tradesmen, where the 'manure-man' could have parked his huge trailer rig and still empty the huge manure heap without blocking the narrow track at all. However he proved to be a lazy man and wanted to minimise the shunting to-and-fro-procedure between the heap and the huge farm trailer, with sides about eight feet high. Over time, he inconvenienced most of us time and time again, as we tried to leave home or arrive back and access our homes beyond the track.

Neighbours used to exchange information about such matters, as we were a very small but close-knit community. One day, I was on the late shift at work which meant I had to be miles away the other side of Henley-on-Thames by 1pm. I went shopping in the morning and had not left myself a great deal of time to get home, change into uniform and rush out again in a ball of steam. As I returned, I found that 'manure-man' had blocked the track by the manure heap, and I had to sit there for a few minutes, gritting my teeth until he spotted me and moved the tractor to let me through. When I raced out again after a record-breaking 20 minutes, in my black trousers, white short-sleeved 'pilot shirt' with HMP black epaulettes with numerals, black tie and shoes, belt-pouches, trailing HMP keychain etc I found that *public enemy number one* had blocked the track again! I parked my car behind his trailer and approached the tractor, whereupon he saw me and switched-off the noisy diesel engine to hear what I had to say. He remained in the driving cab and spoke to me through the opened cab door. Quite patiently, under the circumstances, I asked him if he wouldn't mind in future, parking the trailer so that the track entrance was not obstructed, as we had *right-of-way* over the track on our title deeds. He went 'ballistic' as the modern expression has it. He had no way of knowing, as I stood beside him in my 'shirt-sleeve-order' uniform, whether

Scene of criminal damage and assault on the author and car partly-filmed by timely appearance of friendly, observant neighbours

Defendant re-loads the grab/bucket to carry out his criminal intentions

Caught on film in the act of dumping stables waste onto author's head and car

I was a police officer, prison officer, airline pilot, security officer or fire fighter, neither did he care. He shouted: "I don't know who you think you are but you're a jobsworth!" With that, he slammed the door, started up the tractor engine and then, using his power-steering he began shunting the tractor backwards and forwards towards where I was standing, on ever-tighter steering locks until he almost had me either run over by the huge rear tyres, which were as tall as me, or crushed against the solid post-and-rail paddock fence, which you can see in the photos, by the metal farm gate. I couldn't believe my eyes!

Mr Tom Stacey returns to tractor rig after angry nose-to-nose confrontation with the author

Whilst being polite to an inconsiderate and lazy farm hand from miles away in a different county, I was experiencing the very first recorded case of 'farm-rage' or 'tractor-rage,' by a lunatic who, for all I knew had escaped from the very-nearby Broadmoor Special Hospital at Crowthorne, and was hell-bent on making ME his next victim! Hurriedly I leaped out of the way, fuelled by the adrenalin-rush, whilst rapidly trying to recall whether or not I had ever got around to making my now, all-important last will and testament. (In fact later, in the

Police car finally arrives on the scene

Manure, timber and stone debris dumped from tractor grab bucket

cold light of day when tranquillity had finally been restored, I realised that I had not even made my FIRST will - never mind my LAST!)

I then raced back to my car and swiftly drove past his trailer and parked it beside the manure heap, just inside the track entrance, to prevent his escape, locked it up and got busy with dialling 999 for the police on my mobile phone, which infuriatingly took a minute or two to get through. Amazingly, during the maniacal attempt to run me down or crush me by 'manure man,' I had seen one of my neighbours and her daughter standing near the track entrance, outside their house, snapping away with a camera! I later found out from the police that the daughter had rushed indoors and also dialled 999 to call them. As pictured by my wonderful neighbour, I stood near my car bonnet, speaking to the emergency operator, who was asking me what all the noise was, as 'brain box' was blasting his very loud tractor horn to intimidate me into moving my car to let him out to 'escape.' When he saw I wasn't going to move, he rushed over on foot for a nose-to-nose verbal confrontation and is pictured after this, returning to the tractor. By now, you will get the impression that he had 'totally lost it,' but it was far from over. I had turned around with my back to the scene whilst I again spoke to the 999 operator, to ask her if the Thames Valley Police Force had been disbanded without my knowledge, so that I could concentrate on what she and I were saying.

When I turned back again, after hearing the racing of the tractor engine, to my horror I found that he had loaded the tractor 'bucket' with another scoop of manure etc and had extended the telescopic arms to stretch right beyond and over the full length of my car and up over my head. Using the hydraulic mechanism he then emptied the load from on high all over me, shaking the bucket several times to ensure he hadn't missed any! I had heard of it raining cats and dogs, but this was ridiculous. He returned to the manure heap, refilled the bucket with a huge load, which he then dumped onto my car roof and I saw the roof sag under the unbearable weight. With a final flourish of activity, my intended-assassin then hitched up to his trailer and shunted backwards and forwards in short stages, reversing into and denting my car rear offside wing in the process, and, assisted by two incredulous and spellbound stable girls who opened the farm gate for him, commenced his escape across the field, where he must have known there was another gate at the horsebox car parking area.

Just then two police cars arrived, in the, if you'll excuse the expression, 'nick' of time. They briefly spoke to witnesses, produced a *Polaroid* camera to photograph the manure etc. on my car roof, (but not that on my head), before arresting him for criminal damage and assault, which is where we came in. An officer returned after the offender had been taken to, not Broadmoor Special Hospital but Earley police station, near Reading. This officer took several cups of tea and full statements from myself and my two wonderful neighbours, whose timely intervention had saved my bacon, otherwise it would have been a grey area for the police, his word against mine. After I had washed up the cups and cleaned up the mud and manure on my dining room floor from the track and the officer's boots, I phoned work and told them they would somehow, difficult as it might be, have to manage without me for the rest of the day, as I had narrowly survived a murder attempt by a maniac on the loose.

I then went to the car and field and took some of my own photographs of the huge trailer rig and the car roof, pre-and-post manure, for evidential use at court in due course. My personal photographs are easily distinguishable from those taken by my neighbour and the police, as of course, they are the clearest, sharpest and best-composed!

Later I learned, much to my chagrin, that the culprit, Mr Tom Stacey, not of this parish but of Hook parish, had languished for 2-3 hours in an Earley police station cell, awaiting the completion of the police investigation, and subsequent interrogation on audio tape equipment. It used to be said that police officers once offered to suspects under interrogation, the choice of, 'Do you want it the hard way, or the easy way?' which later became a music hall joke. As it turned out, Mr Stacey made a full confession and told the police he did not know what had come over him, but that he was under pressure at home due to marital difficulties. Ever since then, I've kept one eye on the *BBC South* TV news to see if he'd murdered his wife yet! Fortunately for Mr Stacey, but unfortunately for me, Thames Valley Police, under constant pressure as I know they are these days, took 'the easy way out' and released the offender after serving him with an Official Caution, which I'm told , these days hangs over your head for a year or two in case you offend again, counting in law as a 'sort of criminal record', but not an official one, subject to no recidivism. This course of action can only take place if the offender makes a full admission of guilt. I did not blame the officers for this, as the *Caution* procedure got them back out on the streets again much faster, where they belong. I also knew only too well that, unlike when I carried out my 14 years of police service with just one hand 'tied-behind-my-back', they have to do the job in 2004, with both hands tied!

However it meant that I was denied an official hearing of my case at a Magistrates or Crown Court, as a victim of both assault and criminal damage. (If you look very closely at some of the photographs, you'll notice that chunks of wood, plasterboard and even pieces of brick had been ejected from the bucket, from quite a height and could have caused at least actual bodily harm) This meant that as, presumably, Mr Stacey would have pleaded guilty, or been found guilty, I could have sought a Compensation Order for damage to my car and personal inconvenience, stress etc. Instead, I had to work very hard for months on end in my off-duty time, preparing endless reports and filling-in numerous official forms from Reading County Court in a private claim. Modern County Court procedures include multi-stages and hearings and delayed judicial decisions as to whether your case should appear on the so-called 'fast-track' or 'slow-track' list etc. In the event, whichever option box you tick, you're on the 'slow track', as we all know how slowly the wheels of justice turn.

Eventually, over a year after commencement of the proceedings, after spending small fortunes on photocopying, extra copies of photos, supporting letters from TVP to confirm the police procedures etc., I had my day in court. Mr Stacey, myself and, eventually a District Judge, a different one from the preliminary hearing, sat around the highly polished huge table. He made some notes and got to the stage of calculating the extent of financial reimbursement he would order the Defendant to pay to the Plaintiff, which I could tell was leading to a shortfall, in the Defendant's favour. I then had the satisfaction of stopping the learned judge in his tracks by saying: "What about all of the photo-copying and photographs?" His Honour, in his wisdom, then made my heart sink with his immortal words, "What photographs?" I was then forced to make him look properly and thoroughly through the Court File, with his glasses on, until he found the huge sheaf of photographs and my *submitted to the Court over a year ago itemised expenses list*. He then scrutinised them for several minutes, flicking through the papers whilst he worked out what next to say, finally allowing me to breath again by awarding me judgement to the tune of just under £1,500, which Mr TS immediately paid into the court by cheque, thus prolonging my agony until I received a court cheque after about 7 days.

County Court Judgement awarded by the judge against the defendant, in author's favour, at Reading County Court on 15th November 2002

Prior to standing up to call the proceedings to a halt, the learned judge explained away his professional incompetence over the photos business etc, by claiming that he had only been handed the Court file 'a few minutes' before gracing us with his presence in Chambers no. 1. ("Pull the other leg, Judge, it's got bells on," as my dear mother would have said!) The moral to this report of my personal involvement as a fairly recent victim of criminal damage and assault, is to beware of, and give a wide berth to, any farm tractor/trailer rigs you come across in the Hook to Wokingham areas, after patiently crawling along behind them for 45 minutes or more. In the photographs, I've given you the registration number of the tractor and trailer 'rig', the rest is up to you.

Author's photo - NY City fire fighter bronze tableau

Hopefully, the largest example of deliberate Criminal Damage, as well as far more serious crimes, that any of us will ever see, was the enormous catastrophe at The World Trade Centre in New York, more familiarly known these days as *nine eleven*. The other brutal and outrageous, indiscriminate crimes included serial murders on the most massive scale in modern history, approximately 3000 victims. We were all distressed, shocked and horrified, watching the breaking news, and as the full enormity of the event became clear, we saw pitiful images of many people, singly or in small groups, some hand-in-hand, committing suicide by leaping from multi-storey skyscraper windows, to escape the catastrophic fire which was rapidly consuming the entire buildings known as *The Twin Towers*. Who could ever forget too, the dreadful, heart-stopping moments when we saw the planes fly into the Towers, piloted by religious, fanatical, suicide hijackers?

Author's photo - New York City 9/11 reconstruction site

Who could not be moved, at listening to the recordings of voices of aircraft passengers, calling on their mobiles, their loved ones to say their very last goodbyes, before being blasted into oblivion as the towers were struck, having witnessed already, right in front of their very eyes, horrendous scenes of cabin staff's

PC Norman Brennan, Director, Victims of Crime Trust, patrols New York City with an officer from NYPD

On the first anniversary of the tragic events of September 11th 2001 a delegation of 330 UK police officers visited New York to pay tribute to those who were killed

throats being expertly cut, to assist rapid cockpit entry etc., so as to get at the controls and divert the aircraft onto the doomed, final course bearings? Included amongst that days' shocking and unbelievable unfolding events, were several examples across the USA, of Criminal Damage. We all hope and pray that we will never again see carnage on such a massive scale - deliberately caused by armed criminals.

A fire-raiser aged ten was banned by a court from having matches or cigarette lighters in his possession until his 16th birthday. He had caused almost £80,000 worth of damage in two arson attacks. Exeter Youth Court was told that the boy had 'a fascination for fire.' He set light to a cleaning machine with lighter fluid, after breaking into a council depot, and was lucky to escape unhurt. This blaze did £64,200 damage to the vehicle and the building in which it was stored. He had previously set light to a new house, leaving a £15,500 repair bill. The boy from Honiton, who is too young to be named, was made the subject of a behaviour order and barred from entering any school or college building without permission.

Three youths, who can't be named, shattered the windscreen of a train with a concrete block and nearly killed its driver. Two 14-years-old and one 15-years-old boy pleaded guilty to endangering the safety of persons on the railway, at Westcott, Devon on 14th April 2004. The train was travelling at 70mph from London Paddington towards Exeter when the one-and-a-half-inch thick train windscreen disintegrated. Chairman of the Bench of Magistrates at Exeter Youth Court, in her wisdom, told the youngsters: "The fact no-one was really hurt was a miracle." In spite of the absolute seriousness of the offence, the boys were made the subject of a 12-months referral order and to pay £300 each to train driver Ian Jonas, a father-of-two.

Four members of one family were killed in just 40 seconds in a suspected arson attack on 28th September 2004. The blaze spread so quickly that firefighters could not save them, despite arriving within a minute of the alarm being raised. Ajit Singh, 64, wife Gurdish Kaur, 60, daughter Darshan Kaur, 30, and daughter-in-law Palwinder Kaur, 38, died in the tragedy at the semi around midnight. The couple's grand-daughter Amarjeet Kaur, 20, was saved by a passer-by and was in hospital after suffering ten per-cent burns and inhaling smoke. Their son Singh Sidhu, 36, said: "I can't understand why anyone would do this. My family are good people." Police think petrol may have been poured through the letter-box in Tipton, West Mids. Det. Insp. Carl Southwick said: "We're awaiting a full report but the circumstances are suspicious."

MAD CYCLIST'S REVENGE

A cyclist who developed a hatred for motorists after being splashed by a passing vehicle, took revenge by slashing nearly 2,000 car tyres, a court heard. Ashley Carpenter, 37, who has never passed a driving test, went on a 10-day rampage. Armed with a sharpened Phillips screwdriver, he left his home on his bike during hours of darkness and randomly slashed the tyres of nearly 600 cars. The damage has been estimated at £250,000. Police launched *Operation Cloud* to find him. After his arrest he said he was fed up with the 'inconsiderate manner' of motorists. He pointed out he had nearly been knocked off his bike when a car drove through a puddle and drenched him. Carpenter, unemployed, of Bournemouth pleaded guilty to eight charges of criminal damage and asked for 540 similar offences to be 'TIC.' Bournemouth Magistrates heard that the number of tyres known to have been vandalised was 1,728. On more than one occasion Carpenter damaged several belonging to the same family, and sometimes he returned to puncture tyres that he had already damaged. During a ten day period between December 12th and 22nd 2003, the police were called to 563 reports of damaged tyres. On some cars, all 4 tyres were damaged, and he struck on roads, in private car parks, in public car parks and in peoples' driveways. This scale of offending was unprecedented. After studying CCTV footage, police released pictures to the Press and Carpenter was quickly arrested. As he was arrested he was seen trying to dispose of a small, sharpened screwdriver. Forensic tests later linked the screwdriver to the tyres that were punctured and fragments of tyre rubber were found in his pocket.

Detective Sergeant Mark Monaghan, who led *Operation Cloud* said: "It was a miracle that nobody was hurt or killed if you consider the number of people driving cars with deflated tyres." At Bournemouth Crown Court in

April 2004 he was sentenced to just 16 months imprisonment.

PARKING RAGE OF 'MELDREW' ON PAINT-STRIPPER RAMPAGE

A retired company director who sprayed dozens of cars with paint stripper in protest at them parking in his street, was branded a real-life *Victor Meldrew*. Ian Phillips targeted 29 cars during a ten month vendetta, leaving them with peeling paint costing thousands of pounds to repair. Police, alerted by angry owners, launched a CCTV surveillance operation codenamed *Snakebite* and caught him red-handed. Phillips, 62, from upmarket Mulroy Road in Sutton Coldfield, West Midlands admitted 19 charges of criminal damage. He asked for ten more cases to be considered (TIC). Magistrates at Walsall heard that the damage to the 19 cars he admitted vandalising, cost £8,089 to repair. The others cost another £2,767. Phillips, who has lived in the road for 15 years, was sent to Wolverhampton Crown Court for sentence.

Police in Staffordshire are hunting *Animal Rights* campaigners thought to be responsible for interfering with the grave of Mrs Gladys Hammond, in her 80's, who was buried about seven years ago, in 1997 in Yoxall's St Peters Churchyard. She was the mother-in-law of one of three brothers involved in running a farm, where guinea pigs are bred for scientific research. Commentators stated that this was revolting behaviour, about as low as it is possible to sink in a criminal enterprise. The deceased's son-in-law, Mr Christopher Hall, of nearby Darley Oaks Farm, is reported as saying: "We are shell-shocked at the moment and don't know what to say, very distressed. What sort of people could do such a thing? It's a very emotional time. I have always known that we are dealing with very sick people here, but not as sick as this. This is just a horrible thing to happen".

The desecrated grave was discovered by a local man, resident in the village, whilst visiting his own mother's grave, which is adjacent. He raised the alarm and police screened-off the area for forensic examinations to be carried out. In the meantime detectives commenced house-to-house enquiries in the area, seeking clues that might lead them to those responsible. The man who discovered the grave desecration stated: " I looked inside and saw that the water level inside had changed and what loked like a human bone was visible, then I saw that there was an incomplete skeleton. The coffin side, with its decaying lining material, was also visible. I then spotted a plaque with the inscribed name of Gladys Hammond, which must have come off the coffin lid. I was so shocked and horrified at what I had found, made worse as it was so close to the grave of my own mother." He then arranged for the police to be called. He added: "I haven't been able to sleep since my discovery and I can't eat either. It was in such a mess, I can't believe a human being could possibly do that. Police have sealed-off the area, so grieving relatives can't even get near to the grave."

A police spokesman was quoted as saying: "This is an appalling act committed by depraved individuals who breached the sanctity of a village churchyard in a most shocking way. It is an extremely serious incident against the memory of a much-loved family member, which has left her relatives in absolute distress." The Darley Oaks Farm has been licensed to breed guinea pigs under licence for animal experiments under scientific control for over 30 years. During that period it was targeted from time-to-time with peaceful protests. However, in 2000 the demonstrators cranked-up their intimidation and violence campaign against the Hall brothers. A local MP said, "This is the sickest event in the long series of threats of intimidation and other horrific incidents to have befallen the Hall family. These so-called animal rights activists have been treated with vaccinations and medicines developed through animal testing, so this latest occurrence is not only quite revolting, it is hypocrisy of the worst kind." The Archdeacon of nearby Lichfield, Reverend Christopher Lilley said: "With this act of desecration, a line has been crossed in civilised society. We are upset for many people at this time. Very upset for the family of the lady concerned, who was loved by them. We feel very angry for this pain they are having to bear."

UPDATE: In August 2005, the owners of the guinea pig farm announced that they would close the business at the end of that year. This news has been received by right-thinking and law-abiding members of the public as an outrage and a victory for the Animal Rights Movement, whose members have mounted a protracted campaign of *URBAN TERRORISM* against the long-suffering, government licenced owners of the farm.

Luxury cars belonging to controversial heiress Lady Julia Pilkington (she has annoyed neighbours by romping naked in a hot spa), have been showered with acid. The self-styled aristocrat, who was convicted of harassment, claims that thugs are being paid £500 a time to target her as part of a hate campaign. Both her Mercedes vehicles, which sport personalised number plates with the letters PLK on them, have been left with stripped and blistered paintwork following the attack. One of the cars is a black MLK people carrier, worth up to £60,000, while the other is a canary yellow SLK sports car worth up to £48,000. Acid was also poured on to the alloy wheels and door handles of the MLK, leaving 39-year-old Lady Pilkington, who lives in a penthouse at Southsea, Hants, afraid to touch them. The attacks happened just three weeks after the cars went back on the road, following a similar attack which caused more than £6,000 of damage. Her cars were in a parking area beneath the flats where she lives. Lady Pilkington, who is a member of the Pilkington glass family, has told police she is being victimised after appearing in court over a neighbourhood dispute at her former home. In February Lady Pilkington was sentenced to 42 days in jail for breaching a community service order. The order was imposed by Portsmouth magistrates after she was found guilty of four counts of harassment for pursuing a 'mad vendetta.' She made the lives of her neighbours in Eastlake Heights, Eastney, Portsmouth, hell by repeatedly abusing them and regularly holding late-night sex romps in her open-air spa. Her onslaught left some needing counselling, others too frightened to leave their homes. She breached the order when she turned up to help clear litter from a forest, as part of her community service, wearing a mini skirt, low-cut vest top and gold sandals. Then she refused to change into a pair of dowdy overalls, claiming she was a victim of sexual discrimination. Later she failed to turn up for another session of community work, claiming her 19-year-old whippet Roxy was sick. Lady Pilkington said she would not be bullied into giving up her cars by whoever is behind the attacks and has told police who she thinks is responsible. "I am extremely angry," she said. "They are animals."

Britain's worst graffiti vandal has been ordered to pay just £250 for causing more than £600,000 worth of damage. The 17-year-old, who cannot be named for legal reasons, carried out a two-year campaign across the beautiful Georgian city of Bath, with its soft, paint-absorbing stonework, using the tag-name *Phase*. The teenager caused thousands of pounds worth of damage to the world-famous Royal Crescent and also defaced the city's rugby stadium. Many of the spray 'artist's' daubs were coloured versions of his tag, some up to three ft high and five ft wide. But the youth ran up the highest bill by daubing railway bridges and walls bordering railway lines. After his arrest the teenager was charged with 10 counts of causing criminal damage at a cost of almost £60,000. He asked for a further 98 incidents to be taken into consideration.

Bath magistrates heard how those further acts of vandalism had caused £170,000 in damage. But the figure will rocket when the clean-up cost is included. Network Rail said the price to blast away graffiti on its Bristol to Bath line and the Avon viaduct was a staggering £395,000. The teenager, who also received a police reprimand for possessing amphetamines and Ecstasy while on bail, also spray-painted subways and car parks in nearby Bristol and Box. Specialist cleaners were called in to blast the teenager's scrawls off Royal Crescent, a street of beautiful houses built with the soft Bath Stone. PC Darren Taylor, head of Bath's anti-graffiti task force, said the teenager was the worst known graffiti offender in Britain. The teenager admitted all the charges at an earlier hearing in July which was adjourned for pre-sentence reports. He told the court he had turned his back on graffiti. "I didn't realise it was so serious," he said. "I just thought it could be painted over with normal paint. Now I just think it's completely wrong." The teenager was sentenced to a 12-month referral order, in which he will work with a team tackling youth offences, sign a contract not to re-offend and carry out reparation work to make amends to those companies affected by the vandalism. The court ordered him to pay £250 compensation to Bath and North East Somerset Council, but told the teenager he would never be able to repay local taxpayers. Magistrates declined to impose an anti-social behaviour order on the teenager, because they said they were convinced that he would not re-offend. Chairman of the Bench Kay Millard said: "We do not believe it would be in the public interest." After the case Detective Constable Colin Saysell said that he had noticed a marked drop in graffiti in the city since the 17-year-old had stopped offending. "But it's like a merry-go-round," he said. "There is always somebody to fill his shoes."

A man who threw a bucket of manure over Robert Kilroy-Silk, walked free from court on 3rd February 2005. Unemployed David McGrath threw the bucket of slurry over Mr Kilroy-Silk because of his comments about Arabs and Muslims, the court heard. McGrath, 37, pleaded guilty to causing criminal damage and a public order offence. Education Secretary Ruth Kelly and Mr Kilroy-Silk's driver were also splattered with the manure in the attack in Manchester in December 2004. After covering his victim's £600 suit, shirt and silk tie, McGrath, of Wilmslow, Cheshire, said: "You insulted my brother's religion. You insulted ISLAM." Manchester magistrates were told. The politician and *Sunday Express* columnist had just arrived at Manchester High School for Girls to take part in a recording of Radio 4's *Any Questions* programme. Ms Aoife Ryan, defending, said: "It is an extremely unpleasant scenario, Mr McGrath deeply regrets the actions." Magistrates gave him 12 months conditional discharge on each of the three counts of causing damage to his victims' clothing and the public order offence. He was also ordered to pay £200 compensation to Mr Kilroy-Silk, £100 to the driver and £10 to Mrs Kelly plus £50 court costs.

Two sick thugs who cooked a cat to death in an oven, then joked about 'cat stew' were branded obscene. Darren Glover, 24, was jailed after admitting the attack on four-year-old *Watson*. His accomplice David Anders, 17, will be sentenced later after being found guilty. Anders enticed the cat into the kitchen of a house where a party was being held. The black-and-white cat was then shoved struggling into the burning hot electric oven. A 15-year-old girl at the party asked Glover to release the pet, but Anders said: "Let's make cat stew." The girl told the court: "I can't describe the smell. I have never smelt anything like it before." Glover, who had been drinking, later grabbed the girl menacingly by the throat and said: "Don't say nowt. I have put the cat in the oven." After killing the cat the pair also talked of eating a "bit of cat pie."

Watson's scorched body was found wrapped in a blanket and dumped in a shed by Tracy Dayis, who had been looking after the house in Barnsley, South Yorks, while her mother was away. She made the discovery after finding clumps of fur in the oven. Judith Naylor, prosecuting, told Barnsley magistrates that the pair had "perpetrated one of the most obscene and abhorrent acts." Glover was jailed for four months after admitting destroying a cat by criminal damage. Anders will be sentenced later after being convicted of criminal damage and animal cruelty.

Sentencing Glover, bench chairman Keith Lax said: "This has been an abhorrent act against a defenceless animal. The sentence we can pass is in our opinion totally inadequate regarding the seriousness of the offence." Watson's owner Jody Porter, 25, lives nearby with Charlene Coe, 23. Mr Porter said yesterday: "You can get over losing an animal to an accident, but something like this I cannot comprehend."

On 17th February 2005 Jewish groups welcomed the six-year jail sentence for a racist who smashed up gravestones of Holocaust survivors. Simon Johnston, 20, caused £100,000 of damage to the Jewish cemetery before racially abusing three black men and a child in the street. A total of 62 headstones were desecrated during a five-day rampage, and others were posted with racist stickers. Racist posters and publications were later found in Johnston's flat, and a welcome message on his mobile home linked him to *Combat 18*, a notorious racist group. The prison sentence follows figures released showing record levels of abusive or violent attacks on Jews in Britain in 2004

Jon Benjamin, chief executive of the Board of Deputies of British Jews, said the sentence should act as a clear message to perpetrators of anti-semitic attacks. "We welcome what is quite a substantial sentence for this kind of thing," he said. "This sends out the right kind of signal that it is something that cannot be tolerated and has to be treated very seriously." Mr Benjamin warned that often those who commit racially aggravated criminal damage move on to attacking individuals. Johnston targeted Witton Cemetery in Birmingham between August 19th and 23rd 2004, the city's crown court heard. The racist attacks occurred on August 22nd. Alexander Jacobs, prosecuting, told the court: "Some of these graves were the resting place of Holocaust survivors who found themselves in

Birmingham in their twilight years and were buried there." The defendant, who had been living in Birmingham, after moving from his native Northern Ireland, admitted one charge of racially aggravated criminal damage. At an earlier hearing, he admitted two counts of racially aggravated harassment and another of causing fear of violence.

Johnston's flatmate Carl Jones, 24, failed to appear to be sentenced on racial abuse charges and a warrant was issued for his arrest. Detective Inspector Steve Bimson, from West Midlands Police, said: "This was a despicable crime and the court has dealt with it by delivering a substantial sentence. This is a sign that such offences will not be tolerated." The Community Security Trust (CST) found there were a total of 532 'anti-semitic incidents', defined as malicious acts toward the Jewish community, in 2004. This was a 42 per cent increase on the previous year, and far higher than the worst year on record, 2000, when there were 405 incidents. Among last year's incidents, there were 83 physical attacks on Jews, up 54 per cent on the previous year.

Just like the matter we have just read about, probably the everyday images we most encounter concerning criminal damage offences, is graffiti. Many travellers who frequently use buses will have been forced to get wet or become very cold through having to stand around in a bus shelter with smashed or totally missing glass panels, and staring at criminal graffiti, caused by vandals, probably overnight. Also, there can't be many frequent railway passengers around who have not become sick and tired of seeing graffiti everywhere.

Serious trackside graffiti near Paddington station

Particularly in the London area near main line railway termini, just about every available inch of space on walls, old signal boxes, trackside huts, electricity sub-stations, gates, fences, bridges, stations, trains parked on sidings and at depots, literally anywhere there is a vertical surface available. Apparently some of these vandals, for that's what they are, consider their artistic capabilities to be so wonderful that they become mindlessly addicted to their criminal offending in the name of 'ART.' They are so fanatical that some have been actually electrocuted whilst at work through, presumably, stepping back to admire their work, forgetting there is a live rail behind them! The most common form of graffiti we tend to come across is where the criminal 'artist' has created his motto or personal logo known these days as a 'TAG.'

Not content to just deface the public surface with just ONE 'work of art', it has to be repeated several times over until the paint runs out. There are others on the loose in public whom I suspect crawl out from under their damp stones after dark. These vandals travel on trains too, and slash with knives the seat squabs and back cushions and/or throw these upholstered items from the windows onto the track. However with the introduction of air conditioned carriages and train crew operated doors, opening windows can be made much smaller these days, making it harder to throw cushions and fire extinguishers etc from windows. However they have developed new skills, which presumably take place late night, viz: scratching names and messages etc onto the actual inner pane of double glazed window units. It matters not to these mindless hooligans if the train carriages are brand spanking new or have been in service for years.

Other thoughtless travellers, but without the criminal intent, damage the train and bus seats by regularly stretching out their legs to rest their dirty shoes or boots on the opposite seat cushion. I have noticed that women as well as men tend to have this irritating habit and it is most often observed, when the train or bus is moving in close proximity to a university or college, coincidentally. One wonders if they treat their own or relatives' furniture with the same disrespect! In the case of graffiti, dried paint is very hard indeed to remove, especially, as is often the case, when it is applied over-night and therefore has had some time to set firm and bond onto the previous outer surface. As any police officer will tell you, criminal offenders (graffitists) are very difficult to catch.

Whilst British Transport Police officers are patrolling underground railway sidings at night, on covert surveillance missions, they themselves run the risk of electrocution, particularly so whilst chasing suspects in the dark. However there is no doubt that modern CCTV cameras with their high resolution images are playing a major part, not just in combating hooliganism in general, but particularly offenders who commit crime at or around railway stations.

Returning now to the graffiti and criminal damage to trains, buses, bus shelters, shop windows, telephone boxes etc., evidence of which we all come in contact with virtually every day. In December 2003, on my third visit to the country, I spent two weeks in Toronto, Canada, visiting relations. I travelled on many buses, sometimes several per day. I travelled on their double-decked trains several times too. In that whole two weeks, I cannot recall seeing a single example of graffiti, neither were there any scratched windows on buses or trains. Thinking about it since my return to this country, I can only assume that a ZERO TOLERANCE policy, like New York, is operated by the Toronto City Police.

In early March 2005, whist travelling on a First Great Western Link Company train on the Oxford to Paddington line, I mentioned to the ticket collector that, as practically every window in the long compartment had been deeply-etched with names, tags and slogans etc., sometimes quite skilfully, which must have taken quite some time, had the rail company considered installing secret cameras to catch some of these half-witted vandals? I pointed out that in modern times, secret camera technology is quite brilliant and lenses are available virtually as small as a pinhead. Furthermore, the camera equipment itself is very small, and therefore easily transportable for switching from carriage-to-carriage or to a fresh train. He advised me that most moronic train window glass-etchers, prior to carrying out their wanton, criminal and destructive behaviour, first steal the emergency glass-breaking hammer from the compartment's emergency cabinet. These small hammers are fitted with very strong, sharp points for smashing the double glazed window glass via sharp corner blows. Readers will be aware that no criminal vandal is going to even consider for one moment, the possibility of restoring the hammer to its emergency cabinet – after his glass-etching is completed. Therefore law-abiding, commuting and regular train passengers, will run the possibly life-threatening risk of being unable to smash their way out of the overturned or stricken by fire compartment.

When I was a uniformed bobby on the beat at Tilbury, Essex in the late 1960's, it became the fashionable thing for criminals to go around breaking open the coin boxes and smashing the handsets and just about every small pane of glass in the old red-painted telephone boxes, which were quite few and far between and normally sited in strategic places. As there were no mobile telephones in those days, and not every householder even had a telephone land line installed, this caused considerable mayhem and inconvenience to thousands of people country-wide. A solution to this vast-scale malicious damage, as it was called in those days, was found. Somebody had the inspiration or far-sightedness to arrange for label stickers to be attached to the three glass walls and the doors of public telephone boxes.

The message on the stickers was:

IF YOU ARE CAUGHT CAUSING DAMAGE TO THIS TELEPHONE BOX YOU WILL GO TO PRISON FOR 6 MONTHS

Across the country as a whole there were many arrests for this type of offence. The word soon got round. Magistrates and Judges seemed to enter into the spirit of the 'sticker' campaign and believe it or not, the six months jail sentences were handed out and before long, public telephone boxes were back in full use again. Did I hear you say, "Those were the days?"

In case you didn't hear about these fairly recent cases of serious criminal damage, I will report them verbatim from the *Daily Express* edition of 25th March 2004, both stories appearing inside on page 11.

THE SUNDAY EXPRESS 'BEAT THE GRAFFITI YOBS' CAMPAIGN

By the end of March 2004, the above campaign had been running for some time. Under a banner headline **BLITZ ON VANDALS** on 28th March, the *Sunday Express* reported that a crackdown on vandalism will see utility firms having to foot the bill if they fail to clear graffiti off phone kiosks, bus stops and rail sidings. Companies targeted by vandals will be given 28 days by local authorities, to clear scrawl off their property. The Home Office is also planning £50 on-the-spot fines for those caught defacing property. Shopkeepers will face fines if they sell spray paints to anyone under 16. A Home Office spokesman said: "We see this as a blitz on the vandal." A pilot scheme is to be introduced in 12 towns across the country, which will see telephone and bus companies being forced to clear up the vandals' mess. Home Secretary David Blunkett is expected to announce the measures soon. Graffiti has become an inner-city headache with thousands of youngsters leaving their multi-coloured tags on railway bridges, underpasses, telephone boxes and bus stops. In London alone, the cost of scouring the mess off walls is estimated at more than £100 million per year. Urban blight caused by vandalism has been blamed for generating inner-city crime. Street crimes such as muggings and car theft are more common in vandalised neighbourhoods.

"Graffiti has become a scourge of the modern age and this unsightly scrawl on public and private buildings has no place in a law-abiding society. The latest proposals should go a long way to help stopping this dreadful vandalism." said the Home Office insider. Let's all hope that the pilot scheme works out and therefore it could be adopted country-wide.

It does seem to be a step in the right direction, but obviously it is very unfair that the onus to remove the graffiti has been placed on the property owners, viz: the utilities, who didn't want the graffiti applied to their managed sites in the first place! Is this the start of a new trend called 'back-door justice?' Only time will tell, we will have to wait and see. My own solution to this problem would be for all fresh and new graffiti sites to be neatly sprayed over with dense, thick, black paint, in neat rectangular or square panels, by trained staff in protective clothing and face masks and goggles. If this could be undertaken nationwide, I am sure that the mindless 'Tag-morons', would soon begrudge the waste of their time and money, and risk of death on the railways. Meanwhile, I'm sure the law-abiding members of the public, and even the owners of the walls, fences, garage doors etc – would far rather gaze upon uniformly-shaped, dark panels in a single plain colour, than the nightmare scenarios which we come across almost everywhere these days.

Author's photo of memorial mural at site of 9/11 terrorist atrocity

COUNT 12

PSYCHIATRIC HOSPITALS
& HMP PAROLE BOARDS

DEFECTIVE RISK ASSESSMENTS
PLACE UNSUSPECTING PUBLIC
AT INCREASED DANGER

A staggering 3,623 offences, including nine sex attacks, have been committed by criminals freed early from jail, shock figures released on 8th July 2004 have revealed. The sex assaults could include rape and child molesting. Ministers have been accused of putting the public at risk because of the flawed early release from jail scheme. Shadow Home Secretary David Davis said: "We always opposed the scheme because we knew it would lead to more victims of crime. As a result of this scheme, at least nine people have been victims of sexual offences. This probably means indecent assault and rape of women or offences against children, thanks to this dangerous and irresponsible policy. Tony Blair should look at these figures and hang his head in shame." Government statistics show a total of 3,623 crimes were committed by early release scheme inmates since 1999.

The alarming figure includes nine sexual offences, 462 assaults and muggings, 163 burglaries, 47 robberies and 306 drugs offences. Sexual offences are broken down by the Home Office as rape, indecent assault, underage sex or gross indecency with a child. The scheme was brought in by Labour to ease overcrowding in Britain's 138 jails. Home Secretary David Blunkett is planning to widen the scheme by tagging offenders electronically. At present, in July 2004, only those serving between three months and four years are eligible for early release under the scheme. Some 87,000 prisoners have been allowed out of jail before the end of their normal sentences since 1999.

The senseless knife attacks by a former psychiatric patient have provoked fresh criticism of doctors for putting the rights of the dangerously mentally ill before public safety. The rampage came amid growing unease over the number of killings by 'care in the community' patients, released on the assumption that they can be treated better outside mental hospitals, and that they are no longer a danger. High-profile killings underline the fact that one in 20 of the murders in England and Wales every year is carried out by killers with a psychiatric history. There was the case of *Camden Ripper* Anthony Hardy, 54, who had been in and out of mental institutions. He murdered three women in 2003, including Elizabeth Valad, whose body parts were found in a rubbish bin. He had been released from hospital without surveillance. And Jonathan Zito's murder shocked the capital when he was stabbed and killed by Christopher Clunis, a psychiatric patient, on a Tube station platform in 1992. Concern among the police is so great that Commander Andy Baker, head of homicide at Scotland Yard, accused doctors of refusing to give police vital information about their dangerous patients. He said recently at a forensic science conference: "The right to privacy is superseded by the right to life." Doctors who breach a patient's confidentiality without good reason are at risk of being disciplined by the General Medical Council and in severe cases may be struck off. But the GMC has said that rules already allow doctors to break the confidentiality principle if they think there is a risk of a patient doing harm.

During my police service, I did not personally come across very many persons who were severely mentally ill. There was one time when I had to assist other officers to deliver a young woman, whom ambulance staff had refused to get involved with, to the former Warley Hospital near Brentwood, Essex. In those days, many male and female patients were allowed personal day release and would just wander around the community. They stood out from the rest of the community, as the trousers of the men were as short as today's 'cropped' ones, and all of them, men and women alike, nearly always wore, probably much-recycled, old-fashioned garments in sombre greys and browns. But at least they were kept rigidly under control through receiving their proper regular medication. We managed to look after this woman who had been 'sectioned' at a police station by two doctors, as she was so intent on self-harming herself. We off-loaded her safely from the police van, rang the bell and stood at the main admissions doors, which of course were kept locked. She stood quietly with us, one of our colleagues was a policewoman, of course, until staff arrived and unlocked to let us in.

As we moved forward to climb the steps into the long corridor, she succeeded in thrusting the wrist which was un-held, straight through a mini-glass pane and cut the wrist quite badly. In those days it was very rare indeed to handcuff a woman and even then, although we all carried a pair of the old-fashioned, solid, non-ratcheted *Hyatt* ones, they stayed in our pockets out of sight and were rarely used at all.

This next series of events only took place because the criminal was released too early from his previous custodial sentence. I was on night duty at North Woolwich in London with my usual small band of colleagues on my 'relief', which was Metropolitan Police jargon for 'team of sharp-end officers'. Some of us were upstairs in the police station practising to one day be world snooker champion, during our refreshment break around 2am. One of our colleagues, Les, who was so short he must have worn 4 pairs of socks and shoes with those built-up heels for his police recruitment medical, phoned in from a pre-Dr Who police box, asking for the Black Maria or 'hurry-up-wagon', the smaller one, a Morris J4 van with the 'period-change' school-type bell, to be sent literally just around the corner, near the entrance to the Woolwich under-river foot tunnel. As it was a call for assistance we all piled in to the van, leaving just the Station Officer to hold the fort. There was our little Les, standing near the largest man I had ever seen at that time, a *Guinness Book of Records* contender, lying apparently 'sparko' in the recovery position on the cold pavement. It was Les's intention to arrest him and in the morning, charge him with being 'drunk and incapable.' In most cases of the sort, police would be doing the guy a big favour, because obviously while you are unconscious on the pavement, you can't get yourself safely home or even defend yourself from persons intent on robbing or otherwise harming you. In any case, the usual penalty for 'drunk and incapable' in the East and West Ham Courts in those days, was no more than that for a crown court judge these days, downloading child porn onto his PC, fined £2.00. We took hold of him, or should I say attempted to take hold of him, as without warning, he sprang to life, rapidly got to his feet and formed the malicious intention in his heart, to murder the entire night shift. It took us our whole combined effort to get him into the van, drive about one minute around the corner into the rear police station yard, and somehow, ease him into an empty cell, hold him down on the floor and en masse escape simultaneously at a pre-determined coded signal. In those days we wore full, thick material jackets with black woolly-pullovers underneath and we each lost 2-3 pounds in weight in 15 seconds, I swear it. We had left the metal observation flap open so that we could keep an eye on him, this proved to be a big mistake. Whilst we stood around attempting to re-breathe and put ourselves in the recovery position, he had shot up off the floor like greased lightning, and, with his bare hands, snapped-off the top section of the 2-inch thick bleached-pine wood privacy screen at the far end of the cell, launched himself to the cell door, thrusting his arm and substantial wooden weapon through the 'judas-hole' and whizzing it around like a helicopter tail-rotor, trying to kill us with it! What a monster, I think had he 'come-to-life' again before we went to assist Les, this lunatic could, and would have torn Les in half.

Later on we found out, via the police surgeon, that he had not taken his medication. Later on still, through our Criminal Record Office at the Yard, we found out that a couple of weeks before we had the pleasure of his company, he had thrown a huge, thick, heavy glass pub ashtray across the public bar and split open a girl's head. He had been charged with GBH with intent for that one and the poor girl had been lucky to survive it. At East Ham Court, the CID had opposed his bail due to the very serious nature of the offence, plus another couple of standard objections from the prescribed and authorised list. Presumably working on the principle 'it takes one to spot one', the lunatic magistrate had granted him conditional bail, hence his original presence on the North Woolwich cobbles, 'playing possum' that night. What a terrifying individual. Our entire night shift relief, remained on duty beyond our 0600 hours shift-finish time, to assist with processing him for court and taking his photograph and fingerprints and generally helping the CID. He had breached the conditions of his earlier bail by damaging the police cell at North Woolwich and resisting arrest etc., so 'mob-handedly', we each earnt an unexpected extra crust from the Commissioner of Police For The Metropolis, as the £5.00 overtime payment bought a bit more in those days than it does now.

This next part of the 'Wild man from Hornchurch' saga, you are just not going to believe. When his case was called, he was 'ushered' from the court cells area into the dock, by yours truly, plus my several buddies, plus 2-3 other officers who were employed full-time in the court, known as warrant officers/jailers. This time, as luck would have it, there was a no-nonsense magistrate on duty who, thank goodness, had more than a tad of common sense. He remanded 'Brian' in custody for seven days. Brian's wife was in the courtroom, supplying moral support. As soon as the penny dropped as to the import of what had just taken place, Brian vaulted over the dock surround and raced the few paces for the double doors leading into the ceramic tile floored and walled courts corridor, with the whole tribe of us trying to hang onto him, to prevent his escape. He crashed through the doors and deliberately took a flying head-first leap at the far passage wall, temporarily stunning himself in the process, lucky for us. We jumped on him to overwhelm him and half-carried and half-dragged him away from public view and harm, to the warrant office.

The senior officer present immediately sent for the police surgeon, with a message not to spare the horses. Within a few minutes, a police station-sergeant (3 stripes-and-a-crown, as *Dixon of Dock Green* wore) raced into the warrant office with a huge length of thick, heavy rope once apparently used for berthing the *Queen Mary*. What a relief for all of us as we almost mummified the prisoner within the rope coils, like an anaconda, determined not to take any more chances. When the police surgeon arrived in a ball of steam, he was carrying his Gladstone Bag and expenses claim form in one hand, and a huge hypodermic syringe as big as a fire extinguisher, in the other. Although we all knew that Brian deserved it, especially as we were all bruised and battered by this time, for the sake of his totally normal and human young wife and child, we hoped that the shot that the police doctor was administering with a shaking hand, was not a lethal injection.

We were told later that he had used a 'horse syringe', whatever that might be. The knockout-injection was fast-acting and we were soon able, the 14 of us, to carry the now rope-cocooned Brian to a 'hurry-up' van in the yard and deposit him on the floor. As the powers-that-be had been so impressed with our 'control-and-restraints' techniques and procedures to date, the 'North Woolwich Mob' plus a small team of reserves, were offered the opportunity to earn some further extra coppers towards the babys' new hats, by delivering the said prisoner to the Governor of HMP Wormwood Scrubs, together with the court committal warrant duly signed by the remanding magistrate.

All in a day's (and night's) work. I'll never know how we managed to survive the next night shift, viz: the same night and drive home safely the next morning with matchsticks in our eyes!

The sequel was that Brian turned out to be a career-criminal with convictions for everything from white-slavery to Mars bar theft from *Woolworth*, eventually receiving his comeuppance in the next Court of Quarter Sessions, thereby transferring responsibility for his future well-being from The Metropolitan Police, to HM Prison Service, Strait-Jacket Department. I kid you not, every word is true. Thank goodness, for the sake of the entire human race, that you don't get too many 'Brians' to the pound.

His full name was one I will never forget and I think his marriage lasted about three minutes after his poor, long-suffering young wife, witnessed his court corridor wall head-butting display.

In the course of researching this book, I have encountered several examples of so-called 'nutcases' still at large in the community, I suppose that I should be grateful in a way, that most of them do not sit in the court dock, but are comparatively 'safe' by sitting on the 'Bench.'

During the same era, the entire night shift was 'scrambled' and ordered to report to the Canning Town area, London E16. On arrival we saw that a huge *Missions To Seaman* accommodation block, several storeys high, was the centre of attention. The Mission building bore its name in very tall neon-lit lettering, high above the ground, which could be seen for miles and was quite close to the docks. As it got lighter, being towards the end of our night shift, we could see that what appeared to be the dead body of a man, hanging from a pointed section of a neon-lit giant letter, by his jumper. As we often did in those days, most of the police officers on scene assumed that the poor guy had been mentally ill and had attempted suicide, but been prevented by the snagging of the strong threads of his jumper. An ambulance was on scene and a fire brigade hydraulic long-reach telescopic ladder with platform was in the course of being deployed. This of course took some time to locate it precisely and stabilise it with its outriggers. Police and fire fighters could be seen at a building window, probably the one the man had climbed out of, or jumped from. It was considered too risky to attempt to recover the body through the Mission building windows, as you can imagine the horror if the corpse had been accidentally dropped and crashed to the ground from that height, there would have been local public outcry about the absence of dignity in death etc. and rightly so. By the time the hydraulic platform was almost ready to make the recovery operation, school children with and without parents, were passing by.

The scene was quite horrific as the poor man had cut his throat, I think almost from ear to ear, as well as taken a selection of tablets in a drugs overdose, in his determination to leave this world. There was no other way for the fire and rescue staff to guarantee his safety from falling, other than to fit him inside a very wide, strong leather body-belt, a rescue harness. Once this was painstakingly effected at agonisingly slow speed, so as not to drop him, he was on the end of the rescue cable bent double from the waist, in an inverted U-shape with his hands and legs as the lowest parts of his body. It was at this stage that his head was tilted back through gravity and his gaping slit-open throat was exposed for all to see. As tragedy and death-hardened police officers, even we found it to be quite gory. Would you believe that we had to turn our attention to the awestruck increasing crowds, as mothers of schoolchildren allowed their offspring to gaze upon such an awful sight, instead of shepherding them off to school at a rapid rate of knots. We had to move them all on, unescorted school kids as well. We later found out that he had not been mentally ill at all. As a merchant seaman just returned from his latest voyage, he had popped into the *Mission To Seaman* in the evening, for a bed for the night, before returning home next day. On checking-in at the Mission, he had been handed a letter which turned out to be from his girlfriend, or fiancée, a tragic 'Dear John' letter. He had obviously not prescribed to, or had never been told about the old adage, 'Whilst there is life there is hope'. As this was such a high building, the body had not been spotted until an early-morning workman had happened to glance up and caught sight of it, and reported it.

In recent years there have been other widely reported incidents where under government schemes, mental hospitals have been closed and the patients released back into the community and supposed to be dealt with and cared for locally at clinics or in the home by visiting health workers, who supply the necessary medication indoors. In one case, which received national publicity, one of these uncontrolled patients, without warning, plunged a knife or a pair of scissors deep into an eye socket, which killed a male passenger on the London underground system at Finsbury Park station, North London.

This was a case which gave me personally, great cause for concern when the matter was initially reported on the TV news. My own son works in Central London and uses that station practically every day of his working life for fast journeys to and from work, on the Victoria Line. Your immediate reaction, on hearing about such tragedies occurring at places you know your own family members use every day, is one of shock and horror, in case the victim was one of your own loved ones. There have been other serious cases you will have heard about, where ex-psychiatric patients have run amok in the streets, chopping peoples limbs off or running them through with samurai swords, or pushing them under trains without warning, just as the train thunders past. For some unknown reason, these unfortunate people are not properly risk-assessed, if at all, before being released into the strange outside world with which they may be totally unfamiliar, after possibly years of incarceration in the old-style secure psychiatric hospitals, in which they received their proper medication on a regular basis.

When such patients run amok as described, we hear of the enquiry boards' boring, repetitive findings in which the familiar, oft-used clichés, such as 'lessons-will-be-learned' are mentioned. The actual truth is that the 'lessons' are almost never 'learned', with further tragic consequences to follow in due course over time.

A serial rapist admitted to police when he was arrested, that he should never have been released from prison to commit his latest horrific sex attack. On 19th February 2004, the third victim of brutal Antony Millgate, 45, raped by him nine times over three hours, expressed horror that he may be released again. Millgate was handed two life sentences at Norwich Crown Court for raping the 30-year-old. Sentencing him, Judge Philip Curl said the minimum term to be served is nine years. It emerged in court that Millgate was given eight years for rape in 1983. He was released, but in 1989 was sentenced to 12 years for rape. He attacked his latest victim in October 2003.

The grieving husband of a mother who led two fellow hospital patients in a suicide pact, hit out at psychiatric care chiefs, at her inquest in April 2004. Anne Harris, 29, jumped 200ft from cliffs in Sidmouth, Devon, with Shaun Sheppard, 17, and Jamie Hague, 19. She was a patient at the Cedars Unit at Wonford Hospital in Exeter and joined in drink and drug abuse, the inquest heard. "She said drugs were sold through the window of the ward at night." said Michael, 39, left to bring up three young daughters on his own. The inquest could take 6 weeks.

A mental patient was held by police in April 2004 after his next-door neighbour died in a frenzied knife attack outside his home. Father-of-two Simon Breed, a 51-year-old builder, fell into the arms of his distraught wife Diane, after staggering to his front door with horrific chest wounds. It later emerged that the murder suspect, Theophilos Theophilou, was discharged from a psychiatric hospital just months ago. Friends told how the family man's home in Wood Green, North London, was attacked when a deranged neighbour battered the door with a machete, a year before the fatal assault. But the deceased victim, his wife Diane, 50, a Deputy Head Teacher, and his two sons Sam, 20 and Daniel, 18, were never told the alleged attacker had been released from a mental unit. Health chiefs are now investigating why the 34-year-old patient, who was sectioned to a secure mental hospital for five months, was released into the community without apparent supervision. Oliver Treacy, director of the Enfield Mental Health Trust, said: "I would have expected him to be under the care of either a doctor, nurse or social worker." A police spokesman said a 34-year-old man wanted in connection with Mr Breed's murder was arrested while roaming in London's Hyde Park in the early hours.

The suspect charged with the horrific murder of Detective Constable Michael Swindells, in Nottinghamshire in May 2004, is a former patient at a mental hospital. Glaister Earl Butler, 48, known locally as Earl, has spent the last few months undergoing psychiatric treatment at a Birmingham hospital and is believed to be currently on a course of medication. The Afro-Caribbean was sectioned twice under the Mental Health Act in 1999 and 2001 but was then freed under the controversial so-called 'care in the community scheme' (Which, some say, should be renamed as 'dumped in the community, try and take your medication, there's a dear!'). He lived in a run-down semi-detached home in Nechells, Birmingham. The murder of the police officer incident started when a worker who called at Butler's home,was confronted by a man who was brandishing a knife. Detective Constable Swindells was stabbed to death after chasing the man down a nearby canal towpath. The man was later arrested by police at a cemetery about four miles away from the scene of the stabbing, but only after they had used baton rounds to subdue him.

The widow of a policeman killed by a heroin addict who hoodwinked the Probation Service (which isn't hard, given the pressure the staff are under these days), said the case mocked the Government's pledge to get tough on crime. Tracy Walker spoke out as the Home Office published a report into the death of her husband, PC Ged Walker, 42, which highlighted a catalogue of blunders by probation officers.

PC Walker was killed by David Parfitt, 26, who had been freed early from jail on licence and was part of a pilot scheme that should have involved strict controls. But the report, by the then Inspector of Probation, Professor Rod Morgan, described how Parfitt failed 10 out of 19 drug tests, and dodged seven other appointments. It said overworked probation staff in Nottingham even accepted an excuse that he had been unwell because he had been taking heroin and treated him with leniency. Mr Morgan said he should have been recalled to prison in September 2002, nine days after his release and four months before PC Walker's death. Dog handler PC Walker was killed after being dragged along by a stolen taxi driven by Parfitt. He was thrown into a concrete bollard and suffered severe head injuries. Parfitt was jailed for 12 years at Birmingham Crown Court in December 2003 for manslaughter.

Mother-of-two Tracy, 42, from Nottingham, appealed to Tony Blair for an enquiry: "The report has confirmed all the things we feared, that if the probation service hadn't failed in their duty, my husband would be alive today. The system has failed me and the children, it has failed Ged and it has failed David Parfitt. The Government only masquerades as being tough on crime. This man served just 10 months. He was then released into the care of a probation system that was happy to let him continue to offend." The report said that a day after a warrant was issued for Parfitt's arrest, probation officers allowed him into their offices without telling police. They had been warned he was likely to resume 'heavy drug taking' and had the potential to cause 'serious harm'. But he was not deemed a priority offender and his assigned officer said she was satisfied if he simply turned up for drug tests.

Businesswoman June Everitt, 52 years, was crushed to death under the wheels of her Renault Megane company car, as she tried to stop a thief stealing it. She received horrific injuries when the car reversed over her, dragging her underneath for 35 feet. She had parked outside her lock-up garage near her home in Luton in July 2003, after a shopping trip. It was then that Manny Davis, 30, jumped into the car and reversed over her, causing so much injury that the pathologist's report stated that more than 100 injuries ran 'from head to foot.' Prosecution barrister Nicholas Browne, QC, told the jury at St Albans Crown Court: "This is a case of car-jacking which, within seconds, became a murder."

The prosecution alleged that Davis, who allegedly told police he was a cocaine and heroin drug addict, followed Miss Everitt to the garages to rob her and steal her car. She died in hospital hours later. The Renault Megane was found abandoned several miles away, five days later. Davis had admitted manslaughter but the jury found him guilty of murder. The jury then heard that Davis had 13 previous convictions for burglary, aggravated car theft and driving whilst disqualified, for which he had served several terms of imprisonment. In February 2000, after he had stolen £12,000 in cash and was fleeing from the scene, he crashed into a police vehicle. He dragged the police officer out from behind the wheel, attacked him and drove off. He then hit a Mercedes truck, causing the driver severe head injuries, then colliding with yet another vehicle, injuring that driver. The heroin user was jailed for three years and three months in August 2000, but released in August 2002 - 15 months early.

Detective Superintendent Nicky Dahl, who led the enquiry, said: "We are pleased justice has been seen to be done." When asked if Davis, with his criminal record and drug history was 'a tragedy waiting to happen', Mr Dahl replied: "With a mixture of drugs and the offences he previously committed, it was just a matter of time." Mr Justice Beatson sentenced Davis to life imprisonment and told him he must serve at least 18 years.

At Nottingham Crown Court on 5th April 2004, Steven Barton, 24, pleaded guilty to the murder of toddler Jade Sinclair, aged three years. He had committed this atrocious crime after being freed early from prison. (Where have we heard that before?) The evidence was that Barton kicked, punched and stamped on little Jade in an hour-long attack. He turned up the stereo to drown her screams, then waited for two hours before calling 999. He then travelled to hospital with her, claiming that Jade had fallen down the stairs.

He gave medical staff a bogus name and address and then went on the run. Barton had been released early from a three-year sentence for robbery, but broke the conditions of his licence by failing to keep in touch with his parole (probation) officer. This cruel thug had nine previous convictions, which included one for causing grievous bodily harm to a boy aged just two years. The Judge sentenced him to life imprisonment and ordered that he should serve a minimum of 16 years.

Victim Jade's mother, Natalie Logan, of Lincoln, will be sentenced later, after pleading guilty to wilful neglect of the child, in allowing the earlier attacks. The thought may spring to your mind that, in the case of such mindless cruelty by Barton, with an earlier similar conviction, a 'whole-life' tariff would be most appropriate.

On 12th July 2004, angry relatives of victims who died in the Selby rail crash horror hit out, after the driver blamed for the disaster was freed from jail early. Gary Hart, 39, served just half of a five-year sentence for the carnage which killed ten people. He fell asleep at the wheel of his Land Rover which careered down an embankment on to a main line, derailing one train into the path of another. He was driven away from prison after leaving by a back door to avoid waiting newsmen. "It's heartbreaking. Five years isn't enough for what he did." said Judith Cairncross, whose brother Raymond Robson, of Whitley Bay, Tyneside, died in the tragedy in February 2001.

Seventy people were also badly injured after Hart's vehicle crashed on the M62 in North Yorkshire. The sleep-deprived builder had spent the previous night until 3am talking on the phone to girlfriend Christine Panter, whom he met on the internet. During his trial, the prosecution claimed the father of four had enjoyed sordid cyber-sex with the woman. As Hart made a frantic 999 call, the vehicle was hit by a 117mph express carrying 102 people. It came off the lines and hit a coal train. Six passengers and four crew died. The judge, Mr Justice Mackay, described the disaster as: "the worst driving-related incident in the UK in recent years." Ms Cairncross added: "To know he is going to be out and about is heart-breaking. It brings back all our memories. Yes, he was sentenced under British justice, but it just doesn't seem fair. The fact he has never admitted he was responsible for what happened, hurts. He has shown no remorse, we're the ones serving a life sentence."

Road safety charity *Brake* led criticism of his release, saying it was appalled by the leniency of the sentence. A spokesman branded it: "an insult to the families of his victims." He added: "His tired driving caused the disaster and the deaths of 10 people. We are outraged that he is being freed after two-and-a-half years." Dai Edwards, whose daughter Janine, 24, was badly hurt, said: " It's not right. He will be able to get on with a normal life now, while all those affected by his actions continue to suffer. Ten people died because of that idiot, and it was lucky that others didn't. If he had got just a year off his sentence it would have been generous." Mr Edwards, of Monk Fryston, near Selby, saw the aftermath of the smash after his daughter called him on her mobile. He said: "The carnage was unbelievable. It was like a war scene. Imagine seeing so many people injured and knowing that some people have died. I just can't believe what's happening. It's just a bunch of do-gooders with no understanding of life in the real world who make these decisions."

Hart, who served his time in North Sea Camp prison near Boston, Lincs, applied for parole in January. The Parole Board decided that he was not a risk to the public. Hart served just 91 days for each of his victims and it has emerged he could be driving again in two years. North Sea Camp once held Lord Archer and is being investigated by the Prison Service over claims that inmates enjoy easy access to drugs and alcohol. Hart, of Strubby, Lincs, left in a white Renault people carrier, sitting in the back. Two other people, believed to be his parents, were in the front. He drove past photographers a few miles from the prison. At one point the vehicle stopped and the driver got out to argue with a photographer. The driver, thought to be Hart's father, then returned to the Renault and sped off. The car was accompanied by a film crew, who were apparently making a documentary about Hart. Initially they drove into the prison with Hart's parents but were asked to leave. Hart's wife Elaine, who split from him five months before the tragedy, had been visiting him.

Fellow prisoners claimed that Hart has been boasting about how much money his notoriety will earn him. One said: "He is very arrogant and says he's going to make a lot of money."

Law in 'shambles' as knife man freed early

Britain's criminal justice system was branded 'a shambles' after a serial burglar and sex attacker was freed five years early, to attack a 63 years old woman.

Anthony Murphy, aged 40 years, had been out of prison only a month when he broke into Georgina Blackwell's home and terrorised her with a 10 inch knife. He had been released two-thirds of the way through a 16-year jail term despite an appalling history of preying on weak, vulnerable pensioners. As a Judge jailed him for a further 12 years, it emerged that new laws which mean violent prisoners such as Murphy, can be kept inside until the end of their sentences, *will not apply retrospectively*. Under 'The Criminal Justice Act 2003', only criminals being sentenced now can receive a 'sentence of imprisonment for public protection'. So thousands of dangerous prisoners can still get early release. Luton Crown Court had heard how Murphy grabbed one of claustrophobic Georgina Blackwell's kitchen knives and locked her in a cupboard before ransacking the house at Watton-at-Stone, Herts. He made her write down the pin numbers of her bank cards. Threatening to burn her house down, he escaped with £5,500 worth of valuables but was caught after a struggle when he turned up for a meeting with his probation officer.

Jailing Murphy, Judge Findlay Baker, QC said, "You absolutely terrified that lady by the threat you posed with the knife and the threat you might burn the house down." The Court heard that during one of his attacks in 1992, he carried out a sex act on an 80 year old woman.

Fears are growing over the number of murders by mentally ill offenders. It comes as new research reveals that 'stranger killings', often by mentally unstable people, have quadrupled in the last 30 years. A mental hospital in London is already bracing itself for damaging criticism from a Government watchdog over blunders which led to two dangerous patients escaping, one of whom has now been charged with murder.

Springfield Hospital in south London, rocked by a series of scandals in recent years, was back in the spotlight again after Mar Ricketts absconded from the grounds. He had been transferred there after being found guilty of attempted murder and sent to Broadmoor. He is still on the run. Paranoid schizophrenic John Barrett, who escaped from the hospital in late August 2004, has been remanded in custody by police charged with killing former banker Denis Finnegan as he cycled through Richmond Park in south-west London. The dossier on Springfield Hospital, which is run by South West London and St Georges Mental Health NHS Trust, comes a week after changes to the draft Mental health Bill were proposed by the Government. The report is expected to insist on greater security to prevent patients escaping and closer supervision of care in the community patients. It is also expected to attack under funding and poor staffing levels. A source said: "There have been too many blunders in recent years. The area has one of the highest numbers of mental health patients in Britain and they need to be better supervised."

Ricketts, 38, was sent to Broadmoor in September 1994 after he was convicted of attempting to stab to death Mark Kemp in a random attack at a tube station. Another patient escaped from the grounds in 2002 but was recaptured shortly after. And yet another, Jason Cann, 22, accused of murdering male nurse Mamade Chattum, 34, at Springfield will stand trial in January 2005. Cann denies murdering the married father-of-two, who died from multiple injuries. Police also say a 52-year-old patient died at the hospital in February 2004 after a fellow patient set fire to his clothes. Research by Manchester University has shown that 'stranger killings' have quadrupled in the last 30 years. Researchers blame this on alcohol or drug misuse, not the 'care in the community' policy. Tarique Ghaffur, a Scotland Yard Assistant Commissioner, says dealing with offenders with serious mental health problems must be given top priority. "It's about managing risks and making sure there's closer supervision of people who may pose significant dangers to the community. If it means locking people up, then that's what has to happen. If it means tighter supervision, or surveillance, then that needs to happen. Otherwise it will lead to major public concern." He has ordered a probe into the background circumstances leading to these murders and attacks in London.

Slovakian student, Terezia Sternbergerova, 25, who was to start a university foundation course in art and design, was stabbed to death in Salford, Greater Manchester, by a 21-year-old student, who was sectioned under the Mental Health Act and is unlikely ever to face trial. Terezia's best friend Szilvia Farkas said the suspect should stand trial and is not mentally ill but 'possessed by evil'. Hungarian Szilvia said: "Her family don't feel anger, they feel sorrow. They don't understand why their daughter has been taken away from them. Terezia came to England for a better life. I was her only friend and she was my only friend. It was a really deep friendship. She was my only family. She came from a very small village, very simple people.

We agreed to take precautions, like not to take our purses out with us when we went out and if someone wanted a mobile we would just give it them. We tried to do everything to protect ourselves, but in the end it didn't help Terezia."

Detectives are still hunting the killer of French student Amelie Delagrange, 22, who was killed while walking home across Twickenham Green. They feel there are possible links between her murder and similar attacks in the area, including the killing of 19-year-old gap-year student Marsha McDonnell in Hampton, Middlesex, in February 2004. Police believe the killer is a psychopath, not necessarily someone who has been medically treated, who meticulously plans the attacks. Commander Andy Baker, head of the Metropolitan Police's murder investigations, said: "Of the 40 murders every year linked with mentally-ill people, 20 of them occur in London and represent 10-per-cent of the 200 killings in the capital every year." Only a few of the 20 are high profile cases like that of the Camden Ripper Anthony Hardy.

Hardy, 54, who had been in and out of mental institutions, murdered three women in 2003, including Elizabeth Valad, whose body parts were found in a rubbish bin. He had been released from hospital without surveillance. Jonathan Zito's murder shocked the capital when he was stabbed and killed by Christopher Clunis, a psychiatric patient, on a Tube station platform in 1992. To prevent similar tragedies Commander Baker set up a mental illness working group to unite health professionals and police to share information. Commander Baker stressed: "People with mental health issues are more likely to be victims than perpetrators of crime." His team is also targeting stranger attacks on lone women after the murders of Marsha McDonnell, and Margaret Muller, attacked in Hackney, East London, whose killer is still at large, and Finnish student Suvi Aronen who was killed in 2003 by a loner with a severe personality disorder.

Analysts are conducting psychological interviews with murderers to identify certain patterns of behaviour and hope this will help them better identify, assess and manage potentially dangerous offenders. Under current laws, psychiatrists can only order the compulsory treatment or detention of people with personality disorders if they believe they can provide treatment to relieve their symptoms, referred to as the 'treatability test', but in the future under new Mental Health draft proposals, doctors can make patients have treatment if agreed by an expert tribunal. However, if treatment could not be justified in this way, because the patient was deemed a danger to others, the case would be referred to another agency such as the police. Michael Howlett of the Zito Trust, which campaigns for improvement in the provision of community care for the mentally ill, said: "We're not terribly excited about new legislation, because it is what happens on the ground that is the most important. There just aren't enough resources. We need more people out there visiting patients in their homes and making sure they're OK, making sure they're getting the support they need. The problem is that the more ill people become, the more psychotic they get and the more untreatable they get."

Police have issued an urgent warning about a convicted sex offender Smzil Verleger, 56, who escaped from another mental hospital, the Maudsley Hospital in Camberwell, south London, wearing just his pyjamas. Scotland Yard detective inspector Bryan Davidson, said: " We are worried that, without medication, Mr Verleger may be a danger to the public, particularly women."

On 23rd September 2004 a man was charged with four murders and two attempted killings at a special court hearing held in his cell. Daniel Gonzalez, 24, whose right eye and jaw were red and swollen, lay on his back on the floor with his cuffed hands on his lap, surrounded by three police officers and two prison guards. The extraordinary hearing at London's Highbury Corner magistrates court was held in the cells for security reasons. It began when District Judge Dorothy Quick formally asked the prostrate defendant: "You are Daniel Gonzalez, born on June 21st 1980, and living at Southwood Avenue in Woking, Surrey?" Gonzalez, dressed in a white jumper and grey jogging pants, lying with his feet pointing to the door, made no reply. A police officer sat on the bench next to him and two more stood outside the door. The judge stood in the doorway and told Gonzalez he faced the new charges which were read out. Standing a few feet outside the cell door, the District Judge added: "These are matters that can only be dealt with in a crown court and you will be sent to the Central Criminal Court to face these matters." After Gonzalez had made an unintelligible sound his solicitor Mr Ian Wilkinson moved into the cell. He said there was no application for bail. At the end of the hearing, which lasted only a few minutes, the judge said: "You will be remanded in custody until September 30th, that is all." The cell door was then shut.

He is accused of four killings within a 48-hour period between Wednesday afternoon and Friday morning the previous week. Gonzalez is charged with the murders of Marie Harding, 73, who was found the previous week near her home in Brighton. Mrs Harding, who was married and had two teenaged grandchildren, was a ticket seller for Brighton and Hove Albion Football Club, had her throat cut. Officials at the club described her as 'a lovely, lively woman'. He is also accused of stabbing to death retired paediatrician Derek Robinson, 76, and his wife Jean, 68, at their home in Highgate, north London. He is further charged with killing pub landlord Kevin Molloy, 46, in Tottenham on the same day. Apart from the four murder charges, Gonzalez is accused of the attempted murder of Peter King, 61, in Portsmouth on the Wednesday of the previous week, and the attempted murder of Koumis Constantino, in Hornsey, north London, two days later. He is also charged with burglary at Mr Constantino's address with the intent to commit grievous bodily harm. Gonzalez's lawyer, Mr Wilkinson, made no application for bail and the defendant was remanded in custody until he will appear at the Old Bailey.

Jobless Gonzalez was arrested in the Kings Cross area of north London following the discovery of the blood-soaked bodies of Dr Robinson and his wife on Highgate's exclusive Holly Lodge estate. Just three hours before, Irish-born publican, Mr Molloy, who had run the Rose and Crown pub in Tottenham for nine years until November 2003, was found dead with his throat cut. By late Friday, Metropolitan Police murder squad detectives were liaising with colleagues from Sussex over the death of Mrs Harding. Her body had been found on a lonely footpath near her home in Highdown, West

Sussex, by a dog walker on Wednesday. Senior detectives from the Metropolitan Police also spoke with fellow officers dealing with the incidents involving Mr Constantino in London and Mr King in Hampshire. Special court hearings in the cells are rare. They are normally held for security reasons or because a defendant simply refuses to co-operate with the court and go up to the dock. The court is assembled in the normal way with a District Judge presiding, aided by his or her clerk. Defendants are represented by either a barrister or a solicitor with a lawyer from the Crown Prosecution Service. Apart from police or prison staff, the press is also allowed to attend to report on the proceedings. A legal expert said: "It can be a bit of a squeeze, but in the interests of safety and justice, special arrangements just have to be made."

Errors by social workers allowed a paranoid schizophrenic out on the streets to commit murder, an official report revealed. Paul Khan stabbed grandfather Brian Dodd, 72, to death in a frenzied, motiveless attack. The killer had been branded a danger to the public seven years earlier and committed to a secure hospital unit after slashing the throat of a stranger. He was held there for only four years before experts decided he could be released back into the community.

But in March last year he stopped his medication, took his father's car from their Cardiff home and drove to Prestatyn, North Wales. There he stabbed Mr Dodd, who had driven to a beach car park near his home to walk his dogs. The retired accountant was stabbed 37 times in the neck and head. Alerts should have sounded 12 hours after Khan, 35, disappeared, but his care team failed to tell the Home Office because their boss was away, said the report ordered by Welsh Health Minister Jane Hutt. It identified a series of shortcomings by the team supervising Khan, including the failure to invoke the '12-hour missing rule' when he failed to keep a hospital outpatient appointment the day before the assault. Khan's parents contacted the community health team to say he had disappeared but were told to tell the police themselves. The team only alerted the Home Office three days later which was a 'significant system failure'.

The report said: "Although the offence had already been committed, the failure to implement the 12-hour rule resulted in a situation where Khan was effectively out of the area, without the instruction to recall him being considered or put in place." Chris Davies, director for social care and health with Cardiff Council, admitted 'a clear failure' in not informing the Home Office that Khan was missing. Sian Richards, chief executive of Cardiff Health Board, said: "We strongly highlighted where there were failures. Both Mr Khan's family and Mr Dodd's widow were pleased to see that there was recognition of the failures in the system." Michael Howard, director of the Zito Trust which campaigns for proper treatment of psychiatric patients, questioned how Khan could have been transferred from a secure unit to independent living. He said: "It is a tragedy that Brian Dodd had to lose his life for these failures to be recognized. There also appears to be a lack of training for staff in the management of conditionally discharged patients with complex mental health needs." Khan was jailed for life at Chester Crown Court following a plea of manslaughter on the grounds of diminished responsibility.

A mentally ill killer butchered his former lover as their children slept upstairs, just hours after he was sent home from hospital. The parents of twisted Craig Sexton were so worried about his state of mind they had taken him to see a doctor for treatment. But, after being assessed that afternoon, the 31-year-old was discharged and simply told to return to the unit the next day. Hours later he travelled to the home of terrified mother-of-two Lynda Lovatt who was trying to start a new life, and hacked her to death. The horrifically injured body of 29-year-old Lynda was found with multiple stab wounds in the living room of the home where she lived with her children, after finally plucking up the courage to dump Sexton following 11 years of abuse. An inquiry was promised into how the disturbed monster, who had a long history of psychiatric problems, was let out to kill.

The outraged mother of his victim declared: "It must have been obvious he should have been detained." Beryl Lovatt, who has been left to look after her grandchildren James, seven, and Amy, four, added: "He had a history of mental illness and his parents must have been desperate to take him to hospital. Why was he allowed out? That decision left a family without a daughter and two children to grow up without their mum." For months after the split Sexton bombarded his former lover with abusive text messages and phone calls, Newcastle Crown Court heard. On the afternoon of June 18 this year, Sexton's parents took him from his home in North Shields to North Tyneside General Hospital, where he was seen by a crisis assessment team. He was discharged in the early evening and told to return next day. Instead, he took a ferry across the River Tyne and made his way to Lynda's home in South Shields, where he cornered her and killed her in a frenzied attack. Sexton denied murder but his plea of guilty to manslaughter on the grounds of diminished responsibility was accepted by the prosecution after psychiatric evidence was considered. Prosecutor John Evans said clinical notes and at least two reports 'detail a history of mental illness and psychiatric intervention that included the involvement of the crisis assessment team on the day of the killing'. He added: "The doctors have satisfied themselves that at the time of the killing, the defendant was suffering from an abnormality of mind induced by disease, that abnormality, a depressive illness, occurring against the background of anxious avoidant personality disorder. The condition means that sufferers have an extreme fear of being criticised and because of that have a high level of 'social discomfort'. They also crave relationships where they are not criticised. Judge David Hodson remanded Sexton in custody until January 21, pending further psychiatric reports. Lynda's grieving mother Beryl, 57, said: "Whatever happens he should be locked away and they should throw away the key". She said the grandchildren, who were spared the horror of what went on downstairs while they slept, have nevertheless been deeply affected.

A crazed knifeman went on a rush hour rampage on 23rd December 2004, killing one man and leaving five other victims fighting for their lives. The attacker, a former psychiatric patient, drove around suburbs in north London apparently picking out his defenceless victims at random, most as they walked to work. His last victim, a 58-year-old man, who was married with children, was stabbed to death in a scrap metal yard and industrial unit just beside the North Circular Road in Edmonton. It is believed the murder victim, attacked in Advent Way under a flyover, staggered over a bridge to a factory unit and asked for help before losing consciousness. The rampage lasted for more than an hour and other victims ranged from a 30-year-old woman to a 76-year-old man.

A 30-year-old Turkish Cypriot man was finally arrested after he pulled up in his blood-spattered car outside his home in Tottenham, north London. He is said to have a history of mental problems. He was detained in the street by local unarmed officers after the registration plate of his red Hyundai saloon was reported by an off-duty policewoman who tended one of the victims. A knife was also recovered. Chief Superintendent Simon O'Brien said: "It seems the suspect was getting out of his vehicle, picking people at random, stabbing them and then getting back in his vehicle. We don't know the motivation for the attacks at this stage. "Our thoughts and prayers are with the families of the victims."

Each victim was stabbed once or twice each, usually in the back, and the attacks took place so quickly that some carried on walking thinking they had been punched. The frenzy began at 8.20am when a 33-year-old commuter was stabbed in the back as he walked to a rail station in Edmonton Green. The victim staggered 400 yards to the station to get help, leaving a trail of blood on the street. Station staff found him slumped on some steps and called emergency services. The stabbing happened outside a family medical centre in a quiet residential area five minutes walk from Edmonton Green. Thirty minutes later in Wood Green some six miles away, a 50-year-old man was stabbed repeatedly in a busy street. His condition was described as critical. The attack happened in Gladstone Avenue, just off the High Road.

In 2002 20-year-old Jonathan McMurray was knifed to death in the same road. A memorial stands on the corner of Gladstone Avenue and Pelham Road, yards from where the attack took place. Minutes later and three miles away, a 76-year old man was standing on a traffic island in the middle of the road when he was slashed by the knifeman. The victim, who was in Empire Avenue, a quiet road just off a parade of shops, was able to walk to North Middlesex hospital where he received treatment. By 9.07, and less than 100 yards away, a 30-year-old woman cyclist was found badly injured in Compton Crescent with severe stab wounds to her back. She was transferred to the London Heart Hospital for emergency surgery. She was attacked as she rode her bicycle along a footpath bordering the A10. Four minutes later, but two miles away, at 9.11am, a 49-year-old man was stabbed in the stomach and ribs outside a Shell petrol station in Ecclesbourne Gardens, Green Lanes. He was walking down the street when the attacker jumped out of his car and attacked him. He stumbled into the Select shop at the petrol station and screamed he had been stabbed.

The area is a busy high street with businesses opposite and a parade of shops. Just 200 yards away is the busy North Circular Road where the attacker made his getaway. Then at 9.27am, the 58-year-old man was stabbed to death just beside the North Circular Road in Edmonton. Chief Superintendent O'Brien said the suspect did not resist arrest, adding that he had a 'history of mental illness', thought to be paranoid schizophrenia. Hundreds of officers are working on the case and forensic science teams are at each stabbing. Yasmm Drabu, medical director at North Middlesex, said all five surviving victims had suffered potentially life-threatening stab wounds, including to the stomach and abdomen. The attacks came two days after the fatal stabbing of Turkish Cypriot shopkeeper Mahmut Fahri a mile and a half away in the Green Lanes area, as he chased a pair of thieves who stole two bottles of spirits. Police have established that the suspect in yesterday's knife rampage was not involved in that attack. Police released CCTV footage of the moments before Tuesday's attack in which one man is seen clearly wielding a knife.

On 23rd February 2005, fury erupted over a vicious pervert who brutally raped a 14-year-old schoolgirl just weeks after his early release from prison. Serial criminal Intikhab Alam, 33, was set free on parole less than five years into a nine-year term for a string of violent robberies on call girls. After just four months of freedom he locked the girl in his flat before raping her. Days later he mugged two women pensioners in street attacks. Victim support campaigners said the case highlighted the need for hardened criminals to serve the full sentence handed to them. Norman Brennan from the Victims of Crime Trust said: "The crime which this individual has committed is one of the worst you can commit. We have to ask why we keep releasing dangerous criminals early when they obviously do not learn from their sentences. They should not be allowed out on to the streets to terrorise innocent people and should serve the maximum sentence given. If we do not change the way we deal with these criminals more and more people will be at risk." Alam, from Oldham, Greater Manchester, was jailed for nine years in 1999 after a string of assaults and robberies on vice girls. After having sex with the prostitutes he produced a revolver or knife and demanded cash or jewellery. He was released on licence in September 2003 and began to prowl a Manchester red light district where he spotted the schoolgirl, who had run away from home. He persuaded the youngster to go back to his flat before locking her inside, leaving her 'trapped, frightened and exhausted', Manchester Crown Court heard. Mr Nick Clarke, prosecuting, said: "She foolishly went with him to the flat and when they arrived two sofas were put together as a makeshift bed. She thought he was going to leave her at the flat but he took his top off, apparently showing her his tattoos. She told him she was a virgin but the defendant's response was 'After I've finished with you, you won't be a virgin any more'."

The traumatised girl, who cannot be named for legal reasons, is now scared of being alone or in the dark and has undergone counselling. But she was able to lead police to Alam's flat where his DNA linked him to the attack. Days after the rape, Alam snatched a 68-year-old woman's handbag and he also mugged a 62-year-old woman. Judge Anthony Hammond sentenced Alam to 13 years after he was found guilty of rape and the two street robberies. He was also ordered to serve a further 745 days remaining from his previous jail term. In 1992 he was convicted of fracturing a stranger's skull outside a nightclub and two years later wounded a college student with a bottle.

A grieving family condemned lax treatment of dangerous mental patients, after a paranoid schizophrenic admitted stabbing a retired banker to death. John Finnegan claimed his brother Denis would still be alive if hospital chiefs had cared properly for killer John Barrett. He was backed up by mental health campaigners after the Old Bailey heard that Barrett simply strolled out of a hospital the day before the killing. Denis Finnegan, 50, was cycling through Richmond Park, in South West London, in September 2004, when he was ambushed by 41-year-old musician Barrett and stabbed to death with a kitchen knife. After the killing, Barrett was filmed by the crew of a police helicopter as he casually strolled away. Barrett, who had a history of mental health problems and violence, had voluntarily gone to Springfield Hospital, Tooting, 24 hours earlier. Prosecutor Crispin Aylett said he was admitted to a secure unit because there were no beds available in an open ward. But a consultant psychiatrist later granted Barrett an hour's leave, as long as he stayed in the hospital grounds, a decision which turned out to be 'tragically wrong'. But Barrett, whose behaviour before the stabbing had been increasingly aggressive, just walked out. He went to stay with a friend in Belsize Park, north west London, and later bought a set of kitchen knives at a branch of *B&Q*.

In the past, Barrett had been plagued by 'voices in the head' which threatened to kill him. On the day of the stabbing, the voices ordered him to kill someone else. Barrett then took a taxi across London to Richmond Park. Mr Aylett said: "In what might be described as a lucid, but chilling, process of elimination, he decided that the person he would kill would not be a woman, a child or an elderly person." Barrett had been treated at Springfield Hospital in May 2004. His condition worsened over the August Bank Holiday after he broke up with his girlfriend. He had a number of previous convictions, including one for wounding, after he stabbed two nurses and a patient at the hospital in 2002. He was detained at the hospital but released to 'care in the community' a year later.

On 25th February 2005 he denied murder but admitted manslaughter on the ground of diminished responsibility. He is detained at Broadmoor Hospital and will be sentenced later. After the hearing, John Finnegan, 47, said: "There was a failure in the care of John Barrett. Everybody involved should be ashamed of themselves. If Barrett had been looked after properly, Denis would be here today." Mr Finnegan claimed that a lack of money and a shortage of staff and beds had been to blame. Marjorie Wallace, chief executive of the charity *Sane*, said: "If the public cannot have confidence in the psychiatric services to make risk assessments and monitor those who may pose a risk to themselves or others, how can they retain their faith in the 'Care in the Community' system?"

One potential victim who had a narrow escape was rock singer Simon Fowler, 39. He was approached by Barrett in the park just before the killing. Barrett muttered 'stay lucky', then moved on. "I didn't even begin to imagine the seriousness of what I'd just encountered," Mr Fowler said yesterday. Hospital authorities are holding an internal inquiry.

A man who strangled his wife will be freed just 18 months after being jailed for six years. Her grieving mother, Pamela Spencer, attacked the justice system, saying it was 'absolutely disgusting' that Mark Aldrich will be walking the streets so soon after destroying their lives. And she vowed to fight any attempt by him to take custody of the couple's children, triplets born through IVF six years ago. Aldrich, 41, killed his wife Dilys with his bare hands three years after the couple had the triplets.

He was cleared of murder but convicted of manslaughter in October 2003 at Lewes Crown Court. But Mrs Spencer has been told he will be out before the end of the month, when time on remand and other concessions are taken into consideration. "It's all so wrong. The justice system has let me down," she said. "He did not just take my daughter's life, he ruined my life and her little sons because they do not have a mummy any more. Six years was not enough as it is and now he is going to be out again. I could almost understand if you take a life when someone is attacking you or someone bangs their head during a fight, but he strangled Dilys and that doesn't happen instantly, it takes time. It was a completely inappropriate sentence for his actions. It is wrong." Aldrich, a recruitment consultant, killed his 33-year-old wife at their home in Dartford, Kent, in March 2002. He then put the three boys into his car and fled to his parents' home before calling police.

He later told officers his wife had been threatening and abusive and claimed she had said his parents would never see the children again. He said she had threatened to take them away and he 'lost it and strangled her'. Mrs Spencer, a pensioner from Derby, said: "One of the boys always tells me how he misses his mummy. It is absolutely heart-rending. I just feel there is no justice. I think the system is a farce really and the sooner it's changed, the better for other people. It is too late for my daughter but it is very important for other people." Mrs Spencer said she will contest any attempt he may make to take custody of the children, who are staying with relatives. "I hope he will never be able to have those little boys. They have stability in their lives. We will fight to stop him taking custody. They have got security now," she added.

Prisoners will serve their jail sentences in full under tough new measures to be announced by Tory Leader Michael Howard. He will promise to bring 'honesty' back into the courts, branding current sentencing rules a charade. Mr Howard, who is placing law and order at the heart of Conservative policy for the next election, wants to end the existing system which allows criminals to serve as little as half their sentence. He will announce his initiative during a trip to Tony Blair's constituency of Sedgefield, Co. Durham.

The idea is for judges to lay down a minimum and maximum sentence, with no possibility that an offender will serve less than the minimum. Mr Howard will say: "I believe that as a society, we need to draw a clear distinction between right and wrong. People need to know that if they commit crime they will be caught and they will be punished. For first-time offenders that may mean a caution. For drug addicts, rehabilitation. But for persistent and dangerous criminals, it must mean prison. And when criminals are sentenced to prison, they should serve their sentence in full. Honesty matters. Nothing does more to undermine confidence in our criminal justice system than victims seeing offenders walk free from prison after serving just half their sentence." He will also say: "Like many people in our country, I believe that Britain is heading in the wrong direction. If we are to make the most of our potential we need to change track. We need to restore order to Britain. The decline of responsibility and the proliferation of so-called human rights have left us in a moral quagmire, unable to get a grip on rising crime and disorder. "People will face a clear choice at the next election, a Conservative government that actually gets a grip on crime and disorder, or more talk about the problem from Mr Blair."

Under the current system, prisoners jailed for less than four years are automatically released after serving just half their sentence, irrespective of whether they are a danger to the public. Those jailed for more than four years are freed after serving two-thirds of their sentence and sometimes even earlier. Under Mr Howard's system, prisoners who behave well and no longer pose a danger will be released at the end of their minimum sentence. But prisoners who misbehave or remain a danger to the public will serve their maximum sentence in full. Although the Tories are still consulting on the proposed difference between the maximum and minimum sentences, it is likely to be around 20 per cent. The system will echo the US courts where criminals serve their whole sentence. In the UK, criminals given a long sentence are usually released early and put on parole. The Tory policy will also feature in an advertisement to be published today. In it Mr Howard says: "I believe the punishment should fit the crime. Most criminals aren't stupid. They commit crime because they think they'll get away with it." He calls for more police on the streets and more prisons, and he criticises Tony Blair for downgrading punishments, such as handing out fines for shoplifters. And he continues: "Some people think punishment is a dirty word. I don't. I believe that punishment should fit the crime. I believe that criminals should serve their sentences in full. I believe prison should be a proper punishment." And he calls for the rights of law-abiding citizens to come before those of offenders.

Since Labour introduced its early release scheme, the Home Detention Curfew Scheme, more than 90,000 people have been released from prison early. More than 1,000 have reoffended and committed 3,623 crimes, including nine sexual offences, 163 burglaries, 47 robberies, and 462 other violent crimes. The Tories claim the US system is fairer on victims and sends out a stronger signal to criminals. Mr Howard, who was in favour of reforming sentencing along these lines when he was Home Secretary, has repeatedly attacked the Government for failing to tackle rising crime, despite talking tough. The proposals will require legislation to establish a framework for minimum and maximum sentences. The Tories are hoping to capitalise on widespread public concern that the criminal justice system is failing to protect the law-abiding majority.

There was a public outcry in November 2004 after the Home Office announced new powers that would allow police to hand out £80 fixed-penalty notices for retail theft up to £200, instead of arresting shoplifters and giving them a criminal record. And despite Mr Blair's pledges at the last general election, the most recent Home Office figures reveal that only one in five crimes is solved.

More than a million violent crimes go unpunished every year and the gap between the number committed and the number solved has almost doubled.

I BELIEVE THE PUNISHMENT SHOULD FIT THE CRIME

- Most criminals aren't stupid. They commit crime because they think they'll get away with it.
- They're right - all too often crime pays.
- Put more police on the streets and they'll catch more criminals.
- Build more prisons and fewer criminals will be free to commit crime.
- It's common sense. It's how I will cut crime.
- Some people think punishment is a dirty word. Mr Blair says shoplifters should get off with a fine - the same penalty you get for parking on a yellow line. I don't.
- The Liberal Democrats want to scrap automatic life sentences for murder. I don't.
- I believe the punishment should fit the crime.
- I believe that criminals should serve their sentences in full.
- I believe prison should be a proper punishment. But prison must also try and put criminals on the straight and narrow - teaching them to read and write, getting them off drugs.
- All my political life I have stood up for people who play by the rules. If I am given the opportunity to serve my country, I will ensure that at long last, their rights come first.

Hurrah! At last someone is listening. On the TV news I saw that Tory leader Michael Howard is calling for prison sentences to be served in full to make it clear that, as a society, 'we have to draw a clear distinction between right and wrong'. About time too. Who isn't sickened to see a serious offender imprisoned, only to hear the victims describe their dismay when they realise that in all probability, only half the sentence will be served?

As a JP, I've heard people complain that even though an offender received a six-month sentence, they have seen the person walking down the street three months later. No one has any faith in such a stupid system. Mr Howard also wants to see an ambitious prison-building programme with 20,000 new places created by 2010. The anti prison brigade say this would be too expensive. Not necessarily, if prisons were built to be prisons and not four-star hotels they would not cost so much. The 'anti' brigade are also in favour of electronic tagging. It sounds wonderful but just because someone is tagged it doesn't mean that they can't reoffend, just that they can be located. Contrary to popular myth, tagging is also very expensive. I served as a magistrate for 26 years and know that during the second half of a sentence, an offender is let out on licence, meaning that if an offence is committed during that time the offender should automatically serve the balance of that sentence. I also know only too well that this is not always carried out. You only have to look at the catalogue of offences committed by prolific offenders and study the gaps when they were free to commit offences.

I only hope that if Mr Howard's proposal is taken up, the team that writes the sentencing guidelines don't come up with recommendations to reduce sentences by half, thus defeating the object. I also hope that this will not just be an election issue for the problem of justice, or lack of it, it certainly needs addressing in the long term. Mr Howard also speaks of minimum and maximum sentencing, which has long been a concern of mine. This means that even though maximum sentences are stipulated for a range of offences, there is not a corresponding minimum sentence. I believe there should be. Recently we have heard about all the luxuries enjoyed by prisoners including access to *Sky* TV, games machines, cheap phone calls, etc.

Leicester prison said that allowing prisoners to watch *Sky* TV and so on helped discipline, because such privileges could be withdrawn for bad behaviour. It would be better if the prisoner had to show exemplary behaviour for three months before being allowed to watch *Sky* TV and then have it removed if they were badly behaved. When building new prisons, we should make the accommodation austere, with two long lines of parallel cell blocks with an exercise yard in the centre like a running lane. The prisoners could be let out into the running lane to exercise and this area could be easily supervised by officers from the security cells spaced out along the line of cells. I am sure that a building could be designed at minimum cost with none of the luxuries of Olympic-standard gyms (Yes, I've seen them) and other such frills. After all, if 'Joe Public' sets out to build a house he has to stick to his budget. He can't apply to the public purse for extra cash. Let's hope that all the politicians are looking at the justice system carefully, particularly at sentencing and enforcement of fine payments. Let's hope they have taken on board the fact that the public believes many prisons are no more than holiday camps. It's time too, that treatment for drugs offenders is made readily available in prisons. All too often at their trial, the defence claims that a drug user should not be sent to prison because he or she will not receive treatment there. Why not? It would be far more cost-effective and reassuring for the public. And after all, they would not fail to keep their clinic appointments, would they?

I well remember North Sea Camp in Lincolnshire, a young offenders' institute. It had a strict regime of working on land reclamation in the Fens (imagine that in November, when we went to visit) and education sessions in the evenings, for which they earned the privilege of watching TV. The re-offending rate of former inmates was extremely low, as they were found a place to stay on their release and help in finding work. Yes, it was a success in our eyes. And yes, it was closed.

An extra 14,000 criminals would be jailed over four years under new Tory plans announced on 8th February 2005. Tory leader Michael Howard also said Labour's early release scheme would be scrapped and convicted criminals forced to serve full sentences. Burglars and drug-dealers would face a 'three strikes' policy after which they would be hit with a set minimum jail sentence. "People who break the law must pay a price. In recent years, that clear message has become shrouded in political correctness," he said. He claimed 20,000 extra prison places would be created and average sentences would increase by 20 per cent within four years. Mr Howard also said judges would get powers to sentence offenders to a minimum and maximum sentence. Prisoners who no longer posed a threat would be released after the minimum term has been served. But Lib Dem home affairs spokesman Mark Oaten said Mr Howard was conning the public by suggesting prison works. "With over half of prisoners re-offending, creating more prisons will just create more criminals. The real tough policy is to tackle the causes of re-offending, rather than pandering to a Right-wing agenda."

COUNT 13

FAMILY-ON-FAMILY ASSAULTS
AND DOMESTIC VIOLENCE

As any serving or former police officer will tell you, Domestic Violence has played quite a major part in their working lives, probably since time immemorial. It has always been a 'GREY AREA' due mainly to the uncertainty of the situation which officers know they will encounter on arrival at the doorstep. The complainant, usually a female, but by no means always, especially these days, is likely to be in some distress, having been assaulted to some degree by the partner, who may or may not be present. If the former, it is really difficult to prevent them wanting to get their individual sides of the story told first, so the initial action is to try to separate them, ideally into totally separate rooms and out of earshot of each other.

I think most police officers would adopt my first move, which would be to interview the actual complainant, who is normally the one who arranged for the police to be called. If there are two officers present, then the scenario lends itself to each officer being able to obtain the details from the two partners, separately. Quite often injuries to some degree will be present and immediately apparent, and therefore that officer's first task would be to apply first aid and/or call for an ambulance. However it is true to say that in most cases, the woman will have been assaulted by the man, who is almost always in drink, having arrived home from the pub with the aggressiveness which the consumption of alcohol generates in many. As time spent at the venue develops, the wounded party is normally asked whether or not they wish to press charges against the other. If so, most officers would require that person to commit their story to writing in statement form, at once if possible, so the officer(s) have clear justification for any future action they may take against the other party.

However, in the heat of the moment, as most officers will tell you, just as you place hands on the aggressor who has caused the injury, with a view to removing him or her from the premises to defuse the situation, this is when it invariably gets tricky. Having realised that her partner is about to be arrested or at least taken outside to hear the other side of the story, the original victim can have a rush of blood to the head and turn on the officer(s) with the immortal words: " Take your ******* hands off my old man, what do you think you're doing? etc." They may have been hurt quite badly and are certain to have been at least verbally abused, but at the end of the day, he belongs with her and she suddenly no longer requires a police presence. In fact the police may be sent packing with quite strong language ringing in their ears, from the actual victim! Now the 'grey area' has become very apparent, so police withdraw.

Well that's how most of my cases turned out anyway! It's a no-win situation for the police. However it seems that all of that is about to change. The Government recently declared in mid-2004 that plans are afoot to put new measures in place. These appear to indicate that police powers will be extended so that prosecutions will be accepted in the courts, with or without the consent of the injured party. Most patrol cars have a *Polaroid* camera in their road kit these days, for obtaining an accurate record of the injuries soon after they were inflicted. However bruising itself takes several days to manifest itself in the most photogenic way for Court evidential purposes. Therefore, subject to the victim's consent, several days later, once all of the bruising is at its most graphic and colourful, additional photographs may be taken at home or at the police station. Furthermore, there is the later option to obtain medical documentary and possibly oral evidence of condition, general well-being and injuries sustained, from the GP or the casualty officer at the local 'A and E' department of the hospital.

I think that just about sums it all up. Most domestic violence issues follow roughly the same pattern, only the degree of violence or verbal abuse differs. Additionally, there are all sorts of varying family members, who find the need or compulsion to injure others within the close family unit or extended family, ranging from a simple 'clip round the ear' from father to son, right through to major and even fatal injuries, as we shall see.

In this next real-life scenario, there was a father-on-schoolgirl daughter series of assaults. Later, the wicked father arranged for a non-family-member 'hit-man', a career criminal, to carry out a most vicious assault on his daughter's boyfriend, a lad of roughly the same age. Due to the severity of this assault, both of their lives were to be changed forever.

One day when I was stationed at Ilford, Essex I was working the 'LATE' shift, till 10pm in the CID office when I answered an in-coming telephone call from a ward sister at St Andrews Hospital, Billericay, Essex, which is miles away from Ilford, and was then within the EPD (Essex Police District). I was about to find out that this Essex Hospital then specialised in plastic surgery. The reason for this telephone call was that one of her young long-term patients, an Asian boy, had returned to St Andrews for yet another plastic surgery operation on his face. The poor lad had been travelling backwards and forwards from his home near the North Circular Road, Woodford, for so long, having his face repaired, that he had almost become part of the hospital family. He was a market trader, then aged about 18-19 years, who had become a victim of very serious 'family-on-family violence, simply because he had the audacity to fall in love with a beautiful Asian girl, who was aged around 15yrs, and still at school when the attack took place. The actual attack had taken place very many months before I had actually been drafted into J division Metropolitan Police, from their 'outer K' division.

The reason for the hospital ward sister's urgent but calm call to Ilford CID was that the Asian boy, on entering the hospital, had immediately recognised another in-patient as his *assailant* from some months, if not a few years earlier. On receiving this call, I was a bit taken aback because the case meant nothing to me at the time, as I was working many miles away when the attack was launched. Thanking the ward sister for her call and promising her some swift action, I asked her to ensure that the two parties were kept very much apart from each other until police attendance. I then consulted my Detective Inspector and one or two uniformed colleagues and succeeded in tracking down a very dusty, large brown OHMS envelope, known as a 'Wanted Docket'. This envelope contained a warrant of arrest, description of the assailant, victim's contact details and other useful information, including a victim statement and a 'photo-fit' of the suspect. This was a composite picture made up from a box containing eyes, noses, hair styles, face shapes etc., prepared by a specialist police officer, using information supplied to him by victims. These photos, which were then also known as 'identikit' pictures, after the box of tricks which held the facial parts etc., were frequently shown on the old *Police 5* and similar TV programmes, the main one these days being known as *Crime Watch* of course. I then drove down to Billericay with another officer and had a face-to-face conversation with both the ward sister and the victim, whose name I will never forget but who deserves total anonymity, even after all of these years. After the victim updated us as to the reasons for his having recognised his alleged assailant, after all the elapsed time and so far away from the scene of the crime, we arrested the suspect and took him back to Ilford Police Station. Almost our first important task was to call out the Police Surgeon to examine the prisoner. The reason he had been in the hospital, according to him, was that following some sort of dispute over a woman, two men had arrived at the front door of his lodgings at Barking, Essex, armed with a knife. A struggle on his doorstep had ensued and during the course of his attempting to take the knife away from his attackers, a tendon in his hand had been severed.

He had therefore been treated at St Andrews Hospital by a plastic surgeon and in fact his hand was wrapped up in miles of bandages, lint, padding and waterproof packaging etc., so that it was at least the size of a professional football. The hand was still very sore and the prisoner was terrified of knocking the dressing, therefore he was in no position to attempt escape during the journey. This was just as well, as we only carried the regulation-size handcuffs and would have needed something like a bear-trap to secure his gammy wrist to the uninjured one. The police surgeon certified the prisoner as 'fit to be detained' and his details were entered into all of the requisite official police documents of the time, so that he could claim his 'extortionate' medical fee for turning out. On being arrested at the hospital in Essex, the prisoner had of course been told exactly why he was being arrested and was officially cautioned in accordance with what were then known as 'The Judges' Rules'. Naturally when first arrested, and almost throughout the entire journey from Billericay to Ilford, as well as in the Police Station, he continued to protest his innocence. Part of the Station Officer's task was to receive the prisoner, hear the brief details of why the prisoner had been brought there, and consider if the evidence was there, on which to detain him, or release him altogether for lack of evidence, or allow him 'Police Bail', whereby the prisoner signs a document promising to return at a later date when required and to pay HM The Queen the specified sum of money in default. After quite a late night, I returned to work the next morning and entered what you might call an impromptu 'case conference' with the Detective Inspector and his line manager, the Detective Chief Inspector. It was then considered that the original attack in the street at nearby Goodmayes, all that time ago, was of such ferocity and had caused such horrendous injuries to the victim, that I should be 'struck-off' from my normal routine duties, so as to be able to give my undivided attention to reinvestigation of the matter. Little did I realise then how long it would take until there was enough evidence to take it to court. This totally random and unexpected recognition of the offender by his victim, occurred at a really difficult time for the entire Police Service.

IDENTIFICATION of suspects by witnesses had become a national 'bone of contention'. The whole conduct of Police Identification Parades at Police stations, was being severely criticised by High Court Judges and Defence Lawyers, almost on a daily basis, with vocal assistance from most of the 'do-gooders', local and national associations and various other band-wagon-jumpers too numerous and boring to mention here, not forgetting Rentacrowd. In fact older readers might recall that, at that time, a quite young Mr Peter Hain was arrested and processed by police accused of a bank robbery or the attempt. He was eventually released with his innocence intact and years later, became a Labour MP. Until quite recently he was acting as 'Leader of the House' in Parliament, a very senior position in Government indeed. However after Mr Blair's historic third consecutive time as Prime Minister, Mr Hain was appointed Northern Ireland Secretary in the post-Election Cabinet reshuffle.

Partly due to all of the national controversy over the question of identification, the fact that my prisoner was injured and wearing a huge 'gout bandage' on his hand, plus the fact that the case was so old since the actual commission of the offence, and the victim needed to be extensively interviewed in writing, the Detective Chief Inspector delivered to me the very bad news. My prisoner would have to be released on Police Bail to a date to be fixed, pending the huge amount of investigative work that would be required to progress the case. Although I was forced to grudgingly agree to let the prime suspect, or one of them, I should say, go free, it took the pressure off, as I was free of the constraints of having to keep going back to court asking for yet another remand in custody every 7-10 days. Over the course of the next year or two, I was able to throw myself into the case, totally un-distracted by everyday mundane matters. I really got to know the victim and his wife, and carried out literally thousands of individual visits and enquiries, some large, some small, but totally time-consuming in total. Naturally, from time-to-time I was required to update my senior officers as to what stage the enquiry had reached thus-far.

This is how it all began. When I first met this young Asian boy on the night he had made his identification of his assailant, he had returned to the hospital for his 7th or 8th plastic surgery operation on his face. Naturally each such visit necessitated becoming an in-patient. When I shook hands with him, I saw that his face at the time was probably best described as 'half-destroyed'. Later I would be shown a pre-attack photograph of him and

I can assure you that he was as handsome as his young wife was beautiful. He had met her whilst she was at school and he was just a few years older than her. Her father worked at a *chemicals* manufacturing plant at Stratford, east London, E15. Both families were Sikhs, although not too orthodox, as turbans were not worn much. Her father attended the Sikh Temple, at Barking, Essex and apparently was quite well respected there, and may have held some sort of hold over Asian people who attended there.

After all these years I can't remember if the boy and girl actually met through attendance at the same school or not. They were drawn to each other and held secret meetings where possible, as once her father found out who her boyfriend was, he raised a huge barrier. One theory was that oft-used one, he felt or knew that the boy was of a *lower caste* than he and his family. Having banned her from seeing her boyfriend, he got word that they were *still* seeing each other and he assaulted his young daughter with a broomstick on more than one occasion, because of this.

Eventually, as soon as she came of age, the inevitable happened, they ran away together to get married, their intention being to elope to Gretna Green for a romantic 'anvil' marriage. Both of them had friends and relations in the Leicester area and whilst en route to Scotland, the young lovers got wind of the fact that her father had sent some unpleasant people after them, therefore they were forced to change their plans and got married elsewhere. Her father was absolutely furious, possibly mainly because he felt he had lost face at the Barking Sikh Temple. He may have felt that other worshippers were secretly laughing at him behind their hands. He found it impossible to even consider forgiveness. This was in spite of the fact that the now-married, in a civil ceremony, young couple, had arranged for their recent wedding to be properly 'blessed' or the Sikh equivalent of 'consecrated' at Barking Temple.

He may have taken this as the last straw, even though the young couple had arranged the Sikh ceremony, partly as a peace offering. I believe the girl was just over the age of 16years when the couple wed. Her father was exceedingly angry and made regular threats, even though his wife acted as the peace mediator and was still in regular contact with her daughter.

One dark, damp, misty, very early November morning in 1974, the Asian boy inserted his ignition key in the driver's door of his car, parked in the street at Goodmayes, Essex, where it had been left overnight. He felt a tap on the shoulder and naturally turned round to see who it was, probably expecting it to be a friend. As he turned, a liquid was thrown into his face and as he described to me later: "the image of my attacker's face was BURNT into my brain for ever!"

He fell to the pavement clawing at his face as a seriously strong corrosive liquid burnt into the flesh of his face, chest and at least one of his hands. In fact he was temporarily blinded in one eye, but eventually the sight returned. At the scene, lying unbroken on the pavement, cushioned by the early morning newspaper it had been wrapped in for cover, was a small 'Nescorey' coffee brown glass jar. The victim was rushed to hospital but quite some time was lost, as accident and emergency staff had no way of working out exactly what had been used in the attack. As luck would have it, somehow in all the excitement at the roadside, an unknown local hero took possession of the lid-less coffee jar and its newspaper wrapping and handed it to police. Miraculously, a very small amount of noxious liquid remained in the glass container and the jar was rushed to the hospital to assist casualty staff with liquid identification.

The small residue was later sent to a Metropolitan Police Forensic Science Laboratory where it was scientifically analysed and found to be *a 98per cent concentrated solution of sulphuric acid*. In other words, so strong that there were only 2 parts of water in a 100, the other 98 parts were full, concentrated, lethal corrosive acid. By comparison, from its plastic container label markings, my thick, household bleach at home, appears to be just a 5 per cent concentration. Initially there were medical fears that the corrosive burns to the body were so intensive, they were considered to be life-threatening, due to severe loss of bodily fluids experienced in such traumas. In hospital, he was guarded night and day by police until he had been nursed back to comparatively good health. He became virtually a walking miracle. Within 3 days of the attack, he forced himself to supply a long and very detailed written statement to police. Amazingly enough, for a human being who had been temporarily blinded, not only could he produce a very detailed description of the assailant, but was also able to assist a specialist New Scotland Yard police officer in creation of an 'identikit' or 'photo fit' picture. These were reproduced in large quantities and swiftly distributed around the Metropolitan Police District as well as to Police Forces in adjoining areas. Due to the sheer severity of this attack, it is to my certain knowledge that when notice boards inside police stations and those outside, were regularly 'weeded' of very old 'WANTED' posters etc., those of the 'acid attacker' were destined to long remain.

This was the description which the brave young victim supplied to police: Male, aged about 30-35yrs. Very thin, gaunt, drawn and pale face, almost skull-like. 6 feet 4 inches in height, viz: *exceptionally* tall, head & shoulders above most other males. Very slim indeed, like a 'beanpole'. Woollen, knitted 'bobble' hat - but without a 'bobble'. Black or navy blue, heavy duffel coat with shiny 'vinyl' patches around shoulders and across the back. Huge, tall, *Dr Martin* boots with multi-lace holes for very long laces, (fairly unfashionable now), similar designs worn by the modern Army, 'Goths' and 'Punks'.

Those were the main characteristics, there may have been one or two additional features, such as hair colour, although hardly any hair, if any, would have been showing from under the woollen knitted hat, similar to a so-called 'celeb' Liam Gallagher modern 'beanie' hat!

Due to the well-above-average height of the suspect, one of my very first jobs was to fill in a police-issue descriptive form as fully as possible, which I forwarded to the Criminal Record Office at New Scotland Yard, with the identikit composite attached. From day one, I really thought we had good chances of making an early identification. How many men do you know who are 6 feet 4 inches in height or thereabouts? Certain Criminal Record Office (CRO) files of suspects fitting the general description I had described, were sent out to me on J division and a longish process of elimination had to take place.

As you can well imagine, we re-issued the identikit picture both publicly and through recirculation around police stations, accompanied by updating material, in the vain hope that someone had seen someone like the man described. Police had always worked on the supposition that the girl's father, being a coward at heart, had paid for a 'hit-man' to do the evil deed for him. He had been interviewed at length at Ilford police station on the very day of the original attack and accommodated overnight. He was interrogated for many hours but gave absolutely nothing away at that time, so he had to be released without charge, for lack of evidence. I should add that he was also re-interviewed the very next day after the hospital identification, but to no avail. There's no way Police can hold suspects on the flimsiest of evidence, even though a motive is clearly established very early on in a case. Furthermore, in relation to the coffee jar found to contain the ultra-corrosive acid, you will not have overlooked the fact that earlier on, I advised you that the young girl's father had once worked at *Berk Chemicals*, at nearby Stratford, East London. As you can imagine, there were not too many male persons living within easy reach of our police area who were as tall as I have described. I finished up with not many more than a handful of CRO files and had to visit the police intelligence collators' offices on each division, to update the material contained within the CRO files. After a while, I got really lucky and located a man still living in Barking, *just a few minutes drive from the attack scene*, living in rented ground floor accommodation. Obviously you don't just race round there and accuse him. In any case, as it turned out, I'd already met him, a slim, very tall man, skeletal facial features etc., last seen months earlier wearing a 'gout bandage', the wound having been allegedly sustained in a violent attack by others armed with a knife (A biblical quotation springs to mind, 'He who lives by the sword etc..!'). As luck would have it, in the time between the original attack being carried out in Goodmayes, and my new interest in him after the absolutely bizarre out-of-town coincidence of the identification, he had come to notice of police several times.

He had been accused by his wife, or ex-wife, of regular domestic violence. I raced round to see her in one of those huge multi-storey tower blocks in Barking, beside the A13 London to Southend road. I came away with a wealth of information in my official pocket book. From there, I tracked down a lady RMN (Registered Mental Nurse) who was still employed at Goodmayes Hospital, which specialised in mental illness. I gleaned an amazing amount of intelligence from her, as well as first class direct evidence.

After his marriage had broken down, the suspect suffered a nervous breakdown, or claimed to have, and was admitted onto this wonderfully helpful mental nurse's actual ward. There he proved to be a thorn in their side as, after his initial nervous breakdown had subsided, he was adjudged sane enough to be allowed to return back into the community. However he had become very attached to the place, was 'all-found' free of charge, with a comfortable room, and they just could not get rid of him.

In the earlier days of his temporary admission to this hospital, he had worked at Ford Motor Company at Dagenham, which was not very far from his rented flat at Barking, or the mental hospital at Goodmayes. His former nurse knew him only too well. She described to me how he went to work at Fords, Dagenham, each day, wearing his black duffle jacket with shiny rear patches, which she thought showed the remains of an employer's name, probably removed by using nail varnish. Best of all, but very unfortunately for her, she remembered that prior to leaving the hospital to set off for work, he would take 'hours' laboriously lacing up his *Dr Martin* boots! In fact, she recalled that one morning, he was very grumpy with her after she said something which upset him, whereupon he kicked her in the stomach whilst wearing those huge boots. She happened to be pregnant at the time, not the sort of patient/nurse treatment you expect, or experience very often, but one that you would not forget for a long time to come!

What a load of hard evidence this wonderful lady was able to hand me, music to my ears at that quite early stage of the investigation. She was happy enough to commit everything to paper in the form of a written statement, as had been his ex-wife.The victim and his wife were overjoyed at the way the evidence in the case was finally building up and could hardly believe their good fortune. However by that time, I was long enough in the tooth to advise them that there is 'many a slip,' etc. Amazingly enough, the victim was still working very hard as a market trader, dealing in woollens and childrens' clothing, assisted by his young wife on most days.

He had to be a really early riser as there was much travelling involved, plus the boring round of packing-unpacking-repacking-unloading again at home. About half of his face was still made of 'plastic' as he had already endured the first 7-8 skin graft operations, and the prospect of many more such operations was on the horizon. His facial hair, where flesh and skin fragments had survived the ordeal of the acid attack ordeal, un-burnt, took him hours to shave, 2-3 times per week. Like other plastic surgery patients, he was required to wear for most of every 24-hour period, a very tight, close-woven fabric mask, which pulled in the skin etc very tightly indeed, virtually 'holding it all together.'

His face was very distressing to observe, and every single day of his life he had been condemned to be (quite naturally) stared at, by children as well as adults. I really admired him for getting on with his life so bravely, to provide for his wife and young child, in the face of such awful odds. Thousands of others in the UK are both 'work shy' and 'benefit happy', in complete contrast to our young hero. His 'crime' was to fall in love with a young girl, that's all. Eventually it was time to have a case conference in London at our Prosecution Counsel's chambers at Lincolns Inn. We had re-arrested both the girl's father and the suspected assailant, but neither gave an inch during the interrogations. We had also searched their houses but found nothing at the girl's father's house, of interest. One or two items of the attacker's known clothing items were found during the search of his flat, but of course, in themselves, without the rest of the 'kit', they were quite innocuous, particularly in the eyes of naïve potential jurors at The Old Bailey. I had been able to secure a statement from Ford Motor Company, confirming that he had worked there during the time in 1974 when the attack was carried out. A security officer there also confirmed that he would have been issued with the donkey jacket just as described by the victim, with 'FORDS' or similar printed on the rear.

I had also confirmed that the girl's father had been employed at Berks Chemicals, Stratford and had actually worked in, or had easy access to, *sulphuric acid*, in the *exact concentration* used, at the time the assault was launched. However, all of this simply added up to a modicum of circumstantial evidence. It included written evidence from quite a few Asian men, who knew the father well. There was about a 50-50 split of those supporting the father and those who didn't like him for various reasons. The girl's mother was torn between loyalty to her daughter and her husband, and was obviously intimidated by him into declining to provide a written statement, or even an oral one.

Naturally I needed very full and detailed written statements from the plastic surgeon and ward sister from St Andrews Hospital, Billericay, as well as the Ilford A & E staff who had received the victim straight after the acid-attack. Not forgetting too, the police officer who created the identikit picture and the CID officer who interviewed the victim in hospital and crucially, wrote down in detail and preserved the full description of the 'hit-man'. At that time, as a police officer, if you overlooked recording immediately, word-for-word the exact description of a suspect as supplied by a victim, you were for the high jump if things went against you in the crown court.

We had even obtained a court order to inspect the father's bank accounts for the approximate times that were relevant, hoping to find an entry relating to a large cash withdrawal, for paying-off the hit man, after the wicked event. However, we drew a blank there. No such entry existed, although this did not mean that the 'contract' money had not been handed over at all. At the local Magistrates Court, the magistrates, having heard all of the evidence, decided that there was enough evidence against both men to commit them for trial in *custody* to the crown court. However the father's solicitor made a later successful bail application and the attacker was granted bail later on, after a successful 'judge-in-chambers' application. This is where a Senior Judge sits in his room with all the documents in the case in front of him, sometimes with police and defence counsel present, deciding on whether or not to over-rule the magistrates' decision in respect of the refusal of bail.

At the Central Criminal Court, (Old Bailey), the jury was sworn in, this took most of the first day, as in those days, defence counsels were allowed to object to up to about 10 potential jurors whom they didn't like the look of, or whose demeanour didn't suit their purposes. At the time, as the trial progressed, I almost grew to 'hate' the Defence Counsel, who was none other than John Mortimer, QC, the well-celebrated author of the 'Rumpole of the Bailey' books and popular extended TV series. Many untruths were aired in court, by 'back-up' witnesses on both sides. After trial days one and two, the victim's wife became extremely distressed at the way she saw the trial was going. I went to see her and her husband that evening to give victim-support and comfort, and there-and-then she declared that she would not be attending the Old Bailey any more.

As it turned out, she had made an entirely accurate prediction as to the outcome. On the final day of the trial, when the jury returned from their room to deliver their verdicts, the foreman declared 'Not Guilty' to all counts of the indictment but one. They found the girl's father 'Guilty' of assaulting her with a broomstick, occasioning her actual bodily harm

(ABH). The maximum penalty for that was and is five years imprisonment. However the judge took into account that the case was quite an old one by then, the attack having been made literally years earlier.

He also took into account the term already served in custody on remand, so he awarded a suspended sentence and a fine and costs. The victim and his wife took the jury verdicts very personally, as you can imagine, as both of their lives had been literally ruined for all time, they had not received justice, in their eyes.

Earlier on in the case, the ward sister had confided in me that many patients with serious facial disfigurements such as my young Sikh friend, requiring multi-cosmetic facial-reconstruction operations, eventually give up and can no longer bear the pain, distress, suffering, discomfort and trauma of repeated operations, and commit suicide. For me, the most tragic part of the whole case, was that for legal reasons, so as not to prejudice the jury, they were never allowed to see the identikit picture, which was such a fantastic likeness of the 'hit-man', you would think it was a real photograph. I had a copy of it in my inside pocket throughout the trial, hoping it would bring me luck.

Before the jury verdicts, I would have given anything to have the power to show the identikit picture to the jury, so they could see it 'bore the exact face' of the tall man in the dock, whom they were trying. After the case was over, the court clerk, herself a bewigged qualified barrister, told me in confidence that if both defendants had been convicted of throwing the acid in the young victim's face, the judge had intended to sentence them to 12 years apiece. This gives you an idea of how dreadful an attack even the judge thought it was! Just one of those cases where police officers have to bite their tongues, keep a stiff upper lip and pray that their next jury and judge will smile favourably on them.

This next case is that of a woman who literally burned her sleeping boyfriend to death. Thirty two-year-old mother-of-one Kerrie Hogben, from Eccles, near Maidstone, waited for her boyfriend, Matthew Thatcher, 28, to fall asleep after a drunken row. She then deliberately dropped a lighted cigarette onto his bed, after hurling a beaker of alcohol and other things on the bedding. Mr Thatcher was rescued from the couple's burning home by an Army 'green goddess' fire crew during the national fire strike in 2002 – but he died in hospital from 45 per cent burns and smoke inhalation. Rescuers told the court that their attempts to enter the bedroom had been hampered by a chest of drawers lodged behind the door, which it is thought was knocked over by Mr Thatcher in his desperate bid to escape the flames.

In a previous murder trial, which had to be abandoned for legal reasons, the court heard claims that Hogben only started a relationship with Mr

Thatcher for financial reasons, but she decided to dump him because she did not find him sexually attractive. The court heard that initially Hogben had confided in her niece, telling her it was not her fault. But when they were alone she eventually said it was her who had started the fire. She told her niece she couldn't take it anymore and didn't want to kill him, she wanted to scare him, so that he would go away and leave her alone. Prosecutor Mr Haycroft said that they had asserted that the defendant lived with the victim because it was convenient to her in terms of accommodation and finances.

Tensions in the relationship manifested through drink and on occasion, violence. Hogben admitted manslaughter just hours before a second murder trial was due to start in April 2004. The victim's parents stated that they forgave her and would pray for her. Detective Inspector Gerry Smith who investigated the horrific killing said: "This has been a very difficult case. There is no happiness today, as this enquiry centred around a good, generous man who was killed by a woman described by the judge as 'wicked and dangerous'. Judge Justice Harrison said at Maidstone Crown Court: "It was a wicked and dangerous thing to have done. One which had disastrous consequences resulting in the death of your boyfriend and having a devastating effect on his family." Hogben was jailed for seven years.

Maria, 42, met Kevin Bloomer in 1991 in the pub where she was a barmaid. She was attracted to his cheeky personality. But he showed his violent side when she was expecting their first son in 1992. She says: "I think me getting pregnant was the trigger for Kevin's violence. The first time he attacked me was when I was four months pregnant. We were in a restaurant with another couple. They had a row and her partner stormed out. I said she shouldn't stand for it. Kevin told me to shut up. Suddenly he punched me in the face across the table." It was the first of many assaults Kevin inflicted over nine years on Maria, from Lye, West Midlands. He even attacked her in the street for walking too far ahead. The final straw came when Kevin, 42, slashed mum-of-five Maria in the face with a bread knife. She had 35 stitches. He was jailed for just 13 months for GBH in December 2001.

A widow was left with permanent brain damage when her grandson attacked her with a hammer, then stole her cash. Robert Grimes, 17, battered Irene Henderson, 73, at her home in Ainsdale, Merseyside. At Liverpool Crown Court Grimes was jailed for nine years. An order preventing him from being identified was lifted by the judge on 12th March 2003.

An inquest at Cardiff heard how heart-broken father Richard Greening, 52, threw himself under a train at the spot where his 15-year-old son Ben died after being struck by a train whilst taking a short-cut home. After a week of grieving for his lost son, he apparently snapped and attacked his estranged wife Sarah, 32, with a hammer at their home in Barry, South Wales, causing her severe head injuries. He then stood on the railway track waiting for a train to hit him. The coroner recorded a verdict of accidental death on son Ben, and one of suicide in relation to Mr Greening.

A frightened wife had a premonition of her own murder, and left police a text message naming her ex-husband as the killer. Brave Julie Sheppard, 41, was terrified that her brutal husband Howard Woodin, 47, would carry out his threats to kill her. But she ensured that he would not get away with it, by storing in her mobile phone the evidence which would convict him from beyond the grave. She even warned, correctly, that he would try to claim he acted in self-defence. Julie painstakingly keyed-in her 'statement' to police which read: *"20 march 03, twice 2 day Howard threatened to knife or stab me put hand round my throat tried to push me b-wards into kitchen. Said he would say self def."*

The damning message was found by detectives who called at her home after the killing and examined her mobile phone. There they found the words which she had stored hours earlier, in case she came to any harm. Twisted Woodin attacked his ex-wife so violently he inflicted 26 wounds, *stopping halfway through to change knives when one snapped in two.* Twenty minutes before her death she called 999, but hung up when the violent bully arrived at her home. After rowing about money and the sale of the house they shared in Southsea, near Portsmouth, plumber Woodin launched the frenzied attack. Then he calmly called his solicitor and daughter before finally calling an ambulance operator, telling her that his ex-wife had attacked him and then knifed herself. At his trial he insisted Julie had attacked him first, slashing him in the neck and stomach. He said she turned the five-inch vegetable knife and ten-inch bread knife on herself and had injured herself during a struggle when he tried to disarm her.

However pathologist Dr Hugh White told the jury it was *ludicrous* to suggest Julie could have inflicted the stab wounds found on her face, neck and left shoulder, some of which were five inches deep. There were slashes on the backs of her hands, which experts suggested occurred when she had tried to defend herself from Woodin's frenzied attack. Forensic scientist Claire Galbraith told Winchester Crown Court she believed the wounds were inflicted while Julie was on the floor unable to defend herself. Police Surgeon Dr David Chilvers said Woodin's injuries were superficial and self-inflicted. Woodin had denied murder but was convicted by the jury. Jailing him for life, Judge Michael Brodrick told the killer: "You are a devious, domineering, manipulative self-centred man who is just determined to get your own way."

Detective Sergeant Dave Sackman said after the case that the murder was the most extreme case of domestic violence he had come across in his 22-year police career. He said: "If you were to punch the palm of your hand 26 times and imagine it was stab wounds, it must have been a terrifying last few moments for Mrs Sheppard." Woodin, who dressed in designer clothes and sported a Rolex watch and gold jewellery, met Julie at a singles club in late 1998. They married in February 1999. Despite divorcing in December 2001, they continued to live in the same house, as she was reluctant to sell the property while her children from a previous marriage were still at school.

A mother was stabbed to death along with her two sons because her smoking habit upset her fitness fanatic husband. Patricia Jarvis, 36, had agreed to restrict her smoking to six cigarettes a day, in a pre-nuptial agreement with husband John Jarvis, 42.

When he discovered that she had smoked one more he decided to 'fix' her habit by stabbing her and cutting out her heart with a kitchen knife, 'so she couldn't be resuscitated'. Then, realising that their sons John, 11, and Stuart, 8, had seen the attack, he killed them too. Police found Jarvis, who had tried to stab himself, in bed beside his dead wife. A bible, with a cigarette lighter on top, was open at the Book of Revelations. Prosecutor Iain Goldrein told Preston Crown Court: "The defendant was a strict disciplinarian and she (Patricia) did not smoke in front of him. But when he was working away, she smoked and, just prior to her death, there had been confrontations and arguments about this issue. The defendant was obsessed with the fact that, not only was she smoking behind his back, but that the family and friends knew of this and were lying to him about it. Jarvis found a packet of cigarettes hidden by Patricia at the hotel they ran in Blackpool, and monitored how many were missing each day." He admitted manslaughter on the grounds of diminished responsibility.

The court heard he had developed a mental illness at the age of 19 after a road crash. Their daughter Monique, 13, who had been in a bedroom at the hotel, managed to escape. She is being cared for by her grandfather, Trevor Cook. He said: "What has happened to my family is terrible. John was obsessive about smoking but no one would ever have thought it would lead to three deaths." The judge ordered him to be detained for life.

A woman shot at point-blank range by her jilted lover, has to live with 127 shotgun pellets lodged in her body. Sarah Neale, 35, a legal secretary, of Langham, Rutland, was shot just four days after former boyfriend Howard Rear, 30, a gardener, of Melton, Leics, warned she would 'die a sad, lonely woman'. Rear had refused to accept that his seven-month affair with Sarah was over. Leicester Crown Court heard that on 4th February Rear went to her home with a shotgun. Prosecution counsel Mr Ian Welch said: "As she banged on a neighbour's door, screaming for help, Rear approached her with the loaded shotgun. He told her: 'Sarah, I have to do this.' The judge jailed Rear for 12 years, after the defendant admitted attempted murder.

Invalid Michael Goodwin was usually stuck in a wheelchair. But when he learned that his estranged wife was dating another man, he summoned 'superhuman' powers to get out of his wheelchair and attack his rival with knives. Goodwin, 39, who has suffered from a debilitating spinal disease for 15 years, had taken an excessive dose of a drug prescribed for his disability, and that enabled him to carry out the attack. After finding out that his wife Susan, a financial adviser, was seeing a colleague, he managed to get out of his motorised scooter and walk into the bank office where they worked. Then he threw a large knife at the colleague, Christopher Saxalby, but it missed. Then Goodwin produced a steak knife and threw that at Mr Saxalby too, charging after him. The second knife also missed. Goodwin was eventually overpowered when security staff turned a fire extinguisher on him. Later, he attributed his ability to walk to a huge dose of benzodiazepines.

A probation officer told a Bolton Crown Court that "When people have an overdose, they have an initial spurt of energy and seem to have superhuman strength, and after that they crash." During the incident at the Cooperative Bank in Stockport, Goodwin asked his wife if her boyfriend was 'man enough'. He said he loved her, his life had been torn apart, and she was 'history'. He then told Mr Saxalby that he had gone to the bank with the intention of killing him. Since the incident, Mrs Goodwin had suffered from nightmares, locked and bolted her doors whenever she was at home, and depended on her sleeping tablets.

Goodwin's barrister told the court that he had been dependent on benzodiazepines for 15 years and these affected his mood. On the day of the attack he had taken the overdose. He said: "Dependency on these drugs made this man a brooding and morose individual. He has since stopped taking any prescribed drugs. The man his wife knew, is far removed from the happy, pleasant individual you see today. The drug should not be prescribed for more than 2-4 weeks. He has been on them for years." Goodwin, of Stockport, admitted carrying an offensive weapon, threatening to kill and causing an affray. The judge handed down a two-year rehabilitation order and an anti-social behaviour order forbidding contact with his wife or Mr Saxalby.

Tracy White, 29, was just taking her dog for a walk near her home in

Crawley, W.Sussex. When she turned into the road in which she lived, she saw her estranged husband's car speeding towards her. He was staring straight at her with a fixed expression, so she knew just what his intentions were. Just as she screamed, 'Stephen, no!' the car slammed into her and she was thrown onto the bonnet, before landing with a sickening crunch in some bushes. He had been suffering with depression and was unhappy that she was seeing another man. She was taken to hospital with severe bruising to her stomach, back and legs. Her estranged husband then locked himself in the house and called police to tell them: "I've killed my wife and I'm going to kill myself." It took about two hours to coax him into coming out and he was then arrested for attempted murder. In January 2004 at Lewes and Hove Crown Court he was sentenced to six years for dangerous driving and GBH.

Philip Stone, 34, repeatedly bludgeoned his fiancée, nurse Lisa Kilmartin, 25, with a pickaxe handle which he called his 'attitude adjuster'. He also attacked her with a crowbar, poker, hammer and knife. The monster raped her, cut off the top of one of her fingers, knocked out 3 front teeth and, when he broke her arm, refused to allow her to go to hospital for five months. Lisa has bravely waived her right to anonymity and spoken out about her ordeal, to encourage other terrified women to report domestic violence to the police. "He is pure evil, I know that I am lucky to be alive."

Lisa, who met Stone when she was 17, at first suffered 'slaps and punches', but the violence exploded into sadistic torture when they moved into their home in Wigan. If she put too much sugar in his tea or even asked him how he felt, he would beat her with the 'attitude adjuster', the name he scratched into the wooden pickaxe handle. Stone smashed her engagement ring off with the pickaxe, hurled a knife which lodged in her kneecap and tied her to the bath. She was locked in the house and often forced to stand still in a corner of a room. Lisa said the pickaxe handle was his favourite weapon. "If I did anything that he deemed showed a bad attitude, he would use it on me. When I was pouring with blood he would tie me to the bath because he said he needed to calm down."

Lisa finally called police in April 2003 after Stone assaulted her so badly, she was left with injuries which required 10 days of treatment at Wigan Royal Infirmary. She was too terrified to leave Stone because he threatened to petrol bomb her mother's house if she ever walked out. He was found guilty at Bolton Crown Court of two rapes and four cases of grievous bodily harm, as well as actual bodily harm and false imprisonment. Lisa said: "I want women to realise there is help out there for them. If my speaking out gives just one woman the courage to leave someone like this and report them, I will have helped somebody."

Detective Inspector Steve Crimmins said: "To be the victim of any kind of violence is bad enough, but when the person responsible is your partner, it can make it even harder to get help. The most important thing is that you do not suffer in silence. In this case Stone's behaviour only worsened over time, as the attacks became more frequent. I have the utmost admiration for anyone who can suffer so much and still have the strength and courage to ensure their attacker is punished. I hope that this lengthy sentence will encourage other victims to speak out and get help." The judge sentenced Stone to six life sentences, believed to be without precedent in any case of domestic violence.

A bitter row between two former lovers, over who owned a Mercedes sports car, ended in murder, a court was told. Furious Frank Wade got behind the wheel of the £12,500 vehicle and deliberately ran down Melanie Malcolm as she tried to stop him taking it. Wade, 46, was jailed for life at the Old Bailey for murdering Ms Malcolm, 49, who was also his business partner. The pair, who ran a successful shoe firm, became lovers and started living together. Ms Malcolm bought the Mercedes from the profits of selling a house. But she was banned from driving and let Wade use the vehicle. When the pair split up, arguments started about who owned it. The court heard that Wade claimed she had given him the vehicle, but Ms Malcolm insisted that, though she allowed him to drive it, the car still belonged to her.

In October 2003 Wade threw her out of his house in Kilburn, NW London, and Ms Malcolm asked a recovery company to pick up the Mercedes. Wade got wind of her plan. The prosecutor said: "The defendant arrived at the scene and wanted to drive it away. He got into the car, it was in an ordinary tree-lined street, she went to it and tried leaning on the bonnet to prevent him driving off. He stopped the car, got out and threw her away. He got back into the car and started to drive forward. She leaned across the bonnet and eventually she was in front of the car. As he accelerated, he drove right over her."

In jailing him for life, Judge Brian Barker told him: "This was loss of temper. This car was described as a gift of love, but you used it as a lethal weapon."

The husband and the father-in-law of a woman who vanished more than two years ago have appeared at Winchester Crown Court. David Gibson, 33, pounced on his wife Belinda, 32, smothering her face with a pillow, as his father Leslie Gibson, 66, held her down. With her dying breath, Mrs Gibson gasped 'I love you' to her husband. David Gibson told one of his lovers, who later went to the police, that her words had 'affected him in his task'. But he continued until she went limp. The two men later motored out to sea in an inflatable boat and are thought to have thrown the body into the sea off the Isle of Wight. It was never found. The trial had heard that before the murder, Gibson boasted she was 'fishing bait'. He had claimed she had walked out on him, and he last saw her carrying a suitcase down their road in Sholing, Southampton. The verdicts were greeted with cheers from Belinda's family. But David Gibson screamed: "I did not kill my wife. I am not taking this."

A child killer was a marked man in prison after he was locked away for the horrific murder of a nine-month-old girl. Evil Kenneth Crowston, 26, smashed little Paige Windsor's head on the floor 25 times 'like a battering ram', because she woke him up. The baby died in agony, suffering appalling injuries including brain damage and a split liver. When he feared she may be dead, Crowston even stabbed a needle into the tiny soles of her feet 20 times in a sick, desperate bid to wake her. After he pleaded guilty to Paige's murder, it emerged that Crowston was accused of disfiguring a three-year-old boy four years ago by pouring hot oil over him. He was acquitted due to insufficient evidence.

Prison sources warned inmates were 'desperate' to harm the baby killer after he was remanded to Hull prison prior to sentencing. "It is prisoners' logic that people like Crowston are the lowest of the low and need to pay," said an insider. "He will have to watch his back very carefully." Crowston and girlfriend Julie Fish, 22, were often asked to babysit for Paige. By the time of the attack in June she was spending more time at their home in Scunthorpe, East Yorks, than at the nearby house of her mother Stacey Windsor, 19. Jeremy Baker, prosecuting, told Hull Crown Court that Miss Fish left Paige with Crowston on the morning of her death to go to work. Neighbours Katie Sanderson and Mark Nottingham, who lived in the flat below Crowston, were woken at around 6am by a series of bangs. "The noise they described was of a thudding coming through the ceiling," said Mr Baker. "It was loud and it lasted for about five minutes." Crowston admitted he attacked the tot when she would not stop crying. Her injuries were consistent with her being punched, kicked, and her head slammed against the floor. After the attack, Crowston put Paige back in her pram. She was only taken to hospital after Miss Fish returned, but died in her mother's arms. Miss Windsor and Miss Fish have both admitted child neglect and will also be sentenced. Investigating officer Det. Insp. Tony Garton said: "There's no sense of victory in a case like this."

A newly-wed bride stabbed her husband to death just a week after they returned from honeymoon, a court heard. College lecturer Catherine Osliffe, 34, employed at Garth Prison, Leyland, Lancs, murdered husband

Roger, 35, after they argued over who had sent her a bunch of flowers, jurors were told. Before plunging the knife into his chest, Osliffe allegedly screamed: "We have only been together for a week and I hate you already. I hate you, I cannot stand you." Roger had tipped a water-filled vase of flowers over her as she lay in bed during a violent 5 am argument, the court heard. Osliffe then grabbed a kitchen knife from downstairs before attacking him in the bedroom, the trial was told. She then telephoned for an ambulance claiming that Roger had stabbed himself by accident, it was alleged. But the court heard how fencing contractor Roger managed to tell paramedics before he died: "Cath's done it. I was in bed. I woke up and she stabbed me."

The couple, who wed in church and had enjoyed a honeymoon cruise, were at the end of their first week together as man and wife at their semi-detached home in Whalley, Lancashire. Roger went to watch a football match on TV at a friend's home on June 5 last year and had returned home at 7pm where he argued with his new wife. Michael Shorrock QC, prosecuting, said: "Catherine was going out with her friend and they argued about what she intended to wear. Roger stayed in looking after divorcee Osliffe's five-year-old daughter Bethany, until her eldest daughter Samantha, 14, and school-friend Laura Barnes came home and they babysat. Roger then went out and met Catherine in a nightclub, where they danced and drank until 2am." Mr Shorrock said: "The Osliffes' relationship was stormy and volatile and there were frequent arguments and loss of temper. Their next-door neighbours frequently heard shouting and screaming. "Catherine had received some flowers that day from her mother and there was further dispute over who had sent them to her." Mr Shorrock said: "It would appear that during the evening they were together, there had been some friction between them, but they seemed to be getting on all right. Each of them had consumed a great deal of alcohol." During the 10-minute walk home from the club they again rowed. "An argument started between them about the flowers she had received from her mother," said Mr Shorrock. Once home, the argument continued until after 5am.

Neighbours Janet and David Enefer were awoken by screaming. The couple heard Catherine shouting through their wall: "One week and I hate you." They also heard doors banging. Roger staggered out of the bedroom where the girls saw him bleeding heavily, the court heard. Laura told police that Roger, who was also a divorcee with a six-year-old son Michael, stammered: "Look what she's done to me." Mr Shorrock told the jury: "At 5.37am, half-an-hour after the Enefers were woken up, the defendant phoned the emergency services and reported that her husband had stabbed himself." Paramedics arrived at 5.46am along with the police. Mr Shorrock said: "When they arrived the deceased was lying on the floor in the kitchen with his head resting against the door and there was blood everywhere." Unconscious Roger was taken by the ambulance crew and his wife stayed at home to explain to the police what had happened. She claimed Roger had stabbed himself in an "almighty scuffle" with her after getting the knife. Mr Shorrock said: "She was in a highly agitated state. The defendant told police her husband had stabbed himself and pointed at a knife on the work surface. "Osliffe claimed she was woken by the vase being thrown over her. She stripped the bed, before replacing the flowers on top of the TV. Roger then burst into the room brandishing the knife , shouting: "Me or you." Osliffe recalled a scuffle but could not remember how he was injured. Neighbours reported that she was screaming during the row but he had been talking calmly. She shouted, "You don't understand how much these flowers mean to me." Roger replied, " I know, I don't." Mr Shorrock told the jury, "She was enraged by what had happened. She rearranged the flowers and filled the vase. She had the opportunity to pick up the knife."

Meanwhile, her husband came round in the ambulance, and when asked why he had stabbed himself, he replied that his wife had done it. Roger died at 8.45am in hospital from a three-inch deep lung wound. The couple, who met three years ago, wed at Whalley Parish Curch on April 30. Osliffe, who wore her wedding and engagement ring in the dock at Preston Crown Court, denied murder. The trial continues.

UPDATE: The sequel to this case was that the jury cleared her of murder but found her guilty of manslaughter, on the grounds that she had been provoked. She was jailed for five years.

Nearly two years after Rikki Neave's naked body was found near his Peterborough home, his mother, Ruth stood trial for his murder and was subsequently cleared by a jury. In the third of a series of features to mark the 10th anniversary of Rikki's death, chief Reporter Neil Franklin looks back at a court case which gripped the city.

In life, Ruth Weave treated her six-year-old son Rikki worse than a dog. The little boy was seen to grovel at her feet, on one occasion pathetically crying out: "I love you mummy, I love you mummy," after she had gripped him round the throat. This was not out of the ordinary. On one occasion she was seen dangling him by his feet from a bridge, 15 ft above a river in March. In sharp contrast to the way she treated him in life, Neave showed tenderness to her son when he was dead, when it was too late to give the little boy any hope of a life filled with any love or understanding. After Rikki was found and taken to a mortuary, his mother was seen to show an 'extraordinary' interest in her son's body. She was seen touching him, stroking him, and kissing his cheek. The warped relationship between this mother and son was just one element of the Ruth Neave murder trial which gripped the people of Peterborough for four weeks, and was in turns shocking and sensational.

The trial was held at Northampton Crown Court and was presided over by High Court Judge Mr Justice Popplewell, one of the most respected judges in Britain. Neave faced a charge of murdering Rikki, which she denied. She also faced charges of cruelty to the six-year-old, and two other children, and charges of supplying a class B drug and burglary. Here are extracts from *The Evening Telegraph's* trial diary:

October 3

A packed court room fell silent as prosecution barrister James Hunt QC alleged Rikki was killed in a sacrifice by his mother, who had an interest in black magic and the occult. Mr Hunt said the six-year-old's body was found in a position which mirrored diagrams in books recovered from Neave's home. Harrowing details of the schoolboy's last moments were also revealed. He was strangled by his own clothing being pulled up and twisted around his neck, the zip on his top acting as a ligature. Rikki had not been sexually assaulted and he was allegedly murdered 'elsewhere', before being taken to the woods. The prosecution also claimed that Neave had a fascination with the minds of murderers and wrote a catalogue of manuscripts on the subject.

October 4

Jurors and Justice Popplewell visited the Welland estate, where Rikki lived and died.

October 7

Witnesses revealed disturbing details of alleged acts of cruelty against Rikki by his mother. The court heard Neave regularly assaulted her son in full view of neighbours. She was seen kicking and throwing Rikki, as well as threatening to kill him. In one incident, a witness said she saw Neave laughing as she suspended her son by his ankles 15ft above a river. The jury also heard allegations that Rikki was sent out on late-night drug runs to feed his mother's habit. A witness said Rikki would be sent out to find amphetamines, which his mother described as 'sherbet', from dealers on the Welland.

October 8

On her first day on the Welland estate, Neave claimed she was a High Priestess of the occult who dabbled in black magic, the jury heard. A next-door neighbour said Neave made the bizarre statement over a cup of tea. Details of the Neave family's contact with social workers were revealed for the first time. The jury heard Neave had pleaded with social workers to take Rikki into care and warned them he was in danger if he stayed with her. During cross examination of witnesses, defence barrister Nigel Rumfitt revealed Neave had pleaded guilty to cruelty charges in relation to her son. One witness, Shelley Dickson, broke down in tears as she recalled how Neave punished Rikki for calling her a 'slag' by squirting washing-up liquid into his mouth. A social worker said during one of her visits to Rikki's home, Neave had threatened to 'hang her son from the ceiling'.

October 9

More shocking details of Rikki's contact with social services emerged. Social worker Bryony Smith described how Neave threatened to kill her son, the day before he was reported missing. She said Neave claimed she would 'kill him' if she didn't receive help. The jury also heard Neave was spotted 'hurriedly' walking towards the area where her son's body was found on the day he went missing. Sarah Turner said she bumped into Neave as she walked along Redmile Walk, where she lived. The court was told that Rikki spent his final day alive, absent from school and roaming the streets of the Welland. At about 2am on November 29, the day Rikki was found, a thorough search was made of Neave's home in Redmile Walk by two policemen, who failed to find any evidence as to where Rikki might be.

October 10

The court heard Neave had written a novel called The Perfect Murder which she had given to a social worker. Jurors also heard how, in a conversation with Rikki's aunt soon after his death, Neave had described a way to dispose of a young body. Witness Joan Dickson, who became a close friend of Neave's after the tragedy, said Neave predicted where her son's body would be found. She said Neave made the claim before they were told that Rikki's body had already been discovered in a copse. The trial heard Neave seemed 'high' and 'excited' during a visit to see her son's body in a hospital chapel. On the first occasion, Neave made two attempts to pull back a shroud covering the youngster's body.

October 11

The court heard how Neave stayed at home while friends went out looking for her missing son. Rikki's clothes were found wrapped in the jacket he was allegedly strangled with in a wheelie bin in Willoughby Court, near where his body was found, the jury was told.

October 14

The court heard Neave confessed to killing Rikki to a woman she met in a bail hostel. Women who stayed and worked in the bail hostel said Neave was fascinated with her son's death and regularly talked about it. The jury heard a claim that Neave had paid a friend £5 to call police in a bid to implicate her estranged husband, Dean, in Rikki's death.

October 15

The court heard Rikki had begged his mother to take him away from the Welland because he hated it. The youngster blamed his bad behaviour on the estate. The jury heard that Rikki wanted his stepdad to leave him and his mother alone to live in peace. It also emerged Neave had a number of theories on Rikki's deaths, including that a woman had murdered him and taken his body to the woodland in a wheelchair.

October 16

The jury was read a letter which Neave wrote to her husband, Dean Neave, in January 1993. It said: "What can I do, kill him or kill myself? I can't seem to get Rikki to do anything. I hate him sometimes because all he does is laugh at me. I just want to kill him if I'm truthful, but I can't." In another letter read to the court, Neave said the death of her son had left a 'gaping hole' in her life.

October 17

The defence case opens. The jury heard the death of Rikki had similarities with the attack on another young boy on the Welland Estate. Barrister Nigel Rumfitt said a youngster was attacked and tied to a tree in Belvoir Way five months before Rikki died. The court also heard details of Neave's past, including her parents committing suicide in a joint pact when she was 24. She was put into care at the age of two-and-a-half.

October 18

Neave repeatedly denied killing her son during two hours in the witness box.

October 21

A video of a police interview with a 10-year-old girl was played to the court in which she reported seeing Rikki alive after he was reported missing.

October 22

The court heard that a teenager, who claimed he had killed Rikki, was seen emerging from the woodland where the youngster's body was found. Louis Butcher had told other children on the estate that he had strangled Rikki. He was arrested but never charged.

October 23

The prosecution and defence summed up their cases. Defence barrister Nigel Rumfitt QC said a sex attacker, who had still not been found, could be responsible for Rikki Neave's death. Prosecution barrister James Hunt QC told jurors to have no sympathy for Neave based on her tragic background. Mr Hunt said Neave could also be found guilty of manslaughter if they, the jury, believed she killed Rikki *accidentally*.

October 28

Mr Justice Popplewell sums up the case.

October 29

Jury sent out just after 11am to start its deliberations.

October 30

Neave was cleared of murdering Rikki. But she was jailed for seven years after admitting five charges of cruelty to Rikki and two other children, including her daughter Rebecca. Neave, who broke down after being cleared of murder, then made a direct plea to her former neighbours: "Please help me find my son's killer".

Neave was taken back to Holloway prison where she had been on remand since May 1995.

Ruth Neave indictment summary:

Count 1 Murder. Cleared.

Count 2 Cruelty to daughter Rebecca between May 18, 1986 and July 10 1992. Pleaded guilty.

Count 3 Cruelty to Rikki between March 4, 1986 and July 10,1992. Pleaded guilty.

Count 4 Cruelty to daughter Rebecca between July 10, 1992 and February 14, 1994. Pleaded guilty.

Count 5 Cruelty to Rikki between July 10, 1992 and November 29, 1994. Pleaded guilty.

Count 6 Cruelty to another child between July 10, 1992 and November 29, 1994.

Count 7 Concerned in supplying class B drug (amphetamine sulphate) between July 1992 and November 1994. Pleaded guilty.

A teenager obsessed with satanism was facing life in jail after being convicted of the 'truly evil' ritual murder of his girlfriend. Luke Mitchell, 16, who was a fan of goth rock star Marilyn Manson, was found guilty on a jury's majority verdict of killing 14-year-old Jodi Jones. Jodi was stripped, tied up and stabbed to death with all the hallmarks of a ritual killing. She went missing after going to meet her boyfriend in June 2003. Hours later, her naked and mutilated body was found close to her home. Her death bore similarities to the Black Dahlia murder of 1940s Hollywood actress Elizabeth Short.

Manson has painted graphic images depicting the US killing. During the trial, the prosecution attempted to prove that Manson's work was connected to Jodi's murder. The High Court in Edinburgh was shown a Manson DVD bought by Mitchell. It featured two girls tied together and struggling as hoods were placed over their heads. Mitchell, who was 14 when he killed Jodi, denied murdering her in woods near their homes in Dalkeith, Midlothian. But the judge, Lord Nimmo Smith, told him: "It lies beyond any skill of mine to look into the black depths of your mind. You have been convicted of a truly evil murder, one of the most appalling crimes that any of us can remember, and you will rightly be regarded as wicked."

The murder verdict was met in court with cries of 'Yes' and applause from the public gallery. Jodi's mother Judith wept when the verdict was announced. Mitchell's mother Corinne hung her head. The judge told Mitchell, who will be sentenced in three weeks' time, that he would face 'detention without limit of time'. He added: "What you did was to subject Jodi to a horrible death and one can only hope it was mercifully quick. There must, however, have been a time before she became unconscious when she knew that you, her boyfriend, whom she held in affection and trust and whom she left joyfully to meet, had turned into a fiend. She was loved by her family and you have left them bereft." Sentence was deferred for background reports and to help determine the minimum period Mitchell will have to serve before being considered for release. The trial began on November 18 2004, making it the longest single accused murder trial in Scottish legal history. The jury of five women and seven men took five hours to reach their verdict.

UPDATE: The sequel to the above murder came on 11th February 2005. Mitchell was sentenced to Life Imprisonment with a minimum tariff of 20 years to be served. Not quite the same severity of 'detention without limit of time' which Judge Lord Nimmo Smith had promised at the earlier hearing.

A devoted father killed his five-year-old daughter by throwing her off the top of a multi storey car park before jumping to his death seconds later, an inquest heard on 16th February 2005. Noel White, 39, took his daughter Shanice to the 11th floor of the car park before lifting her over the parapet wall. Diners at a nearby restaurant watched in horror as the little girl fell almost 70ft and died from multiple fractures. Her father, who had earlier been seen walking across the car park beside Beatties department store in Wolverhampton, also died from multiple injuries.

But the inquest heard that the reasons for his actions remained unclear. Coroner Richard Allen said that Mr White had been 'more withdrawn' than usual but added: "I can only conclude that something that I have not been told of had been bothering him. It must have been quite important that he intended to kill himself and his daughter, whom he was devoted to." Work colleague John O'Brien drove labourer Mr White to work on the day he died and thought he was withdrawn. On the way home Mr White, from Wolverhampton, had spoken on the phone to his partner Clare Beardsmore, Shanice's mother, and had sounded 'agitated'. Mr O'Brien said: "He said to her 'I will talk to you about it later,' and then more firmly 'I will talk to you later'."

Sergeant Ralph Howarth, who examined the scene, told the Wolverhampton inquest that the speed at which Shanice fell meant she must have been pushed. He said she also must have been carried over the car park wall. Coroner Mr Allen said: "Mr Howarth concludes that Shanice would not have achieved the speed at which she was travelling unless she had been pushed off and I agree." Mr White arrived back at the home he shared with Miss Beardsmore, his partner of eight years at 4.30pm. She said that when she left two hours later, there did not seem anything unusual about him. She told the hearing: "He was bubbly on the outside but he would never really show me how he was really feeling. "We'd made arrangements to go on holiday and even booked a hire car. That day he was fine when he came back from work and didn't appear any different from any other day." The administration assistant said Mr White had a 'strong relationship' with their daughter, adding: "He was very protective of his girl and he was very fond of her."

She wept as she was shown CCTV footage of Mr White and the little girl in the city centre car park. She said he had always been scared of heights. Witness Deborah Welsh said the pair followed her into the car park at about 6.50pm. She could hear the girl, who was sitting on her father's shoulders, chatting happily. She also heard her ask him where he was taking her.

Mr White's brother Winston, said Noel visited him two days before he died last July. "He was a bit worried, but he didn't say why," he said. "I was very surprised to see him because he was not a regular visitor. I now know that he had come to say goodbye." Recording verdicts of unlawful killing and suicide, Mr Allen said: "This was a very sad inquest to preside over."

A distraught father described on 18th February 2005 how he watched his former partner career into a river in her car, killing herself and her two young children. Kelly Toye, 23, sped off 'like a maniac' after a row with Michael Turner. Mr Turner watched heartbroken as emergency crews pulled them from the freezing water but were unable to save their lives. Fighting back the tears, he told how, minutes before the incident, he and Kelly had argued. She had come to his house with children Brandon, three, and Courtney, six, in a failed bid to get back together with him.

After the row ended, she drove her son and daughter away at 50mph along a dirt track leading towards the River Lea, between Nazeing and Broxbourne, on the Hertfordshire-Essex border. The car flipped upside down into the river and submerged. Visiting the scene, Mr Turner, 30, a breakdown recovery worker, said: "I broke up with her and she wanted to get back together. She couldn't take it when I said no. She drove off like a maniac. I drove after her but couldn't keep up." By the time he reached the river, a mile from his home in Broxbourne, Herts, it was too late. "All I could see was the back lights of the car in the water," he said. Mr Turner could only watch in horror as fire fighters battled in the river for over an hour to free his family from the wreckage. They recovered the bodies of Ms Toye, their son Brandon and her daughter Courtney from a previous relationship. Police are investigating whether Ms Toye deliberately drove into the river or whether her car spun out of control on a bend in the dirt track in icy, foggy conditions. Mr Turner, who alerted the emergency services, said: "I watched three bodies being dragged out of the water. My kid was in that car. "I'm very upset. I would have chased after her faster if I'd known what was going to happen." He later released a statement saying: "They were two children that will be dearly missed, as will their mum, by all family and friends."

A couple and their three children, thought to be relatives of the victims, laid a bunch of red roses on the towpath next to the scene. Kelly, from Harlow, Essex, drove off 20 minutes after police were called to the family row at Mr Turner's home. They arrived following reports of a dispute at about 7pm and left after dealing with it. An Essex Police spokeswoman said that Ms Toye had not been present when police arrived at Mr Turner's house to deal with the row. Minutes later police were called again, to be told a car had been driven into the freezing river.

Terri Hambrook, who lives 100 yards from where the car plunged into the water, said she saw the vehicle speed past on the narrow track. "It must have been going at about 50mph. But I didn't hear it hit the water," she said. Two doctors and a nurse from Chase Farm Hospital, Enfield, joined the rescue as fire crews cut off the doors of the submerged vehicle, which was then winched to the bank. Kelly was freed first, followed by Brandon and

Courtney. They were cut from the mangled remains and passed to paramedics, who battled in vain to revive them.

Essex County Fire spokesman Terry Povey said the difficulty in getting into the submerged car meant it took more than an hour to free Ms Toye and the children. "Our crews had wet suits and entered the water. They had a look around the car and pulled it towards the bank. Unfortunately all the doors and windows were secure. They broke one of the windows and could not reach anyone so they were forced to burst one of the doors open using cutting equipment under water. They managed to get the passenger side rear door open and reached inside for the mother. They pulled her free. We then couldn't find the children, so we had to pull the vehicle to the bank."

Murray MacGregor of Essex Ambulance Service said five crews attended the scene. He said: "They worked hard in very difficult circumstances. Despite 100 per cent effort, we could not save their lives." Courtney's grieving father, website designer Daniel Clark, from Broxbourne, said: "Courtney will be greatly missed. She was a happy child enjoying life just like any other six-year-old. She celebrated her birthday on St Valentine's Day."

A scorned sales boss who shamed his 'naked civil servant' girlfriend by bombarding her family, friends and colleagues with nude pictures of her, narrowly 'escaped jail' on 21st February 2005. Stephen Noades felt 'angry and betrayed' after Wendy Wagstaff, 39, ended their 12-year relationship. He put copies of a photograph taken on a naturist holiday in Crete on the windscreens of hundreds of cars outside her office in Telford, Shropshire. He also sent copies to friends and family. She was off work for three weeks because of her embarrassment. Noades, 50, was convicted of being involved in conduct causing harassment at an earlier hearing at Telford magistrates' court.

He was given a 120-hour community punishment order and a one-year restraining order and told not to publish any material which might cause offence. Chairman of the bench James Edgington said: "It's clear what you did caused great distress and embarrassment to Miss Wagstaff, causing her to take time off from work." But he spared Noades from jail because it was his first offence 'and the course of conduct was over a very short period'. Noades, from Telford, was also ordered to pay £364 costs. The court had heard previously that he had mounted a campaign of 'vindictive retribution'.

Miss Wagstaff, who had worked for the Inland Revenue for 18 years, told the earlier hearing that although she had gone on discreet holidays to naturist resorts, she had been embarrassed to be naked in this country. She had been 'sick to her stomach' when she saw the fliers produced by her former lover showing her naked on a Mediterranean beach. "I was in a terrible state and did not know if he was going to do anything else. I was frightened to go out and felt like a prisoner in my own home." Miss Wagstaff, also of Telford, said: "I had made my feelings clear that I no longer wanted a sexual relationship. I did not like the person he had become, but I did care for him," she said." He kept repeating 'You will hate me'. He was clearly very distressed and I was concerned about him because of his mood." Speaking after the case yesterday, Noades said he was relieved he had not been sent to jail but was thinking of appealing.

He said: "I think in life there are a lot of people who come to a point following an acrimonious break-up where they feel mentally scarred for years. I felt very angry and betrayed by what happened and I did it for closure of the relationship." Noades' solicitor John Macmillan said his client felt the end of the 'intense, true and loving' relationship was like a death.

A plumber, completely naked, chased his police officer wife down the road after suspecting her of having an affair, a court was told on 18th August 2004. Timothy Edmondson, 40, tried to catch wife Sally-Anne as they passed neighbours' homes but she sprinted on. Mrs Edmondson, 36, rang her alleged lover, colleague Sergeant Anthony Adkins, who drove to get her. Edmondson headed back to his house at Rookley, Isle of Wight, put on his clothes and then drove to Sgt Adkins' home to confront the pair. When he got there, he climbed onto the porch roof and began shouting. He tried to reach in through a window and grabbed at a curtain before other officers turned up and took him away.

Prosecutor Francis Phillips said Edmondson had become furious with his wife after returning home from an eight-hour drinking binge. He went to bed but they continued to argue. Mr Phillips said: "He grabbed her by her arms and legs and throat and started strangling her." The policewoman grabbed her clothes and fled the home. Mr Phillips continued: "Mrs Edmondson ran down the street being chased by her husband who, at this stage, did not have any clothes on at all." After his arrest the plumber was found to have 51 microgrammes of alcohol per 100 millilitres of breath. The legal driving limit is 35. Edmondson, now separated from his wife, admitted common assault, drink-driving and criminal damage. He was given two years' community rehabilitation and banned from driving for three years.

A couple were jailed for five years on Friday 13th February 2005 after killing a troubled toddler they planned to adopt, by poisoning him with salt, because he spoilt their dream of a perfect family. Childless Ian Gay and his wife Angela owned a £500,000 house, a Lotus sports car and a cabin cruiser when they took on three-year-old Christian Blewitt to fill the one void in their life. But when the blond youngster, who came from a poor home and had been taken from his natural mother amid fears of neglect, proved difficult, they decided to punish him 'in cold blood', a court heard.

Julia Macur QC, prosecuting, told a jury at Worcester Crown Court: "Christian was their bugbear, putting an end to all their dreams of a rosy future with perfect children. Gay, 37, who had stayed at home acting as a house husband, and his £200,000-a-year career wife Angela, 38, stood emotionless in the dock as they were convicted of manslaughter. The Gays, from Bromsgrove, took on Christian and his younger brother and sister, but after just one week Mrs Gay telephoned a care worker, referring to the boy as 'a brainless vegetable and a zombie'. Christian was later killed by a single overdose of salt.

The court heard that as a baby, Christian had been taken to hospital five times during his first year, suffering with a virus, chest problems, vomiting and coughing. On the day of Christian's collapse in December 2002, he complained of being thirsty, vomited, and was taken to his bedroom where he was found limp five minutes later. Gay drove the boy to hospital in his Lotus at speeds of up to 100mph and later told police he knew of no reason why Christian had excess salt in his body. But the boy died four days later.

A post mortem showed that he had also suffered 11 areas of bruising to his brain, which the prosecution claimed had been caused by him being 'thumped down' in the cot. Blood tests showed that Christian had been fed the equivalent of four teaspoonsful of salt, one-sixth of which would have immobilised him. The Gays met 18 years ago when they were students at City University in London. Mrs Gay, who had a congenital heart problem, confided to her husband on their third date that she could never have children. They married in October 1990, but split up six years later over the child issue.

But they got back together again. By the time they got the children, Mrs Gay was a consultant insurance assessor. She told adoption assessors that she could take 12 months off work without feeling the pinch. But she was back at work within 10 days, a fact which her husband hid from social services.

Gay told the jury that his wife had returned to work 'too early' and office stress had contributed to her disaffection with the children. Mr Justice Pitchers sentenced the couple to five years after they were cleared of murder, but convicted of manslaughter. He said the jury had accepted that they had given Christian the salt knowing it would harm him without realising how catastrophic it would be. He added that by returning to work after Christian was rushed to hospital, Mrs Gay had shown where 'her true priorities' lay.

Christian's mother Tracy Osik, 24, said after the case: "The fact that they only got five years for doing something so wicked is beyond words. This has ruined my life. "I always knew my children would be better off with their mother. But they were taken off my hands for reasons I don't want to go into."

Tracy's mother Susan Osik, 48, from Wednesbury, West Midlands, admitted that her daughter had been 'uncaring'. She added: "Tracy knows who the father is, but she has never told me. Three weeks after Christian was born she wasn't looking after him properly. All his clothes were wet, and he started losing a lot of weight." Mrs Gay's parents Margaret and Royston Swain, from Cradley Heath, said they were completely devastated and insisted there had been a miscarriage of justice. "This couple put their lives in the hands of these jurors and the jury had come back with the completely wrong verdict," they said. "British justice stinks." They said that their daughter had worked hard all her life and was among only a handful of women actuaries in the UK. "She was a perfect mother to the children. She is the favourite auntie of her nephews and nieces," they added.

Detective Inspector Steve Cullen said: "Christian led a brief life, and we can at least be thankful that the period he spent with his first foster parents were happy times." Angela Saganowska, executive director of Sandwell Council, whose social services team took Christian into care, said his brother and sister had now been successfully adopted together. The Gays denied murder, manslaughter and cruelty. The jury were not required to return a verdict on the final charge.

Two women are being killed by a partner every week as domestic violence soars, official figures show. There were 107 deaths in 2003, up 40 per cent on 5 years ago. The revelation comes as a report is published severely criticising probation officers for failing to deal with the problem of violent partners. Chief Inspector of Probation Andrew Bridges said he was 'seriously concerned' at the flawed approach taken by many of his staff. "The facts about the prevalence of domestic violence in society are alarming. Every minute the police receive a domestic violence-related call. Every day thousands of children witness such abuse. Every week two women are killed by a partner or ex-partner." His study found that in only one-fifth of cases, did probation officers have an adequate plan for containing violent partners. In two-thirds of cases, not enough consideration was given to the safety of victims and only 27 per cent were reassessed after an incident took place. The risk of harm to any children in the household was analysed in only 59 per cent of cases. Mr Bridges admitted: "The findings show there is much room for improvement."

The report said that when probation officers attempted to establish an abuser's history, in most cases there was a superficial discussion with the offender, that was then not cross-checked against other information, even previous probation records." The Home Office figures for murders by partners or ex-partners were given in response to a Parliamentary question by Cheryl Gillan, Tory spokesman on domestic violence. She said: "The Government has wasted a lot of time by concentrating on trying to reorganise the Probation Service, which has been really stretched, rather than allowing staff to get on with things that really matter. Domestic violence has been neglected for too long. We must raise its profile as an issue, and make sure the right risk assessments on victims are carried out." Stephen Murphy, Director General of the Probation Service said: " Whilst it is clear there is still a great deal of work to be done, the report recognises the progress of the past couple of years. We are actively working on the development of a national domestic abuse strategy." A Bill to strengthen the law on domestic violence is currently before Parliament.

One-in-six pregnant women are being beaten by their partners, a shock study has revealed. And also domestic violence is one of the biggest KILLERS of mums-to-be. Horrifying figures show 12 per cent of maternal deaths follow abuse during pregnancy. Government statistics reveal that a third of domestic abuse starts when the woman becomes pregnant. One told of a terrible catalogue of abuse which started when she was three months pregnant. Sandra Horley OBE, director of domestic violence charity *Refuge* said: "He punched her in the stomach and stubbed cigarettes on her breasts. Her baby was born prematurely with three fractured limbs." Frances Day-Stirk, of the Royal College of Midwives, who compiled the study, said: "This is an increasingly common occurrence." The 700 midwives quizzed said pregnancy was often the trigger for the abuse. A fifth of the midwives said at least one of their expectant mums was a victim of violence. Midwife Astrid Osbourne of University College London Hospitals, warned: "It makes you more likely to die, as your health is not as robust."

This article in *The Sun* was illustrated with a graphic showing a pregnant woman in her underwear holding on to her 'bulge'. The caption read: "At 18 weeks the baby started kicking – at 22 weeks, so did the father."

The Government advert warns of abuse and quotes the following 'horror facts':

1) More than a third of domestic abuse starts when women are pregnant.

2) 12 per cent of women who died during or after pregnancy reported some form of abuse during pregnancy.

3) Domestic violence in pregnancy is linked to repeated

miscarriages, severe haemorrhaging, premature labour, placenta damage, low birth weight and foetal fractures.

4) Injuries to the mother can lead to rupturing of the uterus, liver or spleen.

5) Abusers focus attacks on abdomen, breasts and genitals.

COUNT 14

FAITH LOST IN THE BRITISH CRIMINAL JUSTICE SYSTEM

The following is the recent history of a career criminal who has had his finger in a whole range of criminal pies in his young life. He was lucky enough to have a serious lottery win, £9.7 million, in November 2002. His name is Michael Carroll, he is 21 years of age and lives in the Swaffham area of Norfolk. He is of heavy build, wears a goatee beard and a 'knuckle-duster' array of jewellery - lump of solid gold something-or-other on every finger of both hands. His gold neck chain hangs low with links as big as custodial security chains. Shaven head and/or baseball cap. You can't mistake him if you happen to see him out in public, the centre finger of his right hand is permanently 'set' in the vertical position, he avoided warnings from others that he would be 'struck' like it, but he gets his kicks by being rude to those he sees 'in authority' over him. The sheer effort of holding up this centre finger on a permanent basis, weighed-down as is the digit by the sheer weight of 'bling-bling' jewellery, has caused his right arm to become as muscular and bulbous as that of *Popeye*, so there's another distinguishing feature to help you to decide to put miles between yourself and him, as quickly as possible .

RECENT DIARY DATES:

November 2002
Lottery win - £9.7 million.

2nd April 2004 (A near-miss for ALL FOOLS DAY)
Kings Lynn Magistrates Court – Fined £1,650 and banned from driving for 6 months, for driving unaccompanied as a learner driver, without L plates and insurance – just two weeks after treating himself to a £49,000 top-of-the-range BMW convertible car. Currently being treated for cocaine addiction after a conviction for possession of drugs. Discovery that burglars targeted him a few days ago while he had been staying in his uncle's modest bungalow at nearby Magdalen. A safe was stolen, containing £20,000 in £20 notes, £40,000 of his characteristic bling-bling jewellery, plus an antique watch worth £30,000. Police suspect the burglars knew he was staying away at his uncle's home and targeted him, via the unlocked back door.

5th April 2004
Reported in the national press that he had been arrested by armed police for allegedly brandishing a hand gun. No weapon was found but blank bullets were seized by police. Carroll was freed on bail. He was arrested at the £250,000 bungalow he bought for his mother in Downham Market. It was revealed that he has already been in court over 30 times in his life.

21st May 2004
Kings Lynn Magistrates Court issued a warrant for his arrest after he failed to turn up for a pre-trial hearing. He is accused of dishonestly handling (the former 'receiving') power tools worth £1,110 and attempting to handle a stolen hedge trimmer. The persistent offender, who appeared at his lottery winnings cheque presentation press conference *wearing his electronic tag*, has a history of missing court dates and appointments due to 'illness'. A sick note spared him from arrest on his 21st birthday. Currently on a 12-month drugs treatment order for possession of cannabis, cocaine and magic mushrooms. He also was charged with allowing his £350,000 villa at Swaffham to be used for the smoking of drugs. He became a cocaine addict after his wife Sandra left him, taking their daughter with her. On the very day he was supposed to be in court, his solicitor handed up the 'sick note' and made his excuses to the Bench. Meanwhile Carroll was tucking into a plate of chips and swigging from a bottle of high-strength lager, in a café a few hundred yards away from the court. A reporter asked him how he would be celebrating his 21st birthday, predictably, he snarled: "Sniffing cocaine". He swore at the reporter and then spat at his feet, before climbing into a cab with his beer can and brandishing his trade-mark one erect finger gesture in defiance.

7th July 2004

This proved to be a really special day in Norfolk and I can almost imagine church bells pealing all over the County, quite late into the evening, communal bonfires, hog-roasts, BBQ's and firework displays. No, this wasn't the start of the Royal Norfolk County Show, it was the day serial offender Carroll finally received his comeuppance. It was reported that, during the three-hour court hearing, he appeared unsteady on his feet. It was felt by those who observed him in this state, that it was not solely caused by the weight of trashy-looking jewellery hanging down in festoons, as he was also glassy-eyed. The magistrates were told that he had virtually ignored a drug treatment and testing order, so they finally ran out of patience, and sent him to where he will probably spend a major part of the rest of his life, hopefully, Norwich Prison. Carroll's cousin had begged the Bench not to imprison him, but to allow him to live with him for 14 days and make sure he completed the drug treatment order, he claimed that he had been the subject of violent threats and attacks by mysterious men wearing balaclava masks. These had left Carroll 'paranoid and frightened', making him feel too scared to leave home to attend his counselling sessions, and supply his mandatory eight urine samples per month, to prove he was 'clean' of drugs. However the Bench declined his cousin's kind offer.

Inside HMP Norwich, all of his so-called 'riches' will count for nothing. All of his trade-mark knuckleduster jewellery, gold 'mayoral chains', designer clothing, ear rings etc. will be removed from him and he will have to subsist on a tax-free small, weekly subsistence allowance, the same as everyone else. Any drugs that manage to find their way through the prison walls to him, will not have been stored in the most hygienic of areas, and he will not take kindly to having to wear uniform provided by Her Majesty, instead of his own tasteless, designer clothing. Carroll's latest jail term sees his life come full circle. Before his massive lottery win, he had served two months of a four-month jail term for criminal damage and driving while disqualified.

Shamed bar manager John Atkinson, of Ulster, scooped a £2million win in the lottery in 1996, but didn't want any publicity. A year earlier he had pleaded guilty to gross indecency after taking part in gay sex orgies at a public loo.

In 1999 Paul Clark from Possilpark, Glasgow won a £250,000 jackpot, only two days after being convicted of supplying heroin. Paul, 29, offered to buy his way out of a jail sentence by paying a substantial fine, but the judge at the High Court in Edinburgh jailed him for 15 months instead.

Reginald Tomlinson, 47, from Derbyshire, won £100,000, but hid the winnings from his wife. He blew the money on cars, a house, and a cannabis factory he set up near his home. In 2001 he was jailed for three years.

Criminal Lee Ryan, 44, had previous convictions when he hit the jackpot with a £6.5million win in 1995. He was jailed for 18 months shortly afterwards for handling stolen cars, and since then he's been arrested for drink-driving.

In August 2004, a serial rapist serving life imprisonment, was *unescorted by HMP staff* whilst away from his bail hostel. Whilst enjoying his short-lived piece of freedom, he bought himself a lottery ticket, allowed under existing HMP rules. He won the princely sum of £7million, Just in time, police rushed around to wherever he was staying and found him with a packed suitcase, apparently about to swan off to Honolulu, or wherever the greatest number of potential future rape victims are to be found around the globe. The police swiftly felt his collar and returned him to one of Her Majesty's more secure lock-ups. He was absolutely furious at his plans being thwarted. His name is Iorworth Hoare, 52, of (write to him c/o HM Prison Service, Home Office, London SW1, if you're preparing a begging letter).

   In the meantime, his former wife is 'suing him for every last penny she can get', and some of his victims are taking legal advice about suing him for damages etc. too. They couldn't do this at the time of all the offences being committed, as apparently he had no money then. Hoare had begun a series of sex attacks while in his 20's and was sentenced to a total of 18 years imprisonment, for five attacks starting in 1973. His crimes included one rape, two attempted rapes and three indecent assaults in Exeter and Leeds. He was jailed for 'life' at Leeds Crown Court after a jury convicted him of trying to rape a 60-year-old teacher. Can you believe that HM Prison Service let this dangerous man, described in court as a 'monster', out of jail in 1993 to marry a woman called Irene Harrison at Wakefield Cathedral of all places? (Did they think he was royalty or something?) Even his own brother has disowned him and hasn't seen him for 20 years. His sympathies are entirely with all of his brother's victims. The 'monster' bought his lottery ticket at a shop near his bail hostel at South Bank, Middlesbrough, where ex-Detective Superintendent (Zero Tolerance) Ray Mallon is now the Mayor. Hoare was on weekend unaccompanied release from Gloucester's Leyhill Prison, presumably conditional upon residing at the bail hostel over the weekend. Prisoners in this country are *banned* from doing the football pools and buying Premium Bonds, but the Lottery appears to have been overlooked.

The true shocking picture of Britain's youth crime epidemic was revealed in juvenile courts up and down the country. Today we shine the spotlight on two of the country's busiest courts, where hundreds of mostly young boys appear before a judge to answer serious charges.

Whereas 50 years ago, teenagers lived in fear of getting a clip round the ear from the local bobby for scrumping apples, today's youths list robbery, sexual assault, drugs and driving offences among their crimes. Shockingly, two of the youngest offenders, both aged 12, were making their first appearance at Camberwell Youth Court in south London, accused of assaulting a young girl. They are part of a growing yob crime wave sweeping Britain.

According to a recent Government report, one in four boys aged between 14 and 17 is a serious or regular offender. Unashamed, these young tearaways show no regard for the law or its processes. Far from donning their school uniforms in the hope of impressing the judge, most of the errant teenagers are dressed in the uniform of the street, tracksuit pants, trainers and a hooded top. In an average week at the busy Camberwell court, about 150 youths pass through the doors of justice. Many of their crimes are fuelled by drink.

Thursday was described as a quiet day at the court as 18 youths aged from 12 to 17 appeared before District Judge Quentin Purdy. A television blares in the waiting room where the youths sit drinking cola, many smoking cigarettes, while they wait for their cases to be called. One of the more serious involves a 16-year-old boy accused of beating up a policewoman and breaking her finger. The youngster, who had no parent with him, was alleged to be part of a gang which had verbally abused and harassed a stranger as he walked past. In a motiveless attack, he is then said to have punched the man before giving chase with another one of the yobs, when the victim fled into a nearby Burger King to escape.

Once inside they hurled chairs and stones at the man, who suffered cuts in the attack. It is claimed the boy, who has a drink problem, then launched a vicious attack on the policewoman when she arrived, punching her in the face and chest and then, when she fell to the floor, kicking her several times.

His case was adjourned until February 4 to allow time for the prosecution to gather more information and he was released on conditional bail, which requires him to sleep at home, wear an electronic tag and comply with a curfew.

At Stockport juvenile court in Greater Manchester, a 14-year-old turns to his mother, fighting back tears, as he is led away by custody officers. He is on his way to a young offenders institute again. Whether he's a teenage tearaway or a victim of circumstance or peer group pressure, this young man is about to spend the next three months locked up. On a relatively busy Friday he is just one of the youths being dealt with for anything ranging from breaching supervision orders to making threats to kill. After being given countless last chances time has run out for this youth who has deliberately missed appointments with the Youth Offenders Team, despite knowing he faces losing his liberty because of his behaviour.

Because he failed to comply with his supervision order, he has now been brought back to be sentenced for his original crime, robbery. He was one of three yobs who threatened a child and stole his mobile phone. When police turned up, the victim was warned: "Don't say anything. If you do I'm gonna bang you out." On his first appearance in court, magistrates took pity on the boy, even though he had been jailed before for robbery. His classification as a persistent young offender qualifies him for special treatment, and with his previous record he was lucky to escape a custodial sentence, but he did. The magistrates are told how, at first, he turned up to his appointments with social workers, but gradually his interest dropped off. He was placed on an Intensive Supervision and Surveillance Programme, legal jargon for last chance saloon. He was tagged but repeatedly removed it.

One youth worker said: "It's strange because a lot of these youngsters like being tagged. They ask *what colour* tags are available. It's become something of a fashion statement." Asked why he stopped attending, the boy shrugs his shoulders. The three magistrates return to deliver their sentence - six months, three of which will be served in the community.

Prosecutor Nick Smart, who specialises in juvenile cases, says that well over 50 per cent of them involve under-age drinking. "It's very common for alcohol to have played some role in the offending," he explains. Labour's answer to spiralling crime rates was revealed, simply recruit more spin doctors to insist violent Britain is under control. Recorded crime has risen by an alarming 16 per cent since 1998 to 5.9 million offences last year. Meanwhile, spending on Home Office press officers rocketed by 477 per cent to £1.9million.

Shadow Home Secretary David Davis, who uncovered the figures in a written Parliamentary answer, said: "Under Labour, gun crime has doubled, drug crime has increased, detection rates have fallen and last year there were one million violent crimes for the first time ever. Labour's only answer is to invest in spin doctors to try and conceal this." The cost of press officers at the Home Office, which recently moved to new £311million headquarters in London's Marsham Street, stands at £1.9million, compared with £329,000 in 1998/99. The cash would pay for 66 extra police officers. Recorded crime has increased from 5,109,089 incidents in 1998/99, the year Labour's crime policies started to take effect, to 5,934,580 in 2004.

The Home Office, using data from the British Crime Survey, insists the risk of being a crime victim, put at one in four of the population, was the lowest in more than 20 years. But new recorded crime statistics, offences logged by police, continue to show alarming increases. Violent crime is up six per cent, sexual offences up 22 per cent, all gun crime is up five per cent and the use of imitation firearms is up 48 per cent. Police logged a five per cent rise in firearms offences in the year to September 2004, reaching 10,670 incidents, 500 more than in the previous 12 months. There was a seven per cent rise in assaults to 268,100 offences in the third quarter, compared with 250,200 in the same period in 2003. Sexual offences rose 22 per cent to 17,000. The increase in press officer numbers, from 16 when Labour came to power, to 39, has been backed by a surge in spending on advertising. In 2003, the latest period for which figures are available, the advertising bill was £12.5million, enough to pay for 430 police officers. In 1997, the bill was £5.2million. A Home Office spokesman said: "The expansion of the Home Office press office followed an external consultant's review of its staffing. Also, the Home Office press office and the prison service press office merged in May 2001."

Tony Blair's law and order policies are failing and Labour has ignored the well-founded concerns of most people about crime, a study claims. Offending behaviour programmes such as 'thinking skills' and 'anger management courses, costing at least £2,000 each, had not cut crime, says independent think-tank *Civitas*. In 2002-3, more than 12,000 courses were completed at a cost of over £25million. An intensive supervision and surveillance programme has cost at least £45million since 2001 but 84 per cent of participants were reconvicted within a year and fewer than half of offenders completed the six-month programme. Drug treatment initiatives were also proving ineffective. *Civitas* claims Britain ignored evidence from America which found similar schemes had not reduced offending. In a further damning indictment of Labour's record, *Civitas* says robberies increased by 12 per cent in 2004, in 10 'street crime initiative areas' where the problem was targeted. There was evidence the initiative had simply 'displaced' crime to other areas. Meanwhile, the number of offenders brought to justice is still 20,000 below the original target of 1.2million by 2005-6. Mr Blair was blamed for trying to appease Labour activists, who believed criminals were victims of circumstance, and most Labour voters who thought they had done wrong and should be stopped. It had 'saddled his Government with self-contradictory policies'. Shadow Home Secretary David Davis said: "This shows Labour's promise to be tough on crime was all talk"

On 10th February 2005 Michael Howard placed restoring law and order to Britain's violent streets at the heart of the Conservative general election campaign. The Tory leader declared: "Punishment is not a dirty word". In a foreword to a crucial chapter of his party's manifesto Mr Howard said Tony

Blair's Government had allowed crime to spiral 'out of control'. He repeated pledges rolled out by the Tory high command over the past month, that there would be more jail places, 40,000 extra police, and that prisoners would serve their sentences in full.

Mr Howard then wrote: "Some people think punishment is a dirty word, I don't. Criminals need to know that if they commit crime there will be a price to pay." The Tories are publishing their manifesto one chapter at a time in a bid to wrestle the spotlight from Labour. Crime is chapter two, following an initial set of pledges to restore discipline and improve standards in the schools. The publication was backed by plans to allow the public to be able to elect US-style police commissioners in place of the current system of appointments to the post of police authority chairman. Mr Howard cited the 'zero tolerance' approach to policing by former New York Mayor Rudy Giuliani and Teesside 'Robocop' Ray Mallon as the way forward.

Speaking in Manchester, after the first shadow cabinet meeting to be held outside London, he said: "I don't just want people to feel safe in their homes, I want them to feel safe everywhere." Labour Home Secretary Charles Clarke hit back by labelling Mr Howard a 'failing leader' following a decision to order Tory MPs to abstain on a key vote on the Government's controversial Identity Card Bill. The Police Federation, representing rank-and-file police, issued a note of caution about elected police chiefs. President Jan Berry said: "Policing must remain fully accountable but independent of political control. It is a service, not a political football to be kicked around every time an election approaches. These plans could result in those with extreme political views dictating what actually happens on the ground."

A war veteran terrorised by burglars killed himself after telling his family that crime-ridden Britain was 'no longer a place I want to live'. Herbert Buckland, 84, hanged himself after being robbed three times by thugs who left him too frightened to leave his home. The tragedy came as MPs severely criticised the police for solving only one-fifth of crimes. RAF hero Mr Buckland's niece Marilyn Dowson, 55, said: "He did not want to live any more after what happened. These burglars are responsible for his death. He lost the will to live. The upsetting thing is that he fought to give us a free country but he has also given a free country to scumbags like this."

Norman Brennan, director of *Victims of Crime Trust*, added: "I ask this Government, how bad does it have to get? This tragedy should be acknowledged by the magistrates and judges who persistently and consistently fail to punish those who blight people's lives. What does it say that a war veteran who has lived a law-abiding life is pushed to the brink and beyond because of persistent burglaries? This sadly sums up the criminal justice system in this country."

Mr Buckland and his wife Barbara were too scared to leave their bungalow in Wroughton, near Swindon, Wiltshire, or even answer the door after they were twice burgled by conmen who wormed their way inside. The couple kept all their doors and windows locked but the final straw came last month when Mr Buckland came face-to-face with intruders who broke in through a bedroom window and stole cash. Mrs Dowson said her uncle told her 'the world was no longer a place he wanted to live' and three days later he was found hanging from the beam of his back door. It was a sad end for a hero who survived being shot down in the Far East during the Second World War, had his rescue boat torpedoed and escaped from shark-infested waters of the Pacific.

Mr Buckland, who was known as Joe, flew with the 20th Squadron and also served in India and Burma. A spokesman for the RAF Association said: "It is an added insult that a man who put his life on the line for his country should lose it because of criminals." Mr Buckland's brother-in-law, Harry Fitchett, 79, said the intruders had 'murdered' the pensioner. "He took his own life because of the burglary and that to me is murder," he said. No one has been caught for any of the three break-ins in a county where one in every 100 homes was burgled last year.

Wiltshire Police perform better than the national average but still only solve just over a quarter of crimes. Officers said the burglaries were 'a heinous and cowardly crime'. Detective Inspector Paul Jennings, of Swindon CID, added: "It is always tragic when someone takes their own life. The police sympathise with the family and the position they find themselves in." The Buckland couple were first targeted by a man posing as a water board official, who distracted them while an accomplice raided their house. A few months later a man knocked on the door and diverted their attention by claiming that children had been messing around with roadworks. As he kept them occupied, another man stole cash. Then on February 24th 2005, burglars forced their way through a locked, double-glazed bedroom window. Mr Buckland, a retired engineer, who was watching TV with his wife, confronted them but they barged past and escaped with a small amount of cash. His granddaughter, who asked not to be named, said: "Even when they thought they were safe by not answering the door and keeping all the windows and doors locked, these scumbags still managed to get into their home. My grandad was smiling and laughing, his death was a massive shock."

Close friend Martin Hynes, 76, said: "He never did any harm to anyone." Mr Buckland was found dead by a carer who called at his home on February

27. His wife had been watching TV and was oblivious to her husband's desperate actions. Friends at Wroughton Working Men's Social Club said the burglaries 'put the fear of God into him'. His best friend Val Davis, 77, who worked with him at the same engineering plant for 25 years, said: "Even though he went through all that in the war, in the end he just couldn't stand up for himself any more. I guess he just gave up."

Brian Ramshaw, 76, added: "From the first moment I met him he struck me as a very friendly and principled man. He loved his wife Barbara and their daughter and was very protective of them both. No one who knew him can understand what drove him to such actions. If only he had shared his problems this tragedy might never have happened."

The Wiltshire coroner, David Masters, opened and adjourned an inquest into Mr Buckland's death.

Fewer than one in every five crimes ends with anyone being punished by the courts, MPs revealed. In a damning indictment of Labour's failure to get a grip on law and order, they said the 'detection rate' for offences was still far too low, three years after drastic improvements were promised. The all-party Commons Home Affairs Select Committee said: "It is still a matter for concern that too few criminals are brought to justice." The MPs also warned that police were spending too long stuck behind desks dealing with mountains of paperwork rather than patrolling streets to protect the public. And the committee attacked ministers for attempting to claim that sitting in the station filling in forms was 'front-line policing'. Even if this duty was included, PCs were still only spending 63 per cent of their time on the beat. The true figure for time spent on patrols, surveillance and dealing with crime was only 53 per cent.

Committee chairman and Labour MP John Denham, a former Home Office Minister, said: "Despite good attempts to reduce bureaucracy, too many officers are still at their desks dealing with paperwork, when they could be out on the beat, policing on the front line and giving the public the visible presence they need and want." The report, which covers the Government's plans for police reform, was seized upon by the Conservatives and victims of crime as evidence of Labour's poor record.

Shadow Police Minister Andrew Mitchell said: "This is yet more evidence of the Government's failure on crime. Gun crime has doubled and last year, for the first time ever, there were a million violent crimes. "Yet Labour's response has simply been to continue to tie our police officers up in increasing amounts of red tape and politically correct bureaucracy." Norman Brennan, director of *Victims of Crime Trust*, said: "I have been telling the Government until I am blue in the face that we need to reduce paperwork, bureaucracy and political correctness. The sad reality is this Government does not care for victims of crime and the safety of society, because if it did it would have got a grip on the problem and dealt with this as a priority. If it reduced paperwork and bureaucracy just by 50 per cent, that would mean tens of thousands of officers spending 50 per cent more of their time on the street." The report reveals that only 19 per cent of reported crimes lead to an offender being punished by the courts.

However, police and the Home Office downplayed the significance of the figure, claiming that boosting the detection rate would involve dedicating more time to 'bulk' offences such as shoplifting at the expense of more serious crime. But they admit the statistic desperately needs improving and have set a target of 25 per cent by 2008. Even if they manage to hit the goal, it will still leave three-quarters of offences technically going unpunished in court. The committee report said: "Some of the original aspirations expressed when the police reform process was launched have not yet been met, in particular, an improvement in the crime detection rate."

Former Home Secretary David Blunkett launched the police reform programme in December 2001. But MPs warned that evidence suggested spending on police training had been 'squeezed' and was 'likely to prove a false economy'. Use of on-the-spot fines for a wide range of minor offences, such as loutish behaviour, had proved successful in freeing up police time to return to the beat. But this was only 'at the the margins' of what could eventually be achieved, the report said. The real potential for saving police time and resources lies in introducing more effective information technology. MPs said there was an 'acute need' for a computer system which would allow police, courts and the Crown Prosecution Service to communicate electronically. "Police officers and staff are entangled in paperwork because they do not have the IT systems they need and want. Redressing this deficiency should be a Home Office priority."

The MPs also said there was a confusing number of organisations overseeing the work of the police, with 'unnecessary overlap' between them. One force complained it had been investigated by 37 different inspections in a single year. Chris Fox, president of the Association of Chief Police Officers, said: "We accept the need to increase the number of detections, as one of a number of tools to continue to reduce crime and the fear of crime. We recognise that victims deserve to see offenders brought to justice for crimes committed. However, while many criminals caught by the police have committed more than one offence, a successful prosecution and conviction will assist in the overall prevention of crime, even where the other offences committed may not be brought to a satisfactory conclusion. We have every confidence that we are catching and convicting the right people." Jan Berry, of the Police Federation, said: "There are still too many officers spending too much time dealing with paperwork when they could and should be on the beat."

A damning second report, by Parliament's Public Accounts Committee, revealed that in some parts of the country fewer than one in 10 criminals spared jail to undergo drug treatment actually *finished* the process. Shadow Home Secretary David Davis said: "Drugs destroy lives and cripple efforts to combat crime. Yet after eight years, the Government flagship policy on drugs is failing, condemning thousands of addicts to more suffering and creating more victims of drug-related crime."

Now that you have read this far into *Judgement Impaired*, no doubt you will have probably already made up your own mind as to whether it is possible for *anyone* to find *justice* in this country, or not. Here is a set of real-life circumstances for you to read about and then, having been made aware of all the evidence in the case, make your own mind up as to whether, in *your* opinion, justice *prevailed*, or not.

HM Royal Marines go back a long way. They were actually originally formed on the 28th October in the year 1664 as The Duke of York and Albany's Maritime Regiment of Foot, also known as the Lord High Admiral's Regiment. Over the centuries since then, the Royal Marines have built for themselves an enviable reputation, not just as *elite troops*, but also famous for their most colourful, much-admired Royal Marines Band Service. There cannot be many readers who have never attended a Sunset Ceremony and stood in awe at the spectacular performance of a Royal Marines Band and its Corps of Drums and buglers.

The Royal Marines are very highly trained as a result of their basic training lasting 8-9 months, instead of just a few weeks, as in Army Regiments etc. There is a tremendous *esprit de corps* amongst not just serving Royal Marines, but former Royal Marines too. The latter can join the Royal Marines Association, which has many Branches spread across the United Kingdom, as well as quite a few Branches overseas, such as Canada, Malta, Australia etc.

Every year without fail, on the Corps Birthday, 28th October, their special day is remembered right across the Corps, no matter where Royal Marines are stationed, around the Globe. Special silver bugles are brought out for the day and special fanfares played. Corps Birthday Dinners are held on the actual day, or, in the case of the Royal Marines Association, usually on the Saturday closest to 28th October.

On 25th October 2003, the Windsor Branch, Royal Marines Association celebrated the 339th year since the birth of the Corps, at the Grenadier Guards Club, Windsor, Berkshire, as they do not have their own premises.

Many successful previous Corps Birthday Dinners, as well as other events such as Burns Nights etc., had been held there for many years without incident.

After the Dinner, drinks and after-dinner speeches had been enjoyed, it was time to toast and honour the long-serving Patron of the Royal Marines Association, HM The Queen. This was followed by communal singing of the first two verses of the National Anthem, with the assembled Branch Officers, Members, Guest of Honour and other guests, all standing to attention in the normal way, and facing their front.

There came a time during the singing of verse two of the Anthem, when a Branch Member, Mr James Adams, a serving Police Officer in the Thames Valley Force, 'broke ranks' by turning around and in a loud voice proclaimed 'The Pope could do a better job than The Queen', or words to that effect. He then fidgeted, smiling and apparently looking around for support from those surrounding him, which was certainly not forthcoming. As the hall in which the Corps Birthday Dinner was being celebrated was quite large, not everyone present heard this outburst by Mr Adams.

However standing immediately behind Mr Adams, and facing him, at the next table, as close as it was possible to get to him, was another member of Windsor and District Branch, Royal Marines Association, together with his two invited guests who had travelled many miles around the M25 motorway from their home in Essex, to attend their first-ever Royal Marines function. They were quite disgusted at the disrespect shown to HM The Queen during the second verse of the National Anthem, by the disgraceful outburst from the member behind them. Later, they were to write in expressing their outrage that the incident had spoiled an otherwise perfect evening.

Within a day or two, the RMA member who had invited the Essex guests, wrote letters to the RMA Branch President, and to the then-Chairman, seeking support, protesting at what had transpired, and with the intention of making all Branch Members present at the Dinner, aware of what had taken place. The second reason for writing was to seek a general apology of some sort, from the offender who had marred the special occasion by virtue of his anti-social and offensive and unacceptable behaviour.

At a subsequent monthly Branch Meeting, the same Member rose to his feet to inform all of those who were then present, as to the circumstances of the RMA Patron, the Queen, having been insulted and the Branch brought into disrepute by the member who had found on the night, that he was unable to behave properly. The Member who had written the two letters, also explained at the meeting, that two messages had been left on the offender's telephone answering machine, requesting him to return the call, but without success.

The matter was quite hotly debated at some length, but unfortunately, the offending member was not present, to present *his* side of the story. From the attitude of some members, together with the responses which had been received from the addressees of the two letters, the letter-writing member began to suspect that some sort of cover-up and/or ranks-closure was taking place. The then-Branch Secretary claimed to have personally dealt with the matter *in a way which would minimise harm to the Branch*, or words to that effect, although no apology whatever had by then been received, or passed on to the membership. The Secretary had also declared that the conduct complained of was most unlikely to be repeated in future.

At a subsequent to that Branch Meeting, both the Complainant Member *and* the person responsible were present at another monthly meeting, but still no apology was made. In fact it could have been settled very simply with a quick 'Sorry' at the Bar, over a handshake and a drink, and soon forgotten.

There came a time when the Complainant wrote to the Branch Secretary, asking if an apology had yet been received, concerning the disrespect shown to the Patron, HM The Queen. Although over the years, all other letters from the Complainant to the then-Branch Secretary, Mr D. Clarkson, had always been promptly answered, this one was totally ignored, thus compounding the Complainant's irritation, and his suspicions re a possible cover-up.

Before much longer, the *next* October's RMA Regimental Dinner was looming up. In desperation. the Complainant wrote a personal letter to the Windsor Branch President, Grenadier Guards Association, seeking his assurance that a repeat of the previous year's unruly behaviour by Mr Adams would not be tolerated. Instead of answering this letter, the Grenadier Guards Association Branch President took it straight to the RMA Branch Officers.

Within a very short space of time, the Complainant letter-writer received a stern letter from the RMA Branch Officers, stating that by a *unanimous decision*, the Complainant had been unceremoniously *expelled* from the Windsor and District Branch, Royal Marines Association.

The officers of the RMA, Windsor & District Branch who put their names and signatures to the whistle-blowing member's exclusion from theBranch letter of the 9th November 2004 were: Mr Allen Mustoo, Branch Chairman; Mr David Clarkson, Outgoing Branch Secretary: Mr John Douglas Best, Branch Vice-Chairman.

The expelled Member is currently, in June 2005, appealing against this, what he sees as an OTT and unjustified decision, to victimise, defame and vilify him (Not just locally, but right across the Royal Marines Association organisation!). Meanwhile, quite bizarrely you may or may not think, the original troublemaker, Mr James Adams, the serving Police Officer in the Thames Valley Force, *remains* a Windsor and District, Royal Marines Association Member!

It would have been useful to have been able to receive *feedback* from my readership, acting as a *Jury*, as to whether JUSTICE came into the equation, as to the Branch's *unanimous* decision to expel, if so, for whom? The perpetrator, or the whistleblower?

Although no *crime* had ever taken place, the *whistleblower* was left with his good character besmirched, possibly forever, as a *victim*, Whilst the *offender* walked free. Where on earth have we heard of *that* happening before?

UPDATE: On 13th July 2005 at Central Office, Royal Marines Association, HMS Excellent, Whale Island, Portsmouth, the author appeared before a full board of all 16 RMA Trustees. Legal advice had previously been obtained.

After questioning of the author by some Trustees and the RMA Chairman, Major Dunn RM, the decision of the Board of 16 Trustees was that **reconciliation** between the author and the Windsor District Branch, RMA, should be **attempted**. That remains the present position as *Judgement Impaired* is prepared for final printing and hard-binding in September 2005.

COUNT 15

ANTI-SOCIAL BEHAVIOUR ORDERS

ASBOs are often targeted at gang leaders such as 13-year-old glue sniffer Ellen Moore, who led a mob of 50 hoodlums in Leeds. She was barred from the city centre for five years and banned from covering her face to escape detection.

But it is not just young people who are targeted. Britain's oldest neighbour from hell, 87-year-old Alexander Muat, was jailed after breaching an ASBO imposed because of an eight-year campaign of terror in which he spat at his neighbours, gave them two-fingered salutes and blocked them in with his car. They are also being used to clear prostitutes from residential areas. A contentious aspect of ASBOs is that conditions are individually tailored. Teenagers have been banished from specific shops, banned from playing loud music, swearing in public and even using particular insults, such as 'grass'. They sometimes seem unworkable.

Redford Taylor, 15, was banned from saying 'Osama Bin Laden' in public until 2010, after he constantly screamed the name at a family from Afghanistan. Last year (2003) a new Anti-Social Behaviour Act gave police powers to disperse groups of youths. *The Children's Society* strongly opposed the change and has serious concerns about ASBOs. Policy manager Sharon Moore said: "Young people rely on the police to keep them safe and are worried the new powers will increase tension. The ASBOs have very strict conditions which they don't see how they can stick to. They are setting young people up to fail." The civil liberties group *Liberty* says the practice of publicising the names of those on ASBOs punishes the yobs' families and has led to siblings being bullied. "I suspect in a year's time they won't be widely in use because these problems will become more obvious," says spokesman Barry Hugill.

The civil rights group *Liberty* is to challenge the legality of a night-time curfew which banned children under 16 from a Cumbrian market town. The scheme was launched during the Easter holidays 2004 in Wigton, to clamp down on anti-social behaviour involving young people. It gave police the power to order any group of two or more young people, whatever their age and whatever the time, to leave the area and not return. The night-time curfew applied to all children under 16, who were not allowed on the streets after 9pm. During the fortnight it was operational, 13 children were returned home by police. The youngest was a 10-year-old found on the streets at 11.20pm. But *Liberty* believes the curfew was in breach of the European Convention and it plans to challenge it in the High Court. Other police forces in Teesside and Middlesbrough adopted similar curfews.

In Redcar, a six-month scheme is under way in three roads on an estate. Officers say it is a direct response to residents' complaints of anti-social behaviour. In Newcastle upon Tyne, Epsom and Cambridgeshire, curfews are also being considered to combat anti-social behaviour. Barry Hugill, *Liberty* spokesman said curfews were becoming 'ubiquitous' and were 'clearly flavour of the month'. He added: "Our research shows that 60% of police forces will be interested in curfews by summer. Effectively what they are doing is subjecting anyone under the age of 16 to a form of house arrest after 9pm. It is disproportionate and is like east Berlin before the Iron Curtain fell." Mr Hugill said Liberty's lawyers were to make a High Court challenge to get a ruling on, whether they were correct in believing the actions of Cumbria police are in contravention of the European Convention on Human Rights, to which Britain is a signatory. He said *Liberty* had no objection to the full force of the law being used against youngsters who behaved badly: "But we think it is wrong to penalise the majority because of the wrongdoing of the minority." A statement for Cumbria police said: "After consultation with the local community and other agencies, it was felt that this was an appropriate measure to tackle the issue, which is of great concern to local people, namely the incidents of anti-social behaviour in a rural town.

"This measure was carried out in accordance with the law. We are now in the process of evaluation, involving the community and different agencies into the success, or otherwise, of the initiative."

There was once a favourite sport on a Manchester street on summer evenings. A group of teenagers, cheered on by a drunken crowd of family and friends, would each take a run up to a parked car, leap on the bonnet, stamp viciously on the roof, jump down from the boot and race round for another go, pausing on the way to kick the doors in. Lesley Pulman used to watch this scene from her bedroom window as the thugs yelled: "Die you bastard." It was her red Vauxhall Astra that was being used as a trampoline but she was too frightened to go out and confront the vandals. Yet sitting quietly behind her drawn curtains, Lesley was fighting these neighbours from hell. Her weapons were a video camera, which was recording every kick and obscene gesture, and a notebook in which she wrote down every detail. Four months later Lesley was the only person brave enough to appear in court when three of the teenagers were put on Anti-Social Behaviour Orders banning them from entering that area of Manchester and from mixing with each other in public. The measure worked, she said: "like magic". Once the ringleaders had been taken out, the rest of the crowd melted away and last summer the house at the centre of the trouble was boarded up and sold. "Without the ASBOs, they would still be here and all the rest of the houses nearby would be boarded up. I thought: 'They will have to kill me because I will not move and I will not live with it'." Lesley says.

ASBOs were introduced in the Crime and Disorder Act 1998, and became available for use five years ago this month (April 2004) as the Government's flagship measure to combat rowdy families and youths whose behaviour was blighting entire communities. Yet the take-up of ASBOs has been patchy to say the least. According to Home Office figures, only 1,623 had been imposed in England and Wales up to September 2003. Critics condemn them as unenforceable, time-consuming and draconian, they have been used to ban children as young as 12 from a city centre. Manchester City Council has been in the forefront of the use of ASBOs, imposing 360 on 221 perpetrators, more than twice as many as London. Wiltshire has used only three and Essex four. There is no one more enthusiastic than Lesley, whose highly public stance led the local paper to name the legislation 'Lesley's Law'. Her story is an inspiring one of lone defiance against the kind of yobbery that cowers numerous communities. It has been a long and stressful process which has taken a considerable toll on her, and graphically illustrates the difficulties of implementing the law.

She is now a size eight, down from fourteen, she says, as she smokes nervously in the spacious living room of the three-bedroom house in New Moston where she has lived since she was a child. A 54-year-old mother of two, she suffers from multiple sclerosis, which is sparked off by stress, and has had two spells in hospital during her fight. Her ordeal began in January

2001, when the four-bedroom house three doors away was bought by two single mothers with a troupe of teenagers, a pair of three-year-old twins and a couple of other children between them. Yobs from other areas were drawn to the house and noisy crowds often gathered outside. "You know immediately you are in trouble. It's like the aliens have landed," says Lesley. "The mothers smoked spliffs in the street and drank Bacardi straight from the bottle while carrying a baby. The crowds often turned belligerent. There were thefts and muggings and windows broken. Kids in school uniforms would come to buy skunk or ecstasy from dealers who arrived on scooters or in cars. They would throw bottles in our gardens and the language was disgusting. They'd say: "This estate is ours now." and it was true in a way. They controlled us through fear. I'd watch old people and young mothers crossing the road to avoid them. Big men didn't like it either. I'd see their legs going fast and their faces turning pale as they forced themselves to walk through them.

"Estate agents started offering us cash because they knew we wouldn't be able to sell our houses with this going on. It was a drip, drip, drip, grinding our community into nothingness. The neighbours felt helpless, but when an Asian family, who had been bearing the brunt of the harassment, came under serious physical attack, Lesley decided she had to act. She had a video camera installed and tried to encourage her neighbours to fill in Incident Diaries. One of the problems with ASBOs is they rely on often terrified victims to act as witnesses. ASBOs are civil orders, similar to injunctions, brought by police and the local authority acting in partnership. Witnesses can submit written statements, but at least one must be prepared to be cross-examined if the Order is resisted, and many are too scared of reprisals. Some councils ask people who only work in the area, to act as witnesses or encourage residents to volunteer en masse.

Manchester has also hired professionals to carry out surveillance. Lesley tramped round her neighbours dissuading enraged men from taking the law into their own hands and bolstering the flagging courage of the five people who were keeping Incident Diaries. She spent hours on the phone reassuring them the yobs didn't know what they were doing and arranged a secret meeting so they could draw strength from each other. She phoned police every time there was a window broken or a theft and was soon targeted as a 'grass'. Her husband Bob, a 57-year-old milkman, had to give up his part-time taxi driving job because it became too dangerous to leave the house.

One night the police took one of the three-year-olds away and the crowd turned dangerously ugly. "The women were always threatening to burn me out of the house. They used to shout: 'There's the biggest f***ing grass in the world'. They would go 'Nee-naw, nee-naw', like a police siren or make snorting noises and call me a 'pig lover.' After it has all kicked off, the police drive away and you are still here, and so are they. You don't live day to day, it's minute to minute. It completely takes over your life. To go on holiday we hired a car and Bob brought it to pick up the luggage from the back gate at 5am. I walked out of the front door later, leaving my car outside so they wouldn't know we were away. When the notice of the ASBO hearing with my name on it was going to be served, I had a panic button fitted. Three days later I heard the letter box rattling and saw them all bent round it. I was convinced they were pouring petrol through and was so scared, I forgot the panic button but dialled 999 and police and firemen swooped from all directions."

Before an ASBO is imposed, the perpetrator must be given a formal warning and the family offered mediation and help from health and social services. In Manchester the warning has proved enough in more than half the cases. After an order is handed out in the magistrates court, the council distributes leaflets informing residents of the details so they can report breaches. Manchester has posted over 185,000 leaflets so far and around a third of its ASBOs have been breached, which is an offence carrying up to five years in prison.

Lesley always predicted the teenagers in her case, Lee Fazackerley, then 16, Ryan Schofield, 15, and Paul Marshall, 17, would breach their Orders, imposed in December 2002. Very soon she was back in court supporting a 20-year-old single mother who was vomiting with fear before giving evidence on a burglary charge against Marshall and Schofield. After the teenagers were jailed, the girl came out of court punching the air in triumph and Lesley felt her efforts were vindicated. She has been given the Ross McWhirter Award for bravery and gets calls from around the country from people wanting advice about how to deal with a similar problem. "People say: 'It's alright for you, you are not frightened', but courage is not the absence of fear, it is the mastery of fear. My heart was always pounding but I felt I had no option. I was more afraid of living with them," she says. Lesley rejects critics claims that it is naming and shaming.

"These people don't feel any shame. Round here people used to feel shame if they didn't donkey-stone their front step. I felt shame when my visitors had to walk through a crowd calling me a 'f****ing grass'. "I see it as a shift in the balance of power. People like that single mother have nothing except aspirations for their kids yet the whole community had to bow to these cretinous scumbags. Now we are saying: 'You come up to our level, we are not going down to yours."

One of two teenage brothers banned from large parts of a seaside town has quit a residential training course two weeks after a judge said it was his 'last chance'. Ben White, 19, who with his younger brother Robert is barred from three housing estates in Weston-super-Mare, Somerset, under an ASBO, was given a 12-month rehabilitation order at Bristol Crown Court in March 2004. White had admitted theft, assault, interfering with a vehicle, and breaches of his ASBO. Passing sentence, Bristol Crown Court Recorder Crowther said the punishment was a 'last chance' and warned White of a future in jail if he continued to 'tyrannise anyone who crossed him'. A condition of the Order was that he completed a 12-week rehabilitation course at a centre on the edge of Dartmoor. But a spokeswoman for the centre said he had 'family problems'.

A couple who waged a campaign of abuse and harassment against their neighbours have been kicked out of town for five years. Paul and Janet Downing, 52 and 48, of Buxton, were warned that if they return without permission they will be jailed. They were made the subject of one of the country's most sweeping Anti-Social Behaviour Orders. Derby County Court decided that the conduct of the couple was so serious they should be barred from Buxton until 2009.

Pensioner Aubrey Mathews has seen child yobs 'take over' his town, causing mayhem every night. Problems in Keynsham, Bristol include youths smashing windows, daubing graffiti on walls and wrecking public telephone booths. "Every day a shop window seems to be boarded-up after someone has thrown a stone through it," he said. "The High Street is covered with glass at weekends. People have always caused trouble drinking alcohol, but these gangs take things a step further by destroying everything in their path. They have taken over the town at night and nothing seems to stop them." Mr Mathews added: "These kids are a blight on Britain and more should be done to stop them. People can't walk the streets without the possibility of being abused. It's time to act. This used to be a quiet town where there was respect but all that has now gone."

Tearaway teenager Robert Alexiuk, 19, faces up to five years in jail, if he swears in his garden. Foul-mouthed Alexiuk was hauled before a court after neighbours claimed he regularly subjected them to a tirade of abuse as they walked past his home. On 25th March 2004 he was ordered to mind his language or face a prison sentence under the terms of an ASBO handed down by magistrates. The court heard how his threatening behaviour and swearing in Monsall, near Salford, Manchester, left neighbours fearing for their lives and property. The five-year Order forbids him from 'interfering with the peace, comfort or convenience of others' while in his front and back gardens. He is also barred from congregating in his garden with more than three people. Alexiuk is allowed to swear inside his house, but only if no-one can hear him from outside. He is already serving a 15-month jail sentence for theft, has convictions for having a stun gun, stealing from cars and damaging a police cell. Police believe he was part of a gang behind soaring crime in his neighbourhood, Manchester magistrates heard. He will be served with the ASBO when he is released from jail. Basil Curley, housing executive for Manchester City Council, which obtained the Order, said: "Alexiuk has been a menace to a peaceful community. This Order gives him a choice, behave or risk going back to prison."

On 28th April 2004, a thug father and son were banned from every single house in Britain. Nigel Wetherick, 47, and his son Michael, 19, from Watchet, Somerset, were handed the first nationwide ban in a double-ASBO after terrorising neighbours with violence and threats. Under the two-year Order, they face jail if they enter any house in England and Wales, apart from their own, without consent. They are also barred from assaulting, harassing, intimidating or distressing anyone. The loutish pair appeared before Taunton Crown Court accused of violent and abusive behaviour in their otherwise peaceful country town of Watchet. A council spokesman said later: "For more than a year there's been persistent intimidation.

We hope this will make these men stop behaving in a threatening way." But defiant Nigel Wetherick said: "We're the ones being victimised. We just want a quiet life. Michael has been in trouble, but he's never beaten anyone to a pulp." An elderly neighbour is still having hospital treatment after an ugly confrontation with Michael. Watchet harbourmaster George Reader and his wife Ann received phone threats after the teenager threw a stone through Mr Reader's window. Ex-cabbie Nigel attacked a man while the victim gave a statement to the police. The prosecution said: "When the Wethericks get in trouble and there are repeated threats, you're entitled to say it's coming from that direction." Nigel received a 180-hour community punishment order for affray. His son was given a two-year community rehabilitation order for affray, criminal damage and possessing a weapon.

For more than 13 years, Alan and Linda Fisher were the epitome of middle-class respectability, living a normal life in a typical English street. But when a children's nursery opened next to their £100,000 home, a court heard that the couple turned into the neighbours from hell. Furious at what they saw as the *Kite Early Years* nursery's flouting of planning laws, they orchestrated a seven-month campaign against staff and children. They blared out Gangsta rap music, songs by foul-mouthed artist Eminem, threw stones into the playground while the children, ranging from babies to five-year-olds, played outside, and unleashed torrents of foul and abusive language within earshot of the youngsters. Magistrates at Worksop, Notts, also heard that Mr Fisher, 48, a joinery firm manager, even brandished a golf club at a female member of staff. The couple, from Worksop, who have two grown-up sons, have now been branded yobs after magistrates issued an ASBO against them. They face five years in jail if they breach the Order.

Mrs Fisher, 43, a community care worker with Nottinghamshire County Council, has also been suspended from her job pending an enquiry. Joanne Gray, 39, of *Granby Nurseries Ltd* which owns the nursery said: "We are pleased and relieved about the verdict and were always confident that the police would be successful with their application for the ASBO." The court heard that the Fishers, who moved into their house in 1991, began their campaign against the nursery when it was opened 12 months ago, caring for 30 children. Mrs Gray said: "We are a community nursery and most of the children live locally so we wanted to be friends with everyone. But the Fishers took an instant dislike to us. It seems they didn't like the idea of little children being next door.

When their campaign started we had only just opened and there were only six children here, all babies, so there was no noise at all. They began playing Eminem music at full volume in the house with the windows open, and they used to stand in the garden just a few yards from where the children play, swearing at the tops of their voices. They were pretending to swear at one another but it was aimed at us. I run three other nurseries in the area and my business has been established for ten years. We are very conscious about getting on with our neighbours and not causing problems." But angry Mrs Fisher claimed that the nursery had used the children to provoke them and denied they had created a problem. She said: "All this has been mind-blowing and bizarre, my nerves are shot. My reputation is so corroded I don't know how I am going to get my job back. It seems that if you challenge or question things, or ask for your rights, then you are in trouble. The nursery used the children as a means to provoke us." Mrs Fisher, who now lives in another house which they own across the road, compared her love of Gangsta rap music to that of any hobby, such as stamp collecting. "I really love Eminem, I love the lyrics, I love rap and Gangsta music. I play his music all the time but I don't play it loud. They tried to say I was playing it to offend the kids but that's my music. Some people like jogging or stamp collecting but I'm into Gangsta rap. As far as swearing and shouting, yes that happened, but in the privacy of our home. We didn't shout or swear to annoy the nursery and, as far as throwing stones at the playground, that never happened. The nursery has been breaching planning restrictions but no one has done anything about that."

Under the terms of the ASBO, the couple are banned from playing explicit music within earshot of staff and children at the nursery, and from using or encouraging others to use explicit language within the vicinity of the nursery. They are also prohibited from acting in a manner intended to harass, alarm or distress staff, parents or children, and were ordered to pay £500 costs. PC David Taylor, of Nottinghamshire Police said: "I was very impressed with the nursery. They took all reasonable steps to make sure everything was OK."

A teenage thug who terrorised residents on an estate has finally been locked up after breaching an ASBO 11 times. Glue-sniffing Michael Cambridge, 17, was given a five-year ASBO banning him from entering the Osmondthorpe estate in Leeds after a shocking reign of terror. But he carried on getting high and went around the estate abusing and threatening residents and vandalising property. He was caught by police several times in a 'crazed state' and was given a succession of second chances by magistrates before being jailed. A man in his forties, who asked not to be named, said: "The police kept arresting him but as soon as he was let out he was back here sniffing glue. He should have been locked up a long time ago." Jim McCauley, chairman of Leeds Magistrates, lifted reporting restrictions, and allowed the thug to be named after he was given a four-month detention order in a young offenders institution. The ASBO, imposed at the end of August 2003, banned Cambridge from anti-social behaviour anywhere in Leeds, associating with certain friends and inhaling toxic substances. It was made after he swore at residents and entered their gardens, taunted security workers, raced through the estate on motorbikes and was caught sniffing glue. He terrified residents as he burgled neighbours, told a friend to torch buildings and threw bricks and stones at homes, including his own.

A couple from hell have been given a LIFE ban from every pub in Britain, and face jail if they break it. The ban is part of an ASBO given to Robert and Lisa Hughes after police had to use CS gas to break up a row. JP's in Pontypridd also put Lisa, 37, under an 8.30pm curfew for assaulting a police officer. Robert Hughes, 38, admitted using threatening behaviour after the incident. Neighbours in Tylorstown, South Wales, welcomed the ban which also stops them playing loud music at their home. One said: "They are the original couple from hell."

Tearaway teenager Melissa Page, 16, of Lipson, Plymouth, has been banned from every police station in her city. Officers were so fed up with the abusive and violent child that they obtained an ASBO excluding her from within 100 metres of their police station. PC Guy James said: "She's been harassing officers and staff. She has no respect for authority." Page was arrested 34 times in 2003.

Natalie Henderson, 16, a gang leader, nicknamed 'Poison Ivy', has been told to stop her reign of terror or face jail. She is one of the ringleaders of a teenaged mob which has plagued a council estate in Seaham, County Durham. In one case her gang pelted a mother's house with snowballs for 90 minutes while her young children were crying inside. They also threw flaming firelighters at passing cars and yelled abuse.

Despite promising to mend her ways, she has pelted cars with eggs, vandalised property and abused neighbours and police, Peterlee magistrates heard. They issued an ASBO which means that if she causes trouble she could be sent into custody. Afterwards, Henderson claimed: "I have been picked on by police." But one resident said: "She's a menace. We call her Poison Ivy." PC Gail Conroy said: "The Order will mean peace for the local people."

The mother of a teenaged yob attacked a neighbour whose complaints led to the boy being banned from a village, a court heard. Lisa Marriott, 36, assaulted Gary Pugh at his home on the same day he and his wife Sara had reported her and her son Aaron Raven, 15, to police. Raven led a gang causing havoc in the Dorset village of Lytchett Matravers, and terrorising elderly residents. He was banned from the village and the shops in nearby Upton. When he was arrested in December 2003, his mother went with him to the police station. As she left the station, an officer heard her say: "My son will put her windows in when he gets out." She went to the Pugh's home later and hit Mr Pugh and his friend Wayne Musson. At an earlier hearing she admitted intimidating a witness. At Bournemouth Crown Court, His Honour Judge Samuel Wiggs, in his wisdom, sentenced Marriott to 60 hours community service and a two-year rehabilitation order, after telling her: "It's clear you have an anger management problem." She was also ordered to pay for damage to the Pugh's front door.

Four yobs who terrorised a community while visiting their 'Granny from hell' have been banned from going to see her. Doris Lewis, 69, let the youngsters, including two schoolgirls aged 14 and 15, run amok. They have been served with ASBOs, the first of its kind, after running wild while under the care of their grandmother. Now they face being locked up if they are caught visiting her council house in Manchester, or surrounding streets. Mrs Lewis, who was warned last year that she faced jail if she failed to keep the children under control, will only be allowed to see them away from the area. Council chiefs successfully applied for the indefinite ASBO ban after their alleged string of crimes, including robbery, were outlined in a court. The grandchildren are Ashley Carter,17, his brother Scott,16, their sister Lois and their cousin Zara Lewis.

Manchester magistrates were told that Ashley Carter, of Blackley, was alleged to have been involved in burglary, criminal damage, assault, robbery, intimidation and indecently exposing himself to a young girl. He was also said to have thrown bricks at a community centre in November 2001. He also shouted homophobic abuse at a resident and threatened to slash him. Scott Carter, who has a police record of vandalism, theft, burglary and deception, formed part of a 19-strong gang including Lois and Zara, which hurled metal bars at a man's house in February 2003. He allegedly told the terrified tenant, who was inside the property: "I am going to petrol bomb your house." Lois, 14, and Zara, 15, joined three other girls who hurled abuse at teachers and banged windows at a primary school for 90 minutes during a staff meeting. Lois was also said to have stolen from a supermarket and been involved with threats and vandalism. Zara, of Harpurney, Manchester, was accused of verbal abuse, criminal damage and theft. Manchester City Council director of housing, Steve Rumbelow, who applied for the ASBO, said the children had been 'simply allowed to run wild when they were in the care of their grandmother'.

Mother-of-nine Mrs Lewis, who has 37 grandchildren, could not be contacted at her home in Collyhurst, north Manchester. She has not breached the ASBO against her because the four teenagers' alleged crimes took place before the injunction was issued. One neighbour, who was too frightened to give her name, said: "You take your life in your hands even going out of your front door when those kids are around. Everyone round here calls Doris 'the granny from hell'.

(**Authors note:** *Cast your mind forward about 4-5 years – these budding career-criminals will be draining the public purse in large measures – they will be filling-in their HMP 'Governor's Application' forms for inter-prison visits so as to 'maintain family ties'. This will tie-up an army of male and female prison officers plus HMP coach drivers or a fleet of taxis, running a circular tour between HMP's Wandsworth, Holloway, Wormwood Scrubs, Dartmoor, Exeter and all stations to Penzance, so that they can hug each other, and exchange drugs and information about their proposed criminal activities when it's time for 'Criminals Reunited' to carry on where they left off! Mark my words.*)

A tough cop who brought peace to a warring housing estate has received death threats from the yobs he managed to defeat. No-nonsense PC Henry Garrod did such a good job in clearing up the troubled Craylands Estate in Basildon, Essex, that Tony Blair heaped praise on his methods. PC Garrod's *zero tolerance* stance put a stop to a summer of unrest which saw cars set on fire and gangs of lawless vandals running wild. But on one occasion riot police had to be called in and 13 residents were arrested after they staged a roof-top protest at PC Garrod's methods. Yobs have daubed estate walls with chilling graffiti that declares 'Garrod is dead'. There have even been rumours that a bounty has been placed on the constable's head. And in a sorry tale of our times, more than 300 estate residents have signed a petition calling for PC Garrod to be removed, simply because he is too good at his job.

His main weapon in the war against the yobs is the ASBO, which places strict conditions on hooligans intent on causing trouble. Those hit with the court orders claim the tactics went too far, despite the fact that the estate is now safe for residents who previously refused to leave their homes at night. But the tough-talking policeman stood defiant. He said: "The existing ASBOs have worked. And there are more in the pipeline for people on the estate and people who enter it. If people who live there think they can create mayhem and remain there as tenants in their council homes,they may be wrong." He added that he was prepared to shackle entire troublemaking families with ASBOs, and that he would carry on regardless. He said: "The law-abiding citizens here don't have a problem with me, but the show goes on because I am determined to stop trouble on this estate."

The Prime Minister toured the Craylands estate accompanied by local MP Angela Smith. Mr Blair praised PC Garrod for his excellent work. PC Garrod said: "Mr Blair was keen to know what it was really like on the estate. He wanted to hear from the residents about their problems and he wanted to know from me what I needed to help me in my new role."

But despite all the improvements, estate resident Terry Reason, 16, hit out at PC Garrod's so-called 'aggressive' policies. The teenager said: "He is totally over the top and he picks on young people. He pushed my mate off his bike and handcuffed him just for riding on the footpath." Another angry resident said: "This is not a bad estate and zero-tolerance policing is not needed. Garrod is just drunk with power and throwing his weight around, we just want to get rid of him." But PC Garrod is being backed by Essex Police, councillors and residents alike.

Local council leader Malcolm Buckley said: "I am very disappointed that the minority of people are making their voices heard and far too loudly. But it will have no effect on the police's determination to fight crime in the area. PC Garrod has our complete support and for these people to protest against him shows that he is doing his job properly." And one Craylands resident who wished to be unnamed said: "Things had got really bad round here before PC Garrod arrived. There were drugs and joy-riders and vandals, it wasn't safe to go out after dark. Most of us are really happy that he is bringing law and order back to the estate."

The policing of a troubled housing estate is being scrutinised following a seven-hour rooftop protest against 'zero tolerance'. Speaking at a public meeting into the problems, police chiefs vowed to review the way the Craylands estate at Basildon is patrolled. But they stressed that the tough approach to crime in the area would continue. More than 100 concerned residents packed out the crunch talks. Residents took to the roofs and streets in Norwich Walk, calling for the removal of the estate's lone officer PC Henry Garrod. Twelve people were arrested in the disturbance. Deputy Divisional Commander Glen Caton told the meeting that the majority of residents supported the 'positive policing' and Mr Garrod's presence. He said that a 'hardcore' minority were responsible for most crime and anti-social behaviour and for wanting him ousted. Mr Garrod was drafted in, in October 2003 following a crime surge in the summer.

According to Insp. Dave Miller crime is now at an 18-month low on the estate, with 55 less incidents being reported each month, a drop of 26 per cent. Sgt. Phil Whitehard, who is conducting the estate review, has been visiting known offenders and other youths on the streets for their views. He said: "I wish they were here tonight because their voice needs to be heard." Police aim to continue using ASBOs where appropriate and evicting constant offenders. Mr Garrod did not attend the meeting because police believe his presence could have been counter productive.

Mr Caton refused to comment on whether the officer's style was under review by his bosses, but said that he was likely to remain at the estate. Under the review, police numbers on the estate are being assessed. Three officers now patrol its streets. In a question and answer session at the meeting held in St Andrews Church from 7.30pm, several residents claimed that there were not enough police and some crime scenes were not attended. One woman claimed to have never seen Mr Garrod on the estate. Another resident claimed he had no problem with a police presence, but that Mr Garrod was 'unapproachable' and that was an 'unsupportable' way for an officer to behave.

Two boys aged 11 who broke into a zoo and terrorised two of its wallabies to death have been named and shamed. Ryan Jones and Keiron Anslow climbed into the wallaby enclosure at Dudley Zoo with a 10-year-old friend and let the animals out of their huts. They gave them such a severe chasing that one of them, a female, broke a leg and had to be put down. Two weeks later the boys were caught on video as they returned to the zoo with a nine-year-old boy and again began chasing the terrified marsupials. One of the boys decided that a baby wallaby, just out of its mother's pouch, 'needed a bath'. The tiny creature was picked up by its tail and repeatedly dunked in a pool of water. Its soaking body was found the next morning by zoo keepers. It had died of shock.

At Dudley Youth Court, district judge Michael Morris lifted a ban protecting the pair's identities to act as a deterrent to other children. An order banning identification of the 10-year-old, who stood beside his friends in court, remained in place because, unlike the other boys, he was not involved in the second incident. Prosecutor Julia Vale told the court that in the time between the incidents, the three boys, all from Kates Hill, Dudley, joked about their actions to police when they were stopped in the street. "In the presence of the police, one of the lads said to another, 'Remember when you killed that wallaby at the zoo?' The other boy admitted it and said they had climbed over the keeper's hut to get into the enclosure. All three found it to be highly amusing. They were laughing and joking about it." Mrs Savage said that a camcorder was set up after the first wallaby's death. When the second wallaby was found dead, staff checked the tape and saw the children climbing into the enclosure.

Jones, Anslow and the nine-year-old, who is below the age of criminal responsibility, were identified and interviewed the following day. The ten-year-old, who did not take part in the second incident, was also questioned. Jones and Anslow both admitted two charges of causing unnecessary suffering and the ten-year-old admitted one charge. All three were made subject to referral orders for 12 months, which involves signing a contract regarding their behaviour and liaising with a Youth Offending Team. Judge Morris ordered Jones and Anslow to pay £450 in compensation to the zoo, while the ten-year-old was ordered to pay £200.

The judge said the barbarity of their conduct had shocked the public. "All three went into the zoo intent on having what they described as fun, which is nothing but the most serious form of cruelty" he added.

After the case, Keiron Anslow was pictured leaving the court holding up an extended middle finger, known as a 'one-fingered-salute', and was spitting obscenities. He is the oldest of five children in a single-parent family. Pictured with him was his co-defendant Ryan Jones, who is one of six children born to a single mother. Their faces were both defiant and neither boy has expressed the slightest remorse for their cruel conduct. Anslow's mother, Dawn, claimed the boy was an 'animal lover'.

Police investigating a string of violent incidents were astonished to find the culprits were four young girls, one of them only 12. The tearaways were responsible for robberies, shoplifting, violent attacks and threatening behaviour. Leisha Banyard and Carrie Syrett, both 16, and 12-year-old Sheridan Rattigan, began their campaign of terror in September 2003 and were joined within two months by Jade Harper, 15. In one incident they robbed a teenage girl on a bus of her mobile phone and £2, before Syrett and Rattigan punched her in the face while Harper and Rattigan chanted,

'Punch the blonde bitch'. Although they returned the mobile phone because it had run out of credits, they intimidated and threatened her after she complained to police.

In another incident, a garage worker discovered £30 missing from her purse after Syrett and Rattigan, who also hit a shop worker in the face with an umbrella, had been on the premises. And a 14-year-old girl was head butted and punched in the face by Syrett, Rattigan and Harper in an unprovoked attack. The four were also accused of about 30 incidents of threatening shopkeepers near their homes in Great Yarmouth, causing damage in shops and stealing from them. On some occasions police were called as they hurled abuse at their victims. Sergeant Mike Jones, of Norfolk Police said: "We were getting lots of complaints from traders and eventually linked them together. Although not all the incidents were serious, the sheer number of them made them a real nuisance. The traders felt very intimidated and although it sounds ridiculous to say young girls can be such a threat, that was how they felt. They were very concerned by what was happening and were being verbally threatened as well as having their shops damaged."

Great Yarmouth magistrates banned Banyard, Syrett and Rattigan for five years from entering 30 shops and arcades in their town centre as well as their local library. Harper was given a two-year ASBO banning her from six premises and from mixing with the others in public. Nationally, almost 90% of ASBOs have been issued to male culprits. The girls face two years in custody if they break their Orders. Robert Glass, prosecuting, said: "Their behaviour was completely unacceptable in any society." Chief Superintendent Ray Adcock of Yarmouth police: said: "The decision sends out a clear signal to young people and parents that anti-social behaviour will not be accepted. No one wants to see young people stigmatised by court appearances but they have persistently harassed shopkeepers and customers. This behaviour must cease."

As they entered the street after the court case, Syrett, 16, was pictured smiling with her tongue out and making a 'one-fingered salute.' Rattigan, 12, was photographed with her face partially covered by her open jacket, making a 'vee' sign and half-smiling. Banyard, 16, was grimacing, threatening and defiant in her photograph.

A blind man who groped young women as they helped him to cross the road has been handed an ASBO. Neil Middlehurst, 49, appeared at Kingston Crown Court and admitted touching the breasts of three women. The ASBO specifies that he can only place his hand on the shoulder of any woman helping him. He was also sentenced to 16 months imprisonment for indecent assault, but he may be eligible for an early release because of the time he spent in custody on remand awaiting trial. *You may feel that the judge could have given far better protection to future potential female victims of Middlehurst. The terms of the ASBO could have specified that Middlehurst can only ever call upon* <u>men</u> *to help him across the road safely. Seems like common sense to me.*

Foul-mouthed drunken alcoholic David Pegler, 50, of Portsmouth, broke an ASBO, just NINE MINUTES after JP's made him the subject of the Order. He walked straight out of court and opened a can of cider in public as the police watched. Now he faces five years in jail for flouting the Order, which he told the magistrates he would break 'for the hell of it' as it infringed his rights.

A schoolboy has been named and shamed after he became the most wanted burglar in a city, at the age of 13. Luke Menzies, who is just 4ft tall, made it to the top of a police hit list after plaguing residents in Bradford with a one-boy crimewave. Bradford Magistrates Court made the tearaway the subject of an ASBO in a bid to curb his serial stealing spree. Detectives described the 13-year old as a 'prolific and persistent' offender who became known to them at nine, and started stealing from the age of eleven. A Bradford police spokesman said: "At one stage he was the number one target in the burglary team's top ten most wanted."

Menzies, whose feet could not even reach the floor as he sat in court, hung his head in shame as his catalogue of crimes was outlined. Since 2002, he has been convicted of 14 offences including assault, burglary, attempted burglary, robbery, theft, shoplifting and vandalism. Harjit Ryatt, applying for the ASBO on behalf of police and the city council, told Bradford magistrates that the Order was needed to 'protect the community'.

The boy's mother, Karen Barnett, sat next to her son as Mr Ryatt reeled-off a shocking list of offences, including locking one woman in her bedroom as he burgled her flat. On other occasions, Menzies was verbally abusive to shop owners, threatened people with violence in the street and vandalised parked cars. He was also once spotted driving a car. Other victims were robbed of shoes, mobile phones and jewellery, and he terrified parishioners by throwing balloons filled with flour at them as they left church. Under the ASBO, Menzies is forbidden from entering Bradford city centre and banned from any public place between 9pm and 7am. If he breaches the Order he could face a custodial sentence.

A teenaged girl whose wild, drunken binges plagued the town where she lived has been locked up for two years after ignoring a last-chance ASBO. Kelly Bowness, 16, from Cumbria, made the lives of neighbours and shop staff a misery. She was made the subject of the ASBO, which imposed a night-time curfew on her, and ruled she should stay away from alcohol. But far from mending her ways, the Order appeared to make her even worse, magistrates in Whitehaven, Cumbria, were told. She harassed shoppers in the town and burned one store assistant with a cigarette. She swore at officers who tried to stop her drinking and went berserk in a police station, it took six officers to bundle her into a cell. Police welcomed her jailing, saying she had been a drain on their resources.

Three youths from well-off families were among a gang of 11 teenage tearaways named and shamed by a court for terrorising a once-sleepy village. They are the largest single group of yobs to be handed ASBOs in one case. They were brought to heel by a joint police and council operation after residents in the village of Yarnfield, Staffordshire, said their community felt like a war zone. Three-year banning orders were handed out to Carl Davis, 16, Reece Colcroft, 16, his brother Brian, 17, John Evans, 15, Nicola Boult, 15, and her 13-year-old sister Tiffany. David Timmis, Harry Keen, Michael Rawlinson and James Tippett, all 16, and Sarah Traynor, 17, received two-year orders.

Eight of the 11 live in the village but Timmis lives in a six-bedroom farmhouse estimated to be worth about £1million in nearby Eccleshall. Keen lives in Barlaston, eight miles away, in a four-bedroom semi with a BMW on the drive and Tippett lives in Cold Meece, two miles away, in a modern six-bedroom house at the end of a tree-lined drive. Magistrates at Cannock, Staffs heard how, in the past year, the gang had hurled abusive language, lit fires, behaved like yobs while drunk and thrown missiles at passing cars. The gang sometimes boasted as many as 27 followers and had left some residents too frightened to leave their own homes.

Ian Colville, prosecuting on behalf of Stafford Borough Council, said they congregated either on the village green or in the car park next to the pub. He added: "There has been damage to the bus shelter, climbing on the phone box, missiles thrown at houses and passing cars and damage to vehicles in the car park. Youths have also banged loudly on people's doors, jumped over hedges causing damage to peoples' gardens and run over private drives. Fires had been lit in the pub car park, there had been threats to burn down fences, and drunken youths had abused residents."

District Judge Elizabeth Harte said the orders covered the village and the whole of the county of Staffordshire. The orders include a ban on drinking alcohol in public, urinating or spitting in public, using the pub car park, using racist or sexually-explicit language and damaging property. The judge said they had behaved in 'a manner which caused and was likely to continue to cause harassment, alarm and distress'. Four solicitors claimed the youngsters, none of whom contested the orders, had modified their behaviour in recent weeks but only one,Sarah Traynor, apologised.

Councillor Stan Highfield thanked the witnesses for having the courage to go to court to protect their community. He said: "More than 50 residents came forward to give evidence and, without those statements, we would not have been able to take such effective action." Councillor Trevor Reeves said: "We will not tolerate bad behaviour and will take strong action to ensure residents can live in peace." Sergeant Kath Hancock said: " This case has been about protecting a community and about allowing people to feel safe on their own doorstep." Residents said they were delighted at the granting of the orders to the young tearaways.

Pensioners Tom Watson, 72, and his wife Phyllis, 75, spent hundreds of pounds extra on their insurance after youths targeted their home. Mr Watson, a former soldier said: "We moved here in the 1970's when it was a lovely place to live. Everybody respected everybody else and we got along together. Then it just went downhill. It got to the stage where we could not go in our own back gardens because of their noise and missiles flying over the fence. I have lost count of the amount of time we have had windows broken, cars damaged and eggs thrown at the house. This destroyed our lives. It made it difficult to get out of the house without feeling threatened and intimidated by the gangs. If we said anything to them, the language we got back in return was unbelievable. Hopefully, this order will improve things for the likes of us: the normal, law-abiding citizens who just want to live their lives in peace." Some residents remain too frightened to be identified because they are still scared of retribution.

One 80-year-old man, who has lived in the village for more than 40 years, was heartbroken when the louts smashed up his greenhouse. He said: "I heard glass smashing and saw a group of these lads hitting golf balls from the village green into my front garden. The balls were crashing against the greenhouse, destroying many of the panes. They were obviously doing it deliberately but there was nothing I could do to stop them. If you try to take on 10 young lads in a big group, who knows what would happen?" The man said there had been a 'few hairy moments' but the level of harassment in the village had been 'much worse'. He added: "I'm glad something has been done about these young idiots at last." One resident who has lived in the village for more than 30 years told how her quiet, peaceful community had been destroyed by young vandals and yobs. Avril Rogers, 61, moved into the village, an overspill from the Potteries based around a green and one pub, *The Labour In Vain*, when life there was tranquil. But in the past year the 3,000-strong population has witnessed an explosion in loutish behaviour by youngsters who have made their lives a misery. Mrs Rogers, who has lived in Yarnfield for 33 years explained: "The past 12 months have been pretty horrific. It has been like living in a war zone. After today we are hoping that this will bring peace and quiet for all of us. The problems were generally the large number of youths hanging around together, and people spitting and the foul and abusive language. Their behaviour went two or three steps beyond what you would consider to be normal and acceptable behaviour for a gang of teenagers. They had no respect for other people and other people's property. Only time will tell if the order will have any effect. This is not a path we wanted to go down, but something had to be done to get the village back to being a community again."

(**Author's note:** *Are you wondering, like me, how many of the 11 sets of parents took the trouble to attend the court hearing? Some of these dreadful kids even lived in huge semi-mansions. It just confirms the old adage 'People who live in large houses, shouldn't throw stones!'*)

Glass dynasty heiress Lady Julia Pilkington has launched legal action against a judge who jailed her. Pilkington, 39, was sentenced to 42 days in February 2004 after she harassed neighbours by having sex romps in her outdoor spa.

Now she has taken steps for a judicial review against District Judge John Woollard, alleging that he did not handle her case properly. Her jail sentence came after she failed to carry out a community punishment order, which entailed clearing litter from a forest and working in a charity shop. Pilkington, from Portsmouth, served her time in Holloway Prison. Since her release in March she has been busy preparing her case and has already sent the paperwork to the Royal Courts of Justice.

A young thug who began a campaign of terror soon after his 10th birthday, has become one of the youngest recipients of an anti-social behaviour order. Ryan Wilkinson's lawless antics with a pack of 17 yobs started just days after he passed the age of criminal responsibility in July 2004. He and his pack held their neighbourhood in a grip of fear, so that grown men were afraid to walk the streets at night and women locked themselves in their own homes. On 9th February 2005, the little thug was named and shamed and made the subject of an ASBO, barring him from four areas of the city where he lives, and banning him from meeting the rest of his gang, all of them older teenagers, for five years.

Despite the ruling, his mother insisted her son was just 'a cheeky-so-and-so'. Single parent Susan O'Driscoll, who has two daughters aged eight and seven, and another son aged two, also complained that banning her boy from some streets would force her to walk further to take him to school. In fact, the youngster has been excluded from school for the past six months because his behaviour in the playground is as bad as on the streets.

Magistrates in Leeds agreed to the ASBO, one of only a handful handed down in Britain to a child of his age, after city officials outlined an appalling catalogue of crime and unruly behaviour. The court heard that in the space of a few months he has:

- Thrown a scooter at a minibus full of children
- Desecrated a church and damaged other properties
- Broken into homes and wrecked houses, and fled across rooftops
- Attacked other youngsters
- Hurled foul-mouthed abuse at residents
- Smashed up cars

Under the ban, Ryan, from the Harehills area of Leeds, will also be subject to a 7.30pm to 7.30am curfew at his family home. If he breaks the conditions during the next five years he could face up to two years in custody.

Neighbours welcomed the ASBO, which they hoped would return law and order to their streets. But Miss O'Driscoll, 35, insisted her son was taking the blame for the misbehaviour of others. "I know he is a cheeky-so-and-so but half of the time he is being mixed up with other lads," she said. "Much of the time he has done what they have said, otherwise he wouldn't be on the ASBO. But he gets the blame for what other lads have been up to."

Les Carter, Leeds City Council's executive board member for community safety, said the measures had been a necessary last resort. "We have already gone to considerable lengths to avoid this drastic action and to help turn this child's life around," he said. "However, we cannot and will not tolerate this type of behaviour. The community is entitled to be protected from him. Whilst I appreciate a 10-year-old is very young to receive an ASBO, this child's actions cannot be ignored." A Leeds social services spokesman said the department had been working with the family for some time, and would continue to do so. "We don't give up on young people in Leeds, so we will continue to do all we can to help Ryan in the future," he said.

A thug aged 11 who carried out a series of robberies was hit with an Anti-Social Behaviour Order on 15th February 2005. Martin Faulkner, who is just 1.5m (5ft) tall, terrorised other youngsters, stripping them of cash and valuables such as MP3 players and mobile phones. He also harassed staff and pupils at his primary school. At Nottingham Youth Court, a judge allowed Faulkner to be identified because of the number of offences he had committed. He told the youngster: "You have admitted a large number of offences, offences someone older than you would be going to prison for, for a very long time." Faulkner, of Nottingham, was given a two-and-a-half year supervision order. The ASBO bans him from entering Nottingham city centre without an adult for two years.

Here is a separate version about Martin Faulkner's behaviour which goes into more detail as to his escapades leading to his ASBO being issued.

A young tearaway who terrorised other children as he carried out 16 street robberies in just two months, has been banned from his city centre. Martin Faulkner, 11, targeted his young victims for sums as small as £4, claiming he had a gang who would move in if they did not pay up. During his reign of fear in Nottingham he also stripped them of mobile phones and music players and spent the money on crisps, sweets and cigarettes. Faulkner's story is a sad indictment on modern Britain. Living in the care of the local authority, the youngster, who is slight and stands barely 5ft tall, has been expelled from school and his education has stalled. He is described as a boy who has been left alone 'literally and emotionally'. But what he lacks in formal education, Faulkner makes up for by being streetwise.

His style was to terrify his victims with increasing use of threats and violence. One victim, 13-year-old Dean Sutherland, was robbed after his mother allowed him to go into the city for the first time with just a friend for company. Nottingham Youth Court heard that Faulkner, who comes from a broken home and uses cannabis and Ecstasy, was also a vandal who intimidated teachers and pupils when he was in school. He also terrorised other residents at his care home. Faulkner, of Nottingham, was given a two-and-a-half year supervision order. Magistrates took the unusual move of allowing him to be identified despite his young age, because of the seriousness of his crime. He was also made the subject of an Anti-Social Behaviour Order for two years, which bans him from entering Nottingham city centre without being accompanied by an adult.

District Judge Morris Cooper lifted the normal reporting restrictions which prevent the naming of young defendants because of an 'overriding need' to inform and protect the public. Police, however, remain convinced that with the right treatment, Martin Faulkner can yet be brought back into line. Officers say they do not condone his actions but recognise the troubled background that has led him into a life of crime.

The mother of tearaway Martin Faulkner claims that social services are partly to blame for her son's criminal behaviour. Mrs Mandy Bell, 36, says she urged social workers to take him into care three years ago because she could not cope. "If only they had given me some hope then he wouldn't be like this," she said. "They only come when it is too late." Martin is one of five children whom Mrs Bell had to four different men. He did not know the identity of his father during his early years, and the biggest male influence on him was an older brother who was also often in trouble. His life of crime can be traced back to the age of eight, when he was expelled from school. He had always been known on his estate as a troublemaker. Mrs Bell suffered from depression and admits that by the time Martin was 10, she had lost control of him. "I tried grounding him, but he just climbed out of the windows," she said. She believes the only answer for her wayward son may be to keep him in a secure unit until he is 18.

Jobless decorator Martin Maloney was never involved in bringing up his son, until he turned up unexpectedly, aged nine, asking for a roof over his head. "I couldn't turn him away," said Mr Maloney, 43. "I first got to know him when he was about seven. But they kept moving to different areas so I never really knew who he was."

His son slept on a camp bed in his one-bedroom flat, but the arrangement added little stability to the youngster's life. He sometimes went back to his mother, or stayed with his brother Gary. He would occasionally sleep rough. "No school would take him," said Mr Maloney. "The police got to know him, but they didn't know what to do with him." Mr Maloney has applied for a larger council home so that he can look after his son when he is released from care. The police also think his son may be redeemable. "He is not past the point where he can be put back on the straight and narrow," said Det. Insp. Paul Murphy, the head of Nottingham City police team.

Neighbours from hell will be forced to take 'life skills' lessons in a crackdown on anti-social behaviour. People evicted from council houses must agree to the programme before getting new homes. Home Secretary David Blunkett is introducing the tough measures because of concern that evicted families continue with their anti-social behaviour when they are rehoused. He aims to use new Government legislation to force them to take part in behaviour lessons. Nuisance families will be expected to take courses in parenting and anger management in return for a new home.

(**Author's note:** *Please ensure that all of the relevant courses are completed BEFORE allocating the new house!*)

A Police Force has come up with a novel way of dealing with any increase in drunkenness caused by new 24-hour pub opening times. They are beaming giant pictures of people convicted of breaching anti-social behaviour orders (ASBOs) on to a town centre's 'wall of shame'. The first two men to be made an example of have both been banned from the centre of Guildford, Surrey, and jailed for defying ASBOs. Photographs of Albert Green, 41, and Jamie Yates, 35, are being projected on to the *Friary Centre*, a shopping precinct at the heart of the town's nightlife area and near its main taxi rank. Green was jailed for two months for repeatedly defying an order imposed for a catalogue of offences including criminal damage, drunken, aggressive and racially aggravated behaviour, intimidation and threats towards residents, shop owners and staff.

Yates was locked up for 56 days for breaching his ASBO twice in the same weekend, after being convicted of numerous offences of drunk and disorderly conduct. Superintendent Kevin Deanus said: "The majority of anti-social behaviour in Guildford town centre can be attributed directly to alcohol. Change to a 24-hour cafe culture is a high-risk strategy. We have invested immense resources to improve public feelings of safety at night which may be lost through round-the-clock drinking. We are not prepared to tolerate anti-social behaviour. Our Wall of Shame highlights how we have successfully tackled the problems of two particularly persistent offenders of alcohol-fuelled disturbance, and made them accountable for their actions." Police believe the photos will act as a warning to possible offenders and reassure law-abiding revellers that they are safe.

"Nobody should have to feel threatened or frightened or have to put up with people acting in an anti-social way," added Mr Deanus. "Together we can stamp out anti-social behaviour and make our communities safer." The pictures will be on show every night and police will be dispensing advice on how the community can tackle anti-social behaviour.

A woman who has tried to kill herself four times has been banned from jumping off bridges or into rivers in a bizarre Anti-Social Behaviour Order. Kim Sutton, 23, who suffers from a personality disorder, is not allowed to 'dip one toe or finger' in a river or loiter around multi-storey car parks and bridges.

The 'inappropriate' ruling was attacked by mental health charities. Magistrates had heard how Sutton first tried to kill herself in August, when she was seen in the River Avon at Bath, Somerset. Two members of the public were preparing to jump in and rescue her when police arrived and hauled her to safety. She was treated in hospital before being arrested and later released. Three months later she was rescued from the same river twice in two hours. On the second occasion she even told council gardener Colin Hall to 'leave me alone' after he dived in to rescue her. Sutton, of Odd Down, Bath, had been found clinging to a railway parapet 'by her fingertips', forcing train services to be halted, and was often spotted on top of multi-storey car parks. After being convicted of three public order offences by Bath magistrates, she was given a 12-month conditional discharge and a five-point Asbo for two years. It bans her from going into rivers, canals or open water, loitering on bridges, going on to railway lines, entering multi-storey car parks unaccompanied, or acting in a way that causes harassment or alarm.

David Holden-White, defending, said her actions were not attempts to seek attention but genuine bids to take her own life. He said she suffered from 'an unstable personality disorder', adding: "She suffers from a burst of emotion and will act impulsively without regard for the consequences."

Chairman of the bench Pamela Gwyther warned her: "You are not to dip one toe, not one finger, in a river or canal." Sutton will face a jail sentence if she breaches the order. Mental health organisations criticised the court for the 'incredible' order, and accused it of not properly protecting the woman's life. Marjorie Wallace, chief executive of mental health charity *Sane*, said: "It seems extraordinary that a person who needs care and treatment should be put under what amounts to a criminal order. "It is quite inappropriate and ineffective, as a person who is very disturbed and intent on either attempting or committing suicide will find other means." She added: "It feels almost like a failure to protect the life of a patient." *Samaritans* spokeswoman Sarah Nelson said: "Criminalising suicide is not helpful. *Samaritans* believe people have a right to take their own life, but hope it can be alleviated, by talking about their feelings and working through them."

Sutton's social worker, Thomas Lockhead, of Bath South Community Mental Health Team, said her health had improved over the past nine months. But he added: "I am concerned that the Asbo might have a perverse incentive, because on some occasions, she finds it desirable to go to prison."

A foul-mouthed family was named and shamed on 1st March 2005, after subjecting neighbours to a five-year campaign of terror and violence. Benefits scrounger Stacey Weedon, 36, and her two daughters, both teenage mothers, were all handed three-year Anti Social Behaviour Orders. Residents had complained the family smashed windows and doors, fought with neighbours, hurled abuse at them and played loud music into the early hours. The orders ban Stacey and her daughters Charlie, 16, and Billie, 15, from threatening or intimidating anyone living in the entire London Borough of Havering. Mrs Weedon's layabout boyfriend Leslie Giggins, 42, was earlier made the subject of a five-year Asbo. The family are now facing eviction from their squalid terrace house in Harold Hill, Romford, Essex. Stratford magistrates heard how one neighbour was so traumatised she was forced to flee her home. And another elderly disabled woman who lived next door, had CCTV cameras installed outside her house.

The abuse became so bad, officials from the local housing association had to be accompanied by a police escort when they visited the family. A squad of eight police officers were put on standby to deal with Giggins. Terrified Sarah Kent told how she was subjected to a savage attack in her home by the three women. She said she came to the rescue of an injured victim after fighting broke out outside. Weedon and her daughters kicked in the front door and battered her with a pottery bowl, as she clutched her petrified four-year-old son to her chest. Ms Kent said: "I got very bad headaches after that." The windows in her car were also smashed, and she was so traumatised she moved out. When she returned to collect her mail her home was pelted with stones. She was later abused by Billie when she went to collect her child from school. She received a hoax call at her house and police were sent round after being told there were stolen goods inside. "I was very, very scared. I have three children and I have to think of them. I was really scared for my life. I had to leave. When I went back they tried to break in, shouting abuse and said they were going to kill me. I can't go back because every time I do, I get abuse."

The court heard that the women also attacked Ms Kent's mother, who runs a stall at Romford Market. Billie, who was seven months pregnant at the time, is alleged to have struck Eileen Kent with an umbrella as she screamed a torrent of abuse at her. The

Devastated garden of a house at Dagnam Park Drive, Harold Hill, Romford, Essex, caused by a whole family of anti-social neighbours - since evicted

stall was overturned in the melee. Eileen Kent said: "Billie came flying round with an umbrella in her hands. My daughter came out and said, 'You can't come here calling my mother a slag. My mother should not be abused by two young girls and by a mother as well'." Pensioner Pauline Meanwell, who walks with a stick, told an earlier hearing: "The filth, rubbish, cruelty to pets, loud music, criminal damage, threats, harassment and abuse to police and fire services, have blighted my life since the day I moved in, in 1999." Mrs Meanwell, who used to lend the family money and give them presents for their babies, added: "We don't talk to other people in the street now because we are scared of the repercussions. We just go into our own houses and if we want to talk it has to be on the phone. We shouldn't have to live like that in our own homes."

Housing association East Homes, sought the orders after receiving repeated complaints from residents, who enlisted the help of local MP Angela Watkinson. But many of the neighbours were too terrified to give evidence against the family for fear of reprisals. Paul Clarke, who was handling the matter for East Homes, told the earlier hearing how maintenance staff needed a police escort to attend the house. Weedon claimed she has split up with Giggins, and says he has moved to Bournemouth.

UPDATE: Jubilant neighbours were celebrating, after a judge gave the go-ahead to evict a family of louts who had waged a five-year campaign of terror and violence against them. Benefits scroungers Stacey Weedon, 36, and her layabout boyfriend Leslie Giggins, will have seven days to quit the terrace house they turned into a slum. Weedon's daughters Charlie, 16, and Billie, 15, who both have children of their own, are also being forced out. The ruling comes just two days after the foul-mouthed family were named and shamed by a court for making their neighbours' lives a living hell. They were blamed for a catalogue of vandalism and abuse. Broken furniture, old TV sets and discarded toys were among the rubbish piled in their back garden. The family, who have all been made the subject of Anti Social Behaviour Orders, were finally brought to justice, after two terrified women victims decided enough was enough, and made a public stand against them.

Disabled grandmother Pauline Meanwell, 56, was so terrified that she was forced to hire her own team of security guards. They stay overnight to protect her property next door to the Weedons in Harold Hill, near Romford, Essex. Divorcee Mrs Meanwell, who walks with the aid of a stick, has also installed CCTV cameras outside her home. Mother-of-three Sarah Kent fled in terror seven months ago and has not been able to return to her home since. It followed a terrifying attack when Mrs Weedon and her daughters kicked in her front door.

The women battered Ms Kent, 31, with household objects, as she clutched her petrified five-year-old son to her chest. The three women later ambushed members of Ms Kent's family at their clothing shop in Romford's indoor market. During the assault, Billie Weedon, who was seven months pregnant at the time, attacked Ms Kent's 26-year-old sister Louise with an umbrella. The neighbours were at Romford County Court, where a bid by the Weedons to be allowed to remain in their property was thrown out. After the hearing, delighted Mrs Meanwell said: "It's fantastic. I am looking forward to living in peace and quiet for the first time in years. I won't have to be always looking over my shoulder and wondering when I'm next going to come under attack. I don't like to see people being thrown on to the streets, but they had a lovely home which they have destroyed. They don't deserve to live in a place like that."

Ms Kent, who has been staying with her parents, said: "They truly are the family from hell. Nobody should have to put up with them. Until now they've just been laughing about all this. They were the ones causing all the problems, but they were still sitting there in their house with all their kids, while people like me were the victims. I've not lived in my home since last August. Now I can finally go back. It's brilliant. Justice has finally been done today, and not before time. Hopefully I can now go back to leading a normal life." The terror campaign by the Weedons began after they moved into the two-bedroom property owned by housing association East Homes, in December 1999. Neighbours complained that jobless Giggins 'ruled the street' through violence, harassment and intimidation. The family were accused of vandalising homes, smashing windows and doors, and bombarding residents with abuse. It became so bad that housing association officials had to be given a police escort. East Homes first began legal action against the family three years ago, after they failed to pay their rent. It is believed that the Weedons, who owe £955 in arrears,were claiming housing benefit but spending the money on other things. In October 2004 a warrant was issued to take possession of the property but the family were given more time to pay. District Judge Timothy Bowles dismissed an application by Mrs Weedon to have the eviction order suspended. The judge told the hearing, held behind closed doors, that he had taken into account the family's intimidation campaign, in reaching his decision. "It seems to me there is clearly concern that the lives of other tenants will continue to be blighted if the Weedons, and in particular Leslie Giggins, remain at the property," he said.

Previously Stratford magistrates handed three-year Anti Social Behaviour Orders to Mrs Weedon and her daughters. Giggins was made the subject of a five-year Asbo in February 2005. Mrs Weedon, who has two younger children with Giggins, claimed the couple had split up and he had moved to Bournemouth. But neighbours insist he is still living at the property. After the ruling Mark Kent, a manager at East Homes, said: "It has been regrettable to have to go this far, but it is important we consider the other tenants' rights to a quiet and peaceful enjoyment of their homes." Bailiffs backed up by police will now be instructed to evict the family. A police source said: "They will have seven days to get their things together and find alternative accommodation, but for practical reason, it's likely to be three weeks to a month before they can be removed."

Stacey Weedon has lost her rights to local authority accommodation and will have to rent or buy a property in the private sector. The family could be split up. A council source said: "Mrs Weedon will not be re-housed by any local authority in the country. Her two daughters both have young children of their own. The eldest girl, Charlie, is 16. She is entitled to immediate accommodation by social services. Billie is only 15 and she may be taken into care." As she left court, Stacey Weedon was unrepentant. "I've got another home to go to anyway," she said.

A Government crackdown on neighbours from hell, first announced four months ago, was dismissed as a tired 'gimmick' on 14th February 2005. The Conservatives said the Home Office spent more on its staff mobile phone bill last year than on yesterday's high-profile blitz of householders who make their neighbours lives a misery. The total pledged to tackle so-called 'neighbours from hell' in 50 hotspots was £1.25million, compared to a total mobile bill of £1.5million in 2003/4. The new Home Office cash is the equivalent of £25,000 for each trouble-plagued area. Shadow Home Secretary, David Davis, said: "These proposals are just a re-hash of existing Government policy on anti-social behaviour. "Ordinary people want workable solutions to difficult, nuisance neighbours, not attention grabbing headlines and gimmicks. The fact that the Home Office's mobile phone bill is higher than the amount of money promised yesterday, shows how seriously this Labour government takes anti-social behaviour."

The Home Office first announced the crackdown in September. It announced the names of the 50 new 'hotspots'. In these areas, rowdy tenants who persistently break the rules will be given a 'final warning' they face eviction. Home Office Minister Hazel Blears said moves to 'rehabilitate' problem families would also include treatment for drugs and alcohol and encouraging children to go to school. The crackdown will target 1,000 of the worst families in the country, the Home Office said. Police and councils will also use warnings such as Acceptable Behaviour Contracts and Anti-Social Behaviour Orders.

During a visit to a family support project in Eccles, Manchester, Mrs Blears admitted: "It's not a lot of money." Yet she insisted: "But it will help in getting people to change their behaviour. Many families are facing eviction. We don't want them to be evicted, we want them to change their behaviour. Mrs Blears also published a study of 100 cases of bad anti-social behaviour, showing a quarter of 'nuisance neighbours' have been evicted from previous homes. In 38 per cent of the families, children were not attending school regularly or at all. Half of the cases involved threatening and intimidating behaviour and some had been dragging on for many years. The longest-standing case had lasted for 18 years. The problems were curtailed in 66 per cent of the cases, according to follow-up studies. But Liberal Democrat Home Affairs spokesman Mark Oaten said: "The solution for nuisance neighbours depends on changing behaviour, not just doling out punishment. Simply evicting troublesome families moves the problem to other locations." The Government has repeatedly vowed to be tough on loutish behaviour but many of the schemes have flopped. Late sitting of magistrates' courts, based on US night courts, were trumpeted by former Home Secretary Jack Straw in 2001, but a £5.4million pilot scheme proved difficult to manage and was dropped. Prime Minister Tony Blair suggested in June 2000 that police should march drunken thugs to cash points and collect £100 on-the-spot fines.

It was never discussed again. Also, one third of ASBOs are breached, which carries a possible prison sentence. Other measures which have been introduced by the Government, include banning sale of spray paint to under-16s, to deter vandals, a new £100 fine for noisy neighbours and the power to confiscate audio equipment and £50 fines for graffiti and fly-posting. The Home Office has yet to publish any research on the effectiveness of its measures. But it has announced that 10,000 parish and town councils in England are to get powers to hand out on-the-spot fines for littering, dog-fouling, graffiti, fly-posting and night-time noise.

COUNT 16

AIR RAGE

My only personal experience in this field would be better classified under the heading of AIR DAMN NUISANCE or even, IN-AIR RAGE EXPERIENCED BY LONG-SUFFERING, LAW-ABIDING PASSENGERS.

I was returning from a fabulous winter holiday in Cyprus, my favourite holiday destination of choice, in January 2002. Unable to obtain a direct flight home, I flew across the Island from Paphos to Lanarka airport, to take on more passengers. The first, very short leg of the journey home was absolute bliss for all on board. However the airline had made the tragic, unforgivable and very costly mistake of allowing onto our oh-so-peaceful *Cyprus Airways* aircraft, a bunch of 6-8 foul-mouthed, noisy, drunken football hooligans in their early 30's, masquerading as golfing enthusiasts.

I regret to report that these thugs gave a first impression to existing passengers that there had been a mass break-out from Nicosia prison on Cyprus - it seemed that only the prison warders were missing. Their loud cavorting, swearing, seat-vibrating, meal-and-drinks spilling, bad-breath-imposing behaviour, was not appreciated one bit. In fact the whole cabin was immersed under a cloud of fear and trepidation, so much so that even strong-charactered, confident, professional wrestlers on board, returning from the 2002 International Wrestling Association AGM in Limassol, concealed their secret notes to cabin crew asking for urgent help, under the guise of filling out duty-free order forms, which were soon to be collected by stewards and hostesses. The noise was appalling and cabin crew were totally out-of-order in supplying even more drinks to the frontal-lobotomists who were sitting in row 26, viz: RIGHT BEHIND ME!

Forget reading your book, your *Cyprus News*, your safety card, looking for drop-down oxygen masks, forget checking whether you're wearing stiletto heels which might puncture the pneumatic escape-chute, forget everything, how can you even THINK with morons like that slouching behind you and kidney-punching you every 3 minutes with their over-sized knees and rugby jokes and songs? If you were lucky, you did not have two black eyes from being poked with their guitar cases, possibly containing sub-machine guns – or their 'golf-bags', 12-feet tall, when they stowed them in the overhead lockers, dislodging everyone else's dainty cabin holdalls. As you can imagine, they were all Essex thugs, mostly from Romford, self-tattooed with *love* on one set of knuckles and *hate* on the other, Popeye-sized fists (Just like working out the age of a fallen tree by counting its annular rings, it is possible to calculate their numbers of convictions resulting in custodial sentences, by reference to their HMP-inked self-tattooed forearms, bodily-piercing sites using HMP paper clips, plus, the number of times they hawk in their throats and eject the resultant puce globules into their paper coffee cups.).

These are what airline flights dreams are made of, or should I say, NIGHTMARES or FLIGHTMARES? Tragically for the other 279 innocent adult and children passengers, there was not a single SKY MARSHAL or AIR MARSHAL on board, to use them for target-practice with non-pressurised-air-cabin-penetrating bullets. Even if there had been, even well-placed head-shots would not have stopped these loud, unruly barbarians.

Dozens of *Tescos* staff were thrown off a flight before take-off after the captain said they were 'drunk and disorderly' and the cabin stank of alcohol. Police helped eject the 37 staff, who were feared 'a potential safety threat'. *Tescos* however, insisted it was 'no more than good-natured banter among colleagues' and 'an over-reaction' by the captain and crew. No one was arrested in the incident at Glasgow airport, but those thrown off the *Flybe* flight were delayed for the night. They returned home to Belfast the following morning. Three other *Tesco* staff and 17 other passengers were on the flight when it finally took off three hours late. The *Tescos* group, which included store managers, accountants and personnel managers, had attended a company meeting in Glasgow.

Flybe defended its decision. A spokesman said: "The captain felt their presence as a group was a potential threat to the safety of other passengers, because of the drunk and disorderly behaviour of a number of individuals.

He discerned a strong smell of alcohol in the passenger cabin."

We should not forget the so-called 'celeb', former Wimbledon football player, now turned 'film star' Mr Vinnie 'Smoking Shotgun Barrels' Jones, 39. He was probably the first two-bit, well-known thug to be arrested for 'Air Rage'. He created a terrifying mid-air attack in which he threatened to have the cabin crew murdered. He too, was 'let off' by a judge living on a different planet to you and me. Volatile Jones was fined £500 and ordered to carry out 80 hours of community service. I'll bet the passengers who experienced Jones's outrageous and frightening behaviour on that plane, on hearing about the result at his trial, were reassured that the judge had seen that justice was done - Some hopes!

When the Acts of Parliament first were updated to allow for severe penalties for unruly and frightening, dangerous behaviour in mid-air, drunken thugs and hooligans were being sent to jail left, right and centre. However judicial complacency has now set in, with the passage of time and ever-increasing liberalism, so much so that you've practically got to almost bring an aircraft down before you get to see the inside of a prison cell. Where will it all end, I expect you're asking yourself?

A man who racially abused a group of Asians on a holiday jet was described by a judge as 'a disgrace to the human race'. Christopher Harper, 51, of Bristol, made a throat-slitting motion to one of five Asians sitting in front of him and asked to see his passport, Bristol Crown Court heard. Harper, who had been drinking, was returning home to Bristol from Malaga, Spain with his 73-year-old father when he began taunting the Asians. He admitted racially aggravated disorder and was sentenced to 200 hours of community service. His father was Bound Over to Keep the Peace after the court heard he told the group: "My taxes are keeping you lot."

On 22nd November 2004 at Manchester Crown Court, a drunken passenger who terrorised passengers on a US Airways flight from Philadelphia, USA to Manchester, in August 2004, paid a high price for his drunken rampage. Aron Berhane, 44yrs, born in Ethiopia, was employed as a baggage handler at Los Angeles Airport, USA. His drunken and terrifying behaviour took place when the trans-Atlantic passenger jet was cruising at 30,000 feet. Berhane had breached security by somehow sneaking a bottle of whisky on board the aircraft and hiding it under his seat in a white bag. In his drunken state he started making adverse, insulting comments about Jews and Muslims, and spat at passengers. A passenger unlucky enough to be seated beside Berhane, Mr Jason Williams, said: "Berhane said Islam was an unfortunate religion, for making people do things like 9/11." He asked Mr Williams which was his religion and he replied that he followed no religion at all. Berhane then tried to make him accept a crucifix, but Mr Williams declined to accept it, which only made Berhane all the more persistent. Mr Williams was unable to calm him down, so drunken Berhane left his seat. Whilst brandishing the crucifix, he tried to press the crucifix against the heads of various children on the flight, which alarmed many passengers. One mother tried to block him from doing this, but he struck out in a chopping motion and in doing so, bruised the mother's forearm. She thought she and her children were being attacked, so she screamed for help, fearing for her life. An air stewardess asked him to return to his seat, whereupon he punched her in the face. She cried out for some help and at least six passengers dashed to her assistance. Whilst they held him, he was handcuffed by the flight crew. During the rest of the flight to Manchester, Berhane berated Jews and Israelis and was rude to other passengers. He was arrested when the flight touched down at Manchester and it was observed that his whisky bottle was by then empty. At Manchester Crown Court he pleaded guilty to affray and drunkenness on an aircraft. He was told by Judge Jonathan Geake: "This is entirely your fault, you were behaving in a bizarre way, terrifying fellow passengers. You must know that these incidents are made all the more worrying since 9/11 for the public. It is nerve-wracking for people to travel in airplanes, particularly in the present climate. You acted quite deplorably. You were so drunk you barely knew what you were doing and you behaved in a most peculiar way." He was sentenced to 9 months imprisonment. His defence barrister Lisa Judge told the court that Berhane had turned to drink because he was a nervous flier.

A drunken pilot who was arrested minutes before he was due to fly a plane packed with 225 British passengers to Turkey, was jailed for six months on 2nd December 2004. It was the first prosecution since new laws to breath-test aircrew were introduced in March 2004. Heikki Tallila, 51, was found drunk in the captain's seat of the *Finnair* Boeing 757 only 23 minutes before take-off, a court was told. Acting on a tip-off, police escorted him off the plane at Manchester airport before breathalysing him. Blood test results revealed that Tallila was more than twice the legal limit for flying. He was immediately suspended by the airline and has now lost his £100,000-a-year job. The pilot, from Espoo, near Helsinki, had drunk six glasses of wine and a beer the day before he was due to fly the plane 1,600 miles to Turkey, Minshull Street Crown Court in Manchester was told. He pleaded guilty to an offence under the new Transport Act 2003 of having excess alcohol in his blood whilst carrying out aviation duties. The arrest was sparked by a bus driver employed by the airport to ferry pilots, cabin crew and other workers from the car parks to the terminal buildings. He called police as the pilot was going through pre-flight checks for the 7.20am flight from Manchester to Dalaman. Mrs Linda Walker, prosecuting, said: "This is the first prosecution under the new Act which came into force in March. It is certainly the first in Manchester and the first to be sentenced, though one other case is pending at Heathrow. Police boarded the plane at 7.35am and saw the defendant sat in the captain's seat. A blood sample showed he had 49 milligrams of alcohol in 100 millilitres of blood. He was then charged." The legal limit for a pilot is 20mg - for a driver it is 80mg. British law states pilots must not drink eight hours before a flight. But *Finnair* crew are banned from drinking 12 hours before a flight. At the time of his arrest, *Finnair* said Tallila had been with the company for 20 years and was said to have a 'very good record'. Passing sentence, Judge John Burke QC, told him: "You had the well-being of over 200 passengers in your care. If you had been a passenger and misbehaved you would have gone to prison for causing problems and alarming your fellow passengers and the crew." Gerard McDermott QC, defending, said: "This defendant is 51 years old and finds himself in a foreign country facing a serious charge, and is likely to lose his flying licence for at least two years and has also lost his job."

A woman airline pilot had drunk the equivalent of eight shots of spirits or four beers before attempting to take off in a packed plane. The pilot, who works for *EasyJet* out of Luton Airport, may even have drunk more, police said. She was breathalysed at 6.45am on a Saturday, several hours after her drinking binge had ended. The pilot, who earns £70,000 a year, was found to be **MORE THAN FOUR TIMES OVER THE LEGAL LIMIT** as she attempted to fly the Airbus 319 from Berlin to Basel in Switzerland. She was suspended on full pay pending an inquiry and has now returned to Britain. German authorities believe she may have been drinking until 3am before rising at 5.30am at her hotel in the German capital. She then travelled to Schoenefeld Airport where she was arrested. One officer said: "It is unlikely that alcohol was her breakfast. The body loses alcohol at a rate of a unit per hour. It is highly likely that she drank much more than this (eight shots of spirit or four beers)." It is understood another crew member alerted police because of her condition. She was stopped, breathalysed and led away before she had reached the cockpit of the plane, which was due to carry some 120 passengers. In a statement, *EasyJet* said: "Throughout our nine years of operations, we have never before encountered an incident such as this. Should the allegations relating to this incident be proven, *EasyJet* would be extremely disappointed and distressed." An alternative pilot was found for the flight and the plane left 20 minutes late. Prosecutors in Berlin have been handed details of the case and a prosecution is 'highly likely', according to a spokesman. The pilot faces two years in jail if charged with, and found guilty of, endangering an aircraft, even though she never made it into the cockpit. Under UK Civil Aviation Authority regulations, pilots must not drink alcohol in the eight hours before reporting for duty. A CAA spokesman said: "Fortunately instances such as these are fairly rare. The rules are clear. You are not allowed to fly if you have more than 20 milligrams of alcohol per 100 milli-litres of blood in the system." *EasyJet*, which has 45 women among its 1,036 pilots, said it banned its crews from drinking for 10 hours before flying.

Former *Stone Roses* singer Ian Brown is still denying he committed the air rage crime that led to him spending two months in prison. Brown was released on Christmas Eve after serving half of a four month sentence for using threatening behaviour towards an air stewardess and the captain of a flight from Paris to Manchester in February 1998. Magistrates heard how he told the stewardess he would 'chop her hands off' and how he banged on the door of the aircraft's cockpit. He told music weekly *NME*: "I got put away for something that I never said. My mother's been reading lies about me. I didn't do it. I didn't swear at the woman, I didn't approach any cockpit. They claim I banged on the cockpit and charged me with endangering lives. I'm saying what they charged me with I didn't do." Brown spent most of his sentence at Strangeways prison in Manchester.

At his trial he admitted telling *British Airways* stewardess Christine Cooper he would 'chop her hands off' - but said it was meant as a joke. He also admitted tapping on the cockpit door, but it was to try to get the names of the crew to complain about their treatment of him. Brown, who started his comeback by making a surprise appearance at a London concert by the group *Unkle*, had his appeal against the case thrown out in November, after Judge Simon Fawcus said he was guilty of 'disgraceful and loutish behaviour'. He was banned by *British Airways* from all the company's flights. He is angry with press coverage of the case, especially the music press, which he feels should have backed him. "The NME and all these papers, they are supposed to be representing the youth which is anti-establishment and all, yet these papers are calling me a hooligan and such. They're taking the words of the captain of the plane and using them against me." he said. Brown, who is nominated for best male artist in the Brit Awards, features on the new *Unkle* single 'Be There', which is due for release. He cancelled a UK tour shortly before he was released, but is now working on a new album to follow his first solo release *Unfinished Monkey Business*. It has a working title of *From The Inside*.

A routine holiday flight home turned ugly for Parkside, Cambridgeshire detective, Simon Flint, as he struggled for 90 minutes to restrain a violent passenger. Simon, 34, was returning from Bangkok to London via Frankfurt with his friend, Jason Finnegan, a Hertfordshire officer, when the air-rage drama began. Six hours into the packed *Thai Airways* flight, Simon noticed a drunken, German passenger 10 rows in front, standing up, shouting loudly and gesticulating at other passengers. The passenger became increasingly violent and as female cabin crew tried to intervene, another man leapt to his feet and grabbed the German round the throat pushing him against the side of the plane. "The situation had got out of hand," said Simon "and I thought the female cabin crew would like some assistance." He alerted Jason, also 34, as to what was happening and both officers identified themselves to cabin crew. The crew cleared the business section of the aircraft of other passengers while Simon and Jason explained through a translator to the passenger that they were going to escort him to the front of the aircraft. "The man refused my requests, and the requests from the Staff. He was at this time gesticulating and shouting at us. I was concerned he would become physical with me or anyone else on the aircraft and put the safety of everybody on the flight in danger," said Simon. Putting the passenger in transport wrist locks, the two officers escorted him to business class where they spent 90 minutes trying to restrain him, efforts that reached a climax as the aircraft came into land and the passenger began to struggle violently. With everyone strapped into their seat belts and Jason able to restrain only one of the man's arms, Simon was forced to unstrap his own belt and stand up to restrain the passenger seconds before touchdown.

"I was standing up as we landed," said Simon, "it was certainly the most interesting flight I've been on and was actually quite scary at times to be honest and I missed the in-flight film! The man was very drunk and just wanted another drink. He was travelling with his wife and she tried to explain to him that he should calm down, but she left him to us when he wouldn't take any notice. German police met the aircraft and took away the passenger, and Simon and Jason were thanked by passengers and crew. Their reward was a tour of the first class area of the aircraft and flight deck and, later, a letter of thanks from the airline and gifts each of a Thai Airways silk tie and travel document case.

An airline passenger has landed taxpayers with a £12,000 bill after he got drunk and caused trouble on a flight to Thailand. Jobless Anthony Seddon-Knight, 56, swore at an air stewardess when she challenged him about an empty whisky bottle under his seat. A court heard a subsequent investigation into the incident by the Civil Aviation Authority cost an estimated £12,000. The authority said it had to hire an investigator to examine what happened aboard the flight and the expert charged by the hour. Minshull Street Crown Court, Manchester, heard Seddon-Knight would not be able to pay a penny towards the costs as he is on benefits. The bill will now probably be picked up by the public purse. Earlier Zabeda Maqsood, prosecuting told the court how the incident occurred on the morning of July 11, 2000 on *Britannia Airways'* flight BY352. There were 316 passengers on board at the time and nine cabin crew. An hour away from landing at Abu Dhabi airport, senior cabin crew member Carol Colleridge and crew member Samantha Ford were handing out meals. They noticed a female passenger sitting in the central aisle with an empty bottle of vodka on her table tray. "The cabin crew spoke to the female who was slumped over," said Miss Maqsood. "There were concerns for her welfare as she was foaming at the mouth. The defendant was sitting next to her. As a result of her condition he was questioned but denied knowing her." It later emerged the woman was Seddon-Knight's partner and both had been heavily drinking. Seddon-Knight was later challenged by other crew members but became increasingly abusive and refused to sit down and co-operate. They were met by police when the plane landed at Abu Dhabi airport and were removed from the flight. Seddon-Knight, of Barlow Lane, Eccles, pleaded guilty to being drunk on an aircraft and was sentenced to a 200 hour community punishment order. In mitigation, defence counsel Mr Peter Cadwallader said the incident was 'entirely out of character'.

A drunken yob who brought terror to a holiday jet at 30,000ft was behind bars on 7th March 2005. Paul Tolley, 38, had downed nine pints of lager before boarding the flight. He was supposed to be on his way to a new life in Spain with his girlfriend. But his air rage attack forced the captain to make an emergency landing and call in security guards to arrest him. Tolley, a labourer, of Scarborough, North Yorkshire, caused trouble before even boarding the *Monarch Airlines* flight from Manchester to Alicante, a judge heard. Passengers complained that Tolley had attempted to light a cigarette in an airport no-smoking area. He and his girlfriend were moved to the second row of seats on the aircraft so they could be closely monitored.

Before the jet took off, Tolley interrupted stewardess Susan Broadhurst's safety announcement to ask her for a date. Steven Johnson, prosecuting, said: "When the drinks trolley was pushed down the cabin he demanded alcohol. He frightened the cabin crew, saying, 'Give me a drink if you know what's good for you'." Miss Broadhurst feared he might 'punch her lights out'. When the captain. Craig Turner, left the controls to ask Tolley to curb his loutish behaviour, he swore and replied: "Just fly the plane." "The most troubling thing was that women and children were on the flight and appeared frightened. Some children were crying." Mr Johnson told Minshull Street Crown Court, Manchester. "Tolley also didn't seem able to say anything without using the 'F' word, saying it practically every other word." Cabin crew believed Tolley was on the verge of assaulting Captain Turner,

Mr Johnson said. Captain Turner locked himself and other crew in the cockpit and diverted the Airbus 321 to Bordeaux. Many of the other 167 passengers shouted 'off, off, off' in relief, as Tolley was led away by French security guards. One woman told police her five-year-old son was plagued by nightmares for a week after the incident, in August 2003, and refused to fly home. Another holidaymaker, Christopher Robinson, said: "There was an element of fear. My wife is a nervous flyer anyway and my children were with me. It's not like coming across something in the street. I had a feeling of helplessness, what would I do if something happened?"

Tolley admitted interfering with an aircraft and was jailed for 11 months. Judge Robert Atherton told him: "You behaved in a selfish and boorish manner, you were trying to throw your weight around on the aircraft, probably fuelled by drink. We all go on flights now and you can't help but reflect at six miles in the air, there is no way out if something goes wrong." After the incident, Tolley and his girlfriend split up. He returned to Scarborough to live in a flat with his mother. Taryn Turner, defending, told the court: "The defendant was flying to Spain to settle with his now ex-girlfriend. His actions were as a result of his consumption of alcohol. He had had nine pints before boarding the flight, and be believes he should not have been allowed on the plane, though he now accepts that the fault is his own.

Over recent years international airlines have witnessed a massive increase in air rage incidents:

19th January 2005 – Tenerife

A Norwegian man had to be tied up after he started to assault passengers on a flight from Trondheim to Canary Islands. The man from Trondelag was reportedly already drunk when he boarded the flight. Passengers restrained the man.

12th January 2005 – Moscow

A flight from Toronto to Moscow was diverted to Iceland because of a man in a state of alcoholic intoxication who provoked a fight, swore wildly and shouted at the crew and passengers.

10TH January 2005 – Orlando

A 66 year old woman was arrested on a flight from Orlando to Albuquerque after she started to act strangely on the flight by laying down her seat, blocking the aisle with her legs, exposing her bra to the cabin crew and placing her hand on the crotch of a sleeping male passenger. While speaking to a flight attendant she said 'I know there is a bomb on the plane' and 'I know we are being hijacked'. After being arrested she then proceeded to tell an airport officer and a US customs agent that she was going to kill the FBI agent who had interrogated her. While being transported to jail she asked how much money the officers made and offered to pay them between several hundred to a thousand dollars if they let her go, the officers asked her if she was trying to bribe them in their capacity as federal agents. She answered 'Yes'.

4th January 2005 – China

A man was arrested in China accused of trying to hijack a passenger jet to Taiwan. The man was detained after he told cabin crew on the flight from Harbin to Xiamen that he wanted to fly to Taiwan and threatened to kill himself. He had a knife which he held to his throat in an effort to convince the cabin staff who, instead, overpowered him.

There were 696 incidents of air-rage in the 12 months to March 2004, according to the Department of Transport.

Most readers will be aware that some sort of *prison cells,* normally referred to as 'THE BRIG', have been installed in HM and Merchant Navy ships almost since time immemorial.

Having read in this chapter about just a few incidents which have shocked and frightened air passengers in recent years, I predict that it is almost inevitable that future passenger aircraft will have such cells incorporated into the cabin space, so that such air rage etc. offenders can be more easily confined, for the safety and peace of mind of all on board.

COUNT 17

FRAUD

Section 15 Theft Act 1968

A person who, by any deception, dishonestly obtains property belonging to another, with the intention of permanently depriving the other of it, shall on conviction on indictment be liable to imprisonment for a term not exceeding ten years.

Whilst serving in the Metropolitan Police, as a very junior CID officer, (A TDC – Temporary Detective Constable) then stationed at Hornchurch, Essex, I had the good fortune, in fact the honour, to be selected and appointed as Exhibits Officer in a very serious fraud. This major fraud had been practiced at the Ford Motor Company at Dagenham, Essex for many years, involving tipper truck drivers, weigh bridge staff and outside contractors. Ford Motor Company (FOMOCO) engines used to be manufactured in the huge foundry there. Cast iron engine blocks used to be created from sand moulds whereby molten metal was poured into the moulds and left until fully set or 'cast', whereupon staff would 'clean them up' by chipping off the odd fragments of metal, from where the molten metal had run awry, leaving the 'clean' engine blocks ready for use. Later, in other departments, pistons, crankshafts etc. would be added until a complete engine was created. It was essential for FOMOCO to buy-in from outside metal and sand contractors, huge quantities of scrap iron and sand, basic 'ingredients' for the foundry engine casting process. Huge, maximum size tipper lorries would arrive at the Fords weigh bridge. Some would be full to the brim with sand, others with scrap metal. The sand would be used, as I have described, for creating the engine mouldings. In the blast furnace, the scrap iron would be converted into molten metal and poured into the moulds.

Each driver of a tipper truck arriving at the weigh bridge would hand in a delivery note from his employer, bearing the firm's name, address etc, vehicle registration number, nature of load, e.g. sand or scrap metal etc. Weigh bridge staff would then weigh the loaded truck on its way in, and again as it left the premises. Tickets would be printed which would specify the 'gross' and 'tare' or unladen weight, in tons or tonnes. Obviously the difference between the two figures on each weigh bridge ticket would result in an invoice being raised for the net amount of scrap metal or sand being purchased by FOMOCO. Tipper truck drivers would leave the premises with their copy of weigh bridge tickets, which would be handed later to their employers. These would be used by the outside contractors to calculate the number of daily runs the tipper driver had made, to calculate his pay. More importantly, the tickets would be attached to contractors' invoices, so that they could claim their payments for each delivered load, from FOMOCO.

However the Ford's weigh bridge operating system was found to be open to abuse. Weigh bridge operating staff discovered that multiple weighings could be made, to the financial advantage of the weigh bridge staff, tipper truck drivers, and sand and scrap metal contractors. A secondary major fraud was run side-by-side with the 'duplicate weighings'. The commodity of sand, weighs far heavier than scrap metal. Therefore there was a huge financial advantage for all concerned if a tipper truck load of sand was described and invoiced as a load of scrap metal, as the latter was purchased by Ford at a far greater price per ton or tonne than its equivalent in sand. As I recall, the first indication to the Security Department at Ford, that all was not as it should be at the Dagenham plant, came when, during routine maintenance I believe, an essential part of the weigh bridge mechanism, a piece of metal known as a 'fishtail', was removed. I believe thistail removal took place when the normal weigh bridge staff were absent, perhaps on a bank holiday, shutdown or suchlike. The very first time after that, when the weigh bridge staff attempted to carry out their fraudulent weighings, in the absence of the fish device, the huge, heavy mechanism of the weighbridge apparently 'bucked and kicked' so violently, it was thought that the office roof would come down, as the building vibrated and shook!

At Hornchurch police station, huge batches of weigh bridge tickets, delivery notes and invoices were delivered and a team of approx 8-10 of us commenced the marathon task of sorting this documentation into approximate date order etc. The eventual aim of the exercise was to match up as many fraudulent, multiple-weighings as possible and then cross-reference them with their individual drivers' delivery notes and contractor-generated invoices for payment. In this way, from a criminal court evidential point of view, we would have continuity and a perfect chain of evidence, as in due course, FOMOCO would produce for our inspection and comparison, the individual sets of documentation to prove that the sand and scrap metal merchants had subsequently been paid for each and every bogus transaction. As stated, this proved to be a mammoth task, as desk top work surfaces were in short supply, for each officer to spread out his next batch of documentation for identification and subsequent reconciliation. Millions of individual documents had been generated during this 'scam' at Ford Motor Company. The size of individual weigh bridge tickets was very small, say, about two inches by five inches. In addition to having the (fraudulent) weight printed on the slips by the weigh bridge mechanism, they bore the purported date of the transaction. Some fraudulent weigh bridge tickets were easily recognisable at once, as the weight printed thereon in tonnes, hundredweights and quarters, would be smudged or slightly double printed, proving to be a tell-tale mark of a 'double or multi-weighing' and thus a criminal deception.

As the enquiry slowly developed, we noticed that identical weighing slips, right down to the exact recording of tonnes, hundredweights and quarters, were submitted by the scrap metal contractors, for perhaps, several different tipper trucks on the same day. In other words, multi-fraudulent weighing tickets had been printed off, by pulling the operating lever as many times as the staff felt like doing so. This meant that assorted, identical tickets, could be apparently 'shared around' the individual tipper trucks in the transport fleets of the various sand and metal contractors, all of whom partook in the vast, multi-million pounds criminal deception. In other words, Ford Motor Company, over time, paid out far in excess of the amount which should lawfully have been claimed by the contractors.

In our CID mini-fraud squad offices at Hornchurch, we spent months and months peering at millions of pieces of paper, placing them in individual piles under various headings, for later reconciliation with their corresponding delivery notes and eventual invoices submitted to Fords for payment by all of the contractors. With all of that paperwork flying about, some of it damp and mildewed with age, it was essential to be able to keep track of it. We therefore invested in thousands of coloured stickers in multi-shapes, for attaching to individual weigh bridge tickets, delivery notes etc. These stickers proved to be an amazing aid and were invaluable in identifying and tracing the whereabouts of a particular ticket or delivery note, at a moments notice, to extract from the system and pass up to the Trial Judge for his inspection. In fact there were so many individual documents, some little more than scraps of paper, that at the eventual fraud trial at the Central Criminal Court (Old Bailey), as Exhibits Officer, I needed a full sized, multi-drawer metal filing cabinet, present inside the court room, from which I could access the system. Eventually, after about two years of diligent, mostly boring, paper sifting and shuffling, the trial was held under His Honour Judge Grant.

Almost from day one of the trial, we got the feeling that the elderly Judge could neither understand, nor keep up with the pace of the trial. Mr Brian Watling, leading Treasury Counsel, was in charge of the prosecution team. The last I heard of him he was a Judge at Chelmsford Crown Court. He was magnificent and had a wonderful understanding of the intricacies of the case, I thought. Naturally, in those days there were no computers available, as these days, all of the reconciliations of the millions of documents would be carried out in computer programmes, taking perhaps weeks instead of our two years approx. As is often the case, the result at Court was a complete disaster and disappointment. As I recall, no jury was required as all defendants pleaded guilty to various offences of criminal deception and/or conspiracy to defraud the Ford Motor Company. Out of approx 17 or more defendants in the dock, only one received a sentence of imprisonment, and that was for so short a term that it was nothing to write home about. Oh well, we all know by now that life is FULL of disappointments!

Our only consolation, as the Ford major-fraud squad team members, was that we received various commendations, both locally and from New Scotland Yard. However the whole exercise had been of enormous benefit to us as individual CID officers and provided us with great experience, which was to stand us in good stead for many years to come. Even to this day, if I have a complicated problem to sort out or unravel, the very first thing I do is to create a chronological SCHEDULE of data, or even a series of schedules. These documents have proved invaluable to me, in seeing clearly what action is next required to progress the matter further to satisfactory conclusion.

Here are some reports of modern frauds, of various types, but disappointingly perhaps, for you, not one of them was on the same scale as the widely-publicised Ford Motor Company, Dagenham weigh bridge major fraud.

At Bournemouth Crown Court on 5th March 2004, a self-styled alternative therapist was on trial for tricking a terminally ill cancer patient. Reginald Gill, 68, of Poole, told Stephen Hall, 43, of Flint, North Wales, he could cure him with a £200 device for minor aches. Stephen refused chemotherapy and was sold the electrical machine for £2,500, by Gill. The latter was found guilty of three counts under the Trade Descriptions Act. Recorder Lorraine Morgan told Gill: "You must have filled his last months with a false hope whilst taking his money." Gill was jailed for 12 months.

At Chelmsford Crown Court on 2nd April 2004, dentist Michael Bolsin, 51, of Harwich, admitted false accounting and furnishing false information. His MO was to submit bogus claims for work on fictitious patients, thus attempting to defraud the NHS of almost £10,000. Judge Ben Pearson told Bolsin: "Over the course of some 18 months you embarked on a sophisticated and determined course of dishonesty." Bolsin was jailed for nine months.

Three gangmasters who ruled an empire of illegal immigrant workers, appeared at Kings Lynn Crown Court for sentence on 2nd April 2004 for money-laundering offences. Rusian Kulish, 28, of Ely, David Mutch, 58, of Soham, and John Carter, 58, of Caldecote, ran an operation in which more than 250 illegal workers from Eastern Europe were employed on farms and in food factories. They supplied workers with false papers and convinced farmers and factory managers that they were running a legitimate operation, the court was told. Police said the scam generated more than £4 million in 33 months, with the three, all from Cambridgeshire, sharing profits of around £1 million which they laundered by buying property.

Kulish was jailed for seven years, Mutch was jailed for six years and Carter was jailed for four and a half years.

Another gangmaster, who with his son, ran a £10million illegal immigrant slave labour racket has been stripped of more than £400,000. Victor Cox, 56, who masterminded the scam with his son Jayson, 35, has been ordered to hand over cash, shares and even half of his detached home. If he fails to do so, by April 2005, a further five-years imprisonment will be added to his seven-year jail sentence, a judge at Canterbury Crown Court has ruled. The gang bosses were jailed in March 2004 after the court heard that more than 1,700 immigrants were being paid just £1 per hour. The father and son lived a millionaire-lifestyle with mansions in Norfolk and expensive Mercedes cars. The son Jayson will face his confiscation proceedings at a hearing in September 2004.

At Sheffield Crown Court on 2nd April 2004, Jim Speechley, 67, former leader of Lincolnshire County Council, who tried to change the route of a bypass to boost the value of his land, was dealt with. He had tried to influence the route of the Spalding to Eye bypass, so it would run closer to a four-acre field that he owned. He had told a highways engineer working on the project, that he did not like the original plan and wanted it altered. He had hoped that a new route would make his land more attractive to potential developers. Judge Simon Lawler QC, told him: "When such conduct is found proved, the court is bound to take a very serious view. It strikes at the very roots of our democracy. We must have confidence in our public servants." Speechley was jailed for 18 months for misconduct in public office. He was also ordered to pay £25,000 costs.

A female impersonator called Paul Downes, 35, from Hockley, Birmingham, was not what he seemed in more ways than one. He claimed he was too ill to work and took benefits of £54 per week. But by night he was paid up to £200 a time to appear in clubs across the country, dressed up in a long, spangly dress, long blonde wig and full make-up. Downes, who appeared at Birmingham Crown Court, soberly dressed as a man, in January 2004, admitted three charges of obtaining benefit by criminal deception and asked for a further 126 similar offences to be TIC.

He began claiming benefits on the grounds of ill health in 1995, but by 1998 he was working under the stage name 'FollyB' as a drag artist. He worked all over the country for a company called *Studio One*. He sometimes worked as a compere too and would work most months and earn £150 - £200 per performance. Before he was caught out, he had accrued £18,959 more than he was entitled to. When he was caught, he made frank confessions. His barrister told the court that since June 2003, Downes had paid back £300 of the money he owes. He was depressed and anxious and ill and is now full of remorse for the way he acted. "He is a very quiet and private man and if he was to go to prison for fraud, he could be at risk from the degradations of other inmates. When he performed he only made an extra few pounds. He is full of remorse. I believe these are exceptional circumstances and Mr Downes throws himself at the hands of the court for a merciful sentence." The judge at the Crown Court placed him on probation for two years and ordered him to undertake 50 hours of community service. After the case, Downes made no comment. (Most unusually, a [secret] hearing was held in the judge's chambers before the case, attended by all parties.)

Matters arising:

1) Would you like to have been a fly on the wall in (secrecy of) the judge's chambers?

2) If you were the investigating Benefits Officer, would you feel justice was done?

3) Do you think the punishment fitted the crime?

4) Was this a case where the sweetest-talking barrister achieved the best result?

5) How many other 'entertainers' are working in the 'black economy' would you think?

6) What proportion of your council tax goes to subsidise people of Mr Downes's ilk?

Conman Ian Bussey, 37, swindled top soccer clubs out of pricey memorabilia by claiming his son had cancer. The scam fooled 28 football clubs, including Chelsea, Everton and Newcastle United. Liverpool sent a signed photograph of Michael Owen. Bussey wrote to 92 clubs saying that he wanted to give his child one last dream holiday at Disneyland. He stated that he would auction off any donated items. At Teesside Crown Court, Bussey admitted forgery. The judge told him it was a 'mean and despicable offence'. However you may well consider that the Judge's 'bark was worse than his bite', as he sentenced Bussey to carry out 150 hours of community service, that's all.

A bride-to-be borrowed £19,500 from her fiancé and spent it marrying another man. Unemployed Rosarie McNamara, 44, posed as a successful business woman after meeting Peter Hart through a lonely hearts advertisement. They became engaged and she even bought a wedding dress to convince Mr Hart that she planned to marry him. She then conned him into lending her £19,500 to settle business debts, but instead, spent most of it marrying an Indian waiter. Mr Hart became suspicious when he discovered her bank details were false. He searched her handbag when she visited his home in Sevenhampton, Wilts., and found her marriage certificate. Mr Hart, who is in his 60's, has now begun civil action to try to recover his money. McNamara, of Bristol, admitted obtaining the £19,500 cash by criminal deception. The Judge at Swindon Crown Court spared her from jail and sentenced her to 100 hours of community service.

In early April 2004, two men were sent for trial at Middlesex Guildhall Crown Court, by Horseferry Road magistrates. Kamel Haddouche, 40, and Mustafa Boukhalfa, 38, both from London, are accused of attempting to steal £25,000 from Princess Michael. Three of the Princess's personal cheques are alleged to have been stolen from Kensington Palace. They were in a cheque book which the Princess had used to pay caterers for a party. Haddouche faces a charge of stealing three cheques on 1st July 2003 and was remanded in custody. Boukhalfa is charged with dishonestly receiving the cheques and dishonestly attempting to obtain a money transfer, by trying to cash cheques at Lloyds Bank Ltd in November 2003. Both men are charged with using a false instrument under the Forgery Act.

Two 'cowboy' gardeners, currently not yet identified, conned a widowed grandmother, aged 76 years, out of £16,000 for fixing her fence. She had accepted the gang's quotation for £750.00 for replacing a few flagstones and fence panels, as it was most competitive. They then claimed that it was more costly than expected and she gave them £250.00 up front. She then spent weeks traipsing to the bank, withdrawing her life savings, in lumps of up to £3,400 at a time. Finally a worried bank cashier advised the widow to tell someone about it. A friend she then confided in, reported the matter to police. Now the victim, left with a rickety fence and a patch of bare earth, refuses to leave the house. Detective Inspector Michael Fraser said: "The people who did this are despicable."

Riccardo Nardi, 36, is a high-flying barrister who has been sacked from his job as legal director of the Association of British Travel Agents (ABTA). He and his wife Samantha have been questioned by the Metropolitan Police and released on bail. ABTA has also launched its own civil claim against the barrister, who is alleged to have embezzled £1.2million over a nine-year period. It accuses him of 'fraud, misrepresentation, and/or breach of fiduciary duty, and/or breach of trust'. ABTA is understood to be claiming £960,000 from Mr Nardi and £265,000 from his wife, who is an aromatherapist. Assets including Mr Nardi's Porsche Boxster car, his wife's BMW and the family's £500,000 home in Bedfordshire, have been frozen by the High Court while investigations are completed. Last year, ABTA gave Mr Nardi, their barrister, the specific brief of tackling fraud against ABTA members, who are responsible for 90 per cent of all package holidays sold in the UK. The British travel industry loses nearly £3million a year from credit card fraud and rogue travel companies. In an interview with a trade publication, Mr Nardi raged against the police and the Serious Fraud Office for having 'totally failed' to tackle the problem! He recently took a prominent role in a high-profile ABTA case involving a string of travel agency failures that had cost consumers and other companies £1.9million. The allegations, against their own barrister, Mr Nardi, are particularly embarrassing for ABTA, which has 7,000 travel agencies and 1,000 tour operators as members, and prides itself on being a champion of consumer rights. A Scotland Yard spokesman said officers had been contacted in early February 2004 and were investigating an allegation of fraud.

Then there was the internationally publicised case of the 'Mad Major', his wife Diana, and their university lecturer friend, who made a serious, some people say convincing, attempt to win £1million from the TV quiz show, *Who Wants To Be A Millionaire?*, hosted by Mr Chris Tarrant. In fact he actually 'won' the money, but the cheque was later stopped by the TV production company, making Ingram the shortest-lived millionaire ever. The then-serving Army Major, Charles Ingram,39, sat in the hot seat and apparently bluffed his way through the various stages of the game, whilst his wife Diana, 38, and their university lecturer friend Tecwen Whittock, 53, sat well away from each other in the audience. There were four possible answers to each question. Correctly answering each stage or round of the game, more or less doubled the accumulating winnings. Several of the production staff had their suspicions during the screening of the show, and an extra camera was secretly trained on Diana Ingram. It was later conclusively proved that, as Major Ingram read out loud each of the four possible answers to each question, a code of coughing, previously worked out, was operated by the co-conspirators in the audience. For instance, at the £32,000 prize level, presenter Chris Tarrant asked Major Ingram: "Who had a hit with 'Born To Do It'?" Ingram said he initially thought it was boy band 'A1', but he changed his mind when his wife coughed twice at the correct answer being read out, which was 'Craig David'. The next bout of coughing came from a different quarter, their apparently 'planted' friend Whittock, who had been a contestant in his own right, or a contestant-in-waiting. Whittock coughed at the £64,000 and £125,000 stages. Meanwhile, Diana Ingram appeared to be fuming at her husband for overplaying his hand.

As he launched into the £1million question, she muttered: "Oh God, don't start." Most bizarrely, after the show, whilst the Major and his wife were in their dressing room, they were overheard engaged in a heated row. Not what you would expect after just winning the wonderful sum of £1million! Later, at a Crown Court trial, all three of the 'team' were found guilty of attempted criminal deception. Once again, most people who had followed the trial were amazed when the judge handed down suspended prison sentences of 18 months to each of the Ingrams and fined them a total of £30,000 with £20,000 costs. In spite of his having brought the Army into the most public display of disrepute one could imagine, they held off from court-martialing him, or otherwise dealing with him, at this stage.

A few months later, he was back in the Crown Court charged with fiddling several insurance companies over alleged burglaries at his home etc. He was found guilty of most, if not all of the counts on the indictment. Virtually the whole world held its breath to see how much immediate imprisonment the judge would order, for this new string of fraudulent offences. 'Surprise,

surprise' the sceptical and cynical would say, he did not go to jail at all. He was given a conditional discharge. After an apparent series of car boot sales of marital home effects and possessions, to assist them to keep going whilst in serious debt, Major and Mrs Ingram almost became celebrities by, it was mooted, going onto the 'dinner party speaker' circuit and financially benefiting in this way. As of April 2004, they continue to appear on quiz shows in their infamous celebrity.

Eventually and most tardily, the Army, totally humiliated and mega-embarrassed, decided it was time for them and the Major to part company, although I recall, he was able to keep his quite considerable Army pension/gratuity in place. Viewers, like myself, who watched the TV documentary of the Major's 'Millionaire' serious fraud public spectacle, were highly amused and entertained by watching the facial expressions and body language of the three conspirators, at each 'fit' of coughing emanating from Diana Ingram and the university lecturer, who later felt it appropriate to resign from his academic post. Older readers, who will remember the early days of televised quiz shows with high-value prizes, are no doubt left thinking that, if the now-defunct sound-proof contestant cubicles were still in use, the attempted 'coughing scam' could never have got off the ground.

UPDATE: On 21st October 2004, both Charles and Diana Ingram appeared at Southwark Crown Court, before Judge Geoffrey Rivlin. They had appealed against an earlier order to pay court costs. His Honour told the Ingrams that they had 'cynically' avoided paying back taxpayers' money. In 2003 they had been ordered by a court to pay £65,000 after trying to cheat their way to the £1million cheque, fully detailed above. On this occasion, Judge Rivlin told the court that the Ingrams had gone there 'effectively to plead poverty', as they asked for a reduction in the £65,000 legal costs order. For reasons best known to himself, the judge cut the outstanding bill from £65,000 to £30,000, but accused them of moving funds around to put them 'beyond the reach of the court'. He said Major Ingram moved £40,000 plus into his wife's account, claiming it was to pay debts. The judge added: "Between them, they cynically manipulated their finances." You may well be of the opinion that, if the judge found clear evidence of their having attempted to deceive the court, as his comments appear to indicate, what on earth was he doing in allowing the taxpayers to fund the other £35,000? Surely he should have just dismissed their appeal out-of-hand?

Following the fairly recent introduction of the new Euro currency, in April 2004 it was reported that police on the Isle of Sheppey in Kent made a raid on a counterfeit currency 'factory'. Counterfeit euros to the face value of more than £150,000 were seized. The factory was one of two addresses police raided and a man and woman, both aged 30, were in the unenviable position of 'helping police with their enquiries.' Police described the quality of the fake Euros as 'very good.' The eventual court case result is awaited with 'bated breath', if the alleged forgers are convicted.

In the case of serious frauds involving the country's economy, such as counterfeiting, VAT frauds and Customs and Excise offences, this countrys' judges all seem to 'read from the same hymn sheet' and award realistic penalties, almost always resulting in immediate imprisonment. What a tragedy it is for victims of most non-fraudulent criminals, such as burglars, muggers and perpetrators of serious violence, that the same degree of salutary severe sentences is predictably, rarely handed down.

The world's 'biggest' record bootlegger appeared at Blackfriars Crown Court in July 2004. He had built up a £15million fortune ripping-off such stars as Madonna, Oasis, the Beatles, Eminem and the Rolling Stones. Mark Purseglove, 33, was in breach of a Court order banning him from making copies of work by the Rolling Stones, Bill Wyman and Mick Jagger. He ignored it. David Martin, head of the British Phonographic Industry's anti-piracy unit said: "In the international bootlegging fraternity, this guy is a legend." He had sold illicit recordings made by corrupt sound engineers and crooked concert-goers. He sold his 'dodgy discs' at music festivals, shops and on line for up to £130 a time. His crimes bought fast cars, smart homes, designer clothes and expensive holidays. A Far East holiday with former *Big Brother* producer Deborah Sergeant cost 'at least' £11,000. She had no idea about his racket. His victims, who presumably lost mega-royalties etc, also included Michael Jackson, Eric Clapton, Pink Floyd, David Bowie and Prince. Had he not pleaded guilty to the indictment counts, Sir Paul McCartney, Ringo Starr, Led Zeppelin's Jimmy Page and Mick Hucknall of Simply Red, had all agreed to give evidence against him (So each of these must have spent quite some time making lengthy statements to Trading Standards officers and Police.). The judge sentenced Purseglove to three-and-a-half years imprisonment. Additionally, if he fails to repay £1,827,937 within eight months (by March 2005), he must serve an extra five years imprisonment. You may well think this particular, unknown judge, handed down a good result. I seem to recall that this particular prisoner was the subject, with a master forger of currency, of a recent TV documentary, during which he seriously bragged about all of his criminal achievements, and had owned industrial premises in which whole banks of electronic copying machines were installed, manned by a whole team of corrupt employees. You may have seen it, in June 2004.

A nanny who worked for Lord and Lady Daventry was paid by them £200 a week and given a Range Rover car, whilst living at their ancestral home. Meanwhile, she was receiving a total of £26,000 from the state by criminal deception. Grandmother Julie Beastall, 43, of Skegby, Notts, had claimed to be a single mother and part-time hairdresser earning £60 per week, over three years, whilst in full-time employment at Arbury Hall, near Nuneaton, Warwickshire, Lord Daventry's ancestral home. The Inland Revenue said they believed she was currently earning as much as £600 a week working for a wealthy couple in London's Kensington. On 5th May 2004 at Nottingham Crown Court, Beastall was jailed for nine months. However she will only have to attend prison at weekends, so she can work as a nanny to pay back the money. This is a government measure recently introduced, 'PART-TIME IMPRISONMENT' (No, I'm quite serious!). Can you imagine Nanny Beastall telephoning her jail from her smart workplace in Kensington on a Friday afternoon and saying: "Sorry, er, I won't be in tomorrow, I've gone down with a serious cold/ migraine /toothache" etc.

(In the old days, as police officers, we used to be plagued with crown court judges who would postpone continuance of a trial at Friday lunch times, as they had planes or trains to catch to their weekend haunts. Bearing in mind that crown court trials never start until 10.30am or 11.00am, justice was always delayed under those circumstances.

Now we've got the ludicrous situation where wealthy parents in affluent areas must baby sit their own kids on Friday afternoons, all weekend and possibly Monday mornings too, as 'Nanny' travels to and from her part-time weekend jail for nine months!)

By the time you deduct from the 'weekends only' jail trips, time spent there on legal visits, family visits, out-of-cell on education, sports activities, exercise, eating three meals a day plus a 'supper pack', prison library trip, Probation Officer interviews, Police interviews re other crimes you are suspected of, studied and 'sussed' the perimeter fence for the easiest climb, collected your free methadone from the health care centre, letter-writing, ringing your emergency cell alarm bell for today's newspaper or a TV guide, throwing rubbish into the prison yard, exchanging drugs and other contraband out of your cell-window on swung lines made of torn-up HMP sheets and pillow cases, fought with prison staff and other inmates, adjusted your prison-issue curtains and carpets to your liking, burnt holes in your prison-issue duvet and cover, graffitied all four walls of your cell, carved your initials on the door, prepared your door-barricade, stuck up all your pictures of naked men or women, illegally wiring-up your personal stereo or gameboy to the ceiling light, smashing your washing sink off the wall, flooding the other 29 cells on your landing, burst the eardrums of every HMP staff member within 100 metres with your loud music, trashed your chair and wardrobe, flung your loo-brush out into the quadrangle, had more time-out-of-cell for your occasional urine test for-drugs, filled in your 'tick-sheet' for next weeks' meal-options, ordered your 'burn' etc from the prison shop, 'swung' a 'poo-parcel' on another line to your near-neighbour on the guise it's crack-cocaine, urinated in the staff tea pot, bullied your pre-selected victims for their deodorants, sweets, burn, cakes, drinks, laid down your rotten fruit to ferment into 'jail-hooch', been to the chapel to exchange 'spliffs', dry-mouthed yourself through serial-spitting from your window, secreted your unauthorised mobile phone, inserted your all-important 'suppositories' in outrageous places, not washed your hands afterwards, written out your Appeal Form, Complaint Against Staff Form, Demand Form for reimbursement of your gold Rolex Oyster Perpetual Watch value £4,800 stolen in jail (which never even existed), IT WILL BE TIME FOR YOUR RELEASE! As they say: "You're having a laugh aren't you? You couldn't make it up, could you?" Quick, pass me *The Samaritan's* telephone number!

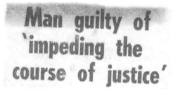

In sharp contrast to the case of the corrupt Immigration Officials weak sentencing by Judge Denis Clark at Liverpool Crown Court (please see *Count 22 – Impaired Judgements* re. Lisa Woods and others), is this case dealt with at Inner London Crown Court. The defendant was a teenaged asylum seeker called Ademola Adeniji, 19, a Nigerian from Camberwell, South London. He was caught running a bedsit passport factory potentially worth millions. He had been found in possession of false passports, driving licences and birth certificates. He was sentenced to three-and-a-half years imprisonment. Well done Judge, that punishment fits the crime much better than the Lisa Woods case and others.

Thousands of forged IDs, licences and travel documents intended for illegal immigrants were seized in a swoop which shut down Britain's biggest fake passport factory, senior detectives said. Forgeries had been sold by the thousand for £2,000 a time. And officers discovered bin bags crammed with fresh orders, along with names and photos of customers. One single order was for 590 documents. Det. Chief Insp. Michael Hallowes, who led the inquiry, said: "This was ID fraud on a massive scale. Thousands of people passed through this gang's hands. The market for fake identity documentation is growing day by day. The documents were destined for illegal immigrants, mainly from North Africa."

The racket was run from a bedsit above a fish and chip shop in Streatham, South London. Police found an assembly line for fake passports with hundreds of pages ready to be slotted into passport covers. The factory was divided into zones, with passports from France, Italy, Belgium, Norway and Portugal. Eleven people from Algeria and Libya were arrested in raids across London under *Operation Maxim*, which targets human traffickers.

Lap-dancing and stripper Karina Clarke, 24, of Streatham, laundered cash from a multi-million pounds tax scam. She banked £5million for trickster Paul Ward, 37, of Leighton Buzzard, who bought tax-free computer chips from Ireland and sold them on in the UK inclusive of VAT. Clarke, at her trial, claimed that Ward used fast cars and flash hotels to convince her he was a legitimate businessman. She agreed to open a bank account to help him cover up the scam. At Southwark Crown Court, Ward was sentenced to six years and six months for the crime that took place in 2001. His assistant Clarke, was jailed for 12 months.

An airport security guard was tricked into helping a thief load £1.1 million in cash onto a bogus security van. Gatwick security controller David Rickman, said that he noticed that the van looked odd and that the collection time was 'a bit unusual', but didn't register that it might be a criminal undertaking. He said that although the Ford Transit looked like a Brinks van on the outside, the inside was different and he had commented on this. As for the collection being made at 2.45am, he told Southwark Crown Court: "Collections are made at all times." The 'guard' fooled the security man with a fake pass before producing the correct paperwork, allegedly secured by Gatwick worker Keith Rayment. "The paperwork appeared correct, so I helped him load the packages in the van," said Mr Rayment. "The outside of the van was all metal with the badges. Inside was wooden-panelled. At the time I thought it was a bit unusual, but it didn't register as being wrong. I didn't speak much to the guy, but I did say something like it was different inside. He muttered something back, I wasn't really listening." The 13 bags of cash, belonging to *Hongkong & Shanghai Banking Corporation*, (HSBC) had been in the vaults of *British Airways World Cargo* when it was taken on 27thMarch 2003. Mr Rickman said: "The guy got in the rear of the van and I passed the packages to him. Once it was loaded, he signed the release note. He then got out of the back, shut the doors and got in the front. I then said to the security agent on the door that he could open it and let the van out. The van left."

The jury heard that the Transit left the airport followed by Flying Squad officers, who stopped it and arrested the two men. The pair are said to be part of a 12-strong gang who carried out a series of hijackings from docks and airports. It is claimed the gangsters plotted their heists at Peacock Gym in the East End of London, where boxers Lennox Lewis and Prince Naseem trained. They may have got away with up to £2million worth of goods. Alleged ringleader Paul Bowers, 37, from Silvertown, and Lewis Nicholl, 55, from Maidstone, both deny conspiracy to obtain property by deception.

An investigation into a huge student visa scam which has allowed thousands of immigrants into Britain, has uncovered up to 500 bogus colleges. Home Secretary David Blunkett has revealed that his officials had swooped on 672 suspect 'language schools'. Only 178 were genuine, 195 were definitely bogus and 299 needed further investigation. The raids back fears that tens of thousands of people have been granted visas or won permission to stay in Britain, by enrolling for courses at colleges which do not exist. Mr Blunkett, who is setting-up a register of bona-fide courses, published the figures as part of a wide-ranging crackdown on immigration scandals. In addition to shutting bogus colleges, people already in Britain who risk being sent home, will be barred from switching visas to anything other than a degree-level college course (Maybe all of the fraudsters will select that option then!).

Genuine foreign students who want to study on courses below degree level, will have to get permission to enter UK before they travel from their own countries and students will only be able to spend a maximum of two years taking lower level courses. The Home Secretary also announced tighter rules to stop temporary immigrants in the UK switching into permanent employment. And clerics will need a basic grasp of English before being allowed to preach in the UK. The move is aimed at clamping down on rogue imams whose controversial teachings have made headlines. Mr Blunkett said it was vital to ensure clerics had the skills needed to preach in a 'diverse and cohesive' society.

After two years the pre-entry requirement will be raised to ensure they can write and speak English. The Home Office is also considering proposals that would require imams and priests who have been in the UK for a year, to demonstrate their knowledge of British civic life, including an understanding of other faiths. Mr Blunkett said: "We have consulted and listened to faith groups and are encouraged that many faith representatives recognise the need for ministers to speak for the communities they represent and, in particular, to communicate effectively with the younger generation. That is why it is essential that ministers coming from overseas can speak English. It is also important that once here, faith leaders play a full role in their communities and gain an understanding and appreciation of civic life. We hope that faith groups will continue to work closely with us during the second half of the year to ensure that overseas ministers of religion, like all immigrants, engage with the communities in which they live."

Rebecca Smith, 19, and her sister Georgina, 18, both of Oldham, appeared at Minshull Street Crown Court, Manchester, together with a male accomplice, Bradley Hadfield, 18. The court was told that the sisters and Hadfield tricked their way into the homes of old people, by claiming they needed to change the six-month-old borrowed baby girl's nappy. Once inside, the sisters and Bradley stole cash and valuables. In some cases they pretended that the baby was disabled and they were seeking charity sponsorship. Judge Adrian Lyon told the gang: "It was a cruel, unpleasant series of offences. You exploited their goodwill and took advantage of them when they were not, perhaps, at their best." The female fraudster Rebecca Smith and Hadfield were each sentenced to three and a half years in a young offender's institution. Georgina Smith, who has a child herself, received two and a half years for burglary and handling offences. All three, who were also given five-year ASBO's, had previous burglary convictions. Detective Constable Dave Moores said after the case that the thieves had "plagued the community."

(**Author's note:** *Section 25 of the Theft Act 1968 deals with offences of 'Going Equipped For Stealing etc." and specifies: "A person shall be guilty of an offence if, when not at his place of abode, he has with him any article for use in the course of or in connection with any burglary, theft or cheat. A person guilty of an offence under this section shall on conviction on indictment [crown court] be liable to imprisonment for a term not exceeding three years. Where a person is charged with an offence under this section, proof that he had with him any article made or adapted for use in committing a burglary, theft or cheat shall be evidence that he had it with him for such use." This wonderful piece of updating legislation simplified all the previous complications under the much-antiquated Larceny Acts of 1861 and 1916 which had been in serious need of renewal.*

Under the old Acts, for instance, there were different penalties for burglars found in possession of housebreaking implements by day, than for night time possession. Police officers also had to carry some sort of watch, because 'night time' was defined in the act as 'the interval between 9pm and 6am'. This meant that you had to know your 'nights' from your 'days', so as to be able to charge the offender correctly on the charge sheet, otherwise the case could be thrown out at some future stage. Thank goodness that in these ultra-busy times when police officers hardly get a minute to themselves and are always under pressure and stress, the one thing they don't have to worry about with burglars is whether it is, officially, day or night. The only exception to this is that they must be capable of working out on a particular day whether they should report for duty on a day shift or a night shift, and I'm sure most of them get it right more often than not. Getting back to the 'cheat' part of going equipped for any burglary, theft or cheat. Quite often burglars and thieves will be in possession of false identification cards or driving licences, passports etc., which they will use to try to trick potential victims. The most common one is where these horrible men produce false ID to show to OAP's, to deceive them into allowing them in to check the gas or water pressures. They get the OAP to turn on all the taps for water pressure 'checks', meanwhile purses, wallets and valuables etc are stolen. These are known as 'distraction burglaries'.

In the case of the above-mentioned Manchester teenaged gang who were all subsequently jailed for their wicked frauds on vulnerable, frail and gullible OAP's, it could be argued that being in possession of the baby, particularly as it was a 'borrowed' baby, was a possible additional, or alternative charge of 'going equipped to cheat. Although, whether under that section, the baby can be described as 'an article' for any burglary, theft or cheat, is debateable and I haven't got time to look it up. In practice, police officers try to charge offenders with an offence that carries the most severe penalty, not that judges or magistrates take much notice of that when it comes to deciding on the sentence. Also, as we all know, the Crown Prosecution Service can't leave anything alone and have to go and change everything. It seems the only practical post-law school experience they need is how to operate a special and quite unique legal calculator, into which all the data extracted from the written statements supplied to them by police, is entered and within a minute there is a paper print-out of the likelihood of a conviction, expressed as a percentage. Very fortunately for us, in my time, the station sergeant or inspector made sure that almost every prisoner was charged with something or other, more or less appropriate to the offending behaviour, and let the **courts** *sort it out. Amazingly enough, a very high percentage of defendants pleaded guilty at the first magistrates' court appearance, wishing to get it over with as quickly as possible. However, as we know, the more serious matters have to be committed to a crown court for trial or sentence, dependant on the offender's criminal history.*

Looking back on those days, the mid-late 1960's and early 1970's, the high percentage of guilty pleas were entered even though sentences fitted the crimes more closely, and were harsher. You might think there is some irony there, perhaps the criminals had more personal respect and personal 'honesty' in owning up to everything and clearing their sheet, in the face of likely sentences far more severe than today's 'pats on the heads, 'don't do it again, sonny, there's a good chap, or next time you'll be painting the Probation Office or the Judges' Robing Room, by the way, your victim's had all of his stitches out now and he's having his second fitting for his dentures next week, after you knocked out all of the original ones he had looked after and flossed for years.").

A retired police superintendent who was shamed after ripping off the British music industry, is counting the £90,000 cost of his crime. John Stewart, 55, had set up a pirate CD factory in his home, using a copier that made 32 discs an hour. At his trial for conspiracy to defraud, he was branded a 'parasite' by a judge after supplying his son's market stall with the counterfeit discs. It emerged that he had agreed to pay back £90,000 in damages and costs to music business body the *British Phonographic Industry*. Stewart had escaped prison in January 2003 when he was given a 16-month suspended jail term after a court heard his home in West Yorkshire was 'like a CD factory'. Police were alerted when the rogue discs appeared on his son Karl's stall and at a council-run car boot fair.

A third man recruited to boost the operation, Gurdeep Sanby, estimated that an average of 600 to 700 counterfeit CDs were being sold every week, netting a £2,000 profit. Following Stewart's conviction, he was sued by the BPI and a civil case was set for the High Court. But Stewart, whose job as a superintendent was dealing with discipline and complaints, agreed to the £90,00 settlement before the hearing. Speaking after the settlement, David Martin, the BPI's Anti-Piracy Director, said he was disappointed that Stewart had not been jailed following his trial. "Stewart had amassed a small fortune at the expense of British record labels who invest millions of pounds each year in new music," he said. "Having built up an illegal retirement fund at our members' expense, for him to get off was quite simply unacceptable. Criminals who venture into music piracy do so because it is perceived to be a high profit, low-risk venture which is often regarded by the courts as a 'victimless' crime. In fact, it is an extremely serious offence where the victims are those people who lose their livelihoods."

Stewart, from Allerton Bywater, West Yorkshire, and his son were described as 'parasites' by Judge James Barry during their trial at Leeds Crown Court. Stewart's warehouseman son Karl, 30, was given a 12-month suspended sentence and was ordered to pay £5,000 costs. Sanby was handed a four-month suspended sentence and ordered to pay £500 costs.

The shambles of Britain's benefits' system was exposed when a court heard how a single mother remained undetected for 11 years while fraudulently claiming nearly £140,000. Marie McGinty's astonishing catalogue of deception showed the ease with which people can claim housing and income support, said a judge. And Shadow Works and Pensions Secretary

David Willetts said the case of the mother-of-three illustrated the failure of the Government to get to grips with benefits spongers. He said: "Under Labour, benefit fraud is costing the taxpayer at least £3 billion annually and some estimates put it as high as £7 billion."

Before they came to power they talked tough about tackling fraud but this has once again been proved to be just that - talk. We will make sure cheats are stamped out quickly." Jailing McGinty, 39, for 30 months at Manchester Crown Court, Judge Anthony Hammond said: "It shows how easy it is to steal from these departments and how the public purse needs to be protected." McGinty's deception spree started when she claimed income support using two false names in 1993 and housing benefit two years later. She continued fleecing the system until June 2004, when she was arrested after surveillance by Department of Work and Pensions officials.

She defrauded the DWP of £45,945 and £36,931 using the names Karen Marshall and Marie Reid and claimed two lots of benefit for her young son by registering him under two different names. She also illegally obtained £22,528 worth of housing benefits from Stockport council after she falsely claimed to be a tenant and claimed a total £35,927 in benefits from Trafford council between 1995 and 2002. Her lawyer Rod Priestly said the system had made it 'easy' for McGinty to falsely claim and revealed that up until last week the DWP was still sending her information about benefits she could obtain. He said the money was not 'frittered away on expensive living' and added: "It was taken up with normal household expenses, which come with having children and being a single mother."

He claimed McGinty, who has previous convictions for deception and driving offences, didn't pocket any money she claimed in housing benefit, because it all went to landlords. McGinty, from Wythenshawe, Manchester, admitted obtaining property by deception. A DWP spokesman said: "This was a sophisticated fraud during which the accused went to great lengths to cover her tracks. Sadly, there are a number of people who tend to defraud over a long period of time. The system is there to help honest people, and while we are doing everything to catch fraudsters, it sometimes takes longer than we'd like. We have served notice of confiscation proceedings in this case and will continue to examine her circumstances when she is released." Anti-Fraud Minister Chris Pond insisted: "We are winning the war on fraud and have saved the taxpayer over £1 billion since 1998 by cutting benefit fraud and error."

A fraudster who boasted of a 'Rolls-Royce' lifestyle after vanishing with almost £300,000, stopped short of buying one of the legendary cars to avoid suspicion. Instead, he splashed out £25,000 on a Volvo which he parked outside his modest terrace house, a court heard. Retired engineer Eric

James spent almost a year travelling the world after he helped to pull off a massive swindle. But James was jailed for four years after he admitted conspiring to defraud the BP-Safeway Partnership out of £1,508,857. Cardiff Crown Court heard that James, 58, was a partner in crime with his brother-in-law Dheej Keesoondoyal, 34, who was a 'bitter and frustrated' accountant working at the BP-Safeway Partnership. He used his inside knowledge to produce fake invoices for work creating petrol stations at supermarket sites. The money was paid into an account set up by James under the title of a fictitious company, *Global Construction and Electrical Contractors*. Prosecutor Martyn Kelly told the court: "Twelve false invoices were created authorising payment for more than £1.5million from the Partnership."

The pair were caught out when James tried to pay a £300,000 cheque into his account. A suspicious bank clerk checked with BP-Safeway and an investigation uncovered Keesoondoyal's link to James. Even then, James still tried to get the money and rang BP-Safeway to complain. Mr Kelly said: "James phoned asking why the cheque had been stopped. He threatened to tell the papers and BBC's *Business Breakfast* about them." Keesoondoyal was arrested after the racket was discovered and most of the money was frozen in bank accounts. But James had vanished with almost £300,000 and £262,643 was still missing when he gave himself up at his home in Aberbargoed, South Wales. Keesoondoyal, of Northolt, Middlesex, was also jailed for four years on the same charge at an earlier hearing.

An asylum seeker who masterminded a benefits fraud that netted more than £100,000 was jailed for five years. Mulele Pongo, 41, faces being deported to the Congo when he is freed. Fellow African Kimbambi Magembo, 44, was jailed for three-and-a-half years at Cambridge Crown Court. The London pair admitted the conspiracy involving counterfeit Giro cheques. Six others, all from the London area, admitted lesser roles. The gang was caught in Soham last June after targeting post offices all over Cambridgeshire.

Fraudsters involved in a £1m scam selling condemned chicken to schools, hospitals and supermarkets have been jailed. The poultry, classed as unfit for humans, should have been incinerated, made into pet food, or used as fertiliser, but instead it was repackaged in a rat infested factory and sold on. Two Milton Keynes men were among five who admitted a charge of conspiracy to defraud and were sentenced at Nottingham Crown Court. Gary Drewett, of St John's Road, Bletchley, was jailed for two and a half years. The 33-year-old who owned a food processing outfit, based in Northampton, supplied meat to national supermarkets as well as adding European health stamps to the produce.

A manager at *MK Poultry* escaped jail. Mark Durrant, 31, of Kingsfold,

Bradville, got a 12 month suspended sentence. Three other men, one from the Midlands and two from the North of England, were also jailed. Judge Richard Benson told them: "You five were involved in what I regard as a wicked fraud. It was dangerous and it was the general public who were in danger. If you had been dealing in Class A drugs rather than chicken, then the sentences you would be receiving would be in double figures. The people who consume drugs know the risks involved. Your victims didn't. Anyone in their right mind would not have eaten the food, had they known what it was."

Another city man, David Watson, 38, of Paxton Crescent, Bletchley, walked free from court at the end of a 12-week trial. The judge discharged the jury after it failed to return a verdict on the involvement of his firm, *S.J Watson Meat Ltd*, based on Clarke Road, Mount Farm, in the scam. There will be no retrial after the prosecution offered no evidence. Ringleader Peter 'Maggot Pete' Roberts is still on the run after he was convicted in his absence of the same charge at the trial. The 68-year-old, from Derby, ran Derbyshire-based *Denby Poultry Products* and masterminded the fraud between 1994 and 2000. The court heard during the trial that Denby bought waste chicken and turkey for as little as £25 a ton. He sold it on for up to £1,792 a ton after being processed. Some of the meat showed signs of diseases including hepatitis and the food poisoning bug E-coli. David Lawton, 55, from Derbyshire, a former manager at *Denby Poultry*, was jailed for four years and three months. Robert Matlock, 59, from West Yorks another former manager was given two years in prison. George Allen, 47, an occasional *Denby* worker from Lancashire, was jailed for 15 months.

An underworld Mr Fix-It who arranged slave labour for hundreds of illegal immigrants smuggled into Britain was jailed for seven years on 11th February 2005. Martin Moo, 59, helped to run an evil trade in human misery involving gangsters in Malaysia who promised a new life in cities with streets paved with gold in return for up to £20,000.

After being flown in posing as tourists, Moo would meet the naive immigrants at airports before directing them to a network of Chinese takeaways and restaurants. But the groups ended up sleeping four to a room in dingy bed-sits, sending every penny of their meagre wages home. Bachelor Moo, who had contacts in all major cities, lived a 'ghost-like' existence, using aliases and insisting he was always paid in cash to avoid detection. But he was trapped after a two-year investigation by the elite National Crime Squad, which ended when he was secretly filmed showing seven immigrants into one of his flats in Blackley, Manchester. Police also secretly taped a conversation Moo had with one of the refugees in which he said: "You won't get sent back, if you are questioned by police you just say you are on holiday. Just do that on pain of death. They can't send you back because of human rights. After five years you have got the "right to work and live here."

Officers collected evidence that he dealt with more than 300 Chinese migrants but believe that hundreds more were involved. So far 30 have been deported. Former chef Moo, who lived mainly in Birmingham and Manchester, would pocket a £350 cut from each refugee. Jailing Moo at Manchester Crown Court, Judge Michael Henshall told him: "The business you were in is an evil trade and the people who came here would then live in constant fear of being denounced to the authorities. They could easily become victims of unscrupulous employers who would exploit them. This was a business which was well run by you and people who worked in it. You were a very important part of a large and sophisticated business."

Moo, who will be deported when he completes his sentence, pleaded guilty to 10 charges of facilitating illegal entry to Britain. Outside court, Detective Superintendent Nick Lewis, who led the investigation, said Moo's arrest had 'cut off the arm' of the Malaysian gang's British operation. "Moo sought to portray himself as a caring man who wanted to help his fellow countrymen, but in fact he exploited the vulnerability and inexperience of foreign economic migrants," he said. "These people paid large sums of money, some tens of thousands of pounds each, thinking the streets of Britain were paved with gold but they ended up living a hand-to-mouth existence. He has so many aliases it is fair to say we don't know for sure who exactly he is." Moo, whose names included Ow Chai Moo and Peter Chai, did not pay taxes, claim benefits or have a bank account in order to dodge the law. Immigrants would answer newspaper adverts in Malaysia offering work in Britain and then paid gangmasters to fly to Britain. All passed through immigration claiming they were holidaymakers, but were met outside by Moo who organized their transport, accommodation and work. He would use libraries, hotels and newsagents to receive faxes from Malaysia giving details of the new arrivals.

Two builders swindled vulnerable pensioners out of £115,000 for bogus house repairs, a court heard on 12th May 2004. Roy Williams and Anthony Bolt overcharged customers in their 70s and 80s by more than 500 per cent for unnecessary work, it was claimed. The work the 'cynical conmen' did was often shoddy and would have needed further costly maintenance, it was alleged. The pair, both aged 52, drove some of their elderly victims to the bank and made them withdraw their savings to cover the charges, Bournemouth Crown Court was told. The jury heard that Williams would turn up at victims' homes and say he was from *ABB Property Maintenance* and work was needed on their roofs. Prosecutor Ian Fenney said he would often go on to a roof and dislodge the chimney. Once the pair started a job they would claim that more work than was first thought was required.

One 85-year-old widow handed over £16,200 for work which should have cost only a quarter of that, Mr Fenney said. In all, the pair were alleged to have conned 21 pensioners in Poole, Dorset, and High Wycombe, Bucks. "These two men have deliberately and systematically defrauded the elderly, quite a double act," Mr Fenney said. Williams, of Poole, and Bolt, of High Wycombe, deny 21 charges of conspiracy to defraud. The trial continues.

On 12th May 2004 an airport immigration officer suspected of selling stolen passports to illegal migrants was arrested. Lucy Denyer, 21, was held when officers swooped on an address in Surrey following a tip-off from the Immigration Service. Denyer, who worked at Gatwick, is being questioned at a South London police station.

A crooked businessman who funded a champagne lifestyle from a £3million fake Ecstasy empire, taunted police by driving a Rolls-Royce Silver Spirit with a 1E number plate. He also owned a £47,000 Lexus, registration number MIDAS. Swaggering father-of-five Carl Metcalfe, 61, ploughed £400,000 into his town's rugby league team, had shares in racehorses and flaunted a £37,000 diamond-studded watch, a court was told. But he was caught in a police sting following a five-year undercover operation and is now serving eight years after being convicted of manufacturing and selling counterfeit Ecstasy, which is known as 'E'.

Metcalfe was arrested along with his wife Valerie, after raids on several properties including *Bronte Villas*, his £300,000 home in Keighley, West Yorkshire, where he was chairman of the *Keighley Cougars* rugby league team. He established his fake drug ring in 1994, spending between £12,000 and £18,000 on three machines to produce realistic-looking Ecstasy tablets and selling them through a company specifically set up for that purpose, Bradford Crown Court was told. He sold slimming and dietary products as a 'front' and sponsored a body-building competition shown live on *Sky Sports* to maintain the scam. Thousands of the tablets, containing legal drugs like ephedrine and ketamine at four times the normal levels, were produced every week and sold through pubs and clubs. He also opened a gym called *Betta Bodies* to boost distribution. A jury was told how Metcalfe spent £150,000 on raw materials, enough to make tablets worth £13million, and between 1994 and 1996 he netted more than £3million from them. He also ran legitimate ventures in double glazing, jewellery sales and CB radio shops. Metcalfe had a fleet of luxury cars and as well as the Rolls-Royce and the Lexus he owned a £43,000 Jaguar XJS. He told his local newspaper in 1996: "I will meet anyone face to face who has positive proof that I have been involved in buying and selling drugs. I have taken on a position of great importance in the town. Do you think I would put that at risk and do you think the rest of the *Cougars* board would take the risk of having a so-called drug baron in charge?"

Metcalfe and his wife were arrested in a raid by a specialist police team. Judge Robert Bartfield told Metcalfe: "Your arrogance was such that you thought you were above the law, taunting the police with the car number plate IE." Valerie Metcalfe, 57, who was company secretary and processed documents for the phoney company, was sentenced to 10 months. Metcalfe will appeal against conviction, his lawyers said.

The fiance of former TV weathergirl Sian Jones was spared jail over a £410,000 con so they can start a family. Richard Van Baaren, 41, used forged papers to try to claim a sheikh's stocks and shares. But his lawyer Edmund Gritt said he and ex-*Five* presenter Sian, 39, "desperately want children, prison will extinguish the possibility of that". Van Baaren, of Isleworth, Middx, was given 240 hours' community service at Southwark crown court in London after being convicted of fraud. The financial expert resorted to the scam after Sheikh Fahad Al Athel's lawyers spent five years snubbing Van Baaren's offer to recover unclaimed shares for them.

More than one in 20 crafty workers have forged their boss's signature on documents ranging from letters to leaving cards. And one in four have signed on behalf of someone who is absent rather than go to the trouble of getting hold of them, says a report by banking giant *Lloyds TSB*. Up to one in five adults admit that they had forged a note to get them off games while still at school. Although small scale and often harmless, it demonstrates just how easy it is to fake someone else's signature, the researchers claim. Many workers may only be scribbling their boss's autograph to lend a more senior look to letters to customers or on requests for extra stationery from suppliers. The practice of faking it is more common among the 25 to 34-year-old age group than anyone else, though this is also the group most likely to lose their cards and so be victims of others faking their signature. The concern comes as up to three in four people reckon they have signed for a purchase in a shop and noticed that the signature is not checked by a member of staff. While it has not mattered at the time, it is an indication of how easy it could be for a criminal to deliberately try to get away with a forged signature. The survey of over 2,000 adults was conducted for the launch of 'Chip and Pin', the new microchip-based system being introduced by credit-card companies to combat increasing levels of fraud. The system will mean that, to verify a purchase, the consumer will have to tap a four-digit pin number into a machine rather than rely on a signature which is often not even checked.

Helen van Orton, senior manager, *Lloyds TSB Cards*, said that even if the signatures are checked, today's crooks are becoming more adept at writing someone else's name anyway. She said: "The recent explosion in card fraud is partly due to fraudsters getting better at imitating signatures, but *Chip and Pin* will help combat this problem. It makes card fraud considerably more difficult. At the end of the day fraudsters can forge your signature, but they can't read your mind."

A trusted City secretary who stole £4.5 million from her bosses' accounts was jailed for seven years. Joyti De-Laurey, 35, who claimed she took the money with the consent of her employers at *Goldman Sachs*, even stole £16,000 from her mother's building society account during her four-and-a-half-month trial. De-Laurey's mother, Devi Schahhou, 68, a GP who was given a six-month sentence suspended for two years, only discovered the money was missing when she learned her account was closed and empty. Her only child had taken it to pay household bills on the days the court was not sitting. De-Laurey's husband, Anthony, 50, a chauffeur, was jailed for 18 months. Both he and his mother-in-law were convicted of helping De-Laurey to launder some of the money. Judge Christopher Elwen said De-Laurey had told a cocktail of lies. "It is clear to me lying is woven into the fabric of your being," he told her, adding that she was 'duplicitous, deceitful and thoroughly dishonest'.

De-Laurey claimed the money she took from the private accounts of Jennifer Moss, her husband Ron Beller and Scott Mead by forging their signatures on cheques and other documents, was a reward for her ultra-efficient organisation of their private and professional lives. All three denied giving any such permission. After she was convicted in April, Mr Mead, a father of five, condemned the secretary he once described as 'the best I have ever had' for revealing his affair, now over, with a solicitor. He said De-Laurey, who at one stage claimed to have cancer and wrote letters to God asking for help in getting 'what's mine', was a liar and a thief. "She violated and abused many people's trust in a most cynical and calculating way," he said. Mr Mead discovered more than £3 million was missing from his accounts when he checked before giving a donation to his old college, Harvard. De-Laurey was confronted, made certain admissions which she later claimed were false and the three launched a High Court action to freeze her assets. The court was told *Goldman Sachs* is now pursuing De-Laurey for the return of the money. She was arrested weeks before she started a new life in Cyprus where she had bought a £750,000 seafront villa and had ordered a £150,000 power boat and a £175,000 Aston Martin. She had already spent nearly £400,000 on Cartier jewellery, and a fortune on clothes, holidays and a course of flying lessons. Jeremy Dein, QC, defending, said her financial difficulties began when a sandwich bar she started with her husband failed. She got a temporary job with *Goldman Sachs* and was hired permanently soon afterwards. "Her inability to grapple with her financial problems set her on the path to the dock," Mr Dein said. "Ironically and sadly, her first bitter experience with financial difficulties coincided with her novel introduction to a 'Dallas'-type world where huge, unthinkable sums of money stared her in the face day in and day out." He said she gave in to 'irresistible temptation'. She was 'spellbound' by the trappings of wealth she saw and heard all around her. He claimed there was strong evidence that she worked in an atmosphere where she was expected to forge signatures on cheques and other documents when her bosses were busy or out of the country. This led her to forge cheques to herself.

Mr Dein said: "The opportunity to steal was put on a plate by others." But the judge said her claim to have had permission to take the money was 'absurd and preposterous'. He said she plundered the accounts 'quite cynically'. De-Laurey, of North Cheam, Surrey, was convicted of 14 charges of obtaining by deception and six of using a false instrument. Her husband and her mother, of Hampstead, north London, were each convicted of four money-laundering charges.

A financial adviser murdered a wealthy spinster after seducing her and stealing her fortune, in a plot similar to a storyline in *Coronation Street*, a court heard. Peter Crittenden, 64, preyed on 'lonely and vulnerable' retired tax inspector Joan Beddeson, it was claimed. The married father-of-three started an affair with Miss Beddeson, 71, after visiting her home when she replied to a newspaper advert placed by his company, a jury was told. Heavily in debt and realising she was worth £500,000, Crittenden persuaded her to hand over £280,000 and make him sole beneficiary in her will, Lord Carlisle QC, prosecuting, told Chester Crown Court. He suffocated the 'reserved and gentle' spinster, with a pillow at her bungalow in Macclesfield, Cheshire, after she asked for her money back.

Lord Carlisle said: "Crittenden was rotten to the core and an expert at recognising vulnerability and naivety, not least in some elderly women." He compared Crittenden to *Coronation Street* character Richard Hillman, played by Brian Capron. Hillman, a serial-killing financial adviser, tried to con widow Emily Bishop before attempting to kill her. Lord Carlisle described Crittenden's claim that, on the night Miss Beddeson was killed in November 2002, he had been in bed with his wife Irene at their Worcester home, as a 'black lie'. The number plate of his car was captured on camera that evening on the M5, he said. Crittenden had used similar methods to con another client, who survived because she did not demand her money back, the jury was told. Crittenden denies murder and theft. The trial continues.

During the second period of seven years of my 14 years police career, spent in the Metropolitan Police, its Fraud Squad was then known as (branch) 'C6'. The branch had its own tie, which included a logo showing a crossed quill pen and sword, signifying 'the pen is mightier than the sword.' Therefore, if you are fiddling your income tax return on your laptop whilst commuting home on the train, do check the ties of male passengers seated near you!

On another occasion I had to conduct surveillance in a factory in the Manchester area, which made and sold the then-newly fashionable vertical blinds, for homes and offices. These were just the vertical equivalent of metal Venetian blinds, which had been around for very many years. A recent audit had proved to the factory owner that the company's finances were in such a poor state that it was bordering on collapse. For a whole week, sometimes with colleagues, from a high vantage point which overlooked the whole rear of the factory complex, using an expensive telephoto lens on a top class camera which, unusually for those times, had a 'rapid-fire' facility, I literally photographed everything and everyone who moved.

Over the course of the week, I observed and photographed various members of staff exiting the factory via the rear doors and placing usually long, bulky items in cars or vans parked at the factory rear. At this time, I knew nothing about how the products were manufactured and then packaged up for delivery, so I could not then identify a criminal transaction from a genuine one. At the end of the week, the multi-photographs sets were shown to the factory owner, who was able to identify and name those members of his staff I had photographed in the rear yard area. The following week I was introduced to the work force as a nephew of the Managing Director, who would one day inherit the business. I was then systematically attached to first one manufacturing process and then others, until I had learnt to make the vertical blinds myself. All of the workers accepted me and we were on first name terms in no time. I quickly learned the names of 'major players' on the factory floor. Over time, I noted that incoming telephone calls were answered by certain members on the assembly lines, and written notes made by them. Furthermore, other workers carrying note pads and price lists, made external phone calls from time to time each day. After several days of internal surveillance on the factory floor, I was debriefed by the MD during a conference.

Having put all of my findings together since first looking at the factory site etc., we quickly discovered the actual reason for the firm's fast-approaching financial demise. It was because the majority of the manufacturing staff, including some Supervisors on the factory floor, were using most of the company's raw materials to run their own private venture of bespoke vertical blinds. These fraudulently produced blinds were labelled with the Northern expression, 'foreigners', meaning stolen goods. The main players were earning fortunes on top of their wages, as all raw materials were supplied to them 'free of charge' by the previously unwitting company. I was able to gain in confidence in my undercover role and was so well accepted and integrated that I was invited out a couple of nights each week, for drinks with most of the conspirators.

This gave me even more opportunity to positively identify the ring leaders, not just by name, but also by personal description. This very serious long-lasting fraud was so well organised that door-to-door canvassers were employed. These people would speak to householders, show them mini-blind working samples and soft material pattern books etc., literally taking orders for made-to-measure vertical blinds in the home, riding on the back of this newly fashionable home and office improvement product, largely utilised for providing privacy inside patio sliding doors. Naturally, the vertical blind factory workers and all accomplices were 'on a winner', since there were no overheads whatever! Literally 'stealing to order'.

Eventually, once enough evidence had been gathered to provide proof of the full extent of this version of a 'major fraud', I said my 'goodbyes', made my 'excuses' and I was extracted from the factory and temporarily accommodated in a very comfortable hotel in the centre of Manchester, quite a few miles away from the scene of the crime. Several days later, a large posse of police officers arrived with a large coach for a daytime raid and most of the manufacturing staff were bussed off to the Police Station. Miraculously, the company survived and, having recruited a mainly brand-new work force, soon re-established profitability.

I have to admit that, prior to the Police raid, I derived great satisfaction in sitting down with all of the surveillance photographs I had taken in the week beforehand, from the high ground, relating a particular photograph to a now-identifiable employee, to the extent of even being able to calculate the actual lengths of packaged blinds being loaded into vehicles, by 'measuring-off' the photographed packages against known bricks-lengths in the factory perimeter wall.

Council bosses at Basildon Council who employed a convicted fraudster, say they did nothing wrong. Bright Oduro-Kwateng, 50, was employed as a council racial equality advisor four years ago, despite having been convicted of using the passports of dead children to allow people from his native Ghana into the country illegally. Despite his dismissal from Greenwich Council for the offence, Basildon Council was still willing to give Oduro-Kwateng a role in the race relations division. Oduro-Kwateng was also named as Basildon Council's individual of the year in 2004. A spokesman for Basildon Council said that having a criminal conviction was no reason not to give someone a job. He added: "At the time of his appointment, Bright was the best candidate for the post and council procedures have been followed correctly at every stage." However, when questioned about the procedures, the spokesman said: "The initial feeling is there are no laid down guidelines with regards to how we deal with somebody with a conviction. The statutory duty is down to the employee and there is no onus on us as to what we should or should not do." Despite this, the UK's advising body for Human Resources professionals, *The Chartered Institute of Personnel and Development*, said councils have to be vigilant when recruiting. The Institute's guidelines read: "Organisations that have a legal obligation to protect vulnerable client groups from people who have committed serious offences, should be particularly vigilant about risk management. Organisations should assess the risk of employing the person with a criminal record, by comparing the applicant's conviction circumstances against risk criteria identified for the job."

The council's senior director, Doug Smith, was not willing to comment about the appointment. In 1998, Oduro-Kwateng appeared at Woolwich Crown Court and was convicted of conspiring to defraud the Home Office.

COUNT 18

EVENTS OCCURRING IN HM PRISONS & HM YOUNG OFFENDERS INSTITUTIONS

During the six years that I was employed on the junior staff work force in one of Her Majesty's Young Offenders Institutions, I found that there was an inherent liberal attitude towards prisoners, pervading the establishment. This liberalism chipped away at staff morale and there was a constant problem in recruiting, and trying to retain, new staff. Discipline amongst Young Offenders (ages 18-21) and Juveniles (ages 15-18) was virtually non-existent. Members of staff, both uniformed and civilian (in the main, teachers) were often assaulted by convicts, over time.

Weak, inappropriate, liberal and pathetic punishment awards were constantly handed-down to trainees by Prison Governors presiding over Adjudication hearings, after staff members had placed offenders 'on report' for breaches of the Discipline Regulations. Additionally, during one of the several-day inspection visits by a team from HM Inspectorate of Prisons, quite strong criticism of Prison Governors was made. Reference was made to inconsistent and often too-low punishment 'Awards' made to prisoners, by various Prison Governors, thus contributing to 'An unsafe working environment for staff and prisoners.'

Arising out of this serious criticism, the next year, a newly installed Deputy Governor carried out random checks of completed Adjudication Papers, after completion, issuing personal criticisms to individual

Governors, who were not 'up to speed' with 'punishments' they had handed-down to young convicts in certain cases. Certain prisoners would 'trash' their cells, by smashing their sinks off the wall, causing serious flooding of several landings, in some cases, smash their TV sets, 'hard-wire' their personal stereos or CD players into the in-cell 240v power supply, create fires in their cell, thrust burning newspaper out of their windows, to the danger to health of staff and other prisoners, graffiti all over their cell walls etc.

Later, the inherent liberalism of the regime even went so far as to dictate that cells were no longer to be described as such, but as 'rooms'. When the Youth Justice Board organisation was set up, as a separately run Agency from HM Prison Service, a diktat was issued that black and white uniforms worn by male and female officers, almost since time immemorial, were to be done away with, as they made staff appear to be 'too authoritarian'.

Instead, we were issued with dark blue or black polo shirts, dark blue tracksuit bottoms, long-sleeved, Winter-weight sweatshirts and blue zipped fleeces, all of which except the tracksuit bottoms, which bore only a crown insignia, were embroidered with the officers rank, name (including first names in most cases) and the name of the HMP establishment. All staff were given a one-off monetary grant of £50 to purchase a pair of trainers, so that black shoes and boots could be dispensed with.

From that time on, it was quickly discovered by staff responding to a general alarm bell activation, rushing to another wing where a fight was in progress, that where colleagues were taking part in a scrummage, whilst trying to separate opposing fighting convict factions, it was quite difficult to distinguish between staff and inmates if the officers were dressed in the newly-issued 'soft', casual clothing, which included tracksuit bottoms, which inmates also wore.

Previously, when all staff of uniformed grades were dressed in 'black and whites', male or female officers in their white shirts or blouses, often long-sleeved, black trousers or skirts, it was easy to make an immediate recognition and identification, in a scrimmage, between staff and fighting prisoners.

There also came a time, widely publicised in the case of HMP Wakefield, where it was suggested by the Board of Visitors (Now, Independent Managing Board) that all convicts should be allowed the respect and personal dignity of being addressed by staff as 'Mr', followed by the surname, or alternatively by their first-given name, or nickname. This 'regime' change was swiftly 'officially' adopted right across the HM Prison Service estate, but in practice, proved almost impossible to enforce. In sharp contrast to all of this, prisoners, wore no identifying names on their clothing whatsoever, and when challenged for discipline breaches, often refused to identify themselves at all, so that a member of staff who knew the convict personally, had to be brought in, usually from the offending inmate's wing, to make the identification.

Also in sharp contrast to the official requirement for staff members to address prisoners by first or nicknames, or as 'Mr', instead of, as previously, just by their surnames, prisoners addressed staff members as 'Guv', 'Boss', 'Miss', '****head', '****' etc. Furthermore, the liberalism extended to inmates being allowed to slouch around, almost at snails-pace, during 'Labour Movement' in low-slung tracksuit bottoms or jeans, revealing 'Plumbers Bums', both hands down inside their trousers, often handling their private parts.

In some education class-rooms, particularly those in which personal computers were in use for 'IT' instruction, illustrated notices were affixed to walls, stating that anyone found touching their private parts during computer keyboard operation, would be sent outside to the washrooms, to wash their hands. Some teachers were so afraid of being assaulted or attacked by convicts, in spite of emergency alarm bells being fitted in most classrooms and workshops, that they failed to lock their classroom doors, so as to allow them a quick exit in case of serious trouble erupting. However, this allowed disinterested or bored prisoners to simply wander out of classrooms into the passageways or toilets and, in contravention of the 'No Smoking Except in Your Own Cell' rules, light up a cigarette, generally in the lavatories, which were 'cleaned' by prisoners, and always looked and smelled disgusting.

Other prisoners could be so rude and disruptive in class that eventually, uniformed prison officers would be summoned, by alarm bell or telephone, to remove the trainees and return them to their accommodation blocks under escort. It was a regular occurrence for some convicts to make inappropriate, comments of a sexual nature, or even indecently assault female staff in classrooms, as well as on the landings where they resided. When I first joined the Prison Service in 1998, various colleagues of the same grade as me, were detailed to furnish me with 'on the job' training, explaining the requirements and job descriptions in relation to the various daily posts that I would be assigned to.

On several occasions during my first few weeks at the Prison Service Establishment, I was required to inspect the inside of the jail's perimeter fence. As it was accommodating quite low-category security risk Young Offenders and Juveniles, there was no stone, brick or concrete wall to contain the convicts. Instead, the outer fence had been constructed from custom-made large sheet-steel solid panels, painted in mid-green. These sat on top of continuous brick and concrete plinths. The metal fence panels were tall enough so that passers-by or nearby residents could not see through or over the panels, for maximum privacy within.

Secured to the top of each fence panel were heavy-gauge square-meshed metal sections, with modern coiled and affixed razor wire over, to discourage prisoners climbing the fence and escaping. As I patrolled the internal fence perimeter with my new colleagues, they would pass on to me various tips which I was advised to make it my business to remember. One of these was to keep a sharp look-out for tennis balls and oranges – it was made known to me that incoming drugs were very easily concealed within a slit-open tennis ball, and an orange which had been partially opened and pith removed from inside, to accept the drugs, and then thrown over the fence to land on the grass of the football pitches, or the inner concrete hard-standing which lined almost the entire inner fence perimeter. This hard standing 'path' was wide enough to accommodate fire engines, which are more than eight feet wide, and other emergency and service and delivery vehicles, to stop them from being bogged down by sinking into soft grass verges and grassed leisure areas.

It was explained to me that so-called 'trusties' or red, green or blue arm-band wearers, aka Wing Orderlies, were allowed outside of the accommodation blocks into designated parts of the grounds, for the purpose of cleaning up wind-blown litter, most of which had been thrown out of their cell windows by prisoners who were too lazy to use their cell rubbish bins. The extent of access to the various parts of the grounds were pre-determined by the colour of the arm band, the 'most-trusted' being the 'red-bands', who were totally unescorted by members of HMP staff whilst employed on outside clearing of litter and cleaning duties.

Additional, *unauthorised duties* were undertaken by 'red-bands' etc, as it was their accepted responsibility to recover any oranges or tennis balls from the grounds, invariably lying in the grass fairly close to the inner perimeter fencing panels. Whilst carrying out this unofficial duty, the 'red-bands' would of course, keep a sharp lookout for any approaching members of the uniformed staff, or civilians, such as teachers, trades training officers etc.

As you can imagine, the *correct procedure*, by the 'red band', having spotted an incoming suspected drugs container, would be to pretend to carry on sweeping right up close to it, create a raised pile of litter, drinks containers, dead leaves, discarded prison clothing etc., which needed to be temporarily sited very close to the suspected drugs container, viz: a hollowed-out orange, or a tennis ball and suchlike. Then whilst bending over to sweep or shovel the litter pile into a black bag, it was a simple matter to pocket the drugs container, or remove the contents and 'trouser' them, placing the now-empty container into the black bag. Actual recovery of the incoming drugs container took literally a few seconds.

The 'red-band' would then, after making sure the coast was clear, make a bee-line for the open window of a cell occupied by one of his wing-mates, and pass the drugs through the approx four inch gap of the restricted window opening, to his buddy inside. On completion of his external cleaning duties, the 'red-band' would ask to be re-admitted onto his wing by a member of staff, who may or may not, usually not, have time to strip-search him.

In an effort to combat this ongoing failure by the Prison Service to stop, once and for all, the 'red-band' cleaners from acting as grounds-to-accommodation-block drugs couriers, I made a suggestion in writing and submitted it for consideration. My idea was that, for a one-off cost, a council type of pedestrian controlled or ride-on mechanical hoover, as used in pedestrian precincts, should be purchased, and driven by a designated member of staff. The entire areas of the prison grounds, inside the perimeter fences could then be literally 'swept' in just a few hours. Drugs containers and larger or heavier items, too heavy to be vacuumed-up, could be separately put to one side or bagged-up by the staff driver. Nothing ever came of the report I had submitted under the staff suggestion scheme, and its very existence was never even acknowledged.

If adopted, my scheme would have dispensed once and for all, with the procedure through which external *trusted* 'red-bands', could collect and distribute drugs which had originally been thrown over the fence.

Drug-taking and dealing was a constant problem and very occasional whole-wing searches were undertaken, sometimes including active or passive drugs dogs. 'Sentries' had to be posted outside each elevation of a residential wing block, to take notes of which convicts were throwing from their windows drugs, mobile phones, weapons, money, items stolen from carpentry and engineering workshops, such as tools, etc. From outside, fortunately, each window was identified by a numbered plate on the wall, otherwise it would have been literally impossible to identify individual down loaders of prohibited items.

On one occasion I was posted outside during a very intense wing-search involving several pooled drugs dogs from other jails. I spotted a small, light-coloured object come flying out of a cell window on an upper landing. After noting the cell number from its external identifying number, I retrieved the item from the grass. It turned out to be a modern plastic barrel-type pencil sharpener, which contains its own sharpening wood shavings. On unscrewing the lid it was found to contain several 'wraps' of cannabis, for which the juvenile convict was later punished under the Discipline Regulations.

Weapons of offence were very easily constructed from everyday items which convicts were allowed to possess in their cells. Two 'C' size large batteries tied inside a knee-length sock, made a formidable weapon, of skull-busting ferocity. A razor blade or two, secured into a toothbrush handle, heated to soften the plastic, were used as weapons or discovered during individual full-scale cell searches, at least weekly in most cases.

Readers may recall that during mid-July 2004, a very angry and dangerous estranged husband visited a house in Highmoor, near Henley-on-Thames, Oxon. It was a fine summer day and he arrived armed with a firearm. His wife, her sister and his mother-in-law and the children, were all enjoying a family barbecue. Within a very short space of time, this man had shot and killed his wife, her sister, and very seriously injured his mother-in-law, although she later recovered. He then went to ground for approx 7-10 days but was eventually flushed-out and arrested from a dense forest in the Nottinghamshire area, after a massive, protracted man-hunt by the local Police Force.

He was remanded in custody to a prison and *risk-assessed*, as is every incoming prisoner, as to his mental state, with a view to being placed on 'suicide watch'. However, in his case, this was found not to be necessary. Soon afterwards he was found dead in his cell, having opened his veins with a prison-issue razor blade, thus defeating justice.

(Local police and an Armed Response Unit from Thames Valley Police, were quite severely criticised at the time, for holding-back emergency ambulances, whose crews might have been able to save the two sisters, who died of their wounds, until they were sure that the scene of the crimes, at Highmoor, was safe and the gunman had withdrawn. Quite often, Police these days, under so much pressure of work, find themselves in a 'no-win'situation.) Eventually, an unarmed, brave, lone Detective Sergeant from The Thames Valley Force, visited the scene, and was able to verify that it was safe for emergency vehicles to attend.

In the case of Juvenile and Young Offender prisoners, unless they were on 'suicide watch', when requiring to shave, usually during lunch breaks, staff members would issue individual razors, marking each cell door involved with a distinctive magnetic sign stating 'RAZOR IN CELL'. Inmates on 'suicide watch' would shave in-cell under the close supervision of a Senior Officer or his nominee, who would stand in the cell open doorway.

Turning now to the ever-present drugs problem inside British jails. It has become almost a 'Music Hall' joke these days, that there are far more drugs inside jails, than outside them. Ongoing attempts to keep the drugs outside the establishment, as well as to detect them once inside, are regularly undertaken. On occasions, attending visitors are 'sniffed' by drug-detecting dogs, when available, which is not often. Visitors include probation officers, lawyers, youth offending team workers, not just family visitors. Establishment uniformed and civilian staff are also subject to occasional random drugs dog confrontations, and physical bodily searches, nearly always by their own colleagues. Most Prison Governors set an example by submitting themselves to such searches too, but the odd one or two, invariably arrogant, power-crazy and with 'holier-than-thou' attitudes, bypass the searching areas – it being apparently beneath their dignity to be publicly searched!

Occasionally, staff are caught red-handed with incoming prohibited items, such as drugs, or are identified by a passive drugs dog sitting down in front of the suspect and refusing to move away, indicating current drugs possession, or quite recent usage. Staff exiting the prison, such as the departing night shift, are also searched. There is a very sensible, common sense rule, whereby prison staff are even prohibited from such innocent-seeming tasks as posting a letter for a convict at an outside post box. This is taken very seriously and is regarded as 'Trafficking'.

Some staff, it is said, do not discourage convicts from using drugs in jail, and/or would take no steps to prevent such unauthorised usage, or to place the offender(s) 'On Report' for a breach of the Prison Discipline. Their thinking is that 'it keeps them quiet' and settles them down to sleep much sooner during the evenings, therefore the officer concerned can enjoy some rare moments of 'peace', until the next cell emergency alarm bell is pressed, by an inmate seeking an envelope for his letter, or a newspaper to read!

In my own experience, cannabis is smoked on the Wings almost daily, usually in the late evenings or early mornings. Some convicts have developed the habit of enjoying a cannabis 'joint' whilst lying on the floor under their beds. They are very aware of the sickly, pungent, unmistakable, tell-tale smell carried around in the thick smoke. They seem to think that by lying under the bed, they are reducing the chances of escaping smoke giving the game away. However the gaps at each side of cell doors are quite wide, certainly wide enough for passing staff members to be spat upon, which is another regular occurrence.

Other smells, too, have to be swiftly investigated, such as smells of burning. Newspapers, bedding, beds, mattresses etc. are often set on fire by disgruntled convicts, or those with mental health problems. Sometimes burning paper or fabric packages are thrust outside via the window gaps, falling to the ground or being blown through the windows of other cells, with the danger of causing injury to others and/or the risk of causing a major fire. This is more or less an ever-present danger, as huge piles of discarded cardboard, paper and other inflammable items are often stacked outside accommodation blocks, against the walls and often under cell windows.

Tall, plastic, wheeled 'wheelie bins' are utilised these days. If these are left by staff and convict cleaning parties with the lids partially or fully open, these are easily set alight, with a huge risk of escalating a fire, to the danger of all in the vicinity.

Naturally in prisons, convicts confined in their cells behind locked doors, can easily be trapped, or not reached in time, during the resulting panic which can set in during a mass attempt at speedy evacuation. With serious incidents like a fire and/or escape attempts being an ever-present threat, just like in a German Concentration Camp, the 'ROLL' is called many times a day, and if found to be incorrect, called again as many times as is necessary to ensure that each and every prisoner is fully accounted for.

Reporting-in as to convict numbers is effected via staff members from each accommodation block or workshops, offices, the library etc, all around the establishment. Internal landlines, personal radios, etc. are utilised for this important procedure, or by staff members attending designated areas to make a personal report face-to-face to the Orderly Officer.

Drugs, tobacco, cigarettes, Rizla cigarette papers and other items falling under the general heading of 'contraband', are easily transferred between convicts This even includes passing goods to a buddy some distance away and even totally out of sight, as well as earshot. Issued HMP bedding sheets, pillow cases, even fabric cleaning cloths, are torn-up into narrow strips to create a 'line', often by joining several such strips together. If the items to be delivered or exchanged, are to be effected via the *external* fabric of the building, the line is 'swung' through the narrow open window gap, backwards and forwards until sufficient momentum is generated for the line to reach its intended destination.

Often a line is caught and retrieved by a recipient or a middleman, via an extended arm or by attempting to 'hook in' the line with an extended toilet brush. The merchandise can either be tied on to the end of the line, or inserted into the inmate's string vest-like laundry bag. Even toilet rolls are utilised as lines, with added weights, such as waxed drink containers, to help counteract the force of the outside wind and assist with target-achievement.

On one occasion, during my watch, a convict who was being bullied, was sent via a swung line, what is known in prisoner-speak as a s**t parcel. This is a prepared parcel of human excrement, which the convict has been told contains drugs or some other type of contraband. You can just imagine the horrendous yelling, screaming and disgusting language which emanates from the convict, who finds he is left with faeces all over his hands, after expecting some items of pleasant value! This would be one of the very few times during his sentence, that a convict would wash his hands properly.

Internal, inter-cell merchandise transfers are effected by using an afro-comb, CD disc, plastic ruler, or other weighty, slim object, tied to the end of the 'line'. Inmates then kneel down, listen to make sure staff are not around, before 'shooting-the-line', as it's called, by hand movement or kicking it, across to a cell immediately, or diagonally opposite, via the gaps under the cell doors. During quieter periods, such as overnight, staff attention can be drawn to attempted 'shot-line' transfers, as the target under-door gap is totally missed, causing the high-speed line weight to ricochet off the door jambs or cell-wall masonry, with quite loud thudding, giveaway sounds.

The secret then is for staff to creep up, sometimes in just socked feet, as shoes or trainers can squeak, usually in the half-dark, identify the culprits area, wait for a successful 'line' to enter its destination cell, and for the line to move as it drawn in by the recipient-trainee, then, if swift enough, grab and confiscate the merchandise and line, noting the cell numbers concerned, for writing-up the incident in official documentation.

Both convicts, once realising that the game is up, then jointly enter a loud, fierce, name-calling tirade against the member of staff, whereby his or her parentage is more than rudely called into question, usually in the most disgusting ways, which can totally unnerve and upset a male or female officer quite new to the job.

The most widely-used phrase, incorporating the most revolting swear words, advises the officer(s) to perpetrate the most disgusting sexual acts against their (alive or dead) mother. On the odd occasions, I have been lucky enough to investigate 'ripping' sounds and, after a near-silent approach, swiftly open the cell door metal observation flap, in time to find inmates tearing-up sheets or pillow cases, blankets etc., as raw materials to construct a line. Under these circumstances, I would place the prisoner 'on report' for committing criminal damage to prison property, and if possible, confiscate the line sections as evidence. The number of sheets, blankets and pillow cases which 'disappeared' over the course of a typical year, had to be seen to be believed, usually reported in the shape of a Governor's Order or Governor's Letter to staff. The severe shortage of these bedding items were normally drawn to the Governor's attention via the member of staff running the Clothing Exchange Store, after a mini-audit.

In an effort to reduce the number of visitors ignoring the drugs warning notices, which threaten police attendance if caught, and still bringing them in, body searches are carried out routinely, and baseball caps and most hats, as well as chewing gum are prohibited. Visitors wearing hats for genuine religious reasons, such as Sikh's turbans, Islamic Imams' skullcaps etc., can still be made to remove them for inspection for drugs, knives, mobile phones etc., but they are normally taken to one side for this purpose, so that the searching can be effected sensitively and in private, so as to prevent embarrassment.

Babys' and toddlers' nappies have often been utilised to bring in prohibited items, therefore female staff conduct such searches as humanely as possible, whilst wearing protective surgical-type gloves. Prams, push chairs and even wheel chairs, nearly always are constructed at least in part, from tubular metal sections, which are hollow and can be used to conceal incoming drugs etc.

Mandatory Drugs Tests (MDT) are frequently carried out. Additionally, inmates wishing to heighten their integrity and hopefully climb up the behavioural regime level, to receive increased privileges, can take part in a voluntary drugs test scheme. All inmates passing a mandatory or voluntary drugs test, by their urine samples testing negative at a Government Testing Laboratory, receive a scrolled 'PASS' certificate on A4-sized paper, which is filed on the wing in their personal records file. Convicts failing such tests, can be sentenced to 'closed' visits for approx one month, whereby they view their family and friends through a glass or Perspex screen, as well as receiving very short visitation durations, usually just 20 minutes, as against one or two hours.

In spite of the glass or perspex screens, evidence is often found whereby masonry or sealant has been scraped away so as to create a small gap through which drugs etc can be passed. HM Prison Service is run very much on a shoestring, so far as staff availability is concerned, meaning that there are constant staff shortages. In practice, this means that the few available staff have their duty time prioritised into the covering of essential tasks, such as inmate movement to and from educational facilities, healthcare centre, meal times, inmate association etc. The result is that cell-searching, urine testing for drugs and other very important tasks, appear very low down the priority list. Many officers can be so hard-pressed due to the constant demands by the Service and the convicts, that their food is taken 'on the hoof', which is a most unsatisfactory state of affairs. A very regular shift pattern arrangement demands that all officers must work an 'A' shift : viz: 0730hrs to 2100hrs, sometimes 2–3 times a week, playing havoc with their social lives.

In the HM Young Offenders Institution in which I was employed, all uniformed staff of officer grade had one weekend off in two, in other words, worked on alternate weekends, with a very occasional 'long' weekend incorporated into the shift pattern or 'detail'. There were frequent opportunities for overtime to be worked, sometimes under special dispensations from the Governing Governor (Also known as 'No.1 Governor'), at enhanced rates of pay.

I must question the apparent lack of professional judgement in respect of a certain matter. There came a time when a Governing Governor, aka *No.1 Governor*, Governor Elaine Jones, implemented a requirement for trainees no longer having to wear fluorescent bibs or tabards, during visits by family and/or friends in the visits hall. This had been a long-standing security requirement and staff on duty supervising visits, found the wearing of the bibs to be most helpful in distinguishing actual convicts from male visitors at their table, of similar.

A further, long-standing arrangement in the Visits Hall at HMYOI Huntercombe, near Henley-on-Thames, Oxon, was that, during weekend visiting times, all Young Offender or Juvenile prisoners were required to sit in a chair at a designated end of tables, all in line and facing the right hand wall of the Visits Hall. This gave supervising prison staff a secondary chance, to be able to easily and readily identify and distinguish serving prisoners, wearing fluorescent tabards, from other young male non-prisoners in the Hall, dressed in ordinary clothing, who were legitimate visitors.

Within a comparatively short space of time, the news was flashed around the jail that the Governor's instruction to abolish the fluorescent orange bibs, had resulted in a trainee and his girlfriend managing to enter a lavatory in an anteroom off the Visits Hall, and somehow barricade the door. This would have been almost impossible in times before the fluorescent bibs were discontinued. I would comment that prior to making the decision to dispense with the requirement for convicts to wear the fluorescent orange bibs, or tabards, the Governor did not give the matter enough thought, or alternatively, failed to carry out a comprehensive *risk assessment*, as it is known within the service. Poor judgement by Governor E. Jones had proved to be a liberal step too far, backfiring on her, with resultant embarrassment.

The number of prisoners *dying* in jails has soared because of a spiralling rate in suicides. Home Office figures show 184 inmates died in custody in 2003, 94 of them by taking their own lives. Among the dead were 15 prisoners aged between 18 and 21. Penal reform groups called for more prisoners to be sent to Secure Hospitals for treatment. The Prison Reform Trust said 50 prisoners committed suicide in the first three months of 2004, and the final death toll was set to top last year's figure.

Inspectors delivered a blistering attack on Britain's overcrowded jails, on 27th January 2005. Anne Owers, OBE, HM Chief Inspector of Prisons, revealed the jail system is at bursting point with almost a quarter more prisoners than it was designed to cope with. In a scathing Annual Report,

Ms Owers warned that if the prison population, which has now reached 73,000, could not be controlled, it may lead to an 'unmanageable crisis'. The report added that inmate suicides are at a rate of two every week, while an investigation has begun into why some children suffer broken bones in detention. Last year, 2004, there were 95 deaths and 17,678 recorded incidents of self-harm.

And Ms Owers revealed that prisons are still failing to give criminals enough education or work. Ministers said the projected prison population in 2011 had fallen to 76,000, compared to an estimate of 109,000 three years earlier. They plan to keep numbers down by releasing all except the worst criminals *halfway through their sentence*, with a greater use of softer community penalties.

But Ms Owers warned: "The levelling off of the prison population is, in reality, the difference between a manageable crisis and an unmanageable one." The report also said restraint techniques used on children were being reviewed, while there were concerns how juveniles were treated in custody. Shadow Home Affairs Minister Cheryl Gillan said: "Under Labour, our prison system continues to suffer. Tony Blair's only solution to overcrowding has been to give criminals *lighter sentences* and let dangerous prisoners out before they've served their sentence." Almost £2.6million of public money was spent in 2003, probing complaints by disgruntled prisoners. Cases included a man who complained, twice, that he had been served a baguette 'smaller than usual'. And one was unhappy at not getting vegan soap.

Uproar broke out in March 2004 over plans to force prison officers to address some of Britain's most evil killers as 'Mister'. The barmy proposal by the Board of Visitors at a jail dubbed 'Monster Mansion', was seen as a move to make the regime politically correct. It would mean that all 740 inmates at Wakefield Prison in west Yorkshire, including sex beasts like Roy Whiting, killer of Sarah Payne, would be afforded the same courtesy as the men who guard them. So too would Ian Huntley, murderer of Holly Wells and Jessica Chapman in Soham, who will soon be transferred to the jail. Prisoners are currently known by their surname only. Sarah Payne's mother Sara, described the idea as 'an insult to the victims' and prison officers' leader Brian Caton condemned it as "bloody stupid".

At Wandsworth Prison in London, the Governor sent a memo to Principal Officers and above, (viz: Governors) to the effect that anyone having a problem with addressing prisoners by their first names, or as 'Mr', should let him know, and he would find 'alternative employment' for them! (The mind boggles!)

Britain's most dangerous criminals are enjoying new high-tech gym equipment bought by the taxpayer, while staff have to pay for their own. Wakefield jail's infamous F-wing, dubbed 'Monster Mansion', is fitted with £5,000 worth of step machines, exercise bikes, cardio-vascular equipment, weights and benches. 'Charles Bronson' and serial killer Robert 'Cannibal' Maudsley are among prisoners using the kit. But when 420 warders at the West Yorks jail asked for a gym, they were told to pay for equipment themselves. An insider said: "It beggars belief. These scum, the lowest of the low, have everything. If they want more gear, why not give them the prison officers' old equipment and let the staff have the new stuff? The warders are furious." Wakefield has a system of enhanced privileges to give inmates an incentive to behave. Fitness fanatic Bronson, 51, is serving life for holding a jail lecturer hostage. Four times killer Maudsley, 50, ate the brain of one victim. The Prison Service said: "Officers have full access to the main gym at no charge."

Prisoners are creaming off millions of pounds in compensation because the Home Office would rather settle out of court than contest claims. The Prison Officers Association condemned the 'immoral practice' and said inmates were ridiculing the justice system. Laughable claims for items such as breakfast turning up half an hour late, and a watch getting lost in the post, are becoming common practice. Now POA General Secretary Brian Caton says that prisoners should be 'made to pay recompense to their victims if they receive compensation'. Norman Brennan of the Victims of Crime Trust said: "It's about time that frivolous claims are refused. Prisoners are afforded most luxuries apart from their freedom. Their victims are left devastated. It's time that some sort of sense is brought back to the criminal justice system because the criminals are running the asylum."

One source said: "Often they don't have anything to do all day apart from plot and scheme about the next compensation claim. If they can get £3,000 or £4,000 by doing nothing, they will do it." Victim Support said it was not its policy to comment on compensation given to prisoners, but privately many victims are angered by the thought of inmates getting rich. The Home Office refused to say how much compensation it pays to prisoners, but the yearly bill runs into millions. It is no longer an offence for an inmate to put in a malicious or false claim against a prison officer, so guards are often suspended for months while an investigation takes place. Even if the claims are fake, the worst a prisoner faces is an extra few days banged up.

Mr Caton condemned the way in which prison officers were treated as 'guilty until proven innocent'. Worse still, when a prison officer is assaulted, the Crown Prosecution Service says it is 'not in the public interest' to pursue charges, said Mr Caton. He added: "It is quite shocking. Often prison officers are stigmatised because they don't get the opportunity to clear their name in court." Convicted child rapist Geoffrey Shepherd, 61, got £1,000 and has been granted legal aid to sue the Home Office, over rejection of his plea for a prison transfer. Gangster Richmond Oduku, 24, who is serving 15 years for supplying heroin, is suing the Prison Service for more than £16,000, because a gold Cartier watch he says he sent to his partner got lost in the post. Hitman Ricardo Blanco, 40, who is serving Life, launched a court bid to sue prison bosses for keeping him in solitary confinement. Taxpayers are also facing a multi-million bill after a landmark judgement in a Scottish court that the prison service must compensate a prisoner who was forced to slop out.

Thousands of criminals must be kept out of jail to stop the prison population soaring, Ministers announced in January 2004. They hope to divert 13,000 burglars, car thieves, drug users and minor offenders from custody over the next six years, and fine them or impose community punishments instead. The Home Office insisted it was not 'going soft on crime' and said the move would help reduce reoffending. But shadow Home Secretary David Davis warned MPs: "The House will need to be reassured that fines and community penalties will not be used to replace custodial sentences, merely because the Home Secretary has already filled our jails.

"Does he still believe that punishment should fit the crime, or does he believe it should fit the number of empty cells?" The proposals were announced as a report ordered by Tony Blair warned that the justice system is failing to 'bear down sufficiently on serious, dangerous and highly persistent offenders'. The report, by businessman Patrick Carter, said only the most dangerous and persistent criminals should be jailed. Others should get toughened-up community punishments. Prisons Minister Paul Goggins said the number behind bars could not be allowed to continue rising, from 72,300 now to an estimated 93,000 in 2009.

But Norman Brennan, director of the Victims of Crime Trust, said this was 'contemptible to victims of crime and law-abiding members of the public'. Tory MP Ann Widdecombe, a former shadow Home Secretary, insisted: "The answer to overcrowding in our prisons is to build fresh jails."

In August 2004, HM Chief Inspector of Prisons, Ms Anne Owers, OBE, stated that 20% of all prisoners at HMP Coldingley, in Surrey, were not doing any work or education. It is claimed taxpayers spend around £8million every day to finance a 'couch potato lifestyle' for the approx 75,000 prisoners in British jails.

Up to 30,000 criminals who would have been sent to jail, are to go free because the Treasury is refusing to fund extra prison cells. The Government has already slashed the predicted size of Britain's prison population in four years' time from 109,000 to 80,000. MPs claimed that the cutback had been motivated by a Treasury refusal to fund extra prison places rather than serve the interests of justice.

The powerful Home Affairs committee of MPs accused ministers of massaging the predicted prison population to fit in with Chancellor Gordon Brown's spending plans.They said the "questionable" figure of 80,000 had been picked because that was how many prison cells the Treasury was willing to pay for. Instead of being imprisoned, convicted criminals who could have expected to be jailed, will now face fines or "softer" community penalties.

Critics accused the Government of failing to build enough jails, and Shadow Home Secretary David Davis said the revelations proved that the country's prisons were in chaos. "The Government has had seven years to deal with the problem of overcrowding. Instead it has ignored prison population projections and not built enough prisons, ultimately putting the public at risk by releasing those who have not undergone proper rehabilitation. The prison system is a complete shambles." In a report on rehabilitating offenders and reducing re-offending, the committee drew attention to the dramatic changes in the predicted prison population in four years. In December 2002 the Home Office said it would be as high as 109,600 by 2009, compared with the current record level of 77,000.

A study published a year later, the Carter Report, revised the figure down to 93,000. Then the Home Office slashed the figure even further to the current total of only 80,000. To cope, the Prison Service is spending £1.3billion to provide nearly 3,500 additional places in existing prisons by 2006. A further 1,290 places will be provided through new jails at Ashford, Middlesex, and Peterborough. The Home Office publicly insists it has all the places it needs to cope because of the changes to sentencing rules it decided to introduce, which will also see greater use of electronic tags, and prisoners being released earlier in return for guilty pleas. But the committee states the 80,000 figure has been selected to suit Gordon Brown, and ministers have bent the new sentencing rules to fit.

The MPs, led by former Home Office Minister John Denham, report: "The scale of the overcrowding problem is massive and the Government's optimistic assessment that by 2009 the prison population will neatly match prison capacity, rests on some questionable assumptions." Critics said the report is yet more evidence of the Government's attempt to avoid sending criminals to jail.

Last year, 2004, the *Daily Express* revealed an admission by ministers that dangerous criminals will be jailed only if it is 'cost-effective'. Judges now have to consider whether a jail term provides better value for money than picking up litter or repairing property damaged by vandals. The Home Office said: "Prison should remain a last resort for those individuals who pose a threat to the community. Short sentences in particular are considered to have a limited rehabilitative value."

Security firm *Group 4* is carrying out another inquiry after losing its second prisoner within a month. Violent burglar Carl Townsend was still on the run after attacking his guards to escape. Just 3 weeks earlier, murderer Gordon Topen, 33, went on the run for nearly a fortnight after giving his guards the slip at Walsgrave Hospital, Coventry. Townsend, 22, who was jailed for three years, feigned illness and beat up his guards when they pulled over on the A508 in Northampton, while heading to Bedford Prison. A *Group 4* spokeswoman said it would change its security measures 'if there are any lessons to be learned'. (*'Lessons will be learned'* – I can't think where I've heard that phrase before.)

In April 2004 a prison inmate won a court case over the practice of slopping-out, in a landmark move which could cost the taxpayer millions of pounds. At the Court of Session in Edinburgh, Lord Bonomy agreed with Robert Napier that the outdated toilet practice breached his human rights. He awarded Napier, once an inmate of Glasgow's Barlinnie jail, £2,450 in compensation. Napier, 24, launched his legal bid in June 2003, claiming conditions in Barlinnie were unacceptable. Slopping-out continues in areas of Barlinnie, Polmont, Perth and Edinburgh jails, and in the whole of Peterhead Prison.

A dangerous convict who has cost taxpayers £100,000 with a string of 'frivolous' claims is suing prison bosses, after he was refused a second mattress for his bed. George Knights, serving nine life sentences for a gun rampage, is demanding £50,000 compensation from the Prison Service for breaching his human rights. The case, which will be heard in the High Court, is the gunman's sixth in two years. He has also tried unsuccessfully to sue the prison service for failing to provide TV channel Five on his set and for refusing to fit an extra plug socket in his cell. Knights, 46, claimed he needed the extra socket to shave, and use his electric toothbrush at the same time. Experts said the total cost to the taxpayer may already have reached £100,000. His latest case could cost a further £20,000.

Knight's latest claim has already been turned down by a High Court judge, but he has been granted an appeal of the Judicial Review. He claims the refusal of a second mattress is an infringement of the Human Rights Act, which prohibits 'torture, cruel and unusual punishment'. The mattress needs to be added to the one already on his prison bed, to stop him suffering symptoms of 'pins and needles' in his legs, caused by deep vein thrombosis, according to his legal papers.

He also wants his cell in the high-security Long Lartin Prison, Worcs, switched to the ground floor, his own toilet, £50,000 in compensation and a legal promise from the authorities 'not to do this to me again'. The taxpayer will have to foot the bill for a video link to Knight's cell for the court hearing, as he is not permitted to attend. Home Office lawyers are to 'vigorously contest the claim'. In papers they submitted to the court they state Home Secretary David Blunkett would supply a second mattress if there was a valid medical reason, but Knights does not fall into that category.

In his application for the judicial review Knights said: "The time for compromise is long over and I am more and more determined to expose this to the public and, if I have to, the International Court of Human Rights." Prior to the case he had brought five private law actions against the Home Office, on top of four judicial review applications. Knights, a former security guard obsessed with guns, was given nine life sentences in 2000. A court heard drivers and pedestrians came under fire as he tried to escape traffic police, who had stopped him for an out-of-date tax disc. He hijacked four vehicles at gunpoint and kidnapped one motorist. Three police and three civilians were hit by gunfire. The terror ended in a three-hour armed siege at Knight's flat in Feltham, Middlesex. Former Conservative Prisons Minister Ann Widdecombe said: "The system should not be such a mug as to allow him to go through with it."

Serial killer Dennis Nilsen took advantage of an agonising loophole in the Human Rights Act to demand **hardcore pornography** to be delivered to his cell. Jailed in 1983 for murdering six young men, he was granted permission to receive explicit homosexual pornography in 2002. Nilsen, who kept the bodies of his victims for days, argued that his 'right to information and freedom of expression' under the Act entitled him to receive the hard-core material in prison. **Rather than contest the claim, the Prison Service agreed to allow prisoners this 'right' which opened the floodgates to similar demands. Previously all hardcore material was forbidden.**

Hook-handed terror suspect Abu Hamza had to be tied to prison officers because handcuffs kept slipping off his stumps. Since his arrest, the Muslim extremist, 47, has had his metal hooks removed. And when he was being escorted to a room at London's Belmarsh Prison for a video link-up to a court, Hamza was tied to two guards using strait-jacket-type restraints on his arms. Purportedly, Hamza lost an eye and at least one hand, during a bomb or mine explosion whilst he was fighting in Afghanistan. There is also the possibility that the other hand was amputated for his involvement in some crime in his country of origin.

Four prisoners went on the run after leaving dummies in their beds, just like the Clint Eastwood movie *Escape From Alcatraz*. They were caught and returned to Norwich jail. One had to be recaptured when he escaped again. A source said: "You'd have thought the warders wouldn't have been fooled a second time."

Soham killer Ian Huntley is to be housed in a 24ft by 12ft 'super cell' at his new jail. Two cells are being knocked into one in Wakefield top-security prison at a cost of up to £100,000, so Huntley can be observed round-the-clock. Special cameras and listening devices will be used to ensure there is no Harold Shipman-style suicide. The GP was found hanged at the west Yorks jail in January 2004. Staff have even been alerted about any mentions on TV of Maxine Carr, Huntley's former girlfriend. A source said: "If there is anything coming on TV about her, we have been told to switch it off or take him away from it, to try to maintain a stable state of mind. For the moment he is 'unnickable'. He is being handled with kid gloves. That is already getting up the noses of staff."

The super cell scheme follows a Home Office feasibility study into how best to handle the child killer. Huntley, moved from Belmarsh in London, after being attacked there, will be on F-wing at Wakefield for Category 43 sex offenders. Initially the cell will have a simple bed, toilet and sink, and personal belongings such as Huntley's own Roberts FM radio. The extra space should make room for a 'buddy', an inmate who would befriend him. Huntley, serving life for the murders of 10-year-olds Holly Wells and Jessica Chapman' has begun his time there in the hospital wing under observation. A Prison Service source said: "He calls staff 'Sir' and is trying to ingratiate himself." Huntley also wants to be a vegan, seen as a way of avoiding standard jail diet. Wakefield has 500 lifers. Inmates include Sarah Payne killer Roy Whiting and Robert Maudsley, nicknamed Hannibal the Cannibal.

Police have confirmed that a 15-year- old boy died at a Secure Training Centre in Northamptonshire, being run by *Group 4* staff, in April 2004. The boy, Gareth Myatt, was being restrained by three staff at Rainsbrook Secure Training Centre. The police officer leading the investigation, Detective Chief Inspector Moffat, said it was his job to enquire into the matter to establish whether, and against whom, criminal charges should be brought. He had interviewed the boy's family, who are devastated. The incident took place at 9.15pm at the unit, which is near Rugby.

The officer said: "It was necessary for staff to exercise their normal techniques, known as C & R (Control and Restraint) during the course of care and physical control of the boy. Whilst that C & R procedure, which is Home Office approved, was being undertaken by two male employees and a female, the boy lost consciousness and died. The director of children's services for *Rebound*, a subsidiary of *Group 4*, stated that the 3 staff members had not been suspended but were removed from operational duties in which there is direct handling of children, whilst the current police investigation is being undertaken.

Witness statements have been taken from staff, and also from some of the 67 detainees at the centre. Copies of the police report will be forwarded to the local Coroner and to the Crown Prosecution Service. The Howard League for Penal Reform called for the staff concerned to be suspended and for the launch of an independent enquiry. Their representative, Frances Crook said, "If a teacher slaps a child in school they are immediately suspended. It is extraordinary that when a child dies under circumstances such as this, the staff involved in the incident carry on working."

Double killer Kenneth Noye's first victim was a Detective Constable who was on surveillance in the grounds of Noye's mansion in Kent. Noye was suspected of having been involved in the massive Brinks Mat gold robbery. Detective Constable Needham was discovered in the grounds, after dark, by one of Noye's dogs. Noye armed himself with a knife and stabbed the officer to death there and then. At his trial, he claimed 'self defence', even though the officer was totally unarmed. The *second tragedy* was that the Jury were naïve enough to believe Noye's pathetic story, giving him the benefit of the doubt and acquitting him.

Many years later, at Swanley, Kent, Noye stabbed his second man to death as he claimed that he had been 'carved up' on a roundabout. Several witnesses saw the murder and took part car numbers etc. Noye went to ground and fled to Spain but was eventually tracked down and identified in a Spanish restaurant by the second victim's girl friend, who had been present at the scene, in fact driving the van, and had watched Noye stab her boyfriend to death. When she made the actual identification of Noye to the Police, she was naturally quite terrified, but wore a special wig etc. as a disguise.

He fought his extradition from Spain, right down to the wire, but appeared at the Central Criminal Court and on this occasion, could not convince the Jury of his innocence of his second murder and was jailed for life. In 2004 he complained that HMP staff at his former jail, made him feel suicidal through closely guarding him on suicide watch, with the light in the cell keeping him awake all night, he said. He was moved from a maximum security jail and sent to a normal wing at Whitemoor jail. He was previously categorised as an exceptional escape risk. But he has been downgraded in a 'reclassification' and the secure unit has been temporarily shut with three other prisoners moved out. He said: "It was worse than 'Guantanamo Bay' and I'm glad to be out of it. It's only purpose was to destroy the mind. I am glad the Home Office has seen sense. I was never in danger of escaping and have no interest in doing so."

Noye's move comes after a judge gave him the go-ahead to launch a Human Rights action over his treatment behind bars. He claimed the 'oppressive' conditions at the Cambridgeshire jail, including sleep disturbance and inadequate exercise, had made him think of killing himself. Noye was particularly upset he had not been able to touch or hold his elderly parents for some time.

But second stabbing victim Stephen's dad Ken attacked Noye's switch. He said: "Where does he want to be moved to, a holiday camp? He murdered my son and he is now paying the price. What human rights did he give my son?" A Prison Service spokesman said: "A number of inmates were reclassified. The prisoners were not deemed as high an escape risk as they were in the past. The unit has been closed, but it is not being shut down."

Noye was jailed for life in 2000 and cannot apply for parole until he has served at least 16 years. He had fled to Spain after killing Stephen on a slip road near Swanley, Kent but was extradited back to Britain. Noye's lawyer is arguing that he was only extradited on condition he did not get a life sentence. Having lost one High Court action, his lawyers are asking the Criminal Cases Review Commission to consider sending the case back to the Court of Appeal on the basis his conviction was legally flawed.

Prim teacher Alexandra Johnston, 49, has been banned from a jail because of an alleged relationship with a male prisoner. She broke the rules governing mixing with male prisoners. Senior Management staff at HMP Dartmoor state that she will not be getting her job back, and will be refused entry to the jail. She was a lecturer at a college in Somerset, known as Strode College. She had been visiting the prison on three days each week, but a prisoner, an armed robber called Robert Isaacs, falsely claimed she had an affair with him. Isaacs, aged 31, alleged that he had sex with Alexandra Johnston, during a spell of 21 months at Dartmoor. He claimed to have had sex with her on a classroom table. Later, he forged some letters purporting to come from her. However, a prison source advised that Johnston was banned from the prison due to a relationship with another prisoner, not Isaacs. He discovered about her relationship from prison gossip and decided to try to cash in on the deal, claiming to have had sex. Later, a Strode College spokesperson stated that Alexandra Johnston resigned from the HMP post at Dartmoor, after she appears to have been caught in the inappropriate and banned relationship. On being interviewed by a Sunday newspaper, she denied having any affairs with prisoners. However she did tell them that she went to visit a prisoner in hospital. A member of the Prison Service stated: "A teacher has been excluded."

HMP North Sea Camp, the seaside jail situated in the bleak fenlands of Lincolnshire, close to the Wash, has a fairly troubled recent history. It has been accused of bullying and drug-taking, having first begun life as a Borstal in the 1930's. It's original young offenders were put to work reclaiming parts of the marshlands, so that a prison farm could be created, to supply prison establishments with freshly grown foodstuffs.

In April 2004, the prison's Governor, Mr Keith Beaumont was removed from his post and sent home, after allegations against him of 'unprofessional conduct' were made. Prison Service officials were commencing an investigation into the matter. In 2002, some of the Jail's many acres were sold off to the Royal Society for the Protection of Birds. There came a time when two separate Crown Court judges contacted the Home Secretary, complaining about the number of prisoners who were escaping. One of its inmates, Lee Smith, 27, whilst on day-release from North Sea Camp, during a six-year sentence for armed robbery, failed to return, claiming he had fears because of his having been offered drugs and drink there.

In April 2004, recovering heroin addict, Ricky Foster, was given an additional 28 days on his sentence, for walking out of the jail. Several prisoners are known to have left the jail without permission, walked a few miles to another area and surrendered themselves to police. They asked to be transferred to another prison. In the year 2002, an official Home Office inspection report was highly critical of HMP North Sea Camp, and revealed that prisoners there were 'coasting' and victims of what might be described as 'benign neglect'.

A prisoner called Stephen Clarke, 38, from Pleasley, Derbyshire, was jailed for life in 1992, for murder. He stabbed to death, by causing 51 separate stab wounds, a male chef called Christopher Vitel, aged 27 at the time of his untimely death. Clarke then dumped the body in a wheelie bin. Using the deceased's car and credit cards, he fled to America where he went on a mad spending spree. Whilst there he met up with a gay friend . On his return to the UK he was arrested for the chef's murder. Clarke has decided he wishes to change sex and has already grown breasts, even though he is now serving his sentence in an all-male jail, HMP Springhill at Grendon Underwood in Buckinghamshire. He is now being prepared for a full-blown sex-change operation, costing £32,000.

The cost of the operation will be borne by the taxpayer. The sister-in-law of Clarke's murdered victim, is complaining in the strongest terms about the planned operation. She said, "Clarke should stay in jail until he rots for what he has done. He should not be having sex-change surgery at the taxpayer's expense. He snuffed out the life of one of the loveliest, most gentle people in the world and the family never received a penny in compensation. In my book, he should not be entitled to any human rights. It is outrageous."

Clarke is currently on day-release from the jail and catches a bus to nearby Aylesbury, where he works as a charity clerk. He already wears his hair at shoulder length and dresses as a female, having been recently seen waiting at a bus stop, wearing a pink head scarf and a trouser suit in burgundy over a pink blouse. His breasts grew following hormonal treatment and he has received counselling to prepare him for the eventual gender-change. He will also need separate treatment for bodily-hair removal etc., at further cost to the taxpayer. A source from inside Springhill Prison is reported as saying: "It was weird when we were told to call him 'Steph', but she is a really nice bloke."

A Home Office spokesman said: "Prisoners requesting treatment to change their sex would have to be treated in accordance with the NHS guidelines."

(**Author's note:** *This prisoner is now in a quandary and a 'grey area' as to whether he can legally use a female lavatory, whilst away from the jail. Perhaps you can visualise a scenario where a female using the same public toilets, sees through his disguise and sends for the police. A probationer police officer, fresh from initial training at a police college, would no doubt have a problem with the best way to tackle this one. The chances are that Clarke would be arrested and the matter sorted out at a police station.*)

In May 2004, information was received that Soham double-murderer Ian Huntley has behaved himself so well in jail that he is to be rewarded with a *Sony PlayStation*. He will also have access to a mail order catalogue and hopes to be allowed to purchase a CD player, to complement the TV he already has in his cell. It soon came to notice that he was being mollycoddled in this way. An organisation called *Phoenix Survivors Group*, through its spokesperson Shy Keenan, said: "We deal with families who have been shattered and torn apart by these people. Some of the families can't even afford to bury their children, let alone afford Playstations."

Spokesperson Lynn Costello, from a charity known as *Mothers Against Murder and Aggression* said: "Someone like Huntley should be seen to be punished. Letting him have PlayStation games, a CD player and a TV, is not a punishment. It's ridiculous how he is being cosseted. Many children cannot afford PlayStations." Huntley is currently serving two life sentences for the dreadful murders of Holly Wells and Jessica Chapman, aged 10 yrs. He will be allowed to purchase his personal entertainment equipment as soon as he reaches what is known as 'enhanced' prisoner status.

In May 2004 he was still being held at HMP Wakefield, Yorks, which is a maximum security jail. An internal prison source stated: "It is very easy to achieve 'enhanced' status and Huntley is assured of this." It is thought that Huntley has settled in well at this prison and has bonded well with other sex monsters in there, including Roy Whiting and Robert Black.

In May 2004, Home Secretary David Blunkett gave permission for a sex monster called Ian Mitchell, 34, to be temporarily released on escorted leave from Chadwick Lodge Secure Hospital, Milton Keynes. He had previously been described by police as 'too dangerous for the public to approach'. He was sent there after being considered unfit to plead to two terrifying sex attacks. Whilst walking with his lone escort, he was not handcuffed or tagged, and whilst taking a bus to Bletchley to look around the shops, his escort sat about 5-6 rows of seats behind him. Eventually Mitchell gave his escort the slip in a shopping arcade.

As police hunted for him, they announced: "This man is a risk to the public and should not be approached." Mitchell managed to remain at large for just under 24 hours before being recaptured approx 150 miles away at Grimsby. Angry local residents near the Secure Hospital declared that they were 'furious, sickened and frightened' by the number of paedophiles and sex offenders released from the hospital to walk the streets. One resident, Joyce Hall, said, "We've never understood why a Secure Mental Hospital is in the centre of our community. There's a hospital next door to it, with a children's wing and a nursery, and it's surrounded by schools. They keep telling us that their patients are not dangerous, just people with a severe personality disorder. Now we know that is rubbish".

At Chadwick Lodge, a female member of staff stated: "If a patient posed a risk to the public, he would not be going on escorted leave." In 2003 the Hospital was criticised for freeing killer Wayne Page, 39, for a day trip to the Chelsea Flower Show.

During the week commencing 17th January 2005, the new Home Secretary Charles Clarke, admitted that 'The Yorkshire Ripper', Peter Sutcliffe, had been granted an application to temporarily leave the Special Hospital for the Criminally Insane, Broadmoor, at Crowthorne, Berkshire. Having been previously refused permission to attend his father's funeral in 2004, due to obvious security considerations, Sutcliffe was allowed to visit the beautiful area of the Lake District at Arnside, a 540 miles round trip. His father's ashes had been scattered in the area. His application to visit the spot, had been originally approved by former Home Secretary David Blunkett 'for compassionate reasons', and was endorsed by his successor Charles Clarke. He was safely returned to Broadmoor afterwards, having been escorted by four members of staff.

The reader can just imagine the adverse publicity this 'humanitarian' day trip generated, given the total lack of compassion or humanitarianism which Sutcliffe had shown to his many female victims, whom he savagely slaughtered using a hammer etc. The MP for Arnside, Tim Collins said there had been 'shock and surprise' among locals that the (serial) killer had been smuggled to the town in a massive security operation. He further said: "They are worried that it has happened once, and it could happen again." Marcella Claxton, who survived a hammer attack by Sutcliffe in Leeds 29 years ago, said: "His just being outside of his prison walls gives me terrible feelings. He has been allowed to go to the coast and taste the sweet sea air, none of the women he murdered will get that chance. I still have nightmares about that man."

MPs from all parties joined the wave of condemnation taken by the Home Office. Tory MP Julie Kirkbride, who was at school with 19-year-old victim Josephine Whittaker, said: "I don't think it's possible that the Home Secretary understands the fear in which women in West Yorkshire lived for many years, that they would be the Ripper's next victim." Labour's Fabian Hamilton, MP for Leeds North-east, where some of Sutcliffe's victims' families live, said the Ripper was the 'most brutal murderer of modern times'. He said: "And my worry is this will cause further grief, further anger and upset for the families."

Tory Andrew Mackay MP, whose seat includes Broadmoor, demanded a statement from Mr Clarke. He said: "This is a very, very bad start for the new Home Secretary and it does make clear that he is not serious about law and order and crime prevention." A Home Office spokesman said: "The decision was made by the previous Home Secretary, David Blunkett. This was subsequently reaffirmed by Charles Clarke. A full and comprehensive risk assessment was made by the authorities and the individual was closely supervised at all times. At no point was there any danger to members of the public." In an extraordinary cloak-and-dagger security operation, Sutcliffe and four guards left Broadmoor at 5.30am. Sutcliffe was given no advance warning that he was making the trip to Cumbria to stop news of it leaking out. He was jailed for life in 1981. Between 1975 and 1981, he murdered 13 women and left seven others for dead in a killing spree that terrified the entire country.

Prison chiefs have spent more than £10,000 doing up a special cell for the Lockerbie bomber ahead of a move from Scotland's toughest prison to a new jail. The £250,000 segregated suite at Barlinnie, nicknamed 'Gaddafi's Cafe', is to be given over to elderly sex offenders who prison authorities fear could be attacked by other inmates. The Scottish Prison Service has spent the cash on new facilities for Abdelbaset al-Megrahi, since announcing his move to Gateside Prison, Greenock, last year. It has cost £6,000 to knock two cells together and another £4,000 to kit it out with satellite TV, hi-fi system, shower and separate cooking facilities. Megrahi, 52, has been held at Barlinnie since 2002, after being found guilty of mass murder following a special Scottish High Court trial at Camp Zeist in the Netherlands.

The single mother of a four-year-old boy has been jailed for 15 months for smuggling heroin to her father in prison. Claire Garside, 34, of Mellow Purgess, Laindon, Essex was told by a judge at Canterbury Crown Court only a custodial sentence could be justified. At her trial in November 2004, a jury heard how Garside had been seen on CCTV handing her father a bag of snacks during a visit to Elmley Prison on the Isle of Sheppey.

When the pack was seized by warders they found it contained 3.8g of brown powder, later analysed and found to contain heroin. Pleading not guilty to supplying a class A drug, Garside claimed she thought the pack contained brewers' yeast, which her father wanted to brew alcohol to pay off prisoners who were attacking him. But the jury did not believe her and found her guilty and **the judge then adjourned sentence to allow Garside to have Christmas with her family**. How kind of him. Judge Michael O'Sullivan said Garside had been manipulated by her father, and he had taken that and her previous good character into account.

Six prison officers won the right to compensation for witnessing the bloody aftermath of a cell murder. Prison bosses admitted the men should not have been exposed to the horror when Jason Ricketts strangled Colin Bloomfield, 35, and hacked his body to bits in Cardiff Prison. Ricketts, 29, was later jailed for life. A judge at Cardiff County Court criticised the Home Office for taking five years to admit liability. Two of the officers have been forced to leave their jobs.

Prison bosses have turned to herbal tea as an unlikely way of bringing peace and quiet to jails. Inmates are swapping sedatives for *Dr Stuart's Botanical Teas*, including a mixture promising 'tranquillity'. Many convicts at Downview jail in Surrey now rely on the soothing effect of a cup of herbal tea rather than a sedative, to help calm them and assist sleep. A Prison Service spokesman said: "They are very, very popular with prisoners. They are so widely used by women in Downview jail that the tea bags have almost replaced sedatives as a way of helping the women sleep."

News of the benefits of a cup of tea has spread far and wide in the prison system since *Dr Stuart's Botanical Teas* were first introduced at Wandsworth men's jail in south London four years ago. The most popular teas requested by the jails are *Tranquillity* and *Valerian Plus*, which are known for their ability to help people to relax. *Tranquillity* is a blend of lime flowers, hawthorn berries, yarrow and fennel, and *Valerian Plus* is a mix of lime flowers, valerian root, hops, passion flowers and fennel. Prisoners in HMP Wandsworth started the trend towards herbal teas in jail when inmates suffering from stress and insomnia asked the prison pharmacy to order supplies.

The teas are also being supplied to High Down men's jail in Surrey and Lewes prison in Sussex. The firm delivers 11 cases of tea or 2,640 tea bags to each jail every month at a cost of £120. The tea is distributed by the prisons' healthcare departments. Tea also offers an alternative to cannabis, common in jails. The Prison Service added: "We are doing very well with them. They are being introduced into more prisons and are proving a good alternative to sedatives and other prescription drugs which can become addictive."

A spokesman for *Dr Stuart's Teas* said: "We were contacted by Wandsworth prison pharmacy department, as the teas had been requested by inmates, especially those coping with stress and sleep problems." The herbal tea initiative has been welcomed by prison pharmacy departments, who are keen for prisoners to enjoy the healthy natural herbal remedies, rather than becoming hooked on other habit-forming drugs, which are also far more costly.

A prison riot that caused £3million damage and left an inmate dead, was sparked by a row over sandwiches. The devastation at Lincoln Prison in October 2002 was Britain's worst since Strangeways erupted into violence in 1991. For eight hours prisoners smashed everything, started fires and looted the pharmacy. The last trials of those involved heard that one reason for the violence was that sandwiches replaced hot meals on the menu. Previous trials could not be reported until after the proceedings.

On 8th February 2005 the Government's handling of the prison system was dealt a huge double blow. In one of the most scathing reports ever compiled, Chief Inspector of Prisons Anne Owers condemned The Mount jail, in Hertfordshire, for its "appalling" conditions. And former Prison Service director general Martin Narey, revealed at an inquiry that he only got the job in 1999 because all other candidates refused even to look at it.

A Jamaican drug smuggler held Britain's 'soft' prison regime up to ridicule on 17th February 2005, as he boasted that he saved £6,000 while having the time of his life in jail. The 'four-star' life enjoyed by Lloyd Seymour Kenlock, cost UK taxpayers £112,000, after he was caught trying to sneak £126,000 of cocaine into the UK. His three-year jail term even made front page news in Jamaica, after he boasted on his return that life in Wormwood Scrubs was 'the best'.

Kenlock said he had saved money from his prison job, sent £1,000 to relatives in Jamaica and enjoyed healthcare which would have cost a fortune at home. The 58-year-old said: "It was wonderful, like a four-star hotel: own bathroom, hot water, heating in winter, own light and no one to come bug you." After he was deported on June 14 2004, he even sent a thank-you letter to the prison staff and offered to present them with a watercolour painting he had made of them. C Wing Governor Alan Parkins refused the gift but replied: "*It is gratifying to know that your experience was as pleasant as it could possibly have been.*"

These comments just sum up the state of the criminal justice system. "Prisoners get lax sentences, they get compensated and when they leave prison they are able to laugh. What sort of deterrent is that? When criminals leave prison the last thing they should want is to go back. Rather than having a tough regime, prisons have just become an occupational hazard for criminals."

Kenlock was sentenced in 2001 after pleading guilty to importing a Class A drug and evading customs. He said that on June 14, 2001, a friend had given him a round ticket from Kingston to London and £500 payment for smuggling the drug. The route is one of the major passageways for smuggling cocaine, which is often turned into deadly crack, in the UK. When he arrived at Heathrow airport customs officers discovered two kilograms of cocaine packed in his suitcase. Mocking the lax treatment he received at the hands of the UK authorities, he said: "They did treat me real nice. They just wanted to know why I was bringing drugs into the country. They gave me food, tea, water, anything except alcohol."

Once he had been sent to medium-high security prison Wormwood Scrubs, he earned £40 a week mending head phones, double the minimum wage of Jamaica. As a result he saved £6,000, more than 12 times the amount he was paid to commit the crime. Kenlock was entitled to free health and dental care, a luxury in Jamaica where most people have to pay for it, and sent money home for his two ex-wives and four children.

He said: "I can't afford health care in Jamaica but in England I got my eyes tested and was given free dentures. I spent four months in a prison hospital because of trouble in my leg. It was superb. I complained I couldn't hear the television because I am partly deaf and the nurses got me one with teletext so I could read the subtitles. In prison you have 100 per cent privacy except when you bathe. I had my own cell and the food was nutritious and healthy but a bit bland for my taste.

"The wardens treated me with compassion, they were kind and patient. Apart from getting no sex, life was better for me there. My time in prison was cool, I couldn't have asked for more. Those who say it is no good are lying."

The cost of keeping Kenlock in Wormwood Scrubs was an estimated £37,305 every year, a total of £111,915. In 2003 there were 2,795 Jamaicans in British prisons, making up the largest ethnic group within the service. Most of them were being held on drug smuggling charges. The total number of foreigners in our jails is 9,000, which costs the public purse £335million a year. These include thousands of illegal immigrants and failed asylum seekers. At any one time there are also up to 600 criminals living in the UK who have served their sentences but have not been kicked out of the country, even though deportation was part of their punishment.

Tory home affairs spokeswoman Cheryl Gillan said: "The number of foreign nationals in our prisons is huge and is growing, and the British taxpayer is picking up the bill. After seven years of talk, Tony Blair's Government has failed to get a grip on this problem. Michael Howard is right to attack the way in which criminals are sentenced in this country. Sentencing policy is a farce. It is, as he says, 'a lie'. It has lost the trust of the general public and destroyed the faith of the victims. The latter increasingly feel that they will be extremely lucky if they get justice. Our courts have become institutions that tend to attend to the needs of the offenders, rather than to the rights of the victims. The fact that criminals rarely serve the sentence that is imposed by the judge, destroys confidence in the system."

As the Tory leader pointed out, criminals sentenced to less than four years are automatically released after serving just half of their sentences. This does not seem to most people to be right or fair. They want certainty. They want to know that the felon will do the time that is imposed on him. They are rightly angry and dismayed when they discover that the man who viciously attacked their daughter and is sentenced to six years, is found back living across the street just three years later. That said, it is understandable that we should wish to encourage prisoners to become reformed characters, to be rehabilitated and to behave well while in prison, the latter is especially important for the welfare of the prison officers. A prisoner behaving properly should be rewarded, they should be given incentives. What better incentive could there be than to promise lopping some time off the sentence?

We should do this but taking off 50 per cent, automatically, is far too much. It is taking the mickey. In any case, the 50 per cent rate of remission was never introduced as a matter of principle. It wasn't the figure hit upon as the optimum period of time in which to gauge whether an offender was indeed reformed. It wasn't a considered assessment of the time necessary to rehabilitate them. Instead it was a cynical and crude attempt to reduce what was then regarded as an overlarge prison population. It was implemented out of expediency. It was designed to appease the noisy liberals. The desire was to save money.

There is still a problem with the number of people in prison. There are more people behind bars in Britain per head of population than any other European country, other than Portugal, though we are well below the US. That has to be rectified. The trouble is that we imprison the wrong people. Obviously, as Michael Howard says, 'persistent and dangerous criminals should be sent to prison'. As he insists: "The public needs protection from them." And it is absolutely true, as he constantly reminds us, that while felons are in jail they cannot commit further offences. But it is not necessary to imprison the army of inadequates and the mentally ill. It is not necessary to impose harsh and lengthy sentences when rehabilitation could be achieved earlier. So, while it is right to ensure that our sentencing policy is realistic, fair, in accordance with public opinion and commands the fear of the criminal and the respect of the law-abiding, we should stop wasting money on the non-violent petty offender and concentrate on the real villains. On the subject of crime, it is amazing, isn't it, that New Labour has been responsible for creating 1,018 new crimes since it came to office? There are new criminal offences created every three days by Tony Blair.

Now, I know he was, as he promised, going to get 'tough on crime' but I hadn't realised he was quite that serious: 1,018! That's amazing. Really tough, brilliant. Except, he's not exactly cracking down on crime. He's not making the streets safer and our lives more bearable Not at all. What he is doing is to allow a £1,000 fine to be imposed for meddling with a vehicle clamp, a £500 fine for obstructing a fire hydrant, a £20,000 fine for staging a church hall concert without a licence and a fine of £2,500 for attending a woman in childbirth if you are not a doctor or midwife. And in each of these and the other new offences which carry a fine, you will be locked up if you fail or refuse to pay. This is very silly. It demonstrates how far we've lost touch with reality and how much power has been put into the hands of the busybodies.

For one thing is certain, the law will be imposed by the diligent 'jobsworth' just like the law was employed to crush Sarah McCaffery for holding an apple in her hand while driving.

The Government needs to get its priorities right. Instead of devising new and unnecessary laws to criminalize hard-working people, it should be concentrating on those responsible for the 22 per cent rise in sexual offences, the 12 per cent increase in assaults and the six per cent increase

in violent crime. But that would be asking too much of Tony Blair. That would be asking him to use a little common sense.

Over the years, I have noticed that most escapes from jail are those whereby at least two prison officers accompany a prisoner to a local hospital, either for casualty treatment, tests etc., or even for an operation. On leaving the jail, prisoners are 'double-cuffed', which means his own set of prison handcuffs are applied, always, well almost always, with the cuffs being secured above the *wrist bone*, so that they cannot be easily slipped off.

A second pair of cuffs are used to link one of the officers to the prisoner. The prison officers take a briefcase to the hospital with them. This always contains a quite long, heavy chain known as a 'closeting chain'. This is mainly used when the

An example of modern style HMP 'double-cuffing' of prisoner to escorting officer

prisoner claims he needs to use a hospital toilet. The closeting chain, in theory, allows him his privacy to use the lavatory, but still be secured to one of the officers.

However, having studied the HMP Key Performance Indicators (KPI's) during my service, as well as published details of methods of escaping, it seems that in many cases, the prisoner wasn't desperate for the loo at all, merely desperate to escape! He had been briefed by his wing mates before he left jail, as to how to slip off the cuff at his end of the closet chain, and enjoy his new-found freedom via the toilet fanlight window. However, when he or she is recaptured, if at all, he will be dressed in what are known as 'Patches'. This is a one piece jumpsuit in bright green and yellow material patches, like a patchwork quilt. A kind of 'see-at-a-glance' recognition uniform kit, for HMP staff.

Additionally he will not be allowed to move around any part of the jail for the rest of his sentence, unless he is always accompanied by two prison officers. Furthermore, he goes nowhere unless express permission for the move is sanctioned via telephone or personal radio from the HMP Gatehouse, Security department, or the Orderly Officer. In the case of escaping HMYOI offenders, as at HMYOI Huntercombe, near Henley-on-Thames, the 'Patches' prison clothing is dispensed with after 2-3 days, once the little dear has promised his modern liberal Governor, that he will certainly not be trying to escape ever again, and that nothing is further from his mind. Other forms of escapes are graduated downwards, by being referred to as 'absconding', or 'being unlawfully at large' rather than 'escaping'.

This situation occurs quite frequently when a so-called 'risk-assessed' prisoner is allowed out of the jail on a daily basis to go out and work in the community. However, hardly any security training, if at all, is handed down to those members of the public into whose care our bright young lad is handed for the day.

In one HMYOI where I worked, on two quite different occasions, involving different convicts, the Project Leaders supervising them, took them somewhere or other in their private cars. On arrival at the external Project venue, or at the visit destination, the keys were left in the cars ignition locks, easy pickings for the convict to wander back to the car as soon as his 'Supervisor', the Project Leader's back was turned. Who could resist such a temptation to drive back to one's old haunts and renew your opportunities for getting some long-awaited 'crack' cocaine smoke down into your lungs? (As they say, 'You couldn't make it up - could you?) Convicts failing to return under licence from 'Home Leave', are recorded as 'Unlawfully at Large'.

Some criminals are born into a criminal culture, where crime is a family business. In these cases, HM Prison Service spends fortunes per year in 'Inter-Prison visits', running criminals around the country in taxis or official vehicles, funded by the taxpayer of course. The liberal thinking regarding this, under the guise of 'maintaining family ties or links', is 'humanitarianism'. However, hardly any regular and repeat offenders within the system, express the slightest *concern* or *humanitarianism* for their multi-victims!

If only the same degree of care and concern was shown by members of HMP Senior Management Teams (SMT) to *staff* members, as to the convicts, life inside for prison officers would be far more pleasant. And as for the endless huge, plastic, four feet high Father Christmas sacks and contents, excitedly brought in by external do-gooders, well, that's another story!

Early in March 2005, a taxi containing a prisoner and two prison officers on the way to a hospital, was stopped by armed men in a car, who at gunpoint, forced the prison staff to remove the prisoner's handcuffs, and for him to escape in their car. A Prison Service spokesperson was reported as stating that prisoners were rarely transported in taxis. What tosh! At the HMYOI where I worked, Huntercombe, taxi firm proprietors must have become millionaires at the frequency with which their services were required. Small fortunes changed hands in 'waiting times' and/or 'wait and return' situations.

One year, a special directive was published, quoting the annual taxi budget and requesting staff exercise more care. In practice, it is much easier for senior staff to quickly pick up a phone, press the 'speed-dial' button to local taxi firms, than to lay on the use of HMP official transport , at all hours of the day or night.

In recent times, it has become the practice in some establishments, to remove the wire protective cage or panel which protects the driver from his oft-violent passenger cargo seated behind him. The reasons given for this include: the prisoners feel *intimidated* or *embarrassed* whilst passing through public areas in the outside world. Naturally the poor official driver would not feel intimidated or embarrassed or distracted from his driving by being spat upon, called names, having apple cores thrown at him, or lighted dog ends flicked at him! (or the HMP van hi-jacked away from him.)

A veteran prison officer was demanding his job back after he claimed he was sacked for calling inmates 'convicts' and describing their meals as 'feeding time'. Michael Summers, 53, who has been awarded six commendations for bravery during his 20-year career, says he was dismissed from his £26,000-a-year post because he was too 'old school' for his *politically correct* bosses. He alleges he was initially told he was being kicked out of the Prison Service because he had taken nearly 200 days off sick in two years. But he claims a Senior Officer later gave him other reasons, including use of offensive terminology.

His case for unfair dismissal will be heard at a later date. It comes three months after staff were urged to call inmates 'Mister' by the Board of Visitors at Wakefield Prison in West Yorkshire. Mr Summers, who was working at Canterbury Prison in Kent when he was dismissed in November 2003, said: "They told me I had acted unprofessionally by referring to prisoners as 'convicts.' I thought they were joking. If you look in the dictionary under convict it says 'a person serving a sentence of imprisonment'. A few of the prisoners were stunned when I told them what had happened. They thought it was a joke as well. I asked them (HMP Senior Staff) to give me other examples. They criticised me for referring to meal times as 'feeding time'. I was told I should have said, 'It's time for the prisoners to have their meals'. The Management turned on me because I was from the old school and they just wanted me out. There was a bullying culture among Management." Mr Summers said his problems started in 2001 when his torment at work caused him to become depressed, and he was diagnosed as suffering from stress. Over the next two years he had to take 171 days sick leave. In November, Governor Helen Rinaldi told him he was being sacked for 'unsatisfactory and unacceptable attendance'. Mr Summers, of Westgate-on-Sea, Kent, said: "I had a doctor's certificate and was trying to get back to work. But the Prison Service did not accept stress as a valid reason for absence. I know several other wardens who are ready to walk out after 20 years service because of the way they are treated by Management." Mr Summers, now working as an £11,000-a-year security guard, added: "I want the Prison Service to be ordered to reinstate me. But if the tribunal rules against that, I will fight for compensation." A Prison Service spokeswoman said she could not comment on individual cases.

(**Author's note:** *Further to Mr Summers's claim that there was a 'bullying culture among management', in fact I had personal experience of this during my six years of employment in HM Prison Service. At the time of writing, I am currently investigating my legal position in respect of this. Also, I heard on the grapevine that in February 2005, an external private company were permitted to run a staff survey at HMP Wandsworth, Apparently, approx 30% of those members of HMP Wandsworth staff who took the trouble to complete and return their survey questionnaires, complained that they had been* **bullied by staff** *)*

Towards the end of 2004, I prepared a very detailed report in relation to my own incidents of perceived bullying during my service at one of Her Majesty's Young Offenders Institutions HMYOI HUNTERCOMBE, near Henley-On-Thames, Oxfordshire. One complaint concerned the fact that a Governor M. Gillan, as Head of Operations, failed to support me fully by non-enforcement of the No Smoking policy. This was a Health and Safety issue, since Employers are legally bound to provide 'a safe working environment for all employees'.

The problems of No Smoking regulations not being enforced applied only, so far as my complaint was concerned, to the actual prison *Gate Lodge*, where entry and exit to the HMYOI was controlled, all keys and radios were issued, and was the 'nerve centre' of the establishment. It was normally manned by 3-4 members of uniformed staff, who, for obvious security reasons, had to keep the single storey building closed and locked at all times, except for when admitting normally senior staff for various reasons.

The Gate Lodge was designated a 'No Smoking' area at all times. Staff posted to the gate lodge duties who were smokers were required to go outside into the open air vehicle lock. However certain staff members repeatedly breached the No Smoking regulations, by smoking *inside* the gate lodge. People smoked cigarettes, a Senior Officer who was a frequent visitor to the gate lodge actually smoked a cigar. Still worse, one day an HMP colleague of my own equivalent grade, returned from outside and put his still-smoking pipe down on the desk right in front of me. It was all a bit of a scandal really, 'No Smoking' signs were taken down, or, if free-standing on lockers etc., were knocked over to lie flat.

Even the Deputy Governor wrote a 'conform or else' letter which was stuck to an inner wall near the back door. Even this was taken down! The only persons who supported me in any way were other non-smokers, one of whom congratulated me on taking a stand. I even co-opted myself onto the Health and Safety Committee and made sure my regular protests and updates re incidents were fully recorded in the Minutes of regular meetings. Eventually I involved the Area Manager through leaving a message at his nearby hotel. Amazingly enough, the very next morning he arrived at the jail, entered the gate house and immediately caught an Officer smoking, and gave him a piece of his mind. To the Officer's personal embarrassment, the news of his 'capture' spread around the establishment like wildfire!

I became so paranoid about the continued infringement of the 'No Smoking in the gate' campaign that I wrote to the *Prison Service News* monthly magazine about it. As a result, a female Senior Officer employed in the Health Care Centre at either HMP Liverpool or HMP Manchester telephoned me and said that she was like-minded. At her prison she was almost hated and they called her by an insulting and disparaging nickname of either 'ashtray' or 'fag ash Lil'. Also, a male officer phoned to say he was having the same problem at his jail. A very good friend of mine, whom I had known for 40 years, had been employed at HMP Reading, and was constantly forced to *passive smoke*, but challenged almost every offending staff member who smoked in his presence.

At my HMYOI, Huntercombe, eventually the Deputy Governor advised me that funding had been agreed for the installing of 'hard wired' aircraft lavatory-style smoke alarms. Earlier versions, battery operated ones installed in the ceilings had their batteries removed. One female officer kept her own ashtray on the floor under a bay window in the gate lodge, and was obviously a regular offender. Even a Principal Officer, the Head of Security, smoked in the gate lodge on occasions. You can imagine that it takes a great deal of courage for a junior member of staff in HM Prison Service to challenge people about three grades higher than yourself!

One day, whilst employed for the whole shift on days as Duty Driver, I went out from the Jail to collect some day release young offenders from their external community Projects, in the minibus. One stroppy individual from the east end of London, Stratford, E15, had been given a packaged sandwich at his work-in-the-community Project. He often played up whilst being transferred out and returned each weekday, seeing himself as a 'leader' amongst his peers. When I facilitated entry into the area between the outer gates, known as the 'Vehicle Lock', I saw that he was brandishing his packaged sandwich, which was unopened. I challenged him over this and asked him to hand it over. This he refused to do, neither for me, nor the more senior Officer in charge of the gate lodge. This left us, in these ridiculously liberal times, with no right to remove it from him by force, therefore I placed him on Governor's Report for 'failing to carry out a lawful order' under the Prison Discipline Code.

The very next morning, Governor M. Crabbe, who was in charge of this convict's Residential 'House' (meaning 'Wing'), came in very early and made it his first job to deal with the Adjudication against the sandwich prisoner. After hearing my evidence, he dismissed the charge and allowed the acquitted convict to leave the jail to go to his community project, as usual, at the normal time. I complained about the acquittal to the No.1, or Governing Governor, Mr P. Manwaring. He was most sympathetic, after I pointed out to him that each morning at the Reception area, where the convicts are searched and processed prior to departure to their outside duties, they must fill out and sign and date a special form to declare that *they will not take anything out of the prison, or bring anything at all back in*, the form even has a space for entering what clothes they are wearing, just in case they abscond, in which case the full description, clothing etc details can be passed on to the Police, to assist with their recapture.

I pointed out to Mr Manwaring that, not only was Governor Crabbe the Residential Governor of the sandwich boy's Wing , and therefore ultimately responsible for his so-called, all-important 'RISK ASSESSMENT', but that he was also in the Senior and responsible position of 'Head of Regimes', and therefore had responsibility for being aware of such very important things as security, such as the convicts having to sign and date the forms I've just described. How embarrassing to be caught out in this way, resulting in a bizarre and perverse Adjudication acquittal of the convict for breach of Prison Security Rules!

In the event, No.1 Governor Paul Manwaring, who literally had an 'ever-open office-door policy', unlike others I could name, wrote to Governor Crabbe, advising him to make an apology to me, over the perverse acquittal. Surprise, surprise, no apology was ever forthcoming and soon afterwards, Governor Crabbe packed his bags and moved elsewhere, to HMP Gloucester or Bristol, I suspect the former.

Any readers who have ever touched any kind of miscarriage of justice, or been aware of one close to home, will be able to imagine how seething I was at the time. Governor Crabbe was officially in command of the official judicial hearing, the Prison Adjudication, and chose to throw out the charge against the convict. You could compare it exactly to the situation where a High Court Judge throws a case out on a point of law of which he was not aware, but it was his duty to know it, and act correctly upon it.

My next written complaint concerns another Prison Governor at the same HMYOI, Mr P. Newton. He rapidly progressed from Senior Officer in the PE Department, to Governor Grade in approximately two years. He was quite a surly, serious man and very rarely smiled. Not a good manager of staff and had no idea as to how to get the best performance from his subordinates. Before we knew it, our Deputy Governor had been promoted and moved on to become No.1 at a different Prison. This meant that Governor P. Newton was temporarily uplifted to Acting Deputy Governor, moving into the large office which went with the temporary posting.

One day, I returned from a week's annual leave to find that I was detailed as Duty Driver again. In the usual way, I drove the 'risk assessed' Project prisoners to their Community venues. On this day, one of the prisoners was a very likeable rogue, as, unusually in prisons, he was very friendly and respectful towards staff. This kid was always smiling, he seemed to be an Arab boy from his colouring. I used to overhear stories he told to his Project travelling mates, in the minibus, that made your hair curl. He lived in west London and was given to 'slight' exaggeration. He once told his chums that he knew of a young man from his home area who had survived not one, but FIVE headshots from a hand gun, for example.

On this particular day, as we approached the Arab convict's Community Project at Didcot, Oxon, a Senior Citizens Home and Day Centre I think, he said to me: "You don't need to walk me in today Guv, I take myself in now, the residents think I'm a student from the College. Can I have my card please?" I replied: "It's the first I've heard of it!"

The normal routine since time immemorial had been that the Duty Driver, in his HMP uniform of some description, walks the convict into the venue and personally hands to the staff member in charge inside, the prisoner's stiff cardboard descriptive card, printed out with action to be taken in the event of an unexplained disappearance, or determined escape etc. At this stage, official responsibility for the young convict passes from the HMP Duty Driver, to the Project Leader or Deputy. So I 'walked' the inmate into his community Project in the usual way, handing his HMYOI security card to a Project Leader. Later that morning Acting Deputy Governor Newton called me to his temporary office in the Admin Corridor. Ever unsmiling, he said: "I hear you frogmarched a trainee into his Project this morning!" You could have heard a pin drop. I was livid, I almost shouted 'FROGMARCHED? I never touched him'.

He then had the gall to try to convince me that there is no harm in **aiding**

and abetting a young inmate of the jail to deceive the Care Home residents and day-visitors into believing he was not a serving prisoner in a Young Offenders Institution. (My words, not his, but that was what he was really saying!) He immediately suspended me from driving duties until further notice, and I had to report to the Senior Officer who prepares the weekly duty lists. I was not posted to Duty Driver again for a week or so. What arrogance and overbearing, officious conduct from an Acting Duty Governor! So much for the so-called encouraged notion to try to turn these boys' lives around from their criminal culture and dishonest behaviour. How dare he suggest that I should encourage the boy to LIE to innocent members of the public, particularly elderly and vulnerable ones with whom he came in contact on a day-by-day basis!

However the most outrageous and bizarre part of this real-life HM Prison Service anecdote I have saved till last. Believe it or not, Mr Newton, a hypocrite if ever there was one, in my eyes, was at the time, the Senior Member of the Prison staff in charge of instruction into C & R techniques (Control and Restraint), which regularly took place just outside the Jail in a designated room known as The Dojo! Therefore, in a manner of speaking, *he* was the CHIEF FROGMARCHER in the establishment, running regular mandatory refresher courses in how a three-officer team should secure and safely march away under control to his cell or the segregation unit, a recalcitrant and ill-disciplined, probably violent, teenaged thug.

However, fortunately for the hard-working HMYOI staff at the sharp end, Mr Newton was destined not to remain there much longer. He was head-hunted over as Deputy Governor to a fresh jail, by the very man whose office he had temporarily occupied for a while, as Acting Deputy Governor. Unlucky for them, but a reason for staff at our jail to celebrate. In fact it is quite normal and seemingly traditional in HM Prison Service for an 'I'll scratch your back if you'll scratch mine' policy to be operated in the Service, by the Hierarchy.

I recall that when Governor E. Jones was finally appointed as No.1 at our jail, after Paul Manwaring's departure, her entourage of 3-4 senior staff with whom she had worked at HMP Wandsworth, swiftly followed, including our then-new Deputy Governor, Nigel Smith. Within a year or two, the other two members of her retinue had been elevated with Governorships. I think it's known colloquially as 'Jobs for the Boys', although one of them was a girl. You know, the same scenario as with Mr Blair and his 'old crony' Government, Former Lord Chancellor Derry Irvine, his replacement as Lord Chancellor, Lord Faulkener etc... (Have I missed any?)

Members of non-management grades at our jail were regularly treated with contempt or disdain, even quite ignorantly. Once I submitted a detailed report to Deputy Governor Nigel Smith (ex-HMP Wandsworth) expressing my concerns at the unreliability of in-cell lighting, with particular reference to night observation lights for checking on the overnight status of convicts, *particularly potentially suicidal ones*. The electrical wiring seemed outdated, lights eventually often came on after some delay, or flickered for 10 minutes before fully powering-up due to faulty starter switches in the fluorescent tubes. As in my report I had put this down to lack of regular maintenance by the electrical section of the HMP Works Department, instead of praising me for drawing his attentions to my concerns, he lambasted me in his reply for jumping to conclusions or making assumptions about the inefficiency of the Works Department.

Furthermore, it was quite the norm for Governors, or Acting-up ones, to totally ignore written reports from junior grades who expressed concern over controversial matters, particularly in relation to events which occurred on the landings overnight. Acting Governor D. Willis and ex-Wandsworth Governor Miss Viv Le Forte both did this to me. These days, I am told that ignoring people in the workplace is looked upon as a form of bullying.

A new monthly magazine was set up by a junior member of the admin staff, who canvassed for contributions to be published.

I took the trouble to create an amusing poem which ridiculed the amount of official, computer-generated posters displayed around the jail, a fair number of which contained *spelling mistakes*. Some of these HMP official A4 size laminated signs were displayed in public areas and, to me, were obviously unprofessional. At the end of my poem, the punch line was 'switch on your integral spell-checker of your PC and it won't happen'. However, my spellchecker poem, submitted for amusement, was destined to backfire on me. Next thing was, I received a written memo from Deputy Governor Nigel Smith for me to contact the female Head Of Security Principal Officer face-to-face. It turned out that a senior female member of the admin secretariat had reported me over its content. Having seen the PO I wrote to Mr Smith, querying the fact that he had said I needed a so-called 'Diversity Course', and asking to meet with him to discuss the matter. It had been claimed that any dyslexic staff members might have taken exception to, or been embarrassed by the poem. In my reply to his letter I had thrown his own catchphrase back in his face, by stating that he had 'missed the point'. The point of my poem was that the people who would most benefit from switching-on their PC spellcheckers, were poor *spellers*, who might be brilliant at every other subject but that. Mr Nigel Smith refused to see me and delegated the matter to one of his junior Governors.

I had also drawn attention to his vetoing of my poem, but his apparent acceptance of advertisements on HMYOI staff notice boards for a forthcoming Ann Summers Sex Party, on Prison property, viz: in the Staff Club, which in fact subsequently took place as planned. Having washed his hands of me, as he saw it, by delegation to a subordinate grade, he was forced to later 'unwash' them, as I took the matter up with the Area Manager. All of a sudden Governor Nigel Smith *did* wish to see me about it after all, although in the event he never did.

In between times though, he managed to mysteriously lose my spellchecker poem, for all time, as I had submitted it to the Prison magazine, obviously now unwisely, without first taking a copy of it. However, having asked around the Service as to his antecedents, I drew some comfort from being told that it was rumoured that, whilst playing a game of scrabble at HMP Wandsworth with HMP colleagues, he had queried and challenged a particular word used in the game by an opponent. Having been overruled after reference to dictionaries or suchlike, and lost his challenge, it was 'alleged' that he had upended the scrabble board in temper! I wasn't there of course, so I can't say if it actually happened or not.

Having had word that the stupid man had *lost* my private property, viz: the poem, I did wonder if during his HMP career he had *lost* any other documentation, I was particularly angry over this, as I write poetry and short articles for publication in minor outlets, and wanted to add the poem to my portfolio.

A previous Governing Governor, Mr Paul Manwaring, thought that Young Offenders and Juvenile convicts should not be embarrassed when discharged from jail after their sentences, by the public recognising them as former jailbirds, by the carriage of their personal property through the streets and on public transport in the blue-printed 'HM PRISON SERVICE' tough polythene bags. He therefore authorised from his 'Establishment Budget', a posh phrase meaning 'FROM THE PUBLIC PURSE', for a whole consignment of posh-looking sports bags or 'holdalls' to be obtained and issued at Reception during discharge routine procedures, to prisoners being released. This meant that members of the public encountering groups of loud, foul-mouthed, youths, all bearing identical sports bags, *without prison markings* in the streets near Stations and Bus Stops in the Prison general area, would not recognise them as being recently released convicts!

Furthermore, if an imate being discharged had too much personal kit to fit into just one prison-issue holdall, he was handed a second, or even third one, to facilitate his journey back to the area in which he could not wait to resume his chosen criminal career. Amazingly, there is never enough money in the HM Prison Service Annual Budget to pay Prison Officers a decent salary, but when it comes to inmates, money is no object.

Having criticised Governor Manwaring, in this manner, of the abolition of HMP strong polythene tote bags, I have to be fair and praise him in other ways. Unlike his successor, he would worry as much about the health and welfare of each member of his staff, just as much as those of the convicts. Also, I cannot fault him on his timekeeping. Invariably, he would be first through the front door of the HMYOI each day. Whereas in the case of his immediate full-time successor, for the last almost three years of my service there, I only set eyes on her once, and that was on a routine 'night visit' to see that all was in order.

Governor Manwaring also had the 'ever-open-office-door' policy during his watch. Regrettably, his successor, Miss Elaine Jones, had to keep hers closed as much as possible to contain the damaging tobacco fumes, thus preventing staff in the corridor passing her office, from *passive smoking*.

Most readers will be fairly familiar with the fact that very many self-harming incidents, some ending in suicide, happen inside Prisons and other custodial establishments. Very recent ones which occurred in Prison include mass-murderer Fred West and Dr Harold Shipman. The Prison Service is often criticised by Coroners during Inquests, for its lack of care in such cases. Other cases occur where convicts are murdered in jail by other convicts.

A classic recent case, enquired into in 2004 and 2005, was that of an Asian inmate who, a very short time before he was due to be released, was murdered in a shared cell at HM Young Offenders Institution at Feltham, Middlesex. His cell mate bludgeoned him to death, I believe, using parts of smashed-up wooden furniture, or suchlike. There appeared to have been a serious error of judgement in the carrying out of the RISK ASSESSMENT in that case. The Young Offender who carried out the murder, was apparently so racist that he had a tattoo on his forehead to visibly indicate this. Furthermore, it was reported in the Press that the same convict had previously been implicated in *another* murder, but the details of that, earlier murder are not to hand. Most right-thinking people would no doubt state that the RISK ASSESSMENT should have been centred on *common sense*, given the known facts of the perpetrator's past violent history.

During the time I was employed at HMYOI Huntercombe, in Oxfordshire, I had to take my turn at monitoring the movements and behaviour of many young convicts, between the ages of 15 and 21 years. This was mainly on the night shift for the second half of my service there. Remanded or convicted youths aged under 18 years, are described as 'juveniles', whilst convicts aged 18-21 years are described as 'young offenders'. Soon after reaching the age of 21years, prisoners are shipped out to main, adult prisons.

Special documentation in respect of suspected or known suicidal tendencies of prisoners, is in existence, including special 'self-harm' printed booklets containing log sheets, so that behaviour and/or concerns can be recorded in writing literally around the clock. However, these booklets are quite *hit and miss*, as loose-leaf continuation sheets can be added at the whim of a monitoring staff member, simply by puncturing and threading onto a woven tag the fresh, additional log sheets, or even blank sheets of A4 paper. In other words, a quite unprofessional, haphazard method of recording essential information about an inmate's mental and/or physical condition.

Unlike the official pocket books of police officers, which are kept under lock and key both before and after use, good housekeeping in respect of the self-harm booklets is rarely practised in HM Prison establishments, it seems.

In the case of one very difficult juvenile convict who was flagged-up for anti-self-harm supervision by Wing staff, on the Juvenile Wing on which I was employed, some Senior Staff had a quite lackadaisical attitude.

A particular inmate who spent his 16th birthday in custody, was already assigned to the *Basic Regime*, meaning that he had few privileges and his cell TV set would have been removed. He could be totally uncooperative and examination of his case history sheets etc. indicated that on one previous occasion he had *set light to his cell*, and on another occasion, he was found in possession of a ligature.

I personally monitored him for several consecutive nights one week, finding that he was given to covering his cell door observation panel glass, with clothing, cardboard or suchlike, so that he could not be seen by monitoring staff. Furthermore, he would apparently lie on his bed, totally disregarding all staff efforts to ascertain if he was currently alive or dead, by ignoring shouts made to him or knocking loudly on his steel door. As his cell was at first floor level, it was impossible, routinely, to look in through his cell window from the outside, to check his condition and demeanour.

On one occasion, he 'played possum' for over three hours continuously, resisting all staff efforts to communicate with him. I therefore placed him 'On Report' for failing to comply with an official direct order, viz: to uncover his door observation panel glass so that he could be seen and monitored randomly and irregularly. A day or two later, I arrived at work to discover that female Governor Viv Le Forte, ex-HMP Wandsworth, had *dealt* with the inmate's Adjudication hearing, at which he had pleaded 'guilty' as charged, by referring him back to the Basic Regime pattern, net result, no punishment whatsoever for the convict, no support whatsoever for the staff member concerned. A most unsatisfactory state of affairs and one in which staff morale is undermined and no real sanction whatever was imposed, in disciplining the young, virtually out-of-control convict.

I was so disgusted that I reported the matter to the Deputy Governor, Mr Nigel Smith, as a clear example of an Adjudication Award by a Prison Governor being so ineffective and inappropriate, as to contribute to an unsafe working environment for both staff, as well as convicts. Deputy Governor Smith's response to my report, effectively was to shrug his shoulders and suggest I should take the matter up directly with HM Inspectorate of Prisons, who had already completed their Annual Inspection just a few days beforehand.

Furthermore, in his written response, he informed me that he would forward a copy of my report to junior Governor Miss Viv Le Forte. Whether he did so or not, I will never know, as she failed to contact me. Written or verbal reports to Governing staff from junior members of the establishment staff, were very often totally ignored for ever. I have since been advised that this is a form of staff-on-staff bullying, and therefore totally unacceptable.

As a result of this apparent deliberate SNUB by Miss Le Fort, and Mr Nigel Smith's perceived cavalier attitude to my having committed my concerns about the suicidal convict, and other unacceptable matters, to previous official reports, I put together a fresh, 16 page report. It contained full details of the matters I have already mentioned earlier in this chapter of *Judgement Impaired*, together with the most recent one, concerning the suicidal, ligature/fire-raising incidents by the incommunicative convict etc.

On 5th October 2004, I sent copies of the full report, which drew attention to the existence of other written reports and bundles of documents etc. to the following recipients: Mr David Blunkett, then Home Secretary; Mr Phil Wheatley, Director General, HM Prison Service; Mr Martin Narey, Commissioner, National Offenders Management Service; Mr Paul Goggins, then Prisons Minister; Ms Ann Owers - HM Chief Inspector of Prisons; The Investors in People Organisation; The Prison Officers Association; My Member of Parliament. Additionally, I had previously written on more than one occasion to Mr Stephen Shaw, the Prisons Ombudsman, who proclaimed on his personal office stationery that he 'investigated complaints'. However he advised me in writing that complaints originating from HM Prison Service members of staff were 'outside my Terms of Reference', or words to that effect. 'Investors In People' organisation replied briefly, but appeared to be incapable of intervening in any kind of staff dispute at all.

Earlier, I had also passed some official reports on to HM Chief Inspector of Prisons as above, but she claimed along the lines of her hands being apparently tied as far as **staff** complaints were concerned.

My Member of Parliament referred my case back to Governor Elaine Jones personally at Huntercombe, so as you might imagine, nothing came of that, as she had been one of the Senior Management Team about whom I had complained in my detailed and comprehensive final report.

The bottom line of my final report was that my treatment by the SMT stated members over the period of my employment there, had amounted to **perceived** Staff-on-Staff **bullying**, in my eyes..

Here I should remind the reader of such incidents as *(1)* Governor Martin Crabbe's ignorance, as Head of Regimes - of the convict daily declaration form, certifying that **nothing at all** must be brought back into the jail on return from Community Project, and *(2)* Acting Deputy Governor Paul Newton's outrageous, overbearing and unacceptable conduct in accusing me of **FROGMARCHING** a very likeable, friendly convict into his Community Project.

Eventually, the Director of Operations, HM Prison Service, Mr Michael Spurr, advised me in two separate letters that he would not be taking any kind of action on my behalf, and that the matters were therefore closed. It was obvious to me through the wording of his letters in reply, that he had apparently not investigated the whole matter thoroughly, if at all, in *that he had seemed not to have spoken to a single Prison Governor mentioned in my final, as well as earlier reports!*

In the light of the then-recent Official Reports instigated by Prime Minister Blair, such as the Hutton Report etc., the only satisfaction I obtained was in responding to the Director of Operations, HM Prison Service, by stating that he had whitewashed the whole matter in *The Spurr Report*, and that was the end of that.

I am left to wonder how many other written complaints from junior members in HM Prison Service over the years, relating to claims of **Staff-On-Staff Bullying** have been left to 'lie on the file', to use a Judicial expression!

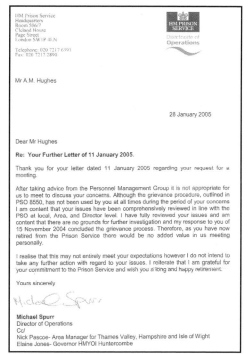

Letter from Michael Spurr, Director of Operations, HM Prison Service, advises that he will not 'further investigate' HMP Governors for alleged 'Staff-on-Staff' bullying on the Author

Convicted cocaine traffickers are getting day-release from jail to work with unsuspecting Customs officers *on the frontline of Britain's drugs war*. Inmates are recruited direct from Prison for shifts at Felixstowe docks to 'help' stem a deadly tide of contraband destined for addicts all over the country. Incredibly these villains are still serving sentences and drive back to jail after work. Even more astonishing, the Customs team have no idea of their new colleagues' dodgy backgrounds. After special training the old lags are put in charge of powerful trucks and given the run of the massive East Coast dock complex. They are directed to suspicious cargo containers and are responsible for moving them to a secure Customs warehouse to be searched for drugs, weapons and explosives. But one of the convicts bragged to our undercover investigator: "It's a joke. Most of us have been done for drug offences and they've chosen to put us to work here of all places. We now know exactly how cargo is checked and could easily make sure a drug consignment gets through.

"When they sent us here we were told to keep hush about being in prison. It's funny walking past police patrols and Customs officers every day."

Several cons on the shocking day-release scheme from nearby Hollesley Bay Prison, Suffolk, work at the port six days a week. The men landed the £270-a-week jobs under the prison's resettlement plan. They were sent to a company called *Orwell Ports Operatives*, a subsidiary of the reputable *Drake International* recruitment firm based at Felixstowe. There they had a week's training on how to operate the specialist trucks used inside the port.

Our undercover reporters watched as five cons from Hollesley Bay - nicknamed 'Holiday Bay' because of its lax regime - were driven to the docks. The crooks had no trouble entering the port. But our team did. Within a minute of driving through the gate they were stopped by a police patrol car. "Nobody's allowed in the port without permission," declared the suspicious officer. "You can't just come in here, it's a port. No Tom, Dick and Harry can just stroll in." Really? The cop was obviously unaware that the guy driving an IMV nearby was drug baron KEVIN RIPPE, currently serving seven years for smuggling cocaine, Ecstasy and super-strength cannabis. Rippe, 40, has been working at the docks since February. He was jailed in November 2002 after detectives planted bugs in his car and home at nearby Harwich, to track smuggled class A and B drugs. Following one large shipment Rippe was heard saying: "That's my class A for Christmas. That should keep Harwich happy for a week or two!" Now he swans freely around Felixstowe sea terminal. And, as the cops continued grilling our man, Rippe chatted to fellow con STEVE TAYLOR, 26, doing six years for similar drug offences. Just a few hundred yards away their pal, portly bald drug dealer

ENZO DEFOE, 37, was busy taking containers off the internal rail line. He is serving three years for possession of cocaine with intent to supply after a stash of it was found in his Land Rover and at his home in Braintree, Essex. Another Hollesley Bay convict, MARK ORRIS, has achieved such a position of trust at the port that he now instructs newcomers in handling the IMV trucks.

One Sunday morning our investigators watched him at work in the Customs inspection area, standing next to a vehicle X-ray machine joking with a colleague - an unsuspecting excise man. The officer's smile will vanish when he learns that ORRIS - from Bramford, Suffolk - is serving four years for unlawful wounding, slashing his victim with a Stanley knife. As ORRIS gossiped, his jailbird buddy KEITH ALLISON - nicknamed 'The Gentleman Thief' - was busy chatting to another Customs man. But bald burglar ALLISON, 53, was definitely not discussing how he was jailed at Norwich Crown Court for five years after getting caught stealing the family silver from a Norfolk farmhouse. The former antique dealer's record goes back 30 years. His targets included Brocket Hall in Hertfordshire, once home to *I'm A Celebrity* jungle star Lord Brocket.

Until recently the port team also included inmate TERRY ROBINSON, doing three years for theft. But insiders say he was removed after it emerged his crime involved the snatch of a container - from the very docks he was working in.

After we alerted Customs about the backgrounds of their workmates, the cons were suspended and the prison launched an inquiry.

Tory home affairs spokesman Cheryl Gillan was shocked by our revelations. She said: "Your story makes a mockery of the whole day release system. These people have learned nothing more than how to commit more crimes."

The Orwell Ports Operatives recruitment agency refused to comment on their role in the scheme. But a dock worker who discovered the truth about the new boys on the waterfront told us: "I was shocked. It's like putting a bank robber to work in Barclays so he can learn all the ins and outs for his next big job. It's totally mad."

(**Author's note:** *The reader may well be wondering whether adult convicts at HMP Hollesley Bay, are trusted enough by the HMP Senior Management Team so as to be able to undertake* **their own** *Risk Assessments and liaise directly with Drake International for day-release positions in the Felixstowe Docks – after re-hashing their CV's accordingly; eg 'Extensive experience in recognising and categorising Controlled Drugs' etc.*

My parting shot in this chapter, is that during my six years employment at HMYOI Huntercombe, I came across many 'Impaired Judgements'. Most of these related to weak, lenient, inappropriate and liberal awards, handed-down to convicts by most, but not all, Prison Governors there, not just in Adjudications in which I was involved, but in other colleagues' Adjudications too. For this reason, many HM Prison Service staff prefer not to place inmates 'on report' *at all* – considering the effort in completing paperwork etc. *as not worth it*.

COUNT 19

THE PUBLIC SPEAKS

While I agree with your view that our compensation culture will continue to mushroom unless society changes its attitude, I fear the sentiment is wishful thinking. Our adoption of the European Convention of Human Rights spawned a rampant new industry which is relentlessly transforming our society into one in which the rights of individuals and politically-correct lobby groups are deemed more important than our traditional cultures and values.

Personal gain has swept aside the erstwhile virtues of community spirit and common sense. This damaging legislation has triggered a proliferation of ambulance-chasing lawyers and civil liberties and human rights groups. Combine this with a judiciary that favours the accused rather than the victim, ably assisted by our barmy legal aid system, and is it any wonder that a culture of 'What's in it for me?' is now rife in our society?

Dr R.Piercy, Retford, Notts

As a retired police officer with 30 years service in a Midlands Force, I agree with the contents of the letter sent by PC Norman Brennan to Her Majesty. For years the Police Service has worked with one hand tied behind its back. It now works with two hands tied. I sincerely believe that Chief Constables are afraid to run their respective forces for the benefit of the people they serve. They are told by the bigwigs at the Home Office (who have probably never walked a beat or patrolled an area) how to do the job. Morale is probably at rock bottom and my ex-colleagues cannot wait to get out of a job gone to the dogs. The criminal justice system is a joke. Magistrates and judges cannot punish criminals as they ought to be punished, because they are told there aren't enough prison places. So crooks are let off with community service orders or with probation – anything other than a real punishment. Good on you PC Brennan for standing up and being counted. Unfortunately no one will take a blind bit of notice until it's too late.

Linda A. Hicken, by e-mail

In the past few years I have seen the rise of a disturbing attitude to victims of crime – that they should just shut up and take it. But why should law-abiding members of the community be victimised twice, once by the criminal and again by our legal system, just for trying to uphold the very laws that are supposed to protect us?

I foresee the day when a woman who has been raped will be arrested for injuring her attacker while trying in vain to defend herself. If individuals choose to step outside the law to commit crime, they do not deserve protection from within the law. And if they sustain injuries while committing crime – whether from those defending themselves and their property or just from a rusty nail in a fence – on their own heads be it. I am neither condoning nor promoting vigilantism, but the letter of the law is now being used by those breaking the law to kill the spirit of the law, and this, as well as the criminal, must be stopped.

Name and address supplied

I note that the Home Office believes that the jail sentences of less than a year are often ineffective. Its spokesman is also quoted as saying, 'During a short prison sentence, virtually nothing constructive can be done with an offender'.

In reply I'd like to say that at least something constructive will have been done, both for the general public and, above all, for the victim of the offence!

The latter will have seen the offender put safely away and unable to commit another crime, at least for the duration of the sentence. If, however, the offender is not imprisoned, there is a very strong possibility of them reoffending and their previous victim feeling even more at risk.

The time has now come to give more support to the victims, whose needs have been seriously neglected for too many years.

Robin Rae, Chipping Sodbury, Gloucestershire

Your correspondent P.Ingle asks 'what can be done to improve the behaviour of today's young people?' I believe that the problem lies in a complete lack of respect and discipline. When I was in school I had to listen to what I was told or I was punished. That punishment included the cane. Police officers were also respected. Can any police officer honestly say that that is still the case today?

Our elders, our parents and our relations were looked up to and not given cheek, as is the case today. I would like to see the reintroduction of detention and punishments, including the cane, to control unruly children. There should be stronger punishments for younger offenders and also the reintroduction of National Service. Perhaps our politicians would like to give their comments? Or are they too busy listening to the namby-pandy do-gooders?

N.R.Williams, Swansea

Never mind calls to bring back the birch. Here is a blast from the past seen at the National Railway Museum in York – South Eastern and Chatham Railway – 'The extreme penalty for throwing stones and other missiles at trains is Penal Servitude for Life'.

Harry White, Atherton, Manchester

LETTER TO HM THE QUEEN APRIL 2004

May it please Your Majesty – I am writing to you as a serving police officer of 25-years and director of the Victims of Crime Trust. When I was growing up, I wanted to do a job where I could benefit society in a positive way, so on 25th September I joined the police service. I took an Oath to well and truly serve my Queen and country and when I first wore my uniform it was the proudest day of my life.

Twenty-five years on, the Criminal Justice System is in crisis and spiralling out of control. A view that is not unique to myself, but shared by many of my colleagues throughout the UK and millions of people in this country. They have seen the decline in the standards and quality of policing and the lack of effective action taken against criminals. Consequently, we now live in a society where law-abiding citizens expect to be mugged, burgled or have their cars stolen, or worse. I have written to you and your Government on a number of occasions over the past 12 years highlighting my concerns about our failing criminal justice system. Sadly, all of my predictions have come true, including the rise in violent and gun crime. I would like to reiterate, that if your Government continues muddling through on its current course, it will destroy the British Police Service and the Criminal Justice System will collapse. It is clear that the Government has lost their way on law and order. I am ashamed to say as police officers, we cannot protect and reassure the public in the way we would like, and therefore we can no longer command the respect and support of the British public that we once took for granted. I did not join the Police Service to allow the criminal to win, so I have decided to make a stand. I personally feel that I must do something about it.

Today, I am using the Victims of Crime Trust 10th Anniversary Conference to launch a nationwide phone petition under the auspices 'Voice for Victims, Communities against Crime'. We will be asking the country to unite with the Trust to ensure that victims of crime and the safety of society, is the foremost concern of the Criminal Justice System. I have written to all of your Chief Constables, suggesting ways they too can help, a copy of which is enclosed. I am presently six months into a year secondment to the Victims of Crime Trust from the police. I intend to spend the next six months travelling around the UK, in order to meet with communities to gather support for the nationwide petition. If after this time I believe I can once again be proud to wear the uniform I have done for so long, I will return to join my colleagues in frontline policing. If not, I will seriously consider resigning from the Police Service.

Your humble servant, PC NORMAN BRENNAN

I would like to congratulate PC Norman Brennan on his courageous stand against the rising tide of crime and for his direct appeal to the Queen to save the justice system from disintegrating. It is said that it takes an ordinary PC to say that that the law and order system is on the verge of collapse, while most of his superiors remain silent. It is also said that trying to reverse this tide will take decades. Crime, in all guises, is now firmly ingrained into the fabric of our society. That is thanks to the liberalism of the misguided socialists who have effectively ruled our country for so many years. Criminals, whether burglars, murderers, benefit fraudsters or con artists, see easy pickings without very much fear of even being caught, let alone 'paying' for their crimes.

So I say good luck to PC Brennan and all that he stands for!

David Heath, Birmingham

Tony Blair's vision of Britain is fast becoming a nightmare for all of us. Seven years of weak government have come at a cost. We have asylum seekers benefiting from a welfare system funded by the contributions and taxes of honest, hard-working taxpayers. Human Rights lawyers are earning huge fees, defending career criminals and illegal immigrants, funded by legal aid.

What's more, the UK is a country where an evil Islamic cleric can preach hatred against the UK and still receive state aid. We have a justice system that favours the criminal rather than the victim. And we live in a country where billions can be found to fund a seemingly unjustified war in Iraq while health, education and transport struggle for funding.

Peter Watts, Aberdeenshire

More custodial sentences should be handed out to crooks, after Prof. John Dilulio calculated that keeping them behind bars saves the country £25K a year per prisoner. And if this is the case, why is Cherie Blair insisting that FEWER women should be jailed? Women should not be treated differently because of their sex. If they commit a crime that warrants it, they deserve to go to prison.

Janet Stringer,Leeds

Traitor was the only word that entered my mind when I read your story about the woman in the Immigration Service selling dodgy passports. It's utter greed and she should be jailed.

Natalie Branch, Basingstoke

Young James Speakman, who confronted Tony Blair over the problems on his estate, is a lad this country can be proud of. At the age of ten he spoke to the Prime Minister about vandalism and burglaries around his home at Fairfield Estate in Leeds. The PM must take note and grant James his wish of wanting 'nice people' on his estate.

Maria Newman, Bristol

I read with increasing anger, of the incredible lengths to which the establishment is going to protect Maxine Carr on her release. I feel great sadness for the families of Ian Huntley's victims, Holly Wells and Jessica Chapman. If those two little girls had been as well protected by the establishment, they might be alive today. Carr deserves nothing from us, least of all protection. She knew what she was doing when she lied for Ian Huntley. Now she is a free woman she should take the consequences.

Deirdre Dickson, Colnbrook

How much taxpayers' money is going to be wasted on rehabilitating Maxine Carr? She is already being given a new identity and police protection. Now we learn she is going to have psychiatric treatment to help her get over her involvement with Ian Huntley. Carr hasn't had to endure a fraction of the torment she inflicted on the families of Holly and Jessica. We should stop wasting money and let Maxine live with her guilt – if indeed she feels any.

Kim Kimber, Leigh-on-Sea

Does anyone really care about Carr's safety? She should rot in hell. To give her all that protection is insane. What must the victims' families be feeling? It's a pity the Government doesn't show so much concern for victims of crime. Instead it chooses to reward criminals. How can we have faith and confidence in a justice system that is geared up to cater for the wellbeing of criminals and works against law-abiding citizens?

Richard Mikula, Nottingham

It will cost millions to protect Carr. What a pity we didn't spend those millions on policing to protect the victims of her partner's vile crime.

Philip Cove, Aylesbury

Why should we be surprised if details of Carr's new identity were stolen from a Home Office official's car just as she is released? She has to be one of the most hated women in Britain. Most people believe she got off very lightly for her part in the case of Holly and Jessica. There are many people baying for her blood. Carr should have taken the offer of a new life in Australia when she had the chance. No doubt she will cost the taxpayer even more money keeping her safe. Many would say she's not worth it.

Dave Shaw, Exeter

Carr should be released under her real name and take the consequences of her actions. People are more likely to shun her than hurt her.

Matt Edwards, Slough

My grandson is on the waiting list to see a counsellor because of anxiety and trauma problems. Every day he waits, his condition worsens but his appointment is still a year off. It angers me immensely that Carr will have a psychiatrist and counsellors available to her. Anyone would think she was someone special who deserved this prompt treatment – but nothing could be further from the truth.

Name and address supplied

Let us hope Maxine Carr never profits from her association with Ian Huntley. If she had told the truth, Holly Wells and Jessica Chapman could be alive today. This serial liar has served less than two years, is costing the tax payer hundreds of thousands of pounds in police protection and has inflicted a life sentence on the parents of those poor little girls.

Bob Littler, Manchester

The whereabouts of Maxine Carr will not be secret for very long. The arrogance of this woman who always seems to be full of self-importance will make her give herself away in a matter of months.

Robert Martin, Hull

Why is Maxine Carr being compared to Myra Hindley? Her biggest crime was to stand by the man she loved not realising what he'd done. Lots of women and men have done that in the past. They cannot believe the person they love could be guilty. How many of us would believe our partner had committed a crime as evil as Huntley's?

Kevin Baker, Poole

It is disgusting that Maxine Carr will get a 'shrink' to help her 'forget' her romance with evil Ian Huntley. Did Holly and Jessica's parents receive the same round-the-clock psychological support to come to terms with the deaths of their daughters? It seems only criminals get help these days, while victims are left to fend for themselves. This country needs to get its priorities right.

Julie Porter, Swindon

The only 'irresponsible rabble' are the judges and barristers who'd sell their grandmothers if they could get legal aid to do it. I'm an 'irresponsible father' who has tried for four years to see my two children and be a good dad to them. I've been in court 30 times and came across judges who wouldn't let me speak and solicitors who bled me dry. Going into a family court is like putting napalm on a burning house. We have a society of single mothers, living on state benefits, while men work for their ex-wives and aren't allowed to see their own children. As a result, we have high teenage crime rate and the highest pregnancy rate among young girls in Europe.

Steve Chimarides, Brighton

Why do we bother voting in elections if the judiciary are running the country? Once again David Blunkett has been foiled by the men in wigs in his attempt to sort out asylum seekers. The only way to stop the judges is to prevent those cases going to court in the first place. And the way to do that is to stop legal aid for non-British citizens. I don't think lawyers would be so quick to defend spurious asylum seekers if there was no guarantee of getting paid.

Stephen Gorham, Bracknell

Smart Justice director Lucie Russell, claims prison doesn't work because criminals who are released reoffend within two years. Actually prison does work – it's releasing people early that causes the problem. Jail costs money but it would be less than the cost of crime to the victims, police, courts and society as a whole. If people are persistent offenders, then the longer they are kept away from the rest of us, the better.

Paul Wakeman, Stourbridge

Ian Huntley having a minder shows how pathetic he is. After committing such a horrendous crime, the man is now too scared to accept his punishment. His poor little victims never had such protection.

Adele Rawlinson, Bury

After the tragic death of DC Swindells it would seem the man accused of his killing may never face trial. Given the number of policemen who have paid the ultimate price in recent years, it is tragic that those who are guilty are either found unfit to plead, or receive such ridiculous sentences they are back in the community within a few years. Is this how the Government is 'getting tough' Mr Blunkett?

Nichola Purcell, Southend

The killing of Michael Swindells is a terrible tragedy. The standard sentence for anyone killing a police officer should be 50 years. And that is 50 years with no remission, no comfy cell with TV and games consoles. We have got to stop what is now becoming a common headline: 'Police Officer attacked in the course of duty.' This won't stop all violence aimed at the police – but it would make the criminals think very carefully before drawing a knife or gun.

Paul Cowell, Canterbury

The death of hero cop Michael Swindells is one more reason why our police need to be armed. You simply cannot fight armed offenders with CS gas and batons.

Jeremy Haydon, Hampton

I am deeply moved by the death of such a brave policeman. But it could have been avoided if cops were able to carry guns. Nowadays kids aged 12 carry knives. Guns are readily available and our police definitely need more protection. The time is right to think of change. I can't think of any other country where the police don't carry guns.

Joe Lanzante, Anerley

With the death of brave DC Michael Swindells, and three cops run over trying to stop a car to interview the driver, it is about time we stopped blaming the police for everything that goes wrong in society. A country gets the police force it deserves. We send them out unprotected and ill-equipped and expect them to perform miracles. If the public gave them support, it would be a much safer Britain for all of us to live in.

Steve Rush, Botley

The death of Michael Swindells is tragic and unnecessary. If he had been wearing an anti-stab vest, he may still be alive today. All police, whether front-line or plain-clothes officers, should be issued with anti-stab vests and it should be obligatory to wear them when on outside duty.

Sharon Sawyer, Catford

There is so much crime in England now I think it is time we armed our police. I think this would then be a much safer country to live in. Something has to be done before there are more deaths.

Paulette Coulter, Haverhill

The tragic death of DC Swindells must reopen the debate on arming our police. Sadly, because he was not a beat bobby, he did not even have a knife-resistant vest. If this was America, Michael would have been armed and probably alive today. How much longer must our brave police be exposed to dangerous criminals when the gun and knife culture puts them at risk every time they go to work?

Pat Holt, Manchester

If ever a case highlighted the need for our police to be armed, it is the death of DC Swindells. It is imperative that criminals know they face the possibility of being shot, and the law must be changed so police officers have the opportunity to defend themselves.

Gavin Upex, Peterborough

I fail to understand why DC Swindells wasn't given a special knife-resistant vest by his force. Just because he didn't pound the beat, didn't mean he would never be faced with a situation where the person he was after had a knife. From now on, every cop should be given body armour whether they are on patrol or sitting behind the front desk. It's the only way to protect our police in these dangerous times.

John McCafferty, Glasgow

When I was a serving police officer, I opposed the the arming of front-line personnel. But after the fatal stabbing of DC Michael Swindells, I've changed my view. Issuing weapons to all operational police would help to stop the proliferation of violence.

John Kenlock, Northampton

Your report on the death of DC Swindells underlined just how dangerous a police officer's job can be. Perhaps if the public were made more aware of the bravery of those in the service, they would be far more appreciative of it.

Jean Elliott, Symington

It's unbelievable that evil Ian Huntley will get his own bodyguard to protect him from attack. It's the children who need protecting with the introduction of 'Sarah's Law' – not the animals who commit these despicable acts. Justice would be partly served by Huntley having to live the rest of his life in fear of retaliation. Now he has everything to worry about.

Peter O'Sullivan, Darlington

Babysitting monster Jamie Thompson should be behind bars for abusing a young child. The judge who let him off with 'community rehabilitation' should be ashamed of himself. What a joke this country's justice system is.

Wayne Kisbee, Peterborough

A big thank you for continuing to point out ridiculous Euro laws. Apart from the fact we have a better road safety record than half the EU, what upsets me is that if we refuse to allow random breath testing, they'll simply impose it. It is only by *The Sun* bringing such nonsense to the public's attention that we can beat the advances of the federal super-state.

Ed Bowden, Harpenden

The threat of imposing random drink tests on Britain should sound alarm bells about what we can expect should we ever sign up to a federal European state.

Louise Ashton, Doncaster

It worries me that there is opposition to the idea of random breath-testing. We all know it's wrong to drink and drive. Surely the possibility of being stopped would be a deterrent strong enough to save a few more lives. If you're sober every time you get behind the wheel of your car, where's the worry?

Peggy Hall, Harrogate

Why doesn't irritating Dutchman Ad Hellemons, President of the European traffic cop's organisation, just go away and leave us alone? – taking his equally annoying colleagues with him? Trying to impose breath tests for drivers in a country with roads as comparatively safe as ours, is meddling for meddling's sake. Drivers have enough to deal with as a result of measures imposed by our Government.

Cathie Hunter, Preston

What's the point of the EU issuing a blanket ruling when member countries have different problems? Our cops say they have enough powers for drink-driving. Surely we should be putting money, time and effort into catching those who dodge road tax, MOT and insurance? And we should overhaul the penalties for killing with a car.

Tony Smith, Chester

It wouldn't bother me if I was randomly breath-tested, since I don't take drugs or drink and drive. However, if this measure is forced on us by Europe it will tie even more of our police force up on targeting motorists. That's the last thing we need.

Diane Stevens, Helston

How would Joe Public know whether he really is being pulled over at random, or because a police officer doesn't like the colour of his skin or thinks he looks like a yob? It could become another wedge driven between the police and the public, as speed cameras have been.

Jane Miller, Nottingham

For once I agree with the European Commission and their attempts to introduce random breath-testing for British drivers. And I despair that the Home Secretary is fighting the road safety measure. Introducing such a policy would force drivers to rethink having one for the road – something they've been able to do with impunity since the police withdrew from our roads to rely on speed cameras.

William Shaw, Lincoln

If anyone is to impose random breath tests on British drivers it should be our Government, not the idiots in Brussels. But before looking at our record, how about the Greeks and Portuguese? Their record is considerably worse than ours.

Robert Townsend, Watford

Police surely have enough to do, without the extra burden of randomly breath-testing motorists. It would be a stab in the dark to actually catch people over the limit and at best might act as a deterrent. If given these powers, why not just do it the easy way and place an unmarked police car on any pub car park and bingo hall. That's where you'll catch the majority of offenders.

Ann Johnson, Brierley Hill

With the hideous number of people injured and killed by drunk drivers, allowing police to carry out random breath tests might be a good thing. I have known people who drink and drive and boast they drive better when they've had a few.

John Emmitson, Fareham

Lee Jones's appeal against his sentence just shows how much remorse he is feeling – none. How can he question such a small fine when he took the lives of three innocent people? He should hang his head in shame for what he did. The sentence he received was disgracefully lenient - Pay up and shut up Jones – you got off lightly.

Jayne Devine, Sheffield

How can Lee Jones contest his conviction for killing three volleyball players? He wasn't punished enough for what he did. My son, daughter and her husband were all with the victims at the tournament before the crash. I have had to deal with their continuing grief at losing three friends. The two who were injured in the same accident will have to go through it all again in court. All we can hope is that Jones will suffer for the rest of his life for what he has done. If I had been the judge he would have been jailed.

Mags Dorren, Dagenham

Lee Jones killed three people and injured two others. He had drunk 4 bottles of beer, been on his mobile phone just seconds before the crash, was driving on the wrong side of the road and was 20mph over the 40mph speed limit. The verdict should have been cut and dried – Jones should have been facing a custodial sentence, but magistrates only had the power to impose a fine. It's an insult to the memory of the lives he snuffed out. The law needs changing so that idiots like Jones are given the appropriate sentence for their actions.

Rose Ford, Camborne, Cornwall

Death caused by careless driving should be punished in the same way as murder. Time and again drivers walk free because magistrates don't have the power to give custodial sentences. The families of the three people Lee Jones killed have every right to be angry at his lenient sentence.

Anne Firm, Rushden, Northants

Lee Jones killed three and received a fine of £1,500 and a five-year ban. Patricia Amos, whose daughter played truant from school, was jailed for 28 days. Where's the justice?

Audrey Peters, Blackburn

Lee Jones may not have set out to kill three people – but he knew he had been drinking and it could affect his driving. Had he killed them with his bare hands, he'd have been jailed for life. He still took away their lives and should be punished accordingly.

Maria Stevenson, Bedford

How many people have to be killed by 'careless' drivers before a law is passed to make it possible to jail criminals like Lee Jones?

If you cause a death, surely that should be enough grounds for imprisonment? A paltry fine and driving ban are no deterrent. If a driver is found guilty of causing another's death by careless driving, their freedom should be taken away.

Sara Nichols, Downpatrick, Co. Down.

Our judicial system seems to have turned into a pantomime. It is high time the overpaid idiots in charge of enforcing our laws were sent back for retraining. We must start giving out sentences that fit the crimes before our justice system becomes a total farce.

Helen Dickson, Spalding, Lincs.

It is disgraceful that Lee Jones can walk out of court a free man after swerving to the wrong side of the road and killing three people. How is it that far more mediocre offences are given severe punishment, while real criminals get a slap on the wrist?

Liam Bennion, Sunderland

The tragedy involving Lee Jones is a sad affair – but it was an accident. Police could not prove he was using his mobile phone at the time he swerved his car and a breath test after he was treated in hospital was negative. This meant he could only be charged with careless driving, in which case justice has been done.

Stephen Gorham, Bracknell, Berks.

In response to the letter from Douglas Wathen, I would like to say that I totally agree with him – it would indeed be wonderful to see a policeman, particularly if you happen to be married to him. My husband is a Detective Inspector and, apart from his usual working duties, he is on call for one week in every four. Not only does this entail all his usual duties, but also being on call 24 hours a day for the next seven days to deal with anything serious that may arise. The other weekend my husband worked an extra 38 hours in one week in addition to his normal working hours. Good money you might think, but unfortunately Inspectors do not get paid overtime. No overtime on an 80-hour week – what joy!

In our household we know exactly what's going on with the police force and yes – I personally think that the police are wonderful. Would a member of any other profession work such hours for no extra pay? I think not. Let us just be thankful that there are still some men and women out there who, day in and day out, readily put their lives at risk, despite getting little thanks for it.

Sheila Bending, Hornchurch

If white racists – BNP supporters for example – visited Arab countries in the Middle East, trying to stir up hatred against Muslims and encouraging violence against non-whites, I think they would find they are at best deported by their Arab hosts but far more likely, and understandably, arrested and severely punished. This is the obscene racism Abu Hamza has been preaching on a daily basis outside a mosque in north London for years and years – and only recently has he been arrested. Britain has taken tolerance to the extreme.

Michael Perry, Basildon, Yorks.

I wonder what D-Day veterans thought of the BBC Panorama programme on 6th June, 60-years later? It showed a typical weekend in the centre of Nottingham and the scenes were something out of Sodom and Gommorah. The streets ran with urine, blood and worse. Drunken men and girls were fighting, swearing and behaving like yobs. The police explained that weekend policing concentrated on the city centre, leaving the outskirts without cover. Labour's Tourism Minister spoke of making Britain's city centres into café societies. I almost laughed out loud at a vision of a French boulevardier strolling through any British town on a Friday night, or sitting enjoying a glass or two, without being savagely beaten by the drunken hordes. It is glaringly obvious that our culture of binge drinking has to be curtailed with an end to so-called 'happy hours' and cheap drinks.

William McCann, Brompton-on-Swale, N.Yorks.

As regards the unacceptable leniency in sentencing of offenders, which we witness every single day of the year on which magistrates and judges sit in judgement. I have come up with the simple and perfect solution – in fact we could turn around the appalling violent crime figures virtually overnight – let's arrange a one-month's job-change for all magistrates and judges, with the police. After all, they were once known as 'Police Courts' in certain parts of the UK. We'll have all the judges and magistrates in the country in police cars, patrolling on foot, experiencing and responding to anti-social behaviour, violent gun and drugs crime, burglaries, murders committed by criminals, some of whom are mentally disturbed, all released from jail or hospital too early, multi drink-drivers, multi drivers who drive totally without documents whilst disqualified, etc. If the judiciary actually succeed in arresting any offenders, we'll have them taken before Senior Police Officers sitting in judgement on the Bench, dispensing justice by sentencing them all to community penalties, referral orders, probation and drink-drive awareness courses.

Then let the judges and magistrates experience the disappointment, amazement, horror and frustration of victims and police officers when all of THEIR prisoners just walk free from courts across the land. During the month's 'TRIAL', we'll arrange for most of those offenders to roll up their sleeves, bend their backs and work-off their aggression, pent-up anger and selfishness, by laying the foundations of the 18 new-build prisons we so badly need. Let's create a new, combined community penalty order for them, to be known as 'Community, Reparation, Rehabilitation, Construction and Restorative Justice Orders.' (CRRCRJ Orders) – It's time for change – let's break the mould once and for all and have the most welcome return of ORDER, JUSTICE and PEACE OF MIND.

Mike Hughes, Oxfordshire

What planet does Judge John Diehl come from? How could he allow criminal Robert McVey an extended adjournment on his robbery trial, so that he could fly off on a two-week holiday? McVey pleaded guilty – he should have lost his holiday and liberty.

Tanya Weedon, Amersham

The murder of detective Michael Swindells proves yet again that our police officers are inadequately equipped for an increasingly violent Britain. I for one would be in favour of armed police. Had DC Swindells had a gun, this tragedy would never have happened.

G.Reilly, Birmingham

My work colleagues and I often talk about leaving Britain. We talk about the general state of our society, the greed, selfishness, materialism, disrespect and impoliteness that exists. But the most talked-about reason for leaving is the yob culture – yob parents and yob drivers who make up the section of society that's out of control. Thanks to 30 years of liberal policies we've reached a state where the police and judiciary seem powerless to protect ordinary citizens. How on earth do we, as a country, get ourselves out of this mess?

J.M. Davis, by e-mail

Your correspondent Harry Williams says that he has travelled to many lands and has not found a better place to live than Britain. I wonder what criteria he is using to measure 'better than'? If it's the weather, then without doubt there are many countries better than Britain, as the million retired people who have moved to Spain and other warmer climes in recent years bear witness. If it's social benefits, then I would agree with Mr Williams, and so would the thousands of refugees, asylum seekers and illegal immigrants who, having travelled through several free and democratic countries, risked life and limb to cross the English Channel by whatever means. If it's league tables for unmarried mothers, divorce, abortion, murder and crimes of violence, drug use, attacks by pupils on teachers and by patients on hospital staff...again, I agree we are better than most at these things. This year I've visited friends who have moved to Malaysia, Mauritius and Madeira. None of them expressed the slightest wish to return to the UK.

Each said that personal security and the standard of behaviour in public were among the most attractive features of the places they now live. Britain might have been the safest place to live, but that was 40 years ago.

Paul Bastier, Windermere, Cumbria

I recently watched a programme on BBC1 about car thefts and car ringing gangs. The Metropolitan Police squad did a wonderful job tracking down the crooks and cars and spent weeks and hundreds of thousands of pounds in the process. When they came to court, the three main participants in a huge network of crime and fraud were sentenced to the sum total of eight years. Two got two years, the third received four years. With good behaviour they will be out in half that time. If that was the most they could be given as a sentence, then the law needs changing rapidly. Talk about crime doesn't pay! With sentences like these it certainly does. It surely doesn't give the police much incentive to keep up their hard slog.

Tom Marriott, by e-mail

Why was a High Court judge allowed to retire on 'health grounds' after he was charged with a paedophile offence, but before he was convicted in court? No wonder the public has no confidence in the 'Establishment'.

Tony Hill, Epsom, Surrey

So a judge can download 75 child porn images on his computer and only expect to receive a minimum sentence because he uses his knowledge of the law to get away with it. It shouldn't matter who it is, the law should be able to come down extremely heavily on child porn offenders. Apparently the images don't show the kids aged 8 to 14 engaged in sex acts. So what? Anyone who downloads any kind of child pornography should go to prison for at least ten years. It might make them think twice about it. It would be interesting to know just how many child offenders he let off lightly.

Paul Cowell, Canterbury

I'm horrified at the shamefully lenient sentence given to the repulsive former judge David Selwood. If only my son Joseph had been afforded the same leniency as this deviant. Aged 16, he was convicted of street robbery in March 2002 and received the maximum sentence of a two-year detention and training order. He was detained at Stoke Heath Children's Prison in Shropshire. Despite being under supposed close observation in the healthcare centre by nurses, just nine days later he was discovered by a passing prison maintenance worker hanging from the window bars of his squalid cell. Joseph had appeared before Judge Bernard Lever at Manchester Crown Court, with 30 self-inflicted slashes across his face, such was his level of distress. Before sentencing, the judge had received documentary evidence of Joseph's vulnerability. He had been the victim of prolonged abuse by a member of his father's family, was suicidal and self-mutilating. Joseph had just one prior conviction, for affray, that being the court's response following a previous suicide attempt. What a shame that there does not seem to be the same level of tough custodial sentencing directed at paedophiles who rob children of their innocence, as sadly there is to children convicted of street robbery. It would appear that our society attaches more value to a mobile phone than to the life of an abused child.

Yvonne Scholes, Meliden, Denbighshire

You don't need to go to France or Las Vegas to find tidy streets, clean toilets and graffiti-free zones. I have just returned from Beauly, near Inverness, where my son lives. We went as far North as Durness and as far West as Gairloch. Everyone in the Highlands seems to take pride in their surroundings. We visited some beautiful places and found public toilets in the most remote beauty spots, and all were clean. Inverness was virtually free of graffiti, and I didn't see any drunken yobs even when we went into town for a meal on Friday nights. My son tells me there are plenty of policemen on duty to keep an eye on any potential troublemakers. There is almost no litter on the streets and no abandoned cars by the sides of the roads. We certainly got a culture shock when we got back. I would appeal to anyone visiting the Highlands please to leave them as they find them.

Mrs Beryl D. Higginbotham, Holyhead, Anglesey

I read with interest last week's prize letter, but must inform Joe Field as follows regarding corporal punishment in schools. The teaching unions banned the use of the cane some ten years before such a ban became law. Therefore, part of the decline in the behaviour of school children (and consequently adults) lies with the teaching profession.

Eric Neal, Coventry

I refer to your article (*PC gets stab-proof vest...to patrol school*) Hengrove is one of 300 schools in the Government's Safer Schools Partnership Programme. Beat officers visit schools dressed and equipped for daily duties. PC Jones was not equipped with stab-proof vest, CS gas and truncheon for our school. His role is not to tackle crime in school or prevent truancy but rather, as with all involved in the Safer Schools Initiative, to build relationships between police and young people. CCTV protects schools from outside threat, not to prevent pupils from absconding. Our perimeter fence, installed after Health and Safety advice, prevents public intrusion. It is not a 'prison-style steel fence'. There is no serious crime. We had a single incident of someone coming on site possessing a small quantity of drugs and two pupils were arrested for minor offences.

Stephen Murtagh, Head Teacher, Hengrove School, Bristol

Am I missing something on the issue of police gathering and sharing information? (*How many more Huntleys have slipped the net?*, June 23) The overwhelming fact seems to be that the problems that allowed Ian Huntley to slip through the net, are essentially national ones and could have been just as bad whichever police forces were involved. It seems ludicrous for Home Secretary David Blunkett to seek a scapegoat – any scapegoat – when it could have been almost any Chief Constable in the frame. The entire affair beggars belief and appears to be a perfect example of amateurism at its best. A 10-year-old could have seen the benefits of a national information gathering system. But if it could have happened almost anywhere, with no national system in place, then surely the person requiring whipping is the man in charge of the Home Office?

Philip Codd, Manchester

In the light of constant criticism over a few bad apples in the police force, it was refreshing to read of the sheer heroism of the two officers who tore open a burning car door to rescue a woman, despite getting burnt themselves. That story along with the other courageous acts described, shows we still have the finest law enforcement agency in the world.

Tom Jenkins, Cardiff

Callous Thomas Rudge who killed a woman while driving under the influence of alcohol – and then tried to blame it on someone else – fully deserves his eight-year sentence. In fact he got off too lightly. In less than five years he will walk away from jail. Judges need to come down more heavily on drink-drivers. A few life imprisonments would deter many.

Jonathan Cooper, East Finchley

So the public picks up another bill because Humberside Police Authority 'forced legal action' by defying the Home Secretary. I don't suppose this is down to David Blunkett's desire to deflect the blame and gain some political points by being seen to 'take appropriate action'? Humberside Police may not be entirely blameless for the tragedy in Soham. However, overall responsibility for the inadequacies of the Data Protection Act, and the general policy of protecting the 'rights' of serious offenders, above those of potential victims against an increasingly ludicrous background of political correctness, lies squarely with this Government. It's a great pity for the nation that the Home Secretary has not 'taken appropriate action' on a few other serious issues, such as the asylum shambles.

David Aitken,Southampton

I would like to thank the *Sunday Express* editor for his recent comments. They reflect much of how I feel about society today. For the past 5 years I have worked as a mid-day assistant at the local senior school. We moved house two years ago due to the behaviour of local children. One boy in particular decided to use his tennis racket to hit stones instead of a ball. He broke my bedroom window. But what I wasn't prepared for was the reaction of his parents (especially as his mother was a teacher and his father a policeman). When I confronted them about the window they flippantly told me: "That's what you have home insurance for." My husband and I were brought up to behave and respect other people and we have brought our two boys up to do the same. Unfortunately I now feel that they are the exception.

Name and address supplied

So David Blunkett is to put 40,000 extra police men and women on our streets. My partner was a police officer for five years and gave it up as a lost cause. An arrest followed by hours of form-filling, resulted more often than not in the offender receiving the most derisory penalty at court. Until the Home Office and courts get tough on offenders, being in the police service offers little job satisfaction.

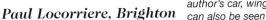

Horse manure dumped on author's car, wing damage can also be seen

Paul Locorriere, Brighton

Convicted armed thug Michael Polizczuk is suing the police for branding him a crook on name-and-shame leaflets. He should realise that this infamy goes with the job. Chief Constable Steve Green was spot-on when he said the legal action was a sick joke.

Judith Harper, Leeds

I have been listening with interest to the current debate on police 'stop and search' activities. During the Sixties, which were more peaceful times, I was regularly stopped at least twice a week by the police when driving home through east London after a late shift. I never once felt it was a threat to my civil liberties, but a reassurance that the police were doing what they were paid for. As someone once said, 'The price of liberty is eternal vigilance'.

S.Askham, Leigh-on-Sea

The claim that car crime has been significantly reduced is, of course, complete and utter rubbish. (*Car crime at 20-year-low, says Minister,* July 1st 2004) Car crime in the area where I work continues upwards and has not fallen in the least. What has fallen is the number of people reporting damaged cars to the police. Why is that? Because all they get when they do so is an incident number from the police, with nothing ever followed up. It is a waste of time reporting the crime to the police.

Malcolm Brown, Buckinghamshire

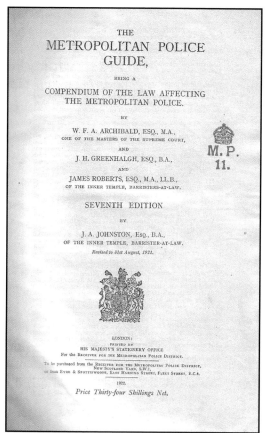

Details from Metropolitan Police Guide 1922 (seventh edition) issued to the Author's grandfather PC Charles Hancock

Our travelling army of moronic lager louts is drinking flat-out to ensure that England tops the table of drunken thugs in Portugal. The arrests we have seen shame every true England supporter. Isn't it ironic that just a few days ago, we honoured those British heroes who liberated Europe from Hitler's jackboot in June 1944? Sixty years on, so-called England football fans are about as welcome in Europe as myxomatosis in a rabbit warren. They are a disgrace to our country and should have their passports withdrawn for life.

Tony Thorn, Bordon, Hants

How can the Government expect so-called football supporters to behave when they travel abroad, when precious little is done to contain drinking and violence at home? The police should introduce zero tolerance for all matches here and ban drinking within a mile of all grounds, as well as inside grounds. This should eliminate the problems.

Ian Oxley, Paignton, Devon

The law against the incitement of racial hatred is obviously aimed at unsavoury groups such as the British Nationalist Party – and rightly so. But there are Muslims in this country who also seem to be less than tolerant about other people's beliefs – or non-beliefs. Over the past few weeks this country has played host to Muslim clerics who were preaching hatred against Jewish and Hindu people. We don't hear their leaders, or others of ethnic minority faiths spreading hatred against those of differing beliefs to their own. Racism must never be tolerated in this country and if extremists of any faith cannot appreciate that, they are surely best residing in countries other than Great Britain.

M.Perry, Baildon, West Yorks.

A Turkish man was jailed on Monday for 36 years for the killing of a British toddler on holiday with his parents. This seemed a just sentence for taking a young life. Now we read of a British mother who, with her boyfriend, inflicted horrific cruelty on her own little son over a long period, so violently that he died with more than 200 injuries to his body. This monstrous pair were put away for a mere five years. The mother should have been jailed for the same length of time as the Turk – and sterilised so that she could never kill another innocent, helpless child.

Mrs Heather Causnett, Escrick, York

As the law stands, millions of homeowners throughout the UK are vulnerable to squatters. If you leave your house unattended and squatters invade your property without obvious evidence of a break-in, and say the door was open, you cannot

Old litigation print

have them removed if they claim squatters' rights. So much for the Englishman's home being his castle. Should anyone have problems with squatters, I advise them to get a friend to break a window or door panel before going to the police. Tell them this is how you found it. If the only way to protect your home is to lie, then so be it.

John Hornsby, Solihull

In 1978, squatters moved into a house I owned in Woodford, Essex. I went to the local authority and provided them with the names of the squatters, obtained by the police. Rate demands were served and the squatters soon left.

Roy May, Palma De Mallorca, Spain

How can the law allow apparently homeless people to take over a £200,000 house? I find it deplorable that this is allowed to happen and people are powerless to do anything about it. Why is there not a change in the law to protect the home owner? These squatters appear to have everything on their side. Those interviewed are on benefits and are now occupying someone else's house and are paying no rent. There needs to be some way of kicking these scroungers out.

Steve Kenyon, Bournemouth

Farmer Tony Martin must be feeling happier now that burglar Brendon Fearon has at last admitted he was right to shoot him. That must now leave the judge who sent Martin to prison as the only person in the country who believes what he did was wrong.

Michael Foley, Romford

Finally, Brendon Fearon is 'man' enough to admit that Tony Martin was right to defend himself against burglary. I hope when Fearon is old and vulnerable he finds himself in a similar situation, and that he gets to know what it's like to be petrified. That would be justice.

Martin Worrall, Paulsgrove, Portsmouth

If Brendon Fearon really thinks Tony Martin was right to use force to protect his home, why didn't he speak out earlier? Maybe then, the honest farmer wouldn't have been jailed for doing so and have to suffer prison.

Mrs Gloria Wilding, Prescot, Merseyside

I hope it is genuine remorse Brendon Fearon is feeling, for breaking into Tony Martin's farmhouse with Fred Barras with such tragic results for all concerned. Fearon's record is appalling. A leopard does not usually change his spots but miracles can happen, so let's hope this is the case here.

Mike O'Dell, Fareham, Hants.

Why did it take being shot and nearly killed for Fearon to recognise the error of his ways? As a father and man in his thirties, he should have known better and many will view his apology as a cynical ploy to create sympathy.

Gavin Upex, Woodston, Cambs.

I laughed like a drain when I read Brendon Fearon getting all poetic saying, 'I know now that the weed of crime bears bitter fruit'. Such words coming from a villain like him are as hollow as an empty Smarties tube. It's no wonder Tony Martin refuses to accept his so-called apology which came five years too late.

Keith Stoddard, Newburn, Tyne and Wear

Author's Family Heritage: Grandfather, Charles Hancock - A Police Constable, Metropolitan Police. Uncle, Stanley Hancock - A B/Constable, Palestine Police and Former Royal Marine in WW2

Bravo to the *News of the World* for backing a scheme to build a centre for victims of crime. Not enough is done to support victims and having a centre run by the Victims of Crime Trust charity is a great idea. I urge all readers to donate to this good cause.

Lucy Maunders, Shirley, Southampton

So Tony Blair is blaming the 1960's for sowing the seeds of today's yobbish society and its bad behaviour. He says it's time to end the 'liberal consensus' on law and order, as his Home Secretary sets out Labour's latest crackdown on anti-social behaviour. The Prime Minister is clutching at straws, blaming the Sixties for the trend of high crime and bad behaviour. Margaret Thatcher tried this ploy when she was in no.10, saying Britain should go back to Victorian values. It is worth mentioning that one of Tony Blair's greatest political heroes and advisers, the late Roy Jenkins, is still blamed by many for bringing in a lot of the liberal laws which caused the permissive society, when he was Home Secretary in Harold Wilson's reforming Labour administration of the Sixties.

Ian Payne, Lichfield, Staffs.

Congratulations to the *Sunday Mirror* for exposing the vile Nazi thugs.

Britain is facing a grave danger if they go unchecked. All those who sacrificed their lives and fought for the world's freedom in World War Two would have done so in vain.

David Barber, by e-mail

I was appalled to learn of the ultra-racist November 9th fascists. I fail to understand how the fact that they use words such as 'different', Aryans rather than 'superior' mean they escape the provisions of the Race Relations Act. We need to take action against these people.

Margaret King, North London

I agree with Carole Malone when she blames the Government for the rise in votes for the BNP. The reason why people support the BNP is that they are frustrated and scared that people like Abu Hamza are allowed to incite racist hatred by encouraging Muslims to kill the infidels. If we were to go and live in any Muslim country we would soon be thrown in jail if we broke their laws or used threatening language. It's about time Blair ignored the politically-correct brigade and stood up to these sick individuals. If nothing is done about the immigration problem, we can expect the BNP to get even more support – and that would be catastrophic.

Metropolitan Police Constable on Point Duty at a London junction, wearing his 'on duty' armband

Mrs J.A.Silcock, Liverpool

Thank you for the coverage given to the thoughts of our Chief Constable, Steve Green, in your newspaper. The response that we have received at the Police Authority has proved that we were right to appoint a Chief Constable who is prepared to listen to the feelings of the community, and get tough on crime and those who cause it. When the Police Authority appointed Mr Green four years ago, its members were impressed by his commitment and determination to make Nottinghamshire a safer place to live and work. Although at times he has been subject to public criticism for the wide-ranging changes he has made to policing in the county, in order to achieve his goals, the Police Authority has been steadfast in its support of his stance. During the same period we have consistently called for further resources for policing, something which the public has also embraced. Crime is reducing and 3,000 more criminals have been arrested this year, compared to the same period in the previous year. Our police officers deserve our thanks and appreciation.

However, it must be recognised that neither the police nor the authority can tackle these issues alone. We need help from the communities themselves and, most especially, from our partners on the crime and reduction partnerships. Only by a consolidated and cohesive approach will the balance ever be redressed. We are proud to see our Chief Constable has spoken out. We know his words echo the views of the majority of the public in our area, and we feel sure that this is the same across the country.

Metropolitan Police officer on Point Duty in falling snow

W.J.Clarke, Chairman, Nottinghamshire Police Authority

I am a serving police officer and fully agree with the comments of the Chief Constable of Nottinghamshire, Steve Green. Liberals and prison reformers state that prison doesn't work. I disagree, as I don't know of any criminal who continues to rob or burgle from inside a prison cell. The problem now is the constant use of short custodial sentences. This means that prolific offenders are in and out of prison numerous times a year. I suggest that we enforce an American-style 'three-strikes-and-you're-out' rule, thereby incarcerating for life, any person who decides to become a career criminal. This will prevent my colleagues from having to listen to me moaning every time I arrest someone with 20 or more convictions. The Government funds 20,000 Community Support Officers at a yearly cost of more than £440million in wages alone. This would be better used on new no-frills prisons.

Name and address supplied

Chief Constable Steve Green has hit the nail on the head. We are now paying a very heavy price for attitudes adopted over many years. There has been a serious breakdown in discipline. Discipline begins at home in a child's very early life, not in early teenage years. This is far too late. Failure to punish yobs properly and excusing their behaviour makes the police's job far harder.

Steve Fuller, Hove, E. Sussex

Congratulations to the *Daily Express* for giving so much coverage to the views of Steve Green. He is a man of real experience and he paints an accurate picture of what is happening on the streets of our towns and cities every night. How much worse must it get before the apathetic public and their mediocre representatives say enough is enough?

Paul Rhodes, London, SW19

How refreshing to read the article about the Chief Constable of Nottinghamshire and know that at least one of our senior policemen is prepared to speak out on crime. When I did my National Service in the late Fifties, I was taught self-discipline, respect for authority and the need to co-exist with one's peers. If we were to reintroduce some form of National Service then most of Mr Green's concerns would be addressed. This service should be run on military lines but not be part of the Armed Forces. Three to six months should be spent on basic training and up to 12 months preparing for a career. I despair for the future of Britain if something is not done soon, to make our youth more accountable for their actions. It can be argued that not all our children need this experience but, as in my case, there is so much to be gained.

R. West, Basingstoke

Chief Constable Steve Green deserves a medal for speaking out. He is saying what millions of law-abiding citizens have been pointing out for years. But as we don't have a voice, we are not heard. I'd like to see all the other Chief Constables in the land joining forces with Mr Green to confirm his views and opinions and give him support. If all of them did this, then the powers-that-be would have to listen.

Derek Bunting, by e-mail

At last a man with some sense. Well said Steve Green, the Chief Constable of Nottinghamshire. His comments on soft sentences and rising violent crime levels were spot on. I have despaired, with the odd exception, at the sentences meted out to the yobs, delinquents, muggers and burglars. Instead of community service, which gives them the idea that they have got away with it, they should be hit hard with a meaningful sentence. Jail would make them think twice about offending again. If need be, build more prisons, because the public want these people to be put away. It's time that those who dish out sentences came into the real world.

Tom Marriott, West Yorks.

I could not agree more with every single word of Chief Constable Steve Green's letter to the nation. We need real deterrents to combat the criminals, hooligans, vandals and the yobs. I only hope that the Home

Secretary and everyone in the Government reads his letter, takes it to heart and acts upon it. The simple fact is that this country is too soft on crime. Figures implying that crime is falling don't reflect the fact that most of us don't even bother to report so-called minor crimes any more. My car has been vandalised 15 times over the last 10 years – it has almost become the norm in the area I used to live in. The same people who vandalise cars also hang around in gangs, intimidating the innocent, spraying graffiti, throwing litter on the floor and generally making an unpleasant nuisance of themselves. When I was a child your neighbour knew you and your parents, and any misbehaviour would get back to them. We are now all too frightened to complain. I admire Steve Green for having the courage to tell it as it is.

Joyce V. Chevill, Hornchurch, Essex

I would like to congratulate Steve Green, Chief Constable of Nottinghamshire, for his open letter to the nation. There are probably very few people who have not been victims of, or witnessed, the violent, thuggish, loutish or offensive behaviour described by Mr Green. The time has come for the good people of this country to make a stand, and tell the politicians we will not tolerate it any more. People who make the lives of others a living misery should be punished. I would rather my taxes be spent on building more prisons to house these criminals, if it means people can live without fear. Unlike the lily-livered politicians running this country, we have, in Mr Green, someone who speaks the truth. Will someone please elect this man as Prime Minister?

Bev Bradley, Huddersfield, W.Yorks.

Most people in the country are cheesed off at having leaders who quite simply don't listen. We are sick of the law pandering to those who break it. I am trying to instil into my young family that they are responsible for their actions, along with the consequences that go with them, be they good or bad. It's difficult in this current climate where people bleat that things aren't their fault and take no responsibility. As so many of your readers have already written, the law needs to be given back its teeth. If there is a lack of prison spaces, then build more prisons. We need to be guided by common sense rather than political correctness and liberal attitudes that harp on about Human Rights. If you break the law then you forfeit your rights. We need more people like Chief Constable Steve Green who points out we have created out-of-control young monsters.

Helen Beere, Basingstoke, Hants.

I have to add my thanks and congratulations to Steve Green, Chief Constable of Nottinghamshire, for his comments on law and order. Why doesn't this Government listen to the people who know what's going on, the people on the front line? Everyone's had enough of louts and thugs destroying their way of life, and we are tired of all the do-gooders making excuses for them. Drink is one of the main causes for this lawless, disgusting behaviour. So what does this Government do? It extends the drinking hours! The silent majority are fed up and will have their say very soon, Mr Blair.

Dennis Jones, Widnes, Cheshire

Nottinghamshire's Chief Constable blames today's appalling yob culture on the fact that this country is too soft on crime. I agree 100 per cent with the thrust of his argument. I believe that 75 per cent of everything we know about life, including how to behave in a civilised, disciplined fashion and respecting the rights of others, is learnt before our first day at school. Society's current, terrible problems are down to poor parenting and the misguided beliefs of the anti-smacking, do-gooding brigade. Go into any supermarket and you can see and hear tomorrow's anti-social yobs, already practising their obnoxious skills, at the tender age of two and three. These are tots who have always got away with murder in the absence of discipline and standards, and are making their parents' lives a living hell. That's what they will do to the rest of society when they have added foul-mouthed abuse, binge drinking and vicious behaviour to their repertoire of selfish, disrespectful and arrogant bloody-mindedness.

Tony Thorn, Bordon, Hants.

At last! A police officer has had the bottle to state what is actually going on in this country, and confirm what we have known for years. We have watched, usually in horror, as lenient sentences are handed down to yobs who have no respect for the law or anyone else. When, as Steve Green puts it, is sympathy going to be afforded to the victims of crime and not the criminal?

Ian Bloomer, Northumberland

Congratulations to the *Daily Express* on your support for the people of this country. The coverage you gave to the Chief Constable of Nottinghamshire can only be admired. How refreshing for someone in his position to stick his head over the parapet. His Police Authority, in supporting him, has given others a lead. The bureaucrats in the Home Office must be chewing on their pencils. I am a former police officer and I'd like you to ask all Chief Constables if they support Steve Green's views. Keep it up! We need a return to real policing and not Community Support Officers with few or no powers. We need value for money from our serving police officers and the removal of those who do not pull their weight.

Stan Dibble, Exeter

You must have had thousands of letters praising Steve Green, the Chief Constable of Nottinghamshire. At the risk of repeating the many congratulatory comments, may I add my own? His inspirational statement has triggered a reaction from the public that has probably surprised few. The majority of ordinary people know what needs to be done, but there is an overwhelming feeling of helplessness. We have seen these outbursts of common sense in the past but (conveniently for the Government in question) they soon go away. Let us not allow this surge to suffer the same fate. Let's build on what Steve Green has started, and the *Express* and its readers have supported, and force a change for the well-being of the citizens of this country. They are thoroughly fed-up with being ignored.

Martyn Redmore, Huntingdon

Surely the way to stop drunken louts causing trouble is to stop the widespread sale of alcohol? Let's put an end to all-day drinking in pubs and stop all supermarkets and other shops from selling alcohol. An identity card should also be needed to buy drink. We need some control over the drink problem. The country has gone too far down the road towards anarchy.

C.A.Smith, Kings Norton, Birmingham

I agree wholeheartedly with your correspondent Steve Fuller. I am 52 and couldn't have wished for more loving parents. However, discipline, good manners and politeness were instilled in both me and my brother as children. Father was the disciplinarian and mother the stickler for good manners, which she in turn had instilled in her by her own mother. My father had only to look at us over his spectacles and we immediately did as we were told. The trouble is, a lot of parents don't have the time or the inclination to teach their children even the rudiments of good manners.   They start school thinking they can do what they like, when they like, as they do at home. Teachers have to deal with this behaviour before they can even begin to teach.

D.Davis, Sleaford, Lincs.

I am utterly disgusted that David Selwood, a supposed Judge put in charge of child porn cases, got off so lightly after being caught with images of naked boys on his PC. If he was anything other than a Judge, he would be in jail. A two-month community order isn't good enough.

Stuart Maynard, Woking

America has televised court cases for years. If it happens here in the UK, it could show how some of our muddle-headed judges arrive at such inadequate sentences. The extra scrutiny from a public already cheesed-off by their leniency might propel them towards a sentence which fits the crime.

Colin Woods, Newcastle upon Tyne

Yet again the British public have been let down. The decision to let nine Afghans stay in the country after they used guns and grenades to force a plane to fly here, sends out a clear message: 'Come to the UK, it's a haven for hijackers.' This case has now cost the British taxpayers £30million. Is this what is meant by being tough on crime?

J.Wooster, High Wycombe, Bucks.

All my life I have lived by the rules. I like to think that all the hard work my parents endured to bring me up, in hardship, has finally paid off. I work hard too, and pay my bills and taxes, like many other good people in this country. It infuriates me that these Afghan terrorists have been handed a life of luxury on a silver salver, at our expense, after committing a major crime.

Alan Gower, Northampton

I am no racist but when I see people who have done wrong and not contributed to our country – and even threatened our country – driving around in cars, when I cannot afford one, it makes my blood boil. Hard-working people are sick to death of seeing their efforts in everyday life go to waste.

Kelly Reynolds, Billericay, Essex

I was not at all surprised to read about the Afghan hijackers living the life of luxury. It seems that yet again the honest citizens of our once great land have been made to look like fools.

David Gwilt, Bentley, W. Midlands

I cannot believe that nine men who terrorised 187 people on an aircraft are being allowed to live in luxury in this country. It is an outrage. I have been off work since July last year with stress and all I am receiving is a meagre £66 per week to live on. I am overdrawn and struggle to pay my mortgage. These men should be locked up and the keys thrown away, as they have endangered the lives of so many and have been allowed to get away with it.

Nigel Flint, Kenilworth, Warwickshire

I would like to see what sort of house, car and benefits would be paid to Hitler if he stepped off a boat at Dover. We would smother him with kindness.

John Yeates, Swansea

Who says crime does not pay? The Afghans are certainly reaping the benefits of their criminal act. Should these men not be treated as terrorists? Is hijacking an airliner not a terrorist act? Now that Afghanistan is no longer under the Taliban, surely these 'criminals' should be sent back. Once again the justice system proves that it is one law for some and another for everyone else.

James Becker, Milton Keynes, Bucks.

Isn't this country a joke? Hard-working people paying tax can't afford the lifestyle being enjoyed by these criminals. I wonder what they would be doing if the incident had happened in America? Is it any wonder that hard-working, honest citizens are trying to get out and move abroad?

Andrea Hodgson, Cranham, Essex

I am speechless with rage about the Afghan hijackers. If I even brandished a gun I would no doubt be in prison for many years to come. Blair and Blunkett have announced another plan to deal with crime. What a message to send out, when we cannot even punish armed hijackers. Britain has become too soft on crime and it will be a miracle if it can be turned around.

Robert Irwin, Northfleet, Kent

I'm all for free speech and all the gentle things about the British way of life. But when it means that those nine Afghans are able to stay and pursue asylum claims, in spite of already costing taxpayers £37million, it's pure insanity. Put them on a plane home and suffer the cost of a Human Rights judgement.

Harry James, Leicester

Leaving aside the rent, council tax and utility bills paid for by the British taxpayers, how is it that the Afghan hijack gang can afford mobile phones and cars on just £42 each per week? Evidently crime pays very well indeed.

Bob Jenkins, Stirchley, Shropshire

Reading that £37million has been spent on the Afghan hijackers made me feel sick. Many people born and bred here cannot afford mobile phones, let alone cars. The Shadow Home Secretary is right – the public feel outraged.

William Ells, Maidstone, Kent

The Prime Minister is wrong to blame the rise of yob culture on 1960's liberalism. Parents and successive governments must bear some responsibility for fostering a society which encourages the young to expect everything to be handed to them. Boredom is too often cited as an excuse for bad behaviour and TV and video games do little to encourage young minds to think for themselves. Neighbourhoods must work together to fight these appalling louts who are interfering with our right to a peaceful existence.

B.Ruffle, Westgate on Sea, Kent

So Tony Blair blames liberalism in the past. Perhaps he'd also like to bring back the birch and hanging? What he fails to grasp is that poverty and crime go hand-in-hand and with the gap between the rich and poor growing wider, so crime has risen in recent years. What happened to Labour's election pledge 'Tough on crime, tough on the causes of crime?'

W.Turner, Bristol

The neighbourhood my family lives in is typical of many in Britain. It's controlled by gangs of 11-year-old yobs, who target my children because I'm an IT consultant, and they see me leaving my house in a suit and carrying a laptop – which makes me stand out. When I confronted them once, my car was vandalised and my windows smashed. I'm desperate to move out of the area but the sky-high property prices elsewhere mean we're effectively trapped. This is my life, Mr Blair.

Karl Whitburn, Carshalton, Surrey

I am in total agreement with the *Daily Express*. Plans for an extra 20,000 Community Support Officers is just policing on the cheap. I was a Special Constable for 13 years, policing in the community with no financial reward. I felt it an insult that these paid support officers were to be introduced. As with other reserve services, such as the Territorial Army and Retained Fire Service, surely the way forward would have been to just pay the Specials? It should also be noted that Specials, who hold full police powers and are trained to a very high standard, are on the decline. Is it any wonder, when paid support officers, with limited powers, wander around being of practically no help, except in handing out parking tickets? It goes without saying that I have resigned as a Special after feeling cheated and undervalued by David Blunkett.

Mike Jefferies, by e-mail

As someone who lives in the Kent town of Chatham may I commend the actions of WPC Caroline Pope for speaking out about the growing problem of asylum seekers that exists locally? She is to be applauded for standing up at a meeting to question the claims that only 293 asylum seekers live in the area. Chatham, like many other towns, is becoming a dumping ground for these people. Only the police seem prepared to acknowledge this seriously growing problem. The *Daily Express* has highlighted time after time the scams that are letting more and more illegal immigrants enter this country. Yet we have a Government that does nothing and just ignores the situation.

John Cherry, Chatham, Kent

It appears to me that we live in the most confusing of times. I don't understand, for example, why a Chief Constable can be forced into suspension, on the premise that he presided over intelligence failures and system flaws, but that the argument is not applicable to a Prime Minister. I also don't understand why, despite the false premise, it was ethically and morally right to have gone to war in Iraq because it removed a murderous regime, but it is not appropriate to apply the same argument in, say, Zimbabwe.

Chris Lee, Ipswich, Suffolk

Just what is going on in the country today? A seriously ill pensioner has her house occupied by squatters days before its sale, to pay for her care. How dare these people enter this woman's home, which she and her husband have worked hard all their life for? The law surrounding squatting needs changing urgently. Law abiding, self-sufficient members of the community and their property need to be protected against these dropouts. Whether squatters deny forced entry or not, if homeowners have asked politely for someone to leave their home and they refuse, then the police should be able to go in and remove them.

C. Jones, Wirral, Merseyside

There was much concern about squatters taking over a sick widow's house days before its sale, to pay for her nursing home care. But shouldn't we really be asking why she had to sell her house to fund her care bills in the first place?

David Williams, Llangollen, N.Wales

I agree 100 per cent with your correspondent, Matthew Riley regarding the misuse of the middle lane on our motorways. Why the police ignore this danger on our motorways I will never know. Hogging the middle lane, when there are no vehicles using the inside one, is not only selfish and inconsiderate driving, but also a potential cause for accidents.

Ray Pritchard, Little Bookham, Surrey

I am pleased to see that killer Alan Pennell, 16, has finally been named as he begins his life sentence. He will face a minimum term of 12 years for the cold-blooded killing of fellow pupil Luke Walmsley, 14, outside a school classroom. The judge made the correct decision in lifting the ban on reporting Pennell's identity, as the public have the right to know the killer's identity. However, I believe that a life sentence should mean just that. In my opinion our politically-correct society now focuses on rehabilitating criminals, instead of helping the victims of serious crimes. A minimum term of 12 years will be of little consolation to the family of the dead boy. It's a sad reflection of society that life does not mean life for premeditated crimes of this nature.

Nick Brown, Reading

I couldn't agree more with the serving police officer who says that career criminals need locking away for ever. It is time that those who dish out the sentences got tough. They need to stand up and be counted and start passing sentences that will deter would-be future criminals. If a future mugger knew he faced a bare minimum of seven years for the offence, without the chance of remission, then maybe he wouldn't be so quick to go out and rob somebody. If that criminal knew that if he carried a gun, replica or real, he faced 15 years behind bars, and if the weapon was real and was discharged, that would jump to 20 years, all without remission, again he wouldn't be so eager to carry a gun. Just because a criminal stands up in court and pleads guilty and says he is sorry should not automatically give him the right to a lesser sentence. My plea to judges is a simple one. Make the punishment fit the crime – please.

J.O'Connor, Bolton, Lancs.

I am writing in support of your correspondent Mike Jefferies. I have been a Special Constable for 21 years. But I have now decided to finish, as I also feel insulted by the introduction of Community Support Officers who have no powers at all. While members of the Specials, who do have the power of arrest, are appreciated by PCs, sergeants and inspectors, we feel that's as far as it goes up the official line. Perhaps Mr Blunkett does not know what a Special Constable is? We found this to be the case with members of the public when we held a promotion campaign in our town. The few members of the public who do recognise what we are and do, feel that we do a good job when we patrol problem areas. It's a shame that the experience of people like Mike and myself is being lost.

Gillian Bestwick, Derbyshire

Former Police Chief Ray 'Robocop' Mallon again tells us all how policing should be carried out. (*'Smash down the criminals' doors...drag them out of their homes'* August 11) His message to police officers is worth repeating: "I want you to go out there and smash the criminals' doors down, tear the doors off their hinges if you have to. Drag the criminal out of his house and bring him back to the police station. Do not even think about the Human Rights Act." Sounds fair enough to me. What rights should criminals have? The do-gooders and bleeding heart liberals scream and stomp their feet on behalf of low-life, but there's deafening silence when it comes to the victims and their Human Rights. Ray Mallon is wasting his time as Middlesbrough's Mayor. We would be better off if he was Prime Minister.

Terry Palmer, Barnsley, S. Yorks.

Regarding the £7million lottery win by convicted rapist Iorworth Hoare.

I would like to know why a serial sex attacker, who has been identified as a danger to women, was out in public buying a lottery ticket instead of being securely locked up? It makes you wonder what the point is of a prison sentence?

A. Powell, Bracknell, Berks.

It's no use politicians bemoaning the fact that a convicted rapist has won a huge sum on the lottery. If they, and their do-gooding predecessors, hadn't changed the law, so that life imprisonment means only a few years, instead of until death, Iorworth Hoare wouldn't have been able to get out of jail to purchase a lottery ticket.

Sue Hudson, London, W

Convicted sex attacker Iorworth Hoare should pay compensation to his victims with his £7million lottery win. He should then be made to pay for his board and lodging while languishing at Her Majesty's Pleasure! Perhaps if all prisoners who have funds were made to pay, there would be more money available to look after the more deserving elderly.

C.Kirby, Eastleigh, Hants.

The decision by benefits scrounger Mike Blake not to work but to concentrate on bringing up his 6 children may seem, at first, to be laudable. But just think about what kind of children he's going to bring up. Our parents are the single biggest influence on our developing attitudes and values. What kind of influence will these parents have on their children? Will they have any real sense of self-respect? Will they have any kind of work ethic? And will they go on to any kind of life outside the benefits system? Sadly, the answer to those questions is more than likely to be 'No'. What message are they sending to their children? That it's OK to take and give nothing in return? That you don't have to stand on your own two feet because someone else will take care of you? That responsible people are mugs? How did we get to a situation like this?

John King, St. Helens, Merseyside

Michael Howard has pledged to free our police from the 'mumbo jumbo' of political correctness. Thank the Lord that finally someone is prepared to speak out for the rules of common sense and decency. In a world of political correctness gone mad, I for one am prepared to stand up and be accountable for my actions and those of my children. We have created a generation of individuals who do not appear to want to take responsibility for their actions. They are quick to blame anyone or anything for their misfortune and feel they are somehow 'owed' by society. I was raised in a supportive family environment. We were far from perfect but there were clear boundaries. I was taught very quickly and clearly about the consequences of my actions. Respect for others, both young and old, was promoted. It isn't rocket science to realise that this ethos needs to be developed inside the home.

Jackie Trundell, Ware, Herts.

Having just read your front page story (*Rough justice*, January 12), I am outraged - what is the justice system in this country doing? There are few people who would not react as Iain Ross did if they were confronted with someone mugging their five-year-old in his own garden, for his trainers. There does not appear to have been any use of common sense in this case. It is of no help to this man that the judge offered his sympathy - he is still left with a criminal record. What punishment was meted out to the offenders, and who will convince the little boy that it is safe to go and play in his garden? Day after day we hear of cases which penalise the victims of crime and not the offenders, and no one seems to be able to do anything to change matters.

Cynthia Tweddle, Hartlepool, Cleveland

Having read the deplorable news of a father being judged a criminal for defending his young son on his own property, I have to ask what is wrong with the legal system and those who administer it? No one can be happy with the increasing yob culture that prevails today. Yet the legal system encourages and reinforces the belief that one can live outside the acceptable rules of behaviour in society. The father in this case is just the perfect example of the victim being prosecuted, while the criminal is allowed to get away with breaking the rules of society we believe we should live by. Do officers of the law believe they are doing society or law-breakers any favours by ignoring their wrongdoing? Two children have just been taught that breaking the law is acceptable. Welcome two more yobs to society, welcome two more children who do not know right from wrong. Labour would have the people believe they have improved law and order. This example proves they have not.

David Mills, Milton Keynes

So, the Home Secretary Charles Clarke loftily tells us that the present law on reasonable force is sound and will not be altered (*Why can't we protect ourselves?* January 13). Instead, we will be 'advised' on how far we will be allowed to go in dealing with criminals. The arrogance is breathtaking. People are being beaten and murdered in their own homes, but Mr Clarke continues to reach out a protecting and sheltering hand to the criminals who plague our society. What do we have to do to rid ourselves of these so-called leaders?

Roger Taylor, Wirrall

I share the sense of shame expressed over the behaviour of urban savages roaming Britain's streets (*Urban savages ruining life in Britain*, January 11). And I am completely confounded by the warped justice dished out by those in positions of authority. A father defending his five-year-old son from attack by two yobs ends up in court (*Rough justice*, January 12). Then there's Home Secretary Charles Clarke, flying in the face of public opinion, telling us that existing legislation covering a citizen's rights to protect property and family is sound and no change in the law is required (*Why can't we protect ourselves?* January 13). So here I am. One of the silent majority, a powerless person writing this letter because I don't know what else to do to show my anger and frustration at the injustice of it all. How many more of us feel the same way?

M Haines, Atherstone, Warks.

I am appalled at the way the legal profession is going in this country, when a magistrate has to resign because she states that all burglars should be jailed for six months (*Forced out.....the JP who dared to speak her mind on burglars*, January 17) The only thing Adoline Smith did wrong in my eyes is that she should have said that at the first offence she would give burglars five years in jail. Harsh maybe, but if burglars knew they were going to be put away for a long time, they would probably think twice about doing it in the first place. Soft sentences never deterred anybody from a life of crime. I think we should have many more magistrates like Mrs Smith and a lot stiffer sentences, and then we might turn the corner on crime. And if it means building more jails, so be it – at least the criminals will be out of action.

Tom Marriott, Leeds

How childish of the England football team to refuse to talk to the Press because David Beckham and David James were heavily criticised after their dismal performance against Austria in the World Cup qualifier. It just about sums up the intelligence of these over-rated drama queens.

Stuart Guthrie, Brixton, SW London

As one of the many thousands of Brits who move abroad every year, when I see the way another country treats its people it makes me wonder why we don't ask serious questions of our Government? Living here in Spain, I pay about £22 a year council tax, the bins are emptied every day and streets are swept. I also have the services of police, firefighters and so on. I pay £25-a-year road tax on my car yet have cheaper petrol and utility bills are less than half what I paid in the UK. So who exactly is Britain looking after and what are the huge taxes spent on?

Brenda Stevenson, Murcia , Spain

Our judicial system is a shambolic mess and a national embarrassment. Judge Michael Roach is rightly exposed for letting off sex offenders with light sentences. Now we learn another High Court judge has been allowed to stay in his job after being caught surfing the Internet for porn. Both ought to be dropped and banned from working in the law.

Paul Marshall, Kings Lynn. Norfolk

A man admits having sex with a 12-year-old girl after befriending her on the Internet yet is given a conditional discharge, leaving him free to roam the Net and streets. This is all too similar to the stories of Ian Huntley, Roy Whiting and others who committed serious sexual crimes. They were only locked up when they went what some judges must think was just a little bit too far – and killed their victims.

William Hall, Liphook, Hants

Roach is one of numerous judges who seem to find it acceptable to limit the punishment of paedophiles to community service instead of custodial sentences. It seems those judges find this repulsive perversion a minor offence. It makes one wonder what sort of web sites they like to visit.

Jane Robinson, Bolton, Lancs

How can we allow fanatics in this country to celebrate 9/11? How can a nation pay and house Omar Bakri so he can insult and spit on them? If the British Government allow this kind of behaviour, all people coming in to this country will think it's OK to bring their own rules and they will not abide by the laws of this country. I love and treasure the freedom and beauty of this place and it is a shame for it to be ruined by these extremists.

Christine Leahy, Willesden Green, London

It beggars belief that Michael Barrett has walked free. What message are we sending to people with this type of deviant behaviour? He should have been sent to prison. Judges who have no understanding of child protection issues should not preside over cases like this.

Sandra Dwyer, Nine Elms, SW London

How can Judge Michael Roach make such ridiculous comments and not be held accountable? He has now given the green light to paedophiles who can convince a court that their victim, not them, made all the moves.

Gary Hughes, Exeter

I do not care how provocative the girl was or how old she looked – it was totally wrong for anyone to have sex with her. Judge Michael Roach must never again be allowed to deal with sex crimes against children.

David Parsons, Chichester, Hants.

Daily Express Readers Poll Results

Should we hang police killers? YES 99% NO 1%

Daily Express Readers Research

Are TV soaps turning children into yobs?

YES At last someone is prepared to speak out about the effect TV's terrible soap operas have on our children. Is it any wonder so many of our young people act like mindless yobs when night after night they see this kind of behaviour being acted out on the small screen? Young characters in soaps are, in the main, ill-mannered, self-centred and full of their own importance. Sadly, the watching public laps up their antics. Soaps need to clean up their act and parents must teach children this isn't the way to behave.

S.Walker, by e-mail

NO What nonsense to suggest that anything that happens in fictional television soapland turns our young people into yobs. It's not the writers of soap operas that should be blamed for the declining standards of the younger destination. The blame for this sad fall in standards has to be placed squarely at the feet of parents who do not discipline their offspring or teach them how to behave properly in public.

M.Woodrow, Merseyside

Sunday Express Readers Poll Results

Would you watch Saddam's execution? YES 42% NO 58%
Is the law soft on travellers on illegal camps? YES 96% NO 4%

Sunday Express Readers Debate

Are Criminals treated too leniently?

YES Swift and harsh deterrence is the only way to bring down rising crime figures. I recently read that Ian Huntley whiles away his time in prison watching TV and playing on his PlayStation. What a tough life he must be having.

Sean Bakersfield, Milton Keynes

NO It is all well and good saying criminals need to be given harsher sentences, but where are we to incarcerate these people? Surely we need to look at different methods of reforming criminals rather than slamming them in a cage.

Kelly Winters, Brighton

Readers' Poll

Are criminals treated too leniently? YES 97% NO 3%
Should people who desecrate our flag be punished? YES 99% NO 1%
Should all muggers be jailed? YES 98% NO 2%

COUNT 20

THE FOURTH ESTATE

A campaigning police officer directly appealed to the Queen to stop crime in Britain from 'Spiralling out of control'. Brave PC Norman Brennan issued an urgent plea to the Head of State to save the law and order system 'from collapse'. In a letter hand-delivered to Buckingham Palace, he complained that tens of thousands of grass-roots officers like him were angry that they cannot 'protect and reassure the public in the way we would like'. He blamed Tony Blair's Government for a system which has seen crime rates rocket since Labour came to power seven years ago. He concluded that, unless there was a dramatic U-turn in policing policy, he would consider what would previously have been unthinkable to a proud bobby, retiring from the force.

Mr Brennan, a British Transport Police Officer for 25 years and Director of Victims of Crime Trust, also condemned the criminal justice system for failing to protect and support the families of murder victims. The trust claims that just £18.66 is spent helping each victim of crime, while around £30,000 is spent each year keeping a prisoner behind bars. The shocking figure was revealed at the launch in London of the Trust's *Ring The Changes For Justice* campaign. Relatives of murder victims, including Sara and Michael Payne, the parents of schoolgirl Sarah, backed the nationwide fundraising petition, aimed at attracting one million telephone donations.

Other high-profile supporters there included Denise Fergus, the mother of murdered toddler James Bulger, Damilola Taylor's father Richard, and Norfolk farmer Tony Martin. Mrs Fergus said she was devastated by the decision (by Lord Chief Justice Woolf) to release her son's killers, Robert Thompson and Jon Venables, and give them new identities after just eight years, costing the taxpayer £2million. She said: "I was shocked when the Government ruled that these boys had done enough to make up for my son's murder. They are supposed to be banned from entering Merseyside but I don't know if they are sticking to that. Now I don't know where they are, they could walk past me in the street." She added: "It's not just for me, it's also for my kids. They're not allowed to play out in the street because I am still so scared that it could happen to me again. We cannot lead normal lives."

Other relatives of murdered victims also voiced their anger against the failing justice system. Dr Janet McKenzie, whose sister Liz Sherlock was run over and killed by thieves who snatched her bag at London's Euston Station three years ago, condemned the status quo. She said her father, who already suffered from high blood pressure when her sister died, had subsequently suffered three heart attacks, the last of which was fatal. Dr McKenzie, who is training as a counsellor in Cambridge, said: "His heart was actually broken even though his spirit was not." She said that her mother had also suffered two strokes following her daughter's death. She went on: "I believe that criminals should have the best possible support in their rehabilitation but there is something wrong in a society in which criminals are entitled to more support than their victims. Society should not be judged only by how it treats its criminals but also by how it treats their victims. Many people have been bereaved who need more expert support."

Clive Elliott, operations director of the Trust, said that every murder affects up to 3,000 people including friends, family and those in local communities. He said that funds from their hotline, which will give 74p from every £1 raised, towards establishing a help centre for families, were vital to help neglected victims escape their own 'life sentences'. Mr Brennan said he had made the dramatic move of appealing to the Queen because these victims are ignored by society. He said: "I see the devastation homicide and crime causes to victims and I do not see anyone helping them. The criminal justice system is failing and failing badly. In medical terms it is in crisis, it is critical and it is fighting for its life".

Tom Morgan, Daily Express, 27th April 2004

Sarah Payne's mother was horrified when England and Wales top judge, Lord Woolf suggested that her killer could walk free early. Eight-year-old Sarah was abducted and murdered by sex beast Roy Whiting in 2000. He was sentenced to life imprisonment in 2001 and then had his tariff altered to 50 years by Home Secretary David Blunkett. But the Lord Chief Justice sparked anger when he revealed plans to release killers early if they show complete rehabilitation. Mrs Sara Payne, of Hersham, Surrey, said: "We are totally against what Lord Woolf is trying to do. If a life sentence is given then it should mean life." She revealed that her troubled partner Michael, who survived an earlier suicide attempt, turned to expensive private counselling after NHS treatment proved inadequate. She said: " We had to pay the fees ourselves as the treatment Michael received on the NHS did not work for him."

James Bulger's mother, Denise Fergus, thought justice had been done when her son's killers were sentenced to 15 years each in prison. The pair, then aged 10 years, had snatched two-year old James from a shopping mall in Bootle, Merseyside, before brutally murdering him in a crime that shocked Britain. (after terrorising and torturing him, they threw or placed his body on a railway line, where he was cut in half by a train.) But the nation was shaken once again when England's top judge ruled the boys could walk free after just eight years in a Secure Home facility. Controversial Lord Woolf said that the boys, now 21, should not face the 'corrosive atmosphere' of an adult prison. *At a cost of £2 million they were given new birth certificates, national insurance numbers and education histories.* But Denise slammed the criminal justice system and lives in fear her son's killers may one day confront her. She said: "The judges and probation officers are very keen to bend over backwards for the killers. But the relatives of the victims are just forgotten."

Helen McCourt's distraught mother, Marie McCourt, has waited 16 years to finally lay her beautiful daughter to rest. But thanks to killer Ian Simm's refusal to reveal where he hid the 22-year-old's body, the campaigning mother knows she may never find peace. Close to tears, she said: "To this day he refuses to give me the right to bury her. He won't tell us where she is buried." Simms is serving life after becoming only the third person in British legal history to stand trial for murder without a body being found. The 47-year-old murderer is eligible for parole soon and Marie is campaigning to keep him behind bars. She has also called for a law to allow Simms to remain in jail until he reveals where Helen's body is hidden.

Tony Martin was jailed for life for shooting dead a gipsy who broke into his farm. There was a massive public outcry when he was jailed. He was handed the sentence in 2000 for the murder of burglar Fred Barras, 16 years. He also injured career criminal Brendan Fearon. Although the offence was later reduced to manslaughter,with a tariff of 5-years, middle England united to protest against the perceived miscarriage of justice. Mr Martin's defence of the right to protect property and his belief that the law was skewed in favour of criminals, struck a chord with huge numbers of people nationwide. But there was further anger when Fearon, 34, received £5,000 in legal aid to sue Mr Martin for his injuries. Mr Martin said: "I've seen the system from both sides. I am not a victim, I am just a miscarriage of justice. The two young girls who were murdered at Soham, they were victims."

A row broke out after it emerged that thousands of pounds of taxpayers' money have been spent on palm trees for a magistrates court. The four 20ft high trees, which cost £7,000 each, decorate the new £30 million court building in Crown Square, Manchester. But despite claims that they create a better atmosphere in the building, which is home to 18 courtrooms, critics hit out. PC Norman Brennan, director of the Victims of Crime Trust said: "When magistrates and judges start getting their sentencing policies right, and hitting those who blight society hard, I'm sure that the public will have no problem spending this amount of money on palm trees. But until then, most people will rightly see it as a waste of money." Graham Brady, Tory MP for Altrincham and Sale West said: "I imagine there will be people who will raise their eyebrows and ask if the best way to spend public money is on trees to cheer up those who are going before the magistrates." Martin Gibbons of *The Palm Centre* in Ham, south-west London said: " The indoor trees are generally cultivated and imported from the Canary Islands and Italy. They sell for between £6,000 and £7,000 each, according to size. I have never heard of a court building having them inside before, I'm surprised they didn't go for something less expensive."

Court bosses defended the trees, saying that they helped to divide the building and were part of the original architect's plans. Neil Milligan, director of corporate services for Greater Manchester magistrates' courts committee said the trees were in an atrium separating the public part of the building from the offices. He said: "The trees were the idea of the architects and came as part of the package, the costing was not broken down for us. If we had not had the trees there would have been some kind of landscaped area in the atrium instead." The court was funded by a Government-backed private finance initiative, which means a consortium pays for the building and its maintenance. The Government then pays a regular charge for the use of the building. The Department of Constitutional Affairs pays 80 per cent of this and the 10 local authorities in Greater Manchester make up the remaining 20 per cent. A spokesman for the Victim Support and Witness Service gave the trees the thumbs-up, saying, "The old court building was very formal and intimidating, but with the new building they are trying to create a better atmosphere. If that can be achieved with the help of the trees then that's brilliant."

(**Author's note:** *this is hardly a* **triumph** *for common sense! How long will it be before names and initials are carved into the tree trunks and the walls of the atrium covered in graffiti?*)

Richard Moriarty, Daily Express, 7th May 2004

There is every chance that in the next few days or weeks Maxine Carr will walk out of Holloway Prison with only a humble electronic tag to take the spring out of her step. That was a short three-and-a-half-years wasn't it? That was a very perfunctory sentence for a woman placed bang in the middle of one of the most horrific murder trials of our times. But then the poor lamb had to wait in custody all that time for her trial to begin. The only person that can wipe the smile off her face, apparently, is Martin Narey, head of the Home Office's National Offender Management Services, (aka HM Prison Service and Probation Service!) He can now overrule prison governors if he feels, get this, that an early release would 'undermine public confidence' in the system. Who is the Home Office trying to kid? As far as the integrity of sentencing is concerned, there is *no confidence* in the system.

Take the extraordinary case of Adrian Carr, the 28-year-old who had a few drinks and fell asleep during Middlesbrough's 4-0 home defeat by Arsenal. He had only done what millions of us have at least come close to doing. Having dated a fan of Early Music for a few years during my teens, I can confess to nodding off at practically every concert hall in London. It took only a couple of glasses of wine, the first few chimes of a harpsichord and a keening counter-tenor and I was sleeping like a baby. But while the keepers of The Wigmore Hall might turn a blind eye, football stewards are less indulgent. Hauled up in front of Teesside Magistrates, our Mr Carr was charged with being 'drunk in a sports ground', given a two-year conditional discharge and ordered to pay £150 costs. The stewards claimed that he was disorientated, that they could not shake him awake and that he had to be carried from the sports ground. Mr Carr denied being drunk and said that he was simply tired after working earlier. Whatever the precise circumstances, the fact is that, for lolling in his seat at a match, not swearing, not fighting, just lying there, Mr Carr now has a criminal record. The real irony for the hapless Mr Carr is that on the very same day he was sentenced, George Best was getting away with far worse. What an insult this latest Best fiasco was, what a slap in the face for all those ordinary, hard-working folk who, by a combination of slight personal error and sheer accursed bad luck, find themselves on the wrong side of the law. George Best, flawed former golden boy of soccer turned loathsome, wife-beating old soak, was not snoozing innocently in Row 30 waiting for the stewards to arrive. He was behind the wheel of his car, **TWO AND A HALF TIMES**

OVER THE LIMIT. George was a lethal weapon. A potential kerb-mounting, child-killing drunk-driver. A head-on collision waiting to happen. And it wasn't the first time he'd been caught doing it. Back in the Eighties, Besty had been jailed for drink-driving. This time round then, he had to go away for longer, didn't he? He had to be taught a real lesson. Not on your life. A 20-month ban and a £1,500 fine is what he got. Oh, and he agreed to go on a drink rehabilitation course which, if he completes it, will reduce his ban by five months. Mind you, if he had hit and killed a child we have some idea what sort of sentence he would have received.

Just four days after George slunk out of Wimbledon Magistrates Court, no doubt vowing, ho, ho, ho, never to touch another drop, one Kamel Kadri was sentenced for the killing of nine-year-old Callum Oakford. Kadri had no licence, no insurance, no MOT and had entered Britain illegally. His sentence? Two years. The original charge against him, that he had caused death by dangerous driving, had to be reduced because there was, apparently, 'insufficient evidence' that he had been negligent. So where is this 'system' that we are all supposed to have so much confidence in? A man can fall asleep at a football match and have the full weight of the law tumble down on his shoulders. But a drunk-driver walks free and hit-and-run drivers who have no right to be in the country, let alone behind the wheel of a car, have the scope for their sentence reduced on a technicality that may have some significance in the legal process, but means not one jot to a nine-year-old boy's heartbroken parents.

There is no consistency here. None. And there is blatant prejudice and unfairness. In George Best's case, as in the air-rage incident involving Vinny Jones last year, the fame of the accused undoubtedly played a big role. What possible other reason was there for letting either of them off with such piffling punishments? These are the sort of blatant injustices which should have us howling 'foul!' from every rooftop. And Maxine Carr? Her proposed early release doesn't so much 'undermine public confidence in the system' as make an absolute laughing stock of it."

Martin Townsend, The Editor, The Sunday Express

Today *The Mail* reveals in chilling detail the real views of the fanatical cleric Abu Hamza who is appealing against David Blunkett's decision to deport him. Hamza's public sermons of hate, dripping with anti-British and anti-American venom, strain the tolerance of any civilised society. But he has carefully said nothing that leaves him open to prosecution. Now comes tape-recorded evidence which shows that his message exhorting supporters to become suicide bombers in this country is being quietly disseminated. This is surely enough proof that Hamza threatens Britain's national security.

But there is no guarantee that Mr Blunkett will win his case. Inevitably the cleric's lawyers claim Mr Blunkett's correct decision to strip Hamza of his citizenship, breaches the cleric's human rights and they are prepared to fight the case all the way to the European Court. That could take years and leave taxpayers with a massive bill. Astonishingly, Hamza will receive legal aid unless Gordon Brown can block the funding. Remember Hamza has already cost this country tens of thousands of pounds in benefits and police protection. And this is by no means the only example of the way Britain cossets our enemies.

Last week, an Algerian known to be a risk to public safety won his claim to be detained under house arrest as he had become psychotic in prison. Contrast this with how other countries deal with the problem. When the Islamist fanatic Abdel Mamour boasted that Al Qaeda would devastate several Italian cities, there was no argument or appeal, just a seat on a plane back to Senegal. No wonder terrorists know Britain is a soft touch. No wonder David Blunkett looks at this part of our criminal justice system with incredulity and despair. Isn't it time we put more emphasis on the need to protect our citizens and less on jumping through judicial hoops to treat those suspected of terrorism with woolly-minded indulgence?"

Daily Mail, 'Comment', 26th April 2004

"As everyone knows, this country faces an immensely grave terrorist threat. The police and security services repeatedly warn that it is only a matter of time before there is a terrorist atrocity in Britain. Yet, even as the Home Secretary David Blunkett, publishes his proposal to introduce identity cards today, there is little sign that those charged with keeping the country safe are prepared to do what it takes. As we report elsewhere, secret tapes reveal that the extremist Abu Hamza is regularly urging British Muslims to commit atrocities in Britain and rise up to dominate the world. Yet he is *still* at liberty. And elsewhere, some in the senior judiciary appear to be going out of their way to send a signal that Britain is just not serious about stopping terror in its tracks.

Last week, the Special Immigration Appeals Commission (SIAC) released on bail an Algerian known as 'G'. He had been locked up in indefinite detention because he was said to support members of Al Qaeda and to have helped young British Muslims train for *jihad* against the West. SIAC said it had no doubt that 'G' had 'actively assisted terrorists'. Nevertheless, it accepted the claim that his unlimited incarceration was making him psychotic and potentially suicidal. Accordingly, it released him under house arrest. Mr Blunkett described this decision as 'extraordinary' and added that others would consider it 'bonkers'. And indeed, it is hard to understand what on earth SIAC thought it was doing. For it actually agreed that 'G' was a serious danger to this country and yet released him on the grounds that he was ill. There are about 5,000 inmates in our jails suffering from mental illness and who might claim imprisonment is ruining their health. No one says they should therefore be released on bail; they would instead be treated or maybe moved to a secure hospital. Yet psychiatrists actually judged 'G' not to be ill enough to be sent to Broadmoor. Instead, a man who is thought to place our society gravely at risk has been released under restrictions which are as inadequate as they are costly to enforce. He will be limited to talking to his family, lawyers and health professionals, opening the way to communicate with terrorists through third parties. How can a body entrusted with decisions critical to our security, and headed by a High Court judge, have arrived at such a perverse decision?

The chairman of SIAC, Mr Justice Collins, has form in repeatedly thwarting government attempts to impose immigration controls. In the two appeals he has now heard under the detention without trial provision (a Libyan, 'M' was released after the Lord Chief Justice approved SIAC's decision), he appears to have bent over backwards to frustrate it. Rights campaigners at Liberty say 'G' was literally driven mad by the prospect of indefinite detention. But this melodramatic claim misses the point. All these prisoners are actually free to leave prison at any time, provided they either return to the country they came from, or find another country that is prepared to take them. They refuse to go home because they claim they will be ill-treated or killed there and not surprisingly, no other country will take them because they don't want to be lumbered with someone accused of being a dangerous terrorist. And here's the nub of this issue. In any sane universe, Britain would simply deport such people as undesirables. Indeed, we used to do precisely that.

But now we can't deport them because the judges say so. This is all because of a key ruling in a case in 1989 in which the European Court of Human Rights extended the prohibition in the Human Rights Convention against torture and inhuman or degrading treatment, to make it also illegal to deport someone if they faced such a prospect at their destination. As a result, it became impossible to deport suspected terrorists who claim they will be executed or ill-treated if they are returned home, even if they themselves have committed atrocities. This means we are forced to keep people here who are a danger to the state. That alone is why the Government was forced to bring in detention without trial for such people, who cannot be deported but are too dangerous to be at liberty. Surely it is this human rights law, preventing deportation, which is bonkers? For it does not protect human rights at all. Instead, it directly threatens the right to life by allowing terrorists to manipulate the legal system to their advantage. Indeed, the Terrorism Act, which allows people to be detained without trial, is itself qualified by an interpretation of the Human Rights Act which limits such detainees to supporters of Al Qaeda and its associates. This obviously leaves wide holes in the legislation through which other suspects, such as the Libyan 'M', can slip. Other countries do not have this problem with human rights. Last week, France deported an Imam simply for having said that Islam permitted wives to be beaten. It could do so because when such countries signed the convention, they entered a number of caveats to protect their national interest. The only country that entered no caveats at all was dozy, complacent Britain. The Government, however, will not face the terrible error it made in introducing the Human Rights Act. It will not accept that it cannot adequately fight terror having given such subversive power to dodgy interest groups and activist judges. As a result, it is constantly wrong-footed by the human rights industry and can do little more than rail in impotent fury. Now Mr Blunkett says he will 'ask' lawyers to look again at the problem of deportation, and says he will change the law to give the Government the right of appeal against such SIAC decisions.

But why is the judicial tail still being allowed to wag the Government dog like this? The former Master of the Rolls, Lord Donaldson, has attacked Mr Blunkett for questioning judges' decisions on the basis that this undermines the rule of law. But what if the judges themselves bring the law into disrepute? The root of the problem, however, lies in the laws Parliament has passed which have encouraged such judicial activism. The failure to deal with foreign terrorist suspects or immigration abuses ultimately boils down to a failure of political will. Similarly, for all their popular appeal, ID cards are yet another displacement exercise. Identification is not the major problem in combating either terrorism or illegal immigration. Even if we know who they are, we still won't throw out illegal immigrants. And the Madrid bombers and 9/11 hijackers used their own names. The problem there was not false identity but lack of adequate intelligence. Terrorism and illegal immigration will only be combated if existing human rights law is repealed, if we pass our own law defining asylum and either prosecute or throw out undesirables. The Government has helped create a judicial monster that is hindering the defence against terror. Mr Blunkett should show political courage, admit to past mistakes and put the bewigged beast firmly back in its box."

Melanie Phillips, Daily Mail, 26th April 2004

"Our prisons are bursting at the seams and the threat of jail riots is never far away. But the answer is not to avoid custodial sentences and let prisoners out bearing electronic tags. Instead, as the Criminal Justice Association says, we should build more jails. Criminals are offending knowing that there is little risk of being caught, or, even if they are, of incarceration. When they do get sent down, they are often let out early. Fines and community service are no substitute for jail. Villains know they can get away with not paying fines and scoff at community sentences. By removing prison as a punishment, we invite them to commit more crime. But we do not just need more jails; we need better jails. At present prisons are woefully poor at rehabilitation. If we built more jails there would be more room to educate prisoners. Many have no legal means of earning a living. Many are illiterate or drug addicts. Prisons should stop them returning to crime by teaching them a trade, helping them find employment and weaning them off drugs. Even if we cannot stop criminals reoffending, at least putting them behind bars keeps us safe."

Sunday Express, 'Opinion', 18th April 2004

"A pressure group launched a blistering attack on community rehabilitation schemes, branding them a 'licence to reoffend'. Despite overcrowding in prisons reaching crisis point, the Criminal Justice Association is against releasing criminals early from prison on a tag. It says the only answer is to lock them up and adopt a New York 'zero tolerance' style policy on crime. The Association says 2,000 criminals who have been tagged have reoffended. Now it is calling on the Home Office to build more prisons. Director Peter Coad said: "Criminals volunteer to go to prison by committing imprisonable offences; victims of crime do not have such a choice."

Sunday Express, 'In Brief', 18th April 2004

Tony Blair famously promised the British people that he would be 'tough on crime and tough on the causes of crime'. But after seven years, Labour is losing its grip on law and order as violent crime, sex offences and youth crime spiral out of control. The PM has attempted to pull the wool over the public's eyes by boasting that overall crime figures have dropped in the past five years. But the story the public is not being told is that the type of crime is getting worse. Here the *Daily Express* gives the real picture. Violent crime has soared by two thirds under Labour. Official figures show the number of violent crimes recorded by police has risen by nearly 64 per cent to 991,800 in 2002/3. Youth crime is out of control. The number of persistent young offenders appearing before courts in England and Wales has increased by 63 per cent since 1996 to 26,116 in 2002. Recorded crime has soared under Labour to 800,000 in 2002/3, a rise of more than 15 per cent. Sex offences have increased by eight per cent. Even though half of those raped still do not report the attack, there has still been a 27 per cent increase in female rape to 11,441 cases. Indecent assaults rose from 21,700 to 24,800. Detection rates are down. From 889,000 burglaries last year

(2003), only 26,300 offenders were convicted. In England and Wales the overall detection rate for crime was 23.5 per cent in 2002/3 and only 12 per cent of the total of recorded offences resulted in charges. Prisons are in crisis. The prison population has reached record levels, leading to chronic overcrowding. Assaults on prison and probation officers increased by two fifths between 1999 and 2003, from 1,816 to 2,511.

There are now an estimated one million hard drug users in Britain. Cocaine use is up by 250 per cent under Labour, while Ecstasy use has doubled. The Prime Minister pledged a major crackdown by appointing drug tsar Keith Hellawell (a former Chief Constable of a Yorkshire police force) in 1997, but he was sacked. In an attempt to hide Labour's failings, Mr Blair has ordered numerous crisis summits in Downing Street. After one set of bad statistics showing muggings (street robberies) had risen by 38 per cent in London alone, he 'took control' to tackle street crime. But it only targeted certain areas and other crimes rose as police concentrated on street crime. Early last year Mr Blair vowed to 'take control of gun crime' after two teenage girls were shot in Birmingham on New Years Eve. But the detection rate for violent crime, including gun crime, actually fell in 2002/3 to 50 per cent from a figure of 69 per cent in 1997.

WHAT LABOUR GOT WRONG

Tony Blair and Home Secretary David Blunkett have spent too much energy focusing on headline-grabbing initiatives and stunts. Meanwhile the worst types of crime have soared and police are being bogged down with targets and bureaucracy. There are an extra 9,000 police officers in Britain under Labour, but nearly 19,000 Home Office pen-pushers.

WHAT TORIES DO RIGHT

The Conservative Party has pledged to recruit an extra 40,000 police officers. They have promised to cut paperwork, so officers can spend more time battling crime on the streets. They have also outlined a possible move to New York-style precinct policing with every neighbourhood given its own dedicated band of officers.

Daily Express, 22nd April 2004

(Their 'Historic Decision To Back The Tories' U-Turn, pages 6 and 7 double-page special feature.)

(Author's questions/ comments on the above Daily Express main feature: *During the Tory Party's 18 continuous years in Government, oft-described as '18 years of Tory Misrule', why did they not tackle the law and order problems of the day? I recall old people being too frightened to go out after dark etc. The Tory Party 'Prime Minister-in-waiting', Mr Michael Howard,* *now the Leader of the Opposition, was the Tory Party's final Home Secretary before they were ejected in huge consecutive general election landslides by Tony Blair's Labour Party. I recall that Michael Howard had some really promising-sounding ideas for tackling the terrible crime figures of his day, but unfortunately was not in the Home Secretary's post for long enough to implement these, as I saw it. I do recall his watchword for quite some time was 'PRISON WORKS', or words to that effect.*

During **18 years in Power***, I would have thought the Tory Party, if 'PRISON WORKS BEST', would have been prudent and wise to have addressed the National Prison Shortage of the day and harnessed a free labour force, viz: all current prisoners who were bricklayers by trade, to assist in their construction, after all, HMP Dartmoor was constructed using French prisoners-of-war all those years ago!*

Furthermore, it is a well-known fact that the Tory Party during their 18 continuous years in Government, converted the National Health Service to one in which bureaucratic pen-pushers outnumbered front-of-house hands-on actual nursing staff at the 'sharp end', by a factor of approx 3 to 1. During the run-up to the last general election, I have to say I had a lot of respect for many Conservative MP's, including some former Government Ministers, who were not afraid to keep repeating in public, such as during TV news interviews: "We know we lost the last one because we failed to listen to the electorate".

To Mr Blair's credit, I think most people, if they are honest, would admit that at least the Labour Government have 'turned around' the NHS. All that seems left to be done, urgently, is to replace the trolleys parked in hospital corridors with unseen/unattended-to patients on board, to be found proper beds and an increased number of inspection/assessment/ treatment cubicles, together with more staff to deal with the situation. There is also the scourge of the MRSA deadly infection syndrome to be eradicated, reportedly by nursing and medical staff washing their hands more often and between patients.

As to the question of the vast number of hours that police officers have to spend in police stations filling out vast numbers of documents for statistical purposes, thus preventing their rapid return to the streets after processing prisoners, successive governments over the years have failed to address this problem. In these days of magnificent electronic technology, I'm amazed that nobody has invented a simple machine with all the required programmes loaded for swift push-buttons or keyboard keys to be activated. After all, when the public want to know if a particular item in Argos stores is in stock and its price, self-help machinery is fitted in the catalogue areas, for instant response. If the machine indicates that the desired product is out-of-stock, customers refer back to the catalogue and select a different product of a different brand-name and keep trying until they get lucky. Comparison can also be made to the electronic wizardry that giant supermarkets incorporate into their point-of-sale outlets. As the cashier activates the bar-code reader for each item from the customer's trolley or basket, the store's copies of the customer till receipts supply the management with a constant regular insight into each individual customer's living habits. By this I mean they can identify whether you favour Braeburn apples over Royal Gala or Golden Delicious, what quantities of them you buy and when, how you pay, viz: cash, debit or credit card, cheque etc. All of the extracted information even assists the store and warehouses in re-ordering and even programmes the mechanisms of the warehouse power train which automatically 'picks' desired items from the storage areas, to constitute a particular lorry-load delivering to various branches. When you consider the absolute 'miracles' which are taking place almost daily in Home Office Forensic Science Laboratories with regard to suspect-identifications from DNA, virtually anything is possible.

If the budget restricts the installation of my custom-designed 'statistics' rapid-use technology, the Home Office could be advised that NCR [No Carbon Paper Required] documentation has been discovered, so that a single multi-use document, with vastly-reduced classifications can be swiftly box-ticked. After all, what on earth do 33 separate Home Office and Government civil servants do with their ex-police service individual copies of data, make paper aeroplanes? It's high-time to break the mould, cut it to the quick and give the few remaining tropical rainforests a chance!)

"We report today that, yet again, crime figures are on the rise. Violent crime rose by 11 per cent in the last 3 months of 2003, 'minor' violent assaults were up 21 per cent, criminal damage increased by 10 per cent and sex offences by six per cent. The survey is 'encouraging', according to Home Office minister Hazel Blears. Admittedly, she was referring to the overall picture, which showed a drop in burglary and robbery. But 'encouraging' is not the word we would choose to use. Rather, the situation is utterly appalling. And yet still conviction rates are falling and the police in some areas appear to have all but given up. This is yet another example of the Government promising to take action but in reality doing nothing. It is less than a week since Lord Woolf, the Lord Chief Justice, said the Government was failing to tackle the problem, or, as he put it: "we are not being sufficiently tough on the causes of crime." Encouraging? Who is right?"

Daily Express, 30th April 2004, Editorial

"Scotland Yard's Flying Squad has moved on from the rough and ready days as portrayed in TV's *The Sweeney*. Foiling an attempt to steal £40million from a Heathrow warehouse is the latest in a long line of successes for this wonderful bunch of detectives, who combine modern methods with good old-fashioned hunches."

Daily Express, 18th May 2004, Editorial

"Police officers who died in the line of duty are to be honoured in their own version of poppy day. The Queen and Tony Blair are expected to attend the first National Police Memorial Day, which will take place at St Paul's Cathedral on 3rd October 2004. Blue ribbons will be on sale to the public in the run-up to the event and proceeds will go towards helping families of dead cops. Jan Berry, chairman of the Police Federation said: "It is only right that there be public recognition of the sacrifice fallen officers have made protecting society." Nearly 4,000 officers have lost their lives while on duty in England and Wales since the police service was set up nearly two centuries ago. And in the past 12 months, five officers have been killed, including Ian Broadhurst, 34, of West Yorkshire Police, who was shot dead on boxing day."

Sunday Express, 16th May 2004, Editorial

"Soaring crime, guns, gangs, drugs and terrorism threaten Britain, and more than any other institution our beleaguered police force is in the front line. Officers face death daily, every time they go on shift they know that it could be their last, and in the past 12 months eight officers have died, five in the line of duty. We are 100 per cent behind the decision to launch an annual police memorial day as a tribute to fallen officers and a blue poppy appeal for the partners and dependents of officers. It is an inspired idea. Our police must go on duty knowing that if the worst happens, their loved ones will at least not suffer financially."

Sunday Express, 16th May 2004, 'Opinion'

"Our hearts go out to the family of the policeman stabbed to death when he was trying to arrest a man in Birmingham. The police have had to endure a good deal of criticism in recent years, which makes it easy to forget that policing is actually a dangerous and difficult job. In many areas of the country, men such as this latest police victim are putting their lives on the line just by doing their job and, in some cases, as with the events of yesterday, they pay the ultimate price. Indeed, the police receive nothing like the support they should. We live in an increasingly violent society, which means that to be a policeman or policewoman has become very much more difficult. And we should not forget that the vast majority of people who serve in the police force are courageous individuals, battling in sometimes very difficult circumstances to keep some semblance of order on our streets. Yesterday's dreadful stabbing reminds us all of quite how much we owe to the men and women out on the beat."

Daily Express, 22nd May 2004, Editorial

"Rogue law firms have been caught milking the legal-aid system for millions by fighting hopeless cases for asylum seekers. A third of legal firms specialising in human rights for immigrants were found to be continually 'over-claiming' from the spiralling legal-aid budget. A flood of lawyers brought 'hopeless' actions on behalf of asylum claimants and charged £30 million in legal aid to which they were not entitled. Firms who profited from the gravy train have now been sacked from legal-aid work but, to add insult to injury, will not have to pay back the £30 million. The astonishing bill was revealed as the Legal Services Commission, which oversees the legal-aid budget, announced figures showing 30 per cent of firms working for it have been axed or are threatened with the sack.

Out of 411 practices which had contracts for asylum work, 141 have either had legal-aid contracts rescinded, or face that fate. They were found to have wasted taxpayers' money fighting asylum cases which had no chance of success. One firm's work was so sub-standard that a High Court judge branded the lawyer involved 'not competent'. The scandal was revealed by Constitutional Affairs minister David Lammy, who admitted to a committee of MP's that dozens of asylum firms were undermining the legal-aid system. A number of the firms sacked by the LSC are appealing against the decision in a bid to retain their right to claim legal-aid cash. Several law firms earn over £1 million-a-year from asylum cases. It is one of the fastest growing areas of legal-aid work, funded by taxpayers. Ministers blame the scale of over-claiming on the explosion in asylum cases since 1998, when the numbers claiming refugee status began to multiply. Many cases last for years because of repeated appeals.

The over-claiming scandal emerged as new figures revealed the mounting overall legal-aid bill for asylum seekers. Virtually all of them are entitled to state-funded lawyers and the total now paid to lawyers for immigration and asylum work is eight times what it was seven years ago. In the 12 months to March 2004, asylum lawyers claimed £204 million from the public purse, compared with £26.1 million in the year to March 1997. Lawyers in asylum and immigration work now claim £1 in every £10 paid out by the LSC, 9.2 per cent of its budget, compared with 3.2 per cent in 1998. Shadow Home Secretary David Davis said: "We need to close the loopholes that allow unscrupulous lawyers to make a mint from our shambolic asylum system."

Padraic Flanagan, Daily Express, 11th May 2004

(**Author's note:** *A clear-cut case of the* **lunatics** *taking over the* **asylum***!*)

IS ENGLAND'S FLAG OF ST GEORGE THREATENING?

Daily Express, 21st May 2004, Reader's letters page

YES. The cross of St George should be a symbol of honour and pride for everyone who is English. Sadly that is just not the case. The fact is that our flag has been hijacked by soccer hooligans and thugs. It has been waved by these idiots across the world as they have brought misery and mayhem to peaceful, cultured towns and cities with their violent menace. I, along with many other English people, hope that one day we will be able to fly the flag with pride. But first we have to get rid of the thugs that drape themselves in it."

S.Green, address supplied

NO. What nonsense to suggest that the flag of St George upsets women and is offensive. There's no doubt that in the past a minority of hooligans attached themselves to our flag. But it is our symbol and we should fly it with pride, by doing that we will take it away from the hooligans. Paula Radcliffe and other English athletes showed their pride in it and in our country at Manchester's Commonwealth Games, so should every Englishman and woman."

M.Rainford, by e-mail

A lot is heard about drug crimes but drink is responsible for a huge number of offences, especially violent ones. Today Home Secretary David Blunkett tackles booze-fuelled crime with a programme aimed at dealing with the drunks who cause mayhem. It is tough for the police dealing with these abuses and often dangerous thugs. But Britain will be a better place when they clear them off the streets.

Daily Mirror, 29th April 2004, Editorial

On the face of it, it looks like a good idea, target pubs that have become a focal point for trouble-makers and, if necessary, have the buildings bulldozed. That is what Lambeth Police Commander Dick Quinn is doing in his particularly troubled area of London, he had had several rowdy establishments closed down and one actually razed. The only trouble with this idea is that if you shut down one seedy establishment, the trouble-makers simply move on. The *Sunday Express* understands the frustrations the police feel when their arrests do not lead to a court appearance, let alone conviction, but this is not the answer. Indeed, there is something unpleasantly 'Big Brotherish' about shutting down public houses just because the police don't approve of them, however many criminals these places might attract. The answer to the problem of an increasingly violent and criminal society is not to shut down isolated trouble spots, it is to reform the whole criminal justice system, starting at the roots. For far too long society has been more concerned with the rights of the criminal than the victim, that imbalance must be shifted back right now. Nor should the system be run by woolly-headed liberals who haven't a clue about the type of people they are dealing with. We need leaders prepared to administer a short, sharp shock where it is needed and a much greater degree of severity when it is merited elsewhere.

Sunday Express, 25th April 2004, Editor

The message from Ecclesiasticus couldn't be clearer: "Wine is as good as life to a man if it be drunk moderately." and that, no doubt, is what the vast majority of us do. I certainly enjoy a beer, or a glass or two of wine, with my meals. However, although moderation in most things is a pretty good maxim by which to live, it is one that an increasing number of people haven't taken on board. The Institute of Alcohol Studies says that Britain's culture of intoxication has spread far wider and to a far younger age group than was previously thought. Alcohol abuse is a frightening and destructive illness at any age but what is particularly worrying is that now it is being seen in children as young as nine.

You may wonder how children aged nine get their hands on alcohol and the answer, in many cases, is from their parents. Andrew McNeil, the director of the Institute, says that parents are so afraid of their children getting into drugs that, on the principle of better the devil you know, they allow them to drink alcohol. So the drinking age, with the knowledge and consent of some parents, is getting younger and younger, with disastrous results. Inspector Piers Quinnell, of Essex Police, reports that anti-social behaviour by drunken children has now become Britain's No. 1 community issue. Sometimes police even find them unconscious and have to take them to hospital. At other times groups of up to 50 drunken children aged anything from nine to seventeen intimidate or attack people.

A spokesman for the Association for Convenience Stores says that many shopkeepers now live in fear of attack by young children if they refuse to supply them with alcohol. He added that, when they are already drunk on alcohol supplied by their parents, asking to see some ID means they get so aggressive that they sometimes throw bricks through shop windows and attack staff. Only last weekend the Prime Minister criticised parents for being too willing to abdicate to teachers the responsibility for disciplining their children. He said that when he was younger, if a pupil was in trouble at school they could expect automatic punishment at home as well. He added: "It is not always the case today but it should be," and he promised teachers firm support in dealing with feckless parents. He's right. And what is right in dealing with cases of trouble in school is also right in dealing with underage drinking.

Inspector Quinnell says it is frightening that, when you tell a parent that their 13-year-old has been found drunk five times, they just say: "Well what do you expect?" What I would expect is for such parents to be told that their children are their responsibility and that if they are encouraging them in underage drinking, or criminal activities, or even condoning such behaviour, they will be firmly held to that responsibility in court if necessary where, let's hope, they will encounter a magistrate or judge who holds strong views on punishing parental responsibility."

Jimmy Young, Sunday Express, 9th May 2004

The public has been saying for as long as I can remember that it is about time we put police officers back on the beat where they belong. I couldn't agree more. For too long politicians refused to listen to the public's demand for beat policing. One of the biggest mistakes that British politicians made after the Second World War was to take heed of the academics and experts who said there was no relationship between crime and the presence of police on our streets. The public knew it was not true. They saw that the absence of bobbies on the beat was making our streets and housing estates feel dangerous and allowing troublemakers to run riot. The sight of the police in panda cars left many neighbourhoods feeling isolated and ignored. For the public, it looked like a retreat and it certainly felt like one.

If anyone had any doubts about the relationship between policing and levels of crime they should remember what happened in New York and London after September 11. In both of these cities, street crime in the outer boroughs went up because local police were, understandably, re-deployed to deal with anti-terror duties. This showed that there was a direct link between the number of police patrolling our streets and the level of crime. I never believed anything else but it is not so long since it was fashionable to think exactly the opposite. I am quite sure that the growth in petty vandalism, graffiti and in street crimes was related to the sense of confidence that criminals felt because they knew that a police officer was unlikely to come around the corner. It wasn't simply that beat policing went into decline. For many years the overall level of police fluctuated, and often fell, making it hard for the police to plan an anti-crime strategy. For example, while Mrs Thatcher steadily increased police numbers, John Major cut them. When Michael Howard was Home Secretary, the number of police officers in London actually fell by more than 1,300. Freedom from crime and the fear of crime are just as important as the right to a good-quality education or a decent pension. One act of anti-social behaviour, unchecked, encourages another. If you feel that you cannot leave your house at night, or that you might be a victim of crime on public transport, or that your local park is too dangerous, then your civil liberties are being infringed. You are being prevented from taking advantage of everything that our society has to offer and, if a street or neighbourhood declines, then it can spiral downwards and it can take months or even years to stop the rot. The response has to be that we should be intolerant of what at first appear to be minor offences such as fly-tipping, small-scale vandalism and mindless anti-social behaviour. When this starts to happen in a street or neighbourhood, the quality of life can plummet.

The presence not only of police officers but also of police community support officers, street wardens, even park wardens and other visible figures of authority, can prevent this vicious circle. It can make it harder for a small minority to make everyone else's life a misery. The Americans called this the 'broken windows' theory, if a house on a street has a broken window and no-one does anything about it, soon all the windows will get broken. I think that that's absolutely right; it's not just about catching criminals, we should be stopping the crime before it happens. I believe that there is now a sea change in British policing and that the public's views are being taken more seriously than at any time I can remember.

Across Britain police numbers are up and the authorities are being given stronger powers against anti-social crime. In London, Sir John Stevens, the Commissioner of the Metropolitan Police, and I, working closely with the Government, have driven the numbers of officers relentlessly upwards. I have provided the Commissioner with 3,500 extra police officers out of my budgets, in addition to the extra anti-terrorism police and community support officers provided by David Blunkett and the Government. That is more than 4,500 extra police in four years. Every poll says this policy has overwhelming public support. And as we have developed this policy, there has been a conscious decision to put officers and police community support officers into new locations where the public had begun to feel unsafe or threatened. For example, we now have units of police officers riding buses, assisted by more CCTV, and there are more police stopping and checking mini-cabs to make sure they are licensed and safe. And by cracking down on apparently small offences, the police often find that they have caught up with someone who is a much more serious criminal. We are today taking the next step, the launch of probably the most important policy that I have ever been involved in. It is every bit as important to me as congestion charging or improving buses. 'Safer Neighbourhoods' is the start of dedicated beat-policing based in specific neighbourhoods, and made possible by a significant boost in police numbers. We've been building up to this over the past four years, but today marks the breakthrough. The rest of Britain will be watching closely to see how this new anti-crime strategy works.

We know neighbourhood policing has worked elsewhere in Britain, but it has not been applied on such a large scale before. Three neighbourhoods in each of the London boroughs will get a team of six extra police, whose only job is to patrol that specific neighbourhood. The first teams start today. They will be dedicated to their neighbourhood and they will get to know their areas in the way the public expects them to, by pounding the beat and being part of the community. I hope that they will become familiar faces in these neighbourhoods, getting to know their local people, understanding what is bothering them and becoming aware of the persistent troublemakers. The higher police numbers mean we can deploy these officers on the beat without switching reserves from specialist operations such as anti-terrorist work or the murder squad and, eventually, I want to see this new policy applied in to every neighbourhood.

For me this is a revolution in crime fighting, but it is also a common-sense response to an age-old problem. And, as is so often the case, the public has been right all along.

Mr Ken Livingstone, Lord Mayor of London
Daily Express, 5th April 2004

Drunken louts have elbowed aside respectable citizens who want to enjoy a quiet drink in peace or simply walk the streets without fear. Cheap booze promotions have turned many of our pubs into loud, uncivilised places, characterised by youngsters who pour as much alcohol as they can down their throats in the shortest possible time. They stand rather than sit, and spill out on to our streets, often swigging as they go. Our towns are becoming lawless alcoholic playgrounds for the young. And these no-go areas are being made more riotous by the spread of new superpubs selling alcohol at knock-down prices. They are a dangerous magnet for our young. We raise our glass to publican Declan Duggan who, as we report today, is campaigning against these blots on our landscape which corrupt our young in pursuit of profit. Cheap drink blights our quality of life, fuels violence and crime, is a strain on our police and fills our accident and emergency departments. Days lost through alcohol damage the economy. It is also a medical time bomb. Youngsters who drink heavily will pay for it in ill-health in later life. Meanwhile, foreign visitors who witness drunken depravity go home shocked at what they have seen.

Frighteningly, the relaxation of licensing laws that is around the corner will give youngsters more opportunity to get drunk. Strict licensing hours have contributed to the 'get-it-down-before-closing-time' mentality, but scrapping them will not change habits overnight. We will not suddenly start drinking the Continental way. Alcohol Concern rightly argues that to create a less destructive drinking culture in Britain, there must be a change in the attitudes of our drink industry, from the big producers to the chain bars and even local pubs.

As well as a curb on irresponsible promotions that encourage binge drinking, pubs and bars must observe the laws which ban sales to under-aged youngsters and those who are already drunk, laws that are frequently flouted. The Government should also spend more of the £7 billion a year that flows into its coffers from drink into educating people about the dangers of its misuse. Most of all, we must teach our young that there is nothing cool about drinking so much that you lose control. Drinking is something to be enjoyed, and you cannot do that if you drink so much that you cannot remember the taste.

Sunday Express, 23rd May 2004, 'Opinion'

"A very elderly couple, he in immaculate tweeds, she in a long dress, the pair of them carrying suitcases, were walking across the main concourse at London's Waterloo station earlier this week. They were both tired. You could see it in their faces. His shoes were brightly shined but the colour had drained out of his face. She stared straight ahead. "The problem is," I heard him say, "that it's very hard to find anywhere to sit." Very hard? I would say impossible at Waterloo during the rush hour. There are just not enough benches. It's the same on virtually every other station in London. It's the same in most streets. Where DOES anyone stop and sit? Where do the very elderly, the very young or the plain exhausted sit down and take a rest?

Britain is still the greatest nation in the world but we are becoming very uncivilised towards our own. We lack the niceties, the detail. We have forgotten how to be gentle with each other or even with ourselves. We are now part of an enlarged European Union. Ten new countries have joined a big club which, let's face it, still looks to Britain to set certain standards, in compassion, in dignity.

Somehow, though, we have forgotten how. Young people get drunk and vomit on the streets. Teenagers use abortion as contraception and fall in and out of sexual relationships with impunity. Our streets are strewn with rubbish, scarred by broken paving and cracked kerbs, despite sky-high council taxes, and every grass verge is a rubbish dump for a multitude of discarded burger-boxes and cigarette ends. No amount of tinkering with the criminal justice system seems to stop the rise of violent crime or make it any easier to send anyone to jail. Hit-and-run drivers get a slap on the wrist. Everyone has an excuse, broken home, childhood abuse. No one needs to take the blame any more.

Police stations don't open all the week and, when they do, the officers inside are too busy with paperwork to be able to deal with inquiries or patrol the streets. Everyone is just getting away with it, whether 'it' is crime, rudeness, shabby workmanship or just plain incompetence. There are no park-keepers. There are few railway station attendants after 9.30am.

Everything is automated or unattended after certain times. No patrols look after this or that open space and, therefore, those open spaces have now gone to the dogs.

In addition, there is nowhere for the elderly or infirm to sit. Whatever happened to our standards, our pride? Recent surveys suggest that women over the age of 50 have lost faith in politics and that, next time around, they will not be voting. We discuss this issue elsewhere in the *Sunday Express* this week but let's just consider what it means. Women over 50, those who are, without question, the most sensible and civilised people in our sad old society, those who have put up with the most and are our most resilient citizens, don't want to know. They are part of the one-third of older people who don't even want to be here any more. They want to live abroad. This, above all, should be our call to action.

Britain needs civilising. It needs strong, positive policies put in place to improve everyone's quality of life. We need full-time, well-paid anti-graffiti patrols, not part-time policemen, not dunderheaded private security firms but responsible, intelligent citizens. We need armies of gardeners to beautify our public verges and parkland, to keep an eye on our common land and public spaces and make sure they don't just become a haven for drug-users, deviants and vandals. We need to staff our railway stations full-time, keep an eye on our bus stations and terminals and make the dead, sodium-lit spaces, where crime and violence breeds, a thing of the past. Nine times out of ten, it will be enough that our towns and cities are merely patrolled and occupied. Most criminals are cowards who can work best on empty, late-night streets. We also need to get tough in our schools. One secondary school teacher recently said that if the hard-core of those trouble-making pupils whose parents allowed them to hide that much-abused label of 'special needs' were actually thrown out, the number of such expulsions would total no more than 30 pupils in every school, but the school itself would be improved beyond measure. Let's take that step. If children don't want to learn, if they only want to make trouble and hold others back, let's throw them out. Where will they go? Don't know, don't care. Let's give the majority a chance and start building a better country from the ground up."

> *Martin Townsend, The Editor,*
> *Sunday Express, 9th May 2004, Editorial*

Home Secretary David Blunkett has told the alcohol industry that more strident powers to beat binge drinking are 'inevitable' if it does not behave responsibly.

> *Daily Express, 11th May 2004*

Instead of eating a hefty slice of humble pie and apologising to customers for a third-rate service, Post Office boss Adam Crozier has dismissed a

Channel 4 documentary, which showed many of his staff to be lazy, thieving, arrogant, good-for-nothings who don't give a stuff about getting our mail to us on time or even at all, by claiming it was not representative of Post Office staff. Well the reporter who got 'inside' the Post Office and worked in various London sorting officers for five months seemed to think it was absolutely typical. He saw barely-literate staff being sent out to deliver letters with only a dog-eared map. He saw postmen rolling cannabis joints before going out to deliver. He saw letters, including Special Deliveries for which we pay upwards of £3.50, lying on the floor while staff trampled on them and played football around them. And he saw workers with criminal records handling cheques, passports etc., admitting they routinely steal them. Odd isn't it?

Every time I write anything critical about soft-lad posties who refuse to deliver in streets which have low-flying pigeons or particularly virulent rhododendron bushes I get rude, vitriolic letters from arrogant union bosses who say I don't know what I'm talking about. Bearing in mind the Royal Mail is two years into a three-year shake-up (and is worse than ever), and is intending to charge us more for its pitifully poor service, Crozier ought to get to grips with what he was put there to do. And if he values the decent, honest postmen he's always talking about, he should root out and sack the louts who are giving them a bad name. I always preface anything I write about postmen by saying mine is a gem, always conscientious, always smiling and willing to do anything for his customers. I've always known he's a rarity. But after this I shall treasure him even more.

Carole Malone, Sunday Mirror, 2nd May 2004

Is it just accidental, or is there some deliberate broadcasting policy to make Manchester the civic template for balanced, even-handed reporting? For every documentary or drama on television that paints Manchester as the hippest place in Britain, a city brimming with Premiership footballers who can earn more per hour than even Bank Holiday emergency call-out plumbers, dotted with trendy nightclubs crammed with either expensively dressed gay men or long-legged blondes hoping to lure a Premiership footballer into a fling that she can auction to the Sunday papers, and full of stainless-steel-and-wenge loft apartments owned by southern buy-to-let investors who can no longer afford London property prices, there is another documentary or drama on television which paints the opposite picture.

These counterbalancing programmes portray Manchester as the sort of place that even Mike Tyson would be scared to walk around alone in broad daylight, where people talk in that unusual way only because they're on crack; where the most common thing to call a 16-year-old schoolgirl is 'mum' and where the local economy functions on a precarious commercial model based on people stealing each other's possessions and then reselling them for a fraction of their actual value, a sort of inverted capitalism.

ONE LIFE: The Trouble with Being Lee (BBC 1) suggests it was the turn of nasty Manchester to show its face on TV. This film's introductory sentence told us that Manchester has one of the highest youth offending rates in England. It homed in on an area called Openshaw, apparently one of Manchester's most notorious estates, which happens to be in the grip of a new culture of young people spending their pocket money (well, other people's pocket money, obviously) on drinking cheap vodka, straight from the neck of two-litre bottles. These young people, having no visible means of support, beyond gravity, tend to rob in order to pay their bar bills. I suppose you have to regard it as some kind of tribute to their city's mercantile history that Mancunians can make a secondary market in almost anything. When one suspicious-looking young man is stopped and frisked by the local bobby, not only is he carrying a DVD player in a black bin-liner, but also two damp pairs of jeans. Openshaw is the sort of place where people steal laundry from each other's washing lines.

The local bobby is PC Lance Thomas, at the vanguard of a new policing policy called 'Embrace', a zero-tolerance approach to drunks, smack heads and nuisance neighbours. It runs in parallel with very visible community policing, designed to demonstrate to troublemakers the benefits of keeping their noses clean, actually and metaphorically. Another element of the policy is referring to Openshaw as a village, rather than as a housing estate; much the same way that London estate agents try to massage an area upmarket by rechristening it a village (three gentrified streets encircled by some of the most derelict, crime-ridden estates in London), or a quartier (suggesting a cosmopolitan feel), which is generated by the plethora of different nationalities who come to the area to be fleeced by the pickpockets), or a plaza (an isolated block of new housing encircled by winds powerful enough to overturn container lorries). Either 15-year-old Lee is the worst troublemaker in the village, or he's just the one that caught the crew's imagination. Thomas says that Lee has: "built a reputation for himself as a toe-rag", and has been trying to explain to the boy that it takes five minutes to earn a bad name, and months to get rid of one. In addition to a bad name, Lee has a conviction for house burglary and is on bail for car theft. One more arrest and he could go to prison. Lee's mother, a nurse, has given up her job to keep a more vigilant maternal eye on her lippy son. Lee had been identified by his youth offending team (YOT) as a risk to the community. But since PC Thomas began keeping a closer eye on Lee as part of 'Embrace', picking him up whenever he was loitering with a bad crowd, drilling in to him the consequences of committing another offence, Lee seemed to turn a corner. He stopped taking drugs, almost stopped drinking vodka, and kept a clean sheet.

When it came to the judge having to pass sentence for Lee's earlier car theft, he decided Lee had responded well enough to the 'Embrace' project to be spared a custodial sentence. By the time the film crew had packed its bags and left Openshaw, Lee had been crime-free for nearly a year. His hopes for his life now? "Just wait till I'm 16. Get into a college course. Got to be a fireman. Get in to be a fireman. Do the job. Get myself a girlfriend. Get make-up money to buy myself my own house. Get myself my own car, a nice car. Have a couple of kids. And then die a happy man, instead of behind bars." Who knows? Next time we meet Lee he might be in a film about the other, nice Manchester.

Joe Joseph, The Times, 19th May 2004

Typical Media Priority Reportage of News

Front page:	Hundreds queue in Scarborough to register with a new NHS dental surgery.
Page 2:	Immigration – EU gipsy crisis – Dutch kick-out 26,000 refugees.
Page 3:	Tycoon dumps supermodel.
Page 4:	GCSE's to go in massive exams overhaul.
Page 5:	(continuation of NHS dentists story from page 1)
Pages 6/7:	Bafta awards – Brits rocked by 'Darkness'.
Pages 8/9:	Confession of rampant army major.
Page 10:	Car advertisement.
Page 11:	Eleven-year-old girl loses leg in 999 car crash.
Page 12:	Editorial.
Page 13:	Whole-page columnist.
Page 14:	Half-page supermarket advertisement.
Page 15:	**Tycoon Death Horror.**
	Daily Express, 18th February 2004
Page 4:	**Wife Murdered In Horror Attack In Poole.**
Page 33:	**Murder Quiz As Girl Found Dead At Pub in Basildon.**
	Sunday Express, 15th February 2004
Front page:	Panic at 10% home loans.

COUNT 21

IN PRAISE OF THE JUDICIARY

LORDS JUSTICE STEYN
LORD JUSTICE RODGER
LORD JUSTICE CARSWELL
LORD JUSTICE BROWN
BARONESS HALE

Five Law Lords stood up for crime victims by ruling that police should be allowed to build the largest possible database of DNA and fingerprints. In a landmark ruling they said the Human Rights case against storing the details of suspects who are later cleared was 'threadbare'. In two test cases brought against South Yorkshire police it had been argued that holding the information would be unfair on people who were acquitted or who had charges against them dropped. But Lord Brown said the rights of crime victims also needed to be taken into account, adding that the benefits of a larger database were 'manifest'. He said: "The more complete the database, the better the chance of detecting criminals, both those guilty of crimes past and those whose crimes are yet to be committed." The decisions by Lords Steyn, Rodger, Carswell, Brown and Baroness Hale, uphold earlier High

Court and Appeal Court rulings in favour of police – at last – common sense prevails!

LORD JUSTICE BROOKE

Appeal Court Judges have outlawed appeals that enable 'unmerited' asylum seekers to extend their stay in Britain. The ruling means the Home Office need not wait until the legal process is exhausted before removing those with hopeless claims. Previously, failed refugees who went to the Court of Appeal were automatically granted a stay of deportation, however weak their case. The ruling is expected to save hundreds of thousands of pounds of public money spent on legal aid and court expenses. Lord Justice Brooke told the Court of Appeal: " The practice of pursuing a further appeal to this court in a judicial review matter in the immigration and asylum field, has given rise to very serious abuse. Appellants are pursuing wholly unmeritorious appeals simply to delay the time when they are to be deported." He said that before cases reached the Court of Appeal, they had already been turned down by two High Court Judges, who give 'anxious scrutiny' to all applications, and the Immigration Appeal Tribunal. But if a refugee made an application to the Court of Appeal within seven days of losing at the High Court, the Home Secretary deferred removal until the legal process was completed. In future, a stay on deportation will be granted only following a special application to a judge. Lord Justice Brooke said the ruling was made following talks with leading judges, including Master of the Rolls Lord Phillips, and called for it to be widely publicised to help cut down on hopeless appeals. The Home Office welcomed the ruling, saying it supported the aims of the Government's immigration policy.

LORD JUSTICE KENNEDY
AND MR JUSTICE TREACY

Yobs who cause misery should not complain when they are named and shamed, High Court judges ruled on 7th October 2004. In a crushing defeat for the human rights lobby, they cleared the way for councils to plaster the photographs of louts on posters and leaflets. Lawyers for Liberty had said publicising the details of three gang members responsible for an 'epidemic' of crime was a breach of the controversial European Convention on Human Rights. But, in a victory for common sense, Mr Justice Treacy and Lord Justice Kennedy said the strategy was 'justified, reasonable and proportionate'. They also attacked delays in the court system caused by bringing the case, which has cost the taxpayer an estimated £250,000. Home Secretary David Blunkett, who announced plans for increased naming and shaming of tearaways, welcomed the verdict. "We are pleased that the judge recognised the rights of the community." his spokesman said.

The case was brought on behalf of Jovan Stanley, 16, William Marshall, 17, and Martin Kelly, 19 who were handed ASBOs after inflicting misery on a housing estate in Brent, London. They were members of a gang blamed for smoking drugs, plunging homes into darkness by removing fuses from a communal fuse box, abusing and threatening residents, aggravated vehicle-taking, assault, carrying offensive weapons and starting fires. A total of seven gang members were hit with ASBOs, which banned them from causing further misery on the estate, by Brent Council and the Metropolitan Police.

But Stanley, Marshall and Kelly complained the right to protection of their private and family life under Article 8 of the Human Rights Act, had been infringed by the wide-ranging publicity which followed Brent's decision to put their faces on leaflets and in a newsletter. The court was told they were seeking a moderate sum in compensation. But, throwing out the claim, Lord Justice Kennedy said: "It was clear that publicity to inform, reassure or inhibit behaviour is unlikely to be effective unless it includes photographs, names and at least partial addresses. Not only do the readers need to know against whom orders have been made, but those responsible for publicity must leave no room for mis-identification." Ann John, leader of Brent Council said: "The young people in this case had been involved in serious and persistent bad behaviour, which was often of a dangerous, threatening and violent nature, and the residents who were affected were terrified in their own homes." Christopher Johnston for the Police, had told the High Court that it was hard to imagine 'the hell of the residents' daily existence' at the hands of the gang. Councils currently can name under-18s who are made the subject of an ASBO but cannot publicise details of those who go on to breach the order.

At the recent Labour Party conference, Mr Blunkett unveiled plans to change the law so that under-18s who break an ASBO can be banned for the first time.

MR JUSTICE JAMES MUNBY
HIGH COURT FAMILY DIVISION

In April 2004, a High Court judge slammed the family justice system saying it 'failed' a father who has not been able to see his daughter for more than two years. The man, who cannot be identified, has been forced to give up his five-year battle for access to his seven-year-old girl after 43 court hearings. His ex-wife has continued to ignore orders allowing him contact with the child. Mr Justice James Munby, a respected Family Division judge, said the courts were making 'victims' of some fathers. Apologising to the man, he said: "We failed them. The system failed them. It is very disheartening. I am sorry there is nothing more I can do." He called for short jail sentences of up to three days for mums who do not comply with contact orders, and said sweeping changes were required. Judge Munby attacked the 'sheer length of the proceedings' in the case and the number of different judges, 16 at 43 hearings, who heard it. Proposing allocating cases special timetables that could be measured in weeks or months, rather than years, he said a sole judge, or at the most two, should hear complex cases. Children should get separate legal representation and skilled social work intervention, he added.

He then said: "There is much wrong with our system and the time has come for us to recognise that fact and to face up to it honestly. If we do not we risk forfeiting public confidence." He said the system made victims of the fathers more than the mums. The couple had separated in 1998, but almost immediately there were problems with visits and since October 2001, the dad's only contact had been through letters and cards. The mum was jailed for two weeks in 2001 for ignoring court orders. Judge Munby's remarks came on a national day of protests in Family Court offices by fathers. Matt O'Connor from civil rights group Fathers 4 Justice said: " It is a jaw-dropping judgement. Twelve months ago such a judgement would have been unthinkable. Let no one forget the outcome was still the same. Another father has lost his child."

LORD COULSFIELD
HIGH COURT JUDGE

Lord Coulsfield, who was the Trial Judge at the Lockerbie bombing trial, and one of Britain's top Judges, has shaken the Home Office by declaring that the British criminal justice system has become a laughing stock, because of releasing convicts from their prison sentences too soon.

The public's confidence has been undermined by Home Secretary David Blunkett's *tagging scheme*. Lord Coulsfield has demanded that prison sentences should 'mean what they say.' He went on to say that Mr Blunkett's 'custody plus' policy, where criminals spend up to three months in jail, followed by 6 months of external supervision in the community, has 'little or no value' in reforming or the deterrence of offenders. This Judge's enquiry, with funding from the Rethinking Crime and Punishment group, has backing by MPs and some victims' groups. It was stated that more than 3,600 crimes were committed by early release scheme offenders, since the policy was introduced in 1999. The figure of 3,600 includes the following categories of offences:

9 sexual offences
462 assaults and muggings
163 burglaries

47 robberies

306 drugs offences

Comment from the Shadow Home Secretary David Davis, was as follows: "David Blunkett is more obsessed with emptying prisons than punishing criminals. Tagging should be used as an addition, not an alternative to prison. Sentences should fit the crime, not the number of cells available." Norman Brennan, director of the Victims of Crime Trust was interviewed and said: "The Judge speaks common sense and David Blunkett should take notice." The existing HDC (Home Detention Curfew) scheme allows convicts sentenced to less than 4 years in prison, to be freed *even earlier* than normal, and the scheme was obviously introduced in the first place to ease serious overcrowding in prisons, which throughout 2004, have been almost at breaking point. The normal release time scale for the less serious offenders is approx halfway through their original sentence. However, if considered trustworthy and suitable for the tagging scheme, they can be released an extra 135 days earlier.

An example of how ludicrous the system can be is illustrated by the behaviour of career criminal Brendan Fearon, who was shot in the leg by farmer Tony Martin, during a raid with others on Mr Martin's farmhouse. Fearon, 34, had been released less than a third of the way through his sentence of 18 months for dealing in heroin. However he breached the tag requirements by driving without insurance, and was returned to jail. Lord Coulsfield went on to say: "It's a framework we think is unfortunate, because it interferes with the court's decision. It is another thing capable of suggesting to the public that what the court says, is not what actually happens." The recent report by the Rethinking Crime and Punishment group in November 2004, said sentencing should be more transparent. Lord Coulsfield said a criminal sentenced to two years imprisonment should serve a full two years behind bars. His enquiry declared that people sentenced to non-custodial punishments, such as fines, probation or community service, should be 'sent down' from the court dock as if being jailed, so that they can arrange their first fine payment or probation session etc. At the moment they can just leave the dock, walk to the back of the court and depart with waiting friends or family. The senior Judge further stated that local residents in the criminal's home area, should have some input into which community service projects should be addressed by the offenders.

LORD CHIEF JUSTICE WOOLF IN COURT OF CRIMINAL APPEAL

A bus driver who strangled a passenger after she refused to have sex with him had his 12-year jail term increased to 20 years under new sentencing guidelines. Lord Woolf, the Lord Chief Justice, and two other senior judges, imposed the extra penalty on Lee Holbrook as they gave new guideline rulings on minimum sentences for murder where the killers have admitted their crimes. Holbrook, now 40, pleaded guilty at Plymouth Crown Court last August, 2004, to murdering Alicia Eborne, 18, a student at Plymouth College of Further Education.

A growing number of cases involving guilty pleas to murder are reaching the courts and until the guidelines, published recently by the Sentencing Guidelines Council, judges had to operate a 'rule of thumb' as to what discount to give. Although guilty pleas generally attract a sentence discount of one third, the council had caused a furore with its draft proposals for England and Wales, suggesting that murderers should also receive such discounts. In its final guidelines it said that only where murderers pleaded guilty at the first opportunity would they be entitled to a discount and this would not be more than one sixth (up to a maximum of five years) with no discount in the most severe cases, when killers would serve a 'whole life' sentence.

The judges, sitting in the Court of Appeal in London, gave their rulings in five representative appeals in which they increased one minimum jail term, reduced another and dismissed three other cases. The guidelines, which came into force on January 10 and are 'designed to promote consistent and effective sentencing across the criminal justice system', say that reductions would have to be weighed carefully by a judge so that they did not lead to an inappropriately short sentence.

A 12-year jail term by Sara Crane, 26, who had pleaded guilty at Kingston Crown Court to killing a neighbour, David Thompson, with a knife. Her lawyer argued that the jail term did not reflect her 'appalling personal life' or her plea of guilty. But appeal judges ruled that her lawyer had failed to take account that Crane had chased her victim up the stairs with the knife and that she had already received three years for robbery.

Emma Last, 19, of Braintree, Essex, pleaded guilty to the murder of a teenage girl who was doused in petrol and set alight. She had her minimum term of 20 years cut to 17. Her co-accused, Kerry Bauer, 21, had her minimum term set at 17 years and the Court of Appeal reduced Last's minimum term to the same level. Last's lawyer had argued that the disparity between the pair was not justified.

Giving decisions in the five appeals, Lord Woolf said that the cases had been heard together 'in order to provide further assistance as to the determination of the minimum term to be served by defendants convicted of murder and sentenced to life imprisonment, prior to their being considered for release on licence by the Parole Board. The common feature of the cases is that in each the defendant pleaded guilty'. He added: "Until recently it was rare for a defendant to plead guilty to murder. This may have been a throwback to a time when the penalty for murder was death. In that situation, the legal profession regarded it as inappropriate to allow a defendant to plead guilty." The guidelines, he said, were 'to assist the judge to reach a just sentence, and in the case of murder, the just minimum sentence', but do not remove judges' discretion. 'They merely indicate the matters to which the judge must have regard when exercising his discretion'.

In the case of Holbrook it was contended on behalf of the Solicitor-General that the 12-year minimum term imposed as the period of detention for punishment and deterrence 'failed adequately to reflect the gravity of the offence, the aggravating features, the need to deter others and the public concern about cases such as this'. Lord Woolf said that the family of Alicia Eborne had prepared a moving statement explaining the impact on them of her death, and the court had taken that into account. There were serious aggravating features in the case, a particularly powerful one being 'that Alicia was murdered because she was going to make a complaint against the appellant relating to the sexual demands which he made on her,' Lord Woolf said.

SUMMARY OF FIVE APPEALS ON RULINGS HEARD TOGETHER

1) Lee Holbrook, now 40, who pleaded guilty to strangling Alicia Eborne, 18, after she refused him sex, had his minimum term increased from 12 years to 20. It was argued in December that the minimum term of 12 years, set at Plymouth Crown Court, was not severe enough.

2+3) Appeals by Edward Quillan, 24, of East Kilbride. Scotland, and his brother James Quillan, 18, of Fleetwood, Lancs, who admitted robbing and murdering bachelor James Fleming, 70, in Fleetwood, were dismissed. James had received a minimum sentence of 19 years and his brother a minimum term of 25 years.

4) The appeal court also rejected an appeal against a 12-year jail term by Sara Crane, 26, who had pleaded guilty at Kingston Crown Court to killing a neighbour, David Thompson, with a knife. Her lawyer argued that the jail term did not reflect her 'appalling personal life' or her plea of guilty. But appeal judges ruled that her lawyer had failed to take account that Crane had chased her victim up the stairs with the knife and that she had already received three years for robbery.

5) Emma Last, 19, of Braintree, Essex, pleaded guilty to the murder of a teenage girl who was doused in petrol and set alight. She had her minimum term of 20 years cut to 17. Her co-accused, Kerry Bauer, 21, had her minimum term set at 17 years and the Court of Appeal reduced Last's minimum term to the same level. Last's lawyer had argued that the disparity between the pair was not justified.

MR JUSTICE HOLLAND
LEEDS CROWN COURT

A judge has condemned laws which prevented him from jailing a sick pervert for longer than a total of eight years. In an extraordinary outburst, Mr Justice Holland said it was 'really quite absurd' that he could not hand Nathan Eyre a longer sentence for grooming a young boy for sexual abuse.

Sitting at Leeds Crown Court, the judge said: "This man provides prostitutes to men and I do not have the power to sentence him. It's really quite absurd. These cases are rarely as serious as this but this case demonstrates the seriousness of it at its extreme. It's extraordinary the judge is hamstrung in this way, to seven years, when it might be ten or even life." Mr Justice Holland hit out after he found that he was powerless to give Eyre the sentence he wanted because his crimes only carried a maximum sentence of seven years. His condemnation of the inadequate sentencing powers for judges dealing with some of the country's worst sex offenders, was swiftly applauded by child protection campaigners, who demanded tougher jail terms for those who prey on the young.

Maggie Bucknall, spokeswoman for the Communities Against Paedophile Accommodation said: "the sentencing guidelines need to be crushed and start again. It is obscene that someone can be given such a minimum sentence when the judge wanted to give more. It is fantastic that the judge has spoken out like this because then people have to sit up and take notice. I just wish others would do the same." Natalie Finlayson, Director of Communications for *Childline*, said: "It is good that the judge recognises the seriousness of what has gone on. He understands the appalling devastation that is inflicted on a child who has experienced such abuse." John Carr, of children's charity NCH, said: " The judge is spot on. Good on him for speaking out."

Eyre, 38, from Leeds, groomed a 14-year-old boy, who cannot be named for legal reasons, to work as a (male) prostitute for two years. He was then abducted and sold on to endure a week-long "blur" of sexual abuse by other men. The pervert was convicted of living off the earnings of prostitution which carries the maximum sentence of seven years. The court heard that Eyre groomed the vulnerable youngster to work as an under-age male prostitute before he was abducted and sold to Raymond Hawthorne in

October 2003. Hawthorne, 40, of Manchester, admitted abduction, indecency with a child, conspiring to live off the earnings of a male prostitute, and conspiring to commit indecent assaults, and was sent to prison for seven years. Leslie Loram, 50, of Rochdale, 'one of Hawthorne's best customers', was jailed for three and a half years, after admitting two counts of buggery and one of indecent assault on the boy. Eyre was sentenced to five years in jail after admitting the offence, and was given an extra three years for a separate conviction of conspiring to sell the boy. Passing sentence, Mr Justice Holland said: "The criminality is really quite breathtaking. It was complete exploitation, selling (the boy) to a man with national connections for extensive further exploitation. From the victim impact statement it is clear the consequences are still continuing and the mental and psychological scars may be with him for the rest of his life."

Neil Davey QC, for the prosecution, told the court the young victim's horrific experience 'just blurred into one week-long episode of sexual abuse'. A Home Office spokesman said the Sexual Offences Act 2003, which came into force in May 2004, was the beginning of a law reform for tough new penalties on those who exploit for prostitution. It introduced new offences of sexual activity with a child and causing or inciting a child to engage in sexual activity that are punishable by a maximum of 14 years imprisonment. The spokesman said: "The Government is determined to combat the stranglehold of pimps and break the links between prostitution and drug markets, trafficking and other areas of organised crime."

JUDGE JOHN McNAUGHT
SWINDON CROWN COURT

A senior Crown Court judge has added his voice to the public concern over reluctance to be out on the streets at night, due to the ongoing breakdown in law and order.

Judge John McNaught, who presides at Swindon Crown Court, recently declared: "I feel nervous if I come back from London on the evening train and have to walk through the town centre to my car. I am wary about walking through the town centre late at night. I don't like walking from the station very much." He said that the fear of street crime was one of the biggest concerns for fellow residents in Swindon, Wiltshire, on the London to Paddington main railway line. The judge, during a speech about the criminal justice system, said that Swindon's Crown Court saw many cases of violence such as fights, attacks and violent muggings. He added that he had no statistics to quote but he had heard of plenty of anecdotal evidence to convince him that people were becoming more and more scared. However the local police appeared to take exception to the judge's remarks, claiming that, due to their efforts, Swindon was one of the safest places in the UK. However civic leaders and Swindon residents praised the judge's observations. Mr Pendlebury, president of the Chamber of Commerce at Swindon, said it was of no surprise to him that people were scared of walking alone after dark. He said: " I have lived in Swindon for 25 years and I have seen it get progressively worse. It used to be a sleepy town with a small-town mentality. When you walked around the town centre at 11pm, it would be a rarity to see anybody else. Now it has all changed. I would not walk through the town centre at night. In truth, I would only ever go through in my car with my doors and windows firmly locked.

"I know people who have been victims of violence and these are people who have contributed in no way whatsoever to what has happened to them. The majority of violence seems to be caused by alcohol when people are turned out of the pubs at night. There are also problems with gangs and drugs, which are things you find across the country, but the problem in Swindon is the lack of places for young people to go and few resources to control it."

Apparently Swindon has the second-lowest crime rate in England. Director of the Victims of Crime Trust, Mr Norman Brennan, a serving police officer with 26 years service, said: "When a judge feels scared to walk the streets, it should tell us there are problems. The sad reality is, it is down to the judges and magistrates, who give lenient sentences to people who commit very serious crimes, that these serious fear factors have arisen."

JUDGE NICHOLAS COLEMAN
NORWICH CROWN COURT

A Crown Court Judge has caused outrage by allowing a paedophile to return to arcades where he preyed on young girls. After admitting numerous sex offences, including the abduction of an eight-year-old girl, Eric Long, 50, was jailed for five years by Judge Nicholas Coleman at Norwich Crown Court in October 2004. He was ordered to be placed on the sex offenders register for life. He was also banned from visiting all amusement arcades in the UK for a total of 15 years.

However, for reasons known only to himself, the judge, in his wisdom, added a clause which allows Long to return to the arcades if accompanied by another adult. However the children's charity *Kidscape* was quick to point out that the 'other adult' could himself be a paedophile, and therefore the judge's ruling was potentially tragic and absurd. Their spokesman, Michelle Elliott, was reported as saying: "The judge should have banned this man from amusement aracades for life. The judge is assuming the other adult is a responsible person, but he could also be a paedophile. It is an absurd ruling that allows him to prey on other children. I am totally baffled by this."

In fact the CPS had called for Long to be banned for life from visiting amusement arcades. Long, from Great Yarmouth, admitted gross indecency, possessing indecent photos and abducting a child. The court had heard how Long had targeted young girls on the seafront of a Norfolk coastal resort, took them to amusement arcades and spent money on them there, to ingratiate himself with them. Two girls, both under 10 years of age, had been persuaded to pose indecently for him. Long appeared naked in the photographs, with the girls. Later, fresh victims came forward and raised the alarm to police.

During sentencing, Judge Coleman said to Long: "You are a man with a serious perversion, trawling the seaside resort of Yarmouth looking for likely children who would pander to your sexual deviancy. These were planned tactics and considerable thought had gone into this. You targeted a particular age group. You have little or no insight as to the consequences of your conduct to those young people. Goodness knows what the long-term effect will be." Katherine Moore, defending, told the judge that Long's wife was divorcing him. She said that Long, who has never been to prison before, in spite of his previous conviction in 1991 for indecently assaulting a girl under 14, had 'lost everything'. "He appreciates now that something must be done to reduce the risk he accepts he now poses."

UPDATE: There is a sequel to this case, which you may find refreshing, as the Judge made a 'u turn', after apparently becoming aware of his mistake, through a major article in a national newspaper. You will appreciate that it is almost unknown for a Judge to admit to having made a mistake. Apparently Judge Coleman had the paedophile Eric Long brought back from prison to court. He said to him: "Following the sentencing of you, my attention was drawn to a newspaper report. It is necessary to review the order (I made against you) because of concerns expressed about its terms. It is clear it is felt the restriction is not clear enough. On reflection, I agree. I note that you do not disagree that the order should be amended to exclude you from any amusement arcade, whether or not accompanied, for 15 years. I did not impose the order for you to be accompanied by another paedophile. Quite the opposite, the court has a duty to protect the public." He therefore officially varied the order against Long accordingly. Afterwards, Michelle Elliott, director of children's charity Kidscape, was re-interviewed after being advised of the judge's revised sentencing. This time, she is reported as saying: "Thank goodness common sense has prevailed. I commend the judge for having the decency to look at the situation again, see a mistake had been made, and change it.

Good for him. Congratulations to the Daily Express for bringing the concerns people had to the attention of the Judge. This action has probably saved a lot of children." The judge was also congratulated later by legal experts. They declared that he had listened to informed public opinion and it was a great credit to him. I'm sure that quite a few readers will consider that he did the right thing too.

JUDGE ANDREW HAMILTON
DERBY CROWN COURT

At Derby Crown Court on 25th October 2004, Judge Andrew Hamilton restored many peoples' faith in the British Criminal Justice System in a landmark ruling against a persistent burglar, shot by the homeowner during his third raid on the farm premises. Judge Hamilton ruled that burglary victim Kenneth Faulkner, 73, 'could not be criticised' for discharging a shotgun at serial criminal John Rae. The judge went on to say that it was a 'pity' that the CPS had even wasted time contemplating the prosecution of the farmer. Mr Faulkner had been arrested by the police but then released without charge. The judge, speaking of the burglary victim, Mr Faulkner, told the court: "Nobody could criticise that man. He was defending his property. For him it has been a most harassing and terrible incident."

The case mirrors that of farmer Tony Martin, well publicised and documented, who shot dead a teenaged burglar, who was part of a gang of three burglars he found on his property during the hours of darkness. Under a totally different judge at another court, Mr Martin was originally found guilty of murder by a jury, and jailed for life. However on appeal, Lord Chief Justice Woolf and other judges reduced the charge to manslaughter and reduced the sentence from life imprisonment to five years. At the time, public outcry was made nationally, homeowners having clung to the belief, held for very many years, that 'an Englishman's home is his castle'.

After Judge Hamilton's findings in the Derby Crown Court case, Malcolm Starr, spokesman for farmer Tony Martin was quoted as saying: " It sounds like this particular judge is in tune with 99 per cent of public opinion. We have been far too lenient on the burglar and the thug that intimidates law-abiding people. It's about time the tables were turned on these people and they were locked up for longer periods. The Government and the opposition parties need to realise that the majority of the public think law and order is the biggest single issue. We need to be tough and afford people the right to protect their properties." Judge Hamilton jailed Rae, 22, for seven years for the farm burglary and dozens of other offences, branding him 'an absolute menace'. Rae had suffered shotgun pellet wounds to the leg during the farm burglary. Rae had revisited the farm for the third time in roughly as many weeks, to steal from it. On the first occasion, Rae had been accompanied by two other burglars. Five shotguns, a longbow, arrows, together with a crossbow and bolts, were also stolen, after they forced open a secure, police-approved gun cabinet at the farm. During sentencing, the learned judge had even more to say to the court about career criminal Rae: "Mr Faulkner had lost his wife, was 73 years of age and lived alone on an isolated property. He believed he was being targeted and he was entirely right. He wrongly believed the original burglars had come back armed with those guns that had been stolen. Very sensibly he took out his shotgun. Nobody could criticise him for what he did. He discharged the firearm when he saw you and a pellet lodged in your leg." After the case, a relative of burglar Rae, whose heart, unlike the Trial Judge's, was not in the right place, said the case sent out the wrong message: "John could have been killed. I think what happened was attempted murder. You can't shoot somebody and then not be charged. Are they saying we can all shoot burglars?"

MRS ZINNIA WATSON
FORMER MAGISTRATE IN WILTSHIRE

The following article from the press was headlined in bold as follows:

JP QUITS BECAUSE SHE CAN'T SEND BURGLARS TO JAIL

It's very important for me that you should hear this story 'straight from the horse's mouth' so to speak, so I'll report it verbatim from its origin.

"A Magistrate has retired early because she is unable to accept new guidelines ordering JPs (Justices of the Peace, viz: Magistrates) to go soft on crime. Zinnia Watson says the last straw was a ruling from Law Chief Lord Faulkener, insisting that house burglars should go to prison only in extreme cases. She branded the system in some counties as 'fairly shambolic' and added: "Sentences are being dumbed down and the public is not being well served." Mrs Watson, a Magistrate for nearly 20 years in Wiltshire, said: "Lord Faulkener has just told us that people who commit house burglary should not go to prison except in extreme circumstances. Burglary was always thought serious enough for the burglar to go to prison, not to be rehabilitated, but because the public deserve to be protected. It is a crime that makes people feel totally unsafe. People have heart attacks. The victim really suffers because they don't feel safe in their homes any more. I couldn't possibly sit there and be lenient with somebody who has just destroyed somebody else's lifestyle. But our hands are tied by the guidelines. There's nothing we can do about it." Mrs Watson said that political correctness and the increasing emphasis on individual (criminals') rights was also making the system unworkable. "It isn't

Lord Faulkener who has dumbed down sentences. It started with Lord Irvine and the move towards Europe. We are taking a lot of laws that are absolutely sound to ridiculous proportions" she said. She spent most of her career in Salisbury, but more recently sat in Chippenham and Devizes. She added: "People used to be Magistrates because they knew their towns really well. Now benches are joined together, I sit in places where I don't automatically know the deprived areas. Crime is increasing because family life has broken down in certain sections of society. The children feel unwanted and the teenagers get into the drugs scene. There is no point in putting people like that in prison. We should have residential rehabilitation centres." She is distrustful of crime statistics which suggest certain offences are being reduced. "The idea of Police warnings (Official Cautions) was to reduce the number of cases that came through the Courts, but some counties are giving far more warnings than was first envisaged," she said.

Mrs Watson obviously speaks from experience and must have had thousands of people appearing before her in Court. How sad that, having given such good (voluntary) service in all that time, she is forced to leave the Bench prematurely, as she feels her hands and those of her colleagues on the bench, have been tied. (I wonder if you are now wondering whether Lord Faulkener, Lord Woolf and Lord Irvine have ever experienced the traumas of a burglary?)

ANONYMOUS CHAIRMAN
OF BENCH OF MAGISTRATES

On 1st November 2004, an anonymous chairman of a bench of magistrates, (Name and Address supplied), wrote the following letter to the *Daily Express* newspaper, and had it published:

"As a chairman of magistrates, I have received full training in the application of anti-social behaviour orders (ASBOs), and know they have a genuine potential to tackle persistent offending. They are already doomed to fail, however.

At the time of my training, we were told that two out of three people who breached the orders had been imprisoned. But this figure is, I believe, already failing. It is this very basic weakness that must be addressed. Certainty must be built in. All those who breach an ASBO must be jailed, if the system is to work. The same weaknesses appear in the excellent Community Penalty programmes, where those in breach must learn to expect custody, instead of magistrates being bullied from on high, to jail only in the most extreme circumstances.

Getting tough would actually reduce the prison population in the longer term."

MR DEREK LEGGETTER
FORMER MAGISTRATES COURT CHAIRMAN

During the last quarter of 2004, the *Daily Express* newspaper launched a 'crusade' to help force through fresh legislation which would allow Magistrates and Crown Courts to hand out tougher sentences. A Mr Derek Leggetter suggested there should be a separate 'special roads constabulary', quite separate from the various Police Forces. Furthermore, he suggests that the Crown Prosecution Service should be disbarred from having anything whatever to do with any cases involving car crimes etc.

Under his proposed scheme, he feels that victims of road crimes would receive a better deal in court. He speaks with some authority, as he sat on the Bench in a North London Magistrates Court for 24 years. He is now running the only road law training course for magistrates in the whole of the United Kingdom. Year-on-year, approx 3,500 members of the public are killed on our roads, by drivers. His research appears to indicate that most of the drivers responsible for these tragic deaths, escape with fines and/or a few penalty points. Currently across the UK, such crimes are invariably investigated by police officers employed in the Traffic Departments of the various police forces. The *Daily Express* crusade has called for a new offence of 'death by driving', and Mr Leggetter apparently supports this. He stated in an interview: "An entirely separate police force is essential, because the existing ones clearly can't cope with a system that doesn't work. We need specially trained officers who will not be wrenched away from traffic, if there is a manpower shortage elsewhere, which is what is happening now. We must then dump the CPS, which has been an absolute disaster when it comes to road crime prosecutions. Magistrates will tell you that day in, day out, they see the CPS solicitor come into court with little or no knowledge of traffic issues. But the guy defending is an expert, because that's what he's paid to do. The defender simply makes mincemeat out of the prosecutor." (This never used to happen when police prosecuted most of their own cases, in pre-Crown Prosecution Service times, as police officers, particularly in the various traffic departments, had an excellent working knowledge of past and current traffic legislation). Mr Leggetter went on to state that magistrates throughout the UK felt frustrated that their hands were relatively tied, in that they cannot issue tougher sentences. He added: " You feel like your hands are virtually tied. If a person comes into court and pleads guilty, you have to cut their sentence by a third. Then any financial punishment has to be set by what they claim they earn. If you don't go along with it, they'll simply appeal and win the day. That shouldn't be happening. Sometimes I would say to a family, sitting at the back of the court, 'we know your feelings and you're not going to be happy with the sentence we give out today. You're not going to get the penalty you want but our hands are tied'. That's the point where the clerk of the court would turn to me and tell me off, saying, 'You can't say that', but I'd say it anyway. Magistrates haven't spoken about this nearly enough, because we've always had to be guarded.

At the moment, the Government isn't listening, so we just have to keep screaming at them. We've got to get rid of trying to equate the penalty for road crime, with the penalty for ordinary crime. If someone gets three years for road crime they complain and say: 'I wouldn't have got that for a burglary'. But the two are entirely separate." He went on to say that the Driving Standards Agency figures suggested police were failing to keep tabs on probably the most dangerous class of driver, those who are newly qualified, young and likely to be quickly banned.

In the mid-90's, new legislation was introduced so that drivers accumulating six points on their licence within 2 years of passing their driving tests, would have their driving licences revoked. The most recent figures for the period November 2003 to July 2004 reveal that as few as half of drivers banned from driving by the courts, have applied for re-tests. Last July the totals were 1,443 revoked, 722 re-applied. Does this mean that all of those other people are driving around without licences? It's a fair assumption that quite a few are. The situation is appalling and the system is obviously failing us."

MR RECORDER STEVENSON
READING CROWN COURT

A judge ordered a wallet thief to be remanded in custody until he is sentenced, in a get-tough stance to protect the public, in February 2004 at Reading Crown Court.

Mark Edwards, 18, had been on unconditional bail since robbing Mark Simms in October 2003. But he was remanded in custody after Mr Recorder Stevenson, QC, learned it happened less than a month after he was given a community service order for another mugging. Turning aside protests from defence barrister Jonathan Woodcock, Mr Stevenson said: "Protection of the public is paramount". Edwards had admitted robbing Mr Simms, stealing a mobile phone from Ben Ashlin and assaulting him, causing him actual bodily harm on 3rd October 2003. He had denied a charge of inflicting grievous bodily harm on Mr Simms and the charge was left to lie on file. Mr Simms was badly injured when he was struck by a piece of concrete, but Edwards, of Hornbeam Drive, Lower Earley, said it was someone else. Edwards's barrister, Mr Woodcock, asked the judge to order a pre-sentence report, but he ordered Edwards to be remanded in custody instead. Edwards had been sentenced to community punishment in September 2003, for a robbery, and Mr Recorder Stevenson, QC, said: "My anxiety is that if he is granted bail until he is sentenced on May 10th, he is likely to commit further offences. Mr Woodcock answered: "Nothing has changed. Nothing makes him more dangerous than at 10.30am this morning. There is not the justification." But Mr Stevenson disagreed and asked court officials to attempt to have Judge Josh Lait, who dealt with the teenager in September, to sentence him again. He said: "Having been sentenced on September 7th, this robbery and the other offences were committed within the month."

Persistent criminal Mark Edwards, did not have far to go, HMYOI and Remand Centre, Reading, virtually backs onto the Reading Crown Court. Reading Jail was the prison where Oscar Wilde, imprisoned for homosexuality, famously wrote his poem *The Ballad of Reading Jail*. It might well do Mark Edwards some good to read it, though I doubt it.

MRS ADELINE SMITH
RECENTLY-RESIGNED MAGISTRATE
FORMERLY OF COALVILLE MAGISTRATES COURT

A magistrate has been forced to quit after demanding that all burglars should serve at least six months in jail. Her treatment caused outrage among campaigners, who branded the move 'a licence for burglars to continue reoffending'.

Adeline Smith spoke out in her local newspaper after her home was targeted by raiders. But the unrepentant veteran JP admitted that her job of 26 years was over when defence lawyers said their clients accused of burglary might not receive a fair trial if she sat on the bench. Her views were backed by the director of the *Victims Of Crime Trust*, Norman Brennan, who said: "Time and time again burglars get away with community service, which gives them a licence to continue. This magistrate clearly understands, like all victims, the devastation this type of crime causes. It's sad her views have cost her her job."

Mrs Smith was suspended just days after Tony Blair turned his back on home owners by refusing to give them greater rights to fight back against burglars. Her outspoken words cost her a seat on the Coalville bench in Leicestershire, when she received a letter suspending her from service following a complaint from defence solicitors to the court clerk. Labour councillor Mrs Smith, 68, said yesterday: "I am disgusted at the way I have been treated, as all I did was speak my mind. "I got a letter telling me not to sit until the issue was resolved. I was put in a position where I had no option but to resign. I have raised the same subject many times at conferences. Anyone who breaks into a person's property should face a minimum fixed term in jail. "I don't think justice is done when a burglar is not sent to prison. At the moment they can be let off with probation or some other non-custodial sentence."

Nick Watson, director of legal services to the Lord Chancellor's Advisory Committee for Leicestershire, said he was told solicitors defending clients charged with burglary had complained they 'might not get a fair trial' before her. A spokesman for the Magistrates Association yesterday insisted appropriate steps were taken after Mrs Smith 'stepped out of line'. He said: "It is important that justice is seen to be done. As a magistrate, you take a judicial oath to treat everyone fairly and equally. If you go public and say something like that then it can make things difficult and jeopardise the perception that justice is being done. This is a very difficult case, and one has sympathy in all directions. But you have to go back to the basics of that oath every magistrate takes."

Mrs Smith, a member of the Leicester Police Authority, who lives in Coalville, insisted she was left with no choice but to resign. She said: "I am a free agent and stand by what I said. Burglary is a terrible crime. I wasn't willing to apologise, and that's why I had to resign. I am ending my membership with the Magistrates Association. I don't want to lose the right to say what I believe is right for the sake of an unpaid job.

"You only have to see these burglars who reoffend time and again to know they have nothing but utter contempt for the law."

In a U-turn which defied overwhelming public opinion, the Prime Minister refused to back Tory proposals to give people stronger powers to use physical force to protect their homes and families. Instead they will be given leaflets on how far they are allowed to go under current legislation, despite a pledge weeks earlier that householders would be allowed to use maximum force against violent intruders.

North-West Leicestershire Labour MP David Taylor, himself a former Coalville JP, said he was appalled that Mrs Smith felt she had been forced out. He said: "When I was sitting as a magistrate I always found Adoline a very experienced, scrupulously fair, knowledgeable and considerate colleague. Any suggestion to the contrary, from whatever source, is grossly unfair and wholly unacceptable. I am dismayed that she felt it necessary to resign."

Mrs Smith's bungalow was raided while she and her husband Harry were away on a two-week cruise around the Canary Islands to celebrate their golden wedding anniversary. The burglars fled with thousands of pounds worth of goods. Mrs Smith added: "When I think intruders have been in my home it makes me feel ill. My view about burglars has always been the same, it's not just because I've been burgled. I've always felt it's a violation of people's homes." Last year 402,000 households were burgled, meaning that one in every 50 homes is broken into each year.

MRS ADELINE SMITH
RECENTLY-RESIGNED MAGISTRATE
FORMERLY OF COALVILLE MAGISTRATES COURT

Here is a separate report about the voluntary resignation of Mrs Adeline Smith, worth reporting as it tends to ram home the message "Offenders' rights come first in the UK".

A magistrate forced to quit after insisting that all burglars should be jailed for at least six months branded British justice 'a lie'. "It's not fair to fool the public, telling them that Joe Bloggs got six months when he will be out in three," said Adeline Smith. "Every time a magistrate sits in court and passes sentence it's a lie. We very rarely pass a maximum sentence, because it's immediately cut in half." Her earlier outspoken comments in a local newspaper which led to her resignation as a JP, stirred a huge groundswell of public support. A total of 98 per cent of readers who voted in a Daily Express telephone poll said they agreed with Mrs Smith's call for tougher sentencing policies. The 68-year-old magistrate, who spoke out after she was targeted by burglars, also revealed that she has been overwhelmed with phone calls and letters from supporters, including magistrates and police officers. She said yesterday that the courts were bamboozling the public with their sentencing system, because the criminals invariably served only up to half of the time for which they had been jailed. She said: "Punishment has gone out of the window. Punishment and prison should be a deterrent, but they are not any more. Sentences are too lenient. It's time we brought proper sentences back."

Mrs Smith, who sat on the bench in Coalville, Leicestershire for 26 years, was suspended after defence lawyers claimed that their clients would not be dealt with fairly if they came before her in court. Statistics suggest that nationally one fifth of all burglary victims have been targeted more than once, and around one in eight had been burgled twice before. One couple who had been burgled twice, bar manager Chris Ryder, 33, and his partner Georgina Sheldon, 29, an office manager, supported Mrs Smith's stance. Chris said they lost £300 in cash and a Sony PlayStation during the first raid, and a crystal bowl full of expensive jewellery during the second. Since then, thieves have tried to break into their ground-floor, three-bedroom luxury apartment in Birmingham on two further occasions. Chris said: "I definitely support the idea of a convicted burglar being given a mandatory six-month sentence, because having your home broken into is a complete violation." The Magistrates Association implied a degree of support for Mrs Smith's views, although it made it clear in a statement issued that it did not comment on individual cases. But it said: "Charges of burglary range from minor opportunistic offences such as taking a pint of milk through an open window to a house being trashed, leading to distress and alarm for the victim." More serious burglaries are dealt with in the Crown Court. The national sentencing guidelines for magistrates courts indicate that magistrates' powers (a maximum six-month sentence) may not be sufficient even in the case of a first-time offender."

Mrs Smith, who resigned in disgust at the Lord Chancellor's Department's handling of her case, fuelled the controversy even more by contrasting the plight of offenders and their victims. She said: "When I read about high-quality prisons being built I get angry, because how many *pensioners* live in luxury of that sort? And if those pensioners had been burgled then they have already been made a prisoner in their own, less luxurious house anyway. Judges were recently asked to consider how full our jails are before passing sentence, but if the jails are full then we should double up in the cells.

"The only things that should be available to inmates are rehabilitation, education and counselling, the things that will help stop them being criminals. "They don't need TVs, Gameboys and the like, just a bare cell and some books. We need to stop spending more on the guilty than the innocent." Mrs Smith was suspended days after Tony Blair turned his back on home owners by refusing to give them greater rights to fight back against burglars. She added: "All this talk of 'reasonable force' is just a load of nonsense. You can't stop and ask a burglar whether they are going to hit you or just swear at you. If you're in your own home then you just have to face them." Mrs Smith's bungalow was targeted while she and her husband Harry were on a two-week cruise around the Canary Islands celebrating their golden wedding. They lost thousands of pounds worth of goods.

The Royal Courts of Justice sign

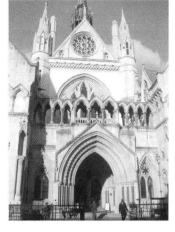

The Royal Courts of Justice Main entrance,Strand

Premier Custody Group cellular vehicle enters The Royal Courts of Justice with prisoner(s) for Appeal

Old Bailey, London EC4 street sign

Main entrance - Central Criminal Court Old Bailey

Defend the poor etc sign above Central Criminal Court - Old Bailey

COUNT 22

IMPAIRED JUDGEMENTS

England's 'soft touch' courts should be locking up far more crooks, a shocking new report claims. We have the most lenient criminal justice system in the western world, says the report by Civitas. The influential think-tank's deputy director, Robert Whelan, blasted the 'criminal justice elite' for treating offenders like clients, and running the courts for their benefit. He said: "The way the criminal justice system is currently run, is an incitement to the professional criminal to continue his life of crime. We need to build more prisons so that criminals know that the system is serious about dealing with them. The problem is not that we're sending too many people to prison, but that we're not sending people to prison soon enough."

Despite some concern about overcrowded jails, the report reveals that, in comparison to the number of crimes committed, our judges send fewer offenders to prison than other EU countries. The Tory's new Crime Policy, launched in mid-August 2004, pledges to build more prisons, in direct contrast to the policies of Tony Blair. Shadow Home Secretary David Davis said: "This report demonstrates all too clearly why we need more prison places to protect the public, something that can't be done at the moment because the prisons are full under this Government. The simple truth is that prison works. One of the reasons we have 800,000 more crimes today than in 1997 is because we have not been tough enough on criminals."

When it comes to tackling crime, the Government, the courts and the entire criminal justice system have quite simply got it wrong, according to Robert Whelan. The Deputy Director of influential think tank Civitas insists: "People say prison isn't the answer, but it depends what the question is. Our problem is not too many people in prison, but too much crime. Do prisons make bad people into good people? No, they don't. But neither does anything else. The fact is that the alternatives to prison really don't work, and at least prison takes them out of society for a while so they are not committing crime." Just days after the Government and the Tories both launched new crime policies, a new report by Civitas reveals that despite all the tough talking from both sides, the system is failing, by allowing criminals to walk free. Most criminals do not believe they will get caught, let alone punished. And with conviction rates for most crimes down to pitifully low levels, they are quite right. Criminologists estimate a tiny minority of just 100,000 people are committing more than half the country's crimes. Their names and faces are well known to the police and the courts, yet most are left to walk the streets with impunity. But since we already have one of the highest prison populations in the western world, why is our country still plagued by rising crime? What is going wrong? The Civitas report, *Crime and Civil Society*, reveals the high prison population is not a result of over-zealous sentencing, but is because our crime rate is much higher than in comparable countries. We simply have more criminals to punish. And far from being too harsh, our judges and magistrates actually jail fewer criminals than their counterparts in any other Western country. Statistics for 17 industrialised countries in Europe and around the world in the year 2000, showed an average of 35.2 crimes committed per each 100 of the population.

In England and Wales, there were an amazing 54.5 crimes for every 100 people. In 2000, the average number of prisoners per 100,000 of the population across the whole of the EU was 87. But in England and Wales, that figure was 124. Across the EU there were 17.7 prisoners for every 1,000 recorded crimes, but in England and Wales, that figure was the far lower 12.7, clear proof that we actually imprison far fewer criminals than our neighbours, not more. Yet according to the International Crime Victims' Survey of the 17 nations, we suffer more crime per head than any other country, we have the worst record for very serious offences and we have the second highest rate for crimes such as robbery, sexual assaults and violence. We expect prison to keep bad people out of circulation so they are not ruining other, law-abiding people's lives. Unfortunately, the people who run the criminal justice system seem to be living on another planet where they think they are running a system for the benefit of the criminal.

The criminal has become the client, but the client ought to be the law-abiding citizen. *An elite group within the criminal justice system are pursuing their own agenda, that is not supported by the majority of ordinary people in this country.* By the time most people actually get sent to prison, they have got a list of charges as long as their arms, and that's just the offences they've been caught for. They should be in prison much quicker. If people find that there is no immediate punishment for their crimes, that they can get away with things, then they will. Ordinary people want criminals to be dealt with firmly by the police and the courts, and they are not getting that at the moment. A study of the US 'get tough' crime policy, found that a 65 per cent rise in the number of burglars jailed between 1981 and 1994 was coupled with a 50 per cent fall in burglaries. In England and Wales over the same period, however, with a more 'softly, softly' approach of more cautions and community sentences in force, the number of burglars in jail fell 72 per cent. And the number of burglaries went up 50 per cent.   And Civitas blames the surge in crime on successive governments' lighter sentencing policies, and the belief that prison only turns criminals into worse offenders. This policy has been accompanied by numerous experiments to find ways of cutting habitual offending.

But Nadia Martin, co-author of the 200 page Civitas report, set to be published in the Autumn, said: " Some people say that if you put people in prison they will become worse criminals, but there's no factual evidence for that at all. The truth is that we are not very good at reforming and rehabilitating criminals, not only in Britain, but worldwide. And we need to keep known offenders from reoffending." There is wide evidence that very little can be done in terms of rehabilitation, to convince repeat offenders to end their life of crime. However, programmes to combat drug addiction, which affects the majority of prisoners, and the teaching of literacy and other skills, such as a trade or vocational qualification, can enable many prisoners to go on to find jobs after leaving a jail. Ms Martin explains: "There is very little evidence that rehabilitation programmes have very much effect at all, and some have a worse effect than prison. Some people are very compassionate about offenders. They want to give them more chances. They say that it's not their fault, they come from single-parent homes, that it's society's fault they haven't been given opportunities. But every individual at every moment has responsibility for their own actions." She believes the problem is not that offenders do not get the opportunity to go straight, but that they are given too many opportunities. "Criminals are fined or face community sentencing instead of prison, but there is very little enforcement of fines in this country, partly because the court system is so completely overwhelmed."

The report also slams the early release programme, which sees most offenders complete only half of their sentence. As MS Martin says: " We do not think that people should be released after only half their term. If they were meant to only serve two years, then they would have been sentenced to two years." Indeed, the failure to enforce punishments has made them laughable to many criminals, in 2000-2001 only 63 per cent of fines were actually collected. And ASBOs only work when criminal youths know they will face the wrath of the prison system if they breach them. The report concludes that offenders should face stiff jail terms for their third offences, arguing that "after giving every opportunity for change, an effective system must be willing to punish individuals who continue to commit crimes."

Shadow Home Secretary David Davis MP said: "The simple truth is that prison works. And it works by taking hardened criminals out of circulation. Criminals need to know that if they commit a crime, then they will be caught, and if they are caught, they will be punished, and for serious crimes, that punishment will mean a prison sentence."

(**Author's note:** *Very inspiring words from a budding Home Secretary in the making! But how come during 18 years of Tory rule, immediately before the Blair Government took office, with Michael Howard as their Home Secretary, not much was done to contain career criminals either?*)

"The smile on Nicholas van Hoogstraten's face outside the High Court last week should have sent a shiver of horror through anyone who cares about Britain's judicial process. The slum landlord tycoon, who terrorised anyone who got in his way, had just been cleared on appeal of the manslaughter of a business associate, Mohammed Raja. The Appeal Court ruled that the judge at the original trial, Mr Justice Newman, had failed to direct the jury properly in his summing up. Thus a man with a sickening track record of violence and a callous contempt for the law, was freed and another high-profile conviction had crumbled, thanks to judicial error. Yet, according to the Lord Chancellor, who is responsible for judicial standards: "England and Wales are well-served by judges of the highest calibre." Can he be right? Well the Lord Chancellor cannot possibly know, because, as he admitted to me a few days ago, he doesn't actually check. But I did, for a Channel 4 documentary to be shown later.

I analysed 19,000 court transcripts and logged every recorded judicial error made by the 600 crown court judges, and corrected at the Court of Appeal. I have uncovered the judges whose performance on the bench is undermining confidence in the system of justice and I have spoken to some of the people whose lives have been damaged by judges who keep getting it wrong.

Take the case of a woman in her mid-thirties whom I will call Mary.

From the age of eight, her father would regularly beat her and indecently assault her. It took Mary 25 years to find the strength to go to the police. Her father pleaded guilty at Nottingham Crown Court and it was left to His Honour Judge Richard Benson to decide sentence. Unbelievably, he ordered that the child-abuser should be given a conditional discharge. He walked free, his name not even on the Sex Offenders' Register. The Attorney General intervened in Mary's case and three Appeal Court judges ordered the abuser's immediate arrest and imprisoned him for 18 months.

GUILTY! From left, judges Gabriel Hutton, David Owen, Richard Benson and Peter Fox

That day in the Royal Courts of Justice, Mary sat through the case before hers, another appeal over a child-abuse case, a man who raped his stepdaughter more than a hundred times, but had been handed a sentence of less than four years. The Court of Appeal accepted the judge had been misinformed that the rapist had surrendered voluntarily. However they increased the jail term to ten years. The name of the judge responsible? His Honour Judge Richard Benson. My research uncovered two more child abuse cases in which the Appeal Court stepped in to increase Judge Benson's lenient sentences. Four child abusers, Four soft sentences.

And his extraordinary leniency didn't end there. *I found 37 cases in which the Court of Appeal has corrected Judge Benson's mistakes*. Richard Benson, 60, has been a circuit judge for ten years, earning £110,000 a year. How then does he defend his record as a member of the judiciary? "I am not a public servant!" boomed his voice down the telephone. Judge Benson had called me, horrified at my suggestion that he should be accountable for his mistakes. His argument, like the Lord Chancellor's, is that the judiciary's independence would be threatened if any form of professional appraisal were introduced. "I would always be looking over my shoulder." he said. Well, yes he would. Just as teachers, doctors and police officers have to 'look over their shoulders' as part of their accountability to society. It seems extraordinary, in an age when the Government has no qualms about naming and shaming poor performers in other public services, that the judiciary should be exempt. Once they get their backsides on the bench, judges have a job for life, no matter how professionally incompetent or unjust they might be. Only one judge has ever been sacked, he'd been convicted of smuggling whisky and cigarettes.

This is not to say that I believe our judiciary is in crisis. In fact, if the Lord Chancellor cared to look, he would find that most serving Crown Court judges have seen their actions overturned on appeal just three times or less in the past seven years. Being appealed is not, in itself, an indicator of incompetence. Indeed, it is often argued that the best judges will be successfully appealed from time to time. But there are a few dozen judges whose regular appearances at the Court of Appeal should be setting the alarm bells ringing in the Lord Chancellor's office.

They don't ring because there are no bells. So he doesn't know the name of the judge who freed a heroin dealer and wrongly jailed a frail woman of 76, *just two of 37 cases involving Judge Gabriel Hutton from Gloucestershire in which the Court of Appeal has intervened. He doesn't know the identity of another judge, who himself sits at the Appeal Court, but has seen his own decisions overturned at least 38 times, His Honour Judge Peter Fox, Recorder of Middlesbrough. And he doesn't know which serving judge has been successfully appealed more than any other, 56 times and counting. The man in question is His Honour Judge David Owen of Manchester*. He has a habit of over sentencing, more than 50 of his prison terms have been reduced on appeal, which does nothing for consistency in sentencing or the deliverance of fair justice.

Transcripts of the Appeal Court hearings give a sense of exasperation with Judge Owen. In just one appeal, his handling of a case is described as 'inadequate', 'inappropriate', 'dangerous', 'irrelevant', 'positively misleading', 'inaccurate' and 'incomplete'. The Lord Chancellor's answer is that if the Court of Appeal 'concludes that there is any reason for wider concern', the Presiding Judge of the Circuit on which the judge sits is informed. It is then up to him or her 'to take appropriate action, whether by way of advice or guidance'. So the system deals only with individual errors, no one stands back and looks at the bigger picture. It protects judges who make repeated mistakes, and accountability amounts to a quiet word over a glass of claret. Calls for some form of accountability are not new.

In 1993 a Royal Commision recommended 'a formal system of performance appraisal'. In 2001, Lord Justice Auld in his report on the criminal court system, said appraisal 'would be of considerable benefit…to bolster public confidence in their professionalism and competence'. Once again, the Government has dismissed the idea out of hand, which is a great pity because the current constitutional reforms offer a golden opportunity. The Lord Chancellor is proposing a new 'independent' committee to appoint judges. He says it would hire judges free from political or other interference. Well, if they can hire them without undermining judicial independence, why, if necessary, can't they fire them too? Perhaps then we would not be confronted with images such as the malign grin that spread across Hoogstraten's face as he climbed into a taxi to freedom outside the High Court last week."

Mark Easton, Home Affairs Editor, Channel 4 News

"I have commented before that, while most judges have had the benefit of an expensive education, many seem to have been missing when common sense was handed out.

What else could possibly account for Judge Michael Roach's decision to allow Michael Barrett, who had sex with a girl of 12, to walk free with only a Conditional Discharge? So serious is the offence that, under laws which came into force in May 2004, sex with a child under 13 is automatically classified as rape, with a maximum penalty of life in prison, and a recommended minimum sentence of eight years. It is true that Barrett committed the offences last year and, since the law is not retrospective, he was charged with the less serious offence of unlawful sexual intercourse. But there is a big difference between a minimum eight-year prison sentence and a conditional discharge. Little girls are born with the ability to flirt and twist men around their little fingers. They start with their fathers and go on from there. It is also true that girls as young as seven enjoy using make-up, and even dressing in a provocative manner. That doesn't alter the fact that every man knows it is a criminal offence to have intercourse with a young girl under the age of consent. This makes it difficult to understand Judge Roach's ruling that the girl was a 'willing participant'.

Her willingness doesn't come into it. However willing, or even eager, she was, Barrett knew having sex with her was against the law. In fact, since on two occasions Barrett stayed with her family and on both occasions she went into his room and consented to sexual intercourse, surely questions could be asked about her parents' responsibility for their 12-year-old daughter? Professor Liz Kelly, of the Child and Women Abuse Studies Unit at London Metropolitan University thinks the sentence sent out a totally wrong message. She said: "This is basically saying that the age of consent doesn't matter.

All adults know they shouldn't be having sex with a 12-year-old. It doesn't matter what the child does, the responsibility is with the adult." After the ruling Barrett said he thought he had been lucky. I think he was considerably more than lucky. The children's charity Kidscape, described the judge's decision as appalling, and the NSPCC said the sentence was lenient. When are we going to widen the background from which our judges are recruited? Having fewer expensively educated, but often elitist and out-of-touch judges, and appointing many more with the highest legal qualifications, together with a great deal more down-to-earth common sense, would do much to improve the standards of our judiciary."

Jimmy Young, Veteran BBC broadcaster and newspaper columnist

"We report today on the dreadful case of Daniel Blackett, a 36-year-old father of two who was gunned down outside his own house. It follows the brutal murders of retired paediatrician Derek Robinson and his wife Jean in London, Marie Harding, a pensioner who was killed yards from her daughter's house near Brighton, and Geraldine Evans, a doctor's daughter from Lytham St Annes in Lancashire.

How does Lord Woolf, the Lord Chief Justice, react to this terrible spate of killings across the country? He announces that some murderers should serve a term of just seven years. It is little wonder that violent crime is soaring. Lord Woolf must not be allowed to get away with this. Murder is murder. What he is suggesting is nothing less than an attempt to undermine the sanctity of human life. What the people of this country want is a harder line on criminals, not something that is tantamount to a murderer's charter. Lord Woolf says they may be released sooner if they 'confess early' and show 'absolute candour'. Does this mean the hit man who lay in wait for Daniel Blackett, or the killer who slashed Marie Harding's throat, will spend just over half a decade in prison if they are quite open about what they have done? These proposals represent not only a monstrous miscarriage of justice but a risk of allowing dangerous people out into the community. They must be quashed right now."

Daily Express, Editorial, 20th September 2004

"Hundreds of years ago, referring to Thomas a Beckett, the Archbishop of Canterbury, Henry II asked: " Will no one rid me of this turbulent priest?" In the same way, Home Secretary David Blunkett probably wishes that someone would quietly and peacefully rid him of the well-meaning, but completely dotty and out-of-touch Lord Chief Justice, Lord Woolf. Lord Woolf is an outstanding example of a very well-educated man, occupying a position of enormous power and influence, who appears to have no common sense whatsoever. Last year he was widely dubbed 'the Burglar's Friend' when he advised judges not to jail first-time house-breakers.

Now he proposes that murderers who plead guilty at the first opportunity, should serve only a reduced sentence. This must sound encouraging to those thinking of committing their first murder. Knock off your nagging husband or wife, nip down to the local police station, if you can find one open, and own up.

Earlier this year Mr Blunkett brought in laws which say that a typical murderer should serve 15 years. Even that sounds lenient to those of us who remember that, when capital punishment for murder was reduced to life imprisonment, it was stressed, and we believed it, that it would mean exactly what it said. We certainly didn't think it would mean 15 years. Yet Lord Woolf and his colleagues, secure from crime in their ivory towers and remote from the real world, now want to see even that slap-on-the-wrist sentence reduced by a third. In Lord Woolf's view, murder – the most foul, serious and abhorrent of crimes, merits a prison sentence of only 10 years. And, if murderers behave themselves inside, they could possibly be out of jail in only seven years. That is totally unrealistic, unjust and an insult to decent, law-abiding citizens. No wonder Norman Brennan, Director of the Victims of Crime Trust, accused Lord Woolf of 'losing the plot at a time when murder is at its highest level since the Second World War'.

Those who speak up for murderers argue that long-term prison sentences are dehumanising, and that prisoners who serve more than 15 years are irreparably damaged by the experience. The overwhelming majority of people who, in the absence of the death penalty, would lock them up and throw away the key, rightly point out that the people they murdered were also dehumanised and irreparably damaged by the experience. Soft-hearted Lord Woolf has always maintained that custodial sentences are not the answer to crime. On the contrary, as Michael Howard says, prison works. When murderers, rapists and burglars are in prison, they can't be out and about, murdering, raping and burgling. The answer to Lord Woolf's complaint that our prisons are overcrowded is, as I've pointed out many times, simple, build more. Law-abiding citizens are fed up with, and frightened by the soft, limp-wristed, liberal establishment's attitude to crime. Lord Woolf is completely out of touch with public opinion. He should apologise and resign. Unfortunately we know that he will do neither."

Jimmy Young, Veteran BBC broadcaster and newspaper columnist

"Our investigation into violent crime makes shocking reading. (Please see introduction to 'Street Violence' chapter) Violent assault is on the rise all over Britain, not just in inner cities. Incredibly, the latest statistics reveal that there are now 16 killings a week. It is bitterly ironic that they come just a week after the Lord Chief Justice Lord Woolf, launched astonishing new proposals for lighter sentencing for murderers. If his scheme is adopted, convicted killers who admit their guilt could be free after seven years. This makes no sense and sends the wrong message to the criminal community.

Serious crime of all sorts is on the increase but, since this Government came to power, the number of murders has leapt by 14 per cent, to 853 in the past year. Criminologists blame the drugs epidemic for driving up the death toll. If this is the case, surely the answer is more police on the streets. Community officers have neither the skill nor experience to tackle violent criminals. Home Secretary David Blunkett must grasp the nettle, and put more traditional police officers back on the beat. As a society we should be moving towards zero tolerance of all crimes of violence, not greater leniency to perpetrators."

Daily Express, Editorial Comment, 27th September 2004

"Drunken drivers who kill deserve no mercy in court, so what can justify the lenient sentence given to Craig Smith who killed 18-year-old Amy Gonzales? Smith, who arguably might have been charged with manslaughter, was convicted only of death by dangerous driving and was jailed for six years. But Appeal Court Judges later ruled that, under 'established sentencing principles', Smith's original sentence was 'manifestly excessive', so they reduced it to five years, meaning he will be out in half that time. Do you think two-and-a-half years in jail is a just punishment for drunkenly slaughtering an innocent young woman? No, nor do I. And who bears the ultimate responsibility for the established sentencing principles that are soft on criminals? Our controversial Lord Chief Justice, Lord Woolf. Thank God he's retiring this year."

Jimmy Young, Broadcaster & Columnist, Sunday Express,
7th November 2004

"Judges in Manchester hand out more lenient sentences than any others in the country, according to official figures. The city tops the table in the number of cases where people have received punishments regarded as too soft by senior law chiefs. Figures from the Solicitor General show that during the last three years, 58 cases from the city's two crown courts, Crown Square and Minshull Street, were referred to the Attorney General's office because they were considered 'unduly lenient'. Of these, 24 subsequently went to the Court of Appeal, with 18 sentences being increased.

The next-highest was Bristol, which saw 48 cases sent for referral and 24 going to the Court of Appeal, resulting in 12 sentences increased. The Central Criminal Court in London saw 30 of its cases referred and 10 ending up before the Court of Appeal. In Liverpool, there were 17 cases referred to the Attorney General, with eight subsequently going on to the Court of Appeal. Minshull Street Crown Court handles about 3,000 trials and 500 committals for sentence a year, while Crown Square handles about 2,000 trials. Oldham West and Royton MP Michael Meacher said: "I find these figures very worrying, because I believe people in Greater Manchester have been outraged by some judicial decisions and want a system which will in future ensure fair justice is done. I believe a more robust policy is needed which will provide an opportunity to review, not only unduly lenient sentences, but the performances where the record clearly reveals a regularity of such referrals involving a particular judge.

"I would propose that an Independent Judicial Commission, which was responsible for the appointment of judges, should also have a remit to review where necessary, a judge's record in the light of public concerns and complaints from the relevant authorities."

A spokesman for the Department for Constitutional Affairs said: "One of the main reasons behind the recent establishment of the Sentencing Guidelines Council, chaired by the Lord Chief Justice, was to address the problem of inconsistency and to draw up a system of guidance for judges. The council will also monitor the extent to which its guidelines are applied.

"It is important to maintain the independence of the judiciary. It would be completely inappropriate for a disciplinary procedure to be applied to judges because their sentences attracted unfavourable press or Government attention, it would be wrong for the Government to monitor decisions made by individual judges.

"Where there are real concerns about a judge's performance, these are addressed by the senior judiciary. There are currently comprehensive arrangements in place to identify concerns about judges' performance, which are highlighted in judgements made by the Court of Appeal. "The senior judiciary pursues these directly with the post-holder."

Martin Dillon, Manchester News, 16th August 2004

THE LORD CHIEF JUSTICE
LORD WOOLF

England's most senior judge sparked a new political row by saying violent criminals should not automatically be sent to jail. Lord Chief Justice Woolf said some violent offenders should be given community penalties instead.

Two years ago Lord Woolf became embroiled in controversy by arguing that some burglars should be spared prison terms. But his latest comments contradict hard-line Home Secretary David Blunkett, who insists that jail is the only punishment for vicious criminals. The Home Office spokesman said: "We must protect the public from dangerous criminals." Britain's top judge has savaged Tony Blair over the failings of every aspect of the criminal justice system. He warns that decent, law-abiding people are being let down. Lord Woolf, the Lord Chief Justice, became the latest senior figure to lambaste the shortcomings of Mr Blair's Government, warning that the public had lost faith in British justice and Labour's law and order shambles. In a damning attack which also cast doubt on David Blunkett'stewardship of the Home Office, Lord Woolf said the public believed that every part of the criminal justice system was failing under Labour. "Unfortunately, it has to be accepted that, for many years now, the public have had little confidence in the ability of our criminal justice system to ensure that justice is done.

"Regrettably, each part of the system has appeared to be failing the public. The inescapable conclusion is that, unless there is a dramatic change in the way we deal with offenders, there is every likelihood of the position getting worse." In a cutting reference to Mr Blair's promise, made while he was shadow Home Secretary in 1992, to be 'tough on crime and tough on the causes of crime', Lord Woolf added, 'We are not being sufficiently tough on the causes of crime'. Lord Woolf said overcrowded prisons made it much harder for the penal system to effectively deal with and rehabilitate offenders. He warned of a 'huge gap' between planned capacity in the country's prisons and the forecast jail population increasing to up to 106,000 by 2010. And in a savage dig at Mr Blair and Mr Blunkett's apparent inability to take a strong lead, he said there had been "no shortage of reviews of the penal process." He went on: "Each report reveals a mind-blowing situation involving vast expenditure with little, if any, long-term improvement in the protection of the public. At any one time there are on average more than 10,000 serving sentences of 12 months or less. This is despite the fact that there is a uniform acceptance that sentences of this sort make little or no contribution to the reduction of crime. My primary concern in painting this sombre picture is not with the offenders who often find their regimes undermined by overcrowding, but with those who will be the victims of crime, because of our inability to tackle offending behaviour." He also appeared to question the performance of the Police and Crown Prosecution Service under Labour, by saying the proportion of criminals detected, brought to court and convicted was "regrettably low". Tory Shadow Home Secretary, David Davis weighed in with his own stinging rebuke. He said, "Labour's record on crime has concentrated on only one thing, headlines. The Home Secretary has to realise that action rather than words is what is needed in the criminal justice system."

On 20th September 2004 the national press was once again reporting that Lord Woolf, in his great wisdom, had introduced even more controversy into the perceived serious breakdown in law and order in this country. He declared that in the very near future, murderers could be freed from jail after only seven years, if they readily admit their guilt and assist the police.

The bombshell proposal, which has sparked outrage among relatives of murder victims and children's charities, is contained in draft sentencing guidelines. Under the plan, killers would effectively be able to plea bargain to reduce their sentences, before their victims are even buried. That could mean the new current minimum 15-year life term for murder, being reduced by 'greater than one third' so long as the murderers fully co-operate once they are caught. Remission for good behaviour while serving their sentences, would then bring the jail time down even further to just seven years. The draft proposal is the work of the 'independent' Sentencing Guidelines Council, which earlier in 2004 sparked outrage when it suggested that 'non violent' muggers should be spared jail. In 2003 there were 853 murders in England and Wales. For those caught, the cost of prosecuting and jailing them is massive. A rise in guilty pleas from the reduced tariff would save hundreds of millions of pounds in court and prison costs, as well as sparing witnesses the ordeal of giving evidence.

But opponents of the Government were quick to seize on the report, arguing that it made a mockery of the Home Secretary's pledge to be 'tough on serious crime'. Shadow Home Secretary David Davis said: "Parliament should set the sentencing guidelines. David Blunkett cannot claim to be tough on crime if he will allow murderers to walk free after just seven years. With over 800 murders a year, up by a sixth in only five years, this reinforces the need for punishments that deter killers." There was also alarm among victims' groups, who feared that a further move towards 'softly, softly' sentencing, was sending the wrong message to killers. Lynn Costello, co-founder of Mothers Against Murder and Aggression, said: " This is giving people a licence to murder. What next? These people are idiots who do not live in the real world." Dr Michele Elliot, Director of the national charity Kidscape, said, "It is a charter for murder and I will be very surprised if there is not public outrage over this. Is this designed to protect the public, or reduce the prison population?" Home Office sources have sought to play down the significance of 'plea bargaining' for killers, by arguing that the principle of reducing sentences in return for early guilty pleas had been around for a decade. However, the Home Secretary no longer has control over the sentencing of killers, and there is little he can do should the courts choose to adopt the proposals. They are also being unveiled by Lord Woolf, the Lord Chief Justice, who is opposed to Mr Blunkett's wish to increase the jail time of the most serious criminals. Mr Blunkett is introducing a so-called three tier law for killers, under which terrorists responsible for atrocities, mass murder, and child killings would spend their entire lives in jail.

However, experts such as Lord Woolf have already said that Human Rights legislation would overturn this law. Some readers may well be thinking that there is no doubt whatsoever that the lunatics have taken over the asylum and that it's high time the men in white coats were sent to take Lord Woolf to secure accommodation, where he can inflict no further fear and intimidation on the millions of law-abiding citizens in this country.

Controversial judge Lord Woolf defended new guidelines which would see killers given reduced jail sentences. The Lord Chief Justice appeared unmoved by the latest accusations that judges are going soft on crime as he spelled out a raft of 'discounted' jail terms. As he revealed full details of the sliding-scale justice scheme, giving a one third discount off sentences for early guilty pleas, there were claims that it was sending out the wrong message to criminals. There was growing concern that the guidelines will undermine public confidence in the courts and went further than the Government intended when it handed over control of jail sentences to a new independent body. It emerged that even killers caught 'red-handed' could still be entitled to a reduced sentence if they admit guilt. Prison terms are to be set for the first time by the new Sentencing Guidelines Council headed by Lord Woolf. Other members include seven judges, victim support groups and police. But their recommendations sparked fury when it emerged murderers, who currently face a 15-year tariff, could have their jail term cut by even more in 'exceptional cases' where offenders demonstrate 'absolute candour', the Council said. The Council said there was even 'no reason' why credit should be withheld from people caught red handed, as they could plead not guilty if they wanted. The cut in sentence is likely to be 'less' than the one-third maximum, but will still be on offer. The papers also revealed repeat offenders will be able to benefit from the rule change more than once, with no limit on the number of times credit will be given for an early plea. Criminals who do not decide to admit guilt until they walk through the court door will still benefit from a one-tenth cut in sentence. In the case of murderers, they will serve 10 years by pleading guilty at the first opportunity, 11 years and three months by pleading guilty at trial, 13 years and six months by changing their pleas to guilty.

Shadow Home Secretary David Davis said: "These guidelines seem to be pursuing every possible angle to try to reduce a murderer's sentence. This completely undermines David Blunkett's claim to be tough on crime. These proposals send the wrong message to murderers and criminals in general. Sentence length should reflect the crime."

Defending the proposals, Lord Woolf insisted the discounts were appropriate, because a guilty plea removes the need for a trial, saves money and saves victims and witnesses reliving the incident. Lord Woolf, who has clashed with Home Secretary Mr Blunkett over prison sentences, confirmed in some cases the draft guidelines would 'almost certainly' allow a one-third reduction for murder. He said: "Unfortunately individuals are encouraged at present to plead guilty very rarely in the case of murder, possibly for historical reasons, because it used to be a capital offence. The tradition used to be in murder cases that you always contest it. There's no reason why that should apply. The draft guidelines encourage those who commit even the offence of murder to take responsibility. The sentence remains life imprisonment. What it will mean is that you will come up for parole earlier than you would otherwise."

But Norman Brennan, Director of the Victims of Crime Trust, accused Lord Woolf of 'losing the plot'. He said: "Lord Woolf has an arrogant contempt for victims of crime and the law-abiding public. It's partly due to the lenient sentencing from judges that violent crime and crime in general is spiralling out of control in the UK." The guidelines are now set to be scrutinised by Westminster's Home Affairs Committee.

Britain's most senior judge has been forced into a humiliating climb down over hated plans to release murderers from jail up to five years early. The Lord Chief Justice, Lord Woolf, will today abandon sentencing guidelines which would have reduced their jail terms by a third in return for an early guilty plea. In the face of furious protests by *Daily Express* readers and MPs, he will water down the proposals dramatically by saying the maximum reduction should be only one-sixth. The Sentencing Guidelines Council's new framework will see the standard 15-year tariff fall to no less than 12 years if a murderer admits guilt. The SGC, chaired by Lord Woolf, said possible reductions would have to be 'weighed carefully' by a judge, so they did not lead to 'an inappropriately short sentence'. "Where it is appropriate to reduce the minimum term having regard to a plea of guilty, the maximum reduction will be one sixth." said the updated paper. It added: "The reduction should never exceed five years." Last night, it emerged that the SGC had employed a top City public relations firm, Luther Pendragon, to attempt to win favourable coverage for the massive U-turn. But the plan backfired when news of the changes to the guidelines leaked out. It had intended to release the details only to friendly newspapers. Shadow Home Secretary David Davis said: "We welcome the Sentencing Guidelines Council backtracking on their previous ludicrous proposal. Sentences should fit the crime and there is no more serious a crime than murder. Murder should not be subject to a cheap discount scheme."

The Home Office, which had also savaged the proposal, welcomed the climb down. A spokesman said: "We are pleased that in the reduction for guilty plea guideline, the SGC acknowledge the unique nature of the crime of murder, and shares our view that it should be treated differently to other offences. The revised guideline goes a long way towards meeting our concerns by ruling out any reduction for the most heinous crimes, halving the maximum reduction for guilty pleas to one sixth in other cases, and emphasising that in all other cases the tariff must adequately reflect the seriousness of the offence. We are confident that the new guideline will ensure that the murder principles will be upheld."

In a hastily-prepared statement, Lord Woolf said he was confident the new guidelines would leave judges 'better placed to deliver sentences which are effective both as punishments and deterrents to offending and reoffending'.

Director of Public Prosecutions Ken Macdonald QC, who sits on the SGC, added: "It represents a tougher regime than existed previously, because the discount is automatically reduced if a guilty plea is not made at the first available opportunity."

On its website, PR firm Luther Pendragon boasts it is 'in the business of making your professional and commercial arguments highly effective'. "Whether you are a local, national or multi-national corporate, a regulated institution or simply a private company with a new direction, we make your case heard in a way that will enhance your reputation, competitiveness and prosperity. We call the process 'issues management'. Other consultancies specialise in communicating with one specific audience, adapting their strategic recommendations to the expertise that their senior consultants can offer. At best, this is qualitatively limited, at worst, it is rather stupid.

To make your case effectively, you should be making a good argument in the markets in which you operate, and enjoy doing so."

LORD DERRY IRVINE
FORMER LORD CHANCELLOR

Referred to as a 'crony' of Prime Minister Tony Blair, who appointed him to the above post as 'Senior Judge' in the jurisdiction of England and Wales - it is widely thought that years ago, Mr Blair was a pupil barrister in Mr Irvine's law chambers in London, this means that he began his legal career there as an 'apprentice' or pupil barrister. ("One good turn deserves another, don't you know old boy? You scratch my back. I'll scratch yours.") You will certainly have heard of Lord Irvine, he is the one who used to sit on the 'woolsack' all day in the House of Lords, in all of his legal pomposity and majesty and long-wigged regalia, pantyhose, buckled shoes etc, wondering where he can find wallpaper for at least £300 per roll, to furnish his lavish apartment supplied by the taxpayer, and to keep him in the manner to which he feels he should become accustomed. Regrettably and highly embarrassing for his Lordship, he has an apparently wayward son, possibly now in his late 30's. The son went to America and got himself in some trouble over a woman, whom I believe he was accused of stalking, and involving, possibly drugs and/or firearms. At the time of reporting this, I think the US matter is still unresolved. Having loosely followed the case at the time, I'm fairly sure he was being kept in custody, as I believe he had threatened the woman.

In January 2003, Lord Irvine sided with his buddy, LCJ Lord Woolf. He was reported widely in the press as saying: "The public sees nothing wrong in burglars escaping jail, even for their second offences." Supporting the lenient approach prescribed the previous month by Lord Woolf, he went on to say: "I don't accept that people are disturbed at first-time burglars, or even second-time burglars, where there are no aggravated elements in the burglary, not going to prison." Asked about LCJ Lord Woolf's ruling, in a guideline judgement, that courts should impose non-custodial sentences on first-time, 'standard domestic' burglars, Lord Irvine said, "I have no difficulty in agreeing with the Lord Chief Justice on that." He insisted in a BBC interview that people had less faith in imprisonment than tabloid newspapers suggested. "In other words, I think that people are more worldy-wise, better informed, than some of the critics of the Lord Chief Justice, credit." In an attempt to put the Court of Appeal's recent burglary guidelines in context, the Lord Chancellor claimed that Lord Woolf, and the other judges sitting with him, had 'sanctioned very substantial sentences of imprisonment for the three burglars whose appeals were in front of them,' and that this had been 'largely ignored'. In fact there were two burglars before the Appeal Court, in the appeal decided just before Christmas 2002, and both had their sentences cut. William McInerney, 22, who had 10 previous convictions for a total of 39 offences and who had at one stage asked for 49 other burglaries to be TIC, had his five-year sentence reduced to 3.5 years. Stephen Keating, 33, with 12 previous convictions, for which he had served two terms of imprisonment, had a four-year sentence reduced to three years. His probation officer said he had 'clearly poor coping mechanisms for his offending', but did not assess him as presenting a serious risk of harm to the public. Lord Irvine's interview with the BBC Radio 4 programme had been planned before the guideline judgement on 19th December 2003, but was recorded in mid-February 2004. He asked rhetorically whether people were better protected 'by ever-increasing jail sentences of imprisonment, with all the cost for the state that entails, or are they to be better protected by giving a vigorous programme of community service a chance?' Lord Irvine went on to discuss the finer points of jail v community service, but I found this too heavy and boring to include. More importantly, Sir David-Calvert Smith, QC, Director of Public Prosecutions, said the guidelines would not discourage the Crown Prosecution Service from bringing cases to court. He said: "Burglary is still sufficiently serious to prosecute, even if it leads to a community punishment." The only difference he saw was that more burglars would be tried by magistrates, so fewer cases would be dealt with in the Crown Court, which has heavier sentencing powers.

Tony Blair has seen many former allies plunge the knife into him in recent years but none of the attacks will have been so deeply wounding as the latest. Derry Irvine's emergence as the leading light in a crushing defeat for Mr Blair's proposed new anti-terror laws in the Lords, is a major landmark in the decline of the Prime Minister as a respected national leader. With the man who shaped New Labour's entire approach to the law and constitution, feeling compelled to oppose plans to give the Home Secretary sweeping powers to restrict the liberty of British citizens, the PM can hardly now portray his critics as foolish or irresponsible. They are the mainstream. Mr Blair has long had a prolific talent for collecting mentors. Indeed, many were crucial to his meteoric rise from goofy ex-public school boy to Labour leader. Gordon Brown took him under his wing in 1983, teaching him many tricks of the trade and living to regret it. Roy Jenkins then became a political father figure and Paddy Ashdown a doting cousin. Experienced and influential Labour hands such as Peter Kilfoyle and Giles Radice also looked kindly on him in the early days. The latter became so emotionally attached, he began referring to Blair as 'the young Lochinvar', after Sir Walter Scott's fictional hero. At one time even that ardent Leftist Michael Foot was charmed into the Blair fan club, singing the young hopeful's praises when he stood unsuccessfully at a by-election in an ultra-safe Tory seat in 1982. "We believe he is going to have a very big future in British politics," swooned Mr Foot, about the only thing he got right during his disastrous tenure as Labour leader. At the other extreme, Margaret Thatcher was lured into the big tent, reportedly commenting of Blair shortly before the 1997 election: "He will not do the country down." And that is before we even consider Bill Clinton and George W Bush. But none of these characters is so central to the Blair story as Alexander "Derry" Irvine, the man who by Blair's own account taught him "how to think", introduced him to his future wife and became his most trusted counsellor.

Irvine could easily have expressed his disdain for the incoherent and sinister legislation placed before the Lords on Monday by abstaining. Instead, he told friends, he found himself voting with his 'conscience'. Some will believe Irvine's vote to have been contaminated by bitterness at the way he was elbowed aside as Lord Chancellor, in favour of another Blair crony from his legal days, Charles Falconer, two years ago. But it seems far more likely that the super-bright Irvine simply considered the PM's anti-terror plans so abysmal that he could not in good faith do anything but help to vote them down. It was in a similar spirit of deep disappointment that Mr Blair's long-term European policy adviser, Roger Liddle, also turned on the PM by calling for him to start 'being honest' with the British public about the Government's real view that transferring powers to Brussels can be a good thing.

Mr Liddle advised the PM from 1997 until last year and now works for that other Blair mentor Peter Mandelson in Brussels. Let us not forget that Mandelson has also publicly lamented how the PM allowed himself to be 'outmanoeuvred' by his Chancellor over single currency policy and is on record criticising aspects of Blair's foreign policy. The roll call of the disenchanted does not finish there. The PM's other departed European adviser, the diplomat Sir Stephen Wall, last year published an excoriating account of his employer's failings, documenting how 'let down' he felt at Mr Blair's U-turn over a referendum on the EU constitution. The mandarin class has turned against Blair, a man in whom it once invested such high hopes. The perceived wisdom about him now is simply that he hasn't been much good.

Lord Butler, considered by colleagues to be the doyen of senior civil servants of the past two decades, has been eloquent in his criticisms of Blair's 'sofa' style of governing. Last year, 2004, Mr Blair's longtime economic adviser, Derek Scott, took him to task for his 'poor grasp' of basic economic principles. A few years back, Jenkins went public on his frustration at Blair's inability to 'make the weather' politically, while Ashdown left politics a disappointed man and Kilfoyle's judgment on his one-time protege is that 'there's nothing there'. Let us not forget that Britain's foremost advocate of high standards in education, Chris Woodhead, initially felt he had found in Blair, a Prime Minister who really got the message, but this week it was announced that he had accepted an invitation to review the national curriculum – for the Conservatives. About the only people from the original gang to remain wholly loyal to the idea of Blair as a heroic and high calibre leader are Falconer, who has a lawyer's gift for knowing on which side his bread is buttered, and that tribally-minded liability Alastair Campbell. The British public is picking up on the mood music from the lost brigade of mentors. There is a thaw in the attitude of Middle Britain towards the Conservatives. When their posters ask 'Are you thinking what we're thinking?' more and more of us are nodding our heads. Mr Blair pirouettes and leaps around as if the surface beneath his feet is as solid as ever but he is skating on very thin ice. His political last supper may come sooner than he bargains. If we could imagine who would be sitting at his high table, clearly it would not be a matter of only one disciple doing him down. Most of those assembled from down the years would be ready to contemplate an act of assassination.

If those closest to him are thinking it, is it any wonder that the rest of Britain is starting to notice that the Emperor has no clothes?

HIGH COURT JUDGE LORD WHEATLEY
THE HIGH COURT IN EDINBURGH

Here is a report of an absolutely atrocious theft which you may have missed. I found it in a copy of the London free newspaper called *Metro*, which is issued at main line stations, dated 25th March 2004.

TEENAGERS ACCUSED OF GRAVE THEFT

A teenaged boy removed a head from a body in a graveyard tomb and then played with it in front of friends, a court heard.

Sonny Devlin, 17, allegedly put his hand in the neck and used the dismembered head as though it were a puppet. Devlin and a 15 year old boy, who cannot be named, both deny charges of 'violation of a sepulchre', in what is thought to be the first grave-robbing trial to be heard in more than a century. The pair, both from Edinburgh, are accused of violating the mausoleum of Sir George 'Bloody' Mackenzie, in the city's historic Greyfriars cemetery. After they finished playing with it, the teenagers discarded the head. The identity of the body in question is not known.

Here are reports of the outcome of the case, from 2 different national daily newspapers, both dated 24th April 2004, first from *The Guardian*:

BOYS AVOID JAIL FOR 'VIOLATING' TOMB AND BEHEADING CORPSE'

'Two teenagers who forced their way into the burial chamber of one of Scotland's most brutal historical figures and cut the head from a corpse, were sentenced to probation at court in Edinburgh on 23rd April 2004. Sonny Devlin, 17, of Edinburgh, and a 15-year-old boy, who cannot be named for legal reasons, took the skull from the mausoleum of Sir George 'Bloody' Mackenzie and played with it in the grounds of Greyfriars Kirkyard.

The youths were charged under ancient legislation used to prosecute Edinburgh's notorious 18th and 19th century grave-robbers. It was the first time for over a hundred years that anyone had been accused of 'violation of sepulchre'. At the High Court in Edinburgh, Devlin was sentenced to three years probation and the 15-year-old to two years probation. The judge, Lord Wheatley, said they had committed a 'gruesome and revolting offence'. He said that although the younger teenager had only been standing guard, he was equally guilty in the eyes of the law. The court had heard how the youths caused around £10,000 worth of damage during the incident on June 30th 2003. The doors of the Mackenzie mausoleum were forced and the mummified head of a male corpse cut off with a penknife. Devlin then put his fist into the neck and talked to the head 'like a glove puppet'. He was later caught after returning to the graveyard to show off to a girl, who did not believe his claim that he had broken into a tomb. Police had been called after the operator of one of the city's ghost tours, challenged the teenagers in the cemetery, after seeing them carrying something in a blanket. Officers who arrived at the scene found the headless remains of a body in the lower level of the vault.

The identity of the corpse is not known, but it was in a mummified state and was thought to have been there for many years. Devlin's lawyer, Jim Stephenson, told the court his client was 'aware of the seriousness nature of the offence and has shown some regret'. Richard Goddard, counsel for the co-defendant, said his client was 'a likeable young man' from a 'fairly complicated personal background.'

The youths were found guilty after a trial in March 2004. Sir George Mackenzie, a former Lord Advocate during the reign of King Charles 2nd, died in 1691. He earned the nickname 'Bloody Mackenzie' for sending hundreds of Protestant Covenanters to their deaths.'

Now for the *Daily Express* reportage of the same event:

BOYS WHO CUT HEAD OFF A CORPSE ESCAPE JAIL

'Two teenage boys who cut off the head of a corpse and played with it in a graveyard escaped jail. Sonny Devlin, 17, and a 15-year-old, who cannot be named, were both put on probation at the High Court in Edinburgh. They were convicted of the ancient crime of violation of a sepulchre in a historic case, the first trial of its kind to come to court in Scotland for more than a century.

Devlin, from Edinburgh, was sentenced to three years probation, with the condition that he carries out 200 hours of community service. His accomplice was given two years probation. The judge told Devlin that the fact he had been drinking was no excuse. Lord Wheatley said: "You committed a gruesome and revolting offence."

(Yet another judge whose bark is worse than his bite? What sort of message is that likely to send around the streets of Edinburgh and Glasgow, to other teenagers? Some deterrent! I'm really thankful that it wasn't the tomb of any of my relatives, aren't you? No comment, for once I'm absolutely lost for words.)

LORD JUSTICE ROSE
MRS JUSTICE HALLETT
MRS JUSTICE DOBBS
SITTING IN THE CRIMINAL COURT OF APPEAL IN LONDON

At Peterborough Crown Court in May 2004, a devastated family wept as a drink-driver admitted killing their teenage daughter in a Christmas Day crash in 2003. Student Amy Gonzales, 18, died four weeks after the crash, just hours after opening her eyes for the first time since the tragedy. Craig Smith, 22, from Eaton Socon, Cambridgeshire, admitted killing Amy by dangerous driving and driving with excess alcohol. More than 20 of Amy's friends and family, wearing sunflower buttonholes, packed the public gallery shouting 'killer' as Smith stood in the dock. Amy's mother Melanie, 43, began sobbing as her daughter was mentioned during the emotionally-charged hearing. Her boyfriend Paul Ray attended, still on crutches after the accident. The court heard that Amy had bought a kebab with Paul, 21, when she was hit by Smith's BMW in the town's High Street, at around 1am on Christmas Day, after attending a church midnight mass with her family.

A subsequent breath test revealed that Smith was **ONE-AND-A-HALF-TIMES THE LEGAL LIMIT**. Smith was jailed for 6 years and disqualified from driving for 15 years.

For the parents and family of Craig Smith's drink-driving victim, Amy Gonzales, there was to be a bizarre sequel to the case, which was to cause a major set-back and re-open all of their misery, grief and sadness. On 4th November 2004, the result of Smith's Criminal Appeal against his 6-years imprisonment sentence was announced. Amy's parents, Kevin and Melanie Gonzales publicly wept aloud, as Smith's sentence was cut from six years to five years, by three Appeal Court Judges, Lord Justice Rose, Mrs Justice

Mrs Justice Hallett

Hallett and Mrs Justice Dobbs. Smith therefore will claim eligibility to be freed from jail in just 2 years. As if to rub salt in the family's wounds, the 3 High Court Judges, in their wisdom, drastically slashed Smith's driving disqualification from 15 years, to just 7 years. Mr & Mrs Gonzales described Smith's Appeal as 'obscene'. Amy's father said: "We keep thinking back to Christmas morning at 1am, when Craig Smith destroyed our family in front of us. We are still struggling to cope with what happened to Amy. The lack of justice in these cases cheapens all our lives. We didn't feel justice had been done last time and we feel we haven't got justice again. As Amy and Paul were fighting for their lives in hospital, he was out drinking again in our local pubs. One was only 20 feet away from where Amy's body had been lying."

His wife found it impossible in her misery, to control her anger and tears, launching a scathing attack against Smith and the totally unfair way in which the Criminal Justice System had caused them even more pain and suffering, by the Appeal Court Judges' liberal and lenient treatment of their daughter's irresponsible killer. She is reported as saying: "We can't understand how somebody with such a callous disregard for human life can only be put away for 5 years. The person who killed our beautiful daughter, our beautiful Amy who everybody loved, we have got to face him." Amy's boyfriend, himself seriously hurt in the horrendous collision, said: "He will only serve two-and-a-half years and I don't think any member of the public will think that was long enough for what he did." Amy and Paul had been to a Christmas Eve midnight mass and were walking to a rendezvous in St Neots to meet her parents, for a lift home. Craig Smith, in his drunken condition, crashed into them as they were crossing the road, in his BMW car.

Amy's parents rushed to the scene and found Amy lying in the road in a pool of blood with serious head injuries. Paul, her boyfriend, was also badly hurt, receiving multi-fractures to his leg. He almost died when, during an operation on his leg, he suffered from a collapsed lung. Smith had gone out drinking straight from work and when questioned, at first claimed that Amy and Paul had run out in front of him, later changing his story to the fact that he 'simply hadn't seen them'.

At the Court of Criminal Appeal, all three judges agreed with Smith's barrister that the six year jail sentence had been 'manifestly excessive', ordering it to be reduced by one year to just five years. Mrs Justice Hallett stated in court that Smith's drunken driving had 'caused untold misery to Amy's family and friends, but, as bad as it was and as horrific in its consequences as it was, it did not justify a sentence so close to the 10-year maximum'.

You may well consider that this is a clear-cut case of the human rights of the offender, taking preference over those of the victim's relatives and of the second victim, Amy's boyfriend Paul. "This has made a mockery of the law", stated Caroline Chisholm, from Brake, a road safety group.

MR JUSTICE McKINNON
MANCHESTER CROWN COURT

When you have finished reading about this case, you may well come to the conclusion that there is little or no justice in the world. This is particularly so in the case of babies and young children who do not live to 'tell the tale' about how they were abused, or, had they survived, would have been too young to give evidence anyway.

On Tuesday 29th June 2004 at Manchester Crown Court, a cruel mother and her brutal internet lover were acquitted of killing her baby son, 21-month-old John Gray, after both defendants denied all knowledge of the toddler's 200 injuries. Love cheat Lorna Gray, 30, and her lover, James McEwan, 27, admitted wilfully neglecting the helpless child in the weeks before his death in March 2003. But the judge, Mr Justice McKinnon, directed the jury to acquit them both of unlawfully killing the child, who died of a ruptured liver caused by a punch.

The judge ruled there was no direct evidence that either of the defendants had inflicted violence on the infant, even though a post mortem examination revealed an appalling catalogue of injury, including damage to the baby's stomach wall, four fractured ribs, a broken arm and bruises. However the judge said the pair can almost certainly expect to go to jail for the cruelty they admitted. The judge said: " It must be clear to everyone the most probable result, if not the inevitable one, is that there will be an immediate custodial sentence", as he remanded them in custody for reports. The baby's distraught father, Dean Gray, 34, of Fife, said: "I did not think she could be capable of leading our own son to his death. She is not fit to be a mother and I can never forgive her."

Mr Gray, who left his wife when he learned she was unfaithful, added: "My son is dead because of her sick sexual fantasy." The court had heard that Mrs Gray, a civil servant, met McEwan while surfing the internet from the home she shared with her husband and three children in Scotland. They began an affair so intense that their sexual obsession led her to travel regularly to the father-of-four's home in Fallowfield, Manchester. She would take baby John with her, but relatives became concerned about marks and bruising on him. Prosecutor Alan Conrad, QC said John once had a black eye and later bruising on his face, chest and testicles and that his mother's explanations were 'unconvincing'. The toddler died on 16th March 2003 'as a direct result of a severe abdominal injury' during a weekend visit to McEwan's home. The child had vomited green bile on the Saturday night and his mother had found him unconscious on the Sunday morning. Paramedics were called an hour later but the child was pronounced dead at hospital. Blows of 'considerable' force had caused the acute injuries and death. They are not compatible with a fall downstairs or other falls. The likely cause is punching with a clenched fist, kicking or stamping.

In police interviews, each defendant denied causing baby John any injuries. They also said they were unaware of any physical abuse of the child. Gray and McEwan denied manslaughter, but, on the 10th day of the trial, admitted child cruelty. They reappeared before the judge for sentence on 20th July 2004, after the judge had the benefit of reading the all-important, so-called 'reports'. (**Author's note:** *These are the 'reports' which contribute to the lack of swift justice in the modern courts, and were rarely found to be necessary in the old days. Then, once the defendant(s) had been found guilty by the jury in the Crown Court, the judge would say to the police officer in the case, or to the prosecution counsel, 'Is anything known?' At this juncture the police officer would take the witness stand, handing up copies of what were then known as 'antecedents' on his way to the witness box. In fact the judge would have known whether or not 'anything was known', even before the jury had been sworn in, as a copy of the antecedents would have been submitted for him at an earlier stage, affixed to his case papers document bundle. The antecedents gave a potted history of a defendant's age, date of birth, schools attended and every known job, with reasons for leaving those jobs, as far as could be pre-verified, marital status, home circumstances etc., and would have been extracted from the defendant by the police officer as soon as he was charged, photographed and fingerprinted. These days DNA swabs would have been taken from the mouth at the same time, no doubt. On separate sheets of paper, but forming part of the same antecedents bundle of documents handed up, would be a list of the defendant's previous* convictions, these days pre-scanned and calculated, so as to omit what are known as spent convictions, viz: those too old to count any more and specifically excluded under an Act of Parliament called The Rehabilitation Of Offenders Act. The police officer, sometimes guided by the prosecution counsel who would be on his feet, would go through the convictions, in open court, for the benefit of all, but most of all, for the judge. Particular prominence and stress would be placed on convictions of a similar nature. It is at this stage that members of the jury often swoon, tut and sigh with shock and horror, as they discover that the person they have just tried is in fact a serial offender, and has committed the same or similar offences, sometimes countless times before, over the years, during the course of his or her criminal career.

It used to be the case, in my time – and probably still holds good – that no details were ever made known to a jury, as to the details of any previous acquittals at crown courts, or not guilty verdicts in magistrates courts, for the same or similar offences. However, I understand plans are afoot to change this.)

Returning now to the tragic case of baby John Gray, battered to death at the tender age of just 21months by 'a person or persons unknown!' The judge told the two defendants that they were guilty of 'the most extreme cruelty'. The two lovers sat in the dock with their heads bowed as the judge said that they had 'kept their own counsel' until today about what truly happened. "You failed to take early action to get him medical attention, when it must have been obvious he was seriously ill. It is not possible to choose between you, you must each take joint responsibility in the sense you were both guilty of the most extreme cruelty." As neither of these two wicked, cowardly adults had been prepared to individually take the blame for inflicting the dreadful multi-injuries on the young infant, the judge had directed the jury to find them not guilty of his unlawful killing, viz: manslaughter, which carries the same maximum penalty as the mandatory one for murder, life imprisonment. Instead, he sentenced them to five years imprisonment each,on the considerably lesser count of child cruelty.

Lorna Gray's barrister had told the court that she had been infatuated by McEwan. He tried to stop her cuddling baby John and called him a 'mummy's boy'. Outside the court afterwards, the boy's natural father, Dean Gray, branded the sentences as unacceptable. He said: "Five years for killing my little boy? His life was worth more than that. I can't understand why it is these two people cannot be held to blame for my son's death. There should be a change in the law. The justice system is failing every child. I hope no other babies suffer at the hands of evil. I had to look at pictures of his bruising. I hope John may be able to find peace in the future.

Right now he won't and neither will my family. This is an absolute disgrace, a travesty of the highest extent. He was my flesh and blood."

Relatives had reacted furiously as the two defendants were led to the cells after sentencing. Fighting broke out and one relative shouted: "We hope you both rot in hell, that's our family you've destroyed." Police were called as fighting went on outside the court.

MR JUSTICE HODGE

The husband of Tony Blair's crony, Margaret Hodge has been made a High Court Judge. This makes Henry Hodge one of only two out of 108 High Court Judges to have started as a solicitor rather than a barrister.

The appointment, with a salary of £150,878 a year, follows continuing controversy over favouritism in the promotion of judges and senior lawyers. Mr Hodge's wife is a long-time friend and ally of Tony Blair, who controversially appointed her Children's Minister in 2002. Her 60-year-old husband has attracted allegations of cronyism as his career has advanced. His North London law firm built up a big trade, much of it on legal aid, during the 1980's and 1990's. It gave Cherie Blair a number of cases to handle in her early years as a barrister. A former chairman of the National Council for Civil Liberties and councillor in Islington, the borough his wife once led, Mr Hodge first won judicial office in 1997 when he was made a Recorder, a junior Crown Court Judge. Two years later he was made a full Circuit Judge, and two years after that was appointed Chief Immigration Adjudicator. He will bring a further liberal voice to a High Court bench already seen as far too willing to block laws passed by Parliament in contentious areas, such as asylum and immigration. The firm he founded, *Hodge, Jones and Allen*, has a record of acting in favourite radical causes, and defended Winston Silcott, who was jailed for the murder of PC Keith Blakelock in the 1985 Broadwater Farm riots, before being cleared on appeal. Mr Hodge has played a central role in efforts by judicial authorities to ensure political correctness on the bench. He was a member of a committee which this year (2004) warned judges not to use words such as 'immigrant', 'Asian', 'postman' or 'man' and 'wife' because they are said to be tainted with prejudice. High Court Judges are appointed by the Queen on the recommendation of the Lord Chancellor, who is supposed to consult among judges and lawyers on the best candidates. But Lord Falconer, himself a target of cronyism allegations because of his closeness to his former flatmate Mr Blair, failed to implement a report this summer which told him the system for choosing High Court Judges should be suspended, and a new method established to remove cronyism suspicions.

The report said High Court Judges appeared to be picked on the basis of who they know and 'the championship of the Lord Chancellor is clearly a factor in determining chances of appointment.' Mr Hodge's wife has been a controversial political figure since her days as leader of the Left-wing Islington Council for ten years until 1992. Her appointment as Children's Minister in 2002 brought a tide of criticism, because of her record over homosexual abuse in Islington children's homes. The council, under Mrs Hodge failed to deal with scandals in the homes and she tried to condemn the journalists who exposed them. In 2003, she attempted to persuade the BBC to drop a story on the abuse in the homes. She wrote complaining that a former resident who spoke about his experience of abuse, was 'an extremely disturbed person'. That former resident, Demetrious Panton, turned out to be an adviser to the Government on its New Deal for Communities. Mrs Hodge was compelled to pay a total of £30,000 in legal costs and payment to a charity nominated by the man she smeared.

MR JUSTICE EADY

Soham liar Maxine Carr sparked uproar on 24th February 2005 after winning the right to police protection for the rest of her life, at an estimated cost to the taxpayer of £50million.

The former fiance of child killer Ian Huntley was granted anonymity by London's High Court after her lawyer claimed that her life was at risk if her whereabouts became known. It is the first time such an order has been made for an offence other than murder. James Bulger's murderers, Jon Venables and Robert Thompson and child killer Mary Bell are the only people to have previously received the full protection of the court. Victims' groups said the decision sets a dangerous precedent. Norman Brennan, director of the Victims of Crime Trust, said: "It sets a worrying precedent in which anyone who complains enough gets police protection at an enormous cost to the taxpayer. You can understand the logic of protecting the likes of the Bulger killers with indefinite injunctions but the only one courting publicity and attention here is Maxine Carr. "If she just went away and stopped whingeing everyone would forget about her and we wouldn't need an order."

He added: "It just reviles me how much money is being spent on protecting her anonymity. Groups like ourselves who have to pick up the devastation left behind by people like Carr and Ian Huntley get nothing." Edward Fitzgerald QC justified her claim to anonymity, telling Mr Justice Eady in the High Court: There is a real or significant risk of injury or worse, of killing, if the injunction is not granted." It means there is now a permanent injunction banning anyone from revealing the 28-year-old's new name or whereabouts. It also guarantees a continuing drain on the public purse to ensure that the order is not broken and that Carr's safety is not compromised.

Carr was convicted of perverting the course of justice when she gave Huntley a false alibi after he killed 10-year-olds Holly Wells and Jessica Chapman. She was cleared at the Old Bailey of the more serious charge of assisting an offender. The former teaching assistant was jailed in December 2003 and released last April, halfway through her 42-month sentence. Carr is still under a three-year supervision order after admitting 20 charges of fraud and deception. She was sacked from a job earlier this year after she was caught stealing food from nuns at a convent. The Home Office has put the cost of protecting her at £1 million a year, though £1.5million has already been spent on Carr in the 10 months since her release from Foston Hall women's prison last year, 2004. The cost of her High Court application, around £100,000 including lawyers' fees, was also met by the taxpayer. She has 21 police officers and an armed response vehicle on call 24 hours a day, at a cost of £700,000 a year before overtime. And there is the £70 per week incapacity benefit she is expected to claim long-term as she fights depression and bulimia. Added to this are the costs of social workers, medical care and lawyers' bills of at least £1,000 a week. The *Daily Express* has also learned the Home Office has been paying for Carr's shopping, accommodation, and telephone bills. Maggie Bucknall of Communities Against Paedophile Accommodation said: "How can Carr be granted anonymity when so many actual victims, such as battered wives who are worried for their lives, get nothing? The woman did what she did and must now face the consequences." This latest order was made because of Carr's Right to Life and Right to Privacy under the European Convention on Human Rights.

JUDGE ANDREW LOWCOCK
MANCHESTER CROWN COURT

A motorist with one of Britain's worst driving records, escaped a jail sentence after telling the judge a prison sentence would not help him.

In defiance of his 30th driving ban, Andrew Haige, 39, got behind the wheel after drinking 14 pints of beer. After smashing into the back of a car, he threatened to kill two witnesses, then lashed out at police officers sent to arrest him. Yet Haige, whose 75 previous motoring convictions include five for drink-driving and 25 for driving whilst disqualified, walked free from Manchester Crown Court. Instead, His Honour Judge Andrew Lowcock, in his wisdom, banned Haige from driving for 4 years (Of course he will abide by the ban!) and made a two-year community rehabilitation order on condition he attends a programme to tackle his drinking. Road safety campaigners condemned the decision, claiming it was only a matter of time before Haige killed someone. Mike Jobbins of the Campaign Against Drinking and Driving said: "It beggars belief that this man has gone free. He may say prison doesn't work, but surely other road users would be much safer if he was locked up? He has defied ban after ban and there is no saying he won't do it again. Luckily, no one was seriously injured but do we have to wait for a fatality before this man is stopped?"

Judge Andrew Lowcock

Manchester Crown Court had heard that Haige, a security guard who has served a jail term for assaulting a police officer, had been drinking all afternoon on 11th February before he got into his car to go to work. Richard Orme, prosecuting said that Haige ploughed into the back of a Toyota Yaris driven by student Katie Green, then cut in front of her. After she sounded her horn signalling him to stop, he pulled over, got out of the car and swore at her. Two men came to assist her, but Haige became violent and threatened to have them killed. Haige, of Levenshulme, Manchester, then got back into his car and drove at one of the men, sending him sprawling on the road. When police arrived he told them: "You'll be eating hospital food." Kicking and screaming he was then arrested. Tests showed that he was 112 microgrammes over the 35 mg limit in 100 millilitres of breath. His offences dated right back to 1983. He pleaded guilty to driving with excess alcohol, driving while disqualified, affray and having no insurance.

His defence counsel told the court he had simply 'forgotten' he was banned from driving, after his wife died of cancer last year. His Honour Judge Andrew Lowcock, in his great wisdom, told Haige: "These were quite appalling offences. You have repeatedly flouted orders of disqualification and don't seem to think they apply to you. You were extremely drunk and had no business being anywhere near a car. You behaved in a quite dreadful fashion and should be utterly ashamed. It seems to me the only person you feel sorry for is yourself. You have had repeated custodial sentences and I think you need help for your problem." After the case, Roadpeace, a road safety pressure group said: "The judiciary's attitude to death and injury on our roads is disgraceful. The number of children and adults killed each year by people flouting the law is nothing short of a national disaster. Yet individuals like this just walk out of court. He has already disregarded 25 disqualifications. Does the judge think he's going to take any notice of the latest one?"

JUDGE JOHN BURKE, QC
MINSHULL STREET CROWN COURT, MANCHESTER

A cab driver who went on a drunken rampage aboard a transatlantic jet escaped jail on 8th April 2004.

New York cabbie Mohammed Ahmed, 47, pinned a steward against the side of the British Airways plane, and repeatedly demanded more alcohol during a flight from John F. Kennedy airport to Manchester. During the flight he tried to urinate in a sick bag in front of the 200 passengers. One crew member was so worried that he blocked the plane's exit door as a precaution. Father-of-three Ahmed was warned about his behaviour by the captain, and others on board were so appalled by his foul-mouthed tirade that they offered to help the crew to deal with him. Ahmed was arrested when the plane touched down and held in police custody for a week. But at Manchester's Minshull Street Crown Court, he was let off with a 12 months conditional discharge, after His Honour Judge John Burke QC, in his wisdom, said he was taking into account his guilty plea to being drunk on an aircraft. The Judge told him: "Your drunken stupidity must have created a feeling of unease to other passengers and caused problems for the cabin crew. It has resulted in hardship to your family, and if you come to Britain and behave like that again in the next 12 months you will go to prison."

The prosecutor told the court that the flight passed without incident until an hour from touchdown, when Ahmed became 'very loud' and began using obscene language. He constantly demanded alcohol, and on one occasion slammed some money down on the counter and pinned a crew member against the cabin wall. He refused to sit down and the crew were forced to work around him. Due to his conduct he was served with a written warning from the captain, but even when the situation was explained to him fully by a Punjabi-speaking steward, he continued his behaviour and refused to sit down. A steward was eventually forced to spend the remainder of the flight sitting beside Ahmed, but as he attempted to placate him he constantly asked for alcohol. The seatbelt signs were illuminated for landing but as the plane touched down and taxied along the runway Ahmed took his seatbelt off and got up. The prosecutor said: "There was a risk of injury to himself or others if he had fallen. He caused the crew much more concern. It was a night flight with the ordinary pressures attached." Ahmed continued swearing loudly even when he was told that police were arriving to meet the plane. He was seated towards the rear of the aircraft, near where cabin staff were busy preparing meals, and when he stood up and started ranting, stewardesses had to work round him. "He caused the crew great difficulty in ensuring a smooth flight." said Prosecutor Mr Booth. Defence counsel told the court, there was no evidence he had endangered the aircraft in any way. "He is clearly overwhelmed by embarrassment and shame. It was wholly out of character. He had been working hard as a taxi driver throughout the night and was under considerable stress as his mother was about to undergo heart surgery. He began drinking and miscalculated the effects of dehydration." A British Airways spokesman said: "There can never be an excuse for violent or abusive behaviour on board an aircraft."

Questions and comments:

1) Thank you so much Judge Burke QC, for offering the protection of your court to the crew, and the many inconvenienced and upset passengers of flight BA 1502 - conditional discharge indeed! – Have I spelt your name correctly, or is it *Berk*?

2) Judge, were you in fact listening to the evidence as it was outlined by the Prosecution Counsel?

3) It's a pity the cabin staff did not accept passengers' offers to assist them in dealing with Ahmed, he needed strapping in his seat with tight cable-tie 'handcuffs'.

4) Ahmed had the services of a (publicly funded) Punjabi interpreter at the crown court hearing and a Punjabi-speaking cabin crew staff member during his in-flight anti-social behaviour. Does he carry a Punjabi interpreter around with him in his New York cab? Wouldn't the interpreter take up a valuable seat required for a fare-paying passenger? What a farce!

5) How differently he would have been treated if arrested on return to JFK airport, New York, by the NYPD and an American court! NYPD may have revoked his cab licence.

6) It's a pity frightened passengers didn't take out a private prosecution against him, they must have been scared to some degree, and fearful for their childrens' safety.

JUDGE ALAN BERG
MANCHESTER CROWN COURT

David Flint, 36, from Miles Platting, Manchester, sunk about as low as it is possible to go. He was in a hospital bed recovering from head injuries at North Manchester General Hospital. In the next bed to him had been 68-year-old Mr Alfred Webster, who had a heart attack and had then died, and his body had been removed from the ward. Flint had struck at 2 o'clock in the morning, as other patients were probably asleep. When he dropped some coins as he rifled the late Mr Webster's bedside locker, he was caught by a nurse. He had also taken Mr Webster's car keys.

He fled from the ward with around £5 but was later caught by hospital security guards. The dead man's sister, Lillian Smiles said: "The thought of going through a dead man's belongings, it's disgusting and it has sickened our family. Even the nurses were shocked and said they had never seen anything like it." Flint had claimed that he was 'paying his respects to the dead'. Speaking after the case, Mrs Smiles, 54, said that her brother, who had a heart attack following a hip-replacement operation, may have been worried about Flint shortly before he died. He had pleaded with her to take his wallet and mobile phone home because he was worried someone might steal them. She said: "That man knew he was dead because there was a commotion on the ward when staff tried to revive Alfred."

In contrast to what Flint had told the nurse about paying his respects to the dead, Flint's defending advocate told the court: "At the time the keys were taken from the deceased person, Mr Flint did not know that Mr Webster had passed away." Judge Alan Berg branded Flint as "A 21st century grave robber." He added: "In the many cases which I have had the misfortune to come across, this case ranks as probably among the meanest, most despicable ever." He then sentenced Flint to just 5 months imprisonment. (A magistrates court would have had the power to sentence him to SIX months!)

JUDGE JONATHAN GEAKE
MANCHESTER CROWN COURT

A bullied boy took bloody revenge on a gang of teenagers tormenting him, by plunging a knife into one of them. The 16-year-old 'exceptional student' and head prefect, who cannot be named, stabbed a 14-year-old fellow pupil in front of horrified classmates when he felt threatened by the 15-member gang. The blade impaled the boy's arm and entered his chest, puncturing a lung. He was rushed into a hospital intensive care unit but has since made a full recovery.

On 5th October 2004, the bullied pupil, known as boy B, sobbed in Manchester Crown Court as a judge decided not to send him to youth custody because of the 'exceptional' nature of the case. Sentencing him to 240 hours of community service, Judge Jonathan Geake called Boy B an 'exemplary student'. He said: "The parents, teachers and everybody present, would expect me to send a message out to the public that the carrying of knives is not to be tolerated in a civilised society. But you have been picked on from time to time in the past, and as you were making your way home on this day you were picked on again. Plainly the victim, young boy C, did not deserve to get stabbed. You lashed out in the heat of the moment and it was a wicked thing to do. This is an extremely sad case for everyone. Boy C has made a robust recovery. His mother is here in court today to see that justice is done. I do not for a moment forget the mother and her son. This is an exceptional case and I hope the mother can find it in her heart to allow this to take place." The stabbing happened on December 1st 2003 when Boy B was a year 11 student at the 1,300-pupil school in the Trafford area of Greater Manchester. The school received funding from a top Premiership football club and won national prizes for sporting prowess. The bullied pupil, described as a keen mountain biker and an 'extremely calm and peaceful young man', had suffered taunts while working voluntarily in the school library. The knife he used was bought over the internet by a classmate, Boy A. Five knives and a police baton were recovered by officers involved in the investigation. Boy B first claimed he had only 'jabbed' at Boy C, who was in Year 10, with a broken protractor. But on the day of the trial he pleaded guilty to unlawful wounding.

Mark Savill, defending, said Boy B was tormented and taunted by the gang. He said: "There had been disputes between pupils at the school, and they used to go to the library to bully him. One or two of these children were saying 'Show us your knife' and the situation began to escalate. There was a large number of pupils around them and Boy C began to taunt my client. He pushed my client and my client pushed him back." Boy B's mother told the judge: "He has never been in trouble. He is very much a family boy and has 10 GCSEs."

Boy A, who admitted affray, was sentenced to 100 hours community service.

JUDGE DAVID PAGET
CENTRAL CRIMINAL COURT
OLD BAILEY

On 10th September 2004 at the Old Bailey in London, a man who masterminded Britain's biggest gun factory, brazenly thanked a judge for helping him to "get away with it".

Stephen Herbert, 45, said he was delighted to receive only six years in jail for selling 574 guns to criminals. The sentence was immediately criticised by gun control campaigners. As he was led out of the Old Bailey dock, Herbert thanked Judge David Paget: "That's lovely. Thanks very much. We got away with that." Judge Paget was criticised a few years ago by children's charities for giving "light"sentences to a group of elderly paedophiles.

But it emerged that Herbert's jubilation may have been premature, when legal sources revealed that the prosecution had decided to apply to the Appeal Court to increase the sentence.

Labour MP Fabian Hamilton, who has campaigned against lax gun laws, said: "I am appalled by the sentence. People like this are as guilty as those who pull the trigger. They deserve life in prison because they are no better than murderers." Herbert and his partner Gary Beard, 47, had faced up to 10 years in jail after pleading guilty to conspiracies to manufacture prohibited weapons, sell them and cause fear of violence with them.

The main gun factory was in Beard's council flat in Sydenham, south London. But the plan was masterminded at Herbert's home in Bermondsey. The court was told that over 14 months, the pair were responsible for putting more than one gun a day into the hands of criminals. They bought £40 replica Walther PPK handguns, and changed them from blank-firing to fully functioning weapons capable of killing. They were then sold on by a shopkeeper, who cannot be named for legal reasons, with adapted ammunition for around £600 each, netting in excess of £350,000. Herbert had convictions for minor offences dating back 30 years, and Beard, a former jewellery maker, had been in court for dishonesty.

Judge David Paget

Judge Paget said the only thing in the two men's favour was that they pleaded guilty. If they had contested the case, they would have faced 9 years in jail. Campaign group Mothers Against Guns said in August 2004: "These converted guns are potentially even more lethal than a genuine firearm, as the bullets shatter on impact. One of our members' sons died with 189 internal injuries from one bullet from a replica gun."

JUDGE STANLEY SPENCE
READING CROWN COURT

PC Pete Scott suffered a breakdown after raider Paul Reilly attacked him in a loft Reilly had broken into, Reading Crown Court heard.

Reilly admitted the assault but claimed he was only acting in self-defence, a claim Judge Stanley Spence accepted, despite PC Scott and a fellow police officer saying it was an unprovoked attack. Judge Spence's decision means that Reilly will be sentenced on the basis that he may have been attacked first, a decision described by Police Inspector Martin Elliott, chairman of the Police Federation as 'bizarre'. The court was told Reilly hid in a loft in George Street, Reading, after officers were alerted to an intruder on 5th April 2003. Giving evidence, PC Scott said Reilly, 27, ignored repeated orders to put his hands out and instead knocked him off his feet and pinned him down. PC Scott said that Reilly, from Oakley Road, Caversham, then leapt on top of him and delivered at least six punches, before grinding his face into some roof lagging. "I was trying to breathe but gagging on the insulation. I realised I was in deep trouble and of the opinion I was going to die." said PC Scott.

The court heard that PC Scott lost a stone in weight following the attack and suffered post-traumatic stress disorder. John Dennis, prosecuting, suggested Reilly wanted to 'get the police officer out of action' in his desperation to escape. Reilly's attack was brought to a halt after former Judo champ PC Steve Purser put him into a headlock and struck him three times on the head with a mini-torch. But Reilly, a night shift worker at the Tesco store in Napier Road, told the court he complied with PC Scott's orders, but was instead beaten by the officers. He claimed this led to a struggle and he was only acting in self-defence. He denied pushing PC Scott's head into the insulation.

Martin Jackson, defending, said Reilly only pushed, not punched, PC Scott and that he lost his balance and landed on top of the officer. Reilly admitted assault occasioning actual bodily harm on the basis of self-defence but the prosecution did not accept this. Because of the discrepancy between the two versions, a court hearing, (known as a Newton hearing) was held, to decide if the basis of the plea was accurate. Judge Spence ruled it was, saying: "I have paid close attention to what was said by all the witnesses, and their demeanour when giving evidence. I cannot be sure the defendant was not acting in self defence when he pushed PC Scott." Commenting on the decision, Inspector Elliott said he was shocked and angered. He said: "My officers stick their lives on the line day in, day out to protect the public. This is not supporting the police service or the public and it is appalling that the judge said he could not make his mind up who he believed. Ninety-nine point nine per cent recurring of police officers are industrious hard-working people, who are paid to tell the truth and take their duty very seriously. This is a bizarre judgement giving the benefit of the doubt to the perpetrator, as opposed to the victims of crime. It is time the judiciary got behind the police force and the public." Reilly also admitted a charge of handling stolen goods on 2nd April and burglary on 5th April 2003, both in George Street, Reading.

JUDGE CHRISTOPHER CRITCHLOW
READING CROWN COURT

The scandal over Britain's 'soft' treatment of internet paedophiles has grown, after an Eton College master escaped jail for hoarding child porn images on his computer.

Classics master Ian McAuslan, 58, received a suspended nine-month prison sentence, the day after former judge David Selwood got a 12-month community order for similar offences. The two cases prompted repeated calls for an overhaul of punishments for paedophiles. One leading barrister said: "There's no doubt that had he been from a more ordinary background, he would have gone to jail. That is completely unfair."

McAuslan taught Latin and Greek at the £20,000-a-year Berkshire school. Bracknell magistrates had sent him to Reading Crown Court, because they did not believe their sentencing powers, of a maximum of six months jail, were adequate. He was unmasked as an internet paedophile when he sent his personal computer to Eton's IT Department for upgrading. Technicians found a library of 200 images of boys, some being raped by men. McAuslan, who joined Eton in 1980, was arrested in February 2003 and confessed to police that he had downloaded the images from the internet. He said he found the pictures 'attractive' and kept them because he wanted to look at them again. He resigned from the school, whose former pupils include Princes William and Harry. He never taught them. James Leonard, defending, said McAuslan had an unblemished 33-year career, and there was no question that he had ever assaulted boys in his care. McAuslan, of Southampton, admitted making indecent images of children and possessing indecent images. His Honour, Judge Christopher Critchlow, said: "You have a fine record as a teacher and you were clearly devoted to your profession. There is no evidence these offences and voyeuristic behaviour led to any involvement with your pupils. Had it done so the consequences would have been more serious."

The learned judge, in his wisdom, as stated, sentenced McAuslan to a suspended nine-month prison sentence and placed him on the Sex Offenders' Register for seven years. No order was made banning him from working with children.

(On 14th July 2004 police destroyed 120 computers belonging to convicted paedophiles, at a scrapyard in Shoreham, W.Sussex, in the latest move to crack down on child abuse.)

JUDGE CHRISTOPHER BALL, QC
CHELMSFORD CROWN COURT

A judge let a child-sex abuser off jail, then blamed his three schoolgirl victims for egging him on. Amazingly, Judge Christopher Ball, QC, said he even considered naming and shaming the youngsters to warn other men not to be lured by THEM.

Pervert Nicholas Caley, 43, a former fireman from Braintree, Essex, admitted having unlawful sex with a girl of 14, and indecently assaulting two 15-year olds. But Judge Ball allowed him to walk free, saying all the girls were sexually provocative, precocious and promiscuous, and agreed to what happened. The comments from the judge, father of two daughters, sparked outrage among anti-abuse campaigners. TV star Esther Rantzen, head of the Childline charity, told *The People*: "I sometimes wonder what world judges inhabit. What he said would be extraordinarily hurtful to the children and their families and displays a lack of understanding of children and paedophiles."

Judge Christopher Ball

Michelle Elliott, director of Kidscape, a charity which helps bullied youngsters, added: " Anyone hearing this would think the judge seems more concerned to protect paedophiles than children." Caley could have got 14 years for under-age sex, and 10 years for each indecent assault. Instead, His Honour Judge Ball, in his great wisdom, gave Caley a 3-year rehabilitation order and a two-year punishment order. He also put him on the Sex Offenders Register for five years. The 54 year old judge told him: "These three young girls instigated this episode. They were drunk. They were provocative in engaging you in sexually titillating talk, advancing to sexual activity, which was completely consensual and indicative of a degree of sexual precociousness and promiscuity. I have considered whether they should be named, so other men in the vicinity are alert to the possible dangers of engaging in any form of social activity with these girls." But he had decided, 'with regret' not to identify them. "Even if they are their own worst enemies, they have to be protected from themselves." he explained.

Esther Rantzen said the judge's comments: " send out the worst message that the English legal system is as out of touch as it ever was." Elizabeth Frank, of the Children's Legal Centre said: " This is a prehistoric attitude. If he had named the girls they could have been targeted." An NSPCC spokesman said: "Sexual abuse should never appear to be condoned by judges." Judge Ball, who has been on the bench for three years, criticised a local newspaper in 2003 for naming a paedophile. He told *The People*: "I'm unable to speak to you about the details of any particular case I deal with."

JUDGE JOHN DIEHL
SWANSEA CROWN COURT

A mother of two who drove more than 30 miles the wrong way along a motorway, walked free from court with a five-year driving ban. Rebecca Denton, 37, of Pontypridd,raced past 13 junctions, believed to be a British record, at 80mph before being stopped.

Denton's 'incredible driving' ended only when she ran out of motorway as it reached a roundabout and turned into an A-class road. There, police laid a stinger device across the carriageway and blocked the road. Denton later told police that she thought that all the other drivers were going the wrong way. Swansea Crown Court heard that Denton, who had a history of depression, collected her friend Martine Williams from a mental hospital in Pontypridd, South Wales, and took her into Cardiff for a night out. After drinking two pints of lager, the pair decided to head for 'a short break' in Tenby, 80 miles west. Denton pulled off the motorway at junction 36 to use the Sarn service station. Paul Hobson, prosecuting, said she rejoined it by driving down the wrong exit slip road, and began heading west on the east-bound carriageway.

Her Toyota Celica was almost hit immediately by Mark Thorpe, who was at the wheel of a petrol tanker. He swerved onto the hard shoulder to avoid a collision and alerted police on a mobile phone. Police cars then drove alongside her in the correct carriageway, signalling across the central reservation for her to stop. "But Williams simply waved at them and Denton fixed her eyes on the road ahead." said Mr Hobson. At Port Talbot the motorway reduced to two lanes. Ryan Jones, driving east in a Renault Clio, pulled out to overtake, only to face Denton's car head-on. He swerved back into the slow lane but Denton's car took off his wing mirror. Further along PC Justin Knight 'bravely volunteered' to park his car in the centre lane with blue lights flashing, hoping Denton would see him and stop. But she did not even slow down. Mr Hobson said that by now Denton appeared to accelerate when she saw a vehicle approaching her. At junction 49, where the motorway ended, police blocked the eastbound carriageway and waved her down.

Mr Robson said Denton was 'heavily intoxicated' but failed to provide a breath sample. Denton admitted dangerous driving. Her plea of not guilty to failing to provide a sample for testing was accepted because, said Mr Hobson, the dangerous driving charge covered the drinking. She also denied assisting a person detained under the Mental Health Act to abscond. Her barrister, John Holmes, said she had a history of depression and had not been taking her medication. Although under the care of a psychiatrist, she was able to lead a normal life in the community.

Judge John Diehl made her the subject of a three-year community rehabilitation order, with a condition she underwent psychiatric treatment. She was also ordered to take an extended driving test before getting her licence back.

MR DAVID SELWOOD FORMER JUDGE AT WINCHESTER CROWN COURT

This man joined the Army and worked hard and was well-respected. He worked his way up to the top in the Army's legal services department and retired as a Major General, which is almost as high as you can go, just two ranks below Field Marshal. On retiring from the Army, probably on age-limit, he managed to get himself appointed as a Crown Court Judge, which probably meant just attending a conversion course, with his extensive legal background. He was appointed to Portsmouth Crown Court and seems to have quite swiftly become the senior judge there. However, the one item

which he had never declared on his CV, was the very important one, that he was a paedophile. He enjoyed downloading images of young boys, child pornography, from the internet. He paid for the services using his credit card and thus became one of the thousands of international child porn downloaders caught up in *Operation Ore.*

Above: Ex-Judge D.Selwood and wife leave Bow St. Magistrates Court after his conviction and sentencing as a Paedophile

Right: Ex-Judge D.Selwood shown in his robes

He was visited by the police at his home in Winchester and was arrested, his computer seized and the evidence discovered. It was widely publicised in the national press in 2004 and the story was put around that he had retired on ill-health grounds. Nobody with half a brain was going to fall for that one. At first, it appeared that there would be a cover-up, under the One Law For The Rich, Another For The Poor Act. However that proved not to be the case. The police charged him with 12 counts of making indecent images of young boys 8-14 years, and one count of possessing 75 indecent images on his computer. Because the indecent images of the boys were classified as level one, the least serious category of child pornography, plus the fact that he has co-operated fully with police throughout, AND had entered an early guilty plea, District Judge Timothy Workman, in his wisdom, sitting at Bow Street Magistrates Court, decided that a slap on the wrist was all that was required in Selwood's case.

His barrister had suggested that a Conditional Discharge would suffice. In the event, District Judge (The new name for Stipendiary Magistrates) Workman sentenced him to a 12 months community rehabilitation order. He was excused having to do any community service due to his age and ill-health and will not have to attend a programme for sex offenders. (Why the devil not?) He was also placed on the Sex Offenders' Register for five years. The reason ex-Crown Court Judge Selwood did not appear at his local magistrates court, is that Bow Street is the most senior magistrates court in the land and is often used for dealing with very high-profile cases and extradition hearings etc. However, you will be wondering why Mr Selwood was not dealt with in a CROWN COURT, like anyone else, for having been found in possession of child pornography? I think the relevant 'legislation' that covers this is *The Old Pals Act*, but I forget which year it was enacted.

Here is the icing on the cake, you'll be pleased I researched this item for you, Whilst sitting in his black and purple robes and horsehair wig, as a still-undetected paedophile Crown Court Judge at Portsmouth Crown Court, in 2002, a paedophile came before him. This man, Paul Hobbs, from Fareham had been convicted of being in possession of hundreds of indecent images of young girls. In his pre-sentence delivery speech, hypocritical Judge Selwood said to the defendant, "Those who search for and download images of this kind, create a market which encourages the abuse of young girls." He then sentenced the man to seven years imprisonment.

It's easy for the imagination to run wild after hearing something like that. Had Mr Hobbs's indecent images been of young BOYS, might the judge have slipped him a covert note via the court usher? Might he have visited him in prison, with the intention of trying to set up an indecent image exchange or trade-off? (Had he done so, Mr Selwood could have walked from his home in Winchester, the short distance to HMP Winchester, which would have been Mr Hobbs's first port of custodial call, after being sentenced.) In all seriousness, we have to face the fact that somebody in the JUDICIAL HIERARCHY pulled a huge string for pervert Selwood, which diverted him from the Crown Court, where you and I would have been tried, to Bow Street Magistrates Court, where even a District Judge has limited sentencing powers.

Will ex-Judge Selwood's exposure as a child pornography pervert prove to be the judicial scandal of the century? – Only time will tell.

DISTRICT JUDGE TIMOTHY WAKEMAN
BOW STREET MAGISTRATES COURT

Here is a second version of the Judge Selwood paedophile saga well worth including for your information:

During mid-April 2004, at his home in the Winchester area of Hampshire, a top Crown Court Judge, David Selwood, the resident judge at Portsmouth Crown Court, was arrested over the nationwide child pornography allegations. The married father of four, who boasts an illustrious military record and a lengthy entry in *Who's Who?* was interviewed at Eastleigh police station, near Southampton. He was quizzed by detectives over allegations of possessing indecent images of children and released on police bail pending further inquiries.

At his £500,000 home in leafy Magdalen Hill, the curtains remained drawn and the senior judge refused to talk to reporters about the allegation, when he answered his intercom. Judge Selwood, 69, would only say: "Thank you for your enquiry, but I am afraid that I am not in a position to say anything at the moment." The former Army Major General had been listed to sit in Court 1 at Portsmouth Crown Court on Thursday 22nd April 2004 but did not attend. He was due to preside over the trial of Francis Snook, 70, of Portsmouth, accused of indecent assault. Legal argument was instead heard by Judge Roger Hetherington. A Portsmouth Crown Court spokesman confirmed: "Judge Selwood has not been at work due to illness. We are not expecting him in next week either." A Hampshire police spokeswoman said: "The police can confirm that a man was arrested at an address in Winchester on Wednesday, in connection with a countrywide paedophile operation. The man was interviewed at a police station in Hampshire and has been subsequently released on bail pending further enquiries."

Judge Sellwood has been married for more than 30 years to his wife Barbara, with whom he has three sons and a daughter. In *Who's Who?* the judge lists a distinguished military career dating back to 1957, when he was a 2nd Lieutenant on National Service. He held military posts in the Army Legal Services in Germany and Cyprus, before being appointed Director of Army Legal Services in the Ministry of Defence in London from 1990 to 1992. The son of a naval commander, he has been a Circuit Judge in Hampshire since 1992 and resident judge at Portsmouth Crown Court since 1996. He is also an author of the Crown Court Index, a respected legal publication which gives advice on crown court issues. Judge Selwood has presided over a number of high profile cases at Portsmouth Crown Court. In 2001 he called a teacher who ran off with a 15-year-old schoolgirl, 'Every parent's nightmare'. He jailed Paul Tramontine, then 33, for 18 months after hearing that the girl's mother could never forgive him. He also made headlines the same year after a legal loophole meant he had to free a man from jail who was branded 'Britain's most dangerous paedophile'.

A spokesman for the Department for Constitutional Affairs said: "We can confirm that he is not currently sitting. We cannot comment on anything which may or may not be pending with this individual."

On 1st June 2004 it was announced publicly on BBC South TV news that Judge Selwood was being retired prematurely on health grounds! (What? No court case? Why on earth not?) I wouldn't mind betting that, like me, certain questions sprang to your mind as you read this report.

1) Did Judge Selwood receive the early morning sledge hammer knocking on his door?

2) Were police covering the rear as well as the front of his house in case he ran off?

3) Was his computer seized by police? How many vile images were downloaded or inspected by him?

4) Was he handcuffed behind his back?

5) Was he videoed for the continuance of the national 'pay-as-you-view' child porn TV documentary?

6) At the police station, was he allowed his single phone call and did he turn his pockets out?

7) In 1992 did he walk straight into his Army-to-Judiciary career change under *The Old Pals Act*?

8) In the last few years, has he sentenced any other 'pay-as-you-view' child porn offenders?

9) If so, could they have been members of a paedophile ring to which he might have belonged?

10) If the answers to questions 1-6 above are 'No', we have a 'one law for rich, another for poor' scenario.

IMPORTANT UPDATE RE THE ABOVE CASE OF (NOW-RETIRED) JUDGE DAVID SELWOOD

On the front page of the *Daily Express* newspaper dated 14th July 2004, beside a picture of him in his wig and robes, appeared the following banner headline: **Was this paedophile let off with a soft sentence because he is a Crown Court judge?** The main full-page article on page 11, carries two eye-catching, bold banner headlines:

1) **OUTRAGE AS HE WALKS AWAY WITH COMMUNITY ORDER**

2) **Paedophile judge is let off with just a slap on the wrist**

As this serious case of a senior judge, who was still sitting as Resident Judge, or 'judge-in-charge' at Portsmouth Crown Court, when he was arrested for downloading indecent images of young boys on his computer, is of such national importance and with far-reaching implications as to what goes on in the dark, murky world of paedophilia, I will now supply you with a verbatim report of the case, straight from the *Daily Express*.

"CHILDREN'S charities hit out at 'soft justice' after a former judge was given a 12-month community order for downloading indecent images of young boys. Experts condemned the sentence as 'little more than a slap on the wrist' and demanded a major overhaul of punishments for internet paedophiles. The NSPCC said: "Behind these indecent images are real children who will have suffered immense trauma. Receiving or downloading abusive images of children perpetuates its production and reinforces the cycle of exploitation. It is important to send out a strong warning to everyone, including those in all walks of life and professions, that they cannot remain anonymous and escape the law by using the internet to access abusive images of children."

David Selwood, 70, looked relieved as he emerged from Bow Street Magistrates Court in central London, holding hands with his wife Barbara. He resigned recently as a £110,000 a year judge at Portsmouth Crown Court. He was once head of the Army's Legal Service, holding the rank of Major General (This is just 2 ranks below the very top rank – Field Marshal), and gave advice to the SAS. While sitting as a judge in 2002, Selwood jailed an internet paedophile for seven years for having hundreds of indecent images of girls on his computer. He told Paul Hobbs, of Fareham: "Those who search for and download images of this kind, create a market which encourages the abuse of young girls."

Selwood admitted 12 counts of making indecent images of boys, aged from eight to fourteen and one count of possessing 75 indecent pictures in his computer. The father of four was arrested at his £500,000 home in Winchester, Hants, after detectives were tipped off by US investigators that he was using his credit card to download pay-per-view paedophile websites. The court heard that the images were considered to be level one, the least serious of the five categories of child pornography. District Judge Timothy Workman was restricted by court sentencing guidelines in punishing Selwood. He dismissed an application by Richard Hallam, defending, to give a conditional discharge. But legal experts said a 12-month community rehabilitation order was hardly a more severe penalty. Selwood was excused working in the community as part of the Order, because of his age and health. He will also not have to attend a programme for sex offenders. District Judge Workman told the court: "The defendant is a man who until now has had an exemplary record and who has throughout his career in both the Army and in the law, provided long and distinguished public service. He is entitled to credit for pleading guilty at the earliest opportunity and for his co-operation throughout with the police investigation. The commission of these offences and the convictions now recorded, are undoubtedly a personal tragedy to him and his family."

Selwood was put on the Sex Offenders' Register for five years, at a hearing last month. A senior lawyer involved in child porn prosecutions said: "This is little more than a slap on the wrist. The sentencing guidelines urgently need to be looked at again. A year's community rehabilitation order in cases like these simply does not represent an effective deterrent." Children's charity *Childline* welcomed the prosecution. Detective Chief Superintendent Jon Hesketh, who led the investigation said: " Mr Selwood disgraced the position of authority he held as a crown court judge." Despite calls that he should face severe financial penalties, Selwood will receive a £35,000-a-year pension plus a lump sum, thought to be around £75,000. He also has a substantial Army pension. Meanwhile, nine people were arrested by detectives and questioned at a London police station as part of the *Operation Ore* inquiry into child pornography on the internet."

MR JUSTICE COLLINS
HIGH COURT JUDGE

Mr Justice Collins

This top judge who caused uproar by freeing a terror suspect, has made a string of bizarre rulings which have infuriated politicians. High Court Judge Andrew Collins, sparked fury after releasing from custody an Algerian who was said to have been made mentally ill in jail, despite the fact that he had been described as a risk to national security. But Mr Justice Collins, 62, has been accused of 'being a law unto himself,' after making a whole series of judgements that have struck down Government decisions and confounded both Labour and Tory Ministers. Before the case involving the Algerian, who has been identified only as 'G', the judge had caused consternation on issues ranging from asylum, to fishing, and even Viagra. Educated at Eton and Cambridge, the married father of two is the son of left-wing cleric Canon John Collins, the 1950s founder of the Campaign for Nuclear Disarmament (CND).

As a barrister before becoming a judge, he represented supporters of Militant Tendency and was counsel to the Hillsborough Inquiry, that was heavily critical of the police. Probably the most shocking of his rulings came in September 2001, when he left the Government's ASYLUM policy in tatters, by stating that four Iraqi Kurds had been unlawfully held at Oakington Immigration Detention Centre in Cambridgeshire. But his record of upsetting Ministers stretches as far back as October 1996, when he decided that the then Home Secretary, Michael Howard, was wrong to stop BENEFITS for asylum seekers who delay making their applications after arriving in Britain. In July 1997, with two other judges, he ruled the

Government was wrong to ban 107 TRAWLERS from fishing in UK waters, leading to compensation of £100 million being claimed. In May 1999 he said that Health Secretary Frank Dobson was wrong to order doctors to limit PRESCRIPTION of Viagra. In November 2001 he insisted that Social Security PAYMENTS for Abu Qatada, Osama Bin Laden's 'Ambassador' in Europe, must be restored, after being stopped by Social Security Secretary Alistair Darling. In July 2002, as Head of the Special Immigration Appeals Commission, he ruled DETENTION of nine suspected al-Qaeda members was in breach of their human rights. The judgement was later overturned by the Court of Appeal. In February 2003 he decided that all asylum seekers have a right to social security benefits, overturning moves to stop illegal immigrants SPONGING off the state.

Mr Justice Collins has refused to comment on the backlash to his release of terror suspect 'G'. He was back in business in the Administration Division of the High Court, where he gave a Bosnian asylum seeker the right to appeal against a decision to boot him out. Mr Justice Collins' clerk said: "The judge does not make any comment on any of these cases." In the case of the terrorist suspect named only as 'G', Home Secretary David Blunkett could barely disguise his anger, as he vowed to strengthen anti-terror laws to prevent other extremists getting bail. He said: "Allowing someone like this bail, is an extraordinary decision which puts massive pressure on our anti-terror and security services and sends a very different signal to the one we have been sending."

The Algerian, a polio sufferer, is now under virtual house arrest, after being freed from Belmarsh top-security prison in SE London. His lawyers had claimed that he had become psychotic while in jail and would try to kill himself if he was kept locked up. The Special Immigration Appeals Commission rejected Mr Blunkett's claim that 'G' is a threat to UK security and should be kept behind bars. The Home Office would only say that its officials 'regretted' the decision to release the 35-year-old, who was one of 12 suspects held under emergency terror laws. The tagging is one of 11 bail conditions. 'G', who cannot walk unaided, will be monitored by phone 5 times a day. He cannot leave home, even to visit a mosque, without a police escort and cannot have visitors without permission. He cannot use a computer or mobile phone.

Tony Blair blasted Judge Collins over the terror suspect's bailing. In a highly unusual move, the Prime Minister slammed the Special Immigration Appeals Commission Panel. The PM's official spokesman said: "We regret the decision. Only 3 months ago the SIAC said there was reasonable suspicion that the appellant was an international terrorist and there was reasonable belief his presence is a risk to national security." David Blunkett vowed to change the law so he can appeal against such judgements. "I have not called it 'bonkers', but no doubt other people will."

Mr Blunkett's reaction was criticised on BBC *Newsnight* by the former Master of the Rolls, Lord Donaldson. He said: "We will always get a few litigants who complain about the judge, but we really don't expect this from people who hold the office of Secretary of State. He seems to show he has no respect for the law."

JUDGE ROBERT PRENDERGAST
INNER LONDON CROWN COURT

Britain's youngest hit-and-run killer was on bail for robbery when he ploughed into a teenager on a stolen motorbike, leaving him fatally injured. David Joyce was only 14 when he careered into 13-year-old Jamie Hussey as he collected conkers. He then fled, leaving his victim in a pool of blood.

As Joyce, now 15 was sentenced to four years in detention on 19th August 2004, for causing death by dangerous driving, it emerged that he had been out on bail, after being charged with being in a gang which attacked two men. He was given bail yet again, after being accused of killing Jamie. Seven months after the teenager's death, he was arrested again, this time for stealing a Mercedes. The teenager, who is from a family of Irish travellers, took his first car at the age of 12, but was only reprimanded by the police at the time.

Jamie's parents Wendy Hussey, 34, and her partner Graham Marriott, 37, sobbed as he was sentenced for killing their son. Later, Miss Hussey, who has five younger children, wept as she said: "He left my son lying in the road like a dead dog and all he got was four years. It's disgusting. When people say time heals, they are wrong. Nothing can take away our pain. How do you explain this sentence to the rest of our children? This boy isn't even remorseful. He stole another car after he killed my son. That is not remorse. He robbed a young boy of his life and we have to live with the consequences for ever."

Keith Burrows, of the Death by Dangerous Driving Campaign, said: "Joyce has flouted the law time and again and is laughing at the law, yet he only gets four years. It is a joke. Judges seem to think these youngsters are the victims because of their age, but they have ripped someone else's life apart." Mr Marriott added: "Jamie was terrific. He was a lovely boy, and we have lovely memories of him, but they are overshadowed by what Joyce has done to our family. We can't get it out of our minds." Judge Robert Prendergast ordered that he serve only two-thirds of his sentence, meaning Joyce will be free in under three years. Jamie had been out with friends close to his home in Bermondsey, South London, in September 2003 when Joyce crashed into him on the Kawasaki 125cc scrambler motorbike. Witnesses saw him careering along a pavement before swerving onto the road, where Jamie and his friends were crossing in a line. One driver heard the bike accelerate as it headed towards them.

Prosecutor Alex Chalk said: " Jamie was wrapped around the front of the motorcycle and it drove on a few feet before the driver fell off. There was a pool of blood around Jamie. He was obviously seriously injured." Passers-by tried to keep Joyce, who lived in nearby Rotherhithe, at the scene, but he swore at them and drove off. Jamie suffered serious head injuries and died three days later. A jury had earlier found Joyce and his co-defendant Liam Lawless guilty of the robbery. They attacked two men in May 2003, beating one up and stealing a £450 mountain bike from them. At Inner London Crown Court the judge recorded 'NO SEPARATE PENALTY' on Joyce for this offence. He also did not impose a separate penalty for stealing the motorbike which killed Jamie.

Joyce pleaded guilty to taking the Mercedes and other offences. At the time of sentencing for killing Jamie by dangerous driving, he had outstanding offences for aggravated vehicle taking, failing to stop for a police officer, driving without insurance, driving without a driving licence and giving false details.

JUDGE SUSANNAH WOOLLAM
BLACKFRIARS CROWN COURT

A drink-driver who fled after killing a couple in a high-speed crash, was jailed for just four years, on 27th September 2004. Simon Oakley, 32, a commodities broker, from Richmond, Surrey, was driving his Range Rover at 90mph when he ploughed into Valerie and Dick Hunt's Ford Escort, knocking it off the slow lane of the M3. He had drunk two gin and tonics, a Pimms and a pint of beer at a wedding reception, then ran off. When he was found six hours later, it was estimated he was **MORE THAN TWICE THE DRINK-DRIVE LIMIT** at the time of the crash.

Mr and Mrs Hunt's family described former grammar school boy Oakley as 'a pitiful coward', as they saw him sentenced at Blackfriars Crown Court. "Two wonderful human beings are just as dead as they would have been if this man had shot or stabbed them," said Carl Waldron, 43, Mrs Hunt's son from her first marriage. "I cannot forgive him, not after he ran away and left them for dead." Grandmother Mrs Hunt, 65, a retired civil servant, was driving her 50-year-old second husband home to Sunbury, SW London on 11th May 2003. The couple were killed 'almost instantly', the court heard. Oakley told the police he felt a 'mighty bang' and after getting out to investigate, he 'panicked.' At 6am, after sleeping in a hedge, he turned himself in. He admitted two counts of causing death by dangerous driving while over the limit.

Judge Suzannah Woollam told him: "You've deprived three children of their mother in circumstances of horror and deprived grandchildren of the happiness of knowing their grandparents." She added that Oakley had prolonged the suffering of the family by at first contesting the charges against him.

JUDGE FRANK CHAPMAN
WOLVERHAMPTON CROWN COURT

Judge Frank Chapman

Picking out a suspect with a shock of dyed hair and pierced ears from an identity parade should have been easy enough. But when every member of the line-up was made to wear hats and cover their ears with sticky tape, things suddenly got much harder. In fact, not one of the witnesses managed to pick out the alleged bag-snatcher, prompting the exasperated judge in the case to lament: "You might as well have a row of people with bags over their heads." Police had disguised the line-up, to ensure the suspect's bleach-blonde hair and earrings in both ears, would not sway the witnesses. But Judge Frank Chapman ridiculed their efforts, insisting the hair and ears should have been on view.

"They are the identifying features." he said. The suspect was applying for bail, when the identity parade came to light. Michael Burrows, prosecuting, said the defence could argue that their client should be freed on bail, because he was not picked out by anyone at the ID parade. But he then drew attention to the fact that members of the line-up were made to wear disguises. Martin Liddiard, defending, said he shared the prosecution's concerns over the parade but argued his 20-year-old client should be granted bail. However Judge Chapman ruled that bail should be refused and the man was remanded in custody.

The suspect, who went to public school, before being discharged from the Army with a leg injury, denies two charges of robbery, one of aggravated burglary and one of going equipped to steal. Later a spokesman for West Midlands Police defended the force's policy on ID parades. She said: "In the West Midlands there are three identification suites with permanent staff. They work to high standards and try to cater for the individual circumstances of each case." She said the Force would not comment in more detail about Judge Chapman's comments because the case was proceeding to trial.

JUDGE ROBIN ONIONS
WOLVERHAMPTON CROWN COURT

A boy who became Britain's youngest armed robber when he held up a grocery store with a sawn-off shotgun when he was only 12, walked free from court. The boy, now 13, who cannot be named for legal reasons, pointed the double-barrelled shotgun at the terrified shopkeeper before demanding cash and cigarettes. But he escaped detention when Judge Robin Onions placed him under a supervision order for three years.

He will be electronically tagged and will have to report to officers working for the local council for 25 hours a week. Passing sentence at Wolverhampton Crown Court on 19th August 2004, Judge Onions told the boy, who is said to be a talented footballer: "What you have done is very, very serious and if you are brought before me again you risk facing life detention or life in prison. Because of your age and because of the fact that you had no previous convictions, I feel a supervision order will help you to become an upstanding member of the community. You will start school again in September but I do not want you boasting of this. It is not something to be proud of."

The court was told how the baby-faced bandit burst into the store wearing a scarf round his face and a hooded top over his head. Jurors watched in horror as CCTV footage showed him pull the shotgun from under his jacket before threatening shopkeeper Jasbir Singh Guliani. The 20-minute footage, shown earlier in August 2004, showed the courageous store owner keeping the youngster talking before armed police stormed the shop. It was not until after the boy was arrested that they discovered the illegal weapon was not loaded. The court had earlier heard that the boy, from West Bromwich, West Midlands, had carried out the robbery as 'part of a game'. He had pleaded guilty at an earlier hearing to possessing a firearm with intent and attempted armed robbery.

Sentencing him, Judge Onions said: "This offence has a very bizarre quality about it. You have pleaded guilty to two offences of having a firearm with intent and attempted armed robbery. At the time you were only 12 years old although you have recently just turned 13. You claim to have found the shotgun at the home of a friend or relative. You took the gun and then you kept it for three weeks. You also claim that another member of your family dared you to commit this offence. Something you have also claimed is that you did this because you did not want to lose face. That is a remarkably poor reason. I have seen the video and you entered the store carrying the gun with a hood over your head. The shopkeeper, Jasbir Guliani, was very frightened, as he did not know if the gun was loaded.

Shortly after you entered the store, Mr Guliani's mother and father also entered the store and helped calm the situation. They took control and quickly realised they were dealing with a young boy. You were told to put the gun away and you did so before they contacted the police. When the police arrived they dealt with the situation and they pointed the gun at you. Understandably you were very frightened. You then knew how it felt to have a gun pointed at you."

The youngster, who is not much more than 4ft tall, was brought into court wearing a white sports shirt and white trousers. The court heard how he had written a letter to the Guliani family, telling them how sorry he was for what he had done. He wept as the letter was read out, it said:

I'm so sorry for what I have done. I never meant it to turn out the way it has. When I was doing this, I did not think what the penalty would be. If I could rewind what happened like a video tape I would not be playing it again. I cannot say enough about how sorry I am, I have been extremely stupid.

JUDGE MICHAEL STOKES
LEICESTER CROWN COURT

A drugs baron did a runner while on a £10 million heroin charge, after a judge freed him on bail so he could go off to Amsterdam. John Barton assured Judge Michael Stokes he would come back to face trial, after travelling to Europe's drugs capital with his solicitor 'to prepare his defence'. But Barton, 48, took advantage of the extraordinary decision to bail him with his passport, and he failed to come back. Now he is on Interpol's 'Most Wanted' list but is unlikely ever to serve time in a UK jail. Judge Stokes defended his decision to free Barton, telling the *Sunday Mirror*: "There has to be a reason not to allow somebody bail and if the prosecution say they have no objections, how can the judge do otherwise?" The former carpet salesmen's legal team told the judge, during a hearing in the run-up to his trial at Nottingham Crown Court, that the court would be in breach of the Human Rights Act, if Barton was not allowed to travel abroad to prepare his defence. Judge Stokes feared Barton, if found guilty,  would have clear grounds to appeal on the basis of not

Judge Michael Stokes

receiving a fair trial. So he agreed to hand back his passport. Astonishingly, the prosecution did not ask for any special restrictions to be placed on Barton's trip and the convicted thief was allowed complete freedom to travel around Amsterdam. Barton, charged with trying to smuggle 100 kilos of high-grade heroin into the UK, flew to Holland in January 2003.

After a few days, his solicitor, John Barnes, returned home expecting Barton to follow soon afterwards. Instead he simply vanished. It is only now that his dramatic flight from justice can be revealed because of legal reasons. A police source told the *Sunday Mirror*: "The decision to give Barton back his passport was unfortunate. The police and customs were very concerned he would do a bunk, using contacts in Amsterdam to disappear. Our worst fears became a reality. It was a bit embarrassing on the opening day of the trial to hear that the main suspect had not returned. The judge looked extremely angry. The judge was put in a difficult position because of the legal argument. He did not want to give Barton a reason to appeal on the basis that he did not have a fair trial."

Barton was convicted in his absence in April 2003 after a three-month trial at Nottingham Crown Court. He was jailed for 19 years for conspiring to import heroin. A second trial relating to Barton ended in April 2004. Hotelier Robert Briggs-Price attempted to smuggle eight million cigarettes into the UK. He wanted the profits to pay Barton to bring the Dutch heroin into Britain. Briggs-Price, 49, was convicted of conspiring to import drugs and is now serving 17 years. Barton was arrested in June 2000 after a huge police and customs surveillance operation. British police began following him after Dutch detectives photographed him, handing over a bag of cash to a supplier in March 1999. They arrested and jailed the man before he could supply the heroin to Barton, who made plans to recoup his outlay using the same crime gang. Customs officers set up a round-the-clock surveillance operation using a fleet of unmarked cars. They also read his phone bills to discover his contacts. Customs found that Barton, a bankrupt since a second-hand car dealership crashed in 1998, was renting a £1,500-a-month mansion in Caunton, Nottinghamshire. The divorced father-of-one lived in the £500,000 three-storey property with girlfriend Mary Gosling and her three children.

Friends revealed he had a succession of flashy cars, including a Bentley, and owned 3 racehorses. Despite the trappings of wealth, Barton did his best to avoid drawing police attention to himself. He rarely used mobile phones and met drug contacts in remote service stations, pubs and cafes. But unknown to Barton, police working undercover for 10 months had infiltrated Briggs-Price's gang. They even offered to set up transport for the deal, via a contact in Ireland, also an undercover officer. But the deal never went ahead and although Barton backed off, armed police arrested him at his home.

Because of the complexity of the case, Barton spent 16 months in custody. Then in October 2001 he was freed on bail and was handed back his passport for a holiday to Cuba. He returned and turned up for all his court appearances, it was only on the eve of his full trial that he disappeared. Mary Gosling said: "I had no idea he was going to go as suddenly as he did. I don't want anything more to do with him. I haven't heard from him since he left and I don't want to. I have moved on with my life."

One of Barton's co-accused in the trial, who was found not guilty, said: "I don't think I will see him again, he's not the type to get homesick. I don't envy him. It's not the type of life I would want to live, always looking over your shoulder every day, wondering if you're going to get nicked." Judge Stokes believes Barton had been lulling the authorities into a false sense of security. He said: "Barton did turn up on four occasions. But of course, with the benefit of hindsight he was creating the illusion he could be trusted. When it came to the big one he wasn't there."

JUDGE MICHAEL STOKES, QC
LEICESTER CROWN COURT

If you don't recall the nationwide publicity which this next case generated at the end of the Crown Court trial, you probably were out of the country on business, or on holiday. If you did miss it, you will hardly be able to believe your eyes when you've finished reading about it.

Jamie Thompson, 38, a Post Office security guard, from South Wigston, Leicestershire, had a girlfriend, who can't be named for legal reasons, to protect her child, a little girl then aged 12 months. For some reason, she suspected that Thompson, her then boyfriend, was ill treating her child whenever she trusted him to temporarily look after her. She set up a secret video camera in her lounge to check it out, for her own peace of mind. She then left the room for just five minutes. When she heard her little girl's screams she rushed back into the lounge and played back her secret video recording. The tape, which was played to the Crown Court, showed Thompson walking into the lounge and yanking the child from where she had been sitting on the sofa. Clutching one of her legs he was depicted swinging the child around as she screamed hysterically. He then taunted her, saying: "Again? Do you want me to do it again?" The tearful girl shook her head and begged "No." She screamed in terror as he grabbed her and again swung her about like a rag-doll and dangled her upside down. The girl was not injured but was distressed and traumatised. Her mother called the police.

When he was arrested, Thompson at first claimed that he was playing with the girl and that she was just as likely to laugh as cry, during their 'games'. He was later forced to admit what he had done 'in the face of the overwhelming evidence' of the video footage, the court was told. The prosecutor told the court that the child had previously been happy and trusting but became nervous and introverted when near Thompson. Her mother suspected that he was mistreating the child when left in his care. She therefore trained the secret video camera on the lounge settee area and left the room. He said that 'What she saw when she returned will – in her words – stay with her for the rest of her life'.

At an earlier hearing at Leicester Crown Court, James Varley, representing Thompson, said that his client, a post office security guard, was suffering from post traumatic stress disorder after an armed robbery at work in 1999, when a raider threatened to chop off his head with an axe. When the baby cried, it triggered traumatic memories of the incident, during which the raider held the axe against his throat. He added: "He suffered in that attack, and now he makes someone else suffer. But that video is as abhorrent to him as it is to the rest of the court." Since the first (axe) attack, he had been the victim of a second robbery, this time at gunpoint. Sentencing Thompson, the judge said to him: "What you did to this child was quite appalling. My one real concern is that I am not fully satisfied that you acknowledge the gravity of what you did. The child was absolutely terrified and the damage you may have done to that child is incalculable. But there's another important principle in this case. Defendants who are under severe stress or a genuine mental condition or disorder at the time of the offence should not be sent to prison. His Honour Judge Michael Stokes, QC, in his infinite wisdom, ordered Thompson to serve a two years community rehabilitation order and to be treated for post traumatic stress disorder.

After the trial, the child's mother said: "The sentence is far too lenient. I feel let down after everyone saw what happened in the court. I really did not think he would be let off so lightly. The only stress he has been under is the stress of finding an excuse to save his own neck. My daughter now behaves apprehensively with strangers. She's still withdrawn. I hope she will get over it." She went on to say that she was outraged by the judge's comments. "The first I ever heard about this robbery was when he used it as an excuse in court. I can never forgive him for what he has done. I really didn't think he would be let off after the judge had seen the video, but he has got off with just a bit of counselling. He deserves to be punished for what he did. That video was just five minutes of my little girl's life. She suffered brutal, systematic abuse for months. It's as if he's been let off for what he's done. It's as though they can say anything and get away with it. 'Oh, I'll just make up some story that I had such and such and I'll get away with it'. It's given him a second chance."

(**Author's note:** *If you couldn't understand my compulsion to write this book, before you read about this wicked child-abuser who has beaten the* *system, I'll bet you can now. Every day that goes by, dreadful people like this defendant, hire silver-tongued solicitors and lawyers, funded by the Legal Aid system of course, to twist the facts or invent a story to suit, to get them off the hook, THEIR RIGHTS being considered OVER AND ABOVE YOURS as a victim, or a victim's friend or relation, in this so-called criminal justice system, which has failed all law-abiding and decent people for far too long.)*

JUDGE JEFFREY RUCKER
TRURO CROWN COURT

A sick ex-schoolmaster who launched vile sex attacks on young boys has been jailed, after originally going free. Joseph Denley, now 79, was convicted of 41 offences committed over 21 years from 1962, when he was Deputy Head of a primary school. Yet Judge Jeffrey Rucker gave the brutal pervert a suspended sentence, telling him he would have gone to prison if he had been younger.

Now the Appeal Court has branded the sentence too soft and jailed Denley for two years after the case was taken up by a *News Of The World* Children's Champion. At the original trial, 21 former pupils of Marazion primary school, Cornwall, told of their torment. Truro Crown Court heard that Denley punished boys by calling them to the front of the class and putting his hands down their shorts. He humiliated youngsters by making them stand in a corner wearing a dunce's hat and beat them so hard that the rulers he hit them with snapped. Victim Frank Twyning, 50, now Cornwall County Council's Treasurer, said: "Denley would abuse me while I stood beside him at his desk. We all lived in fear of being hurt or humiliated. You didn't know if it was best to be in his good books or his bad books. If you were in his good books he would sexually abuse you, if you were in his bad books he would be violent."

Fellow victim Kevin Richards, 45 said: "Denley took a boy into the cupboard brandishing a long cane. When he came out the cane was in shreds from whacking him." Judge Rucker told Denley, from Penzance, "You were a bully who inflicted cruel forms of torture and punishment." But the judge let him off with a two year suspended sentence and a £2,500 fine. It was then that Phoenix Survivors, the support group for victims of paedophiles, stepped in to persuade the Attorney General to launch an appeal. The Group welcomed the jail term. "The original sentence was an insult to all of Denley's victims," said founder and spokeswoman Shy Keenan, winner of our Children's Champion award. "Too many sex offenders get lenient sentences because they are elderly. A paedophile will not stop offending at 79, he will go on and on abusing until he drops dead."

HIS HONOUR JUDGE WASSALL
TRURO CROWN COURT

Now for a report about a man at the very top of his profession, who carried out an appalling, deliberate and wilful attack whilst under the influence of drink. A leading heart disease expert, Professor James Scott, 57, of Chalfont St Peter, Bucks, and from Imperial College, London, highly qualified, committed this disgraceful offence of GBH (Grievous Bodily Harm) in a

Professor James Scott of Imperial College, London - caused serious GBH to a Hotel Manager's arm whilst in drink in Scilly Isles and walked free from Truro Crown Court

clear, public display, whilst acting in complete disregard for the all-important Hippocratic Oath, which all members of the medical profession have to swear to and then uphold its provisions.

You may well be of the opinion, when you've heard all of the facts, that in Professor Scott's case, he in fact must have sworn a *Hypocritic* Oath instead. This man is in charge of a £25million research budget and has won every honour in his chosen profession, short of the Nobel Prize. He is one of only two medical researchers elected as *Fellows of the Royal Society* and is a world-acknowledged expert in cardio-vascular research. He is the clinical professor of the National Heart and Lung Institute and Director of Imperial College's Genetics and Genomics Research Institute. So much for his medical qualifications and attributes, which must now have been seriously blighted by his behaviour on this occasion.

Just after Christmas 2003, Scott had gone with his fiancée to the Isles of Scilly intending to marry her on 30th December. However, the day before the planned wedding, he got drunk at the New Inn on Tresco, Isles of Scilly and slapped his fiancée, mother-of-three Vivienne Dignum, 55, and tried to throw a glass of wine over her. Hotel staff moved them to different rooms to defuse the situation but Scott carried on causing trouble. Hotel duty manager Mr Robin Lawson was attacked by Scott as he raised his arm to try to prevent Scott getting to his fiancée's room. Prosecution counsel Mr Ron Ede told Truro Crown Court that Hotel manager Mr Lawson heard two loud cracks, followed by a third, as Scott twisted his arm in apparent retaliation for frustrating his attempts to reach his fiancee's room. In fact the arm was found to be broken in three places through excessive rotation by Scott. Mr Lawson was immediately consumed by pain from the injured right arm, which he realised was useless and hanging down. The proposed wedding was then cancelled and Scott was arrested and flown to the mainland for questioning, but the couple have since made up and were due to marry within weeks. Scott admitted causing grievous bodily harm and was put on probation for three years under a community rehabilitation order.

He was ordered to pay £180 costs and attend courses to tackle his alcohol problem, and anger management. No order of compensation was made to the victim, after the judge was told that a civil action is pending and Scott has already offered an interim payment of £5,000. The judge said he would have gone to jail if the injury was intentional. He told Scott: "I have to sentence you on the basis that this was reckless and not intentional and I have to consider your record of achievement which goes beyond the exceptional. The only greater recognition of your work would be a Nobel Prize."

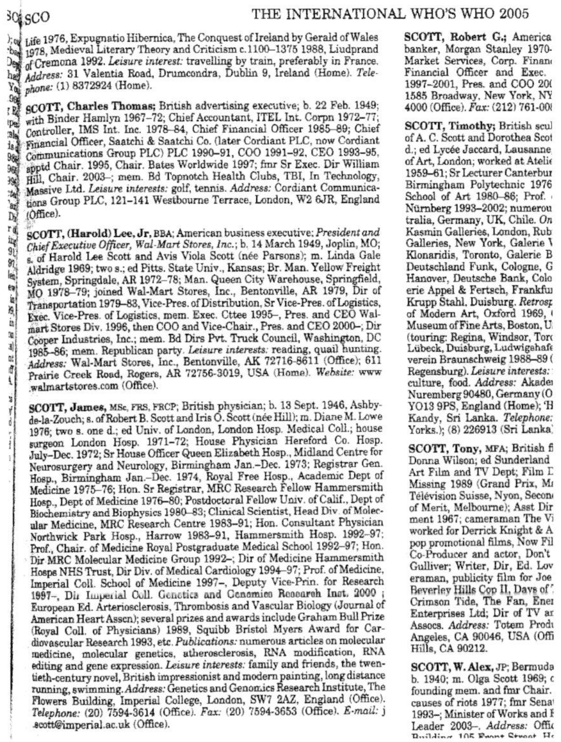

The following is a reproduction of a printed Who's Who page:

> 30 SCO THE INTERNATIONAL WHO'S WHO 2005
>
> Life 1976, Expugnatio Hibernica, The Conquest of Ireland by Gerald of Wales 1978, Medieval Literary Theory and Criticism c.1100–1375 1988, Liudprand of Cremona 1992. *Leisure interest:* travelling by train, preferably in France. *Address:* 31 Valentia Road, Drumcondra, Dublin 9, Ireland (Home). *Telephone:* (1) 8372924 (Home).
>
> **SCOTT, Charles Thomas;** British advertising executive; b. 22 Feb. 1949; with Binder Hamlyn 1967–72; Chief Accountant, ITEL Int. Corpn 1972–77; Controller, IMS Int. Inc. 1978–84, Chief Financial Officer 1985–89; Chief Financial Officer, Saatchi & Saatchi Co. (later Cordiant PLC, now Cordiant Communications Group PLC) PLC 1990–91, COO 1991–92, CEO 1993–95, apptd Chair. 1995, Chair. Bates Worldwide 1997; fmr Sr Exec. Dir William Hill, Chair. 2003– ; mem. Bd Topnotch Health Clubs, TBI, In Technology, Massive Ltd. *Leisure interests:* golf, tennis. *Address:* Cordiant Communications Group PLC, 121–141 Westbourne Terrace, London, W2 6JR, England (Office).
>
> **SCOTT, (Harold) Lee, Jr,** BBA; American business executive; *President and Chief Executive Officer, Wal-Mart Stores, Inc.;* b. 14 March 1949, Joplin, MO; s. of Harold Lee Scott and Avis Viola Scott (née Parsons); m. Linda Gale Aldridge 1969; two s.; ed Pitts. State Univ., Kansas; Br. Man. Yellow Freight System, Springdale, AR 1972–78; Man. Queen City Warehouse, Springfield, MO 1978–79; joined Wal-Mart Stores, Inc., Bentonville, AR 1979, Dir of Transportation 1979–83, Vice-Pres. of Distribution, Sr Vice-Pres. of Logistics, Exec. Vice-Pres. of Logistics, mem. Exec. Cttee 1995–, Pres. and CEO Wal-mart Stores Div. 1996, then COO and Vice-Chair., Pres. and CEO 2000–; Dir Cooper Industries, Inc.; mem. Bd Dirs Pvt. Truck Council, Washington, DC 1985–86; mem. Republican party. *Leisure interests:* reading, quail hunting. *Address:* Wal-Mart Stores, Inc., Bentonville, AR 72716-8611 (Office); 611 Prairie Creek Road, Rogers, AR 72756-3019, USA (Home). *Website:* www.walmartstores.com (Office).
>
> **SCOTT, James,** MSc, FRS, FRCP; British physician; b. 13 Sept. 1946, Ashby-de-la-Zouch; s. of Robert B. Scott and Iris O. Scott (née Hill); m. Diane M. Lowe 1976; two s. one d.; ed Univ. of London, London Hosp. Medical Coll.; house surgeon London Hosp. 1971–72; House Physician Hereford Co. Hosp. July–Dec. 1972; Sr House Officer Queen Elizabeth Hosp., Midland Centre for Neurosurgery and Neurology, Birmingham Jan.–Dec. 1973; Registrar Gen. Hosp., Birmingham Jan.–Dec. 1974, Royal Free Hosp., Academic Dept of Medicine 1975–76; Hon. Sr Registrar, MRC Research Fellow Hammersmith Hosp., Dept of Medicine 1976–80; Postdoctoral Fellow Univ. of Calif., Dept of Biochemistry and Biophysics 1980–83; Clinical Scientist, Head Div. of Molecular Medicine, MRC Research Centre 1983–91; Hon. Consultant Physician Northwick Park Hosp., Harrow 1983–91, Hammersmith Hosp. 1992–97; Prof., Chair. of Medicine Royal Postgraduate Medical School 1992–97; Hon. Dir MRC Molecular Medicine Group 1992–; Dir of Medicine Hammersmith Hosps NHS Trust, Dir Div. of Medical Cardiology 1994–97; Prof. of Medicine, Imperial Coll. School of Medicine 1997–, Deputy Vice-Prin. for Research 1997–; Dir Imperial Coll. Genetics and Genomics Research Inst. 2000 ; European Ed. Arteriosclerosis, Thrombosis and Vascular Biology (Journal of American Heart Assocn; several prizes and awards include Graham Bull Prize (Royal Coll. of Physicians) 1989, Squibb Bristol Myers Award for Cardiovascular Research 1993, etc. *Publications:* numerous articles on molecular medicine, molecular genetics, atherosclerosis, RNA modification, RNA editing and gene expression. *Leisure interests:* family and friends, the twentieth-century novel, British impressionist and modern painting, long distance running, swimming. *Address:* Genetics and Genomics Research Institute, The Flowers Building, Imperial College, London, SW7 2AZ, England (Office). *Telephone:* (20) 7594-3614 (Office). *Fax:* (20) 7594-3653 (Office). *E-mail:* j.scott@imperial.ac.uk (Office).
>
> **SCOTT, Robert G.;** American banker, Morgan Stanley 1970- Market Services, Corp. Finan. Financial Officer and Exec. 1997–2001, Pres. and COO 200 1585 Broadway, New York, NY 4000 (Office). *Fax:* (212) 761-00...
>
> **SCOTT, Timothy;** British scul d.; ed Lycée Jaccard, Lausanne of Art, London; worked at Atelie 1959–61; Sr Lecturer Canterbur Birmingham Polytechnic 1976 School of Art 1980–86; Prof. . Nürnberg 1993–2002; numerou tralia, Germany, UK, Chile. On Kasmin Galleries, London, Rub Galleries, New York, Galerie V Klonaridis, Toronto, Galerie B Deutschland Funk, Cologne, G Hanover, Deutsche Bank, Colo erie Appel & Fertsch, Frankfu Krupp Stahl, Duisburg, *Retrosp* of Modern Art, Oxford 1969, (Museum of Fine Arts, Boston, U (touring: Regina, Windsor, Toro Lübeck, Duisburg, Ludwigshafe verein Braunschweig 1988–89 (Regensburg). *Leisure interests:* culture, food. *Address:* Akade Nuremberg 90480, Germany (O YO13 9PS, England (Home); 'H Kandy, Sri Lanka. *Telephone:* Yorks.); (8) 226913 (Sri Lanka
>
> **SCOTT, Tony,** MFA; British fi Donna Wilson; ed Sunderland Art Film and TV Dept; Film D Missing 1989 (Grand Prix, M Télévision Suisse, Nyon, Secon of Merit, Melbourne); Asst Dir ment 1967; cameraman The Vi worked for Derrick Knight & A pop promotional films, New Fil Co-Producer and actor, Don't Gulliver; Writer, Dir, Ed. Lov eraman, publicity film for Joe Beverley Hills Cop II, Days of ? Crimson Tide, The Fan, Ener Enterprises Ltd; Dir of TV ar Assocs. *Address:* Totem Prod Angeles, CA 90046, USA (Offi Hills, CA 90212.
>
> **SCOTT, W. Alex,** JP; Bermuda b. 1940; m. Olga Scott 1969; c founding mem. and fmr Chair. causes of riots 1977; fmr Sena 1993–; Minister of Works and F Leader 2003–. *Address:* Offi Building, 105 Front Street, H

'Who's Who 2005 entry of Professor James Scott

Certain questions need answering, you might well agree:

1) Is this a clear-cut-case of one law for the rich and another for the poor?

2) Is this judge clearly guilty of failing to protect the public, in this case, victim Mr Lawson?

3) Will Professor Scott be punished by the General Medical Council?

4) Will he be internally disciplined by his employers, Imperial College, London?

5) With his vast medical qualifications and experience, Professor Scott of all people, must have known at the very start, that if you deliberately 'corkscrew' someone's arm in an unprovoked assault, to a rotation factor of three, not only will you most certainly break the arm, but you run the serious risk of also shattering or cutting the brachial artery, leading to severe, life-threatening trauma.

6) How on earth can a so-called learned Crown Court Judge state publicly in open court that Professor Scott's fuelled-by-drink-and-temper action in respect of the victim's arm, was NOT INTENTIONAL? (The arm could only have been left attached by tendons, muscles and sinews!)

7) Why was not Scott charged with 'causing grievous bodily harm with intent' (to cause GBH), which is one-step higher than (simple) GBH and, like Attempted Murder, carries life imprisonment? (Nobody could ever convince me that Scott in his temper, corkscrewing that poor man's arm, had no intention of causing grievous bodily harm). What are your considered views?

MRS JUSTICE RAFFERTY
LEWES CROWN COURT

Mother-of-two Miriam Keating behaved like a 'loud-mouthed offensive fishwife' after she was refused an upgrade on a flight from Jamaica to Gatwick, a Judge said at Lewes Crown Court. Keating, 46, of Glasgow, hurled obscenities at cabin crew, lit up a cigarette and staggered along the aisle on the Air 2000 flight. Her Honour Judge Mrs Justice Rafferty, in her wisdom, told Keating that she came 'very, very close' to being jailed. (Oh, not those dreaded 'cop-out' words from legal jargon again!) She was fined £1,500 for being drunk and smoking on an aircraft.

MRS JUSTICE RAFFERTY
LEWES CROWN COURT

The families of two young nannies killed by an uninsured drunk-driver condemned British justice after he was jailed for just five-and-a-half years. Relatives of Vicki Browne, 19, said they were disgusted that Graham Travers is likely to be freed in just three years, after killing two women and maiming a third.

Vicki's mother sobbed: "The sentence was an act of sheer stupidity and an insult to us all. We accept that none of this was intentional but five-and-a-half years is not acceptable. The family feels cheated. We expected justice for the death but what we have got is an insult. Is this all Vicki's life was worth?"

Mrs Browne said the family would urge the CPS to take the case to the Court of Appeal in a bid to get the sentence increased. Vicki and Natalie McCabe, 20, accepted a lift home from the 21-year-old barman in a borrowed Ford Mondeo after a night out. The killer was **ONE AND A HALF TIMES OVER THE DRINK-DRIVE LIMIT**, had no insurance and no driving licence. As he raced along the Hove seafront he hit a barrier. The third passenger, Becky Smith, 20, survived but had to have part of a leg amputated. Travers crawled from the wreckage and ran off.

Mrs Justice Rafferty, in her wisdom, told Travers: " Your driving was an exercise in arrogance. Like a petulant child you indulged your temper, but you did so using that most dangerous of weapons, a motor car. It's not accurate to say you have ruined three lives, those of your victims, since you have blighted many more. Nothing this court can do can right your wrongs." Travers had admitted causing deaths by dangerous driving and having no driving documents. In jailing him for just five-and-a-half years, Mrs Justice Rafferty was guided by current sentencing policy and had to give him 'CREDIT' for his guilty plea and the ONE-OFF nature of the offences. The maximum offence is TEN YEARS, but Mrs Justice Rafferty appeared not to have considered the death of *two* young girls and the maiming of another, whilst driving in drink etc. was worth more than what she gave. Who cares if he pleaded GUILTY or not, the evidence sounds as if it was overwhelming, especially as he ran away full of guilty knowledge, and to escape arrest no doubt?

A leading barrister said: "The judge has to work within sentencing guidelines and give the defendant credit for pleading guilty. If he had fought it and he was convicted, she would have jailed him for seven or eight years. Bad as this case is, there are even worse cases, particularly by repeated offenders. Five-and-a-half years is a stiff sentence when the maximum is ten".

(**Author's note:** *These lawyers and sentence advisory groups all live in a different world to the rest of us, don't you agree? Pity we can't do anything about it. What was wrong with making an example of the irresponsible person and giving him 10 years?*)

JUDGE CHARLES KEMP
LEWES CROWN COURT

It's not often that an action replay of an attempted murder and theft/robbery can be scrutinised by investigating police officers. When the attempted murder is followed by nothing short of a miracle, it is rarer still.

These actual events took place at Crawley railway station in West Sussex. The victim in this case, a youth named John Gibbs, was deliberately pushed off a railway platform onto the live rails, by an absolute thug called Stuart McLean, 23. The voltage passing through the live rails is 750 volts, viz: approx 3 times the normal domestic voltage of 240 volts. Most of the incident was captured on various CCTV cameras installed for safety etc at the station. Detective Constable Mark Chambers told Lewes Crown Court that McLean launched his assault on Mr Gibbs after making a completely untrue sexual allegation against him. The pair started to fight and McLean threw Mr Gibbs onto the tracks. The miracle occurred when Mr Gibbs lived to tell the tale, after actually coming in contact with a live rail. He received an electric shock but managed somehow to push himself off the live rail, before scrambling across the rest of the tracks and up onto the opposite platform. The cowardly McLean then fled the scene, leaving his accomplice, Craig Baker, to jump down onto the track to steal Mr Gibbs's bag containing a video recorder and cash. As well as the CCTV security cameras, the murderous attack was witnessed by other passengers waiting on the platform and by workmen who were installing a new ticket machine. An ambulance was called and the victim was examined by paramedics. He was found to be totally unharmed physically and was allowed to go home.

At the trial, McLean, of Horsham, admitted endangering the safety of a rail passenger. He was remanded on bail by the judge, yes, that's right, out on bail, not in custody, for one month for pre-sentencing reports to be prepared. The judge warned him that a jail sentence was, wait for it, possible! Minka Braun, defending, said McLean himself had been the victim of a horrendous attack when he was thrown off a railway bridge, breaking his back. "He fell into a deep depression and turned to drink." During the trial, McLean had claimed that prior to the attack, he had consumed 12 pints of beer and that the victim had stumbled onto the line by accident, during a struggle, but he later accepted that he had deliberately pushed him.

UPDATE: The sequel to this dreadful case is that once again, in a matter of great importance, this case could very easily have been a case of murder, a crown court judge has let the side down and passed a most lenient and inappropriate sentence.

At Lewes Crown Court on 19th August 2004, Judge Charles Kemp sentenced McLean to just 18 months imprisonment. How do you think the victim and his parents and family feel about that? This judge should be ashamed of himself, he has not made sure that justice is done, or seen to be done. He has not shown the victim and his relations the protection of the court and perhaps most importantly has not sent out a clear message, as a deterrent, to young hooligans not to fool about on railway platforms where live rails are adjacent.

JUDGE CLARK
LIVERPOOL CROWN COURT

Home Office worker Lisa Woods, 35, was part of an international crime ring selling fake passports which fetch up to £45,000 in the Middle East, Liverpool Crown Court was told. Executive Officer Woods, Stephen O'Toole, 45, of Aintree and Alison Saunders, 27, of Litherland, countersigned photographs for each other to get passports which were sold to foreigners.

One was bought by a Lebanese citizen who paid £15,000 through a Dutch contact. The prosecutor said that Liverpool Passport Office was alerted in June 2001 by an application accompanied by a photograph countersigned on the back by Saunders. Applications signed by Woods and O'Toole were also noted. All three said they had known the applicants for years as friends.

The prosecutor said one photograph was traced to an inmate in Sudbury Prison, Suffolk, who had surrendered his passport for bail. Another was of a man with a criminal record. The court was told that Woods, of Croxteth, Liverpool had been sacked. The trio were told by Judge Denis Clark: "These false passports in the hands of terrorists are like gold, that is how valuable they are. People dealing in this dangerous trade must stop." His Honour Judge Clark, whose bark is far worse than his bite, having stated to the three defendants that trade in false passports is so dangerous due to modern terrorism threats, in his great wisdom, jailed immigration official Woods for six months and O'Toole for 12 months. Saunders was given a 100-hour community service order. Terrorists in the forged/false passport-supply chain, reading the Judge's sentences, must be laughing up their sleeves and reaching for their camcorders, blindfolds, orange jumpsuits, hoods and sharp beheading knives. How pathetic, for handing-down sentences so weak as to be of no deterrent value whatsoever. If anything, you may feel that other Home Office Immigration Officials may be encouraged to jump on the lucrative 'False Passports' scam bandwagon.

JUDGE DAVID LYNCH
LIVERPOOL CROWN COURT

Judge David Lynch, on 15th November 2004 at Liverpool Crown Court, let the side down by failing to jail a defendant who was in breach of his ASBO. Great-Grandfather Alexander Muat, 88, a retired RAF engineer, had terrorised his neighbours yet again. In 2003, Muat became the oldest person in the country to be made the subject of an ASBO. He breached the ASBO three times by threatening a neighbour with a chair leg and twice swearing at other neighbours. When the ASBO had been originally made, Muat had been warned that the penalty for breaching it, was immediate jail. However liberal Judge David Lynch said to Muat: "The only reason I am not sending you to prison is because of your age." This Judge, in his infinite wisdom, therefore totally undermined the ASBO system, thus failing to send out the necessary message to other anti-social behaviour offenders across the country.

JUDGE ANTHONY WEBB
CANTERBURY CROWN COURT

A judge at Canterbury Crown Court has praised a veteran investigator of

The People newspaper for trapping a child-porn pervert. Roger Insall caught Lawrence Frape, 43, raking through sordid photographs of naked young girls, and secretly filmed him. He went into action after receiving a tip-off from Frape's neighbours in Dover, Kent, who were alarmed by his disgusting behaviour. Frape pleaded guilty to making indecent pictures. His Honour Judge Anthony Webb, in his wisdom, said: "I thank the national newspaper and reporter involved for acting responsibly in handing over its material to the police." He then, disappointingly, rather than jailing Frape, ordered him to have treatment and go on the Sex Offenders' Register.

JUDGE BATHURST NORMAN
SOUTHWARK CROWN COURT

This next case of serious, unprovoked violence took place in the London area. You may have already heard or read about it. It is almost too horrendous to commit to print, and I am quoting from the *Daily Mail* newspaper of 10th February 2004, amazingly deep inside the newspaper, on a double spread on pages 36 and 37. Personally, I feel it easily warranted pages 1, 2 and 3, as the case is just about as close to a murder as it's possible to be. You may well be of the opinion that the Crown Court Judge acted outrageously when sentencing and you may think that it's high time he was retired, as the last thing he is doing is protecting the public. The three-inch high bold headlines in this case, asked the question:

CAN THIS BE JUSTICE?

"Adyl Kanata had lain in intensive care for many days before his father was able to reach his bedside. The boy could neither hear nor see and had made no sound since being admitted to hospital, stabbed and beaten beyond recognition by an unknown assailant. But when his father, already in tears, reached down and touched his son's paralysed arm, Adyl emitted a terrible, unearthly cry. Who can say whether it was tactile recognition, pain or heart-rending coincidence?

That was almost 3 years ago. Adyl, now 23, is silent again and remains in hospital in what is called a 'persistent vegetative state', he exists in an immobile, twilight world, dependent on specialist care. His life was wrecked as the result of a chance encounter on the morning of 5th May 2001. For this is the story of not one, but two young men, from very different backgrounds and of the moment their paths crossed. It confirms the cheapness of life on our inner-city streets, yet it highlights the endurance of a mother's love in the face of brutality. It also calls into question the wisdom of an elderly judge, who, according to Adyl's family, has destroyed their faith in British justice.

Adyl grew up in a cosmopolitan, middle class family in the great Moroccan port city of Tangiers. His father, Homman, is Spanish, while his mother, Maria, is from Marrakesh. Both worked for the Moroccan Customs Service and were able to provide Adyl and his two sisters with a comfortable upbringing. Like his multi-lingual parents, Adyl was good at languages, mastering Arabic, Spanish, Berber and French. His ambition was to be a translator, and to this end, at the age of 18, he told his parents he wished to spend a period improving his English in London.

Everyone was against it, especially his father, because it was so far away, and he had read about English football hooligans. His mother explained: "His father wanted him to study in the Moroccan capital, Rabat, or in Madrid. I was the only one who supported my son's wish." As Adyl had a Spanish passport, studying in London was not a problem. He found a language college near the City, took a room with a West Indian family in Notting Hill Gate and a job as a waiter in Knightsbridge, near Harrods. Every Saturday he phoned home to his father in Morocco and his Dad implored him to take care. Adyl told his Dad not to worry as 'people here are ok.' His mother recalls that Adyl spoke as though London was some kind of paradise.

On Friday 4th May 2001, Adyl finished his restaurant shift and later met up with his friend Ashraf. Ahead of them lay a night of music, chat and laughter. It would end, instead, in horror and bloodshed. At 3.15am the next day, after an enjoyable night out, Adyl, Chris and two other friends called Yousaf and Ibrahim went to buy some food at an all-night Texaco garage on Hackney Road, East London. As they queued inside, a white car drew up on the forecourt. The driver filled its tank with petrol and then entered the shop. Instead of joining the back of the queue, the newcomer, a big man, pushed in front of Adyl and his friends. Adyl protested, but the queue jumper, Daniel Barker, became angry and threatened Adyl. Then he walked back to the car and spoke to its occupants, before seeking something in the white car boot. Despite the confrontation, Adyl continued to queue, testament, says his mother, to how safe he felt in London. Now Barker re-entered the shop, carrying a steel wheel lock 'like a baseball bat'. With him came his front-seat passenger, brandishing a knife. This second man, who has never been identified, began plunging the knife into Adyl's chest and stomach, although, at first, it seemed to witnesses, and probably the victim himself, that he was merely being punched. Adyl hardly moved as Barker then began to beat him around the shoulders with the tool, while his friend, Ibrahim, was also stabbed. The two men attempted to flee their assailants.

Adyl got as far as the pavement, where he was caught once again by Barker, who was seen to 'savagely' smash him about the head and neck with the steering lock, even after he had collapsed. Again and again the blows came down and when the defenceless student lay bleeding and unconscious on the pavement, Barker and his accomplice ran back to their car and drove off at speed. Later that day, Adyl's father was waiting for his son to call him on his mobile phone as usual. But this time it was the brother of Adyl's friend Ashraf who rang. He told Adyl's Dad: "Your son has been stabbed. You must come. I do not know whether you will find him alive or dead!" Adyl's father, so close to his only son, went into a shock from which he has never fully recovered. As a result, it was his two daughters, closely followed by their mother, who rushed to Adyl's bedside. The three women could barely recognise him. "Seeing my son like that was the worst thing in the world," says Mrs Kanata. "I could not bear to be told any more at that time." While Ibrahim, the other victim that night, made a full recovery from his injuries, Adyl's mother knew that his recovery, if there ever was one, would not be quick. So she resigned her job, losing her pension rights, in order to remain with him. Daniel Barker remained at large for 18 months after the attack. The two CCTV cameras on the garage forecourt weren't working that night and the police had only the film from the camera shooting over the cashier's shoulder inside the shop. That posed several problems. No one could say for sure the make of the car the attackers had escaped in. One witness said it might have been a white Renault Clio. Barker's then-girlfriend owned a similar model. In August, the police released a grainy CCTV image of one of the attackers. There was no response from the public and detectives later spoke of a 'climate of fear' surrounding the case. A small group of people knew who was responsible but did not dare come forward.

Then police approached a London TV news programme and when the enhanced CCTV footage was shown, in September 2001, the police incident room received two anonymous phone calls, both named the attacker as Barker. Police discovered that, unlike many of his contemporaries, Barker had no previous convictions, not even a driving offence, but behind this mask of innocence was a clever and dangerous young man, who, police suspected, was probably involved in the criminal underworld. Barker had associates who were involved in major drugs-dealing. More than once, he had been a suspect in cases involving violent assaults and intimidation, but they had never gone to trial. "He is the classic East End villain who kept his nose clean." said one police source. Barker is 6ft 3inches tall and powerfully built. Few would wish to stand in his way, yet in the early hours of that fateful day, Adyl did just that, in the most banal circumstances. Now, his almost meticulous avoidance of trouble with the law was beginning to unravel. But when the police broke down his door a few days later to arrest him, he wasn't there and he didn't surface again until December 2002. Even then, it was only because of the heightened terrorist alerts at airports following September 11th.

Special Branch officers were on the alert for single men travelling with little baggage. One man fitted that bill, on a flight to Malaga from Stansted, it was Barker. At the time of his arrest he was carrying £1,400 in cash, a small bag with a clean shirt and trousers, and a one-way ticket. He had recently become a father again, with a different woman and travel documents found later suggest that he had travelled to Spain at least ten times in the 19 months after the attack on Adyl. Barker was to claim that the trips were merely social, although one wonders how an unemployed man, who allegedly suffered from claustrophobia, managed to afford or even tolerate such journeys. Was he trying to hide, or could he have been involved with drug running?

Either way, he denied all knowledge of the Hackney attack, providing a string of false alibis and insisting: "I never stabbed anyone." Nevertheless, a jury at Southwark Crown Court found him guilty in February 2004 of wounding with intent (This offence is just one step down from attempted murder). Barker's ability to 'keep his nose clean' before the attack had apparently paid off. It was the minimum possible term and the Crown Prosecution Service are appealing against the sentence. But though Barker has destroyed the life of a bright and sociable young man and still refuses to identify his accomplice in the assault, he was handed a sentence of just five years by Judge Bathhurst-Norman (The maximum penalty for unlawful wounding with intent to cause grievous bodily harm is life imprisonment). Judge Bathhurst-Norman said to Barker: "This was a most horrendous attack on a young man whose only fault was that he objected to you queue-jumping. I have no doubt at all that you instigated the attack." For Adyl's mother, who has had her son snatched away to a living death, this is no kind of justice. When Adyl was transferred to The Royal Hospital for Neuro-Disabilities in Putney, (which was previously known as 'The Royal Home For Incurables') in late 2001, she was told it was very unlikely his condition would ever improve. Instead of wallowing in self-pity and grief, she made the selfless decision to dedicate her life to her son. Aided by admiring detectives, she got a National Insurance number and a bank account and was given indefinite leave to remain here, by the Immigration Authorities. She was also given council accommodation in a condemned block of flats, full of prostitutes and drug dealers, in Barker's home area of Bow, the other side of London from Adyl's hospital bedside. it is a far cry from her comfortable existence in Tangiers, Morocco, but Mrs Kanata was determined to stay with her son whatever the circumstances and soon got a job as a ward housekeeper at his hospital. For the past two years she has risen at 5am each day to spend a few precious moments with her son before her shift begins. Such devotion and dedication has had a devastating effect on family life. While her younger daughter stays with her in East London, her husband has had to keep his job in Morocco, visiting Adyl in UK when he can. The family's savings are gone, spent on air fares and Mrs Kanata's living expenses. She has received an interim payment from the Criminal Injuries Compensation Board, but, given the permanency of Adyl's condition, much more is needed. And what of the future? No hospital in Morocco is willing or able to look after Adyl. Until Judge Bathurst-Norman's lenient sentence, she was prepared to spend the rest of her life with her son in England. Now, though, she is so disgusted that she is exploring a possible transfer to a Spanish hospital. Doctors say that despite his injuries, Adyl could well live into middle age. He and his heart-broken family will continue to suffer for the rest of his life. Barker, on the other hand, could be free in three years. "My son was stabbed. With his sentence, the judge stabbed me" says Mrs Kanata. "I am full of anger. My son was effectively killed. My family was destroyed. I will live the rest of my life like this. Nothing will satisfy me or compensate my son. I will die with my heart full of pain."

Questions you might have liked to hear an answer to:

1) Did Judge Bathurst-Norman have Adyl's mother called to the witness box in his court, to hear what Mrs Kanata had to say about the terrible effects of Barker's wicked and criminal conduct on her and her family, before deciding on what sentence to pass on Barker?

2) Would the Judge have been satisfied with the 5-year sentence if it had been passed by another Judge, and Judge Bathurst-Norman knew the victim or his family?

3) Is Judge Bathhurst-Norman living in the same wicked world as we are?

4) How would you have felt in Mr and Mrs Kanata's places?

JUDGE PAUL DODGSON
SOUTHWARK CROWN COURT

A drunken steelworker who kicked his wife in the face after she failed to stack the fridge with beers 'escaped jail' for the 'disgusting' assault. Paul Cook received a community rehabilitation order at London's Southwark Crown Court and was ordered to pay £250 in compensation to his wife Theresa for her 'horrific' injuries. She left him after the attack.

Judge Paul Dodgson 'spared 47-year-old Cook from jail' to 'give him better access to an anti-domestic violence group'. So now you know where to go girls, if your cruel husband or partner kicks you in the face because the fridge is empty. Go to Southwark Crown Court and ask for Judge Paul Dodgson. He'll arrange for your 'ex' to pay you £250 for some retail therapy. You'll also know where your other half is most definitely not going, i.e. to jail. What an encouragement for members of the fair sex who are being regularly beaten up by their partners, but too scared to make the first move, to come forward. It's beyond me.

JUDGE GREGORY MITCHELL QC
SOUTHWARK CROWN COURT

At Southwark Crown Court on 7th October 2004, there could hardly have been a dry eye in the courtroom. Former college secretary, Carol Nicholls, 46, from Laindon, Essex, with a previous conviction for 13 counts of obtaining property to the value of £100,000 by deception in March 1989 by credit card fraud, was convicted of further fraud. On this occasion, a jury found her guilty of 19 counts of false accounting and obtaining money transfers by deception.

The total value she defrauded from her employers this time, was £37,000. The jury acquitted her of two further counts of obtaining property by deception. Nicholls had deceived her college professors into signing payments for freelance photographic work which she had not in fact carried out. The prosecutor told the court that Nicholls was able to use her knowledge of the accounting system at her college, to cash in on lax accounting practices, to the extent that she more than doubled her annual salary in just 10 months. She claimed she earned the money legitimately, after working on prestigious projects carried out by the Queen Mary University, in London's East End. The matter came to light after the books were audited in 2002. It was then discovered that she was being paid far more than she was entitled to. She spent the money on home improvements, including a conservatory, new kitchen units and a new central heating system. Her defence counsel, Caroline Moonan, told the court that the fraudulently obtained cash had been spent on 'necessities', rather than being squandered away. In his great wisdom, His Honour Judge Gregory Mitchell QC, allowed Nicholls to *keep the money* and ordered that a court costs figure of £1,600 should be waived. His Honour was clearly influenced by the fact that frauds woman Nicholls had, regrettably, lost her job due to her criminal behaviour at the college.

He had also heard that she is caring for a partially-sighted partner who suffered a brain haemorrhage. Instead of setting an example to other serial frauds persons, by jailing Nicholls, Judge Mitchell QC, decided that a community penalty was far more appropriate in this particular case. He sentenced her to a 240 hours community punishment order. After the case, a college spokesman outside the court said: "We are very fortunate in having staff who are generally highly responsible, and it is a shame that this employee abused the trust placed in her."

JUDGE DAVID GOODIN
IPSWICH CROWN COURT

A jealous husband drove the family car at his wife after accusing her of having an affair with his daughter's tennis coach. Furious Paul Martins pinned helpless wife Kay against their front porch with such force that the injuries meant doctors had to amputate her leg. Martins had confronted the 43-year-old hairdresser over her relationship with coach Simon Jordan, who is 18 years her junior.

Ipswich Crown Court was told he first slapped her, then threw her clothes out of the window before jumping behind the wheel and ploughing into her. The blow demolished a pillar which collapsed on to her and broke her right leg in two places. But despite the ferocity of the attack, Martins, 47, of Carlton Coleville, Lowestoft was spared jail, after his estranged wife asked for leniency. At Ipswich Crown Court on 31st August 2004 he was given an 18-month prison sentence, suspended for two years, after admitting a charge of inflicting grievous bodily harm. He was also ordered to pay £475 costs. The feuding couple,who also have two sons aged 16 and 14, are now getting divorced and are living at separate addresses.

Lyndsay Cox, prosecuting, said the couple's 17-year marriage got into difficulties after their nine-year-old daughter took up lessons at nearby Gorleston Lawn Tennis Club. "A friendship developed between the tennis coach and Mrs Martins. The defendant was upset by it and told his wife there was to be no further contact. However, during the summer holidays Mrs Martins saw the trainer, and they met on a fairly frequent basis. On

October 21st 2003 she saw him at the tennis club. Her car was seen by mutual friends and on October 22nd she returned home. Martins told her that her car had been seen. When he pressed her she admitted she had been meeting with him. He slapped her across the face and told her to pack her bags and go. He was very upset and emotional." He said Martins then threw his wife's mobile to the floor and threw some clothes from the house before driving off.

She went into the garden to retrieve the clothing and then became aware his car was returning at some speed. It struck the front porch and her leg was pinned between the vehicle and the structure. The defendant got out of the vehicle and said, 'Oh my God, what have I done?' Martins told police that he had not known his wife was in the porch and had not meant to crash his car into her. Simon Spence, defending, said the incident was the result of 'reckless behaviour rather than trying to cause his wife harm.' He said Martins, who used to work for Norwich Union, had not worked since the accident because of depression, and described the case as a 'human tragedy for all concerned.' "Mrs Martins herself has expressed the view she does not wish to see her ex-husband go to prison. It would enable him to pick up the pieces of his life and continue caring for his children, but remind him that one must act within the law." Judge David Goodin told Martins that such a case would normally result in a prison sentence, but he would make an exception for the sake of his children. "To send you immediately to prison would be to damage your children who are innocent bystanders in this tragic affair," he said. Blonde Mrs Martins, who had a prosthetic limb fitted two weeks after the attack, said: "I don't want to say anything, I just want to put all this behind me."

JUDGE PETER CHARLESWORTH
LEEDS CROWN COURT

A banned motorist driving a defective van with no insurance or MOT was jailed for four years on 17th September 2004 after killing a mother-to-be. Nick Craven, 28, who had never taken a driving test and had already been disqualified three times, was on bail awaiting sentence for other driving offences when he rammed into 25-year-old Fay Lee's family saloon. Fay, a teacher, was 14 weeks pregnant and died shortly after the crash when Craven's Ford Escort 'banger', which had bald tyres, failed to stop at a junction and hit the Renault Megane driven by her husband Ken. Craven admitted causing death by dangerous driving, attempting to pervert the course of justice, driving while disqualified and without insurance at Leeds Crown Court. His 'insulting' four-year sentence was 10 years less than the maximum. Judge Peter Charlesworth said he had rarely read more moving and heartrending statements from the victim's mother, husband and sister. He told Craven, of Skelmanthorpe.West Yorks: "For whatever reason you just didn't see the junction and I'm prepared to accept you didn't deliberately drive straight on knowing you had to give way. "The fact is you should not have been on the road at all and the van you were driving should not have been on the road. You were on bail at the time and you didn't care that the courts had told you not to drive. You didn't have an MOT or insurance and you didn't care whether you had a defective van." The crash happened near Wakefield as Craven returned from a night out at a pub with a friend. The court heard he had drunk two-and-a-half pints of lager although he was not over the limit when breath-tested at the scene in August 2004. Mr and Mrs Lee were returning home in Ardsley, South Yorks, from a night out and in a tragic twist of fate he took a wrong turn. Craven, who escaped unhurt, gave police a false name and claimed the van's brakes had failed. Among Craven's previous offences the court heard that in 1997 he was jailed for two months for driving while banned and without insurance. A spokeswoman for road safety charity Brake said: "This is an insult to Fay's family. This man should have received the maximum sentence. Four years is nothing against the life of a pregnant woman."

JUDGE CHRISTOPHER HODSON
COVENTRY CROWN COURT

Judge Hodson was the trial judge in a five day trial at Coventry Crown Court in August 2004. Professional footballer for West Bromwich Albion, and international player Lee Hughes, had pleaded not guilty to causing death by dangerous driving, but guilty to failing to stop after an accident and failing to report one. He caused a tragic and horrendous fatal car crash after a

Lee Hughes

post-big-match drinking binge with friends and others. He raced his £100,000 Mercedes sports coupe around a bend 'like a madman'. Having survived the crash which left one father-of-two dead and another wheelchair-bound with 2 broken knees and an injured hip, he was thought to have downed six shots of whisky at two pubs. This superfit and healthy, so-called professional 'star', with one previous conviction under his belt already, for drink-driving, fled the scene and literally vanished off the face of the earth for 36 hours. During that time, police had even broken into his house with a breathalyser kit, but he could not be found. He seemed totally unrepentant at the carnage he had left behind, not knowing whether the occupants of the other car were alive or dead. Apparently he wriggled and ducked and dived throughout the trial, and bit his lip when he discovered that the jury had not believed a word of it. He had obviously run off, or was picked up near the scene to beat the breathalyser. The minute West Bromwich Albion management learnt he had been convicted on the major charge, they sacked him. Judge Christopher Hodson told Hughes (no relation), "While I realise that your football career is at an end, be reminded that Douglas Graham's life is at an end." The maximum penalty for causing death by dangerous driving has, (since this accident) recently been increased from ten to fourteen years. His Honour Judge Hodson, in his wisdom, sentenced Hughes to just six years imprisonment, to the complete and utter horror of the surviving relations of Mr Graham, and the now-crippled Mr Albert Frisby, 59. He banned him from driving for ten years and sentenced him to four months imprisonment concurrent on the failure to stop and failure to report charges. He was also ordered to pay £8,467 in costs.

After reading about what a cowardly act he performed in running away from the scene, as well as making the grieving relatives suffer through a not guilty plea trial, you might well think that Judge Hodson could not have found a more deserving case for the then-maximum penalty of 10 years to be imposed, as there could not have been anything decent to be said in his favour. Instead, out-of-touch with reality Judge Hodson gave him more than a 40 per cent "discount", as it's bizarrely referred to, but for what?

As a sequel to the above report of Lee Hughes' disgraceful driving conduct, arising out of all the huge publicity generated around this country, if not internationally, has come this report from the victim of Hughes' *previous* drink-driving hit-and-literally-run accident. In a carbon copy of the crash which killed a father, Hughes fled from the scene of another, earlier accident when he knocked down cyclist Laurence Shannon. Mr Shannon, 53, revealed how the millionaire striker, who later failed a breath test, admitted going to a pub following the accident, but despite warnings that Hughes would 'one day kill someone', charges were dropped. In return, the former West Bromwich Albion footballer, who already had a previous conviction for drink-driving, was ordered by police to undertake a short driving improvement course. Mr Shannon said: " I warned the police back then that one day he was going to kill someone, but instead he got a slap on the wrist. After he knocked me over, he left me for dead and went off to, of all places, the pub. What kind of person does that? Afterwards they dropped the charges on the condition that he underwent a better driving course. I was absolutely outraged when I found out that was all he got for nearly destroying my life, and I was even more horrified to hear that he would be allowed back on the road.

I knew for certain Hughes was an accident just waiting to happen and all I could do was just pray that when it did nobody would be seriously hurt. Now it is too late and I can't imagine the pain that the victim's family are going through, but I am also disgusted because I just feel this was a tragedy which could and should have been prevented." Mr Shannon, a factory worker, said he was also left for dead, after being struck down in April 1999 by Hughes, who was behind the wheel of a BMW. He was cycling along a main road when Hughes smashed into him from behind. The impact threw him ten feet in the air over the top of the car. But instead of stopping to see if Mr Shannon was injured, Hughes ran off. Shaking with emotion, Mr Shannon said: "As I was lying there, a passer-by said that the driver was making a run for it. I just couldn't believe what I was hearing. There I was lying in the gutter and the driver was running off."

Mr Shannon escaped with a broken shoulder but was badly cut and bruised and deeply shocked. In another startling similarity between the two cases, Hughes later turned up at the hospital and gave himself up to police. He used exactly the same excuse for leaving the scene, claiming he panicked because of the shock. Mr Shannon added: " He told police that he became hysterical, so much so that he felt the urge to run up to the local pub. While he was there he must have been trying to forget about the accident over a pint, while I was lying helpless in the road. It was obvious my life had meant nothing to him and he was prepared to make up any excuse to try to worm his way out of the blame." Hughes, who failed the initial breath test, but passed a subsequent one, was reported for driving without due care and attention and failing to stop and report an accident.

After a four month wait, Mr Shannon was informed that charges had been dropped. Instead police offered Hughes the opportunity of a motoring course. A letter from West Midlands Police said: " Detailed consideration was given by the police to the circumstances of the accident, the previous driving record of Mr Hughes and it was decided on evidence that he was required to enrol in the National Driver Improvement Scheme. This he did and successfully completed."

Mr Shannon, who needed months of physiotherapy, received £20,000 compensation from Hughes after his insurers admitted liability, but the disgraced player never apologised to him. Bizarrely, within a week or so of Hughes having been convicted by the jury on this current matter and sentenced to his term of imprisonment, Hughes's father wrote to a national newspaper, complaining that his son Lee, had been made a scapegoat! Furthermore, readers will almost certainly not be surprised to learn that Lee Hughes, after taking up occupancy of his new 'home' in jail, failed his first drugs test !

HIGH COURT JUDGE JOHN WEEKS QC
IN THE HIGH COURT SITTING AT BRISTOL

This judge may be highly qualified in the legal department, but is sadly lacking in the brains and common sense departments. In August 2004, in his infinite 'wisdom', His Honour refused to grant an eviction order against a team of 16 families of gypsies, who had bought a three acre plot of land at the tiny village of Minety, Somerset and in breach of unapplied-for planning laws, bulldozed across fields to lay water, electricity and concrete roads, paths, hard-standings etc., thus blighting the naural charm and beauty of the village. The offending gypsies were represented on legal aid by a firm of legal aid fees-rich solicitors.

The local council and the village residents had to fund their own application. In a classic speech of balderdash and utter tripe the Judge said in court: "There is clearly a strong public interest in upholding planning laws and there has been a flagrant and deliberate breach of planning control. However, the immediate hardship and suffering which will be felt from the order sought, is sufficient to outweigh the public interest in enforcing it." Apparently his reasoning included considerations about their human rights and their potential inability to educate their children. (Since when were gypsies and travellers or tinkers concerned about child education?) If by 'education', they meant how to go to the toilet unhygienically all over the place, tear up gates and fences for sing-song bonfires and BBQ's, crush down the

Judge John Weeks

crops and leave 28 tons of rusty scrap iron and old car tyres behind when they move, then 'education' needs clearly defining. Some Minety villagers have staked out the entrance gates area to Judge John Weeks's huge mansion and vast swathes of land, with caravans and placards stating 'How do you like it, m'lud?'

Councillor Doreen Darby from the planning committee of North Wiltshire District Council said: "The law is an ass and it is braying rather loudly at the moment. The gypsies have driven a horse and caravan through the planning laws".

UPDATE: On 2nd August 2004 Judge Weeks, QC, was quick to afford himself the kind of protection he denied the villagers of Minety. The *Daily Express* tried to take a photograph of the judge's £3.5 million turreted, sandstone mansion,which is approached by a 100ft drive and enjoys uninterrupted views of the Somerset countryside. But he angrily turned them away as they approached the imposing building, which is on the site of a deserted medieval village and has parts dating back to the 13th century. "You know that you can't approach judges, this is unethical," he said, before complaining that the press actions amounted to a 'gross intrusion' of his privacy. The married father of three, who lists 'walking his dog' as his hobby in *Who's Who*, refused to answer questions about his decision, which has enraged the residents of the once-beautiful village of Minety. It is not the first controversial ruling made by the Oxford-educated judge. He once found in favour of a couple who complained about a neighbour's sewage system, but then ordered them to pay legal costs for both parties. In another bizarre ruling, he refused to allow a family haulage business to drive its lorries down a lane to where the firm was based, but could only use the route for 'agricultural purposes.'

RECORDER JEREMY STUART-SMITH QC
BRISTOL CROWN COURT

A woman involved in an acid attack in a Bristol pub has been jailed for (only) four years at the city's Crown Court. Leanne Jackson, 26, had previously pleaded guilty to a series of wounding offences after the attack in December 2003. The charges relate to injuries sustained by five people when Jackson threw drain cleaner in the *Inkerman* pub in St Paul's, Bristol. The victims were treated for burns and the effects of inhaling fumes. Jackson suffered burns during the incident. The cleaner was 96% sulphuric acid and was thrown by Jackson after she was thrown out of a private birthday party at the pub. The mother of two, of Byron Street, was told by Recorder Jeremy Stuart-Smith QC: "The injuries you caused to other people were horrific. This was deliberate even if it was done on the spur of the moment. You certainly did know it was a dangerous substance that could cause really serious harm." Prosecutor Fiona Elder said some victims had suffered significant injuries and were permanently scarred by the acid.

She said: "Any splashing to anyone caused erosion immediately to their skin or clothes. Almost all of the burns the doctors looked at in relation to the victims were severe and permanent." The charges related to five different people and Jackson asked the judge to consider 23 (TIC) further counts of actual bodily harm. Victims of the attack described the sentence as 'ridiculous'. Attack victim Pauline Williams, 39, of St Pauls, said: "I wanted her to get longer, at least 10 years. What she has done has affected me for the rest of my life and I'm going to see the results of it every day when I look at my face in the mirror." The court had heard that Jackson had a previous conviction for carrying an offensive weapon and attacking someone with a hammer.

JUDGE MICHAEL ROACH
BRISTOL CROWN COURT

A judge's decision to free a man who had sex with a 12-year-old girl after grooming her over the internet, sparked outrage among child protection campaigners. Judge Michael Roach said the girl had encouraged a physical relationship and described it as an 'exceptional case'. But campaigners said the judge's comments would encourage paedophiles who groom internet victims. Michael Barrett, 20, admitted having sex with the girl after meeting her in an internet chatroom. But sentencing Barrett to a two-year conditional discharge, the judge said: " It seems to me that whilst you did what you did, in contrast to many cases, there was no sexual coercion. The girl was a willing participant and her family allowed you to stay in their

home that night, after which you had second thoughts and you took the view that you had to do something about it and went to the police. I trust you to behave yourself now after the reports I've read about you, which have been very positive and encouraging. Set yourself straight."

Judge Michael Roach

Barrett, who was also ordered to sign the Sex Offender's Register for two years, visited the girl twice at her parents' home and confessed to having unprotected sex on both occasions. The trainee croupier walked free from Bristol Crown Court on 6th September 2004 and admitted: "I think I have been lucky. I just want to put this behind me. I have no intention whatsoever of doing anything like that at all again." But Dr Michele Elliott, founder of national charity Kidscape, labelled the judge's decision as 'appalling'. She said: " What this is saying is that having sex with a child is not really serious and that 12-year-old girls don't really have to be protected, even though it says so in law. Basically this man has got off with a slap on the wrist. This sends out a terrible message to young girls that they can go ahead and have sex, and it is certainly not heeding the dangers of the internet. It is also saying it is OK for anybody to have sex with 12-year-old girls, as long as they don't rape them, or as long as they groom them, so they think they have given informed consent. The law is clear. You don't have sex with 12-year-old girls and this should always incur a prison sentence."

Under new laws brought in this year, 2004, penetrative sex with a child under 13 is classified as rape and carries a maximum life sentence, but the Act is not retrospective. So Barrett, described as being 'younger than his years', could only be sentenced on the charge of unlawful sexual intercourse. He had admitted two counts of unlawful sexual intercourse (USI) with the girl, who lives in Greater Manchester. Liz Atkins, of NSPCC, said: "This does appear to be a very lenient sentence that sends out the wrong message. Even under the old law there was a clear distinction and a child under 13 can't give informed consent to any sexual act." Labour MP Dan Norris, a former Child Protection Officer, said: "The judge needs to be on trial, this is wholly unacceptable." Margaret Gregor, head of the Zero Tolerance Trust said: " This further highlights the need for judges to have training in how to deal with such cases."

MR RECORDER ECCLES
PRESTON CROWN COURT

A father who let his 11-year-old son drive down a motorway causing a horrific crash has been jailed. Giovanni Fronte, 53, asked his son Stephen to take the wheel so he could have a nap. The lad, who had been allowed to drive along the M6 earlier in the day at speeds of up to 85mph, was more cautious because it was dark and the road was wet and slippery. But Fronte, a former sergeant in the Italian Air force dozed off. When he woke, he thought they were about to miss the junction they needed. Stephen panicked and swerved towards the exit at around 65mph, skidded onto the hard shoulder and veered back onto the motorway. Their Hyundai hit another vehicle and smashed into the central reservation. The accident, on Boxing Day 2003, left two elderly people in the other car badly injured. The elderly lady sustained five broken ribs and a fractured sternum (breastbone). Hotel boss Fronte and Stephen were also badly hurt, but managed to swap places before police arrived. Fronte later admitted the youngster was driving.

Mr Recorder Eccles told him at Preston Crown Court: "This was an unbelievable thing to do. To allow an 11-year-old boy to have control of a car is absolutely absurd. The idea of a child of this age behind the wheel of a car beggars belief and it is terrifying that you even considered it. The fact an accident occurred is no surprise. I do not believe anybody could sensibly consider what you have done. For an offence this serious, custody is the only option.

He jailed Fronte, of Blackpool for 6 months. He had pleaded guilty at an earlier hearing to aiding and abetting dangerous driving. He was also banned from driving for two years. Stephen said afterwards: "It was dark and raining when I was driving. I saw a sign for the turning then I started to spin. I can't remember much else." The boy and his father had been returning from a Boxing Day meal in Manchester.

JUDGE GRAHAM COTTLE
EXETER CROWN COURT

A drunken lout was jailed for (just) five years for killing a caring pensioner who dared to ask him to pick up a glass he had smashed. Daemion Cain-Purcell, 23, flattened 65-year-old retired accountant Patrick Parkes with a single punch and left him dying on the pavement while he went to a pub for another drink. Sentencing the thug, Judge Graham Cottle said: "Your needless act of violence ended the life of a man who was much loved by his family and friends, and respected in his local community. His only crime was to remonstrate with you when you displayed the sort of loutish and drunken behaviour that is all too typical of youth today."

Mr Parkes and his wife Ann were walking home after dinner at the *Royal Fowey Yacht Club* in Cornwall when he spotted Cain-Purcell throwing his empty beer glass away in a car park. Despite being more than 40 years older than Cain-Purcell and his three friends, Mr Parkes told him to pick up the broken glass. Exeter Crown Court heard he started doing so, but then gave up and instead confronted Mr Parkes and punched him in the face after shouting abuse at him. Father-of-three Mr Parkes was a highly respected volunteer coastguard in Fowey and an active member of the sailing club, where friends described him as a true English Gentleman. Cain-Purcell was unemployed and homeless and was sleeping on friends' floors while spending most of his time drinking. He already had six convictions for violence and public order offences and just 19 days earlier he had been put on probation and ordered to do community service, after admitting a vicious assault on a shopkeeper who refused to serve him drink. Cain-Purcell of St Austell, admitted manslaughter and was jailed for five years by Judge Cottle, who said he was amazed that the killer was not already in jail for the earlier attack.

The judge told Cain-Purcell: "Mr Parkes was a man of 65 who posed no conceivable threat to you. Your victim could have walked away, but he was obviously the sort of man who had the courage to speak out and he paid the ultimate price when he did so. It was your response to punch him to the ground with so much force that his head hit the ground and he suffered fatal injuries. You showed your attitude when you were interviewed by police at a time when he was lying in hospital seriously injured. You told them, 'If you don't want to get knocked out, don't run or walk quickly towards me, simple'." Geoffrey Mercer, QC, prosecuting, said Mr and Mrs Parkes were walking home along the Esplanade in Fowey at 10.45pm on a Saturday night in January 2004 with their friends Gerry Williams and his wife. "The defendant was drunk. He later told police he had drunk four or five pints of

Guinness, four or five pints of lager and seven or eight glasses of Jamieson's." Sarah Munro, QC, defending, said: "This was not a gratuitous or unprovoked piece of violence (Oh-really?). It was only one punch which could only have led to a black eye, but in this case led to a tragedy." She read a letter from Cain-Purcell apologising to the victim's family. Afterwards, Mr Parkes's son Jeremy, a 34-year-year-old lawyer, said: "A loving family man has died as a result of an act of mindless drunken violence. In these days of ever increasing acts of wanton, drunken thuggery, we hope this sentence and the judge's comments will act as some kind of deterrent."

(**Author's note:** *The way the defence QC related a black eye possibility to an actual murder or manslaughter in the street, as 'not a gratuitous or unprovoked piece of violence', I find to be outrageous. How dare she minimise her violent career-criminal client's brutal conduct in that almost-dismissive way? As for the judge, in spite of his long, impassioned diatribe, in which he commented on weak sentencing by his immediate predecessor 19 days earlier, he turns out, when it comes to the crunch, to have a bark worse than his bite, like all-too-many of his judicial colleagues these days. Bearing in mind that the offence of manslaughter carries a maximum sentence of life imprisonment, his award of a paltry five years imprisonment to vicious, ne'e'r-do-well Cain-Purcell, had no deterrent value to any other brutal street-yobs whatsoever. He'll be out in two-and-a-half years or less, wearing his tag like a prestigious trophy, enjoying a very short-term of freedom, before his excessive binge-drinking further addles his brain and steers him towards his next victim. What a dreadful event for Mr Parkes's widow and friends to have witnessed, after going out for a nice, peaceful meal in convivial and familiar surroundings. Sadly, in these tragic circumstances, the trial judge has failed everyone – his performance on this occasion would not withstand an inspection by the Audit Commission or anyone else – don't you agree?*)*

JUDGE PHILIP CURLE
NORWICH CROWN COURT

During the hot summer of June 2003, near the Vauxhall Holiday Centre in Great Yarmouth, Norfolk, four girls were intent on attending a disco there. Kristine Errington, 12, suffered severe head injuries and died 36 hours later, after Shaun Moyse, 24, of Great Yarmouth, lost control of his high-powered BMW 325I convertible sports car, and mounted the pavement. He had owned the car for just 4 days. He was accused of driving 'like a bat out of hell' just prior to the accident. Victim Kristine's sister Leanne, 14, was knocked out and suffered head and shoulder injuries. The other two girls, miraculously, were unhurt.

The jury at Norwich Crown Court was told how Moyse had been driving 'aggressively' before the crash, revving up at traffic lights and giving the impression he wanted to race. It was claimed by one witness that after leaving the traffic lights, he drove at speeds up to 80mph. He then 'floored' the accelerator whilst trying to speed away from a roundabout, swerved out of control in the 130mph sports car on the wet road, hit the central barrier before hitting the girls, finally rolling down an embankment. Moyse had pleaded not guilty to causing death by dangerous driving, telling the jury that he felt the back of the car slide on the roundabout and had tried to brake. It was suggested to him that he might have put his foot on the accelerator instead of the brake, as the car had an automatic gear box, with two rather than three pedals. The parents of the dead girl broke down in tears as the jury found Moyse not guilty of dangerous driving. Mrs Errington said later: "We are absolutely devastated by this decision. We had all hoped that he would be found guilty of causing Kristine's death by dangerous driving, but even if he got 50 years in jail, it would never bring my daughter back. She was a happy, loving daughter who adored life and we are devastated by her loss."

Moyse's lawyer, Guy Ayers told the court, "We do not want anyone to think he has not been affected. He appreciates the devastating effect on the family who have lost their child." In a photograph accompanying the article, Moyse was shown grinning outside the court, although no mention was made as to whether he was pictured before, during, or after the trial. Crown Court Judge Philip Curl described the matter as 'a bad case of careless driving which had tragic results'. However the learned judge, in his wisdom, decided that the loss of Kristine's life was worth only a monetary penalty of £1,500 and a 15 months driving ban! You may be wondering if once again, this judge lives in 'the real world'. If ever there was a case of 'boy racer' running wild, you may think this was it. Would you have liked to be a 'fly-on-the-wall' in that jury room? I know I would.

JUDGE ALASDAIR DARROCH
NORWICH CROWN COURT

In 2003 it was reported in *The Times* newspaper that Judge Alasdair Darroch, at Norwich Crown Court, you might think, dealt totally inappropriately with drug addict Gary Callaby, aged 29 years. This man targeted the homes of people he knew, or where he had worked as a decorator. He broke in and stole jewellery and other property. Apparently his victims were left devastated by his raids on their homes in East Anglia. Callaby of West Raynham in Norfolk, admitted 3 burglaries, a theft and asked for four other burglaries to be TIC. In sentencing Callaby, His Honour said: "If the latest decision of (LCJ) Lord Woolf had not come out, it would have been a prison sentence. The offences you committed were very serious with two aggravating features. They occurred over a period of time, and you misused the information you obtained from customers." Callaby was given a 12-month drug treatment order. The Judge told him that if he breached the drug treatment order he could expect to go to jail for 18 months.

As usual, there was no mention of recompense, restitution or compensation for any of the eight victims in the case, in fact such 'awards' seem to be virtually unheard of these days. The above sentence was passed just two weeks after Lord Chief Justice Woolf told the Courts not to jail first-time burglars who would normally have received up to 18 months in prison. As stated, this 'guidance' from Lord Woolf and others, will be fully reported further on into the book.

JUDGE SIMON BARHAM
NORWICH CROWN COURT

A paedophile who had 85,000 child porn pictures on his computer has been banned from internet chat rooms for ten years. Christopher Dunkley, 36, from Great Yarmouth, is the first to be outlawed from the internet under a new law introduced in May 2004. Norwich Crown Court was told that Dunkley had gone into chat rooms to share his sexual feelings for boys and show his pornographic pictures. The prosecutor said: "He had been using chat rooms on the internet and had installed a webcam (internet web camera) on his PC so that they could see each other. He had been using the chat rooms to talk to others sharing his sexual views. He had been showing pornographic images of young boys being sexually abused at various levels. He was living-out his sexual fantasies and getting his sexual thrills from the internet. There is concern about Dunkley using the internet. He had begun to use a friend's computer to enter the chat rooms."

Police raided a flat in Norwich and found the perverted images on a computer. One of three CD ROMS in Dunkley's wardrobe contained 304 child porn images. Dunkley admitted 19 charges of making indecent images of children over three years and six charges of distributing them. Norwich Crown Court was told that Dunkley had been jailed for two years ten years ago, for indecently assaulting a boy in a public toilet. Judge Simon Barham told Dunkley: "This is necessary to protect the public from you." and jailed him for two-and-a-half years. One shocking image found on his computer was of an 18-month-old boy being abused by a man. Dunkley was also put on the Sex Offender's Register. His internet chat room ban was issued under the Sexual Offenders Act 2003.

The Crown Prosecution Service said: "We have not heard of a judge making this order before."

(**Author's note:** *This sick pervert was sentenced for the current child pornography matters on 21st July 2004. As a former police officer and cynic, the thoughts crossed my mind, firstly, whether this sentencing judge might have actually known recently-convicted paedophile, former Winchester Crown Court Judge David Selwood and secondly, whether this child-sex pervert Dunkley, might have shared some of the above-mentioned sick child-porn images with Mr Selwood. Who will ever know now? It makes you think, doesn't it? Obviously the grossly over-stretched police haven't the time to literally cross-reference ALL of their findings on individual paedophiles' computers with EVERY OTHER paedophiles perverted images.*)

JUDGE RONALD MOSS
LUTON CROWN COURT

A church-going MOD civil servant who killed a mother of four, when he crashed his car at 100mph during a suicide bid, has been jailed for just five years at Luton Crown Court. The sentence was branded as 'pitiful' by the victim's husband, Andrea Murphy, 40. He said: "We put our faith in the legal system and it let us down. I walked out of court in disgust."

Alistair Moffatt, 48, of Stotfold, Beds, attacked his wife with a knife and a jar of coffee at his home, after finding out she was in love with another man and had an affair. He then left home and tried to kill himself by driving his Ford Mondeo into a railway bridge at around 100mph. But his car struck a ramp that was hidden by vegetation and crashed into a silver Vauxhall Tigra travelling in the opposite direction, causing a major explosion. Driver Caroline Murphy, 39, also of Stotfold, suffered multiple fatal injuries as the car was sent spinning into the air. The court heard that despite trying to take evasive action, Mrs Murphy stood no chance. In police interviews Moffatt, who was not badly hurt, said he had intended to kill himself but had not wanted to harm anyone else. Judge Ronald Moss said to Moffatt: "Mrs Murphy was an innocent party. Your mind may have been in turmoil, but you had the choice whether to drive that way. There was no need for you to drive to commit suicide. There were other ways of doing it, rather than putting members of the public at risk. No judge can ever reflect the loss of a person's life in a sentence." Moffatt had pleaded guilty to the attempted murder of his wife and causing the death of Mrs Caroline Murphy by dangerous driving on 26th June.

JUDGE STEPHEN HOPKINS, QC
CARDIFF CROWN COURT

A babysitter, James Laidler, 35, a jewellery shop manager, of Penylan,

Cardiff, has appeared at Cardiff Crown Court. He was left in charge of an eight-months-old baby girl whilst her mother went to run some errands. He was alleged to have slapped the baby with 'full force', leaving a hand-shaped bruise on her face. He initially claimed the tot had smacked her head on the cot while crying. But prosecutor Harry Baker told the court: "But he then started shaking violently and said, 'I've hit her'." Judge Stephen Hopkins, QC told Laidler: "It is clear you have an explosive and uncontrollable temper." He sentenced the violent babysitter to eight months imprisonment.

JUDGE GABRIEL HUTTON
GLOUCESTER CROWN COURT

A judge who jailed a man for five years for causing the death of two men by dangerous driving, has given him his driving licence back four years early. Douglas Belassie, 59 then of Clanfield, West Oxon, now of Wokingham, Berks, was banned from driving for 10 years in December 1996 by Judge Gabriel Hutton at Gloucester Crown Court. Police had calculated that Melassie had driven home from the Cotswold Sailing Club, near Cirencester, at speeds up to 86mph, before losing control of his car on a bend near Fairford, Glos. Trent Carter, 29, and his lodger, ex-paratrooper Glenn Cooper, 22, were killed in the collision. Sentencing Belassie in 1996, after a jury had found him guilty, Judge Hutton told him it was one of the worst examples of dangerous driving he had come across. "Your driving was clearly of the most aggressive and dangerous kind and is probably accounted for by the fact you had taken drink, even though the amount of drink was not above the legal limit." Re-applying for his driving licence to be returned early to him, Belassie told the judge that he would never get behind the wheel of a car again, but added: "I have to cycle 16 miles to work every day and it would make life a lot easier if I had a small motorcycle." Naturally his application was granted. I wondered if relatives of his two dead victims were present in the court, to oppose the application, with impact statements? (Just ask the courts for anything, nothing is too much trouble – unless you're a VICTIM)

JUDGE JAMIE TABOR QC
GLOUCESTER CROWN COURT

Organised criminal gangs have infiltrated banks in Gloucestershire as part of a scam to fleece thousands from accounts, a court has heard. A fraud ring is using leaked confidential details about the state of customers' bank balances to get their hands on ther savings. Well-placed staff in banks are thought to be passing on detailed information, including the name of account holders and how much money they have, to contacts in the underworld. A shadowy figure is thought to be masterminding the scam and has contacts in banks in several parts of the country, including London. The sophisticated operation has targeted Cheltenham and a Crown Court judge has called for a police investigation to stem the flow of leaked information.

Judge Jamie Tabor

Gloucester Crown Court heard that Alan Thomas arrived at the Cheltenham branch of the Halifax armed with in-depth information about an account belonging to Wayne McDonald. The 41-year-old from Clovelly Road, Gloucester, was also carrying a false passport in Mr McDonald's name but bearing his own photograph. Thomas, who was described as 'small fry' in the operation, tried to withdraw £5,000 from the account but was caught after suspicious staff raised the alarm. Judge Jamie Tabor QC, who was dealing with the case, revealed he has dealt with three similar cases in as many months in the Cheltenham area. He said: " This type of activity seems to be increasing and it has got to be stamped out." Thomas admitted attempting to obtain £5,000 and was jailed for four months. Anwen Walker, prosecuting, said alert staff were concerned about the unusually large size of the withdrawal and started asking security questions. He began struggling to answer the questions and used his mobile phone to speak to another person to ask for help. "The woman cashier became more and more suspicious until Thomas realised the game was up and left." said Miss Walker. But he was later found by police hiding in the canteen at Littlewoods. He admitted using a credit card and passport to try to obtain money. Thomas is due to appear in court in London later to be sentenced for a similar offence he committed at the Chelsea branch of NatWest. When Thomas was questioned by detectives he said that a man known to him only as 'Dino' had set up both attempted scams. David Maunder, defending, said it appeared there was a shadowy figure behind the scenes, with the ability to forge documents and gain information about accounts.

Judge Tabor said: "There is a leak at the banks. You have to find an account where there are riches, and then you have to have a sophisticated fraudulent copying of passports and ID and then you find persons who go down and act on your behalf." The judge said he had some sympathy for Thomas, until he realised he had travelled to Cheltenham to commit the offence after being arrested and bailed in London. Mr Maunder said Thomas, a married father of two, succumbed to temptation when his work in the telecoms industry began to dry up and his earnings fell.

(**Author's note:** *Judge Tabor said: "This type of activity seems to be increasing and it has got to be stamped on and stamped out." You may well consider that Judge Tabor himself has done little or nothing towards stamping it out, with his paltry sentence of just four months imprisonment imposed on Thomas. Under the Theft Act 1968 the offence probably carries at least two years imprisonment and, in any case, a magistrates court could have sentenced Thomas to SIX months. Perhaps you are thinking that some judges sitting at Gloucester Crown Court live in a totally different world to the one that we live in.*)

JUDGE JAMIE TABOR QC
GLOUCESTER CROWN COURT

In December 2003, Judge Jamie Tabor QC, sitting at Gloucester Crown Court, dealt with a husband and wife couple. Deborah Major, 43, and her husband Kevin, both living in Gloucester. They were convicted of forcing a child to pose nude for pornographic pictures. His Honour Judge Jamie Tabor QC, in his great wisdom, apparently felt that the best way to protect children and the public from paedophiles, was to keep them out of jail. Deborah Major was ordered to carry out community work for 12 months and to sign the Sex Offenders Register for five years. Her husband Kevin was placed on probation for three years and told to attend a sex offenders' rehabilitation course. However just six months after her conviction, Deborah Major was recognised by someone who knew her, and her sickening history, as she was working as a cleaner at Barnwood Park High School for Girls in Gloucester

The discovery followed hard on the heels of the Bisham enquiry into the Soham case, in which Ian Huntley gained employment as a school caretaker leading to his access to Holly Wells and Jessica Chapman, whom he later murdered, after his credentials were not thoroughly checked by the police and the school authorities. A furious parent at Barnwood Park School said she was shocked that procedures were so lax following the Soham enquiry. She said: "It is unbelievable, I feel very angry about it. When I drop my daughter at school, I expect them to take full responsibility. After all we've heard about the Ian Huntley case, how can a sex offender still gain access to children like this?"

A spokesman for Gloucester County Council said it was up to the contract cleaning company to carry out checks on the staff it puts into schools. He said: "The safety of all children in our schools is of paramount importance to us. We insist that all staff, including those employed by contractors working in schools, have Criminal Record Bureau checks."

RECORDER MICHAEL SOOLE QC
SNARESBROOK CROWN COURT

This case involves a woman who was driving her Mazda sports car. This is the very popular, most common sports car you ever see in this country, in fact it is listed in the *Guinness Book Of Records* as the biggest-selling sports car of all time. They only seat two persons and as you probably know, they are very low and the driver sits almost 'on the ground'. The older models used to have retractable headlights, like a 'frog-eyed Sprite'. Mrs Rachel Doige, 46, of Woodford Green, Essex, was pulled over by stunned police officers, after they saw her race past Chingford police station in the red Mazda, with her terrified husband Clayton Doige, spread-eagled on the hood of the car, with his feet braced against the pop-up headlights. He was dressed just in shorts and a t-shirt. When the officers stopped her, Mrs Doige refused to take a breath test, telling them: "You'll pay for this, I'm a personal friend of your station commander." She was arrested and found to be **ONE AND A HALF TIMES OVER THE LEGAL LIMIT**, after drinking wine with a friend at a tennis club.

Her husband had jumped onto the car to try to stop her driving away after an argument about how much she had been drinking. She drove around for a mile or so, later claiming that she was too frightened of what her 17-stone husband might do to her, if she stopped the car to let him get off. A jury at Snaresbrook Crown Court, after deliberating for just 20 minutes, found her guilty of one count of dangerous driving on 18th February 2004. She had pleaded guilty to failing to provide a specimen for a breath test. Her counsel told the court that she had admitted having problems with her 'decision making' at the time of the offence and had sought counselling. He called for Mrs Doig to be 'spared jail' (Those oh-so-familiar-words we are sick and tired of hearing from benches of weak magistrates and judges!) as she 'has already been punished'. He said her marriage was 'destined to end' and that she had already moved out of her home at Hawkdene, Chingford.

Handing down her sentence, Recorder Michael Soole, QC, told the beautician, who had recently returned from carrying out voluntary work in India, that she was: "Lucky to escape a jail term for risking the lives of the public and your husband." Instead he sentenced her to a 60-hours community punishment order, fined her £250 with £500 costs and disqualified her from driving for five years.

RECORDER CHRISTOPHER WILSON-SMITH QC
DORCHESTER CROWN COURT

At Dorchester Crown Court on 4th November 2004, a paedophile 'escaped jail'. William Turton, 31, of Yeovil, Somerset, in his defence, had claimed that he was 'high on pot' whilst having sex with a girl aged 14 years. He already had a conviction for having under age sex. He admitted that during his commission of the current offence, he had sex with the girl, after ordering her to remove her clothes, while her parents slept close by. But the Recorder told Turton he believed that the girl was a willing partner. He said: "If you had not had cannabis, you would have pushed her away." Instead of jailing Turton, he handed down a three-year community rehabilitation order. Michelle Elliot from the children's charity Kidscape, said: "This is appalling. It gives any child molester the perfect excuse."

JUDGE DAVID RADFORD
SNARESBROOK CROWN COURT

Recently, at Snaresbrook Crown Court, based on the guidance given by the Lord Chief Justice, that most burglars should be given Community Sentences instead, Judge David Radford appears to have taken him at his word. He allowed Danny Coulson, aged 28 years, a drug addict, to walk free from Court, in spite of confessing to a total of 18 burglaries. His Honour Judge Radford, in his wisdom, sentenced him to a 12 months drug test and treatment order and an 18 month community rehabilitation order. In the press report of this matter, there was no mention of whether any or all of the 18 burglary victims were in Court, for the Judge to question them as to their traumas and post-burglary sufferings. Because of this, you might feel that British 'JUSTICE' is only available to *offenders*, whose human rights are always considered in great detail by the Judiciary?

JUDGE HENRY GLOBE
LIVERPOOL CROWN COURT

Disqualified and uninsured driver and convicted car thief Andrew Thompson, 27, from Anfield, Liverpool, appeared at Liverpool Crown Court on 4th June 2004, after a hit-and-run accident, before Judge Henry Globe. Thompson has never had a driving lesson in his life. He decided to borrow his friend's high-powered Ford Mondeo car, but was spotted by police and decided to make a run for it. After jumping red traffic lights to escape from police, he ploughed into 74-year-old father of seven Jim Barrett, who was crossing a road. He then crashed into some bollards. Although Thompson was himself injured in the crash, he crawled to a friend's house. The car was later set alight and a trail of blood he left on the pavement was washed away to hide his tracks.

Thompson pleaded guilty to causing death by dangerous driving. The judge said to him: "It is clear Mr Barrett was a quiet family man and by your actions you have affected the lives of a great many people. You are 27 years of age and have never had any lessons. You were driving while disqualified and have no insurance. This is almost as bad a previous convictions list as I have ever seen." (there being 42 previous convictions in total, including 17 convictions for driving whilst disqualified since the age of 16. At the time of this horrific accident, Thompson had just been released from his 15th jail sentence). The judge jailed Thompson for seven years. After the case, Mr Barrett's tearful daughter Sharon, 32, said she saw the white Mondeo being driven wildly just before her father was killed on 22nd February 2003. She went on to say: "Thompson is a scumbag, a known crook who is despised around here, and will never be forgiven for what he has done."

Merseyside CID Detective Chief Inspector Paul Robinson said that the sentence did not reflect the damage Thompson had caused. "The sentence will never reflect the impact of this tragedy upon the family. The family have lost a father of seven and grandfather of 20. He was a fit and healthy man who would do anything for anybody."

JUDGE ROBERT MOORE
SHEFFIELD CROWN COURT

A distraught mother slammed the 'disgusting' sentence handed out to a drugged-up learner driver, who killed her 14-year-old daughter Jade, when he crashed a 'banger' he had bought hours earlier for £50. Lisa Foster, 35, hit out after uninsured Gareth Frost, 18, from Wickersley, Rotherham, pleaded guilty at Sheffield Crown Court. He was 17 at the time and had taken two ecstasy tablets, smoked cannabis and had been drinking, before climbing behind the wheel of his 14-year-old 'rust-bucket' Austin Metro, the court was told. He had not passed his test, was not insured and had no driving licence, when he offered to take four teenagers, including Jade, for a ride in the car, which also had defective brakes and no MOT certificate. Soon afterwards he crashed into a lamp-post at 70mph, the vehicle skidding for 50 yards before flipping onto its roof. Jade suffered serious head injuries and died at the scene. The other three escaped with minor injuries. Witnesses described the car as 'cheap and in poor condition' when they saw it swaying from side to side before veering out of control in Maltby, South Yorks. Judge Robert Moore told him: "You have taken away one life and ruined the lives of two families." Afterwards, Mrs Forster said: " Jade had her whole life ahead of her and it has been snatched away. She was killed by someone who had taken drugs and was driving a car that wasn't fit for the road. He hasn't even passed his test. Even the police were amazed how light the sentence was. In my eyes he is a killer and should have got 10 years. It is disgusting. It was said in court that he showed remorse and regretted Jade's death, but I haven't had a word from him, not even a simple 'sorry'. I made myself go to the court. It was agony but I wanted to see the boy who took my daughter's life. I have never seen an ounce of remorse from him. Jade was a lovely girl and always had a smile on her face. She was so bubbly and full of life. On the night she died she went out with her friends and one of them knew the driver of the car and they thought it would be fun to have a ride in it."

Acting police inspector Graham Sayner said: "The maximum sentence in a case like this is 10 years and Frost was given a quarter of that. I can understand why Jade's family will not be happy." His Honour Judge Robert Moore, in his wisdom, had sentenced Frost to just two-and-a-half years youth custody, and banned him from driving for three years. Mrs Forster, who has three other children said: "He should have got at least 10 years. He'll be walking the streets in 15 months but I have to serve a life sentence and will never see my pretty girl again."

JUDGE ANTHONY BRIGGS
TEESSIDE CROWN COURT

Army sergeant John Smith, 30, of the First Battalion, King's Regiment, with two previous convictions for assault, went for a boozy night out with his wife and pals in Richmond, Yorkshire. However the father-of-two got involved in a fight when one of his friends was attacked. Passer-by William Wells, 30, tried to break up the fight, but Sgt. Smith punched and kicked him unconscious. In 1998 he had received a sentence of 80 hours community service for assault and affray and two years ago, 2002, the sergeant was court-martialled for causing bodily harm. He is stationed at Catterick Garrison, N.Yorks. At Teesside Crown Court he pleaded guilty to unlawful wounding (GBH).

A Major from his unit told the judge that the Army and his country needed him, especially as the Army was so under-manned, for another tour of duty in Kosovo and then back to Basra in Iraq. The Major said: "As a soldier he is particularly competent and respected by his men." Unfortunately, there is the usual sad ending for the victim in the case. His Honour Judge Anthony Briggs in his wisdom said: "You behaved disgracefully, this is your last chance." as he fined our hero £1,000 with £800 costs and ordered him to pay his victim £1,000 in compensation.

In the days of my military service with the Royal Marines, if you were unable to behave yourself whilst you were away from your unit and got in trouble with the civil police and courts, you received what was then known as 'consequential punishment' from the military, in addition to any civil penalty, for bringing the Queen's uniform and your unit into disrepute. How times have changed, when your assistant Commanding Officer turns out in his best uniform to speak up for you in court, knowing you're a thug of the first order, who cannot be trusted with a couple of pints of beer, never mind an SA80 semi-automatic rifle! I wonder what penalty Sgt. Smith will suffer next time he's on the loose in a pub or club? In my day he'd be tearing around Colchester Army 'Glasshouse' with a ten-pounds in weight, decommissioned rifle held at arms length above his head in double-quick time, as well as scrubbing his barrack-room floor with a toothbrush! Those were the days!

JUDGE TREVOR FABER
BIRMINGHAM CROWN COURT

The torment of three children at the hands of their parents was exposed when one child begged to be adopted, Birmingham Crown Court was told. The eight-year-old wrote to his teacher pleading to be given to a nice family. School staff were close to tears as they read of the suffering of the pupil, his 13-year-old sister and their 14-month-old brother. In a childish scrawl, the boy poured his heart out, explaining: "My family are not being like a family. I think I should be adopted by another family, you would think that it would not be fair, but I am telling the truth."

The youngster's cry for help was read out in public in the court, when his parents appeared on child-cruelty charges. The case was brought as a direct result of the boy's letter to his teacher. His note recounted graphic examples of his ordeal at home. He wrote: "My dad flushed my head in the toilet and my mum hits me with a spoon and a belt." Unusually, you may think, the local Social Services department intervened before there was a tragedy and the police were called in. The mother, a 34-year-old immigrant from southern Africa, admitted two counts of child cruelty and her partner, 32, admitted one count. The parents cannot be named for legal reasons. The father had denied flushing the boy's head down the toilet, but his barrister admitted he should have done more to protect his children.

Sentencing the parents, His Honour Judge Trevor Faber, in his wisdom, ordered them to each serve two-year community rehabilitation orders. The judge praised the boy's courage and said he had wisdom beyond his years. "It is impressive that he had such common sense and that he was doing so well at school." The judge told the parents that the mother's different cultural background, where child-beatings are said to be accepted, was not an excuse. He said: "These offences come at the bottom end of the scale, but are still regarded seriously by the courts, who have a duty to protect children. You have accepted that you hit your children with a wooden spoon and a belt. While you grew up in a country where this behaviour is accepted, in this country this kind of behaviour is rightly regarded as abhorrent and unlawful."

JUDGE TONY LANCASTER
NEWCASTLE CROWN COURT

Two men who caused the death of a moped rider while racing each other at speeds of up to 100mph, have been jailed. Steven Hoggett, 19, and Csaba Nemeth, 22, were racing home after work, when Hoggett's car clipped Derek Miller's moped, Newcastle Crown Court heard. Mr Miller, 59, from Sunderland, was thrown from his machine during the April 2003 incident. The victim's widow hit out at the sentences, saying both men should have been jailed for longer.

Hoggett, of Hawkins road, Murton, County Durham, had admitted causing death by dangerous driving, but both he and Nemeth, of Rosedale Street, Sunderland, had denied causing death by dangerous driving by racing. The court was told the pair were travelling at around 100mph and were just seconds apart in the moments before the collision. Nemeth's Toyota Corolla managed to swerve round Mr Miller's moped, but Hoggett's Citroen Saxo ploughed into the back of it. After being convicted by a jury they were both sentenced to three years and nine months imprisonment and banned for four years.

Judge Tony Lancaster told the two defendants: "I am aware of the views of Mr Miller's family. Their feelings for a severe sentence are understandable, borne out of anguish, but human life cannot be restored by the length of a prison sentence. The jury found you had been racing with each other. That is a feature which makes the offence worse and makes your driving highly culpable, a feature I must reflect in the sentence I pass." Mr Miller's widow Sylvia, 54, said after the sentence: "It's not enough. We would have liked a life sentence for a life. We knew that would never happen, but we thought six or seven years at least. The sentence is so disappointing for the loss of a life."

JUDGE BARRINGTON BLACK
HARROW CROWN COURT

One *serial* graffiti vandal is Michael Arthur Potter, then aged 19 years, from Kenton, Middlesex. He was caught red handed on CCTV after carrying out approx £10,000 worth of graffiti damage on the London Underground. His 'face' was circulated and apparently a near-neighbour identified him to police. Potter's form of graffiti was to spray underground trains on the Central Line, Bakerloo Line and Northern Line with his 'TAGS', *SUKA* and *KCD* ('Kicking cops to death'). Apparently on one occasion, Potter left behind his offensive graffiti marks at 40 separate sites on one tube train in one night.

He eventually appeared at Harrow Crown Court, Middlesex before His Honour Judge Barrington Black. Jailing Potter for 12 months, His Honour said to him: "If I had the power to take you by the scruff of the neck and make you clean every piece of filth off public transport in the city I would do so, but I don't believe it would or could be done by you." The judge added: "Apart from the expense to the owners and the public of cleaning these mutilated forms of transport, to my mind to inflict and expose on the general public offences of unsightly writings and drawings is both impertinent and arrogant, to say nothing of the offensive comments you found it necessary to make about the police force. It is not art. Art is something people choose to view. You were imposing your marks on a long-suffering public." Judge Black then said to Potter: "I believe these are serious offences and the public have correctly had their attention drawn to your escapades. It may be others will be deterred from the ruination of our city." His Honour sentenced Potter to 12 months imprisonment, and I'm pretty sure that he suspended the second half of it. Knowing from experience how difficult it is to catch the 'Potters' of this world, I was so incensed that I actually wrote to

Judge Barrington Black

Judge Barrington Black at the Harrow Crown Court, as I felt that a much longer sentence had been called for, with *none* of the sentence suspended. I referred to his handling of the Potter case and that he and other judges and magistrates could make a considerable difference to the almost total breakdown of law and order, virtually overnight, if he and they did their jobs properly, particularly so as we paid judges so much money every year. I suspect that this did not go down too well with Judge Black, and I feel there is a very good chance that he felt compelled to commit criminal damage to my letter! In any event, he decided not to answer it! (I failed to keep a copy of it in my angry rush to catch the post, otherwise I would have reproduced it here).

Most bizarrely, within a very short space of time indeed, after sentencing Potter, he had him brought back to Harrow Crown Court. (This very rarely happens in British courts). He is reported as saying to Potter, on this second occasion: "In the course of my sentencing, I said that the fact that the public were so disgusted by the preponderance of graffiti that, if I had the power, I would compel you to clean up the mess yourself." The judge said he had been aware of community service work involving gardening and painting and decorating local schools but felt that such punishment was 'too mild a palliative for the scourge of graffiti'. However, since then, he had been told by the Probation Service of a community project in another part of London, which did make graffiti offenders clean trains and property damaged by the illegal practice, information was not available to me at the time of the original sentence, therefore I am prepared to put my money where my mouth is." He told Potter: "It is rare to transfer someone to another district for community service." The judge then set aside the previous sentence of 12 months imprisonment and substituted one of 200 hours of community service instead. He was also ordered to pay London Underground £1,000 in compensation. Judge Black said to Potter: "I see a look of relief on your face, I'm not surprised. I take into account the ten days you have already spent in custody and you have thus experienced the clang of the prison gate. You have no previous convictions and are well thought of by both teachers and employers. You pleaded guilty at the first opportunity and I am told you are full of remorse."

A London Underground spokesman said: "We are pleased that Potter will experience at first hand the result of his crimes, and be forced to clean up the mess he has created. Graffiti is a personal attack on every Londoner's quality of life. It costs an estimated £10 million every year to fight graffiti and this money would be much better spent improving our service." Sergeant Paul Guile of the British Transport Police graffiti squad said: "The victims are not just the London Underground but also the good people of London using the service. BTP and London Underground will always seek stringent sentencing for persons brought before this court for this type of crime."

I personally feel that this important case raises a number of questions, which you might wish to consider:

a) Was Judge Black right to bring Potter back for a reduced sentence?

b) In a totally overstretched Probation Service, as we've heard, how did they find the time to phone around seeking an out-of-area placement for community service for Potter?

c) Was justice done in this case?

d) What were the costs from the public purse of the second hearing at the Crown Court?

e) Is Judge Black's bark worse than his bite?

f) As a good speech maker, would he be better employed in a theatrical environment?

g) Have the public been let down yet again by the Judiciary?

h) Were the offender's requirements prioritised over those of the victim?

i) Is this yet another all-too-familiar case of weak sentencing?

j) Do you think Potter graffiti-damaged his prison cell?

Well now that you've had a chance to perhaps answer one or more of the above questions, here is a report about Judge Black's then intended appearance on 19th June 1999 at the University of Leeds, Rupert Beckett lecture theatre, where he was to deliver the annual convocation lecture headed up: *Too fair, too far, to whom?*

> "Guilty people are going free because the legal system is 'too fair' to the accused. There are far too many acquittals because the direction to a jury that they should be 'satisfied so that they are sure' is setting a virtually impossible standard for conviction. After all, is there anything in this rapidly-changing world of which anyone can be satisfied so that they are sure? Another reason for guilty people walking free is that there are not sufficient numbers of mature jurors. The age of jurors should be raised, 18 is far too low and many of the professionals currently excused should be made to serve. Government proposals for human rights legislation and plans to change access to jury trials."

Those are the points that Judge Black intended to argue at that University lecture hall in 1999. I'm sorry I missed the lecture, are you? (Apparently Judge Black is an 'old boy' of that university).

Since researching and following-up on Judge Barrington Black's subsequent re-hashing of the vandalism on tube trains saga, ('Now-you're-in-jail – now-you're-not') I am pleased to report that some time in his past judicial career, Judge Black was employed as the Chief Metropolitan Magistrate at Bow Street Magistrates Court in London. I believe this is the most senior magistrates court in the land, presumably dating back to the days of the *Bow Street Runners*. I think I am correct in stating that Bow Street Magistrates Court has only ever used, certainly in recent years, Stipendiary Magistrates, who are paid to do the job on a full-time basis, unlike most ordinary magistrates who are in the main, part-time, and unpaid volunteers. You have probably noticed that very serious cases, such as hoped-for extraditions and paedophilic former Crown Court Judges like Mr David Selwood, are at least commenced there, if not finalised. I am sure that former Stipendiary Bow Street Magistrate Barrington Black did a superb job during his posting to that ultra-busy court in the very heart of London.

JUDGE PHILIP RICHARDS
CARDIFF CROWN COURT

A millionaire businessman and Rotary Club member was spared jail after a court heard how he blew his fortune on drugs and sex binges with a vice girl half his age. Company director David Vaughan, 52, admitted squandering £2,000 a day on prostitute Sarah Harding, supplying her with crack cocaine, jewellery, and designer clothing. The pair were arrested in Cardiff's *Big Sleep* hotel, voted one of the world's 25 'coolest' hotels and which has Hollywood star John Malkovitch among its shareholders. Vaughan, a father of three, had moved Harding, 26, into the hotel's £150-a-night penthouse suite in a sordid recreation of the *Pretty Woman* movie, starring Richard Gere and Julia Roberts. But staff became suspicious about them and alerted police, who raided the room and found crack cocaine pipes and drugs with a street value of more than £1,000.

Judge Philip Richards fined him £12,500 but spared him prison after describing the case as a 'personal tragedy'. He told him: "You have destroyed the reputation you had. Your marriage broke down and you resorted to taking cocaine at a devastating level. This is a personal tragedy. If I had formed any other view it would have meant a lengthy prison sentence."

Cardiff Crown Court heard how 'pillar of the community' Vaughan went off the rails after his marriage broke down. He spent £100,000 on sex and drugs. Vaughan told detectives that Harding would not have been with him but for the money he lavished on her, admitting that he gave the pretty brunette whatever she wanted. Prosecutor Jonathan Austin said: "In the few weeks before his arrest, Vaughan admitted his spending had been extremely heavy. He had been taking £2,000 a day out of his bank, spending money on clothes, make-up and jewellery for the young woman. They had apparently been together in the hotel room for a few days, spending £1,000 a day on drugs. "When asked where he had got the money he told officers he had assets worth in excess of £1.5million. He said there was a Spanish property he used as a holiday home and he had a very valuable house worth £750,000." The court heard that Vaughan, director of an electrical contractors, began using cocaine after the break-up of his 28-year marriage to Patricia, 52. Christopher Rees, defending, said up until the split four years ago Vaughan was a successful company director. He said: "It is a sad situation that Vaughan finds himself in. He was arrested in a hotel room with a 26-year-old girl which is a far cry from the previous life he had led. Through his hard work he had built up a firm employing 50 people. He was a valued member of the local Rotary Club and was known for his charitable work. But in 2000 his marriage failed, he was no longer living in the family home and he went through a breakdown." He said Vaughan began drinking heavily and was introduced to drugs for the first time in his late 40s. He became addicted to cocaine and by 2002 was 'suffering badly' from his abuse of the drug. He checked into a clinic in a bid to tackle his addiction but relapsed within months of being treated.

Mr Rees said Vaughan and his wife were going through a 'messy' divorce, and she now had their luxury home near Cwmbran, South Wales. He said: "Vaughan is not going to be left with much, he has spent over £100,000 on his drug habit in the last four years. As a result he has had to break into his personal equity plan and pension. He realises his wife is going to have her share, which leaves him with nothing, he is back at the bottom." Miss Harding was not charged and did not appear in court.

DISTRICT JUDGE PAUL FIRTH
BLACKBURN MAGISTRATES COURT

A furious outcry broke out after a drink-driver who killed an unborn baby was let off with a two-month jail sentence. David Hornby, 31, lost control after getting behind the wheel of his defective vehicle, following a drinking session, colliding with a car containing pregnant mother Eileen Winstanley. In a harrowing statement, Mrs Winstanley told a court how she had lost her precious baby 'for the sake of a taxi fare'. She also recalled the devastating moments after the baby was stillborn following the crash, and how she held him to say goodbye. Hornby, of Bolton, Greater Manchester pleaded guilty at Blackburn Magistrates Court to driving with excess alcohol, driving without due care and attention and with two defective tyres. He had told police he had three or four pints of Guiness before driving his Audi A4 with two bald tyres, one of which was massively under-inflated. He collided head-on with a car driven by Mrs Winstanley's husband Jason, after losing control on a bend near Bolton in December 2003. Seconds after the crash, passenger Mrs Winstanley, who was six months pregnant, 'felt strange' and collapsed. She was taken to hospital and doctors, who initially felt the baby's heartbeat, carried out a scan, but within minutes he had died. Mrs Winstanley, who is in her 30's, then had to endure an emergency caesarean section operation to remove the child. "They told us we had lost the baby and Jason just sat there and sobbed. The baby hadn't done anything to anyone and I felt that the least I could do was to give him a kiss and a cuddle from his mum. I felt I should have been able to look after him better. I kept asking to see him and eventually they brought him to me. He was beautiful, lots of curly hair and I could even see his eyelashes and finger nails. I held him close to me and prayed the heat from my body would bring him back to life. It seems so cruel, his life had been destroyed for the sake of a taxi fare. I saw another couple leaving the hospital with balloons tied to their car and I wished it could have been me. I still wish they could have saved my baby, why did it have to happen?"

District Judge Paul Firth said that had the baby been born alive, and then died as a result of Mrs Winstanley's injuries, Hornby would have faced a more serious charge of causing death by careless driving whilst under the influence of alcohol. As the law makes a distinction between those cases and a baby being stillborn, Hornby could only be charged with a lesser offence carrying a maximum six-months jail term. (As we know, the more serious charge of causing death by dangerous driving, now, in 2005, carries a maximum penalty of 14 years, meaning that it can only be tried by a judge and jury in a crown court).

The District Judge went on to say: "It is right that the law makes that distinction, but I believe it is also right that I acknowledge that this is just as much a death as any other child's death. Some years ago a Lord Chief Justice made a statement on which I can't improve. He said: "No court can restore a human life. Nor can its loss be measured by any sentence. No time, no sentence imposed on any offender can reconcile the family of a deceased person to their loss, nor will it cure their pain." The couple, who have a daughter Elizabeth, buried their dead child two days before Christmas Day, 2003. Hornby gave a reading of 82mg of alcohol in his blood against the legal limit of 80, but the sample was not taken until three hours later because he was treated in hospital. Hornby was sentenced to just two months imprisonment and disqualified from driving for two years. Why on earth, we ask ourselves, was he not given the maximum sentence of six months?)

PETERBOROUGH MAGISTRATES COURT

The 'disgusted' father of a teenager killed in a car crash has hit out at the £200 fine handed out to the driver. Victoria Martin, 18, admitted driving without due care and attention when her car plunged off the road into a ditch killing two of her friends. Claire Hilbert, 17, of Sawtry, Cambs, and Nicola Judge, 18, from Yaxley, were in the back seat of the Vauxhall Corsa. Claire's father Andy Hilbert, 38, said the fine and five penalty points were "a total injustice. We are absolutely numb, we just can't believe it. Victoria Martin has destroyed two families. We're disgusted with Peterborough Magistrates and the whole system and we will be appealing against it." Passenger Jonathan Harris, 17, said the car was travelling at 70mph on a dual carriageway.

JANET POWELL – CHAIRMAN
SOUTH SOMERSET MAGISTRATES COURT

This court report is about a disgraceful drunken driver, who after learning of his court sentence, was reported as saying: "I'm chuffed to bits with the result, I thought I'd go down. I'm off to get p**** to celebrate, but I won't be driving." What a shameful mentality! Shane Trim, 30, a window cleaner from Yeovil, Somerset, was so drunk when he left a pub after a 24-hour bender, that he could not remember where he had parked his Ford Escort van. When he finally found it, he crashed into a lamp post nearby. The father-of-one, who only held a provisional licence anyway, staggered away from the scene but fortunately, right-thinking witnesses pointed him out to police and he was arrested. A breath test revealed that he was **THREE TIMES OVER THE LEGAL LIMIT**. Trim's marathon drinking session around Yeovil started on the evening of Friday 9th April 2004, after a row with his girl friend over money. He said he visited every pub in town and drank 17 pints, before the session ended at *The Wine Vaults* at 11pm THE NEXT DAY.

At an earlier hearing at the South Somerset Magistrates Court, Trim had admitted drink-driving, driving without insurance and driving not in accordance with his driving licence. He could have been jailed for up to six months and fined £5,000. However Janet Powell, the learned Chairman of the South Somerset Magistrates, in her wisdom, told Trim that they had taken into account his remorse and guilty plea! He 'escaped jail', as the expression is repeated every day country-wide by Magistrates and Judges AD NAUSEUM, and instead was sentenced to 100 hours of community service and banned from driving for just two years and four months. He was also fined £40 and ordered to attend a drink-driving rehabilitation programme for 12-months. No doubt Trim spent more than the trivial £40 fine on beer during his irresponsible drinking session. We can expect that the citizens of Yeovil are thanking their lucky stars that Trim hit a lamp post and not a moving vehicle or pedestrians etc.

MS J GOLDTHORPE – CHAIRMAN
CALDERDALE MAGISTRATE COURT

Joan Goldthorpe is the Bench Chairman of Calderdale Magistrates Court, in Halifax, West Yorks. She is yet another example of the Head of a Bench of Magistrates lacking in wisdom and common sense and by no means qualifying for the mark of judicial respect, 'learned'. In fact, in keeping with probably the majority of lay, unpaid magistrates up and down the country, her bark is by far worse than her bite, if her sentencing in this pathetic case is anything to go by. Stephen Taylor, 48, from the Hipperholme district of Halifax, Yorks, was before the court for driving whilst disqualified, driving without insurance, driving without an MOT certificate and was **MORE THAN THREE TIMES OVER THE LIMIT**, when his Vauxhall Astra car was stopped by police. The Court had heard that Taylor had been previously convicted of 10 drink-driving offences and been previously disqualified from driving for motoring offences no less than 22 times. He had also been jailed on several previous occasions. Bench Chairman Goldthorpe told Taylor: "I have never seen such an appalling record! Our first thought was to send you to prison, but you have been there in the past and it hasn't done any good at all, so we are punishing you in a different way." She then 'sentenced' Taylor to a three-year community rehabilitation order and 100 hours of community service, ordered him to pay £40 in costs and disqualified him from driving for 5-years. What an absolute disgrace and a complete let-down for everyone involved in the case.

Mr Michael Jobbins, chairman of the Campaign Against Drink Driving said: "There is no doubt this man should have been sent to jail again. If he is behind bars, he would not be behind the wheel of a car and likely to kill someone." Mr Jobbins, whose 25-year-old daughter was killed by a drunk driver, added: "I think the magistrates involved in cases like this should be made accountable for their actions. Do we have to wait until this man kills someone before he is locked up? Families who lose loved ones should be allowed to sue." (Presumably Mr Jobbins meant sue the magistrates.) Mr John Foran, Tory Councillor for the district of Halifax where the defendant Taylor lives said: "I would jail him for a long time. When people drive drunk, without insurance or an MOT, they not only put themselves at risk, but anyone they might crash into and injure or even kill. Uninsured drivers are a huge problem now because people consider it an acceptable risk. If the insurance premium costs £500, they would rather run the risk of getting caught, pay the £100 fine handed out by our namby-pamby courts and do the same again."

PORT TALBOT MAGISTRATES COURT

At Port Talbot Magistrates Court in Wales, Mark Jones, 19, of Briton Ferry, South Wales, appeared for driving offences including no insurance. The Learned Magistrates, in their wisdom, let him off with fines of £400 after Jones agreed to sit in silence for 30 minutes. (How sweet, such empathy!) They gave him a conditional discharge for having been found in possession of the cannabis drug. Wasn't that a good day's work by their worships? With such lenient, unrealistic, impractical and inappropriate 'deterrents' as that, you can imagine that there is no way that Mark Jones will ever offend again!

MR DAVID STEVENS – CHAIRMAN
BODMIN MAGISTRATES COURT

Unemployed drug-addict Hayley Matthews, 25, appeared before magistrates at Bodmin, Cornwall in June 2004 and was fined £83.00 (Yes, £83.00!) for killing a pedestrian in a hit-and-run accident from which she fled the scene. The court had heard that Matthews was driving her car near Redruth, Cornwall one night in August 2003 when it left the road. Marc Downing, 22, a holidaymaker returning to campsite was killed, having suffered multiple injuries, in spite of paramedics' efforts to save him. Matthews pleaded guilty to driving with no tax, failing to stop, failing to report an accident, two counts of defective tyres and having no insurance. She was also banned from driving for 2 years. Her solicitor told the court that she had suffered shock and distress as a result of the accident.

Chairman of the Bench at Bodmin, Mr David Stevens, in his wisdom, told Matthews: "We accept that you have suffered emotional upset. An inquest has said this was not your fault, but there was a sense of irresponsible behaviour on your part and we must take that into account." Mr Downing's grieving family joined road safety campaigners in condemning the court's decision. His mother, Denise, from Ipswich said "It's absolutely diabolical, I'm speechless. It's no wonder people take the law into their own hands. How are parents like myself supposed to accept that? Our son was killed and that's all his life is worth is it? It's an insult, an absolute insult." Brigitte Chaudry, spokesman for road safety pressure group Road Peace said: "Our young people are being slaughtered on the road and everybody just shrugs their shoulders. This woman left the scene with this poor man dying after she had run over him. The very fact that someone escapes from the scene after knocking another person down means they should face a stiff penalty. The message being given is that you can kill, you can break the law, and it is fine. Your feelings will be taken into account but your victim's won't." (**NB** on the same day, the same Bench of magistrates dealt with a case which was heard immediately before the Matthews case. It concerned a Robin Conway, 19, a telecoms engineer, who they fined £443 for careless driving and banned for 2 years, after his car left the road and hit a tree)

Soon after the above-mentioned case of Hayley Matthews was disposed of in court by the imposition of the £83 fine, TV presenter Fiona Bruce, who normally presents *Crimewatch* on BBC1, interviewed Elliott Griffiths of the Magistrates Association, on BBC TV, on the subject of 'wholly inadequate sentences', particularly in the case of 'hit and run' crimes. I transposed the relevant part of the interview to share with you, as follows:

> *FB* "Do you think the law at the moment as it stands, adequately reflects the outrage of victims, or relatives of victims, that someone has failed to stop when someone has been injured, or in the worse case, has died, they have not stopped out of sheer common decency to help that person?"

EG "It is a problem. It is very difficult, if not impossible to come towards satisfying the victims' families when circumstances like that have happened. Almost whatever we do to the defendant is unsatisfactory."

FB "But can you see, or would you welcome a change in the law which would reflect the fact that someone who is driving and who hits someone, even if it isn't their fault, has an onus, a legal onus to stop and help?"

EG "Well they have an onus to stop, but it is of course, to exchange details with the...

FB "What the insurance details? Not much use if they're lying dead in the road."

EG "That's right."

FB "You see, why people feel magistrates are too soft... do you think they are? Are people like you too soft?"

EG "No I don't think we are too soft. As I say, we've got sentencing guidelines and that leads us to the sentences that we mete out."

FB "But you see, someone's got £83 (fine), a man has lost his life, this person wasn't insured, wasn't taxed, hadn't got an MOT. You can see how the relatives and the mother of this particular individual is incensed, is insulted by that."

EG "I can certainly see that, yes."

FB "And does £83 sound, on the face of it, reasonable?"

EG "It does not sound reasonable".

JEAN WOOD – CHAIRMAN
PLYMOUTH MAGISTRATES COURT

A mother who was **ALMOST FIVE TIMES OVER THE DRINK-DRIVE LIMIT** while on a school run with her two children, was jailed on 27th August 2004 for just 4 months. Kay Wright, 43, was stopped by police with her sons aged 15 and 11 in her Nissan Micra car, and was so drunk that she stalled it twice, before she got out. Shocked officers found she was obviously drunk as soon as they stopped her in the centre of Plymouth at 4.10pm, magistrates were told. The housewife had an alcohol reading of 152 micrograms in 100 millilitres of breath. The legal limit is 35. She was arrested and appeared in court the next day, where she was banned from driving pending a sentencing hearing, but she was arrested again 10 days later for breaking the disqualification. Wright, of Plymouth, admitted drink-driving, and driving while disqualified and without insurance. She was jailed for a total of four months and banned from driving for three years by Plymouth magistrates. Chairman of the Bench Jean Wood told her: "This was a very high alcohol reading and you had two children in the car with you on your way home from school. With this amount of alcohol it meant you were a substantial risk to other road users and in particular to your own children in the car. You then drove in breach of the interim disqualification and while on bail." Mike French, prosecuting said Wright was arrested in a spot check. "As the Nissan Micra was being driven into the check area the defendant stopped and stalled. She managed to start the engine and drove off the road and stalled once again. As soon as she got out the officers saw she was heavily in drink. She later gave a very high reading on the intoximeter."

She was brought to court the next day and after she admitted the offence, she was made subject of an interim disqualification. While still subject to this, she was stopped by police officers. She said she had foreign students staying with her and had got up late and in an irrational moment, drove her car to take them to college. Ken Papenfus, defending, said Wright was suffering from depression and an acute alcohol crisis at the time, but is now addressing the issues and is no longer a danger." He added: "She was struggling with an alcohol problem and trying to maintain her family."

Readers might be wondering why, with such an appalling level of alcohol in her bodily system, together with the aggravating factors of having later driven whilst disqualified and without insurance, the Bench did not apply the maximum penalty within their powers, of six months imprisonment. They were very generous too, by only awarding a comparatively short period of disqualification from driving, viz: 3 years.

NORWICH MAGISTRATES COURT

On 14th October 2004, the bench at Norwich Magistrates Court, in their wisdom, made a most controversial decision and many people were outraged when it was made public. The implications were enormous. A very serious career criminal, Kevin Page, 23, from Norwich, with a total of 112 criminal convictions, walked free from the court instead of receiving an immediate custodial sentence from the magistrates, or alternatively, being committed to the Crown Court for sentence, as the magistrates powers would normally not have been sufficient enough to adequately sentence Page. Police and champions of victims' rights, were quick to attack the leniency of the magistrates' decision, which has been seen as an encouragement to consistent offenders to continue their criminal habits. Page was first convicted during his teenaged years. During his abysmal serial offending, he has caused serious damage and stolen property running into tens of thousands of pounds in value. Having been handed down 13 separate custodial sentences, which in total came to six years, this caused barely an interruption to his criminal ways.

The Norwich magistrates, instead of jailing him for damaging a car by breaking into it, placed him under the new Prolific and Priority Offender Scheme for just 18 months. This means that he retains his liberty to continue re-offending, as the mood takes him, but will be under the 'scrutiny' of probation officers and other agencies. Page, like most career criminals these days, is a drug addict. At the time of breaking into the car, Page had only regained his liberty for approximately four weeks, after serving a jail sentence in respect of a previous matter, and was subject to a Community Rehabilitation Order. This means he was already subject to probation service supervision when he broke into the car.

Local police are furious and outraged at what they see as a totally unrealistic sentence. Their view appears to be that he is a prime example of needing almost continuous imprisonment to protect the public. Serving police officer, Mr Norman Brennan, who is a Director of the Victims of Crime Trust, stated that Page should have been taken off the streets. He is reported as saying: "This individual, having committed no fewer than 112 offences, should have gone to prison for a long, long time. How many chances do the courts have to give persistent criminals, before they say enough is enough? The public have the right to be protected and the criminal justice system has a duty of care to give them that respite. Locking up persistent offenders would allow officers to stop chasing the same criminals, and have more time to patrol and reassure the public."

Sarah Francis, a Chief Inspector in Norfolk Police said: "The Prolific Offender scheme was inadequate for some criminals. The strategy should not mean that persistent offenders escape punishment or a period in prison, which actually may assist in his rehabilitation. We are all for attempts to prevent people re-offending, but we want to give the public some respite from someone who is a persistent offender. Sometimes you have to ask whether letting people straight out into the community is the right way forward."

It transpired that Page had no qualifications when he left school. He is a regular car thief, during his criminal career he has stolen at least eight cars and of course there may be others which he has got away with. Roughly 100 of his past crimes are for thefts from cars. He was arrested in September 2004, when a SOCO (Scenes of Crime Officer), lifted Page's fingerprints from inside a Fiat car. It had been broken into and a large number of compact discs had been stolen. This was the offence to which Page pleaded guilty and was made the subject of David Blunkett's new Prolific Offender scheme, by the Norwich magistrates. His father was interviewed and claimed that his son was 'very pleased at being let off' by the bench. He claims he deserves a chance.

Readers may well be of the opinion that car owners resident in the Norwich area deserve a chance as well! No doubt, the words of former Tory Home Secretary Michael Howard, spring to mind — 'prison works'. David Blunkett's latest initiative, the Prolific and Priority Offender Scheme was launched in September 2004. He claimed that it would concentrate the police's crime-fighting initiatives on the 5,000 serial and career criminals in the UK, who are suspected of committing one million crimes per year. Prime Minister Tony Blair presented the concept of CCTV cameras being installed near career criminals' homes to track their movements, and 24-hour police surveillance on the most prolific drug dealers, hooligans and criminals who steal cars and/or break into them. However, for some reason these particular initiatives have not been implemented. Focus appears to have been made instead on satellite tracking technology and drug treatment schemes. However only three areas are currently equipped to use the satellite technology, these being Greater Manchester, Hampshire and West Midlands. No mention was made in court as to whether Page was ordered to be fitted with any kind of TAG, or at least an after-dark curfew being imposed.

MR TONY BAKER – CHAIRMAN
IPSWICH MAGISTRATES COURT

The tough new conditions for serial drink-drivers to regain a licence are aimed at habitual offenders such as Donald McKeller. He was caught at the wheel while **NEARLY THREE TIMES OVER THE LIMIT**, after celebrating his 29th birthday nearly four years ago, his third drink-drive offence. McKeller, of Nacton, Suffolk, was already serving a five-year ban for drink-driving when stopped. Even before the hearing outside Ipswich Magistrates Court, he was drinking a can of lager. As he was jailed for six months and banned from driving for five years, magistrate Tony Baker told him: "You have shown a complete disregard for court orders. You have two previous convictions for driving while disqualified and now you have three convictions for driving with excess alcohol."

Tests showed McKeller had 101mg of alcohol in 100ml of breath. The legal limit is 35mg. He admitted drink-driving, two charges of driving while disqualified, three counts of driving without insurance and two offences of driving a vehicle without an MOT certificate. With a disgraceful, irresponsible driving record like that and being mockingly pictured drinking lager before going into court for his case to be heard, Mr Tony Baker's bench of magistrates should have committed McKeller in custody to a Crown Court for sentence, as their own powers were insufficient to hand down a substantial-enough sentence, don't you agree? Having said that, when magistrates carry out that procedure, there is a certain risk attached to it. It is far from unknown for Crown Court Judges, in their great wisdom, to pass a sentence of Probation or even a small fine etc.

MR JOHN SUDWORTH – CHAIRMAN WAKEFIELD YOUTH COURT

This next case of theft, dealt with at court in early April 2004, caught the eye through its bizarre banner headline:

BOY SPARED PRISON FOR WEARING A DRESS

The secondary headline read:

JP praises tearaway's drag act

Persistent offender Adam Zemlik, 17, of Lupset, Wakefield, Yorks, appeared at Wakefield Youth Court, admitting taking a Ford Sierra motor car and interfering with another motor vehicle. He already had 14 previous convictions for 30 criminal offences to do with motor vehicles, including taking cars and stealing from them, all in the space of a year. He had previously spent two months in a Young Offenders Institution. However he went on a *Prince's Trust* course, which are designed to help young people put their lives back on track. He borrowed a long, black, sleeveless dress and paraded around the streets in drag to help old folk, collecting cash for an Away Day for them. The presiding magistrate at the youth court, Mr John Sudworth, told him: "For a young man your record is terrible. If it wasn't for the *Prince's Trust* report you would probably be going into custody." West Yorkshire Police were granted an anti-social behaviour order, (ASBO) banning Zemlik from mixing with a gang which has targeted vehicles across Wakefield. Presiding Magistrate John Sudworth sentenced Zemlik to a 100-hour community service order

Questions arising:

1) Had you been a victim of these car crimes, would you have been impressed with the sentence of 100 hours community service, with this young man's appalling record?

2) Given the opportunity, might you have had something to say to the Bench afterwards?

3) Weren't you impressed with the 'drag act' story from his solicitor?

4) Did you think that failing to return this 'career criminal youth' to jail will prevent him from re-offending in the future?

BRADFORD MAGISTRATES COURT

At first it had seemed like an extreme case of road rage, when driver Leslie Arliss, 39, caused £150,000 damage by shunting 11 vehicles outside his home. He agreed that he was drunk but insisted his foot became trapped under the accelerator of his Range Rover, as he went to fetch a tape and started the engine. He admitted drink-driving and driving without due care and attention, after causing the chaos in Queensberry, West Yorks, in December 2003. Although the total damage bill reached £150,000, Bradford Magistrates ordered Arliss to pay just £920 compensation and banned him from driving for three years. He agreed to go on a drink-impaired driver's course. I'll bet the 11 wrecked-car drivers thought that was wonderful, their faith in the British Criminal Justice System restored at last!

DISTRICT JUDGE DAVID KITSON
LEEDS MAGISTRATES COURT

Football boss Terry Yorath was spared jail despite mowing-down a woman while **THREE TIMES OVER THE DRINK-DRIVE LIMIT**. But a judge's decision to show mercy was labelled a 'disgrace'. His victim, Raziya Aslam, 27, said Yorath was 'selfish and irresponsible', while campaigners said the former Wales manager should have been jailed. Miss Aslam suffered a shattered pelvis when Yorath, 54, ploughed into her in his X-type Jaguar as she walked home from a karate class. Yorath, who had been on a heavy drinking session, lost control of his sports car on the A61 in Leeds and smashed into the central reservation before mowing her down. But he was fined just £500 and handed a community rehabilitation order. Miss Aslam said after the case at Leeds Magistrates Court: "It was such a selfish, irresponsible and dangerous

Serious drunken-driver Terry Yorath, Manager, Leeds United Football Club

thing to do. He was putting his own life at risk, as well as other people's. Drink-driving makes him a threat to himself and to the public. He should be counting his blessings because he walks away with his life intact, while this will affect me forever."

Mike Jobbings, chairman of the Campaign Against Drink Driving, said: "It is an absolute disgrace that this man has been let off with a slap on the wrist. Jail was the only answer. With that amount of alcohol in his body,

Yorath could have killed several people." Yorath, who played for Leeds United in the 70s and is the father of ITV sports presenter Gaby Logan, was found to have 120 microgrammes of alcohol in 100 millilitres of breath after the crash on 24th June 2004, **THREE AND A HALF TIMES THE LEGAL LIMIT** of 35. He admitted drink-driving and driving without due care, and faced up to six months jail.

But Yorath, of Leeds, escaped heavier punishment, after the court heard that he turned to drink when his 33-year marriage to wife Christine, 53, ended. District Judge David Kitson was told that his life had been 'beset by tragedy', including the death of his son Daniel, who dropped dead with a heart defect aged 15 while playing football in 1992. The judge told Yorath that his crime merited jail, but his remorse, personal problems and guilty plea had spared him. Yorath, now assistant boss at League One club Huddersfield Town, was also banned from driving for 30 months and must attend a course for drink-drivers. Richard Manning, defending, said: "He is very keen that he does get some help." Afterwards, Yorath told the *Daily Express*: "People should feel sorry for the girl, not me. What I did was so stupid. I feel very ashamed and I let my family down. I will never drink and drive again." Miss Aslam, from Leeds, who is still off work and on crutches, said of the crash: "I didn't stand a chance in the middle of the blur. I wondered if I would ever walk again."

(**Author's note:** *You have probably noticed the all-pervading theme and scenario running through most of what you have read in the book so far. In the public galleries of crown courts and magistrates courts throughout the land, sit cripples in wheelchairs, widows and widowers dressed in black, with sobbing children at home desperate to know why Daddy or Mummy isn't coming home any more. In stark contrast to that, seated in huge, comfortable chairs with a backdrop of crested oak-panelled walls, sit the judiciary. Their eyes and ears are hanging on every word leaving the lips of the defence counsel or solicitor, on his or her feet before them.*

Their handkerchiefs or official paper tissues are close at hand, dabbing at their eyes, together with jugs of iced lemon-water, as they struggle to contain themselves from shedding tears of anguish, as the terrible tales of woe unfold. By the time every last detail has been elucidated at great length, to include that the defendant's cat aged 16 yrs died on the day of the offence and that the washing blew off the line and had to be re-laundered, which temporarily upset the balance of the defendant's mind, causing pre-occupation and distraction from the driving matter in hand, the judge or magistrates have forgotten every word of the victims' **crime impact statement**, *hospital and undertakers' bills, or the fact that the cyclist left for dead in a pool of blood in the gutter, by that totally* *irresponsible person sitting in the dock, preparing for jail with a toothbrush in the pocket, nearly didn't make it. When WILL the judiciary in this country knuckle down properly and restore the balance, so that law-abiding victims' human rights take* **preference** *over those of criminal offenders? In this particular case, the District Judge told Yorath that his crime 'MERITED JAIL' but 1) his remorse, 2) personal problems and 3) guilty plea 'had spared him'. No apparent reference to* **the crippling of the victim** *at all*)

WEST ALLERDALE MAGISTRATES COURT

A drunk-driver escaped a ban by convincing a court that he was *sleep-walking*. Former Army sergeant William Bough, 46, of Garstang, Lancs, admitted driving three miles while **TWO AND A HALF TIMES OVER THE LIMIT** before he crashed. But he told magistrates he had no memory of getting in his car.

Bizarrely, his case was backed by a psychologist, who said he was having drink-induced sleeping problems. Bough had drunk four beers, two glasses of wine and three large whiskies. But he claimed the last thing he remembered was going to sleep at his mother's home in Workington, Cumbria. Bough said: "I remember getting ready for bed. The next thing I remember is being in the back of an ambulance. I must have gone downstairs, opened the front door, started the car and put the lights on. But the first recollection was in the ambulance and in hospital." He was rushed to West Cumbria Hospital after crashing his Proton car into a wall at Lillyhall on the A595. He was found by police fully clothed but without his glasses on. Later he gave a urine sample and was found to be way over the limit.

Clinical psychologist Elspeth Desert told West Allerdale Magistrates he had no intention of driving after getting into bed. After clearing Bough, the presiding magistrate said: "We accept Mr Bough's action was involuntary due to *sleepwalking*." The court heard that Bough was suffering from post-traumatic stress disorder. But the decision was condemned by anti drink-drive campaigners. Jack Sparrow, of the Campaign Against Drink-Driving called the decision 'bizarre'. He said: "This is setting a ridiculous example and others will try it on now."

A police spokesman agreed it was 'unusual' and said the Cumbrian force had not yet decided whether to appeal.

HARROGATE MAGISTRATES COURT

On 17th September 2004 magistrates provoked outrage after allowing a drunken businessman, who drove 16 miles on the wrong side of a motorway, to walk free without even being fined. Philip McAteer, 33, clocked up to

70mph and was oblivious to a police patrol car which followed him for 12 miles with its lights flashing, as he sped south on the north-bound carriageway in the early hours. But the horse dealer escaped jail after claiming he was 'preoccupied' with financial problems, and was instead banned for just 12 months and given a 200-hour community order. Road safety campaigners condemned the decision by JPs in Harrogate, North Yorks, which they claimed 'sent out completely the wrong message'.

McAteer, who admitted dangerous and drink-driving, was **ONE AND A HALF TIMES OVER THE LIMIT** when he was eventually stopped on the A1(M) in his Land Rover Freelander 4x4, after police were alerted by a series of frantic phone calls from other motorists. He was first spotted on the wrong carriageway shortly after 3 am in May 2004 near Thirsk, when an HGV driver saw two headlights coming towards him. Four miles further south, another driver tried to overtake the vehicle in front of him, only to be confronted by the Freelander travelling at 40 to 50mph. One clip from a video shot from the following police car showed 10 cars and 6 HGV's passing inside McAteer as he drove in the outside lane. After he was stopped and a breath test gave a reading of 53 microgrammes of alcohol against the legal limit of of 35, he told police: "I'm sorry sir." His lawyer, Richard Reed, claimed he was 'only slightly over the limit' and was driving steadily when the road was quiet. He said McAteer, of Cockfield, Durham, had been 'preoccupied' with problems in his private life. He would have stopped earlier if the police car had been driving directly behind him in his line of vision. After McAteer was ordered to pay just £80 towards costs, a spokeswoman for road safety charity Brake condemned the sentence. She said: "We are appalled. A conviction for dangerous driving carries a sentence of up to two years in prison and an unlimited fine, but this driver has escaped without paying a penny. It sends the completely wrong message to drink-drivers that they can continue to get away with it until they kill or injure someone."

TIMOTHY BURRELL – CHAIRMAN
HARROGATE MAGISTRATES COURT

A woman charity worker was jailed for three months on 7th October 2004, after she was found to be **MORE THAN FIVE TIMES OVER THE DRINK-DRIVE LIMIT** following a 10-hour drinking binge. As she began her sentence, Toni Hird was described as the country's worst female drink-driver. When she was arrested she was already serving a 32-month ban following a previous drink-driving conviction. Hird, 33, was detained after she drove her BMW at just 5mph in the middle of a busy road in Harrogate, N.Yorkshire. Her driving was so erratic that cars coming towards her in the opposite direction were forced to take evasive action. A spokesperson for the road safety charity Brake said: "It is one of the most extreme cases we have seen, in terms of the extent to which somebody is over the legal drink-drive limit, particularly for a woman. It is an absolutely appalling case. Drink-driving is a growing menace in our society." Harrogate Magistrates Court heard Miss Hird's marathon binge began at a party, before she returned home and carried on drinking. She set off to collect her dry cleaning but was stopped close to her home after she was spotted by police driving erratically at 5pm on September 4th 2004. A breath test showed she had an alcohol level of 176 microgrammes per 100 millilitres of breath. The legal limit is 35. She was also banned from driving for five years, after pleading guilty to driving with excess alcohol and not having insurance. She had been banned from driving just six months earlier following the previous conviction. Jailing Hird for just 3 months, chairman of the bench Mr Timothy Burrell told her: "This was an exceptionally high reading, aggravated by a driving disqualification and a blatant disregard for a court order for a similar offence in March 2004."

(**Author's note:** *With a fairly recent previous conviction already for drink-driving, and with a blood-alcohol reading as high as that, wouldn't you have expected the bench to hand down the maximum sentence within their power, viz: SIX months?*)

FAREHAM MAGISTRATES COURT

This next case leads to a decision by a bench of 'learned' magistrates that is almost beyond belief, one could say they frequent *NEVER NEVER LAND*.

Keith Gray,52, a dock worker, of Portchester, Hants pleaded guilty to false representation, at Fareham Magistrates Court, Hampshire. Over a period of time he fraudulently received the sum of £18,500 in council tax and housing benefits, by failing to disclose that he was receiving a pension.

The magistrates, in their wisdom, ordered him to carry out 140 hours of community service. He was also ordered to pay restitution of £18,500 to Fareham Council at £50.00 per month. As this will take him **30 years** if he keeps up his payments, does the learned bench have a direct line to the Almighty, to confirm that this defendant will live that long, viz: to the age of 82? Once Mr Gray becomes a senior citizen at age 65 years, in the year 2117, will he be able to maintain the payment rate from his meagre state pension? Amazingly, Angela Crane, fraud investigation manager for Fareham Council said: "We are happy with the rate of recovery. This is a good result for us." (Until I read her comment, I had thought it was PUBLIC MONEY that Mr Gray had fraudulently obtained in unauthorised benefits!)

FAREHAM MAGISTRATES COURT

Safety groups branded a decision to allow a footballer caught speeding at 110mph to keep his licence 'obscene and ridiculous'. Magistrates ruled that Diomansy Kamara, Portsmouth's £2.2 million striker, could remain on the roads after accepting a ban would 'make it difficult for him to get to training'. But the ruling has sparked disbelief and fury among road safety organisations, which accuse it of being an insult to the memory of those killed by dangerous drivers. Zoe Stow, of Road Peace - the charity for those bereaved and injured in road crashes - said: "This is totally obscene. The reason given for keeping his licence is utterly ridiculous. "What kind of message does this send out to all the youngsters who see this man as a role model? The magistrates have made utter fools of themselves. It's nothing but an insult to the families of those whose lives have been taken."

Police clocked the Senegal striker in his powerful Audi A4 as he sped along the M27 to his apartment at the exclusive marina development of Port Solent near Portsmouth. When he was pulled over the 24-year-old, who had just joined the club from Italian side Modena, told officers he was unaware of the speeding laws in Britain. And magistrates spared Kamara a ban after being told he could not use public transport or get a lift from teammates to get to training. But Ms Stow said: "What kind of excuse is that for a man with his money and his position? He or the club could easily have paid for his transport. It's an absolute disgrace." Kamara, who earns £15,000 a week, was fined £1,000, ordered to pay £43 costs and had his licence endorsed by six points. The French-speaking star needed an interpreter when he attended Fareham Magistrates Court. The court heard the star was caught on October 28 last year in Whiteley, near Fareham, while returning from training in Eastleigh, Hants. His lawyer, Ryan Seneviratne, said Kamara had only been in the country for two months at the time and was not sure of the speed limit. He added that his Italian-registered car's speedometer was marked in kilometres per hour rather than miles. Mr Seneviratne said: "Ignorance is not a defence, but ignorance is the reason why he was breaking the limit on this occasion. "If he is banned it will be difficult for him to travel to training on public transport as he does not speak English. He added that none of the player's teammates lived near him. After the hearing, Portsmouth chairman Milan Mandaric vowed to warn the club's other foreign signings about the country's driving laws. Mandaric, who was himself caught speeding in July 2003, said he would be speaking to all new players in future about the law and their duty as role models.

DUDLEY MAGISTRATES COURT

A lottery winner who scooped a £250,000 prize was so greedy she continued to claim benefits. Gail Poole kept up her money-grabbing con for an astonishing 18 months. After being caught she admitted that she had been motivated purely by greed. On 21st April 2004, Poole gasped and held a hand bearing a large diamond ring to her face, as she was told her deception had almost landed her in jail for six months. Instead, magistrates in Dudley, West Midlands, fined her £3,500, after she admitted seven charges of swindling Dudley Council out of almost £1,000 in council tax benefits.

The court heard that Poole failed to declare her lottery windfall when her numbers came up in 2003. Prosecutor Tim Holder said the fraud came to light during a routine benefits audit and Poole, 47, and her husband Anthony, of Quarry Bank, Dudley, were investigated. "It transpired that they had savings in excess of the £16,000 limit. One account alone held more than £200,000 in it, yet claims were still being made for council tax benefit." Simon Jessup, defending, said the fraudulently obtained money had since been repaid. After their lottery win, the Pooles continued living in their former council house for another two-and-a-half years, to avoid financial penalties if they should sell it within an agreed time limit, according to neighbour Arthur Mason. "They had to wait a year or so before they could move because it was a council house," he said

COUNT 23

KNOWN SUPPORT ORGANISATIONS
FOR CRIMINALS

CRIMINAL CASES REVIEW COMMISSION . . . . .QUEENSWAY, BIRMINGHAM

INQUEST . . . . .LONDON, N4 2PJ

MIND . . . . .BROADWAY, LONDON, E15 4BQ

JOINT COUNCIL FOR WELFARE OF IMMIGRANTS . . . . .LONDON, EC1V 9JR

NATIONAL ASSOCIATION OF PRISON VISITORS . . . . .BEDFORD, MK40 2PB

PHILEMON TRUST . . . . .SHEPHERDS BUSH, LONDON, W12 9BH

GAMBLERS ANONYMOUS . . . . .LONDON, SW10 0EU

PRISON LINK . . . . .ASTON, BIRMINGHAM, B6 6AJ

NACRO . . . . .LONDON, SW9 0PU

JUSTICE . . . . .LONDON, EC4V 5AQ

BODY POSITIVE . . . . .LONDON, SW5 9EB

IRISH COMMISSION FOR PRISONERS OVERSEAS . . . . .LONDON, N4 3AG

GRIP . . . . .KEMPTOWN, BRIGHTON, BN2 5JS

LIBERTY . . . . .LONDON, SE1 4LA

NATIONAL ASSOCIATION CITIZENS ADVICE BOARD . . . . .LONDON, N1 9LZ

HOWARD LEAGUE FOR PENAL REFORM . . . . .LONDON, N19 3NL

THE NEW BRIDGE . . . . .LONDON, SW1P 2BD

PRISON FELLOWSHIP . . . . .MALDON, ESSEX CM9 4EW

OPEN DOOR PROJECT . . . . .LONDON, SE10 8TJ

PRISONERS FAMILIES AND FRIENDS . . . . .LONDON, SE1 1DB

WOMEN'S LINK . . . . .LONDON, EC1A 2EJ

PRISON PHOENIX TRUST . . . . .OXFORD, X1 1PJ

RELEASE . . . . .LONDON, EC1V 9LT

THE SAMARITANS . . . . .SLOUGH, SL1 1ST

TERENCE HIGGINS TRUST LIGHTHOUSE . . . . .LONDON, WC1X 8JU

PARTNERS OF PRISONERS FAMILIES SUPPORT . . . . .MANCHESTER, M8 7HF

JEWISH VISITATION COMMITTEE . . . . .LONDON, N12 0US

HALOW . . . . .COVENTRY, CV1 5BN

GRUPO AMIGA . . . . .LONDON, EC4V 2BB

THE BOURNE TRUST . . . . .LONDON, SW9 6DE

BARS . . . . .MILTON KEYNES, MK4 4DA

PROP (NATIONAL PRISONERS MOVEMENT) . . . . .LONDON, WC1N 3XX

ADFAM NATIONAL . . . . .LONDON, SE1 0EE

FEDERATION OF PRISONERS' FAMILIES GROUP . . . . .LONDON, W6 0LE

PRISONERS ADVICE & INFORMATION NETWORK . . . . .LONDON, WC1N 3XX

SCOTTISH FORUM ON PRISONS & FAMILIES . . . . .EDINBURGH, EH12 5DR

NATIONAL PRISONERS MOVEMENT . . . . .LONDON, WC1N 3XX

PRISONERS' WIVES & FAMILIES SOCIETY . . . . .LONDON, N1 0NG

STONHAM HOUSING ASSOCIATION . . . . .LONDON, SE1 0LR

VISITORS TRAVEL EXCHANGE . . . . .LONDON, N5 2EA

SSAFA . . . . .LONDON, SE1 2LP

PRISONERS' ADVICE SERVICE . . . . .LONDON, EC1N 7RJ

SERIOUS OFFENDERS FAMILIES ASSOCIATION (SOFA) . . . . .HULL, HU5 3AR

WISH - WOMEN IN SPECIAL HOSPITALS . . . . .LONDON, EC4V 2BB

APEX CHARITABLE TRUST . . . . .LONDON, EC2Y 5DA

WOMEN IN PRISON . . . . .LONDON, N5 2EA

SOCIETY OF VOLUNTARY ASSOCIATES (SOVA) . . . . .LONDON, SE1 4LD

CAMPAIGN AGAINST DOUBLE PUNISHMENT . . . . .MANCHESTER, M40 8WN

PRISONERS' RESOURCE SERVICE (PRS) .LONDON, SW191ZU

CREATIVE & SUPPORTIVE TRUST . . . . .LONDON, NW1 0JR

AFTERMATH . . . . .SHEFFIELD, S4 7RT

PRISON WATCH . . . . .DERBY, DE24 0HS

ANGULIMALA . . . . .WARWICK, CV35 8AS

FEMALE PRISONERS WELFARE PROJECT . . . . .LONDON, EC4V 2BB

ALCOHOLICS ANONYMOUS . . . . .STONEBOW, YORK, YO1 2NJ

CONSEQUENCES . . . . .SHEFFIELD, S6 3YW

COUNT 24

KNOWN SUPPORT ORGANISATIONS
FOR VICTIMS

THE VICTIMS OF CRIME TRUST . . . . .2, YORK ST. TWICKENHAM TW1 3LE

CAMPAIGN AGAINST DRINK DRIVING (CADD) 01235 227261

HOMICIDE SUPPORT UNIT 0191 440 3431

JUSTICE FOR VICTIMS 020 8549 6762

JUSTICE FOR VICTIMS (Scotland) 0141 554 4238

NORTH OF ENGLAND VICTIM'S ASSOCIATION (NEVA) 0191 423 2210

SUPPORT & CARE AFTER ROAD DEATH & INJURY (SCARD) 01484 384702

THE ZITO TRUST (Mental Health) 01497 820011

JUDGEMENT IMPAIRED

AUTHOR'S RECOMMENDATIONS
MARCH 2005

- Reintroduce Approved Schools, Detention Centres, Attendance Centres and 'boot camp-style' Borstals for young offenders and juveniles - many Borstal inmates enjoyed the disciplined regimes - and, for the first time in some cases, order came into their lives.
- Introduce fixed-by-law *minimum* sentences for most crimes - irrespective of the offender's antecedents and offending history to date. (it's *working* with gun crime)
- All new-build prisons must have the modern-style non-opening windows, to prevent & disrupt passing of drugs etc from cell-to-cell, or from 'red bands' working in the grounds, to cells - essential to incorporate drugs treatment and rehabilitation wings in new-builds, these convicts must have no contact whatever with prisoners on other wings.
- Ligature fixing-point-free windows and totally flush walls, ceilings and door frames - sink units to be filled and lavatories to be flushed by floor-mounted, railway toilet-style stainless steel foot pumps.
- All visits halls to have US-style closed visits with view-family-through toughened glass screens, with fixed-to-floor seats on convict side and telephone handset communication from both sides.
- Increase use/convert/new-build of military-style dormitories in HMP's - Double-up occupancy of en-suite cells in existing establishments, with steel bunk beds bolted to floor.
- Install strong loo-privacy screen if thought desirable or necessary.
- For Police and Home Office etc. statistical documentation - introduce an NCR paper, multi-page, multi-purpose, tick-box only form - alternatively utilise civilian staff in police stations to transpose or programme computers from tickbox format - thus freeing-up front line police officers for operational street duties.

- Abolish the maximum age limit for Special Constabulary recruits – leave to Chief Constables' discretion as to physical fitness of individual applicants - police officers retire early and a whole bank of valuable, long-term police experience could be utilised – many police pensioners would flock to Police Forces in response to this. Consider half-normal pay scale for these very experienced personnel.

- Call Youth Offending Team managers to account monthly for their achievements or failures - introduce key performance indicators (kpi's) for this purpose.

- Dispense with central sentencing advisory panels who are far too liberal and out-of-touch, and replace with a senior Parliamentary Committee of legally-qualified MP's with modern investigative and forensic techniques.

- Ban all taxis for prisoner movements, such as hospital visits and inter-prison visits for maintaining family ties - too easy to hijack prisoner from escort staff by forcing unshackling at gun point.

- Prisoner-possession of a mobile telephone to be a serious HMP disciplinary offence. (many drugs deals arranged this way)

- **Absolutely all detected drugs offences in HM Prison Service** to be dealt with by specially trained Visiting Magistrates Boards only (internal adjudication awards by individual governors are ludicrously liberal, lenient, and of virtually no deterrent value whatever and prison-wing to prison-wing and convict-to-convict communication systems are amazingly super-swift, far-surpassing modern comms systems! - Viz: news of meaningful and salutary warning awards by Visiting Magistrates would have far more deterrent value).

- All custodial establishments must have *2 drugs dogs* - one active, the other passive - each with its own separate handler-officer (currently at some custodial establishments, just one prison officer dog handler has access to 1 active & 1 passive dog - but of course, can only use 1 dog or the other at any one time). This would obviate non-availability of lone handler on alternate weekends off duty, under normal shift patterns (High quantity of drugs ingress occurs on visiting days - which are mostly on Saturdays and Sundays - *totally unacceptable* if every visitor to prisoners at these vulnerable-to-drugs-ingress times is left unscreened by drug-sniffer dogs.).

- Immediately abolish Civil Service cross-hierarchal transfers into HM Prison Service - the Service currently ends up with totally inadequate, inexperienced, gentle and delicate-natured, junior prison governors, who are brilliant at paper-shuffling, but lack the essential, focused man-management skills - unique and essential for the prison environment - which can only be learned from several years working on the actual wing landings. (short, cross-hierarchal conversion courses are a total waste of time and money)

*Author as a Royal Marines Corporal/coxswain of an LCA on deck of
LST 3516 HMS Striker in Persian (now Arabian) Gulf in the early
1960's. (A landing craft (assault) mk 2 - 43 feet long - is shown
hoisted on its davits, viewed stern-on.)*

ABOUT THE AUTHOR

THE CAREER of Michael Hughes reads like something out of a Boy's Own Adventure Story.

Enlisting in the Royal Marines' elite 40 Commando, RM, Hughes saw active service in the Troodos Mountains of Cyprus during the EOKA conflict and, after 7 years service, joined the Essex Constabulary. Another 7 years service in some of the toughest dockside areas of the County were to pass before he transferred to the Metropolitan Police.

There he rose to the rank of detective sergeant and helped investigate a multi-million pounds fraud against the Ford Motor Company, as well as several headline-hitting murder investigations, including the sensational gangland executions of Billy Moseley and Michael Cornwall, a case which would attract controversy for almost 30 years.

After his police service, during which time Hughes was commended on many occasions by the Commissioner of the Metropolitan Police, Deputy Assistant Commissioners, the Chief Constable of Essex Constabulary, Crown Court judges and Magistrates Courts Benches, he retired to be employed both as a private investigator and then at one of HM Young Offenders Institutions.

It is difficult to imagine a tougher slice of down-to-earth experience of the British criminal justice system and Hughes provides a wealth of inside information to pass on to the readership of *Judgement Impaired*.

Hughes lives in the Oxfordshire area and spends his time walking, river cruising, attending military and police functions, appreciating the music of HM Royal Marines Band Service, and writing.

Author, seen fourth from left, back row, pictured with his colleagues on a CID course at Essex Police HQ, Springfield Chelmsford in the late 60's

1923 photo showing the first outside radio link to Scotland Yard, using Morse Code, from a Metropolitan Police mobile unit at Epsom Downs. Photo: London Police Pensioner magazine

NOTES AND SOURCES

COUNT 1 - BURGLARY

42 - Mail on Sunday - 23.5.05 - Adam Lusher & Karen Miller - Lord Chichester & Perovetz

44 - Daily Express - Richard Moriarty - 22.1.04 - Mark Patterson

45 - Daily Express - 4.2.05 - Paul Broster - Dad's throat slashed

46 - Daily Express - 28.2.04 - Nick Fagge - John Bale

47 - Daily Express - 23.1.04 - Bruce Forsyth

49 - The Times - David Leaman - Digital photo

49 - Daily Express - 16.3.04 - Andrew Williams and Cookson

49 - Daily Express - 6.5.04 - Roy Safe - Pigeons' throats slashed

50 - Daily Express - Greg Swift - 11.5.04 - OAP Joan Rice & burglar Engel

50 - Daily Express - Jane Young - 11.5.04 - Callie Rogers - Lottery

50 - Daily Express - 5.6.04 - Kevin Skelly - Footprints in the snow

51 - Daily Mirror - Rod Chaytor - 22.5.04 - Jack Charlton's hotel room raided

51 - Daily Mirror - Jan Disley - 26.5.04 - home with 41 locks

52 - Daily Express - John Twomey - 25.9.04 - Burglars drive Army Major to suicide

53 - Daily Express - Richard Moriarty - 3.12.04 - Dean Ward - 8 years

54 - 9 X Hanoi burglars

55 - Daily Express - Richard Moriarty - 5.2.05 - Marathon runner Danny Scott

58 - Lord Chief Justice Woolf - Rose lecture

60 - Andrew Turner - Isle of Wight MP - 30.12.02

61 - Police Magazine - March 2003 - Wig-clad Woolf

67 - Daily Express - John O'Connor - 9.2.04 - Retired Commander, New Scotland Yard

70 - Mail on Sunday - March 2004 - 'The law must protect us - not the individual'

71 - Daily Express - Rachel Baird - 1st & 23.1.04 - 13 thousand spared prison

79 - Daily Express - James Slack - 3.2.05 - Burglars have no rights etc

80 - Daily Express - James Slack - 5.2.05 Tackle burglars first then ask questions

85 - Daily Express - Mark Reynolds -

4.3.05- Tony Martin - BBC Pays burglar Fearon

COUNT 2 - PAEDOPHILIA

94 - Sunday Mirror - 25.7.04 - Alan Green

95 - Daily Mirror - Rod Chaytor - 2.3.04 - Thomas Titley

96 - Daily Mirror - 2.4.04 - John Kinsey

96 - Daily Mirror - 6.3.04 - Ian Taylor

96 - Daily Express - 30.3.04 - Christopher McCoy

96 - The Sun - Ian Hepburn & Mike Sullivan - 23.2.04 - Sun Crime Team 'Beasts'

99 - Daily Express - Geoff Marsh - 3.4.04 - Toby Studebaker

100 - Daily Express - John Twomey - 14.7.04 - Judge David Selwood

101 - Daily Express - John Twomey - 14.7.04 - version 2 of ditto above

103 - BBC & Forensic Science Service - 9.2.04 - Sarah Payne

107 - Daily Express - 7.5.04 - Kevin Fisher - wheelchair-bound paedophile

108 - The Sun - Harriet Harkell - 12.6.04 - Zondo - Cardiff Crown Court

108 - Daily Express - John Twomey - 9.6.04 - Dr Robert Wells - paedophile Police Surgeon

110 - The People - Phil Nettleton - 27.6.04 - Steven Castle

111 - The Sun - 14.5.04 - Mike Hardy

112 - Daily Express - 29.7.04 - Irvin Gale

112 - The Sun - 29.5.04 - Robin Woods

112 - The Sun - 14.5.04 - Brian Darwent

112 - The Sun - 29.5.04 - Martin Taylor

112 - Daily Mirror - Geoff Wakeman - 28.5.04 - John Keeler

113 - The Sun - Tom Carlin - 20.7.04 - Stephen Mertens

113 - The Sun - Charles Rae - 21.7.04 - BT figures

114 - Daily Express - Robin Perrie - 21.8.04 PC Lee Doggett - flasher

114 - Daily Express - 26.8.04 - Jonathan Rees-Williams

114 - Daily Express - 10.9.04 - Frank Newberry

115 - Sunday Mirror - Andy Gardener - 25.7.04 - Christopher Dunkley

116 - Daily Express - John Twomey -

5.10.04 - William Goad

117 - Daily Express - 29.5.04 - Lord Berriedale

118 - Daily Mail - Sam Greenhill & Sabi Phagura - 26.4.04 - Child rescuer Stuart Wilson

118 - Daily Express - Mark Blacklock - 7.1.05 - John Temple

119 - Daily Telegraph - John Steele - Commodore David White

120 - Daily Express - Geoff Marsh - 4.2.05 - Commander Tom Herman

121 - Daily Express - Paul Broster - 8.2.05 - John Harrison

122 - The Sun - George Pascoe Watson - 29.5.04 - Paedos will sit lie detector test

123 - Daily Mirror - Gary Jones - 21.7.04 - Matthew Brereton

123 - Daily Mirror - Brendon Williams - 21.7.04 - Richard Brunstrom, Chief Const. N.Wales

124 - Daily Express - James Slack - 3.3.05 - Rupert Massey

125 - Daily Express - 11.8.04 - Eric Blackledge

COUNT 3 - VIOLENCE IN THE STREET, PUBS & CLUBS

127 - Daily Express - Tom Whitehead - 2.3.05 - Peter Grice - Furious chef

128 - Mail on Sunday - Richard Creasy - 2.5.04 - Apparent road rage death

129 - Daily Mirror - 2.3.04 - Fiance bayoneted

129 - Daily Express - Aidan McGurran - 15.3.04 - Trevor Griffith stoned

130 - Berkshire Co. Uk - 12.12.03 - Vicious Slough bouncers

130 - BBC News - 19.2.03 - James Pinsent

130 - Daily Mirror - 22.5.04 - Lee Sharkey - Chain saw attacker

131 - Daily Express - Paul Broster - 18.3.04 - Victim Martin Brierley etc

132 - Daily Express - 4.5.04 - Vipaul Presannae murder

132 - Daily Express - Mark Lister - 5.6.04 - Amy Exley & Christopher

133 - Daily Express - 14.7.04 - Accidental self-harm to testicles

133 - Daily Express - Geoff Marsh - 16.2.05 - Tory MP's son David Amess in club violence

COUNT 4 - HOMICIDE

146 - The Sun - John Coles - 3.4.04 - OAP wife-murderer Alan Wickenden

147 - Daily Express - John Chapman - 3.4.04 - Ian Madden

147 - Daily Express - Jeremy Armstrong - 6.4.04 - Christopher Hoyland

148 - Daily Express - 6.4.04 - Spencer & Allen

148 - Daily Express - 2.4.04 - Michael Timperley - rubbish skip violent death

148 - Daily Mirror - 6.3.04 - Keith Newnham

149 - Daily Express - 13.3.04 - D & B Elener

149 - Daily Express - 7.4.04 - S Rogers & B Stone

149 - The Guardian - 24.4.04 - Curtis Rowe

149 - Daily Mirror - Tom Morgan - 20.4.04 - Jason Dockrill

149 - Daily Mirror - Don Mackay - 22.5.04 - Palwhinder Dillon

150 - Daily Mirror - Steve McGomish - 29.5.04 - Jason Ward

150 - Daily Express - Tony Brooks - 26.1.05 - Murderous scythe attack

150 - Daily Express - Jo Wiley - 29.9.04 - Horrific wife and son murders & suicide

152 - Daily Express - John Chapman - 22.10.04 - Michael Robinson

153 - Daily Express - Myra Philp - 22.1.05 - Goth Luke Mitchell girlfriend murder

154 - Daily Express - Mark Blacklock - 29.1.05 - Wife's body in the lake killer, Gordon Park

158 - Daily Express - Cyril Dixon - 17.2.05 - Nicholas Rose

158 - Daily Express - James Slack - 31.1.05 - The terrifying threat by knives

160 - Daily Express - John Twomey - 5.3.05 - Betty Marshall & James Long

161 - The Sun - 26.2.05 - David Gaynor

161 - Sunday Express - David Stephenson - 27.2.05 - Chilling footage of Dr Harold Shipman interviews

162 - Daily Express - 7.3.05 - Shipman's widow awarded £35,000

COUNT 5 - ROBBERY & THEFT

167 - Daily Express - Paul Broster - 24.4.0 - Eddie Poole

176 - Daily Express - John Chapman

- 2.9.04 - Teenage brutal robbers McPherson, Barrett, Silcott etc

185 - Daily Express - Doug Watson - 8.4.04 - Colin Sadd

192 - Daily Express - Mark Blacklock - 25.3.04 - Evil sons steal dead father's credit card

193 - Daily Express - 9.6.04 - Callous thief, Broad Green

193 - Daily Express - 1.5.04 - Distraction thefts

194 - Daily Mirror - Richard Smith - 27.4.04 - Dishonest customers empty faulty ATM @ Tescos, N. Cheam

195 - Daily Mirror - Paul Byrne - 29.4.04 - Faulty Halifax ATM at Urmston cleared by dishonest customers

195 - The People - Phil Nettleton - 2.5.04 - Chocaholics distraction theft of lorry & cargo

196 - Sunday Mirror - 2.5.04 - John Radcliffe Hospital, Oxford - theft of surgical equipment

196 - Sunday Mirror - 29.4.04 - Broad daylight theft of Bournemouth garden hot tub

196 - Daily Express - Geoff Maynard - 29.6.04 - Nicholas Sims - Thief

196 - Daily Express - 28.1.05 - Magistrate steals a Rolex watch

197 - Daily Express - John Chapman - 20.4.04 - Theft of Royal Mail by temporary postman

197 - Daily Express - 27.4.04 - A & J Jarvis

198 - Daily Express - John Twomey - 10.2.05 - theft of luxury Mercedes cars

199 - Daily Express - 10.2.05 - Theft of shower from hotel room

199 - Daily Express - Tom Morgan - 26.2.05 - Senior Police Officer bike thief

205 - Daily Express - Sarah O'Grady - 3.5.04 - 'Research indicates'....

206 - Sunday Express - 2.5.04 - 'Nation of shoplifters'

COUNT 6 - DRUGS - THE SCOURGE OF OUR SOCIETY

212 - Daily Mirror - 24.5.04 - Falling cost of cocaine

212 - Daily Express - 21.4.04 - Portable drugs test kit

212 - The Times - Louis Smith - (date n/k) - Home test drugs kits

213 - Daily Express - Vanessa Feltz - 18.8.05 - Parents drugs test kits for teenagers

214 - Sunday Express - 13.6.04 -

Red-card zone - violent Lambeth

215 - Daily Mail - Beezy Marsh - 27.9.04 - Dr Peter Harvey

216 - The Sun - Ian King - 21.7.04 - Cozart company drugs tests

216 - Mail on Sunday - 11.7.04 - Yale University School of Medicine 3 million cannabis users

217 - Daily Express - 13.8.04 - Journal of Epidemiology

217 - Daily Express - James Slack - 14.8.04 - Drugs epidemic in HM Prisons

218 - Sunday Mirror - Paul Gilfeather - 25.7.04 - Cannabis arrests fall by one third

219 - Daily Express - 19.5.04 - Drugs sniffer dogs in schools

219 - The Sun - Alastair Taylor - 27.5.04 - HMP staff member smuggles in cocaine in bra

219 - Daily Express - Geoff Marsh - 16.3.04 - Adam Gregory

220 - Daily Express - 25.3.04 - Julian Halloran

220 - Evening Standard Metro Magazine - 25.3.04 - Michael Connell, Thailand

221 - Daily Mirror - Jan Disley - 1.4.04 - 9-year old boy

221 - The Sun - 17.4.04 - Onandi Lowe

221 - Daily Mirror - 24.4.04 - Lincoln White

222 - Daily Mirror - 2.5.04 - Pat Brailsford - bravely holds criminal in headlock

222 - The People - 16.5.05 - Huge HM Customs drugs seizure - Poole, Dorset

222 - Daily Express - 12.6.04 - Pigeon breeder caught with cannabis claims it to be bird seed.

222 - The Sun - John Coles - 18.5.04 - Michael Edwards - 16th birthday party

222 - Daily Express - Simon McWhirter - 5.4.04 - Lee Robins

223 - The Sun - Jamie Pyatt - 24.5.04 - Protest by Eton College pupils caught with drugs

224 - Daily Mail - 26.5.04 - Gareth Frost

224 - Daily Express - Geoff Maynard - 10.6.04 - Jack Elliott

225 - Daily Mirror - 24.5.04 - Liverpool Police seizure

225 - The People - 30.5.04 - Nigel Clack

226 - Daily Express - John Twomey - 9 & 10.7.04 - Julian Whiteway-Wilkinson

227 - Daily Express - 16.7.04 - Drugs smuggled into UK sewn into stomachs of dogs

227 - Daily Mail - Liz Hull - 16.7.04 - Chemist grilled re supplies to Harold Shipman

228 - News of the World - Fred Burcombe - 18.7.04 - Nicky Booth

230 - Daily Express - Tom Morgan & Sarah White - 23.7.04 - Royal love-rat James Hewitt drugs deal

231 - Daily Express - Mark Blacklock - 24.7.04 - Frazer Goodwillie

232 - Daily Express - 24.7.04 - Lord Freddie Windsor

232 - Daily Express - Geoff Maynard - 23.7.04 - Selina Hakki - robs by date-rape drugging male victims

233 - Daily Express - 28.8.04 - Queen's Troop, Household Cavalry fail random drugs tests at barracks

234 - Daily Express - Kirsty Walker - 12.5.04 - David Blunkett - "Don't grumble".

234 - Daily Express - James Slack - 12.1.05 - Full cost of organised drugs crime

235 - Daily Express - 24.2.05 - Naomi Campbell drugs problem

COUNT 7 - SCHOOLS - CRIMES COMMITTED BY PUPILS, STAFF & PARENTS

239 - Daily Express - Sarah White - 22.6.04 - Ta'lisha Edwards - assaulted teacher & excluded

240 - Daily Express - 21.6.04 - Richard Walters

240 - Daily Express - 12.6.04 - Oldbury Wells School - sniffer dogs

240 - The Sun - 24.5.04 - Rhyl High School

241 - Daily Express - Geoff Maynard - 15.5.04 - 50 screaming schoolgirls without tickets halt train

241 - Daily Express - Padraic Flanagan - 8.6.04 - Sarah Fisher

242 - Daily Express - Joel Wolchover - 7.4.04 - Jo Redmond

243 - Daily Express - Gregg Swift - 11.6.04 - PC P Jones

244 - Daily Express - 10.4.04 - Mike Wilson - Grove School

245 - Daily Express - 10.4.04 - Melanie Symonds

245 - Daily Express - 10.4.04 - Andy Mather

246 - Mail on Sunday - James

Tapper - 2.5.04 - Winston Silcott, convicted murderer lectures children

247 - Sunday Express - David Paul - 4.7.04 - Moorside High School

248 - The Guardian - Jamie Wilson - 24.7.04 - Jennifer Abbot

249 - Daily Express - Martin Stote - 28.7.04 - Alan Pennell - knife-crazy school killer

251 - Daily Express - Dennis Rice - 2.9.04 - Eli Frankham, gipsy parent - terrifies School staff

252 - Daily Express - Richard Moriarty - 29.9.04 - Georgina Corby

253 - Daily Express - Richard Moriarty - 9.11.04 - David Morgan

254 - Daily Express - Tony Brooks - 3.2.05 - Linda Walker

255 - Sunday Express - Marthe Gomer - 30.1.05 - College Principals 256 -Metro Magazine - Suzy

256 - Austin - 6.10.04 - 'No kissing etc' new rule introduced

256 - Daily Express - 14.12.04 - Anthony Gatenby

258 - Sunday Express - Tim Shipman - 30.1.05 - Explicit photos on the net

258 - Daily Express - Geoff Maynard - 10.2.05 - David James

259 - The Sun - 26.5.04 - Stanley Johnson

259 - Daily Express - John Chapman - 12.2.05 - Oliver Sabine

260 - Daily Express - Tom Price - 12.2.05 - Ampleforth College drugs problem

261 - Daily Express - 24.2.05 - John Hurst

261 - Daily Express - Geoff Marsh - 28.2.05 - Gavin Lister

262 - Sunday Express - Tim Shipman - 30.1.05 - 'New Education Secretary....'

263 - Daily Express - Tom Whitehead & Chris Riches - 3.2.05 - 'Foul-mouthed football.

265 - Daily Express - Tom Morgan - 24.2.05 - Wayne Rooney

265 - Daily Express - 3.2.05 - 'More than 100 obscenities ...'

266 - Daily Express - 3.2.05 - 'The handful of outstanding...'

266 - Daily Express - Nick Fagge - 28.7.04 - Teachers reluctant to discipline

267 - Sunday Express - Lucy Johnston - 9.1.05 - 'The no. of school children......'

269 - Daily Express - Patrick O'Flynn - 1.3.05 - 'Violent gangs

are running amok....'

270 - Daily Express - 1.3.05 - 'England's top education official....'

270 - Daily Express - Padraic Flanagan - 1.3.05 - 'A boy of 6 was so .....'

271 - Daily Express - James Slack - 3.3.05 - 'A muslim schoolgirl...'

271 - Daily Express - 3.3.05 - 'Tricky decision...'

273 - Daily Express - 3.3.05 - The jilbab is banned in France

COUNT 8 - RAPE & SEXUAL OFFENCES

279 - Daily Express - 1.4.04 - Matthew Thomas

280 - Daily Express - 26.3.04 - Clare Newson

280 - Daily Mirror - 28.9.04 - Scott Locket

280 - Daily Express - 27.3.04 - Lance Smit

281 - Daily Mirror - Don Mackay - 1.4.04 - A Kunowski - serial sexual predator

285 - Daily Express - Sarah white - 3.5.04 - A Imiela - serial sexual offender, railwayman

288 - Daily Express - David Pilditch - 24.2.04 - G Coutts

290 - Daily Mail - Stephen Wright - 23.3.04 - Delroy Lindo

291 - Brian Parnell

297 - The Sun - Sinead Desmond - 10.7.04 - Daniel Owen

299 - Daily Express - Mark Brown

299 - Daily Express - John Twomey - 25.8.04 - Milton Brown

300 - Daily Express - John Twomey - 24.12.04 - Night stalker

303 - Daily Express - Richard Moriaty - 24.12.04 - Merdina & Bregu

304 - Daily Express - Wayne Gaskin

304 - Daily Express - Tony Brooks - 22.1.05 - Vakil Singh

305 - Daily Express - Geoff Marsh - 15.2.05 - ATM gang rape

306 - Daily Express - Mark Reynolds - 21.2.05 - Guinara Gadzijeva

307 - Sun Express - Julia Hartley - Brewer - 30.1.05 - Ministers have dropped plans

COUNT 9 - VIOLENCE & OTHER CRIMES - COMMITTED BY SELF-STYLED CELEBRITIES, PROFESSIONAL FOOTBALLERS AND SUPPORTERS

314 - Daily Mirror - Steve McComish - 28.5 04 - Gary Charles

314 - Daily Express - 13.5.04 - Darren Bent

314 - Daily Express - 13.5.04 -
Steven Gerrard & Milan Baros

314 - Daily Mirror - 1.4.04 - Terrell
Forbes

315 - Daily Mirror - Tom Parry -
28.5.04 - Ben Upton

315 - Daily Express - Geoff Maynard
- 13.5.04 - Lee Ryan

316 - The Sun - John Sadler -
18.5.04 - D Beckham

317 - Daily Express - Sarah White -
3.7.04 - Felicity Thorpe

319 - Daily Express - 15.7.04 -
Trevor Sinclair

319 - Daily Express - 11.8.04 - T
Repka

319 - Daily Express - Martin Evans -
12.5.04 -'The Football Factory'
film

321 - Daily Express - 26.3.04 - W
Rooney

321 - The People - David Brown -
2.5.04 - Neil Coyle

321 - Daily Express - Richard
Moriarty - 22.5.04 - 'Boy of 10'

322 - Daily Express - 19.5.04 -
Fabrice Fernandes

322 - The Sun - Andrew Parker -
27.5.04 - Kelly Adams

325 - The Sun - Jamie Pyatt & Mike
Sullivan - 14.5.04   Stan Bowles

325 - Daily Express - David Pilditch
- 13.5.04 - Stan Collymore

326 - Sunday Mirror - David
Hudson & Martin Coutts -
2.5.04 - G Souness

326 - Daily Express - Geoff Marsh -
23.4.04 - Frank Partridge

326 - Daily Express - Paul Broster -
13.7.04 - Bevan Williams

328 - Daily Express - 17.2.05 - Gary
Carragher

328 - Sunday Express - Roddy
Ashworth & Tim Shipman -
Alan Sugar

329 - Daily Express - Richard
Moriarty - 21.2.05 'Early
evening football matches...'

COUNT 10 - HIT-AND-RUN AND OTHER DRIVING OFFENCES

339 - Daily Express - 25.2.04 -
Brumwell & Hodgson

340 - Daily Mirror - Jeremy
Armstrong - 6.3.04 - Paul Lee

340 - The Sun - Martyn Sharpe -
17.4.04 - Daniel Wilkinson

341 - Daily Express - Paul Broster -
24.8.04 - Lee Elton

342 - The Sun - 12.6.04 - Free
Health Club Membership for a
criminal

342 - Daily Telegraph - Richard
Savill - 24.3.04 - Lee Jones

343 - Daily Express - 13.1.04 -

Simon Teesdale

344 - Daily Express - Paul Broster -
20.3.04 - Stephen Johns & Red
Cross - Ivon Flagg

345 - Daily Express - Sally
Guyoncourt - 1.5.04 - Peter
Cassidy

345 - Daily Express - 13.3.04 -
Father Colin Murphy

345 - Daily Express - 17.2.04 -
Stephen Wallace

346 - The People - Phil Nettleton -
11.4.04 - Sean Huntroyd

346 - The Sun - 17.4.04 - Dane
Bowers

347 Daily Express - Mark Blacklock
- Chris Till

347 - Daily Express - Geoff Maynard
- Norman Preston & Graham
Travers

349 - Daily Express - Nick Fagge -
23.4.04 - Tracey Edwards OBE

349 - Daily Express - Allison
Burroughs - 20.3.04 - Andrew
Bartlett

350 - Daily Express - Craig Smith

350 - Daily Express - Dennis Rice -
13.7.04 - Tracie Ward

351 - Daily Express - 17.7.04 - Lt
Simon Trimble RAF

351 - Daily Express - Jo Willey -
16.7.04 - Les McKeown

351 - Sunday Mirror - 25.7.04 -
Daniel Beldom

352 -Daily Express - Geoff Maynard
- 7.5.04 - Dave Gough

352 - Daily Express - 8.5.04 - David
Moran

353 - Daily Express - Amy Vickers -
2.7.04 - Caroline Murphy

353 - Daily Express - 10.7.04 - Tara
King

354 - The Sun - Robin Perrie -
26.5.04 - Shamsi Ahmed

355 - Daily Express - Robert
Desmond - 19.2.04 - Kamel
Kadri

356 - Daily Express - Sinead
McIntyre - 21.7.04 - Jodie
Duffin - miraculous recovery
after hit-and-run

357 - Daily Mirror - Jeremy
Armstrong - 2.4.04 - Police
'sting' traps car thieves

358 - The Recorder Group - Matt
Knight - Elo Okpokpor

358 - Daily Express - John Chapman
- 5.2.05 - Sonja Oliver

360 - Daily Express - Nick Fagge -
19.2.05 - Citroen Saxo & Xsara

360 - Daily Express - Nick Fagge -
19.2.05 - Mark Stockdale

362 - Daily Express - John Twomey -
12.2.05 - Michael Duncan &
Neil Honnor

362 - Daily Express - Chris Riches -
14.1.05 - Nathan Rowe

363 - Daily Express - Richard
Moriarty - 7.1.05 - John Smee
aged 13 yrs

364 - Daily Express - Geoff Maynard
- 8.4.04 - Steve Cram

365 - The People - 27.6.04 - Daniel
Baptiste

365 - The Sun - 18.5.04 - Richard
Dark

365 - Daily Express - Richard
Moriarty - 8.6.04 - Paul
McDonald

366 - Daily Express - Martin Stote -
2.3.05 - A Chisango

367 - Mail on Sunday - Christopher
Leake - 18.4.04 - 'Police have
launched...'

367 - Mail on Sunday - Christopher
Leake - 18.4.04 - The Home
Office plans

367 - Mail on Sunday - Christopher
Leake - 18.4.04 - The Drugs
Test equipment

368 - Daily Express - Tom Morgan -
Inspector Justin Pedley 'no
insurance etc car-crusher',
Government's alleged war, Ernie
Harbon, Christopher Harris,
Charles Bartlett

370 - Daily Express - Lyndon
Herring - 4.5.04 -

COUNT 11 - CRIMINAL DAMAGE

381 - Photo/picture credit NYPD
officer & PC Brennan -
11.9.2002 - Daily Telegraph -
Press Association -
Constabulary magazine

382 - UK police on city hall steps -
Constabulary magazine

382 - Daily Mirror - 1.5.04 - Fire-
raiser aged 10 yrs

382 - Daily Mirror - 15.7.04 - Train
driver's windscreen smashed at
speed

383 - Daily Mirror - Rod Chaytor -
29.9.04 - 4 persons dead in
arson attack

383 - Daily Express - Richard
Moriarty - 25.3.04 - Mad
cyclist's revenge on cars

384 - Daily Express - 25.3.04 -
Parking rage of 'Meldrew'

384 - Daily Express - Martin Stote -
9.10.04 - Grave-robbing

385 - Lady Pilkington - her cars
paint-stripped

386 - Daily Express - Tom Morgan -
14.8.04 - Serious graffiti on
beautiful Bath stone

387 - Daily Express - 4.2.05 - Kilroy-

Silk - drenched in manure

387 - Daily Express - Paul Broster - 4.2.05 - Mindless youths microwave a pet cat

388 - Daily Express - Padraic Flanagan - 17.2.05 - Simon Johnson - graves desecration

392 - Sunday Express - Stuart Winter - 28.3.04 - Sunday Express 'beat graffiti yobs' campaign

COUNT 12 - PSYCHIATRIC HOSPITALS & PRISONS - DEFECTIVE RISK ASSESSMENTS PLACE THE UNSUSPECTING PUBLIC IN INCREASED DANGER

395 - Staggering 3,623 offences

402 - Daily Express - 20.2.04 - Anthony Milgate

402 - Daily Express - 20.4.04 - Anne Harris

402 - Daily Express - Padraic Flanagan - 20.4.04 - T Theophilou

402 - Daily Express - 24.5.04 - Glaister Earl Butler - Murdered De Michael Swindells

403 - Daily Express - Martin Stote - 26.3.04 - David Parfitt

404 - Daily Mail - Sinead McIntyre - 26.3.04 - Manny Davis

404 - Steven Barton

405 - Daily Express - John Chapman - 13.7.04 - Gary Hart

406 - A Murphy

407 - Sunday Express - Andrea Perry - 12.9.04 - 'Fears are growing...'

409 - Daily Express - John Twomey - 24.9.04 - Daniel Gonzalez - serial murderer

411 - Daily Express - Tony Brocks - 3.12.04 - Paul Khan

412 - Daily Express - Mark Blacklock - 23.12.04 - Craig Sexton

413 - Daily Express - Nick Fagge & Padraic Flanagan - 24.12.04 - Crazed knifeman

414 - Daily Express - Paul Broster - 24.2.05 - Intikhab Alam

415 - Daily Express - John Twomey - 26.2.05 - John Barrett

416 - Daily Express - Tom Whitehead - 7.3.05 - Mark Aldrich

417 - Sunday Express - Julia Hartley-Brewer - 6.1.05 - 'Prisoners will serve in full...'

COUNT 13 - FAMILY-ON-FAMILY ASSAULTS & DOMESTIC VIOLENCE

434 - Daily Express - Geoff Marsh - 22.5.04 - Kerry Hogben

435 - The Sun - Sophie Sturt - 27.5.04 - Kevin Bloomer

435 - Daily Express - 13.3.04 - Robert Grimes

435 - Daily Express - 8.5.04 - Richard Greening

436 - Daily Express - Mark Blacklock - 7.5.04 - Julie Shepherd / Howard Woodin

437 - Daily Express - Tony Brooks - 25.5.04 - Jarvis

437 - Daily Express - 19.4.04 - S Neale & H Rear

438 - Daily Express - Tony Brooks - 9.4.04 - Michael Goodwin

438 - Take It Easy Magazine - Stephen & T White

439 - Daily Express - Paul Broster - 12.7.04 - Stone - v - Lisa Kilmartin

440 - Daily Express - Geoff Maynard - 15.7.04 - Wade - v - Malcolm

440 - Daily Express - Sally Guyoncourt - 24.7.04 - D & B Gibson

441 - Daily Express - Paul Broster - 16.12.04 - Crowston

441 - Daily Express - Paul Broster - 25.1.05 - Osliffe

443 - Peterborough Today & Evening Telegraph - 7.2.05 - Neave family witchcraft slaying

448 - Daily Express - John Twomey - 12.2.05 - Luke Mitchell - Goth murder

449 - Daily Express - Martin Stote - 17.2.05 - Noel White

450 - Daily Express - Sarah White - 19.2.05 - Toye - v - M Turner

451 - Daily Express - Martin Stote - 22.2.05 - S Noades

452 - Daily Express - Geoff Marsh - 19.8.04 - T Edmondson

452 - Daily Express - Martin Stote - 14.1.05 - I & A Gay

454 - Daily Express - James Slack - '2 women being killed by a partner every week...'

455 - The Sun - Sharon Hendry - 27.5.04 - 'One in six pregnant women........'

COUNT 14 - FAITH LOST IN THE BRITISH CRIMINAL JUSTICE SYSTEM

457 - Daily Express - R Moriarty - 7.7.04 - Michael Carroll

457 - Daily Express - John Twomey - 2.4.04 - Michael Carroll

458 - Daily Mirror - Damien Fletcher - 7.8.04 - John Atkinson

459 - Daily Mirror - Damien Fletcher - 7.8.04 - Paul Clark, Reginald Tomlinson & Lee Ryan

460 - Daily Express - Mark

Blacklock & Dennis Rice - 12.8.04 - Iorworth Hoare - wins Lottery in jail

460 - Sunday Express - Andrea Perry & Eugene Henderson - 30.1.05 - Judge Q Purdy - Camberwell Court

464 - Daily Express - Tom Whitehead - 10.3.05 - Mr H Buckland

462 - Daily Express - James Slack - 17.2.05 - Labour's answer

463 - Daily Express - Alison White - 14.2.05 - 'Tony Blair's law & order.....'

463 - Daily Express - James Slack - 11.2.05 - M Howard

COUNT 15 - ANTI-SOCIAL BEHAVIOUR ORDERS

473 - Daily Express - 3.4.04 - Ellen Moore - 13 yrs

473 - Daily Express - 16.11.04 - Alexander Muat - 87 yrs

473 - Daily Express - 3.4.04 - Redford Taylor - 15 yrs

474 - The Guardian - Helen Carter - 24.4.04 - Liberty - appealing against night-time youth curfew

474 - Redcar - 6 month scheme

475 - Daily Express - 3.4.04 - Lesley Pulman - brave ASBO witness

478 - Daily Express - 10.4.04 - Ben White & Robert

478 - Daily Express - 8.4.04 - Paul & Janet Dowling

478 - Daily Express - 24.2.04 - OAP Aubrey Matthews

478 - Daily Express - Paul Broster - 26.3.04 - Robert Alexiuk

479 - Daily Mirror - Geoff Lakeman - 29.4.04 - Nigel & Michael Wetherick

479 - Daily Express - Richard Moriarty - Alan & Linda Fisher - ASBO campaign against day nursery

481 - Daily Express - Geoff Marsh - 4.5.04 - Michael Cambridge, 17 yrs

481 - The Sun - 27.5.04 - Robert & Lisa Hughes

481 - Daily Mirror - 28.5.05 - Melissa Page

482 - Daily Express 29.5.04 - Natalie Henderson

482 - Daily Express - 12.6.04 - Lisa Marriott & son

482 - Daily Express - Paul Broster - 12.6.04 - Doris Lewis & family

483 - Daily Express - Anna Pukas - 29.4.04 - PC Garrod

485 - Daily Mail - Andy Dolan - 25.6.04 - Ryan Jones & Kevin Onslow

486 - Daily Mail - Tahira Yaqoob -
25.6.04 - Banyard, Syrett &
Rattigan

487 - Daily Express - 8.7.04 - Blind
man gropes ladies as he crosses
road

488 - The People - 27.6.04 - D
Pegler

488 - Daily Express - Paul Broster -
10.7.04 - Luke Menzies, 13 yrs

488 - Daily Express - Mark
Blacklock - Kelly Bowness

489 - Daily Express - Martin Stote -
27.7.04 - Davis,Colcroft & Boult
etc

491 - Daily Express - 2.6.04 - Lady
Pilkington

491 - Daily Express - Mark
Blacklock - 10.2.05 - Ryan
Wilkinson

492 - Metro Magazine - 16.2.05 -
Martin Faulkner

493 - Daily Express - Martin Stote -
19.2.05 - Martin Faulkner

494 - Sunday Express - Dennis
Cassidy - 20.2.05 - Albert
Green & Jamie Yates

495 - Daily Express - Tom
Whitehead - 26.2.05 - Kim
Sutton

496 - Daily Express - Tom
Whitehead & David Pilditch -
5.3.05 - Romford neighbours
from hell

497 - Daily Express - Photo credit -
Jonathan Buckmaster & Tony
Sapiano

500 - Daily Express - James Slack -
15.2.05 - 'Government
crackdown.....'

COUNT 16 - AIR RAGE

505 - Mail on Sunday - Claire
Newbin - 4.7.04 - Vinnie Jones

505 - Daily Express - 19.6.04 -
Christopher Harper, Bristol

505 - Daily Express - Richard
Moriarty - 23.11 04 - Aron
Berhane USA to Manchester
flight

506 - Daily Express - Richard
Moriarty - 3.12.04 - Heiki Tallila

507 - Daily Express - Mark Reynolds
- 13.1.05 - Female pilot drunk -
Berlin to Basle flight

508 - BBC News Online - 1.1.99 -
Ian Brown - Pop singer

508 - Cambridgeshire Police -
August 2003 - Flint, Finnegan &
German passenger

509 - Manchester News - 4.2.05 -
Seddon-Knight

510 - Daily Express - Paul Broster -
8.3.05 - Paul Tolley

504 - Daily Express - Geoff Maynard

- 14.5.04 - 37 drunken Tesco
staff removed from flight

511 - AD Aerospace & Flight Vu
magazine - various mid-air
incidents

COUNT 17 - FRAUD

516 - Reginald Gill - Therapist

517 - Daily Mirror - 3.4.04 - Dentist
Michael Bolsin

517 - Daily Express - 3.4.04 - Kulish,
Mutch & Carter

517 - Daily Mirror - 22.7.04 - V & J
Cox

517 - Daily Express - Cyril Dixon -
3.4.04 - Jim Speechley

518 - Daily Express - Martin Stote -
17.1.04 - Paul Downes

519 - Daily Express - 9.4.04 - Ian
Bussey

519 - Daily Express - 10.4.04 -
Rosarie McNamara

519 - Daily Express - 9.4.04 -
Haddouch & Boukhalfa

520 - The Sun - 17.4.04 - Cowboy
gardeners

520 - Daily Mail - Charlie Bain -
16.4.04 - R Nardi

520 - Sunday Express S2 magazine -
Nigel Blundell - Mad Army
Major & wife

522 - Daily Mirror - 24.4.04 -
Counterfeit Euro factory

523 - Daily Express - 8.7.04 - Mark
Purseglove

523 - Daily Express - 6.5.04 - Julie
Beastall

525 - Daily Express - 21.7.04 -
Ademola Adeniji

525 - The Sun - Steve Kennedy -
18.5.04 - Thousands of forged
ID's, driving licences etc

526 - News of the World - 18.7.04 -
Karina Clark & P Ward

526 - Daily Mail - 16.7.04 - David
Rickman

527 - Daily Express - James Slack -
23.7.04 - Huge student visa
scam

528 - Rebecca & Georgina Smith

530 - Daily Express - Paul Broster -
30.4.04 - John & Karl Stewart

530 - Daily Express - Tony Brooks -
9.2.05 - Marie McGinty

531 - Daily Express - Frank Corless
- 26.8.04 - Eric James

532 - Daily Express - 8.5.04 - M
Pongo & Magembo

532 - Milton Keynes News - 24.9.03
- G Drewett condemned meat
fraud

533 - Daily Express - Paul Broster -
12.2.05 - Martin Moo

534 - Daily Express - Geoff Marsh -
13.5.04 - R Williams & A Bolt

535 - Daily Express - Tony Brooks -
29.4.04 - Carl Metcalfe

536 - Daily Mirror - Cameron
Robertson - 23.6.04 - R Van
Baaren & Sian Jones

536 - Daily Express - John Chapman
- 27.4.04 - Lloyds TSB cards

537 - Daily Telegraph - 15.2.05 -
Joyti De-Laurey vast bank fraud

538 - Daily Express - Paul Broster &
Ron Quenby - 14.5.04 - Peter
Crittenden

540 - Basildon & Wickford
Recorder(Echo) - Oduro-
Kwateng

COUNT 18 - EVENTS OCCURRING IN PRISONS & HMYOI'S

553 - News of the World - 18.7.04 -
No. of prisoners dying in jail

553 - Daily Express - James Slack -
27.1.05 - Inspectors delivered

554 - Daily Express - Tony Brooks -
20.3.04 - Uproar broke out

555 - Daily Express - Britain's most
dangerous criminals

555 - Sunday Express - Andrea
Perry - 30.5.04 - Prisoners
creaming off £ millions

555 - Sunday Express - Andrea
Perry - 30.5.04 - Cash scam in
HMP's

555 - Daily Mirror - Jeremy
Armstrong - 29.5.04 - HMP
convicts' new gym

556 - Daily Express - Rachel Bird -
7.1.04 - 1000's of criminals

558 - Daily Express - Dawn Knight &
James Slack - contented jailbird
Kenlock

558 - Daily Express - James Slack -
2.5.04 - Dangerous convict
George Knights

559 - News of the World - 18.7.04 -
Cleric Hamza can't be cuffed,
they slip off his stumps

559 - Daily Express - James Slack -
20.8.04 - Dennis Nilsen

560 - Daily Mirror - Jeremy
Armstrong - 27.4.04 - Super cell
for child double-killer Ian
Huntley

560 - The People - 2.5.04 - Lags flee
on dummy run

561 - Daily Mirror - Gary Jones -
2.4.04 - murderer Kenneth
Noye

562 - The People - 27.6.04 -
Alexandra Johnston

563 - The Sun - Ian Hepburn -
1.10.04 - Stephen Clarke

564 - The People - Phil Nettleton -
PlayStation for child-killer Ian
Huntley

565 - The Sun - John Askill - 1.5.04 - Ian Mitchell

567 - Daily Express - James Slack - 27.1.05 - Herbal tea enjoyed by convicts

567 - Daily Express - 24.1.05 - Jail move for Lockerbie killer
567 - Daily Express - 26.1.05 - Jail horror witnessed by 6 HMP staff
568 - Daily Express - 29.1.05 - £3 million jail riot caused by sandwiches in lieu of hot meal
568 - Daily Express - 9.2.05 - HMP The Mount
574 - Daily Express - John Twomey - 15.6.04 - Michael Summers
586 - News of the World - Mazher Mahmood - HMP Hollesley Bay convicts on day release to HM Customs

COUNT 19 - THE PUBLIC SPEAKS
589 - Daily Express - 10.5.04 - Dr R Piercy
589 - Daily Express - 29.4.04 - Linda A Hicken
590 - Mail on Sunday - 8.3.04 - (Name & address supplied)
590 - Daily Express - 27.4.04 - Robin Rae
591 - Daily Express - 28.4.04 - N R Williams
591 - Daily Express - 9.6.04 - Harry White
591 - Daily Express 28.4.04 - PC Norman Brennan
592 - Daily Express - 28.4.04 - David Heath
592 - Daily Express - 6.5.04 - Peter Watts
593 - The Sun - 18.5.04 - Janet Stringer
593 - The Sun - 18.5.04 - Natalie Branch
593 - The Sun - 18.5.04 - Maria Newman
593 - The Sun - 18.5.04 - Deirdre Dickson
593 - The Sun - 18.5.04 - Kim Kimber
594 - The Sun - 18.5.04 - Richard Mikula
594 - The Sun - 18.5.04 - Philip Cove
594 - The Sun - 18.5.04 - Dave Shaw
594 - The Sun - 18.5.04 - Matt Edwards
594 - The Sun - 18.5.04 - (Name & address supplied)
594 - The Sun - 18.5.04 - Bob Littler
594 - The Sun - 18.5.04 - Robert Martin

595 - The Sun - 18.5.04 - Kevin Baker
595 - The Sun - 14.5.04 - Julie Porter
595 - Daily Mail - 26.5.04 - Steve Chimarides
595 - The Sun - 26.5.04 - Stephen Gorham
595 - Paul Wakeman - Stourbridge
596 - Adele Rawlinson - Bury
596 - The Sun - 26.5.04 - Nichola Purcell
596 - The Sun - 26.5.04 - Paul Cowell
596 - The Sun - 26.5.04 - Jeremy Hayden
596 - The Sun - 26.5.04 - Joe Lanzante
596 - The Sun - 26.5.04 - Steve Rush
596 - The Sun - 26.5.04 - Sharon Sawyer
597 - The Sun - 26.5.04 - Paulette Coulter
597 - The Sun - 26.5.04 - Pat Holt
597 - The Sun - 26.5.04 - Gavin Upex
597 - The Sun - 26.6.04 - John McCafferty
597 - Daily Mirror - 26.5.04 - John Kenlock
597 - Daily Mirror - 26.5.04 - Jean Elliott
597 - The Sun - 24.5.04 - Peter O' Sullivan
598 - The Sun - 24.5.04 - Wayne Kisbee
598 - The Sun - 27.5.04 - Ed Bowden
598 - The Sun 27.5.04 - Louise Ashton
598 - The Sun 27.5.04 - Peggy Hall
598 - The Sun - 27.5.04 - Cathie Hunter
598 - The Sun - 27.5.04 - Tony Smith
599 - The Sun - 27.5.04 - Diane Stevens
599 - The Sun - 27.5.04 - Jane Miller
599 - The Sun - 27.5.04 - William Shaw
599 - The Sun - 27.5.04 - Robert Townsend
599 - The Sun - 27.5.04 - Ann Johnson
599 - The Sun - 27.5.04 - John Emmitson
599 - The Sun - 30.3.04 - Jayne Devine
600 - The Sun - 30.3.04 - Mags Dorren
600 - The Sun - 30.3.04 - Rose Ford
600 - The Sun - 30.3.04 - Anne Firm
600 - The Sun - 30.3/04 - Audrey

Peters
600 - The Sun - 30.3.04 - Maria Stevenson
600 - The Sun - 30.3.04 - Sara Nichols
601 - The Sun - 30.3.04 - Helen Dickson
601 - The Sun - 30.3.04 - Liam Bennion
601 - The Sun - 30.3.04 - Stephen Gorham
601 - Sunday Express - 30.5.04 - Sheila Bending
601 - Sunday Express - Michael Perry
602 - Daily Express - 9.6.04 - William McCann
603 - The People - 30.5.04 - Tanya Weedon
603 - The People - 30.5.04 - G Reilly
603 - Daily Express - 7.6.04 - J M Davis
603 - Daily Express - Paul Bastier
604 - Daily Express - 14.6.04 - Tom Marriott
604 - Tony Hill - Epsom
604 - The Sun - 22.6.04 - Paul Cowell
604 - Daily Mail - 16.7.04 - Yvonne Scholes
605 - Daily Mail - 16.7.04 - Mrs Beryl D Higginbotham
605 - Sunday Express - 23.5.04 - Eric Neal
605 - Daily Express - 23.6.04 - Stephen Murtagh
606 - Daily Express - 24.6.04 - Philip Codd
606 - The Sun - 9.7.04 - Tom Jenkins
606 - The Sun - 9.7.04 - Jonathan Cooper
606 - Daily Express - 6.7.04 - David Aitken
607 - Sunday Express - 4.7.04 - (Name & address supplied)
607 - The Sun - 7.7.04 - Paul Locorriere
607 - The Sun - 7.7.04 - Judith Harper
607 - Daily Express - 5.7.04 - S Askham
607 - Daily Express - 5.7.04 - Malcolm Brown
608 - Daily Express - 21.6.04 - Tony Thorn
608 - Daily Express - 21.6.04 - Ian Oxley
608 - Sunday Express - 11.7.04 - M Perry
609 - Daily Mail - 23.7.04 - Mrs Heather Causnett
609 - Daily Mail - 23.7.04 - John Hornsby
610 - Daily Mail - 23.7.04 - Roy May

610 - Daily Express - 23.7.04 - Steve Kenyon

610 - News of the World - 18.7.04 - Michael Foley

610 - News of the World - 18.7.04 - Martin Worrall

610 - News of the World - 18.7.04 - Mrs Gloria Wilding

610 - News of the World - Mike O'Dell

610 - News of the World - 18.7.04 - Gavin Upex

610 - News of the World - 18.7.04 - Keith Stoddard

611 - News of the World - 18.7.04 - Lucy Maunders

611 - Daily Express - 20.7.04 - Ian Payne

611 - Sunday Mirror - 25.7.04 - David Barber

612 - Sunday Mirror - 25.7.04 - Margaret King

612 - Sunday Mirror - 25.7.04 - Mrs J A Silcock

612 - Daily Express - 26.7.04 - W J Clarke

612 - Photo/picture credit - 'LPP' (London Police Pensioners magazine)

613 - Daily Express - 26.7.04 - (Name & address supplied)

613 - Photo/picture credit - 'LPP' (London Police Pensioners magazine)

613 - Daily Express - 26.7.04 - Steve Fuller

614 - Daily Express - 26.7.04 - Paul Rhodes

614 - Daily Express - 26.7.04 - R West

614 - Daily Express - 23.7.04 - Derek Bunting

614 - Daily Express - 23.7.04 - Tom Marrriott

614 - Daily Express - 23.7.04 - Joyce V Chevill

615 - Daily Express - 23.7.04 - Bev Bradley

615 - Daily Express - 27.7.04 - Helen Beere

615 - Daily Express - 27.7.04 - Dennis Jones

616 - Daily Express - 27.7.04 Tony Thorn

616 - Daily Express - 27.7.04 - Ian Bloomer

616 - Daily Express - 29.7.04 - Stan Dibble

617 - Daily Express - 29.7.04 - Martyn Redmore

617 - Daily Express - 28.7.04 - C A Smith

617 - Daily Express - 28.7.04 - D Davis

617 - The Sun - 19.7.04 - Stuart Maynard

617 - The Sun - 19.7.04 - Colin Woods

618 - Daily Express - 15.7.04 - J Wooster

618 - Alan Gower - Northampton

618 - Kelly Reynolds - Billericay

618 - David Gwilt - Bentley, W Midlands

618 - Nigel Flint - Kenilworth

618 - John Yeates - Swansea

618 - James Becker - Milton Keynes

619 - Andrea Hodgson - Cranham, Essex

619 - The Sun - 23.7.04 - Robert Irwin

619 - The Sun - 23.7.04 - Harry James

619 - The Sun - 23.7.04 - Bob Jenkins

619 - The Sun - 23.7.04 - William Ells

619 - Daily Mirror - 21.7.04 - B Ruffle

620 - Daily Mirror - 21.7.04 - W Turner

620 - Daily Mirror - 21.7.04 - Karl Whitburn

620 - Daily Express - 22.7.04 - Mike Jefferies

620 - Daily Express - 22.7.04 - John Cherry

620 - Daily Express - 22.7.04 - Chris Lee

621 - Daily Express - 22.7.04 - C Jones

621 - Daily Express - 27.7.04 - David Williams

621 - Daily Express - 22.7.04 - Ray Pritchard

621 - Daily Express - 28.7.04 - Nick Brown

622 - Daily Express - 30.7.04 - John O'Connor

622 - Daily Express - 30.7.04 - Gillian Bestwick

622 - Daily Express - 17.8.04 - Terry Palmer

622 - Daily Express - 16.8.04 - A Powell

623 - Daily Express - 13.8.04 - Sue Hudson

623 - Daily Express - 13.8.04 C Kirby

623 - Daily Express - 13.8.04 - John King

623 - Daily Express - 13.8.04 - Jackie Trundell

624 - Daily Express - 14.1.05 - Cynthia Tweedle

624 - Daily Express - 14.1.05 - David Mills

624 - Daily Express - 14.1.05 - Roger Taylor

625 - Daily Express - 14.1.05 - M Haines

625 - Daily Express - 18.1.05 - Tom Marriott

625 - The Sun - 13.9.04 - Stuart Guthrie

625 - The Sun - 13.9.04 - Brenda Stevenson

626 - The Sun - 13.9.04 - Paul Marshall

626 - The Sun - 13.9.04 - William Hall

626 - The Sun - 13.9.04 - Jane Robinson

626 - The Sun - 13.9.04 - Christine Leahy

626 - The Sun - 13.9.04 - Sandra Dwyer

626 - The Sun - 13.9.04 - Gary Hughes

626 - The Sun - 13.9.04 - David Parsons

COUNT 20 - THE FOURTH ESTATE

629 - Daily Express - Tom Morgan - 27.4.04

630 - Daily Express - Richard Moriarty - 7.5.04

633 - Sunday Express - Martin Townsend

634 - Daily Mail - Comment - 26.4.04

635 - Daily Mail - Melanie Phillips - 26.4.04

637 - Sunday Express - Opinion - 18.4.04

638 - Sunday Express - In Brief - 18.4.04

638 - Daily Express - Law & Order feature - 22.4.04

639 - Daily Express - Editorial - 30.4.04

642 - Daily Express - Editorial - 18.5.04

642 - Sunday Express - Editorial - 16.5.04

642 - Daily Express - Editorial - 22.5.04

643 - Daily Express - Padraic Flanagan - 11.5.04

644 - Daily Express - S Green - 21.5.04

644 - Daily Express - M Rainford - 21.5.04

644 - Daily Mirror - Editorial - 29.4.04

644 - Sunday Express - Editor - 25.4.04

645 - Sunday Express - Jimmy Young - 9.5.04

646 - Daily Express - Ken Livingstone - 5.4.04

648 - Sunday Express - Opinion - 23.5.04

649 - Sunday Express - Editor - 9.5.04

650 - Daily Express - Binge drinking warning to Alcohol Industry - 11.5.04

650 - Sunday Mirror - Carole Malone - 2.5.04

651 - The Times - Joe Joseph - 19.5.04

653 - Daily Express -Typical Media Priority Reportage of News - 18.2.04

653 - Daily Express - Typical Media Priority Reportage of News - 24.5.04

COUNT 21 - IN PRAISE OF THE JUDICIARY

655 - Daily Express - 23.7.04 - LJ Steyn, Rodger, Carswell etc

656 - Daily Express - James Slack - 8.10.04 - LJ Kennedy & Treacey

657 - Daily Mirror - Don Mackay - 2.4.04 - Mr Justice Munby

658 - Daily Express - James Slack - 16.11.04 - LJ Coulsfield

659 - The Times - Frances Gibbs - 28.1.05 LCJ Woolf

662 - Daily Express - Edward White - 17.9.04 - Mr Justice Holland - Leeds

663 - Daily Express - John Twomey - Judge J McNaught - Swindon

664 - Daily Express - Sally Guyoncourt - 16.10.04 Judge N Coleman - Norwich

666 - Daily Express - Martin Stote - 26.10.04 - Judge Andrew Hamilton - Derby

667 - Daily Express - Martin Stote - Mrs Z Watson JP - Wilts.

668 - Daily Express - 1.11.04 - feature by an anonymous Chairman of a Bench of Magistrates

669 - Mr D Leggetter, ex- Chairman of a Bench of Magistrates

670 - MrRecorder Stevenson - Reading Crown Court

671 - Daily Express - Sarah White - 17.1.05 - feature by Mrs Adeline Smith JP - Coalville

673 - Daily Express - Martin Stote - 18.1.05 - ditto as above

COUNT 22 - IMPAIRED JUDGEMENTS

677 - Sunday Express - Julia Hartley-Brewer - 15.8.04 - Civitas Report

680 - Channel 4 News - Mark Easton - 'The smile on etc Van Hoogstraten..'

683 - Sunday Express - Jimmy Young - 12.9.04 - I have commented before

684 - Daily Express - Editorial - 20.9.04 - We report today on

685 - Sunday Express - Jimmy Young - 26.9.04 - 100's of years ago

686 - Daily Express - Editorial - 27.9.04 - Our investigation into violent crime

686 - Sunday Express - Jimmy Young - 7.11.04 - Drunken drivers who kill

687 - Manchester News - Martin Dillon - 16.8.04 - Judges in Manchester

688 - Daily Express - James Slack - 2.7.04 - England most senior judge

691 - Daily Express - James Slack - 16.12.04 - Britains most senior judge

694 - Daily Express - Patrick O'Flynn - Tony Blair has seen many former allies plunge the knife

696 - Evening Standard Metro magazine - 25.3.04 - Teenagers grave theft

697 - The Guardian - Kirsty Scott - 24.4.04 - 'Two teenagers...

698 - Daily Express - 24.4.04 - Two teenage boys who cut...

698 - Daily Express - Gonzales & Craig Smith

700 - Lorna Gray & James McEwan

703 - Daily Mail - Steve Doughty - 2.8.04 - Mr Justice Hodge

704 - Soham liar Maxine Carr

705 - Daily Mail - Jaya Narain - 16.3.04 - Haige

707 - Ahmed - Air rage

708 - Flint D - grave robber

709 - Daily Express - Geoff Maynard - 6.10.04 Bully boys A-D etc

710 - Daily Express - John Chapman - 11.9.04 - S Herbert & Beard

711 - Reading Evening Post - 9.2.04 - PC Scott TV Police

712 - Daily Express - John Twomey - McAuslan

713 - The People - Damien Fletcher - 30.5.04 - Nicholas Coley

714 - Daily Express - Jo Willey - 3.9.04 - Rebecca Denton

715 - Daily Express - Sarah Westcott - 24.4.04 - D Selwood

721 - The Sun - Nic Cecil, Tom Carlin & Kathryn Lister - 4.4.04

723 - Daily Mail - Sinead McIntyre - 20.8.04 - David Joyce

724 - Daily Mail - Charlie Bain - 28.9.04 - Simon Oakley

725 - Daily Mail - 8.1.04 - Dyed hair @ ID parade etc

726 - Daily Express - Martin Stote - 20.8.04 - 12 yrs old off-licence robber with shotgun

727 - Sunday Mirror - Andy Gardner & Anil Dawar - 2.5.04 - John Barton

729 - Jamie Thompson

731 - News of the World - Luke Mendham & Lucy Panton - 30.5.04 - Joseph Denley

732 - Daily Express - Padraic Flanagan - 13.5.04 - Prof J Scott

733 - International Who's Who 2005 - Prof J Scot's entry

734 - Daily Express - John Twomey - 19.3.04 - Travers & McCabe & Miriam Keating

735 - Daily Express - Geoff Maynard - 24.7.04 - Stuart McClean - Railtrack - live rail contact

736 - Lisa Woods

737 - Lawrence Frape

738 - Daily Mail - Richard Pendlebury - 10.2.04 - Adyl Kanata & Barker

743 - Paul Cook

743 - Basildon Yellow Advertiser - 14.10.04 - Carol Nicholls - Guilty of 19 counts fraud - walks free

744 - Daily Express - Cyril Dixon - 2.9.04 - Paul Martins

745 - Daily Express - Tony Brooks - 18.9.04 - Nick Craven

746 - Daily Express - Martin Stote - 10.8.04 - Lee Hughes

747 - Sunday Express - Michael Knapp - 15.8.04 - Lee Hughes (2nd version)

749 - Daily Express - Greg Swift - 3.8.04 - Minety gipsies

750 - BBC News Website - 6.9.04 - Leanne Jackson

751 - Daily Express - John Chapman - 8.9.04 - Michael Barrett

752 - News of the World - Neil Michael - 18.7.04 - Giovanni Fronte

753 - Daily Express - Rony Brooks - 31.7.04 - Cain-Purcell

754 - Daily Express - Geoff Maynard - 26.4.04 - S Moyse

755 - Gary Callaby

756 - C Dunkley

757 - A Moffatt

757 - James Laidler

758 - Oxford Mail/Herald - 20.8.02 - D Belassie

758 - Western Daily Press - Michael Ribbeck - 3.9.04 - Alan Thomas

760 - News of the World - 18.7.04 - D & K Major

761 - Rachel Doige

761 - Daily Express - 5.11,04 - Wm Turton

762 - D Coulson

762 - Daily Express - Paul Broster - 5.6.04 - A or G Thompson

763 - Daily Express - Tony Brooks - 26.5.04 - G Frost

764 - The Sun - Chris Riches -
    17.4.04 - Violent Army Sgt
    John Smith
765 - 8 yrs old bo
766 - Hoggett & Nemeth
766 - M A Potter graffiti on tube
769 - Daily Express - Dennis Rice -
    13.1.05 - David Vaughan
771 - Daily Express - Paul Broster -
    1.5.04 - David Hornby
772 - Daily Express - 3.7.04 - V
    Martin
772 - Daily Express - Geoff Maynard
    - 11.5.04 - Shane Trim
773 - Daily Express - Tony Brooks -
    10.5.04 - Stephen Taylor
774 - Daily Express - 26.3.04 - Mark
    Jones
774 - Daily Express - Cyril Dixon -
    Hayley Matthews
776 - Daily Express - Paul Broster -
    28.8.04 - Kay Wright
777 - Daily Mail - Andrew Levy &
    Matthew Hickley - 15.10.04 -
    Kevin Page
779 - Daily Express - 16.8.04 -
    Donald McKeller
780 - Daily Express - Geoff Marsh -
    10.4.04 - Adam Zemlick
781 - L Arliss
781 - Daily Express - Paul Broster -
    25.8.04 - Terry Yorath
783 - Sunday Mirror - Andy Gardner
    - 3.10.04 - W Bough
783 - Daily Express - Tony Brooks -
    18.9.04 - P McAteer
784 - Daily Express - David Pilditch
    - 8.10.04 - Toni Hird
785 - Keith Gray
786 - Daily Express - Mark Reynolds
    - 28.1.05 - Diomansy Kamara
786 - Gail Poole